NORTHERN
MEXICO
HANDBOOK

NORTHERN
MEXICO
HANDBOOK

INCLUDING THE COPPER CANYON
SECOND EDITION

JOE CUMMINGS

MOON
TRAVEL
HANDBOOKS

NORTHERN MEXICO HANDBOOK
SECOND EDITION

Published by
Moon Publications, Inc.
P.O. Box 3040
Chico, California 95927-3040, USA

Printed by
Colorcraft Ltd.

Please send all comments,
corrections, additions,
amendments, and critiques to:

**NORTHERN MEXICO HANDBOOK
MOON TRAVEL HANDBOOKS
P.O. BOX 3040
CHICO, CA 95927-3040, USA
e-mail: travel@moon.com
www.moon.com**

Printing History
1st edition—1994
2nd edition—October 1998

ISBN: 1-56691-118-4
ISSN: 1098-6693

Editor: Don Root
Map Editor: Gina Wilson Birtcil
Copy Editor: Asha Johnson
Production & Design: David Hurst, Carey Wilson
Cartography: Brian Bardwell, Chris Folks and Mike Morgenfeld
Index: Valerie Sellers Blanton

Front cover photo: Incised meanders, Copper Canyon © Richard D. Fisher,
Sunracer Photography and Publishers

All photos by Joe Cummings unless otherwise noted.

Distributed in the United States and Canada by Publishers Group West

Printed in China

"The glittering treasure you are hunting for day and night lies buried on the other side of that hill yonder."
—B. Traven, *The Treasure of the Sierra Madre*

ᥴᕽ

CONTENTS

ABBREVIATIONS

a/c—air-conditioning
ATV—all-terrain vehicle
B&B—bed and breakfast
Chih.—Chihuahua
Coah.—Coahuila
COTP—Captain Of The Port
d—double occupancy
Dgo.—Durango
FNM—*Ferrocarriles Nacionales de Mexico*
G.T.—*gran turismo*
kg—kilograms
km—kilometers
N.L.—Nuevo León
Nte.—*norte* (north)
NP—new pesos

Ote.—*oriente* (east)
pp—per person
Pte.—*poniente* (west)
q—quadruple occupancy
RV—recreational vehicle
s—single occupancy
s/n—*sin número,* used for street addresses
   without building numbers
Sin.—Sinaloa
S.L.P.—San Luis Potosí
Son.—Sonora
t—triple occupancy
Tamps.—Tamaulipas
Zac.—Zacatecas

MAP SYMBOLS

MEX. FEDERAL HIGHWAY	━━━━ DIVIDED HIGHWAY	● HOTEL / ACCOMMODATION
MEX. STATE HIGHWAY	━━━━ MAIN ROAD	■ POINT OF INTEREST
U.S. STATE HIGHWAY	──── OTHER ROAD	○ TOWN / VILLAGE
U.S. HIGHWAY	─ ─ ─ UNPAVED ROAD	○ CITY
U.S. INTERSTATE	─·─·─· TRACK / TRAIL	▲ MOUNTAIN
PEMEX GAS STATION	══╪══ BRIDGE	⋰ WATERFALL
✈ AIRPORT	━╍━ RAILROAD	WATER
	─··─··─ STATE BORDER	
	━ ━ ━ INTERNATIONAL BORDER	

ACCOMMODATIONS
PRICE KEY

Shoestring: under US$15
Budget: US$15-35
Inexpensive: US$35-55
Moderate: US$55-80
Expensive: US$80-120
Premium: US$120+

MAPS

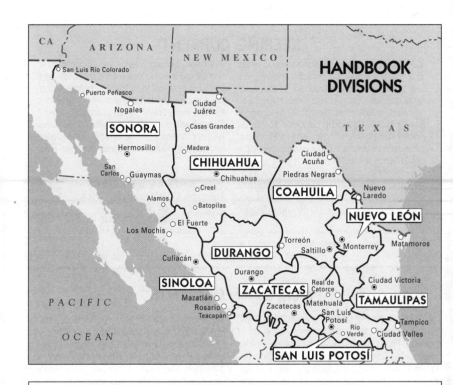

THE STATES OF NORTHERN MEXICO

STATE	CAPITAL	SIZE (IN SQUARE KILOMETERS)	POPULATION (1995)
Chihuahua (Chih.)	Chihuahua	244,938	2.8 million
Coahuila (Coah.)	Saltillo	149,982	2.2 million
Durango (Dgo.)	Durango	123,181	1.4 million
Nuevo León (N.L.)	Monterrey	64,924	3.5 million
San Luis Potosí (S.L.P.)	San Luis Potosí	63,088	2.2 million
Sinaloa (Sin.)	Culiacán	58,328	2.4 million
Sonora (Son.)	Hermosillo	182,052	2 million
Tamaulipas (Tamps.)	Ciudad Victoria	79,384	2.5 million
Zacatecas (Zac.)	Zacatecas	73,252	1.3 million

KEEPING CURRENT

Between the time this book went to press and the time it got onto the shelves, hotels have opened and closed, restaurants have changed hands, and roads have been repaired (or fallen into disrepair). Also, prices have probably gone up because of this, all prices herein should be regarded as approximations and are not guaranteed by the publisher or the author.

We want to keep this book as accurate and up-to-date as possible and would appreciate hearing about any errors or omissions you may encounter while using *Northern Mexico Handbook*.

If you have any noteworthy experiences (good or bad) with establishments listed in this book, please pass them along to us. If something is out of place on a map, tell us; if the best restaurant in town is not included, we'd like to know. Found a new route to a hidden canyon or historic mining town? Share it with other Northern Mexico travelers. All contributions will be deeply appreciated and properly acknowledged. Address your letters to:

Joe Cummings
Northern Mexico Handbook
c/o Moon Travel Handbooks
P.O. Box 3040
Chico, CA 95927-3040 USA
e-mail: travel@moon.com

ACKNOWLEDGMENTS

I am grateful for the generous assistance of the following people and organizations in and out of Mexico: Fernando Domínguez Arvizo, Walter Bishop V., Laura Castro G., Laurel Cooper, Doug Elliott, Hall Elliot, José Salcido Gómez, Cathy Le Jehan, Ernie Lewis, David Lida, Ron Mader, David Maung, Stuart H. Maule, Gloria J. McDonagh, Stephanie Meyer, Marlene Páez Millán, Bob Mirrielees, Sandra Molyneaux, Cecilia Morfín, Luz Carmen Parra, Marcela Puente, Juan Quezada, Cliff Ross, Adolfo Salido, Paul Sherman, Shooka Shemirani, Molly Sweeney, María Guadalupe Trujillo, Paul Van Vleck, and Mike Williams. Hard-working research assistants Jennifer Bartlett, Chris Humphrey, and Alex Peterson were of considerable help and brought new perspectives to this update. My wife Lynne gave up her "day job" as an interior designer to assist in both research and the preparation of the update manuscript, and for this help as well as her companionship I will always be thankful.

BOB RACE

INTRODUCTION

Much of the wildness once associated with the American Southwest survives in the sparsely populated Northern Mexico mainland. Here vaqueros still cobble their own boots, horses and burros remain important forms of transportation, and legends of silver barons, *bandidos,* revolutionaries, lost gold mines, and ancient Amerindian cities abound.

Of late the region is more accessible than ever to anyone willing to take the transborder plunge. Many of the nine northern states—Sonora, Sinaloa, Chihuahua, Durango, Zacatecas, San Luis Potosí, Coahuila, Nuevo León, and Tamaulipas—now boast four-lane highways that have cut travel-time in half, connecting border towns with formerly remote destinations in the in-

terior and along Mexico's two main coastlines. Yet despite the completion of these asphalt ribbons, Northern Mexico remains largely undiscovered by the tourist hordes.

Cloud forests, canyons inhabited by Tarahumara Indians, tropical lagoons, state-of-the-art museums, deep limestone caves, precipitous waterfalls, austere Mennonite colonies, chile farms, and beach resorts are just a taste of what Northern Mexico has to offer. And the unique *norteño* culture that has developed over the centuries endows the top half of Mexico with a spirit that may seem both familiar and surprising to first-time visitors—a mixture of tranquility and independence that brings many of us back time after time.

THE LAND

GEOGRAPHY

The nine states of mainland Northern Mexico comprise approximately 1,040,000 square km, or about 52% of the total surface area of the

Republic of Mexico. Of Mexico's 31 states, the four largest—Chihuahua, Sonora, Coahuila, and Tamaulipas—are northerners, a fact that proud Northern Mexicans are quick to point out.

Northern Mexico's border with the U.S. extends for 3,133 km (1,942 miles) from the Gulf of

Mexico in the east to the Río Colorado, a dammed-to-a-trickle river that separates Sonora from Baja California Norte in the west. To the east, more than half of the U.S.-Mexico border is formed by the Río Bravo, known in the U.S. as the Rio Grande.

Mountain Ranges

Three major cordilleras (mountain chains), each comprised of numerous smaller mountain ranges, dominate the Northern Mexican landscape and determine much of the region's climatic variation and biodiversity. Together the three encircle a major system of plateaus and basins known in Mexico as the Altiplano or "High Plains," thus forming the basic topographic framework for all of Northern Mexico.

Two of these cordilleras constitute the Sierra Madre or "Mother Range," so called because the two arms reach down the east and west flanks of continental Mexico as if to cradle the vast center. In many ways, life in these Northern mountain chains represents Mexico at its most traditional. In the Sierras Madre most people still use the horse or burro for transportation and farm work, plow their fields with oxen, and grind their own corn and wheat for handmade bread and tortillas. Because the highlands are less arable than the plains below, fighting for land—the source of most political conflict in Mexico—is historically less common here. As a result, the vagaries of 20th-century Mexican politics have largely eluded the Madreans.

The western Sierra Madre or **Sierra Madre Occidental,** Mexico's most extensive cordillera, runs 1,300 km (800 miles) along a northwest-southeast axis more or less parallel to the Sea of Cortez and Pacific Ocean coastlines. Basically a continuation of a chain that begins with Alaska's Endicott Mountains and extends through the Rocky Mountains of the U.S. and Canada, the Sierra Madre Occidental reaches a breadth of 300 km in places, and is interspersed with peaks over 3,000 meters (9,800 feet) high.

This cordillera is composed primarily of igneous rock, with rugged cliffs, steep canyons, and high waterfalls along the eastern escarpment and gentler slopes descending the western side toward the coastal plains. Extensive pine and oak forests blanket the uppermost elevations. Suspended between the western and eastern flanks is an interior savanna that has been

NORTHERN MEXICO LOCATION

© MOON PUBLICATIONS, INC.

JOE CUMMINGS

Barranca de Urique

used as a natural highway for human and animal migration since prehistoric times.

By contrast, the eastern Sierra Madre or **Sierra Madre Oriental,** extending roughly 1,200 km parallel to the Gulf of Mexico coast, is a sedimentary chain of predominantly limestone peaks pocketed with caves and vertical pits called *sótanos,* some as deep as 1,400 feet. Although averaging only 150 km in width, the Oriental cordillera reaches heights in excess of 3,800 meters (12,000 feet).

Humid winds from the Gulf of Mexico coil off the Oriental peaks and condense to provide lush, semitropical vegetation along the cordillera's eastern escarpment; one of the more remarkable features of the Oriental chain is an extensive cloud forest on Gulf-facing slopes south of Ciudad Victoria (see "Reserva de la Biosfera, El Cielo," under "Vicinity of Ciudad Victoria" in the State of Tamaulipas chapter). By contrast, the western side of the cordillera is more arid as a result of desertic influences from the Cortez coastal plains.

Linking the lower portions of the two Sierra Madre cordilleras is a lesser chain of mountain ranges known as the Sierra Transversal de Zacatecas, La Breña, y San Luis Potosí. Running west to east across the states of Zacatecas and San Luis Potosí, this largely volcanic chain separates the northern Altiplano from its counterpart in the south. The highest peaks here top out at 2,500-3,000 meters.

PRINCIPAL PEAKS OF NORTHERN MEXICO

NAME	HEIGHT	STATE
El Potosí	3,810 meters (12,496 feet)	Nuevo León
San Rafael	3,770 meters (12,366 feet)	Coahuila
El Morro	3,710 meters (12,170 feet)	Nuevo León
Picacho San Onofre	3,554 meters (11,657 feet)	Tamaulipas
El Jabalí	3,409 meters (11,182 feet)	Coahuila
Epazote	3,227 meters (10,585 feet)	Durango
La Ascensión	3,210 meters (10,530 feet)	Tamaulipas
Grande	3,190 meters (10,463 feet)	San Luis Potosí
El Oso	3,170 meters (10,398 feet)	Durango
Páfilo	3,168 meters (10,390 feet)	Durango
Las Nopaleras	3,130 meters (10,266 feet)	Coahuila
Alto las Taunitas	3,110 meters (10,200 feet)	Chihuahua
Las Chorreas	3,070 meters (10,070 feet)	Durango

Altiplano

The vast plateau between the Sierra Madre Occidental and Sierra Madre Oriental is commonly known as the Altiplano, or less commonly as the Altiplanicie Septentrional or Llanuras Boreales—both of which roughly translate as "northern high plains." After Tibet and

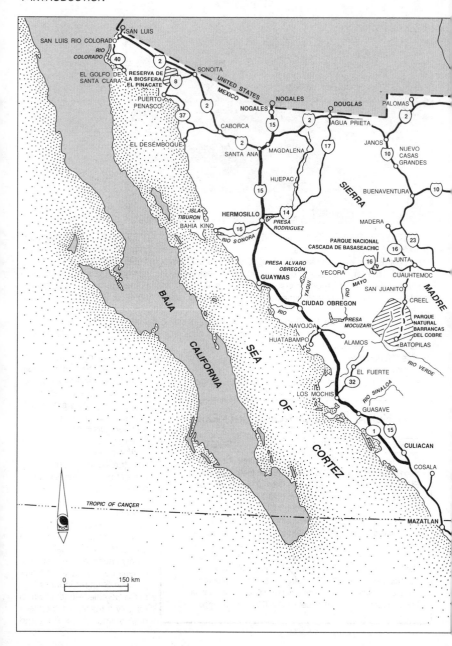

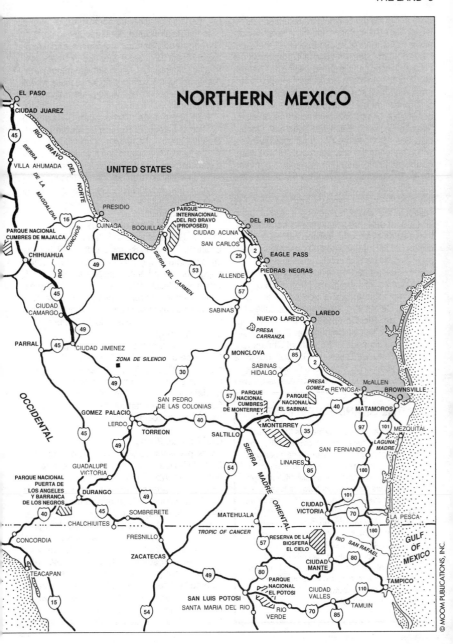

NORTHERN MEXICO

Bolivia, it is the third highest inhabited plateau in the world. At its northern end the Altiplano averages 1,000 meters above sea level, but as it moves south toward the Sierra Transversal, the plateau ascends to around twice that height. Much of the Altiplano consists of interior chaparral, savanna, scrubland, and desertland.

The central plains also encompass a number of large basins called *bolsones* (Spanish for "bags" or "purses"). Rainwater flows down mountainsides into these basins to form shallow lakes, which are often the only source of surface water on the Altiplano during long periods between rains. The paucity of rivers on the plains also means a lack of drainage; minerals suspended in the runoff—mainly gypsum and salt—tend to collect in the lowest points of a *bolsón*. During times of sparse precipitation and hot weather, these lakes evaporate, leaving behind gypsum dunes (as at Cuatrociénegas) or salt flats (such as El Salado de San Luis).

The plateau can be divided topographically into a number of subregions. Mexico's Río Conchos has transformed a portion of the Chihuahuan Desert into a verdant oasis called the **Cuenca del Río Conchos,** an area now supporting the cities of Chihuahua, Delicias, Camargo, and Jiménez in the state of Chihuahua. Opposite Presidio, Texas, the Río Conchos joins and revives the Río Bravo (Rio Grande), whose flow upstream from the confluence is heavily usurped by El Paso-area agriculture.

In the **Región Lagunera,** occupying parts of Durango and Coahuila, the Nazas and Aguanaval Rivers have been dammed to create several large lakes. The lakes provide major water resources for the surrounding fertile plain, where wheat, corn, cotton, and vinifera are cultivated in abundance.

Part of the larger Chihuahuan Desert (see "Deserts," below), **El Bolsón de Mapimí** straddles the states of Chihuahua and Coahuila in the center of the Altiplano and is characterized by a stark flatness and desert climate. Intense, sporadic precipitation is quickly lost to subsurface infiltration and evaporation. Gypsum, one of the principal precipitates left behind, has been exploited economically.

El Salado de San Luis, a *bolsón* system centered in San Luis Potosí, extends into parts of Coahuila, Tamaulipas, and Zacatecas. It is similar in climate to Mapimí. As the name El Salado suggests, the primary precipitate here is salt, which is collected from salt wells at the area's southern edge. In both Mapimí and El Salado, campesinos use the locally abundant lechuguilla, yucca, and candelilla plants to make fiber products and candle wax.

To the west of the Bolsón de Mapimí is the **Comarca de los Indios Pueblos** ("Pueblo Indian District"), a desert area that is nonetheless irrigated by several rivers originating in the Sierra Madre Occidental. The valleys lining the Río Casas Grandes, in particular, have become thriving agricultural centers.

Gulf Coastal Plains

These plains form a wide coastal belt along the Gulf of Mexico from the Río Bravo delta to the port of Veracruz. Blessed with a mild and moist climate, the plains are traversed by several rivers that feed into the Gulf, creating a major agricultural and ranching center.

Most of the Gulf coast from the U.S. border to Tampico is fringed by sandy barrier islands and peninsulas, a result of gradual coastal erosion. The one short stretch between La Pesca and Tampico not protected by barrier islands is marked by broad, straight, low-relief beaches.

Openings between barrier islands are known as *bocas* (mouths). Major openings along the Gulf coast north of Tampico are Boca de Sandoval

---

THE GRAND SOUTHWEST

Deserts are loosely defined as those areas averaging fewer than 25 cm (10 inches) of rain per year; by this definition, certain portions of nearly every state north of the Isthmus of Tehuantepec can be classified "desert," although rainfall varies considerably between locales.

Nearby desert regions in the U.S. are even more extensive and cover large parts of Nevada, California, New Mexico, Arizona, and Texas—thus forming the core of the great American Southwest. In distinguishing a "natural Southwest region," biologists at the University of Arizona allocate roughly half the area to Northern Mexico and the other half to the United States. In Mexico this area is known as *el Gran Suroeste,* "the Grand Southwest.'"

(or Boca Madre), Boca de San Antonio, and Boca de Jesús María. These openings introduce saltwater from the Gulf of Mexico into the **Laguna Madre de Tamaulipas,** a 230-km-long intracoastal waterway enclosed by barrier islands.

Laguna Madre's brackish waters mingle with flows from the Ríos San Fernando and Soto la Marina to provide an unusually rich estuarine environment. Just north of Tampico, the Río San Rafael feeds the small Lago San Andrés, while the city itself sits on the northern edge of Lago Pueblo Viejo, an intracoastal lagoon formed by a meeting of the Gulf and Río Pánuco.

Sea of Cortez Coastal Plains

Wedged between the Sea of Cortez and the Sierra Madre Occidental, these narrow coastal plains extend from the Río Colorado delta in Sonora south to just north of Tepic, Nayarit. Al-though the Sea of Cortez coast is drier than its Gulf counterpart, irrigation systems using the Concepción, Sonora, Yaqui, Mayo, and Fuerte Rivers have created highly productive farming centers near Caborca, Hermosillo, Ciudad Obregón, Navojoa, and Los Mochis.

Deserts

North America holds four major deserts: the Great Basin, Mojave, Sonoran, and Chihuahuan. The first two are entirely within U.S. boundaries, while two-thirds of the Sonoran Desert and three-fourths of the Chihuahuan Desert lie in Northern Mexico.

The **Chihuahuan Desert** is the largest of the North American deserts, covering approximately 453,000 square km or 36% of the continent's total desert area. Centered on the Altiplano between the two arms of the Sierra Madre, the

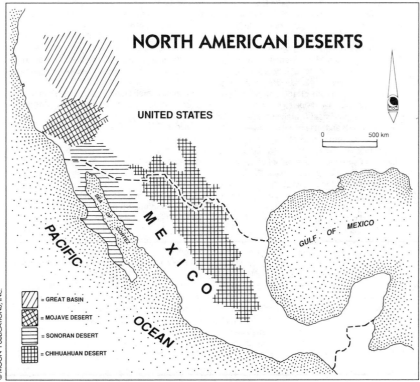

Chihuahuan is a high desert; elevations range from 700 meters above sea level in the lower basins to as high as 2,200 meters (7,200 feet) at the desert's southern end. The topography includes alluvial plains, *bajadas* (outwash plains), and low mountains.

Rainfall—most prominent in the winter months—ranges from just under 20 cm (eight inches) a year at lower elevations to 25 cm (10 inches) or more in desert grasslands near mountain ranges. This makes the Chihuahuan Desert one of the "wetter" North American deserts. Temperature ranges are extreme, varying from 40° C (104° F) in midsummer to well below freezing in winter. Citing these weather patterns, desert specialists typically classify the Chihuahuan

THE SEA OF CORTEZ

The Sea of Cortez was apparently named by Francisco de Ulloa after he sailed the entire perimeter of this body of water in 1539 and 1540 at the command of the most infamous of all Spanish conquistadors, Hernán Cortés. Four years previously Cortés had himself sailed the sea in an aborted attempt to colonize the peninsula. The name Mar de Cortés henceforth appeared intermittently on maps of the region, alternating with Mar Vermejo (Vermillion Sea, in reference to the color reflected from huge numbers of pelagic crabs) until the Mexican government officially renamed it the Gulf of California (Golfo de California) early in this century. Sailors, writers, and other assorted romanticists, however, have continued to call it by its older name.

The sea is roughly 1,125 km (700 miles) long, with an average width of 150 km (93 miles). Oceanographers have divided it into four regions based on the prominent characteristics—depth, bottom contours, and marine productivity—of each zone. The northern quarter of the gulf, between the Colorado River delta and the Midriff Islands, is shallow in relation to the zones farther south because of silt deposited by the Colorado River, which has also rounded the bottom contours. The sea here is highly saline due to evaporation and there is a tidal range of up to 10 meters (30 feet). Before the damming of the Colorado River, the tidal bore created when the seaward river currents met the incoming tide was powerful enough to sink ships.

The second region south encompasses the Midriff Islands, where basins reach depths of 820 meters (2,700 feet) and strong currents bring nutrients up from the bottom while aerating the water. This leads to a unusually high level of biological productivity, otherwise known as "good fishin'."

From the Midriff Islands to La Paz, basin depth doubles, silting is minimal, and water temperatures begin decreasing dramatically. The final sea zone below Culiacán is oceanic, with trenches and sub-marine canyons over 3,600 meters (12,000 feet) deep. Between the tip of Baja California Sur and Mazatlán, the Sea of Cortez meets the Pacific Ocean.

Of the 25 named islands in the Sea of Cortez, the largest is Isla Tiburón ("Shark Island"), a geological remnant of the mainland with an area of around 1,000 square kilometers. Because of their isolation, the Cortez islands feature a high number of endemic natural species; at least half of the 120 cactus varieties found on the islands are endemic. The Sea of Cortez is biologically the richest body of water on the planet, with over 800 species of marine vertebrates and over 2,000 invertebrates at last count. The reported number rises with the publication of each new marine study.

In order to protect the Cortez ecosystem from coastal industries and overfishing, the Mexican government plans to ask the United Nations for International Biosphere Reserve status for the northern Sea of Cortez and its surrounding shores. Whether or not the request is granted, the government has stated it will take steps to upgrade protection for the sea, which is finally being recognized as one of Mexico's greatest natural assets.

Two species native to the Cortez, **totoava** and **vaquita dolphin,** are of particular concern. According to government sources, gill-netting for the totoava (with a 70- to 100-ton yearly harvest) has severely threatened the vaquita, which is now thought to be the most endangered marine mammal in the world. The current vaquita population is estimated at only 200-500 individuals. Since the passage of new Mexican laws in 1993, the use of gill nets in the upper Sea of Cortez has become illegal. If the law is fully enforced, the vaquita may be able to bounce back as successfully as the California gray whale has (from around 250 worldwide in the 1930s to over 20,000 in the 1990s) since the U.S. Marine Mammal Protection Act of 1972.

Desert as a "warm-temperate desertland" comparable to the Saharan, Arabian, Indian, Mojave, and Iranian Deserts.

Most of this desert is underpinned by a layer of hard limestone (commonly known as caliche) and covered by a thin soil that supports over a thousand endemic plant species, predominantly grasses, yuccas, and agaves. Indicator plants—dominant species occurring only or mostly in the Chihuahuan Desert—include creosote bush, tarpaper bush, whitethorn acacia, lechugilla, peyote cactus, candelilla, and crucifixion thorn. Although cactus species are common, other desertscrub plants tend to outnumber them. Noticeably lacking are the various columnar cacti normally associated with the Sonoran Desert to the west; instead, locally dominant cacti include prickly pear, cane cholla, and other low-growing varieties. In spite of their low profile, the Cactaceae of the Chihuahuan Desert number some 250 species, more than in any other North American desert.

The **Sonoran Desert** is the third-largest North American desert, occupying about 221,000 square km or 21.5% of the continent's total desert area. It extends 12° in latitude, from the upper California-Nevada border south to the tip of the Baja California peninsula. On mainland Mexico it is limited to the Sea of Cortez coastal plains and the Río Colorado-Río Sonora alluvial plains of Sonora—essentially it is curtained from the Chihuahuan Desert by the Sierra Madre Occidental.

Like the Kalahari, Central Australian, and Patagonian Deserts, the Sonoran is classified as "tropical-subtropical" due to the relatively narrow differential between average summer and average winter temperatures.

The surface of the Sonoran Desert features a mix of volcanic, sedimentary, and metamorphic

rock. Volcanic activity from as recent as 1,300 years ago has left a number of striking craters and lava fields in the Pinacate region of northern Sonora. The topography is also unique for the number of year-round rivers traversing the desert from the Sierra Madre Occidental to the Sea of Cortez.

CLIMATE

Temperatures

Mexican geographers often divide their nation into three broad climatic zones: *tierra caliente* (hot land), sea level to 900 meters (3,000 feet); *tierra templada* (temperate land), 900-1,800 meters (3,000-6,000 feet); and *tierra fría* (cold land), over 1,800 meters (6,000 feet).

The Gulf of Mexico and Sea of Cortez plains are the lowest regions and have the warmest average year-round temperatures. In Ciudad Obregón, Son., for example, the average high temperature is 18° C (65° F) in January and 34° C (93° F) in July. The northern Altiplano is also hot in summer—parts of Coahuila, Nuevo León, and Tamaulipas often exceed 40° C (104° F) in July and August. And the hottest zones of all are found in the interior Sonoran Desert and in the Chihuahuan Desert's Bolsón de Mapimí, where the annual high and low are over 38° C (68° F) apart.

The coolest temperatures are found in the Sierra Madre mountain ranges. At higher altitudes in both cordilleras, the median annual temperature is 10° C (50° F); annual highs average 18° C (64.5° F), annual lows around 0° C (32° F). In January, snow is not uncommon in the Sierra Madre Occidental above 1,800 meters.

Precipitation

Generally, the highest rainfall in Northern Mexico occurs at the southern edge of the Sierra Madre Oriental, where the cordillera intersects with the Gulf coastal plains below the Tropic of Cancer, i.e., from the Huasteca region of San Luis Potosí east to Tampico, Tamaulipas. Here annual precipitation usually exceeds 150 cm (58.5 inches), most of this occurring in late summer. A similar weather pattern occurs on the Pacific coast in the vicinity of Mazatlán.

A dry, steppe climate dominates major parts of Zacatecas, Coahuila, Nuevo León, northwestern

---

ESTIMATING TEMPERATURE CHANGES

For every degree of latitude farther south you travel, figure a temperature increase of 2° C (3.5° F). For each 100-meter increase in altitude, figure a temperature drop of 2° C.

San Luis Potosí, northern Durango, and the western Sierra Madre Oriental, with less than 75 cm (29 inches) annual precipitation below the Tropic of Cancer and less than 60 cm (23 inches) above the parallel. Most of this rainfall occurs during the summer months.

The Sonoran and northern Sinaloan plains and the center of the Altiplano (eastern Chihuahua and most of Coahuila) feature a dry, desertic climate with annual rainfall of fewer than 25

cm (10 inches). Rains are sporadic and intense, usually occurring in the early fall and spring.

Light, sporadic rains distributed year-round are typical in central and northwestern Tamaulipas and in northern Nuevo León. In the southern half of Tamaulipas rainfall tends to be more concentrated in the summer months. Throughout this zone the average annual precipitation is around 60 cm (23 inches). A similar pattern occurs on the lower western slopes of the Sierra

RIO GRANDE/BRAVO

The fifth longest river in North America, the Rio Grande—called Río Bravo in Mexico—has its source at 3,660 meters (12,000 feet) above sea level in Colorado's Rocky Mountains. From there it flows southeast through Colorado and New Mexico, then along the Texas-Mexico border for more than half its length until it empties into the Gulf of Mexico, for a total distance of 3,052 km (1,896 miles). Its principal tributaries are the Pecos, Devil, Chama, and Puerco Rivers in the U.S. and the Salado, San Juan, and Conchos Rivers in Mexico. All are important sources of water in a region that generally receives little rainfall. The major portion of the river's volume, however, is provided by Mexican tributaries; the only U.S. affluent of significance is the Pecos River in Texas.

Archaeological evidence indicates that Amerindian groups had inhabited rock shelters along the river for 10,000-12,000 years before the Spanish *entrada.* Still-visible Coahuiltecan pictographs on the walls of Seminole Canyon near Ciudad Acuña are at least 4,000 years old. The Upper Rio Grande Valley near Ciudad Juárez is the oldest irrigated region in Mexico and the oldest continually cultivated area in North America. The Patarabueyes, a Pueblo Indian group, had been tilling the flood plains since at least A.D. 1200 when the Spanish arrived at La Junta in the 1600s.

The Spanish first explored the river, which they originally called Río de las Palmas, in the 1500s, settling on the riverbanks in the 17th and 18th centuries. By the mid-19th century, steamboat traffic extended northwestward from the Gulf of Mexico as far as Camargo, roughly 170 km (105 miles) upriver.

Nowadays water from the river is so heavily diverted for agricultural use on both sides of the border near Ciudad Juárez/El Paso that the Rio Grande nearly comes to a halt until it is joined farther down

by Mexico's Río Conchos at Ojinaga, Chihuahua. Then, for 150 km (93 miles) or so, the Rio Grande follows the southern boundary of Big Bend National Park, flowing through three high-walled canyons (the Santa Elena, the Mariscal, and the Boquillas) that are favorite destinations of river runners.

One of the most pristine sections of the lower Rio Grande is a 70-mile stretch between the Mexican village of Guerrero and the Colombia Bridge north of Laredo. A *San Antonio Express-News* reporter who recently spent four days kayaking this reach wrote that he was amazed by the variety of indigenous wildlife, including great blue and white herons, snowy and cattle egrets, owls, four-foot alligator gars, carp, catfish, bass, white-tailed deer, javelinas, and mountain lions—almost everything native to South Texas except humans.

Major cities along the Rio Grande/Río Bravo's course include Albuquerque, El Paso, and Brownsville in the U.S., and Ciudad Juárez, Nuevo Laredo, Reynosa, and Matamoros in Mexico. Two major international dams, the Presa Amistad (near Ciudad Acuña) and Presa Falcón (near Nuevo Laredo), have been built along the river to provide water storage through protracted dry periods and to prevent flooding downriver during heavy rains.

Albuquerque, New Mexico, is the only U.S. city that dumps sewage into the river as a matter of standard practice; many Mexican municipalities do. According to the U.S. Environmental Protection Agency, all the major human centers along the river—except, surprisingly, Ciudad Juárez-El Paso—have sewage problems of varying degrees.

Since the passage of NAFTA, the Mexican and U.S. governments have promised to share the US$35 million tab for a new water treatment plant in Nuevo Laredo, Mexico. Similar projects are planned for Matamoros, Ciudad Acuña, and Reynosa.

Madre Oriental and lower eastern slopes of the Sierra Madre Occidental.

The higher elevations (coniferous zones) of the Sierra Madre cordilleras receive up to 120 cm (47 inches) of annual rainfall, most of it falling during the summer months.

BIOTIC COMMUNITIES

Although Northern Mexico is often described simply as a region of "mountain islands and desert seas," the geographic interplay of mountains, valleys, basins, seas, and rivers—not to mention nearly 10 degrees variation in latitude and 16 degrees in longitude—has formed over 30 major biomes (separate, ecosystem-based biotic communities) that can be broadly grouped into five biogeographic provinces: Chihuahuan, Tamaulipan, Madrean, Sonoran, and Sinaloan. The vegetational zones across these divisions encompass forests and woodlands, scrublands, grasslands, desertlands, and wetlands.

Forests and Woodlands

In Northern Mexico, forests and woodlands are for the most part found in the Sierra Madre cordilleras. At the higher elevations in Coahuila, Durango, and Chihuahua, two types of **Madrean montane conifer forests** are common: ponderosa pine forest and, on scattered peaks in the 2,000- to 3,000-meter range, a mixed conifer

AVERAGE TEMPERATURES AND PRECIPITATION FOR SELECTED CITIES

CITY	JAN.	APRIL	JULY	OCT.
Chihuahua, Chih.	9.4°C/49°F 25 cm/.1 in	18.3°C/65°F .76 cm/.3 in	25°C/77°F 7.9 cm/3.2 in	18.3°C/65°F 3.6 cm/1.4 in
Ciudad Obregón, Son.	18.3°C/65°F .69 cm/.27 in	25°C/77°F .41 cm/.16 in	33.9°C/93°F .69 cm/.27 in	29.4°C/85°F 1.45 cm/.57 in
Creel, Chih.	5°C/41°F 4.83 cm/1.9 in	10°C/50°F 1.4 cm/.55 in	17.2°C/63°F 13.5 cm/5.3 in	12.2°C/54°F 6.6 cm/2.6 in
Culiacán, Sin.	19.4°C/67°F 1 cm/.4 in	23.3°C/74°F 0 cm/0 in	28.3°C/83°F 14.7 cm/5.8 in	26.7°C/80°F 4.06 cm/1.6 in
Durango, Dgo.	11.7°C/53°F 1.3 cm/.05 in	18.3°C/65°F .25 cm/.01 in	20.6°C/69°F 12.5 cm/4.9 in	17.8°C/64°F 3 cm/1.2 in
Guaymas, Son.	17.8°C/64°F .76 cm/.3 in	22.8°C/73°F .25 cm/.1 in	30.5°C/87°F 4.57 cm/1.8 in	27.2°C/81°F 1.02 cm/.4 in
Hermosillo, Son.	15.5°C/60°F .25 cm/.1 in	22.7°C/73°F .25 cm/.1 in	32°C/90°F 7.1 cm/2.8 in	26°C/79°F 4 cm/1.6 in
Mazatlán, Sin.	19.4°C/67°F 1.3 cm/.5 in	21°C/70°F 0 cm/0 in	27.2°C/81°F 16.7 cm/6.6 in	26°C/79°F 6.1 cm/2.4 in
Monterrey, N.L.	15°C/59°F 2.03 cm/.8 in	23.3°C/74°F 2.8 cm/1.1 in	27.2°C/81°F 7.4 cm/2.9 in	22.2°C/72°F 11 cm/4.3 in
San Luis Potosí, S.L.P.	12.8°C/55°F 1.3 cm/.5 in	20.6°C/69°F .51 cm/.2 in	19.4°C/67°F 5.8 cm/2.3 in	17.2°C/63°F 1.8 cm/.7 in
Tampico, Tamps.	18.3°C/65°F 5.3 cm/2.1 in	25°C/77°F 1 cm/.4 in	27.8°C/82°F 14.7 cm/5.8 in	25.5°C/78°F 17.8 cm/7.0 in
Torreón, Coah.	12.2°C/54°F 1.3 cm/.5 in	21°C/70°F .51 cm/.2 in	26.6°C/80°F 5.3 cm/2.1 in	23.3°C/74°F 2.3 cm/.9 in
Zacatecas, Zac.	9.4°C/49°F 1 cm/.4 in	15°C/59°F .25 cm/.1 in	13.9°C/57°F 8.9 cm/3.5 in	13.3°C/56°F 2.3 cm/.9 in

forest of Douglas fir, white fir, limber pine, and aspen.

At 1,000-2,000 meters along these same slopes, **Madrean evergreen woodland** is encountered. Mild winters and wet summers produce several varieties of evergreen oaks (live oaks) at this elevation, along with alligator-bark juniper, one-seed juniper, and piñon pine (Mexican pinyon). Although often called a "transition" forest, the Madrean evergreen woodlands are florally distinct from the vegetational zones above and below them. In Mexico these areas are sometimes called *encinal,* meaning woodlands dominated by evergreen oaks (encinos). Another commonly heard term is "pine-oak woodland."

Tropical-subtropical deciduous forests occur on the lower (300-1,050 meters) and warmer foothills of the Sierras Madre. On the Occidental side, the **Sinaloan deciduous forest** is mostly confined to steep canyon areas in southern Sonora and northern Sinaloa, and is particularly profuse in the vicinity of Alamos, Sonora. Usually bordered by Madrean evergreen woodland, the forest is characterized by tropical elements, including hydromorphic fig, lianas, orchids, and bromeliads; common trees include Coulter acacia, bursera (torote), palo colorado, copalquín, cassia, and several trees endemic to Sinaloa whose names only keen botanists and locals know, such as Jarilla chocola, a semitropical tree common in the sierra foothills. Most of these

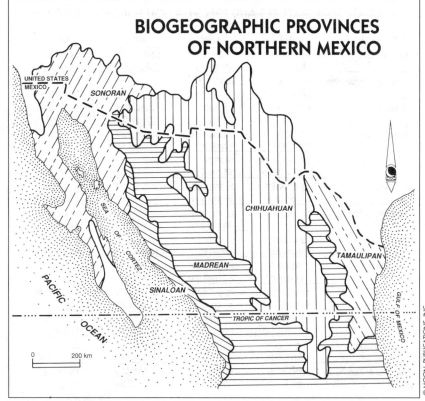

BIOGEOGRAPHIC PROVINCES OF NORTHERN MEXICO

UNITED STATES
MEXICO

SONORAN

SEA OF CORTEZ

CHIHUAHUAN

MADREAN

TAMAULIPAN

PACIFIC

SINALOAN

GULF OF MEXICO

OCEAN

TROPIC OF CANCER

0   200 km

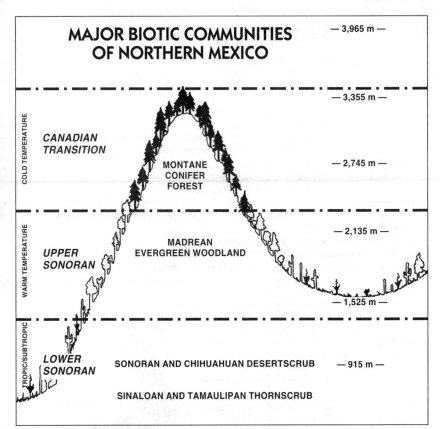

MAJOR BIOTIC COMMUNITIES OF NORTHERN MEXICO

— 3,965 m —

— 3,355 m —

COLD TEMPERATURE

CANADIAN TRANSITION

MONTANE CONIFER FOREST

— 2,745 m —

— 2,135 m —

WARM TEMPERATURE

UPPER SONORAN

MADREAN EVERGREEN WOODLAND

— 1,525 m —

TROPIC/SUBTROPIC

LOWER SONORAN

SONORAN AND CHIHUAHUAN DESERTSCRUB — 915 m —

SINALOAN AND TAMAULIPAN THORNSCRUB

plants are drought-deciduous; that is, they alternate periods of growth with periods of dormancy through two wet and two dry seasons. Hence the Sinaloan deciduous forest typically features a heavy summer foliage while looking rather bare during the arid winter months.

The Sierra Madre Oriental's counterpart is the **Tamaulipan semideciduous forest,** which extends from the Rio Grande Valley in Texas southward to Ciudad Victoria, along the lower eastern escarpment of the cordillera. Common vegetation includes honey mesquite, Texas ebony, granjeno, winged elm, hackberry, and huisache. In many areas tree branches are festooned with Spanish moss, especially near rivers where Montezuma bald cypress (called *sabino* in

Mexico) is the dominant tree.

A bit further south along the eastern Sierra Madre Oriental is the little-known **Tamaulipan cloud forest,** the northernmost cloud forest habitat in the Americas. (Mexico has two other cloud forests, one each in Veracruz and Chiapas.) It lies just above the southern reaches of the Tamaulipan subtropical deciduous forest in the area of Gómez Farías, Tamps., at an elevation of 900-1,500 meters (3,000-5,000 feet). As its name suggests, this forest receives much of the water necessary for growth from cloud cover (formed by moist air from the Gulf) that blankets the area most of the year. Dominant trees here are evergreen oaks, sweet gum, wild cherry, magnolia, maple, hickory, beech, and Mexican alder.

(continues on page 18)

NORTHERN MEXICO WILDLIFE[†]

Common Name; *Scientific Name;* Common Habitat

MAMMALS

antelope jackrabbit; *Lepus alleni;* Sinaloan thornscrub, savanna grassland

Apache squirrel; *Sciuris nayaritensis;* Madrean evergreen woodland

Arizona pocket mouse; *Perognathus amplus;* Sonoran desertscrub

big brown bat; *Eptesicus fuscus;* Madrean conifer forest, riparian tropical-subtropical deciduous forest

blacktailed jackrabbit; *Lepus californicus;* semidesert grassland, Sonoran desertscrub

bobcat; *Felis rufus baileyi;* Sinaloan thornscrub

cactus mouse; *Peromyscus eremicus;* Sonoran desertscrub

California myotis; *Myotis californicus;* Sonoran desertscrub

cliff chipmunk; *Eutamias dorsalis;* interior chaparral

coati; *Nasua nasua;* Madrean evergreen woodland, Sinaloan deciduous forest, Sinaloan riparian evergreen forest/woodland

coyote; *Canis latrans;* semidesert grassland, Sonoran desertscrub

deer mouse; *Peromyscus maniculatus;* Madrean conifer forest

desert bighorn sheep; *Ovis canadensis mexicana;* Chihuahuan desertscrub

desert cottontail; *Sylvilagus auduboni;* Chihuahuan and Sonoran desertscrub, Chihuahuan and Sonoran riparian scrubland

desert muledeer; *Odocoileus hemionus crooki;* Chihuahuan and Sonoran desertscrub

eastern cottontail; *Silvilagus floridanus;* Madrean conifer

elk; *Cervus elaphus;* Petran and Madrean conifer forests, Madrean evergreen woodland, interior chaparral

feral burro; *Equus asinus;* Sonoran desertscrub

gray fox; *Urocyon cinereoargenteus;* Sonoran desertscrub

gray wolf; *Canis lupus;* Madrean conifer forest

jaguar; *Felis onca;* riparian tropical-subtropical deciduous forest, Sinaloan riparian evergreen forest/woodland

jaguarundi; *Felis yagouraoundi;* Sinaloan and Tamaulipan thornscrub

javelina (collared peccary); *Dicotyles tajacu;* Sinaloan thornscrub, semidesert grassland, savanna grassland, Sonoran desertscrub

kit fox; *Vulpes macrotus;* Sonoran desertscrub

margay; *Felis weidii;* Sinaloan deciduous forest

Merriam's kangaroo rat; *Dopodomys merriami;* semidesert grassland, Chihuahuan and Sonoran desertscrub

Mexican cottontail; *Sciurus truei;* Sinaloan deciduous forest

Mexican grizzly bear; *Ursus arctos;* Madrean evergreen woodland

Mexican longnosed bat; *Leptonycteris nivalis;* Madrean evergreen woodland

mule deer; *Odocoileus hemionus;* Madrean conifer forest, interior chaparral, semidesert grassland

blacktailed jackrabbit

BOB RACE

[†] Rather than an exhaustive listing, this is a selective presentation of noteworthy (either very common or very unusual) fauna found throughout Northern Mexico.

NORTHERN MEXICO WILDLIFE

Common Name; *Scientific Name;* Common Habitat

MAMMALS (continued)

ocelot; *Felis pardalis;* Sinaloan and Tamaulipan thornscrub, Sinaloan riparian evergreen forest/woodland

pronghorn; *Antilocapra americana;* semidesert grassland

raccoon; *Procyon lotor;* riparian scrubland, riparian tropical-subtropical deciduous forest

ringtailed cat; *Bassariscus astutus;* Sonoran desertscrub

Sonoran pronghorn; *Antilocapra americana sonorensis;* Sonoran desertscrub

Texas antelope ground squirrel; *Ammospermophilus interpres;* Chihuahuan desertscrub

white-tailed deer; *Odocoileus virgianus;* Madrean conifer forest, Madrean evergreen woodland, Sinaloan deciduous forest, semidesert grassland, montane riparian wetland

BIRDS

bald eagle; *Haliaeetus leucocephalus;* riparian tropical-subtropical deciduous forest

belted kingfisher; *Megaceryle alcyon;* montane riparian wetland

black-bellied tree duck; *Dendrocygna autumnalis;* Sinaloan riparian evergreen forest/woodland

black brant; *Branta nigricans;* interior and maritime marshlands

black-crowned night heron; *Nycticorax nycticorax;* interior and maritime marshlands

blue-winged teal; *Anas discors;* interior and maritime marshlands

broad-tailed hummingbird; *Selasphorus platycercus;* montane riparian wetland

burrowing owl; *Athene cunicularia;* semidesert grassland, Sonoran desertscrub

bushtit; *Psaltriparus minimus;* interior chaparral

cactus wren; *Campylorhynchus brunneicapillus;* semidesert grassland, Chihuahuan and Sonoran desertscrub

canyon wren; *Catherpes mexicanus;* interior chaparral

caracara; *Caracara cheriway;* savanna grassland

Colima warbler; *Vermivora crissalis;* Madrean evergreen woodland

curved-bill thrasher; *Toxostoma curvirostra;* semidesert grassland, Chihuahuan and Sonoran desertscrub

eared trogon; *Eupilotis neoxenus;* Madrean conifer forest

elf owl; *Micrathene whitneyi;* Sonoran desertscrub

emerald toucanet; *Aulacorhynchus prasinus;* cloud forest

Gould's turkey; *Meleagris gallopavo mexicana;* Madrean conifer forest, Madrean evergreen woodland

goshawk; *Accipter gentilis;* Madrean conifer forest

great blue heron; *Ardea herodias;* riparian tropical-subtropical deciduous forest

greater yellowlegs; *Totanus melanoleucus;* interior and maritime marshlands

green parakeet; *Aratinga holochlora;* Sinaloan riparian evergreen forest/woodland

Harris' hawk; *Parabuteo unicinctus;* Sinaloan thornscrub, Sonoran desertscrub

imperial woodpecker; *Campephilus imperialis;* Madrean conifer forest

ladder-backed woodpecker; *Picoides scalaris;* semidesert grassland, Sonoran desertscrub

lilac-crowned parrot; *Amazonia finschi;* Sinaloan riparian evergreen forest/woodland

long-billed marsh wren; *Cistothorus palustris;* interior and maritime marshlands

mangrove cuckoo; *Coccyzus minor;* mangrove   *(continues)*

NORTHERN MEXICO WILDLIFE

Common Name; *Scientific Name;* Common Habitat

BIRDS (continued)

masked bobwhite; *Colinus virgianianus ridgwayi;* savanna grassland, Sonoran desertscrub

Mexican duck; *Anas platyrhynchos diazi;* interior and maritime marshlands

Mexican jay; *Aphelocoma ultramarina;* Madrean evergreen woodland

military macaw; *Ara militaris;* Sinaloan riparian evergreen forest/woodland

Montezuma quail; *Crytonyx montezumae;* Madrean evergreen woodland

mourning dove; *Zenaida macroura;* semidesert grassland, Chihuahuan and Sonoran desertscrub, Chihuahuan and Sonoran riparian scrubland, riparian tropical-subtropical deciduous forest

pectoral sandpiper; *Calidris melanotos;* interior and maritime marshlands

roadrunner (paisano); *Geococcyx californianus;* semidesert grassland, Chihuahuan and Sonoran desertscrub

prairie falcon; *Falco mexicanus;* semidesert grassland

pygmy owl; *Glaucidium gnoma;* Madrean conifer forest

roseate spoonbill; *Ajaia ajaia;* mangrove, tidal scrubland

sandhill crane; *Himantopus mexicana;* interior and maritime marshlands

Scott's oriole; *Icterus parisorum;* Chihuahuan desertscrub

Sinaloa wren; *Thryothorus sinaloa;* Sinaloan thornscrub

snow goose; *Chen caerulescens;* interior and maritime marshlands

thick-billed parrot; *Rhyncopsitta pachyrhyncha;* Madrean conifer forest

violet-crowned hummingbird; *Amazilia violiceps;* Madrean evergreen woodland

warbling vireo; *Vireo gilvus;* montane riparian wetland

white-necked raven; *Corvus cryptoleucus;* Chihuahuan desertscrub

white-winged dove; *Zenaida asiatica;* Sinaloan and Tamaulipan thornscrub, Sonoran desertscrub, riparian tropical-subtropical deciduous forest, riparian scrubland

wild turkey; *Meleagris gallopavo;* montane riparian wetland

willet; *Catotrophorus semipalmatus;* interior and maritime marshlands

yellow-billed cuckoo; *Coccyzus americanus;* riparian tropical-subtropical deciduous forest

AMPHIBIANS AND REPTILES

Arizona alligator lizard; *Gerrhonotus kingi;* Madrean conifer forest, interior chaparral, montane riparian wetland, interior and maritime marshlands

Arizona coral snake; *Micruriodes euryxanthus;* Sonoran desertscrub, semidesert grassland

beaded lizard; *Heloderma horridum;* Sinaloan deciduous forest

boa constrictor; *Constrictor constrictor;* Sinaloan deciduous forest, Sinaloan riparian evergreen forest/woodland

bolson turtle; *Gopherus flavomarginatus;* Chihuahuan desertscrub

canyon treefrog; *Hyla arenicolor;* montane riparian wetland

chuckwalla; *Sauromalus obesus;* Sonoran desertscrub

Coahuila box turtle; *Terrapene coahuila;* interior and maritime marshlands

desert box turtle; *Terrapene ornata luteola;* semidesert grassland

NORTHERN MEXICO WILDLIFE

Common Name; *Scientific Name;* Common Habitat

AMPHIBIANS AND REPTILES (continued)

desert iguana; *Dipsosaurus dorsalis;* Sonoran desertscrub

desert striped whipsnake; *Masticophis taeniatus;* interior chaparral

desert tortoise; *Gopherus agassizi;* Sonoran desertscrub

fringe-toed lizard; *Uma notata;* Sonoran desertscrub

giant toad; *Bufo marinus;* Sinaloan riparian evergreen forest/woodland

gila monster; *Heloderma suspectum;* Sonoran desertscrub

iguana; *Iguana iguana;* Sinaloan deciduous forest

leopard frog; *Rana pipiens;* Sinaloan riparian evergreen forest/woodland

Mexican garter snake; *Thamnophis eques;* montane riparian wetland

Mohave rattlesnake; *Crotalus scutulatus;* Chihuahuan desertscrub

mountain skink; *Eumeces callicephalus;* Madrean conifer forest

mountain treefrog; *Hyla eximia;* montane riparian wetland

red diamondback rattlesnake; *Crotalus ruber;* Sonoran desertscrub

regal horned lizard; *Phrynosoma solare;* Sonoran desertscrub

reticulated gecko; *Coleonyx reticulatus;* Chihuahuan desertscrub

reticulated gila monster; *Heloderma suspectum suspectum;* Sonoran desertscrub

rosy boa; *Lichanura trivirgata;* Sonoran desertscrub

roundtail horned lizard; *Phrynosoma modestum;* Chihuahuan desertscrub

sidewinder; *Crotalus cerastes;* Chihuahuan and Sonoran desertscrub

softshell turtle; *Trionyx ater;* interior and maritime marshlands

Sonoran green toad; *Bufo retiformis;* savanna grassland, Sonoran desertscrub

Sonoran mountain kingsnake; *Lampropeltis pyromelana;* Madrean conifer forest, interior chaparral

southwestern earless lizard; *Holbrookia texana scitula;* semidesert grassland

Tarahumara salamander; *Ambystoma rosaceum;* montane riparian wetland

Texas banded gecko; *Coleonyx brevis;* Chihuahuan desertscrub

Texas lyre snake; *Trimorphodon biscutatus vilkinsoni;* interior chaparral

Trans-Pecos rat snake; *Elaphe subocularis;* Chihuahuan desertscrub

tree lizard; *Urosaurus ornatus;* Sinaloan thornscrub, Sonoran desertscrub, riparian tropical-subtropical deciduous forest

western diamondback rattlesnake; *Crotalus atrox;* Chihuahuan desertscrub

western rattlesnake; *Crotalus viridis;* Madrean conifer forest, interior chaparral

FISH ††

blue catfish; *Ictalurus furcatus;* riparian scrubland

channel catfish; *Ictalurus punctatus;* riparian scrubland

Chihuahua chub; *Gila nigresens;* interior and maritime marshlands

Chihuahuan shiner; *Notropis chihuahua;* riparian scrubland

desert pupfish; *Cymatogaster macularius;* interior and maritime marshlands

European brown trout; *Salmo trutta;* montane riparian wetland   *(continues)*

NORTHERN MEXICO WILDLIFE

Common Name; *Scientific Name;* Common Habitat

FISH (continued)

gila trout; *Salmo gilae;* montane riparian wetland

golden shiner; *Notemigonus crysoleucus;* montane riparian wetland

largemouth bass; *Micropterus salmoides;* riparian tropical-subtropical deciduous forest, Sinaloan riparian evergreen forest/woodland

Mexican golden trout; *Salmo chrysogaster;* montane riparian wetland

Mexican stoneroller; *Campostoma ornatum;* riparian scrubland, riparian tropical-subtropical deciduous forest, Sinaloan riparian evergreen forest/woodland

mosquitofish; *Gambusia affinis;* riparian scrubland, riparian tropical-subtropical deciduous forest

rainbow trout; *Salmo gairdneri;* montane riparian wetland

smallmouth bass; *Micropterus dolomieui;* riparian tropical-subtropical deciduous forest

speckled chub; *Hybopis aestivalis;* riparian scrubland

striped bass; *Morone saxatilis;* riparian tropical-subtropical deciduous forest

Tamaulipan shiner; *Notropis braytoni;* riparian scrubland

tilapia; *Tilapia* various species; Sonoran riparian deciduous forest

†† For saltwater fishing see "Fishing," p. 50

Scrublands

Drier mountain slopes in northeastern Chihuahua, Coahuila, and Nuevo León feature interior chaparral (sometimes described as "Mediterranean-type" terrain) at elevations of around 1,500-2,450 meters (5,000-8,000 feet). Occasionally chaparral occurs along the lower borders of Madrean evergreen woodlands. Typical interior chaparral species encountered near the Sierra Madre Occidental include shrub live oak, manzanita, mountain laurel, hollyleaf buckthorn, and desert olive. These are often mixed with Sonoran thornscrub elements such as catclaw and mesquite, as well as crucifixion thorn, jojoba, yucca, and other desertland species.

In Coahuila and Nuevo León, interior chaparral near the Sierra Madre Oriental is typically dominated by various shrub live oaks (Coahuila shrub oak, Pringle oak, Vasey oak), Texas madrone, silktassel, sugar sumac, chaparral ash, and various sages. As in the Occidental ranges, small numbers of thornscrub and desertland species are often found in these eastern chaparrals.

Tropical-subtropical scrublands at lower elevations toward or below the Tropic of Cancer usually take the form of thornscrub (also known as thorn forest or, in Mexico, as *matorral).* A transitional community between desertscrub and woodlands, thornscrubs are characterized by thorny, multitrunked trees and shrubs with a canopy between two and eight meters in height.

As with interior chaparral, separate versions exist for the Sea of Cortez and Gulf of Mexico sides of the continent. The west coast version, **Sinaloan thornscrub** (or Sinaloan thorn forest), covers much of southern Sonora and northern Sinaloa with brasil, bursera, acacia, paloverde, hopbush, brittlebush, guayacan, tree ocotillo, and palo blanco, interspersed with cactus (particularly pitahaya or organ-pipe cactus, *hecho,* and prickly pear) and herbaceous shrubs. Many Sinaloan thornscrub species are drought-deciduous, alternating periods of growth with periods of dormancy through two wet and two dry seasons.

On the Gulf side, **Tamaulipan thornscrub** (or Tamaulipan thorn forest) is centered in northern Tamaulipas but now extends into southern Texas, where it has invaded former grasslands destroyed by overgrazing. Like its Sinaloan counterpart, Tamaulipan thornscrub is found below 1,000 meters between desertscrub communities and either tropical deciduous forests or Madrean evergreen woodlands. Because the coastal plains of Tamaulipas receive significantly more rainfall than the western plains of Sonora and Sinaloa, fewer of the Tamaulipan species are drought-deciduous. Dominant trees and shrubs include mesquite, acacia, cenizo, huisache, hackberry, strangler fig, and breadnut tree, interspersed with small cactus species.

Grasslands

Large tracts of land in the Altiplano consist of **semidesert grasslands** (often incorrectly called desert grasslands), or in Mexico *pastizal,* a transitional zone of dominant perennial grass-scrub that occurs between desertscrub and either chaparral or evergreen woodland. This type of grassland is found mostly within Chihuahuan Desert areas of 1,100-1,400 meters (3,600-4,600 feet) in Chihuahua, western Coahuila, Nuevo León, and Zacatecas. In northeastern Sonora, it also occurs just above Sinaloan thornscrub.

Tobosa grass and black grama are major indicators for semidesert grassland, and are often mixed in with other grasses (buffalo grass, various other gramas), scrub (acacia, mesquite), and various cacti and succulents (particularly ocotillo, yucca, sotol, barrel cactus, and prickly pear).

In areas where rainfall is more plentiful, usually farther south toward the Tropic of Cancer, grasses intensify to produce **savanna grassland.** Perennial grasses are thicker in a savanna and are interspersed with woody trees and shrubs.

THE BURRO

L ong-eared, slow-plodding, dim-witted—the quintessential beast of burden: this is the city person's image of *Equus asinus*. But to rural Mexicans the donkey or burro is an image of strength and surefootedness. Compared to the horse, its taller, more graceful-appearing cousin, the burro is a far more useful animal in mountainous or arid domains. On slopes, rocky surfaces, or sand it moves with more agility and is able to keep a load—whether human or inanimate—more balanced. Standing only about 3.5 feet high at the shoulder, burros can also cover greater distances on less water and food than horses; they actually seem to prefer rough forage such as dead cactus or thorny paloverde over nutrient-rich grasses.

JOE CUMMINGS

Although a burro's coloring may vary from light to dark brown, its withers are almost always marked with a cross of darker hair. This cross is said to be a symbol of divine protection for having carried Mary and the infant Christ from Egypt to the Holy Land. Amid the arid plains of Northern Mexico, a burro certainly takes on a biblical aura.

Unknown numbers of wild burros roam northwestern Mexico, particularly in desertscrub areas of the Sonoran Desert and in the canyons of the Sierra Madre Occidental. Ranchers or campesinos will occasionally capture a wild burro for domestic use as they are fairly easy to tame (the burro's legendary stubbornness can often be attributed to mistreatment by its owner; a well-cared-for animal is usually quite loyal). The wild male burro or "jack" is considered the best stud for producing a mule, so ranchers occasionally turn mares loose to breed with them. Mules produced from such a union are especially hardy.

Trekkers occasionally hire burros or mules as pack animals in Northern Mexico's canyons and sierras. For long forays, it is sometimes cheaper to purchase one outright rather than pay a daily hire rate; prices range from around US$40 for a poor animal to around US$75 for an exemplary one—if you can find a rancher willing to sell one. If the price doesn't include an *aparejo* (a leather-and-wood pack saddle for carrying cargo), you'll have to buy one or have one made—they're inexpensive. Also useful are a pair of *cascateles,* square wooden crates that hold materials to be fastened to the *aparejo.* If possible, have a veterinarian inspect the animal for diseases before agreeing on a purchase.

Desertlands

At elevations below the semidesert grasslands lie the deserts, of which Northern Mexico holds two: the Sonoran and Chihuahuan. It isn't mere aridity that makes a desert distinctive but also the range of biologic responses to aridity. Because periods of rain are so infrequent, resident species have adapted to make use of "ephemeral habitats"—those that exist only temporarily—to carry out the breeding and feeding necessary for survival; typically desert plants and animals are dormant or torpid between seasons of activity. What distinguishes one desert from another is the range of endemic or dominant species present.

The driest areas of the warm, temperate Chihuahuan Desert between the Sierras Madre produce low **Chihuahuan desertscrub,** typified by lechugilla, tarpaper bush, creosote bush, ocotillo, shrub mesquite, various yuccas and agaves, saltbush, sandpaper bush, cholla, acacias, sage, and a number of Cactacaea that grow close to the ground such as barrel cactus (biznaga), rainbow cactus, hedgehog cactus, peyote cactus, prickly pear, and desert Christmas cactus. Tall cacti tend to be absent from the Chihuahuan desertscape.

West of the Sierra Madre Occidental and north of Guaymas, the subtropical Sonoran Desert features **Sonoran desertscrub.** Like their Chihuahuan neighbors, the Sonoran desertlands feature a number of agaves, yuccas, acacias, ocotillos, and barrel cacti. Because of longer wet seasons and warmer temperatures, most of the Sonoran varieties of these plants are larger; this is especially true of ocotillos and yuccas. The peculiar **cirio** or "boojum tree," a 12- to 15-meter (40- to 50-foot), candle-shaped succulent related to the ocotillo, is a Sonoran endemic that grows only in a limited area north of Bahía Kino (and across the Sea of Cortez in Baja California). Sonoran desertlands also produce numerous endemic tree species, including *torote blanco* (elephant tree), paloverde, smoke tree, and *palo fierro* (ironwood).

For many visitors, Sonoran desert vegetation is generally typified by three large, tall, columnar cacti species that impart the classic Southwestern desert look: pitahaya or organ-pipe cactus, saguaro, and cardón. As the world's tallest cactus, the cardón can reach as high as 18 meters (60 feet) and weigh as much as 12 tons, though more commonly it tops out at 7.5-9 meters (25-30 feet). The giant, pale-green trunks feature 11-17 vertical ribs and sometimes measure three feet thick. The cardón is often confused with the smaller saguaro cactus; one major difference is that the branches of the cardón tend to be more vertical than those of the saguaro.

Wetlands

Although Northern Mexico is generally thought of as arid territory, a remarkable number of wetland habitats exist around rivers, seacoasts, lakes, springs, *tinajas* (rock pools), and seasonal streams and basins. You'll find **montane riparian wetlands** along mountain rivers of the Sierras Madre; **riparian deciduous forests** and **riparian evergreen woodlands** along lower slope riverbanks; **riparian scrublands** where streams run through scrublands; **maritime marshlands** along the Gulf of Mexico and Sea of Cortez coasts; and **interior marshlands** surrounding lakes and desert *bolsones* (drainage basins). The Gulf coast also has areas where interior and maritime marshlands commingle along barrier-island lagoons.

Wetlands biology is extremely complex; saltmarshes, for example, represent the most concentrated biomass on the planet (exceeding even tropical rainforests). To begin to enumerate even the basic indicator species for each of these habitats is well beyond the scope of a travel guidebook. Certain characteristics for some of these biomes are described under the corresponding destination sections later in this guide; readers with a keen interest in Northern Mexico wetlands should scan the "References" section at the end of this book for further sources.

prickly pear cactus

HISTORY

PRE-CORTESIAN HISTORY

Paleo-Indian and Desert-Archaic Cultures
Scattered evidence of human habitation in Northern Mexico dates back at least 10,000 years. Human skeletons, metates (grinding stones), and pictographs found in parts of Mexico near the Río Bravo river system and further west in Chihuahua indicate a Paleo-Indian (or Clovis-Folsom) presence—among the earliest known cultures in North America. The Paleo-Indians of Northern Mexico are believed to be descendants of Asian tribes that migrated across the Bering Strait to North America from the Asian continent some 50,000 years ago.

The distribution of artifacts suggests that the Paleo-Indian groups were nomadic and small in number, and that they relied on small game and forage for food. It isn't known whether their cultures later evolved into more advanced cultures or whether they were supplanted by other migrants, but by the time the Ice Age ended around 5000 B.C., the slightly more advanced Desert Archaic culture had developed in pockets across the north.

Archaic Indian groups such as the San Dieguitos of the Río Colorado delta or the Chihuahua Cochise of the northern Sierra Madre Occidental spent much of the year wandering in small migratory bands of 15 to 20, searching for freshwater sources, hunting, fishing, and gathering edible wild plants. Archaeological remains include circles of stones, stone tools —choppers, raspers, knives, spear points, ax heads, mortars (metates) —and simple pottery.

Gradually the Amerindian cultures of Northern Mexico breached a cultural watershed as the development of agriculture allowed nomadic groups to slow or halt their wanderings. Current evidence indicates that the earliest agriculture in Northern Mexico or the U.S. Southwest can be traced

Clovis points

LOUISE FOOTE

to the La Junta culture centered around present-day Ojinaga, Chihuahua, in the upper Río Bravo (Rio Grande) valley; the flood plains here are considered to be the oldest agricultural region in North America. Early agricultural techniques were also developed by the Río Sonora culture in the extensive Sonora River valley. Ceramic technology evolved along with agriculture, to the point that pottery became a trade item among tribes. By the early centuries A.D., a number of groups in northwestern Mexico were actively employing these more advanced technologies.

Oasis and Arido America
The most abundant evidence of early cultures in Northern Mexico dates to Oasis America, a term Mexican archaeologists commonly use to categorize the loose association of Indian groups—including the Pueblo cultures of the American Southwest and the Paquimé (or Casas Grandes) culture of northwest Mexico—spread over a vast area centered around Chihuahua's Río Casas Grandes from as early as A.D. 900 through the Spanish *entrada*. Oasis America was distinct from Arido America—the less-sophisticated Desert-Archaic cultures that remained in northeastern Mexico and Texas through the Spanish *entrada*—as well as the advanced Mesoamerican cultures of Southern Mexico and Central America.

The Oasis America cultures built multistory, cubelike houses in mountain caves or on semidesert plains, and produced beautiful ceramics that were prized by neighboring Mesoamericans. In Mexico, the major remains of this period are found in the state of Chihuahua at Paquimé (Casas Grandes), Cuarenta Casas, and the Río Papigochic area.

Some Mexican archaeologists include Oasis America and the earlier Arido America within the larger "Gran Chichimeca," a proto-historic Amerindian diaspora that extended from southern Kansas to the Tropic of Cancer and from the Sea of Cortez to the Gulf of Mexico. *Chichimeca* is actually a derogatory Aztec term meaning "sons of dogs" and is employed by Mexico City historians with an Aztec bias—a bias that colors all official, i.e., Mexico City-centered, history.

Between Oasis America-Arido America and the Aztec- and Maya-dominated Mesoamerica was a belt—termed Mesoamerica Marginal—that extended across southern Durango, Zacatecas, San Luis Potosí, and Querétaro. As cultural/commercial liaisons developed between Oasis America and Mesoamerica, the cultures here blended characteristics of both north and south. Archaeological remains of Mesoamerica Marginal include the ruins of Chalchihuites (Zacatecas), La Quemada (Zacatecas), and Tamuín (San Luis Potosí).

By the 11th century, contact with Mesoamerica had advanced to the point that the Paquimé Indians of western Chihuahua were incorporating the ceremonial platforms and I-shaped ball courts of Central Mexico's Aztecs and Southern Mexico's Maya into their capital city. Oasis American cultures in northwest Mexico continued to expand and flourish well into the 13th century, then gradually began to stagnate and decay. By the time the Spanish arrived in the early 16th century, much of Oasis America was either in a state of decline or had disappeared.

SPANISH CONQUEST OF MEXICO

Following 700 years of conflict with the Moors over control of the Iberian Peninsula, Spain emerged in the 15th century as the most powerful nation in Europe. Convinced that a Roman Catholic God was destined to rule the world with Spain as His emissary, the Spanish monarchy sent Christopher Columbus in search of a new route to the Far East. His mission was to make contact with a mythical "Great Khan" and establish an alternate trade route to the Orient, since the Arabs (Moors) controlled the overland route through the Middle East. Along the way as many pagans as possible were to be converted to Christianity. Once the Arab trade monopoly was broken, the Holy Land would be returned to Christian control.

Columbus's landfall in the West Indies in 1492 was followed by Pope Alexander VI's historic 1493 decree giving the Spanish rights to any new land discovered west of the Azores, as long as the Spanish made "God's name known there." Hence, the Spanish conquest of the New World started as a roundabout extension of the Holy Crusades.

A succession of Spanish expeditions into the Caribbean and Gulf of Mexico led to the rapid conquest of Mexico and Central America. Conquistador Hernán Cortés subdued the Valley of Mexico Aztecs in three years (1519-21), and the allegiance of other Aztecs and Mayans followed quickly. Spain's first missionaries, the Franciscans, arrived in 1522. At first the Indians were enslaved, but another papal bull issued in 1537 by Pope Paul III discouraged slavery. Consequently Spain's policy changed from "conquest" to "pacification"—an ambiguous policy all too often abused.

Basically, the Spanish mission system worked thus: The padres, always in the company of armed escorts, approached groups of natives and offered them the protection of the Church and the Spanish crown in return for a willingness to undergo religious instruction. Those who agreed were congregated at a suitable spot and directed to build a mission. The mission in turn became both a refuge and a place for natives to learn European farming techniques and other trades, as well as Catholic ways. Those who rebelled were punished, and those who organized rebellions were executed. Once pacification was complete, the mission became a secularized church community (pueblo) and the missionaries moved on to new areas. The system worked well among the docile cultures of Central Mexico but was often unsuccessful among the nomadic, fiercely independent Indians of Northern Mexico.

Northern Mexico Colonization

Missionary zeal wasn't the only motive driving the Spanish conquistadors. The rugged terrain of the conquered New World was thought to contain vast mineral caches, perhaps even gold and silver. When a substantial vein of silver was discovered at Taxco, Gro., in 1522, Spanish hopes seemed confirmed and an all-out effort to find more of the precious metal—often under the guise of missionization—began less than a year after Cortés's arrival.

As the conquistadors took control of Central Mexico, the Amerindian populations fed them myths about cities of gold and silver to the north, an obvious ploy (which the Spanish leadership never fully seemed to recognize) to rid themselves of the conquistadors. The mythical cities were never found, but during one push northward a huge silver deposit called La Bufa—much larger than the one found at Taxco—was discovered in Zacatecas in 1540.

After the opening of La Bufa mine in 1546, Zacatecas became an important point of departure for further exploration and missionization of the north. So thorough was their hunt for silver that the Spanish uncovered every large deposit in Mexico, and soon New Spain was minting its own silver coins and financing the colonization of the entire continent.

Many of the largest silver caches—along with gold deposits—were found in the Sierra Madre Occidental regions of western Chihuahua, Durango, and eastern Sonora. The Spanish crown took one-fifth (the origin of the popular term "El

Quinto") of all treasures, and the Spanish officers in charge of mining the silver usually took a fifth for themselves as well—a possible precursor of Mexico's infamous *mordida* or minor-bribe tradition.

Meanwhile, the missionization of northeast Mexico was proceeding poorly. The nomadic people of Arido America were no more amenable to Spanish rule than they had been to Aztec rule. This was due partly to hostility toward outsiders, and partly because the people of the northeast were much less homogeneous in culture, language, and dialect. The Spanish had managed to gain a foothold on the Río Pánuco near Tampico, but two Cortés expeditions into the Río Bravo area in 1528 were forced to return south the same year.

Sometime in the late 1520s (the exact date is unknown), the legendary Álvar Núñez Cabeza de Vaca and a Moorish slave named Esteban (considered the first African to arrive in the New World) departed from Cuba to explore the Gulf of Mexico coast. After their ship ran aground

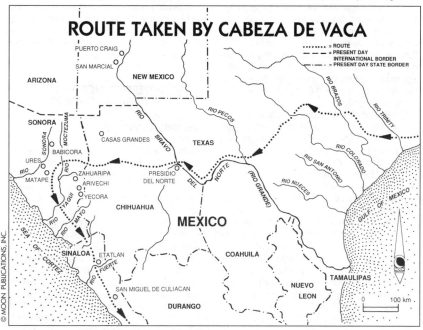

ROUTE TAKEN BY CABEZA DE VACA

on the Florida coast, they attempted to reach New Spain on animal-hide boats and became stranded on Galveston Island, Texas. Although their reception by the Karankawa of Galveston Island was less than warm, Cabeza de Vaca and Esteban ended up living with various Amerindian tribes throughout the American Southwest as they traveled westward on foot for the next nine years.

During this remarkable journey Cabeza de Vaca learned six Amerindian languages and developed a widespread reputation among the Indians as a healer, but in 1536 he headed south into Sonora and rejoined his own people. He later became an outspoken critic against the Spanish treatment of Amerindians and was eventually banished by the colonial administration to a remote Latin American outpost.

Tantalized by Cabeza de Vaca's second-hand stories of gold cities, the colonial government commissioned Francisco Vásquez de Coronado to explore the lands to the north. Coronado's explorations (as far north as Oklahoma and Kansas) never yielded any gold or silver, but along the way he left missionaries in the upper Rio Grande valley to "pacify" the people. This eventually led to the discovery of El Paso del Norte, the "northern pass" in the mountains of northern Chihuahua, through which a well-worn trade route eventually developed (culminating in the booming El Paso-Juárez transborder metropolis).

Other Spanish settlements in northwest Mexico followed. Italian-born Padre Eusebio Francisco Kino managed to establish 25 missions in Sonora and Arizona, where he is said to have converted thousands of Amerindians to "the one true faith," Roman Catholicism. In 1701 Kino accompanied an expedition from northwestern Sonora to the mouth of the Río Colorado, confirming an earlier claim that Baja California was a peninsula. Around this same time, missionaries in northeastern Mexico were able to push northward into Coahuila, Nuevo León, and Tamaulipas (and beyond into Texas and Louisiana). No gold or silver was discovered in this region, but Spanish settlers found the terrain well-suited to large-scale farming and cattle ranching, activities that were ultimately more stable and profitable than prospecting for shiny metals.

In 1746 José de Escandón, a highly regarded military officer and colonial administrator, received an assignment to survey the Gulf of Mexico coastal plains from Río Pánuco north to the Nueces River in Texas. The following year Escandón began sending colonists to the area and named it the state of Nuevo Santander after his home province in Spain. Other Spanish *empresarios* established similar colonies in the northeast, which soon became Mexico's cattle kingdom.

The New World's first cowboys or vaqueros (those who work with *vacas,* or cows) bred horses to use in ranch work. Although the colonists had met with hostile Indians from time to time, the Indian population in this area—or what was left of it after European-borne diseases decimated a large portion—wasn't a major problem until Spanish horses got into the hands of the Plains Indians to the north. With the increased mobility, Comanches began moving southward from the Rocky Mountains. They displaced the Apaches, who moved deeper into Northern Mexico, displacing in turn the more peaceful Jumano and Coahuiltecan tribes. Although some Apache groups were lured into the mission system, the Spanish continued to battle the Apaches right up until Mexican independence.

INDEPENDENCE AND CHANGING BORDERS

Independence from Spain

By the end of the 18th century the Catholic Church in Mexico had amassed huge amounts of wealth and had become a lender to the colony's growing entrepreneurial class. At the other end of the economic spectrum, the increasing numbers of mestizos (Mexican-born residents of mixed Spanish and Amerindian ancestry) were denied land ownership and other rights, and generally were treated as second-class citizens.

Fearing that the Church was becoming too powerful, King Charles III of Spain decreed in 1804 that all church funds were to be turned over to the royal coffers. As padres all over Mexico were forced to comply with the decree (calling back large sums of money that had been lent out to entrepreneurs), economic chaos ensued. Mexicans blamed their economic and social problems on Spain's remote rule; when Napoleon invaded Spain in 1808, limiting authority to Spanish loyalists in Mexico City, the disaffected clergy began planning a revolt.

Mexico's struggle for independence from Spain began on 16 Sept. 1810 (celebrated annually as *diez y seis* or Mexican Independence Day), when mestizo Padre Miguel Hidalgo y Costilla issued a call for independence known as the *Grito de Dolores* ("Cry of Dolores") in Guanajuato. Although the rebels who gathered around Padre Hidalgo soon captured Zacatecas, Valladolid, and San Luis Potosí, Mexico wasn't completely free of Spanish rule for another 11 years. When Hidalgo was captured and executed by loyalists, another padre took his place and the fighting continued until Mexico City acceded to the demands of the rebels in 1821.

The Plan de Iguala and the Constitution of 1824

The 1821 Plan de Iguala treaty between Spain and Mexico guaranteed three political underpinnings of the new regime: the religious dominance of the Catholic Church, a constitutional monarchy, and equal rights for mestizos as well as Mexican-born Spaniards. Former Viceroy Agustín de Iturbide, author of the Plan de Iguala,

Agustín de Iturbide, emperor of Mexico, 1822-24

was appointed emperor of the new republic but his reign lasted only two years before he was overthrown by another junta that established a short-lived federal republic called Los Estados Unidos de México—the United States of Mexico —in 1824.

Over the next six years the Mexican republic endured two more coups and it wasn't until 1829 that all Spanish troops were expelled from Mexico. In 1832 all non-Dominican missions were secularized and converted to parish churches. Another change in policy involved the encouragement of Anglo-American immigration to the northeastern Mexican state of Coahuila y Texas.

Santa Anna and the Republic of Texas

In 1833 Antonio López de Santa Anna, a megalomaniac general in charge of enforcing the expulsion of Spanish troops, seized power and revoked the Constitution of 1824, thus initiating a series of events that eventually led to a war with the United States and the resultant loss of huge amounts of Mexican territory (see "The Mexi-

can-American War and the Gadsden Purchase," below). During the first 50 years of Mexican independence, Mexico changed governments 50 times; Santa Anna—who called himself the "Napoleon of the West"—headed 11 of these regimes.

Mexican citizens everywhere were angry at the revocation of their republican constitution by a self-appointed dictator. Particularly upset were the Anglo-American immigrants who had voluntarily left behind their U.S. citizenship in order to take Mexican citizenship under that constitution and live in the northern half of Coahuila y Texas. In 1836 the "Texicans" declared an independent Republic of Texas, fought and lost San Antonio's famous Battle of the Alamo, and then routed Santa Anna's defending troops in San Jacinto, Texas.

Defeated and captured, Santa Anna signed an independence treaty in which he reportedly agreed to the Rio Grande border between Mexico and the new Texan republic. He then was allowed to return to Mexico City. There matters lay until the U.S. granted statehood to the near-bankrupt Texan republic in 1845. Later the Santa Anna government claimed that they had never recognized the Río Bravo (Rio Grande) as the Texas-Mexico border and that Texas extended only as far south as the Nueces River (about 160 km/100 miles north of the Rio Grande at the widest gap). In addition, Mexico claimed that Texas had been granted independence in 1836 with the condition that its government never seek annexation to the United States.

The Mexican-American War and the Gadsden Purchase

Which side violated the independence treaty? Modern history books on each side of the Rio Grande tell the story differently; yet neither wields a copy of the treaty as proof. Logic suggests both parties violated the treaty, the Mexicans by changing the agreed border, the Texans by ignoring the promise to remain independent of the United States. At any rate, when the U.S. Army moved in to claim the area south of the Nueces River (and west, including about half of present-day New Mexico and Colorado), Santa Anna retaliated by sending troops across the Río Bravo/Rio Grande, thus starting the Mexican-American War.

After a series of skirmishes along the Río Bravo (during which 200 Texans of Irish descent from San Patricio, Texas, deserted the U.S. Army and fought for the Mexican army), U.S. president James Polk ordered the army to invade Mexico. Mexico City finally fell to U.S. troops in Sept. 1847 and Santa Anna signed the Treaty of Guadalupe Hidalgo in Feb. 1848. In the treaty, Mexico conceded not only the Rio Grande-Nueces River area of Texas but also the territories of Nuevo México and Alta California—which together included the present-day states of Colorado, Nevada, and California, and parts of New Mexico, Arizona, Utah, and Wyoming—for a payment of US$25 million and the assumption of US$3 million in claims lodged against the Mexican government by citizens living in those territories.

In retrospect, it is likely that the annexation of Texas was part of a U.S. plan to provoke Mexico into declaring war so that the U.S. would have an opportunity to gain more of the Southwest—such expansionist tactics were common all over the Western world in the 19th century. The war so damaged Mexico's already weakened economy that in 1853 Santa Anna sold southern Arizona and a section of New Mexico's Mesilla Valley to the U.S. for another US$10 million as part of the Gadsden Purchase (known in Mexico as el Tratado de Gadesden or Venta de la Mesilla). Altogether Mexico lost 51% of its territory as a result of the war; U.S. president Abraham Lincoln later called it "the most unjust war there ever was." Moral recriminations aside, the ultimate political cause for Mexico's loss of territory in the 19th century was a lack of national cohesion (coups d'état were putting a new Mexican president in office an average of every 7.5 months) at a time when its more powerful northern neighbor was engaged in active expansion.

For the Mexican population, already strongly dissatisfied with Santa Anna, this additional loss and threatened further loss of territory (at least three postwar American filibuster groups tried to take additional lands from Baja California and Sonora) was the final straw; in 1855 Santa Anna was overthrown by Zapotec Indian lawyer and populist Benito Juárez.

CIVIL WAR, REVOLUTION, AND REFORM

Benito Juárez and the War of Reform

The second half of the 19th century was to be even more turbulent for Mexico than the first. Church wealth was a continuing issue. The liberals, under Benito Juárez, promulgated a new constitution in 1857 and passed a law further restricting the financial powers of the Church. All Church property, save for church buildings, had to be sold or otherwise relinquished. This led to civil war (the "War of Reform") in 1858, with self-appointed governments in Mexico City and Veracruz vying for national authority. A reactionary opposition group took control of Mexico City, and fighting continued until 1861, when the liberals won and Juárez was elected president.

Juárez immediately had to deal with the 1862 French invasion of Mexico, which came in response to Mexico's nonpayment of debts to France. Napoleon III's first invading force was defeated at Veracruz, but the following year the

TERRITORIAL LOSSES

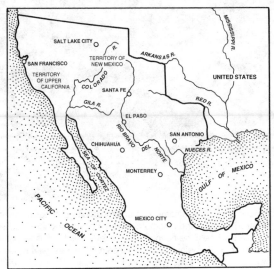

MEXICO BEFORE 1836

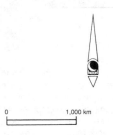

0   1,000 km

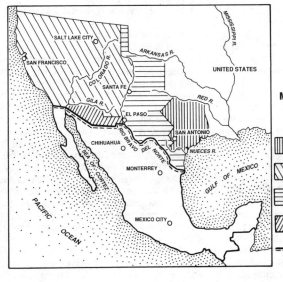

MEXICO FROM 1836 TO THE PRESENT

1836 : TEXAS DECLARES INDEPENDENCE.
1845 : ANNEXED BY THE UNITED STATES.

1848 : TREATY OF GUADALUPE HIDALGO - CEDED TO THE UNITED STATES.

1848 : NUECES RIVER/RIO BRAVO TERRITORY DISPUTE.

1853 : GADSDEN PURCHASE.

PRESENT MEXICO/UNITED STATES BORDER.

Joining Pancho Villa and Zapata in Mexico City is John (Jack) Reed, the gringo in the back wearing the sombrero and wire-rim glasses. You know, Warren Beatty in Reds.

COURTESY MUSEO DE LA REVOLUCIÓN, CHIHUAHUA

French captured the port and continued onward to take Mexico City, where they installed Austrian Ferdinand Maximilian and his wife Carlota as emperor and empress of Mexico. Under U.S. pressure, the French gradually withdrew from Mexico. Maximilian was executed (Carlota returned to Europe, widowed and estranged), and Juárez was back in power by 1867.

Over the next four years Juárez initiated many economic and educational reforms. Upon his death in 1872, Juárez's political opponent, Porfirio Díaz, took over and continued those reforms, albeit in a much more authoritarian manner. Díaz (or his cronies) would rule Mexico for the next 28 years, suspending political freedoms such as open elections and a free press but modernizing the country's education and transportation systems.

Foreign Investment in Northern Mexico
Díaz and the "Porfiriato" encouraged foreign investment on a large scale, and in the 1880s vast land tracts in the north were sold to American or European mining, farming, manufacturing, oil, and railway concessions. Mineral excavation in turn-of-the-century Northern Mexico boomed—gold, silver, copper, lead, zinc, and gypsum were the main finds, along with graphite, mercury, nickel, and sulfur. Foreign oil companies established themselves in Tamaulipas, Veracruz, and Tabasco, and employed large numbers of ex-

patriates. A large proportion—perhaps most—of the income generated by these operations left the country. This money was then used by foreigners to purchase more mines, oil rigs, plantations, and textile factories in Mexico. By 1920, an estimated 75% of Mexico's industrial wealth was concentrated in the hands of foreigners.

The Mexican Revolution and U.S. Prohibition
By the early 1900s, it was obvious that the gap between rich and poor in Mexico was becoming increasingly wide due to the extreme procapitalist policies of the Díaz regime and the total lack of a political voice for workers and peasants. In response to the situation, a liberal opposition group formed (in exile, using Texas as a base) and organized strikes throughout the country, which forced Díaz to announce an election in 1910. His opponent was Francisco Madero, a liberal from Coahuila who was educated at the University of California at Berkeley in the United States. As it became clear that Madero was garnering mass support, Díaz imprisoned him on trumped-up charges June 21, 1910—election day.

Following Díaz's reelection, Madero was released on bail with the provision that he remain in the city of San Luis Potosí. He did—until October—at which time he fled to Texas and began organizing the overthrow of the Díaz government. The rebels, with the assistance of Chihuahua's colorful bandit-turned-revolutionary Francisco "Pancho" Villa and peasant-hero Emiliano Zapata, managed to gain control of the Northern Mexican states of Sonora and Chihuahua. Unable to contain the revolution, Díaz resigned in May 1911 and Madero was elected president. The opposition, however, broke into several factions—the Zapatistas, Reyistas, Vasquistas, Villistas, and Felicistas (named for the leaders of each movement)—and Madero was executed in 1913.

For the next six years the various factions played musical chairs with national leadership and Mexico remained extremely unstable. The U.S. supported the Constitutionalist army commander-in-chief, Venustiano Carranza, who formed a government in Veracruz. The notorious Pancho Villa (born Doroteo Arango in Durango) opposed Carranza from his own provisional capital in Guanajuato.

Angered by U.S. support of Carranza, Villa began raiding American border towns. The U.S. response was to send Gen. "Blackjack" Pershing and nearly 5,000 U.S. cavalry troops into Mexico in an attempt to roust Villa. This "punitive expedition" lasted from March 1916 until Feb. 5, 1917; Villa eluded General Pershing but Carranza finally emerged as president.

Carranza then held a historic convention that resulted in the Constitution of 1917 (the current Mexican constitution). It established the *ejido* program, which returned to local communities lands traditionally cultivated by the peasantry but taken away or purchased by rich ranch and plantation owners under Díaz. Three years later opponent Álvaro Obregón (a Sonoran who had served as army chief of the División Noroeste during the revolution) and his supporters overthrew Carranza, who later was assassinated while attempting to flee Mexico City.

The Mexican Revolution, which had claimed the lives of 10% of all Mexicans, was officially over and the country began to rebuild. Obregón managed to hang onto the office for four years and establish important educational reforms. He was followed by Sonoran Plutarco Elías Calles in 1924. Calles instituted wide-reaching agrarian reforms, including the redistribution of three million hectares of land. He also participated in the establishment of the National Revolutionary Party (PNR), the forerunner of the Institutional Revolutionary Party (PRI), Mexico's dominant party today. In 1928, just as Obregón was elected president a second time, he was assassinated by a religious fanatic.

In the same year that Obregón originally took power in Mexico City, the U.S. government amended its own constitution to make the consumption, manufacture, and sale of alcoholic beverages a federal offense. This proved to be a disastrous experiment for the U.S. (ushering in an era of organized crime), but was a boon to Mexican border development as Americans rushed into Northern Mexico border towns to buy booze from the restaurants, cantinas, and liquor stores.

With American dollars flowing into Mexico, the border towns added casinos and brothels to the assortment of liquor venues, becoming world-renowned as sleaze capitals in the process. This reputation persisted long after Prohibition ended in the U.S. in 1933 and long after the Mexican government outlawed gambling (but not prostitution, which is still legal in proscribed districts) in 1938.

Nationalist Reforms and World War II

The year 1934 proved a turning point in modern Mexican history as PNR candidate Lázaro Cárdenas ascended to the presidency. (With Mexico's legacy of election-fixing, it's difficult to use the word "elect" in the usual democratic sense—see "Government," below, for further explanation.) Cárdenas instituted the most sweeping social reforms of any national leader to date, effecting significant changes in education, labor, agriculture, and commerce.

His land reforms included the redistribution of nearly 50 million acres among newly created *ejidos,* agricultural collectives in which land is owned jointly by peasant communities—a legacy that is as hot a debate topic today as it was then. Foreign-owned oil interests were expropriated and a national oil company, Petróleos Mexicanos (PEMEX), was established. Even though foreign investors were compensated for expropriations at fair market value (under a treaty signed by both the U.S. and Mexico), these reforms frightened off prospective investors for many years. It has been only recently that Mexico has been able to reattract foreign capital. Cárdenas also reorganized the PNR as the Mexican Revolution Party (PRM—Partido de la Revolución Mexicana), which soon changed its name to the current-day Institutional Revolutionary Party (PRI—Partido Revolucionario Institucional).

Since the Cárdenas period, Mexican political history has been characterized by comparatively subtle shifts. Mexican leadership succession also has stabilized, a process often referred to as the oxymoronic "institutionalization of the revolution" (meaning the PRI has so far won every national election).

CONTEMPORARY NORTHERN MEXICO

Northern Mexico only began to emerge from its provincial past with the construction of a national railroad system in the late 19th century; at that point, communications between the central and northern states expanded rapidly. During WW II, the Mexican economy was boosted by increased U.S. demand for materials and labor, and also by the scarcity of imported goods in Mexico, which forced the nation to increase domestic production. In addition, Mexican troops fighting in the Pacific for the Allies needed materials, both imported and domestic. This exchange of products between the U.S. and Mexico favored the development of Northern Mexico by sheer virtue of proximity.

Northerners took advantage of their increasing prosperity to reinvest in regional human resources, building Mexico's top universities and technological research centers. Today these educational centers train many of the best and brightest from all over the country.

Another boost to Northern Mexican political and economic development came in the 1980s, when Pres. Miguel de la Madrid proclaimed a new era of modernization and plupartyism—equivalent in word if not in deed to Soviet president Gorbachev's roughly concurrent perestroika/glasnost proclamation. The already-modernizing north—heavily allied with PAN (Partido Acción Nacional, the nation's conservative opposition party)—benefitted from a relaxation of PRI's hold. The era of optimism was extended by Pres. Carlos Salinas de Gortari, who was a strong supporter of the much-debated NAFTA (North American Free Trade Agreement; see "Economy," below, for more information on the treaty).

In 1880 only three northern cities—Monterrey, Saltillo, and Hermosillo—were among Mexico's 25 largest. By the 1980s, 10 of Mexico's 25 largest cities were located in the north. In the early '90s Northern Mexico was clearly poised to take further advantage of upward shifts in the economy.

THE CRISIS OF 1994-95

Although the economy went for a roller-coaster ride in the 1970s and early '80s, when the government nationalized banks and devalued the peso, things brightened considerably in the late '80s and early '90s under Salinas's market modernization. Then in 1994 everything seemed to go wrong.

Trouble in Chiapas

On Jan. 1, 1994, the day NAFTA took effect, a group of several hundred armed Lacandón Indians under the leadership of a masked, pipe-smoking mestizo dramatically seized four towns in the state of Chiapas in a series of well-coordinated attacks. They retreated swiftly in the face of overwhelming Mexican armed force but not before 145 people had been killed in armed skirmishes. Calling themselves the Zapatista National Liberation Army (EZLN), the guerrillas were not only protesting NAFTA—which they believed would have negative effects on the rural Southern Mexican economy—but were also airing traditional grievances regarding fraudulent regional elections and land seizure from Lacandón peasants.

Although perceived by the world at large as an organization created in direct response to NAFTA, the EZLN had actually been training in the jungles of Chiapas near the Guatemalan border for 10 years, using U.S. military manuals translated into Spanish and Tzeltal (a Maya dialect).

Assassination and Corruption

While the EZLN and Mexican government were negotiating in Chiapas, another event unfolded to create even more difficulties for the Salinas government. Luis Donaldo Colosio, the PRI's prime presidential candidate groomed to take Salinas's place, was shot to death by a factory worker while campaigning in Tijuana on March 23, 1994. In the ensuing federal investigation, deputy attorney general Mario Ruiz Massieu and Salinas's brother, Raúl, were implicated in the assassination plot.

Then in May 1994 the government seized 117 kg of cocaine base during a raid on a ranch in Quintana Roo owned by a PRI senator, and around the same time a senior Ministry of Tourism official who was involved in deciding whether to legalize gambling casinos was arrested and charged with illegal enrichment.

Colosio's campaign manager, Yale University graduate Ernesto Zedillo Ponce de León, was elected to the presidency in the August 1994 election, widely considered the cleanest in Mexico's history. But the decisive PRI victory proved a short-lived high point for the party, as Mexico City politics continued to unravel. First investigators uncovered a trail of corruption that threatened to implicate Mexico's former *wunderkind*, Carlos Salinas. In order to avoid testifying against his own brother—or perhaps to protect himself— Carlos fled the country. Raúl Salinas was subsequently found to have amassed a US$24-million fortune through illicit means.

In a state-of-the-nation address, President Zedillo acknowledged that corruption was deeply rooted in Mexican institutions and in the general social conduct of the nation. He confirmed the determination of his administration to confront official corruption and to encourage the creation of a new culture of respect for law, beginning with the behavior of public officials. Zedillo also signed the Organization of American States (OAS) Corruption Convention, which was ratified unanimously by the Mexican Senate. Mexico's attorney general, appointed from an opposition party, dismissed over 1,250 officials for incompetence or corruption, and completely revamped hiring, training, and internal accountability.

Mass firings of state and local police took place for dereliction of duty. Often these positions were taken over by military officers, who are presumed to be less corruptible than civilian law-enforcement agents. Whether any of this will make a difference is difficult to tell; virtually every president who has taken office in Mexico during the last 25 years has vowed to fight corruption.

Economic Turmoil

By the end of 1994 the events in Chiapas, the Colosio assassination, and glimpses into high-level Mexican corruption had resulted in an extreme loss of investor confidence in Mexico, leading in turn to a stock sell-off and a domestic run on the U.S. dollar. To protect draining reserves, Mexico City responded by allowing the peso to float, sending the currency into a deflationary tailspin.

Over the months of January and February 1995 the peso dropped from an exchange rate of three per U.S. dollar to around eight, bringing the worst recession the country had seen in 60 years. The Clinton administration, along with the International Monetary Fund, bailed out the government with loans to pay off international debt, but Mexicans of all economic classes—especially those involved with international business— suffered heavy losses and a substantial drop in standard of living.

Northern Mexico, because of its ties to the U.S. economy and access to the U.S. dollar, weathered "the crisis" better than most parts of the country. By the beginning of 1997 most sectors of the Mexican economy showed signs of a recovery, though foreign investor confidence remains shaky as scandals in law enforcement, the military, and the drug arena continue to surface on an almost weekly basis. Many observers, both Mexican and international, now see the rosy Salinas years as an elaborate setup of smoke and mirrors that masked overvaluation of the peso, corruption, and other economic and political ills that are only now being addressed by the sober Zedillo administration. Hope seems to be rising out of despair in yet another demonstration of Mexico's uncanny ability to survive. In Northern Mexico, people just shake their heads and blame it all on the *chilangos* of Mexico City.

GOVERNMENT

Political System

Mexico's federal system allows for some degree of autonomous rule by state governors and legislatures. The nine states of mainland Northern Mexico, along with Baja California Norte and Baja California Sur, are considered among the most politically progressive states in the nation, in the sense that PRI candidates aren't automatically elected.

Several northern governors and big-city mayors—particularly in Chihuahua, Tamaulipas, San Luis Potosí, and Sinaloa—have been members of PAN, the nation's main opposition party. PAN is usually described as a conservative party because of its probusiness stance, yet in the context of Mexican politics it is more reform-minded than either the PRI or PRD.

In the south the leftist PRD (Partido Revolucionario Democrático) has made a few inroads in local elections and in Mexico City. PRD spokesperson Cuautémoc Cárdenas, winner of Mexico City's first-ever mayoral election in 1997, has become a popular symbol of resistance in the country despite the fact that his rhetoric does not substantially differ from that of the dominant party.

Of the five other officially recognized parties, none is electorally significant so far. And the PRI continues to win every national election. The next presidential election, to be held in 2000, may be a serious runoff since the traditional PRI base was seriously eroded by the events of 1994-95 (see "History," above).

In spite of occasional opposition victories, Mexican politics has been notorious for election fraud ever since it adopted a republican system in 1917. Hard-boiled cynics insist that all high political offices are part of a ruling dynasty extending outward from the presidency in Mexico City (even municipal mayors in Mexico are called *el presidente* and the local seat of government is the *palacio municipal*). Wags point out other symbolic evidence—the president wears an imperial sash and sits upon a throne when making official proclamations—and the fact that whichever candidate the incumbent endorses always wins the next election.

The *presidentes municipales* appoint city *delegados* to represent federal power at the local level; smaller communities may even have *subdelegados.* These *delegados* and *subdelegados* are the highest authority within their jurisdictions and are part of a chain of command that reaches back to the president of Mexico.

At the national level there is a bicameral Congreso de la Unión (National Congress), divided into a 128-seat Camara de Senadores (Senate) and 500-seat Camara de Diputados (Chamber of Deputies). Elections for congressional positions are held every three years.

Pres. Ernesto Zedillo de Ponce de León
Elected in 1994 as a stand-in for assassinated presidential candidate Luis Donaldo Colosio, Zedillo has an academic and public-service background similar to his predecessor, Carlos Salinas. While Salinas was a Harvard grad, Zedillo graduated from Yale University with a Ph.D. in economics. He served as staff economist for Banco de México, then served stints as education secretary and secretary of budget and planning under Salinas. His last post was campaign manager for Colosio, who was assassinated on March 23, 1994 while campaigning in Tijuana.

Zedillo is strongly in favor of continued denationalization of state enterprises. His 1978 Yale dissertation focusing on Mexico's foreign debt problems alienated several government officials by stating that the country's national debt problems were "caused more by Mexican government mismanagement than by the intransigence of foreign lenders." Though loyal to his party,

Federal Judicial Police destroy marijuana crop in the Sierra Madre Occidental.

Zedillo has continued to buck against the PRI establishment and is currently out of favor with his own party for cleaving to Salinas's now-unpopular market reforms. Unlike Salinas, he seems keenly interested in cleaning up government corruption, yet another threat to the PRI. Zedillo's six-year term ends in 2000.

Democratization

In an excellent four-part series published in the *Dallas Morning News,* authors Alfredo Corchado and Tracy Easton of the *News* Mexico City bureau concluded that in Mexico, a truly democratic system is thwarted by "the lack of democratic culture in a country dominated by authoritarian regimes for 500 years." Despite this "deep-structure" view, most observers agree that Mexico is moving ever so slowly toward a more democratic system. Electoral fraud in particular has come under ever-increasing scrutiny and for the most part the election process is getting better.

In this arena, Northern Mexico has taken the lead. In a functional sense democracy is defined very differently in Northern and Southern Mexico. Relatively more industrialized states like Chihuahua and Nuevo León, for example, boast a well-established two-party system complete with polling booths even in the smallest towns. Meanwhile in southern states like Oaxaca and Chiapas, local elections are still determined by a simple show of hands under the watchful eye of the PRI. The political paternalism of the south—where the PRI distributes chickens, free paint and building materials, and other "gifts" just before elections—is absent in most of the north.

Even as the whole country progresses in this vein, built-in impediments remain. *No Re-elección,* a basic tenet of the Mexican Revolution, means that no president or legislator can be reelected to an immediate second term. Legislators may be reelected after sitting out one term but presidents get one *sexenio* (six-year term) and that's it. Many political analysts inside and outside the country think the prohibition on reelection of legislators is one of the primary flaws in the system, since it allows elected legislators to ignore their constituency. At the same time it strengthens the presidency by packing the Mexican Congress with inexperienced members.

One of the more encouraging steps toward more popular participation was the 1996 estab-lishment of voting rights for Mexican citizens living abroad. In the same legislative package, Mexico announced that it will now allow and recognize dual citizenship, enabling many Mexicans living in the U.S. and elsewhere to have a say in national elections.

The 1997 midterm elections for Mexico City mayor, national legislature, and some state gubernatorial selections was the greatest display of multiparty politics the republic has ever seen, leading President Zedillo to claim that "democracy has finally arrived in Mexico."

ECONOMY

Production, Resources, and Income

The political and economic crises of 1994-95 rocked all sectors of the Mexican economy, costing a million jobs and inflicting a net economic contraction of around seven percent. By the middle of 1997 that trend had been reversed, a recovery was in full swing, and the economy was growing at 4-7% percent per annum. Foreign investment in 1997 totaled US$7.2 billion; among the major beneficiaries were the petroleum and natural gas, aviation, and telecommunications industries. Per capita income figures for the northern states are well above the Mexican national average, which is just US$2,750 per annum if measured in raw terms, or a much better-looking US$7,188 if figured by the purchasing-parity method, which compares raw income with the ability to buy a standard "basket" of consumer necessaries. By the latter calculation, Mexico ranks well ahead of Brazil (US$5,675) and Turkey (US$5,550) but behind Thailand (US$7,535).

Northerners have a saying to explain their higher productivity (about double the national average): "In Southern Mexico the people want; in Central Mexico they think; in Northern Mexico we work." While this folk axiom may be partially true, the added reality is that Northern Mexico is blessed with a variety of natural resources that are either absent or less accessible in other regions.

Agriculture, ranching, timber, mining, fishing, and manufacturing are Northern Mexico's main revenue-earners. In all of these sectors, Northern Mexico leads the nation in production statistics.

Sinaloa, for example, grows over 75% of Mexico's soy and virtually all of its *córtamo* (safflower); the Región Lagunera (Torreón-Lerdo-Gómez Palacio) produces about a third of the nation's cotton; Coahuila and San Luis Potosí lead in horse breeding; and Durango and Chihuahua alone account for half the nation's timber output. In mineral production, Sonora is first in copper, producing nearly all of the nation's output; Zacatecas leads in silver with a third of national output; and Chihuahua produces the most lead and zinc.

Fishing boats work both coasts, but Sonoran fisheries (centered in Guaymas) are the most productive; the Sea of Cortez yields large annual harvests of shrimp, oysters, tuna, seabass, and lobster. On the Gulf of Mexico coast, commercial fishermen rely primarily on oysters, sardines, and red snapper.

Manufacturing is mostly concentrated in the Saltillo-Monterrey and Torreón-Lerdo-Gómez Palacio areas and in the larger border towns. Despite NAFTA the stars of the manufacturing sector remain the *maquiladoras* or in-bond industries, which combine third-world labor costs with first-world capital and management. *Maquiladoras* currently employ 18% of the country's manufacturing work force and constitute the second most important source of foreign exchange after petroleum. Most are located in former special export-processing zones along the border, although since 1988 the *maquila* program has been expanded to all of Mexico. Gradually such joint-venture enterprises are spreading farther south into the interior, relieving some of the social and environmental pressures concentrated along the border (see "*Maquiladoras*" and "North American Free Trade Agreement," below).

The System

On a macroeconomic level, Northern Mexico finds itself caught between two economic systems. Because of its proximity to the U.S., the regional economy has tended to be American-influenced. But it is nevertheless subject to the same vicissitudes of the Mexican economy as the rest of the country, most pointedly a weak currency and steady inflation. Although the country's current-account balance rose from a deficit US$6.2 billion in 1982 to a surplus of US$4 billion in 1987, the inflation rate that same year hit 146%. Because of its regional ties to the U.S., particularly Texas and the Southwest, Northern Mexico's economy weathered this period better than many other areas in Mexico. A similar phenomenon occurred during the 1994-95 period, when a negative balance reappeared; the current estimated US$1.8 billion deficit is improving quarter by quarter.

During the Salinas administration the nation moved closer to U.S.-style, growth-led economics, thus lessening the schizoid nature of the north's regional economy. One of the biggest steps taken by the Salinas government was the reprivatizing of the national banking system, the telephone system, and several other state industries (PEMEX is the major exception). Still, the eight largest employers in Mexico are government agencies connected with education, social security, PEMEX, or defense. Despite overall budget deficits, social spending increased nine percent in 1996 to comprise a stiff 56% of Mexico's national budget.

Inflation reached a high of 52% in 1995 during all the turmoil but is now running 15-18% per annum and dropping. Mexico in 1997 managed to repay the final US$3.5 billion of its US$13.5 billion emergency loan package from the U.S. government three years ahead of schedule. A portion of the IMF loan was also repaid ahead of schedule. Exports for 1995 totaled US$80 billion, three times greater than in 1992; foreign debt stands at US$118 billion. On a microeconomic level, the official national minimum wage hovers at US$3.50 per day, attractive to foreign manufacturers looking for cheap labor but just barely enough for survival in today's Mexico.

Some optimistic economists predict that if Mexico continues its current economic reforms, it may become Latin America's fastest-growing economy by the year 2000. Growth in Northern Mexico will probably be slower, however, since much of the current and projected growth is in areas of Mexico that are "catching up" with the north.

Border Economy

The border is also the focus of a mostly undocumented shadow economy supported by both legal and illegal migrant Mexican labor in the United States. Mexican labor migration has become so integrated into the regional econo-

LA FRONTERA

The border means more than a customs house, a passport officer, a man with a gun. Over there everything is going to be different; life is never going to be quite the same again after your passport has been stamped and you find yourself speechless among the money-changers.

—Graham Greene, Another Mexico

Like novelist Greene, we often think of international borders as a thin line separating entirely different worlds, a geopolitical reference point that symbolizes a great gulf between cultures. But the reality along the United States-Mexico border is that this jagged line—extending 3,326 km from the Gulf of Mexico in the east to the Pacific Ocean in the west—acts more as a glue binding cultures together.

Rather than defining the periphery of separate cultures to the north and to the south, one of the world's longest international borders actually forms the center of a third, hybridized culture that's neither American nor Mexican. Here First World meets Third World; northern European, Protestant capitalism meets southern European, Catholic feudalism. This newer world has its own name, "La Frontera"—the frontier—and its own culture, *fronteriza*. White Anglo-Saxons dine on tacos and breakfast burritos regularly and celebrate the availability of inexpensive, handmade leather boots, while mestizos (Mexicans of mixed Spanish and Indian ancestry) patronize Pizza Hut and use installment plans to purchase Japanese-made washing machines at WalMart—all without ever crossing the border.

When residents on either side refer to La Frontera, they're talking about an area that extends as far as a hundred miles north and south of the border. Despite the fact that Mexico ranks as the U.S.'s second largest trading partner, this wide swath contains some of the poorest areas in either country. The burgeoning twin-plant (*maquila* or *maquiladora*) industry along the Mexican side of the border, in which American—or increasingly Canadian, European, or Japanese—technology and management exploits cheap Mexican labor, was supposed to be the hope of the future for the borderland. Goods produced at these plants are granted special trade status since they're established in "export processing zones" using U.S. capital. The *maquilas* have been heavily criticized in recent years for their contribution to regional air and water pollution as well as worker exploitation.

As the number of *maquilas* increases, more unemployed Mexicans migrate to Northern Mexico in hopes of landing steady, though low-paying, jobs. Once on the border there's the attraction of higher-paying work just over the river, so labor tends to flow back and forth according to supply-and-demand forces in the border labor market. Many Mexicans work on the U.S. side during the day and sleep at home in Mexico at night. Human taxis wade across carrying passengers on their backs for 25 cents a trip during "commute" hours.

Many Americans, often goaded by local Congressmen seeking reelection, fear that illegal Mexican immigrants are stealing jobs from them. "Operation Rio Grande," the latest and one of the most expensive U.S. Immigration and Naturalization Service (INS) efforts ever undertaken in American history, spills millions and millions of taxpayer dollars into a high-tech cat-and-mouse game that will at best produce dubious results in terms of its effects on American economics. Every empirical study ever carried out on the economics of migrant labor has concluded that Mexican immigration, illegal or otherwise, does not pose a true economic or political crisis for the United States.

The evidence, in fact, clearly indicates that the influx of Mexican workers provides strong economic benefits for U.S. border states and beyond, benefits that greatly outweigh the undocumented immigrants' use of public facilities and services. As essayist Paul Theroux pointed out in his book *The Old Patagonian Express,* the U.S. farm lobby isn't keen to enforce immigration laws. "[I]f there were no Mexicans to exploit, how would these [American farmers] be able to harvest their crops?" Mexico's official government response to Operation Rio Grande stated that the venture "puts a serious cloud over the commitment [of both countries] . . . to jointly promote a more human vision of the border." Alas politics rarely follows either economic or diplomatic wisdom.

my that it is now considered largely responsible for the competitive and stable pricing of U.S. consumer goods. Economists use the term "commodity migrants" to describe social behavior in which labor transports itself to where capital demands it.

That Mexican labor is essential to U.S. production is also indicated by the cyclical nature of migration statistics relative to upturns and downturns in the U.S. economy. Intertwined with the shadow economy, the entire border economy tends to move with the U.S. economic tide.

An even more shadowy aspect of the border economy is linked to the production and trafficking of illegal drugs. As succinctly described in the 1997 International Narcotics Control Strategy Report:

Taking full advantage of the 2,000-mile border between Mexico and the United States and the massive flow of legitimate trade and traffic, well-entrenched polydrug-trafficking organizations based in Mexico have built vast criminal empires that produce illicit drugs, smuggle hundreds of tons of South American cocaine, and operate drug distribution networks reaching well into the continental United States. Mexico is the principal transit route for South American cocaine, a major source of marijuana and heroin, as well as a major supplier of methamphetamine to the illicit drug market in the U.S. The drug trade and other criminal activities generate huge cash proceeds; given the intimate ties between the two countries' financial systems, and the absence of adequate controls in the Mexican system, Mexico has become a major money laundering center and the preferred international placement point for U.S. dollars. Drug cartels launder the proceeds of crime in legitimate businesses in both the U.S. and Mexico, favoring transportation and other industries which can be used to facilitate drug, cash, and arms smuggling or to further money laundering activities.

What the above summary leaves out is the fact that the U.S. underground economy itself launders three times as much drug money as Mexico, according to money-laundering experts.

For the most part the north is simply an unavoidable conduit for drugs passing through from Guerrero, Michoacán, and South America (primarily Colombia). Remote, mountainous areas of Chihuahua, Sinaloa, and Durango, however, are major sites for the cultivation of marijuana. Rumors say opium poppy (from which heroin is derived) is grown in the latter two states, although it is more commonly cultivated further south.

Ejidos

One unique feature of the Mexican economy is the *ejido* institution, considered a mainstay of PRI policy. The *ejido* has its roots in the Spanish *reconquista,* the period during the late 15th century when Spanish Christians retook the Iberian Peninsula from the Moors. The Spanish crown honored Spanish nobles who had fought against the Moors with land tracts confiscated from the latter. In Nueva España the Spanish monarchy continued the tradition by offering communal land to conquistadors in return for dominating the Indians. In his reforms of 1863 and 1867, Benito Juárez, Mexico's first president, converted church and *ejido* lands into individually owned plots in an attempt to give peasants land rights.

Following the Mexican Revolution the *ejido* concept became a way of restoring lands that had been taken (usually legally purchased) from peasants by rich *hacendados* (big ranchers and plantation owners) during Spanish colonization and early Mexican independence.

Today's *ejido* is a land tract held in common by a peasant community. The property may include not only cultivated fields but also school properties, urban zones, water and forest resources, and any other facilities or resources either native to the land or produced by collective efforts. *Ejidos* are granted to *ejidatarios* by the government without rents or fees of any kind and originally were nontransferrable, nonattachable, and inalienable, i.e., *ejido* lands couldn't be sold, used as loan collateral, or taken away by local, regional or national legal bodies.

According to Mexican law, *ejidos* are considered neither state property nor private property but are entities of the "social interest sector." How they are used is solely the concern of the peasant communities that hold them, but around 95% of them are "individual" *ejidos* in which the common holdings are divided into individual plots and cultivated by individual *ejidatarios* and their families. The remaining five percent are "collective" *ejidos* that pool all land resources for collective production. The number and total acreage of Mexico's *ejidos* is not well documented but by 1970 they were estimated to encompass around 46% of national farmlands. According to every survey that has been conducted nationwide, *ejido* lands are the most unproductive of all agricultural lands in Mexico.

Various bits of *ejido* legislation enacted since the Revolution have alternately strengthened and weakened the program. In the 1980s, laws were passed that allowed *ejidatarios* to lease their lands to neighboring private estates for agricultural or livestock purposes. In the '90s, the government established regulations that now permit the sale of *ejido* lands. For the first time ever individuals living in *ejidos* have property rights.

Has the *ejido* program been successful? On the one hand, it has kept hereditary lands in the hands of peasant communities who have worked them for hundreds of years—without them, many *ejidatarios* would probably become landless migrant workers. On the other hand, because *ejido* production is notoriously low (as are fixed prices for agricultural products), the need for cash to survive in Mexico's cash economy has forced many *ejidatarios* to work as laborers on private neighboring lands. As a result, it has been estimated that *ejidatarios* are among the poorest and most exploited of Mexico's rural workers.

Maquiladoras

Since 1974 the *maquiladora* (also called "twin-plant" or "in-bond" factory) industry—in which foreign-owned companies build manufacturing facilities in Mexico, train Mexican workers, and export the profits—has grown at an average annual rate of approximately 17%. As many as 200 new *maquiladora* plants come on line in any given year, and the current total stands at around 3,000. The benefit to Mexico has been direct employment for over 600,000 Mexicans, along with the generation of around US$3.5 billion in annual revenue—second only to PEMEX as a source of national income.

Maquilas were once restricted to special "export processing zones" within 12.5 miles of the border, but in order to compete with other world labor markets the Mexican government has opened up the entire country to *maquilas*. *Maquila*-made products enjoy duty-free status when imported to the foreign company's country. Conversely, parts and raw materials imported into Mexico for use by the *maquiladoras* are tax exempt.

One of the intentions of the *maquila* program has been to slow the flow of migrant labor to the U.S. and Canada by enticing Mexicans to stay at home and work at foreign-owned companies. By allowing foreign capital to use inexpensive Mexican labor without paying taxes on the export of finished products, it's supposed to be a win-win situation; Mexico gets jobs and U.S. business makes a profit. But as long as the apparent standard of living is higher in *El Norte*, *maquila* jobs are not going to satisfy everybody.

North American Free Trade Agreement

Enter the much ballyhooed North American Free Trade Agreement, which in Mexico is called El Tratado de Libre Comercio. Ratified by the U.S. Congress in January 1994—and by the Canadian and Mexican governments much earlier—NAFTA will eliminate nearly all taxes and tariffs on goods exchanged between the U.S., Canada, and Mexico by 2009.

In Mexico—particularly Southern Mexico—NAFTA is more unpopular than in either the U.S. or Canada. In the minds of most Mexicans the agreement is linked to their number-one public enemy, exiled ex-president Carlos Salinas. The term "NAFTA" has become a little-understood buzzword that serves as a Mexican scapegoat for the country's recent economic crisis. Many businesspeople in Northern Mexico, however, still hope that NAFTA will live up to its promise.

North of the border feelings are mixed. NAFTA opponents in the U.S. and Canada claim that jobs in their countries will be lost as American and Canadian companies rush to set up shop in Mexico, leaving closed factories behind. Supporters counter that even before the treaty, American and Canadian companies had long been moving manufacturing operations to Mexico (and elsewhere) to take advantage of the large, inexpensive, and productive labor force as well as the growing Mexican demand for imported goods. With or without NAFTA, say the supporters, Mexico will continue to attract foreign manufacturers, traders, and investors. But without NAFTA, American- and Canadian-made products would have difficulty competing in the Mexican market due to high tariffs and other trade barriers, or in the world market due to high labor costs.

Furthermore, say NAFTA supporters, if the U.S. were to liberalize trade restrictions on Mexican products, the Mexican economy would presumably improve and *maquilas* would become unnecessary from the Mexican perspective. As the economic gap between the two countries diminished, say NAFTA advocates, illegal immigration to the U.S. would become less and less of a problem. As President Salinas said before his downfall: "I want to export goods—not people; if I do not create jobs for Mexicans in Mexico, they will merely walk across the border looking for jobs in the U.S., and then the American worker may lose *his* job."

Most experts agree it's still too early to judge if NAFTA has had a net positive or negative effect on any of the three countries involved. Predictions of job flight from the U.S. haven't been borne out; as of May 1996 American analysts figured the treaty had netted around 3,000 jobs on the U.S. side, a number not considered significant either way.

Trade between the three countries has grown considerably since 1 Jan. 1994, but that growth can likely be attributed to the fact that most tariffs between the countries had already been reduced or eliminated by a combination of GATT (the pre-NAFTA General Agreement on Tariffs and Trade) and unilateral trade liberalization on the Mexico side.

Complaints from Florida tomato and California avocado producers about Mexican competition have little to do with the treaty since nearly 90% of the winter crop of both of these products has always come from Mexico. NAFTA has merely made such situations more topical and has given growers in all three countries an outlet for international grievances. This is exactly one of the roles the treaty was designed to play.

And Mexico's 1994-95 economic crisis held back growth in that country, leaving as yet untested the theory that an improved Mexican economy will result in the purchase of more U.S. and Canadian exports.

In many ways, NAFTA recognizes a preexisting economic reality, namely the "silent commercial integration" that Mexico and the U.S. have cultivated over the past 150 years as a result of sharing a 3,000-km border. In spite of Mexico's number-two ranking among international trade partners, it has yet to be offered "most favored nation" status by the United States. With competitive trade blocs emerging in East Asia and the European Community, a North American trade alliance makes good long-range economic sense.

THE PEOPLE

DEMOGRAPHY

North vs. South

Northern Mexicans see themselves as almost a breed apart from their compatriots to the south. They're proud of being *norteños* (northerners), and this pride is evident in the many ways they manage to declare their northernness through language, dress, food, and custom.

First, some stereotypes: northerners wear wavy-brimmed, Texas-style Stetson headgear and boots; southerners wear flat-brimmed *sombreros* and sandals; northerners eat wheat tortillas; southerners prefer subsidized corn; north-

erners are comparatively punctual; southerners pay no attention to time; northerners are tall and fair-skinned; southerners are short and dark. Such statements are often heard in Mexico, but any foreign visitor traveling cross-country will quickly note both the relative inaccuracy of these stereotypes and the kernels of truth that have propagated them.

Ask a *norteño* what distinguishes the northern character from the southern and the most common answer will be that northerners are more hardworking, more self-reliant, and better looking! To the average *norteño*, southerners seem to rely excessively on fate and the Mexican government to see them through their lives. A special scorn is reserved for *chilangos,* a derogatory term used by *norteños* in reference to Mexico City politicians or businesspeople who come and try to tell the northerners how to run things. Ask a northerner to imitate *chilango* speech and they'll mimic a high, mincing voice.

The reciprocal view from the south—heavily influenced by the Mexican academic bias toward the Mesoamerican cultures of Southern Mexico—is keyed to the superiority southerners feel in being descended from the Aztecs and Mayans. Many Mexico City scholars still refer to the pre-Cortesian Amerindian cultures of the north as *los bárbaros del norte,* viewing them as the least civilized of Mexico's ancient cultures. To southerners, *norteño* speech sounds like a low growl.

A more significant difference between north and south is the average standard of living. With the exception of Mexico D.F., Northern Mexico states have a higher degree of literacy—as high as 95% in Nuevo León—than those of the south. In contrast, such southern states as Chiapas, Oaxaca, and Guerrero have literacy rates under 70%. The average number of households with running water and electricity is also greater in the north, and the incidence of malnutrition is far less.

Criollo vs. Mestizo

The tension between north and south dates to a caste system that existed in colonial New Spain and that to some degree still exists in a subtler and more simplified form throughout modern Mexico. In colonial Mexico the most privileged were the *gachupines* (pure-blooded Spaniards born in Spain), followed by *criollos* (pure-blooded Spaniards born in Mexico), mestizos (mixed Indian-Spanish born in Mexico), and *indios* (pure-blooded Indians). In many cases the Spanish lumped together *indios* and mestizos as simply *indígenas.* One of the ironies of the colonial caste system was that the *gachupines* themselves were descended from a 700-year mixing of Moors and Iberians, the conquerors and the conquered—a pattern the Spaniards repeated in the New World.

Their profound knowledge of how to survive in the desert made the Amerindian cultures of Northern Mexico more difficult for the Spaniards to subdue than any other indigenous groups in continental Mexico. Nevertheless, by the late colonial era, when Spaniards and *criollos* were settling the north in larger numbers, most of the Indian population of the region (which had been sparse to begin with) had been eliminated through disease or colonial violence. Hence a relatively larger proportion of Northern Mexico's population traces its ancestry to criollo or Spaniard (rather than mestizo or Indian) origin. Today the average *norteño* physiognomy tends to be more European than Amerindian.

To at least some degree, these physical differences play into the racial prejudices held by

AMERINDIANS OF NORTHERN MEXICO

GROUP	PRIMARY LOCATION	CURRENT APPROXIMATE POPULATION
Huastec	San Luis Potosí, Hidalgo, Tamaulipas, Veracruz	91,000
Tarahumara	Sierra Madre Occidental, Chih. & Dgo.	62,000
Mayo	Sonora	56,600
Tepehuan	Durango, Chihuahua, Zacatecas	17,600
Huichol	southeast Durango, Nayarit, Jalisco	14,800
Cora	southern Durango, Nayarit	10,200
Yaqui	Sonora	9,700
Seri	coastal Sonora	500
Papago & Pima	Sonora, Sinaloa	490
Kikapú (Kickapoo)	Coahuila	200

north and south. The Mexican government recognizes *mestizaje* ("mestizo-ism," or "mixing") as the root cultural characteristic of Mexico, yet distinguishes between two kinds of mestizos, the *indomestizos* of the south ("in whom indigenous characteristics predominate") and the *euromestizos* of the north ("in whom European traits prevail"). Also recognized are smaller groups of *afromestizos* in the southern Gulf coastal regions (particularly Veracruz), where African slaves were brought in by the Spanish toward the end of the colonial era to fill labor shortages caused by the rapidly shrinking indigenous population.

In many ways the schism between mestizos and Spaniards (or criollos) that led to the Mexican independence struggle was less of an issue in the north than in the south because of the northern frontier context. In addition to coping with the rugged terrain, Northern Mexicans have borne the brunt of the nation's Indian wars, revolutions, and U.S. invasions. This almost continual confrontation with the outside world has engendered a high degree of self-reliance and solidarity among *norteños*.

This self-reliance contrasts strongly with the traditional paternalism of Southern Mexico, where each person tends to participate in a web of "patron-client" relationships in which one is either taking care of someone or being taken care of—in either case for reciprocal services rendered. This relationship is mirrored in the enormous faith Southern Mexicans show for their patron saints and the relative importance of *compadrazgo* or "godparenthood." Although the north-south differences are not nearly as strict as this sociological explanation may imply, the tendencies are nevertheless observable.

Population Density and Growth

One reason highway traffic in Northern Mexico is pleasantly light compared to that farther south is simply that the northern states are the nation's least densely populated. Eight of the nine northern states fall below the national average of 46 persons per square km, ranging from a low of 11 persons per square km in Sonora to a high of 42 in Sinaloa; Nuevo León exceeds the national average at 55 persons per square km. Most of the latter state's population is found in the metropolitan Monterrey area.

Mexico's population growth rate is currently estimated at 1.8% per annum, relatively low for a developing country, particularly relative to Latin America. The overall rate for the north is even lower, perhaps due to the relatively higher levels of income and education.

Indígenas

Of the estimated nine million Amerindians who inhabited Mexico when the Spanish arrived in 1518, only a relatively small proportion survived the conquest. The principal causes of their decline in absolute numbers as well as in cultural varieties and cultural vitality include: the sudden changes in the socioeconomic and cultural order brought about by the conquest; the onslaught of diseases (smallpox, chicken pox, measles, malaria) brought from Europe and Africa, against which the indigenous populations had no natural defense; the violent form in which the conquest was accomplished and the local populations were kept under control; and the

JOE CUMMINGS

Chihuahua vaquero

exploitation and marginalization to which the Indians were subjected for over 300 years.

By 1568, only 47 years after the defeat of the Aztecs, the Indian population had declined to an estimated 2.5 million. Later, at the beginning of the 17th century, the total population of New Spain was approximately 7.6 million, of which the predominant proportion were mestizos; the indigenous population had shrunk to just 750,000.

Today the Mexican government classifies as *indígena* those persons who are monolingual in an "aboriginal" language; those whose first language is aboriginal but who also speak Spanish; and those who speak no aboriginal languages but whose "physical and cultural characteristics are aboriginal." According to this classification system, there are 56 indigenous groups (with 90 indigenous languages) in Mexico today, most of whom live in the southern states, with a total population of approximately 5.2 million (six percent of the nation's total population).

Around 240,000 *indígenas* reside in the nine states of Northern Mexico. Most numerous are the Huastecs of San Luis Potosí; the Tarahumaras of the Sierra Madre Occidental; the Tepehuanes of Durango, Chihuahua, and Zacatecas; and the Yaquis of Sonora. The Papagos, Pimas, Mayos, and Seris of Sonora, along with the Kikapús of Coahuila, are fewer in number (500 or less per group) and are considered in danger of cultural extinction.

Since no individual living in Mexico today can truly be considered more "indigenous" than another from a biological perspective, and since all races living in the Americas now or in the past were originally migrants from other parts of the world, the use of the term "indigenous" in the Mexican context is strictly political and without any anthropological basis. For Mexicans (and for many other North and South Americans as well), it is merely a way of ranking racial origins based on the temporal concept of "who came first," and according social privilege solely on the basis of race. In this way the *indígenas* concept extends the old Spanish caste system in new and subtle forms.

Immigrants

For Northern Mexicans, *mestizaje* is more than a blend of Spanish and Indian heritages; North-

ern Mexico remained a frontier area much longer than most of the nation and hence attracted an international mix of people who arrived in the New World long after the Spanish. Transmigration via the U.S. has also had a substantial influence on Northern Mexico's ethnic makeup.

During the late 19th and early 20th centuries, large groups of Mennonites and Mormons, fleeing religious persecution in the U.S. and Canada, immigrated to the fertile plains of the north. These groups—for the most part of northern European descent—have had a huge impact on Mexican farming practices and have become somewhat integrated into the overall social fabric, particularly in Chihuahua and Nuevo León.

Other immigrants who pioneered the Northern Mexican frontier included Chinese laborers, who came to work in 19th-century mines and railroad camps and many of whose descendants are now successful city merchants; and Greek farmers, who turned the Valle de Culiacán into one of the most productive farm areas in all of Mexico. Many of these newcomers intermarried and their descendants have added much to Northern Mexico's multicultural spirit.

The north also historically harbored Mexican intellectuals, artists, and dissidents fleeing political oppression in the south (and gravitating toward Chihuahua, Hermosillo, Durango, Mazatlán, Monterrey, and Tampico). Their legacy contributes to the liberal, independent character of today's Northern Mexico.

RELIGION

The original inhabitants of Mexico were indoctrinated in the ways of Roman Catholicism by Spanish missionaries between the 16th and 19th centuries. That Catholicism is now the majority religion in Mexico (around 90%) is an amazing achievement considering that it was laid over a vast variety of native belief systems in existence for perhaps thousands of years, and considering that the Mexicans eventually forcefully expelled the Spanish.

Most of the small existing Protestant population consists of Indians in the south who were missionized by North Americans in the 19th and 20th centuries. A few colonies of Mormons and Mennonites also thrive in the state of Chihuahua.

Although many Spanish Jews arrived in the early European migration to Mexico, the Spanish Inquisition forced most to convert to Catholicism.

Mexican Catholicism

In contrast to their Christian counterparts in Canada, America, and northern Europe, Mexican Catholics tend to be devout practitioners of their faith. Mexican Catholicism, however, has its own variations that distinguish the religion from its European predecessors. Some of these variations can be traced to preexisting Indian spiritual traditions that were absorbed by the Catholic faith and are localized according to tribe.

One variation common to all of Mexican Catholicism is the Virgin of Guadalupe cult, which began in 1531 when a dark-skinned Virgin Mary appeared before the peasant Juan Diego in a series of three visions at Tepeyac, near Mexico City (which coincidentally was a sacred Aztec site dedicated to the goddess Tonantzin). Many Mexican churches are named for Our Lady of Guadalupe, who has become so fused with Mexican identity that the slogan *¡Viva Guadalupe!* is commonly used at political rallies. The affectionate Mexican nickname for Guadalupe is La Morenita, "Little Darkling." She has become, as Mexican-American cultural commentator Richard Rodriguez puts it, the "official private flag of Mexico," and one way in which Catholicism has been absorbed by indigenous cultures rather than vice versa.The official feast day for Guadalupe, Dec. 12, is fervently celebrated throughout the country.

At one time most of Northern Mexico was under the ecclesiastical jurisdiction of the Guadalajara diocese; now there are regional dioceses centered in many Northern Mexican cities. The rural areas of Northern Mexico hold fewer churches per capita than those of the south; to accommodate its parishioners, a country church *(iglesia)* here might hold as many as 18 masses a day.

Roadside Religion

Occasionally along Mexico's roadways you'll see small roadside crosses (sometimes in clusters) or shrines. Often placed at fatal accident sites, each cross marks a soul's point of departure from this world. Larger shrines containing Christ or Virgin figures have been erected to confer blessings or protection on passing travelers. They can vary from simple enclosures made of vegetable-oil cans to elaborate sculptural designs.

CONDUCT AND CUSTOMS

Although Mexico is an extremely heterogeneous country with pronounced regional differences in food, music, language, and life perspectives, a few generalizations can be made about how the "Mexican character" may appear to outsiders.

Time and Appointments

Of the many stereotypes about Mexican culture, the one about the Mexican sense of time being highly flexible is probably the most accurate. The whys and wherefores are too numerous and complex for the context of this book; read Octavio Paz's *The Labyrinth of Solitude* for a glimpse of an explanation. However, it's important to realize that the so-called *mañana* attitude is a generalization; in many cases Mexi-

mission church, Cerocahui, Sierra Tarahumara

can individuals are punctual—especially when it comes to doing business with Americans. Furthermore, *norteños,* it is said, tend to be more punctual than their southern counterparts.

If you make an appointment with a northerner for dinner, a party, or other social engagement, you should figure that the actual meeting time will be around two hours later than verbally scheduled. As with business engagements, if the person involved has dealt frequently with Americans, this might not *always* be the case. Also, Mexicans will typically accept an invitation rather than say no, even if they don't plan to attend the scheduled event. This is because, within the Mexican social context, it is usually worse to refuse an invitation than to not show up. To avoid disappointment, prepare yourself for any of these scenarios.

When hiring a fishing boat or any sort of guide in Northern Mexico, you can expect a modicum of punctuality—most Mexicans in the tourist industry have adapted themselves to the expectations of gringo tourists. Again, business and social appointments differ.

Siesta

The stereotypical afternooon siesta, when everyone goes off to sleep for a couple of hours, is fast becoming history throughout Mexico. Nevertheless, a vestige of the siesta lingers in the hours kept by offices and small businesses, which are typically closed from 2-4 p.m. or 3-5 p.m. The first hour is reserved for *comida,* the midday meal, while the second hour is for relaxing or taking care of personal business. This long lunch hour is usually offset by longer evening hours; most Mexican offices and businesses stay open until 7-8 p.m.

No matter what hours are posted for small businesses, the actual opening and closing times may vary with the whims of the proprietors. This is also true for tourist information offices. Banks, on the other hand, usually follow their posted hours to the minute.

Meal Times

If you'll be meeting Mexican acquaintances for meals, whether at a restaurant or in their homes, be aware that customary eating times differ from those north of the border.

The first meal of the day, *desayuno* (break-fast), is usually taken at about the same time as the average American breakfast, say 6-8 a.m. Around 11 a.m., another breakfast/early lunch called *almuerzo* is sometimes eaten; on weekdays it's light, on weekends and holidays it may be more substantial. The *comida,* largest meal of the day, is eaten around 2-3 p.m. In small towns, workers will often go home for this meal and not return to the workplace until around 4-5 p.m.

After work, around 8-10 p.m., *la cena,* the final meal of the day, is eaten. *Cenas* are usually as light and informal as *desayunos,* so it is not often that guests are invited to a home for this meal. On weekends and holidays, the *cena* may become a grander occasion, however.

For information on what Mexicans typically eat at these meals, see "What to Eat," under "Food and Drink" in the On the Road chapter.

Terms of Address and Titles

Mexicans frequently use titles of respect when addressing one another. At a minimum, *señor* will do for men, *señora* for married women, and *señorita* for unmarried women or girls. When in doubt about a woman's marital status, *señorita* can be used.

Professional titles can also be used for variety and to show additional respect. *Maestro* (master) or *maestra* (mistress) are common and can be used to address skilled workers (cobblers, auto mechanics, seamstresses, etc.) and any teacher except those at secondary schools, colleges, and universities (who are *profesores*).

College graduates are *licenciado* (men) or *licenciada* (women), while doctors are *doctor* or *doctora.* Other professional titles include *arquitecto* (architect), *abogado* (attorney), *ingeniero* (engineer), and *químico* (chemist).

Body Language

Mexicans tend to use their arms and hands a lot during verbal communication. Learning to "read" the more common gestures can greatly enhance your comprehension of everyday conversations, even when you don't understand every word being spoken.

One of the more confusing gestures for Americans is the way Mexicans beckon to other persons by holding the hand out, palm down, and waving in a downward motion. This looks similar to a farewell gesture in the U.S. and Canada

IS THIS YOU?

An American woman recently wrote to us about her guided train tour along the rim of Chihuahua's Copper Canyon, complaining that: "They made us put used toilet paper in wastebaskets rather than in the toilets. . . . No one spoke English on the train. . . . There were army soldiers on the train and I thought we were going to be killed. I will never go back to Mexico and will be telling all my friends how dangerous it is."

It's a shame the woman's tour guide didn't take the time to explain that: (1) it is customary in most of Mexico not to put used toilet paper into the toilet bowl but rather in trash bins placed next to the toilet (this is because most Mexican plumbing systems aren't designed to accommodate wads of paper); (2) most Mexicans speak Spanish, not English; and (3) the soldiers on the train were stationed there for her protection and for the protection of her fellow passengers.

Still, if these are the kinds of things that might bother you, then you probably shouldn't visit Mexico.

but means "come here" in Mexico. Holding the palm upward and crooking the fingers toward the body, the typical American gesture for "come here," is a vaguely obscene gesture in Mexico.

Extending the thumb and forefinger from a closed hand and holding them about a half-inch apart means "a little bit" in America but in Mexico usually means "just a moment" or "wait a minute" (often accompanied by the utterance *"Momentito"* or *"Poquito"*).

The wagging of an upright forefinger means "No" or "Don't do that." This is a good gesture to

use when children hanging around at stoplights or gasoline pumps begin wiping your windshields and you don't want them to. But don't overdo it—they only need to see a few seconds of the wagging finger (otherwise you'll look out of control!).

Mexicans commonly greet one another with handshakes, which are used universally, including between the sexes and among children and adults. Mexican males who are friends will sometimes greet one another with an *abrazo* (embrace), and urban women may kiss one another on the left cheek. Foreigners should stick to the handshake until they establish more intimate relationships with *norteños*. Handshakes are also used upon parting.

Dress

Compared to their southern counterparts, who tend to be more conservative, *norteños* are relatively tolerant about the way visitors dress. Nonetheless, invisible lines exist that, out of respect for Mexican custom, shouldn't be crossed.

Number one is that beachwear is not considered suitable dress for town visits. Beach resorts are the most obvious exception to this general rule since during peak seasons tourists may outnumber the locals in these towns, so the locals are used to gringo immodesty. In downtown Mazatlán, however, beachwear will result in indignant stares if you wander far from the beach strip.

Upon entering a church or chapel in Mexico, men are expected to remove their hats (many Mexican males remove their hats when passing in front of a church). More tradition-minded Mexican women will cover their heads when inside a church, but younger women usually don't and foreign females aren't expected to. Shorts, sleeveless shirts/blouses, sandals, and bare feet are considered improper dress (for both men and women) in churches, even for brief sightseeing visits.

BOB RACE

ON THE ROAD

SIGHTSEEING ITINERARIES

Many of the places described in this guide can be reached within one or two days by car or bus from the U.S. border. Still, the total area covered encompasses over half of Mexico's surface area; time and money constraints will compel most visitors to make advance decisions as to which parts to see and which to leave out.

Most visitors entering Northern Mexico by road approach either from the northwest (San Luis Río Colorado, Nogales, Agua Prieta) or from the northeast (Piedras Negras, Nuevo Laredo, Matamoros), hence the following suggested itineraries are divided by angle of entry. Persons with more money than time can fly to any of Northern Mexico's many airports, thus avoiding the northwest-northeast thoroughfares. Road travel, however, is the best way to experience the most of what these regions have to offer. Driving in Northern Mexico is mostly a pleasant experience due to the relatively high quality of roads and overall lack of traffic.

These are only suggested itineraries, to be adjusted according to individual tastes and energy. Some people are content to spend two weeks or more in one place; others prefer to see and experience as many different places as they can, regardless of time spent in each locale. In Mexico it usually pays to be a little underambitious with your travel plans; don't try to see too much in too short an interval or your travels may quickly become a tedious chore.

Northwest

If you have only five days to spend, consider staying within the state of Sonora, where you can explore Pinacate National Park, the historic Jesuit missions, the beaches of Bahía Kino and San Carlos, or the colonial city of Alamos. Or head straight for the state of Chihuahua's *barrancas* (canyons) if hiking or canyoneering is your particular interest, and—if time permits—stop off in the state capital of Chihuahua on your way out for a little culture and history.

With eight days to explore, you could add parts of Sinaloa, including colonial El Fuerte, the former Sierra Madre mining center of Cosalá, and the beaches of Mazatlán.

Ten days would allow the addition of a foray into Chihuahua's Sierra Tarahumara (Copper Canyon) area via the spectacular Chihuahua al Pacífico rail journey from Los Mochis, Sinaloa.

If you have two weeks for the northwest, consider making a Sonora-Sinaloa-Durango-Chihuahua loop, taking in the best along the way: the Sonora missions and Alamos; Mazatlán; the scenic Mazatlán-Durango mountain highway; historic Parral; and the Copper Canyon. The scenery along this loop encompasses parts of the Sonoran Desert, the Pacific Ocean, the Sierra Madre Occidental, and the Chihuahuan Desert.

Northeast

For the naturalist, a five-day trip would allow plenty of time to explore the Gulf of Mexico coast from Matamoros, N.L., to Tampico, Tamps., an area known for good fishing, deserted beaches, intracoastal lagoons, marshes, and barrier islands. Depending on your interests, an enjoyable five-day sojourn alternatively could be spent exploring the Monterrey-Saltillo area in Nuevo León—shopping in the markets and malls of these two very different cities and visiting the Cumbres de Monterrey National Park (which includes Horsetail Falls, the caves of Villa de García, and Huasteca Canyon).

With eight days to spend, the above Gulf Coast and Monterrey-Saltillo itineraries could be combined. A good 10-day trip might include these along with a visit to Ciudad Valles and the lush Huasteca region of San Luis Potosí. If colonial architecture is your major interest, substitute the city of San Luis Potosí for Monterrey in your 10-day trip. More nature? Slot in a visit to the desert springs of Cuatrociénegas, Coahuila.

If you have two weeks, consider a loop that takes in the Gulf of Mexico coast, Monterrey-Saltillo (and/or Cumbres de Monterrey National Park), the Región Huasteca, San Luis Potosí, and the exquisitely restored silver city of Zacatecas.

North Central

If you enter Mexico via Ciudad Juárez or Ojinaga (opposite the West Texas towns of El Paso and Presidio, respectively), you'll miss out on the coastal attractions along the Sea of Cortez or Gulf of Mexico. Nevertheless, this is the most direct route to Casas Grandes, the Sierra Tarahumara (Copper Canyon area), Parral, Durango, and the quaint winemaking town of Parras de la Fuente in the Región Lagunera. Any of these destinations could be accomplished within a five- to seven-day trip.

An ambitious eight- to 10-day circuit from Juárez/El Paso or Ojinaga/Presidio might head south to Chihuahua's state capital, then to the Sierra Tarahumara, Durango, and Zacatecas, returning north through Saltillo, Las Cumbres de Monterrey National Park, and Monterrey to Laredo, Texas. From Juárez/El Paso, you could also toss in a stop at the Paquimé ruins in Casas Grandes.

A desert-mountain-sea alternative along the same route might divert west from Durango to Mazatlán, then up the Sea of Cortez coast to Hermosillo, from where you can return by road to El Paso via Agua Prieta. This loop takes in the Chihuahuan Desert, the Sierra Madre Occidental, the Sea of Cortez, and the Sonoran Desert.

The Grand Tour

Road warriors with flexible schedules can comfortably drive through all nine states of Northern Mexico from coast to coast—taking in all the sights mentioned above—within a month. A schedule of five or six weeks would allow more time to explore sidetrack destinations like Real de Catorce, S.L.P., and Coahuila's Sierra del Carmen, as well as more time for resting and soaking it all in.

An itinerary that would lead you through the best of Northern Mexico would include: Pinacate National Park, Son.; the Sierra Tarahumara (Urique and Copper Canyons, Basaseachic Falls), Chih.; the Paquimé ruins at Casas Grandes, Chih.; Alamos, Son.; Mazatlán, Sin.; the Mazatlán-Durango drive along Mexico 40; Zacatecas and Guadalupe, Zac.; San Luis Potosí, S.L.P.; El Potosí National Park, S.L.P.; the Región Huasteca, S.L.P.; La Pesca, Tamps. (plus Tampico for seafood lovers); El Cielo, Tamps.; Monterrey, N.L.; Cumbres de Monterrey National Park, N.L.; Saltillo, Coah.; and the Colombia-Matamoros drive parallel to the Río Bravo/Rio Grande along Mexico 2.

OUTDOOR RECREATION

Some of Northern Mexico's major attractions fall under this heading—from hiking in the Sierras Madre Occidental and Oriental to marlin fishing in Mazatlán. For the most part, Northern Mexico's outdoor recreation can be enjoyed at little or no cost simply because user demand is so low; when fees are involved they're usually quite reasonable.

HIKING AND BACKPACKING

National Parks and Preserves

Northern Mexico has several types of officially designated protected areas, including *parques nacionales* (national parks), *parques naturales* (literally "natural parks," a designation similar to that of "natural area" or nature reserve in the United States), *reservas de la biosfera* (biosphere reserves), and *áreas de protección de flora y fauna silvestre* (wildlife protection areas). While the legal definition for each of these varies considerably, in practice all are multiuse areas containing some portions that are well-protected and others where some habitation and exploitation is permitted. Enforcement remains a major problem due to lack of funding and staffing, though overall the country has done amazingly well considering the political and economic situation.

Foreigners with a keen interest in Mexico's natural environment often argue about which places are "officially" protected areas and which aren't. For the record, the following list is taken directly from official government documents prepared by the Secretaría de Medio Ambiente, Recursos Naturales y Pesca (SEMARNAP, the Ministry for Environment, Natural Resources, and Fishing). SEMARNAP is the main government organ charged with creating and administering such zones.

Chihuahua: Parque Nacional Basaseachic Falls, Parque Nacional Cumbres de Majalca, and Parque Natural Barranca del Cobre

Nuevo León: Parque Nacional Cumbres de Monterrey, Parque Nacional El Sabinal, and Monumento Natural Cerro de la Silla

Durango: Parque Nacional Raymundo, Parque Nacional Puerta de los Angeles y Barranca de los Negros, Parque Natural La Ciudad, Reserva de la Biosfera de Mapimí (also covers parts of Chihuahua and Coahuila), and Reserva de la Biosfera La Michilía

Coahuila: Parque Nacional de los Novillos, Parque Natural la Amistad, and Área de Protección de Flora y Fauna Silvestre Cuatrociénegas

San Luis Potosí: Parque Nacional El Gororrón, Parque Nacional El Potosí, and Reserva de la Biosfera Sierra del Abra Tanchipa

Tamaulipas: Parque Natural Camargo, Reserva de la Biosfera El Cielo

Sonora: Reserva de la Biosfera El Pinacate y Gran Desierto de Altar (also covers part of Baja California), Reserva Especial de la Biosfera Isla Tiburón, Reserva Especial de la Biosfera Cajón

JOE CUMMINGS

del Diablo, Reserva de la Biosfera Alto Golfo de California y Delta del Río Colorado

In addition, Rancho Nuevo, Tamps., is considered a special wildlife sanctuary for sea turtles, while the cloud forest at El Cielo, Tamps., has been double-honored with International Biosphere Reserve status by the United Nations as well as the domestic equivalent. The Reserva Especial de la Biosfera Islas del Golfo de California covers all the islands in the Sea of Cortez (or Gulf of California). And an international park is under discussion for an area along the Texas-Coahuila border that would link Big Bend National Park in the U.S. with Mexico's Sierra del Carmen.

At most of these officially protected areas, public facilities are few and rudimentary—in some cases ("natural parks" or *parques naturales*) they're nonexistent by definition. Some of these public lands are described in detail in later sections of this book.

Trails

The Sierras Madre Occidental and Oriental are full of hiking trails—from wide, 150-year-old paths created by Indians or immigrant shepherds to smaller, more recent trails worn by hikers. On the lower, subtropical slopes toward both coast lowlands, trails are much more scarce—it's a good idea to scout an area first and ask questions locally about the best way to get from point A to point B. Although it's sometimes tempting to venture off established trails, this is a good way to get lost; it can also add to the destruction of delicate ecosystems. Light trails that don't seem to go anywhere may be animal trails that connect surface water sources.

Maps

Topographic maps, which chart trails and elevation differentials, are essential for extended hiking and backpacking. **Map Link,** 25 E. Mason, Santa Barbara, CA 93101, tel. (805) 965-4402, fax (805) 962-0884, and **Map Centre,** 2611 University Ave., San Diego, CA 92104, tel. (619) 291-3830, carry fairly complete lines of Mexico topographic maps in two scales—1:250,000 (contour lines every 50 meters on plains and every 100 meters in mountains), and 1:50,000 (contour lines every 10 meters and 20 meters, respectively). They're sold separately (around

US$6 each) according to region. Map Link will mail out a catalog on request.

These same topographic maps are also available in Mexico from any Instituto Nacional de Estadística Geografía e Informática (INEGI) office for about US$3 per sheet (see "Maps and Information" under "Getting Around," below). Some topos may be out of print, in which case you can usually obtain a photocopy of archival prints from an INEGI office for US$8. These maps not only show trails and contour lines, but villages not normally marked on other maps. In Mexico they're mostly used by the military, *narcotraficantes,* and surveyors.

Although you won't need a great deal of Spanish to read the INEGI maps, you might need to know the following translations for the map legend:

brecha: gravel road

vereda: path

terracería transitable en todo tiempo: all-weather dirt road

terracería transitable en tiempo de secas: dirt road passable only in dry weather

carretera pavimentada: paved highway

carretera de más de dos carriles, caseta de pago: toll highway of more than two lanes

Equipment

For hikes of a day or less, you'll just need sturdy footwear (light, high-topped hiking boots are preferable to sneakers in rocky terrain) and whatever food and water you plan to consume for the day.

Longer hikes obviously require more preparation and more equipment. Whether in the desert or the mountains, bring enough clothing to remain comfortable at both ends of the thermometer—Northern Mexico days tend to be warm, nights cool. If you plan to hike in the high sierras, bring a sleeping bag good for temperatures down to -4° C (25° F). For camping at lower elevations, make sure whatever tent you bring has plenty of ventilation. Good hiking boots are essential; thick lug soles are preferable as they provide protection from sharp rocks and desert plants. Bring along a first-aid kit that includes an elastic bandage—to use for sprains and snakebite treatment (see the special topic "Snakebite Prevention and Treatment")—and a pair of tweezers for removing thorns and cactus spines. Also bring a flashlight, compass, waterproof matches, a knife, flashlight with extra batteries, foul-weather gear, and a signal device (mirror or whistle). If you'll be hiking along the coast, a telescoping fishing rod and light tackle are handy additions, as surf fish are usually plentiful (see "Fishing," below, for details on what to catch).

Water
Always carry plenty of water—a minimum of one gallon per person per full day of walking during hot weather, three quarts in winter. Although there are streams and springs in the sierras, the water level varies considerably and you shouldn't count on finding year-round sources of water along the way except in canyon bottoms. If you need drinking water from one of these sources, always boil it first for at least 10 minutes or treat it with purification tablets, iodine crystals, or with a water filter designed to remove impurities. Even if you know of reliable water sources along the trail, it's a good idea to bring along a water purification system just to be sure. Bring enough food for the duration of your hike plus one or two days extra.

Camping Do's and Don'ts
In addition to all the usual rules for choosing campsites, here remember not to camp beneath coconut palms (a falling coconut could knock your tent in or fracture your skull) or in arroyos (danger of flash floods).

Open fires are permitted just about anywhere in Mexico except within city limits. Even in the desert, fuel is plentiful (dried ocotillo and cactus skeletons make excellent fuels), but imitate the locals and keep your fires small so as not to waste any. Never leave hot coals or ashes behind—smother the embers with sand (or water if you can spare it) till cool to the touch.

Pack out all trash that won't burn (including cigarette butts—they take 10-12 years to decompose), bury human waste six inches down, and don't use soap in streams or springs.

Desert Hiking
For hikes in the Sonoran or Chihuahuan Deserts, special precautions are appropriate in addition to those outlined above. Water is the number-one concern; desert hiking requires at least one gallon of water per day per person—some people recommend at least two gallons per day if you plan to hike while the sun is high. On extended excursions of more than a night or two, the weight of anything beyond two gallons (water weighs about 3.7 kg per gallon) is prohibitive and you'll need to obtain advance information on reliable water sources along the trail. While hiking, keep your mouth closed and breathe through your nose to keep the mouth and throat from drying out. This will also keep you cooler, as the nasal cavities are designed to moderate outside air temperatures as the air passes into your lungs.

Sun protection is especially essential in the desert. Wear long-sleeved clothing with light, reflective colors (white is best), sunglasses, a wide-brimmed hat, and sunscreen. Between 11 a.m. and 3 p.m., it's best to take shelter from the sun if possible, especially during the hotter months. Most of Mexico's deserts have a modicum of shade available in the form of mesquite trees, overhanging cliffs, or leaning boulders. But it's also a good idea to carry your own shade in the form of a lightweight opaque tarp (a poncho can double as a tarp and rain protection—yes, it does rain in the desert occasionally).

Anyone contemplating an extended desert hike for the first time might consider reading at least one of the books on desert travel listed in the References section at the end of this book. These contain important information on a variety of desert survival topics, from how to test the edibility of plants to making your own water with an improvised solar still.

HUNTING

The Mexican government allows licensed hunting in season, as regulated by SEMARNAP. Hunting is popular in Northern Mexico among foreigners and Mexicans alike but is for the most part restricted to various species of rabbit, quail, dove, pheasant, duck, and goose. White-tailed deer and mule deer are also hunted but permits are limited in number and expensive by Mexican standards. Occasionally a special hunt for the rare desert bighorn sheep *(borrego cimarrón)* is held; bighorn permits cost as much as US$12,000 and aren't usually issued to foreigners (earlier in this century, bighorn hunting by foreigners nearly wiped out the entire population).

Hunting regulations, which include bag limits on both size and number, are strictly enforced. Hunting seasons vary according to species, but no hunting is permitted anywhere in May, June, and July. Current SEMARNAP hunting-season calendars can be obtained through any Mexican embassy or consulate abroad. A maximum of two rifles per hunter is allowed, along with two boxes of American shells per gun. With the proper hunting permit, additional shells may be purchased in Mexico through the Alcampo chain; only .22 caliber bullets and 12-, 16-, 20-, and 40-gauge shotgun cartridges are legally available. Signs that say *Prohibido Cazar* mean "Hunting Prohibited."

SEMARNAP hunting permits come in six types: Type I—waterfowl, Type II—doves, Type III—other birds, Type IV—permitted mammals, Type V—limited, and Type VI—specials. To apply directly to the Mexican government for a permit, contact SEMARNAP, Aquiles Serdán 28, piso 7, Mexico, D.F. 06500. Permits are valid for only one Mexican state at a time; allow at least two months for processing.

In addition to the SEMARNAP hunting permit, foreign hunters need a consular certificate, special visa, and military gun permit. The consular certificate may be obtained from any Mexican embassy or consulate upon presentation of a letter from the hunter's local police or sheriff's office verifying that the hunter has no criminal record. This certificate is also necessary for obtaining the military gun permit, which is issued by army garrisons at the Mexicali, Nogales, Ciudad Juárez, and Nuevo Laredo border crossings. Gun permits costs a steep US$150-170 each nowadays, a tax that deters all but the most serious or wealthy hunters.

Finally, a new regulation requires that all foreign hunters be accompanied by a licensed Mexican hunting guide. The average guided hunt costs US$100-135 a day.

The whole process of obtaining the required permits and a guide is very time consuming, even if you speak perfect Spanish. You're better off arranging the guide and all the necessary paperwork through a U.S. broker service or Mexican hunting outfitter; a list of the latter can be requested from any Mexican consulate. This costs a bit more than applying directly through SEMARNAP because you have to pay either membership dues or a surcharge, but the procedure is guaranteed to be much smoother and quicker.

Organizations dedicated to helping hunters obtain Mexican permits and guides include: **Mexican Hunting Association,** 3302 Josie Ave., Long Beach, CA 90808, tel. (213) 421-6215; **Joan Irvine Travel,** 1600 West Coast Hwy., Newport Beach, CA 92663, tel. (714) 548-8931; and **Sunbelt Hunting and Fishing,** P.O. Box 3009, Brownsville, TX 78520, tel. (210) 546-9101 or (800) 876-4868. (The California outfits specialize in northwestern Mexico trips while the Texas agency focuses on northeast Mexico.) Certain hotels and sporting goods stores in regions near well-known hunting grounds—e.g., Ciudad Victoria, Tamps.; Hermosillo, Son.; Chihuahua, Chih.; Los Mochis, Sin.; and Torreón, Coah.—also outfit hunters.

FISHING

Mexico's reputation as one of the best sportfishing regions in the world is well deserved. Although it's most famous for deep-sea fish, especially the Mazatlán area's acrobatic billfish (marlin, sailfish, and swordfish), Northern Mexico also offers fishing opportunities for surf casters, lake trollers, small boaters, and sport divers.

Onshore Fishing

Onshore or surf fishing can be enjoyed anywhere along the coast where you can get a line into the water (unless you see a rare *Prohibido Pescar* sign). Surf fishing is good along the Gulf of Mexico coast between Playa Bagdad and Lago Morales (La Pesca), and on the Sea of Cortez and Pacific Ocean south of Los Mochis, but fish can be taken in just about any surf zone along either coastline. Common onshore fish along the Sea of Cortez and Pacific coast include surfperch, cabezon, sand bass, ladyfish, halibut, corvina, opaleye, leopard shark, triggerfish, and croaker. On the Gulf of Mexico side, look for flounder, croaker, redfish (red drum), sand seatrout, ladyfish, and black drum. All of these are excellent food fishes.

Note: One fish commonly caught along the Sea of Cortez and Pacific coast is the puffer, called *bolete* in Mexico. Be warned that the meat of the puffer is toxic to humans and can cause poisoning. Two species are common to the region: the bullseye puffer, which has a brownish body with black spots; and the golden puffer, which is either all golden or a dark purple-black with white spots and white fin trim, depending on its stage of maturity. The bodies of both species expand like balloons when they're disturbed (the easiest way to identify them).

Inshore Fishing

Anyone with access to a small boat, either a trailered skiff or a rented *panga,* can enjoy inshore fishing at depths of around 50-100 fathoms. The *panga,* Mexico's most popular type of fishing boat, is an open fiberglass skiff that's usually five to six meters long and powered by a 40- to 50-horsepower outboard motor.

Common inshore catches on the lower Sea of Cortez and Pacific coast include many of the surf fishes mentioned above, plus various kinds of groupers, Mazatlán jack, seabass, bonito shark, sculpin (scorpionfish), barracuda, rockfish, lingcod, sierra, pompano, amberjack, red and yellow snapper, pargo, and cabrilla (cabrilla must be released if caught—see "Legal Requirements," below). Larger gamefish occasionally taken inshore include bluefin and yellowfin tuna, yellowtail, dorado, jack crevalle, and roosterfish.

Inshore fishing on the Gulf of Mexico coast includes the excellent bay, *boca,* and lagoon fishing along the barrier islands between Tampico and the U.S. border, where the onshore Gulf fish listed above are common, as is snooker. Farther off the windward side of the barrier islands, typical Gulf catches include silver and spotted seatrout, sheepshead, ling, kingfish, skipjack, bonito, tarpon, Florida pompano, blue runner, and mackerel. All are good eating.

Offshore Fishing

The bigger game fish are found in deeper waters —over 100 fathoms (about 180 meters or 600 feet)—and require bigger tackle and more technique, e.g., specialized trolling methods prescribed for each type of fish. Larger boats—fishing cruisers—are usually necessary simply because of the distances involved from shore to fishing areas.

Because of the special equipment and techniques involved in offshore fishing, many visitors hire local fishing guides (who usually provide boats and tackle) to take them to offshore fishing grounds. A sometimes less expensive alternative is to sign up for fishing cruises that take out groups of tourist anglers on a big powerboat.

Mazatlán is the west coast center for offshore sportfishing. Most offshore anglers are after striped, blue, or black marlin, sailfish, swordfish, wahoo, dorado, roosterfish (papagallo), yellowtail, and tuna. Offshore fishing on the Gulf of Mexico side brings in sailfish, blue marlin, barracuda, red snapper, grouper, amberjack, and warsaw. All of these fish are large, powerful fighters and require skill in handling rod and line. The billfish are known as the most acrobatic, performing high leaps and pirouettes when hooked, although the wahoo and roosterfish will also "greyhound," performing a series of long, low jumps while swimming rapidly in one direction.

Of the billfish, only the swordfish is considered particularly good eating; the other billfish are thought of as traditional trophies to be stuffed and mounted in someone's den or living room. To their increasing credit, many sportfishers these days are releasing billfish after the fight is over; many sportfishing outfitters discourage (or even forbid) the taking of these beautiful creatures unless a fish has been badly damaged in the fight. The wahoo, dorado, roosterfish, yellowtail, and various tunas all make excellent eating.

Fishing Seasons

Fish bite somewhere in Mexico waters year-round. Water temperature, ocean currents, weather patterns, fish migrations, and other changing variables, however, mean that you usually won't find the same type of fish in the same spot in December, say, as in July. All the variables interact to provide a com-

marlin

BOB RACE

plex set of fishing conditions that not only vary from month to month but also from year to year. An unusually dry year in the American Southwest, for example, can lessen the outflow of nutrients from the Colorado River into the Sea of Cortez, thus diminishing the proliferation of plankton and other small marine creatures at the bottom of the Cortez food chain. This, in turn, will affect populations of larger fish from seabass to whale sharks (a Cortez resident and the largest fish on the planet).

All the various "fishing calendars" in print (including the ones in this book) can serve only as general guidelines. The happiest sportfishers drop line with the knowledge that a certain amount of luck is always involved. It also helps to ask around once you've arrived at a fishing area —try local sporting goods stores, bait shops, and other anglers. In the most popular fishing areas, professional guides are available.

A few generalizations with regard to fishing seasons are possible. The greatest variety and number of offshore, onshore, and inshore fish are swimming the widest range of Mexican waters between April and October, when the water temperatures are relatively warm. During the winter, many Sea of Cortez and Pacific species migrate south and are available only in the Mazatlán area.

Fortunately for winter anglers farther north, however, exceptions abound. The widely distributed California yellowtail, for example, is present year-round, migrating up and down the Sea of Cortez (Altata to Mazatlán in winter, central to northern Cortez in summer) and the lower Pacific coast. Wahoo generally spend Dec.-April near Mazatlán, moving up the southern Cortez in the warmer months. On the Gulf of Mexico coast, redfish, black drum, and sheepshead are plentiful Jan.-Feb., flounder and speckled trout Oct.-November. Most other Gulf of Mexico species are present in some numbers year-round.

As a final caveat, remember that an unusually warm winter will mean better fishing all along the Sea of Cortez/Pacific coast; likewise a particularly cold winter will force many fish south, making even Mazatlán and the Gulf of Mexico less productive than average.

Equipment

Although bait and tackle are available at shops in Hermosillo, San Carlos, Los Mochis, Mazat-

lán, La Pesca, and Tampico, supplies vary and you can't count on finding exactly what you want. Therefore you ought to have your gear squared away, according to the type of fishing you plan on trying, before your arrival in Northern Mexico.

A full fishing kit containing tackle for every conceivable Mexico sportfishing possibility would probably weigh in excess of 150 pounds. But seasoned Mexico anglers claim you can get by in just about any situation with four basic rigs: two trolling rods with appropriate reels and 50- to 80-pound test monofilament line (for offshore fishing), one medium-duty eight- or nine-foot rod and spinner with 20- to 30-pound mono (for surf casting and onshore fishing), and a six-foot light spinning rig loaded with four- to eight-pound line (for bait fishing, freshwater fishing, or light surf casting). Two trolling rigs are recommended because these are the ones used against the fish most likely to yank your outfit into the sea; it's always best to have a spare.

Bait

What a fish will take at any given moment is highly variable, hence the properly equipped angler is ready with an array of natural and artificial bait. Live or frozen bait (including everything from squid to mackerel to clams) is usually available near the more frequented fishing areas; you can also easily catch your own with a light rig. A cooler is necessary for keeping bait fresh— hired boats will usually supply these. Among the vast selection of artificial lures available, the most reliable seem to be those perennials that imitate live bait, such as spoons, leadheads, candybars, swimmers, and, for offshore fishing, trolling heads. Bring along a few of each in different colors and sizes and you'll be ready for just about anything. A few highly specialized lures, such as marlin heads and "wahoo specials," can be purchased in San Carlos, Mazatlán, and La Pesca.

Tide Tables

Serious onshore-inshore anglers will want to bring along a set of current tide tables so they can decide what time to wake up in the morning. (For information on where to obtain Pacific and Cortez tables, see "Charts and Tide Tables" under "Boating," below.)

Freshwater Fishing

Arid Northern Mexico has a surprising number of lakes, rivers, and streams with angling opportunities. Common catches throughout the region include catfish, crappie, largemouth and smallmouth bass, sunfish, trout, walleye, and white bass. Particularly good fishing venues include the reservoirs of northwestern Mexico and those of the lower Río Bravo and Río Soto de la Marina valleys in northeastern Mexico. State governments periodically stock many of these lakes with gamefish. Presa Vicente Guerrero (Lake Guerrero) in Tamaulipas is known throughout North America for its excellent largemouth bass fishing. More detail on inland fishing is given in the destination chapters.

Small- to medium-size spoons, plastic worms, and spinners are the basics for Mexico lake fishing—bring a wide selection for experimentation.

Fishing Licenses

The red tape surrounding fishing in Mexico is minimal. The basic requirement is that anyone over 16 who intends to fish must have a Mexican fishing license; technically, this includes all persons aboard boats equipped with fishing tackle, whether they plan to fish or not. This is important to remember for anyone going along on fishing trips as a spectator.

A single license is valid for all types of fishing, anywhere in Mexico, and is issued for periods of one week (US$22), one month (US$28), or one year (US$35). A license is usually included in the price of sportfishing cruises but not necessarily on *panga* trips—if you don't have a license, be sure to ask if one is provided before going out on a guided trip. The cost of the Mexican license has been rising steadily over the last few years but it remains less expensive than most fishing licenses in the U.S. or Canada. Rates are reviewed quarterly and adjusted accordingly, so those given above could rise or decrease a bit every three to six months.

Fishing licenses are available from a number of sources, including tackle shops and Mexican insurance companies near the U.S.-Mexico border. They can be obtained by mail from the Secretaría de Pesca, 1010 Second Ave., Suite 101, San Diego, CA 92103, tel. (619) 233-6956, fax 233-0344; or from California branches of the American Automobile Association (AAA).

Mexican Regulations

The general daily bag limit is 10 fish per person, including no more than five fish of any one species. Exceptions include perch and carp, of which up to 20 a day can be taken. Certain fish varieties are further protected as follows (per-day limits): one full-grown billfish (marlin, sailfish, or swordfish); two each of tarpon, shark, halibut, roosterfish, and dorado. For inland fishing the limit is five fish per day, whether one or more species.

Bag limits are the same for divers as for rod-and-reelers; only handheld spears and band-powered spearguns (no gasguns or power-heads) are permitted. The use by nonresident aliens of gill nets, purse nets, and every other kind of net except handling nets is prohibited, as are traps, explosives, and poisons.

The taking of shellfish (clams, oysters, abalone, shrimp, and lobster) by nonresident aliens is also officially prohibited; however, it is generally recognized that taking a reasonable amount of these (no more than can be eaten in a meal or two) is permitted by custom. This regulation is in place to protect the Mexican fishing unions; even buying shellfish from local sources is prohibited unless purchased from a public market or *cooperativa*, in which case you should obtain a receipt to show in the event of an inspection.

Totuava, sea turtles, and cabrilla are protected species that cannot be taken by anyone.

Mexican fishing regulations are subject to change at any time—be sure to check with the Mexico Department of Fisheries for the latest version before embarking on a fishing expedition.

Other Precautions

Fishing, boating, diving, and other aquatic activities can have long-term effects in lagoons and on delicate shore ecologies—use special care when traversing these places. Never drop an anchor or a fishing line on a coral reef, as such contact can cause irreversible damage to reef systems.

U.S. Customs and California State Regulations

Once you've bagged a load of fish in accordance with Mexican fishing limits, you still have to conform to U.S. Customs regulations if you cross the U.S.-Mexico border with your catch. Fortunately, the U.S. regulations conform with Mexican bag limits, so that whatever you've legally caught south of the border may be transported north of the border. The state of California further requires anyone transporting fish into the state to present a completed "California Declaration of Entry" form, which is available at the border. In order to facilitate the identification of the transported fish, some part of each fish—head, tail, or skin—must be left intact (in other words, you can't just show up at the border with a cooler full of anonymous fish fillets).

BOATING

From sea kayaks to huge motor yachts, pleasure boats of all kinds are used in Northern Mexico. The most heavily navigated area is the Sea of Cortez/Pacific Ocean coast between Bahía Kino and Mazatlán, but even these waters are relatively uncrowded compared to the marinas and bays of the United States. Along the Gulf of Mexico, pleasure boating is much less popular in spite of the many opportunities offered by the barrier island system running from the U.S. border south to Tampico.

Because of the relative safety of Sea of Cortez boating, this is the most popular coast, particularly for smaller crafts—kayaks, skiffs, and motor- or sail-powered vessels under 35 feet. The Cortez waters are relatively calm most of the time, but late summer and early fall *chubascos* (Pacific hurricanes) can whip up sizable and sometimes treacherous swells. South of Mazatlán in the open Pacific, and anywhere along the Gulf of Mexico coast, high winds and challenging swells come and go year-round.

The major difference between the two coasts is the number of available, safe anchorages. The Gulf of Mexico side features only four anchorages that provide protection when winds become treacherous: Mezquital in the northern Laguna Madre, La Pesca at the southern tip of the Laguna Madre barrier island system, Lomas del Real in Lago San Andrés, and Tampico. Over on the Cortez side, however, dozens of protected anchorages line the east coast and the Cortez islands. The Sea of Cortez thus offers not only safer boating waters but a wider selection of places to drop anchor on a whim.

Open-ocean Pacific or Gulf of Mexico sailing is not for the novice. The relative absence of assistance and boat-repair facilities make the Gulf coast especially risky for first-timers.

It is now possible for boaters to navigate from ports in California, British Columbia, or Alaska to Baja California's Ensenada marina and then arrange for overland transport of their boats (on hired trailers) from Ensenada to San Felipe on the Cortez side. From San Felipe you can then undertake a crossing to San Carlos on the mainland. The Ensenada tourist office, Blvd. Costero and Calle Rocas, Ensenada, Baja California Norte, tel. (66) 72-30-22, fax 72-30-81, has details on the service.

Cartopping
The most popular boats for short-range cruising, fishing, and diving are those that can be transported on top of a car, RV, or truck, e.g., aluminum skiffs in the 12- to 15-foot range. The primary advantage of this type of boat is that it can be launched just about anywhere. Larger, trailered boats are restricted to boat launches with trailer access. The most appropriate outboard motor size for a 12- to 15-footer is 15-20 horsepower—larger motors are generally too heavy to be carried separately from the boat (a necessity for cartopping).

If you decide to transport a skiff (or sea kayak) on top of your vehicle, be sure to use a sturdy, reliable rack or loader with a bow line to the front bumper and plenty of tie-downs. The rough road surfaces typical of Mexico's highways can make it difficult to keep a boat in one place; crosswinds are also a problem in many areas. Frequent load checks are necessary.

BOB RACE

Trailering

Larger boats that must be trailered because of their weight and then floated from the trailer at a launch site are much less versatile than car-top boats. Along the Cortez coast there are fewer than 25 launches with trailer access. Another disadvantage to boat trailering is that Mexican road conditions can make towing a slow, unpleasant task. On the other hand, if one of these spots happens to be your destination and you plan to stay awhile, then the added cruising range of a larger vessel might be worthwhile.

Charts and Tide Tables

The best nautical charts available for Mexico waters are those originally published by the U.S. government. The nautical surveys that resulted in this series were carried out between 1873 and 1901—as a result, many place-names are out of date.

The charts can be purchased individually from the Defense Mapping Agency , Washington, DC 20315-0010, tel. (800) 826-0342 or (301) 227-2495. Two of the Coastal Series are out of print, however, and only the Pacific and Sea of Cortez charts are readily available. A less expensive source of these charts is *ChartGuide: Mexico West,* a compilation of all the nautical charts from San Diego to Guatemala, including those currently unavailable from the DMA. ChartGuide has extensively updated the charts by marking anchorages, boat ramps, hazards, even fishing and diving spots. The spiral-bound volume can be ordered from U.S.-based ChartGuide, Charlie Davis and Assoc., 5151 Oceanus Dr., No. 107, Huntington Beach, CA 92649, tel. (714) 891-5779, fax 892-7510. It is also available in some California marine supply stores. Charts for the Gulf of Mexico are difficult to come by—try asking around at marine supply stores along the Texas Gulf coast.

Tide tables are published annually; to cover the entire Mexico coastline you'll need three sets, one each pertaining to the Pacific, Sea of Cortez, and Gulf of Mexico tides. The Pacific/Sea of Cortez tables can be purchased from marine supply stores in California, the Gulf tables in Texas. Map Link, 25 E. Mason, Santa Barbara, CA 93101, tel. (805) 965-4402, fax 962-0884, or **Map Centre,** 2611 University Ave., San Diego, CA 92104, tel. (619) 291-3830, may also be able to order charts and tide tables.

Boat Permits

A temporary import permit is required if you plan to take a boat to mainland Mexico, whether by land or water. The permit can be obtained from the Registro Federal de Vehículos office at each of the major border crossings.

In addition, any nonresident foreigner operating a boat in Mexican waters who intends to fish from the boat is required to carry a Mexican fishing permit. Even if you transport a boat to Mexico with no fishing tackle and no plans to fish, it's a good idea to obtain a permit anyway—first, because you might change your mind when you see all the fish everyone else is pulling in, and, second, because you never know when you might end up carrying a passenger who has fishing tackle. *All* boats used for fishing require a permit, whether cartopped, trailered, deflated and carried inside a motor vehicle, or sailed on the open seas. The permits can be obtained by mail from the Mexico Department of Fisheries *(Secretaría de Pesca),* 1010 Second Ave., Suite 101, San Diego, CA 92103, tel. (619) 233-6956, fax (619) 233-0344. A boat permit is valid for 12 months; fees vary according to the length of the craft.

Fuel, Parts, and Repairs

Only San Carlos and Mazatlán on the west coast, and La Pesca and Tampico on the Gulf of Mexico coast, have permanent marinas that offer fuel year-round. Elsewhere you must count on your own reserves or try your luck at canneries, boatyards, and fish camps along the way (prices at these sources will probably be well above the official PEMEX rates). Often you'll have to go ashore at places other than marinas and haul your own fuel back to the boat—come prepared with as many extra fuel containers as you can manage.

Finding marine supplies and repairs in Mexico is much more challenging than finding fuel. San Carlos, Mazatlán, La Pesca, and Tampico are the best places for both—there's usually someone around who can work minor miracles. To a limited extent, parts (but not necessarily competent repair) are also available for established-brand (e.g., Johnson, Mercury, Evinrude) outboard motors in smaller ports. As with all other motorized conveyances in Mexico, it's best to bring along plenty of spare parts (especially props, filters, water pumps, shear pins, hoses, and belts) to avoid getting stuck in the middle of nowhere. Don't forget to bring along at least one life jacket per person—statistics show that in 80% of all boating fatalities, the victims weren't wearing PFDs (personal flotation devices).

Watermakers

Ocean cruisers should consider equipping their boats with a desalinator in order to avoid relying totally on stored fresh water. Recovery Engineering, tel. (800) 548-0406 in the U.S. and Canada, offers a line of reverse-osmosis desalinators that run off 12-volt power sources and produce as much as 3.3 gallons of drinking water per hour from seawater. For life rafts they also manufacture a handpumped survival version that weighs only 2.5 pounds.

Emergencies

Along both coastlines, the Mexican navy, all COTPs, ferry vessels, and commercial ships monitor VHF radio channel 16 and may be able to respond to pleas for emergency assistance.

Citizen-band (CB) radio is commonly used as a substitute for a telephone system in the remoter marine areas; it's also heavily used by RVers, the Green Angels, CB clubs, and other boaters, so it's one of the quickest ways to get attention. As in the U.S. and Canada, channel 9 is the most used, and channels 1, 3, 4, 7, 9, and 10 are also monitored. Special radio permits for foreign visitors are no longer required for CB radios with a transmission power of five watts or less.

SEA KAYAKING

Kayaking is one of the best ways to experience coastal Mexico, bar none. Coves, inlets, water caves, and beaches that are inaccessible to skiffs or 4WD vehicles are easily approached in a kayak, especially on the Sea of Cortez. The Cortez is, in fact, a truly world-class sea kayaking environment, as more and more kayakers are discovering every year. It's also an excellent place to learn sea kayaking skills, since the seas are generally calm.

The most popular kayaking areas along the Cortez coast are still on the Baja California side. (Moon's *Baja Handbook* contains detailed infor-

mation on Baja kayaking.) However, a growing number of kayakers have launched from the eastern Cortez shore, particularly in the Bahía Kino and San Carlos areas. The Gulf Current, which runs counterclockwise around the Cortez, favors trips planned in a south-north direction if you launch from the east coast, with pickup arranged at the north end. A few intrepid kayakers have accomplished voyages across the currents from Bahía Kino, Son., to Bahía de los Angeles on the Baja side by using the "Stepping Stones" route from island to island (the Seris once followed the same route in reed canoes). Extended Cortez trips are fairly easy when the weather's good, since campsites can be chosen from a huge selection of beaches. If you bring along some light fishing gear, you're virtually guaranteed not to go without food.

Besides Bahía Kino and San Carlos, several other areas along the Sonora and Sinaloa coasts have strong, untapped potential as kayaking destinations, especially Bahía San Jorge and the Río Concepción estuary between Puerto Peñasco and El Desemboque, Son.; Isla Tiburón near Kino; and the series of river estuaries, bays, and islands west of Culiacán, Sinaloa. Another potential kayak playground, especially for novice paddlers, is the Laguna Agua Brava, a lovely 110-km-long lagoon that is part of a *marismas nacionales* (national marine reserve) south of Mazatlán at Teacapán.

The coastal islands near Mazatlán are well worth paddling to, but kayaking in the Pacific is for the experienced sea paddler only. The high surf and strong currents require equal quantities of strength and expertise.

Open-sea kayaking in the Gulf of Mexico is almost as challenging as in the Pacific, though surf zones tend to be tamer. Kayakers will find paddling on the massive Laguna Madre between Mezquital and La Pesca very similar to paddling in the barrier island lagoon of the same name that extends from Corpus Christi to South Padre Island in Texas. This is a good area for less experienced kayakers, yet the variety of wildlife will keep almost any kayaker enthralled.

Maps and Tide Tables

Nautical charts are of little use for kayak navigation—a better choice would be 1:50,000-scale topographic maps, available from Map Link or

Map Centre (see "Maps" under "Hiking and Backpacking," above, for phone numbers and addresses). Tide tables are also invaluable (see "Charts and Tide Tables" under "Boating," above, for sources).

Types of Kayaks

The four basic types of sea kayaks all come in the 4.2- to 6.4-meter (14- to 21-foot) range necessary for extended paddling. The traditional closed-cockpit, hardshell boat comes in single (one-person) and double (two-person) models and is made of either molded polyethylene plastic or fiberglass. A "glass" boat is lighter and faster; a polyethylene boat heavier and slower, though it holds up on rocky beaches much better. This type of kayak is easily cartopped, but a sturdy, secure rack is necessary on rough roads. Touring models can carry up to 115 kg (250 lbs.) of gear in built-in hatches, an attribute that makes them a good choice for extended overnight kayaking. Because of the sealed cockpits, they're also very good in the cold waters of the Pacific and the northern Cortez.

Folding kayaks are much easier to transport and are popular among kayakers who fly to their destinations, or who want to keep boats inside their vehicles rather than on top. The disadvantages are that a folding kayak costs more and is a bit slower because of a wider beam, up to 86 cm (34 inches) compared with a 60-cm (24-inch) beam on a hardshell boat. Assembly and disassembly—the hull is usually hypalon, a synthetic rubber, stretched over aluminum tubing—is not as easy as the sales representative claims. For carrying convenience, however, it can't be beat. The wider beam also means the craft will carry up to twice the payload of a hardshell.

Gaining popularity in recent years, especially in San Carlos and Mazatlán, are open-deck kayaks. The advantage to these is that the paddler sits on top of the deck rather than underneath it, which makes it much easier to exit and thus somewhat safer overall. Like the closed-cockpit variety, some models feature hatched stowage compartments that carry up to 115 kilos. Open-cockpit kayaks are easier to paddle and more stable than traditional kayaks; just about anyone can paddle one with little or no practice. They cost several hundred dollars less than the closed-deck versions, but are also a bit slower

because of a wider beam and higher center of gravity. They also make excellent dive stations for short scuba- or free-diving trips; a few models, such as the Aquaterra Kahuna or Scupper Scrambler, are designed specifically to carry scuba gear. As with other hardshell kayaks, they're easily cartopped.

Inflatables are the lightest of the touring kayaks, which makes them even easier to transport than folding kayaks. However, inflation requires an air compressor or electric air pump since the craft's rigidity depends on air pressure of two to four pounds per square inch. Like the folding kayak, an inflatable's main advantage is ease of storage and transport.

Accessories

Paddle styles are very much a matter of personal choice; as a general rule, Aleuts or asymmetrical paddles are useful on the windy Gulf of Mexico and Pacific, traditional shapes on the Cortez. Whatever you decide on, bring a spare. Other essentials include a paddle leash, a 15-meter (50-foot) parachute-cord towline, a waterproof flashlight, and, in winter, a wetsuit. A detachable two-wheel cart or "skate" for the stern is helpful for transporting a kayak short distances on land; you can easily store it in one of the hatches.

Foot-controlled rudders are really not necessary for Sea of Cortez kayaking for much of the year since winds and currents are usually moderate. The exception is from November to March when wind and swells are up. Also keep in mind that parts and service for a broken rudder are virtually nonexistent in Mexico. On the Pacific and Gulf sides, or if you're going to attempt a cross-Cortez route to the mainland, a foot-controlled rudder is a good idea. Bring spare parts.

If you can manage the extra weight, include a kayak sail rig to give your arms a rest during a good breeze.

WINDSURFING

Both of Northern Mexico's coasts offer outstanding windsurfing possibilities. The Sea of Cortez is a high-wind paradise Nov.-March, particularly from the central coast southward. As with kayaking, the favorite spots are Bahía Kino and San Carlos in Sonora, where conditions are perfect for beginning and intermediate board-sailors. Any of the channels between the Sea of Cortez coast and the larger offshore islands (e.g., Canal Infiernillo opposite Isla Tiburón) usually see good sideshore wind action, although sometimes that's coupled with strong currents—if you don't see other sailboards out, try to find someone who knows the currents before launching.

Farther south, the surf and open-ocean blasts of Mazatlán will delight those in the advanced class. The Pacific shoreline generally demands a more experienced boardsailor, although there are bays near Mazatlán suitable for almost any level. Novices and intermediate boardsailors can also enjoy the lagoons and river estuaries along the northern and central Sinaloa coast or the lengthy Laguna Agua Brava south of Mazatlán. Boardsailors with sturdy transport—4WD or high-clearance trucks—can choose from dozens of smaller bays that pocket the entire Sea of Cortez/Pacific coast and are connected to Mexican highways by dirt roads of varying quality.

The best windsurfing area along the entire Gulf of Mexico coast is the extensive barrier island-lagoon system between the U.S. border and Tampico. This region offers open-sea windsurfing on the windward side of the barrier islands—complete with surf and high winds—combined with the calmer pleasures and long runs of the intracoastal Laguna Madre.

SURFING

Mexico is one of the last refuges of "soul surfing," an experience that has all but disappeared from the crowded surfing beaches of North America. Instead of fighting for a wave, Mexican surfers will typically take turns, making sure that everyone gets a ride now and then. Two reasons persist for the laid-back atmosphere: Mexico attracts a lot of older North American surfers who are either fed up with the agro scene up north or are simply investigating new territory; and there are many fewer surfers on Mexican beaches, hence heated competition is simply less imperative.

Northern Mexico surfing is mostly restricted to points south of Culiacán, Sin., where the Sea of Cortez meets the Pacific Ocean, and to the northern Gulf of Mexico coast. On the Sea of Cortez/Pacific side, most of the best surf areas

are below *puntas* that offer right point breaks stoked by prevailing northwesterlies during the winter months. Interspersed with the point action are plenty of reef and beach breaks, some of which arrive with the southwestern summer swells. As with all other coastal recreation, more places are accessible to those with high clearance vehicles or 4WD, although so many good surf spots are easily accessible by ordinary passenger cars that a heavy-duty rig isn't obligatory.

In summer the Sea of Cortez/Pacific surf is mostly small to flat except when a tropical storm comes up from the south. When this happens, there's usually high wave action at Mazatlán. Mazatlán, in fact, is the focus of most surfing activity in Northern Mexico, although plenty of other good surf areas lie between Altata to the north and San Blas, Nay., to the south.

Tropical depressions coupled with strong south winds can bring high surf to the Gulf of Mexico coast any time of year. Although the surfing possibilities here are vastly underexplored, Texas surfers agree the best action is off the jetties near La Pesca. Why would Texans head hundreds of miles south to La Pesca from their home surf at Port Aransas, Mustang Island, and Galveston Island? Simply because La Pesca is more pristine in every way—fewer people, less trash, and cleaner water.

Equipment
Fortunately, surfing is one of the more low-tech sports of modern times, so the fact that surf shops are scarce in Mexico is not a major problem. For any extended trip down the Sea of Cortez/Pacific coast, carrying both a short- and a longboard would prepare you for the wide variation in surf. Besides wax and a cooler, about the only other items you need bring are a first-aid kit for routine surf injuries (most surf spots are far from medical assistance—don't forget butterfly bandages) and a fiberglass-patching kit for bad dings. Boards can also be repaired at just about any boatyard on the coast, since most Mexican *pangas* are made of fiberglass and require a lot of patching. Mazatlán has a couple of surf shops where boards can be rented or repaired.

Information
A Mexican publisher called Lúcan has recently published a large "Mexico Surf Spots Map" that

plots 160 surfing destinations in Mexico, with terse descriptions of each break ("right point," "reef break," "beach break south swell only," etc.). Eighty-five of those listed lie along the coast of Baja California and Baja California Sur, while the remaining 75 are plotted along Mexico's Pacific coast from Punta Patole north of Mazatlán all the way to Puerto Madero near the Guatemalan border. Unfortunately the Gulf of Mexico is completely neglected. This map is difficult to find outside Mexican surf shops.

The *Surf Report,* P.O. Box 1028, Dana Point, CA 92629, tel. (714) 496-5922, fax 496-7849, publishes occasional information on Mexican surf locales. Issues on the coasts of Sinaloa and Nayarit were last published in December 1993, so an update is probably due out any day now.

SNORKELING AND SCUBA DIVING

Because the Sea of Cortez has one of the richest marine ecosystems in the world, the underwater scenery can be especially vivid and varied. Sea lions, numerous whale and dolphin varieties, colorful fish, manta rays, and schooling hammerhead sharks are all part of a thick food chain that is stimulated by cold-water upwellings amid the over 100 islands and islets that dot the Cortez. The largest proportion of Cortez sealife consists of tropical species that have found their way north from Central and South American waters.

The mainland side of the Sea of Cortez provides opportunities for diving, but they are not as well known or as well promoted as those on the Baja California side. With the exception of Puerto Peñasco, the northern Cortez is avoided by many divers because of strong tidal surges, speedy currents, and overall lack of underwater marine variety (relative to the central and southern Cortez). A dive shop in Puerto Peñasco rents diving equipment and organizes trips to nearby Isla San Jorge, a little-known dive destination in the northern Cortez.

The next northernmost diving area is Bahía Kino and San Carlos, where tidal conditions and visibility are suitable for recreational diving. The Midriff Islands are the main attractions here. Isla Tiburón and smaller islets nearby are the most accessible of these; others require long-range

boats and an experienced appraisal of local currents and tidal changes. Rock reefs are abundant throughout these islands.

Below the Midriffs, tidal conditions calm down considerably and the water is generally warmer. Marine varieties began multiplying, and spearfishing is excellent in many areas. Coastal islands, bays, and points here are suitable both for snorkeling and scuba diving; rock reefs, boulders, volcanic ridges, and sand flats are common throughout. The southern Cortez features vast submarine canyons as well as more remote volcanic and continental islands that are best explored by experienced scuba divers.

The best diving is in the Mazatlán area, where rock and island reefs are fairly common. The west and southwest sides of these islands offer the greatest proliferation of sealife, including kelp beds, coral reefs, and encrusted sea pinnacles amid scenic sand flats, and the fast-running currents make for good visibility in offshore areas. But heavy swells and surging along the Pacific coast means that diving here should only be undertaken by experienced scuba divers or with an experienced underwater guide.

Above Mazatlán, onshore water temperatures usually hover between 21 and 29° C (70-85° F) year-round; farther south, as the warm Cortez meets the cool Pacific, temperatures drop a few degrees. Water visibility is best July-Oct., when it exceeds 100 feet; however, this is also when the air temperature is warmest, often reaching well over 32° C (90° F). In Mazatlán, several dive operations offer trips and equipment rental.

Equipment

Divers shouldn't count on finding the equipment they need in Mexico, even in the resort areas—most equipment sold or rented at the dive shops is imported from the U.S., so stock can vary from season to season. Purchase prices are also generally higher in Mexico than north of the border. Average equipment rental fees are: mask and snorkel US$5, fins US$5, belt US$5, buoyancy compensator vest US$10, regulator US$15, tank rental US$8, air refills US$4.

For Pacific and central Cortez diving, a light wetsuit may be needed late Nov.-April, while shorties or just an ordinary swimsuit will suffice the rest of the year. From the Midriff Islands north in the Sea of Cortez, heavier suits are necessary Dec.-March.

Because divers and anglers occasionally frequent the same areas, a good diving knife is essential in case you have to deal with wayward fishing line; in fact, bringing two knives would be a good idea so you'll have a spare. Also bring extra CO_2 cartridges for flotation vests, rubber slings for spear guns, O-rings, and a wetsuit patching kit.

Air

Dependable air for scuba tanks is usually available in Puerto Peñasco, San Carlos, and Mazatlán. Always check the compressor first, however, to make sure it's both well maintained and running clean. This will lessen the risk of a contaminated air supply. Divers with extensive Mexico experience will usually carry a portable compressor not only to avoid contaminated air but also so that they can travel to areas where tank refills aren't available.

ENTERTAINMENT

BASEBALL

El béisbol is the most popular spectator sport in the northwest (Sonora, Sinaloa) and northeast (Nuevo León, Tamaulipas), where you'll typically find more (and larger) community fields and stadiums than in many areas of the United States. Baseball was first brought to Mexico by U.S. railroad workers working along the Sonoran/Sinaloan coast and today several cities in Northern Mexico have professional teams. The Latin American World Series between Mexico's Pacific Coast League and the Caribbean League (Puerto Rico, Dominican Republic, Cuba) is held each February; the event has alternated between Hermosillo, Son., Culiacán, Sin., Mazatlán, Sin., and various Caribbean capitals. Several famous ballplayers on professional U.S. teams (e.g., Fernando Valenzuela, Teddy Higuera, Ismael Váldez) have come from Mexican teams.

The regular Pacific Coast League season runs Oct.-Jan., perfect timing for visiting American farm-leaguers who want to stay in shape between the end of U.S. baseball season and spring training. The larger Mexican League plays during the summer. Although the nation's hottest teams—usually made up of Northern players based in Mexico City—play in the Mexican League, the overall quality of PCL ball is reputedly better. The atmosphere at a typical game is reminiscent of American ball, with *tacos y cerveza* replacing hotdogs and beer.

Tickets for baseball games are usually easy to obtain at the stadium on game day; exceptions include play-off and Latin American World Series games. Inquire at local tourist offices for schedules and stadium locations.

BULLFIGHTS

La corrida de toros ("the running of bulls") is especially popular in the north-central states of Zacatecas and San Luis Potosí, and in Ciudad Juárez, Chih., which has the best of the border *corridas.* Aficionados agree that Zacatecas and San Luis Potosí host some of the finer bullfights in the country. Mazatlán has a *plaza de toros* (bullring) but it is kept in business mostly as a tourist attraction—Sinaloans prefer baseball!

Regular bullfight columns appear in the sports sections of Mexican newspapers. Before a big *corrida,* these columns will critique the bulls as much as—or even more than—the matadors themselves, assessing weight (the average is over 500 kg), bloodlines, and other variables. Local tourist offices are good places to find the current *corrida* schedule. In most areas of Mexico, summer is the bullfight season. An exception is Mazatlán, where the bulls run during winter and spring to coincide with the tourist season.

KATHY ESCOVEDO-SANDERS

SOMBRA Y SOL

Called *la corrida de toros* ("the running of bulls"), *la fiesta brava* ("the brave festival"), *la lidia de toros* ("the fighting of bulls"), or *sombra y sol* ("shade and sun," in reference to the stadium seating), the bullfight can be seen as sport, art, or gory spectacle, depending on the observer's social conditioning.

To the aficionado, the *lidia* is a ritual drama that rolls together courage, fate, pathos, and death in one symbolic event. But no matter how you may feel toward the bullfight, it is undeniably an integral part of Mexican history and culture. Every town of any size has at least one *plaza de toros* or bullring; occasionally a small bullring will be improvised for a rural fiesta. In Northern Mexico you'll find major stadiums in Ciudad Juárez, Mazatlán, Monterrey, Zacatecas, and San Luis Potosí. The latter two cities are considered the heartland of the Mexican bullfight in terms of both bulls and toreros (bullfighters).

History

Ritualistic encounters with bulls have been traced as far back as 3000 B.C. when, on the Greek island of Crete, the Minoans would perform ritual dives over the horns of attacking wild bulls. A closer antecedent developed around 2000 B.C. on the Iberian peninsula, where a breed of fierce, wild bulls roamed the plains. Iberian hunters—ancestors of the Spanish and Portuguese—figured out how to evade the bulls at close quarters while delivering a fatal blow with an ax or spear. When the Romans heard about this practice they began importing wild Spanish bulls and accomplished bullfighters for their Colosseum games—possibly the first public bullfights.

During the Middle Ages, bullfighting became a royal sport that was practiced on horseback by the Spanish and the occupying Moors, who both used lances to dispatch the wild bulls. As the toreros began dismounting and confronting the bulls on the ground, the game eventually evolved into the current *corrida*, as performed in Spain, Portugal, Mexico, and throughout much of Latin America.

In the early years the only payment the torero received was the bull's carcass after the event. Nowadays bullfighters receive performance fees that vary according to their status within the profession.

El Toro

The bulls used in the ring, *toros de lidia* ("fighting bulls"), are descendants of wild Iberian bulls that for over four centuries have been bred especially for their combative spirit. They're not trained in any way for the ring, nor goaded into viciousness, but as a breed are naturally quick to anger. The fighting bull's neck muscles are much larger than those of any other cattle breed in the world, making the animal capable of tossing a torero and his horse into the air.

Bulls who show an acceptable degree of bravery by the age of two are let loose in huge pastures (averaging 10,000 acres per animal) in Zacatecas, San Luis Potosí, or Guanajuato to live as wild beasts until they reach four years, the age of combat. By the time *el toro* enters the ring, he stands around 127 cm (50 inches) high at the withers (even higher at the shoulder) and weighs 500 kg (1,100 pounds) or more.

The carcass of a bull killed in the ring does not go to waste, at least not from a meat-eater's perspective. Immediately after it's taken from the ring, it's butchered and dressed, and the meat is sold.

El Torero

The bullfighter is rated by his agility, control, and, as surprising as it may seem, his compassion. The torero who teases a bull or who is unable to kill it quickly at the moment of truth is considered a cruel brute. In order to be judged a worthy competitor by the spectators, he must excel in three areas: *parar,* or standing still as the bull charges (as opposed to stepping away from the bull, even as little as an inch)—only the cape and the torero's upper body should move; *templar,* or timing and grace—the movements must be smooth, well timed, and of the right proportion; and *mandar,* or command, the degree to which he masters the entire *lidia* through his bravery, technique, and understanding of the bull, neither intimidating the animal nor being intimidated by it.

Standard equipment for the torero is the *capote de brega,* the larger cape used in the first two-thirds of the *lidia;* the *muleta,* a smaller cape used during the final third; the *estoque* or matador's sword; and the *traje de luces* or "suit of lights," the torero's costume originally designed by the Spanish artist Goya.

La Lidia

The regulated maneuvers or *suertes* followed in a bullfight date from 18th-century Spain. Anywhere from four to eight bulls may appear in a corrida (typically six), and one torero is on hand for every two bulls scheduled. The order of appearance for the toreros is based on seniority. Toreros who have proven their skills in several bullfighting seasons as

(continues)

SOMBRA Y SOL (continued)

novilleros (novice fighters) are called matadores de toros (bull killers). Ordinarily each torero will fight two bulls; if he is gored or otherwise put out of action, another torero will take his place even if it means facing more than his allotment of bulls.

Each lidia is divided into three tercios or "thirds." In el tercio de varas, the bull enters the ring and the matador performs capeos, a cape maneuver that doesn't expose the matador's body to the bull's horns, but is meant to test the bull or lead it to another spot in the ring. He then "lances," a cape maneuver that exposes the matador's body to the horns and brings the bull closer to him, while two horsemen receive the bull's charge with eight-foot varas or lances. The varas have short, pyramid-shaped points that are aimed at the bull's neck muscle but do not penetrate very deeply on contact.

The purpose is both to punish the neck muscle so that the bull lowers its horns, and to give the bull the confidence of meeting something solid so that it won't be frustrated by the emptiness of the cape as the lidia proceeds. Usually only two vara blows are administered but more are permitted if necessary to produce the intended effect (the lowering of the head). The crowd protests, however, when more than two are administered, as they want the matador to face a strong bull.

In el tercio de banderillas, the bull's shoulders receive the banderillas—26-inch wooden sticks decorated with colored paper frills, each tipped with a small, sharp, iron barb. They can be placed by the matador himself or more often by hired assistant toreros (called banderilleros when performing this function). The purpose of the banderilla placement is to "correct" the bull's posture; the added punishment also reportedly makes the bull more crafty in his charges. Placed in pairs, up to six banderillas may be applied to the bull, varying in number and position according to the needs of the individual animal.

At the end of the tercio de banderillas, signaled by a bugle fanfare, the matador takes up his muleta and sword and walks before the box of the juez or judge presiding over the killing of the bull. He looks to the juez for permission to proceed with the killing of the bull and, after receiving a nod, offers his brindis or dedication. The brindis may be made to an individual, to a section of the plaza, or to the entire audience. If the dedication is to an individual, he will present his montera (matador's hat) to that person (who will return it, with a present inside, to the matador after the lidia). Otherwise, he tosses his hat onto the sand

after waving it at the crowd; he remains hatless for the final tercio, a gesture of respect for the bull.

The final round of the lidia is called el tercio de muerte, "the third of death." The main activity of this tercio is la faena, "the work" involving cape and sword, during which a special set of passes leads to the killing of the bull. For the first two tercios there is no time limit; for the last, however, the matador has only 15 minutes to kill the bull, or he is considered defeated and the bull is led from the ring (where it is killed immediately by the plaza butcher).

In a good faena, a matador will tempt fate over and over again, bringing the bull's horns close to his own heart. The time for the kill arrives when the bull has so tired from the faena that it stands still, forelegs squared as if ready to receive the sword. Then, with his cape the matador must draw the bull into a final charge while he himself moves forward, bringing the sword out from under the cape, sighting down the blade, and driving the blade over the horns and between the animal's shoulders. A perfect sword thrust severs the aorta, resulting in instant death. If the thrust is off, the matador must try until the bull dies.

It is not necessary to kill the bull in one stroke (quite an extraordinary accomplishment); the matador's honor is preserved as long as he goes in over the horns, thus risking his own life, every time. If the bull falls to its knees but isn't dead, another torero on hand immediately comes forward and thrusts a dagger (puntilla) behind the base of the skull to sever the spinal cord and put the beast out of its misery. When the bull is dead, the lidia is over. If the matador has shown bravery and artistry, the crowd will let him know with their applause; an unusually dramatic performance will see lots of hats and flowers thrown into the ring.

Practicalities

It's usually a good idea to buy tickets for a corrida in advance if possible—check with the tourist office to find out where they're available—since it's not unusual for an event to sell out (in which case you might still be able to buy a ticket from a scalper or revendedor). In a large stadium, the spectator sections are divided into the sol (sunny side) and sombra (shaded side), then subdivided according to how close the seats are to the bullring itself. The sol tickets aren't bad, since the corrida usually doesn't begin until around 4 p.m.; bring a hat, sunglasses, and sunscreen, plus plenty of pesos for beverages (tequila, beer, and soft drinks are usually available)

CHARREADAS

Decreed the national sport of Mexico in a 1933 presidential edict, the *charreada* or Mexican-style rodeo is popular throughout Northern Mexico and was the initial inspiration for American rodeo. Private *charro* associations stage the *charreadas* in skillet-shaped rings called *lienzos charros*. The contests of equestrian and ranching skills are open to everyone, but *charrería* (the art of *charro*) is an expensive pastime requiring the maintenance of trained horses and elaborate clothing—somewhat analogous to polo in the Anglo world.

Unlike in American rodeo, *charros* and *charras* (gentleman and lady riders) compete for team, not individual, awards. Each team fields six to eight persons, who singly or in combination perform a series of nine *suertes* (maneuvers or events); upon completion of all *suertes,* the team with the most points wins. Another difference is that *charreada* points are usually scored for style rather than speed. Live mariachi music adds drama and romance to the events.

One of the more thrilling *suertes* is the *paso de la muerte* in which a *charro* leaps from the back of a horse onto the back of an unbroken mare—while both horses are at full gallop! In the *coleadero,* a *charro* leans down from his horse, grasps the end of the steer's tail with one hand, wraps the tail partially around his leg, and throws the animal to the ground. In the *terna en el ruedo,* three mounted *charros* rope a wild bull and bring it to the ground within 10 minutes or three casts of *la reata* (origin of the English word "lariat"); points are scored for complexity and style of the rope work, not speed.

Also striking is the *escaramuza charra,* a women's event featuring rapid, precision-timed, and carefully choreographed and executed equestrian moves by a group of 6-10 riders. This extremely colorful and popular event owes its name to the Italian *scaramuccia,* a 16th-century cavalry maneuver.

In the bull-riding event or *jinete de toro,* the rider must stay atop the bull until it stops bucking, then dismount with the cinch in hand, landing on both feet simultaneously. By contrast, the American rodeo counterpart to this event only requires a cowboy to stay mounted eight seconds or more.

A serious *charreada* regular maintains four *charro* suits: the *traje de faena* or plain working outfit; the *traje de media gala,* a semiformal suit with embroidery; and two *trajes de gala* including the silver-buttoned *traje de etiqueta* or "dress suit" and the *traje de ceremonia,* an elegant tuxedo outfit for special ceremonies. Each *traje* consists of a broad-brimmed sombrero, tight-fitting trousers of cloth or leather, a short-waisted jacket, boots, and—when the *charro* is mounted—deerskin *chaparreras* ("chaps"). *Charras* generally dress in *coronela* or *china poblana* outfits, turn-of-the-century styles featuring full, embroidered blouses and long, billowing, brightly colored skirts with layers of lace and petticoats.

MUSIC

Norteña
When most North Americans think of Mexican music they think of brass-and-violins mariachi music, which is a style from the state of Jalisco in Central Mexico. In Northern Mexico, mariachi music is generally reserved for weddings, banquets, and tourists. By far the most commonly heard music in Northern Mexico is *la música norteña,* a style that's representative of ranchero life yet has a wide appeal throughout Northern Mexico and beyond, including as far north as Chicago and as far south as Colombia and Venezuela.

Norteña music shares common roots with the Tex-Mex *conjunto* music enjoyed in Texas and New Mexico and made famous by Flaco Jimenez (from Texas), Ramón Ayala (from Monterrey, Mexico), Los Lobos (from California), and the Grammy-winning Texas Tornadoes (a group comprised of Jimenez, Freddie Fender, and the remnants of Doug Sahm's Sir Douglas Quintet).

In Mexico this music is typically played by an ensemble led by an accordion and *bajo sexto,* a large Mexican 12-string guitar. Originally, these two instruments were supported by a string bass and sometimes a trap drum set; later, electric bass and guitar were occasionally added, along with alto sax and keyboards. Most *pura* (pure) *norteña* bands still maintain the traditional accordion, bajo sexto, and acoustic bass lineup. The music itself encompasses an exciting mix of Latinized polkas and waltzes, *rancheras* (similar to American country and western songs), and *corridos* (Mexican ballads), as well as modern Latin forms like *cumbias* and salsa.

The most popular *norteña* band among Northern Mexicans in recent years has been Los Tigres del Norte. Although based in San José, California, most of the band members were born in Sinaloa. Like many *norteña* bands, Los Tigres sing songs that reflect the daily lives and sentiments of Northern Mexican peasants, sometimes with a political edge. In 1988 Los Tigres won a Grammy award in the U.S. for best Mexican-American album for ¡*Gracias! . . . America . . . Sin Fronteras* ("Thank You! . . . America . . . Without Borders"). Some of the songs recorded by Los Tigres and other *norteña* groups have been banned by the Mexican government and can only be heard from bootleg tapes that circulate at cantinas or local fiestas. In Mexico, *norteña* lyrics often chronicle the tragedies and triumphs of *mota* (marijuana) smugglers and

other *narcotraficantes* on the run from law enforcement.

The major recording and touring center of *norteña* music is an area that stretches across Tamaulipas, Nuevo León, Coahuila, Chihuahua, Durango, and southern Texas, but live *norteña* music often can be heard at fiestas throughout Northern Mexico and in bars and cantinas in larger towns and cities. In districts where bars tend to cluster, you'll find *trobadores* strolling from bar to bar most evenings playing *norteña* music; although bar districts usually aren't the nicest areas of town to hang out, this does offer an opportunity for the curious to hear some local sounds.

Other Styles

Also *muy popular* in the North is brassy **banda,** a style that originated in turn-of-the-century Sinaloa and is currently undergoing a big resur-

NOT SO GENTLE BALLADS OF THE NORTH

By Chris Humphrey

Across the north of Mexico concerned citizens and morally inclined politicians have raised an outcry against a wildly popular form of pop music, which, they claim, praises violence, promotes drugs, and corrupts the youth.

The music causing the uproar is not the thumping grooves of gansta rap, but a lyrical subculture of traditional *música norteña* known as *corridos norteños*, often played to a polka beat. The *corrido,* or Mexican ballad, is a traditional storytelling song that originated during the wars for Mexican independence in the early 19th century and came into national prominence in the 1910-20 Mexican Revolution, when *corridos* served as one of the main ways common people learned of events during the decade-long civil war.

But these days, rather than tell of the exploits of legendary generals or cattle-rustling outlaws, *corridos* sing of their modern-day counterparts in the deserts and mountains of the Mexican north—drug smugglers.

It's commonly suspected that the writers of *narcocorridos,* as the current songs are popularly known, get much of the material for their songs from the

smugglers themselves, either from anonymous letters, phone calls, or by paying the musicians to play at their private parties.

Teodoro Bello wrote 11 of the 19 songs on *Jefe de Jefes* ("Chief of the Chiefs," or "Boss of the Bosses"), the latest hit album by top *norteña* band Los Tigres del Norte, and has written *corridos* for several other bands. Bello concedes he has gotten some background information from inside the industry, as it were. "Sometimes someone will call me and say, 'Hey, Don Teodoro, I'd like it if you wrote a song about this or that,'" Bello says. "If I like the story, I'll do it. But if I don't think it's real, I won't use it, because the *corrido* can't be made up."

Most of his material, Bello says, comes from the newspapers, not *narcotraficantes.* As he diplomatically points out, most drug traffickers are not very interested in having attention called to them, and might not appreciate songwriters talking about private matters. "You can't go around writing songs about things that people wouldn't want to hear; that could be a problem," he said.

Many of the songs on *Jefe de Jefes* defend Bello's assertion that he is merely the composer of what he calls a "musical newspaper." The lyrics read like a thumbnail sketch of Mexican politics for the past couple of years.

gence throughout Mexico. *Banda* ensembles consist mostly of brass instruments and drums playing loud instrumental march music against the familiar two-step or waltz rhythms found in *norteña* music. La Banda Sinaloense carries the banner for this style (lots of bands manage to work "Sinaloa" or "Sinaloense" into their names). A permutation known as *tecnobanda* adds or substitutes electronic keyboards and may add vocals as well.

Rock en español has followers in the larger cities of the North, particularly Monterrey and Mazatlán. Although lyrically descended from Latin American *nuevo canto* folk/rock music, *rock en español* takes its major musical inspiration from Anglo-American rock and Anglo-Jamaican ska. Mexico has become the international center for this movement, with Mexico City the epicenter. Since the late 1980s, Maldita Vecindad ("Cursed Neighborhood") has been very successful, blending ska, punk, rock, jazz, and traditional Mexican elements; their first major hit was "Mojado" (Wetback), a tribute to transborder Mexican workers. Also extremely popular are the rock fusion/art group Los Jaguares, and Café Tacuba, a band that mixes alternative rock sounds with some Amerindian instrumentation and wild live performances. All the major groups working in this style come from the state of Mexico except for ¡Tijuana No!, possibly the most political of all the current bands (the name signifies a plea not to flee Tijuana for the U.S.). One of their most recent CDs, "Transgresores de la ley" (Lawbreakers) is more or less a tribute to the EZLN.

Música folklórica, ethnic folk music, is also popular on a localized level, with various *son* or song forms and instrumentation tied to particular regions of the North. Such *son* traditions are less common in the North than in the South, al-

---

The title song, written by Bello, is a not-so-veiled reference to drug trafficker Amado Carillo Fuentes, the mythical "Lord of the Skies" (so called for his fleet of smuggling jet planes) who died in mysterious circumstances in August. Other numbers include "El General," about former antidrug czar Gen. Jesús Gutiérrez Rebollo, arrested earlier this year for supposedly taking protection money from Carillo, and "El Prisionero," about Mario Aburto, arrested for shooting presidential candidate Luis Donaldo Colosio in 1994.

But the kind of songs critics claim glorify drug trafficking and violence are more like "Lo Que Siembra Allá En La Sierra" ("What They Harvest There In The Mountains"), which tells the story of a wily drug producer outwitting those chasing him:

I know my life is dangerous
But I like the good life
The girls give me caresses
The mountains give me money
I'm going to enjoy life
And not take anything with me when I die

Drug trafficking is a major industry and many *narcotraficantes* are celebrities, if infrequently seen ones, in many northern states. Authorities there say songs like this one encourage young people to admire the drug traffickers.

The state governments of Sinaloa (the birthplace of many famed drug traffickers), Baja California, Sonora, and Chihuahua have all issued calls for local radio stations to stop playing *narco-corridos,* and many stations have complied. No laws have been passed trying to censor the music yet, but the Sinaloa government may write a new law aimed at *narco-corridos,* according to government spokesman Silviano de la Mora. "It will be based on the Federal Radio and Television Law, which prohibits music supporting violence," de la Mora said.

Much like the U.S. rappers, who say they are merely portraying the realities of the inner city, Bello says *corridos* tell people what's going on in their country and are not responsible for creating drug traffickers.

"It's not my fault that these people exist, but unfortunately they do," Bello says. "If I was born back during the Revolution, I'd write songs about Pancho Villa, Emiliano Zapata, or Francisco Madero, because they were important people in Mexico then. It's not my fault that now the *narcos* are important."

Asked if it would ever be possible to ban *narco-corridos,* Bello is unequivocal. "No chance," he asserts. "The truth is not always easy to come by in Mexico, and *corridos* tell the truth about what is happening. So people will always find a way to write them, play them, and listen to them."

Los Tigres del Norte

DAVID MAUNG

though the Huastecs of southeastern San Luis Potosí and southern Tamaulipas are famous for their *huapangos* (a native dance form with possible links to the Spanish fandango). If this sort of music interests you, a Mexican record label called Discos Corasón produces a series of tapes and CDs focusing on folkloric music of Mexico and the Caribbean. Corasón's three-CD set *Antología del Son de México, An Anthology of Mexican Folk Music,* is a good place to start. It's distributed in the U.S. by Rounder, America's largest independent record label.

FESTIVALS AND EVENTS

Mexicans love a fiesta and *norteños* are no exception. Any occasion will suffice as an excuse to hold a celebration, from a birthday or promotion to a chile harvest. Add to all the civic possibilities the vast number of Mexican Catholic religious holidays, and you've got the potential for some kind of public fiesta at least every week of the year, if not all 365 days. Besides the national religious holidays, 115 Catholic saints are honored each year on individual feast days (nine or 10 each month). Any town, pueblo, *ejido,* or colonia named for a saint (e.g. Santa Ana, Villa de Santiago, San Fernando, etc.) will usually hold a fiesta on the feast day of its namesake. Individuals named for saints, too, will sometimes host parties on their *día de santo* (saint's day).

The primary requisites of a fiesta are plenty of food (especially tamales, considered a festive dish), beer, liquor, music, and dancing. More elaborate celebrations will include parades, exhibitions, *charreadas* (Mexican rodeos), and occasional fireworks.

Following are some of the more memorable yearly events and public holidays observed throughout Northern Mexico. Smaller festivals and events that are held only locally are mentioned later in the text in the corresponding destination section. Actual dates may vary from year to year, so be sure to check with the appropriate tourist office in advance if you need current dates for the time of your visit.

Government offices and some businesses close on national holidays. These closings are not always mentioned in the text; you may want to call ahead to find out.

January
New Year's Day: January 1 (official holiday)
Día de los Santos Reyes: January 6—see "Las Posadas" under "December"

February
Constitution Day: February 5 (official holiday)
Carnaval: This pre-Lenten festival is held in late February or early March as a last celebration of the carnal pleasures that Catholics are supposed to forgo during the 40-day Lent season preceding Easter (the fiesta's name derives from the Italian *carne vale,* "flesh taken

away"). In Mexico, Carnaval is traditionally observed only in port towns; in Northern Mexico the festival is celebrated most grandly in Mazatlán and Tampico. Like New Orleans's Mardi Gras, Carnaval features lots of music, dancing, costumes, parades, and high-spirited revelry. See the Mazatlán section for more information.

Flag Day: February 24 (official holiday)

March

Birthday of Benito Juárez: March 21 (official holiday)

Spring Break: Not a Mexican holiday at all, but an annual ritual for American college and university students (mostly Southern Californians and Arizonans) who go on the rampage in Puerto Peñasco, San Carlos, and Mazatlán. The spring break season usually straddles late March and early April. Unless you're one of the revelers, these towns should be avoided at all costs during these weeks.

April

Semana Santa: Easter Week or "Holy Week" (the third week in April) is second only to Christmas as the most important holiday period of the year. One of the most prominent Semana Santa customs is breaking *cascarones,* colored eggs stuffed with confetti, over the heads of friends and family. Besides attending mass on Good Friday and Easter Sunday, many Mexicans take this opportunity to go on vacations. Mexican beach resorts can be overcrowded this week with the large influx of both Mexicans and Americans.

May

International Worker's Day: May 1 (official holiday)

Cinco de Mayo: Held on May 5, this festival commemorates the defeat of an attempted 1862 French invasion at Puebla de los Angeles on Mexico's Gulf of Mexico coast. Features music, dance, food, and other cultural events.

Mother's Day (Día de las Madres): May 10

June

Navy Day: June 1 (official holiday)

September

Mexican Independence Day (Fiesta Patria de la Independencia): Also called *diez y seis,* since it falls on the 16th of September, this holiday celebrates the country's independence from Spain, as announced in 1821 in the town of Dolores. Festivities actually begin on the 15th and last two days. The biggest celebrations are centered in the state capitals, and include fireworks, parades, *charreadas,* music, and folk-dance performances.

October

Día de la Raza: Celebrated as Columbus Day north of the border, the 12th of October in Mexico commemorates the founding of the Mexican race (as heralded by the arrival of Columbus in the New World).

November

Día de los Muertos: The "Day of the Dead" is Mexico's third most important holiday, corresponding to Europe's All Saints Day except that it's celebrated on the first and second days of November instead of only the first. Some of the festivities are held in cemeteries where families clean the headstones and crucifixes of their deceased relatives *(los difuntos),* decorate them with flowers, and play games unique to this fiesta. In some areas the faithful will spend an entire day and night beside the family graves in a cemetery. Even roadside shrines throughout Mexico are laid with fresh flowers and other tributes to the dead. Offerings of *pan de los muertos* ("bread of the dead") and food and liquor are placed before family altars on behalf of deceased family members, along with papier-mâché skulls and skeletons. The event is also referred to as Fiesta de Todos los Santos (All Saints Festival) and Festival de los Fieles Difuntos (Festival of the Deceased Faithful).

Anniversary of the 1910 Revolution: November 20 (official holiday)

December

Día de Nuestra Señora de Guadalupe: The feast day of the Virgin of Guadalupe, Mexico's patron saint, is December 12; special masses are held that day throughout Mexico. The nearest Sunday to the 12th will also

*Day of the Dead,
Durango*

JOE CUMMINGS

feature special events such as mariachi masses, food booths, and games. The celebrations at the border city of Ciudad Juárez are particularly well attended.

Las Posadas: Beginning on the 16th of December, Mexicans hold nightly *posadas*—candlelight processions terminating at elaborate, community-built nativity scenes—in commemoration of the Holy Family's search for lodging. The processions continue for nine consecutive nights. Other activities include piñata parties where children break open hanging papier-mâché figures filled with small gifts and candy. Churches large and small hold continuous Christmas masses beginning at midnight on the 25th (Día de la Navidad).

Las Posadas culminates on January 6, which is Día de los Santos Reyes (literally "Day of the King-Saints," referring to the story of the Three Wise Men). On this day Mexican children receive their Christmas gifts and family and friends gather to eat a wreath-shaped fruitcake called *rosca de reyes* (wreath of kings), baked especially for this occasion. Hidden inside each *rosca* is a small clay figurine *(muñeco)* that represents the infant Jesus. While sharing the *rosca* on this day, the person whose slice by chance contains the *muñeco* is obliged to host a *candelaría* or Candlemas party on February 2 for everyone present.

At the *candelaría* (which commemorates the day the newborn Jesus was first presented at the temple in Jerusalem), the host traditionally displays a larger Christ-infant figure and serves tamales and *atole,* a thick, hot grain drink flavored with fruit or chocolate.

SHOPPING

You'll have ample shopping opportunities while traveling through Northern Mexico, from roadside craft vendors to bustling municipal markets and big-city department stores. A few things to remember: *Solo mirando* means "just looking." Prices are sometimes marked in pesos, sometimes in U.S. dollars—when in doubt, ask. In shops that take credit cards, you'll get a better rate of exchange by charging your purchases.

Markets

One of the main shopping venues in Mexico is *el mercado,* the market. Virtually every town and city has at least one, sometimes housed in a centrally located *mercado municipal* building provided by the city government. Stalls within the municipal market are rented by vendors hawking everything from fresh meat to furniture. Sometimes smaller street vendors cluster near the municipal market. Large cities like Monterrey have several daily markets scattered around the city; smaller village communities may have only an open space or plaza where vendors gather one day a week or on weekends. Even if you're not looking to buy anything in particular, Mexican markets are worth strolling through for their color and ambience.

Market goods sometimes have price tags attached, sometimes not. When price tags are absent, you can usually expect to haggle a bit. Even when a price tag is apparent, it doesn't hurt to try for a lower price by bargaining. Generally speaking, you'll have much better luck if you make an effort to negotiate in Spanish, however poorly. Usually more than one vendor in the same market will be offering the same wares; comparing prices at different stalls can help you determine the best price.

Department Stores

Among the several Mexican department store chains found in Northern Mexico, one of the best is **Sanborn's.** Along with the usual department store fare, the typical Sanborn's contains a pharmacy with common American-brand medicines, a selection of English-language books and magazines, a *cafetería* with good Mexican food, and clean restrooms. **Woolworth Mexicana** is found in several Northern Mexican cities and is a more downscale alternative to Sanborn's with many of the same features.

Purchasing something at a Mexican department store is usually a two-step process. First you present the item(s) to a uniformed attendant, who rings it up at a cash register. Then the cashier hands you a receipt (but not the item) and takes the purchase to another counter where you must show your receipt in order to receive your purchase.

Unlike in Mexican markets, where price-haggling is expected, department store prices are always fixed.

Good Buys

Contrary to myth, the ubiquitous **designer goods** seen in the downtown shopping districts of major cities as well as in larger border towns are usually legally licensed products. Gucci, Fila, Ralph Lauren, Ellesse—among other well-known labels—have granted permission for the manufacture of such items in Mexico; retail prices are typically 30-40% less than in the label's country of origin. Some world shoppers say they can tell the difference between, for example, a Ralph Lauren shirt made in Mexico and one made in the U.S. (or more likely Hong Kong, Thailand, Malaysia, etc.), but for most of us the money saved tends to outweigh these small variations.

Silver and gold jewelry are bargains in Mexico, mainly due to lower labor costs rather than lower costs per ounce. Well-crafted silver *(plata)* pieces are particularly plentiful and relatively inexpensive throughout Northern Mexico. Look for .925 stamped into silver products; this means they're 92.5% silver, the highest quality. You will also come across *alpaca,* an alloy of copper, nickel, and zinc that looks like silver and costs a third to a half less than real silver. Zacatecas has the best silver selection and prices in Northern Mexico.

The states of Zacatecas, Durango, Nuevo León, and Tamaulipas are known for producing the finest *charreada* **suits and accessories** in Mexico, including sequined sombreros, embroidered jackets, and fancy spurs and saddles. **Leatherwork** is excellent throughout Northern Mexico but is especially well regarded in Zacatecas, Coahuila, Nuevo León, and Tamaulipas.

Among the various kinds of Indian arts and crafts available throughout the region, look for high-quality **baskets** *(cesta, canasta)* handwoven by the Seris, Yaquis, and Papagos of Sonora or by the Tarahumara of the Sierra Madre Occidental; **ceramics** fashioned by the Guarojillos (near Alamos, Sonora) and from the Casas Grandes area of Chihuahua; and **woodcarvings** by the Seris and Guarojillos. Handwoven *sarapes* ("serapes"), *jorongos* ("ponchos"), blankets, and rugs can be found in many Northern Mexican states, but Saltillo, Coah., is known to have the best quality and variety. For **rebozos and shawls** *(chales)*, the state of San Luis Potosí is best, particularly the small town of Santa María del Río.

Folk and religious art can be found in the former colonial provincial capitals of Mazatlán, Chihuahua, Zacatecas, and San Luis Potosí. *Retablos,* religious paintings on wood or tin, cost US$6-10 new, US$15-75 for older pieces. Now that folk art has become a standard element of modern Mexican interior design, some of the larger department stores carry limited folk art selections. FONART stores in the larger border cities usually offer a wider variety than department stores, but quality varies greatly from year to year.

Generally speaking, **liquor** is significantly less expensive in Mexico than in the U.S. or Canada. Quality liquors typically cost around US$9 per liter (as low as US$5 for a fifth); the best buys are tequila, rum, and brandy. Top brands include Herradura (the only tequila still made entirely by traditional methods), Bacardi Añejo (an aged rum usually not available north of the border), and Don Pedro Reserva Especial brandy.

Vanilla, extracted from the seed pod of the orchid *Vanilla planifolia* (first cultivated by Mexico's Aztecs), goes for around US$10-15 a liter. If you see vanilla that costs less than US$10 per liter, it probably isn't genuine vanilla but rather tonka bean extract, which has a very similar taste and smell. The cheaper tonka bean substitutes may contain traces of kumarin, a blood thinner used (in larger amounts) as rat poison and banned for human consumption in the United States. "Tropical World" is the most reliable brand of genuine vanilla—look for the Vanilla Association stamp.

Mexican coffee costs around US$5-12 per kilo depending on the brand and quality. Prices are lower in the Huasteca coffee-growing region of southeast San Luis Potosí. A reliable Mexican coffee brand called Café Combate is sold in whole-bean or ground form at stores of the same name in some cities. Some beans come laced with sugar, so if that doesn't sound appealing be sure to avoid coffee labeled *con azucar* (with sugar). Some grocery stores will grind beans for you on the spot.

Tarahumara basketry and woodcarving

JENNIFER BARTLETT

Many **pharmaceuticals** that would ordinarily require a doctor's prescription in the U.S., Canada, or Europe are readily available over the counter in Mexico. It is perfectly legal to purchase Mexican drugs over the counter and consume them in Mexico; however, once you return home you're subject to the drug laws of your home country. Popular over-the-counter purchases by visiting Americans include Retin-A (acne, face wrinkles), isoprinosine (herpes), and ribavirin (herpes again). It's not a good idea to purchase or use any over-the-counter drug in Mexico without a doctor's counsel.

Complaints

The **Procuraduría Federal del Consumidor** or Consumer Protection Agency solicits complaints about purchases and contracts and will defend consumer rights through legal action if deemed necessary. Branch offices in Northern Mexico include Ciudad Juárez , tel. (16) 12-3970; Ciudad Victoria, tel. (131) 2-9682; Culiacán, tel. (67) 3-3555; Chihuahua tel. (14) 13-4770; Durango, tel. (181) 8-0721; Hermosillo, tel. (62) 4-7517; Mazatlán, tel. (69) 2-5200; Monterrey, tel. (8) 340-5073; Saltillo, tel. (84) 5-5544; San Luis Potosí, tel. (48) 2-1802; Tampico, tel. (12) 12-2252; Torreón, tel. (17) 2-6406; and Zacatecas, tel. (492) 2-0460.

Complaints can also be made by mail directly to the central office in Mexico City at Carmona y Valle 11, Col. Doctores, Mexico, D.F. Complaints need not be filed in Mexico.

ACCOMMODATIONS

Places to stay in Northern Mexico run the gamut from hostels to plush resort hotels. Commercial campgrounds are not as numerous but visitors who bring along the appropriate gear will find camping opportunities in wilderness areas. RVers can avail themselves of almost any open space as well as the occasional RV/trailer park.

HOTELS AND MOTELS

Rates

Hotels and motels in Northern Mexico are considerably less expensive than their counterparts in the U.S., Canada, or Europe; the largest number of them fall into the US$15-55 range. You can save money by planning your stay by the times of year and week. In tourist areas, particularly beach destinations, midweek rates are lower than weekend rates. Conversely, in business destinations such as Hermosillo, Chihuahua, Durango, and Monterrey, hotel rates are lower on weekends.

In the sierras, some places charge high season rates May-October. Along the Sea of Cortez and Pacific coast it's generally the opposite, with rates highest Dec. 15-Apr. 15. To save money on accommodations, try traveling in the off-season for each region; except for the inland deserts and coastal plains, much of the region is livable year-round (on the Cortez coast, summer temperatures of 37° C/100° F are usually mitigated by sea breezes and relatively low humidity).

Except during peak periods such as Christmas, spring break, or Easter, you can usually bargain down the rack rate on a hotel room. When checking in, be sure to clarify whether the room rate includes meals—occasionally it does. Asking for a room without meals *(sin comidas)* is an easy way to bring the rate down, or simply ask if there's anything cheaper *(¿Hay algo más barato?)*.

Rating System

At one time each state in Mexico was required to use a SECTUR rating system to classify all accommodations by price and facilities. There were seven classes, from *clase económica* (C.E.) to *gran turismo* (G.T.), but the majority of places fell in the one- to five-star classes between these extremes. Except for five-star and G.T.-class hotels, which had no upper rate limit, the rating system limited the maximum room tariff that a hotel, motel, or guesthouse might charge. Two-star hotels in Nuevo León, for example, once had an upper rate cap of US$28, three-star places could charge up to US$53, and four-star establishments were limited to a maximum of US$82. One-star places were capped at US$20; *clase económica* rates weren't monitored.

In reality, hotels/motels charged whatever the market would bear, which was usually less than

BUYING OR LEASING PROPERTY IN MEXICO

The Mexican government allows both resident and nonresident foreigners to own Mexican real estate—both land and buildings—within certain restrictions. Under the Constitution of 1857, land ownership by direct title is only permitted in areas that are more than 100 km (62 miles) from any international borders and 50 km (31 miles) from any seacoasts.

However, since 1973 the Mexican government has offered a way for foreigners to acquire lots that fall outside the geographic limits, including coastal property. For property of this nature, the Ministry of Foreign Affairs issues permits to foreigners allowing them to create limited real estate trusts, administered by Mexican banks, with themselves as beneficiaries. Originally, these trusts were valid for 30-year nonrenewable terms only. In 1989 the government further liberalized real estate regulations so that the trusts (called *fideicomisos*) can be renewed at the end of each 30-year term for an additional 30-year term, with no limit on the number of renewals. *Fideicomisos* can be bought and sold among foreigners—at market rates—just like fee-simple property.

Mortgages are now available through certain banks in Mexico with financing for up to 70% of appraised property values and with terms of 15 to 20 years. Interest rates run around three percent higher than in the United States. Closing costs for a mortgage deal are as much as 25% higher.

Before you rush off to acquire Mexican land by purchase or bank trust, you should be aware that a lot of people get burned in Mexican real estate deals. It's best to negotiate through an established, reputable real estate agent. Local or state tourist offices in Northern Mexico often carry information on residential property and can assist with locating real estate agencies.

Is buying property in Mexico a risky proposition? Depends on how seriously you take the Mexican Constituion. Article 27 of this document mandates that "the nation" owns all property, a principle that obviously stacks the deck against private property and leaves all lands open to government seizure. Under Pres. Lázaro Cárdenas, many foreign-owned properties were expropriated in the 1930s as part of the push toward nationalization of all industry; in every single case, however, the owners were compensated for the land at market prices.

Probably the riskiest property purchases involve *ejido* lands (see "Ejidos" in the "Economy" section for an explanation of this collectively-owned property entity). Although at the moment *ejidatarios* (*ejido* shareholders) have the full right to sell their *ejido* parcels—just as they did under the presidency of Benito Juárez in the 19th century—there is no guarantee they won't later turn around and seize (or be granted by decree) their *ejidos*—as happened under the presidency of Lázaro Cárdenas and has happened in Chiapas since 1995. In the 1930s large numbers of *campesinos* took back lands that their families had previously sold to *hacendados*. In Chiapas, during the 1995 Zapatista rebellion and shortly thereafter, farmlands that had legally been purchased by middle-class Mexicans (some of whom had saved their entire lives to afford them) were seized by persons who considered the land their birthright despite a lack of history of occupation.

In a political system that sanctions inextricable links between ethnic/class divisions and land, any purchase of *ejido* property carries some historic risk. Some real estate experts advise prospective buyers to stay away from all *ejido* property. Others find the risk tolerable, depending above all on the *ejido* location—the southern states of Mexico are historically riskier than those of the north.

The best Mexican real estate advice we've heard: Never invest more than you can afford to lose.

Time-Shares

As many as 40% of Mazatlán's visitors at any given time are staying in time-shares, a purchase arrangement in which a room, apartment, or condominium is "bought" for a specified annual interval—usually a week or two. Hotels offering time-share programs include El Cid Mega Resort, Pueblo Bonito, Los Sábalos Resort Hotel, Torres Mazatlán, Hotel Costa de Oro, and The Inn at Mazatlán.

Are time-shares a good value? Most real estate experts will respond negatively, pointing out that although time-share property may be bought and sold like any other real estate, the rate of return (appreciation) on investment is the worst of any type of real estate investment. On the other hand, thousands of people—reasoning that they can only get away to a lovely spot like Mazatlán once a year—are quite satisfied with the arrangement, perhaps looking at it as a long-term vacation lease rather than as an investment.

Other purchasers have become sharply dissatisfied with the dishonest, often deliberately misleading sales tactics often used to market time-shares. The "free breakfast" offered in return for reviewing a time-share property always turns into an hour spent with an agent trying very hard to sell you a time-share property. These agents are prepared with answers for your every objection and will soon put you in the company of a "closer," a person trained to get your signature on the dotted line by almost any means.

Other scams involve young Mexican men who trawl the beaches for tourists to sign up for drawings for free city tours, restaurant coupons, and a "big surprise." With these, you get a phone call at your hotel room the next day saying you've won a free cruise—usually from San Diego to Los Cabos, Mazatlán, and Puerto Vallarta—and that all you have to do is go to Hotel X for a 75-minute tour of the property. You're assured that the tours are for hotels, not for condos, that no time-shares are involved (they simply call it by another name), and that no one will try to pressure you into anything. Assuming you make it through the tour without signing your life away, conditions attached to the cruise certificate or other "prize" always render it nearly worthless.

Such scams are an American import; enforcement of consumer protection laws in Mexico and the U.S. have caused their number and frequency to decrease substantially. On a recent trip to Mazatlán, in fact, I wasn't approached once by a time-share tout, so perhaps the hard-sell era is over. Just in case, keep in mind this simple but direct warning printed on a card placed on the nightstand of every room at Hotel Playa Mazatlán: "There are no free breakfasts in Mazatlán; you will be requested to listen to a sales promotion, and afterwards a high-pressure salesperson will try to close the 'deal.'"

the maximum allowable rate. SECTUR dropped the official scale during the freewheeling Salinas years, but most states still employ the system, albeit unpredictably. The ratings aren't that useful for pinning down exact rates, but do give an idea of the relative price range to expect.

Trying to judge the facilities using the rating system is even more difficult. While the facilities of a two-star hotel are always significantly more humble than those of a five-star, I've found that in some instances the difference between a two-star and a three-star or a three-star and a four-star isn't readily apparent.

This book uses the following scale to categorize accommodations prices:

Shoestring: under $15
Budget: $15-35
Inexpensive: $35-55
Moderate: $55-80
Expensive: $80-120
Premium: $120+

Unless otherwise specified, where rate ranges are quoted in this book, the lower figure represents the rate for the least expensive single room, while the upper figure is the rate for the most expensive standard double room. Other room choices may be available at rates between those two figures, and suites may be available at higher rates. If a single price is listed, it reflects the average price of a standard room, single or double occupancy. All listed rates are per room, per night.

Shoestring

In rural areas and small towns, room rates in very basic C.E. hotels may be as low as US$5-10. City lodging under US$10 per night is rare unless you stay at a youth hostel, *casa de huéspedes*, or *pensión* (described separately below), where bathrooms are usually shared. Shared bathroom facilities are usually indicated by the term *baño colectivo*.

Budget

In the economic range (one- to two-star according to most state rating systems), you'll find simple but clean rooms with private bath and double bed for around US$15-22 a night. Soap, towels, toilet paper, and purified drinking water are usually provided, but in some places you may have to ask. Rooms in this price range may not have air conditioners or heaters; you can often obtain a *calentador* or space heater on request for especially cool nights. In cities and large towns, the cheaper hotels tend to be found near the *mercado municipal*, railway station, or intercity bus terminal.

Inexpensive
Government ratings for this price range may vary from two to four stars depending on the state. Some are older Mexican-style hotels that are just a bit larger than those in the budget range, while others are American-style motels. Most everything in this range will come with heating and air conditioning.

Moderate, Expensive, and Premium
Higher-end places (five-star and G.T. classes) are found mostly in state capitals and in the beach resorts of San Carlos and Mazatlán. Prices for "international-class accommodations" average US$55-120. Some of these places are good values in this range, while others are definitely overpriced.

The most reputable luxury chain in Northern Mexico is Fiesta Americana, which has hotels in many larger cities. Other chains in this category include Camino Real, a smaller chain, and Holiday Inn International, which offers hotels in Monterrey (three locations), Mazatlán, and Hermosillo.

GUESTHOUSES AND HOSTELS

Casas de Huéspedes and Pensiones
The casa de huéspedes (guesthouse) and pensión (boardinghouse) are the cheapest places to stay in Mexico, aside from youth hostels or very basic campgrounds. Unfortunately for budgeters, they aren't very plentiful. The typical casa de huéspedes offers rooms with shared bath for US$5-8 or with private bath for US$8-12. A pensión costs about the same but may include meals. At either, most lodgers are staying for a week or more, but the proprietors are usually happy to take guests by the night.

The main difference between these and budget hotels/motels (besides rates) is that they are usually located in old houses or other buildings that have been converted for guesthouse use. Soap, towels, toilet paper, and drinking water are usually provided, but as with budget hotels and motels, you may have to ask.

Youth Hostels
Northern Mexico has youth hostels (villas deportivas juveniles) in the cities of Ciudad Obregón (Son.), Durango, Monterrey, Zacatecas, and San Luis Potosí. Accommodation is in shared dormitory-style rooms where each guest is assigned a bed and a locker. Bathing facilities are always communal and guests must supply their own soap and towels. Rates are only US$1.30-1.50 per bed per night, and food is available at hostel cafeterias (except Monterrey) for around US$2 per meal.

Staying at youth hostels is a great way to meet young Mexicans and improve your Spanish (English is rarely spoken). About the only drawback is that the hostels tend to be inconveniently located some distance from the center of town, so transport can be a problem if you don't have your own wheels. City buses, however, are usually available.

In spite of their nomenclature, youth hostels welcome travelers of all ages. All that's required is membership in any national hostel association affiliated with Hostelling International, formerly known as the International Youth Hostel Federation (IYHF). Temporary or yearly memberships are available directly from individual youth hostels, or you can contact the relevant organization in your home country for membership information in advance. Hostelling International can provide an international directory that lists all hostels operated in Mexico; those relevant to this guidebook are listed under the appropriate destinations.

CAMPING

Northern Mexico has plenty of space for campers. Because the population density of the region as a whole is low, it's fairly easy to find off-the-beaten-track campsites that offer idyllic settings and precious solitude—often for free. For travelers who like the outdoors, it's also an excellent way to slash accommodations costs.

Campgrounds and RV Parks
Campgrounds charge fees ranging from around US$1.50 for a place with virtually zero facilities to a high of US$15 for a developed RV park with full water, electrical, and sewage hookups plus recreation facilities (e.g., boat ramps). Most campgrounds charge around US$3-5 for tent camping, US$6-12 for full hookups.

Many motels and hotels will allow RVers to park overnight for a minimal fee. For about US$10 you should be allowed to use showers and toilets in any unoccupied rooms.

Though lacking permanent toilet and bathing facilities, wilderness areas hold a virtually limitless selection of free camping spots, from beaches to deserts to mountain slopes. You won't necessarily need 4WD to reach these potential campsites, as there are plenty of turnouts and graded dirt *ramales* (branch roads) off the main highways that can be negotiated by just about any type of vehicle.

RV Electrical Problems: Mexican circuits are rarely grounded and two-prong electrical outlets are the norm. Bring adapters to convert three-prong plugs to two-prong. To guard against electrical shock, always ground your unit by attaching a piece of wire between a metal part of your rig and a a metal stake in the ground. If the power doesn't work or you get a shock from touching the exterior of your rig, reverse the plug in its outlet.

Always check with the management to confirm voltage before plugging in; in some parks you may find outlets with a 220V (rather than the usual 110V) source. This is relatively rare, and most parks supply transformers to step voltage down from 220V to 110V. If you have a 220V/110V transformer, bring it along just in case.

FOOD AND DRINK

Many of the most popular Mexican dishes worldwide (especially in Texas and the American Southwest) are actually from Northern Mexico, where ranch-style cooking tends to prevail. Burritos, fajitas, *huevos rancheros, chiles rellenos, frijoles a la charra, cabrito, carne asada, filet tampiqueña (carne a la tampiqueña), tacos al carbón*—all are part of *cocina típica norteña.*

But Northern Mexican food isn't a single, monolithic cooking style. Each state has its local specialties that form recognizable subregional cuisines. Areas along the Sea of Cortez/Pacific and Gulf of Mexico coasts produce delectable seafood dishes, while in the Altiplano beef and *cabrito* reign supreme. And as you would expect, the farther south you go the more Southern Mexican influences you will find; by the time you reach Zacatecas and San Luis Potosí, the local cooking styles are a full blend of North and South.

WHERE TO EAT

Your selection of eating venues depends largely on where you are in Northern Mexico at any given moment. You'll find the greatest range of places to eat in the larger towns and cities, which offer everything from humble sidewalk taco stands to five-star hotel restaurants.

Small towns may hold only two or three restaurants *(restaurante, restorán)* that serve basic Mexican dishes or, if near the coast, seafood.

Most hotels also have restaurants and in small towns they may be among the best choices. Sometimes the best meals on the road will come from what you improvise after a visit to a local *tienda de abarrotes* (see "Buying Groceries," below).

Back in the city, one of the main nonrestaurant choices is the *taquería,* a small, inexpensive diner where tacos are assembled before your eyes (sort of the Mexican equivalent of the old-fashioned American hamburger stand). Taquerías tend to be found in areas of heavy foot traffic (near bus terminals, for example); the good ones will be packed with taco-eaters in the early evening.

Another economic choice is any *lonchería*, a small, cafe-style place that usually serves *almuerzo* (late breakfast/early lunch) and *comida* (the main, midday meal). *Lonchería* hours are typically 11 a.m.-5 p.m. Municipal markets will often have a row of *loncherías* serving inexpensive basic meals and *antojitos* (snacks or one-plate dishes). Some *loncherías* offer *comida corrida,* a daily fixed-price meal that includes a beverage, an entree or two, plus side dishes and possibly dessert.

A *comedor* is usually a more basic version of a *lonchería.* Cafes are similar to *loncherías* except that they may open earlier and serve *desayuno* (breakfast) in addition to other meals. A *cafetería* is a larger coffee shop (often attached to a large department store or pharmacy) with a full menu. Table service is the norm; Mexican *cafeterías* rarely serve food in what North Americans might call "cafeteria-style."

Ordering and Paying

You don't need much Spanish to get by in a Mexican restaurant. Stating what you want, plus *por favor* (please), will usually do the trick (e.g., *dos cervezas, por favor,* "two beers, please"). The menu is called *el menú* or, much less commonly in Northern Mexico, *la carta.* As a last resort, you can always point to what you want on the menu.

La cuenta is the bill. A tip *(la propina)* of 10-15% is expected at any restaurant with table service; look to see if it has already been added to the bill before placing it on the table.

WHAT TO EAT

Tortillas

A Mexican meal is not a meal without tortillas, the pancake-like disks that are eaten with nearly any nondessert dish, including salads, meats, seafood, beans, and vegetables. Food experts have cataloged 166 kinds of tortillas in Mexico. Very large, thin wheat tortillas known as *tortillas de agua,* or *sobaqueras* for example, are a favorite in Sonora. In some places—especially Sonora and Chihuahua—you may encounter *coyotas,* thick wheat tortillas similar to *gorditas.* *Huaraches* are large oval-shaped wheat flatbreads that look somewhat like flattened footballs (or North Indian *naan*); these are topped with chopped, fried meats, onions, tomatoes, and spices and served as a complete *antojito.*

Corn tortillas *(tortillas de maíz)* are more common in Southern Mexico, where Indian populations (the first corn cultivators) are larger and the climate is well suited to growing corn. In the North the geography is more conducive to wheat cultivation, which requires less rain than corn. Culturally, wheat ties the *euromestizos* of the North to their European roots, while corn is identified more with Mesoamerica and the *indomestizo* culture. Economics also plays a role in tortilla consumption. Since corn is heavily subsidized by the government, corn tortillas are much cheaper than wheat tortillas; hence the poorer sectors of society often have little choice

but to make or buy corn tortillas.

Both corn and wheat tortillas, however, are consumed in great quantity throughout the North. Among *norteños* it is said that meat and poultry dishes taste best with flour tortillas while vegetable dishes go best with corn. Some restaurants will offer a choice of the two (if you order tortillas without specifying, you may get *"¿De harina o de maíz?"*—flour or corn?—as a response).

Common variations on the standard corn tortilla include the *gordita,* a small, thick tortilla filled with spiced meat and vegetables, especially popular in Durango, and the *sope,* a small, tart-shaped corn flatbread topped with a similar mixture plus crumbled cheese.

Although prepackaged tortillas are available in *supermercados,* most Mexicans buy them fresh from neighborhood *tortillerías* (see "Buying Groceries," below) or make them at home. Many restaurants and cafes, and virtually all *loncherías* and *taquerías,* serve only fresh tortillas (tortillas made the same day or the night before they're served). If you're used to prepackaged tortillas (which is what most Mexican eateries in the U.S. or Canada serve), you're in for a pleasurable surprise when you raise a fresh, hot, homemade tortilla to your nose for the first time. When buying directly from a *tortillería,* remember that tortillas are always sold by the kilo, not by number of tortillas.

Incidentally, there are two sides to a tortilla, an inside and an outside, that dictate in which direction the tortilla is best folded when wrapping it around food. The side with the thinner layer (sometimes called the *pancita* or belly) should face the inside when folding the tortilla. If you notice that the outside of your tortilla is cracking and pieces are peeling off onto the table, it's probably because you've folded it with the *pancita* outside instead of inside (where the food would have kept it from flaking off).

Antojitos

This word literally means "little whims," thus implying "snacks" to many people. However, it also refers to any food that can be ordered, served, and eaten quickly, in other words Mexican fast-food (like burgers and hot dogs in America). Typical *antojitos* include tamales, enchiladas, burritos, *chimichangas,* quesadillas,

ANTOJITOS

birria—lamb or goat stew in a sauce spiced with chiles, cinnamon, cloves, cumin, and oregano

burrito—also called *burro* or *burra;* a flour tortilla rolled around meat, beans, or seafood fillings. Most common in Sonora and Chihuahua, where *carne machaca* (shredded, dried meat) is the most popular filling

chalupa—also known as a *tostada;* a crisp corn tortilla topped with beans, meat, etc.

chiles rellenos—mild poblano chiles stuffed with cheese, deep-fried in egg batter, and served with ranchero sauce (tomatoes, onions, and chiles)

chimichanga—sometimes spelled *chivichanga;* a Sonoran tortilla doubled over, filled with meat and/or vegetables, rolled (or folded again), then deep-fried; found almost exclusively in Sonora

enchilada—a corn tortilla dipped in chile sauce, then folded or rolled around a filling of meat, chicken, seafood, or cheese and baked in an oven

enfrijolada—same as *enchilada* except dipped in a sauce of thinned refried beans instead of chile sauce

entomatada—same as *enchilada* except dipped in a tomato sauce instead of chile sauce

flauta—literally "flute," a small corn tortilla roll, usually stuffed with beef or chicken and fried

gorditas—a small, thick, corn tortilla stuffed with a spicy meat mixture

huarache—literally "sandal," a large, thick, oval flatbread made from wheat flour and topped with chopped fried meats, chiles, onions, and spices

menudo—a thick soup made with cow's feet and stomach (and less commonly, intestines) and seasoned with *chiles de árbol,* oregano, and fresh chopped onion; reputedly a sure hangover cure

pozole—hominy stew made with pork or chicken and garnished with radishes, oregano, onions, chile powder, salt, and lime

picadillo—also known as *salpicón;* a spicy salad of chopped or ground meat with chiles and onions

quesadilla—a flour tortilla folded over sliced cheese and grilled; ask the cook to add *rajas,* strips of green chile pepper added for extra flavor

sope—a small, thick, round corn cake with dimpled edges, topped with a spicy meat mixture and crumbled cheese

taco—a corn tortilla folded or rolled around anything and eaten with the hands; *taco dorado* is the fried version

tamal—plural *tamales;* cornmeal *(masa)* dough wrapped in a corn husk and steamed; sometimes stuffed with corn, olives, pork, or turkey; common in San Luis Potosí

torta—a sandwich made with a Mexican-style roll (*bolillo* or *birote*); one of the most popular is the *torta de milanesa,* made with breaded, deep-fried veal or pork

---

flautas, chiles rellenos, chalupas, picadillo, tortas, and tacos.

Visitors who identify these terms with dishes at Mexican restaurants in their home countries are sometimes confused by the different shapes and forms they may take in Mexico. Tacos can be rolled as well as folded, and enchiladas can be folded (or stacked) as well as rolled; shape is irrelevant. An "enchilada" (literally "chilied") is any *antojito* made with a tortilla that has been dipped or cooked in a chile sauce; an "entomada" (or "entomatada") is the equivalent made with tomatoes. A "taco" is any type of plain tortilla that surrounds other ingredients. In some eateries you can order tacos either *suave* (heated soft tortillas stuffed with meat and vegetable fillings) or *dorado* ("golden"; thin corn tortillas stuffed tightly with meat, then deep-fried whole and served with lettuce and grated cheese).

Breakfasts

Menus at tourist restaurants are sometimes confusing because some of the same "breakfast" dishes may end up on more than one section of the menu. This is because Mexicans have two kinds of breakfasts, an early one called *desayuno,* eaten shortly after rising, and a second called *almuerzo* that's usually taken around

11 a.m. To further confuse the issue, Spanish-English dictionaries usually translate *almuerzo* as "lunch," while bilingual menus often read "breakfast."

The most common Mexican *desayuno* is simply *pan dulce* (sweet pastry) or *bolillos* (torpedo-shaped, European-style rolls) with coffee or milk. Cereal is also sometimes eaten for *desayuno,* e.g., *avena* (oatmeal), *crema de trigo* (Cream of Wheat), or *hojuelas de maíz* (corn flakes).

The heavier eggs-and-frijoles dishes known widely as "Mexican breakfasts" in the U.S. and Canada are usually taken as *almuerzo,* the late breakfast (which is most typically reserved for weekends and holidays). Eggs come in a variety of ways, including *huevos revueltos* (scrambled eggs), *huevos duros* (hard-boiled eggs), *huevos tibios* (coddled eggs—but not "soft-boiled" as sometimes translated), *huevos escafaldos* (soft-boiled eggs), *huevos estrellados* or *huevos fritos* (eggs fried "sunny side up"), *huevos a la mexicana* (also *huevos mexicanos,* eggs scrambled with chopped tomato, onion, and chile), *huevos rancheros* (fried eggs served on a tortilla), and *huevos divorciado,* two *huevos estrellados* separated by beans, each egg usually topped with a different salsa.

Eggs also come *con chorizo* (scrambled with ground sausage), *con machaca* (with dried, shredded meat), *con tocino* (with bacon), or *con jamón* (with ham). All egg dishes usually come with frijoles and tortillas. The biggest *almuerzo* package on the menu is typically called *almuerzo albañil* ("brickmason's *almuerzo*") or *huevos albañil* ("brickmason's eggs"); this means eggs with one or more varieties of meat on the side.

One of the cheapest and tastiest *almuerzos* is *chilaquiles,* tortilla chips in a chile gravy with crumbled cheese on top. Eggs and chicken can be added to *chilaquiles* as options. Visitors from Texas (especially Austin) will notice a strong similarity to Tex-Mex cafe-style *migas* ("crumbs"), though the latter always includes eggs. Another economical choice is *molletes,* a split *bolillo* spread with mashed beans and melted cheese, served with salsa on the side. *Molletes* are usually only US$1-1.50 an order; they're often served with juice and coffee as a "university breakfast" *(desayuno universitario)* for US$2 or less.

Entrees and Styles of Preparation

The main dish or *el plato fuerte* of any meal can be a grander version of an *antojito,* a regional specialty from another part of Mexico (*mole poblano,* for example), or something the *cocineros* (cooks) have dreamed up themselves. Typical entrees are centered around meats, poultry, and seafood.

Common meats include *carne de res* (beef), *puerco* (pork), and *cabrito* (kid goat). *Jamón* (ham), chorizo (sausage), and *tocino* (bacon) are usually reserved for *almuerzo.* Throughout the northwest, *machaca* or dried, shredded meat is very popular, especially in burritos. Steak may appear on menus as *bistec, bistek, biftec,* or "steak." *Venado* (deer meat or venison), *liebre* (hare), and *conejo* (rabbit) are commonly served in the sierras.

Poultry dishes include *pollo* (chicken), *pavo* (turkey), and, less frequently, *pato* (duck) and *codorniz* (quail). Quail is particularly popular in the northeast.

Most entrees are prepared in one of the following styles:

adobo, adobada—marinated or stewed in a sauce of vinegar, chiles, and spices

a la parilla—broiled or grilled

a la veracruzana—seafood (often *huachinanga* or red snapper) cooked with tomatoes, onions, and olives

albóndigas—meatballs

al carbón—charcoal-grilled

al mojo de ajo—in a garlic sauce

al pastor—roasted on a spit

al vapor—steamed

asada—grilled

barbacoa—pit-roasted

con arroz—steamed with rice

empanizada—breaded

encebollado—cooked with onions

enchilada—cooked with chiles

enfrijolada—cooked in a bean sauce

entomado—cooked with tomatoes

frito—fried

guisado—in a spicy stew

machaca—dried and shredded

Cabrito

Kid goat is an almost exclusively Northern Mexican dish that is most popular in Nuevo León and also common in Coahuila and Chihuahua. Restaurants specializing in *cabrito* are easy to spot because their windows will display several *cabritos* in a row roasting on angled spits. Spit-roasted kid *(cabrito al pastor)* is by far the most common way this delicacy is served. Of the several cuts offered on a typical menu, most aficionados agree the *pierna* or leg is the best overall, followed by *riñon* or kidney.

Many a visiting gringo, intent on trying *cabrito* but not wanting to spend much the first time out (and not really knowing the difference between one cut or another), has chosen to order *cabecita* because it's the cheapest cut on the menu (typically around US$3). Surprise of surprises, *cabecita* ("little head") is the goat's head! The minimal meat on this cut consists of the cheeks, brain, and tongue—all very tasty. In the Nuevo Laredo area of northern Tamaulipas, *machitos* — goat-tripe burritos, if you will—are popular.

Fajitas

The latest fad to sweep Mexican restaurants in the U.S., fajitas are strips of meat cooked in a style that originated in the Nuevo Laredo area of Tamaulipas. The name means "little belts" or "little skirts" and refers to a beef cut known in English as "skirt steak," often considered an unusable cut by butchers outside Mexico. In Northern Mexico, ranchero cooks usually slice skirt steaks into strips, grill them quickly over a very hot fire, and serve them with fresh flour tortillas, *salsa fresca* (called *pico de gallo* in some parts of Northern Mexico), grilled onions *(cebollas asadas),* guacamole, and beans. Restaurants in Nuevo Laredo often sell fajitas by the kilo.

Outside of Tamaulipas and Nuevo León, fajitas are sometimes called *arracheras;* Coahuila restaurants occasionally distinguish between skirt steaks cooked in strips and those cooked whole, calling the former "fajitas" and the latter "arracheras." As fajitas gain in popularity throughout Northern Mexico (partly as a result of their increasing popularity in the U.S.), the presentation is becoming more sophisticated. Most cooks now marinate skirt steaks briefly before cooking in order to tenderize the naturally tough meat.

In resort areas, restaurants catering to tourists now offer chicken, shrimp, and sirloin fajitas, so the original meaning of the term "fajita" is changing to indicate any meat, poultry, or seafood marinated, quickly grilled, and served with tortillas and salsas.

Seafood

Pescado (fish) entrees on the menu are often seasonal or dependent on the "catch of the day." Often just the word *pescado,* along with the method of cooking will appear (e.g., *pescado al mojo de ajo*). If you need to know exactly what kind of fish, just ask, *"¿Hay qué tipo de pescado?",* although in some cases the only response you'll get will be something generic like *"Pescado blanco"* ("white fish").

On the Sea of Cortez/Pacific coast, *tacos de pescado* (fish tacos) are popular. If you've never tried one, you're most likely wondering, "What's the big deal—a fish taco?" Eat one, though, and you're hooked for life. Short, tender, fresh fish fillets are quickly dipped in batter and fried, then folded into a steaming corn tortilla with a variety of condiments that include *salsa fresca* (chopped tomatoes, onions, chiles, and lime juice), marinated cabbage (similar to coleslaw in the U.S.), guacamole, and sometimes a squirt of mayonnaise *(mayonesa). ¡La última!* Any kind of white-fleshed fish can be used—the best fish tacos are those made from yellowtail *(jurel).* In Mazatlán a fish taco may be made with shredded fish prepared in a ceviche or *picadillo* style instead of fried fish fillets.

Shellfish dishes *(mariscos)* are popular on both coasts but especially along the Gulf of Mexico. Typical offerings include *ostiones* (oysters), *almejas* (clams), *callos* (scallops), *jaibas* (small crabs), *cangrejo* (large crabs), *camarones* (shrimp), *langosta* (lobster, Sea of Cortez/Pacific only), *langostina* (crayfish, also called *cucarachas*), and *abulón* (abalone, Sea of Cortez/ Pacific only). These can be ordered as *cocteles* (cocktails—steamed or boiled and served with lime and salsa), *en sus conchas* (in the shell), or ceviche (marinated raw in lime juice, onions, and chiles until "cooked" by the acidic juices); or ordered in many of the ways listed under "Entrees and Styles of Preparation," above.

Carnitas

This dish from the state of Michoacán belongs in a category all its own and is usually sold only at butcher shops or at specialty restaurants. The usual method for producing *carnitas* is to slowly braise an entire pig in a huge pot, along with a variety of flavorings (a closely guarded secret among *carnitas* purveyors). The result is chopped into thin slices and eaten with stacks of tortillas, pickled vegetables and chiles, guacamole, and various salsas.

Carnitas are always sold by weight, even in *carnitas* restaurants. You can order by the *kilo*, (one kilogram, about 2.2 pounds), *medio* (half kilo), or *cuarto* (one-fourth kilo), or sometimes in *cien gramos* (100-gram increments). Figure on a quarter kilo (about a half pound) per hungry person and you shouldn't have much left over.

Beans

The beans (frijoles) most preferred in Northern Mexico are pinto beans, usually dried beans that are boiled until soft, then mashed and fried with lard or vegetable oil (usually the former). Often this preparation is called *frijoles refritos* or "refried beans," although they're not really refried except when reheated. Sometimes the beans are served whole, in their own broth, as *frijoles de olla* (boiled beans) or with bits of roast pork as *frijoles a la charra* (ranch-style beans). Frijoles can be served with any meal of the day, including breakfast. In San Luis Potosí, black beans are almost as common as pintos and are always served with *platillos huastecos* (Huasteca dishes).

Cheese

Even the lowliest restaurant or cafe will usually have some cheese *(queso)* around, so if your appetite isn't stimulated by the *iguana guisada* simmering on the hearth, you can usually ask for *chiles rellenos* (mild poblano chiles stuffed with cheese and fried in an egg batter) or quesadillas (cheese melted in folded flour tortillas). A meal of beans, tortillas, and cheese provides a complete source of protein for travelers who choose to avoid meat, poultry, or seafood for health, economic, or moral reasons.

Northern Mexico is famous for its cheeses, the most common of which are Sonora's *queso cotijo* (also called *queso añejo*), Chihuahua's *queso menonita* (called *queso chihuahuense* outside the state), and *queso asadero* (produced in several states but most common in eastern Chihuahua). All three cheeses can usually be found in supermarkets throughout Northern Mexico.

Queso menonita (Mennonite cheese) is a mild, white cheddar produced in wheels by Mennonite colonists in Chihuahua. It's a common ingredient in dishes stuffed with cheese, such as enchiladas or *chiles rellenos*, which won't receive high, direct heat. *Queso asadero* ("griller cheese") is a braided cheese somewhat similar to mozzarella or Armenian string cheese, made by combining sour milk with fresh milk. *Asadero* melts well (without burning or separating) at high temperatures, and as such is well suited to *chile con queso* (hot, blended chile-cheese dip), *queso fundido* (hot melted cheese topped with chorizo or mushrooms), and other dishes in which the cheese is directly exposed to high heat.

Cotija or *añejo* is a crumbly, aged cheese that resists melting and is commonly used as a topping for enchiladas and beans; the flavor and texture are what you might expect from a cross between feta and Parmesan.

Many ranchos produce their own *queso fresco,* "fresh cheese" made from fresh cow's, goat's, or sheep's milk. To make *queso fresco,* the rancheros first cure the milk with homemade rennet (from a calf's fourth stomach) until the milk separates, and then press the curds with weights (sometimes under flat rocks lined with cloth) to remove excess moisture. In more elaborate operations, the initial pressing is then ground up and re-pressed into small, round cakes. This type of cheese is not usually found in stores; if you want to buy some, look for *Hay queso* signs as you pass ranchos. If you're extremely fortunate,

> *"Hey you fellas, how 'bout some beans? You want some beans? Goin' through some mighty rough country tomorrow, you'd better have some beans."*
>
> —"Howard" (Walter Huston), in *The Treasure of the Sierra Madre* (1948)

you might even come across *panela,* an extra-rich cheese made from heavy cream.

Vegetables
Although vegetables are sometimes served as side dishes with *comidas corridas,* with restaurant entrees, or in salads *(ensaladas),* they're seldom listed separately on the menu. When they do appear on menus it's usually at restaurants in towns that are near farming areas. The best place to add vegetables to your diet is at a market or grocery store (see "Buying Groceries," below).

Soup
The general menu term for soup is *sopa,* although a thick soup with lots of ingredients is usually a *caldo* or *caldillo. Menudo* is a soup of hominy *(nixtamal)* and cow's feet and stomach (or, less commonly, intestine) in a savory, reddish-brown broth, served with chopped onions, chiles, and crumbled oregano. It's seen throughout Northern Mexico and is highly prized as a hangover remedy. *Pozole* is a similar soup with a much lighter-colored broth; some varieties of *pozole* are made with chicken instead of tripe.

Other tasty soups include *sopa de tortillas, sopa azteca,* and *sopa tlapeño,* all variations of artfully seasoned chicken broth garnished with *totopos* (tortilla wedges) and sliced avocado.

Salsas and Condiments
Any restaurant, cafe, *cafetería, lonchería, taquería,* or *comedor* will offer a variety of salsas or sauces with their food. Sometimes only certain salsas are served with certain dishes, while other times one, two, or even three salsas are stationed on every table. Often each place has its own unique salsa recipes—canned or bottled salsas are rarely used. The one ingredient common to all salsas is chile peppers, though these vary in heat from mild to incendiary.

There are as many types of salsas as there are Mexican dishes—red, green, yellow, brown, hot, mild, salty, sweet, thick, thin, blended, and chunky, to name a few. It would take a separate book to describe them all. The most typical is the *salsa casera* or "house salsa," a simple, fresh concoction of chopped chiles, onions, and tomatoes mixed with salt, lime juice, and cilantro. This is what you usually get with the complimentary basket of *totopos* (tortilla chips) served at the beginning of every Mexican meal (including *almuerzo*). Another common one is *salsa verde,* "green sauce," which is made with a base of tomatillos (small, tart, green, tomato-like vegetables). Some salsas are quite *picante* (spicy hot—also *picosa*), so it's always a good idea to test a bit before pouring it over everything on your plate.

Whole pickled chiles are sometimes served on the side as a condiment, especially with tacos and *carnitas.* On Sonoran tables it's common to see a bowl of *chiltepines,* small, round, fiery red peppers. Salt *(sal)* is usually on the table, although it's rarely needed since Mexican dishes tend to be prepared with plenty of it. Black pepper is *pimiento negro,* and if it's not on the table it's normally available for the asking. Butter is *mantequilla,* sometimes served with flour tortillas.

In *taquerías,* guacamole—mashed avocado blended with garlic, chiles, salt, and other optional ingredients—is always served as a condiment. In restaurants it may be served as a salad or with tortilla chips. In Sinaloa and Durango, "guacamole" sometimes refers to a very spicy paste of tomatillos and green chiles that may resemble avocado guacamole—always taste before heaping it on your plate. Toasted and ground avocado leaves are also used as a seasoning in Sinaloa and San Luis Potosí.

Desserts and Sweets
The most popular of Mexican desserts, or *postres,* is a delicious egg custard called flan. It's listed on virtually every tourist restaurant menu, along with *helado* or ice cream. Other sweet alternatives include pastries found in *panaderías* or bakeries (described under "Buying Groceries," below), and the frosty offerings at the ubiquitous *paleterías.* Strictly speaking, a *paletería* serves only *paletas,* flavored ice on sticks (like American popsicles except in a much wider range of flavors),

BOB RACE

but many also serve *nieve* (snow), which is flavored grated ice served like ice cream in bowls or cones.

Another common street vendor food is *churros,* a sweet fried pastry something like a donut stick sprinkled with powdered sugar. Perhaps Northern Mexico's best *churros* are those sold by vendors in the city parks of Torreón, Coahuila.

Dulcerías, or candy shops, sell a huge variety of sticky Mexican sweets, usually wrapped individually. Often brightly decorated, *dulcerías* are oriented toward children and sometimes carry inexpensive toys as well as sweets. The larger ones sell piñatas—colorful papier-mâché figures filled with candy and small gifts and hung at parties (where children are allowed to break them with sticks, releasing all the goodies inside). Traditionally, piñatas are crafted to resemble common animals, but these days you'll see all kinds of shapes, including Power Rangers, Batman, and "Teenage Mutant Tortugas de Ninja."

Vegetarians

It's difficult but not impossible to practice a vegetarian regime in Mexico. Lacto-vegetarians can eat quesadillas (ask for corn tortillas, which unlike most flour tortillas do not contain lard), or *enchiladas de queso* (cheese enchiladas). With some luck, you'll stumble across restaurants that can prepare a variety of interesting cheese dishes, including *queso fundido con champiñones* (melted cheese with mushrooms, eaten with tortillas) and quesadillas made with *flor de calabeza* or squash flower. Some places make beans without lard *(sin manteca)* but you'll have to ask to find out. Pizza restaurants are common throughout Northern Mexico. Many larger towns have at least one vegetarian/health food store (usually called *tienda naturista*) with small dining sections as well as bulk foods.

Ovo-lacto-vegetarians can add egg dishes and flan to their menus. Vegans for the most part will do best to prepare their own food. Look for shops with signs reading *semillas* (seeds) to pin down a good selection of nuts and dried beans. Of course you'll find plenty of fresh fruits and vegetables in markets and grocery stores (see "Buying Groceries," below).

BUYING GROCERIES

The cheapest way to feed yourself while traveling in Mexico is the same way you save money at home: Buy groceries at the store and prepare your own meals. While they may not have any dining spots to speak of, even the smallest towns in Northern Mexico will have at least a small grocery store or corner market. A ripe avocado *(aguacate),* a chunk of *queso,* and a couple of *bolillos* can make a fine, easy-to-fix meal.

The humblest stores are the small, family-owned *tienda de abarrotes,* which are usually recognizable by the single word *abarrotes* ("groceries") printed somewhere on the outside (*tienda* means "store"). These stock the basics—tortillas, dried beans, flour, herbs and spices, bottled water, a few vegetables, possibly *bolillos* and cheese—as well as limited household goods like soap and laundry detergent. As at the 7-Eleven back home, the food at the average *tienda de abarrotes* is not particularly inexpensive.

A better deal, where available, is the government-sponsored CONASUPO (an acronym for Compañía Nacional de Subsistencias Populares). CONASUPOs carry many of the same items as the typical *tienda de abarrotes* but at government-subsidized prices. Not every item is cheaper, however, so it pays to shop around. Larger, supermarket-style CONASUPOs are called CONASUPERs.

Privately run supermarkets can be found in larger towns and are usually called *supers* or *supermercados.* Like their American counterparts, they're usually well stocked with a wide variety of meats, baked goods, vegetables, household goods, beer and liquor, and so on. Supermarket prices are often lower than those of smaller grocery stores.

Most towns and cities have *mercados municipales* (municipal markets), large, warehouse-type structures where meat, fruit, and vegetable producers sell their goods directly to the public. Prices are often very good at these markets but it really helps if you speak some Spanish and know how to bargain. Although they're usually centrally located, municipal markets are sometimes difficult to find simply because they look so inconspicuous on the outside—you may have to ask around.

Another common *tienda* is the *ultramarinos,* which is primarily a place to buy beer and liquor but which also sells a few deli-style food items.

Panaderías

Although you can often buy a few bakery items at the aforementioned stores, the best place to buy them is at their source—a *panadería* or bakery. Many of the *panaderías* in rural Northern Mexico still used wood-fired *hornos* (ovens), which make the *bolillos* (Mexican rolls), *pastels* (cakes), and *pan dulce* (cookies and pastries) especially tasty. *Pan de barra,* American-style sliced bread, is also occasionally available but it never measures up to crusty *bolillos.* To select bakery items from the shelves of a *panadería,* simply imitate the other customers—pick up a pair of tongs and a tray from the counter near the cash register and help yourself, cafeteria-style.

Tortillerías

Unless you make them yourself, the best tortillas are found where they make them fresh every day. Restaurants, *tiendas,* and home cooks will purchase from the local *tortillería* to avoid spending hours at a *metate* (grinder) and *comal* (griddle). The automated process at a *tortillería* uses giant electric grinders and conveyor belts to transform whole corn into fresh tortillas, which you purchase by weight, not number. A kilo yields about 40 average, 12-cm (five-inch) tortillas; you can order by the *cuarto* or *medio* (quarter or half kilo). The government-subsidized prices are low.

Prices

Here are some sample grocery prices taken from a supermarket in Los Mochis, Sin., in late 1997 (in U.S. dollars-per-kilogram—2.2 pounds —unless otherwise specified):

whole chicken: 2.00
ground beef: 3.60
queso cotijo añejo: 4.00
queso chihuahuense: 4.00-5.00
queso asadero: 6.00
avocados: .40
papayas: .80
tomatoes: 1.00
bananas: .80
onions: .66
broccoli: 1.00
corn on the cob: .25
rice: .40
milk, two liters: 1.00
18 eggs: 1.15
purified water, one gallon: .80
tequila (most brands), one liter: 8.00-9.00

NONALCOHOLIC BEVERAGES

Cold Drinks

The water and ice served in restaurants in Northern Mexico are always purified—it's not necessary to order *agua mineral* (mineral water) unless you need the minerals. Likewise, the water used as an ingredient in "handmade" drinks, e.g., *licuados* or *aguas frescas,* is also from purified sources.

Licuados are similar to American "smoothies" —fruit blended with water, ice, honey or sugar, and sometimes milk or raw eggs, to produce something like a fruit shake. In Northern Mexico, *tuna* (not the fish but the prickly pear cactus fruit) *licuados* are particularly delicious. Other tasty and nutritious additives include oats *(avena)* and wheat germ *(trigo).* Any place that makes *licuados* will also make orange juice *(jugo de naranja).*

Aguas frescas are the colorful beverages sold from huge glass jars in markets, on the streets of larger cities, or at carnivals, especially during warm weather. They're made by boiling the pulp of various fruits, grains, or seeds with water, then straining it and adding sugar and large chunks of ice. *Arroz* (rice) and *horchata* (either melon or pumpkin seeds, or almonds) are two of the tastiest *aguas; cebada,* a concoction of barley mixed with cinnamon and vanilla, is also good and is a specialty of Sinaloa. *Licuados* and *aguas frescas* are often sold from colorful storefronts invariably named "La Flor de Michoacán" or "La Michoacana."

American soft drinks *(refrescos)* such as 7UP, Coke, and Pepsi are common; their Mexican equivalents are just as good. An apple-flavored soft drink called Manzanita is popular.

aguas frescas

JOE CUMMINGS

Hot Drinks

Coffee is served in a variety of ways. The best (when you can find it) is traditional Mexican-style coffee, which is made by filtering near-boiling water through fine-ground coffee in a slender cloth sack. Instant coffee *(Nescafé)* is often served at small restaurants and cafes—a jar of instant coffee may be sitting on the table for you to add to hot water. When there's a choice, a request for *café de olla* ("pot coffee") should bring you real brewed coffee. One of the better Mexican brands found in supermarkets is Café Combate. You can also buy green, unroasted beans in any grocery store and roast them yourselves in a dry iron skillet to get fresh-roasted coffee.

Café con leche is the Mexican version of café au lait, i.e., coffee and hot milk mixed in near-equal proportions. Coffee is particularly good in San Luis Potosí, where *café con leche* is a local specialty. *Café con crema* (coffee with cream) is not as available—when it is, it usually means non-dairy powdered creamer rather than fresh cream.

Hot chocolate *(chocolate)* is fairly common on Mexican menus. It's usually served very sweet and may contain cinnamon, ground almonds, and other flavorings. A thicker version that is made with cornmeal—almost a chocolate pudding—is called *champurrado* or *atole*.

Black tea *(té negro)* is not popular among *norteños* although you may see it on tourist menus. Ask for *té helado* if you want iced tea. At home many Mexicans drink *té de manzanilla* (chamomile tea) or *té de yerba buena* (mint tea) in the evenings. Both *manzanilla* and *limón* ("lemon," actually dried lemongrass) teas are sometimes available in restaurants if you ask, and these make a nice herbal substitute if you're avoiding caffeine. In Sinaloa *té de damiana*—the flavor resembles a blend of mint and chamomile—is popular. Some *norteños* claim the herb *damiana* has aphrodisiac qualities; others say it's a sedative.

ALCOHOLIC BEVERAGES

Drinking laws in Mexico are minimal. The legal drinking age in Mexico was raised from 15 to 18 years less than a decade ago, and it's illegal to carry an open container of alcoholic beverage in a vehicle. That's about it—booze of every kind is widely available in bars, restaurants, grocery stores, and *licorerías* or liquor stores.

Cerveza

In northwest Mexico, particularly Sonora, the most popular and most available beer brand is Tecate (brewed in Tecate, Baja California Norte), while farther south toward Mazatlán it's Pacífico (from Mazatlán). Both are good-tasting, light- to medium-weight brews, with Tecate holding a slight edge (more hops) over Pacífico. You can't compare either of these with their export equivalents in the U.S., since Mexican breweries produce separate brews for American consumption that are lighter in taste and lighter on the alcohol content—it's always better in Mexico.

As you move east to the more populated areas of Northern Mexico, a greater variety of labels is available, including such major Mexican brands as Corona (now partially owned by Anheuser-Busch), Dos Equis (XX), Superior, Carta Blanca, Bohemia, and Negro Modelo. It's really a matter of personal taste as to which of these brands will most satisfy a visiting beer drinker; beer connoisseurs most often cite Bohemia as the country's best brew. To order Dos Equis, *norteños* usually ask for "lager."

The cheapest sources for beer are the brewery's agents or distributors (look for signs saying *agencia, cervezería,* or *depósito*), where you can return deposit bottles for cash or credit. Each *agencia* sells only the brands carried by its affiliated distributor, e.g., Cervecería Modelo distributes Corona, Pacífico, Negra Modelo, and Modelo, hence where you can buy one of these brands you'll often find the others.

You can buy beer by the bottle *(envase),* can *(bote),* six-pack *(canastilla),* or case *(cartón),* The latter is the best deal; a 24-bottle case of

RODOLFO GAONA tomando
La deliciosa Cerveza Moctezuma XX

Pacífico will cost less than US$6 once you have a case of empty returnable bottles on hand. Also popular are large, liter-size bottles of Tecate called *caguamas* or "sea turtles." The Pacífico equivalent is known as a *ballena* or "whale." When buying beer at an *agencia* or *depósito,* specify *fría* if you want cold beer; otherwise you'll get beer *al tiempo* (at room temperature).

Wine

Northern Mexico—particularly the Región Lagunera and Zacatecas—is one of Mexico's major wine production areas, and regional wines are commonly served in restaurants. A broad selection of varietals is available, including cabernet sauvignon, chardonnay, chenin blanc, petite sirah, pinot noir, barbera, and zinfandel. These and other grapes are also blended to produce cheaper *vino tinto* (red wine) and *vino blanco* (white wine). When ordering wine in Spanish at a bar, you may want to specify *vino de uva* ("grape wine"), as *vino* alone can refer to distilled liquors as well as wine. *Vino blanco,* in fact, can be interpreted as cheap tequila.

Liquor

Tequila is Mexico's national drink and also the most popular distilled liquor in Northern Mexico (see the special topic "Tequila"). The second most popular is brandy followed closely by *ron* (rum), both of which are produced in Mexico for export as well as for domestic consumption. Among brandies, Presidente is the biggest seller, but Don Pedro Reserva Especial is better quality. A favorite rum drink is the *cuba libre* ("free Cuba"), called *cuba* for short—a mix of rum, Coke, and lime juice over ice. An alternative made with Mexican brandy is called *cuba de uva* ("grape cuba"). Other hard liquors—gin, vodka, scotch, etc.—may only be available at hotel bars and tourist restaurants. Drinks that contain imported liquor typically cost about twice as much as those that contain domestic (*nacional* or "national" on most bar menus) liquor.

In rural areas of Chihuahua and Coahuila, a contraband liquor called lechugilla, illegally distilled from the heart of the *Agave lechugilla* (a succulent considered an indicator plant for the Chihuahuan Desert), is common. Clear and colorless, lechugilla (or *"leche"* as it is sometimes nicknamed) can register a strength of

TEQUILA

Mexico's national drink has been in production since at least the time of the Aztecs. The Spaniards levied a tax on tequila as early as 1608, and King Carlos IV granted the first legal concession to produce tequila in 1795 to Don José María Guadalupe Cuervo. The liquor's name was taken from the Ticuila Indians of Jalisco who mastered the process of distilling an extract from the *Agave tequiliana weber* or blue agave, a process still employed by tequila distilleries today. Native to Jalisco, this succulent is the only agave that produces true tequila as certified by the Mexican government (look for the initials NOM—for *Norma Oficial Mexicana*—on the label). All liquors labeled "tequila" must contain at least 51% blue agave distillates. Sugarcane juice or extracts from other agaves usually comprise the rest.

Despite the fact that tequila sales are booming today (exports nearly doubled between 1983 and 1993), much of the tequila-making process is still carried out *a mano* (by hand). In the traditional method, the mature heart of the tequila agave, which looks like a huge pineapple and weighs 50-150 pounds, is roasted in pits for 24 hours, then shredded and ground by mule- or horse-powered mills. After the juice is extracted from the pulp and fermented in ceramic pots, it's distilled in copper stills to produce the basic tequila, which is always clear and colorless, with an alcohol content of around 40%. True "gold"

tequilas are produced by aging the tequila in imported oak barrels to achieve a slightly mellowed flavor. The *reposado* or "rested" type is oak-aged for at least two months, while *añejo* or "aged" must stay in barrels at least a year. Inferior "gold" tequilas may be nothing more than the silver stuff mixed with caramel coloring—always look for *reposado* or *añejo* on the label if you want the true gold.

José Cuervo, Sauza, and Herradura are well established tequila labels with international notoriety. Of these three, Herradura is said to employ the most traditional methods and hence tequila connoisseurs generally prefer it over the other two. Smaller, much more expensive "boutique" tequila-makers use 100% blue agave, rather than mixing in sugarcane distillates. To celebrate the company's 200th anniversary, Cuervo recently introduced La Reserva de la Família Cuervo, which carries a price tag of around US$75 a bottle. Tres Magueyes's Don Julio Reposado is also setting new standards for smoothness and quality. Many tasters claim a label called Reserva del Patrón (sold simply as "Patrón" north of the Mexican border) is the finest and smoothest tequila tipple of them all. Other fine tequila labels include El Jimador, Ecuario Gonzales, Don Felipe, and our personal favorite, Las Trancas. To emphasize the limited production nature of these private reserve distillations, they are usually sold in numbered bot-

---

nearly 100 proof, with a flavor that resembles a mix of tequila and grain alcohol. Good-quality lechugilla may taste no stronger than tequila at first swallow, but the fire in the belly and resultant intoxication are always more intense. In "dry" areas of the Sierra Tarahumara where alcoholic beverages are prohibited by law (e.g., Urique, Batopilas), it may be the only liquor available.

In northern Chihuahua a similar liquor called sotol (from a desert succulent of the same name in the *Agave* family) is the moonshine of choice. Sinaloans make their own moonshine called *caña* ("cane") from sugarcane; the taste, as might be expected, is similar to that of high-proof rum. *Bacanora* is the Sonoran equivalent, made from mezcal or hearts of Sonoran agave. The generic term for all contraband liquors is *aguardiente*.

CANTINAS AND BARS

Traditionally, a true cantina is a Mexican-style drinking venue for males only, but in modern urban Mexico the distinction between "bar" and "cantina" is becoming increasingly blurred. In large cities, an upscale bar-restaurant with "cantina" in its name may have plenty of women downing drinks with the *machos*.

In small, rural towns, the more traditional cantina is the kind of place you'll occasionally stumble upon, usually on the outskirts of town, where blinking Christmas lights festoon a *palapa* roof and palm-thatch or *carrizo* walls. Inside are a few tables and chairs—and a handful of *borrachos;* generally the only women present will either be serving the booze or serving as hired "dates." The only drink choices will be beer,

tles with very fancy labels. As with wine, it's all a matter of personal preference; try a few *probaditos* ("little proofs" or shots) for yourself to determine which brand best tickles your palate. The fancier tequilas may be served in brandy snifters instead of the traditional tall, narrow shot glass.

Mezcal and the Worm

The distillate of other agave plants (also known as magueys or century plants) is called mezcal. The same roasting and distilling process is used for mezcal as for tequila. (Tequila, too, is a mezcal, but no drinker calls it that, just as no one in a U.S. bar orders "whiskey" when they mean to specify scotch or bourbon.) The caterpillar-like grub you see floating at the bottom of a bottle of mezcal is the *gusano de maguey* ("maguey worm"), which lives on the maguey plant itself. They're safe to eat (just about anything pickled in mezcal would be) but not particularly appetizing. By the time you hit the bottom of the bottle, though, who cares?

Tequila Drinks

The most common way to drink tequila is straight up, followed by a water or beer chaser. Licking a few grains of salt before taking a shot and sucking a lime wedge afterwards will make it go down more smoothly (the salt raises a protective coating of saliva on the tongue while the lime juice scours the tongue of salt and tequila residues). In Chihuahua the ordeal is simplified in a drink called the "Pancho Villa," simply chilled tequila mixed with salt and lime.

Tequila con sangrita, in which a shot of tequila is chased with a shot of *sangrita* (not to be confused with *sangria,* the wine-and-fruit punch), is a slightly more elegant way to accomplish the same process. *Sangrita* is a bright red mix of orange juice, lime juice, grenadine, red chile powder, and salt. A drink called the *vampiro* ("vampire")—popular in Nuevo León, Coahuila, and Chihuahua—takes this a step further, mixing tequila and *sangrita* together in the same glass with a wedge of lime.

An old tequila standby is the much-abused margarita, a tart Tex-Mex cocktail made with tequila, lime juice, and Cointreau (usually "Controy" or triple-sec in Mexico) served in a salt-rimmed glass. A true margarita is shaken and served on the rocks, rather than blended with ice in the "frozen" style. Crushed or blended ice tends to kill the flavor.

Debates as to the origins of the margarita continue. The most probable story claims it was created in Ciudad Juárez in 1942 by bartender Pancho Morales at a bar called Tommy's Place, where a customer requested a "magnolia." When Pancho inquired as to the recipe, the only requested ingredient he had on hand was Controy, so he offered the customer an improvised cocktail in which he blended the liqueur with tequila and lime juice. Morales christened the drink after another flower, the *margarita* ("daisy" in Spanish). See the description of El Kentucky Club in the "Ciudad Juárez" section for a more colorful story.

Mexican brandy, and cheap tequila or *aguardiente.* Often when you order tequila in a place like this, you'll be served a large glass of *aguardiente,* considered an acceptable substitute.

Bars, on the other hand, will only be found in hotels and in the larger cities or resort areas. They have developed largely as social venues for tourists or for a younger generation of Mexicans for whom the cantina is passé. A bar, in contrast to a cantina, will offer a variety of beers, wines, and distilled liquors. By Mexican standards, bars are considered very upmarket places to hang out, so they aren't extremely popular—many young Mexicans would rather drink at a disco where at least the drinking is accompanied by dancing.

A sign outside of a bar reading "ladies bar" means that the bar admits women. This doesn't always mean the bar in question is a place a lady would want to enter; a peek inside will usually tell the tale.

Bar Lingo

bartender—*cantinero/cantinera*
beer—*cerveza* (*una fría*—"a cold one")
bottle—*envase, botella* (*casco*—empty bottle)
draft beer—*cerveza de barril*
a drink—*una copita, un tragito*
drunk, drunkard—*borracho*
glass—*vaso, copa*
hangover—*la cruda*
no ice—*sin hielo*
with ice—*con hielo*
snacks—*botanas*

GETTING THERE

BY AIR

Mexico is ranked eighth in the world—right between China and Japan—for the number of airports in the country that can be reached by scheduled commercial flights. Major international airline connections into Northern Mexico are handled by **Alaska, Aeroméxico** (on some routes in conjunction with American Airlines), **Aero California, Mexicana,** and **TAESA,** via several major U.S. cities, as well as major cities worldwide.

Direct flights to Northern Mexico destinations are substantially less expensive than those that connect through Mexico City. For convenience and price, the best U.S. cities from which to fly to Northern Mexico are Los Angeles, Las Vegas, Phoenix, Tucson, El Paso, Harlingen (Texas), Houston, McAllen (Texas), and San Antonio. If you can get a cheap flight to one of these cities and use it as a gateway, you'll probably save a considerable sum. Sample roundtrip fares for nonstop flights include: Los Angeles-Chihuahua US$343; Los Angeles-Monterrey US$495; Tucson-Los Mochis US$224; Tucson-Mazatlán US$328; McAllen-Tampico US$196; McAllen-Monterrey US$128; San Antonio-Monterrey US$152; Phoenix-Guaymas US$216; Dallas-Chihuahua US$196; El Paso-Chihuahua US$96. Figure just over half the roundtrip fare for the corresponding one-way fare.

Note that air tickets to Mexico that are purchased in the U.S. are guaranteed (by U.S. federal law) against fare increases no matter which carrier you use. On the other hand, tickets purchased in Mexico have no such guarantee; you're liable for price increases before departure, payable at airport check-in. Hence if you plan to fly within Mexico and have a good idea of your itinerary, you may want to consider buying the tickets in the U.S. in advance to guard against this.

Air fares to Mexico are always less expensive in the fall and summer than in the winter and spring. A complete list of airlines serving Northern Mexico with their cities of origination

and destination, appears in the Transportation Appendix.

BY LAND

Most foreign visitors to Northern Mexico arrive via one of the many gateways along the U.S.-Mexico border between Yuma, Arizona, and Brownsville, Texas. The major crossings connect with major Mexican highways. From west to east these are: Nogales/Nogales (Mexico 15); El Paso/Ciudad Juárez (Mexico 45/49); Eagle Pass/Piedras Negras (Mexico 57); Laredo/Nuevo Laredo (Mexico 85); McAllen/Reynosa (Mexico 97/101); and Brownsville/Matamoros (Mexico 101). Interspersed between these major points of entry are at least a dozen smaller, less-used crossings. For information on border formalities, see "Immigration, Customs, and Crossing the Border," below.

Reaching the Border
Those who plan to use public transportation in Mexico can easily reach the U.S.-Mexico border by bus or train. Intercity buses in the U.S. generally depart more frequently and are less expensive than trains. **Greyhound Bus Lines** is the major carrier; a bus pass may be more economical than buying single-journey tickets. Outside the U.S., a Greyhound *Ameripass,* which allows unlimited bus travel within specified dates, can be purchased from travel agencies at a discount (e.g., a seven-day pass bought outside the U.S. costs around US$125; in the U.S., around US$150-170). Several smaller, regional bus lines also provide service to U.S. border towns.

Local express buses in large border towns provide convenient connections between the downtown areas on both sides of the border. El Paso's "Border Jumper," for example, links downtown El Paso with downtown Ciudad Juárez. For information on these kinds of bus services, refer to the appropriate city section.

U.S. Rail
The only long-distance passenger rail line in the U.S. is **Amtrak,** which brings passengers very

close to the border at San Diego, California, El Paso, Texas, and Del Rio, Texas. Connections with a number of other Amtrak lines to points in the U.S. farther north or east can be arranged. Amtrak has special fares on occasion—always ask before booking.

Outside North America, some international travel agencies sell a **USA Railpass** which allows unlimited U.S. rail travel within specified dates. A rail pass called *All Aboard America* is sold inside the U.S. at slightly higher prices. For schedule information or bookings inside the U.S., call (800) 872-7245 (800-USA-RAIL).

Mexican Rail
Mexico's national rail service has its western-most terminus in Mexicali, Baja California Norte, providing one alternative for getting to mainland Mexico from Baja (this can also be accomplished farther south in Baja via one of the ferry services—see "By Ferry from Baja," below). Information on rail travel from various Mexican border cities can be found under "Getting Around," below, as well as under the appropriate destination sections.

We have received several complaints from readers who have used U.S. companies advertising Mexican rail tickets by mail. Generally it is safer—and much cheaper—to book in Mexico on your own. This warning does not include tour companies running Copper Canyon train tours, which by and large are reliable (though some are better than others).

See the Transportation Appendix for Northern Mexico's railway schedule.

Driving to Northern Mexico
Most people visiting Northern Mexico by land (except border day-trippers) drive their own vehicles. The red tape for driving into Mexico is fairly minimal and shouldn't prevent or discourage anyone from attempting it. If you find the traffic at the larger border gateways daunting, consider using one of the many smaller crossings available. An easy-to-obtain temporary vehicle import permit is required for stays of longer than 72 hours. See "Driving in Northern Mexico" and "Immigration, Customs, and Crossing the Border," below, for information on road travel inside the country and details on red tape, respectively.

BY FERRY FROM BAJA

Three ferry services currently run to mainland Mexico from Baja California—one each from La Paz to Topolobampo and Mazatlán, and one from Santa Rosalía to Guaymas.

The old passenger-vehicle ferries are still a good way for anyone driving on the mainland to reach southern Baja without having to make a time-consuming U-turn at the top of the peninsula. It's also a way for drivers from the U.S. West Coast to return from mainland Mexico's Sea of Cortez/Pacific coast without covering the same territory twice. In the reverse direction, many West Coasters use the ferry services as an alternative way of reaching the mainland since it allows them to see Baja on the way to Mazatlán or other points farther east or south.

The ferry system was privatized a few years ago and is now operated by Grupo Servicios Maritimos y Turísticos (SEMATUR). As service continues to evolve, we can expect classes, fares, and departure schedules to change regularly. Keep this in mind when making plans according to the below-mentioned information.

Fares and Classes
Passenger fares are based on class. The three classes include *salón* (reclining seats in various general seating areas), *turista* (shared bunk rooms), and *cabina* (private cabins with toilet facilities). Some ferryboats also have an additional *especial* class featuring larger deluxe cabins. Fares for children under 12 are 50% of adult fares.

Vehicle fares are based on the vehicle's length —the longer the rig, the higher the fare. Sample tariffs range from US$28 for a motorcycle on the La Paz-Topolobampo route to as much as US$713 for a trailer rig over nine meters (30 feet) long on the La Paz to Mazatlán route. Passenger and vehicle fares are separate.

You must drive into the cargo hold yourself; this is usually the most unpleasant part of the journey, as most of the vehicles crossing are Mexican 18-wheeled trucks; the fuel fumes that accumulate in the hold while everyone gets in position (as directed by the ferry crew) can be intense. Soldiers and/or federal police are present on the piers at both ends of the journey, searching for arms and illegal drugs with the help of trained dogs.

Note: Signs at the ferry ticket offices warn that passenger tickets will not be issued to pregnant women.

Reservations

Whether it was the fare increases or the reorganization of management under private auspices, ferry reservations are now somewhat easier to make than they were several years ago. *Salón* seats are sold on a first-come, first-served basis; *turista* compartments can be reserved three days (or more) in advance; a *cabina* can be reserved a month (or more) in advance. During holiday periods (especially Semana Santa, when you might want to avoid ferry service altogether), you should try to arrive as early as possible during the allowable booking period for advance tickets. Reservations must be confirmed 15 days before departure date for the La Paz-Mazatlán and La Paz-Topolobampo routes, 10 days before departure for the Santa Rosalía-Guaymas route.

SEMATUR operates ticket offices at each of its ferry piers for advance as well as day-of-departure sales. Mexican travel agencies authorized to handle ticket reservations and sales include Viajes Pedrín, tel. (113) 2-0112, in Ciudad Constitución, B.C.S.; Viajes Mario's, tel. (115) 7-0788, in Guerrero Negro, B.C.S.; Viajes Transpeninsulares, tel. (112) 2-0399, Viajes Perla, tel. 2-8666, and Viajes Cabo Falso, tel. 2-4131, in La Paz, B.C.S.; Festival Tours, tel. (68) 18-3986, in Los Mochis, Sin.; Turismo Coral, tel. (69) 81-3290, and Viajes Attiq, tel./fax (69) 14-2400, in Mazatlán, Sin.; and Festival Tours, tel. (5) 682-7043, in Mexico City.

SEMATUR also has a toll-free information and reservation telephone number in Mexico: (800) 6-9696.

Santa Rosalía-Guaymas

Ferries depart Santa Rosalía for Guaymas every Sunday and Wednesday at 8 a.m. In the opposite direction, ferries leave every Tuesday and Friday at 11 a.m. The westbound crossing takes approximately seven hours and the eastbound about eight.

Passenger fares are US$14 *salón,* US$28 *turista. Cabina* and *especial* aren't usually available on this route, but occasionally a larger ferry from another route will be used. When available, a *cabina* costs US$41.70, *especial* US$56.

Autos/trucks under five meters (15 feet) cost US$145; autos/trucks with trailers cost US$192-500, depending on the length. Motorhomes are no longer accepted along this route. You can wheel the Harley on for US$37.

La Paz-Topolobampo

Topolobampo is a small port town that serves the Los Mochis area. An interesting way to reach the Barranca del Cobre (Copper Canyon) area from Baja California is to ride this ferry to Topolobampo, then take a half-hour bus ride to Los Mochis, where you can catch the *Chihuahua al Pacífico* train to the canyons (or farther on to Chihuahua). Ferries on this route are mostly devoted to cargo, with a smaller *salón* section. During holiday periods, more passenger space is usually made available.

The ferry usually leaves La Paz Mon.-Sat. at 11 a.m. and arrives in Topolobampo about 7 p.m. Westbound, the ferry departs Topolobampo the same days at 10 p.m., arriving at La Paz around 8 a.m. On Monday, Tuesday, Friday, and Saturday, only *salón* class is available and the fare is US$14. When other classes are made available, *turista* costs US$28 and *cabina* US$42.

Motorhomes are charged US$191; autos under five meters (15 feet) cost US$128. Motorcycles pay US$28. Trailer rigs cost US$167-434.

Mazatlán-La Paz

At the moment this is the most full-service passenger-vehicle ferry available between Baja and the mainland. Three of the four craft that regularly ply this route offer *salón, turista, cabina,* and *especial* classes plus a restaurant/bar, disco, video lounge, and cafetería. On Wednesdays (eastbound) and Thursdays (west-bound) only *salón* class is available.

Ferries depart both ports daily at 3 p.m., arriving on the other side at around 9 a.m. Fares are US$21 *salón,* US$42 *turista,* US$63 *cabina,* and US$83 *especial.*

Vehicle tariffs are: autos under five meters (15 feet) US$210; motorhomes US$314; motorcycles US$47; trailer rigs US$273-713.

GETTING AROUND

MAPS AND INFORMATION

Road Maps

Among the many Mexico maps available to visitors, two are particularly well suited to general-purpose Mexico road travel.

American Automobile Association's (AAA) Mexico map is available free to members from most AAA offices (if you're not a member, ask someone to obtain one for you). While lacking the topographic shading of AAA's Baja California map, the excellent graphics on the Mexico map nonetheless make it easy to read, and it's accurate and detailed enough for most Northern Mexico auto trips. The map's coverage extends well into the U.S. border states to aid drivers in navigating toward the Mexico gateway of their choice. Distances on the AAA map are marked in km for Mexico, miles for the U.S. portion (scale: one inch=93.3 km or 58 miles).

For those planning to spend much time on Northern Mexico's back roads, a Mexican road atlas is recommended. The best one currently available is the annual 127-page *Guía Roji por las Carreteras de México,* published in Mexico but available through **Treaty Oak,** P.O. Box 50295, Austin, TX 78763, tel. (512) 326-4141, **Map Centre,** 2611 University Ave., San Diego, CA 92104, tel. (619) 291-3830, and **Map Link,** 25 E. Mason, Santa Barbara, CA 93101, tel. (805) 965-4402, fax 962-0884, as well as many travel bookstores abroad and in Mexican department stores. This atlas contains 38 double-page maps with a scale of 1:1,000,000 (one inch=25 km), along with color graphics to indicate forests and woodlands, desertlands, and marshlands. Best of all, the atlas includes a fairly complete network of unpaved roads, villages, and *ejidos* that don't appear on the AAA or any other large-scale, single-page maps. Another plus is that the atlas includes 15 city maps; unfortunately only three of these (Monterrey, Mazatlán, and San Luis Potosí) are in Northern Mexico.

Two map companies in Mexico City produce individual state maps oriented toward highway travel. The easiest to find (in Mexico as well as bookstores abroad) are the 1:800,000 scale **Guía Roji** maps, which are easy to read and adequate for most purposes. More detailed yet less commonly seen are the 1:100,000 scale **HFET** maps, which include some topographic shading and contour lines, plus regional inset maps, a town and city index, and annotations on history, culture, and economics. HFET (the initials stand for Hector F. Esparza Torres, a one-man map company in Mexico City) also produces many city maps as well as the tiny *Microatlas de los Estados de la República Mexicana,* a handy shirt-pocket atlas that contains separate maps showing the major paved roads in every state. Both Guía Roji and HFET remainders are generally available through Treaty

road to Urique

JOE CUMMINGS

Oak (which specializes in maps of Mexico and Latin America), Map Centre, or Map Link. In recent years several state tourist offices in Northern Mexico have contracted HFET to produce accurate, up-to-date maps of their states and major cities, most notably Chihuahua, Sinaloa, and Coahuila.

Topographical Maps

Since differences in elevation often determine backcountry route selection, hikers, kayakers, mountain bikers, and off-highway drivers should consider using topographic maps. These can be obtained in advance from Treaty Oak, Map Centre, or Map Link in the U.S. (see "Road Maps," above), or in Mexico from any regional office of the Instituto Nacional de Estadística Geografía e Informática (INEGI). In Northern Mexico, INEGI maintains major offices in Aguascalientes, Durango, Hermosillo, Monterrey, and San Luis Potosí (addresses and telephone numbers vary; refer to individual cities throughout this handbook); each of these regional offices stocks maps for at least three contiguous states. INEGI also has smaller offices in every state capital and even in some smaller towns, especially along the border. The INEGI office in Piedras Negras, Coah., for example, carries useful topographic maps for northern Coahuila (along with maps for the rest of the state, Nuevo León, and Tamaulipas).

For more information on what's available in topographic maps, see "Maps" under "Hiking and Backpacking" in the Outdoor Recreation section, above.

Tourist Information

Mexico's federal tourist bureau, the Secretaría de Turismo (SECTUR), has offices in every state capital and representatives in some smaller towns where tourist traffic is considered significant. The tourist offices usually stock a variety of free brochures, maps, hotel and restaurant lists, and information on local activities, but some offices are better staffed to handle visitor queries than others. Each state also maintains its own state tourism office, often a better source of destination-specific information than SECTUR. Mazatlán, Chihuahua, Monterrey, and Ciudad Juárez have city visitors bureaus in addition to the federal and state offices, so they are particularly well stocked with

useful information. The addresses, phone numbers, and hours of each office are listed under the appropriate destination sections of the book.

If you would like to contact the national office directly, you can call or write the Secretaría de Turismo de Mexico, Presidente Mazaryk No. 172, Mexico, D.F. 11570, tel. (5) 250-0151, 250-0123, or in the U.S. (800) 482-9832, fax (5) 250-6610. SECTUR also maintains an Internet site at www.mexico-travel.com.

Outside Mexico the government maintains 12 Mexican Government Tourism Offices (MGTO) to handle requests for tourist information. Seven of these are located in the U.S.; see the chart for contact information.

Newsletters

In addition to the U.S.-published travel club newsletters mentioned above, two published in Mexico are worth a look. **AIM,** an acronym for Adventures in Mexico, issues a homespun bimonthly newsletter that, although aimed mostly at American retirees living in Mexico (or those considering such a move), contains a great deal of practical information on Mexico travel. visas, and living costs. Unlike most Mexico travel newsletters, *AIM* doesn't ignore the negative aspects of Mexico travel and living; each issue closes with a brief commentary on the country's political and economic situation. Subscriptions cost US$16 (C$19 in Canada) for one year; write to AIM, Apdo. Postal 31-70, Guadalajara, Jal. 45050.

Travelmex, Apdo. Postal 31-100, Guadalajara, Jal. 45050, publishes an eight-page newsletter containing travel features and road reports; an annual subscription (six issues) costs US$15.

Two U.S.-based newsletters of general Mexico travel interest include **Mexican Meanderings** (bimonthly, US$18, P.O. Box 33057, Austin, TX 78764), and **The People's Guide Travel Letter** (quarterly, US$15, 15100 S.E. 30th St., Suite 806, Bellevue, WA 98006).

BY PLANE

Domestic flights in Mexico are generally less expensive than international flights from the U.S. to Mexico flown over comparable distances. The "Airlines Serving Northern Mexico" chart in the Transportation Appendix will give you an idea

MEXICAN GOVERNMENT TOURISM OFFICES ABROAD

USA*

10100 Santa Monica Blvd., Los Angeles, CA 90067; tel. (310) 203-8191, fax (310) 203-8316

405 Park Ave., Suite 1401, New York, NY 10022; tel. (212) 755-7621, fax (212) 755-2874

70 E. Lake St., Suite 1413, Chicago, IL 60601; tel. (312) 565-2778, fax (312) 606-9012

2707 North Loop West, Suite 450, Houston, TX 77008; tel. (713) 880-5153, fax (713) 880-1833

2333 Ponce de Leon Blvd., Suite 710, Coral Gables, FL 33134; tel. (305) 443-9160, fax (305) 443-1186

Mexican Embassy, 1911 Pennsylvania Ave., Washington, D.C. 20006; tel. (202) 728-1750, fax (202) 728-1758

*Toll-free number for MGTO in the U.S.: (800) 446-3942

CANADA

999 W. Hastings St., Suite 1610, Vancouver, B.C. V6C 1M3; tel. (604) 669-2845, fax (604) 669-3498

2 Bloor St. West, Suite 1801, Toronto, Ontario M4W 3E2; tel. (416) 925-0704, fax (416) 925-6061

1 Place Ville Marie, Suite 1526, Montreal, Quebec H3B 2B5; tel. (514) 871-1052, fax (514) 871-3825

UK

60/61 Trafalgar Square, 3rd floor, London, WC2N 5DS; tel. (171) 734-1058, fax (171) 930-9202

JAPAN

2-15-1 Nagata-Cho, Chiyoda-Ku, Tokyo 100; tel. (813) 580-2962, fax (813) 581-5539

FRANCE

4 Rue Notre Dame des Victories, Paris 75002; tel. (331) 42-86-5630, fax (331) 42-86-0580

GERMANY

Wiesenhuettenplatz 26, D60329 Frankfurt, AM Main 1; tel. (4969) 25-2413, fax (4969) 25-3755

ITALY

Via Barberini 3, Rome 00187; tel. (396) 487-2182, fax (396) 482-3630

---

of possible connections. In many cases you can save money by flying in and out of a Mexican border city rather than its U.S. counterpart, e.g., flights out of Ciudad Juárez and Tijuana are often cheaper than those out of El Paso and San Diego, respectively.

Sample one-way economy fares on domestic flights include: Ciudad Juárez-Torreón US$175; Hermosillo-Monterrey US$200; Durango-Mazatlán US$60; Monterrey-Tampico US$110; Ciudad Obregón-Durango US$180; Reynosa-Tampico US$112; Tijuana-Chihuahua US$190.

Private Flights

Northern Mexico is dotted with a couple hundred or more airstrips—many of them unpaved—that are used by privately owned and small commercial aircraft. Air traffic over the North is light, and the paperwork for crossing the border is minimal. As if that weren't enticing enough, aviation gas is sometimes cheaper in Mexico than in the U.S. or Canada. Many pilots land immediately after crossing the border in order to fill up on the less expensive stuff and then stop again before leaving Mexico. Keep in mind, however, that fuel is available at or nearby only a fraction of these airstrips—careful itinerary planning is crucial.

An outfit calling itself Baja Bush Pilots, tel. (619) 297-5587 in San Diego, publishes a 384-page guide, *Airports of Baja California and Northwest Mexico* by Arnold Senterfitt (1291 E. Vista

Way, Vista, CA 92084), that contains aerial photos, sketch maps, and descriptions of virtually every landing strip in Sonora and Sinaloa. While some pilots fly to northwest Mexico without this book, they're few and far between. Rumors say Senterfitt may soon be selling the rights to this guide to another publisher. If you can't find the book through the above address or phone number, try **Nelly's Pilot Supply,** 1424 Continental St., San Diego, CA 92173, tel. (619) 661-6099, at Brown Field near San Ysidro, California.

Planes that fly into Mexico are required to carry Mexican liability insurance. Lewis and Lewis, 8929 Wilshire Blvd. #200, Beverly Hills, CA 90211, tel. (310) 657-1112, offers inexpensive annual aircraft policies. Another company dealing in such policies is Thaddeus Smith & Associates, 12443 Lewis St., Suite 201, Garden Grove, CA 92640, tel. (714) 938-9469. Every pilot must show a valid insurance policy at the border to clear customs. In addition, U.S. Customs requires an annual inspection for planes flying into the U.S. whether American- or foreignowned; the inspection costs US$25 but is good for an unlimited number of entries per year.

Nothing similar to the Senterfitt guide yet exists for the north-central and northeastern regions, where foreign pilots rely on word of mouth. Smaller Texas or New Mexico airfields are a good place to begin inquiries about these less-explored (by plane) regions.

BY BUS

Intercity Buses

Public transportation in Northern Mexico is reliable and covers virtually every town and city in the region. On long-distance trips, first-class or *primera* buses offer a/c and reclining seats, sometimes even hostess service. Shorter first-class trips may or may not have a/c, but the buses are always tolerably comfortable—toilets are available on-board and seats usually recline. Schedules are often scrupulously kept and even smaller bus terminals may feature public phones, restrooms, and cafes.

Between state capitals and other large cities, a faster class of service called *expreso* or "express" is available for about 25-35% above the cost of ordinary first class. Even more elite are the newer *ejecutivo* ("executive") and *de lujo* (deluxe) buses, which feature more sophisticated suspension systems, wider, plusher seats, on-board video, and faster service for about double the usual first-class fare.

In more remote areas, intercity buses may consist of old school buses in questionable mechanical condition—they function but you can't count on strict time schedules. These will be called *segunda* or "second class." Terminals on these routes may be little more than a wooden stall or just a worn patch by the side of the road. Mexicans sometimes refer to this type of bus as a *pollero* or "chicken bus," both because the passengers are packed in like chickens in a coop and because it's not unusual for rural passengers to be accompanied by a live chicken or two. For visitors who want to see and experience back-road Mexico, the *polleros* provide an excellent opportunity to get to know local villagers and campesinos.

All fares—from express buses to *polleros*—are inexpensive by international standards. For most routes you can expect to pay less than US$0.05 per km for a basic first- or second-class ticket. A ticket on a first-class bus from Chihuahua to Parral (a distance of 300 km), for example, costs just US$7 first class, US$5 second class; a more basic, rural bus along the Mazatlán-Teacapán route (about 100 km) costs only US$2.

Reservations aren't accepted for many buses—you simply show up at the bus terminal around the time you want to leave. Several departures a day are usually available on any given route. All the Spanish you need for riding a bus is *"boleto"* (ticket), the name of your destination (have a map handy just in case), and a reasonable command of spoken numbers for when they quote the fare (although the fare is always posted somewhere on the ticket office wall). (Refer to the "Spanish Phrasebook" at the back of this handbook.)

City Buses and *Colectivos*

Larger towns and cities have comprehensive city bus systems with fares averaging US$0.12-0.25 (collected in pesos only). City buses come in a variety of sizes and shapes, from 12-passenger vans (usually called *colectivos*) to huge modern vessels with automatic doors. In some cities, painted school buses are the norm. The destination or general route (typically a street name) of the bus is usually painted somewhere on the front or displayed over the front windshield.

Printed bus schedules are hard to come by or may be nonexistent. If you can't figure out which bus to take by comparing the destination sign with a map, ask other waiting bus passengers. If your Spanish isn't up to that, make inquiries at the tourist office.

BY TAXI

Route Taxis

Also in larger cities and towns, you're apt to find *taxis de ruta,* specially licensed cars (usually large American station wagons that hold up to 12 passengers) that follow set routes similar to and often paralleling the bus routes. Unlike the city buses, they can be flagged down anywhere along their route. The destination is usually painted in whitewash on the windshield, but the locals often distinguish the route by the taxis' two-tone color scheme (e.g., a *roja y crema* may run from the central bus station to a market on the outskirts of town, while a *negro y azul* may go from the cathedral to the main shopping district). Other than the terminating points of the route at either end, there are no predetermined taxi stops, so passengers must let the driver know where they want off. As on the city buses, route-taxi fares are the same no matter where you disembark, but they're usually a bit higher than bus fares.

Hire Taxis

Regular hire taxis usually congregate at hotels and designated taxi stands. Sometimes fares are posted at the hotel or taxi stand, but often you'll have to ask for fare quote. If possible, try to find out the fare (from hotel staff or a friendly resident) in advance of approaching a taxi driver so you'll feel more secure about not getting ripped off. If the quoted fare doesn't match what you've been told in advance, you have the options of negotiating for something closer to the correct fare or trying another taxi driver. The author's experience, however, has been that city taxi drivers in Mexico usually quote the correct fare immediately.

Smaller towns don't have buses or route taxis, but sometimes you'll find a few regular hire taxis

hanging out by the town plaza. They're generally used for reaching out-of-town destinations, since anyplace in Mexico without a city bus system is small enough to get around on foot. Although the locals pay a set fare based on distance, gringos are sometimes quoted a much higher fare. Dig in and negotiate until it's reasonable—even if you can afford the higher fare, you owe it to other foreign visitors not to encourage price-gouging. In most situations, however, we've found the first price quoted is fair.

BY TRAIN

Mexico's national railway (Ferrocarriles Nacionales de Mexico or FNM) had its beginnings in the late 19th and early 20th centuries, when various U.S. companies built lines along and leading to the Sea of Cortez/Pacific coast with imported materials. The first line ran between Culiacán and the small seaport of Altata.

All railways were nationalized during the 1930s, and until recently Mexican trains had a terrible reputation. In the 1980s, FNM renovated 14 train routes with the all-first-class Servicio Estrella Azul (Blue Star Service). Unfortunately FNM has not been able to keep up with competition from Mexico's private bus companies and many of these Blue Star lines have been discontinued. Of the remaining passenger lines only a few can be recommended for anyone except hardcore rail buffs. Most of the better lines run through the North.

First-class passengers have a choice of *primera regular* (first-class coach), *primera especial* (first-class reserved, a/c), *camarote* (single sleeper with toilet facilities), and *alcoba* (double sleeper with toilet facilities). For a surcharge over the regular fare of 12-17%—depending on total distance traveled—up to two stopovers per ticket may be arranged en route. Children under 12 get a 50% discount on all fares.

Luggage allowances for rail passengers are 50 kilograms (110 pounds) per adult ticket holder, 25 kilograms (55 pounds) for children ages 5-11. Excess baggage and cargo charges are reasonable.

Although the national routes are fairly extensive, they are actually of limited use to travelers except for long overnight hauls, when a train bunk is definitely more comfortable than a reclining bus seat. For short to medium hauls, buses are much faster and departures are much more frequent. From Monterrey to San Luis Potosí, for example, it costs around US$10 whether by reserved first-class seat on the Regiomontano train or by *expreso* bus. The Regiomontano takes nearly eight hours to complete this route and offers only one daily departure (leaving at 7:50 p.m. and arriving at 3:45 a.m.), while an express bus takes less than six hours and offers several day or evening departures to choose from.

However, for train enthusiasts or for those who aren't in a hurry, Mexican trains provide a pleasant alternative to road travel. The scenery along the railroads is typically better than that along highway routes, and you'll have more of an opportunity to meet Mexican passengers than on a bus since you can walk around comfortably on the train.

Even if you're not a train fan, one rail trip that shouldn't be missed is the *Chihuahua al Pacífico* route between Chihuahua's state capital and Los Mochis on the Sea of Cortez coast. This 13-hour journey across the Sierra Madre Occidental winds through spectacular vistas of craggy mountain peaks, conifer forests, piñon-oak woodlands, precipitous cliffs, plummeting canyons, and sparkling rivers—easily among the top five rail trips in the world under a thousand kilometers. For details on the trip, refer to the Sierra Tarahumara ("Copper Canyon") section.

For overnight trips (only necessary if you're heading for Mexico City) in the winter, bring along a blanket or sleeping bag for added warmth. Toilet tissue is another handy item to have, as train restrooms are sometimes short.

The most useful lines in Northern Mexico include: **El Pacífico** (special first-class reserved) from Nogales to Guadalajara with stops in Hermosillo, Ciudad Obregón, Navojoa, Culiacán,

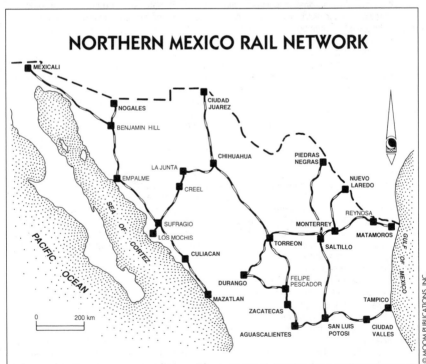

NORTHERN MEXICO RAIL NETWORK

and Mazatlán among others (this train also connects with a shorter line from Mexicali, Baja California Norte); the **Chihuahua al Pacífico** (special first-class reserved) from Los Mochis to Chihuahua via several stops in the Copper Canyon area; the **Chihuahua-Los Mochis,** a slower second-class version of the Chihuahua al Pacífico (also known as *el pollero*); **El División del Norte** (special first-class reserved and second-class coach) from Ciudad Juárez to Mexico City via Chihuahua, Torreón, and Zacatecas; **El Regiomontano** (special first-class reserved, single and double sleepers) from Monterrey to Mexico City via Saltillo and San Luis Potosí; **El Coahuilense** (special first-class reserved and second-class coach) from Piedras Negras to Saltillo (connects with the Regiomontano); **El Tamaulipeco** (first-class reserved seat) along the Monterrey-Reynosa-Matamoros route (also connects with the Regiomontano); and the **México-Nuevo Laredo** (special reserved first class and second class) via San Luis Potosí, Saltillo, and Monterrey.

Reservations and Information

First-class seats and bunks can be reserved in advance by writing to the Chief, Commercial Passenger Department, FNM, Gran Estación Central de Buena Vista, Mexico City, D.F. 06358, tel. (5) 547-1084. Upon receipt of your reservation, a time limit for purchasing your ticket(s) will be assigned; the purchase can be made in person at the departure station or by mail with a cashier's check or international money order (in Mexican currency) for the amount due. Unless you have a lot of lead time, you'll do better to make reservations and buy tickets in person a couple of weeks ahead of planned departure; the Mexican post office is a slow way to do business.

For current fares and schedules, you can request a copy of the "General Information and Condensed Schedules of Main Trains" from La Gerencia de Tráfico de Pasajeros, FNM (see above address).

BY BICYCLE

Plenty of cycle touring and mountain biking opportunities are available in Northern Mexico, though it seems that American and Canadian cyclists have yet to discover them. The interior of the region in particular—from the eastern escarpment of the Sierra Madre Occidental all the way across to the western edge of the Sierra Madre Oriental—is a potential recreational cycling mecca. The traffic is relatively light, the scenery is striking (which helps fight boredom), and cyclists can pull over and camp just about anywhere.

Touring or mountain biking? If you're only heading straight down the flat, paved roads of the Sea of Cortez or Gulf of Mexico coastal plains, a touring bike would be the best choice for weight and speed. Other appropriate routes for tour biking include the border trip along Mexico 2 from San Luis Río Colorado to Ciudad Juárez (crossing the northern Sonoran Desert, the Continental Divide, and nearly half the northern Chihuahuan Desert) or from Ciudad Acuña to Playa Bagdad on the Gulf of Mexico coast in Tamaulipas (through Chihuahuan Desert grasslands and Tamaulipan thorn forest to the beach).

On the other hand, the mountain-fringed interior has so many great off-road rides that anyone who really wants to see Northern Mexico (and has the time) should consider the mountain-bike option, since off-road riding requires a stronger frame, higher clearance, and wider tires.

Equipment and Repairs

Whether you're riding a mountain or a touring bike, you'll need the same basic essentials to handle long-distance riding in Northern Mexico. If you plan to camp along the way, you'll need the usual camping and first-aid gear, selected to fit your panniers. Helmets are particularly important since a head injury can become even more serious when you're in the middle of nowhere; they'll also keep direct sun off your scalp. Don't forget to bring sunglasses and plenty of high-SPF sunscreen.

A rearview mirror is a must for keeping an eye on motorists coming from behind on narrow roads. A locking cable is preferable to a clunky U-lock for long-distance trips since they weigh less—bicycle theft isn't much of a problem in most areas. The only other security you might need is a removable handlebar bag for carrying camera and valuables—the bag can be taken with you when stopping off at restaurants or *tien-*

das, and it's also a reachable spot for on-the-fly snacks.

Water will be an uppermost consideration on overnight trips. No matter what the time of year (spring and fall are the best pedaling seasons), cyclists should try to carry about a gallon of water a day, divided among four one-liter bottles so if one is punctured, all your water won't be lost. The one-liter bottles used for cycling are typically more puncture resistant than the bottles designed for camping. Punctures are of particular concern in Northern Mexico because of spine-bearing trees and plants.

The aforementioned puncture threat means that your bike should be outfitted with heavy-duty tires and tubes. Bring along two or three spare tubes, one spare tire, a tire gauge, and a complete tire repair kit. You should also carry duct tape and moleskin to use as booting material against sidewall cuts (often caused by sharp rocks along the road).

Check rack nuts and bolts daily and retighten as necessary. Applying Loctite should lessen the need for retightening—carry a small supply along with extra nuts and bolts. Bailing wire can be used for improvised repairs if you run out of nuts and bolts or get a minor break—carry eight or 10 feet along with wire cutters.

You'll find bike shops in most major cities. Although the Mexicans who run these shops can sometimes perform miraculous repairs using nothing that resembles the bike's original parts, it's safer to come prepared with spares, especially for parts that aren't easily jury-rigged. At a minimum, carry a spare freewheel, a rear derailleur, and all the wrenches and screwdrivers necessary to work on your bike. If in addition you bring along several extra spokes, cables, and a spare chain, you'll be ready for just about any repair scenario.

Transporting Your Bike

Most bus lines will take the bikes of paying passengers in their luggage compartments for no additional cost, but bikes may have to be boxed. Some airlines and bus companies sell bike boxes for around US$10. If you aren't able to store this box for your return from Mexico, you should be able to pick up a box from a larger Mexican bicycle shop along the way. Or build your own from discarded cardboard boxes.

DRIVING IN NORTHERN MEXICO

Millions of Canadians and Americans drive in Mexico every year without so much as a fender-bender or parking ticket. Sanborn's Mexican Insurance of McAllen, Texas, one of the largest insurers in the Mexican insurance business, says claims are filed on a mere two percent of the auto policies issued by the company. By contrast, the national average for U.S. auto insurance is two to five times that amount.

This is not to say that driving in Mexico is totally free from anxiety. But drivers who prepare themselves and their vehicles, and who take appropriate precautions while driving Mexican roads, will probably discover that Mexican driving is for the most part a comfortable proposition.

The Mexican government is currently seeking to increase the number of visitors entering the country by land by upgrading facilities and highways along the following corridors and circuits: Nogales-Mazatlán, Ciudad Juárez-Creel (Copper Canyon)-Topolobampo, Colombia-Matamoros (Lower Rio Grande/Río Bravo Corridor), and Nuevo Laredo-Monterrey-Saltillo-Reynosa. The announced goal is to provide 2,338 km of better highways in the North by the year 2000. State governments are also engaged in promoting "two-nation vacations" through logistical partnerships between U.S. and Mexican border states, especially between Sonora and Arizona, and among Coahuila, Nuevo León, Tamaulipas, and Texas. Part of this project involves constant road improvements in these states.

INSURANCE

One legal preparation that should be undertaken before driving into Mexico is acquiring Mexican vehicle insurance. No matter what your own insurance company may tell you, the Mexican authorities don't recognize foreign insurance policies for private vehicles in Mexico.

While vehicle insurance isn't required by law in Mexico, it's a good idea to carry a Mexican policy anyway; without it, a minor traffic accident can turn into a nightmare. Short-term (as little as one day's worth) insurance can be arranged at any of several agencies found in nearly every border town between the Pacific Ocean and the Gulf of Mexico. Annual policies permitting multiple entries are also available at far lower per-day rates.

Reliable Brokers

One of the most popular and reliable Mexico insurers is **Sanborn's Mexico Insurance,** P.O. Box 310, McAllen, TX 78502, tel. (956) 686-0711 or (800) 222-0158, fax (956) 686-0732, which has offices in or close to virtually every town along the U.S.-Mexico border except Tijuana and some of the smaller border crossings. For short visits Sanborn's offers a combination of service and convenience that's hard to beat. Coverage for a vehicle valued at US$20,000-25,000, plus US$50,000 property damage, US$80,000 liability, and medical payments of US$2,000 pp (up to US$10,000 per occurrence) costs US$12.30 per day or US$795 per year. Sanborn's offers additional legal-assistance coverage for US$58.76 a year.

In addition to its insurance policies, Sanborn's also offers membership in **Sanborn's Amigo Club,** P.O. Box 310, McAllen, TX 78502, tel. (956) 686-0711, toll-free (800) 222-0158, fax (956) 686-0732, which provides 10-20% discounts on hotels and restaurants throughout Mexico (especially the northeast), a quarterly newsletter, a list of RV parks in Mexico, and a health guide.

Another good source of Mexican insurance is **International Gateway Insurance Brokers,** tel. (800) 423-2646, whose premiums for a similarly valued vehicle (US$20,000-25,000) are US$11 a day or US$402 per year, with a combined single limit for damage and liability of US$100,000, a US$500 deductible on collision, a US$1,000 deductible on theft, and medical liability limited to US$4,000 pp or US$20,000 per occurrence. International Gateway offers additional legal-assistance coverage for US$2 a day.

In California, one of the most popular and least expensive insurers is **Oscar Padilla Mexican Insurance,** 1660 Hotel Circle N, Suite 735, San Diego 92108, tel. (619) 688-1776 or toll-free (800) 258-8600, fax (619) 688-1948, which has insured motorists visiting Mexico since 1951. Premiums for a one-year, multiple-entry, comprehensive policy for Mexico start at around US$130 for under US$5,000 in coverage and rise to US$516 for US$100,000 worth of coverage; liability only costs US$72 per year. Padilla's unique "Phone-A-Policy" program allows repeat visitors to activate Mexican vehicle insurance with a 30-second toll-free phone call.

Limited-Territory Policies

Most companies charge lower premiums for "limited territory" trips that stay within Baja California (Norte and Sur) and various specified states of northern mainland Mexico. If you plan to confine your travels to the areas covered by these policies, you can save some money this way. Sanborn's limited-territory policy—which covers Baja California (north and south), Sonora, Chihuahua, Durango, Coahuila, Nuevo León, Sinaloa, and Tamaulipas—costs US$12.39 per day, US$367 annually.

International Gateway charges US$287 for a one-year, multiple-entry, limited-territory policy covering US$25,000 and valid in Baja California (north and south), Sonora, Chihuahua, and Sinaloa; no daily rates are available. Oscar Padilla charges US$161 for an annual Baja, Sonora, Chihuahua, Sinaloa, and Durango policy. Differences in premiums usually reflect differences in coverage—be sure to check the small print carefully when comparison shopping.

Annual Per-use Policies

Drivers who will be making more than one trip into Mexico each year should consider an annual policy in which you're charged only for those days you're actually in Mexico. Some agencies in Mexico offer this coverage; of course, this requires a trip south of the border in order to obtain such a policy in the first place, so you'll need a day or two's worth of border insurance for the trip.

One U.S. agency that can arrange Mexican liability insurance on a per-use basis is **Anserv Insurance Services,** 1761 Hotel Circle S, Suite 250, San Diego, CA 92108, tel. (800) 262-1994 in California, (800) 654-7504 elsewhere, fax (619) 296-4715. Their rates run as low as $61 per year for 60 days of use per year.

Additional Tips

Whichever policy you choose, always make photocopies of the policy and keep originals and copies in separate, safe places. It's also a good idea to carry a photocopy of the first page (the "declaration" or "renewal of declaration" sheet) of your home-country policy, as Mexican customs law has in the past required that you cross the border with at least six months' worth of home-country insurance. At the moment that law has been rescinded, but there's no guarantee all the Mexican customs officers will be aware of the repeal when you roll across the border.

CHOOSING YOUR WHEELS

Trailers and RVs vs. Campers and Vans

Mexico is a popular destination among the trailer/RV crowd because you can pull off the road and boondock just about anywhere outside the cities, with few restrictions. The restrictions that do exist are largely physical—numerous places simply can't accommodate a wide trailer or motorhome due to narrow roadways, steep grades, or sharp curves.

Probably the rig most suited to Mexico travel is a well-equipped camper or van. With a bed, two five-gallon water containers, a small propane stove and refrigerator, and a portable toilet, you can travel just as independently as someone driving a 40-foot motorhome. Add a deep-cycle

RV battery under the hood and you can run a variety of electrical appliances for at least a week without running your engine. For extra power, a solar panel can be mounted on top of the cab or camper.

As long as you're tricking out your rig, consider installing oversized tires to get more traction and road clearance, overload shocks to protect your vehicle and its contents on rough roads, and a rollbar over the front seats. Whether or not you've got high clearance, skid plates under your fuel tank, engine, and transmission are items to consider.

What's the perfect Mexico rig? Such a beast doesn't really exist, of course, since we all have individual needs, but probably the nearest-to-perfect rig for enjoying most of what Northern Mexico has to offer would be one that combines features of a self-sufficient camper (as described above) with a rugged 4WD vehicle that has a turning circle of 20 feet or less. To achieve this kind of optimal functionality, ambitious drivers have successfully tried everything from jeeps to three-ton diesel cabs (which have a remarkably short turning radius) as bases for custom-built campers.

Motorcycles

Parts of Northern Mexico are excellent for motorcycle touring. The winding sierra roads are especially challenging and since traffic is generally light you can really stretch out and enjoy the ride.

RVers can traverse the Sierra Madre Occidental by hiring a flatcar on the Chihuahua al Pacífico train.

JOE CUMMINGS

As with automotive travel in Mexico, prede-parture planning is very important. You should be able to carry enough gear in two panniers and a backpack (tied down on the rear) for a transcon-tinental trip. Motorcycle mechanics aren't easily found outside larger towns, so it's best to be as self-reliant as possible for a safe and successful trip. Besides the usual camping and first-aid gear, bikers should carry any tools needed for routine maintenance, as well as spare brake shoes, a tire-repair kit, spare levers, an extra battery, a clutch cable, spare light bulbs, a one-gallon reserve gas can, and a spare helmet visor.

For a transcontinental trip, any bike smaller than 600cc is too small. A four-stroke gets better mileage than a two-stroke, an important consid-eration given the situation with gas stations in Mexico. Experienced Mexico bikers replace stan-dard fuel tanks with larger five-gallon tanks to extend their fuel range.

All of the same driving precautions that apply to four-wheel driving should be followed by bik-ers as well. Special care should be taken when negotiating blind curves, since buses and trucks in Mexico aren't used to seeing motorcycles on the highway.

Car Rentals
Cars can be rented in any state capital, in Mazat-lán, and in the border cities of Ciudad Juárez and Nuevo Laredo. Various Volkswagen models are usually the only choice; most rental places charge a basic daily rate of around US$26 for a VW bug, US$45-50 for a VW Golf or Nissan Tsuru II (Sentra), US$50-65 for a VW combi (van), US$61-68 for a Jeep Wrangler, plus per-km fees ranging US$0.10-0.30. The bug, inci-dentally, is one of the best non-4WD passen-ger cars for Mexico travel since the engine is air-cooled (no radiator boil overs) and the road clearance is just a bit above average.

If you're planning on driving long distances, you can save money by arranging a flat rate with no per-km costs *(kilometraje ilimitado)*. If you can rent by the week, the savings increase considerably. A new, made-in-Mexico VW bug (no a/c or radio) rents for as little as US$140 per week, with unlimited free kilometers—but only in larger cities. In smaller cities, rates are high. Some companies also charge extra for a/c or automatic transmission.

Travel agencies will often quote significantly higher rates than these. Even the rental agencies themselves may list higher rack rates, but near-ly all of them are open to negotiation.

Avis International, tel. (800) 331-1212 in the U.S. and Canada, or (800) 7-0777 in Mexico, often has the best deals on weekly rentals in Mexico out of large border cities like Tijuana, Ciudad Juárez, Nuevo Laredo, and Monterrey. Advance bookings made in the U.S. seem to be less expensive than those made in Mexico.

Rentals from the U.S. side are sometimes a bit cheaper but there may be a geographic limit, e.g., the lower state lines of Sonora, Chihuahua, Coahuila, or Tamaulipas—beyond which the rental vehicle is prohibited.

HAZARDS AND HIGHWAY SIGNS

Driving Precautions
The number-one rule for Mexico driving, no mat-ter what kind of road you're on, is: *Never* take the road for granted. Any highway in Mexico, in-cluding toll roads, can serve up 100 meters of smooth, seamless blacktop followed immedi-ately by 100 meters of contiguous potholes or large patches of missing asphalt. A cow, horse, or burro could be right around the next curve, or a large dog could leap out in front of your ve-hicle just as you fasten your eyes on a turkey vul-ture arching its wings atop a tall saguaro cactus.

The speed limits set by the Mexican govern-ment—80 kph (about 50 mph) on most high-ways, 110 kph (about 68 mph) on some four-lane highways—are very reasonable for high-way conditions. Obey them and you'll be much safer than if you try to keep the speedometer needle in the spot you're accustomed to. Wan-dering livestock, relatively narrow highway widths on two-laners (19-25 feet), and lack of consistent highway maintenance mean that you simply can't drive at U.S.-Canada speeds in this neck of the woods.

You'll notice a conspicuous lack of shoulders along many roadways. This doesn't mean turnouts don't exist—gravel turnouts are fairly regular and in many areas you can drive direct-ly onto the roadside from the highway—it just means that you can't count on a safe margin at one side of the highway or the other in an emergency situation. At the very least, an emergency turnout will raise a lot of rocks and dirt—small dangers in themselves. In some spots (e.g., in the Sierras), leaving the highway might launch you and your vehicle into a 1,000-foot (or greater) freefall—guardrails may be flimsy or nonexistent.

Yet another reason not to take the road for granted is the high number of blind curves (sometimes unmarked) and blind hilltops in areas of varied elevation. Never assume a clear path around a curve or over a hilltop—potential obstructions include an 18-wheeler or bus passing in the opposite direction (oblivious to the risk of passing blind), wandering livestock, a rock slide, or a road washout. To be on the safe side, keep toward the outside edge of your own lane. Some commercial trucks in Mexico drive as if they're exempt from all speed limits, flying at least 40 km over the posted limit.

Rule number two: Never drive on the highways at night. Except in metropolitan areas, lighting is nonexistent along the highways. In addition, reflectors and even painted lines are absent from many highway sections; even if no other vehicles besides your own occupy the road at night, you could easily overshoot an unexpected curve. Add to this the fact that many poorly maintained local vehicles have nonfunctioning headlights, taillights, or brake lights, and it should be obvious that trying to make highway miles after sundown is crazy. Local drivers may do it, but they're used to local conditions and know the roads relatively well. And in spite of local savvy, a high proportion of car accidents in Mexico—around 80% according to insurance companies—occur at night.

Note: A left-turn signal from the vehicle immediately in front of you usually means it's okay for you to pass, rather than indicating a left turn (which the driver would signal by sticking out his left arm while activating the turn signal). Drivers usually pull off onto the right shoulder to let traffic pass before making a left turn.

Specific Hazards
Vados: When you see road signs marked *Vado* or *Zona de Vados,* slow down. *Vado* is most often translated as "dip," but in Northern Mexico it can mean more than a simple dip in the road—it's any place where the road intersects an arroyo

or dry stream wash. The danger lies not only in the sudden grade drop but in the potential for running into a recently accumulated body of water. Some *vados* have a measuring stick (marked in meters) next to them so that if water is present, you'll know roughly how deep it is. If you come to a *vado* full of water and no measuring stick is in place, get out of your vehicle and measure the depth yourself using a dead branch or other suitable object before attempting to cross.

Vados aren't always signposted, so keep an eye out for them—they can appear in relatively flat terrain. Even in dry weather, some *vados* are particularly treacherous while others are mild. The *vados* in rural northwest Mexico are particularly hazardous—driving over them at a high rate of speed can severely damage the undercarriage of a passenger car.

Topes: In towns, pueblos, *ejidos,* or anywhere else people live in Mexico, you'll also encounter *topes* or speed bumps. Often they're unpainted and unposted, and can really sneak up on you. Some *topes* are real industrial-strength tire-poppers, so always take it very slow when traversing them. *Topes* in northeast Mexico are sometimes labeled *boyas* ("buoys"). Similar in purpose are *vibradores*, sections of raised ribs across the road.

Highway Signs
One of the pleasures of driving in Northern Mexico is the relative absence of signs cluttering the roadside—in fact, billboards are virtually nonexistent. The Mexican government does have a system of highway signs, however, based on common international sign conventions followed throughout most of the world (except the U.S.), and these can be very helpful as long as you know what they mean. Most symbols are self-explanatory, e.g., a silhouette of a man holding a shovel means "men working" (women never work on road crews in Mexico).

Along major highways as well as on many secondary roads, driving progress can be measured with the assistance of regularly spaced **kilometer markers**—usually black lettering on a reflective white background. These are normally calibrated according to distance intervals between two towns, so that sometimes the numbers run only as far as the next town and then start over. The markers can be a significant navigational aid, especially when you want to take note of a remote off-highway spot for a future trip.

Cautionary sign captions that are especially helpful include: Curva Peligrosa (Dangerous Curve), Despacio (Slow), Camino Sinuoso (Winding Road), Grava Suelta (Loose Gravel), Zona de Baches (Pothole Zone), and Zona de Vados (Dip Zone—see "Specific Hazards," above). Other common highway signs include: Desviación (Detour), No Tire Basura (Don't Throw Trash), Conserve Su Derecha (Keep to the Right), Conceda Cambio de Luces (Dim Your Lights), No Rebase (No Passing), and No Hay Paso (Road Closed).

If you're having tire trouble, look for homemade signs reading *llantera, desponchadora,* or *vulcanizadora,* all of which indicate tire-repair shops. My favorite Mexican traffic sign is *No maltrate las señales*—"Don't mistreat the signs!"

ON THE HIGHWAY

Much of the time Mexican roads appear similar to two-lane roads in less populated areas of the American Southwest. The two main differences are: 1) road conditions vary more from one section of highway to another; and 2) once you're away from towns and cities, you're often farther from any significant population center than on any comparable section of U.S. highways, so accidents or errors of judgment may have greater ramifications. Drivers from western Canada may feel more at home on desolate sections of Mexican highways than Americans—except that the terrain is completely different from anything in Canada!

Another difference is that two-lane (and even some four-lane) routes often lead right through small and medium-sized towns rather than passing around them. In more populated regions of Mexico this means slowing down to a 30 kph (18 mph) crawl every 20 km or so; fortunately the North has far fewer of these areas than the South.

Mexican highways often present an intriguing mixture of old and modern. Horse-drawn cart tracks sometimes parallel four-lane highways, and cattle may roam freely across rural blacktops. The best roadways are the *autopistas* or freeways, which are multiplying in number each year. Also known as *carreteras rojas* or "red highways" (for the color usually assigned them on highway maps), most are financed by long-term private investment projects that are repaid through public tolls. Toll roads usually have phone boxes placed at intervals; from these boxes stranded drivers can call the nearest *caseta de cobro* or toll booth and request assistance. The larger toll operations may have their own ambulances and mechanics; others will relay calls for assistance to the appropriate authorities.

Toll Roads

At the moment there are major tollways from Nogales to Mazatlán (Mexico 15), Ciudad Juárez to San Luis Potosí via Torreón and Zacatecas (Mexico 49), and Reynosa to Monterrey (Mexico 40). All of these, not coincidentally, run a basic north-to-south course; the highway investors realize a significant portion of the tolls will be paid by foreign visitors from the U.S. and Canada, as well as by transportation companies moving goods back and forth between Mexico and America. Most toll roads charge a basic auto fee (e.g., US$2 or the peso equivalent) for a two-axle vehicle, plus that same amount again for every additional axle on the vehicle.

Different toll roads charge different tolls for equivalent distances. Mexico 15-D, a 1,274-km (791-mile) four-lane highway between Nogales and Mazatlán, is often cited as the most expensive toll road in the country. On a price-per-kilometer basis, however, it's actually one of the least expensive; at US$26 for the basic car/van toll, it works out to just over US$0.02 per kilometer. The 536-km (333-mile) Reynosa-Torreón toll road (Mexico 40), on the other hand, charges US$35, or more than US$0.06 per kilometer. Nuevo Laredo to Monterrey, a distance of 224 km (139 miles), costs US$11.75 or around US$0.05 per kilometer. (Tollways in Central and Southern Mexico can be more expensive, e.g., the 169-km *autopista* between Aguascalientes and Guadalajara costs almost US$0.12 per km or US$20 total.)

When deciding between *cuota* (toll) and *libre* (free) highways, remember that the four-lane tollways usually offer a considerable savings in time and gas over their nontoll, two-lane equivalents. In sparsely populated areas, for example between Torreón and Saltillo, there's hardly any time difference between the toll and free highways—but you'll feel a lot safer on a divided highway.

If you plan to travel in Northern Mexico on a strict budget, you may consider avoiding the tollways as a way to conserve money. In fact, the money spent on the average highway toll would usually buy at least one bus ticket, sometimes two. Of course with more than two persons in your vehicle, it may be less expensive to drive.

OFF THE HIGHWAY

Like the highways, Mexico's unpaved roads vary considerably, from rutted jeep tracks to elevated, graded, gravel boulevards—the trouble with the latter is that they tend to degenerate quickly between gradings into washboard surfaces that can be impossible to drive on at anything but very low speeds (5-10 mph), unless you want to risk crushed vertebrae and a dropped transmission.

The effect of these unpaved roads on you and your vehicle depends a lot on what kind of vehicle you're driving. Some off-highway navigators drive pickups with customized shocks and suspension that enable a driver to "float" over even the worst washboard surfaces (see "Choosing Your Wheels," above, for more on this topic). Other drivers, like many of the local residents, can't afford heavy-duty, customized rigs, so they learn to drive slowly and appreciate the scenery.

The best unpaved roads in Northern Mexico are probably those that have evolved more or less naturally, i.e., with little or no grading. When the weather's right (not wet), some of these roads ride better than a run-of-the-mill, potholed highway. Roads like this, however, will sometimes start out nicely but get increasingly worse with each passing kilometer to the point that even the most intrepid explorers are forced to turn around. At other times, a road will suddenly improve after a long stretch of cavernous potholes and caved-in sides. Weather is a big determining factor; even the best ungraded, unpaved roads are often impassable during or following a hard rain.

How do you know when to turn around? It helps to ask others before embarking on a road that doesn't see much traffic, even though the element of risk is always present when driving down a dirt road for the first (or even the hundredth) time. A good road map can also assist with such decisions. The *Guía Roji por las Carreteras de México,* (see "Road Maps," under "Maps and Information" in the Getting Around section, above) is the best Mexican road atlas currently available. The AAA map is also good, classifying unpaved roads into four categories: gravel, graded, dirt, and poor. Using one or the other in conjunction with local input will greatly enhance the decision-making process with regard to off-highway travel. A topographic map could be of considerable value to a 4WD navigator as well, since sometimes it's the steep grades that signal defeat.

OFF-HIGHWAY VEHICLE (OHV) DRIVER RESPONSIBILITIES

In order to help preserve Northern Mexico's wilderness areas, consider these *Tread Lightly!* guidelines when operating your 4x4, dirt bike, ATV (all-terrain vehicle), or mountain bike:

Travel only where you and vehicles are permitted. Never blaze your own trail.

Respect the rights of hikers, campers, and others to enjoy their activities undisturbed.

Educate yourself by obtaining travel maps and regulations from public agencies, complying with signs and barriers, and asking owners' permission to cross private property.

Avoid streams, lakeshores, meadows, muddy roads and trails, steep hillsides, and animals.

Drive and travel responsibly to protect the environment and preserve opportunities to enjoy recreation on wildlands.

*Tread Lightly! is a U.S. Forest Service-sponsored program established to promote the environmentally responsible use of OHVs. For information, contact Tread Lightly! Inc., 298 24th St., Suite 325-C, Ogden, UT 84401, tel. (801) 627-0077, fax (801) 621-8633.

Getting Stuck

Even with the best planning, it's always possible to get stuck in muddy or sandy areas. Anyone engaging in serious off-highway driving should carry a sturdy shovel for digging out mired wheels. You can also try jacking the vehicle just high enough so that you can fill in the hole created by a spinning wheel, or simply push the vehicle off the jack so that the stuck wheel lands slightly ahead of the hole. Another handy trick for negotiating soft ground is to let the air out of your tires to a pressure of around 12-15 pounds per square inch. This really works, but you should also carry along a 12-volt air compressor (one that will plug into the cigarette lighter) for pumping the tires back up after you're on firm ground again.

Organized Trips

4-Wheeling, 11 Melody Hill Lane, Aliso Viejo, CA 92653, tel. (714) 707-1340, fax 707-1346, is a 4WD club that organizes off-highway trips in Baja and northwest Mexico, including the challenging Sierra Tarahumara. Dedicated to safe and ecological off-highway driving, the trips are led by recognized expert Harry "Silver Coyote" Lewellyn.

CITY DRIVING

Towns founded during the Spanish colonial era were invariably constructed in a grid pattern, as decreed in the king of Spain's *Royal Ordinance for the Laying Out of New Cities, Towns or Villages.* This design continues to be followed by Mexican city planners and makes navigation easy no matter what the size of the city—if, that is, you have a map in hand and can tell the difference between north, south, east, and west.

Larger cities add diagonal streets that cut across the grid at 45-degree angles. These diagonals help drivers traverse the city more quickly but also pose the greatest potential for confusion if you're unfamiliar with the city; you might consider avoiding the diagonals until you're sure you've got your bearings.

Traffic Offenses

Although Mexican traffic police really don't go out of their way to persecute visiting foreign drivers, it may appear that way when you're the foreigner being stopped. As a rule of thumb, the more cautiously you drive, the less likely it is that you'll inadvertently transgress local traffic codes. But if you're caught in the act of violating a traffic law, what can you expect?

If you are stopped by a *tránsito* or traffic cop, the first rule is to behave in a patient, civil manner—the cop just might let you off with a warning. The author has been stopped three times for traffic violations in Mexico—guilty all three times: wrong way on a one-way street (didn't see the sign), running a stop sign (again, didn't see it), and speeding (no excuse). Each time I was let off with just a warning. Usually, if officers decide to make a case of it, they will ask you to follow them to the nearest police post or station, where a fine will be assessed and collected on the spot —a request that's perfectly legal. If the cop suggests (or hints at) being paid on the spot, he or she is going for *la mordida,* the minor bribe.

In Mexico, requests for *mordida* from foreigners—for traffic offenses, at least—have become increasingly rare, and the government is trying hard to stamp it out altogether. If confronted with such a situation, you have two choices. First, Mexico's Attorney General for the Protection of Tourists recommends that you insist on going to the nearest station to pay the fine, and that as you pay you request a receipt. Such a request may result in all charges being dropped. Your second choice (if you don't feel like taking a trip to the station) is to negotiate the "fine" on the spot. Doing so, however, won't contribute to the shrinking of the *mordida* phenomenon.

In the author's experience, turning the wrong way on one-way streets and running stop signs are the two most common traffic violations among foreign drivers in Mexico. In some towns the stop *(Alto)* signs seem almost intentionally hidden. Also, vertical signs aren't posted at many intersections; only a broad stripe painted on the pavement indicates where vehicles are supposed to stop. The best practice is to assume that you're supposed to stop at every single intersection in a city (which is pretty close to the truth), except at green traffic lights. This can be generalized for most other urban areas.

Another common offense is going the wrong way on an unmarked, one-way street. Always look carefully at the cars driving or parked on a street to determine which direction is legal before turning.

A few other things to be aware of:

It is illegal to turn left at a traffic light that is equipped with a left-turn arrow unless this arrow is lit (even if the arrow isn't red and the straight-ahead light is green).

At urban traffic circles, drivers turning left usually do so in front of the circle instead of going around counterclockwise from the right as they would in the United States.

In situations where you have parked illegally, the police may remove your license plates, forcing you to come to the station to pay the parking fine.

FUEL, PARTS, AND REPAIRS

Fuel

The only automotive fuel commercially available in Mexico is that sold at government-owned PEMEX stations. The total number of PEMEX stations in Mexico increases each year, but they're still somewhat scarce outside large cities. A good rule of thumb is to top off your tank whenever it reaches the half-empty mark and there's a PEMEX station at hand.

Four kinds of fuel are available: a leaded fuel rated at 81 octane ("Nova"); an unleaded with an octane rating of 87 ("Magna Sin"); a high-test unleaded rated at 89 ("Premium"), and diesel. For the moment, Premium is not common except in larger cities, but its use will probably spread if the economy stays on an even keel for a while. All four fuels are priced by PEMEX according to standard rates and shouldn't vary from station to station. All are roughly equivalent in price to their U.S. or Canadian equivalents, depending on where you're accustomed to purchasing fuel. The price should always be marked (in pesos) on the pump. The pump readout often accommodates only three or four digits, so a 50-peso sale may appear as 5000, 500, 50.00, or 50.0 (although this sounds like it could be a problem when paying up, it's not once you're used to seeing it). The more modern pumps are calibrated for the new peso and even zero out automatically when the fuel nozzle is lifted from the pump.

Take care not to be cheated—make sure the pump is zeroed before the attendant starts pumping your gasoline/diesel. This seems to be less of a problem than in previous years; stations in the border towns are still the most likely places to overcharge. It helps if you get out of your vehicle and keep an eye on the pumping procedures. If you're confused by the pump readout, currency conversion, and price per liter, carry a handheld calculator to make sure it all adds up—a calculator held in clear view will deter most potential grifters.

At press time, PEMEX prices were US$0.43 per liter for Premium, US$0.38 per liter for Magna Sin, US$0.32 per liter for Nova, and US$0.25 per liter for diesel. Since PEMEX is government-owned, you don't see the week-to-week price fluctuations common in countries where oil companies are privately owned and where rates are influenced by small changes in international oil prices. Inflation still influences the price, however, so you can expect the price, in pesos, to increase 10-15% per year; if the peso deflates against the dollar, the price for fuel in dollars should remain fairly stable.

Fuel must be paid for in cash at virtually all PEMEX stations except for a couple of stations in Monterrey, where only Mexican bank cards such as Carnet are accepted. It's probably only a matter of time before Carnet acceptance at PEMEX stations spreads to other cities across the nation, with perhaps Visa and MasterCard close behind. For the moment, be sure to carry plenty of pesos for fuel purchases. Mexican currency is the overwhelming preference of most PEMEX stations; some stations near the U.S.-Mexico border take U.S. dollars, but the rate is always rounded down.

Rumors about the quality of PEMEX fuels sometimes suggest that an extra fuel filter or an additive is necessary. This may have been the case 10 or more years ago, but nowadays PEMEX fuel seems to perform well with all types of vehicles, without such measures. The main problem with PEMEX fuel remains its availability. Stations are sometimes widely spaced (or abandoned), and not all stations carry unleaded gasoline. Generally speaking, the more affluent a town is, the more PEMEX stations it will have. You can further judge the prosperity of a town by the number of PEMEX stations offering Premium and Magna Sin—to feed the late-model American cars that wealthier Mexicans tend to purchase.

At the moment Magna Sin is readily available in the more populated areas of Northern Mexico and is increasingly common even in rural areas—mainly because Mexican federal law requires that all cars manufactured after 1991 be fitted with catalytic converters. The most obvious lack of unleaded—from the average visitor's perspective—has always been in the Copper Canyon area, where for many years the nearest PEMEX station with Magna was in La Junta, Chihuahua. Creel, the center for most Copper Canyon excursions, finally installed a Magna pump a couple of years ago, so it's no longer absolutely necessary to top off in La Junta on the way in (though it's still recommended, since you never know when the single Creel station might run out of fuel).

In a pinch, leaded gas can be used in vehicles that are supposed to take only unleaded (i.e., those fitted with anti-smog catalytic converters) without an appreciable difference in performance. You shouldn't be forced to burn more than a tankful of leaded here and there, if at all, since roughly every other PEMEX station seems to dispense unleaded. Many auto experts advocate adding a can of octane booster to your tank in cases where you have to run a tank of leaded in an unleaded-only vehicle. (The author has occasionally burned a tank or two of Nova, with octane booster, in his unleaded-only vehicle without noticeable ill effects.) **Note:** If you're driving a new car still under warranty, using leaded fuel may void the warranty. If this is a potential concern, check your car's warranty before

GREEN ANGELS

The Secretaría de Turismo operates a fleet of around a thousand green trucks called Angeles Verdes (Green Angels) that patrol Mexico's highways and offer professional assistance to anyone with automotive problems. Founded in 1960, this is the only such highway assistance program in the world.

Each truck carries a first-aid kit, shortwave radio, and a variety of common auto parts as well as extra gasoline; they are usually staffed by two uniformed employees, one of whom may speak some English. The drivers will perform minor repairs for the cost of the parts and can provide towing for distances

up to 15 miles. If they can't remedy the problem or tow your vehicle to a nearby mechanic, they'll give you a lift and/or arrange for other assistance. They can also radio for emergency medical assistance if necessary.

The trucks patrol their assigned highway sections (a total of 233 routes nationwide) at least twice a day. The Mexican government has announced plans to triple the number of Green Angel trucks by the end of the decade.

Although the Green Angels patrol only during daylight hours, the following telephone numbers can be called day or night, 24 hours a day.

Coahuila
Piedras Negras: (84) 3-0137
Saltillo: (84) 14-3175, 12-2182

Chihuahua
Ciudad Juárez: (16) 14-6692, 14-0670
Chihuahua: (14) 17-8972

Durango
Gómez Palacio: (17) 14-4474, 14-0731
Durango: (18) 11-5681

Nuevo León
Guadalupe: (83) 67-1205
Monterrey: (8) 340-3114, 340-2113

San Luis Potosí
Ciudad Valles: (138) 2-2949
Matehuala: (488) 2-0858
San Luis Potosí: (48) 14-0906, 12-2178

Sonora
Agua Prieta: (633) 8-0934
Caborca: (641) 6-4850
Ciudad Obregón: (641) 6-4850, 6-7793
Hermosillo: (62) 14-6304, 15-3197
Nogales: (631) 3-1266
Puerto Peñasco: (638) 3-4129

Zacatecas
Fresnillo: (408) 2-2575
Zacatecas: (492) 2-6824
Toll-free from anywhere in Mexico: 91-800-9-0329

making the decision to use Nova in the more remote areas of Northern Mexico. Carrying a spare five-gallon can will get you through most situations where fuel is tight.

Other availability-related problems include long lines at small-town stations and the occasional selling out of one or all types of fuel at a particular station. To notify customers, the hose will usually be draped over the top of a pump when it's empty. If you're low on fuel and all of the nearest stations are empty, ask if there's a *bodega* (storage facility) nearby. Foreign visitors are legally permitted to buy gasoline directly from a *bodega* in such a situation.

Oil

Motor oil is widely available at *tiendas, supermercados,* and PEMEX stations throughout Northern Mexico. If your vehicle takes anything lower than 30-weight, however, you had better bring along your own, since most places stock only 30- or 40-weight oil.

Parts and Repairs

Good auto shops and mechanics are available in all larger towns and cities and especially in the state capitals. Elsewhere, if you have a breakdown, it's either do-it-yourself or rely on the mercy of passing drivers. In areas where you can find a mechanic, the following makes can usually be serviced: Chevrolet, Dodge, Ford, Nissan, Toyota, and Volkswagen. For anything other than these makes—even for short trips— you should carry spare filters, plugs, points, hoses, belts, and gaskets.

Diesel mechanics can be harder to find. A list of qualified diesel shops in Mexico can be obtained by contacting San Antonio's Mexican Government Tourism Office, MGTO, Centre Plaza Bldg., 45 N.E. Loop 410, Suite 125, San Antonio, TX 78216, tel. (210) 366-3242 or (800) 232-4MEX. This office specializes in Mexican road tourism.

Although plenty of visitors drive the length and breadth of Mexico without so much as a spare tire, anyone driving long distances should consider bringing the following extras, regardless of the vehicle type:

✔ air filters
✔ battery cables
✔ brake, steering, and transmission fluids
✔ fan belts
✔ fuel filters
✔ funnel
✔ fuses
✔ lug wrench and jack
✔ radiator hoses
✔ spare tire
✔ spark plugs
✔ oil filters
✔ one or two five-gallon gas cans
✔ one five-gallon container of fresh water
✔ two or three cans octane booster
✔ emergency flares
✔ all-weather tarp or "space blanket"
✔ fire extinguisher
✔ 60-foot tow rope
✔ tire gauge
✔ 12-volt air compressor

(For a glossary of Spanish automotive terms, see the "Spanish Phrasebook" at the back of this book.)

IMMIGRATION, CUSTOMS, AND CROSSING THE BORDER

ENTRY REGULATIONS

U.S. and Canadian Citizens

U.S. and Canadian citizens visiting Mexico solely for tourism, transit, or study purposes are not required to obtain a visa. In fact, for Mexico visits of less than 72 hours all that's needed is one proof of citizenship—an original birth certificate (or certified copy), an original voter-registration card, a certificate of naturalization, or a passport. Driver's licenses aren't accepted as citizenship proof.

All U.S. or Canadian citizens crossing the Mexican border for more than 72 hours or going farther south than border checkpoints (20-40 km/12-25 miles south of the border in most places) must have in their possession a validated "tourist card" (*forma migratoria turista* or FMT), which isn't actually a card but a slip of paper in duplicate form. These are available free at any Mexican consulate or Mexican tourist office, from many travel agencies, from AAA offices in the U.S., on flights to Mexico, or at the border.

The tourist card is valid for stays of up to 180 days and must be used within 90 days of its issuance. Your card becomes invalid once you exit the country—you're supposed to surrender it at the border—even if your 180 days hasn't expired. If you'll be entering and leaving Mexico more than once during your trip, you should request a multiple-entry tourist card (usually available from Mexican consulates only).

Validation: Once you cross the border with your tourist card, it must be validated by a Mexican immigration officer. This can be arranged at any *migración* office in Mexico (all *municipio* seats have them), but is most conveniently accomplished at the border crossing.

Make sure you receive enough days to cover your visit. Some immigration officers, especially those at airports near tourist resorts, may fill in your FMT for 30 days, figuring that's sufficient for most holidays. If you want more than 30 days, it's best to mention it to the officer in advance.

Minors: Until 1991, Mexico had a regulation requiring children under the age of 18 who crossed the border without one or both parents to carry a notarized letter granting permission from the absent parent, or both parents if both were absent. This regulation is no longer in effect, but we've heard that some Mexican border officers (as well as airline check-in crews) are still asking for the letter, unaware that the regulation has been rescinded. Hence unaccompanied minors or minors traveling with only one parent should be prepared for all situations by carrying a notarized letter. In cases of divorce, separation, or death, the minor should carry notarized papers documenting the situation.

In reality, minors with tourist cards are rarely asked for these documents. Children under 15 may be included on their parents' tourist card but this means that neither the child nor the parents can legally exit Mexico without the other.

Citizens From Other Countries

Tourists from countries other than the U.S. or Canada may need visas in advance of arrival in Mexico. Citizens of Australia, New Zealand, the Republic of Korea, Singapore, and most European Community countries can usually obtain free, no-photo visas at the Mexican border, but be sure to check with a Mexican embassy or consulate first—visa regulations change from year to year. Of late, Andorra was the only one E.C. country whose citizens were required to obtain visas in advance.

If you apply in person at a Mexican consulate, you usually can obtain a tourist visa on the same day of application.

Foreign visitors who are legal permanent residents of the U.S. do not need visas to visit Mexico for tourist purposes. A free tourist card can be obtained by presenting your passport and a U.S. residence card to any travel agency or at the airport or border crossing.

Overstays

If you overstay your visa and are caught, the usual penalty is a fine of US$50 for overstays up to a month. After that the penalties become more severe. It's very rare that a Mexican border official asks to see your FMT or visa when you're leaving the country. Your main risk comes if you get into trouble with the police somewhere in the interior and they ask to see your immigration documents. Having expired papers will only further complicate your situation in such cases, so the best policy is to stay up to date in spite of the apparent laxity of enforcement.

Pets

Dogs, cats, and other pets may be brought into Mexico if each is accompanied by a **vaccination certificate** (which must show that the animal has been vaccinated or treated for rabies, hepatitis, pip, and leptospirosis) and a **health certificate** (International Health Certificate for Dogs and Cats). The latter must be issued no more than 72 hours before entry and signed by a registered veterinarian.

Since 1992 the requirement that the health certificate be stamped with a visa at the border or at a Mexican consulate has been repealed. The certificate is still necessary; the "visa" isn't.

When you recross the border into the U.S., the U.S. Customs Service will ask to see the vaccination certificate.

Inmigrante Rentista Visas

Special visas (FM-2 status) are issued to foreigners who choose to reside in Mexico on a "permanent income" basis. This most often applies to foreigners who decide to retire in Mexico, though it is also used by artists, writers, and other self-employed foreign residents. With this visa you're allowed to import one motor vehicle as well as your household belongings into Mexico tax-free.

The basic requirements for this visa are that applicants must forgo any kind of local employment while residing in Mexico and must show proof (bank statements) that they have a regular source of foreign-earned income amounting to at least US$1,365 per month (plus half that for each dependent over the age of 15, e.g., US$2,047 for a couple). A pile of paperwork, including a "letter of good conduct" from the applicant's local

police department, must accompany the initial application, along with an immigration tax payment (currently US$60) and various applications fees totaling an additional US$75 or so.

The visa must be renewed annually but the renewal can be accomplished at any immigration office in Mexico (almost every *municipio* in Northern Mexico has one). After five years in Mexico, an *inmigrante rentista* is eligible to apply for *inmigrado* status, which confers all the rights of citizenship (including employment in Mexico), save the rights to vote and hold public office.

Many foreigners who have retired in Mexico manage to do so on the regular 180-day tourist visa; every six months they dash across the border and return with a new tourist card (issued at the border) on the same day. This method bypasses all the red tape and income requirements of the retirement visa. If you own a home in Mexico, however, some local immigration officials may interpret the law to mean you must have an FM-2 or FM-3 visa—not an FMT or tourist visa—to be able to stay in that home for any period of time whatsoever. Although it's clear from a straight reading that Mexico's immigration laws do not require any special visas for home ownership, each immigration district is like an individual fiefdom at the mercy of the local immigration chief.

Retirees disinclined to make a run for the border every six months can alternatively obtain an FM-3 *visitante rentista* visa, which allows one-year stays with none of the privileges (i.e., tax-free importation of vehicle and household goods) of the FM-2 visa. This varies again, according to the local preferences of the people in charge—some districts allow the one-time importation of household goods. FM-3 status permits a lower minimum income than FM-2 status, at the moment around US$853 per individual plus US$426.50 per dependent; like the FM-2 it must be renewed annually but unlike the FM-2 you must keep renewing it annually indefinitely. For most people the FM-3 visa isn't worth the hassle of application and annual juggling of financial statements, especially since the tourist card is freely available at the border. However, local conditions—such as an immigration chief who misinterprets residency or home-ownership laws —may make it desirable.

Monthly income requirements for both *rentista* visas are keyed to the Mexican daily minimum wage (400 times minimum wage for the FM-2, 250 times for the FM-3, hence figures may vary according to the current dollar-peso exchange rate.

BORDER CROSSINGS

Between San Luis (Yuma), Arizona, and the Gulf of Mexico are 21 official U.S.-Mexico border crossings. Border facilities at most gateways are open 24 hours, although the smaller crossings (Sasabe, Naco, Palomas, Colombia, Ojinaga, Piedras Negras, Nueva Ciudad Guerrero, Camargo, Díaz Ordaz, Nuevo Progreso) maintain more limited schedules—usually weekdays

7 a.m.-9 p.m., Sat.-Sun. 8 a.m.-5 p.m.—depending on size and border traffic.

Nuevo Laredo is the largest port of entry along Mexico's entire border and also the most heavily used commercially since it connects Mexico with U.S. Interstate 35, which extends north through the middle of the U.S. to Dallas, Kansas City, Minneapolis, Duluth, and the Canadian border. Ciudad Juárez is the second most used gateway. At any of the border crossings, you'll find the shortest waits (15-30 minutes at Ciudad Juárez or Nuevo Laredo) between 10 a.m. and 3:30 p.m. or after 7-8 p.m. on weekdays. Weekends are the worst days in either direction, except late at night or before dawn. If you're on your way out of Mexico and find yourself near the border during rush hours, it might be best to find a restaurant or other spot on the Mexico

OFFICIAL U.S.-MEXICO BORDER CROSSINGS

The following list includes only those crossings with U.S. and Mexican immigration posts.

San Luis Río Colorado, Son. (road; opposite San Luis, AZ): 24 hrs.

Sonoyta, Son. (road; opposite Lukeville, AZ): 24 hrs.

Sasabe, Son. (road; opposite Sasabe, AZ): 8 a.m.-8 p.m. Mon.-Fri., 10 a.m.-2 p.m. Sat.-Sun.

Nogales, Son. (road; opposite Nogales, AZ): 24 hrs.

Naco, Son. (road; opposite Naco, AZ): 8 a.m.-midnight daily

Agua Prieta, Son. (road; opposite Douglas, AZ): 24 hrs.

Palomas, Chih. (road; opposite Columbus, NM): 24 hrs.

Ciudad Juárez, Chih. (bridge; opposite El Paso, TX; there are also three bridge crossings southeast of El Paso near Fabens and Fort Hancock): 24 hrs.

Ojinaga, Chih. (bridge; opposite Presidio, TX): 7:30 a.m.-9 p.m. Mon.-Fri., 8 a.m.-4 p.m. Sat.-Sun.

Ciudad Acuña, Coah. (bridge; opposite Del Rio, TX): 24 hrs.

Piedras Negras, Coah. (bridge; opposite Eagle Pass, TX): 24 hrs.

Nuevo Laredo, Tamps. (bridge; opposite Laredo, TX; plus second crossing northeast at Colombia, Tamps.): 24 hrs.

Nueva Ciudad Guerrero, Tamps. (bridge; opposite Salineno, TX): 7:30 a.m.-9 p.m. Mon.-Fri., 8 a.m.-4 p.m. Sat.-Sun.

Ciudad Miguel Alemán, Tamps. (bridge; opposite Roma, TX): 24 hrs.

Camargo, Tamps. (bridge; opposite Rio Grande City, TX): 7:30 a.m.-9 p.m. Mon.-Fri., 8 a.m.-4 p.m. Sat.-Sun.

Díaz Ordaz, Tamps. (ferry; opposite Los Ebanos, TX; bridge to be constructed): 7:30 a.m.-9 p.m. Mon.-Fri., 8 a.m.-4 p.m. Sat.-Sun.

Reynosa, Tamps. (bridge; opposite Hidalgo/McAllen, TX): 24 hrs.

Nuevo Progreso (Río Bravo), Tamps. (bridge; opposite Progreso, TX): 7:30 a.m.-9 p.m. Mon.-Fri., 8 a.m.-4 p.m. Sat.-Sun.

Matamoros, Tamps. (bridge; opposite Brownsville, TX): 24 hrs.

side and wait it out. Waits are always much longer going north.

If you're on foot, crossing is usually a breeze. Public and chartered buses also get through more quickly than private vehicles because of special traffic lanes provided them.

At all other crossings, wait times are rarely more than 5-15 minutes.

Unofficial Crossings

All along the lengthy U.S.-Mexico border are places where locals cross back and forth at will without immigration checks on either side. Some of these spots are deliberately tolerated by immigration officials of both nations. The rowboat crossings at Paso Lajitas, Chih., opposite Lajitas, Texas, next to Big Bend National Park, and at Boquillas del Carmen, Coah., opposite the park itself, have long been places where park visitors and local tradespeople have been allowed to cross without any border formalities. If the proposed international park linking Big Bend with Mexico's Sierra del Carmen is ever realized, Boquillas del Carmen, Coah., will become the main gateway to the Mexican half of the park. Northeast of Ojinaga, Coah., is a small Mexican town called San Antonio del Bravo where the residents regularly collect their mail at the Candelaria, Texas, post office, reached by a narrow footbridge over the Río Bravo/Rio Grande. Dirt roads from all these towns lead into the interior of Coahuila and Chihuahua.

CUSTOMS

Entering Mexico

Officially, tourists are supposed to bring into Mexico only those items that will be of use during

---

MEXICAN CONSULATES

UNITED STATES

Arizona: 541 10th St., Douglas, AZ 85607, tel. (520) 364-3107, fax 364-1379

486 Grand Ave. (at Terminal St.), Nogales, AZ 85621, tel. (520) 287-2521, fax 287-3175

1990 W. Camelback, Suite 110, Phoenix, AZ 85015, tel. (602) 242-7398, fax 242-2957

553 S. Stone Ave., Tucson, AZ 85701, tel. (602) 882-5595, fax 882-8959

California: 331 W. Second St., Calexico, CA 92231, tel. (760) 357-3863, fax 357-6284

830 Van Ness Ave., Fresno, CA 93721, tel. (209) 233-3065, fax 233-5638

2401 W. Sixth St., Los Angeles, CA 90057, tel. (213) 351-6800, fax 389-6864

Transportation Center, 201 E. Fourth St., Room 209, Oxnard, CA 93030, tel. (805) 483-4684, fax 385-3527

1010 8th St., Sacramento, CA 95814, tel. (916) 441-3287, fax 441-3176

532 North D St., San Bernardino, CA 92401, tel. (909) 889-9836, 889-8285

1549 India St., San Diego, CA 92101, tel. (619) 231-8414, fax 231-4802

870 Market St., Suite 528, San Francisco, CA 94102, tel. (415) 392-5554, fax 392-3233

828 N. Broadway St., Santa Ana, CA 92701-3424, tel. (714) 835-3069, fax 835-3472

Colorado: 48 Steele St., Denver, CO 80206, tel. (303) 331-1110, fax 331-0169

District of Columbia: 1911 Pennsylvania Ave., Washington, D.C. 20036, tel. (202) 728-1750

Florida: 1200 N.W. 78th Ave., Miami, FL 33126, tel. (305) 716-4977, fax 593-2758

823 E. Colonial Dr., Orlando, FL 32803, tel. (407) 894-0514, fax 895-6140

Georgia: 3220 Peachtree Rd. NE, Atlanta, GA 30305, tel. (404) 266-1913, fax 266-2309

Illinois: 300 N. Michigan Ave., 2nd Fl., Chicago, IL 60601, tel. (312) 855-1380, fax 855-9257

Louisiana: World Trade Center Building, 2 Canal St., Suite 840, New Orleans, LA 70130, tel. (504) 522-3596, fax 525-2332

Massachusetts: 20 Park Plaza, Suite 506, Boston, MA 02116, tel. (617) 426-8782, fax 695-1957

Michigan: 600 Renaissance Center, Suite 1510, Detroit, MI 48243, tel. (313) 567-7709, fax 567-7543

Missouri: 1015 Locust St., Suite 922, Saint Louis, MO 63101, tel. (314) 436-3233, fax 436-2695

their trip. This means that you can bring in practically anything as long as it doesn't appear to be in large enough quantities for resale. Firearms and ammunition, as well as boats, however, require special permits (see "Outdoor Recreation," above, for permit information).

Other limits include: three liters of liquor or wine; two cartons (20 packs) of cigarettes or 50 cigars or 250 grams of tobacco; one still camera and one other camera (still, video, or movie), plus 12 rolls of film for each. These limits are rarely enforced. Professional photographers and others who would like to bring more cameras and film into Mexico can apply for dispensation through a Mexican consulate abroad.

Auto Permits

Foreign-registered motor vehicles (cars, trucks, RVs, motorcycles, etc.) do not require permits for border-town visits of less than 72 hours. For longer visits, however, you *must* obtain a **temporary vehicle importation permit** at the border if you're going anywhere besides Baja California or Sonora. To receive this permit, you simply drive your vehicle to a Mexican customs office at an official border crossing and present the following: a valid state registration for the vehicle (or similar document certifying legal ownership), a driver's license, and a credit card (Visa, MasterCard, American Express, or Diner's Club) issued outside Mexico.

If you are leasing or renting the vehicle, you'll also have to present a leasing or rental contract made out to the person bringing the vehicle into Mexico. If the vehicle belongs to someone else (e.g., a friend or relative), you must present a notarized letter from the owner giving you permission to take the vehicle into Mexico. Contrary

---

New Mexico: 400 Gold SW, Suite 100, Albuquerque, NM 87102, tel. (505) 247-2147 or (800) 926-2898, fax (505) 842-9490

New York: 8 E. 41st St., New York, NY 10017, tel. (212) 689-0456, fax 545-8197

North Carolina: P.O. Box 19627, Charlotte, NC 28219, tel. (704) 394-2190

Oregon: 1234 S.W. Morrison, Portland, OR 97205, tel. (503) 274-1442, fax 274-1540

Pennsylvania: 111 S. Independence Mall East, Bourse Building, Suite 1010, Philadelphia, PA 19403, tel. (215) 625-4897, fax 923-7281

Texas: 200 E. Sixth St., Suite 200, Austin, TX 78701, tel. (512) 478-2866, fax 478-2866

724 E. Elizabeth St., Brownsville, TX 78520, tel. (956) 542-4431, fax 542-7267

800 N. Shoreline Blvd., Suite 410, North Tower, Corpus Christi, TX 78401, tel. (512) 882-3375, fax 882-9324

8855 N. Stemmons Freeway, Dallas, TX 75247, tel. (214) 630-7341, fax 630-3511

300 E. Losoya, Del Rio, TX 78841, tel. (830) 775-9451, fax 774-6497

140 Adams St., Eagle Pass, TX 78852, tel. (830) 773-9255, fax 773-9397

910 E. San Antonio St., El Paso, TX 79901, tel. (915) 533-3644, fax 532-7163

3015 Richmond, Suite 100, Houston, TX 77098, tel. (713) 524-2300, fax 523-6244

1612 Farragut St., Laredo, TX 78040, tel. (956) 723-6369, fax 723-1741

600 S. Broadway Ave., McAllen, TX 78501, tel. (956) 686-0244, fax 686-4901

511 W. Ohio, Suite 121, Midland, TX 79701, tel. (915) 687-2334, fax 687-3952

127 Navarro St., San Antonio, TX 78205, tel. (210) 227-9145, fax 227-1817

Utah: 458 E. 200 South, Salt Lake City, UT 84111, tel. (801) 521-8502, fax 521-0534

Washington: 2132 Third Ave., Seattle, WA 98121, tel. (206) 448-6819, fax 448-4771

CANADA

British Columbia: 1130 W. Pender St., Vancouver, B.C. VGE 4A4, tel. (604) 684-3547

Ontario: 60 Bloor St. W, Suite 203, Toronto, Ont. M4W 3B8, tel. (416) 922-2718

Quebec: 2000 Mansfield St., Suite 1015, Montreal, Que. H3A 2Z7, tel. (514) 288-2502

UK: 8 Halkin St., London, tel. (171) 235-6393, fax 235-5480

to rumor, you aren't required to present the "pink slip" or ownership certificate unless the state registration certificate is for some reason unavailable. It also helps to bring along a few photocopies of your registration and driver's license as these may be needed in the import-permit process. This will save having to stand in a separate line for photocopies at the customs office, as is necessary at some border crossings.

Once the Mexican customs officials have approved your documents, you'll proceed to a Banjército (Banco del Ejército or Military Bank) office attached to the customs facilities, where your credit card account will be charged US$10-11 for the permit fee. **Note:** This fee must be paid by credit card; cash is not accepted. If you don't have a credit card, you'll have to post a bond (one to two percent of the vehicle's blue-book value) issued by an authorized Mexican bond company, a very time-consuming and expensive procedure. Banjército is the bank used for all Mexican customs charges; the operating hours for each module are the same as for the border crossing at which it's located.

Once the fee has been charged to your credit card, the permit is issued, with a validity period equal to that shown on your tourist card or visa. You may drive back and forth across the border—at any crossing—as many times as you wish during the permit's validity. You are supposed to surrender the permit at the border when your trip is over, however.

Always carry your vehicle import permit with you when driving your vehicle in Mexico. The permit may be checked at interior immigration checkpoints; and the police may ask to see it during routine checks, or if you've been stopped for a traffic offense.

In the U.S., further information on temporary vehicle importation can be obtained by calling the Mexican Government Tourist Office at (800) 446-8277 (toll free). The American Automobile Association (AAA) advertises a service in which U.S. motorists with credit cards are supposed to be able to obtain both tourist cards and auto permits from AAA offices in Texas, New Mexico, Arizona, and California. In reality, however, all AAA does is fill out the papers for you and put them in a fancy folder. Any travel agent with the forms on hand (available by request from any Mexican consulate) can perform the same func-

tion, and in fact AAA is not authorized to validate your papers. You still have to stop at the border and stand in line to get the "For Official Use" parts filled in. When we went to AAA for these papers, the staff wrote in the wrong places on the forms and gave wrong information about the maximum stay allowed; then when we turned up at the Agua Prieta border post, the Mexican immigration officials weren't at all interested in seeing government papers printed only in English and we had to start from scratch anyway. Going to AAA to start you paperwork simply adds another step to the whole process. Of course if you're a member you might as well stop by for one of their lovely Mexico maps.

Insurance: Although it's not yet required by Mexican law, any visitors planning to drive their own vehicles in Mexico should carry Mexican vehicle insurance. Foreign insurance policies aren't valid in Mexico; without insurance, if you get in an accident that's judged your fault, you can be jailed until you pay damages. See "Driving in Northern Mexico," above, for details on how to obtain Mexican insurance.

Returning to the U.S.
Overseas visitors need a passport and visa to enter the United States. Except for diplomats, students, or refugees, this means a nonimmigrant visitor's visa, which must be obtained in advance at a U.S. consulate or embassy abroad. Residents of Western European and Commonwealth countries are usually issued these readily; residents of other countries may have to provide the consulate with proof of "sufficient personal funds" before the visa is issued.

Upon arrival in the U.S., an immigration inspector will decide on the time validity of the visa—the maximum for a temporary visitor's visa (B-1 or B-2) is six months. If you visit Mexico from Texas (or from anywhere else in the U.S.) for stays of 30 days or less, you can reenter the U.S. with the same visa, provided the visa is still valid, by presenting your stamped arrival/departure card (INS form I-94) and passport to a U.S. immigration inspector. If your U.S. visa has expired, you can still enter the country for a stay of 29 days or less on a transit visa—issued at the border—but you may be required to show proof of onward travel, such as an air ticket or ship travel voucher.

Customs: Visitors returning to the U.S. from Mexico may have their luggage inspected by U.S. Customs officials. The hassle can be minimized by giving brief, straight answers to their questions (e.g., "How long have you been in Mexico?" "Do you have anything to declare?") and by cooperating with their requests to open your luggage, vehicle storage compartments, and anything else they want opened. Sometimes the officers use dogs to sniff luggage and vehicles for contraband and illegal aliens.

Nearly 3,000 items—including all handicrafts—made in Mexico are exempt from any U.S. Customs duties. Adults over 21 are allowed one liter (33.8 fluid ounces) of alcoholic beverages and 200 cigarettes (or 100 cigars) per person. Note that Cuban cigars may not be imported into the U.S. and they will be confiscated at the border if discovered. Since an estimated nine out of 10 cigars sold as Cubans in Mexico are fake, it's not worth the hassle. All other purchases or gifts up to a total value of US$400 within any 31-day period can be brought into the U.S. duty-free.

Plant and Animal Prohibitions: The following fruits and vegetables cannot be brought into the U.S. from Mexico: oranges, grapefruits, mangoes, avocados (unless the pit is removed), and potatoes (including yams and sweet potatoes). All other fruits are permitted, including bananas, dates, pineapples, cactus fruits, grapes, and berries of all types.

Other prohibited plant materials are straw (including packing materials and items stuffed with straw), hay, unprocessed cotton, sugarcane, and any plants in soil (this includes houseplants).

Animals and animal products that cannot be imported include wild and domesticated birds (including poultry, unless cooked), pork or pork products (including sausage, ham, and other cured pork), and eggs. Beef, mutton, venison, and other meats are permitted at up to 50 pounds per person.

Customs regulations can change at any time, so if you want to verify the regulations on a purchase before risking duties or confiscation at the border, check with a U.S. consulate in Northern Mexico before crossing. Now that NAFTA is in effect, expect sweeping changes in customs regulations—toward more leniency—in both directions.

Returning to Canada
Duty-frees include 200 cigarettes (50 cigars, or 250 grams of tobacco) and 1.14 liters of booze. Exemptions run from C$20 to C$500 depending on how long you've been outside Canada. To reach the maximum exemption of C$500 you must be gone at least one week. Since Canada is also signatory to NAFTA, customs legalities will change over the next decade.

Returning to the U.K.
Duty-frees include 200 cigarettes (50 cigars, or 250 grams of tobacco) and one liter of beverage with an alcoholic content of over 22% or two liters under 22%, plus two liters of wine. The maximum total value of exempted items is £136.

Returning to Australia
Duty-frees include 200 cigarettes (or 250 grams of tobacco, including cigars) and one liter of alcohol. The maximum total value of exempted items is A$400.

HEALTH AND SAFETY

By and large, Northern Mexico is a healthy place—sanitation standards are relatively high compared to those in many other parts of Mexico, and the water quality in many areas is superior. The visitor's main health concerns are not going to be with food or water sources, but with avoiding mishaps while driving, cycling, hiking, boating, diving, surfing, or otherwise enjoying Mexico's great outdoors. Health issues directly concerned with these activities are covered under the relevant sections in this book.

FOOD AND WATER

Visitors who use common sense will probably never come down with food- or water-related illnesses while traveling in Northern Mexico. The first rule is not to overdo it during the first few days of your trip—eat and drink with moderation. Shoveling down huge amounts of tasty but often rich Mexican foods along with pitchers of margaritas or strong Mexican beer is liable to make anyone sick from pure overindulgence. If you're not used to the spices and different ways of cooking, it's best to ingest small amounts at first.

Second, take it easy with foods offered by street vendors, since this is where you're most likely to suffer from unsanitary conditions. Eat only foods that have been thoroughly cooked and are served either stove-hot or refrigerator-cold. Many gringos eat street food without any problems whatsoever, but it pays to be cautious, especially if it's your first time in Mexico.

Doctors usually recommend that you avoid eating peeled, raw fruits and vegetables in Mexico. Once the peel has been removed, it is virtually impossible to disinfect produce. Unpeeled fruits and vegetables washed in purified water and dried with a clean cloth are usually okay. After all, plenty of Mexican fruit is consumed daily in Canada and the United States.

Hotels and restaurants serve only purified drinking water and ice, so there's no need to ask for mineral water or refuse ice. Tap water, however, should not be consumed, except in hotels where the water system is purified (look for a notice over the washbasin in your room). Most grocery stores sell bottled, purified water. Water purification tablets, iodine crystals, water filters, and the like aren't necessary for Mexico travel unless you plan to do extensive backpacking (see "Hiking and Backpacking," above, for details).

If you plan to stay in one place for a long period, consider paying a deposit on a large, five-gallon, reusable plastic water dispenser filled with purified water. These are available at local purified water companies all over Mexico. The first bottle, with reusable plastic dispenser included, costs about US$5.70, while refills cost just US$0.75. Siphons (sifóns) designed for these dispensers cost around US$2.50 and are available at some groceries or sometimes directly from the purified water companies. Since a single gallon of water in a disposable plastic jug from a grocery store may cost US$0.75-1.00, using the recyclable five-gallon dispensers not only saves money but reduces landfill.

Turista

People who've never traveled to a foreign country may undergo a period of adjustment to the new gastrointestinal flora that comes with new territory. There's really no way to avoid the differences wrought by sheer distance. Unfortunately, the adjustment is sometimes unpleasant for some people.

Mexican doctors call gastrointestinal upset of this sort *turista* since it affects tourists but not the local population. The usual symptoms of *turista* (also known by the gringo tags "Montezuma's Revenge" or the "Aztec Two-Step") are nausea and diarrhea, sometimes with stomach cramps and a low fever. Again, eating and drinking only in moderation will help prevent the worst of the symptoms, which rarely persist more than a day or two. And if it's any consolation, Mexicans often get sick the first time they go to the U.S. or Canada.

Prevention and Treatment: Many Mexico travelers swear by a preventive regimen of Pepto-Bismol begun the day before arrival in the country. Opinions vary as to how much of the pink stuff is necessary to ward off or tame the evil flora, but a person should not exceed the recommended daily dosage. Taper off after four days or so until you stop using it altogether.

Another regimen that seems to be effective is a daily 100-milligram tablet of doxycycline (sold as Vibramycin in the U.S.), a low-grade antibiotic that requires a prescription in most countries. It works by killing all the bacteria in your intestinal tract—including the ones that reside there naturally and help protect your bowels from outside intruders as well as new arrivals. It's available without a prescription in Mexican *farmacias,* but you should check with your doctor first to make sure you're not sensitive to it—some people have problems with sunlight or upset stomach while taking doxycycline. Also be sure to take it with plenty of water and a meal. Some physicians believe that when you stop taking this drug, you're particularly susceptible to intestinal upset because no protective bacteria is left to fight off infections.

Neither Pepto nor Vibramycin is recommended for travelers planning trips of three weeks or longer.

If you come down with a case of *turista,* the best thing to do is drink plenty of fluids. Adults should drink at least three liters a day, a child under 37 kilos (80 pounds) at least a liter a day. Lay off tea, coffee, milk, fruit juices, and booze.

Eat only bland foods—nothing spicy, fatty, or fried—and take it easy. Pepto-Bismol or similar pectin-based remedies usually help. Some people like to mask the symptoms with a strong over-the-counter medication like Immodium AD (loperamide is the active ingredient); however, though it can be very effective, it isn't a cure. Only time will cure traveler's diarrhea.

If the symptoms are unusually severe (especially if there's blood in the stools or a high fever) or persist more than one or two days, see a doctor. Most hotels can arrange a doctor's visit or you can contact a Mexican tourist office or U.S. consulate for recommendations.

SUNBURN AND DEHYDRATION

Northern Mexico visitors are probably afflicted more by sunburn than by all other illnesses and injuries combined. The sunlight in Mexico can be intense, especially in the Altiplano and along the Sea of Cortéz/Pacific coast. For outdoor forays, sun protection is a must, whatever the activity—the longer you'll be in the sun, the more protection you'll need.

A hat, sunglasses, and plenty of sunscreen or sunblock make a good start. Bring along a sunscreen with a sun protection factor (SPF) of at least 25, even if you don't plan to use it all the time. Apply it to *all* exposed parts of your body—don't forget the hands, tops of the feet, neck, tops of the ears, any thinned-out or bald areas on your scalp, and places where you part your hair. Sunscreen must be reapplied after swimming (no matter what the label says) or after heavy perspiring.

If you're going boating, don't leave shore with only a bathing suit. Bring along an opaque shirt—preferably with long sleeves—and a pair of long pants. Since you can never know for certain whether your boat might get stranded or lost at sea for a period of time (if, for example, the motor conks out and you get caught in an offshore current), you shouldn't be without extra clothing for emergencies.

It's also important to drink plenty of water or nonalcoholic, noncaffeinated fluids to avoid dehydration. Alcohol and caffeine—including the caffeine in iced tea and cola—only increase your potential for dehydration. Symptoms of dehydration include darker-than-usual urine or inability to urinate, flushed face, profuse sweating or an unusual lack thereof, and sometimes a headache, dizziness, and general feeling of malaise. Extreme cases of dehydration can lead to heat exhaustion oreven heat stroke, in which the victim may become delirious or convulse. If either condition is suspected, get the victim out of the sun immediately, cover with a wet sheet or towel, and administer a rehydration fluid that replaces lost water and salts. If you can get the victim to a doctor, all the better—heatstroke can be serious.

Rehydration Formula: If Gatorade or a similar rehydration fluid isn't available you can mix your own by combining the following ingredients: one liter purified water or diluted fruit juice; two tablespoons sugar or honey; one-quarter teaspoon salt; and one-quarter teaspoon baking soda. If soda isn't available, use another quarter teaspoon salt. The victim should drink this mixture at regular intervals until symptoms subside substantially. Four or more liters may be necessary in moderate cases, more in severe cases.

MOTION SICKNESS

Visitors with little or no boating experience who join offshore fishing cruises sometimes experience motion sickness caused by the movement of a boat over ocean swells. The repeated pitching and rolling affects a person's sense of equilibrium to the point of nausea. Known as "seasickness" *(mareo),* it can be a very unpleasant experience not only for those green at the gills but for fellow passengers anxious lest the victim spew on them.

The best way to prevent motion sickness is to take one of the preventives commonly available from a pharmacist: promethazine (sold as Phenergan in the U.S.), dimenhydrinate (Dramamine), or scopolamine (Transderm Scop). The latter is available as an adhesive patch worn behind the ear—the time-release action is allegedly more effective than tablets. These medications should be consumed *before* boarding the vessel, not after the onset of symptoms. It's also not a good idea to eat a large meal before getting on a boat.

If you start to feel seasick while out on the bounding main, certain actions can lessen the likelihood that it will get worse. First, do not lie down. Often the first symptom of motion sickness is drowsiness, and if you give in to the impulse you'll almost certainly guarantee a worsening of the condition. Second, stay in the open air rather than below decks—fresh air usually helps. Finally, fix your gaze on the horizon; this will help steady your disturbed inner ear, the proximate cause of motion sickness.

BITES AND STINGS

Mosquitoes and *Jejenes*

Mosquitoes breed in standing water and since standing water isn't that common in arid Northern Mexico, neither are mosquitoes. Exceptions include estuaries and marshes when there isn't a strong enough breeze around to keep them

SNAKEBITE PREVENTION AND TREATMENT

Although 13 rattlesnake and one coral snake species can be found in Northern Mexico, the overall risk of being bitten by a poisonous snake while hiking in Northern Mexico is low, mainly because such creatures avoid contact with all large mammals, including humans. Most of the unfortunate who are bitten by snakes in Mexico are local ranchers who spend a great deal of time in snake habitats, or small children who may not know to retreat from a coiled rattler.

Nonetheless, anyone spending time in the Northern Mexican outback, including campers and hikers, are advised to follow a few simple precautions.

Crotalus atrox, *as sketched by William Emory in the 1850s*

Prevention

First of all, use caution when placing hands or feet in areas where snakes may lie. This primarily includes rocky ledges, holes, and fallen logs. Always look first, and if you must move a rock or log, use a long stick or other instrument. Wear sturdy footwear when walking in possible snake habitats. High-top leather shoes or boots are best. Rancheros wear thick leather leggings when working in known snake territory; these are sometimes available for purchase at *zapaterías* (shoe stores) or at leather and saddle shops.

Most snakes strike only when they feel threatened. Naturally, if you step on or next to a snake, it is likely to strike. If you see or hear a rattlesnake, remain still until the snake moves away. If it doesn't leave the vicinity, simply back away slowly and cautiously. Sudden movements may cause a snake to strike; rattlers rarely strike a stationary target. Remember also that a rattler can't strike a target that is farther away than three-fourths of its body length. Use this rough measure to judge when it may be safe to move away from one, leaving plenty of room for error.

If you'll be hiking in wilderness areas far from professional medical treatment, by all means carry an elastic bandage or two, the type used for sprains. The old "slice and suck" method of treating snakebite has been discredited by most medical experts.

Don't attempt to kill a rattler unless you have a genuine need to use it as food (great barbecued)—as nasty as they may seem, snakes are as important to the desert ecosystem as the most beautiful flowering cactus.

Treatment

If bitten by a snake, it is important that you remain calm in order to slow the potential spread of venom in your body until you are able to discern whether the

at bay. The easiest way to avoid mosquito bites is to apply insect repellent to exposed areas of the skin and clothing whenever the little buggers are out and biting, usually between dusk and dawn.

The most effective repellents are those that contain a high concentration of DEET (N,N-diethyl-metatoluamide). Those with an aversion to applying synthetics to their skin can try citronella (lemon-grass oil), which is also effective but requires more frequent application. Carl Lumholz, while traveling in northwestern Mexico in the early 1900s, successfully used a French-Canadian recipe consisting of 17 parts olive oil, two parts oil of pennyroyal, and one part carbolic acid.

Some of the same conditions that bring out the mosquitoes will produce *jejenes,* tiny flying insects also known as "no-see-ums" among Americans—you almost never see them while they're biting. The same repellents effective for mosquitoes will usually do the trick for *jejenes.*

For relief from the itchiness of mosquito bites, try rubbing a bit of hand soap or lime juice on the affected areas. A German-made cream called Andantol relieves itchy insect bites and is available in many Mexican pharmacies. *Jejene* bites will usually stop itching in less than 10 minutes if you refrain from scratching them. Excessive scratching of either type of bite can lead to infection, so be mindful of what your fingers are up to.

---

snake in question is a rattler, and so that you can follow the necessary steps for treatment in a cool-headed manner if it is.

First, immediately following the bite, try to identify the snake—was it a rattler or a coral snake? At the very least, memorize the markings and physical characteristics so that a physician can administer the most appropriate antivenin. If you can kill the snake and bring it to the nearest treatment center, all the better, but this could expose you or your fellow hikers to the risk of another bite (not to mention the exertion of energy—that alone could cause the venom to spread faster).

Second, examine the bite for teeth marks. A successful bite by a poisonous pit viper (which includes copperheads, cottonmouths, and rattlesnakes) will have one or two large fang punctures in addition to smaller teeth marks, while a bite by a nonpoisonous snake will not feature fang punctures. A coral snake bite will usually feature a series of small, closely spaced punctures made by the "chewing" motion of smaller fangs (coral snakes have to chew or bite their victim's flesh repeatedly in order to inject sufficient quantities of venom). In general, nonpoisonous bites cause relatively small, shallow marks or scratches.

If you suspect that the bite is poisonous, *immobilize the affected limb and wrap it tightly in an elastic bandage.* This will slow the spread of venom through the lymph system and mitigate swelling. Be careful that the bandage isn't wrapped so tightly that it cuts off circulation—you should be able to insert a finger under it without difficulty. Keep the arm or leg below the level of the heart. The victim should avoid all physical activity if possible since increased circulation will accelerate the absorption of the venom. For this same reason, aspirin, sedatives, and alcohol should be avoided. Do not apply cold therapy—ice packs, cold compresses, and so on—to the bite area or to any other part of the victim's body.

Get the victim to a hospital or physician if possible. Where feasible, carry the victim to restrict physical exertion. Even when wrapping the limb appears successful in preventing symptoms, the bite will need medical attention and a physician may decide that antivenin treatment is necessary. (However, it's possible for a poisonous snake to bite without injecting any venom—up to 20% of reported bites are "dry bites.")

Snakebite victims who require antivenin treatment will usually receive the broad-spectrum North American Antisnakebite Serum for pit viper poisoning (or a similar antivenin for coral snake poisoning)—where available. Your home physician may be able to provide a prescription for the serum in advance of your outdoor trip if convinced that you'll be in areas where antivenin is unavailable or medical treatment is inaccessible.

In cases where it's been determined that a bite is venomous and the serum isn't available, the best you can do is follow the treatment outlined above and keep the victim immobile and cool until the symptoms—pain in the affected limb, abdominal cramps, headache—have subsided. (For some bites, wrapping the limb in an elastic bandage will prevent all or most of the worst symptoms.) The victim should drink plenty of water. Don't panic—remember that few rattlesnake or coral snakebites turn out to be fatal, even when untreated.

Wasps, Bees, and Hornets

Although stings from these flying insects can be painful, they aren't of mortal danger to most people. If you're allergic to such stings and plan to travel in remote areas of Northern Mexico, consider requesting antiallergy medication from your doctor before leaving home. At the very least, carry a supply of Benadryl or a similar over-the-counter antihistamine. Dramamine (dimenhydrinate) also usually helps mitigate allergic reactions.

For relief from a wasp/bee/hornet sting, apply a paste of baking soda and water to the affected area. Liquids containing ammonia, including urine, also help relieve pain. If a stinger is visible, remove it—by scraping if possible, or with tweezers—before applying any remedies. If a stung limb becomes unusually swollen or if the victim exhibits symptoms of a severe allergic reaction —difficulty breathing, agitation, hives—seek medical assistance.

Ticks

If you find a tick embedded in your skin, don't try to pull it off—this may leave the head and pincers under your skin and lead to infection. Covering the tick with petroleum jelly, mineral oil, alcohol, gasoline, or kerosene will usually cause the tick to release its hold in order to avoid suffocation.

Burning the tick with a cigarette butt or hot match usually succeeds only in killing it—when you pull the tick out, the head and pincers may not come with it. Stay with the suffocation method and if it doesn't come out, use tweezers.

Scorpions

The venom of scorpions (alacranes) varies in strength from individual to individual and species to species, but the sting is rarely dangerous to adults. It can be painful, however, and can result in partial numbness and swelling that can last several days. In Mexico, the small yellow scorpions inflict more painful stings than the larger, dark-colored ones.

The best treatment begins with persuading the victim to lie down and relax to slow the spread of the venom. Keep the affected area below the level of the heart. Ice packs on the sting may relieve pain and mitigate swelling; aspirin also helps.

Children who weigh less than about 13 kg (30 pounds) should receive medical attention if stung by a scorpion. Doctors in Mexico usually have ready access to scorpion antivenin (antialacrán), but it should only be administered under qualified medical supervision.

Scorpions prefer damp, dark, warm places— dead brush, rockpiles, fallen logs—so exercise particular caution when placing your hands in or near such areas. Hands are the scorpion's most common target on the human body; campers should wear gloves when handling firewood.

Other favorite spots for scorpions are crumpled clothing and bedding. In desert areas of Northern Mexico, always check your bed sheets or sleeping bag for scorpions before climbing in. In the same environments, shake out your shoes and clothing before putting them on.

Centipedes

Called cientopiés ("100 legs") in Spanish, these slow-moving insects aren't as common as scorpions but have a similarly painful bite. Unlike scorpions, they prefer dry, rocky realms; you're most likely to see them when hiking in the desert. They're also less quick to inflict their bite except when mightily disturbed. Treatment is the same as for scorpions; none of the species in Northern Mexico are known to be deadly, but some people react more strongly than others.

Poisonous Sea Creatures

Various marine animals can inflict painful stings on humans. These include jellyfish, Portuguese men-of-war, cone shells, stingrays, sea urchins, and various fishes with poisonous spines.

The best way to avoid jellyfish and Portuguese men-of-war is to scope out the water before going in—if you see any nasties floating around, look for another beach. You can avoid stingrays by shuffling your feet in the sand as you walk in shallow surf—this will usually cause rays resting in the sand to swim away.

To avoid cone-shell and sea-urchin stings, wear shoes in the water; several sport-shoe manufacturers now produce specialized water shoes, e.g., Nike's Aqua Socks. You can also often spot cones and urchins in clear waters, especially if you're wearing a diving mask. Anglers should take care when handling landed fish to avoid poisonous spines.

centipede

JOE CUMMINGS

The treatment for stings from all of the above is the same. Remove all tentacles, barbs, or spines from the affected area; wash the area with rubbing alcohol or diluted ammonia (urine will do in a pinch) to remove as much venom as possible; and wrap the area in cloth to reduce the flow of oxygen to the wound until pain subsides. If an acute allergic reaction occurs, get the victim to a doctor or clinic as quickly as possible.

MEDICAL ASSISTANCE

The quality of basic medical treatment, including dentistry, is relatively high in Mexico's cities and larger towns; ask at a tourist office or at your consulate for recommendations. Every state capital has good hospitals, as well as public clinics or Red Cross (Cruz Roja) stations in nearly every other town.

Emergency Evacuation
Aeromedical Group, U.S. tel. (510) 293-5968 or (800) 854-2569, Mexico tel. 95 (800) 010-0986, provides emergency 24-hour airlift service (or, in the border areas, ground ambulance service) from Baja to U.S. hospitals in the San Diego area. Payment can be made with a credit card or through your health insurance company. Providing similar services are **Critical Air Medicine,** tel. (619) 571-0482 or (800) 247-8325 in Alta California, (800) 633-8326 elsewhere in the U.S., or 00 (800) 010-0268 in Mexico, and **Aeromede-**

vac, tel. (619) 284-7910 or (800) 832-5087.

Medical Air Services Association, 9 Village Circle, Roanoke, TX 76262, tel. (817) 430-4655 or (800) 643-9023, offers a yearly membership plan that covers unlimited emergency air transportation from anywhere in Mexico to anywhere in the U.S. or Canada. MASA membership rates start at US$120 per year. The service is available to Sanborn's Mexico Club members at discounted rates. For information on club membership, contact Sanborn's Insurance, P.O. Box 310, McAllen, TX 78502, tel. (956) 686-0711 or (800) 222-0158, fax (956) 686-0732. A similar program is available from **SkyMed International,** 442 Civic Center Plaza, Suite 101, Scottsdale, AZ 85251, tel. (800) 475-9633 or (602) 946-5188.

SAFETY

Violent crime is much less common in Mexico than in the United States. According to Interpol statistics, U.S. murder figures typically run 14% higher than Mexico's in the average year. Yet Americans themselves seem to be the most paranoid of all visitors to Mexico.

Historical reasons, to a large degree, account for this paranoia. Chief among these is the general border lawlessness that was the norm in the early 20th century—an era of border disputes and common banditry on both sides of the border. Americans living along the border came to fear the Mexican *bandidos* who stole livestock and occasionally robbed the Anglo ranchers themselves, while the Mexicans in turn feared American cattle rustlers, horse thieves, gunslingers, and the infamous Texas Rangers (known as *rinchos* in Northern Mexico), a private militia whose conduct at the time fell somewhere between that of the Hell's Angels motorcycle gang and the Los Angeles Police Department.

Soon after this era had begun to cool down, and as politics on both sides of the border stabilized, the U.S. Prohibition experiment sent millions of Americans scrambling into Mexican border towns to get the booze they weren't legally permitted in their own country. In this illicit atmosphere, boozers were soon rubbing elbows with gamblers and pimps, and it wasn't long before Mexican border towns gained an even more unsavory reputation.

Once Prohibition was lifted, Americans no longer had reason to come to Mexico solely for drinking purposes, and the border towns began cleaning up their acts. Among the uninformed and inexperienced, however, the border-town image not only remains but also sadly mixes with the equally outdated *bandido* tales, preventing many Americans from enjoying the pleasures of life south of the border.

To add a personal testimony to cautionary advice and statistics, neither the author nor anyone in the author's acquaintance has ever been robbed anywhere in Northern Mexico. On one occasion, however, the author left two shirts and a pair of slacks in a hotel closet in Loreto, Baja California Sur, one morning and didn't remember leaving them until arriving in La Paz in the evening. A phone call that same day and a visit to the hotel a week later were unsuccessful in retrieving the clothes—the management claimed they were never turned in by the cleaning staff. The moral of the story is that the author now tries to be extra careful to not leave things behind in hotel rooms.

Precautions

In general, visitors to Mexico should take the same precautions they would when traveling anywhere in their own country or abroad. Keep money and valuables secured, either in a hotel safe or safety deposit box, or in a money belt or other hard-to-get-at place on one's person. Keep an eye on cameras, purses, etc., making sure you don't leave them behind in restaurants, hotels, or campgrounds. At night, lock the doors to your hotel room and vehicle.

Private campgrounds usually have some kind of security (if only a night watchman) to keep out intruders. Secluded beach or wilderness campsites seem to be safe due to their very seclusion—in Mexico it is rare for any crime to occur in such areas. Nonetheless, don't leave items of value lying around outside your tent, camper, or RV at night.

Isolated areas of the Sierra Madre Occidental in the states of Sinaloa and Durango can be dangerous due to the proximity of plantations where marijuana (and possibly opium) is commercially cultivated for regional drug cartels. Never venture into the mountain areas without a reliable local guide.

If you happen to stop over in Mexico City, you must also be cautious about flagging taxicabs. Stolen taxis driven by thieves occasionally pick up unwary passengers—both Mexican and foreign—and rob them of their money and valuables. Take only cabs from taxi queues at hotels or established taxi stands *(sitios)* and you should be okay.

Help: SECTUR maintains a 24-hour traveler's-aid hotline for emergencies of all kinds: tel. (5) 250-0123 or 250-0151.

MONEY

CURRENCY

The unit of exchange in Mexico is the *peso,* which comes in paper denominations of N$10, N$20, N$50, N$100, and N$200. Peso and *centavo* coins are available in denominations of five cents, 10 cents, 20 cents, 50 cents, N$1, N$2, and N$5.

The N$ symbol (standing for "new pesos" to differentiate from pre-1993 "old pesos") is often used for indicating peso prices. Occasionally you may also encounter the $ symbol for pesos. While it's highly unlikely you'll ever confuse dollar and peso prices because of the differing values, you should ask when in doubt. Sometimes the abbreviation m.n. will appear next to a price —this means *moneda nacional* ("national money") and also refers to pesos.

Since coins smaller than one peso are scarce, payments often must be rounded off to the nearest peso or at least to the nearest 50 centavos. For a marked price of N$8.55, for example, you actually have to pay only N$8.50; for a N$8.75 price you may have to pay N$9. Any denomination over N$50 is difficult to break, so change them at every opportunity to secure a good supply of smaller notes. Small change is commonly called *morraya.*

Some border towns will take U.S. dollars as well as pesos. Paying with pesos, however, usually means a better deal when the price is fixed in pesos; if you pay in dollars, the vendor can determine the exchange rate. If a can of motor oil, for example, is marked at N$15, and the bank rate is N$8 per dollar, you'll pay less than US$2 for the oil with pesos changed at the bank. However, if you ask to pay in dollars, the vendor may charge US$2.50 since vendors have the right— by custom rather than law—to charge whatever exchange rate they wish. Then again, if you're bargaining for price, it really doesn't matter what currency you use.

Old Pesos vs. New Pesos

Mexico's "old pesos" were discontinued in favor of "new pesos" in 1993. Old pesos were legal

tender until Jan. 1, 1996, when they were called out of circulation. It's highly unlikely you'll come across any of the old currency, but if it's ever offered as change you shouldn't accept it as it's legally worthless. Old peso notes came in denominations of 1000, 5000, 10,000, etc.—each bill shows three more zeros than the corresponding "new" peso bills. Of course the new peso is now simply known as the peso.

Deflation

The Mexican peso has been in a deflationary spin since 1976 when the government decided to allow the national currency to "float" on the international money market. From 1976 to 1987 the exchange rate slid from eight pesos to the dollar to over 2,000. In 1988 the Bank of Mexico instituted measures to slow the decline to less than a centavo per day by the end of 1992. Following the switch to the new peso in '93, the peso actually gained in value against the U.S. dollar, until the 1995 devaluation sliced it down again. This was bad news for peso-spending Mexicans, but good news for dollar-holding bargain hunters.

At the moment the currency seems fairly stable, coming full circle to its 1976 value of around eight pesos to one U.S. dollar. This will undoubtedly slide further bit by bit—or all at once if the Mexican federal reserve tries too aggressively to prop the value up.

The relatively stable exchange rate means that changing money in Mexico is much less stressful now than just a few years ago; there's no need to check the exchange rate every day. Of course the devaluation continues to work in favor of the dollar-holder; the dollar bought roughly 40% more in 1997 than it did in 1994.

CHANGING MONEY

Banks

Banks offer the best exchange rate and they all offer the same rate, as set by the Bank of Mexico. This rate is usually posted behind the counter where foreign exchange is handled. They accept a wide range of foreign currencies, including American dollars, Canadian dollars, Swiss francs, German marks, English pounds, and Japanese yen. Either cash or traveler's checks are accepted, though the latter usually get a slightly better rate. The main drawbacks with banks are the long lines and short hours (Mon.-Fri. 9 a.m.-1:30 p.m., with the currency exchange service usually closing around noon-12:30 p.m.). With privatization, some banks are extending their hours.

Retirees age 55 and older living in Mexico may open an interest-bearing "Friendship Senior Checking Program" account at California Commerce Bank in Los Angeles that allows them to cash CCB checks at any branch of Banamex. Checks are free, and neither bank charges for check cashing. CCB is owned by Banamex but fully insured under FDIC.

Moneychangers

The second-best rate is at the *casa de cambio* or private moneychanging office. The *casa de cambio* (also called *servicio de cambio*) will either knock a few centavos off the going bank rate or charge a percentage commission. It pays to shop around for the best *casa de cambio* rate since some places charge considerably more commission than others. The rates are usually posted; *compra,* always the lower figure, refers to the buying rate for US$ (how many pesos you'll receive per dollar), while *vende* is the selling rate (how many pesos you must pay to receive a dollar). As with banks, the difference between the buying and selling rate is the moneychanger's profit, unless they charge commissions on top of it.

Moneychangers are usually open much longer hours than banks; some even have evening hours, which makes them immeasurably more convenient than banks. U.S. dollars are generally preferred, though many *casas* will also accept Canadian dollars. However, Canadians should always keep a reserve supply of U.S. dollars for instances where Canadian currency isn't accepted. Moneychangers will usually accept traveler's checks; some of the border-town *casas,* however, only take cash.

Only the larger towns and tourist centers have moneychanging offices. In smaller towns you'll have to resort to a bank or local merchant. Many store owners will be glad to buy dollars at a high-

ly variable and sometimes negotiable rate. Few will take traveler's checks, however, unless you make a purchase.

Moneychangers at Mexican airports (except in Mexico City) offer notoriously low rates. Try to buy pesos in advance of your trip if arriving by air, or pay with dollars until you can get to a bank or reasonable *casa de cambio.*

Hotels

Hotels, motels, *pensiones,* and other lodging places generally offer the worst exchange rates. If you're trying to save money, avoid changing currency where you stay, and pay for your room in pesos if possible—or better yet with a credit card—since the same low rate often applies to room charges paid in dollars.

Credit Cards and Debit Cards

Plastic money (primarily Visa and MasterCard) is widely accepted at large hotels, at restaurants catering to tourists or businesspeople, at car rentals (you can't rent a car without a credit card), and at shops in tourist centers or large cities. Usually card displays at the cash register or on the door will announce that *tarjetas de crédito* (credit cards) are accepted. If in doubt, flash one and ask *"¿Se aceptan tarjetas de crédito?"* or simply *"¿Está bien?"* A reference to *efectivo* means "cash." Credit cards are not accepted at most PEMEX stations.

Paying for goods and services in Mexico with credit cards that are paid through U.S. or Canadian banks can save you money, since the exchange rate will usually have dipped further in the dollar's favor by the time the transaction is posted at your bank. Many shops and some hotels, however, will add a 3-6% surcharge to bills paid with a card, which more than offsets the exchange rate differential. Cash advances on credit card accounts are available at Mexican banks.

Many banks now also accept MasterCard or Visa debit cards ("cash" or "check" cards) as well as ATM (automatic teller machine) cards on the Plus or Cirrus systems. Using such cards to obtain pesos from ATMs in Mexico is a much more convenient way to obtain travel funds than cashing traveler's checks. Some banks that issue ATM cards charge transaction fees for use of another bank's ATMs; check with your bank to see if these are reasonable. So far Mexican banks don't charge a fee for withdrawing cash from their ATMs with cards from other banks, but this may change over time.

MONEY MANAGEMENT

Estimating Costs

Inflation in Mexico is currently running at around 15-18% per annum, in large part due to the continued weakening of the peso on international markets but also because of a slight relaxation of wage and price controls. This means that when estimating your travel costs based on prices quoted in this book, some allowance must be made for ongoing inflation. Although peso prices will increase in direct proportion to the inflation rate, this isn't necessarily so for prices figured in dollars, since the dollar is continuing to gain in value against the peso.

Because of fluctuations in the peso-dollar ratio, and in an effort to keep prices up-to-date, all prices in this book are quoted in U.S. dollars. This doesn't mean, however, that there won't be any increase in prices by the time you arrive, book in hand. A couple of phone calls to hotels or other services for price quotes should give you an idea of rate increases, if any, and you can apply this difference as a percentage to all other prices for a rough estimate of costs.

Overall, the cost of living in Mexico is 30-50% lower than in most parts of the U.S. and Canada. Spending is virtually limitless while traveling, however; the key to keeping expenses down is to live as much like the locals as you can. If you're contemplating a long-term stay in Mexico, you might try reading a few issues of *AIM* (Adventures in Mexico), a well-edited bimonthly "newsletter on retirement and travel" that devotes a lot of space to analyzing and comparing prices in various Mexican cities. Subscriptions cost US$16 (C$19 in Canada) for one year; write to *AIM*, Apdo. Postal 31-70, Guadalajara, Jal. 45050.

Tipping and Taxes

A tip of 10-15% is customary at restaurants with table service unless a service charge is added to the bill. Luggage handling at hotels or airports warrants a tip of US$0.50, or the equivalent in pesos, per bag (a few hotels have a no-tipping policy, which will be posted in your room). The tipping of chambermaids is apparently optional according to Mexican custom—some guests tip and some don't. Remember that these folks typically earn minimum wage; even a small tip may mean a lot to them.

PEMEX station attendants don't need to be tipped unless they wash your windows, check the oil, or perform other extra services beyond pumping gas—the equivalent of US$0.25-0.50 in pesos is sufficient. When the change due on a gasoline purchase is less than five pesos, many drivers let the attendant keep the change.

In 1997 President Zedillo raised the 10% *impuesta al valor agregado* (IVA) or "value added tax" to 15% on all goods and services, including hotel and restaurant bills as well as international phone calls.

Student Discounts

A Tarjeta Plan Joven ("Youth Plan Card") entitles the holder to discounts on air and rail tickets, hotels, cultural activities, museums, books, and various other educational goods and services. The card is available to anyone who can show proof of current enrollment in a college or university. Obtain it from the Agencia Nacional de Turismo Juvenil, Glorieta Metro Insurgentes, Local CC-11, Col. Juárez, México, D.F., CP 06600, tel. (5) 25-2600. Along with the card you'll be issued a 100-page booklet listing the various discounts available.

Bank Accounts

For long-term stays in Mexico—six months or more—visitors might consider opening a Mexican bank account. Now that peso deflation has been virtually halted, a *small* peso account seems safe; Mexico hasn't had a single bank failure in 60 years. Interest earnings are refreshingly high compared to current rates in the U.S., Canada, or Europe. You can also open a U.S. dollar account at many banks, then convert to pesos at your leisure; these are much safer in the sense that you won't lose out if the peso dives, but they don't earn much interest.

Bancomer, BanCrecer (BanOro), Bital, and several other banks will accept personal checks drawn on U.S. banks from their account-holders. Probably the biggest advantage is that you won't have to worry about the short foreign-exchange hours kept by Mexican banks; you can bank right up till closing or use an ATM card.

COMMUNICATION

THE MEDIA

Newspapers

Every state capital in Northern Mexico publishes at least one Spanish-language daily newspaper. Monterrey's *El Norte* is widely recognized as being the best and is available in cities throughout the North. Even if your Spanish is minimal, city newspapers are worth looking at for current information on museum exhibits and local cinema. Check the comics section for American comic strips with translated dialogue balloons and titles—Lorenzo y Pepita (Blondie), El Fantasma (The Phantom), and Hombre Araña (Spiderman) are Mexican favorites.

Along the border and in Mazatlán, English-language dailies from U.S. cities are sometimes sold in hotel lobbies or city newsstands. Elsewhere, *USA Today* and the *International Herald Tribune* are occasionally available. You may also come across *The News*, an English newspaper published in Mexico City and heavily oriented toward Mexico City residents. A newer English-language daily from Mexico City, the *Mexico City Times*, is harder to find outside the capital. Each Saturday the *Times* features the *Guardian Weekly*, a 20-page supplement featuring international news from the British daily of the same name, while on Monday the paper includes the eight-page *New York Times Weekly Review*.

Radio and Television

Communities in a wide swath of the border area pick up radio and TV broadcasts from both sides of the border. Further south the U.S. stations begin to fade, and in the more remote areas you may find yourself out of range of even Mexican broadcast media. In urban areas, a variety of radio stations can be picked up. Consider bringing along a shortwave radio if you're a news fanatic.

Mexican TV offers a mix of American dramas and sitcoms dubbed in Spanish, as well as Mexico's own versions of the same formulas. Mexico's famous *telenovelas*—soap opera series that run several months rather than several years—are exported all over Latin America. Immensely popular Ed Sullivan-style weekend variety shows like *Siempre en Domingo* ("Always on Sunday") mix circus acts, scantily clad female *cantantes*, celebrity interviews, and Latin rock groups.

Many hotels and motels have their own satellite dishes with as many as 50 channels from Mexico and the U.S. on tap.

CB Radio

Visitors are permitted to operate CB radios with five watts of transmission power or less. Three channels are specially designated for visitor use: channel 9 for emergencies, channel 10 for communication among visitors, and channel 11 for local information broadcasts.

POSTAL SERVICE

The Mexican postal service is reliable but relatively slow. Delivery time has been shortened by 75% since 1989, the year a full government subsidy for Sepomex (Servicio Postal Mexicana) was discontinued and the Ministry of Communications and Transport ordered the agency to become self-sufficient. Average delivery time from Mexico to the U.S. or Canada is about 10 days, while to Europe you must figure two weeks. Mail sent to Mexico from outside the country generally reaches its destination more quickly.

Most towns in Mexico have a post office *(correo)* where you can receive general delivery mail. Have correspondents address mail in your name (last name capitalized), followed by a/c Lista de Correos, the town name, and the state, e.g., Joe CUMMINGS, a/c Lista de Correos, Alamos, Sonora, Mexico. Mail sent this way is usually held 10 days. If you want your mail held up to 30 days, substitute the words "Poste Restante, Correo Central" for Lista de Correos in the address, e.g. Joe CUMMINGS, a/c Poste Restante, Correo Central, Alamos, Sonora, Mexico. If you have the postal code for the town or city, insert it just after the state name. Since delivery time is highly variable, it's best to use poste restante just to be safe.

In small towns and villages, residents don't often use street addresses, simply the addressee's name followed by *domicilio conocido* ("known residence") and the name of the town or village. Even in large towns and cities, addresses may use the name of the street without a building number (*sin número,* abbreviated as "s/n"), or will mention the nearest cross streets (e.g., *ent. Abasolo y Revolución,* or "between Abasolo and Revolución").

The usual post office hours are Mon.-Fri. 9 a.m.-6 p.m., Sat.-Sun. 9 a.m.-noon. Offices in large cities and state capitals may stay open to 6 or 7 p.m., and some small town *correos* close for a 2-4 p.m. siesta.

Many foreigners who are seasonal residents have their mail sent in care of a hotel or RV park. You can rent boxes at larger Mexican post offices but the initial application process often takes several weeks. Some towns have private mail companies (e.g., Mail Boxes, Etc.) that also rent boxes but with minimal red tape.

The Mexican post office offers an express mail service called Mexpost. International rates are relatively high; a Mexpost express letter to the U.S. or Canada, for example, costs US$15, to Europe US$20. Mexpost claims to deliver almost anywhere in Mexico within 48 hours, to major cities around the world within 72 hours. A Mexpost parcel cannot exceed 1.05 meters along any one dimension or weigh more than 20 kilos.

UPS, Airborne Express, DHL, FedEx, and other courier services now operate in Mexico. So far DHL and UPS seem to offer the lowest prices and best services. Local companies such as Estafeta and Aeroflash have also entered the business. I recently mailed a package successfully from Parras de la Fuente, Coah., to Chiang Mai, Thailand, using Aeroflash.

TELEPHONE SERVICE

Local Numbers

Most telephone numbers in Mexico consist of five or six digits, though Mexico City, Monterrey, and Guadalajara feature seven-digit numbers. There's no standard way of hyphenating the numbers; a five-digit number may appear as 211-13, 2-11-13, or 2-1113, while a six-digit number may be rendered 341720, 341-520, 34-17-20, or 34-1720.

TelMex

The national telephone company, TelMex, privatized in 1990 and has improved its services considerably over the last few years. Local phone calls are relatively cheap—a one-peso coin will pay for a phone-booth call—as are long-distance calls *within* Mexico. If you can find a working phone—many public phones seem permanently out of order—connections are usually good, though you may have to wait a while to get through to the operator during busy periods like Sundays and holidays.

A public pay-phone service from TelMex called Ladatel (acronym for "Larga Distancia Teléfono") offers phone booths where you can pay for local and long-distance calls with coins, credit cards, or debit cards. The only credit cards currently accepted are those issued by Banamex, Bancomer, or Carnet in Mexico. You can purchase debit cards in denominations of five, 10, 20, 30, and 50 pesos at many pharmacies, convenience stores, supermarkets, bus terminals, and airports.

If you don't want to use a phone booth or a hotel phone (hotels usually add their own surcharges to both local and long-distance calls), you can make a call during business hours from a TelMex office. Only large towns offer TelMex offices with public telecommunications facilities; a small town might have a private telephone office (usually called *caseta de teléfono*) in the corner of a local shop, where you can make calls. Like hotels, private telephone offices add surcharges to calls.

Competing Services

In January 1997, the Ministry of Communications and Transport began allowing other telecommunications companies to compete with TelMex for long-distance services. So far the companies that have been legally permitted to set up shop in Mexico include Iusatel, Avantel (MCI), Alestra (AT&T), and Miditel. Each of these has its own access code for direct dialing; see the "Telephone Codes" chart for a list. AT&T has already begun laying fiber-optic line in several parts of the country in an effort to come online with superior infrastructure right from the beginning. If trends follow what we've seen in phone service deregulation in other parts of the world, we can expect phone services in Mexico to improve while costs come down over the next few years.

**Domestic Long-Distance
and Toll-Free Calls**
At the moment, TelMex long-distance rates anywhere within Mexico—regardless of distance—

cost a flat rate of about US$0.29 per minute most of the time, half that after 8 p.m. Mon.-Sat. and all day Sunday. To make a long-distance call within Mexico, dial 01 plus the area code and number. To reach toll-free (800) numbers in Mexico, dial 01 first.

International Calls
To direct dial an international call via TelMex,

TELEPHONE CODES

Long-distance operator (national): 020
Time: 030
Directory Assistance (local): 040
Mexico City area code: 05
Police, Red Cross, Fire: 060
Spanish-English emergency information: 07
International operator: 090
Long-distance direct dialing from Mexico via TelMex:
   station to station (in Mexico): 01 + area code + number
   person to person (in Mexico): 02 + area code + number
   station to station (U.S. and Canada): 00 + 1 + area code + number
   person to person (U.S. and Canada): 09 + 1 + area code + number
   station to station (other international): 00 + area code + number
   person to person (other international): 09 + area code + number
Other long distance companies (precede code with 010 for Mexico long distance, or with 000 for international):
   Iusatel: 333; or 01-800-81-918 for customer service
   Avantel: (MCI) 111; or 01-800-921-2020 for customer service
   Alestra: (AT&T) 288; or 01-800-455-34 for customer service
   Miditel: 100; or 01-800-91-277 for customer service
   Example: To make a long distance call outside Mexico using MCI, dial 000 111 + area code + number.

Northern Mexico area codes (see individual destination descriptions for other towns and cities):

Chihuahua, Chih.: 14	Guaymas, Son.: 622	Saltillo, Coah.: 84
Ciudad Juárez, Chih.: 16	Hermosillo, Son.: 62	San Luis Potosí, S.L.P.: 48
Ciudad Victoria, Tamps.: 131	Mazatlán, Sin.: 69	Tampico, Tamps.: 12
Culiacán, Sin.: 67	Monterrey, N.L.: 8	Torreón, Coah.: 17
Durango, Dgo.: 18	Nogales, Son.: 631	Zacatecas, Zac.: 492
	Nuevo Laredo, Tamps.: 87	**Mexico country code:** 52

To call Mexico direct from outside the country, dial 011 + 52 + area code + number. Example: to call the number 20-0361 in Chihuahua from the U.S., dial 011 (international code) + 52 (Mexico country code) + 14 (Chihuahua area code) + 20-0361 (the phone number in Chihuahua).

Help: SECTUR (the Ministry of Tourism) maintains a 24-hour traveler's aid "hotline" for emergencies of all kinds: 01 (5) 250-0123 or 250-0151.

dial 00 plus the area code and number for a station-to-station call, or 09 plus area code and number for a person-to-person or other operator-assisted call. Long-distance international calls are heavily taxed and cost more than equivalent international calls from the U.S. or Canada. (TelMex international rates run about the same as AT&T's, sometimes cheaper depending on time of day and call destination.)

For international calls via other service providers, you'll need to first dial an access number connecting you with your phone company of preference. From Mexico, you can reach AT&T by dialing 01-800-462-4240, a toll-free call that connects you with a USADirect system. For MCI the number is 01-800-674-7000, for Sprint 01-800-977-8000. For Canada Direct, dial 01-800-010-1990, and for BT Direct dial *791 ("star" 791). The appropriate long-distance operator can then place a collect call on your behalf or charge the call to your account if you have a calling card for that service. If you try these numbers from a hotel phone, be sure the hotel operator realizes the call is toll-free; some hotel operators use their own timers to assess phone charges.

You can also try a brand new system for making direct international calls via TelMex's competitors; dial 000 plus the company code (see the Telephone Codes chart) plus the area code and number.

Collect Calls

For international service, calling collect often saves hassles. In Spanish the magic words are *por cobrar* (collect), prefaced by the name of the place you're calling (e.g., *"a los Estados Unidos, por favor—por cobrar"*). This will connect you to an English-speaking international operator. For best results, speak slowly and clearly. You're supposed to be able to obtain an international operator directly by dialing 09, but this number doesn't always work.

Warning

Since the deregulation of Mexican telephone service, several private, U.S.-based long-distance phone companies have set up shop in Mexico to take advantage of undiscerning tourists. Often the same company operates under several different corporate names in the same area, charging at least 50% more per international call than TelMex, AT&T, MCI, or Sprint —as much as US$10-20 for the first minute, plus US$4 each additional minute, even on weekends. A percentage of these charges usually goes to the hotel or private phone office offering the service. At most private phone offices it's cheaper to use TelMex, even if you have to pay a service charge on top of TelMex rates, than to use these fly-by-night U.S. companies.

Always ask which telephone company is being used before you arrange an international call through a hotel or private phone office. And beware if next to a phone you see an English-language sign reading "Call the U.S. or Canada Collect or With a Credit Card" or "Just Dial Zero to Reach the U.S. or Canada."

ON-LINE SERVICES

A number of on-line service providers offer information on different aspects of Mexico, and the number of World Wide Web sites with data on the country is multiplying daily. You can expect a general search under the single keyword "Mexico" to turn up at least 50,000 references, perhaps many more. Many of these are commercial sites established by tour operators or hotels. The ratio of commercial to noncommercial sites is liable to increase over time if current Internet trends continue.

You'll do better to narrow down your search by starting out with a few known URLs (universal resource locators) and working from there using links to other resources. See the chart, "Useful Internet Sites with Information on Mexico." All URLs are subject to change without notice; a couple of them even changed addresses while we were compiling this section. You can of course use your own Web browser to conduct searches. Webcrawler (http://query.webcrawler. com) and Yahoo (http://www.yahoo.com) work well for blind searches.

Moon's own Web site (http://www.moon.com) contains occasional excerpts from this book and other Moon titles, ordering information, an on-line travel newsletter, and links to various other related sites.

On-line in Mexico

If you're bringing a computer and modem to Northern Mexico with hopes of staying on the infobahn, note that on-line options are limited to a handful of local Internet service providers and a few international ones. Baud rates can be slow—you'll probably have trouble logging on at speeds of 28.8 kbps or greater, bottle-necked by low bandwidth and line interrupts in the Mexican phone system. With fiber-optic cables on the way in many parts of the country, this could change rapidly, though much depends on the kind of equipment installed at any given town linked with fiber optics.

CompuServe Interactive, America Online, and IBM Global are the only international providers so far that provide local access phone numbers in Mexico. AT&T and MCI may be entering the market soon. As usual outside the U.S., CompuServe Interactive (CSi) claims the largest market share at 45%, with some 18,000 subscribers as of 1997. So far it is the most reliable service because it has the most highly developed computer networking infrastructure. CSi is available at baud rates up to 28.8 kbps (14.4 kbps in everyday practice).

RJ11 phone jacks are the standard in newer hotels, but in older hotels, motels, and *casas de huéspedes* the phones may still be hard-wired; you might want to bring either an acoustic coupler or a pocketknife and pair of alligator clips for stripping and attaching wires. You can also take your laptop to a local phone office in Mexico and ask to plug into their system. Most phone offices are cooperative if you're polite and explain what you're up to. We've encountered a few small-town offices that seemed to fear that our laptop would suck all the electric power in the town dry, or that we would call Mongolia and charge it as a call to Mexico City. Sometimes a good bit of explanation is necessary. If the office telephone is hard-wired, ask if they have a fax machine, since all fax units use standard RJ11 jacks.

We've seen a few cybercafes in Mexico City and La Paz offering public terminals where you can send and receive e-mail or browse the Web, but so far haven't found anything similar in mainland Northern Mexico. Monterrey should have something of this nature in the near future if not already.

MEASUREMENTS AND TIME

Electricity

Mexico's electrical system is basically the same as that in the U.S. and Canada: 110 volts, 60 cycles, alternating current (AC). Electrical outlets are of the American type, designed to work with appliances that have standard double-bladed plugs. Small towns in some rural areas may from time to time experience brief interruptions of electrical service or periods of brownout (voltage decrease). In a few villages, gasoline-powered generators are the only source of electricity and they may be turned off during the day.

Measurements

Mexico, like most countries in the world, uses the metric system as the official system of weights and measures. This means that the distance between Nogales and Mazatlán is measured in kilometers, cheese is weighed in grams or kilograms, a hot day in Monterrey is 32° C, gasoline is sold by the liter, and a big fish is two

meters long. A chart at the end of this book will help Americans make the conversions from pounds, gallons, and miles to kilos, liters, and kilometers (or vice versa) when necessary.

Norteños used to dealing with American tourists will often use the Anglo-American and metric systems interchangeably. Even rancheros in remote areas occasionally use *millas* (miles) as a measure.

In this book, distances will be given in kilometers, followed by miles in parentheses. Heights are given in meters—American users can simply multiply by three for a close equivalent in feet. Boating and fishing terms (boat lengths, line test) are quoted in feet and pounds since that's the norm in Mexico due to American influence in these spheres.

Time

The states of Sonora and Sinaloa belong to the mountain time zone, as followed in the U.S. and

Canada. The rest of the mainland to the east follows central time (Greenwich Mean Time + 7). This means you should set your timepieces an hour ahead when crossing the Sonora or Sinaloa state lines going east, or an hour back when crossing west.

In 1996 Mexico began observing daylight saving time, so you must reset your clocks in the spring and fall as in the U.S. and Canada ("spring" forward an hour the first Sunday in April, "fall" back an hour the last Sunday in October).

The time in Mexico is commonly expressed according to the 24-hour clock, from 0001 to 2359 (one minute past midnight to 11:59 p.m.) rather than the Anglo-American 12-hour system. A restaurant that posts hours of 1100-2200,

for example, is open 11 a.m.-10 p.m. Signs may be posted using either system.

Business Hours
The typical small business will be open Mon.-Fri. (Saturday for retail businesses) 9 a.m.-2 p.m., closed until about 4-5 p.m., and then re-opened until about 7-8 p.m. Official government offices typically maintain an 8:30 a.m.-3 p.m. schedule (although Secretary of Tourism offices will usually open again 5-7 p.m.).

Most banks are open Mon.-Fri. 8:30 a.m.-1:30 p.m., but remember that the foreign currency-exchange service usually closes down around noon (probably to lock in the exchange rate before afternoon adjustments).

LEGALITIES

Legal Codes and Enforcement
All foreign visitors in Mexico are subject to Mexican legal codes, which are based on a combination of Roman and Napoleonic law updated with U.S. constitutional theory and civil law. Unlike Anglo-American judicial systems, the Mexican judiciary system doesn't provide for trials by jury (instead, the judge decides) nor writs of habeas corpus (though you must be charged within 72 hours of incarceration). Furthermore, bail is rarely granted to an arrested foreigner—for many offenses, not even Mexican nationals are allowed bail. Hence, once you are arrested and jailed for a serious offense, it can be very difficult to arrange release. The lesson here is: Don't get involved in matters that might result in your arrest—this primarily means anything having to do with drugs or guns.

The oft-repeated myth that in Mexico an arrested person is considered guilty until proven innocent is no more true south of the border than north. As in the U.S. and many other countries with civil law, an arrested person is considered a criminal *suspect* until the courts confirm or deny guilt. You have the right to notify your consulate if detained.

Mexican federal police or *federales,* as well as the Mexican army, occasionally set up roadblocks to conduct searches for drugs, mostly under pressure from the United States. In Northern Mexico such roadblocks have become in-

creasingly common in the states of Chihuahua, Sinaloa, and Durango. If your vehicle is stopped by a roadblock, it's best to be as cooperative as possible. If you notice any irregularities or if you object to the way in which the procedure is carried out, make note of the incident (including whatever badge numbers, names, or license tag numbers you can obtain *discreetly*) and later file a report with the Mexican Attorney General for Tourist Protection (see "In Case of Arrest," below, for more detail).

La Mordida
In the past, Mexican police had a reputation for hassling foreigners, especially those who drove their own vehicles in Mexico. Tales of the legendary *mordida* or minor bribe (literally "bite"), supposedly a necessary part of navigating one's way around Mexico, swelled way out of proportion to reality but were nonetheless based on real incidents.

For several years now, the Mexican police have for the most part ceased singling out foreigners for arrest, partly as a result of anticorruption efforts by the federal government but, more importantly, because of a conscious effort to attract more tourists. The vast majority of foreign visitors who drive in Northern Mexico these days complete their trips without any police hassles. (See also "Driving in Northern Mexico," above.)

Military

In recent years the Mexican government has replaced many federal police officers around the country with active-duty army officers in an effort to clean up corruption among nonmilitary law-enforcement agencies. Opinions are sharply divided as to whether this is having a net positive or negative effect, but it's a fact that you can see more military around the country than at any time in Mexico's history since 1920. Road-block inspection points or *puestos de control* along major and minor highways have become increasingly common. All manner of vehicles—buses, trucks, private autos—may be stopped and searched at such inspection points and if you get caught in one the best thing to do is simply be patient till it's over, usually in five minutes or less. For the most part, soldiers stationed at these checkpoints perform their duties in a serious but respectful manner. Typically they speak very little English and this usually works in favor of the non-Spanish-speaking foreign visitor as it means they can't ask too many questions.

In rural areas, particularly in the Sierra Madre Occidental, you may also encounter military squadrons camped by the side of the road or moving around the countryside. In most cases in Northern Mexico they will be pursuing suspected *narcotraficantes,* trying to intercept drug shipments, or searching for marijuana or opium poppy plantations. In such cases soldiers rarely approach foreign visitors, although roadblock inspection points may also be established in these areas.

Drugs

Marijuana, and to a lesser extent opium, is cultivated in remote areas of the Sierra Madre Occidental in the states of Sinaloa, Chihuahua, and Durango. For the most part, drug plantations are well hidden from the view of tourists, hikers, and other passersby, hence there is little danger in traveling in these areas if you don't poke your nose too far off the beaten path.

The main area where you need to be careful not to stray off the main trails is between Urique and Batopilas in the Sierra Tarahumara. In recent years Mexican soldiers have patrolled this area regularly, however, so the fields are being pushed farther back into seldom-visited areas. Occasionally an overzealous hiker in the Sierra Tarahumara region may stray far from the trail and stumble onto a pot patch; the best thing to do if this happens is immediately leave the vicinity. Should you be accosted by a grower or guard, make it clear that you're merely a *turista* and didn't intend to disturb the farm; better yet, pretend you don't know what the stuff is.

Given the stiff penalties for contraband drug possession in Mexico, it would be foolish of any foreign visitor to attempt to purchase either marijuana or opium in Northern Mexico.

In Case of Arrest

If you get into trouble with the Mexican law, for whatever reason, you should try to contact your nearest consulate in Mexico (when there is one —embassies and consulates for each town are listed in this book under the respective destinations). SECTUR and state tourist offices can also be of help in some instances. These agencies routinely handle emergency legal matters involving visiting foreigners; you stand a much better chance of resolving legal difficulties with their assistance.

Conservemos el jaguar

MEXICO N$1.3

G. NORMA G. VERGARA   T.I.E.V.

THE STATE OF SONORA

Unsuccessful early Spanish incursions into the area now encompassed by the state of Sonora left it terra incognita until the 17th and early 18th centuries. The first Europeans to settle in the area were Jesuit missionaries intent on converting and baptizing the various resident O'odham or Papago Indian groups, including the Tohono O'odham, Hiached O'odham, and Gila River Pima, many of whom today claim to be descendants of the semimythic Hohokam of the Greater Southwest. To the Spanish these peoples were collectively known as the "Pima," and the area they inhabited was called "Pimería." The name for the state derives from the Pata Indian word Xunutta ("Place Where Corn Grows"), which became corrupted to "Sonota" and finally to "Sonora" by the Spanish.

The discovery of gold in Alamos brought a steady stream of nonmissionary settlers up from the south and by 1824 the former province of Sonora y Sinaloa had become the state of Occidente. During Occidente's eight-year existence, the capital alternated between the important mining centers of Alamos, El Fuerte (Sin.), and Cosalá (Sin.).

Occidente was eventually divided into the separate states of Sonora and Sinaloa. In both states the main centers of activity tended to be along the lower western slopes of the Sierra Madre Occidental, a storehouse of mineral wealth.

Luckily, at about the time the mines played out, fishing on the Sea of Cortez and agriculture on the Yaqui and Sonora River plains expanded to support the local economy. Today the state holds the nation's most important fisheries and produces about a third of Mexico's annual *ajonjalí* (sesame) crop, as well as an assortment of grains, vegetables, grapes, oranges, and olives.

A more recent contributor to the state economy is tourism; Sonora draws visitors with a warm year-round climate, 916 km of coastline, and an average of 360 days of sunshine per year.

Sonorans take pride in the fact that their state is the birthplace of three former presidents: Alvaro Obregón, Abelardo Rodríguez, and Plutarco Elías Calles. Presidential candidate Luis Donaldo Colosio, assassinated while campaigning in Tijuana in 1994, also hailed from the state.

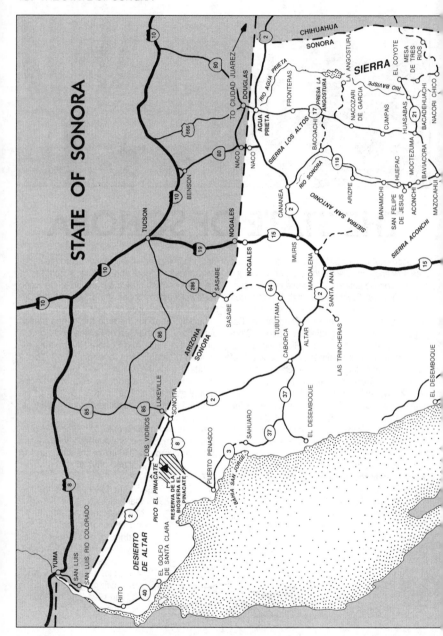

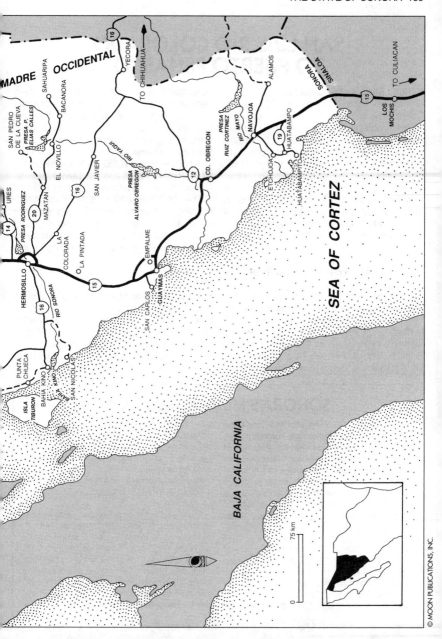

SAN LUIS RÍO COLORADO TO PUERTO PEÑASCO

Sonoita-San Luis Río Colorado

On Mexico 2 between Sonoita and San Luis Río Colorado you may encounter an agricultural checkpoint for "white mosquito plague." Here a Mexican official may check your papers, then use a vacuum cleaner-type contraption to blow compressed air beneath the dashboard of your vehicle—ostensibly to destroy white mosquito larvae. In spite of this slight red tape, the Sonoita-San Luis Río Colorado drive is worthwhile as it passes prime Sonoran Desert scenery, offers views of the Sierra del Pinacate to the south, and provides easy access to El Pinacate Biosphere Reserve.

EL PINACATE NATIONAL PARK

Between San Luis Río Colorado, Sonoita, and Puerto Peñasco is one of the most spectacular volcanic regions in the Americas. Reserva de la Biosfera El Pinacate y Gran Desierto de Altar, marked on some maps as "Parque Nacional del Gran Desierto del Pinacate," is a 2,000-square-km natural area holding more than 10,000 vol-

canic apertures, of which only about 500 have been studied and classified. The extensive lava fields and huge craters dot a volcanic desert region known in Mexico as El Desierto de Altar. This striking landscape has inspired at least three early 20th-century Western novels: *Desert Gold* (Zane Grey, 1913), *Dust of the Desert* (R.W. Ritchie, 1922), and *The Devil's Highway* (Harold Bell Wright and John Lebar, 1932).

The park is named for the 1,270-meter (4,166-foot) **Pico El Pinacate,** which in turn is named for the *pinacate,* an endemic beetle that sits vertically on end when threatened. The peak is part of the Sierra del Pinacate, a mountain range roughly 24 km long and about half as wide.

History

Pico El Pinacate and the second-tallest peak in the range, Pico Carnegie (1,254 meters/4,113 feet, just northeast of Pico El Pinacate) are the remnants of a great volcano dubbed Volcán Santa Clara by Padre Kino, who visited the area in 1701 and 1706. Though no one yet knows for sure, Santa Clara may have erupted as far

SONORA'S MINIMAL RED TAPE

The Sonoran state government introduced a new program in 1995 that enables motorists to bring foreign-registered vehicles into the state without going through the time-consuming federal temporary import permit process at the border. All you need is a passport or other proof of citizenship (such as a birth certificate or voter-registration card), plus a photo ID, and the regular FMT tourist card required for all visits to Mexico. You can cross the Arizona-Sonora border anywhere you like, but must proceed to the "Only Sonora" booth at Km 21 on Mexico 15, south of Nogales, to take care of the minimal paperwork. At this booth you'll show your driver's license and the title or registration (or lease/rental contract in the case of leased or rented cars) for the vehicle and fill out a "Promise to Return Vehicle" letter that you must sign. The staff then applies a

hologramic decal to the windshield of your vehicle and provides a "Temporary Import of Tourist Vehicle" card, which you must return when you leave the state. That's it: no credit cards or posting of bond are necessary.

For further information on this program call (800) 4-SONORA in the U.S. or Canada, or 01-(800) 62-55 in Mexico.

If you will be proceeding farther south or east into the states of Sinaloa or Chihuahua, you will need the regular temporary vehicle import permit; see "Entry Regulations" under "Immigration, Customs, and Crossing the Border" in the On the Road chapter for details on Mexican customs requirements. If you're heading west into Baja California, you won't need any papers at all other than your own vehicle registration and tourist card.

back as 10,000 years ago. The area's most recent volcanic eruption—relatively small—took place in 1935 near Cráter El Elegante.

Following Kino's visit, Pinacate wasn't visited by another European until 1882. The first extended exploration of Pinacate was carried out by the MacDougal-Hornaday expedition in 1907. Although Volcán Santa Clara was the first extinct volcano recognized in North America, it is the last to be studied in detail. Much about the area remains a geological mystery.

The forbidding terrain here has been inhabited by Amerindians for at least 10,000 years. Stone sleeping circles (low, semicircular walls used as windbreaks) and ground mesquite beans found in lava caves suggest Pinacate was a habitat for the paleolithic San Dieguitos. The later Sand Papagos believed the larger craters to be an abode of the god of fire. When Padre Kino crossed Pinacate, the Papago residents he encountered wore rabbit fur, gathered roots and insects, fished in the gulf, and farmed corn, tubers, and beans on the sand flats.

Today a few Papagos and a small number of hardy Mexicans live on *ejido* lands adjacent to

park boundaries. Their houses are typically patchwork constructions of discarded wood, cardboard, and corrugated metal, along with various desert materials such as ocotillo or sotol branches.

Since 1979 Pinacate and the surrounding Desierto de Altar has been a U.N.-designated Biosphere Reserve, an internationally recognized honor bestowed on natural environments considered of global significance.

Flora and Fauna

According to the International Sonoran Desert Alliance, Pinacate is a habitat for over 560 plant species, 56 mammal species, 43 reptile species, 222 bird species, and four fish species. Protected here are the rare Sonoran antelope and desert bighorn sheep, who find water and shelter in volcanic craters during the winter. *Paisanos* (roadrunners) are common; some of the biggest specimens seen in Mexico or the U.S. Southwest are here.

The desert serves as an important habitat for rattlesnakes, so watch out for them, especially at night when they're usually more active. Also

Papagos gathering fruit of the pitahaya cactus, as sketched by U.S. border surveyor William Emory in the 1850s

keep an eye out for the gila monster (in Spanish called *escorpión*), a large lizard with beadlike orange and black scales; its bite is venomous.

Geologic Features

Pinacate's remarkable landscape varies wildly from sand dunes to black cinder cones to red-rimmed craters, interspersed with classic Sonoran Desert vegetation. The largest sand dunes are found to the south and west, the most impressive lava fields to the northeast. In total the reserve contains 10 giant craters and over 400 cinder cones. If you're into vulcanism, you'll have plenty of opportunity for identifying maars, calderas, fumaroles, pressure ridges, lava tubes, lava levees, and other arcane features that don't mean much to those who don't know tuff from tough.

The six largest **craters**—Elegante, Sykes (Volcán Romo), Molina, Cerro Colorado, Celaya, and Badilla—are fairly accessible from the northern park entrances off Mexico 2. Cráter El Ele-

gante is the largest (1,440 meters/4,723 feet rim to rim, 240 meters/787 feet deep) and most visited of these. You can walk Elegante's rim in two to three hours. Get an early morning start as the exposed trail tends to get hot, even in winter. The view into the crater is stupendous. Along the way you'll see exemplary cholla, mesquite, ocotillo, saguaro, cenizo, paloverde, and torote, and perhaps spot some bighorn sheep tracks. The sheep themselves are shy and rarely seen by human visitors.

Although it's thrilling to imagine you're strolling along the edges of extinct volcanoes, the visible crater rims are not actually the edges of the original calderas but rather are "rim beds" formed by falling debris after eruption. The "craters" are depressions left after the cone collapsed and all the gases had been expelled.

Between Cráter El Elegante and the Sierra del Pinacate lie the youngest and visually most spectacular **lava fields** in the region. The terrain here is typical flow breccia, in which lava hardened on top while remaining molten below— the surface still has a "fluid" appearance. Contrary to popular myth, the lava fields here are crossable on foot, although the 16-km (10-mile) hike from one end to the other will totally ruin all but the sturdiest footwear.

The park's massive **dune fields** are best reached via a six-km (3.7-mile) unpaved road that heads west from Mexico 8 near Km 73. Don't try driving on the dunes and don't lose sight of your parked vehicle unless you bring a compass and take a cautionary heading. Near the dunes are the **Papago Tanks,** a set of *tinajas* (rock pools) that provide the park's only year-round source of water; annual rainfall here averages a scant 7-10 cm (three to four inches) a year.

Permits

A permit is legally required to visit the reserve. These are available free at the Sonoita border crossing and at ranger facilities near the southern end of Pinacate, about 30 miles from Sonoita at Km 52 on the highway to Puerto Peñasco. Many people visit Cráter El Elegante on day-trips without a permit. The staff at the ranger station are very helpful, speak a little English, and provide bilingual brochures describing the flora, fauna, and volcanic geography of the area.

Camping

A night spent under the stars in Pinacate is a special experience—coyotes and cactus owls provide the soundtrack; kangaroo rats dance in the moonlight; and St. Elmo's Fire occasionally flashes off the peaks. Camping is permitted anywhere in the reserve, as long as camps are established at least a kilometer from any road or crater. Camps are limited to three persons per site. Because the occasional dope smuggler uses park trails as a nighttime route to the border (in order to avoid Mexico 2), probably the safest area to camp is at one of the *ejidos* along the park's north edge on the south side of Mexico 2—ask for permission first. There are also two official campgrounds signed "El Tecolote" (8.3 km/five miles northeast of Cráter Elegante) and "Cono Rojo" (23.3 km/14 miles northwest of the information center), each with zero facilities. Remember: no rock-collecting; pack out all trash; no plants or wildlife should be disturbed; no hunting or gathering.

Bring at least one gallon of water per person per day; summer temperatures can reach 48° C (118° F).

Getting There

The main road into El Pinacate National Park from Mexico 2 (near Los Vidrios at Km 51) is black cinder, passable by ordinary passenger car for the first 6.5 km (four miles). Here the road jogs right at a quarry (a small wooden sign reads "Elegante/Puerto Peñasco") and becomes rougher and sandier. Vehicles without high road clearance should be left here—the deep, sandy *vados* ahead can be tough going. Though it's not absolutely necessary, 4WD certainly comes in handy. From this junction it's 9.5 km (six miles) to another right turn toward Elegante—look for white road markers—then less than a kilometer more to the base of the cone. It's worth the hike (if your vehicle can't make the drive and you're well prepared for desert hiking) to view the gigantic, four-meter chollas along the way, plus stands of torote, creosote bush, saguaro, and biznaga.

This same road connects with Mexico 8, the highway to Puerto Peñasco from Sonoita, between Km 51 and 52. The route isn't straightforward, however, and the selection of branch roads along the way has caused many a driver to

get lost or end up back on Mexico 2—a compass helps. If you're coming from Puerto Peñasco, look for the water tower on the left.

The most colorful time to visit Pinacate is in the spring when the sand verbena, cactus, and paloverde trees are in bloom.

Another entrance to Pinacate can be found along Mexico 2 at Km 71, 72 km (44 miles) southwest of Sonoita. For the most part the road leading into the interior from this entrance is limited to high-clearance vehicles, preferably with 4WD. This is the road to take for the MacDougal, Sykes, and Molina Craters.

Further Information

Two of the best sources of information on Pinacate are the International Sonoran Desert Alliance (Alianza Desierto Sonorense), P.O. Box 687, Ajo, AZ 85321, tel. (520) 387-6823, fax 387-5626, and PRONATURA, 240 E. Limberlost, Tucson, AZ 85705, tel. (602) 887-1188. Write either organization for a Sierra del Pinacate map and guide containing information on the region's flora, fauna, geology, and history. The Sonoran Desert Alliance is currently developing a project to create a bilateral/binational "borderlands management area" that would link the Pinacate biosphere reserve with U.S. parklands throughout southern Arizona.

SAN LUIS RÍO COLORADO

Squeezed into the northwesternmost corner of the state on the east bank of the Río Colorado, this border town was originally settled by boat via the Río Colorado and Sea of Cortez. The river once watered a vast delta region, but has been slowed to a trickle by 10 dams erected upriver in the United States. Although the entire river originally belonged to Mexico, local farmers now depend on metered flows from the U.S. side to irrigate their fields.

The town itself is essentially a collection of shops catering to local cotton farmers and border traders. Several *maquiladoras,* including U.S. audio-component manufacturer Bose and Korean TV/VCR/computer-monitor giant Daewoo, have arrived in the last few years, fleeing overdeveloped maquila centers to the west in Tijuana and Mexicali.

Crossing the Border

Compared to Nogales or Agua Prieta to the east, few visitors enter Northern Mexico via San Luis Río Colorado—all the more reason to choose this gateway if you're coming from the U.S. West Coast and prefer to avoid heavy border traffic. The crossing here is open 24 hours.

On the immediate U.S. side of the border is San Luis, Arizona. San Luis is even smaller than its Mexican counterpart, little more than a farming community. If you're planning to stock up on food or other supplies for a Sonora road excursion, you'll do better to stop at one of the large supermarkets in Yuma on your way to the border. Opposite the Del Sol market in San Luis, Arizona, is an agency that sells Mexican insurance.

Once across the border, be sure to check in at the customs office if you need a temporary vehicle importation permit (see "Customs" under "Immigration, Customs, and Crossing the Border" in the On the Road chapter).

You Bet

The **San Luis Turf and Greyhound Club,** a block west of the border, offers off-track betting on televised greyhound and horse races throughout the U.S. and Mexico, as well as sports book, a full bar, and food service.

Accommodations

Budget: Motel Continental, tel. (653) 4-2386, and **Motel Río Colorado** are both on Av. Obregón and both in the US$20-30 range.

Inexpensive: The best lodging in town is **Hotel San Angel Valle Grande,** Av. Obregón 1050, tel. (653) 4-0101, which offers a/c, satellite TV, pool, and jacuzzi. Rates: US$40-45.

Food

Since this town doesn't get many border tourists, few eating places offer facilities designed to attract gringos. For steak and Sonora's famous *carne asada,* locals recommend **Restaurante El Herradero,** Av. Obregón between Calles 11 and 12, tel. (653) 4-4060. For Mexican fare, **Restaurante Tres Amigos,** Obregón at Morelos, tel. (653) 4-1386, is also good. If you're in the mood for something quick and cheap, look for the street vendors and burrito stands along Calle 2 and Av. Obregón. **Taquería El Rey,** Obregón at Calle 12, serves the best tacos.

Services

You can change money at one of the several *casas de cambio* on Calle 2, the main north-south street; **Servicio de Cambio San Luis Río Colorado Viejo** is the most efficient. Three banks can also be found along Calle 2.

Whether you're heading south or east, San Luis Río Colorado is a good place to top off with Magna Sin (unleaded gas). Although several PEMEX stations in town post Magna Sin signs, the only place that consistently carries unleaded fuel is the station at Calle 4 and Revolución.

Highway 2

San Luis Río Colorado is the Mexican mainland's western terminus of national highway Mexico 2, which extends in pieces all the way east to the Gulf of Mexico. Between here and Caborca (352 km/218 miles southeast), Mexico 2 runs roughly parallel to an old Indian trail that was used to link a permanent water source in Sonoita with settlements at the junction of the Gila and Colorado Rivers.

The trail was used by Spanish explorers during the 16th and 17th centuries to travel between Northern Mexico and Alta California. It was called Camino del Diablo ("Devil's Road") by the Spanish; as many as 500 European travelers died of thirst or heatstroke along its inhospitable cinder tracks before the road was finally paved between 1955 and 1960. Today the San Luis Río Colorado-Caborca stretch is a comfortable drive that passes through prime Sonoran Desert scenery.

EL GOLFO DE SANTA CLARA

This little-known spot doesn't appear in any state-published tourist brochures but enjoys almost a cult status among a small group of repeat visitors. Poised at the northernmost tip of the Sea of Cortez near the mouth of the dried-up Río Colorado, El Golfo is a true oddity, a fishing village at the edge of one of North America's driest deserts.

Although the 114-km road from San Luis Río Colorado to El Golfo is paved all the way, the village itself has only a small network of sand roads. Drivers with non-4WD vehicles should deflate their tires to 10-12 pounds per square inch; even 4WD vehicles frequently get mired in deep sand caused by constantly shifting winds; tidal changes also occasionally leave cars and trucks flooded with sea water. A retired local fisherman makes a living towing naive visitors out of the sand and salt water.

Southeast of town via one of these roads is the main attraction, a long stretch of sandy beach with well-spaced *palapas*. Dunes in this area are popular with ATV riders. At high tide, the dunes become sandy beaches; at low tide, broad mudflats are exposed and large clams are plentiful. The difference between high and low tides here can be as much as 7.5 vertical meters (25 feet), which at most local beaches translates to roughly a mile between high and low tidelines. That makes it one of the highest tidal variations in the world.

On the way to El Golfo you'll pass a brick-works and several small farming towns. About halfway from San Luis Río Colorado to El Golfo, **Riito** offers a few *tiendas* with classic Sonoran storefronts, a CONASUPO, and a PEMEX station. You can cut across to Baja California at Riito via a paved east-west road that runs between Mexico 5 (Baja) and the road to El Golfo. El Golfo is, in fact, a favorite side destination for Baja hands coming up or down Mexico 5 between Mexicali and San Felipe.

Just north of El Golfo is an intriguing area of mesa-type lava and ash formations left from Pinacate's oldest volcanic outflow (see "El Pinacate National Park," above).

Climate

From May through mid-September, this desert delta becomes an inferno, with temperatures soaring over 38° C (100° F). Heavy evaporation from the Sea of Cortez produces yet another El Golfo anomaly—a humid desert. The best time to visit is Nov.-April.

Accommodations and Food

At the beach southeast of town you'll find the rustic but clean and well-run **Nuevo Motel del Golfo,** Av. Almejas and Calle 1, tel. (653) 8-0221, which offers seven two-bed rooms and four rental trailers at budget rates (US$30 for one to four persons). Also available are 24 full-hookup RV sites; US$12-18. Owner Raúl speaks perfect English and knows the Mexican coast well. Nearby **El Capitán** boasts 150 RV sites for US$10 bare or US$20 with electricity.

La Cabina Restaurant, on the beach next to El Capitán, has good seafood as well as campsites (US$4), basic budget rooms (US$17), and *palapa* shelters on the beach.

The best seafood in El Golfo is served at the simple but very clean **El Delfín.** Don't miss the delicious *burritos de machaca de manta raya,* fresh flour tortillas wrapped around dried and shredded manta ray.

Nevería Blanca Nieve, on the main drag next to the beach, has ice cream and popsicles. Pick up groceries and supplies from **Mercado Las Brisas** or the town's **CONASUPO.**

Events

Visitors come from far and wide for Día de la Marina (Marine Day), held annually on June 1 in coastal towns all over Mexico. This is El Golfo's biggest celebration of the year, and the sand streets are crammed with food vendors hawking *mariscos,* cold beer, fresh fruit, and other snacks, as mariachi and *norteña* musicians stroll by.

Driving

The PEMEX station here usually has Magna Sin. Auto service is available at the **Off Road Tire Shop,** which is also a good spot for local information; Jesús, the proprietor, speaks excellent English.

Even if you have a 4WD, take care exploring the area as the deep sand here can mire just about any vehicle. Anyone trailering a boat to El Golfo should bring along a current set of Cortez tide tables, as the tidal range is extensive.

SONOITA

In 1698 the Spanish founded Misión San Marcelo de Sonoyta here next to an oasis known to the Papago as "Sonoydag." Although the mission was destroyed in a 1751 Pima revolt, Sonoita remained the only dependable source of water for travelers along the harsh Camino del Diablo, a vital overland link between California and Central Mexico until well into the 19th century. On some maps, the town name is still spelled "Sonoyta."

With all the facilities today available in Lukeville, Arizona (see "Puerto Peñasco," below), few travelers stop off in Sonoita for more than the usual border formalities. The Sonoita border crossing is open daily 8 a.m.-midnight.

Motel Excelsior, Benemérito de las Américas 45, tel. (651) 2-1041, is a bit shabby but okay.

Rooms come with a/c and TV, and a pool and restaurant are on the premises. Rates: US$25 s, US$28 d. Magna Sin gasoline is available at a PEMEX station on Mexico 2 in town.

PUERTO PEÑASCO

Known as "Rocky Point" to thousands of Arizonans, Puerto Peñasco (Spanish for "rock port") is a curious amalgam of Mexican fishing port and American beach playground. As at El Golfo de Santa Clara, the beaches here tend to be flat and desert-sandy, with extreme tidal variation. Unlike tiny El Golfo, however, this is a "real" town in terms of population, with a reported 40,000 residents (although it feels more like 4,000) and several distinct districts.

The original Puerto Peñasco, founded as a fishing village in the 1920s, sits atop a broad, rocky cape (a basaltic lava flow from Pinacate's Volcán de Santa Clara) overlooking the Sea of Cortez on one side and a small natural harbor on the other. Urban features include a small fish market, a couple of charming hotels and restaurants, a simple *malecón* (waterfront promenade), and a sprinkling of older Mexican homes. Along the highway from Sonoita is a newer, larger commercial district with stores, offices, more restaurants, and railway and bus stations, all mixed in with newer, less-well-built houses. Puerto Peñasco's Mexican population is mostly restricted to these two urban districts, while American tourists and retirees are congregated in nearby beach areas.

Just west of the commercial district are **Playa Hermosa** and **Playa Bonita,** sandy, northern extensions of the harbor with three beach hotels and a couple of RV parks. Olive ridley sea turtles hatched eggs on Playa Bonita in 1995, extending their known range north by many kilometers. After about eight km (five miles), the north end of Playa Hermosa/Bonita runs into the even longer **Sandy Beach,** access to which is controlled by a gringo consortium at Cholla Bay, an expatriate community at Sandy's north end.

Neither tourist cards nor temporary vehicle import permits are required for visits to Puerto Peñasco, which is part of the little-publicized Sonoran Free Trade Zone. If you plan to fish here, however, you will need a Mexican fishing permit (see "Fishing" under "Outdoor Recreation" in the On the Road chapter for details).

Climate and Seasons

The primary tourist season here runs Nov.-May, when U.S. snowbirds take refuge from the cold north. The winter months are generally comfortable, with daytime temperatures averaging 18-24° C (65-75° F). The occasional two- or three-day cold snap causes temperatures to plummet as low as 6° C (43° F).

In summer, the normal daily high is around 30-35° C (86-95° F), with occasional hot spells over 38° C (100° F). That's too hot to make year-round residents out of the snowbirds, but weekend visitation is common year-round.

SIGHTS

Cholla Bay/Sandy Beach

For most visitors, Cholla Bay is either love or hate at first sight. Largely responsible for the gringoization of Puerto Peñasco (starting with the Anglicizing of local place-names), this expat enclave holds a ragtag collection of beach homes ranging from tacky to charmingly rustic. Access to both Sandy Beach and Cholla Bay is via a 6.5-km private road flanked by signs that make it clear you're entering a quasi-colony. Most of the residents are seasonal, and you get the overall impression that at least some of them have chosen this spot as an escape from zoning and environmental laws in the United States. On the up side, several Cholla Bay residents have volunteered time and money to Puerto Peñasco social services.

On weekends and holidays Nov.-May, the Sandy Beach area is jammed with visiting Arizonans who park their campers and RVs in long rows along the beach; the sand dunes behind the beach are buzzing with ATVs and dune bug-

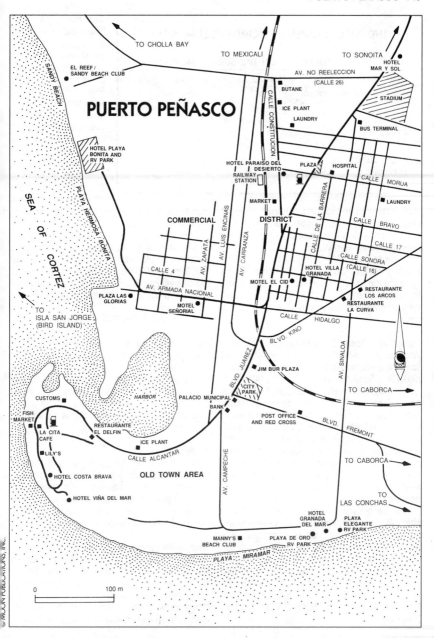

INDIAN CULTURES OF NORTHWEST MEXICO

	NORTE	CENTRO SUR	NORESTE
A.D. 1700-?	Pima	Mayo, Seri, Yaqui	Apache, Opata
A.D. 400-1100	Trincheras		Paquimé (Casas Grandes)
A.D. 0-200		Huatabampo	
400-200 B.C.	San Dieguito Río Sonora		
6,000-4,000 B.C.		Clovis-Folsom	
10,000 B.C.	Clovis		Clovis

gies. Vendors line the road with tourist curios, seashell displays, and "I got wasted in Rocky Point" T-shirts. During the week, however, Sandy Beach is nearly empty.

To get to Cholla Bay/Sandy Beach from Puerto Peñasco, take Calle 26 east off Blvd. Juárez opposite the baseball stadium; this road meets the private Cholla Bay access road. A road also runs southwest directly from Mexico 8 north of town.

Desert and Ocean Studies Center (CEDO)

Another gringo enclave spreads southeast of town from **Playa Miramar.** Several modest RV parks line the shore here, flanked by the beach housing developments of Las Conchas and the newer Estero La Pinta. Occupying the Moroccan-looking structure at Las Conchas, the Desert and Ocean Studies Center (CEDO), a nonprofit foundation, has been dedicated to research, education, and conservation relating to the northern Sea of Cortez and the coastal Sonoran Desert since 1979. Inside, displays include a skeleton of a fin whale and other marine and desert artifacts.

Another attraction on the premises is Earthship CEDO, a building volunteers constructed out of waste materials such as old tires and aluminum cans. Visitors are welcome to tour the Earthship, which is extremely energy efficient because of insulation strategies and placement of windows relative to the sun. For further information, contact CEDO, P.O. Box 249, Lukeville, AZ 85341, tel. (638) 3-5403 in Puerto Peñasco.

Beaches

The area's most pristine and least-visited beaches will be found southeast of Miramar off the road between Puerto Peñasco and Sahuaro (on the way south to Caborca). Only the first 18 km (11 miles) of this road are paved, after which it's 26.5 km (16.5 miles) of sand, dirt, and gravel. Deserted beaches are only 15-20 minutes from the main road via rough vehicle tracks leading to the coastline.

Sunsets over the Sea of Cortez can be spectacular from any west-facing point in Puerto Peñasco. On clear days you may be able to spot 3,000-meter (10,000-foot) Picacho del Diablo, the highest peak in Baja California's Sierra de San Pedro Mártir, on the other side.

ACCOMMODATIONS

Each district in Puerto Peñasco is represented by a smattering of hotels; most visitors interested in staying on the beach head for the Playa Hermosa/Bonita area. Some lodgings close June-Sept., so be sure to call or write in advance if you plan to attempt a summer visit. Those hotels that stay open in summer usually slash their rates by 30-50%.

Budget

Toward the center of the commercial district are **Hotel Villa Granada** and **Motel El Cid.** Both are on the run-down side and best considered as backup when all else is full (as is often the case during spring break). Rates: around US$25 d plus US$3 for each additional person.

Budget/Inexpensive

Just off the highway into town, **Hotel Paraíso del Desierto,** Calle Constitución at Calle Morua, tel. (638) 3-2175, is an adequate place to stay. The simple rooms have a/c and TV, and there's a pool on the premises. Rates: US$22-39 weekdays, US$35-45 weekends. Farther north along the highway (at Km 94), **Hotel Mar y Sol,** tel. (638) 3-3190, has satellite TV and a/c; rates are on a par with Paraíso del Desierto. At Playa Miramar, the new **Fiesta de Cortez Hotel** offers good rooms. Rates: US$32-45 weekdays, US$42-57 weekends, US$67-95 holidays.

Inexpensive
In the "old town" near the harbor are a couple of good choices for visitors who care more about being in Mexico than they do about getting a suntan. The four-story **Hotel Costa Brava,** tel. (638) 3-3130, fax (638) 3-3621, overlooks the *malecón* and is within walking distance of the fish market and a couple of seafood restaurants. All rooms have Sea of Cortez sunset views. Parking is enclosed; service is friendly and efficient. Rates: US$35-40 s/d. Two-night, three-day packages for two adults and two children are sometimes available for US$60.

The commercial district holds several hotels in this price category, only one of which is overwhelmingly commendable. The top choice, for overall value and a good location (within walking distance of Playa Hermosa), is **Motel Señorial,** Calle 3 and Av. Armada Nacional, tel. (638) 3-2065. The large, clean rooms have satellite TV and a/c, while the recently renovated restaurant and piano bar add a touch of class. Rates: US$45. Summer rates as low as US$20 d.

At Sandy Beach, **El Reef/Sandy Beach Club,** is an all-around recreational facility that rents a few beachfront rooms. Rates: around US$50.

Down at Playa Miramar the two-story, characterless **Hotel Granada del Mar** has clean, simple rooms without TV. The adjacent disco might annoy guests seeking a quiet beach holiday. Rates: US$44 s/d in back, US$55 oceanfront, US$66 with kitchen. Also at Playa Miramar, **Manny's Beach Club,** tel. (638) 3-3605, Arizona tel. (602) 387-6921, rents a few small, a/c rooms behind the club. Rates: around US$50.

Inexpensive/Moderate
Perched high above everything else in Puerto Peñasco is the **Hotel Viña del Mar,** tel. (638) 3-3600, Arizona tel. (602) 327-2059. For sunset views the Viña del Mar is tops. Facilities include enclosed parking and a pool. Rates: US$45-60 for most rooms, US$85 for suites.

Moderate
At efficient and clean **Hotel Playa Bonita,** tel. (638) 3-2586, all rooms have TV and a/c; common facilities include tennis courts and a swimming pool. During the summer Playa Bonita runs a special in which for every three-night stay you get a fourth night free. Rates: US$56 weekdays, US$75 weekends, oceanfront rooms US$75.

Expensive/Premium
Closer to town is the new, five-story **Plaza Las Glorias,** tel. (638) 3-6010, fax (638) 3-6015, which dwarfs the competition. All rooms face the Sea of Cortez and offer the luxuries expected at this price level. A pool and spa offer added enticements. Rates: US$100-150 weekends, US$85-135 weekdays.

Notes
The manager of the new **Best Western Playa Inn,** Av. Sinaloa 18, refused to give us any information about the hotel or to let us have a look around. We can't recommend staying at a hotel whose management presents such an attitude to the public.

According to the SECTUR office in Hermosillo, a franchise of the Super 8 motel chain should be opening soon in Puerto Peñasco.

Beach House Rentals
At Your Service Property Management, tel. (638) 3-2275, fax (638) 3-6312, and **Rocky Point Vacation Rental,** U.S. tel. (520) 326-9292, can arrange rentals in local absentee-owner houses and townhouses for US$295-345 for two weekend nights, or around US$775-875 for six nights.

RV Parks and Camping
RV parks are numerous here. The highest concentration of RV slots is at Playa Miramar, where you'll find full hookups for a uniform US$14 per vehicle with two persons, beachfront spaces for US$18, plus US$1-2 per extra person per day. Weekly rates of US$75 (US$100 beachfront) and monthly rates of US$250 (US$300 beachfront) are available. Seniors may be able to get a 10% discount at some places. Rates typically include utilities, though hot showers may be metered. When no boat ramps are available, a boat launch will cost around US$10. As with hotels,

some of these parks close June-Sept., so be sure to call or write in advance if you plan to attempt a summer visit.

The largest and probably the most popular park is the 300-space **Playa de Oro RV Park,** Apdo. Postal 76, Puerto Peñasco, Son. 83550, tel. (638) 3-2668; facilities include a convenience store, restaurant/bar, boat ramp, and boat storage. Other Playa Miramar parks include **San Rafael RV Park,** Apdo. Postal 58, tel. (638) 3-2681 or 3-5044, 60 spaces; **Playa Miramar Trailer Park,** Apdo. Postal 2, tel. (638) 3-2587, 147 spaces; **El Señorial RV Park,** tel. (638) 3-3055, 69 spaces; and **Playa Elegante RV Park,** Apdo. Postal 101, tel. (638) 3-3712, 225 spaces.

Attached to Hotel Playa Bonita at the beach of the same name is 220-space **Playa Bonita RV Park,** Apdo. Postal 34, Puerto Peñasco, Son. 83550, tel. (638) 3-2596. This is one of the better-run RV parks in Puerto Peñasco; facilities include a coin laundry, hot showers, recreation room with satellite TV, convenience store, and boat ramp.

Beach camping is permitted at Sandy Beach for a nominal per-person fee; showers are available at El Reef/Sandy Beach Club. North of Cholla Bay or southeast of Playa Miramar are more secluded beach areas where camping is free.

FOOD

Seafood is one of Puerto Peñasco's big draws, especially for landlocked Arizonans. Jumbo shrimp is sold on the streets and at the fish market in the old town for around US$20 per two-kilo (five-pound) bag. At the market you'll also find oysters, clams, snapper, squid, and flounder for sale.

On Blvd. Kino in the commercial district are two gringo favorites, **Restaurante Los Arcos,** tel. (638) 3-3596, and **Restaurante La Curva,** tel. (638) 3-3470, both of which offer a menu of Mexican standards, steak, and seafood for US$8-12 per entree. La Curva also does burgers, potato skins, and other American food for US$5-8. **Restaurante Puesta del Sol** at Playa Bonita is also popular among gringos for steak, seafood, and Mexican standards.

In the old town, a less gringoized and less expensive alternative to the above is **La Cita Café,** on Paseo V. Estrella near the Hotel Costa Brava. This diner-style place has been in business since 1957 and serves simple Mexican and seafood dishes for breakfast, lunch, and dinner; shrimp dishes are particularly good here. **Lily's Restaurant** nearby is a favorite gringo spot for seafood, especially fish tacos, and boasts excellent sunset views. Nearby on Calle Alcantar, **Restaurante El Delfín,** tel. (638) 3-2608, is slightly more upscale and is open 7:30 a.m.-9 p.m.

The restaurants at **Hotel Costa Brava** and **Hotel Viña del Mar** in the old town are each highly regarded for seafood. The latter has a particularly good Sea of Cortez view.

For quick burritos or *tacos al carbón,* the **Asadero Sonora** on Calle Constitución (opposite the railway station) is Puerto Peñasco's best bet. **La Flor de Michoacán** at Calle 17 and Av. de la Barrera has good *aguas frescas, licuados,* and *paletas.*

Espresso Express, on the beach road by Playa Miramar, next to Manny's, is a small and friendly cafe with shell-covered floors; pastries, Mexican food, and coffee drinks are served.

For groceries, the **Jim Bur** supermarket on Blvd. Juárez will take care of most needs. Farther into town is a bakery, **El Buen Gusto,** at Calle Bravo and Av. Cuauhtémoc, with a good selection of *pan dulce, birote,* donuts, pies, and cakes. Fresh fruits, vegetables, and dairy products are available at **Frutería Las Delicias,** Calles 16 (or Blvd. Sonora) and de la Barrera.

In Cholla Bay, **Abarrotes Patricia** is the main outlet for groceries and fishing supplies. As you might expect, prices are a bit higher than in town.

ENTERTAINMENT

The relaxed outdoor bar at **Manny's Beach Club,** Playa Miramar, is a popular gathering place for all ages. During the week, the bandstand usually features a lone musician playing honky-tonk keyboard; on weekends a combo plays.

Bar Las Margaritas at Hotel Viña del Mar offers sports betting and large-screen TV; the same hotel has a disco. **J.J.'s Cantina** is *the* spot at Cholla Bay for early evening happy hour. Although it has a clubby atmosphere (all the patrons seem to know each other), outsiders are welcome.

RECREATION

Fishing

Puerto Peñasco's main gamefish are black seabass, dorado, pargo, pompano, mackerel, seatrout, shark, and the occasional yellowtail. A fishing tournament is held in June; for information contact **Cholla Bay Sportsmen's Club,** c/o John Fowler, P.O. Box 5, Lukeville, AZ 85341.

Fishing charters are available from **Pasitos Tours,** at Blvd. Juárez near the fish market (P.O. Box 251, Lukeville, AZ 85341), tel. (638) 3-2083, as well as from **Rojo's,** at Cholla Bay near J.J.'s Cantina, tel. (638) 3-3956. At the Puerto Peñasco harbor you can rent *pangas* by the day— around US$50-70 for two to four persons.

Fishing tackle, bait, and boat or motor parts are available at the **Proveedora de Pesca,** Blvd. Kino and Calle Prieto.

Windsurfing

The Puerto Peñasco area has excellent windsurfing, especially during the winter and early spring months. Experienced boardsailors can put in just about anywhere along the coast; novices should stick to Cholla Bay or the estuaries north and south of Puerto Peñasco. Unbelievably, no place in town rents sailboards these days, so bring your own rig.

Diving

Although not exactly a world-class diving destination, the Puerto Peñasco coastline does provide a few spots of interest to snorkelers and scuba divers. Nearby Isla San Jorge (known among the Cholla Bay crowd as "Bird Island") offers rock reefs with soft corals, plus nearby sea pinnacles amid scenic sand flats. A colony of sea lions at the island adds another dimension to the underwater sightseeing. Rocky areas near the old town and at the north end of Sandy Beach are suitable for snorkeling and beach diving.

China Sea Sailing and Diving Co., next door to La Cita Café on Paseo V. Estrella, tel. (638) 3-5450, sells air, rents snorkels, fins, masks, tanks, regulators, and diving accessories, and can arrange dive trips to Isla San Jorge.

TRANSPORTATION

By Bus

From Puerto Peñasco's bus terminal at Blvd. Juárez and Calle Cárdenas, the **TNS** line, tel. (638) 3-2019, runs first- and second-class buses to Sonoita, Hermosillo, San Luis Río Colorado, and other points in northern Sonora, as well as to Mexicali and Tijuana.

By Train

A spur line of FNM's first-class del Pacífico train passes through Puerto Peñasco westbound to Mexicali (Train No. 1), and eastbound to Caborca and Benjamin Hill (Train No. 2). At Benjamin Hill, the spur links up with the main del Pacifico line running north to Nogales and south to Mazatlán and Guadalajara. Travelers heading south from Puerto Peñasco will find it quickest to take the train to Benjamin Hill then buses south from there.

The Puerto Peñasco railway station is at Calle Serdán and Calle Ferrocarril, tel. (638) 3-2610; for reservations in Mexicali call (65) 7-2386.

Driving

The main gateway to Puerto Peñasco is the border town of Sonoita, opposite Lukeville, Arizona, exactly 100 km (62 miles) from Puerto Peñasco via Mexico 8. This road is usually in super condition, partly because the original roadbed was constructed by the U.S. Army Corps of Engineers during WW II to provide defense access to the Sea of Cortez (at the time considered vulnerable to Japanese submarine attack). The drive takes about an hour and a half if you observe the speed limits.

Magna Sin (unleaded gas) is available at the PEMEX stations in Sonoita and on Blvd. Juárez in Puerto Peñasco.

Puerto Peñasco to Caborca

A 160-km route (Sonora 003 and Sonora 37) leads south and east from Puerto Peñasco to Caborca, a scenic drive that parallels the railway much of the way. This two-lane highway is paved *most* of the way; an unpaved, 26.5-km (16.5-mile) stretch between the town of Sahuaro and Puerto Peñasco is sandy and rough in places, and suitable only for vehicles with high road clearance. About two km before the western end of the dirt stretch (around 20 km/12 miles from Puerto Peñasco) is a Mexican customs check where you must present a tourist card and auto permit.

The scenery along this little-used route includes a long section of desertscrub (predominantly ocotillo and cholla) near Bahía San Jorge, and an equally long stretch toward Caborca of cultivated fields of grape, olive, and citrus. The entire Puerto Peñasco-Caborca route can be driven in two to three hours, depending on road conditions along the unpaved portion.

INFORMATION AND SERVICES

In Lukeville, Arizona
The **Gringo Pass** complex, on Arizona Hwy. 85, tel. (602) 254-9284, has a post office, trailer park, coffee shop, grocery store, coin laundry, moderately priced motel, Mexican insurance, propane, and Puerto Peñasco tourist information—in short, just about everything you'd need for a Puerto Peñasco vacation.

Mail and Phone
In Puerto Peñasco, the Mexican government post office is at Blvd. Fremont and Calle Coahuila. Many seasonal residents shuttle back and forth between Lukeville and Puerto Peñasco at regular intervals for mail service. International calls can be made from the public pay phone next to Restaurante La Curva or from any of the several private long-distance phone offices in town; as with mail, many long-termers use Lukeville for telephone service.

PUERTO PEÑASCO TELEPHONE NUMBERS

Police.	3-2626
Red Cross	3-2266
Immigration	3-2526
Customs	3-2693
Green Angels	3-4129
COTP	3-3035
Puerto Peñasco area code	638

Money and Insurance
Bancomer, just south of Jim Bur Plaza and Palacio Municipal on Blvd. Juárez, is the best place to change money or open a bank account. Outside of banking hours you can buy pesos at **Video Distribuidora,** Av. 19 and Calle 23.

If you've been foolish enough to drive into Mexico without Mexican insurance—or if your current policy is running out—stop in at **Alejandro Portugal M. Insurance,** at Blvd. Juárez and Calle Morua (Calle 20), tel. (638) 3-2390.

Other Information
The *Rocky Point Times,* a free newspaper distributed at all the gringo spots in town, contains a mix of information for tourists and residents—probably the paper's best feature is the monthly tide tables. A *Rocky Point Souvenir Map Poster,* available at Hotel Playa Bonita and tourist-oriented restaurants, contains lots of printed information on the opposite side of the cartoonlike, distorted-scale map.

The Sonora state **tourist office,** tel. (638) 3-4129, has a branch in Jim Bur Plaza. In the U.S. you can also dial (800) 4-SONORA for general information on Puerto Peñasco and the state of Sonora.

Street names in Puerto Peñasco can be confusing since many streets have both a name and a number. Calle Constitución and Av. 12 are one and the same, as are Av. Juan de la Barrera and Av. 15; Av. Sinaloa and Av. 18; Calle S. Morua and Calle 20; Av. Campeche and Av. 10.

CABORCA AND VICINITY

East of Sonoita and the Sea of Cortez, the Sonoran Desert gets increasingly green as it joins the alluvial plains of the Río Sonora system and the foothills of the Sierra Madre Occidental. This was one of the earliest parts of northwest Mexico to become missionized by the Spanish Jesuits; their legacy in the area includes several historic mission chapels and a number of nonnative fruit orchards. The Yaqui and other Amerindian groups originally inhabiting the region have been almost totally displaced by Mexicans, who constructed irrigation systems to create an agricultural oasis here.

PADRE EUSEBIO FRANCISCO KINO

During his remarkable 24-year missionary career in Northern Mexico, Jesuit priest Eusebio Francisco Kino managed to establish some 30 pueblos in Sonora and Arizona, baptize over 4,000 natives as Roman Catholics, successfully petition the Guadalajara diocese against Indian slavery in the northwest, introduce cattle ranching and the cultivation of fruits and wheat to Sonora, and refute the hypothesis that California was an island.

Born Eusebio Chino in Segno, Italy, in 1645 and educated in German schools, the young Kino became seriously ill at age 18 and made a vow to St. Francis Xavier that he would dedicate his life to religion if saved. Upon his recovery he joined the Society of Jesus and was sent to Nueva España as a Jesuit *misionero* attached to the Guadalajara diocese (which at the time included all Spanish territories to the north and west). After unsuccessful attempts to missionize Baja California, Kino convinced Guadalajara's crown representatives to issue a *cedula* (royal decree) against Amerindian slavery in the mines, then proceeded to Cucurpe, Sonora, in 1687 to found the first Jesuit mission in the northwest. From Cucurpe he gradually assembled a mission circuit that extended north to Arizona's Santa Cruz River valley (near Tucson), west to Caborca, south to Magdalena, and east to Cocóspera.

In 1701 Kino accompanied an expedition from northwest Sonora to the mouth of the Río Colorado, thus confirming the claim that Baja California was a peninsula and that Alta California could be reached by land. Along the way he traversed parts of El Desierto de Altar and the Sierra del Pinacate, producing the first historical descriptions of this volcanic terrain. In 1706 he completed the first Spanish survey of Seriland and Isla Tiburón on the Sea of Cortez. Wherever he traveled, Kino produced detailed maps and notes that have become part of a rich Sonora/Arizona legacy frequently tapped by present-day historians. His 1701 map of northwest Mexico was so functionally accurate that it wasn't superseded for 150 years following his death. Ironically, Kino died in 1711 while dedicating a chapel in Magdalena to his patron saint, Francisco Xavier.

Iglesia de
San Diego, Pitiquito

JOE CUMMINGS

Caborca, a prosperous agricultural center of 100,000 residents, is surrounded by a soothing blend of rolling hills, lush Sonoran Desert, and cultivated fields of grain, grapes, melons, broccoli, peaches, and olives. The town was once a Papago ranchería (the name is a Spanish corruption of the Papago word *kavork*, meaning "rounded hill"), and today features a tidy, modern downtown and an older section of pastel-colored adobes.

The main attraction here is **La Concepción de Nuestra Señora de Caborca,** a twin-towered neoclassical church completed by the Franciscans in 1809. It's also known as "Misión Padre Kino," although the original 1693 mission built by Kino was destroyed in a 1695 Pima attack.

In 1857 Caborca residents used this church as a fort to defend the surrounding valley against an American freebooter invasion led by Henry Crabb. The invasion was defeated, Crabb and his men were executed, and every year on **April 6** a local festival commemorates the victory. Bullet holes from the battle are still visible on the church's facade.

Other Caborca festivals of note include the *Fiesta de Uva* (Grape Festival) in September and the **Feria del Algodón** (Cotton Fest) in late November.

Accommodations

Few tourists spend the night in Caborca, though the town is well equipped with hotels, among them: **Motel San Carlos** (budget), Av. Quiróz y Mora across the street from more expensive Motel El Camino; **Hotel Plaza** (budget), also on Av. Quiróz y Mora and facing the Plaza de Armas; **Hotel Rivera** (budget), Calle 5 and Av. B; **Motel Los Arcos** (budget), Calle 8 and Carreta; and **Motel El Camino** (inexpensive), Av. Quiróz y Mora near the San Carlos. The new **Motel Toxa** (inexpensive to moderate) at Km 103 on the highway east of town is clean but overpriced and without much style.

Food

The main street through town, Calle 4, is lined with small restaurants and cafes serving classic Sonoran cuisine. **Asadero Bífalo,** on Calle 4 between Av. I and Av. J, is known for first-rate *carne asada* from its own *carnicería* across the street, plus quesadillas, *chiles toreados, cebollas asadas,* and fresh guacamole. The casual dining room is very clean and service is excellent. **Cafetería Plaza,** adjacent to the Hotel Plaza on Av. Quiróz y Mora between Calle 4 and Calle 3 (opposite the Plaza de Armas), serves standard Mexican/Sonoran fare in simple, clean surroundings.

Nearby Missions

About 11 km (seven miles) southeast of Caborca via Mexico 2, in Pitiquito, is **Iglesia de San Diego,** one of the earliest Sonoran mission churches still standing. Built in 1786 by Franciscan missionaries on a site first established by Padre Kino around 1706, the folk baroque-style church is famous for a set of macabre interior murals. Among the subjects depicted are a set of scales, a huge human skeleton, and a bird's head. If you can manage a visit on Nov. 13, the *día de santo* for San Diego, you'll see the little town of Pitiquito at its most animated.

Misión San Pedro y San Pablo Tubutama, in Tubutama, 73 km (45 miles) northeast of Caborca via Sonora 64, is another church built on the site of a Kino mission. The original mission chapel was completed in 1691, destroyed by a Pima rebellion in 1695, and again destroyed in 1751. Whitewashed like the Kino missions of southern Arizona, the current Franciscan chapel dates to 1783 and is one of the more impressive missions in northern Sonora, with a cruciform, barrel-vaulted floor plan, a folk-baroque facade, and a small collection of religious art.

On **June 29,** the church's saints' day, a modest festival is held.

At **Oquitoa** (from the Papago *hókito* or "boundary"), between Tubutama and Caborca off Sonora 64, is a relatively minor mission church dating to 1730. In overall layout it's not as grand as Tubutama but the facade shares many of the same design characteristics, including arched ridges and simple, neoclassic niches. Church bells hang from arches surmounting the facade rather than in a separate belltower.

Alternate Route: Tubutama, Oquitoa, and Caborca can be reached by car from the U.S. via the border town of Sasabe, Arizona. On the U.S. side, Arizona Highways 86 and 286 from Tucson lead to Sasabe, meeting Sonora 64 on the Mexican side. The first 45 km of Sonora 64—until Sáric—are unpaved but passable by ordinary passenger car.

NOGALES/AGUA PRIETA TO HERMOSILLO

NOGALES, ARIZONA

The twin border towns of Nogales make up the main border entry point for visitors heading down Mexico's Sea of Cortez/Pacific coast by road. Before leaving Nogales, Arizona, visitors interested in regional history might want to stop in at the **Pimería Alta Historical Society Museum,** at Grand Ave. and Crawford St., tel. (602) 287-4621, just 150 meters north of the border. Many of the exhibits pertain to northern Sonora as well as southern Arizona. The museum is open Friday 10 a.m.-5 p.m., Saturday 10 a.m.-4 p.m., and Sunday 1-4 p.m.; admission is free.

Nogales, USA, is also a good place to buy pesos, as the moneychangers usually offer better rates than on the other side of the border. And you'll find a **Mexican consulate** at 60 Terrace Ave., tel. (602) 287-5221.

Accommodations and Camping
Budget: Mission Motel, 820 Grand Ave., tel. (602) 287-2472, seems constantly under renovation but remains basic. The **Best Western Siesta Motel,** 673 Grand Ave., tel. (602) 287-4671, offers standard motel rooms and a pool.

Inexpensive: Closest to the border is the **Americana Motor Hotel,** 639 Grand Ave., tel. (602) 287-7211 or (800) 974-8079; all rooms come with mini-refrigerators and there's a pool.

Campground: The nearest campground with full hookups is **Mi Casa RV Park,** 2901 N. Grand Ave., tel. (602) 281-1150, 4.5 miles north of the border. Rates are US$10 for tents and campers, US$17 for trailers/RVs.

Border Transportation
Visitors planning to use public transportation can reach Nogales from Tucson by a/c bus via **Citizen Auto Stage,** tel. (602) 287-5628 in Nogales, (602) 792-0972 in Tucson. The company offers 10 roundtrip departures daily. From Tucson International Airport you can get a taxi (US$7) to the highway bus stop at US 89 and Valencia Rd. to meet the Tucson-Nogales bus.

Buses into Mexico can be picked up at the Nogales, Arizona, bus terminal, 35 N. Terrace Ave., tel. (602) 287-5628. **TNS** offers daily departures to Mexico City, Chihuahua, Hermosillo, Ciudad Obregón, Mazatlán, Culiacán, Navojoa, Cananea, and Los Mochis.

Nogales Taxi, tel. (602) 287-3325, and Carillo's Taxi, tel. (602) 287-3356, provide taxi service to (and across) the border.

Mexican Vehicle Insurance

If you're driving your own vehicle and don't already have a policy valid for Mexico, you can arrange reliable, moderately priced insurance at **Sanborn's,** 2921 N. Grand Ave., tel. (602) 281-1873, fax 761-1215, just off I-19 at Mi Casa RV Park.

Crossing the Border

See "Entry Regulations" under "Immigration, Customs, and Crossing the Border" in the On the Road chapter for Mexican immigrations and customs requirements.

The main Nogales crossing is open 24 hours. You can park your car at private parking lots on the U.S. side within walking distance of the border for US$3 per day.

NOGALES, SONORA

One of the oldest border towns in Mexico, Nogales (originally "Los Nogales," in reference to a landmark stand of walnut trees) was founded in 1880 along a trade route that had been used by the Hohokam and Pima for at least 2,000 years. Its strategic location at Nogales Pass resulted in successive military occupations led by Mexican generals Álvaro Obregón, Plutarco Elías Calles, and Pancho Villa in the early 1900s.

Tourism came to Nogales with U.S. Prohibition in the 1920s and '30s. Today booze is less of a tourist draw; visitors come instead for the town's boot shops, handicrafts, Mexican kitsch, and Sonoran restaurants. A vestige of Prohibition's gambling heyday lives on in the **Nogales Turf Club,** part of the Hotel Fray Marcos de Niza on Av. Obregón. Other contributors to the local economy include over 70 nearby factories, many of them *maquiladoras.*

An almost charming assemblage of pastel-colored structures built on hillsides, Nogales isn't bad-looking for a Mexican border town. Avenida Obregón is the main tourist center of restaurants, hotels, curio shops, and pharmacies. One of the Tijuanalike aspects of this strip is the opportunity to have your photo taken sitting atop a burro.

On the northwest corner of Ochoa and López Mateos, 1891-vintage **Parroquía Purísima La Concepción** features twin bell towers and stone-block construction.

As a hospitality gesture, the Nogales municipal government allows foreign visitors (except those from adjacent Santa Cruz County, Arizona) to use metered parking spaces without putting money in the meters. Of course, the locals never put money in these meters either; parking meters are almost universally ignored in Mexico.

Accommodations

Nogales has nine hotels and motels, but frankly the only reason to spend the night here rather than on the U.S. side is that hotel rooms are generally US$10-20 cheaper; hard-core punters may enjoy being closer to the Turf Club. Many of the hotels on this side cater to Mexican business travelers and are in the US$17-25 range; often they are booked up during the week.

Budget: In this category, the **Hotel San Carlos,** tel. (631) 2-0627, on the west side of Calle Juárez just before it terminates at its north end—not far from the border—offers enclosed parking, clean a/c rooms with hot-water showers, phones, TVs, decent mattresses, and a solid middle-class clientele.

Pseudocolonial, three-story **Hotel Granada,** downtown on Av. L. Mateos, offers a bit more character at about the same rates, but street noise could be a problem. Considerably nicer is the classic pink art-deco **Hotel Fray Marcos de Niza,** Av. Obregón at Calle Campillo downtown, tel. (631) 2-1651, fax (631) 2-1491. The staff is friendly, service superb, and the Nogales Turf Club (with off-track betting/sports book) is adjacent to the lobby. Other facilities include a travel agency, coffee shop, and restaurant. Most of the hotel's 112 rooms are in a nine-story, modern tower. Another hotel that welcomes visitors from the north is the clean and traditional **Hotel Olivia,** on Av. Obregón near Restaurant El Cid. Downstairs are the classic Pancho Villa Bar and a simple Mexican coffeeshop. Both Hotel Fray Marcos de Niza and Hotel Olivia are within walking distance of the border.

Motel Miami, Calle Ingenieros at Campillo, tel. (631) 2-5450, also conveniently located a short walk from the border, has adequate but somewhat musty rooms.

Inexpensive: South of town at Km 7.5 on Mexico 15, the modern and efficient **Hotel Plaza**

Nogales, tel. (631) 4-1510, offers modern a/c rooms, tennis courts, a coffee shop, restaurant, pool, cable TV, and gift shop.

Food

The main bar and restaurant areas are along Av. Obregón west of the railway and highway leading from the border. **Restaurante Olivia,** at Av. Obregón 125, downstairs from the Hotel Olivia, is a local favorite for *chimichangas,* tacos, and tamales costing around US$2-4. For typical Sonoran cuisine, including *menudo estilo sonorense,* head for similarly priced **Cafetería Leo's** on the southwest corner of Campillo and Obregón. It's simple but good, there are plenty of

tables, and the menu also features burgers and Mexican breakfasts; open 24 hours.

Arizonans flock to the well-appointed and a/c **El Cid Restaurant** at Av. Obregón 124 for seafood, steaks, and Mexican standards; strolling mariachis, clay-tile floors, and lots of Mexican tile enhance the atmosphere. **Restaurante El Greco** at Av. Obregón 152 is similar. Figure on spending US$7-17 per entree at these places—expensive by Mexican standards. **El Oasis La Gran Fonda,** at Av. Obregón 401, has the look of a Grupo Anderson restaurant (of Carlos n'Charlie's fame) but actually offers good atmosphere and Mexican food for a decent price—around US$5-10 per entree.

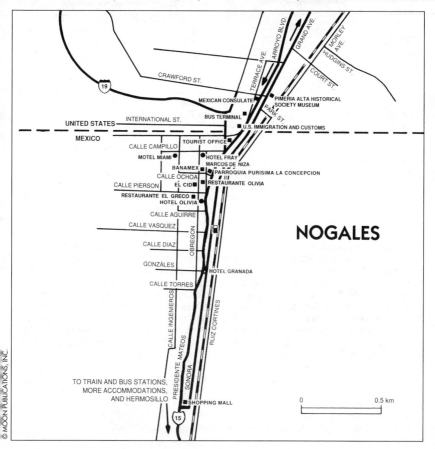

JOE CUMMINGS

Sonoran chilero

Vegetarians will find inexpensive sustenance at **Restaurant Vegetariano Quetzal,** almost opposite the Hotel Granada on Av. López Mateos. **Panadería La Espiga de Oro,** a better-than-average Mexican bakery, has two branches on Av. López Mateos.

Information and Services

Tourist information is available at the **Delegación de Turismo de Nogales,** in the Edificio Puerta de México next to the border crossing, tel. (631) 2-0666 or 2-6446. The town's private business sector maintains its own **Consejo Municipal de Turismo** at Calle Campillo 85, tel. (631) 2-5803.

You'll find a **post office** at the corner of Campillo and Juárez near the border crossing; a **Banamex** with an ATM on Av. Obregón and Calle Ochoa; and several *casas de cambio* along Calle Juárez offering competitive dollar-peso exchanges.

Transportation

Bus: At the border you can catch a white city bus down Av. Obregón to the Nogales bus terminal,

opposite the railway station on Av. L. Mateos; by foot this is roughly a 30-minute walk from the border. The terminal has a snack bar, long-distance phone service, moneychange booth (offering slightly lower rates than downtown), and a magazine/newspaper stand. TNS, Caballero Azteca, and Transportes del Pacífico run first- and second-class buses from Nogales to Caborca, Cananea, Hermosillo, Guaymas, Obregón, Navojoa, Los Mochis, Huatabampo, Puerto Peñasco, Tijuana, Mazatlán, Culiacán, Zacatecas, Guadalajara, and Mexico City.

Train: The useful del Pacífico line runs to and from Guadalajara twice a day in each direction. A second-class train (No. 4) departs at 7 a.m.; the first-class train (No. 2) leaves at 3 p.m. Fares are: Hermosillo US$5.20 first class, US$2.85 second class; Guaymas US$7.80/US$4.40; Ciudad Obregón US$10/US$5.60; Culiacán US$18/ US$9.40; Mazatlán US$22/US$12; Guadalajara US$34/19.

Fuel: Magna Sin is readily available at all of the PEMEX stations in town, as well as the PEMEX stations along Mexico 15 at Km 5 (Super Servicio Nogales) and Km 20.6. The latter is a huge, modern, 24-hour station.

DOUGLAS/AGUA PRIETA

Agua Prieta (Douglas on the Arizona side) is the second-most-popular border crossing from Arizona. A clean, whitewashed border town surrounded by windswept desert, it has virtually nothing of interest for the average visitor but is a gateway for explorations along Mexico 2 (west to Cananea and Magdalena, east to Janos and Casas Grandes) or Mexico 17 (south along the Río Sonora). Both routes thread through grassy hills and gorgeous valleys.

Douglas (117 miles southeast of Tucson, Arizona) was founded in 1901 as a copper smelter site; the smelter has since closed and the economy is now dependent on border trade with Agua Prieta and the employment provided by around 50 *maquiladoras* in the area.

Downtown Douglas is a short walk or taxi ride from the border crossing, which is open 24 hours. See "Entry Regulations" under "Immigration, Customs, and Crossing the Border" in the On the Road chapter for Mexican immigration and customs requirements.

Accommodations

Budget: In Douglas the top choice is the historic **Gadsden Hotel,** tel. (602) 364-4481, which was built in 1907, rebuilt in 1928, and now contains an Italian marble staircase, Victorian chandeliers, and a 42-foot stained-glass mural. Rates: standard rooms for US$32, the "governor's suite" for US$85. For something more modern, you can choose among **Motel 6,** 111 16th St., tel. (602) 364-2457, **Border Motel,** 1725 19th St., tel. (602) 364-8491, and **Thriftlodge,** 1030 19th St., tel. (602) 364-8434. On the Mexican side, adequate choices in the budget range include **Hotel Ruíz,** Calle 10 at Av. 6, tel. (633) 8-2499; and **Arizona Motel,** Calle 18 at Av. 6 (near the bus station), tel. (633) 8-2533.

Inexpensive: Also on the Mexican side, the best place to stay is the efficient **Hotel La Hacienda,** Calle 1 at Av. 6, tel. (633) 8-0621. Rooms have a/c, and a good restaurant is attached. Rates: US$40 s, US$44 d.

Camping: Campers and RVers can check into Douglas's **Double Adobe Trailer Park and Campground,** at Double Adobe Rd. and Hwy. 80, 17.5 miles northwest of town in McNeal, tel. (602) 364-4000; full hookups cost US$10, tent/camper spaces US$5, weekly and monthly rates available. **Saddle Gap RV Park,** tel. (602) 364-4637, and **Twin Buttes Trailer and RV Park,** tel. (602) 364-7075, also on Hwy. 80, offer similar rates.

Transportation

Douglas is served by **Douglas Municipal Airport,** tel. (602) 364-3501, in town, and **Bisbee-Douglas International Airport,** tel. (602) 364-2771, eight miles north of town on US 666. **Bridgewater Transport,** tel. (602) 364-2233, offers bus service to and from Tucson and Bisbee. For taxi service, call **Gadsden Taxi,** tel. (602) 364-5555.

Agua Prieta's new, high-tech bus terminal is a 25- to 30-minute walk from the border (taxis to the bus terminal cost US$4). **TNS** offers daily bus departures to Hermosillo, Ciudad Juárez, Chihuahua, Los Mochis, Ciudad Obregón, Guaymas, and Navojoa.

Information and Services

Douglas's friendly **chamber of commerce,** 1125 Pan American Ave., tel. (602) 364-2477, has lots of information on surrounding Cochise County, Arizona as well as Sonora; the office is open Mon.-Fri. 9 a.m.-5 p.m. Should you need automotive assistance in Agua Prieta, contact the local **Green Angels** unit, tel. (633) 8-0934, headquartered at the Palacio Municipal.

Naco

Mexico 2 can also be accessed from the small border town of Naco, Arizona, 32 miles west of Douglas (11 miles south of Bisbee) via Arizona Highways 80 and 92. The border crossing here is open daily 8 a.m.-midnight. A 15-km paved road leads south from Naco, Sonora, to Mexico 2.

MAGDALENA

This important agricultural center about an hour's drive from the border via Mexico 15 has an older side worth exploring for its simple Sonoran bread-loaf architecture, beautiful leafy plaza, and **Misión San Francisco Xavier,** site of Padre Kino's death in 1711 at age 66.

The padre's remains were discovered in 1966 by archaeologists excavating the town plaza. The plaza now holds Kino's monument/mausoleum; visit at night when Kino's bones are lit.

The mission itself is nothing special. Only the foundation and door are original; all else was rebuilt in 1832. The local myth that beneath the church floor lie 500 pounds each of gold and silver is nothing more than that—a myth common to old Spanish missions and one that results in much senseless vandalism. The only things now found under the mission floors are four priestly cadavers.

A special festival commemorating San Francisco Xavier, centered around the church, is held each year Sept. 22-Oct. 4. Pilgrims from all over northern Sonora—including Seri, Papago, Yaqui, and Pima people—flock to Magdalena to participate.

Native son Luis Donaldo Colosio, shot by a deranged factory worker in 1994 while campaigning for the Mexican presidency, was born and buried in Magdalena.

Accommodations

Budget: At the north end of town, **Motel La Suite,** tel. (632) 2-3627, has good a/c rooms. Rates: US$20-35. At Magdalena's south end,

Motel Kino, tel. (632) 2-3693, offers similarly priced rooms, as well as **RV parking** with full hookups for US$12.

Near the mission is the humble but friendly **El Cuervo Hotel,** Av. 5 de Mayo 316, tel. (632) 2-0748. Rooms have a/c, English is spoken, and a restaurant and cantina are attached. Rates: US$20 s, US$24 d.

Food
Standing out among the numerous standard eateries is the **Home Plate Café,** Calle Allende Ote. 115. The spartan decor is a heartfelt tribute to *el béisbol,* while the food is solid *mexicana* (no menu, but the *comida corrida* is good) and the coffee is cheap. At the north end of Magdalena on Mexico 15, **El Toro** reportedly offers excellent steak and shrimp, good service, and nice decor; it's open daily noon to 2 a.m.

Transportation
TNS offers **buses** to Hermosillo, Navojoa, Huatabampo, Chihuahua, Ciudad Obregón, Mazatlán, Guaymas, and Culiacán; smaller bus companies go to Cananea and other nearby towns. The bus terminal is at Calle Niños Héroes 107.

Magna Sin is available from at least three stations in town.

Vicinity of Magdalena
Mission buffs might consider exploring two nearby Kino sites. **Misión San Ignacio** is about four km north of Magdalena off Mexico 15. The whitewashed church was built in 1720 on a site founded by Kino in 1693. Original artifacts inside include the *retablo* and a spiral staircase of mesquite leading to the bell tower.

A 48-km (30-mile) paved road heading southeast out of Magdalena ends at the small mission town of Cucurpe, where the decaying but nonetheless impressive **Misión Cucurpe** rests on a hillside. The dating for this one is uncertain, though it's definitely older than the 1821 bell in the tower might indicate. If the church is locked, ask around town for a key.

SANTA ANA AND VICINITY

Santa Ana is an important road junction where Mexico Highways 2 and 15 meet. In late July,

many Yaquis convene in Santa Ana to perform the *danza de venado* or sacred deer dance at a regional Fiesta de Santa Ana.

Several hotels and motels along the highways intersecting at Santa Ana offer rooms in the budget to inexpensive range. **Motel San Francisco,** tel. (632) 4-0322, at the Mexico 15/2 junction near Km 165 is at the higher end of this range and is probably the best. Nearby and next to the bus terminal, **Motel Elba,** tel. (632) 4-0316, is at the lower end. Both have attached restaurants with very good reputations for quality and service. The gringo-run **Kennedy's,** at Km 164, does *pollo asado estilo Sinaloa y New Hampshire.*

Punta Vista RV Park, tel. (632) 4-0769, at the south end of town on Mexico 15 is little more than a gravel lot with two-way hookups, but Edgar, the owner, speaks excellent English and can arrange guide service to nearby missions and other attractions.

Next to the Magdalena toll booth are a taquería, gas station, and map of the mission routes.

Las Trincheras
Southwest of Magdalena is a mysterious archaeological site featuring a 120-meter (400-foot) series of overgrown stone terraces along a mountainside. Similar terraces have been found elsewhere in Sonora but this is the largest example. Archaeologists don't know who built them or why, but neither agriculture nor defense seems to be a workable explanation. Local residents may be able to direct you to nearby petroglyph sites.

To reach Las Trincheras, drive west of Magdalena 31 km (19 miles) via Mexico 2, then south 20 km (12 miles) on a signed unpaved road to the town of Trincheras; or take a train between Caborca and Benjamin Hill, getting off at the Trincheras station.

Benjamin Hill
Pronounced "Ben-HA-min Heel" and named for a general of British descent who fought on the side of the *constitucionalistas* in the Mexican Revolution, this town south of Santa Ana is little more than a railway junction where the Mexicali-Benjamin Hill line meets the El Pacífico. Travelers heading north to Puerto Peñasco will find the train from here quicker than buses, which run via Sonoita or Nogales. From Benjamin Hill south, however, buses are generally faster.

Several cafes opposite the railway station offer basic Mexican fare. Magna Sin and ice are available at the highway PEMEX station. **Benjamin Hill Hotel,** just out of town on Mexico 15 (at Km 125), is the only place to stay. Inexpensive.

RÍO SONORA VALLEY

At Cananea, 84 km (52 miles) southwest of Agua Prieta, Mexico 2 meets Sonora 118 (sometimes also signed Sonora 89), a highway south that parallels the scenic Río Sonora for 217 km (134 miles). The same route used by Spanish explorers (including Coronado) and missionaries centuries ago is now lined with picturesque riverside farming towns and villages set amid rolling hills. The area is most colorful following the summer rains—when wildflowers are blooming and the trees are in full canopy—or later in the fall as the leaves of the alamos (cottonwood trees) turn copper.

One of the most prominent local agricultural products is chile peppers, including the large, red, dried variety often presumptuously called "New Mexico chile" in the United States. Beginning in October, strings *(ristras)* of chiles hanging out to dry are a common sight. At the south end of the valley, the famous wild *chiltepín* grows in abundance—look for racks of small, berrylike chile pods.

One of the most scenic and interesting drives in the entire state traces a loop through the Río Sonora and Río Bavispe Valleys along more or less parallel Sonora 118 and Mexico 17 from Cananea to Agua Prieta via Nacozari and Moctezuma or vice versa. AAA's Mexico map

THE *CHILTEPINES* OF SONORA

One of the most characteristically Sonoran chiles is the *chiltepín* (pronounced "chill-teh-PEEN"), a small spherical chile pepper used as a primary ingredient in Sonoran-style red chile sauces or eaten in its dried form as a condiment. The most prized variety in Mexico measures only five to eight mm in diameter; nonetheless it is one of the world's hottest chiles, rated at an average 70,000-100,000 Scoville units by weight. By comparison, a Tabasco chile measures only 30,000-50,000 units, a jalapeño a mere 2,500-5,000 units.

Bowls of dried *chiltepines* are a common sight on Sonoran tables, and to a lesser extent in Sinaloa and Chihuahua as well. The tradition of using whole *chiltepines* as a condiment dates back to at least the mid-1700s, when German Jesuit priest Ignaz Pfefferkorn noted that "[The *chiltepín*] is placed unpulverized on the table in a salt cellar and each fancier takes as much of it as he believes he can eat. He pulverizes it with his fingers and mixes it with his food." The name may derive from a Nahuatl term meaning "flea chile"—descriptive of size as well as "bite," or perhaps from the Spanish *chile pequín,* meaning "little chile." In some parts of Mexico, like the Región Huasteca, it is in fact known by the latter term.

Whatever it's called (even botanists disagree as to which variety of *Capsicum annuum* it actually is), the *chiltepín* is closely related to the original wild capsicum, thought to have come from Bolivia or Brazil. Jesuit padres described the use of these tiny chiles in Sonora as an indigestion remedy among the Papago Indians in 1794, and until recently the Papagos made annual pilgrimages into the sierra foothills to gather them. Today they are still highly valued among the Tarahumaras, who build stone walls around *chiltepín* bushes to protect them from animals.

Like Brazil nuts, pine nuts, and wild rice, *chiltepines* grow best in the wild—when cultivated they tend to elongate like their domesticated cousins and lose some of their characteristic heat. Wild *chiltepín* bushes flourish in interior chaparral at around 1,500-2,000 meters, often beneath mesquite, shrub live oak, and other thornscrub and desertscrub species. Under optimum conditions, *chiltepín* bushes become trees that may proliferate into small forests. In Sonora the total harvest—most of it from the Río Sonora valley (including tributaries such as Río Moctezuma)—reaches over 20 tons per year, around six tons of which is exported to the United States. Due to the *chiltepín's* recent popularity among chile fanatics, the going price tripled around 1990 and quarter-ounce packets now sell for around US$2-3 each in Tucson, Arizona.

To buy *chiltepines* at their source, or simply to view the colorful fall harvest, visit the south end of the Río Sonora valley (especially the towns of Mazocahui, La Aurora, and Cumpas) beginning in late October.

Río Sonora valley

JOE CUMMINGS

is sufficient for this trip, though even better for side trips onto branch roads is the Secretaría de Comunicaciones y Transportes (SCT) Sonora map; the only place we've seen this map for sale has been Hermosillo. These two maps are often in disagreement as to the numbering of state and federal highways in Sonora; the SCT map is more accurate but in some places it, too, clashes with local highway signage.

Cananea

Like Douglas, Arizona, and Agua Prieta to the north, this town owes its existence to copper mining. A large deposit known as Cobre Grande still produces a great deal of copper—virtually the entire national output—and its mine complex dominates the town physically as well as economically. Locals simply refer to the mine as *la compañía*.

American William Cornell Greene started the mine and the Cananea Consolidated Copper Company during the Porfiriato in 1896, but by the early 1900s he was faced with a miners' rebellion that became one of the causes célèbres leading to the 1910-20 Mexican Revolution. On Calle 3 is the brick jail that Greene used for the incarceration of Mexican strikers. It's now the **Museo de La Lucha Obrera** (Museum of the Worker's Struggle); a sign out front reads "Cárcel de Cananea" (Cananea Jail). Exhibits include old photos of the mine, displays of mine interiors, local Indian artifacts, and various tidbits on the geology and anthropology of the region. Sergio,

a 56-year veteran of the mine, is usually around to dispense information. The museum is open daily 8:30 a.m.-5 p.m.; entry is free.

After many years of government mismanagement, the copper mine reentered the private sector in 1990; company facilities now cover 6,632 hectares and employ 3,000 local residents. Brick and wood houses set over rolling hills still lend an American feel to the town.

Four-story **Hotel Alameda,** at Av. Sonora 135 (around the corner from the museum), offers shoestring rates and is next door to a good, inexpensive restaurant. **Motel Valle de Cobre,** on Mexico 2 coming in from Nogales/Magdalena, could use some serious sprucing. Rates are budget to inexpensive. Just across Mexico 2, **Motel El Mesón** features a similar brick courtyard design but is in better condition; rates are inexpensive.

Several restaurants, cafes, and grocery stores line the highway through town, and regional buses stop along the highway to pick up passengers for Magdalena, Agua Prieta, Arizpe, Ures, and Hermosillo.

Arizpe

Originally founded in the 1600s, Arizpe today is a sleepy little town of 3,500 residents. But it wasn't always so. From 1776 until 1788, Arizpe was the capital of all of northwestern colonial Mexico—an administrative division known as the Internal Western Provinces that included Alta and Baja California, Sonora, Chihuahua,

Coahuila, Durango, Arizona, and New Mexico. And from 1832 to 1838 the town served as the capital of Sonora.

The town's colonial character has been preserved by the fact that it lies in a gorge a bit away from the highway. Remnants of the era include whitewashed, baked-bread style adobes, some still sporting heavy wooden doors; red cobbled streets; a pretty plaza; and a simple, single-towered church, **Nuestra Señora de la Asunción,** with a facade of rough-hewn stone. The back and sides of the church are said to consist of the original adobe bricks molded in 1648. Inside the church are the uniformed remains of Capt. Juan Bautista de Anza, who set out from Arizpe on a long colonizing mission that ended with his founding of Yerba Buena (now San Francisco), California, in 1776. Each year in late May, Arizpe celebrates de Anza's journey.

In mid-May, about a week before the de Anza celebration, is the **Fiesta de San Isidro Labrador**—residents carry an image of the saint through the streets, accompanied by fireworks. The **Fiesta de San Francisco de Asís,** held for four days in October, is also big in Arizpe; highlights include dancing in the plaza and copious consumption of beer and *platillos regionales.* One event in Arizpe history that is remembered but not celebrated occurred in the late 1800s, when a band of Apaches led by chiefs Cochise and Magnus Coloradus—today considered the Idi Amin of the Plains Indians—massacred a large number of townspeople.

Arizpe sometimes charms people into wanting to stay longer than planned. The friendly, tin-roofed **Hotel de Anza,** tel. (634) 1-0112, just north of the plaza on Lerdo de Tejada, has immaculate budget-priced rooms each with a/c, hot shower, and fan. Rates: US$20 s/d.

Kankun Kafe, on Juárez and Degollado near the hotel, serves basic *norteña* fare with excellent Sonoran tortillas. **Café Plaza,** a block south of the plaza, is a more casual spot without a printed menu; it's open for breakfast and lunch and serves good Sonoran tortillas, burgers, and fresh cheese *(panela).* Locally grown sugarcane is made into tasty *dulces* each November and March; the sweets are often flavored with *membrillo* (a type of guava), avocado, and other regional produce.

Buses leave from the edge of the plaza for Ures, Hermosillo, and Cananea once or twice a day.

Huépac

Around 56 km (34 miles) south of Arizpe, Huépac is another fading Sonoran colonial outpost. Founded in 1679, the town features a tidy plaza fronting **Misión San Lorenzo,** a church originally built by Jesuits in 1639. Notable in the interior are stone pilasters carved with various motifs, including floral designs, a crown, a heart and cross, and angelic figures. The **Fiesta de San Lorenzo,** held August 8-12, features colorful processions, music, and mock battles between the Moors and Christians. **Motel Misioneros** offers basic accommodations. Food is limited to several grocery shops in town, plus two homes off the highway between Kms 40 and 45 that sell *comidas caseras* roughly 7 a.m. to 7 p.m.

Aconchi

At the foot of the Sierra Aconchi, nine km south of Huépac, is the small town of Aconchi (pop. 1,600), renowned for its chiles and for a nearby hot springs. Twin-towered **Misión San Pedro Aconchi** dates to the 18th-century Franciscan presence in the area; a unique black Christ figure surmounts the altar, a purely Mexican indication that hot springs are in the vicinity. *Artesanos* in Aconchi make rustic wooden furniture. **Casa de Huéspedes Lupita** and a very basic, no-name **hotel**—both off the main street through town—rent shoestring-priced rooms.

The **Agua Caliente hot springs** can be reached from a signed dirt road running west from the north end of Aconchi. Once you're on this road, take the first fork left, then follow the road as it curves south, crossing up to three streams depending on the season. The total distance from town to Agua Caliente is 6.3 km (3.9 miles); a sturdy, high-clearance vehicle is recommended. If you're coming from north of Aconchi, you can also reach Agua Caliente from the village of San Felipe de Jesús, which is four km north of Aconchi. Take the "main" dirt road west and northwest from the village (about 9.5 km or six miles) to the hot springs.

Pumped by solar panels, the springs feed into a series of pools and tubs of varying temperatures; a German woman manages the complex. A large bust of the late presidential candidate and Sonora native Luis Donaldo Colosio was added to the grounds in 1996. Huge mesquite trees shade a picnic/camping area that offers barbecue grills, picnic tables, toilets, and showers. Modest fees are charged for day-use (less than US$1) and camping. For day-use the park is open daily 7 a.m.-7 p.m. The gate may be closed midweek—local patronage is mostly limited to the weekends (almost exclusively Sunday)—but the caretakers will open it and you'll have the place all to yourselves.

Baviácora and Mazocahui

Toward the junction of Sonora 118 are the tidy adobe towns of Baviácora and Mazocahui, both regional centers for the chile trade. You can buy a large *ristra* of dried red chiles for around US$3.50 from any of the many *chileros* who grow and dry the treasured capsicum along the way—fall is the main chile-drying season. *Chiltepíns* can also sometimes be seen here.

Though these towns were founded in the 17th century, neither offers much of obvious historical interest to the potential visitor. In Baviácora, a substantial rock chapel called **Misión de la Purísima Concepción,** was founded by Fray Bartolomé Castaños in 1639 but renovated several times since then.

Posada Familiar Baviácora (the sign reads "Motel Posada") near Km 21 has six clean rooms, including one with a/c; shoestring to budget rates. **Restaurante San Francisco** on the plaza serves Mexican food 8 a.m.-9 p.m. daily.

The drive along Sonora 89 between Mazocahui and Baviácora parallels the Río Sonora through a particularly pretty stretch of river vistas, rock formations, valleys, and side canyons.

Nacozari de García

This clean and prospering mining town roughly midway between Agua Prieta and Moctezuma on Mexico 17 has yielded valuable mineral deposits of one kind or another since the 17th century. The Spanish unearthed gold ore here in 1660, most of which had been played out by the late 1800s when American interests arrived. The Americans converted the mines to copper extraction, and today La Caridad is the third-largest copper mine in the world. This mine and the

EDWARD S. CURTIS

Chiricahua Apache chief Goyahkla, known to most of the world as "Geronimo." Goyahkla and his Apache followers sought refuge in the northern foothills of the Sierra Madre near the Sonora-Chihuahua border before surrendering to the U.S. government in 1886.

Cobre Grande in Cananea together produce 85% of Mexico's copper.

Despite the industrial aspect of the mines, Nacozari (an Indian word meaning "place where nopals abound") presents a more pleasant face to the world than Cananea. The older sections of town consist of simple rock houses—or occasionally two-story wooden houses with upper verandas—built in and around a canyon; many streets are steep and winding. Local *corridos* sing of a legendary 1907 episode when a mining train carrying dynamite caught fire in town; mine worker Jesús García drove the train to the outskirts where it exploded and he died a hero; the town added "de García" to its name to commemorate this brave and selfless act. A 1909 obelisk and replica of steam engine No. 501 in the town square also pay homage to García. A short-line freight train still runs between Nacozari and Agua Prieta, where it connects with the U.S rail network.

Hotel Ana Cristina, near the entrance to town, is a modern-looking place with attached restaurant and budget rooms. **Hotel Imperial,** deeper into town and valley, offers a nice view of town and also falls into the budget category. Among the services available are two PEMEX stations, a hospital, and several grocery shops.

Moctezuma

Eighty-one km (49 miles) south of Nacozari de García, Moctezuma was founded by Jesuit missionaries in 1664 as San Miguel Arcángel. The current name came in 1828 as part of a national push to rid Mexico of its colonial past and celebrate its Mesoamerican roots. It's doubtful, however, that such roots ever extended into this corner of the country, where peaceful Pueblo Indian settlements were destabilized by the Spanish *entrada* and later terrorized by the Apaches.

Today Moctezuma is a poor town of decaying 18th- and 19th-century adobes. **Iglesia de la Candelaria** on the main square was constructed in 1626, restored following a destructive earthquake in 1887, and remodeled yet again in 1982. It's painted bright white, and four Greco-Roman pilasters on the facade lend a distinctive look to its classic Sonoran "wedding cake" profile.

Although they rarely see foreign visitors, **Hotel Marta** and **Hotel La Copa** near the plaza will rent shabby rooms at shoestring prices. Dining options include three taco stands and one *pollo asado* stand in town near the highway junction to Hermosillo, plus a couple of *tiendas* where you can pick up basic groceries. Southwest of town on Mexico 14, between Kms 143 and 144, a small whitewashed building signed **Café Luz** serves basic Mexican truck-stop fare.

From here to Hermosillo, Mexico 14 winds through a relatively lush corridor of *matorral,* farms, and volcanic rock formations.

Ures

When Cabeza de Vaca and his Amerindian followers from the American Southwest arrived in Ures in 1536, the natives offered 600 deer hearts to the travelers. De Vaca's comment on the local population: "They are a substantial people with a capacity for unlimited development." Under Spanish rule, Ures prospered (on the backs of the natives, whose population today is not so substantial), and in postcolonial Mexico went on to serve as the state capital twice in the 19th century.

A way station between Mazocahui and Hermosillo on Mexico 14, present-day Ures is a town whose natural charm has been partially obscured by Mexican highway culture. A few remainders of the town's glory days are in evidence, chiefly the **Plaza de Armas** and scattered 18th- and 19th-century architecture. The 19th-century Franciscan, twin-towered **Misión San Miguel Arcángel** has been restored and whitewashed.

Machaca vendors line the highway through town, as Ures is deservedly famous for the Sonoran-style dried and shredded meat. The town is also well known for *panocha,* a candy made from sugarcane—most available following the annual cane harvest each fall. Hermosillo residents often drive up to Ures for the *carne asada, machaca,* and *rajas poblanas* (roasted chile strips) at **Restaurante La Diligencia de Ures.**

Hotel Misión d'Sales, opposite the bus terminal on the main road, has budget rooms. Many TNS buses running along Mexico 17 stop in Ures.

HERMOSILLO

Set amid sweeping plains of golden grasses and green-tufted hills, with tall, serrated peaks rising abruptly in the background, this bustling city serves a dual role as Sonora's state capital and foremost agricultural center. A pleasant mix of modern Mexico and old Sonora, Hermosillo holds diverse restaurants, supermarkets, ice-cream parlors, discos, a university of 20,000 students, and an American consulate.

Before the *entrada,* a Pima Indian settlement called Pitic ("Place Where Rivers Meet") lay at the confluence of the Sonora and San Miguel Rivers—a site now flooded by Presa Rodríguez on the eastern edge of the city. In 1700, the Spanish superimposed a colony called Santísima Trinidad del Pitic on the site; because of confrontations with Pima and Seri it was nearly a century before the colony was considered "safe" for settlers.

In 1828 the city's name was changed to Hermosillo in honor of a general from Jalisco who was a hero in the war for independence from Spain. As New Spain became Mexico, and Mexico subdivided its territory into smaller states, Hermosillo became in turn the capital of the state of Occidente, then of Sinaloa y Sonora, and finally of Sonora.

Because it offers all the conveniences of "home," Hermosillo is a common stopover for American visitors heading down the coast. A few Americans have chosen to live here, not only for the modern amenities but also because Hermosillo enjoys the lowest consumer price index of Mexico's 35 largest cities—and it's less than two hours from the Sea of Cortez.

For a city of over half a million, the traffic here moves quite well. If you avoid commute hours, you can breeze through town in 10-15 minutes. But Hermosillo is worth a longer stopover—for downtown strolls along the laurel-lined avenues and visits to the cathedral, regional museum, and ecological park.

The best time of year for a visit is Oct.-May. During Semana Santa (the week before Easter), local Yaquis give native dance performances in the city's Barrio del Coloso. In summer Hermosillo bakes, reaching sweltering Tucson-like temperatures as high as 44° C (111° F).

SIGHTS

Many of the city's prominent sights are found along or near a major north-south boulevard variously labeled as Blvd. Kino, Blvd. Rodríguez, and Blvd. Rosales.

Plaza Zaragoza

Hermosillo's city heart since 1865, this spacious downtown plaza features a lofty, Florentine-style *kiosco* (kiosk) built in the early 1900s. At either end of the plaza are the city's two greatest architectural attractions, the Palacio de Gobierno and Catedral de La Asunción (see below).

To reach the plaza from the city's northern entrance, drive or catch a city bus southwest along Blvd. Kino until it becomes Blvd. Rosales. The plaza is bounded at the north and south by Blvd. Hidalgo and Calle Dr. Paliza, both of which run west off Blvd. Rosales.

Palacio de Gobierno

Sonora's capitol was originally constructed as a Casa Municipal in 1859, using Yaqui labor and stone quarried from Cerro de la Campana. Governor Don Carlos Rodríguez had the neoclassic, brick and adobe structure rebuilt in 1881, hoping to turn it into the Instituto Sonorense de Bellas Artes (Sonoran Institute of Fine Arts). The governor's dream was never realized as political complexities forced him to leave office before his term ended. His successor converted the building into the Palacio de Gobierno in 1884.

The Palacio was almost completely destroyed by fire in 1948. In recent years it has been extensively restored and is now one of the most impressive government buildings in Northern Mexico. An interior courtyard is planted with trees and displays murals with regional themes.

Catedral de La Asunción

This huge, white, twin-towered cathedral with a striking, tiered facade sits opposite the Palacio de Gobierno at the other end of the plaza. The original adobe chapel on this site, completed in 1778, had decayed so much by 1877 that 800 local

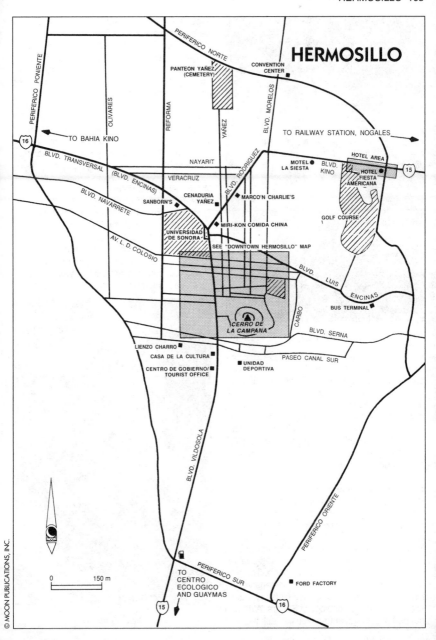

Catedral de La Asunción

to open the underground cells where prisoners were kept in solitary confinement.

Hours are Tues.-Sat. 10 a.m.-5 p.m., Sunday 9 a.m.-4 p.m.; admission is US$1.20 all days except Sunday, when it's free. A small public library onsite, tel. (62) 13-1234, is open Mon.-Fri. 8 a.m.-2 p.m.; admission to the library is free.

To reach the museum from downtown Hermosillo, take Blvd. Luis Encinas east to Calle Jesús García Final, then turn right (south) on Jesús García and continue eight blocks toward Cerro de la Campana until you see the museum on the right.

Museo Regional de la Universidad de Sonora

This museum, part of the campus of the University of Sonora at the intersection of Blvd. Rosales and Blvd. Luis Encinas, opened its doors in 1974 and contains numerous historical and archaeological exhibits from northwestern Mexico. Among them are the 500-year-old mummies of a Pima mother and child from Yécora, a

women petitioned the Catholic diocese to have it replaced. The current neoclassical edifice was constructed in 1908 with a tall, single bell tower; the south tower was added in 1912. Between the two is a huge cupola. The tiered columns, niches, and arches give the impression of a very elaborate wedding cake. One slightly unorthodox detail of the cathedral iconography are the *caravacas,* crosses featuring two crossbars, affixed to the tops of both towers.

Museo Regional de Sonora

Perched just above the foot of Cerro de la Campana, the imposing 19th-century stone building that houses this museum served as a state penitentiary from 1907-79. In 1985 Mexico's Instituto Nacional de Antropología e Historia (INAH) turned it into a museum devoted to regional research, conservation, and education. The museum's 18 rooms feature comprehensive exhibits on the astronomy, geology, history, natural history, and anthropology of Sonora. Although not part of the regular tour, you can ask the staff

Yécora mummy

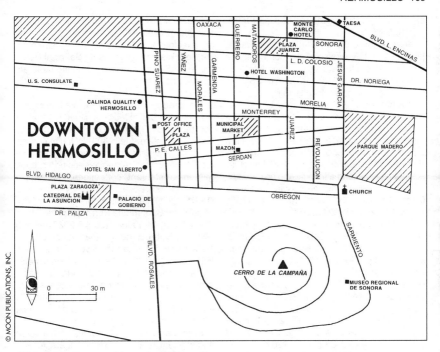

DOWNTOWN HERMOSILLO

© MOON PUBLICATIONS, INC.

0   30 m

1900-vintage topographic map of Hermosillo, a deck of cards made of leather by Spanish colonists and decorated with Seri motifs, and original musical scores by composer Silvestre Rodríguez. Open Mon.-Fri. 9 a.m.-1 p.m. and 4-6 p.m., Saturday 9 a.m.-1 p.m.

Centro Ecológico de Sonora

Created in 1984, this part-zoological, part-botanical gardens just south of town exhibits regional flora and fauna on 2,470 acres of desert. A 2.8-km (1.7-mile) asphalt path weaves through the center's various displays, which cover around 300 plant and 200 animal species, many of them indigenous to Sonora.

The center is open Wed.-Sun. 8 a.m.-5 p.m.; admission is US$0.80. The turnoff for the center is three km (1.9 miles) south of town off Mexico 15 (watch for a sign reading "Parque Ecológico"), after which you must follow a two-km access road east to the main entrance and parking lot. Except for city taxi, no public transportation to the center is available.

ACCOMMODATIONS

Hermosillo's hotels are concentrated in two separate areas: the *zona hotelera* along Blvd. Kino at the north end of the city, where the higher-end hotels and restaurants tend to be; and the downtown district close to Plaza Zaragoza and the municipal market, offering less expensive lodgings that are also more convenient for city explorations on foot. Only one RV park is available in town, but more options lie to the west (details below).

Downtown

Shoestring: The city's best low-budget choice is the friendly **Hotel Washington,** Calle Dr. Noriega Pte. 68 (between Guerrero and Matamoros), tel. (62) 13-1183, fax (62) 13-6502. It's near downtown eating and shopping, and the rooms—built around a courtyard—are simple but clean. The hotel doesn't have hot water or a parking lot, but parking can be arranged at one of the nearby security garages. Rates: US$9 s, US$10.50 d.

Nearby **Monte Carlo Hotel,** on Calle Juárez, tel. (62) 12-0853, offers simple rooms with a/c and TV. The attached Mexican restaurant is also a bargain. Rates: US$13 s, US$14 d, US$16 t, US$17 q, and US$19-21 for suites.

Budget: Hotel Kino, Calle Pino Suárez Sur 151, tel. (62) 13-3131, offers 144 plain rooms in a rambling 1863-vintage, three-story building. Street noise could be a drawback. Rates: from US$19. The colorful old **Hotel San Alberto,** Rosales at Serdán, tel. (62) 13-1840, has character, ambience, and a friendly and helpful staff. Guests receive a complimentary full breakfast. On the down side, the rooms are old and musty. Rates: US$21 s, US$24 d, US$27 t, US$30 q.

One of the better downtown hotels is the three-story **Hotel La Finca,** Calle Matamoros at G. Madrid, tel. (62) 17-1717. Rooms at the clean and efficient La Finca surround a courtyard with a pool and jacuzzi. A small parking lot is attached. Rates: US$26 s, US$31 d. The remodeled, three-story **San Andrés Hotel,** Calle Oaxaca 14 (at Juárez), tel. (62) 17-4305 or 17-3099, fax (62) 17-3139, lacks charm but is efficient and has a safe parking lot. Rooms feature a/c, phone, and satellite TV. Rates: US$24 s, US$26 d.

Inexpensive: The bland, high-rise **Calinda Quality Hermosillo,** Rosales at Calle Morelia, tel. (62) 17-2396, U.S. tel. (800) 221-2222, offers standard-looking rooms. Rates: US$39-50 s/d.

Hostel: Quakers or those affiliated with the sect may be able to stay at an eight-bed Quaker-sponsored hostel called **Casa Herberto Sein,** in an older colonial-style building at Calle Felipe Salido 32, tel. (62) 17-0142. Inspired by Mexico City's Casa de los Amigos hostel, it's reportedly under the care of the Pima (Tucson) Friends Meeting, which is involved with development work in the Sierra Madre. Call for further information and reservations.

Zona Hotelera (Blvd. Kino)

Budget: At Km 2, the one-story, 46-room **San Martín Motel,** Blvd. Kino at Calle San Javier, tel. (62) 10-4105, fax (62) 10-4109, is good value for the *zona hotelera.* Rooms are clean and come with a/c, carpet, phone, and satellite TV. Rates: US$25 s/d/t/q. **Motel La Siesta,** Blvd. Kino at Calle Carpena, tel. (62) 14-3043, is a one-story American-style motel whose comfortable rooms come with satellite TV, phone, and small refrigerators. Rates: US$23-35. Next door, the **Best Western Hermosillo Señorial Hotel,** tel. (62) 15-5155, offers very comfortable a/c rooms, a pool, and a restaurant. Rates: US$29 s, US$34 d, US$46 t, US$77 q.

Moderate: The **Holiday Inn Valle Grande,** Blvd. Kino at Calle R. Corral, tel. (62) 14-4570, fax (62) 14-6473, Mexico toll-free tel. (800) 6-2333, U.S. toll-free tel. (800) HOLIDAY, rents comfortable standard rooms with all the modern conveniences. Amenities include a pool, gardens, restaurant, coffeeshop, and complimentary buffet breakfast. Suites available. Rates: US$78 s/d. Other hotels in this price range include **Hotel Bugambilia Hermosillo,** Blvd. Kino 712, tel. (62) 14-5050 or (800) 6-2333, fax (62) 14-5252; **Hotel Gándara,** Blvd. Kino, tel. (62) 14-4414; and **Araiza Inn,** Blvd. Kino 353, tel. (62) 10-2717, fax (62) 10-4541. All feature pools and security parking; the Araiza Inn also has a lighted tennis court. Room tariffs seesaw depending on whether special rates are currently available; it's worth calling in advance to see which hotels are offering discounts.

Premium: The city's top hotel is the modern and efficient, 218-room **Hotel Fiesta Americana Hermosillo,** Blvd. Kino 369, tel. (62) 69-6000, fax (62) 59-6060, Mexico toll-free tel. (800) 0-0999. A popular choice for visiting business executives, the five-star Fiesta Americana offers very comfortable rooms with all the amenities. Facilities include an attractive lobby bar, a popular disco, heated pool, two restaurants, and security parking. Rates: US$125 s/d during the week; less on weekends.

Northeastern Outskirts of Town

East of the San Martín Hotel, the **Motel Costa del Sol** (near the Café Combate distributor, north of Km 3), **Autoparador Motel,** and **Motel Costa Rica** all offer similar rooms in the budget range.

FOOD

Sonoran cuisine—centered around ranchero-style cooking—is well represented in Hermosillo. The state claims to have the highest quality beef in Mexico; *carne asada* (grilled beef)—

JOE CUMMINGS

making Sonoran-style tortillas

served with Sonoran *sobaqueras* (huge, paper-thin flour tortillas) and pickled chiles—is a big favorite available at virtually every restaurant in town. In addition to the *sobaqueras,* smaller, thicker flour tortillas called *coyotas* are also common. Supposedly originating in Hermosillo's Villa de Seris, *coyotas* are baked in an oven instead of on a *comal* (griddle).

Other local specialties to look for include *cocido* (a stew of garbanzo beans, beef or pork, corn, onions, tomatoes, potatoes, and other vegetables), *burros de machaca* (burritos made with dried, shredded beef), and *chimichangas* (similar to a burrito with additional vegetable ingredients, deep-fried whole). These latter dishes aren't always found in the *zona hotelera* restaurants; check out the *taquerías* and *loncherías* downtown. The municipal market's well-worn lunch counters are an inexpensive place to experiment—you'll find them on the southern end of Matamoros between Monterrey and P.E. Calles.

At the most typically Sonoran eateries you'll see bowls of red, berrylike *chiltepines* on the tables or counters—local customers munch these fiery peppers as a condiment along with their meal. Before dipping into the bowl, be sure to have on hand a glass of water or a *soda,* as Sonorans tend to call soft drinks.

Also very popular in Hermosillo are *tacos de cabeza* (literally "head tacos," featuring beef cheek and tongue), commonly sold by street vendors—some of whom take in as much as US$1,000 a day. Although some vendors set up for lunchtime, prime taco stand hours are dusk to midnight.

Because Hermosillo is close to the Sea of Cortez coast, seafood restaurants are also available as alternatives to the typically beef-oriented Sonoran menu.

The following list represents places selected for quality, reliability, and location—you'll find dozens of other restaurants to sample in the city if you have the time and inclination.

Carne Asada and Steak

Sonora Steak Restaurant Bar, Blvd. Kino 914, Col. Pitic, tel. (62) 10-0313. Sonoran beef, chicken, fresh fish, pasta, and salads. Modern Sonoran-style architecture. Open Sun.-Wed. noon-2 a.m., Thurs.-Sat. noon-3 a.m.

Restaurante Xochimilco, Calle Obregón 51(Jardines de Xochimilco, off Blvd. Vildósola, in the Villa de Seris district at the south end of the city), tel. (62) 13-3489. Established in 1949, this is the most famous restaurant in Hermosillo for *carne asada, costillas* (ribs), and *tripitas* (tripe, served as an appetizer). Most customers purchase a *paquete,* which includes *carne asada* or *costillas,* tortillas, beans, and *tripitas* for one price. *Trobadores* wander from table to table. Open daily 9 a.m.-midnight.

Xochimilco Steak, Blvd. Kino 908, tel. (62) 14-5906. Conveniently located in the hotel zone, this more "international" version of the original Xochimilco features aged steaks. Open daily noon-midnight.

La Carreta, Periférico Sur (South Loop), 300 meters west of Blvd. Vildósola, tel. (62) 15-0130. In addition to *carne asada,* this buffet-style restaurant offers a wide selection of other Sonoran specialties, including *carne con chile* (beef in a chile sauce), *picadillo* (spicy meat salad), and *tamales de elote* (fresh corn tamales). Open daily noon-5 p.m.

Steak del Herradero, Blvd. Navarrete, Col. La Huerta, tel. (62) 15-8406. Rustic ranch-style decor. The specialty is American-style steaks served on hot platters. Open daily noon-midnight.

Mexican

Cenaduría Yáñez, Calle Yáñez 7 (off Blvd. Rodríguez), tel. (62) 14-1872. This very simple family-run restaurant is probably the best all-around eatery in the city for value, quality, and selection of *platillos típicos.* Among the menu selections are *tacos, enchiladas, pozole, menudo, machaca, chimichangas, quesadillas,* and *gorditas.* Very inexpensive *comidas corridas* are also available. Service is excellent but restaurant Spanish is a must (see the "Spanish Phrasebook" at the end of this book). Inexpensive. Open daily noon-midnight.

Restaurante Elba, Calles Olivares and de Niza, Col. Los Arcos, tel. (62) 18-4622. Specialties include Mexican-style *milanesa* (breaded veal), *enchiladas suizas,* and fried shrimp. Open daily 7 a.m.-11 p.m.

Marco n' Charlie's Sonora Bar & Grill, corner of Blvd. Rodríguez and Calle San Luis Potosí, tel. (62) 15-3061. Although it's part of the mostly tourist-oriented Grupo Anderson chain (Señor Frog's, Squid Roe, etc.), this particular permutation has one of the chain's best kitchens (and decors) and caters almost exclusively to Hermosillenses (especially upscale couples). The menu changes periodically, but always features authentic interpretations of regional specialties; tortillas are handmade on the premises. The bar is a good place for evening drinks and *botanas.* Open Mon.-Sat. 1 p.m.-midnight.

Puro Tamal, Blvd. L.D. Colosio 413, tel. (62) 60-6400. Fresh *tamales* for under US$1, to go or delivered. Choose pork, pineapple, or cheese and chile varieties. Open daily 10 a.m.-5 p.m.

San Martín Hotel, near the northeastern outskirts of town at Blvd. Kino and Calle San Javier, tel. (62) 10-4105. Serves a US$4.50 buffet for breakfast, lunch, and dinner.

Taquería Acuarios, Blvd. Rodríguez 136 (between Zacatecas and Tamaulipas). A lively nighttime taco place specializing in *tacos caramelos* (tacos stuffed with beans and cheese). Open Mon.-Thurs. 7 p.m.-2 a.m., Fri.-Sat. 9 p.m.-4 a.m., and Sunday 6 p.m.-1 a.m.

International

Henry's, Blvd. Kino 904, tel. (62) 14-7393. One of the hotel zone's classiest restaurants; housed in a converted mansion with a menu that includes chateaubriand, filet mignon, and other continental dishes. Open Mon.-Sat. 1-11:30 p.m., Sunday 1-6 p.m.

Sanborn's, Blvd. Luis Encinas and Navarrete, tel. (62) 15-7515. Truly international, the menu features an ample selection of tasty continental, American, and Mexican dishes at reasonable prices. Breakfasts start at US$2 and are particularly good—try the *huevos ahogados con rajas poblanas* (eggs smothered in roasted chile strips). Open daily 7:30 a.m.-9 p.m.

Swiss Haus, Calle Dr. Paliza 62, tel. (62) 17-5040. Pricey but good; specialties include oxtail soup, pâté, and fondues.

Seafood

El Corral, Calle Puebla and Garmendia, tel. (62) 12-3979. Lots of informal business transactions take place over El Corral's popular seafood cocktails (scallop, shrimp, octopus, oyster, clam, or squid—depending on the season), *caldo largo* (seafood soup), fish tacos, or *pargo frito* (fried snapper). Open daily 8 a.m.-6 p.m.

Restaurante Los Arcos, Calle Ocampo and Michel, Col. Centenario, tel. (62) 13-2220. Specializes in more unusual seafood dishes such as *caguama* (sea turtle—legally harvested), *filete de mero a la Culichi* (broiled seabass fillet), marlin tacos, and baked crab.

Vegetarian

Restaurante Jung, Calle Niños Heroes 75, tel. (62) 13-2881, off Blvd. Luis Encinas near the corner of Calle Matamoros. As is common in Mexico, Jung is actually a combination natural foods and herbal medicine shop, health library, and vegetarian cafe. Many dishes are attempted equivalents of Mexican standards, others are international. You can buy fresh yogurt and whole-wheat bread here as well. Open Mon.-Sat. 8 a.m.-8 p.m., Sunday 9 a.m.-5 p.m. Second branch at Blvd. Morelos 245, tel. (62) 10-2309.

Pizza and Italian
La Fabula is a national chain with nine locations in town. Reliable American-style pizza, spaghetti, and sandwiches; US$3-8. Open daily for lunch and dinner.

Pizzeria La Romana, Calles Yáñez and Morelia, tel. (62) 13-1955. Good all-around pizza, lasagna, and pasta dishes. Open daily noon-11 p.m.

Chinese
Hermosillo boasts more Chinese restaurants than any other city in Northern Mexico. For the most part they are very similar, specializing in large servings of Cantonese dishes oriented toward Mexican tastes.

Miri-Kon Comida China, Blvd. Rodríguez and Calle G. Madrid, tel. (62) 13-1697. Judging from the crowds, this is one of the most popular Chinese eateries in the city. It is also the only one focusing primarily on Mandarin (or northern Chinese) cuisine. Open noon-midnight daily.

Restaurante Bar Jo-Wah, Calle P. Suárez 190, tel. (62) 13-1399. A huge, ornate banquet-style restaurant that specializes in Cantonese seafood. Open noon-midnight daily.

Restaurante Lai-Wah, Blvd. Rodríguez 6, tel. (62) 14-5555. Jo-Wah's main competitor features a similar menu with an equally ample seafood section. Open noon-2 a.m. daily.

RECREATION AND ENTERTAINMENT

Cultural
Hermosillo's **Casa de la Cultura,** on Blvd. Vildósola, tel. (62) 17-1263, hosts weekly performances of ballet and folkloric dancing, films in the Sala de Cine (Sat.-Sun. noon, 4 p.m., and 6 p.m.), gallery exhibitions, and the occasional outdoor musical or drama event in the central courtyard.

Foreign films are sometimes shown at the University of Sonora's humanities department (departamento de humanidades), Blvds. Rosales and Encinas.

Discos and Bars
The **Hotel Fiesta Americana,** Blvd. Kino 369, tel. (62) 69-6000 or (800) 0-0999 toll free in Mexico, has a small but popular video disco that's packed on weekends.

Nova Olimpia, at Calle Soria and Fronteras, tel. (62) 17-3013, is larger, flashier, and requires semiformal dress (sports jackets for men). Nova features live music Mon.-Thurs., disco on weekends, and is open 9 p.m.-2 a.m.

Opposite Araiza Inn on Blvd. Kino, **Freedom** is a semicasual bar that attracts a younger Hermosillo crowd. Also popular with the young and affluent is **Marco n' Charlie's Sonora Bar & Grill,** corner of Blvd. Rodríguez and Calle San Luis Potosí, tel. (62) 15-3061 (also see "Food," above).

Charreadas
The **Asociación de Charros de Hermosillo,** tel. (62) 18-6067, maintains the **Lienzo Charro el Sonorense** (charro arena) at Blvd. Paseo del Vado and Comonfort. During the Sept.-May season, the association organizes monthly charreadas (usually on Sunday) with charro associations from other Sonoran towns. Weekly practice sessions take place on Tuesdays, Thursdays, and Sundays at 8 p.m. at the charro stadium, and are open to the public. Escaramuza practice for charras takes place on Wednesdays and Fridays at 10 a.m.

Fishing and Hunting
Freshwater fishing is possible at several northern Sonora lakes; the sportfishing season for lake bass and tilapia is Feb.-May. Hermosillo's own lake, Presa Rodríguez, is hardly worth throwing bait or lure into, but anglers hone in on Presa Plutarco Elías Calles (Presa Novillo) in San Pedro de la Cueva, 130 km (80.6 miles) east of Hermosillo.

Deportes Alcampo, at Calles Dr. Noriega and Garmendia near the municipal market, sells an extensive selection of sporting goods, including fishing and camping gear. Bird-hunting trips with English-speaking guides can be arranged here.

Baseball and Basketball
When world-famous pitcher Fernando Valenzuela was called up to the Baltimore Orioles in

1993, he had just finished a season playing for the Hermosillo Naranjeros ("Orange-pickers"), one of the best teams in Mexico's Pacific Coast League. In 1976 Hermosillo won the Caribbean World Series, which is held here every few years, always in February. (The playoff rotates between Hermosillo, Mazatlán, Culiacán, and several Caribbean capitals.)

The Naranjeros play at Hermosillo's **Estadio Hector Espino** (named for one of Mexico's most famous ballplayers), which is at the intersection of Blvd. Luis Encinas (Blvd. Transversal) and Periférico Poniente. This is one of the nation's nicest ballparks; during the PCL season (Oct.-Jan.), advance tickets can be purchased at the stadium. Ask at the state tourist office (see "Services and Information," below) for a current schedule of home games.

Hermosillo also fields its own basketball team, Los Seris, which plays at the **Unidad Deportiva** off Paseo del Canal y Comonfort. Check with the tourist office for the latest home-game schedule.

SHOPPING

Hermosillo's traditional shopping district is centered around the 1920-vintage **Mercado Municipal José María Pino Suárez,** at Calle Matamoros between Calles Monterrey and P.E. Calles. The latter two streets, along with nearby Serdán and Juárez, are lined with specialized shops selling leather goods, clothing, Mexican curios, sporting goods, shoes, household goods, and just about anything else you can think of. Street parking is scarce during the day; rather than circle endlessly, park in the inexpensive pay garage next to the market.

Also in the downtown area are several hat and boot shops at the corner of Calles Guaymas and Sonora, next to a *zócalo* (town square). **Mazón,** an a/c department store at the corner of Guerrero and Serdán, is moderately priced for household goods and clothes.

A newer shopping district has grown up around the intersection of Blvd. Luis Encinas and Calle Reforma in the center of the city. Among the several department stores in this area are **Sanborn's** and **Mazón Boulevares,** both at Blvds. Encinas and Navarrete. Sanborn's has the best selection of English-language books

and magazines in town, as well as a small but high-quality selection of arts and crafts.

Other stores specializing in handicrafts include **Arte Típico,** at Calle 12 de Octubre (between Campeche and Quintana Roo), and **Los Tilliches,** at the Hotel Fiesta Americana on Blvd. Kino. You'll also find some handicrafts at the *Mercado Municipal.* Among the best local buys are Seri *canastas* (large baskets) made from fibers of the torote prieto, a desert tree. The famous Seri ironwood *(palo fierro)* sculptures are found in a number of stores around town; **Artesanía Sonorense de Palo Fierro,** at Calles Serdán and P. Suárez, has the largest selection.

TRANSPORTATION

Air
Aeroméxico, Blvd. Navarrete 165, tel. (62) 16-8206, operates direct flights to Chihuahua, Ciudad Juárez, Ciudad Obregón, Guadalajara, La Paz, Los Mochis, Mexicali, Mexico City, Tijuana, and Tucson.

TAESA, Blvd. Navarrete 168-L-5, Plaza Valles, tel. (62) 18-4745, has daily flights to Mexico City and Mexicali.

Noroeste, Blvd. Navarrete 331, tel. (62) 60-4004, flies to and from Mexicali, Cd. Obregón, and Culiacán.

Mexicana, Blvd. Rosales and Palancares, tel. (62) 17-1103, flies nonstop to Chihuahua, Ciudad Obregón, Culiacán, La Paz, Mexicali, and Mexico City daily.

Transportation between the airport and downtown Hermosillo (10 km) costs US$6.50 by taxi, US$4 by *colectivo.*

Taxis
Taxis are plentiful throughout the city, especially in the hotel zone and around the central shopping district. Rates run around US$1 per km for the a/c VW bugs, a little more for sedans.

Buses
Local buses ply the city streets from dawn to midnight. The network is extensive, and the fare on most buses is US$0.12. As elsewhere in Mexico, destinations are displayed on the front of the vehicle. Several small, modern shuttles run the north-south route between the hotel zone

along Blvd. Kino and the downtown area along Blvd. Rosales.

Hermosillo's main long-distance bus companies include Transportes Norte de Sonora (TNS), Transportes Futura, and Transportes del Pacífico, all of which use the **Central de Autobuses de Hermosillo** on Blvd. Transversal (Luis Encinas), tel. (62) 17-0401. Together these bus lines offer first-class (and deluxe, where two fares are shown) transportation to the following destinations: Magdalena (US$5), Nogales (US$6.50), Sonoita (US$12), San Luis Río Colorado (US$19), Navojoa (US$9), Los Mochis (US$12-13), Mazatlán (US$29), Tepic (US$42), Guadalajara (US$45-52), and Mexico City (US$65-75).

In addition, Unión de Autotransportes de Paisaje Foráneo offers daily buses to Agua Prieta (US$8), Nacozari de García (US$6), Arizpe (US$5), Baviácora (US$3.50), and Cananea (US$6.50). Transportación Foranea de la Sierra Sonorense also goes to Agua Prieta (US$8) and Nacozari de García (US$6). For buses to Bahía Kino, use Transportes de la Costa de Hermosillo, at Av. P.E. Calles 99, tel. (62) 12-2194.

The Central de Autobuses has a post and telephone office, a restaurant, and a Guadalupe shrine in the waiting room. Several taco stands line the street opposite the terminal.

Train

Hermosillo's railway station, tel. (62) 14-3829, sits on the del Pacífico line, 2.4 km (1.5 miles) north of downtown, but there is a ticket office at Blvd. Transversal and Calle González, tel. (62) 17-1711 or 13-8701.

The del Pacífico No. 1 (first class) train to Nogales/Mexicali departs at 7:45 a.m. while the No. 2—the same train in reverse—leaves for points south to Guadalajara at 7:45 p.m. Sample fares include Nogales US$5 first class, US$3 second; Mazatlán US$17/10; Empalme (Guaymas) US$3/1.25; Mexicali US$12/7.

Driving

With the four-lane toll highway from Nogales and the well-tended two-lane from La Junta, Chih. (an alternative to taking the Chihuahua al Pacífico train), Hermosillo is easier to reach by road than ever before.

Coming from Nogales/Santa Ana, Mexico 15 links Blvd. Kino at the north end of town with

Blvd. Vildósola at the south end, where it continues on to Guaymas and points farther south. The city is bisected in the east-west direction by Blvd. Luis Encinas (also known as Blvd. Transversal west of Mexico 15); if you follow Blvd. Luis Encinas west it joins the highway to Bahía Kino. A *periférico* joins these two main arteries as a loop or bypass, although first-time visitors to Hermosillo may find the loop's permutations a bit confusing due to the many intersections along the way. If you stick to the main boulevards you'll probably manage better.

Fuel: PEMEX stations are abundant in prosperous Hermosillo and finding Magna Sin is never a problem. If you're just passing through, probably the best place to fill up is at the large **El Sahuaro** station 3.2 km (two miles) south of town; besides unleaded fuel, the station has clean restrooms and ice.

Auto Rental

The following agencies rent cars out of Hermosillo: **Avis,** Blvd. Kino and Villareal, tel. (62) 15-9920; **Hertz,** Blvd. Rodríguez and Guerrero, tel. (62) 14-1695; **National,** Hermosillo Airport, tel. (62) 14-0936; **Budget,** Blvd. Rodríguez and Tamaulipas, tel. (62) 14-3805; and **Optima,** Hotel San Andrés, tel. (62) 17-3099, with a second location at Av. Niños Héroes 18, tel. (62) 13-0204. Cars can also be rented at several hotels and travel agencies in the *zona hotelera.* Rates start at around US$25 per day plus per-km charges for a VW bug.

SERVICES AND INFORMATION

Tourist Offices

The Sonora state tourist office, tel. (62) 17-4664 or 17-0044, is on the third floor of the Edificio Sonora at the Centro de Gobierno on Paseo del Canal and Comonfort, which is near the southern outskirts of town. SECTUR, tel. (62) 17-0857, also has an office on the lower floor of the Palacio Gobierno downtown.

Maps

Topographical maps for Sonora, Chihuahua, and Sinaloa can be purchased at the INEGI office at Paseo Comonfort and Paseo Río Sonora Sur, tel. (62) 13-0264.

HERMOSILLO TELEPHONE NUMBERS

Police	18-6416
Red Cross	06
Highway Patrol	18-9099
Hospital	13-2556
Green Angels	14-6304, 15-3197
cellular	(62) 58-0044
toll-free	(800) 6-2555
Cruz de Oro	13-6616
U.S. Consulate	17-2375
Hermosillo Area Code	62

Money

Along with the many banks found throughout the city, Hermosillo also has a number of *casas de cambio.* Downtown, try **Casa de Cambio Sonora,** 211B Calle Matamoros, or **Casa de Cambio Express,** 31A Calle Matamoros. The **Banamex** at the corner of Serdán and Matamoros has an ATM.

U.S. Consulate

Visiting American citizens can take care of consular business (reporting lost or stolen passports, voting in absentia, etc.) at the U.S. Consulate on Calle Morelia, tel. (62) 17-2375 or 17-2382.

Internet Access

Arroba Cafe-Internet, Blvd. Rodríguez 96 (at the corner of Garmendia), offers daily Internet service 9:00 a.m.-11:00 p.m. Connection costs US$4.30 an hour with a minimum charge of US$1.25 for 15 minutes. E-mail: cafe@acnet.net. Website: www.cafe-arrobba.com.mx. Similar services are offered by **WebChat Cafe & Internet,** Blvd. Luis Encinas and Reforma, tel. (62) 14-1155, www.webchat-cafe.com.mx/.

BAHÍA KINO

This eight-km-long, sand-fringed bay opposite Isla Tiburón lies 117 km (72.5 miles) west of Hermosillo—about an hour and a half drive through Sonoran Desert scenery and the small highway town of Miguel Alemán. Opinions are mixed on how worthwhile a destination Bahía Kino is. The bay itself is beautiful, and the hills rising from the cardón-studded desert to the east add to the setting; sunsets can be spectacular. But the development along the bay is haphazard, ranging from a ramshackle collection of block houses in the fishing village of **Kino Viejo** ("Old Kino") to a characterless string of American beach homes and built-over trailers known collectively as **Kino Nuevo** ("New Kino," or simply "Kino Bay" to most Americans).

The public beach roughly at the middle of Bahía Kino has *palapas,* and vendors selling chilled coconuts; on weekends and holidays it is usually crowded with Hermosillo day-trippers. At the north end of Kino Nuevo is **Cerro Prieto,** a spiky desert hill with excellent bay views (the base of the hill can be reached by dirt road from Kino Nuevo).

The **Museo de los Seris** in Kino Nuevo, at the corner of Calle Progreso and Av. Mar de Cortés (the main street paralleling the beach), has good displays of Seri clothing, folk utensils,

reed kayaks, and other cultural artifacts, plus historic photos taken earlier this century. The museum is open Tues.-Sun. 10 a.m.-1 p.m. and 2-6 p.m.; admission is free but donations are gratefully accepted.

Although about a quarter of the population living in Kino Viejo are Seris, most Seris now live farther north along the coast in Punta Chueca and El Desemboque. Seri ironwood sculptures and torote-fiber baskets can be purchased from vendors in Kino Viejo or at the aforementioned villages.

The area's best coastal features are found north and south of these main settlements—down dirt and gravel roads leading to deserted coves and beaches—as well as across the bay on Isla Tiburón. Unless you've come for the fishing, how much you enjoy a Kino visit may largely depend on whether you have the time and means to explore beyond the main bay developments.

Climate

Bahía Kino's high season for gringos is Dec.-April, when days are generally warm and nights are cool. Summers can be hot and are a popular time for Hermosillo beachgoers. The only rain to speak of (less than 7.5 cm/three inches per annum) falls mostly July-September.

Bahía Kino, as seen from Cerro Prieto

JOE CUMMINGS

FISHING

Although Kino sportfishing isn't what it used to be, offshore it's possible to land marlin, sailfish, and dorado during the summer, or tuna, yellowtail, *cochito* (triggerfish), and seabass the remainder of the year. Inshore and onshore brings in *pargo* (dog snapper), surfperch, ladyfish, sand bass, and shark.

MEXICAN LOBSTERS

O f the several species of lobster scooting about in Mexico's seas, the two most numerous are: *Panulirus interruptus* (known as red lobster or *langosta roja*), found as far south as the 25th parallel on both the Pacific and Sea of Cortez sides; and *P. inflatus* (blue lobster or *langosta azul*) in the Pacific and lower Cortez as far south as Tehuantepec, Oaxaca. None of the lobster species found in Mexican waters are related to the cold-water type (genus *Homarus*) found off the coast of the northeastern U.S. and southeastern Canada. Mexico's warm-water lobsters are sometimes referred to as "spiny lobsters" because their shells bear spiny projections (the *Homarus* shell is smooth). Spiny lobsters also have smaller pincers than the cold-water varieties.

Adult spiny lobsters reach up to 61 cm (24 inches) in length and weigh as much as six kilograms (13 pounds). Most varieties are nocturnal and tend to frequent depths of 5-30 meters. During the daytime they stay beneath or between rocks to hide from their natural enemies (sharks, octopi, rays and a few larger finfish). Their diet consists mostly of crustaceans, mollusks, and other small sea organisms.

Lobstering is a major part of the fishing industry in Mexico, the world's eighth largest harvester of lobster. An average 700 metric tons are harvested annually; about half of the total catch is exported, earning around US$8 million in foreign revenues. The official lobstering seasons are: March 16-Sept. 30 (red lobster) and June 1-Sept. 15 (blue lobster). It is illegal to take lobsters out of Mexico unless accompanied by a receipt that shows they were purchased from a store or a *cooperativa de pesca* (fishing cooperative).

Favorite surf-casting spots are the beach at Kino Viejo and the rocks next to Caverna del Seri Trailer Park. Onshore fishing is even better if you're willing to head north or south from Bahía Kino, ferreting out sandy roads leading to deserted rock points. *Pangas* can be rented in Kino Viejo for offshore fishing trips. Larger fishing cruisers are available in Kino Nuevo—check with the Kino Bay Sportsman's Club. Typical rates are US$120 per day or US$300 per three days, but these are sometimes negotiable—some boat pilots will go as low as US$80 a day if you pay for the gas.

The local headquarters for gringo anglers is **Club Deportivo Bahía Kino,** Apdo. Postal 84, Bahía Kino, Son. 83340, tel. (624) 2-0321, in a large Quonset hut at the north end of Kino Nuevo; open Mon.-Sat. 8 a.m.-noon and 1-5 p.m. Also known by its English name, Kino Bay Sportsman's Club, this membership organization sells fishing licenses, arranges boat charters, and organizes parties for local *americanos.*

PRACTICALITIES

Motels

Bahía Kino's accommodations tend to be weatherworn, musty, and overpriced.

Budget: At the bay's south end between old and new Kino, **Posada del Mar,** tel. (624) 2-0155, has large a/c rooms with lukewarm showers. The pool and sea-view terrace almost compensate for the lack of upkeep. Rates: US$23-36. In Kino Viejo you may be able to stay at **Islandia (Isla) Marina,** which offers a few basic, three- to four-person cabins with kitchens. Rates: US$22 a night. Trailer parking is also available. **Bella Vista Trailer Park** (see "RV Parks," below) also offers a few simple a/c rooms. Rates: US$25 s/d in winter, US$35 in summer.

Budget/Inexpensive: For midweek visits one of the best deals in town is toward the north end of Kino Nuevo at **Kino Bay Motel,** on Av. Mar de Cortés across from the beach, tel. (624) 2-0216. The Kino Bay offers clean, well-kept rooms with kitchenettes. Rates: US$26 Sun-Thurs., US$40 on weekends.

Inexpensive: On the beach right in the middle of Kino Nuevo, **Saro's** offers 16 basic but cozy apartments with a/c. Rates: US$35 a night, ne-

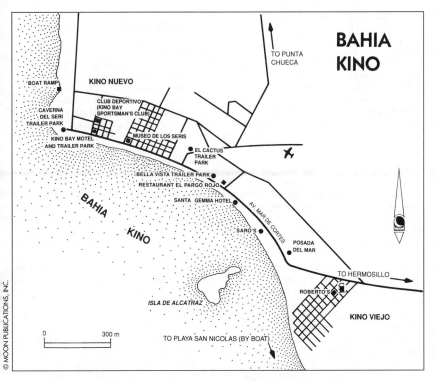

gotiable for longer stays.

Moderate: Farther north along Av. Mar de Cortés, the **Santa Gemma Hotel,** tel. (624) 2-0026, is right on the beach and offers 14 renovated bungalows with a/c, kitchen, and fireplace. Rates: US$75 a night.

Bed and Breakfast
The Anchor House, tel. (624) 2-0141, offers comfortable rooms with attached bath in a private beach house. Rates are US$60-70 per couple, including tax and breakfast. Write Apdo. Postal 80-83340, Bahía Kino, Sonora, for reservations.

RV Parks
Kino accommodation fares better if you bring your own. Across from the beach at Kino Nuevo's north end, **Kino Bay Trailer Park,** tel. (624) 2-0216, has 179 sites, a decent restau-

rant/bar, coin laundry, boat ramp, propane, and a small general store. Rates are US$15 for two persons, US$2 for each additional person; monthly rates are available.

Not far from Restaurant El Pargo Rojo and Santa Gemma Hotel, **Bella Vista Trailer Park,** tel. (624) 2-0139, is a new, family-run place on the beach with full hookups for US$14.50 a day; weekly and monthly rates available.

Near Club Deportivo, **Kunkaak Trailer Park,** tel. (624) 2-0088, has 54 sites and a coin laundry for US$12.50; it's the only real competition for Kino Bay Trailer Park. Monthly rates available.

El Cactus Trailer Park, tel. (62) 16-1643, is on the road to the airfield, well away from the beach, and costs US$11. Monthly rates available.

If staying in Kino Viejo appeals, try for a spot at **Islandia Marina,** tel. (624) 2-0081, right on Kino's main fishing beach. RV/trailer spaces, some with *palapas* or pull-through shelters, cost a bargain US$10 per day.

Food

Several simple restaurants in Kino Viejo offer seafood fresh from local fishing boats. During the Oct.-May shrimping season, fresh shrimp is especially abundant.

Restaurante Marlín is an old favorite catering to gringos as well as Hermosillenses. **Restaurante Doritas,** on the main street in from the highway, has good breakfasts and *antojitos.* Prices at either place run US$4-10.

More local in ambience are two rustic, *palapa*-style places in Kino Viejo: **Restaurante Las Gaviotas** and **Costa Azul,** adjacent to one another on the south side of the village. In the evenings, live *norteña* bands sometimes play for small groups of fishermen here; US$3-8 a meal. A newer spot, **Roberto's,** a *palapa* place a block south of the PEMEX station under a water tower, specializes in Mexican *antojitos* as well as seafood. A house specialty is *tortitas de camarón,* fried shrimp cakes. Open for breakfast and lunch; meals run US$2-5.

If you tire of seafood, shuffle over to **Taquería Sahuaripa,** one block west and three blocks south of the PEMEX station. At night this outdoor Mexican *antojitos* stand is jammed with locals who come to devour delicious tacos, *chimichangas, chiles rellenos,* and other dishes priced at US$1 or less per item—and to watch the three attractive sisters who do the cooking.

In Kino Nuevo, **Restaurant El Pargo Rojo,** in a pink building with *palapa* roof, caters to the retired gringo community with great seafood (US$5-10 a plate) and margaritas.

You can buy fresh oysters at the *ostionerías* on the north end of Estero Santa Cruz, southeast of Kino Viejo, for around US$2 per dozen. Bring your own hot sauce, limes, and beer.

Transportation

Buses run eight times daily between Hermosillo (from the terminal on Av. Serdán, between Jesús García and González) and Bahía Kino. The fare is about US$3. At Bahía Kino the buses usually stop at the PEMEX station at the edge of Kino Viejo and farther on along Av. Mar de Cortés in Kino Nuevo. The Kino Viejo PEMEX station usually carries Magna Sin.

VICINITY OF BAHÍA KINO

Isla Tiburón

Measuring 47 km (29 miles) long and 24 km (15 miles) wide, Isla Tiburón (Shark Island) is the largest island in Mexico and an officially designated *reserva especial de la biosfera* or "special biosphere reserve." As a continental island—a chunk of the mainland left behind as activity on the San Andreas Fault separated Baja California from the rest of Mexico—Tiburón's desert landscape is much like that along the Bahía Kino coast. Most of the island is covered in Sonoran *matorral,* while red, white, and black mangroves grow along the shoreline of Canal del Infiernillo. Two small sierras, Menor and Kunkaak, hold peaks rising as high as 1,200 meters (4,000 feet).

Once an important Seri Indian homeland, the island is now a national wildlife refuge protecting bighorn sheep and other Sonoran Desert species extinct or nearly extinct on the mainland. The island's two springs also help support populations of hares, coyotes, bobcats, foxes, deer, pelicans, sea swallows, and petrels. Clams are found along the rocky shores, while squid lurk just offshore. In total the island and its surrounding waters harbor 52 land mammal species, 39 reptile and amphibian species, and 10 marine mammal species. Reported resident and migratory bird species number 178.

The island was named for the huge schools of hammerhead sharks that used to congregate in the Canal del Infiernillo. The sharks were all but fished out by 1963, when Pres. Adolfo López Mateos declared the island a *reserva natural y refugio para la silvestre* (natural reserve and wildlife refuge). The Seris were forced from the island in 1975 in an effort to enforce protection of the island, but they are still legally permitted to fish along the island's shores. Unfortunately, they also occasionally harvest mesquite and mangrove to make charcoal, exacerbating habitat loss for local land and marine wildlife.

The island can be reached by powerboat from Kino Nuevo in about 45 minutes. Inquire at the Club Deportivo Bahía Kino or in Kino Viejo for charters, which typically cost US$40 pp for drop-off and pick-up service. The charter includes a SEMARNAP permit, required for all non-Seri visitors to the island. Visitors with their own boats should apply to the SEMARNAP office in Hermosillo for the necessary permit.

Sometimes a stop at **Isla Pelicano,** a smaller island between Kino and Isla Tiburón, can be arranged.

Playa San Nicolás

This stunning cove south of Bahía Kino is remarkably pristine and unvisited, considering its proximity to civilization. For years rumors of an upcoming hotel development have simmered, but for now it's one of the Sonora coast's nicest beaches, to some extent preserved by bad roads and general anonymity.

You'll need your own transportation—rugged transportation—to get here. Heading west on Mexico 16 toward Bahía Kino, take the signed turnoff south between Km 94 and 95. The Playa San Nicolás sign reads "12 km" but with detours around washed-out sections, it's more like 22.5 km one-way. The first part of the road is wide and graded but eventually the road veers west before the village of Valle Verde and turns into a bumpy, sandy ride all the way to the cove.

The drive, however, is almost as rewarding as the beach itself. Unless it has been a particularly dry year, you'll pass desert basins—including the huge Salinas Santa Cruz—filled with shrimp and frequented by waterfowl. Total driving time is around 60-90 minutes, depending on road conditions, your vehicle, and your off-highway driving skills. Don't attempt this trip without 4WD if it has recently rained heavily.

A recent report says the road may be closed, i.e., gated; rumors are divided between those who say it's because of pending development and those who say it's a security measure to stop *narcotraficantes* from using the beach as a transfer point for contraband. If you can't get in by road, ask in Bahía Kino about boat charters.

THE SERIS

Seri Villages

Around 450 Seris live north of Bahía Kino in the villages of **Punta Chueca** and **El Desemboque** (also known as Desemboque del Seri), which are supported primarily by fishing and the manufacture of baskets and ironwood carvings. These two villages are respectively 29 km (18 miles) and 90 km (56 miles) north of Kino via a coastal dirt road. The first leg to Punta Chueca is passable by ordinary car, while the stretch beyond to Desemboque requires a sturdy vehicle with good road clearance.

In spite of their small numbers, the Seris (who call themselves *konka'ak,* or "people") have resisted government efforts to integrate them into Mexican society. About half are bilingual in Spanish and their native tongue; a few have also learned English from the steady trickle of Bahía Kino tourists who manage to find their way north.

History

The probable ancestors of the Seri came to the upper Sonoran coast and Isla Tiburón some 500-1,000 years ago. They were the first culture to inhabit the region in any numbers and are associated with a style of "eggshell" pottery known as Tiburón Plain Ware. Apparently these early residents passed down their pottery techniques from generation to generation, for by the time the Spanish reached the area the Seri were produc-

WILLIAM DINWIDDIE

Seri woman, 1894

ing pottery with the highest ratio of carrying capacity to wall thickness in North America. An early anthropologist noted a Seri pot that held 15 liters but weighed less than two kilograms; a comparable Papago pot of four-liter capacity was said to weigh 17 kilograms. Unfortunately, the sophisticated ceramic technique used to produce such wonderful pots has not survived.

The Seris lived in cliff and cave dwellings and relied on hunting and foraging for food. They were said to be the tallest of all Indian groups in Mexico, and apparently they were also renowned for their running skills; the name "Seri" is of Opata Indian origin and means "they who run swiftly." Despite their seminomadic ways, by the 17th century the Seris had become the most powerful Amerindian culture in northwestern Mexico. When the first Spanish missionaries settled among the Seris in the early 18th century, Seri homelands extended well inland from the Río Yaqui into Pimería Alta. The Jesuits were able to missionize a large number of Seris early on, but by the 1740s the Seris had grown tired of constant maltreatment by Spanish soldiers. After warning the padres to leave, the Seris attacked Spanish settlements throughout the area, killing perhaps hundreds of Spaniards. They then retreated to the coast.

The Spanish made repeated unsuccessful attempts to attack and exterminate the Seris, who turned out to be adversaries as fierce and accomplished as the Yaquis. Among all the Amerindian groups in Mexico, only the Seris used poison-tipped arrows, which they could shoot with a force sufficient to penetrate the eight layers of deerskin the Spanish soldiers wore as frontier armor. German missionary Ignaz Pfefferkorn described the efficacy of the arrows: "The smallest wound inevitably causes quick death. At the most, two days may elapse before the wounded person is a corpse. The flesh becomes coal black and falls from the bones in pieces, as though decayed."

In spite of the military prowess they demonstrated in defense of their coastal homelands, the Seris dwindled in number. In 1844 a Mexican army officer counted 421 Seris on Isla Tiburón and along the nearby coast; no one knows how many may have lived here when the Spanish arrived. Concerned for the Seris' welfare (and perhaps vexed by the tribe's insular social habits

and perceived rebellious nature), the Mexican government began forcing them to leave their Isla Tiburón homeland in the 1960s. By 1975 all habitation of the island was forbidden. Today's Seri population numbers about 500, up from a low of 164 in 1934.

Customs

The Seris worship sea deities personified by dolphins, whales, and sea turtles, as well as an earth deity who appears in the form of a mole. Their biggest festivals are centered around the arrival of the *caguama* or sea turtle in May and the fruiting of the pitahaya cactus in July.

Ritual face-painting is still practiced during Seri festivals and in association with rites of puberty and spiritual protection. Female puberty in particular is celebrated; upon first menstruation, girls participate in rites of passage—during which they may consume only liquids—for eight to 10 days, culminating in submersion in the Sea of Cortez and coronation with flower garlands.

The residents of Punta Chueca and El Desemboque will paint their faces in the traditional way for tourist photos; the going rate is US$2 a shot. The natural pigments are mixed from local ingredients, poured in seashells, and applied to the face with a bird feather. Whether a Seri is painted or not, you should always ask permission to take a photo before snapping away; photographers who haven't asked first have on occasion been stoned.

The early Seris dressed in an odd costume of pelican skins with feathers intact. Nowadays Seri men wear standard Mexican attire, while the women generally wear long, full skirts and tie their heads in colorful scarves.

Crafts

Basket connoisseurs agree that the Seris produce the finest basketry in Mexico. Before the Río Colorado was dammed, the Seris used to ford the river in huge, watertight baskets woven from the fiber of torote, a desert tree. Baskets of this caliber, material, and size—called *coritas*—are still available but may cost hundreds of dollars and take months or years to make. Smaller baskets—in a dozen different types—are more affordable.

A more recent Seri handicraft tradition involves the carving of ironwood (*palo fierro*, another Sonoran Desert tree) into smooth, graceful figures—often dolphins and manta rays, or abstracts with a marine motif. Because it sinks when tossed into the sea, ironwood is traditionally used as a talisman by Seri fishermen to calm the Sea of Cortez. Thus to avoid spiritual offense, the Seris won't cut a live ironwood tree, preferring instead to work with fallen, dead wood. Many Seris have stopped carving altogether, as local non-Seri artisans are now cutting down live ironwood trees (causing the supply of wood to dwindle) and carving them with power tools.

Along with the modernization of the production process, the souvenir industry has extended the range of ironwood sculptural subjects to include just about anything under the sun.

Also popular with tourists are inexpensive necklaces made from limpet shells and from the vertebrae of sharks and snakes. Environmental groups may claim the use of such materials for ornamentation is an irresponsible exploitation of wildlife, but all of the animals whose shells and skeletons are thus used by the Seris were originally taken for food or were found dead.

GUAYMAS AND VICINITY

As early as 1539, Spanish explorers recognized the strategic and commercial potential of Guaymas's large natural harbor, protected from high winds and swells by Isla Pájaro. But because the area was occupied by fierce Guaymenas, the Spanish didn't gain a foothold until the 18th century. In 1701, Padres Salvatierra and Kino founded a short-lived mission settlement here. The mission was soon destroyed by the natives, but another attempt was made in 1769. This time the town, called San José de Guaymas, survived.

The port was thrice occupied by foreign military forces: first by U.S. naval troops during the 1847-48 Mexican-American War, then very briefly by freebooter William Walker in 1853, and again in 1865 by the French under Emperor Maximilian. A major turning point in the area's economic development was achieved when a rail line connected Guaymas with Nogales on the U.S. border in 1881.

Today Mexico's seventh-largest port handles around four percent of the nation's total maritime cargo, most of which is shipped straight across the Sea of Cortez to Santa Rosalía (where it continues by road to the western United States). The northernmost passenger ferry connecting mainland Mexico with the Baja peninsula also makes this run.

The city's large commercial fishing fleet brings in around one percent of Mexico's annual harvest. Shrimp is the biggest earner; during shrimping season vendors stand on street corners and along the Bahía Empalme bridge east of town, hawking pink crustaceans by the bucketful. Oysters are another important source of income—the

bayfront is even constructed of oystershell landfill.

Guaymas itself isn't a major tourist destination. Most visitors are on their way west to Bahía San Carlos or to points south such as Alamos and Mazatlán. Others are on their way to or from the ferry dock south of town. Busy Bahía de Guaymas is the city's main attraction. Although it's not beautiful in the travel-brochure sense, neither is it without its charms. Weather, time of day, and shipping activity contribute to a constantly changing seascape, and the bay islands—bristling with profuse stands of saguaro—seem to change color every few hours. The scene has changed almost not at all since John W. Hilton wrote in his 1947 *Sonora Sketch Book:*

> *Yes, I like Guaymas. I like the fishing, and I like to just ride out in the blue bay and look back at the white town against great, red-lava hills, and see the little red islands, studded with giant cacti that grow right down to the shoreline, I like to watch the rookeries of great sea birds of all sorts that inhabit these little islands, and hear their strange cries as they rise and wheel overhead.*

Sunset bay cruises can be arranged through **Gary's Boat Trip,** tel. (622) 6-0049 or 6-0074.

In town, the main points of sightseeing interest are the **Palacio Municipal,** built in grand 19th-century Romanesque style, and the nearby **Parroquía de San Fernando,** a picturesque church next to the small but verdant Plaza 13 de Julio. Also impressive is the dome-porticoed, neoclassical **Antiguo Edificio Banco Comermex**

Plaza 13 de Julio,
Guaymas

(Old Banco Comermex Building), on the southwest corner of Av. Serdán and Calle 21.

The nearest beach is **Playa Miramar** at Bahía Bacochibampo, a palmy stretch of sand around a small bay that almost looks as if it could have been lifted from the South Seas. Most of the city's nicer homes are in this neighborhood. Follow signs to "Colonia Miramar" just six km west of town.

People driving through town rarely venture off Av. Serdán, the main business street lined with banks, restaurants, dentists, and supermarkets. Off-the-main-drag explorations are easier once you figure out that the east-west streets are *avenidas* numbered with Roman numerals, while the north-south streets are *calles* numbered with regular Arabic numerals.

One of the best times to visit Guaymas is during Carnaval, held the week before Lent (for a description of Carnaval, see "Festivals and Events" under "Entertainment" in the On the Road chapter). Another big festival in Guaymas is Día de la Marina (June 1), when homage is paid to mariners lost at sea.

Tours
Ecogrupos de Mexico, a tour company specializing in nature excursions, runs a seven-day trip out of Guaymas that first takes in local Seri communities and the little-known Oasis Nacapules, then continues by boat to the Sea of Cortez islands of San Pedro Nolasco, San Pedro Mártir, San Esteban, Rasa, Partida, and Angel de la Guarda. Each of these islands is an im-

portant habitat for various indigenous and migrating bird species, as well as for rare reptiles and native cacti. While at sea, you can observe dolphins, sea lions, and other marine mammals.

During the boating segment of the trip, passengers sleep and eat all meals on board. This unique trip costs around US$1,700. In Guaymas, you can contact Ecogrupos by phone at (622) 1-0194 or by fax at (622) 1-2030. In the U.S., contact Points of Exploration, 325 W. 16th St., Suite 4W, New York, NY 10011, tel. (212) 691-0733 or 649-3428.

Ecogrupos also offers diving and whale-watching trips in the Sea of Cortez aboard their cruiser *Baja Treasure.*

ACCOMMODATIONS

Hotels and Motels—In Town
Shoestring: Cheap digs in town are available near the municipal market at four-story **Hotel del Puerto,** Diagonal Yáñez 92 (at Calle 18), tel. (622) 4-3408. Its basic but tidy rooms have private baths and a/c; some have TV. Rates: US$9 with a/c, US$12 with a/c and TV.

Budget: At the west end of downtown, the three-story **Hotel Santa Rita,** Av. Serdán at Calle Mesa, tel. (622) 4-1464, has adequate rooms with a/c and TV, plus secure parking. Rates: US$14 s, US$16 d, US$18 t. A block down the street, **Motel Santa Rita** (not to be confused with the hotel of the same name), tel.

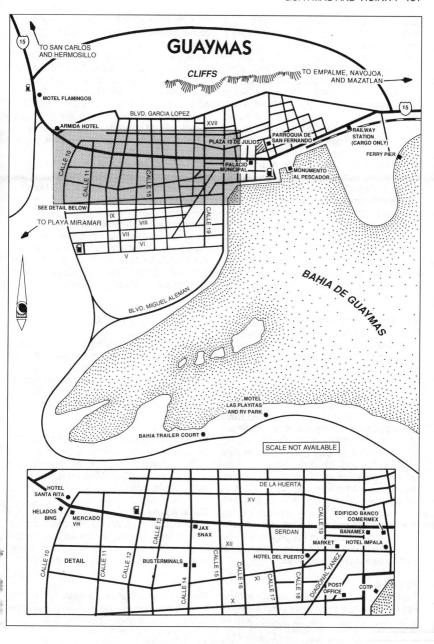

GUAYMAS

15 TO SAN CARLOS AND HERMOSILLO

CLIFFS TO EMPALME, NAVOJOA, AND MAZATLAN →

15

MOTEL FLAMINGOS

BLVD. GARCIA LOPEZ

ARMIDA HOTEL

CALLE 10

CALLE 11

CALLE 15

CALLE 19

XVII

PLAZA 13 DE JULIO

PALACIO MUNICIPAL

PARROQUIA DE SAN FERNANDO

RAILWAY STATION (CARGO ONLY)

FERRY PIER

MONUMENTO AL PESCADOR

SEE DETAIL BELOW

TO PLAYA MIRAMAR

IX

VIII

VII

VI

V

BLVD. MIGUEL ALEMAN

BAHIA DE GUAYMAS

MOON

MOTEL LAS PLAYITAS AND RV PARK

BAHIA TRAILER COURT

SCALE NOT AVAILABLE

DETAIL

HOTEL SANTA RITA

HELADOS BING

MERCADO VH

DE LA HUERTA

XV

CALLE 13

JAX SNAX

SERDAN

CALLE 19

EDIFICIO BANCO COMERMEX

BANAMEX

MARKET

HOTEL IMPALA

CALLE 10

CALLE 11

CALLE 12

DETAIL

BUS TERMINALS

CALLE 14

XII

CALLE 15

CALLE 16

HOTEL DEL PUERTO

CALLE 17

XI

CALLE 18

DIAGONAL YANEZ

POST OFFICE

COTP

X

(622) 4-1919, offers clean rooms with a/c, a restaurant, and secure parking. Rates: US$16 s, US$19 d, US$21.50 t, US$24 q.

At the other end of town near the harbor, the larger **Hotel Impala,** tel. (622) 4-0822, offers similar rooms at similar rates. Slightly more expensive is the well-run **Motel Flamingos,** west of town on Mexico 15, tel. (622) 1-0961, where rooms surround a parking lot and pool. Rates: US$18 s, US$20 d, US$27 t, or US$34 q.

If you're planning to stay awhile, consider moving round the other side of the bay to **Motel Las Playitas,** tel. (622) 1-5196, which offers kitchenettes. Rates: US$22 for one to four guests, US$25 with kitchenette.

Budget/Inexpensive: The best highway hotel Guaymas offers is the modern and efficient **Armida Hotel,** on Mexico 15 at the west entrance into the city, tel. (622) 2-5320, Mexico toll-free tel. (800) 6-4706, U.S. toll-free tel. (800) 732-0780. Rated at four stars by the state, the Armida has rooms with phone, TV, and a/c. Amenities include a pool, bar, video disco, and three restaurants. Rates: US$25-42.

Hotels and Motels—Playa Miramar
Shoestring: Inland a bit off Playa Miramar, two-story **Hotel Leo's Inn,** tel. (622) 1-0104, offers plain rooms with small balconies and sea views for a bargain US$4.50 s/d. The only amenities are private bath and ceiling fan. Who knows how long these rates will last.

Moderate to Premium: Toward the upper end of the rate scale is the 60-year-old **Hotel Playa de Cortés,** on Playa Miramar, Bahía Bacochibampo, tel. (622) 1-1224, fax (622) 1-0136, U.S. tel. (800) 782-7608. Originally built by the Southern Pacific Railroad, this faded but pleasant resort-style hotel offers a range of room rates depending on which wing you choose. Facilities include spacious grounds, tennis courts, a dock, small sand beach, and pool. It's also the only hotel in Sonora we've seen with handicapped access. Rates: US$56 in the original low-rise, US$76 in the oceanview high-rise, and US$136 for the newer deluxe bungalows.

RV Parks
Top choice in Guaymas is the trailer park at **Motel Las Playitas,** on the peninsula at the south side of the bay, tel. (622) 1-5196. Spaces with full hookups cost just US$10 per day; monthly discounts are available. Unfortunately the grounds have become overgrown and the facilities need some upkeep, but you can't beat the location. If Las Playitas is full, try **Bahía Trailer Court,** tel. (622) 2-3545, off the same road to Las Playitas; US$10 per night or US$190 per month. Although not as cozy as Las Playitas, the Bahía does have a boat ramp. Small houses built over trailer slots sometimes rent by the month independently.

Hotel Playa de Cortés at Playa Miramar, tel. (622) 1-1224 or (800) 782-7608 in the U.S., fax (622) 1-0136, has a set of shaded, full hookup slots with rates of around US$14, including use of all hotel facilities (see "Hotels and Motels— Playa Miramar," above).

Empalme Accommodations
If you find yourself stuck in Empalme for the night, waiting for (or arriving from) a late train, try the **Hotel Baluarte,** at Av. Revolución and Calle 4, tel. (622) 3-1380, which offers basic but adequate rooms; shoestring to budget.

FOOD

As Sonora's primary fishing port, Guaymas takes pride in its fresh seafood—virtually every menu in town features a section devoted to *pescados* or *mariscos.* Many of the city's old seafood standbys have closed since the 1994-95 economic crisis and so far we haven't seen many replacements.

Seafood
Restaurant Bar Gary's, Av. V and Calle 10, tel. (622) 2-5481. An old favorite for shrimp dishes, deviled crab, and squid salad. Also serves a range of continental and Mexican dishes. Open daily noon-midnight

Carne Asada
La Cobacha, tel. (622) 4-2799, on Mexico 15 east of Motel Flamingos, opposite a Tecate *agencia.* Specializes in Sonoran-style *carne asada paquetes.* Open daily noon-midnight.

Chinese
Restaurante Jo-Wah. Yet another spinoff from Hermosillo, specializing in Cantonese-style seafood. Huge servings. Open daily noon-11 p.m.

Mexican
Mercado VH, Av. Serdán between Calles 10 and 11. The cafeteria attached to this supermarket offers an inexpensive but tasty menu featuring many *platillos típicos,* tacos, burritos, enchiladas, *chiles rellenos,* Mexican soups, and breakfasts. Excellent value. And, you can buy fresh tortillas at **Señor Maíz,** the supermarket's *tortillería.*

El Sauce y la Palma, Calle 13, four blocks south of Av. Serdán. A clean restaurant with good *tacos de carne asada,* burritos, tamales, and other *antojitos.*

Other
Jax Snax (Jax Pizza), corner of Av. Serdán and Calle 14. Small, casual spot with decent pizza, spaghetti, salads, and draft beer. Open daily 8 a.m.-11 p.m.; US$4-8.

Pizza Hut, near the northwest entrance to town, near El Viga and Ley. Standard American-style pizza; US$3-8.

Helados Bing, Av. Serdán and Calle 10. A branch of Mexico's best ice-cream parlor chain. Open 11 a.m.-11 p.m.

El Pescador monument

SHOPPING

Guaymas is a good place to stock up on supplies for a long-term stay in San Carlos or elsewhere in the vicinity. **Mercado VH** at Av. Serdán and Calle 10 is a huge grocery/department store with everything from tortillas to cassette tapes, plus a concession that carries camping, fishing, and diving gear.

On the highway just north of town is the **Plaza de Viga,** a huge, modern shopping center with attached Ley supermarket, cinema, and various shops selling shoes, toys, and other mall goods.

The **Mercado Central,** on Av. Rodríguez between Calle de Alemán and Calle 19, has the usual selection of household goods and fresh foodstuffs.

INFORMATION

Limited tourist information is available at the Palacio Municipal; there is no longer a tourist office in town. In the vicinity of the Palacio Mu-

nicipal are several banks—the Banamex on Av. Serdán west of the Palacio is the best for foreign-exchange services.

TRANSPORTATION

Air
Guaymas International Airport, tel. (622) 2-3334, is at Km 2 along the Guaymas-San Carlos highway off Mexico 15. **Aeroméxico** fields direct flights to Hermosillo, Los Angeles, and Mexico City, as well as nonstop flights to La Paz and Tucson; the airline has a ticket office in town at Calle 16 and Av. Serdán, tel. (622) 2-0123. A *colectivo* from the airport into town costs US$3.25 pp, while a private taxi costs US$7.

Bus
The main intercity bus terminals are on Calle 14 Sur between Av. XII Pte. and XIII Pte. (Av. Rodríguez). TNS, tel. (622) 2-7007, commands a terminal on one side of the street, while Trans-

portes del Pacífico, tel. (622) 2-0575, is on the opposite side. Together these companies and their affiliates run first- and second-class buses to every major town in Sonora and Sinaloa, plus Guadalajara, Mexico City, and Mexicali. Regional bus lines Transportes del Río Sonora and Autobuses de Guaymas serve smaller towns nearby.

Buses to San Carlos (US$1) leave every half hour from Calle 19 and Diagonal Yáñez near the municipal market. If you need transportation to the Empalme railway station, catch a red bus along Calle 20.

Train
Although Guaymas has no passenger railway station, the Empalme station is only 9.5 km (six miles) east of town across Bahía Empalme. The Pacífico No. 2 train heads for points south (Ciudad Obregón, Culiacán, Mazatlán, Tepic, and Guadalajara), while in the opposite direction the No. 1 train goes to Hermosillo and Nogales. Sample fares: Mazatlán first class US$14.50, second class US$8; Nogales US$8/4; Guadalajara US$26/14.50. The northbound train leaves at 5:55 p.m., southbound at 9:40 p.m. These trains often run one to two hours late. See the railway schedule in the Transportation Appendix for further departure and arrival times.

Ferry
Tickets for the ferry to Santa Rosalía are sold at the SEMATUR ferry pier, tel. (622) 2-3390, fax 2-3393, east of town off Av. Serdán—turn right (south) just before the big power plant. Advance tickets may be purchased here daily 7 a.m.-2 p.m.

Two passenger ferries are currently running out of Guaymas: the 550-passenger *Benito Juárez* and the smaller *Puerto Vallarta*. For fare and schedule information, see "By Ferry from Baja" under "Getting There," in the On the Road chapter.

Sometimes tickets are sold for a second men-only crossing to La Paz on Tuesdays, a trip referred to as *carga negra* or "black freight" because of the sunburnt faces of the mostly seamen passengers. Presumably women aren't sold tickets for the *carga negra* boats because no separate onboard facilities are available for women.

Auto Rental
Budget, at the west end of Blvd. García López, tel. (622) 2-5500, or at the airport, tel. (622) 2-1450, and **Hertz,** at the airport, tel. (622) 2-1000, have cars for rent starting at US$24 per day plus kilometer charges.

SAN CARLOS

About 11 km (seven miles) northwest of Guaymas lies one of the most scenic coastal areas in Northern Mexico. Beautiful Bahía San Carlos is backed by the 600-meter (2,000-foot) Sierra de Bacochibampo, faces several offshore islands, and is the first coastal area south of the U.S. border where you begin seeing palm trees with regularity. Just offshore, the abundant marinelife produced by the **Guaymas Trench**—a sea canyon some 1,500 meters (5,000 feet) deep—attracts sportfishers from all over North America. And a well-protected bay with full-service marina has made San Carlos the pleasure-boating capital of the eastern Sea of Cortez.

Thanks to government designation as a tourist zone, San Carlos has been spared the commercial fishing and shipping operations that give Guaymas a workaday edge. Instead, over the last decade San Carlos has developed into a small but full-blown vacation and retirement colony. Permanent, year-round residents here number around 2,000; in peak tourist seasons the population may swell as high as 6,000. The area has enough markets, hotels, restaurants, and trailer parks—not to mention a country club—to make a visit pleasant, but so far they're few enough in number that the area almost never feels crowded.

Sights and Beaches
The heaviest concentration of retirement/vacation homes blankets hilly **Peninsula del Caracol** at the bay's east end. Many of the Caracol homes are custom designed and have magnificent sea views; the neighborhood even has its own private police patrols. On the bay side of the peninsula is a small, sandy cove with shady coconut palms, while a part of the peninsula known among gringos as "Pelican Point" has a good beach at its tip. Access to the beach is via **Club de Playa,** which is reserved for the private use

San Carlos

of guests from the Plaza Las Glorias marina resort. To use the club facilities (restaurant, pool, restrooms) you must have a PLG-issued card, but the beach itself is open to all; simply pass through saying you're just going to the beach *(solo a la playa)*.

Without a doubt the nicest beach in San Carlos is **Playa los Algodones** ("Cotton Beach"—a reference to the fine white sand), west of the twin peaks known as Tetas de Cabra or "Goat Teats." Two resort hotels, a condo development, and a marina share the beach, which was once used as a location setting for the American films *Catch 22* and *Lucky Lady*. If you're driving here, take either the small road between San Carlos Plaza Hotel and Club Med or another access road just beyond the Club Med wall. The beach is open to the public.

A small airstrip at San Carlos has lately become the focus for a small group of ultralight-aircraft enthusiasts. During the cooler months, they sometimes organize festivals that also include hot-air balloonists and sports parachutists.

Climate and Seasons

Temperatures average a mild 21° C (70° F) in winter, zooming to 40°C (104° F) or higher in summer. The area's scant rain falls mostly in late summer. Early fall—when the ocotillo leaves come out following summer rains—is one of the best times to visit. Peak tourist seasons are Nov.-April (mostly American snowbirds) and July (mostly Mexicans).

Hotels and Motels

Most of San Carlos's lodgings are strung out along Playa San Francisco, a long, stony beach parallel to the Guaymas-San Carlos highway.

Budget: Totonaka Trailer Park, on the approach from Guaymas, tel. (622) 6-0323 or 6-0481, rents basic efficiency apartments for around US$25. **MaRosa Hotel,** toward the marinas, tel. (622) 6-1363, offers several plain, kitchenette-equipped rooms above a complex of shops for US$26 s/d.

Inexpensive: The first hotel you'll come to on approach from Guaymas is the **Hotel Fiesta San Carlos,** at Km 8.5, tel. (622) 6-0229, which has nice grounds on the beach, a tiny pool, and clean-appearing but musty-smelling rooms. All rooms come with complimentary American breakfast. Rates: US$37 s, US$46 d, US$57 t, US$69 q.

Next up, across the road from the beach, the **Hacienda Tetakawi,** tel. (622) 6-0220, fax (622) 6-0248, has a set of new suites facing the bay. Rates: US$40-55.

When available (it's often full, especially Dec.-May), a good choice is the clean and well-run **Motel Creston,** tel. (622) 6-0020, farther along on the beach side of the road. Facilities at the Creston include a small but well-maintained pool, a few barbecue grills, and a palm-shaded courtyard. Rates: US$25 s/d in the off-season, up to US$55 in high season (Dec. 19-May 1).

On the highway beyond the country club, a turnoff to the left (Km 11.5) leads to a nearly private beach and **La Posada de San Carlos,** tel. (622) 6-0072, U.S. tel. (706) 226-0015, one of the first San Carlos tourist developments. Facilities include an airy restaurant, two pools, a beach *palapa* bar, and two tennis courts. Rates: US$35 for a standard room in the original single-story building or in the back of the newer high rise, US$50 for a high-rise ocean view, US$55 for ocean view and balcony, US$60 for a beach-front motel-style unit, US$70 for a larger beach-front unit, and US$80 for a family bungalow.

Luxury Resorts

Playa los Algodones, San Carlos's prettiest beach, is the site of two resorts and a couple of just-getting-off-the-ground condo developments. All rooms at the **San Carlos Plaza Hotel Resort,** tel. (622) 7-0777 or (800) 6-4368 toll-free in Mexico, fax (622) 6-0778, have sunset and ocean views, satellite TV, phone, servibar, and all the other amenities you'd expect at one of Sonora's top hotels. The attractive beachfront pool-and-*palapa* design takes maximum advantage of the natural setting. Other facilities include tennis courts, an outdoor jacuzzi, restaurant, coffeeshop, lobby bar, and a full range of watersport equipment rentals. The resort was originally built as a Howard Johnson and is often still referred to by that name. Rates are erratic de-pending on the season, room orientation (incredibly there are 10 classes of rooms) and your negotiating abilities. Many of the rooms in the high season are taken by package tourists. In the low season (May-Nov.), you can get a room for US$67, otherwise you'll be quoted twice that.

Farther on, past the Costa del Mar condo project, **Club Med Sonora Bay** occupies an extensive, fenced-in section of the beach (though the beach is open to the public) and offers seven-day packages for around US$700 depending on the season (add 20% for single rooms), including all meals and recreational activities (boating, diving, windsurfing). You can spend the day here for US$60 pp, including all meals and activities. Club Med's rooms are nowhere near as nice as the San Carlos Plaza but the all-inclusive rates and exclusive veneer still appeal to some vacationers.

Plaza Las Glorias, tel. (622) 6-1021 or (800) 342-2644 in the U.S., a brand new luxury hotel overlooking Marina San Carlos, offers 87 state-

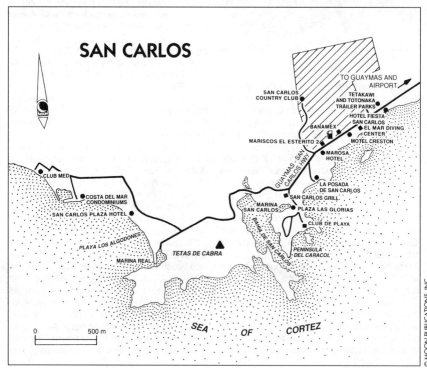

© MOON PUBLICATIONS, INC.

of-the-art rooms for US$105 s/d, plus 18 more-expensive suites. All rooms come with kitchenettes (but no utensils) and look out over the bay and marina. Facilities include a large pool, fitness center, restaurant, and access to Club de Playa, a private beach club at Pelican Point. Plaza Las Glorias also rents condos, tel. (622) 6-0949, fax (622) 6-0939, and sells residential lots.

Apartments, Condos, and Houses

Inexpensive: The **Ocean View Apartments** (no phone) stand at the crest of a hill near Marina San Carlos. Each of the spacious, one-bedroom apartments comes with a/c, cable TV, and large kitchenette. The owner is a Texan. Rates: US$50 a day, US$300 a week (low season US$250) or US$600 a month.

Moderate/Expensive: The new, clean, bayview condos at **Marina Real,** tel. (622) 9-0986, fax (622) 6-0024, or (800) 332-1608 in the U.S., include washer-dryer and satellite TV. Facilities include a tennis court and pool. Rates: US$60 for a studio (up to four people), US$80 for a one-bedroom unit (up to six), and US$100 for a two-bedroom unit (up to eight).

Inexpensive to Premium: West of Motel Creston on the other side of the road (about 20 minutes' walk from the beach) are **Solimar Hotel and Country Club** and **Loma Bonita Condominiums Hotel and Vacation Club,** both condotel developments offering a wide range of accommodations. If you stay at the Solimar you'll have privileges at San Carlos Country Club, which boasts an 18-hole golf course, pool, and 14 tennis courts. Rates: hotel rooms cost around US$35-40 per night, studio condos US$50-60, one-bedroom condos US$70-80, two bedroom units US$100-125.

You'll get the best rates at these lodgings by booking through one of the local rental/real estate agencies. **Star Realty,** tel. (622) 6-0000, fax (622) 6-0990, is one reliable agency that arranges both house and condo rentals. Houses typically rent for US$50-60 a day, US$250-400 a week, or US$600-1500 a month, for one to four persons.

RV Parks

Two parks cluster together across from the beach near Hotel Fiesta San Carlos. The well-established **Tetakawi Trailer Park,** tel. (622) 6-0220, has spaces with full hookups and satellite cable TV for US$18 per day, US$113 per week, or US$300 per month. **Totonaka Trailer Park,** tel. (622) 6-0323, next to Tetakawi, is priced similarly; the Totonaka has a pool for guests and a coin laundry open to the public. Both parks offer refunds of your Mexico 15 highway toll if you stay five nights or more.

Food

The restaurants in San Carlos are generally casual affairs, heavy on gringo influence, with good but not outstanding food. Popular **Rosa's Cantina** on the main road along Playa San Francisco specializes in *tortas,* tacos, enchiladas, *carne asada,* and pecan pie. Rosa's is open daily 6:30 a.m.-9:30 p.m.; a bulletin board inside carries community announcements and sale notices for boats and real estate.

Slightly more upscale is **San Carlos Grill,** on the road to Playa los Algodones just past the Marina San Carlos turnoff. The menu features all the gringo favorites, including steak, seafood, continental, and toned-down Mexican.

Restaurant El Bronco near Km 10 specializes in mesquite-grilled beef and salmon. It's open Tues.-Fri. 5-11 p.m., Sat.-Sun. 1-11 p.m. Nearby **Jax Snax** does hamburgers, pizzas, and Mexican breakfasts; open daily 7 a.m.-11 p.m.

The best seafood in San Carlos is available at **The Reef,** a nicely appointed spot opposite the Loma Bonita condos. Open for lunch and dinner. **Mariscos El Esterito II,** just south of the PEMEX near Km 10, is a simpler Mexican-style *palapa* place with fresh harvests from the sea, inexpensively priced. Open 10 a.m.-8 p.m.

Near Motel Creston, the friendly **Bananas Restaurant Bar** features laid-back, *palapa*-roof ambience, paintings by local artists on the walls, draft beer, and Mexican breakfasts from US$1. Open at 7:30 a.m., closing time varies.

Ranas Ranas is a Grupo Anderson-style fun-food-and-booze house near Hacienda Tetakawi on the beach side of the road. The other place for wild nights is **Tequila's,** next to Plaza Las Glorias. Entrees at either place average US$4-10.

Piccolo Restaurant, Av. Creston 305, offers good basic Italian dishes food and crisp service. Open Tues.-Sun., noon-10 p.m.

Groceries are available from several small markets in town; **Super Frutería y Carnicería Bahía San Carlos** near Marina San Carlos and

Plaza Las Glorias is the best-stocked. On the bottom floor of the MaRosa Hotel, **El Mejor Pan** sells bread and baked goods, while **Pescadería San Carlos** offers fresh fish.

Boating
At the northeast end of Bahía de San Carlos—said to be the largest natural harbor in Mexico—**Marina San Carlos,** tel. (622) 6-0230, fax 6-0565, is the main center for local boating activities. Rates for slips or moorings (400 total) at the marina are US$3 per day up to 10 feet, US$11.50 per day 10-50 feet, or US$85 per month. Facilities include electricity, running water, boat ramp, lockers, bathrooms, showers, VHF radio, telephone, fax, crane, dinghy service, 24-hour security, and dry storage. Several places near the marina sell and repair boats and outboard motors.

At the east end of Sonora Bay (Playa los Algodones), the newer **Marina Real,** tel. (622) 9-0986 or (800) 332-1608 in the U.S., fax (622) 6-0024, offers 325 slips at similar rates. For several years now the Sonoran government has been saying more marinas are planned for the area, but so far two seems to handle all the yacht traffic.

During the second week of October, sailors compete in the **Cristóbal Colón (Christopher Columbus) Regatta.**

Fishing
Because of the nearby Guaymas Trench, San Carlos waters offer the best sportfishing along the Sonora coast. Offshore catches include marlin, sailfish, dorado, pargo, cochito, and grouper; inshore are triggerfish, seabass, seatrout, sierra, and others. The best overall fishing season (especially for billfish) is early summer, although there's something biting all year round. At Marina San Carlos, **Cortez Explorer,** tel. (622) 6-0858, fax 6-0808, offers sportfishing trips for US$65-100 pp per day. **Gary's,** near Km 10, tel. (622) 6-0049, can arrange fishing guides and boat charters as well. A deep-sea fishing tournament is held at San Carlos each September.

Diving
Rocky shoreline outcroppings and offshore islands provide good snorkeling and diving op-

portunities. **El Mar Diving Center,** tel. (622) 6-0404, U.S. fax (602) 898-0194, near Motel Creston, and **El Centro de Deportes de Sonora,** tel. (622) 6-0929, opposite the PEMEX station in town (with a branch on the beach at La Posada de San Carlos), arrange dive trips and offer equipment rental and air. A locally moored yacht called *Baja Treasure,* tel. (622) 1-0319 or (800) 471-4720 in the U.S., offers live-aboard dive excursions. Cortez Explorer (see "Fishing," above) schedules scuba-diving trips as well.

Other Sports
The marine and terrestrial environments around San Carlos are perfect for sailing, windsurfing, sea kayaking, and mountain biking. **El Centro de Deportes de Sonora,** tel. (622) 6-0929, offers instruction, equipment rental, and guided tours for all of these, plus the occasional whale-watching excursion. **Cortez Explorer** (see "Fishing," above) also rents sea kayaks and mountain bikes.

The **San Carlos Country Club,** tel. (622) 6-0339, has 14 world-class tennis courts and an 18-hole, 6,617-yard golf course with Sea of Cortez views. Public play is permitted upon payment of daily use fees.

Transportation
Buses run between San Carlos (near the mini-market district by Marina San Carlos) and Guaymas (Calle 19 and Diagonal Yáñez near the municipal market) every half hour; US$1. Taxis from Guaymas airport cost around US$10 to the Playa San Francisco hotel strip, US$20 to Playa los Algodones.

Marina San Carlos has a **PEMEX** station.

Information and Services
A **Tourist Information Center,** tel. (622) 6-1222, in Edificio Villa Mar, on the Corredor Escénico San Carlos (San Carlos Scenic Road) from Guaymas, dispenses maps and tourist brochures for the area. **Star Realty** in San Carlos, tel. (622) 6-0000, is also a good source of information.

Almost opposite Motel Creston, next to the PEMEX, **Banamex** offers foreign currency exchange during regular banking hours, plus ATM service.

SOUTHERN SONORA

CIUDAD OBREGÓN

Obregón got its start as a railroad station in 1921, when it was still called "Cajeme" after a Yaqui chieftain who led a revolt against the Mexican authorities in the 1880s. In 1924 the city's name was changed to honor the late revolutionary general and Mexican president Alvaro Obregón.

With the damming of the Río Yaqui, a half-million acres of former desert surrounding Ciudad Obregón have become a major agricultural producer, yielding tremendous amounts of wheat and cotton for domestic and international markets. As a result this city of 400,000 has one of the highest per capita incomes in Mexico, as evidenced by the palatial houses and groomed lawns in several residential districts.

Other than the Yaqui Museum, Ciudad Obregón has little of tourist interest. For bass anglers it serves as a supply point for trips to nearby Presa Alvaro Obregón. It is also an important transit point for people arriving by air on their way to colonial Alamos. Those interested in Yaqui Indian culture can use the city as a base for visits to the Río Yaqui Valley homelands.

Museo de los Yaquis

This small museum housed in the public library (Calle Allende and 5 de Febrero) next to the Palacio Municipal contains ethnological exhibits on the Yaquis, whose name means "those who shout about the river." Displays include historical photos, costumes, household articles (among them reed bird cages, "indispensable to the Yaquis"), and a facsimile of a Yaqui dwelling. A few Yaqui crafts, including *pascola* masks, are on sale near the entrance. The museum is open Tues.-Sun. 9 a.m.-1 p.m. and 3-6 p.m.; admission is less than US$1.

Zona Indígena Yaqui

Fifteen km southeast of Guaymas begins a Yaqui reservation that extends southward some 80 km (50 miles) to Ciudad Obregón. Much admired and feared for their tenacity, the Yaquis managed to fend off both the Spanish and the Mexicans throughout most of their history, but in the 1900s many Yaqui families were deported to the Yucatán peninsula. The "indigenous zone" is a Mexican gesture toward the restoration of Yaqui homelands. The Yaquis originally occupied a much wider territory.

Most of the Yaquis living in the zone are bilingual in Spanish and their mother tongue. They make their homes in the Río Yaqui Valley and support themselves through agriculture, fishing, and the gathering of cactus fruit and other edible desert plants. Some settlements still maintain traditional leadership councils consisting of *gobernador, pueblo mayor, capitán,* and *comandante,* all of whom are chosen by the pueblo from persons over 50 years of age who have proven their standing in the community.

The towns of Cruz de Piedra, Pótam, Vícam, and Bácum are worth visiting during Semana Santa or Día de los Muertos to observe native dances such as the famous *danza del venado.*

LA DANZA DEL VENADO (DEER DANCE)

Dances revolving around deer symbolism are common among the Amerindian tribes of Northern Mexico, but the Yaqui/ Mayo version is the most famous. Dancers who portray the deer are trained in the proper movements from a young age and have the title "Maso" (deer) added to their names. The costume and dance ornaments—including deer antlers—must be handled with care and proper etiquette to evoke the spirit of the dance. Musical accompaniment is played on Yaqui flute, harp, violin, and percussion instruments.

Basically the dance is a dramatic representation of life-and-death cycles in which a deer—a revered animal that symbolizes "good" in Yaqui culture—is hunted by coyotes (also sacred but feared). In the drama, the deer kills one of the coyotes in self defense; the coyote is reincarnated as a bow hunter, which in turn kills the deer in a poignant finale.

Bácum also has a mission church, Iglesia de Santa Rosa de Lima, of minor interest for its modern Yaqui artwork.

Presa Alvaro Obregón

This huge impound of the Río Yaqui 42 km (26 miles) north of the city is a major bass-fishing destination. The main boating and fishing access is via **Marina del Rey** at the lake's southern end, where you'll find cabins and trailer spaces (with sewer hookups) for rent, plus a small cafe-store where boats and fishing guides may be hired. In season, hunting trips for white-tailed deer, white-winged dove, and quail can also be arranged. From Marina del Rey the lake extends some 48 km (30 miles) northward; the only other access is via the fish camp of Alamos (not to be confused with colonial Alamos farther south) near the northern end, accessible by an unpaved road that curves around the west side of the lake.

Accommodations

Hotels in this city tend to cost more than you might expect, probably because of the steady business traffic.

Shoestring: The city's hostel, **Villa Deportiva Juvenil,** tel. (64) 15-1560, is west of the city center at Laguna de Nainari. Dorm beds cost just US$1.20 per night, and reservations can be made as many as 15 days in advance. The hostel is 15 minutes from downtown by city bus. Three casas de huéspedes—**Yaqui, Rosa,** and **Vallarta**—are on Calle Coahuila Sur, not far from the bus terminal. Accommodations are basic (no a/c), with baños colectivos. Rates: US$8-10.

Budget: The city's nicer, and more expensive, hotels are lined up along Blvd. Miguel Alemán (the main avenue through town, linked to Mexico 15), in an area signed "Zona Hotelera." **Day's Inn Motel Costa de Oro,** tel. (64) 14-1776, and **Hotel Valle del Yaqui,** tel. (64) 13-3969, are modern and efficient middle-class places on Miguel Alemán. Because of the competition, one or more of these establishments is usually running "promotional" specials. Rates: around US$25-32; specials as low as US$21. The new four-story **Obregón Plaza Hotel,** tel./fax (64) 14-3830, on Alemán in the same area, has nice rooms. Rates: US$31 s, US$34 d.

Inexpensive: Also new and more luxurious is the very comfortable **Holiday Inn,** tel. (64) 14-

0940, fax (64) 13-4194. Rates: US$51 s/d, US$83 suite; weekend specials as low as US$34 are occasionally available.

Food

A good Mexican coffeeshop meal at reasonable prices can be had at **Café Las Espigas,** on Blvd. M. Alemán near the Hotel Valle de Yaqui and behind a PEMEX station. Open 24 hours; meals run $2-5.

For fresh seafood, try **Mariscos La Palapa** at Blvd. Miguel Alemán 628, open late morning through early evening. Good comida sonorense—e.g., carne asada, cocido, quesadillas made with huge tortillas de agua—is available at a number of places in town, including: **Restaurante El Bronco,** Calle Sinaloa 219; **Restaurante Los Apaches,** Calle Veracruz Sur 253; and **Merendero de José Luis,** Calle Durango and No Re-Elección. Figure on spending around US$4-8 a meal. A combinación at movie-postered Merendero de José Luis includes salsa dina (a spicy soup), beans, Sonoran quesadilla, and carne asada for US$8; good seafood here, too.

Cheaper, more casual fare can be had at a number of good, clean taquerías in town, including: **Taquería Sonora,** on 5 de Febrero and Galeana; **Taquería Mazatlán,** on 5 de Febrero and No Re-Elección; and **Taquería San Juan,** across the street from the bus station.

The lavish-looking **Restaurant Beijing,** on Blvd. M. Alemán Nte., serves some of the best Chinese food in Northern Mexico. The extensive menu includes some Sichuan (spelled "Tsy Chon") dishes. The chop suey con mariscos, a pleasing blend of vegetables and seafood, is recommended.

Large American chain fast-food joints have crept into town—Dominos, Jack in the Box, Pizza Hut, Baskin Robbins, KFC, and Jack in the Box can all be found along Blvd. M. Alemán.

Shopping

A half-dozen leather shops in the vicinity of the bus terminal fashion handmade saddles, bridles, chaparreras, and other accoutrements for the working vaquero.

Transportation

Air: Noroeste, Calle Sonora 228, tel. (64) 13-9525, and **Aeroméxico,** Av. No Re-Elección

Ote. 509, tel. (64) 13-2190, offer direct flights to Ciudad Obregón from Chihuahua, Culiacán, and Hermosillo. Aeroméxico also flies to and from Guadalajara; most people flying in from abroad use this connection, since Guadalajara is served by a wide selection of international flights. **Aero California,** Av. M. Alemán Nte. 548, tel. (64) 13-7878, fields nonstop flights to and from Los Mochis, Sin., with connections to Matamoros, Mexico City, Monterrey, San Luis Potosí, Tijuana, Torreón, and Tucson.

The airport is about 22 km (13.5 miles) south of the city off Mexico 15. Taxis to and from town cost US$8.50, *colectivos* US$3.50.

Bus: Tufesa, TBS, Estrellas del Pacífico, and **TNS** operate buses to major towns throughout Sonora and Sinaloa, plus Tepic, Guadalajara, Mexico City, Tijuana, Tecate, and Mexicali. All leave from the huge Central Camionera at the south end of town. Sample fares: Nogales US$13, Culiacán US$12, Alamos US$2.50, Guadalajara US$39, Tijuana US$33, Mazatlán US$22.

The regional **Autobuses de Los Mochis** runs buses to Huatabampo, Nogales, Culiacán, Guasave, and Los Mochis.

Crucero, a joint venture between Mexico's Estrella Blanca and the U.S.'s Greyhound Lines, runs daily buses to and from Los Angeles in the U.S. for US$60 one-way, US$115 roundtrip.

Train: Ciudad Oregon's railway station is west of the highway opposite Calle Hidalgo. First- and second-class trains run north to Hermosillo, Nogales, and Mexicali, and south to Mazatlán, Tepic, and Guadalajara. See the "Railway Schedule" in the Transportation Appendix for schedule information.

Car Rental: Local agencies include: **Budget,** Blvd. M. Alemán Nte. 669, tel. (64) 14-1188; **Hertz,** Blvd. M. Alemán at Allende, tel. (64) 14-7140; **Avis,** Calles Hidalgo and 5 de Febrero, tel. (64) 14-8144; and **Facil,** Calle Hidalgo Ote. 903, tel. (64) 13-1832. Rental rates run higher than usual, from $37 a day for VW bugs to US$130 for Chevy Suburbans.

Fuel: Several PEMEX stations carry Magna Sin and Premium, among them a 24-hour station in the center of town. Another PEMEX at the south end of town on Mexico 15 (near the Juárez statue) has a car wash and oil-change service.

Information

Ciudad Obregón's helpful, English-speaking tourism office is at Calle Cajeme Ote. 952, tel. (64) 13-0093.

NAVOJOA

Started as a Mayo Indian mission pueblo in the 17th century, Navojoa (pop. 100,000) has grown into an important center for cotton production. The many wheat fields and flour mills in the vicinity have also earned the town its reputation as "Mexico's Breadbasket." Light manufacturing contributes to the local economy as well.

Today Navojoa's Mayos, closely related in language and custom to the Yaquis, have for the most part assimilated into mainstream Mexican culture. To supplement incomes earned by farm labor, a few Mayos still produce traditional handicrafts such as sarapes and baskets, which you can find for sale at the municipal market at Calles Morelos and Allende. Mayo dances (including a version of the deer dance almost identical to that of the Yaquis) are performed during festivals, particularly on Día de San Juan (June 24), Día de los Muertos (Nov. 2), Día de la Virgen de Guadalupe (Dec. 12), and Semana Santa (the week before Easter).

Among Mexicans, Navojoa is known as the birthplace of the late president and revolutionary war hero Alvaro Obregón, who is buried in nearby Huatabampo.

American guitar manufacturer **C.F. Martin** has a plant on the highway about five km south of town, tel. (642) 3-5052, where Martin guitar strings and the "Backpacker" travel guitar are made. Tours of the plant are available by appointment only. Note that the strings and guitars are made strictly for export and cannot be purchased on site. Even "seconds" are either exported at a discount or destroyed.

For most visitors, Navojoa serves as a launching point for side trips to the little-known beach at Huatabampito and the quaint ex-mining town of Alamos.

Accommodations

Shoestring: The best budget deal in town is **Hotel California,** tel. (642) 1-2878, on Blvd. Gral. Pesqueira, the main road through the middle of town (connecting with Mexico 15). The small but clean rooms have a/c, hot water, and TV. Rates: US$12 s, US$14.50 d. In the same general vicinity, the newer **Hotel Sicomoro,** Gral. Pesqueira at Guadalupe Victoria, tel./fax (642) 2-0201, has small, modern two-bed rooms set around a courtyard parking lot and pool. All rooms come with a/c, phone, and cable TV. Laundry service is available, and a restaurant and bar are on the premises. Rates: US$9 s/d.

Budget: North of town next to the Río Mayo on Mexico 15, the sprawling, ranch-style **Motel Del Río,** tel. (642) 2-0331, offers spacious, comfortable, a/c standard rooms and larger rooms with kitchenette and extra beds for higher prices. The well-kept, landscaped grounds include a pool. The Del Rio fills with hunters beginning in November. Rates: from US$26 s/d up to US$80. Other budget places include **Hotel Belem,** Blvd. Gral. Pesqueira 411, and the courtyard-style **Hotel Colonial,** also on Blvd. Pesqueira, toward the southern edge of town, tel. (642) 2-1919.

Food

Navojoa is renowned for *pollo asado* (grilled chicken), so you'll find many *tacos de pollo asado* stands and restaurants in town. Friendly **Helio's Pollos Asados,** across the street from the Hotel California, serves exemplary *pollos al carbón* and has a couple of outdoor tables. **Pollo Asado El Tapatío** is another good place on Gral. Pesqueira.

One of best and most convenient places to eat for folks passing through is **Tip's,** on the main highway through town. This clean, efficient, a/c restaurant offers a wide range of *antojitos,* steaks, soups, and salads at reasonable prices. **Restaurante Quinta El Asadero,** near Motel Del Río on Mexico 15, is good for *carne asada.*

Carimali Pizzas, on Gral. Pesqueira, is more popular than the nearby **Pizza Hut.** For groceries, your best bet is **Super-Mercado VH,** on Blvd. Gral. Pesqueira.

Transportation

You'll find two bus terminals at Av. Guerrero and Calle Rincón. One is for **Autobuses de Guaymas** (ADG) buses, which are painted with red, white, and blue stripes. These go to Guaymas (six times daily; US$4), Hermosillo (hourly; US$6.50), Ciudad Obregón (hourly; US$1.60),

and Huatabampo (hourly; US$1.20). The other terminal, for **Transportes del Pacífico,** has better buses to Hermosillo (hourly; US$10.50 special first class, US$9 regular first class), Mazatlán (once daily; US$22/19), Nogales (once daily, US$19/16), Guaymas (thrice daily; US$6.50/6), Ciudad Obregón (six times daily; US$1.60/1.50), and Guadalajara (once daily; US$64/54).

Fuel: Navojoa has three PEMEX stations, including a huge one just north of town that's equipped with restrooms and a mini-market. Filling up with Magna Sin usually isn't a problem.

Information and Services

On Av. Gral. Pesqueira in the middle of town are a couple of **casas de cambio,** as well as a **Banamex** with exchange services and an ATM. A new **SEMARNAP** office in town can issue hunting and fishing permits; check with Hotel Del Río for details. The hotel also screens an 11-minute video on Alamos in the lobby; visitors are usually welcome to watch.

ALAMOS

This Sonoran colonial paragon set in the foothills of the Sierra Madre Occidental was visited by Spanish conquistador Coronado in 1531 but didn't take root until silver was discovered in 1683. Originally named "Real de los Frailes" (Mining Camp of the Friars—a reference to two nearby peaks that resemble monkish figures) and later "Real de la Limpia Concepción de los Alamos," the town had reached a population of 30,000 by 1781. Sonora's first printing press was established here in 1828, and in the mid-19th century Alamos served as capital of Occidente, a province of New Spain that encompassed most of northwestern Mexico. At its peak it was the wealthiest town in Sonora and attracted immigrants from all over the Pacific, including a number of Chinese and Japanese (the latter even founded a silk factory) who were expelled in 1916 for wielding too much economic power.

A series of rebellions by Yaqui mine laborers, followed by the 1910-20 revolution, brought all mining to a halt by the 1920s and the town quickly declined. A few American artists and prospectors began poking around the town ruins in the 1940s as word of a lost mining town in the Sierra

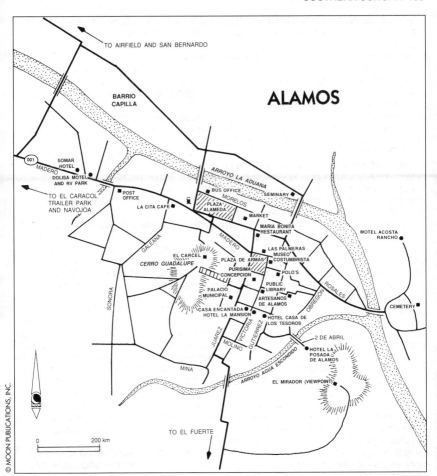

Madre slowly trickled out. Today Alamos counts only around 6,000 residents, including a total of approximately 250 Americans and Canadians who have restored charming Sonoran-style **casonas** (mansions) in the center of town. Fewer than a dozen non-Mexicans actually live here year-round. In a twist on the usual pattern, Alamos has managed to hold onto a traditional feel partially because of (rather than in spite of) the gringo presence. American interest in Alamos flared briefly following an article that appeared in *Town and Country* magazine in 1991.

The expat group here is a different breed from that found along the coast; although most gringo homeowners—like their San Carlos-Bahía Kino counterparts—are only winter residents, many speak Spanish and take an interest in cultural events. Cynical visitors might say that these casa lords are turning Alamos into a gringo fantasy of what they think Mexico *should* be. Some may find the social atmosphere a bit rich as well; a local English-language publication suggests that Americans come to Alamos because, among other reasons, "Household and garden help is available so that one can live graciously," and "The attitude of the natives . . . make[s] contact with service people pleasant."

Romanticists, on the other hand, may find Alamos almost a living dream. Declared a National Historic Monument by the Mexican government, the town has no billboards and no neon; every sign and exterior renovation must be approved as stylistically compatible before being displayed. And the streets are swept cleaner here than almost anywhere else in Mexico. (For an idea of what Alamos might look like without the expat influence, visit El Fuerte in Sinaloa.)

Because Alamos has been isolated from the rest of the Mexican world for so long, a few of the older native residents still speak a dialect mixed with 17th-century Spanish that has managed to survive over three centuries. Most of the Mexican population now lives on the outskirts of town; downtown residences have almost all been purchased by Americans, several of whom are involved in (or have retired from) the U.S. motion-picture industry.

There is little to do in Alamos beyond wandering the narrow cobblestone streets, admiring the stately architecture, and soaking up the atmosphere of Old Mexico. The entire town can easily be seen on foot in less than two hours.

Climate and Travel Seasons

Alamos lies at an elevation of 450 meters (1,500 feet) in the western foothills of the Sierra Madre Occidental. Five distinct seasons are recognizable. The May-June "foresummer" is dry and hot; trees are leafless and dormant, the cicadas are practically shrieking, and only the toughest gringos hang out in town. During the summer rainy season, July-Sept., heavy showers and electrical storms can dump 13 cm (five inches) of rain in 10 weeks, filling the three arroyos that cradle the town and causing local vegetation to green and flower. In late September and October it's dry and hot again save for the occasional *manga* or waterspout, then in November it cools off for the mild winter season, when gentle rains bring spring blooms.

As the winter months offer the most pleasant weather, that's when the town's population peaks. Visitors and seasonal residents start arriving around Thanksgiving, reach their greatest numbers Dec.-Jan. (when you'll need advance room reservations), and are mostly gone by the end of March.

Plazas

The town's visual centerpiece is the tidy **Plaza de Armas,** surrounded by houses that have been converted into inns, restaurants, and a museum. During the winter, music ensembles perform folk music and opera in the plaza's wrought-iron kiosk, which was built in Mazatlán in 1904.

Commercial life revolves around a small municipal market and line of shops adjacent to the **Plaza Alameda,** between Calles Rosales and Morelos. Shaded by large *alamos* (cottonwood trees), this plaza is the focus of the traditional Mexican evening promenade.

La Parroquía de la Purísima Concepción

This large stone church on the Plaza de Armas was completed in 1786, after the adobe original—built during the mining heyday of the late 17th century—was destroyed in a 1772 Yaqui uprising. Its single bell tower holds four bells, one of which was forged locally while three hail from Spain; the exterior clock came from Rome. Inside the church is a late baroque-style altar. Among other unique features are the porcelain plates set into the bell tower exterior; these were supposedly donated by the women of Alamos in 1804. Although many of the plates were shot out during the revolutionary period, a few can still be seen.

Beginning with a church festival on Dec. 8, Purísima Concepción stays very active throughout the Christmas and New Year's season, which coincides with the high tourist season.

Museo Costumbrista de Sonora

This small museum off the Plaza de Armas on Calle Victoria contains historical exhibits on Alamos mining (one room is plastered to look like a mine interior), fashion, printing, coin minting (silver coins were once produced here), and the early cultivation of wheat, tobacco, and citrus. Open Wed.-Sun. 9 a.m.-6 p.m. Admission is US$0.25.

Restored Homes

From the outside, the many restored mansions in Alamos appear similar. Most are imposing, block-like, single-story structures with grand entryways and tall, iron-grilled windows. The most elaborate casas feature *portales,* sheltered walkways characterized by Doric columns topped with Roman arches. Behind the facades, the houses follow a U- or L-shaped plan around a courtyard, where residents have expressed their individual tastes with varied interior-design schemes—some traditional and some innovative. The least successful renovations mix motifs from all over colonial Mexico instead of sticking with the understated Andalusian style brought to Alamos directly from Spain in 1770.

The best way to view the interior restorations without collecting individual invitations is to join one of the **House and Garden Tours** given during the high season each Saturday at 10 a.m., starting from the public library at Calle Comercio 2. The cost is US$8 pp, which includes coffee and cookies served at the library. Weekday tours can sometimes be arranged by stopping in at the library a few days ahead of time. Leila Gillette's self-published book, *The Stately Homes of Alamos* (1996), provides a detailed account of the town's colonial history and relates several legends about local houses and their previous inhabitants. The book is available at local shops.

El Cárcel
Promoted as a tourist attraction, this ancient-looking stone jail sits on Cerro Guadalupe in the middle of town. Only six inmates at a time can be held here, with maximum sentences of three years—more serious offenders are sent to Ciudad Obregón or Hermosillo. Inmates support themselves by making hatbands, bolos, and belts from horsehair; these can be purchased from the yard in front of the jail. The main reason to visit the jail is to take advantage of city views from the hill. To get there, ascend the stone stairs at the end of the alley next to the Palacio Municipal (off Calle Juárez).

Town Tour
Rotund Alamos native "Candy Joe" (José Trinidar) leads two-hour, English-language walking tours (US$5 pp) that take in historical sights as well as one or two restored casa interiors. You can usually find Joe at his crafts and jumping-bean shop on Plaza de Armas. English-speaking guide Emiliano Grajeda has also been recommended—he can be contacted through any of the hotels in town.

El Mirador
Drive or walk south on Calle Juárez and follow signs reading "Camino al Mirador" to reach a hill with the best view of town. Several barbecue grills and a gazebo have recently been built at the summit.

La Aduana
This almost abandoned mining town near Alamos is famous for its simple **Iglesia de Nuestra Señora de la Balvanera.** The church was built at the site where a saint dressed in white robes and blue shawl supposedly appeared in a vision atop a pitahaya cactus; when the vision-

Plaza de Armas,
Alamos

JOE CUMMINGS

seers approached the cactus, the saint vanished but a rich silver vein was suddenly visible nearby. A "miracle" cactus grows out of the side of the church about three to four meters off the ground, as if to remind the faithful of the event. Among the Mayos, this church is very holy; Mayos and other believers will walk here from Navojoa to honor the Virgin of Balvanera (12-21 Nov.), and again during the Festival Guadalupana (12 Dec.).

A small *artesanía* near the church sells native handicrafts, including small pouches fashioned from goat scrotums.

To reach the village, take the signed dirt road at Minas Nuevas, seven km (4.5 miles) south of Alamos on Sonora 001, and then proceed east about 3.5 km (two miles). The road is rough, winding, and sandy in spots, and there is one stream crossing.

Hotels and Motels

Shoestring: Next door to Los Portales is **Hotel Enriquez,** Calle Juárez 4, tel. (642) 8-0280, which offers basic but livable rooms with shared bath. Rates: US$10 s/d. On the outskirts of town, **Somar Hotel,** tel. (642) 8-0195, offers 16 adequate rooms around a courtyard/parking area. Some of the nicer rooms have a/c and cost a bit more. Rates: US$10-13 s/d, US$12-14 t, US$14-16 q, non-a/c; US$16-20, with a/c.

Budget: Facing Plaza de Armas, **Hotel Los Portales,** Calle Juárez 6, tel. (642) 8-0211, is owned by the town's first gringo resident, Levant Alcorn. The eight simply furnished rooms with private baths surround an empty courtyard. In the early evenings, guests, friends, and staff sit in rocking chairs under the exterior portal to watch the passing street show and catch up on town events. Rates: US$24/26 s/d, US$21 s/d in the low season.

Two more choices are found on the outskirts of town. The friendly **Dolisa Motel & RV Park,** tel. (642) 8-0151, fax (642) 8-0131, sits on the road to Navojoa near the town entrance. In true motel style, Dolisa's 10 rooms angle around the parking area (at all other places in town you must park on the street outside). All rooms come with a/c, TV, and a fireplace. Rates: US$21 with one double bed, US$24 two beds, US$26 three beds. **Motel Acosta Rancho,** tel. (642) 8-0246, fax (642) 8-0279, is on the northeastern outskirts of town about one km from the plaza (bear left at the cemetery, proceed along the cemetery wall, then left again at the little bridge). The six rooms are often occupied by visiting hunters but nonhunters are welcome. From early November to early March, dove- and quail-hunting packages (including room, meals, and guided hunts) can be arranged. Each of the large, clean, recently refurbished rooms has a private bath. Rates: US$30 s/d.

Moderate: Two beautifully restored colonial casas share the west end of Calle Obregón, two blocks south of Plaza de Armas. **Hotel Casa de los Tesoros** (Apdo. Postal 12, Alamos, Son. 85760), tel. (642) 8-0010, fax (642) 8-0400, built as a convent in 1789, holds 14 antique-furnished rooms each with fireplace, private bath, and five-meter-high ceiling. The lovely courtyard is surrounded by *portales* set with chairs and low tables beneath lazily spinning ceiling fans; it's a favorite meeting place for local gringos during the 6:30-7:30 p.m. cocktail hour, when guitar ensembles play *música romántica* and the occasional Sonoran ballad. The courtyard's bar/kitchen is flanked by dining tables at one end and a pool at the other. Rates: US$65 s, US$75 d including breakfast, discounted in summer to US$45/50 s/d without breakfast.

One block west of Los Tesoros on Calle Obregón is the well-restored **Hotel La Mansión,** tel./fax (642) 8-0221, originally built in 1683 as the home of a silver magnate. The 12 large rooms surrounding the courtyard are named instead of numbered and are tastefully furnished with art and antiques—the nicest rooms in Alamos. Each has a fireplace and private bath. The courtyard contains a tropical garden of banana trees, fan palms, mango, avocado, bougainvillea, hibiscus, and taro; the dining room has been relegated to a corner room. Former presidents Carlos Salinas and Miguel de la Madrid have each stayed at La Mansión since its 1986 renovation. Rates: US$45 s, US$55 d, US$65 t or suite, meals not included.

Hotel La Posada de Alamos, Calle 2 de Abril Prolongatión Sur, tel. (642) 8-0045, in a quiet southeastern corner of town across Arroyo Agua Escondida, features eight large rooms in a partially restored hospital from the colonial era. Apparently it's mainly used for overflow from Hotel La Mansión and Casa La Encantada when package tours are in town. Rates: US$55-75.

Bed and Breakfast

Expensive: Casa Encantada, Calle Juárez 20, tel. (642) 8-0482, fax (642) 8-0221, U.S. reservations tel. (800) 422-5485, occupies a 250-year-old Andalusian-style casa and offers 10 comfortable rooms decorated with Guatemalan fabrics. Although the architecture is similar to that of Alamos's other casa inns, owner-managers Rod and Statia Carey have created a casual, family-style atmosphere that contrasts with the slightly more formal, Mexican ambience of La Mansión and Los Tesoros.

All rooms have fireplaces and private baths; rates include a continental breakfast of homemade breads, juice, and coffee, plus a self-service cocktail hour with *sangría* and tapas. The courtyard has a pool, and guests may borrow bicycles at no extra charge. Rates: In the Nov.-March peak season, standard courtyard rooms cost US$80 s/d, larger deluxe rooms are US$85 s, US$90 d, and luxury suites and private *casitas* run US$119 s/d. Subtract US$10-20 from these rates during other times of year.

Rooms for Rent

Artist Robert Bloor offers a few rooms for rent at his colonial-era home at Av. Obregón 18, just down from Casa de los Tesoros. Called **Casa Obregón Dieciocho** after its address, the house is also known simply as "Roberto's." The large apartment suites surround a courtyard decorated by the owner. Each suite has a refrigerator; one unit sleeps four and has a kitchen. Rates run US$47 s, US$55 d, including tax; weekly and monthly rates can be negotiated. Breakfast is available for an extra charge, and there is off-street parking in the courtyard. Bloor, a painter-sculptor originally from Vancouver, B.C., has lived in Alamos for 40 years.

Nearby at Obregón 12, **Carlota R. de Salazar,** tel. (642) 8-0180, rents large but simple rooms in an old colonial for around US$200 a month. Señora Salazar speaks no English. Just off the Plaza de Armas, **Bienes Raices Fraser & Pratt,** tel. (642) 8-0467, fax 8-0118, can arrange local rentals and show houses and lots that are for sale.

RV Parks and Campgrounds

RVers with large rigs may find the streets of Alamos a bit too narrow for comfortable navigation. If you think your rig might fit this category,

consider staying at one of the two friendly, well-run RV parks outside town. **El Caracol RV Park,** tel. (642) 8-0117, is 14.5 km (nine miles) down the Navojoa-Alamos highway at Km 37. Trailer slots with full hookups cost US$8, campers and vans are US$7.50, and tent sites run US$4. Amenities include a pool, hot showers, restaurant, and laundry. Buses to Alamos stop at El Caracol. **Dolisa Motel & RV Park,** near the town entrance (within walking distance of downtown), tel. (642) 8-0151, fax (642) 8-0131, charges US$12 for trailer slots with full hookups, US$10 for campers, and US$5 for vans or tents. Amenities here include a coin laundry, hot showers, and spots shaded by mango and citrus trees. At both these parks, the rates listed above are good for two persons per site; add US$1-1.50 for each additional person. Both places offer weekly and monthly discounts.

The **Motel Acosta Rancho** (see "Hotels and Motels," above) charges US$10 for full hookups, US$8 for campers or small- to medium-sized trailers, US$5 for vans or tents. To reach Acosta you'll have to drive through town—make an exploratory trip by foot or taxi first if you think you might have trouble getting your rig down the narrow streets.

El Real de Alamos, tel. (642) 8-0002, on the highway to Navojoa charges just US$5 a night for rustic spaces with water only.

Food

One of the most consistently popular restaurants in town is **Las Palmeras,** tel. (642) 8-0065, a small, family-run place on Calle Cárdenas facing the Plaza de Armas. House specialties include pan-fried *tamales de elote* (corn tamales) and *queso fundido* (melted cheese topped with chorizo), plus daily meal specials that might include *carne asada,* ham, fish, or chicken; prices are reasonable. Las Palmeras is open daily 7 a.m.-10 p.m.

Just west of the plaza in an old, simply decorated casa on Calle Zaragoza, the friendly **Polo's,** tel. (642) 8-0001, offers delicious Mexican breakfasts, sandwiches, and dinners of *carnes* and *antojitos.*

The fanciest eatery in town, **Maria Bonita Restaurant,** on the corner of Calles Juárez and Rosales, features a nice outdoor seating area with a fountain as well as a semiformal indoor, a/c dining room. Menu prices—for steaks, seafood, and Mexican specialties—are commensurate with the decor. The funky bar next door, under the same management, has live music—mostly *norteña*—on some evenings.

La Cita Café is a small indoor-outdoor place with inexpensive Mexican breakfast and lunch.

The courtyard dining area at **Hotel Casa de los Tesoros** (see "Hotels and Motels," above) is open to the public for breakfast, lunch, and dinner (US$7-15). If you're not a guest at the hotel you should make reservations for lunch and dinner. Mayo dances are performed for diners every Saturday at 6:30 p.m.

For less formal meals, **Taquería Blanquita** in the municipal market building serves passable *tacos de carne asada, menudo,* and tostadas from dawn to dusk. **Asadero Los Sabinos,** on Calle 2 de Abril next to Arroyo Agua Escondida, sets up as a *carne asada* stand in the afternoons and early evenings.

Si Fech Jugos Naturales, in a corner of the market building, offers *licuados, refrescos,* and *tortas.* You'll also find several small grocery stores around the Alameda near the market, and a couple of *tortillerías* attached to the market itself.

Shopping

Every Sunday folks from near and far come to Alamos for an open-air market held at Arroyo La Aduana, north of Plaza Alameda. Everything from fresh chiles to household goods is bought and sold at the market.

At the municipal market adjacent to Plaza Alameda, open daily, vendors sell crafts, foodstuffs, and clothing. **El Vaquero,** a shop on the west side of the market facing the plaza, carries fine, locally made saddles, basketry, belts, chaps, and a good selection of hats made by Guarojillo from the Río Mayo area. An unformed *palma real* costs US$8; take it to a hat shop in Navojoa and have it blocked and formed for another US$3-4. Synthetic straw hats are less expensive.

Artesanos de Alamos, on Calle Comercio near the church, is a nonprofit artisans' co-op selling dolls, gourds, masks, toys, rustic furniture, and other regional crafts. Some of the items for sale are made by the Guarojillos (a small tribal group living in southeastern Sonora's Alam-

os and Quiriego *municipios*), who work mostly in palm, wood, and clay to produce musical instruments and pottery. **Artesanías El Nicho,** Calle Comercio 4, carries a variety of folkcrafts, including huge fountains, lamps, tableware, ceramics, and *puta* dolls made for local residents. Some items are nice, while others are mere kitsch.

Jumping Beans: Facing Plaza de Armas, near Restaurante Las Palmeras, is Candy Joe's **Curios Artesanías** shop. In addition to a modest collection of minerals and Mayo crafts (mostly pascola masks, water gourds, and dolls), Joe is the main dealer in town for "Mexican jumping beans." Called *brincadores* locally (*Sapium bilocualare* to botanists), these little beans only occur within a 1,000-square-km (400-square-mile) area around Alamos. Between October and March, a species of moth lays eggs on the *Sapium's* flowers. After the flowers drop the beans (or seeds), the moth eggs hatch inside. The movement of the moth larvae inside the beans makes them hop around. Alamos ships around 22,700 kg (50,000 pounds) yearly, most of it to international destinations; local pickers are paid US$4-8 per kilo.

In season, Candy Joe keeps a cardboard box full of jumping beans to show passersby; the movement inside the box sounds like gentle rainfall. You can buy the beans from Candy Joe for US$3 per 15. Once the eggs have hatched, the average bean will hop for around six months. Mexicans will place *brincadores* in a circle and bet which will hop out of the circle first.

Recreation

Opinions differ regarding the bass fishing at **Presa Ruíz Cortines** (Presa Mocuzari), northwest of Alamos. Some say they're still jumping while others say the lake has slowed down considerably. Hunting for quail, dove, duck, and blue pigeon is also popular around the lake. The signed turnoff for Mocuzari is about halfway between Alamos and Navojoa; from Sonora 001 it's roughly 20 km (12 miles) by gravel road to the south end of the lake. It's possible to camp near the lake, though most sportfishers camp at El Caracol (see "RV Parks and Campgrounds," above) or stay in Alamos. It may also be possible to rent a cabin from someone in Mocuzari, a village near the end of the gravel road by the lake.

At the southeast outskirts of Alamos, near Arroyo Agua Escondida, **Centro Recreativo Camuca** offers a public swimming pool open May-October. Admission is US$1 pp.

Transportation
Air: The nearest commercial airport is outside Ciudad Obregón, 120 km (74.4 miles) from Alamos. Taxis to/from the Ciudad Obregón airport cost US$60 one-way. Inquire about airport shuttles when making hotel reservations; most places will arrange pickup for US$10 pp.

Alamos has its own 1,200-meter (4,000-foot) municipal airstrip (unicom 122.8); buzz the town once and a taxi will make a pickup for US$10—this includes a return trip to the airstrip later.

Buses: A local bus company called **TBC,** tel. (642) 8-0096, has a small office on the north side of Plaza Alameda—look for a white building with brick trim around the door arch and windows. From here buses depart hourly on the half hour 6:30 a.m.-6:30 p.m. for Navojoa; US$1 per passenger. TBC also operates buses to Hermosillo (US$8.50), Ciudad Obregón (US$2.50), and Guaymas (US$5.50); these buses leave Alamos (for each destination) at 4 a.m., 5 a.m., 8 a.m., and 10 a.m. An a/c *primera* for Nogales on the border leaves from Alamos at 9 p.m., arriving in Nogales at 6 a.m. (US$22).

Driving: It takes about an hour to drive the 53-km (33-mile), two-lane road from Navojoa to Alamos. Depending on which section of the road you find yourself on, this road may be signed Sonora 001, Sonora 162, or Sonora 2. Cars can be rented in Ciudad Obregón.

From Alamos it's possible to drive north and east to Bahuichivo in the Copper Canyon area via the tiny lumber and mining towns of San Bernardo, Chínipas, and Témoris. The road alternates between graded gravel and rough dirt surfaces and takes the better part of a day. Don't attempt this trip unless you have a rugged, high-clearance vehicle (and don't attempt it at all during the late summer rainy season); bring spare fuel and water.

An even rougher road heads south approximately 100 km from Alamos to El Fuerte, Sin., a stop on the Chihuahua al Pacífico railway line through the Copper Canyon. Along the way the road passes Presa Miguel Hidalgo.

Fuel: Alamos has one PEMEX station, near Plaza Alameda; both Magna Sin and Nova are available.

Information and Services
A small tourist office on Calle Juárez, next to Hotel Los Portales on the Plaza de Armas, tel. (642) 8-0450, dispenses hotel brochures and town maps.

The local police can be reached at tel. (642) 8-0209, the Red Cross at tel. (642) 8-0225. A couple of *larga distancia* offices are near Plaza Alameda; the best one sits near the bus station on the north side of the plaza.

Alamos is still lacking a bank or place where you can reliably change money, so be sure to stop off in Navojoa for pesos before arrival. A **Banoro** may soon be opening next to La Cita Café.

SOUTH OF NAVOJOA

Playa Huatabampito
The nearest beach to Ciudad Obregón and Navojoa is Playa Huatabampito, a flat, 20-km stretch backed by sand dunes. The beach fronts Bahía Santa Barbara, an estuary where the Río Mayo feeds into the Sea of Cortez. A couple of *palapa* restaurants offer fresh seafood, and beach camping is possible, using nearby Huatabampo (pop. 45,000) as a supply point. FONATUR reportedly has development plans for Huatabampito, but for the time being it's just miles of sand and a few *palapas*.

To reach the beach, take Sonora 49 southwest from Navojoa for 36 km (22 miles), through heavily cultivated farmland to the town of Huatabampo. From here follow another road southeast toward Yavaros, but take a turnoff south (signed for Huatabampito) after roughly 11 km (6.8 miles).

Buses to Huatabampito run from the main drag (Av. Guerrero) in Huatabampo several times daily. Buses to Huatabampo are available in Navojoa and Ciudad Obregón.

Masiaca and Las Bocas
Forty-four km (27 miles) southeast of Navojoa along Mexico 15 is a turnoff onto a gravel road that leads in either direction. To the east a few km is **Masiaca,** a Mayo village famous for rug-

weaving. In the opposite direction, the road leads southwest approximately 15 km (9.3 miles) to **Las Bocas,** a fish camp with a long, flat beach similar to Playa Huatabampito. Surf casting and inshore fishing are said to be good here; since Las Bocas is far from any major city, competition for the catch is slim. *Pangas* can be rented from local fishermen. A sand road paralleling the shore leads a few km south to another fish camp/beach, **Camsahuiroa.**

THE STATE OF SINALOA

Coming from an Amerindian word for "round prickly pear," Sinaloa's name suggests a desert province, yet this is one of the most fertile and well-watered areas in Mexico. Eleven major rivers drain the western slopes of the Sierra Madre Occidental and traverse the state en route to the Sea of Cortez. Along the way these waters irrigate vast tracts of land that enable roughly half the state's population to earn a living from agriculture.

Sinaloa produces 85% of the country's vegetable exports, including over 75% of the nation's total soy and 33% of its total sesame output in a typical year. Other major crops include wheat, sorghum, corn, rice, safflower, sugarcane, tomatoes (over a quarter of Mexico's production), bell peppers, potatoes, garbanzos, and chiles. Bananas, mangoes, avocados, and other tropical fruits are cultivated in the southern end of the state. (Haas avocados were developed here by Antonio Haas.) Ranching, poultry, and forestry also make significant contributions to the state economy.

Not surprisingly, food packing has become the state's primary industry, with manufacturing a very distant second. Fishing is also a major

source of livelihood, thanks to the state's 656-km (407-mile) shoreline; sardines, tuna, and shrimp lead the offshore catch. The many bays, estuaries, and marshes where river systems meet the Sea of Cortez produce a combination of inshore saltwater and freshwater fisheries as well.

Although the first Spanish settlers came in search of gold and silver—concentrating on the mountainous, eastern half of the state—later immigrants from all over the world focused on the fertile river valleys and coastal plains. Today the state's population is a melting pot of Spanish, French, English, American, Lebanese, Greek, and Chinese ancestries.

Most tourists come to Sinaloa to lie on the sunny beaches of Mazatlán (the closest major beach resort to the U.S. border) or to catch the Chihuahua al Pacífico railway at Los Mochis and ride east through the mountains to Chihuahua's "Copper Canyon." But other places worth visiting in Sinaloa include the bustling state capital of Culiacán; the sleepy *lagunas* in the southern tip of the state; and the historic former mining towns of El Fuerte, Cosalá, and Copala, high in the Sierra Madre.

LOS MOCHIS AND VICINITY

This booming agricultural and shipping center (pop. 250,000) lies at the junction of Mexico 15 and the Chihuahua al Pacífico rail line, just a half-hour drive from Topolobampo—Mexico's deepest port. Both Los Mochis and Topolobampo were founded as part of a utopian colony by American Albert K. Owens in 1872. Owens's utopian experiment ultimately failed, but in 1893 Benjamin Johnston established another American colony at Los Mochis—this one with capitalist objectives. Johnston built a major sugar mill (now owned by Mexico's largest sugar company) and laid out the American-style, no-diagonals town grid still in use.

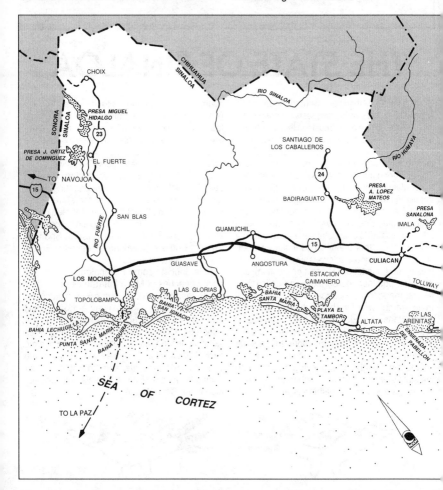

The boxy modern architecture, one-way streets, and businesslike atmosphere of today's Los Mochis aren't particularly endearing to out-of-town visitors. For most tourists, the town is simply a necessary stopover while waiting for the morning train across the Sierra Madre Occidental to Creel or Chihuahua. Others spend a short time here after arriving at nearby Topolobampo by ferry from La Paz, Baja California Sur.

Those with time to explore the town can wander down **Av. Obregón,** a colorful street filled with cut-rate shops, mazelike markets, *servicios de cambios,* and funky cafes; or stop in at the **Museo Regional del Valle del Fuerte,** at Av. Obregón and Rosales, offering displays on regional history and anthropology as well as rotating art exhibits (open Tues.-Sun. 10 a.m.-1 p.m. and 4-7 p.m., US$0.75 admission).

ACCOMMODATIONS AND FOOD

Hotels and Motels
Shoestring: For atmosphere on a low budget,

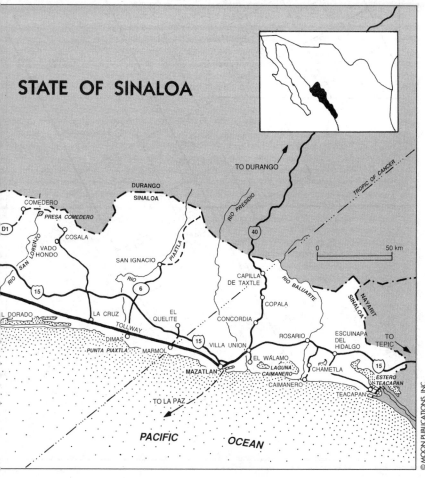

STATE OF SINALOA

TO DURANGO

TROPIC OF CANCER

DURANGO
SINALOA

RIO PRESIDIO

COMEDERO
PRESA COMEDERO

D1

COSALA

RIO SAN LORENZO

VADO HONDO

SAN IGNACIO

RIO PIAXTLA

40

RIO

6

CAPILLA DE TAXTLE

RIO BALUARTE

NAYARIT

0   50 km

SINALOA

L DORADO

LA CRUZ

EL QUELITE

TOLLWAY

15

COPALA

CONCORDIA

ROSARIO

ESCUINAPA DEL HIDALGO

TO TEPIC

DIMAS

PUNTA PIAXTLA

MARMOL

15

VILLA UNION

EL WALAMO

CHAMETLA

15

MAZATLAN

LAGUNA CAIMANERO

ESTERO TEACAPAN

CAIMANERO

TEACAPAN

TO LA PAZ

PACIFIC   OCEAN

© MOON PUBLICATIONS, INC.

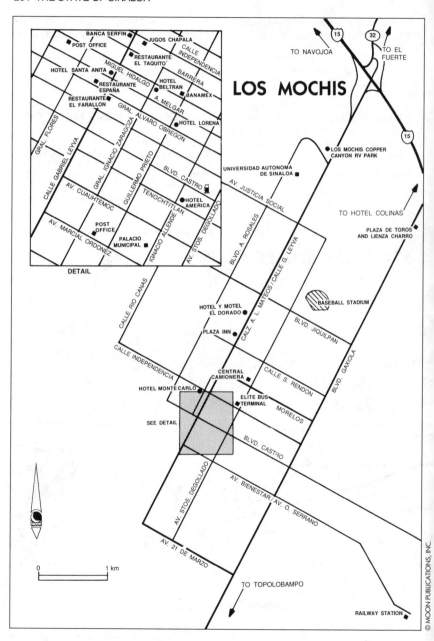

plus good off-street parking, consider **Hotel Monte Carlo,** Angel Flores at Independencia, tel. (68) 12-1344, one block behind the Hotel Santa Anita. This blue, three-story hotel looks like a vestige from the era when sugar was king in Los Mochis. Old, somewhat musty rooms with fan and a/c surround an open courtyard with a fountain. Rates: US$12 s, US$13 d, US$16 t.

Budget: Near the municipal market, **Hotel Lorena,** Av. Obregón at Calle G. Prieto, tel. (68) 12-0239, fax (68) 12-4517, offers pleasant rooms with a/c, cable TV, and private bath. No off-street parking. Rates: US$15 s, US$21 d, US$25 t. Nearby **Hotel Beltrán,** Calle Hidalgo at Zaragoza, tel. (68) 12-0710, is similar. **Hotel América,** tel. (68) 12-1355, is a plain hotel off of Calle Allende and Blvd. Castro, two blocks north of the Palacio Municipal. Simple, clean rooms with a/c and TV. Off-street parking is available. Rates: US$14.50 s, US$20 d, US$24 t.

Budget/Inexpensive: Two blocks north of the Plaza Hotel on Gabriel Leyva, **Hotel & Motel El Dorado,** tel. (68) 15-1111 or (800) 6-9009 toll-free in Mexico, is a modern four-story affair with a pool, travel agency, restaurant, hotel parking, and a friendly staff. Rates: rooms in the larger hotel portion in front cost US$27 s/d, US$32 t including tax; rooms in the smaller motel rent for US$36 s/d, US$39 t including tax.

Moderate: The comfortable and popular **Hotel Santa Anita,** Apdo. Postal 159, Los Mochis, Sin. 81200, tel. (68) 18-7046, fax (68) 12-0046, U.S./Canada tel. (800) 896-8196, has well-maintained rooms with cable TV, phone, a/c, and private bath. Rates: US$60 s, US$72 d, US$86 junior suite. Rates usually drop by around US$12 from March to September. Conveniently located at the heart of downtown, the Santa Anita is part of the Balderrama hotel chain, which operates several properties along the Chihuahua al Pacífico train route. Overflow visitors from the Santa Anita—along with those on hunting packages—are lodged just north of downtown at Balderrama's similarly priced **Plaza Inn,** Calle G. Leyva at Cárdenas, tel. (68) 12-0075. The Plaza Inn is a bit far from the downtown action but has a pool and a popular disco. Rates: US$66 s, US$77 d, US$93 t.

Hotel Colinas, tel. (68) 11-8111, fax (68) 11-8181, just off Mexico 15 near the entrance to town, offers rooms with a/c, satellite TV, and phone. Facilities include four tennis courts and two pools (one with huge, amusement park-style water slides). Rates: US$47 s, US$57 d.

RV Parks

The popular **Hotel Colinas RV Park** has a pleasant *palapa* area for socializing, and RV guests may use the hotel facilities (described above). Sites with full hookups cost US$11 per night for two persons, plus US$2 for each additional person. **Los Mochis Copper Canyon RV Park,** tel. (68) 12-0021, off Mexico 15 on the northern outskirts of town, is similarly priced and a bit quieter. Hot showers, a laundry, and a night watchman are all part of the deal.

Sixteen km (10 miles) north of town on the Río Fuerte, just off Mexico 15 at Km 18, the **Río Fuerte Trailer Park,** tel. (68) 12-0075, offers full hookups for US$14, electricity and water only for US$10.

Food

What it lacks in charm, Los Mochis makes up for in the restaurant department. At the splurge end, the dining room at the **Hotel Santa Anita,** tel. (68) 18-7076, is well known for its delicious shrimp flambé and **sopa de tortillas.** Entrees range US$4-15. **España** (also known as "Madrid"), at Av. Obregón and Calle G. Leyva, offers elegant decor, attentive service, and Spanish/international cuisine. Lunch specials include a four-course international meal for US$5.

For an extensive yet inexpensive selection of regional Mexican dishes, head for the paragon **El Taquito** on Calle G. Leyva between Independencia and Hidalgo downtown. It's open from early in the morning till late at night, but is especially good for *almuerzo* (late breakfast), when you'll have a choice of the "Sonorense" (eggs with *machaca*), "Taquito" (with ham), or "Sinaloense" (with *chilorio,* a venison or pork sausage with chiles), each with coffee, fruit, potatoes, toast, and tortillas, for US$3. The specialties of the house—served anytime—are *taquitos* (soft tacos) and *tacos dorados* (fried tacos).

Jugos Chapala, around the corner from El Taquito on Calle Independencia, features a variety of *licuados* made from fresh Sinaloa fruits.

Restaurante El Farallón, at Av. Obregón and Flores, and **El Bucanero,** Calle Allende Nte. 828 (at Calle Cano), are highly favored for seafood. Entrees run US$4-10 at each.

At night you'll find a dozen *tacos de carne asada* vendors along Calle Independencia east of Calle G. Leyva selling tacos for under US$1; **Tacos La Doña,** next door to Jugos Chapala, serves theirs with 10 varieties of salsa. On weekends *pollo asado* and *mariscos* vendors line the canal parallel to the Los Mochis-Topolobampo road a bit south of town.

RECREATION AND ENTERTAINMENT

Hunting and Fishing
At the Hotel Santa Anita, **Balderrama Tours,** tel. (68) 18-7046, fax (68) 12-0046, can arrange hunting trips for geese, doves, ducks, deer, and wild pigs, as well as fishing trips in nearby lakes or in Topolobampo's Bahía Oguira. Other companies that can outfit hunting and fishing trips include **La Torcaza Club,** tel. (68) 5-2624, and **Wingshooters,** tel. (68) 15-2121.

Nightlife
The **Fantasy** disco at the Plaza Inn, Calle G. Leyva at Cárdenas, is one of the more popular nightspots in town. For a quiet drink, the **Closet Bar** at Hotel Santa Anita is a good choice. The larger **Bar La Hacienda** at the Santa Anita features live music most nights.

The *muy macho* **Ballena Bar** across the street from Santa Anita serves only *ballenas,* one-liter bottles of Pacífico—so you can get some weight-lifting in while you drink.

TRANSPORTATION

Air
Los Mochis airport is served by **Aeroméxico,** Calle G. Leyva Nte. 168, tel. (68) 15-2570; and by **Aero California,** Calle Hidalgo Pte. 440, tel. (68) 15-2250. Aeroméxico offers nonstop flights to and from Chihuahua, Guadalajara, Hermosillo, La Paz, Mazatlán, Mexico City, and Tijuana. Aero California flies to and from Ciudad Obregón, Culiacán, Guadalajara, Hermosillo, La Paz, Los Angeles, Los Cabos, Mazatlán, Mexico City, Tijuana, and Tucson.

Transportation between the airport and downtown (20 km) costs US$10 by taxi, US$3 by *colectivo.*

Bus
The **Elite** bus terminal is at Av. Juárez and Degollado, while **TNS** and **Transportes del Pacífico** have adjacent terminals at Calle Morelos 327 (four blocks north of Av. Obregón). Together the three bus lines offer routes all over northwestern Mexico. Sample fares and departure frequencies: Culiacán (hourly, US$6.50), Mazatlán (hourly, US$16), Mexico City (every two hours, US$58), Nogales (every three hours, US$21), Tijuana (every 45 minutes, US$47), Ciudad Juárez (four times daily, US$43).

From Av. Obregón you can catch frequent local buses to Topolobampo and Culiacán. The 24-km trip to Topolobampo takes about 45 minutes and costs US$0.75 pp; a taxi between the two towns costs US$8.

City buses ply the main avenues—look on the bus windshield for the name of its principal road destination. Most routes begin and end along Calle Degollado between Independencia and Castro.

Train
The main reason foreign visitors come to Los Mochis is to board or disembark from the 674-km (418-mile) Chihuahua al Pacífico train excursion. The Los Mochis railway station, tel. (68) 12-0853, is around two km (1.2 miles) east of downtown on Av. Onofre Serrano (approximately one km from Blvd. M. Gaxiola).

Special first-class reserved seats on train No. 73 to Chihuahua cost US$40 pp, or US$46 with up to two stopovers along the way; this train departs Los Mochis at 6 a.m. daily and usually takes around 13 hours to reach Chihuahua. The second-class No. 75 ("El Tarahumara," or more colloquially *el pollero*) costs just US$7, leaves Tuesday, Thursday, and Saturday at 7 a.m., and is supposed to reach Chihuahua at midnight (but it often takes up to three hours longer).

Other first-class fares along the Chihuahua al Pacífico route, from Los Mochis, include: Bahuichivo US$16; Posada Barrancas/Divisadero US$19; Creel US$23; La Junta US$27; Cuauhtémoc US$33. Add 15% for stopovers (maximum of two permitted on one ticket); children ages 5-11 get a 50% discount on all fares.

Tickets for either train can be purchased at the station an hour before scheduled departure, but first-class tickets are more easily arranged in advance through **Viajes Flamingo,** tel. (68) 12-1613, in the Hotel Santa Anita. Fares cost the same whether booked at the station or at this agency, which is the only authorized ticketing agent for FNM in Los Mochis.

Hotel Santa Anita offers van transportation from the hotel to the railway station every morning at 5:15 a.m. for US$3 pp, including continental breakfast. The Santa Anita can also arrange long-term parking in a security lot behind the hotel for US$4 per day. Other hotels in town may provide similar services.

Since the most scenic sections of the Chihuahua al Pacífico train journey begin east of El Fuerte (over 100 km northeast of Los Mochis), some visitors drive or take a bus to El Fuerte and board the train there. Because the train leaves El Fuerte around 7:30 a.m. (as opposed to 6 a.m. in Los Mochis), this means rising a bit later in the morning as well. It is also an hour quicker to drive to El Fuerte than to take the train—but you still might want to book your onward ticket at Viajes Flamingo or the railway station in Los Mochis rather than in El Fuerte if traveling in the Nov.-March high season. If you're driving, the main drawback to this alternative is the lack of security parking in El Fuerte.

Ferry

Tickets for the SEMATUR ferries between nearby Topolobampo and La Paz, Baja California Sur, can be reserved and purchased at **Festival Tours,** on Guillermo Prieto between Cuauhtémoc and Blvd. Rosendo G. Castro, tel. (68) 18-3986, the only travel agency in Los Mochis authorized to distribute ferry tickets.

For details on the ferry service, see "By Ferry from Baja" under "Getting There" in the "On the Road" chapter.

Car Rental

Hertz, tel. (68) 12-1122, **Budget,** tel. (68) 15-8300, and **Aga,** tel. (68) 12-5360, each have offices along Calle G. Leyva as well as at Los Mochis International Airport. Typical rates (not including additional per-kilometer charges) include: VW bug, US$37 daily, US$235 weekly; Nissan Tsuru II (Sentra), US$53/US$331; Jeep, US$74/US$453; Chevy Suburban, US$129/US$787.

TOPOLOBAMPO

This small port town, called "Topo" for short, is a scruffy, nondescript burg spread over the hills above Bahía Oguira (also spelled Ohuira). But its harbor happens to be the world's third deepest (and Mexico's deepest), with a consistent, navigable depth of 12 meters (40 feet). So far the harbor's potential has yet to be fully tapped. It was opened only in 1991 as a cargo port, and shipping volume is far below that of Guaymas or Mazatlán.

Fishing is the main local business—Topo's commercial fleet supports nearly 30 fishing cooperatives—and PEMEX also has a large storage and shipping facility here. The state hopes to transform the 24-km Los Mochis-Topolobampo corridor into an industrial zone; several textile-manufacturing and food-processing plants are already in place. Overall, Topo has an industrial feel.

The last of Topolobampo's hotels folded a couple of years ago since virtually all overnight visitors to the area chose to stay in Los Mochis, a much tidier city.

Sights and Recreation

For the visitor, the main points of interest are offshore. **Bay tours,** arranged in town at the docks, stop off at Roca El Farallón, a breeding ground for various birds and sea lions; bottle-nosed dolphins often frolic around the tour boats. One local cooperative takes up to 10 persons in a *panga* on a two-hour bay tour for US$13, or a cruise all the way to **Playa Maviri** and back for US$30. The humble seafood restaurants on Playa Maviri are superb, and are accessible by road (US$13-14 by taxi from Topo) as well as boat.

Or you could hire a *pangero* for drop-off and pickup at the lovely white-sand beaches of **Isla Santa María,** northeast of Bahía Oguira. Other nearby islands worth exploring include the relatively pristine **Isla San Ignacio** and **Isla Macapule,** both of which are more easily accessible from Bahía San Ignacio, the next bay south from Bahía Oguira (between Los Mochis and Guasave). Surrounding tidal estuaries are excellent for **birding.**

Fishing *pangas* can be rented at Club de Náutico, near the ferry terminal, for tries at yellowtail, grouper, and roosterfish (year-round) or marlin and dorado (summer).

Food

Seafood aficionados can head for the simple tables at **Chicho's** and **Grecia,** two rustic seafood places flanking the harbor. Sitting on the top floors of two otherwise undistinguished-looking buildings, these restaurants serve a variety of fresh shrimp, oyster, crab, and fish platters at budget prices. Cleaner and slightly higher-class **Restaurant El Capitán Morgan,** across the street from Chicho's on the water, features fresh seafood platters as well as Mexican and Sinaloan dishes.

Transportation

Buses run frequently during daylight hours between Topo and the municipal market area in downtown Los Mochis. The 24-km trip takes about 45 minutes; fare is US$0.75 pp. A taxi between the two towns will cost around US$8.

Although the **Chihuahua al Pacífico train** (see the Los Mochis transportation section, above) terminates in Topo, very few people choose to board here rather than Los Mochis, as the scenery between Topo and Los Mochis is unimpressive.

Ferries bound for La Paz leave from the **Atracadero de los Transbordadores,** tel. (68) 12-0141 or 12-0321, near the PEMEX storage facility. Tickets can be booked at the pier or from Viajes Flamingo in Los Mochis. The ferry leaves Sun.-Thurs. at 9 a.m. and takes about 18 hours to reach La Paz. For further details, see "By Ferry from Baja" under "Getting There" in the On the Road chapter.

If you're **driving** to Topo, follow Blvd. Gaxiola south out of Los Mochis until it meets the four-lane highway to Topo. Once you hit the Topo outskirts, follow the Topolobampo Sur signs to get into town, otherwise you'll end up at the pier and PEMEX facility.

EL FUERTE

The area around El Fuerte ("The Fort") was originally home to the warring Zuaque, Sinaloa, and Tehueco tribes. Spanish settlers first arrived here in 1564, and a Franciscan mission was established in 1590. To subdue the indigenous population, the Spanish built the eponymous fort on a bend in El Gran Río Zuaquen in 1610. Eventually the river took on the name Río Fuerte, although locally many residents still call it the Río Zuaque.

The most important river system in northwestern Mexico, the Río Fuerte irrigates an extensive agricultural zone running through parts of Sinaloa, Chihuahua, Sonora, and Durango. Its major tributaries include the Alamos, Choix, Septentrión, Batopilas, and Urique Rivers, all of which descend from the western slopes of the Sierra Madre Occidental. The Fuerte alone feeds a basin of 33,600 square km, with annual catchment of nearly five million cubic meters. Already partially impounded by Presa Hidalgo, the Fuerte recently received its second dam, Presa Huites, in the state's bid to generate more hydroelectric power and a higher irrigation capacity.

Nestled in the lower Sierra Madre Occidental, El Fuerte (pop. 25,000) is well known for offering good inland sportfishing at nearby lakes and for the Chihuahua al Pacífico railroad, which makes a stop in town. Savvy travelers begin their eastbound rail journeys (or end their westbound journeys) in El Fuerte rather than Los Mochis, simply because the best rail scenery begins east of here.

ocelot

Less known is the fact that El Fuerte was once the Sinaloa state capital (1824-26) and today remains a thriving repository for colonial-Mexican history and traditional Sinaloan culture. In its early days, the town was an important way station on the Camino Real, and during the silver boom it served as a regional banking and supply center for Sierra Madre mining camps. Although business has slowed considerably, El Fuerte today performs much the same function for local ranching and agriculture.

The downtown architecture is exemplary of 18th- and 19th-century provincial colonial construction; check out the *palacio municipal*—still bullet-pocked from the Mexican Revolution days—and the many L- and U-shaped casas sporting iron-grille windows and *portales* built around tidy courtyards. Don't go expecting another Alamos, Son., however; this is Alamos without the moneyed gringo stewardship. Paint peels from the old casas, which for the most part remain authentic and free from San Miguel de Allende or Alamos affectations.

Also unlike staid Alamos, the markets and cobblestone streets of El Fuerte are bustling with activity. During the day, pedestrian activity centers around the municipal market, and *tamboras sinaloenses*—brass-and-drum bands that perform a lively German-Mexican musical blend peculiar to Sinaloa—sometimes practice in the streets. In the evenings the locals converge around the well-kept, shady plaza.

Though somewhat insular in ambience, El Fuerte is a town that "grows" on those who stay around awhile.

Accommodations
Shoestring: Opposite the municipal market, **Hotel San José** (no phone) is a classic truck-drivers' dive with merchandise piled in the small lobby. Upstairs rooms look better and are quieter. No hot water. Rates: A room with one bed and private bath costs US\$5.30, two beds with bath US\$8, one bed with shared bath or two cots with shared bath US\$4, while one cot with a shared bath is just US\$2. Southeast of Hotel San José, at Juárez and Flores, **Hotel El Oasis** (no phone) is a modest motel-like structure offering basic rooms around a courtyard and prices just a bit higher than at the San José.

Budget: For lower budgets, the best deal in town is the friendly **Hotel San Francisco,** tel. (689) 3-0055, a one-story, provincial-style casa on Av. Obregón (the main downtown street) near the municipal market. It offers clean, simple rooms, each with private bath. Rates: US\$22 s, US\$30 d. Also on Av. Obregón is the passable **Hotel Montesclaros,** a newer place without much atmosphere. Rates: US\$17 s, US\$24 d.

Moderate: El Fuerte's main tourist center, **Hotel Posada del Hidalgo,** Hidalgo 101, tel./fax (689) 3-0242, U.S. tel. (800) 876-3942, occupies a huge colonial mansion near the old-town plaza. Originally built in 1895 as the palatial home of grandee Rafael Almada, the inn has a garden courtyard on one level and a pool and dining room on another. Its 39 large rooms are furnished with antiques, many of which were shipped from San Francisco in the 19th century. The late Pres. Venustiano Carranza spent a

EL FUERTE

Río Fuerte

MONTESCLAROS

HOTEL DEL FUERTE

MIRADOR DE MONTESCLAROS

GABRIEL

MONTESCLAROS

LEYVA

SCHOOL

BANAMEX (BANK)

16 DE SEPTIEMBRE

TEMPLO DEL SAGRADO CORAZÓN

HOTEL POSADA DEL HIDALGO

HOTEL SAN JOSÉ

CONSTITUCIÓN

DEGOLLADO

PLAZA DE ARMAS

HIDALGO

To El Fuerte Railway Station and Los Mochis

OBREGÓN

JUÁREZ

ROSALES

PALACIO MUNICIPAL

MORELOS

ZARAGOZA

INDEPENDENCIA

5 DE MAYO

To Presa Miguel Hidalgo

HOTEL SAN FRANCISCO

EL MESÓN DEL GENERAL

SCALE NOT AVAILABLE

© MOON PUBLICATIONS, INC.

night here in 1913. Most rooms have a/c and all come with hot showers. Rates: US$65 s, US$70 d, US$80 t. This hotel is part of the Balderrama chain based in Los Mochis; reservations can be made through Hotel Santa Anita in Los Mochis.

The Río Fuerte riverbank and ruined walls of the Spanish fort are just a short walk from the Hotel Posada del Hidalgo, and a sunset stroll along the dirt road paralleling the river can lead to some rewarding vistas. The hotel can arrange one- to two-hour guided walking tours, horseback rides, and river tours.

Behind the Posada del Hidalgo is the equally historic **Hotel del Fuerte,** Montesclaros 37, tel. (689) 3-0226. The former Paloma Blanca Lodge has upgraded its facilities from rustic accommodations for hunters and sportfishers to a full-scale inn. The well-restored mansion offers 12 rooms around a courtyard. All meals included. Rates: US$65 s/d.

Another place catering to anglers and hunters, **Villa del Pescador,** Robles 103, tel. (689) 3-0160, U.S./Canada tel. (208) 466-2140 or (800) 796-5411, offers eight simply furnished rooms, all with private bath, around a colonial-style courtyard and small pool. Meals can be arranged at a dining area on the premises. Moderately priced walk-in rates are available, although most guests book hunting or fishing packages. If the lodge appears to be closed, ask a taxi driver in town for help; most know how to contact the lodge manager, who will come and check you in.

RV Park/Campground

About 9.6 km (six miles) southwest of El Fuerte, near Presa Domínguez, is a rustic campground run by twin brothers **José and Pepe Castillo,** tel. (689) 3-0836. RV slots with full hookups cost US$10 per night; tent space is US$5.

Food

El Mesón del General, housed in a historic courtyard building at Juárez 202, about a block from the plaza, is open for dinner only. The restaurant specializes in delicious fresh bass *(lobina)* prepared in various styles, as well as seafood and steak. Moderate prices.

The small, clean, a/c **Restaurante Las Cazuelas,** next door to Hotel San Francisco, serves a good selection of Mexican standards at moderate prices. It's open for breakfast, lunch,

and dinner. **Pollos Asados Tarahumara,** almost opposite the Hotel San Francisco, sells tasty and inexpensive barbecued chicken.

The white-tablecloth dining room at Hotel Posada del Hidalgo is quite good (fresh bass is the specialty) although service can be a little slow—especially if a rail-tour group is staying at the hotel.

Restaurant Paseo de las Aves occupies a large two-story ranch house more or less behind the town amid some fields. The house specialty is *carne asada* and other roast or grilled meats—including local quail—prepared in a huge barbecue pit. To find this place, take Paseo de las Aves three blocks past Posada de Hidalgo heading toward Presa Hidalgo. Turn left at the sign for the restaurant, then cross an arroyo and follow the dirt road through fields till you see a second sign on the left—a short road leads from there to the restaurant. The latter turnoff is only about one kilometer (half mile) from the first left back in town.

Taco vendors near the municipal market serve the usual *carne asada.* El Fuerte is famous for *agua de cebada,* a delicious *agua fresca* made with sweetened barley, vanilla, and cinnamon.

Fishing and Hunting

Northeast, west, and northwest of El Fuerte, respectively, are **Presa Huites** (an impoundment of the Río Fuerte), **Presa Miguel Hidalgo** (also on the Río Fuerte), and **Presa Josefa Ortíz de Domínguez** (on the Río El Cuchujaqui). All three reservoirs are well stocked with largemouth bass and catfish. Simple shoestring/budget rooms are available at two hunting-and-fishing lodges near Presa Hidalgo—**Chico's Lodge,** tel. (689) 3-0158, and **Hidalgo Lodge,** tel. (689) 3-0657. Villa del Pescador in El Fuerte runs the **Lake Huites Lodge** at Presa Huites. Most visiting sportfishers, however, use El Fuerte for a base since it's less than hour's drive from these lakes.

The same area is popular for hunting Canada goose, various duck species (canvasback, mallard, pintail, redhead, teal, wigeon, and others), quail, and white-winged dove. Waterfowl season runs Nov.-Feb., while quail and dove are in season Oct.-March.

In El Fuerte, **Villa del Pescador,** Robles 103, tel. (689) 3-0160, U.S./Canada tel. (208) 466-2140 or (800) 796-5411, can arrange fishing and hunting trips in various locations in the surrounding foothills. It also maintains a colonial-style villa in town with accommodations for 16. For further information write to Villa del Pescador, 2704 Pascoe Ln., Nampa, ID 83686. Bonded hunting and fishing guides are also available for hire through the Hotel Posada del Hidalgo in El Fuerte.

Transportation

Air: The nearest commercial airport is in Los Mochis. A 1,469-meter (4,818-foot) airstrip near town can accommodate small planes; buzz the town once for taxi pickup.

Bus: Buses to and from Los Mochis (US$2.50) run frequently throughout the day. The El Fuerte terminal is on Calle Juárez almost opposite Hotel San José.

Train: The first-class Chihuahua al Pacífico eastbound train departs El Fuerte at 7:26 a.m.; tickets cost US$31. The second-class train leaves at 9:40 a.m. and costs only US$5.90. The westbound first-class train passes through El Fuerte at 6:15 p.m.; the second-class at around 9:15 p.m. The railway station is about six km east of town; taxis to the station cost US$4 (negotiation is necessary). If you're planning on an eastbound morning departure, go to the taxi stand at Av. Obregón and Calle Juárez (opposite Bancomer) the night before and arrange a taxi to the station for the following morning. The Posada del Hidalgo and Hotel San Francisco will make taxi arrangements on request. You can also take the 6:30 a.m. bus from the center of town to meet the 7:26 a.m. train for only US$0.55.

CHOIX

About 50 km northeast of El Fuerte via Sinaloa 23 lies the small town of Choix (pronounced "choice"), virtually the end of the road in this neck of the woods. East of here there's not much left but hard trails into the western escarpment of the Sierra Madre Occidental.

Several thermal springs in the area (at nearby Chuchaca, Apuche, Agua Caliente de Baca, and Agua Caliente Grande) all have *balneario* facilities of some sort. And Amerindian rock art can be viewed at various caves in the vicinity, including Cueva Pinta, Cueva San Pantaleón, Cueva Reparito, and Cueva Vinatería. Ask around in Choix for a guide to take you to the caves; the sites can be difficult to locate, and *narcotraficante* activity in the area makes the use of a guide doubly advisable.

Simple shoestring-priced rooms are available at the **Hotel Real de Minas,** Obregón 28, tel. (686) 6-0155, fax 5-6189. Rates: US$14 s/d.

CULIACÁN AND VICINITY

Originally founded in 1531 by Nuño Beltrán de Guzmán, one of the most hated and feared of all conquistadors (he was excommunicated from the Catholic Church for his cruelty to Indians), Culiacán was the first permanent settlement in northwestern Mexico and an important base for early Spanish explorations in this region. The city's name means "Where Two Waters Meet," a Nahuatl reference to the confluence of the Humaya and Tamazula Rivers. In typical Mexican fashion, the river formed by this junction is deemed a third river, in this case the Río Culiacán.

Irrigation has turned the river valleys surrounding Culiacán into a major agricultural zone producing huge crops of tomatoes, eggplants, green peppers, cucumbers, peas, garbanzos, and other vegetables. Bright yellow marigolds are another important source of foreign income; purchased by Purina in the U.S., the flowers are added to chicken feed to make egg yolks come out more yellow. The city also has six industrial parks with a total of 78 plants in operation—over half engaged in food and beverage processing or packing.

In addition to being a farming center, Culiacán is the seat of Sinaloa's state government and home to 440,000 residents according to the last official census (unofficial estimates place the population as high as 600,000). As the state's largest and most modern city, sprawling Culiacán radiates commerce, activity, style, and power. Several universities maintain campuses here, including the Universidad Autónoma de Sinaloa and the Instituto Tecnológico de Estudios Superiores (ITESM). Few visitors spend more

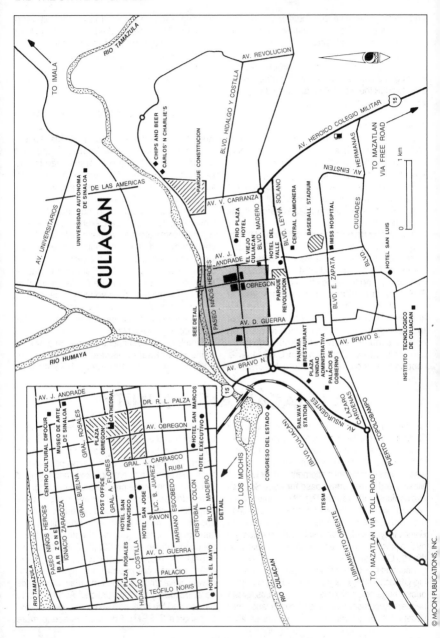

TO IMALA

RIO TAMAZULA

AV. REVOLUCION

CHIPS AND BEER
CARLOS' N CHARLIE'S

PARQUE CONSTITUCION

BLVD. HIDALGO Y COSTILLA

AV. HEROICO COLEGIO MILITAR

15

TO MAZATLAN
VIA FREE ROAD

AV. EINSTEIN

1 km

AV. HERMANAS

UNIVERSIDAD AUTONOMA DE SINALOA

DE LAS AMERICAS

AV. V. CARRANZA

RIO PLAZA HOTEL

EL VIEJO CULIACAN

BLVD. MADERO

HOTEL DEL VALLE

BLVD. LEYVA SOLANO

BASEBALL STADIUM

CENTRAL CAMIONERA

IMSS HOSPITAL

CIUDADES

HOTEL SAN LUIS

CULIACAN

AV. UNIVERSITARIOS

RIO HUMAYA

SEE DETAIL

PASEO NIÑOS HEROES

AV. J. ANDRADE

OBREGON

PARQUE REVOLUCION

AV. D. GUERRA

BLVD. E. ZAPATA

BLVD.

INSTITUTO TECNOLOGICO DE CULIACAN

AV. BRAVO N.

AV. BRAVO S.

PANAMA RESTAURANT

PLAZA UNIDAD ADMINISTRATIVA

PALACIO DE GOBIERNO

RAILWAY STATION

CONGRESO DEL ESTADO

TO LOS MOCHIS

15

BLVD. CULIACAN

RIO CULIACAN

AV. INSURGENTES

AV. LAZARO CARDENAS

PUERTO TOPOLOBAMPO

LIBRAMIENTO ORIENTE

TO MAZATLAN VIA TOLL ROAD

ITESM

DETAIL

AV. J. ANDRADE

CENTRO CULTURAL DIFOCUR

MUSEO DE ARTE DE SINALOA

PLAZA OBREGON

CATHEDRAL

DR. R. L. PALZA

AV. OBREGON

HOTEL SAN MARCOS

HOTEL EJECUTIVO

GRAL. ROSALES

GRAL. BUELNA

GRAL. A. FLORES

GRAL. J. CARRASCO

RUBI

POST OFFICE

HOTEL SAN FRANCISCO

HOTEL SAN JOSE

LIC. B. JUAREZ

PAVON

MARIANO ESCOBEDO

CRISTOBAL COLON

BLVD. MADERO

HOTEL EJECUTIVO

PASEO NIÑOS HEROES

BAR ZONE

IGNACIO ZARAGOZA

RIO TAMAZULA

PLAZA ROSALES

HIDALGO Y COSTILLA

PALACIO

TEOFILO NORIS

AV. D. GUERRA

HOTEL EL MAYO

© MOON PUBLICATIONS, INC.

than a night here, however, and then only when they've underestimated the time it takes to reach Mazatlán farther south. Mexico 15 drivers can circumvent the city via a marked bypass road.

Several city projects underway promise to provide at least a few hours of distraction in the near future. The ambitious Tres Ríos project aims to build a 46-km riverfront district with promenades, park areas, and floating restaurants by the end of the century. The project also entails building a new dam (to eliminate recurring problems with flooding) and 10 new bridges, dredging the rivers, and widening city boulevards. In the meantime, a small riverfront promenade or *malecón* already exists along the Río Tamazula off Paseo Niños Heroes.

SIGHTS

Museo de Arte de Sinaloa
One local sight worth visiting is this relatively new art museum containing over 300 works by Diego Rivera, Rufino Tamayo, Pedro Coronel, and famous Sinaloan artist López Saenz. The museum is just southwest of the Centro Cultural DIFOCUR between Rosales and Buelna. Open Tues.-Sun. 10 a.m.-1 p.m. and 4-7 p.m.; admission is US$0.50 adults, US$0.20 children under 12. For information call (67) 13-9933.

Cultural Centers
In the northern part of the downtown area, **Centro Cultural DIFOCUR,** off Av. Obregón near the Río Tamazula, tel. (67) 15-0311, is Culiacán's most well-endowed cultural center. The center hosts foreign cinema, dance, and musical performances; lectures; contemporary art shows; and occasional historical or cultural exhibits. A bookstore, small museum, and modern art room are open 4-7 p.m.

The older **Casa de la Cultura,** at Flores and Noris (opposite Plaza Rosales), houses a small gallery with works by local artists.

Parks
Culiacán has several large city parks. **Parque Revolución,** off Av. Obregón between Villa and Leyva Solano, holds an amazing amalgam of shade trees, *juegos de video* (video games), food vendors, and sparking lovers. **Parque Con-**stitución, east of downtown at Buelna and Guerrero, boasts a zoo (open 9 a.m.-6 p.m., admission US$0.50) with regional fauna; the park also reportedly contains the world's second-largest meteorite (47 tons).

Malverde Shrine
Not far from the Palacio de Gobierno, near the railroad tracks on the city's west side, stands the famous shrine to Jesús Malverde, a Robin Hood-style bandit who was executed by local authorities on this spot in 1909. Because many drug lords pray at the shrine, both for bountiful marijuana or opium harvests and for protection from the bullets of law enforcement agents or rival *narcotraficantes,* Malverde is nicknamed *el narcosantón* or the "Big Narco Saint." The walls of the simple shrine are pinned with braids of human hair and photos of people who claim to have received miracles by praying to Malverde, who is believed to have the power to cure disease and speed recovery in medical crises. A small band usually hangs out near the shrine to perform *corridos* about Malverde for pay.

How a man who robbed from the rich and gave to the poor and needy has come to be equated with the *narcotraficante* culture becomes easier to understand when you realize that many schools, clinics, and other public services in Sinaloa's Sierra Madre towns have been funded partially or entirely by Mexican drug lords.

ACCOMMODATIONS AND FOOD

Hotels
Because Culiacán doesn't get many tourists, hotel rates are especially moderate.

Shoestring: The cheapest downtown place, **Hotel San José,** Calle Juárez Pte. 233 (at Calle Rubi), offers basic rooms with *baño colectivo.* It's run-down and dark. Rates: US$5.50 s, US$7.50 d, US$9 t.

Budget: In the downtown area, the best hotel for location and value is the clean, friendly, and efficient **Hotel San Francisco,** Blvd. Hidalgo y Costilla Pte. 227, tel. (67) 13-5863, two blocks west of Av. Obregón. Each rooms has a/c, TV, and phone. Rates: US$15 s, US$18 d, US$21 t. Another branch with similar rates is the **Hotel**

Francis, nearby at Calle Escobedo Pte. 135, tel. (67) 12-4750.

A number of hotels in the vicinity of the bus station charge about the same rates as the San Francisco but are poor value and best avoided. Near the bus terminal and somewhat better is **Hotel Del Valle,** Blvd. Leyva Solano at Andrade, tel. (67) 13-9080, where rooms have a/c, TV, and phone. Rates:US$16 s, US$20 d, US$22 t.

The new **Río Plaza Hotel,** on Blvd. Hidalgo y Costilla about four blocks east of the cathedral, tel. (67) 16-9206, is a small, colorful, two-story place that's a better deal than most of its competitors in the same price range. Rooms come with a/c, TV, and private, marbled bathrooms with hot-water showers. A secure parking area is on the premises. Rates: US$17 s, US$19 d. Another economic but decent choice is **Hotel El Mayo,** Blvd. Madero Pte. 730, tel. (67) 15-2230, where rooms have a/c, cable TV, and private bath. Rates: US$16 s, US$20 d, and US$24 t.

Moving to the top of the budget range, **Hotel San Marcos,** Calle Carrasco Nte. 44, tel. (67) 13-7876, has newly remodeled rooms. Suites available. Rates: US$34 s/d, US$44 for a suite. **Hotel Executivo,** Blvd. Madero at Av. Obregón, tel. (67) 13-9310, offers decent facilities for rates on par with Hotel San Marcos.

On Mexico 15 northwest of the city, **Motel Tres Ríos,** tel. (67) 50-5280, fax (67) 13-9300, is another popular tourist lodge. Recently renovated, the facilities include a/c, TV, pool, and parking. Rates: Rooms in the new wing go for US$35 s/d; rooms in the older section are US$27 s/d.

Inexpensive/Moderate: The popular Balderrama-owned **Hotel San Luis Lindavista,** on Av. Las Palmas, tel. (67) 16-710, fax (67) 15-0815, overlooks the city near the Instituto Tecnológico de Culiacán. Amenities include a swimming pool and security parking. Rates: US$59 s/d for rooms in the newer section; US$40 s/d for those in the older section. To reach Hotel San Luis by car, drive south on Av. Obregón—follow signs to ITC—until the institute is on your right; the hotel will be visible on the hill to the left.

RV Park/Camping

Motel Tres Ríos (see just above) offers 40 RV spaces with full hookups for US$11 a night, or with electricity and water only for US$8.

Food

Downtown Culiacán is chockablock with inexpensive *cafeterías* and fast-food eateries. **Panama,** opposite the north end of Parque Revolución on Calle Fco. Villa, has a good selection of Mexican *antojitos* served buffet-style. There's another Panama branch on Av. Lázaro Cárdenas almost opposite the city hall. Both locations are open daily for breakfast, lunch, and dinner. Another inexpensive, popular buffet-style place is **Chic's,** opposite Hotel Executivo. Both are open for breakfast, lunch, and dinner. **Woolworth,** across from the cathedral on Obregón, contains a good, economical cafe serving Mexican favorites as well as burgers and sandwiches. It's open daily 9 a.m.-10 p.m.

At the casual and popular **Jugos California,** on Calle Flores near the municipal market, the house specialty is a roast chicken *(pollo asado)* platter that comes with tortillas, salad, salsas, and beans for under US$3. As the name suggests, fresh *licuados* (*nopal con naranja* or "prickly pear with orange" is a unique one) and *aguas frescas* are available, along with *comida corrida,* tacos, *tortas,* and tostadas. Jugos California generally is open early to late for breakfast, lunch, and dinner.

Chinese restaurants are well represented in Culiacán due to the relatively high Chinese presence. **Tai Pak,** on the corner of Ruby and Juan José Ríos, is one of the better downtown examples.

Steak and seafood are the emphases at **Restaurante Los Arcos,** at Blvd. Xicotencatl and Lago de Cuitzeo, two blocks east of Parque Constitución. The restaurants at Motel Tres Ríos and Hotel San Luis are popular among visiting gringos.

Carlos'n Charlie's, on Niños Héroes next to the nightclubs along the river, is a clean, hip place to drink a few beers or eat regional Mexican cuisine.

El Viejo Culiacán, on Calle Andrade between Colón and Madero, tel. (67) 12-9020, serves traditional Sinaloan food in a colorful adobe lined with wood accents and old photos of Culiacán. House specials include *asado de res* (a stew of beef, potatoes, zucchini, and lettuce, served with tortillas) and *cabrerá* (very tender beef served on a hot metal plate). Open daily for lunch and dinner.

LITTLE CHICAGO

Besides serving as Sinaloa's state capital, Culiacán is also well-known—in Mexico at least—as a major center of operations for Sinaloa's notorious *narcotraficantes*, who move marijuana and heroin out of the Sierra Madre Occidental and into world dope markets. Mexicans have dubbed the city "Little Chicago," likening the local gangster activity to that of 1920s' and '30s' Chicago. Shootouts between police and traffickers or between rival gangs are not uncommon; the city averages two murders a day, high for Mexico. Of course it's not only Culiacán's proximity to the sierra that makes it attractive to mobsters; the police here are notoriously corrupt, as is readily apparent to anyone who visits local police offices. Law enforcement officers at the federal police headquarters in Culiacán, for example, drive late-model Jeep Cherokees (as their personal vehicles) and wear plenty of heavy gold jewelry, expensive watches, and alligator-skin boots.

The city's reputation for *narcotraficante* activity may be on the wane with the recent demise of cartel capo Amado Carillo Fuentes (who died while undergoing surgery to conceal his physical identity) and imprisonment of Juan García Abrego. At any rate, drug gangster activity doesn't appear to affect Culiacán's security with regard to tourist visitation as long as you stay away from narco-business. We have found the city to be as safe as any other Mexican city of its size.

RECREATION AND ENTERTAINMENT

Hunting
The Valle de Culiacán swarms with geese, ducks, white-winged doves, quail, and blue pigeons; local farmers welcome hunters to help keep the populations down. Motel Tres Ríos can arrange hunting guides. A list of guides and outfitters is also available from the Culiacán tourist office (see "Information," below).

Shopping
The main shopping district is centered around Av. Obregón and the municipal market on Blvd. Hidalgo y Costilla. Along neighboring streets you can find a large selection of department stores, shops, and mall vendors selling virtually everything.

Nightlife
Disco-going is a popular activity in fashionable Culiacán practically every night of the week. Most au courant are **Morocco,** at Hotel San Luis; **Baccos,** at Hotel Executivo on Calle Buelna; **O'lydia,** at Motel Tres Ríos (the largest disco in northwest Mexico); and four others along the river on Paseo Niños Heroes—**Banana Rana's, Magic House, Chips & Beer,** and **Canta Show.**

Downtown movie houses showing the latest American and Latin American films include: **Multicinemas,** Calle Buelna and Xicotencatl; **Cine-**

DAVID MAUNG

shrine to Jesús Malverde, patron saint of narcotraficantes *and others in trouble with the law*

ma **Culiacán 70,** on Calle Buelna; and **Cine Diana,** on Av. Obregón.

TRANSPORTATION AND INFORMATION

Air
At Culiacán International Airport (12 km west of the city center), **Aeroméxico,** Av. Rosales Pte. 77, tel. (67) 15-3772, and **Aero California,** Blvd. Madero and Av. Obregón, tel. (67) 16-0250, field nonstop flights to and from Chihuahua, Guadalajara, Los Angeles, Mexico City, La Paz, Los Mochis, Tijuana, and Ciudad Obregón. The standard taxi fare between town and the airport is US$10.

Bus
Transportes del Pacífico, Elite, Tufesa, Futura, and **TNS** operate from the Central Camionera at Blvd. Leyva Solano and Calle Corona, with buses to virtually all towns and cities in Sinaloa and Sonora plus Mexicali, Tijuana, Tepic, Guadalajara, and Mexico City. First-class buses to Nogales and Mazatlán cost US$26 and US$10, respectively. Express buses to Los Mochis (leaving every 15 minutes 5 a.m.-7 p.m.), as well as local buses to Altata and El Dorado, leave from just outside the station. The bus-terminal cafeteria offers probably the largest selection of American-brand beers in northwestern Mexico.

Train
The FNM station, tel. (67) 14-7059, is on Av. Insurgentes opposite the Plaza Unidad Administrativa and the Palacio de Gobierno. For scheduling information on Del Pacífico train No. 1 (special first class reserved), see the "Railway Schedule" in the Transportation Appendix. Second-class train nos. 3 and 4 pass through at 12:35 a.m. (southbound) and 2:40 a.m. (northbound). Sample fares: Guadalajara US$16 (first class), US$8.50 (second class); Nogales US$19/US$10; Mazatlán US$4/US$2.50; Mexicali US$26/US$14.

Driving
Traffic in Culiacán is intense, and many downtown streets are one-way. To reach the downtown area coming south via Mexico 15, turn left (east) at the first traffic circle (about two km/1.6 miles south of the Cuauhtémoc Brewery) onto Blvd. Madero.

A trunk highway encircles the city, connecting old Mexico 15 with the new toll highway between Culiacán and Mazatlán. From downtown Culiacán you must drive west on the trunk highway (follow signs to "Costa Rica," a Culiacán suburb) to reach the toll road (US$5 to Mazatlán).

Auto Rental
Budget, tel. (67) 14-7737, and **Aga,** tel. (67) 13-2262, rent cars at the airport. Cars can also be rented through Hotel San Luis Lindavista.

Information
The useful state tourist office, tel. (67) 17-8419, is on the second floor of the Palacio de Gobierno, off Av. Insurgentes near the railway station.

OUTSIDE TOWN

Beaches
Around 60 km west of Culiacán along the coast lies a system of bays, estuaries, and barrier peninsulas. Sonora 280 leads west to **Altata,** a dingy gray beach on Bahía Altata with a few *palapa* restaurants and beach homes. Better is the sand-and-palm **Playa El Tambor** 15 km north of Altata by gravel and sand road, next to the shrimp camp of Dautillos. Surfers' note: January and February usually bring high, surfable breaks to El Tambor.

Farther south, near the farming/sugar-refining community of El Dorado (53 km/33 miles from Culiacán), is **Playa Las Arenitas,** a fair beach on the fishing bay of Ensenada del Pabellón.

Imala
About 24 km (15 miles) east of Culiacán via unpaved road, the village of Imala has a rustic *balneario* (spa) with thermal baths. The first pool is the smallest and hottest, while three other pools become progressively larger and cooler. Palm trees provide shade and you'll find cabañas (for changing), restrooms, and small brick cabins for rent. If you visit midweek you'll probably have the pools to yourself. The gardener may ask for a donation for grounds upkeep (US$1 is standard).

You'll need your own wheels to reach Imala. The road begins next to the monument at the entrance of the Universidad de Sinaloa in northeastern Culiacán—count on a 50- to 60-minute drive at a leisurely pace. Villages passed along the way include Aguamita and Jotagua (if in doubt you're on the right road, stop and ask). The *balneario* gate is directly across the plaza from Imala's 17th-century church.

A few km east of Imala via a rough dirt road is **Presa Sanalona,** a little-known bass-fishing spot.

Presa López Mateos

Impounded by the nation's third-highest dam, Presa López Mateos is Mexico's fifth-largest lake and is the most popular freshwater fishing locale in the area. Supplies and rustic facilities may be available at the village of El Varejonal at the lake's southern tip. Gringo anglers who have dropped lines here have stayed at Culiacán's Motel Tres Ríos (see "Accommodations and Food" under the Culiacán section, above), where fishing guides can be arranged.

To reach the lake, take the signed turnoff at La Campana, 31 km north of Culiacán on Mexico 15, then proceed northeast 25 km (15.5 miles) to El Varejonal.

COSALÁ

Founded in 1562, the Sierra Madre town of Cosalá is the oldest in the state. The name is a Spanish corruption of Quezala, a Sinaloa Indian term for "place of the macaws." Cosalá was once a boomtown boasting silver deposits so rich that the surrounding area was referred to as the "silver mountains." Although it's hard to believe given today's laid-back ambience of benign neglect (*"muy tranquilo,"* say the locals), the town published the state's first newspaper in 1826 and temporarily served as Sinaloa's state capital in 1827, when its population exceeded 20,000.

Blessed with a moderate year-round climate and reliable water sources, the town has a small but dedicated following among savvy travelers who find it reminiscent of Taxco or a provincial Italian village. The steep, cobblestoned streets are lined with tile-roofed stucco buildings—many of them over two centuries old.

Town Sights

Barrel-vaulted, brick-and-stone **Capilla Cosalá,** built by Jesuit padres in 1607, is the city's oldest structure, though many visitors miss it. On the plaza is the folk baroque **Iglesia de Santa Ursula,** whose interior is decorated with silver ore donated by miners. Opposite the church, the **Museo de Minería e Historia** contains artifacts chronicling the town's 400-year history. Another attraction is the city hall's 200-year-old clock, which uses a rock counterweight, raised by pulleys, to propel the clock hands in 24-hour cycles.

Shopping

If you're in the market for a one-of-a-kind Mexican saddle, check out the shop of renowned saddlemaker **Arcadio García** (on the right as you enter town from below). One of García's saddles was presented to former U.S. president Ronald Reagan by the Mexican government. Two blocks off the plaza is a small **municipal market.**

Vado Hondo

About 15 km southwest of Cosalá in the Arroyo del Sabinal is Vado Hondo ("Deep Dip"), a lovely and rustic *balneario* where you can soak in deep blue-green pools or do a little hiking in the surrounding arroyo. Once you've found the village called Vado Hondo, follow a rough dirt road paralleling a tributary of the Río Elota as it leads through the village and continues up the arroyo three or four km to the *balneario*.

In addition to the natural pools, Vado Hondo features natural water slides cut into the rock and small cascades that make the spot a favorite of local picnickers. We suggest leaving your car at the village just after you cross the river, and walking the three km to the pools. You'll pass chickens, burros, cactus fences, tropical birds, papaya trees, and cornfields before crossing two cattle guards (if you're driving, watch out for the second cattle guard as it's rather deep). At the lower part of the *vado* is a small littered park; the further up the river you walk, the more clean, pristine, and secluded the river and pools become. Trails lead up two tributaries of the river.

Presa López Portillo (Presa Comedero)

Open less than 10 years, Presa Comedero, an impoundment of the Río San Lorenzo set in beautiful subtropical mountain scenery, has quickly become one of Mexico's top bass-fishing spots. Hunting for deer, dove, and quail in the area is also highly reputed.

The only facilities on the lake are operated by **Comedero Sportsman's Lodge** in conjunction with fishing or hunting packages. For information, call or write Ron Speed, Malakoff, TX 75148, tel. (214) 489-1656, fax 489-2856.

The lake is reached via a 48-km (30-mile) dirt road running north from Cosalá.

Accommodations and Camping

Shoestring: Hotel Conde near the plaza offers basic rooms for around US$4.50-6.50 per night. Nicer in ambience if a slight bit run-down is the similarly priced **Hotel Colonial,** an 11-room inn with colonial-style courtyard also close to the plaza. At both of these hotels, bathroom facilities are shared with other guests. Relatively new **Hotel "Ray" 4 Hermanos,** a green-and-white two-story place not far from the plaza, rents rooms set around an open courtyard. All rooms have private bath and a/c; some have TV. Rates: US$10.50 s/d.

You can camp at Vado Hondo, where there's plenty of shade and water.

Food

The restaurant at the Hotel Ray (see above) serves good, basic Mexican dishes. Home-style fare is available from informal, signless cafes near the plaza; usually these are open for breakfast and lunch (about 8 a.m.-5 p.m.) only.

Getting There

Cosalá is reached via Sinaloa D1, which runs northeast from Mexico 15 beginning exactly halfway between Culiacán and Mazatlán (103 km/64 miles from either city). From the Mexico 15 turnoff, the two-lane, paved road runs 55 km (34 miles) to Cosalá. By car the trip takes 1.5-2 hours from Culiacán or Mazatlán.

Buses to Cosalá run from Mazatlán and Culiacán several times daily 8 a.m.-3 p.m. only; the trip takes about three hours.

MAZATLÁN AND VICINITY

Whether viewed from land or sea, by day or night, Mazatlán's lengthy *malecón*—scalloped by sandy, palm-fringed beaches and backed by green hills and glittering shoreline hotels—is one of the nation's most enduring seaside images. Northernmost of the several major beach resorts on Mexico's Pacific Coast, this tropical gem lies within a long day's drive from the U.S. border on the Nogales-Mazatlán tollway.

The city is a favorite vacation destination for Mexicans and foreigners alike. In fact, only a third of Mazatlán's tourists come from abroad, so prices are lower and the "tourist trap" ambience is less apparent here than at any other major resort in the country. Besides claiming Mexico's longest uninterrupted city beach (26 km/16 miles), Mazatlán takes pride in its well-preserved historical and cultural heritage. Away from the beachfront you'll find classic Mexican plazas, cafes, and markets, as well as colonial and Republican architecture more commonly associated with the country's interior highlands.

With a metropolitan-area population of approximately 400,000 (estimates vary wildly), Mazatlán is large enough to offer an abundance of cultural and entertainment venues, yet small enough to get around in easily. And thanks to the steady flow of immigrants who have disembarked on the city's shores from all over the world during the

last four centuries, Mazatlán is a remarkably tolerant place. Small wonder then, the city boasts a very high percentage of repeat visitors.

INTRODUCTION

History

The area wedged between today's Bahía de Puerto Viejo (Old Port Bay) and the natural harbor formed by the Infiernillo, Astillero, and Urias estuaries was once inhabited by the Totorame, a Mesoamerican Marginal tribal group known for finely crafted, polychromatic ceramics. When Nuño de Guzmán sent 25 Spanish explorers here in 1531 from Culiacán, the Chibcha people they encountered were probably Totorame descendants, although disagreement remains as to whether the Totorame culture still existed at that time.

Guzmán moved on to establish his west coast base in Culiacán, reporting only that the native name for the area was "Place of Deer," or *mazatlán*. Since this is a Nahuatl word, most likely the name actually originated with the Spaniard's Aztec interpreter.

The first colonists to settle here in any numbers were primarily *mulatos* (mixed-race colonists whose physiognomy was predominantly Amerindian or African), and so the set-

Mazatlán in 1882

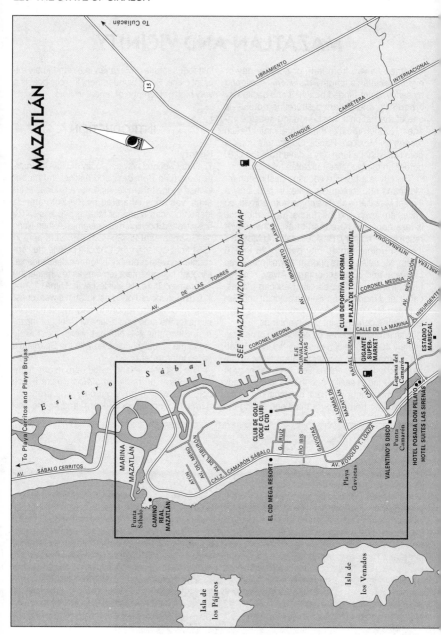

MAZATLÁN

To Culiacán

LIBRAMIENTO

CARRETERA INTERNACIONAL

ETRONQUE

15

AV. DE LAS TORRES

SEE "MAZATLÁN/ZONA DORADA" MAP

LIBRAMIENTO

AV. PLAYAS

CLUB DEPORTIVA REFORMA
PLAZA DE TOROS MONUMENTAL

CORONEL MEDINA

CORONEL MEDINA

EJE CIRCUNVALACIÓN PLAYAS

CARRETERA INTERNACIONAL

AV. REVOLUCIÓN

AV. INSURGENTES

CALLE DE LA MARINA

RAFAEL BUENA

GIGANTE SUPER-MARKET

ESTADIO T. MARISCAL

CAL.

Laguna del Camarón

To Playa Cerritos and Playa Brujas

Estero Sábalo

MARINA MAZATLÁN

AV. SÁBALO CERRITOS

Punta Sábalo

CAMINO REAL MAZATLÁN

CALZ. CAMARÓN SÁBALO

EL CID MEGA RESORT

AV. DEL TIBURÓN

ATÚN

G. RUIZ

RÍO IBIS

GAVIOTAS

AV. LOMAS DE MAZATLÁN

CLUB DE GOLF (GOLF CLUB) EL CID

AV. RODOLFO T. LOAIZA

Playa Gaviotas

VALENTINO'S DISCO

Punta Camarón

HOTEL POSADA DON PELAYO
HOTEL SUITES LAS SIRENAS

Isla de los Pájaros

Isla de los Venados

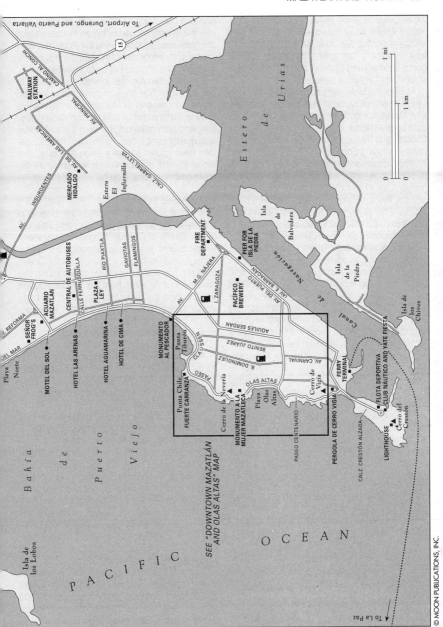

© MOON PUBLICATIONS, INC.

tlement was originally called "Pueblo de los Mulatos." After a flood destroyed the town, a new settlement called San Juan Bautista de Mazatlán took its place. In the early 17th century, this became an important Spanish port for exploration of the Baja California peninsula.

As gold and silver were discovered in the nearby Sierra Madre Occidental in the late 18th century, Mazatlán rose to eminence as a supply depot (and bullion shipment point) for mines at Rosario, Copala, and Pánuco. During the mining era, pirates—including England's Sir Francis Drake and Thomas Cavendish—visited the bay frequently to prey upon gold- and silver-laden Spanish galleons en route to Manila. In the opposite direction, these galleons arrived filled with silks, spices, and gems from the Orient, along with pearls from Baja California (source of Mazatlán's tourist catchphrase, "Pearl of the Pacific").

As the Spanish colonial era wound to a close and Mazatlán's importance as a Spanish port declined, German immigrants moved in and began supplying equipment to local farmers and ranchers. By the time Mexican independence was declared in 1821, the town claimed only 500 residents. Small and relatively remote, Mazatlán managed to avoid many of Mexico's 19th-century conflicts, although the U.S. Navy occupied the town briefly during the Mexican-American War (1846-48). The French also attacked in 1864, but valiant Mazatlecos managed to defend their town successfully against Napoleon III's imperial forces.

As Sinaloa's mild climate, fertile soils, and stable politics attracted an increasing number of immigrants—including many of Greek, Lebanese, American, Chinese, and Japanese descent—the city grew in importance as a trade center. In 1831 Sinaloa was granted statehood (separating from the former state of Sonora y Sinaloa), and from 1859 to 1873 Mazatlán served as the state capital.

The late 19th century brought railroads to Mexico's Pacific coast and the town was transformed almost overnight. With increased access to national and international markets, the local fishing industry flourished, more workers and tradespeople arrived, and the city expanded steadily.

Like most large cities in Mexico, Mazatlán suffered enormous setbacks during the 1910-20 Mexican Revolution as the country sought to narrow the enormous gap between the haves and the have-nots created during the Porfiriato. With renewed development of the port during and following WW II, the city began to grow again.

Fishing lured the first tourists to the area in the '40s and '50s. When sportfishers returned home with reports of Mazatlán's mild tropical climate, picturesque beaches, trophy-size gamefish, and tasty seafood, the town's resort status was quietly established. Pleasure visits to Mazatlán have grown steadily since the '50s, and today tourism is second only to fishing as the main source of local income.

Climate and Seasons

One of the reasons for Mazatlán's popularity is the city's near-perfect climate. Located just south of the Tropic of Cancer, the city enjoys warm temperatures year-round, although it's not far enough south to fog your glasses. Pacific Ocean breezes buffet the coastline, moisturizing the dry air that drifts south from the Sonoran Desert and keeping the mercury from rising too high. Water temperatures along the beach hover between 20° C (68° F) and 24° C (76° F) year-round, while air temperatures average 19.4° C (67° F) in January, 27.2° C (81° F) in July.

Another important climatic influence is the Sierra Madre Occidental, which prevents tropical storms off the Gulf of Mexico from reaching this far west while at the same time blocking the Altiplano's desert heat.

Most of the area's annual precipitation falls June-Oct., which leaves mostly clear skies the remainder of the year. For those of us from temperate zones, the only time of year the weather may feel consistently uncomfortable is July-Sept., when frequent rain and summer temperatures combine to produce hot and muggy afternoons (though it's not as bad as, say, southern Texas). As elsewhere in Mexico, room rates and other prices generally drop to their lowest from August to mid-October, so some budget-conscious visitors make a point of vacationing in Mazatlán this time of year.

July is Mazatlán's biggest month in terms of tourist visitation—in July 1992, 132,000 tourist arrivals were recorded, of whom around 110,000 were domestic visitors. The city's second highest tourist month is December, when foreign arrivals outnumber domestic tourists (but don't worry, in Mazatlán the local population always greatly exceeds the tourist population). Except during Carnaval (late February or early March), these are the only two months of the year when advance hotel reservations are absolutely necessary.

SIGHTS

No matter how you choose to transport yourself around the city (see "Getting Around," below), the first thing to get straight is how the 24-km (15-mile) waterfront avenue changes names six times. Starting from the southern tip of the peninsula at the causeway to Cerro del Crestón, **Calz. Crestón Alzada** becomes **Paseo Centenario** at Cerro del Vigia, which turns into **Av. Olas Altas** at Playa Olas Altas and then almost immediately becomes **Paseo Claussen** (some buildings along this stretch will be listed under both street addresses) upon curving around Cerro del Nevería. At Playa Sur the name changes to **Av. del Mar** for a long stretch along this beach and Playa Norte, and finally becomes **Calz. Camarón Sábalo** as it enters the Zona Dorada.

Sometimes the entire non-Zona Dorada stretch is referred to as "Paseo Costero."

Zona Dorada ("Golden Zone")

Much of the city's tourist industry is focused in the "Golden Zone," which runs southward from **Punta Sábalo** (next to the Camino Real) to **Punta Camarón**. Strung out along both sides of Calzada Camarón Sábalo (sometimes called Avenida Camarón Sábalo), the main avenue running parallel to the beach, are all of Mazatlán's five-star hotels and restaurants, along with most of the city's tourist-oriented souvenir shops, car rental agencies, and beach recreation facilities. The zone is even patrolled by its own *policía turística*.

Two new marinas currently under construction at the north end of the Zona Dorada (along Estero Sábalo) will, when completed, form the largest marina complex in Mexico and one of the largest in all of Latin America. Eventually the complex will include four new five-star hotels along with several condo developments (the first condo phase has sold out in advance of construction).

For most tourists, the Zona Dorada is where the action is. Some may find it a bit too glitzy, preferring the more low-key Playa Norte or Olas Altas areas (see "Beaches," below) farther south. Very few, however, manage to visit Mazatlán without taking a stroll through at least part of the zone; most stroll-worthy is the concentration of hotels, restaurants, bars, and shops found in a loop formed by Av. R.T. Loaiza off Calz. Camarón Sábalo, between Av. de las Gaviotas and Calz. R. Buelna.

Harbor

Mazatlán's estuarial harbor, which has a navigable depth of 10 meters, is the city's true economic heart. Although it's only ranked 10th among Mexico's ports in terms of total maritime cargo, along the Pacific coast it is the largest commercial port between Los Angeles and Panama City. Mazatlán is also the nation's greatest shipper of tuna and shrimp, the bulk of which is exported to the U.S. and Japan via this harbor. A fleet of 500 boats hauls in an annual 63,000 tons of tuna, 57,000 tons of sardines, 18,500 tons of shrimp, 140 shrimp farms. The facilities here can handle five oceanic freighters at a time, offering 50,000 square feet of warehouse space as well as plenty of open storage area. Of the nine quays ringing the harbor, four are devoted to receiving and processing tuna, one is for shrimp, and one is used exclusively for freezing and packing.

El Centro (Downtown)

Arguably, three beach resorts in Mexico—Acapulco, Puerto Vallarta, and Mazatlán—can claim colonial histories. Of the three, Mazatlán has the best preserved architecture, some of it within just a few blocks of Playa Olas Altas. The recently formed Old Mazatlán Association—the only such organized effort anywhere along Mexico's Pacific coast—is taking further steps to preserve and promote the 200-year-old downtown.

An interesting walking route through old Mazatlán can be taken from Playa Olas Altas. Starting at Paseo Claussen, walk east along Av. Constitución to **Plazuela Machado** (see description below). A left onto Av. Carnaval at the east end of the plazuela, an immediate right back onto Av. Constitución, and another left on Av. Juárez will take you to **Plaza Republicana**.

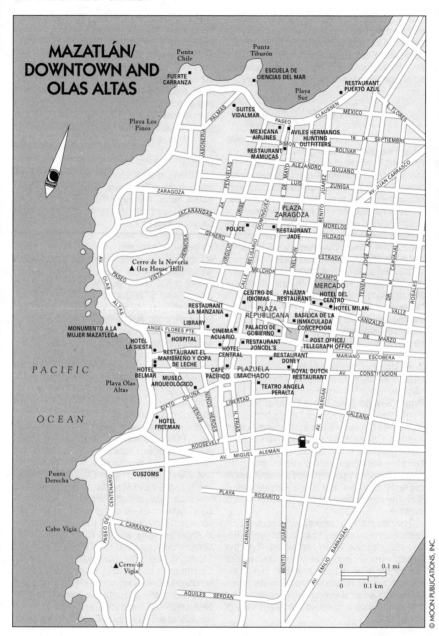

MAZATLÁN/ DOWNTOWN AND OLAS ALTAS

Punta Chile

Punta Tiburón

FUERTE CARRANZA

ESCUELA DE CIENCIAS DEL MAR

Playa Sur

RESTAURANT PUERTO AZUL

Playa Los Pinos

SUITES VIDALMAR

MEXICANA AIRLINES

AVILES HERMANOS HUNTING OUTFITTERS

RESTAURANT MAMUCAS

PLAZA ZARAGOZA

POLICE

RESTAURANT JADE

Cerro de la Nevería (Ice House Hill)

MERCADO

CENTRO DE IDIOMAS

PANAMA RESTAURANT

HOTEL DEL CENTRO

RESTAURANT LA MANZANA

PLAZA REPÚBLICANA

HOTEL MILAN

BASÍLICA DE LA INMACULADA CONCEPCIÓN

LIBRARY

CINEMA ACUARIO

PALACIO DE GOBIERNO

POST OFFICE/ TELEGRAPH OFFICE

MONUMENTO A LA MUJER MAZATLECA

HOTEL LA SIESTA

RESTAURANT EL MARISMEÑO Y COPA DE LECHE

HOTEL CENTRAL

RESTAURANT JONCOL'S

RESTAURANT DONEY

HOTEL BELMAR

CAFE PACÍFICO

MUSEO ARQUEOLÓGICO

PLAZUELA MACHADO

ROYAL DUTCH RESTAURANT

PACIFIC

TEATRO ANGELA PERALTA

Playa Olas Altas

OCEAN

HOTEL FREEMAN

Punta Derecha

CUSTOMS

Cabo Vigía

Cerro de Vigía

0   0.1 mi

0   0.1 km

© MOON PUBLICATIONS, INC.

Two blocks further north on Av. Juárez is the **central market.** If you continue north along Av. Juárez, you'll end up on Av. del Mar at Playa Sur (the south end of Playa Norte). Walk or catch any bus south along Av. del Mar if you need to return to Playa Olas Altas.

Plazuela Machado and Teatro Angela Peralta

At Av. Constitución and Av. Carnaval, this centerpiece of the city's restoration efforts is named for Juan Nepomuceno Machado, an early Filipino settler who donated the land for the plaza in the 1900s. A century ago the plaza was the commercial center of the city; now it's making a gradual comeback as a somewhat gentrified entertainment venue, with chic cafes along the north side and the elegantly renovated **Teatro Angela Peralta** around the corner from the west end. Several famous Mexican artists have moved into this neighborhood, including Antonio López Saenz and Carlos Bueno.

Constructed between 1860-75 as the Teatro Rubio, the theater was restored to its original Italianate Victorian grandeur at a cost of US$5 million and reopened in Oct. 1992 for dance, musical, and theatrical performances. The theater's renovators renamed the former opera venue in honor of famous 19th-century opera diva Angela Peralta (dubbed "the Mexican nightingale" by the press), who died of yellow fever in the Hotel Iturbides next door after giving her first and last Mazatlán performance. An accomplished composer and an opera impresario, Peralta brought Giuseppe Verdi to Mexico City in 1873 to conduct her performance of *Aida*. Her remains are interred at the Rotunda de Hombres Ilustres in Mexico City.

For a daytime entry fee of US$0.40 you can have a look around the theater. If you peek into the performance hall you might catch a rehearsal for an upcoming musical or theatrical show. Upstairs in the theater complex is an exhibit of paintings by local artists as well as a photo history of the theater's renovation. If you have the chance to catch an evening performance at the theater, you'll be amazed by the fine acoustics.

Along the east end of the plaza, the **Portales de Canobbio** provide a good example of the arcade-style architecture once common in urban colonial Mexico.

Plaza Republicana

Two and a half blocks north of Plazuela Machado, bounded by Calle 21 de Marzo, Av. Juárez, Calle Flores, and Calle Nelson, is the city's main, everyday plaza. At the north end of the plaza is the **Basílica de la Inmaculada Concepción,** the city's largest and most important religious edifice. Built between 1875-90 on the site of an Indian shrine, the church was granted *basílica* status in 1935, when the two steeples were added. Architecturally, its lumbering neo-gothic style is unimpressive, but the gilded baroque altar inside is worth a look.

Plaza Republicana is ringed by shoe service stands where the workers don't just shine shoes but will perform repairs and recondition a pair of shoes from soles to uppers; you can leave your shoes here and pick them up a half-hour or so later—looking almost new again. Under the large wrought-iron kiosk in the center of the leafy plaza is **El Jardín,** a simple *cafetería* with *tortas,* hamburgers, breakfasts, and soft drinks; take an outside table to watch the passing show of people.

Plazuela Zaragoza

This large, busy plaza at Av. Zaragoza, Calle Nelson, and Calle 5 de Mayo is known for its cluster of flower vendors. The day before the Day of the Dead (Nov. 1-2), the plaza is packed with flower wreaths and customers. Four blocks east is the city's oldest church, **Capilla de San José,** constructed by Italian priests between 1831-42.

Museo Arqueológico

This well-run museum at Av. Sixto Osuna 76, tel. (69) 85-3502, between Playa Olas Altas and Plazuela Machado features exhibits on the pre-Cortesian history and culture of Sinaloa, including collections of petroglyphs, sculpture, and early Totorame pottery. Open Tues.-Sun. 10 a.m.-1 p.m. and 4-6 p.m. Admission is US$0.50.

Acuario Mazatlán (Mazatlán Aquarium)

Over 50 saltwater and freshwater tanks (containing a total volume of 123,175 liters/32,500 gallons) display around 250 fish species in this modest aquarium. Also on the premises are a marine museum, a small botanical garden, and exhibits of birds, deer, rabbits, seals, and dolphins. Sea lion shows, held three times daily, are a hit with children. The aquarium, tel. (69) 81-

MAZATLÁN/ ZONA DORADA

MARINA MAZATLÁN

To Playa Cerritos, Punta Cerritos, and MEX 15 North

Estero Sábalo

Punta Sábalo

MARINA EL CID BEACH HOTEL & YACHT CLUB

CAMINO REAL MAZATLÁN

HOTEL PUEBLO BONITO

SEÑOR PEPPER RESTAURANT-BAR

PLAYA ESCONDIDA TRAILER PARK

Calz. Camarón Sábalo

Playa Sábalo

Blvd. De Marlin

SAN BARTOLO TRAILER PARK

Av. Del Atún

HOTEL OCÉANO PALACE
DOUBLETREE RESORT CLUB

Av. Del Mero

Av. Del Tiburon

FIESTA INN

Av. Del Puerto

Av.

Estero Sábalo

EL QUIJOTE INN

BANRURAL (TOURIST OFFICE)

MAR ROSA TRAILER PARK

Cala Camarón Sábalo

P A C I F I C   O C E A N

Av. Circuito Del Campeador

EL CID MEGA RESORT

CLUB DE GOLF EL CID

HOTEL INN AT MAZATLÁN

Av. G. Ruiz

Av. Circuito

HOTEL COSTA DE ORO

Del Campeador

HOTEL ROYAL VILLAS RESORT

THE RAQUET CLUB LAS GAVIOTAS

BALBOA TOWERS

Río Ibis

APARTAMENTOS FIESTA

Río Nilo

Albatros

APARTAMENTOS LOS GIRASOLES

Sierra De Venados

Av. De Las Gaviotas

BANAMEX

HELADOS BING

BUDGET RENT-A-CAR

BANCOMER

LAS PALMAS TRAILER PARK

De Mazatlán

Punta Codo

HOTEL SUITES LAS PALMAS

SUITES LINDA MAR

BANCA SERFÍN

LA CASA CONTENTA

Av. Lomas

Sierra Nevada

Sierra Grande

MOTEL MARLEY

SUITES LAS FLORES

PURA VIDA

AEROMEXICO

Av.

CINEMA

Playa Gaviotas

R.T. Loazia

Calz. Camarón Sábalo

Sierra Quemada

Rafael Buelna

HOTEL PLAYA MAZATLÁN

LOS SÁBALOS RESORT HOTEL

Playa Camarón

| 0 | 500 yds |
| 0 | 500 m |

LA POSTA TRAILER PARK

VALENTINO'S DISCO

MOTEL SAN DIEGO

Punta Camarón

To Playa Norte and Downtown

To MEX 15 and Airport

© MOON PUBLICATIONS, INC.

7815, is a half block east of Av. del Mar at Av. de los Deportes 111, behind Motel Del Sol. Open daily 9:30 a.m.-6:30 p.m.; admission is US$2 adults, US$0.75 children.

Acuático Mazagua

Kids will also enjoy this water park with its water slides, water tubes, large swimming pool, and wave pool. The park is on Estero del Yugo, near Playa Brujas and just east of Calz. Camarón Sábalo on the Entronque El Habal-Cerritos. Open daily 10 a.m.-6 p.m.; admission US$8. Call (69) 88-0205 for information (Spanish only).

Mercado José Pino Suárez
(Mercado Central)

Two blocks north of Plaza Republicana off Av. Juárez is Mazatlán's central municipal market. Also known as Mercado Central, the huge complex was originally built in 1895 on the site of a former bullring and features classic *fin de siglo* architecture. This is a very typical, well-stocked Mexican market, with vendors selling a wide variety of fresh produce, meats, cheeses, herbs, flowers, arts and crafts, and household utensils. Upstairs are several cheap *comedores*.

Beaches

Mazatlán's beaches begin well north of the city and extend southward almost to the tip of the peninsula carved by the Pacific Ocean and the Estero del Astillero. Naming of the beaches can be arbitrary, with each beach sometimes having two or more different names; but generally speaking, what separates one beach from the next is a *punta* or point whose name just about everyone agrees on. As fishing and tourism are Mazatlán's only major industries, the beaches stay fairly clean.

Starting from the northernmost end, right at Mazatlán city limits, **Playa Cerritos** ("Little Hills Beach") runs south from Punta Cerritos and is named for the low dune formations that run along the beach. Condo development has almost totally obscured all views of this beach from the road heading north, though there are still a few sizable coconut groves left along the way. If you're driving, follow the Marina Mazatlán signs around the marina and continue heading north and you'll start seeing signs for condos and time-that use the name "Cerritos." On Sundays , Mexican families picnic on the big wide median strip that runs down the middle of Calz. Sábal Cerritos. Cerritos makes a nice walking and sunning beach; swimmers should check the surfline carefully before plunging in as the steep sand berms signal strong undertow.

The northern end of Playa Cerritos next to Punta Cerritos is known as **Playa Brujas. Restaurant Playa Brujas,** a simple open-air *palapa* place serving *mariscos* and cold beer— overlooks the beach and features live music on weekend afternoons. This is the perfect place to kick back with a cold Pacífico and a plate of shrimp, local style. A good right point break draws surfers practically year round. The road dead

*Playa Gaviotas,
Mazatlán*

JOE CUMMINGS

ends right at Punta Cerritos, but just east of the rocky point is a large cove that curves around into a less developed beach called **Playa Delfín,** where there are more *marisquerías* (seafood vendors) and *cocos helados* (chilled coconuts) stands. On some maps this beach is labeled Playa Cerritos and in fact that's what it was called until recently when condo/hotel developers began co-opting the name for use along the stretch where the northern end of Playa Sábalo meets the southern end of Playa Brujas. The area near the vendors is very rocky and is a mooring for fishing *pangas,* hence it's not very clean, but if you continue around the cove east and then north the sand reappears and it look cleaner. This beach's undeveloped remoteness makes it quite suitable for camping.

Playa Cerritos blends into **Playa Escondida** ("Hidden Beach"), also known as Playa Sábalo-Cerritos, around a small headland to the south, an area with a thin string of newer hotels and condo developments, plus a trailer park. In front of El Quijote Inn a strong left break challenges surfers and bodyboarders during northwest swell.

Next south is **Playa Sábalo** ("Ladyfish Beach"), a lovely stretch of golden sand extending from craggy Punta Sábalo ("Punta Roja" on some maps) in the north to gentle Punta Codo in the south. Under certain weather conditions, hard shore breaks and a stiff undertow make swimming a bit hazardous on this beach. Although part of the Zona Dorada, development along Playa Sábalo isn't quite as end-to-end as farther south.

Below Punta Codo, also in the Zona Dorada, **Playa Gaviotas** ("Sea Gulls Beach") looks much the same as Playa Sábalo except that it's thicker with hotels, condos, and restaurants. Offshore

protection offered by Isla de los Venados also keeps the surf gentler and makes the beach less steep. Playa Gaviotas and the Zona Dorada come to a sudden halt at rocky Punta Camarón, topped by the striking white domes and turrets of the Valentino's restaurant-bar-disco complex.

South of Punta Camarón begins the city's original *malecón,* a 9.5-km (six-mile) seawall promenade along **Playa Norte** ("North Beach"). Although not as fine-sanded as beaches farther north, Playa Norte is the city's most popular beach, attracting a friendly mixture of fishermen, local volleyball players, regular strollers, boogie-boarders, and tourists. At night the string of bars and seafood restaurants opposite Playa Norte along Av. del Mar fills with local residents and a few Zona Dorada escapees.

Fishing boats anchor at Playa Norte's south end (sometimes called Playa Sur or "South Beach," also Playa Los Pinos) near Punta Tiburón, after which a headland of rocky beaches swells around to cozy Bahía Olas Altas and Mazatlán's southernmost beach, **Playa Olas Altas** ("High Waves Beach"). The city's oldest tourist lodge, Hotel Belmar, still stands opposite the middle of the beach. High-divers plunge headlong into the surf from a 13.5-meter (45-foot) platform on **Punta de las Clavadistas** ("Divers Point") on weekends and holidays. Divers must time the tide and swells accurately, as even at high tide the water below the platform measures only two meters (six feet) deep between waves.

Although it's a favored surfing spot (consistent left point break both summer and winter), the breakers at Playa Olas Altas are generally a bit too strong for average swimmers.

Las Tres Islas

This cluster of three volcanic islands just off-shore offers opportunities for daytime getaways by boat. The clear waters and pristine beaches of **Isla de los Venados** (also known as Isla Venado or "Deer Island") and **Isla de los Chivos** ("Goats Island") are popular for swimming, snorkeling, and scuba diving (but no goats in sight). Birders flock to **Isla de los Pájaros** ("Birds Island"), an important nesting ground for around a hundred species, especially the native brown pelican.

Amphibious boat transportation to these islands can be arranged from Playa Gaviotas 200

SURF FLAG CODES

Color-coded flags on Mazatlán's beaches are used to signal the following surf conditions:

Green	calm
White	jellyfish
Yellow	surf/tide caution
Red	surf/tide danger

meters north of Hotel Playa Mazatlán or from Aqua Sports Center in front of El Cid Mega Resort. The crossing takes only about 15-20 minutes and costs US$10 roundtrip. If you plan to stay awhile, make an appointment for the return trip—and don't pay till you've been picked up!

Isla de la Piedra

Not really an island at all, "Stone Island" is a peninsula just opposite the harbor canal with 16 km (10 miles) of mostly undeveloped beach and Mexico's third largest coconut grove (about 8,000 acres). Overnight camping is permitted, and there are a few *palapa* restaurants near the boat landing. At the northwest end of the bay, a right point break known as "Escollera" can develop a nice tube and is usually considered Mazatlán's best wave. A beach break a little further south is also good.

Several companies arrange all-inclusive daytrips to Piedra. **Viajes El Sábalo,** tel. (69) 83-1933, at Los Sábalos Resort Hotel, for example, has daily departures from a dock off Av. del Puerto at 10 a.m. on its 15-meter (50-foot) motor catamaran *El Sábalo,* which sails by the lighthouse and pelican rookeries before landing at the beach for the afternoon; the boat returns around 4 p.m. The per-person price of US$30 includes lunch, beverages (including beer), and guide services. **Catamaran Renegado,** tel. (69) 81-7040, offers similar trips. Almost any travel agency in town can arrange a "jungle tour" of the island—similar to the catamaran tours except you ride on slower motor launches—for US$20 pp.

Launches holding up to eight persons can also be arranged on your own from a pier on Av. del Puerto (Av. Emilio Barragan), a little southeast of the intersection with Av. M.G. Nájera. for about US$15 roundtrip total.

The peninsula's seeming remoteness is about to come to an end with the development of the US$2 million Estrella del Mar million master-planned golf and beach resort on 818 ocean-front acres of Isla de la Piedra.

Cerro de la Nevería

Just inland from Punta de Clavadistas on Playa Olas Altas, "Ice House Hill" is named for a tunnel that was used to store ice shipped from San Francisco in the 19th century. During the city's earlier history it served as a lookout point for Spanish sentries guarding against pirates and foreign naval attack.

During the Mexican Revolution, Gen. Venustiano Carranza ordered a biplane to drop a crude, pigskin-wrapped bomb of dynamite and iron onto a munitions dump atop Cerro de la Nevería, a 1914 event that made Mazatlán the second city in world history (after Tripoli, Libya) to be bombed from the air. The airsick bombardier reportedly missed the hill entirely, dropping the bomb on a nearby street and killing two civilians.

Paseo Vistahermosa, off Calle Morelos in Old Mazatlán, leads around the top of the hill to both Pacific Ocean and city views.

At the seaward base of the hill facing the city is the **Monumento a la Mujer Mazatleca** (Monument to Mazatlán Women), a five-meter-high sculpture representing the local feminine ideal.

Cerro de Vigia

This hill south of Playa Olas Altas is surmounted by **Pérgola de Cerro de Vigia,** a garden plaza with an 1875 English cannon and a cityscape view over Old Mazatlán. A little below the plaza, the little-known Café El Mirador offers chairs and refreshment noon-9 p.m. daily. Paseo del Centenario, off Blvd. M. Alemán in the Olas Altas district, winds up the hill to the plaza.

Cerro del Crestón

A causeway at the southwest end of Av. del Puerto leads to Isla del Crestón, topped by 154-meter (515-foot) El Faro, reportedly the world's second tallest lighthouse. A 25-minute hike from the end of the road, along a winding path, leads to the summit.

Other Sightseeing

Built by the Spanish and stocked with an English cannon, the **Fuerte Carranza** (Carranza Fort) at Punta Chile, west of the Playa Sur's southern tip, was used to defend the city against the attempted 1864 French invasion.

Mazatlán's famous Pacífico beer is brewed at the independently owned **Pacífico Brewery,** at Calle Ocampo and Av. Leyva, tel. (69) 82-7900, east of downtown; beer aficionados may be able to arrange tours with help from the state tourist office (see "Information," below).

ACCOMMODATIONS

Mazatlán boasts around 10,000 tourist rooms to choose from. Nearly half are upscale hotels; around 2,000 are condos, apartments, and timeshares; and the remainder are budget-to-moderate accommodations.

Hotel occupancy, especially for less expensive accommodations, remains very high throughout Nov.-April—Mazatlán's "high season"—when advance reservations are recommended. Rates are also highest during this period, although shopping for package deals usually brings substantial savings over "rack rates." Two- to seven-night packages taken before Dec. 25 run as low as US$25 per night at mid-class places or US$40-50 per night at luxury properties. Add US$20 to these rates for high-season packages.

Because seasonal, package, and rack rates vary so widely, it's virtually impossible to nail down a single set of rates for Mazatlán's hotels. Establishments are categorized below by average rates, not including tax, during high season—but not necessarily peak season (late December through early February) months.

Shoestring

Mazatlán's first tourist lodgings were built along Playa Olas Altas in the 1940s but are now separated from the beach by Paseo Claussen near Playa los Pinos downtown. The oldest continuously operating beach hotel in the city, the five-story pink and white **Hotel Belmar,** Av. Olas Altas Sur 166, tel. (69) 85-1111, fax (69) 81-3428, is still popular among budget-conscious travelers. Its well-worn, not entirely clean double rooms all have rusty a/c, ceiling fans and cable TV. Facilities include a pool and sidewalk restaurant. Rates: US$9 s/d in the interior, US$10 with ocean view; extra guests in the same room are charged US$3 per head. The Belmar always fills up for Carnaval in late February or early March.

Right at the southern end of the Zona Dorada, across from the beach, **Motel San Diego,** Av. Del Mar at Rafael Buelna, tel. (69) 83-5703, offers relatively clean if small rooms with a/c and TV. The San Diego has its own parking lot. It's low on atmosphere but you won't find anything cheaper in the Zona Dorada. Rates: US$10-13.

In Old Mazatlán downtown, **Hotel Del Centro,** Calle Canizales Pte. 705 (at Av. Juárez), tel. (69) 81-2673, offers basic but adequate rooms; a/c and TV available. Rates: US$8-11, plus US$2 extra for a/c, another US$2 for TV. Only a couple of doors up from Del Centro, the very similar—right down to the rocking chairs in the lobby—**Hotel Milan,** Calle Canizales Pte. 705, tel. (69) 85-3499, offers rock-bottom singles (just US$6.50); otherwise the rates are the same as at Del Centro. This pair is just a block south of Mercado José Pino Suárez and a block north of the basílica.

Near the Mazatlán bus terminal are **Hotel Fiesta,** a three-story green building at the corner of Ejercito Mexicano and Ferrusquilla (right across from the bus station), and **Hotel Emperador,** on Río Pánuco (opposite another side of the terminal). Neither one can be recommended for atmosphere but they'd do in a pinch if you can't find anything else. Rates: around US$7 s, $9 d.

On the Highway: In the junction town of Villa Unión just south of Mazatlán are a couple of basic US$10-15 hotels. **Hotel del Piñon** looks the best. Just off the highway in Villa Unión, and thus quieter, the **Hotel Galindo** is housed in a two-story white building with a tree-studded open courtyard. Rooms are simple yet clean, with fans and private bathrooms. Rates: US$8 s/d.

Budget

Playa Olas Atlas: The popular **Hotel La Siesta,** Olas Altas Sur 11, tel. (69) 81-2640 or 81-2334, fax (69) 13-7476, Mexico toll-free tel. (800) 6-9770, is built around the semi-outdoor El Shrimp Bucket, Carlos Anderson's first Mexican chain eatery. Rooms in this three-story white and terracotta structure have a/c, TVs, and phones, and surround a large courtyard. Because of the courtyard restaurant, this hotel can get noisy at times, but the restaurant noise tends to subside by 10 or 11 p.m. La Siesta books out quickly for Carnaval. Rates: US$15/18 s/d.

Zona Dorada: Between the luxury high-rise hotels along Playa Gaviotas and Playa Sábalo are a number of smaller inns and apartment complexes with reasonable rates. One of the best deals in this area is the quiet **Hotel Plaza Gaviotas,** Calle Bugambilias 100 (on the opposite side of Calz. Camarón Sábalo from the beach), tel. (69) 13-4322, fax (69) 13-6685. The spacious, simple but comfortable rooms (most with balconies) are built around a pool and shady garden; all have a/c and satellite TV. Rates: US$23-35 s/d.

At the southern heart of the Zona Dorada, opposite the huge Hotel Playa Mazatlán, is the 11-story **Torre Tropicana Hotel,** Av. R.T. Loaiza 27, tel. (69) 83-8000, fax (69) 83-5361. Large but less-than-clean rooms, many with balconies, have a/c, phones, and TV. Moderately priced junior suites with kitchenettes are available. Amenities include parking, a fitness center, and a restaurant/bar. Torre Tropicana is popular with spring-breakers and Carnaval-goers because it's inexpensive and close to the action. Rates: US$23-28; more for the suites.

Almost opposite the flagship Hotel Playa Mazatlán on Av. R.T. Loaiza, a short walk from the beach, is **Azteca Inn,** tel. (69) 13-4477 or (800) 6-9770 toll free in Mexico, fax (69) 13-7476. Look for a three-story, mint green, white, and orange exterior. The lobby's bamboo furniture, bright artwork, and live plants give it a tropical feel. Rooms have TV and a/c, and a pool and jacuzzi are on the premises. It's often booked out. Rates: US$22 d.

Hotel Suites Las Palmas, Calz. Camarón Sábalo 305, tel. (69) 16-5448 or 16-5449, fax (69) 13-4958, features rooms with small refrigerators and two-story, two-bedroom suites with kitchenettes. Although it's on the opposite side of Calz. Camarón Sábalo, this newer hotel has lushly landscaped grounds, a huge organic-shaped pool plus a smaller standard pool (both with kiddie wading sections), a laundry, two restaurants, and a travel agency. Rates: standard rooms US$31 s/d, suites US$46, plus tax.

Playa Norte: Lined up along busy Av. del Mar are numerous three- and four-star hotels built in the 1960s and '70s, all with a/c rooms, swimming pools, restaurants, and security parking.

Next door to Señor Frog's and only 3.5 blocks from the bus terminal is one of Playa Norte's best values, **Hotel Las Arenas (Sands),** Av. del Mar 1910, tel. (69) 82-0000, fax (69) 82-1025, where all rooms come with refrigerators, phones, and TVs. Rates: US$20 s/d in the low season, US$28-35 Dec. 19-March 15. Nearby **Motel del Sol,** Av. del Mar 800, tel. (69) 85-1103, fax (69) 85-2603, features 21 clean and nicely furnished a/c rooms, some with kitchenettes. Rates: US$25 s/d, US$33

with kitchenette. Similar in price and facilities are **Hotel Club Playamar,** Av. del Mar 840, tel. (69) 82-0833, fax (69) 82-5641, and **Hotel Posada de Don Pelayo,** Av. del Mar 1111, tel. (69) 83-1888, fax (69) 84-0799, now a Days Inn property.

Downtown: In the historic downtown area, the modern **Hotel Central,** Calle B. Domínguez Sur 2 (between Calle Flores and Mariano Escobedo next to Plaza Hidalgo), tel. (69) 82-1888, offers clean, a/c rooms, some with plaza views. A small restaurant serves inexpensive Mexican standards. The hotel is within walking distance of all the major plazas as well as the Centro de Idiomas language school. Rates: US$24-28 s/d.

Apartments: Perhaps the most economical way to vacation in Mazatlán—besides camping—is to rent an apartment where you can cook at least some of your own meals. Rents vary from a low of US$160 per month for a studio to US$500-750 per month for a two- to three-bedroom place. The main areas for vacation apartments are the Zona Dorada and Playa Olas Altas; apartments in the former district tend to be a bit more expensive than in the latter, though not substantially so. Check the classified ads in the *Pacific Pearl* newspaper to see what's available.

Suites Vidalmar, Av. Las Palmas 15 (opposite Punta Tiburón at the south end of Playa Sur), tel. (69) 81-2190, rents simple but well-maintained one-bedroom apartments by the night. The units have bay views and kitchenettes; other amenities include a pool and covered parking. Rates: US$16 s, US$20 d. Other small apartment complexes in this area have similar rates; a few one- or two-bedroom places—usually booked a year in advance—rent for as low as US$300 per month.

Apartamentos Fiesta, Calle Río Ibís 502 (at Calle Río de la Plata, four blocks east from central Playa Sábalo in the Zona Dorada), tel. (69) 13-5355, features 10 apartments—some with kitchenettes—around a lush tropical garden. Studio apartments rent for around US$200-250 per month, one-bedroom apartments with kitchenettes for US$300-400. Call or write well in advance to reserve a spot in this popular complex.

Inexpensive
Zona Dorada: On Playa Sábalo at the Zona Dorada's quieter north end, the stark, white, boxlike **Hotel Océano Palace,** tel. (69) 13-0666, fax (69)

13-9666, U.S./Canada tel. (800) 352-7690, has many rooms with ocean views and some with kitchenettes. An open-air restaurant overlooking a waterfall pool is the hotel's best feature. Groups and conventioneers use Océano Palace so it's often booked out. Rates: US$39-46 s/d April 12-Dec. 19; US$10 more the remainder of the year. Farther south on Playa Sábalo is the similar **Hotel Costa de Oro,** tel. (69) 13-5344, fax (69) 14-4209, U.S./Canada tel. (800) 876-5278.

On Punta Codo between Playa Gaviotas and Playa Camarón, the small **Motel Marley,** Calle R.T. Loaiza 226, tel./fax (69) 13-5533, and **Suites Linda Mar,** Calle R.T. Loaiza 222 (Apdo. Postal 214, Mazatlán), tel./fax (69) 13-5533, share the same owner and offer similar apartment-style accommodations in a quiet area. All apartments come with kitchenettes and a/c; Motel Marley has a small pool. Favorites among migrating snowbirds who spend their winters surf casting a few yards in front of the apartments, both properties fill up early every year. Rates: US$40 s/d for one bedroom, US$51 t/q for two bedrooms.

Between Motel Marley and Suites Linda Mar is the similar **La Casa Contenta,** Av. R.T. Loaiza 224, tel. (69) 13-4976, fax (69) 13-9986, offering one-bedroom apartments and larger bungalows. Often full November to May. Rates: US$49 apartments, US$122 bungalows, including tax. Rates are discounted 30% in May and June.

Right on Playa Gaviotas, **Motel Los Arcos,** Av. R.T. Loaiza 214 (next to a *lavandería* near Casa Contenta), tel. (69) 13-5066, offers kitchenettes in seven two-story buildings, some right on the beach. The management is friendly and spirited; a wooden plaque in the office says "Treasure the mosquito-eating geckos." Rates: US$39 s, US$49 d. **Suites Las Flores,** Av. R.T. Loaiza 212, tel. (69) 13-5011, fax (69) 14-3400, U.S./Canada tel. (800) 452-0627, offers studio apartments and more expensive suites—all with kitchenettes—in a seven-story, featureless building. Rates: US$45 s/d studios; suites from US$65 s/d.

Balboa Towers, Calz. Camarón Sábalo at Guerrero, tel. (69) 13-7144, fax (69) 13-5655, is a combination time-share and hotel with nicely decorated, spacious, and airy apartments and expensive suites, all with TVs, balconies, and fully equipped kitchens. Other facilities include an ocean terrace restaurant, cocktail lounge, two pools, a gym, sauna, and parking. Rates: studio units US$39 with mountain views, US$51 with ocean views. One- and two-bedroom suites available in the expensive price range.

Doubletree Resort Club, Calz. Camarón Sábalo at Calle Atun, tel. (69) 13-0200, fax (69) 16-6261, houses 118 faded but livable rooms. Go for the second-floor rooms, which have larger patios facing the beach. Rates: US$46 s/d rack, often negotiable to as low as US$28.

Playa Norte: Best Western's low-rise **Hotel Aguamarina,** Av. del Mar 110 (at Río Piaxtla), tel. (69) 81-7080, fax (69) 82-4624, U.S./Canada tel. (800) 528-1234, features clean, comfortable rooms with phones and satellite TV; some have balconies. As with all the hotels in this area you must walk across Av. del Mar to reach the beach. Rates: around US$55 s/d.

Hotel de Cima, just a bit farther south at Av. del Mar 48, tel. (69) 82-7300, fax (69) 82-7311, has well-kept but not fancy premises plus an underground tunnel linking the hotel with Playa Norte (thereby saving guests from having to dash across busy Av. del Mar). Large standard rooms have a/c, TV, and phones; some also have ocean-view balconies. Rates: US$40 s/d. Four two-bedroom units are available for US$50 each.

Other Playa Norte hotels in the inexpensive category include: **Hotel Hacienda Mazatlán,** Av. del Mar and Calle Flamingos, tel. (69) 82-7000, fax (69) 85-1579; **Hotel Las Jacarandas,** Av. del Mar 2500, tel. (69) 84-1177, fax (69) 84-1077; and **Hotel Suites Las Sirenas,** Av. del Mar 1100, tel. (69) 83-1888, fax (69) 84-0799.

Apartments: Next door to the less expensive Apartamentos Fiesta, **The Racquet Club Las Gaviotas,** Calle Ibis at Bravo, tel. (69) 13-5939, is a real find for the tennis enthusiast since there are seven well-maintained courts on the premises. The large one- and two-bedroom apartments have fully equipped kitchenettes, and the grounds hold a lush garden surrounding a swimming pool. Rates: US$450 per month one-bedroom, US$650 two-bedroom. In the same neighborhood, **Apartamentos Los Girasoles,** Av. Gaviotas 709 (about five blocks from the beach and next to a kindergarten), tel. (69) 13-5288, features small but comfortable Mexican-style apartments with kitchens. The well-maintained courtyard pool and garden add considerably to the ambience. Rates: US$800 a month.

Moderate

Most of the city's upscale accommodations are found along Playa Sábalo and Playa Gaviotas in the Zona Dorada. Each hotel has a distinct high season (Dec. 20-April 11 or thereabouts) and low season (the remainder of the year) rate schedule; the difference between high and low tariffs is often substantial. Some of these hotels also offer "time-share" sales in which you purchase room or apartment space for one, two, or more weeks per year (see the special topic "Buying or Leasing Property in Mexico," for more information).

The venerable **Hotel Playa Mazatlán,** Av. R.T. Loaiza 202, tel. (69) 13-4444, fax (69) 14-0366, U.S./Canada tel. (800) 762-5816, was the first hotel to build on Playa Gaviotas and is still the most successful due to its reputation for good service, reasonable rates, efficient maintenance, and outstanding location just a few steps from the sand. It's also popular for its twice-weekly Fiesta Mexicana (see "Entertainment," below) and Sunday evening beach fireworks, as well as for its location in the heart of the Zona Dorada action. Some rooms have ocean views. Package deals may be available—call and ask. Rates: US$57-61 low season, US$68-78 high season.

The relatively new **Fiesta Inn Mazatlán,** Calz. Camarón Sábalo 1927, tel. (69) 89-0100, fax (69) 89-0130, Mexico toll-free tel. (800) 5-0450, U.S./Canada tel. (915) 326-6900, offers 117 rooms each with balcony and ocean views, a/c, bathtub, color TV, and IDD telephones. Other facilities include a business center (with fax, computers, and bilingual secretarial service), restaurant, and bar. Rates: US$55-75 depending on time of year.

El Cid Mega Resort

This famous resort at the middle of Playa Sábalo, tel. (69) 13-3333, fax (69) 14-1311, U.S./Canada tel. (800) 525-1925, features four hotels with over a thousand rooms, a convention center, 12 restaurants, six palm-shaded swimming pools, an 18-hole golf course, 17 tennis courts, a theater, disco, and shopping mall. A veritable town unto itself

with as many as 4,000 residents (half employees, half guests) at one time, El Cid is the kind of place you can easily get lost in. Three of El Cid's hotels fall in the moderate range: **Castilla Beach Hotel and Tower, El Moro Beach Hotel and Tower** (both US$76 for standard s/d), and the Granada Hotel (US$61 s/d). Suites in the expensive to premium price ranges are also available at these hotels. El Cid's newer Marina Hotel starts in the expensive range (see below for details).

Expensive

North on Punta Sábalo is the nicely landscaped **Camino Real Mazatlán,** tel. (69) 13-1111, fax (69) 14-3789, where all of the large, luxurious rooms have ocean views. Set on its own private cove, with a pool, tennis courts, and open-air lobby, the Camino Real is currently Mazatlán's top hotel. Rates: US$100-120.

Another classy spot is the **Hotel Inn at Mazatlán,** Calz. Camarón Sábalo 6291, tel. (69) 13-5500, fax (69) 13-4782. All 126 spacious and well-appointed rooms and kitchenette suites come with ocean views and balconies. An indoor-outdoor beachside restaurant and classic curved pool complete the picture. Many of the rooms and suites are now time shares but are rented out like hotel rooms when the owners aren't in town. Rates: $85-120 a night depending on the season and room.

Expensive/Premium

Just south of Hotel Playa Mazatlán is the less distinguished **Los Sábalos Resort Hotel,** Av. R.T. Loaiza 100, tel. (69) 83-5333, fax (69) 83-8156, U.S./Canada tel. (800) 528-8760. Suites here are clean but not fancy—some might say they're overpriced. Several restaurants and bars are in the building, including the famous Joe's Oyster Bar. Many tour packagers use this hotel. Rates: US$72-192.

The relatively new **Marina El Cid Beach Hotel & Yacht Club,** Calz. Camarón Sábalo s/n, tel. (69) 13-3333, fax (69) 14-1311, U.S./Canada tel. (800) 525-1925, features 210 luxury rooms and suites in Mediterranean-style buildings adjacent to a deluxe 90-slip marina. Well-kept grounds surround two pools. Guests have access to all El Cid Mega Resort facilities, including an 18-hole golf course, 17 tennis and two squash courts, a spa, 12 restaurants and bars, a grocery store, and a business center. Employees use golf carts to transport guests and their luggage from one part of the marina-hotel complex to another, and shuttle vans run to other El Cid properties and facilities (El Moro Beach Hotel, Castilla Beach Hotel, Granada Hotel, and El Cid Golf and Country Club). All rooms come with kitchenettes, room safes, and glittering white interiors. Time share arrangements are available. Rates: US$104 d, or US$165 for a master double with a larger kitchen and larger living room.

Hotel Royal Villas Resort, Calz. Camarón Sábalo 500, tel. (69) 16-6161, fax (69) 14-0777, just north of Balboa Towers, offers spacious and beautifully appointed one- and two-bedroom suites, each with kitchen and private balcony overlooking the ocean. Other facilities include a large free-form pool, health club, sauna, and game room. Rates: junior suite US$116, one-bedroom suite US$149, deluxe one-bedroom suite US$177, deluxe two-bedroom suite US$293.

Premium

One of the best-run and most popular luxury properties on the beach is the blue-and-white, Moorish-style **Hotel Pueblo Bonito,** Playa Sábalo 2121 (off Calz. Camarón Sábalo at the northern end of the Zona Dorada, just south of the Camino Real), tel. (69) 14-3700, fax (69) 14-1723, U.S. tel. (800) 937-9567. All of the spacious suites enjoy ocean views and come with balconies, kitchenettes, and separate sitting areas. On the premises are three restaurants, two large pools, lush landscaping with live flamingos, a garden jacuzzi, gym, and sauna. Rates: US$130-160, not including tax.

RV Parks and Camping

At any given time, Mazatlán has seven or eight trailer parks in operation with a total of around 500 spaces, all of them near the northern beach strip. Rates are generally US$10-13 per rig per night for two people, plus US$1-2 for each additional person; monthly rates of US$300 (or lower in the off-season) are usually available.

Slots can fill up quickly during the annual Dec.-April snowbird migration—write or call in advance to be sure of a space if you plan to arrive that time of year. Where available, Apdo. Postal (post office box) addresses are listed below with phone numbers. Another reason to contact these parks in advance is that some may close down during the June-Oct. off-season.

The huge, 236-space **Playa Escondida Trailer Park and Bungalows,** Apdo. Postal 682, tel./fax (69) 88-0077, at Playa Cerritos costs US$13 per night for full hookups, US$8 for tents/campers. Monthly rates run $350. Only six spaces are on the beach side of the road, the rest are on the opposite side of the road from the beach, bordered by closely spaced rows of coconut palms, very lush. Facilities include hot showers, barbecue grills, coin laundry, direct TV, volleyball, a saltwater pool, and recreation hall. Nineteen one- and two-bedroom block-built bungalows with small kitchenettes (some units with a/c) near the beach cost US$23-32 a night.

Also at Playa Cerritos is **Mar A Villas Trailer Park,** tel. (69) 84-5310, a fairly basic place right on the beach amidst an attractive palm jungle. Spaces with full hookups cost US$10 daily for stays of less than a month, US$8 daily for a month, or US$7 daily if you pay in advance. Showers and toilets are available. When we visited last, a survey of license plates in the park indicated that every single rig hailed from either British Columbia or Ontario. The park can be hard to spot; it's right next to the Quintas del Mar condo development.

Mazatlán's most expensive RV facility, **Mar Rosa Trailer Park,** Apdo. Postal 435, tel. (69) 16-5967, at Calz. Camarón Sábalo 702, has 65 unsheltered beachfront spaces with full hookups including cable TV for US$17 per day in the off season, US$19 beginning Dec. 1. Despite the lack of shade and high rates, this park tends to fill up with clients loyal to the Mexican and German management, who keep the place open year-round and makes sure the showers and toilets are clean and functioning. Besides hot showers and a small store, Mar Rosa has a few apartments for rent—a plus when a long-term RVer decides to invite friends or family for a visit.

On Calz. Camarón Sábalo opposite Playa Sábalo (near the Hotel Océano Palace) is **San Bartolo Trailer Park,** tel. (69) 83-5755, a relatively small, 48-space park with full hookups for US$13 a day. San Bartolo is closed June-October.

The well-kept, shady, secure, and often full **Las Palmas Trailer Park,** at Calz. Camarón

Sábalo 333, tel. (69) 13-5311, farther south in the Zona Dorada near Hotel Suites Las Palmas, has 66 spaces with full hookups for US$13 per day, $320 monthly. Facilities include a coin laundry and hot showers.

Amidst a tropical setting of mango, papaya, avocado, and banana trees, **La Posta Trailer Park,** Apdo. Postal 362, at Calz. R. Buelna 7, tel. (69) 83-5310, fax 85-1485, near the PEMEX station a couple of blocks east of Calz. Camarón Sábalo, offers 210 full-hookup slots for a budget US$10 per day, tent/camper spaces for US$6. Because La Posta is so large, this is your best bet when arriving in town unannounced during high season. On the premises are a large pool with sundeck, coin laundry, convenience store, *palapas,* and hot showers.

Primitive, free beach camping is possible at Playa Delfín north of Playa Cerritos, at the north end of Cerritos itself (or Play Brujas), on Isla de la Piedra, and on Isla de los Venados.

FOOD

Culiacán may be Sinaloa's state capital, but Mazatlán is the state's food capital, with more restaurants per capita than anywhere in Northern Mexico outside Monterrey. It would take an entire book just to cover the city's restaurants; the following list represents the best places in each category. In addition to bounteous seafood, Mazatlán specialties to look for include *asado a la plaza* and *pollo asado a la plaza,* a well-seasoned stew of beef or chicken and potatoes served with radish, lettuce, other vegetables. A little more difficult to find (try the markets) is *nieve de garrafa,* a traditional homemade ice cream that comes in little aluminum containers; flavors include avocado, coffee, peanut, hibiscus, and corn.

Not described are the chains and fast-food places, many of which are in the Zona Dorada. Burger King, McDonald's, and KFC all have toeholds in town. At the intersection of Calz. Camarón Sábalo and Av. R.T. Loaiza are several fast-food purveyors, including **Helados Bing** (Mexican ice-cream chain), **Dairy Queen** (burgers and ice cream), **TCBY** (frozen yogurt), and **Rin Rin Pizza** (pizza and pasta).

Mexican
Las Cazuelas, Calle 21 de Marzo 723, a couple of blocks south of Mercado José Pino Suárez downtown. Popular, cheap, and very salt-of-the-earth spot for multi-course *comida corrida*

SIERRA CEVICHE

Ceviche (alternative spellings include "cebiche" and "sibiche") is a seafood appetizer made of fish or shellfish marinated in lime juice until "cooked." It's very popular throughout Pacific Mexico, and for every cook, you'll find a different recipe—it can be a wonderful experience in one restaurant and a poor excuse for getting rid of fish scraps in another.

Since it's easy to make even while camping on the beach (no fire necessary), ceviche offers an excellent alternative to the usual fried, baked, or grilled fish dishes with which most Mexico anglers are acquainted. One of the best fishes to use for ceviche is the sierra, a common type of mackerel usually caught inshore-offshore. John Steinbeck, during his 1941 Sea of Cortez expedition, pronounced it "the most delicious fish of all." Other good candidates for ceviche are halibut, shark, shrimp, lobster, or just about any other fish whose flesh is not too "dry" (the oilier the better, since the lime juice counteracts the oil). Always use only the freshest fish available.

Serves four

1/2 pound fresh sierra fillets, thinly sliced

1/4 cup fresh lime juice

one avocado, peeled and cut into half-inch cubes

eight ripe, red cherry tomatoes cut in half (or one large ripe tomato)

one serrano chile, minced (or more if you want it *really* hot)

two tbsp. fresh cilantro leaves, minced

one tbsp. olive oil

1/2 tsp. salt (optional)

Put the sliced sierra into a large bowl, mix with the lime juice, and marinate in a cooler for a half-hour. Drain; gently toss with the remaining ingredients. Best served with fresh tortilla chips (or spread over *tostadas,* whole fried corn tortillas) and cold *cerveza.*

ALEX PETERSON

climbing for coconuts, Isla Piedra, Mazatlán

(US$1.80) or traditional *antojitos*. Open daily 11 a.m.-5 p.m.

Cenaduría El Tunel (no phone), Av. Carnaval, almost opposite the Teatro Angela Peralta since 1945. Consisting of a narrow hallway lined with tables and a traditional kitchen in an Old Mazatlán *casa*, this little hideaway serves authentic Sinaloan and Mexican dishes like *chilorio* (Sinaloan-style sausage made with pork or venison mixed with chiles), *asado a la plaza*, *enchiladas, tacos, tostadas,* pozole, and homemade mole, a thick sauce of chocolate, sesame, chiles and spices. Inexpensive. Open 3 p.m.-6:30 p.m., closed Wednesday.

Cenaduría Tonita, Calle Guerrero 73, a block east of Calle Flores downtown. The only *cenaduría* in the city to be invited to join plaza vendors during Carnaval. House specialties include *carne asada, asado a la plaza,* and *pollo asado a la plaza.* Inexpensive. Open Tues.-Sun. 4-10 p.m.

Copa de Leche Restaurant Bar, Av. Olas Altas Sur 33, tel. (69) 82-5753. Also known as Antojitos El Farol, this casual indoor-outdoor

Mexican cafe has been a local favorite for sunset- and peoplewatching for 30 years. Despite its prime location, prices are very reasonable. Open 7:30 a.m.-11 p.m.

Restaurante Doney, Calle M. Escobedo 610 at Av. 5 de Mayo downtown, tel. (69) 81-2651. A Mazatlán institution since 1959, Doney offers moderately priced Mexican home-style cooking in a beautiful old house decorated with historical photos and a brick-domed ceiling. Specialties include *(carne) asada al carbón,* steak *tampiqueña,* traditional Mexican *antojitos* (tacos, enchiladas, etc.), and *chilorio,* a spicy, Sinaloa-style sausage. Doney's *comida corrida* (served weekdays noon to 4 pm), a complete meal of soup, entree, side dishes, and dessert, is an especially good deal. Live piano music in the evening, Open daily 8 a.m.-10:30 p.m.

Fonda Santa Clara, Olas Altas 66, tel. (69) 81-6451. This new spot specializing in traditional Mexican dishes, including breakfast, is getting more business than the nearby favorite Copa de Leche lately. Paella to go. Moderate prices. Open daily 7 a.m.-11 p.m.

Guadalajara Grill, Av. Sábalo 335, tel. (69) 13-5065. This 1992 addition to the Grupo Anderson empire features reliable if not inspirational Mexican dishes with the usual dramatic flair. Moderate to expensive. Open daily 7 a.m.-1 a.m.

Restaurant Joncol's, Av. Flores between H. Frias and Carnaval, tel. (69) 81-2187. The odd name is explained by the fact that this coffeeshop-style place was founded in 1948 by a Swede named Karl *Jon*sson and an American named Oses *Cole*, who married sisters from Central Mexico. Along with seafood and Sinaloan specialties, the sisters cook some dishes from the states of Zacatecas and Hidalgo. A long menu of seafood includes delicious *camarones a la plancha* (broiled shrimp). An occasional special includes *pavo al horno,* roast turkey. The daily *comida corrida* draws a steady local clientele. Open daily 7 a.m.-10:30 p.m.

Panama Restaurant y Pastelería, Calz. Camarón, Sábalo opposite Hotel Las Palmas, tel. (69) 13-6977; also at Calle Juárez and Canizales, tel. (69) 85-1853, a block north of the basílica, and at Serdán and Morelos, tel. (69) 82-8508. This immensely popular homegrown chain specializes in fruit juices, Mexican breakfasts, *pan dulce,* pies, sandwiches, burgers, pasta, some seafood and Mexican dishes—in other words it has it all. Moderate prices and clean, modern, a/c dining rooms have contributed to Panama's success. Open daily 7 a.m.-11 p.m.

Pollo Kawa, Av. Alemán 308, tel. (69) 82-8444. If you're looking for good Sinaloa-style barbecued chicken, look no farther. In addition to traditional barbecued birds in whole, half or quarter portions, Pollo Kawa also prepares chicken as mole (chocolate-sesame sauce), *empanizado* (breaded and fried), *gorditas* (stuffed corn tortillas), *tostadas de pollo, enchiladas de pollo,* chicken soup, and *pollo a la plaza* (stewed with potatoes and vegetables, a Mazatlán specialty). If chicken isn't your thing, the restaurant also cooks *carne asada* and pizzas, and spaghetti. Sides include a tasty bean soup; *licuados de coco* (coconut smoothies) are also a house specialty. Big outdoor section, plus an indoor a/c section. Near the harbor. Open daily 11 a.m. to 10 p.m.

Señor Frog's Bar & Grill, Av. del Mar 30, tel. (69) 82-1925, Playa Norte (halfway between Valentino's and the Monumento al Pescador). Carl Anderson's second chain venture is still one of his most popular. In fact it gets downright raucous here most nights, with the waiters and waitresses vying with the patrons to see who can act more outrageously. Specializes in the restaurant's own brand of Mexican food, barbecued ribs, stuffed shrimp, and very potent margaritas. *Bandido*-garbed waiters wearing *bandoleros* stuffed with shot glasses and carrying bottles of tequila roam the restaurant in search of victims. Open daily noon-1 a.m.

Tacos Luna, Calz. Camarón Sábalo, Zona Dorada. This indoor-outdoor taco bar, a very popular late-night spot for both locals and tourists, has a good selection of tacos—your choice of marlin, shrimp, ceviche, *carne asada, pollo asado, carnasa* (cheek, tongue, or brains), or *carne de puerco adobado* (adobo pork)—plus delicious and inexpensive quesadillas, *queso fundido,* guacamole, *alambre con queso,* (kabob with cheese), and ice-cold beer. Open daily from 1 p.m.-6 a.m. A similar place on the same strip is the **Taco Factory.**

Terraza Playa Mazatlán, Hotel Playa Mazatlán, Zona Dorada, tel. (69) 83-4455. This casual, popular, open-air restaurant facing the beach offers gut-busting breakfasts and Mexican buffets at moderate prices. The "Fiesta Mexicana" on Tuesdays, Fridays, and Saturdays at 7 p.m. is a one-price deal that includes cocktails, beer, music, dancing, folkloric performances, and a huge buffet with steaks, fried chicken, Mexican standards, and seafood. Not the best but one of the easiest for visitors with limited Spanish. Open for breakfast 6-11 a.m., lunch noon-4 p.m., and dinner 6-11 p.m.

Taquería La Carreta, Av. M.G. Nájera about four blocks from the *malecón.* Of the several taco stands strung out along Nájera—sometimes dubbed "Avenida Taco"—La Carreta is one of the cleanest and best. Offers all three of Mexico's classic taco styles: *carne asada* (grilled beef), *de cabeza* (cow head—meaning choice of tongue, cheeks, brains, or eyes), and *al pastor* (spit-roasted, marinated beef).

Seafood
Seafood is what Mazatlecos do best, and Sinaloan seafood at its best includes *pescado zarandeado* (fish marinated in a zesty sauce and barbecued), *caldo sudador* (red snapper soup), *camarones con mango* (mango shrimp), and *marlín ahumada* (smoked marlin). If you're not sure what to choose, most seafood places offer a mixed seafood grill *(parrillada de mariscos)* that contains a selection of fresh fish and shellfish—oysters, shrimp, crab, swordfish or red snapper, and whatever else might be the catch of the day.

Shrimp is particularly plentiful since no other port in Mexico takes in as many of the pink crustaceans—an average 16.8 million kilograms (37 million pounds) per annum from a fleet of over 800 shrimp boats. Aside from those listed below, you'll find a number of *palapa*-roofed *marisquerías* along the band of beach between Playa Sur and Playa Norte.

Chiquita Banana, Camino Real, Zona Dorada, tel. (69) 13-1111. Despite the cutesy name, this is one of Mazatlán's nicest restaurants, with an open-air, *palapa*-style arrangement overlooking the beach. House specialties include oysters and shrimp á la orange. Expensive. Open daily noon-11 p.m.

Restaurant Mamucas, Calle Bolivar Pte. 404 at 5 de Mayo (behind the Mexicana Airlines office), tel. (69) 81-3490. This no-nonsense seafood place, in business for 40 years, specializes in fresh snapper served Veracruz style, smoked marlin, and a mixed seafood grill for two. Moderate prices. Open daily noon-11 p.m.

Mariscos Los Compadres, just south of Calle G. Nelson on the east side of Paseo Claussen. An informal *palapa*-roofed seafood place distinguished by a loud and brassy Sinaloa-style *banda* that performs nightly. One of the most popular (and inexpensive) waterfront restaurants among local and visiting Mexicans. Open daily 10 a.m.-midnight. **Mariscos El Camichin,** on the corner of Juárez and Paseo Claussen, is very similar.

Restaurant El Marismeño, Olas Altas 1224, corner of Constitución, tel. (69) 82-4900. The well-prepared seafood served here comes direct from the restaurant's own boats; the corner location in a restored historic building (just south of Hotel La Siesta and near Copa de Leche) is used to full advantage. Moderate prices. Open daily 11 a.m.-11 p.m.

The Marisquería, on the beach between the Fiesta Inn and the Doubletree on Calz. Camarón Sábalo, Zona Dorada, tel. (69) 13-5932. A large, *palapa*-style restaurant esteemed for its mixed seafood grill prepared at tableside. Moderate prices. Open daily 11 a.m.-11 p.m.

Puerto Azul, right on the beach at Playa Norte/Sur (off Av. del Mar and Miramar) near the Monumento al Pescador, tel. (69) 82-4031. A rustic but intimate decor combined with attentive service, great food, and simultaneous sunset and city views make this a personal favorite. Menu highlights include *pescado zarandeado* barbecued over an open wood fire near the entrance, *chinchulines* (marlin tacos), assorted ceviches, and *alambres de camarones* (shrimp kabob). The English menu has some particularly amusing translations. Moderate prices. Open daily 10 a.m.-11 p.m.

El Shrimp Bucket, Paseo Claussen 11 (in the courtyard of Hotel La Siesta), tel. (69) 81-6350. A festive, indoor-outdoor restaurant famous for shrimp served in every conceivable fashion, including the ever-popular fried shrimp served in a terra-cotta bucket. Breakfasts are also good here. This was Carlos Anderson's first chain restaurant endeavor (but not his first restaurant, which was Mexico City's Sí Cómo No); Grupo Anderson now has over 50 Mexican restaurants (in four countries), each of them known for their whimsical themes and original recipes. Moderate prices. Open daily 6 a.m.-midnight.

International

Café Pacífico, corner of Av. Constitución and Calle H. Frias on Plazuela Machado. This nicely decorated and fully stocked bar-cafe in a restored turn-of-the-century Victorian features European pub-style food and Spanish *botanas.* Pool tables in back, happy hour 11 a.m.-4 p.m. Open daily 10 a.m.-2 a.m.

Casa de Tony, Calle M. Escobedo 111, tel. (69) 85-1262. Often cited as the city's "best" (read "expensive") restaurant, Tony's serves gourmet steak, seafood, continental, Mexican, and daily specials in the courtyard of an elegantly restored Old Mazatlán mansion. Open daily 6-11 p.m.

Ernie Tomato's, Av. R.T. Loaiza. Good pizza, pasta, and Italian in a casual, a/c atmosphere staffed with energetic younger Mexicans. Moderate to high prices. Open daily for lunch and dinner.

Restaurant Jade, corner of 5 de Mayo and Morelos, tel. (69) 82-0626. Good, basic Cantonese served in very tidy surroundings since the 1950s. Jade's sister eatery is **Restaurant Janito,** Calle Serdán 1811, tel. (69) 81-2923. Both open Tues.-Sun. noon-10 p.m.

La Rioja, Calz. Camarón Sábalo 550, tel. (69) 16-6180. Good Spanish cuisine, including *paella valenciana,* served in an expensively decorated, Spanish-owned restaurant. Expensive. Open daily noon-midnight.

Royal Dutch Restaurant, Constitución and Juárez near Plaza Machado, tel. (69) 81-2007. A Dutch-owned place in a historic building; features large breakfasts, continental dishes from all over Europe, soups, salads, sandwiches, seafood, some Mexican dishes, and good pastries and coffee, all served at tables on an interior patio. English, Spanish, Dutch, and German spoken. Moderate prices. Open daily 8 a.m.-9:00 p.m.

Señor Pepper Restaurant-Bar, tel. (69) 82-1322, opposite the Camino Real on Calz. Camarón Sábalo. Probably the most elegant restaurant in the Zona Dorada, with polished-brass ambience and tuxedoed waiters. Despite the name, house specialties are prime-grade steak, pork chops, lobster, and shrimp, mostly prepared and served American- or European-style. Expensive. Open daily 6 p.m.-midnight.

Restaurante El Sheik, tel. (69) 86-4449, on Punta Camarón, where Calz. Camarón Sábalo turns into Av. del Mar. The architecture is postmodernist Moor, the decor gleaming silver and white tablecloths, the cuisine international and national with an emphasis on seafood, grilled rib-eye, and brochettes. Flaming coffees and liqueurs are a house specialty. Excellent ocean and coastline views. Expensive. Open daily 6 p.m.-midnight.

Sushi Club, north end of Av. R.T. Loaiza near Calz. Camarón Sábalo. A small outdoor sushi bar with tasty and inexpensive *makis, temakis,* and *nigiris.* Open Tues.-Sun. 1 p.m.-11 p.m.

Vip's, tel. (69) 14-0754, opposite the Aeroméxico office at Calz. Camarón Sábalo and Av. Lomas de Mazatlán. One of the best values in the Zona Dorada, this super-clean, a/c wonder serves a wide selection of reasonably priced soups, salads, breakfasts, Mexican specialties, and seafood in a coffee shop-style atmosphere. A good choice for those put off by the zone's tourist-oriented restaurants but too timid to eat at funkier places. Open daily 7 a.m.-10 p.m.

Vegetarian
Restaurante Vegetariano La Manzana, Calle B. Domínguez, diagonally opposite Centro de Idiomas. A small shop/cafe sells curative herbs, vitamins, yogurt, fruit, teas, and a few fresh-baked items. The cafe section is open for lunch only, when a *comida corrida* including soup, salad, entree, and fruit or vegetable drink costs US$4. The owner, a Mexican woman of French-Chinese descent, speaks good English. Open daily 1-3 p.m. for lunch, 8 a.m.-5 p.m. for retail.

Tienda Naturalista, Calle Flores Pte. 208, near Plaza Republicana. Another shop/cafe with imaginative *comidas corridas* and natural food items. Inexpensive. Open daily 1-3 p.m. for lunch, 8 a.m.-5 p.m. for retail.

Restaurant Pura Vida, Calle Laguna 777, Zona Dorada, tel. (69) 81-6585. This funky, tourist-oriented place specializes in fresh juices and tropical fruit smoothies described as "immune system fortifiers," "stomach degreasers," and the like. The moderately priced menu also features breakfasts and innovative, health-oriented dishes like "Greek tacos" made with feta cheese and whole wheat tortillas, vegetarian sandwiches, and *pesadillas* (wheat tortilla topped with chop suey). Open 7:30 a.m.-10 p.m.

Groceries
Mazatlán's biggest supermarkets are the **Gigante** at Calz. R. Buelna and Calle la Marina and **Plaza Ley** on the highway. **El Arbol, Sábalo Real,** and **Super Las Palmas** are smaller, more expensive mini-markets for tourists on Calz. Camarón Sábalo. **Supermarket Las Flores,** just opposite Suites Las Flores, is the best mini-market in the Av. R.T. Loaiza area as it has more fruit and vegetables than the other little supermarkets on that strip. **Panaficadora Al' Mor,** directly opposite the Hotel Suites Las Palmas on Calz. Camarón Sábalo, near a little strip of car rental places, offers a good selection of *pan dulce* and other Mexican bakery items.

The freshest produce is available at the municipal market on Av. Juárez in Old Mazatlán. Ripe Sinaloan mangoes are plentiful in the summer, while Haas avocados (originally cultivated by Mazatlán native Antonio Haas) are available year-round.

ENTERTAINMENT

Nightlife
Discos: Like other Mexican beach resorts, Mazatlán is awash in discos, most of them in the Zona Dorada. Cover charges typically run US$5-10, while hours are roughly 9 p.m.-4 a.m. Not many people arrive before 11 p.m. or midnight.

Walking along Calz. Camarón Sábalo toward Playa Norte, you can't miss **Valentino's Disco and Canta Bar,** tel. (69) 83-6212, a disco with banks of pulsating videos and three dance floors housed in a white edifice that looks like something from the planet Krypton, perched on Punta Camarón at the south end of Playa Camarón. A karaoke section was recently added. The clientele here tends to be a mix of upscale Mazatlecos and Zona Dorada tourists. Women are admitted free on many nights. **Bora Bora Beach Club** in the same complex features live pop music in a tropical ambience, along with a bar, several dance floors, two swimming pools, and a volleyball court. Bora Bora often stays open till 4-5 a.m.

El Caracol Tango Palace, tel. (69) 13-3333 at El Cid Mega Resort captures the El Cid crowd; a unique feature here is a brass firehouse pole used for rapid transits from the upper seating level to the dance floor. **Señor Frog's** (see "Food above") is a popular dance spot for tourists, as is the similar **Mundo Banana,** Calz. Camarón Sábalo 131, tel. (69) 86-4770.

Bars: The Valentino's-El Sheik complex also features **Mikonos,** a sedate piano bar popular for cocktails and appetizers on the sea-view terrace. Relatively new **Tony's Bar & Grill,** at the triangular junction between Av. R.T. Loaiza and Calz. Camarón Sábalo, is a popular outdoor bar frequented by locals as well as tourists; an electric ensemble plays good Latin and rock.

Amadeus Café at the corner of Calles B. Domínguez and Escobedo, is a charming, up-market *peña* with live folk and jazz nightly except Sunday. In spite of the name, there's a full bar as well as a moderately priced menu of Mexican *antojitos.* Service is excellent and credit cards are accepted. Open Mon.-Sat. 6 p.m.-1 a.m.

Time Out at Calz. Sábalo 1446, opposite Pueblo Bonito, is an American-style sports bar with big-screen satellite TV. Billed as the "Unofficial Home of the Chicago Cubs," the **No Name Café,** tel. (69) 13-2031, opposite Suites Las Flores on Av. R.T. Loaiza, is another hangout for armchair jocks. At **Club Derby,** tel. (69) 82-9065, is a race and sports book club in Hotel de Cima where you can bet in dollars or pesos, beginning at 10 a.m.

During the high season, the most popular Zona Dorada bars are the super-casual **Jungle Juice, Gringo Lingo,** and **Joe's Oyster Bar,** all three on the Av. R.T. Loaiza loop. Mostly these are places for hanging out and listening to music, though some people dance as well.

Theater and Dance: Teatro Angela Peralta, on Av. Carnaval next to Plazuela Machado, hosts ballet, dance, musical, and theater performances year-round. In spring the theater serves as headquarters for the Sinaloa International Cultural Festival, in which some 1,500 performers participate. Tickets for theater performances are available at the theater box office during the day or an hour before curtain time.

Although it's not highbrow entertainment, many tourists enjoy the **Fiesta Mexicana** held Tuesdays, Fridays, and Saturdays at 7 p.m. at the Hotel Playa Mazatlán's Terraza Playa restaurant, call (69) 13-4444 for reservations. A single admission price includes beverages, food, and Mexican dance performances (see the Terraza Playa Mazatlán entry under "Food" for more detail).

Plaza Music: Musical entertainment in Mazatlán that doesn't cost a centavo is occasionally played in the kiosks of Plaza Zaragoza and Plaza Republicana. Many kinds of music are aired but if you're lucky, you'll be able to listen to an ensemble playing local *perrada* or *tambora sinaloense,* a type of brass-and-drum band music originally brought by German immigrants but adopted and adapted by local Mazatlecos. Around the turn of the century, *perrada* became the "music of the people" when string music was still for the elite; during the 1910-20 Mexican Revolution it became a rallying soundtrack for the *constitucionalistas.*

Today the usual instrumentation for a *tambora* ensemble is three clarinets, two trumpets, two bass horns, and a sousaphone or tuba, which together play a combination of European marches and Mexican tunes—sometimes fused into one composition. In recent years this type of music—known as *banda* throughout the rest of Mexico—has become very popular again nationally.

Events

Carnaval: The city's most attended annual event officially begins a week before Ash Wednesday (late February to early March), the start of Lent. Attracting as many as 400,000-500,000 participants, Mazatlán's Carnaval is estimated to be the third largest in the world after Río de Janeiro's and New Orleans's.

Throughout the celebrations, Mazatlecos party well into the night; some wear full masquerade as in New Orleans and Río, while virtually everyone participates in the breaking and throwing of confetti-filled eggshells called *cascarones.* In Carnaval's early years, perfumed flour filled the *cascarones;* in 1898 city officials convened and decided to replace the "immoral flour" with confetti. This is considered the "official" advent of the city's Carnaval, though written records dating to as far back as 1823 mention this brilliant and sumptuous festival, and a Carnaval newsletter was published in 1851.

The primary focus of the street action is the "Carnavaldome" on Av. del Mar on Playa Norte (which is blocked off to vehicular traffic Thurs.-Tues.), a temporary assortment of stages and booths accommodating continuous music (*tropicale,* mariachi, rock, and *norteña*), food vendors, outrageous costume-wearing, and all-night dancing throughout the festival. Av. del Mar is also the site of two pyrotechnics displays, the traditional *castillo* (a castlelike fireworks platform unique to Mexico) on Saturday night, and an offshore fireworks finale representing a mock naval battle (in commemoration of Mazatlán's 1864 victory over the French navy) on Sunday night. Admission to the nightly Carnavaldome street dance typically costs less than US$2.

The main events kick off the Friday evening before Shrove Tuesday ("Mardi Gras" in New Orleans) with the *juegos florales* ("floral games") in the city baseball stadium. During this well-attended event, a city committee crowns the Flower Queen and bestows literary awards upon contestants who have written the best "flowery verse." Top prize is the prestigious Clemencia Isaura Poetry Award, a 72-year tradition that honors the best unpublished work from anywhere in Mexico.

Saturday evening activities begin with the coronation of La Reina de Carnaval ("Carnaval Queen") and El Rey Feo ("Ugly King") at the Estadio Teodoro Mariscal, an event that usually includes concert performances by major Latin artists. This is followed by the Quema de Mal Humor, or "Burning of Bad Humor," in which an effigy (usually modeled after an unpopular politician of the day) is hanged and burned. Sunday is the biggest Carnavaldome night, while the Monday following this weekend is El Día del Marido Oprimido, the "Day of the Oppressed Husband," in which married men are allowed 23.5 hours of freedom to do whatever they wish.

Two large costume parades, one on Sunday at 6 p.m. and the other on Tuesday at 4 p.m., feature dozens of floats representing various mythological figures from Aladdin to Zeus, plus the newly crowned Carnaval "royalty." *Tambora sinaloense* bands come from all around the state to participate in the parades, which may feature as many as 10 *tambora* ensembles per day. Because of their prime location along the main parade routes, the streetfront rooms at Hotel La Siesta, Hotel Freeman, and Hotel Belmar are booked out months in advance of Carnaval.

At the turn of the century, Plazuela Machado was the central focus of Carnaval. Now that the plaza area has been restored, Carnaval activities have returned with a gastronomic fair held every evening Fri.-Tuesday. Prominent dishes on hand include Mazatlán's famous *pescado zarandeado* and barbecued shrimp.

Several of the events described above, including the Saturday evening coronation ball, require admission tickets that cost US$3-20 each.

Sinaloa Cultural Festival: Since 1987 this yearly event has brought a month-long series of performing arts to the state from late Oct.-late November. Although performances are also held in Los Mochis, Guasave, and Culiacán, the main focus is Mazatlán, and in particular the Teatro Angela Peralta. The variety of performances generally encompasses opera, ballet, symphony, jazz, flamenco, rock, folkloric dance, and drama. Headline performers have included such Latin greats as Willy Colón, Celia Cruz, and the late Lola Beltrán.

Bullfights and *Charreadas*

Mazatlecos are much deeper into baseball than bullfighting, but for the sake of visitors (Mexicans as well as gringos), *corridas de toros* are held from late December through April at 12,000-seat Plaza de Toros Monumental, located on the north side of Calz. R. Buelna midway between the highway and the beach. Advance tickets can be purchased at the plaza or at the kiosk near Valentino's. The program begins promptly at 4 p.m.

During the rest of the year, Plaza Monumental hosts occasional Sunday *charreadas.* For information on scheduled plaza events, call (69) 93-3598 or (69) 84-1777.

Shopping

Downtown: The city's best bargains are found in the traditional shopping district surrounding the **Mercado Público José Mario Pino Suárez** or Mercado Central, bounded by Juárez, Ocampo, Serdán, and Valle. Amid the usual fresh produce, meats, herbs, and curios are a number of quality handicraft vendors. Just outside the market, **Artesanías Marina Mercante** offers a decent selection of crafts from all over Mexico. Around the corner, **Huarachería Internacional**

at Ocampo and Juárez sells a variety of Mexican sandals at reasonable prices.

Guayaberas, near Plaza Republicana at Calle Flores Pte. 613, has an extensive selection of *guayaberas,* the Yucatán-style men's shirt now popularly worn throughout tropical Mexico. Prices start at around US$10. Also along Calle Flores is a string of **photo shops** with the city's best prices on film and processing.

NidArt, at the east end of Plazuela Machado, is an artist-owned gallery that deals in unique leather sculptures.

Another major urban market, **Mercado Hidalgo,** bordered by R. Buelna, 13 de Abril, Av. de las Americas, and E.P. Arce in working-class Col. Juárez, has many of the same articles found at the Mercado Central at slightly lower prices—or at least the vendors are more open to bargaining.

The city's largest and most modern shopping mall is 28,000-square-meter, a/c **La Gran Plaza,** containing over 120 stores, a food court, and parking for a thousand vehicles.

Zona Dorada: Packed in among the hotels and restaurants are dozens of shops catering almost exclusively to tourists. Much of what is offered is of the "Mexican vacation" souvenir variety, e.g. T-shirts, beer mugs, and other logo-emblazoned items from branches of Señor Frog's Official Store—which seem to be on every other corner. **Mazatlán Arts and Crafts Center,** tel. (69) 13-5243, opposite Hotel Suites Las Flores and next door to the No Name Café, contains a large selection of blankets, rugs, woodcarvings, hats, leather goods, and other crafts from around the country. With some bargaining, prices can be surprisingly good here, although you should probably compare downtown prices before going on a spending spree.

Mazatlán Art Gallery, tel. (69) 14-3612, on Sábalo in Plaza Balboa, sells contemporary paintings, lithographs, and sculptures by Mexican artists, some of them quite well known.

The best selection of foreign newspapers—including *USA Today* and the *Los Angeles Times* during the high season, foreign magazines and English-language best-sellers can be found at **Kioskito de Tin Marín,** a kiosk newsstand opposite the Dairy Queen on Calz. Camarón Sábalo.

Many shops in the Zona offer beachwear, much of it either cheap/tacky or expensive/tacky;

among the most wearable Mexican-made designs are those found at the **Aca Joe** outlet at Calz. Camarón Sábalo and Paseo Díaz Ordaz.

Pharmacies: Farmacia Benavides, just north of Cinema Gaviotas on Calz. Camarón Sábalo, is the biggest pharmacy in the Zona. Three pharmacies in the city are open 24 hours—**Parque Zaragoza,** Calle. G. Nelson 2200, tel. (69) 82-8378; **Atlantis,** 5 de Mayo s/n, tel. (69) 81-4545; and **Cruz Verde,** Calle M.G. Nájera 477, tel. (69) 81-2225.

SPORTS

Baseball
The local pro team, Los Venados de Mazatlán (Mazatlán Deer), participates in the 10-team Pacific Coast League roughly Oct.-April. Los Venados were league champions in the '86-87 and '92-93 seasons. Mazatlecos are avid baseball fans and if you are, too, you owe it to yourself to check out a Venados game in their home town if you can. Compared to American audiences, Mexican ball fans behave politely. Cervecería Pacífico owns the team as well as the well-designed and well-maintained Estadio Teodoro Mariscal on Calle T. Mariscal, about 500 meters east of Playa Norte off Av. Revolución. Weekday games begin at 6 p.m., weekend games at 8 p.m.

Unreserved grandstand tickets *(central general)* cost US$2.60, unsheltered sideline seats *(laterales)* US$1.30, reserved center section *(central numerado)* US$6.60, and boxes *(palco)* US$8. Lots of cold Pacífico and Corona are sold in the stands, along with peanuts and popcorn. Tickets go on sale beginning at 4 p.m. on game days or in advance at the team headquarters at Av. M.G. Nájera 821, (69) 81-1966 or 81-1710. The hot ticket of the season is the game played with Mazatlán's biggest baseball rival, Los Tomateros de Culiacán.

Surfing
Mazatlán is really the first place along the Mexican mainland's Pacific coast with steady wave action. Starting in the north, decent beach and reef breaks are sometimes happening at **Punta Cerritos.** Farther south, depending on the season, **Punta Camarón** ("Valentino's") yields left

and right point breaks on either side. Boogie-boarders can sometimes catch decent beach breaks toward the north end of **Playa Norte,** though generally the action here is limited.

"The Cannons" at **Punta Chile** near the old fort (also called Playa los Pinos) is one of the best and most challenging summer point breaks in the area. Almost any time of year high surf can also break at the north end of **Playa Olas Altas.**

North of Mazatlán at Punta Piaxtla (see "Vicinity of Mazatlán," below) is a secluded beach area with occasional strong breaks.

The city's main shred-shed is **Palm Surf Shop** on Calz. Camarón Sábalo next to Las Palmas Trailer Park, where they sell, rent, and repair boards and sell surfing accessories. Open 10 a.m.-2 p.m. and 4-8 p.m. daily. Surfboards and boogie boards can also be rented at various sports centers in the Zona Dorada.

Kayaking

The Mazatlán area offers several kayaking possibilities. Experienced kayakers can easily explore **Las Tres Islas** offshore (see "Las Tres Islas," under "Sights," above, for details on the islands) from Playa Gaviotas. When the Pacific surf is rough, launching is easier at Playa Norte, even though this means a longer paddle. Another good spot for kayaking is the Isla de la Piedra peninsula, which has a number of interesting inlets and islets on the landward side.

Farther south along the coast are two large estuarial systems, **Laguna el Caimanero** (Laguna del Huizache) west of Rosario (put in at Agua Verde or Caimanero) and **Laguna Agua Grande** at Teacapán, with nearly limitless kayaking venues. (See "Vicinity of Mazatlán" for more information on this area.)

Kayaks can be rented at the Camino Real's Ocean Sport Center and at El Cid's Aqua Sports Center.

Windsurfing

Sideshore breezes through the channel between Playa Gaviotas/Playa Sábalo and Las Tres Islas make this area a popular windsurfing spot. Hot-shots can find higher winds and more chop at Playa Cerritos and farther north at Playa Brujas or Playa Delfín.

Several Zona Dorada hotels offer a limited selection of windsurfing equipment suitable for novices. Experienced boardsailors in need of equipment will find the best selection of rental gear at Aqua Sports Center.

Parasailing

If you take a stroll along Playa Gaviotas, sooner or later you'll be approached by someone offering a parasail experience ("Wanna get high?"), in which you're harnessed to a parachute connected by a long line to a motorboat. The boats run parallel to the beach so that—theoretically at least—you can launch and land on the sand.

Opinions are divided as to how safe a sport this is, though vendors claim they haven't lost a customer yet. The winds are usually steadiest (and thus more predictable) in the mornings—if winds are strong you might think twice before strapping in. The ride—and the beach view from the air—is thrilling; vendors typically charge US$20 for a 10- to 15-minute ride.

Diving

Although Mazatlán isn't a great area for snorkeling or scuba diving, the rocky offshore islands provide opportunities for viewing rock corals and tropical fish. Maximum visibility in good conditions is about 10 meters (30 feet).

The best-equipped place for dive equipment is **Aqua Sports Center,** tel. (69) 13-3333, ext. 341, next to El Cid Mega Resort. In addition to providing air and equipment rental (snorkel, mask, and fins go for around US$7 a day), the staff at Aqua Sports offers scuba instruction and guided dive trips. Equipment and instruction are also available at Ocean Sports Center.

Boating

Two huge boating facilities, Marina El Cid and Marina de Mazatlán, have recently been developed at Estero de Sábalo northeast of Playa Sábalo. Together they form the largest marina complex (about 561 hectares) in Mexico and one of the largest in all Latin America.

The US$200 million project is being built in six phases, beginning with an outer harbor four meters (12 feet) deep and ending with an inner harbor with navigable canals, four new five-star hotels, and a condominium complex. American-managed **Marina Mazatlán** covers 1,458 acres and when completed will boast 1,200 slips, commercial and residential lots, a 27-hole golf course,

EL BÉISBOL

by Tom Huhti and Joe Cummings

While many North American ball fans recognize the Latin Caribbean (Dominican Republic, Puerto Rico, and Cuba) as a baseball powerhouse, Mexico has been generally underappreciated except for a brief episode of "Fernandomania" in the L.A. basin in 1980. Yet the south-of-the-border giant has embraced the Grand Old Game as passionately as—and for as long as—any country outside the United States. And unlike other Latin American or Caribbean lands, which depend on exporting their best talent to the U.S. (and which schedule their own games during the U.S.'s off-season to accommodate migrant players), Mexico has succeeded in remaining independent enough not only to keep many of their hottest players at home, but also to maintain a summer league scheduled head-to-head with the *Yanqui* season up north.

Today Mexico boasts the largest organized baseball system in Latin America, with a 15-team, nationwide Mexican League (Liga Mexicana) that plays during the summer and a 10-team Mexican Pacific League (Liga Mexicana del Pacífico) during the winter. Despite its name, the latter is centered on the northwest coast of the Sea of Cortez, with only one ball club technically linked to a true Pacific city. Together these leagues maintain the year-round loyalties of millions of fans throughout Mexico; on the amateur level, an estimated four million Mexicans play baseball, third behind only the U.S. and Japan.

The Sierra Transversal belt that separates Northern from Southern Mexico also divides Mexico loosely into baseball and soccer camps. Roll into an otherwise unimpressive Northern Mexican hamlet on any given afternoon and you're likely to see Little-Leaguers shagging flies in pristine stadiums that shame more than a few U.S. minor league AA ball clubs. Of the 49 Mexican players to have played pro ball in the U.S., all but seven were from the North; as might be expected, average player statistics are also slanted in favor of Northern ballplayers.

In part the North's affinity for the grass diamond is due to the obvious proximity to baseball's country of origin. Nuevo Laredo's Tecolotes ("Owls")—a Mexican team that actually plays on both sides of the border—is a good example of what can go right between two contiguous nations. Yet for the most part Mexican baseball has aligned itself with the annual Caribbean World Series rather than looking toward the U.S. minors (and rather than restricting itself to Mexican playoffs), showing a stronger affinity for Caribbean ball in spite of the geographic distance between Northern Mexico and the principal Caribbean ball clubs. Mexican teams have twice won the Caribbean World Series—both champion teams hailed from Northern Mexico (Hermosillo in 1976, Mexicali in 1986).

To a large degree, the Mexican leagues have been forced to remain aloof from U.S. ball by the pro sports industry on both sides of the border. In the 1940s, a U.S. baseball commissioner instituted a ban on any American player who "defected" to a Mexican team in the off-season. The ban was lifted the following year (during the winter many U.S.

EL BÉISBOL TALK

base robada—stolen base
blanqueo—shutout
caminar—walk
carrera—run
cuadrangular—home run
elevado—fly ball
entrada—inning
equipo—team
jardín—outfield
lanzador—pitcher
lanzamiento descontrolado—wild pitch
lanzamiento ilegal—balk
palco—box seats
pasaporte—walk
paso de conga—"conga step," 1-2-3 inning
poncho—strikeout
torpedero—shortstop
temporada—season.
¡Bésela!—Kiss it! (equiv. to "Kiss that baby goodbye!")
el día de los fanáticos—fan appreciation day

minor- and even major-league "scrub" players head south with bat and glove), but Mexican baseball fans haven't totally forgotten the insult.

On the opposite side, if a U.S. ball club desires to woo a Mexican player north, Mexican teams require that the player's contract be purchased outright—for a steep sum meant to compensate for gate revenues lost to migrating talent (one American club owner lamented that you can hire five Dominican players for the price of one Mexican). In a sense it's unfair to compare U.S. and Mexican league politics, since the difference in pay scales means better Mexican players tend to move north while the lesser U.S. talent moves south, putting Mexico at the disadvantage.

Since Sonora's Baldamero Melo Almada became the first Mexican national to play in the U.S. (for the Boston Red Sox in 1933), nearly 50 Mexican players have been drafted by U.S. teams. Of those who have become big-name players—among them Ruben Amaro, Jorge Orta, Cy Acosta, Aurelio "Señor Smoke" López, Ismael Váldez, and Teodoro ("Teddy") Higuera—undoubtedly the brightest star so far has been pudgy screwballer Fernando Valenzuela, who caused a national frenzy in 1980-81 on the way to winning Rookie of the Year, the Cy Young Award, and the pride of the U.S. Hispanic population. In Mexico, a pandemonium approaching presidential occurs every time Valenzuela makes a public appearance. In the U.S. he is one of the few ballplayers to inspire an American pop song (F. Sternwheeler's "Fernando de Sonora" in 1981). In the 1990s Valenzuela earned a pitching spot with the Baltimore Orioles in a valiant comeback attempt.

At last count, eight players from Mexico were on the rosters. Yet the biggest and best of Mexican baseball—Ramón Araño, Angel Castro, Epitacio Torres, and, likely the greatest Mexican player of all time, Hector Espino (who holds the Mexican home-run record)—almost never set foot in the United States due to a combination of national pride and the Mexican leagues' prohibitive price tags.

Mexican Pacific League Teams
Tomateros de Culiacán; Mayos de Navojoa; Venados de Mazatlán; Naranjeros de Hermosillo; Cañeros de Los Mochis; Aguilas de Mexicali; Algodoneros de Guasave; Yaquis de Ciudad Obregón

---

dry dock and marine repair facilities, and yacht, beach, golf, and tennis clubs. The marina is purportedly "hurricane safe" has been named a "safe haven" by Lloyds of London. So far 200 slips are operational; rates of US$3 per foot per month (or US$4.50 including power and water) make this marina the least expensive along Mexico's entire Pacific coast. Check in and check out cost US$10 each. All docks include showers, bathrooms, laundry, fax, phone, mail, locked gates, and 24-hr. security. A fuel dock is under construction. Slip rates will increase to US$5 a foot by the end of 1998. Call or fax (69) 16-3614 for further information

Marina El Cid is a much smaller project with 100 slips currently operational and 50 more planned for the future. Facilities include a marine supplies shop, tel. (69) 13-0525, diesel and gasoline fuel dock, port captain visits for check-in, showers, laundromat, beach club access, 24-hour security, parking, and a deluxe hotel (see "Accommodations" earlier in this section). Room service from the hotel is available with rental of dock space. Daily rates run US$24 for up to 59 feet, while monthly rates are US$7 per foot up to 59 feet, US$9 per foot to 75 feet, and US$11 over 76 feet. Electrical services and TV cable are extra; there's a 10% discount for stays of over three months.

Boats can also be anchored or launched at the **Centro de Ciencias del Mar** at Isla del Crestón for US$17 per day. If you're planning to launch or anchor more than two days in a month, a US$34 one-month anchor permit will save money. For trailered boats, another public launch ramp is available at the end of the sportfishing pier at

---

MAZATLÁN WATER SPORTS EQUIPMENT

Aqua Sports Center
El Cid Resort
Calzada Camarón Sábalo
tel. (69) 13-3333, ext. 341

Ocean Sport Center
Camino Real
Punto de Sábalo
tel. (69) 13-1111

Club Náutico, tel. (69) 81-5195, where an all-day launch permit (no anchoring) costs US$20.

Hobie catamarans can be rented for US$20 an hour from the Aqua Sports Center.

Fishing

Mazatlán rivals Cabo San Lucas as western Mexico's sportfishing capital. Approximately 7,000-9,000 billfish (swordfish and striped marlin Dec.-April, blue and black marlin May-Dec.) are caught offshore each year, along with tuna (year-round), skipjack, Pacific snapper, mackerel, and snook (summer), and dorado (year-round except Jan.-February).

At least 10 sportfishing fleets *(flotas deportivas)* offer guided fishing trips from the city's sportfishing piers on Isla del Crestón (at the west end of Av. del Puerto). **Bill Heimpel's Star Fleet** is the oldest, largest, and best known. Party boats cost around US$60 pp including all bait and equipment, while charter boats taking six to eight anglers cost US$240-300 a day (6:30 am to 2:30 p.m.). Several of Star Fleet's clients have set three IGFA records, including a black marlin weighing 619 kilograms (1,362 pounds) that was hooked in 1990. For information call or (69) 82-3878 or (800) 426-6890 in the U.S. and Canada, or fax (69) 82-5155, (512) 377-0454 in the U.S./Canada. **Aries Fleet,** at Marina El Cid, tel. (69) 16-3468, operates eight well-maintained fishing cruisers with similar rates.

Less expensive is **Flota El Dorado,** tel. (69) 81-6204, which charters 38-foot boats with guide plus bait and tackle for six anglers for just US$175. El Dorado also offers a half-day *lancha* trip for up to four persons for US$70.

Panga **Fishing:** If billfish aren't your thing or if you simply prefer fishing closer to shore, *pangas* (small fiberglass launches with outboard motors) are a less expensive alternative to party boats and fishing cruisers. From **Playa Norte** local *pangeros* will take one or two sportfishers out to hook dorado or red snapper for around

US$50 per boat. You must provide your own bait and tackle; these can be arranged through local fishermen if necessary.

Super Sport Pangas, associated with the Star Fleet, has *pangas* for US$60 pp or US$75 for two persons (only one line each), with a three-person limit.

Fishing Supplies: Artículos para Pesca de Mazatlán, Mexico 15, tel. (69) 82-6838, and **Alcampo,** Mexico 15, tel. (69) 82-8865, deal in fishing tackle, rods, and reels.

Hunting

The Presa Comedero area north of Mazatlán is a popular hunting spot for a wide variety of game, including pintail, gadwall, bluebill, brandt, widgeon, cinnamon teal, green-winged teal, bluewing, dove, quail, deer, and wild pig. In Mazatlán the **Aviles Brothers,** Paseo Claussen and 5 de Mayo, tel. (69) 81-3728 or (800) 633-3085 in the U.S. and Canada, are the most experienced outfitters; English-speaking guides are available. Packages must be booked in advance because of the time needed to arrange permits.

Tennis and Golf

The city's best tennis facility is **The Racquet Club Las Gaviotas,** tel. (69) 83-5939, Calz. R. Buelna, which has three clay courts and four hard courts. Court time costs US$10 per hour; opening hours are 6 a.m.-10 p.m. **Club Deportiva Reforma,** tel. (69) 83-1200, is also on Calz. R. Buelna and has eight hard courts with rates and hours similar to those at The Racquet Club. Hotels with tennis courts (usually guests only, but try calling) include Torres Mazatlán, Costa de Oro, Camino Real, and Los Sábalos.

El Cid Mega Resort, tel. (69) 13-3333, has an 18-hole, par 72 golf course open only to El Cid and Camino Real guests; greens and caddy fees total around US$50. **Club Campestre,** at Km 1195 on Mexico 15, tel. (69) 84-7494, has a nine-hole course open to the public daily 7 a.m.-6 p.m.; fees cost around US$12 per day.

Gym

Fitness Central, next to Cinema Gaviotas at Calz. Camarón Sábalo 216, is an American-owned fitness center with the best facilities in Mazatlán. It's open 24 hours and offers daily, weekly, and monthly rates.

yellowfin tuna

Zen Center

If you're interested in studying Zen, you may be able to stay in the palm-thatched huts at **Casa Zen,** Apdo. Postal 881, Mazatlán, Sinaloa, 82000 (or 20749 Parthenia St., Canoga Park, California 91306) on Isla de la Piedra. In addition to a daily meditation schedule, Casa Zen offers short courses in vegetarian cooking, gardening, bread-making, carpentry, arts and crafts, and navigation. After getting a *lancha* from the Mazatlán harbor to the island, you can walk to Casa Zen in 15 minutes or take *pulmonía.*

INFORMATION

Tourist Offices and Publications

The very efficient **Coordinación General de Turismo del Estado de Sinaloa,** tel. (69) 16-5160, on the fourth floor of the Banrural building, directly across from Mar Rosa Trailer Park, has stacks of printed information on Mazatlán and the surrounding area. The bilingual staff can also answer just about any inquiry.

A privately run consortium, the **Mazatlán Tourism Trust,** at Calz. Camarón Sábalo 333, tel. (69) 14-1955, fax 14-1977, also dispenses tourist information and is more convenient to Zona Dorada visitors. If for no other reason, stop by the office for a free copy of the *Mazatlán Coupon Catalog and Guide,* which contains coupons for room upgrades, restaurant and gift shop discounts, an events calendar, a city map, and a list of hotels, restaurants, shops, and attractions. In the U.S. and Canada, you can call (800) 438-4825 to have this booklet sent to any address in these two countries.

Another useful publication is *Pacific Pearl,* a giveaway bilingual monthly newspaper with short features on local history and culture, plus a listing of current events and restaurant specials. *El Sol de Pacífico,* the city's main Spanish-language daily, also publishes *The Sun,* a monthly, bilingual tourist-oriented newspaper. The small, magazine-like *Inside Mazatlán* is similar in content. These publications can be picked up at almost any hotel in the Zona Dorada.

Library: The city's main public library, on Plazuela de los Leones at Av. Flores and Niños Héroes, has a large collection of Spanish-lan-

CONSULATES IN MAZATLÁN

Canada
Av. R.T. Loaiza 202
tel. (69) 13-7320

Finland
Calle Venus and Roosevelt 136
tel. (69) 81-3907

France
Calle Jacarandas 6
Col. Loma Linda
tel. (69) 82-8552

Germany
Av. Jacarandas 10
tel. (69) 82-2809

Italy
Av. Olas Altas 66-105
tel. (69) 85-1478

guage books and periodicals, plus the all-English **Benjamin Franklin Library** upstairs. It's open Mon.-Fri. 8 a.m.-8 p.m., Saturday 9 a.m.-noon.

Maps: A number of free maps of the city are available in hotels or from the tourist office; these are usually adequate for most visitors. If you're planning extensive explorations of the city, or if you plan to drive downtown, try to find a copy of the *Planos Turísticos de Mazatlán, Culiacán, and Los Mochis,* produced by Mexican urban map genius HFET but sponsored and published by SECTUR. It's for sale at the state tourism office cited above—or at least until they run out.

Post and Telegraph

Mazatlán's central post office is at Av. Juárez and Calle 21 de Marzo opposite the Palacio de Gobierno. The telegraph office is next door.

Mail Boxes Etc. has a branch on Calz. Camarón Sábalo near Banca Serfín; it's open Mon.-Fri. 8 a.m.-7 p.m. and Saturday 9 a.m.-3 p.m.

American Express cardholders can receive mail at **American Express Travel Services,** Calz. Camarón Sábalo 310, tel. (69) 13-0466. This office is open Mon.-Fri. 9 a.m.-1 p.m. and 4-6 p.m., Saturday 9 a.m.-1 p.m.

MAZATLÁN TELEPHONE NUMBERS

Tourist Police	84-8444
State Tourist Office	16-5160
Red Cross	81-3690, 85-1451
Fire Dept.	81-2769
Immigration	81-3813
Weather	81-4527
Federal police	85-5440
Highway Patrol	80-6681
SEMATUR (ferry)	81-7020
Railway Station	84-6710, 84-6627
Bus Terminal	82-8321
Mazatlán Area Code	69

Language Study

The **Centro de Idiomas,** Calle B. Domínguez 1908, tel. (69) 82-2053, fax 85-5606, in Old Mazatlán offers a variety of intensive Spanish-language courses in a converted century-old house. Taught by warm, conscientious, native-speaker instructors, classes run two to four hours per day Mon.-Fri., with special activities every Saturday (e.g., aquarium visits, bay cruises). Courses begin every Monday of the year except Easter Week and Christmas vacation.

Group classes cost US$132 per week for the intensive, four-hours-per-day course, US$100 for the two-hours-per-day schedule. Individual one-on-one instruction costs more. Homestays with Mexican families—strongly encouraged—cost US$130 per day (including three meals) On-site registration costs US$30, advance registration by mail is US$105.

Money

Banks are plentiful in Mazatlán. A few have extended hours to accommodate tourists, including **Banamex** at Calz. Camarón Sábalo 434 in the Zona Dorada and **Bancomer** at Av. Juárez and 21 de Marzo downtown, both of which are open Mon.-Fri. 9 a.m.-1:30 p.m. and 3:30-5:30 p.m.

Two reliable moneychangers in the Zona Dorada are **Casa de Cambio Mazatlán** on Av. R.T. Loaiza and **Casa de Cambio Sanchez** at Calz. Camarón Sábalo 109.

GETTING THERE

Earlier this century Mazatlán was a six-day Pacific steamer trip from San Francisco; nowadays it's a day's dive from the U.S. border or just an hour or two by plane.

Air

Rafael Buelna Airport, tel. (69) 81-0865, 20 km (12.4 miles) southeast of the city, is served by several international, national, and regional airlines, including: **Aeroméxico,** Calz. Camarón Sábalo 310, tel. (69) 14-1621 (nonstops to/from Ciudad Juárez, Durango, Guadalajara, Los Mochis, Mexico City, and Tijuana, with connections to/from Hermosillo and Phoenix); **Aero California,** El Cid Mega Resort, tel. (69) 13-2042 (nonstops to/from Guadalajara, La Paz, Los Angeles, and Mexico City, with connections to/from Tijuana via La Paz); **Alaska,** airport, tel. (69) 85-2730 (nonstop flights to Mazatlán from Los Angeles and San Francisco, with connections to/from Seattle/Tacoma); **Continental,** airport, tel. (800) 9-0050 (direct flights to Mazatlán from Houston); **Delta,** airport, tel. (69) 82-4155 (nonstops to/from Los Angeles, with connections to/from Vancouver and Seattle via Los Angeles); **Mexicana Airlines,** Paseo Claussen 101-B, tel. (69) 82-7722 (nonstops to/from Denver, Guadalajara, Los Cabos, La Paz, Mexico City, Monterrey, and Torreón); and **Noroeste,** El Cid Mega Resort, tel. (69) 14-3833 (nonstops to/from Culiacán and Durango).

Airport Transportation: Most of the Zona Dorada hotels operate airport shuttle buses; some collect a US$4-5 fare, while others are free.

A taxi between the Zona Dorada and the airport costs around US$12, *colectivo* (share taxi) US$4 pp. Several times daily, city buses also go to the downtown area for around US$0.40.

Bus

Mazatlán's main bus terminal (signed both "Terminal de Autobuses" and "Central Camionera"), tel. (69) 82-8321, is on Calle Ferrusquilla, 3.5 blocks east of Hotel Las Arenas on Av. del Mar. The terminal is rather shabby given the overall important role Mazatlán plays as a west coast transportation junction. There are a couple of snackbars in the terminal (and lots of cheap restaurants in the vicinity)as well as a Western

Union office, but that's about it. Taxi fares, which are posted in the terminal, average around US$2 to most places in the city.

Transportes del Pacífico and **TNS** runs first-class buses every hour to Esquinapa (US$2.60), Nogales (US$36), Hermosillo (US$29), Guaymas (US$25), Ciudad Obregón (US$22), Navojoa (US$19), Los Mochis (US$15), Culiacán (US$8), and Tepic (US$9), plus once daily to Guadalajara (US$17) and Mexico City (US$39). Luxury bus lines with executive services to major Mexican cities include **Elite, Transpacífico,** and **Transportes Chihuahuenses.** Fares for these run about 10-25% higher than first-class bus fares on Transportes del Pacífico. Chihuahuenses runs once-daily buses to Durango (US$14), Chihuahua (US$33), Juárez (US$46), and Monterrey (US$39)

Train

The Tren del Pacífico line between Mexicali and Guadalajara is notorious for arriving well behind schedule and the unheated cars can become very drafty in the winter. For all but hard-core rail buffs, private bus lines are a much faster and more comfortable alternative.

If you're determined to travel by rail, Tren del Pacífico No. 2 leaves Nogales at 7 a.m. and arrives in Mazatlán around 4:30 a.m. In the reverse direction, train No. 1 is scheduled to depart Mazatlán at 10:55 p.m., arriving in Nogales at 9 p.m.; both trains connect in Benjamin Hill with the trunk line to/from Mexicali. Actual departure and arrival times vary considerably. The one-way fare to/from Nogales is US$16; this is less than the total cost of vehicle tolls along the newly completed four-lane highway! If you're starting from Mexicali, it's US$20. Trains to and from the following cities are also available: Guadalajara, Tepic, Culiacán, Navojoa, Cd. Obregón, Hermosillo, Empalme, Caborca, and Puerto Peñasco.

The railway station is in the Emiliano Zapata district off Camino al Conchi, not far from the intersection of Av. G. Leyva and the highway bypass (Entronque Carretera Internacional). The station's advance ticket office, tel. (69) 84-6710, is open Mon.-Sat. 8 a.m.-12:30 p.m. and 3-5 p.m., Sunday and holidays 8 a.m.-noon.

Ferry

A passenger-vehicle ferry runs between La Paz, B.C.S. and Mazatlán daily except Saturday from the Muelle Transbordador, at the southern end of Av. Carnaval on the Canal de Navigación leading into the main city harbor. SEMATUR, tel. (69) 81-7020, 85-5314, has a ticket office at Paseo Claussen 310 in the Olas Altas area where advance tickets can be purchased weekdays 8 a.m.-2 p.m.

For complete information on fares and departure times, see "By Ferry from Baja," under "Getting There" in the On the Road chapter.

Driving

The Mazatlán-Culiacán segment of the Nogales-Culiacán Carretera Internacional toll road was finally inaugurated in Nov. 1992, the last link in one of Mexico's finest highways. Mexican engineers reportedly built the highway with reference to specifications used by California and Texas state highway departments.

This shortens the old route from Culiacán by 26 km, though some drivers still prefer the old road because it passes through more scenic countryside (and saves the steep Culiacán-Mazatlán toll). The total car toll (two axles only) from Nogales to Mazatlán along Mexico 15D costs US$26.

Motorists coming from Durango and other points east will arrive via Mexico 40, one of the most scenic and harrying drives in Northern Mexico. Allow five to six hours to complete the 318-km (197-mile) road trip between the state capital of Durango and Mazatlán; the middle section through the Sierra Madre Occidental is known as Espinazo del Diablo or "Devil's Backbone" because the road is so precipitous and winding. Although most of the highway is paved, wide swaths of mud occasionally wash onto sections of road high in the mountains during the late summer monsoon season (when this road is best avoided). Gasoline is available in La Ciudad, 146 km (90.5 miles) west of Durango and again in Concordia just 15 km short of Mazatlán. For more information on this route, see "Durango to Mazatlán" in the Durango chapter.

GETTING AROUND

City Bus

Two city buses (urbanos) will serve all the needs of the typical visitor. Bus route No. 9 ("Sábalo/Cerritos-El Centro") runs between the northern end of the Zona Dorada and the central market, while the blue beachfront bus ("Sábalo-Paseo Costero") runs only along the waterfront from north to south. The Cerritos-Juárez bus stops at Gran Plaza mall and at the baseball stadium. Fares are a bargain US$0.22 each way and buses run frequently roughly 5:30 a.m.-10 p.m.; after 8 p.m. the fares cost a few centavos more. *Aurigas,* smaller covered Japanese pickup trucks with benches in the back, supplement the main bus routes with jump-on-anywhere ease.

Taxi

Cabs are plentiful in the downtown area and in the Zona Dorada. The standard fare to anywhere in town is US$1.50-2.

More popular than the standard taxicab are three-person, open-air, VW-powered carts called *pulmonías* (literally "pneumonia"), which cost about the same as a regular taxi. Bargaining is permissible, though most drivers will quote the standard fare right off.

Driving

Although gridlock is rare, traffic around the city is fairly turgid. Mid-afternoon is the worst time to be on the road. Make sure you have a good map before attempting downtown forays (see "Information," above).

Vehicle Rental

The following agencies offer auto rental: **Aga,** Calz. Camarón Sábalo 316, tel. (69) 14-4405; **Avis,** Las Palmas, tel. (69) 14-0040; **Budget,** Calz. Camarón Sábalo 402, tel. (69) 13-2000; **Hertz,** Calz. Camarón Sábalo 314, tel. (69) 13-6060; and **National,** Calz. Camarón Sábalo 7000, tel. (69) 13-6000; Calz. Camarón Sábalo s/n, tel. 86-4562; and airport, tel. 82-4000.

Rental rates vary slightly from company to company. The average rate for a no-frills VW bug is US$24 per day or US$140 a week; or for a Nissan Tsuru II (Sentra) US$53/300 per day/week; for a Jeep Wrangler US$61/364 per day/week; or for a VW combi (van) US$67/400 per day/week. With 200 free km, the bug costs US$55 per day, the combi US$99, the Tsuru II US$72. Most companies add surcharges for a/c and for automatic transmission over and above these rates (the VW bug has neither). Rates at Budget and National tend to run 10-15% higher than those at the other companies, although National advertises VW beetles for US$24 per 24 hours if you pick the car up between 6 p.m. and 8 p.m. and return it the same time the next day.

Several agencies in the Zona Dorada rent motorscooters for US$12-15 per day. For getting around town, this is a considerable savings over car rental.

LOCAL TOURS

Harbor Tour

The most popular tour in Mazatlán is the three-hour harbor cruise operated by **Yate Fiesta,** tel. (69) 85-2237, from the Isla del Crestón pier daily at 11 a.m.; mid-Dec.-April there's a second departure at 2 p.m. Passengers get a look at the shrimp fleet, packing docks for tuna, shrimp, and sardines, and Isla de la Piedra. The cost is US$8 per adult, half that for children ages 5-10. On board is a pay bar.

Jungle Tours

Most tours advertised as "jungle tours" in Mazatlán are boat excursions from the inner bay pier through inland mangrove-lined waterways to Isla de la Piedra. Along the way you'll get a look at the city's shrimp fleet and the seafood packing docks; at Isla de la Piedra you may be able to see iguanas, armadillos, pelicans, and herons. The average jungle tour costs US$20 pp, which includes transportation to/from your hotel, the boat ride, a *pescado zarandeado* lunch, and beverages (including beer). **King David Co. (Viajes Attiq),** Av. R.T. Loaiza 214, tel./fax (69) 14-2400, operates such tours each Tuesday, Thursday, and Saturday at 9:30 p.m. (hotel pickup at 9 a.m.).

Marlin Tours, Privada Laguna 300, Zona Dorada, tel. (69) 13-5301, operates a longer "jungle tour" to Teacapán's Laguna Agua Brava for US$45 pp (including continental breakfast, lunch, and drinks) on Tuesday, Friday, and Saturday.

Birds

Xico Tours, tel. (69) 85-1996, leads birding tours of the nearby Sierra Madre Occidental (tufted jay, eared trogon, yellow-eye junco, summer tanager, white-eared hummingbird, tufted flycatcher, black hawk) and Teacapán (ibis, stilt, jacana, loggerhead shrike, hooded oriole) for US$45 pp. Viajes Attiq (see "Jungle Tours," above) can take reservations for Xico Tours.

Other

Marlin Tours (see "Jungle Tours," above) also offers tours of the city (daily, US$11), Concordia-Copala (daily, US$28), and Rosario and Teacapán (Tuesday, Friday, Saturday, US$37).

VICINITY OF MAZATLÁN

El Quelite

This small town 39 km (24 miles) north of Mazatlán is famous as one of the last places in Mexico where *ulama,* a pre-Cortesian, Mesoamerican ball game, is still played. Surviving only in Sinaloa, *ulama* is played with a solid, rubberlike ball made from the fiber of a regional plant called *aguama* mixed with the milk of another plant, *machaguana.* This mixture is cooked over a fire until it thickens into a rubbery mass called *hule,* then cooled in a wooden mold until it forms a sphere. Between games, the 4.5-kilogram (10-pound) *hule* must be kept in its wooden mold in order to keep its shape.

Once a religious game (in which the winners were sacrificed) played by priests or the highest warriors, today's secular *ulama* is played on a rectangular sand court called a *tachtli* or *taxtli* that measures 50 by 40 meters. *Tahures* (players) wear protective leather pads and can strike the ball using only their elbows, shoulders, hips, and ankles. Other customary playing garb includes cotton shorts, over which is worn a deerskin loincloth *(fajado)* tied with a leather belt. The players' feet are bare.

Two teams of six players each (one of whom serves, but doesn't field the ball) compete in each match, which is refereed by two umpires *(veedores).* A point is scored each time a team brings the ball forward of a designated line, while points are lost each time the ball touches any part of a player's body other than the legal strike areas. The first team to score eight points wins.

El Quelite's court, El Taste, is at the far end of town. Matches are generally played on Sundays, and visitors are welcome to watch. Other towns in southern Sinaloa where *ulama* is still

played include Llanitos, Escuinapa, El Chilillo, Villa Unión, Las Moras, and La Savila.

Dimas

This rail junction town near the coast around 65 km (40 miles) north of Mazatlán via Mexico 15 has little to recommend it unless you surf. A beach break at the Río Piaxtla rivermouth can happen any time of year. According to *Surf Report,* further south between Dimas and Marmol are more surf breaks, including a summer swell left and right outside break that reforms closer to shore. Just south of Marmol, a beach break known as "Ruco's" is also reportedly good at times.

Barras de Piaxtla

Surfers into high waves and serious solitude should seek out Punta Piaxtla near the village of Barras de Piaxtla. The *barras* ("bars") in the name refer to basalt cliffs along the left bank of the Río Piaxtla where it empties into the sea; over a distance of several kilometers these cliffs gradually descend from a height of 47 meters (155 feet) to smooth sand beaches. The main surf can be found on the south side of *el faro* (the lighthouse), and the locals say that during storms the waves are way overhead. On the coast about seven km south of Barras de Piaxtla is an Amerindian rock art site called **Piedras Labradas;** it's sometimes submerged by the tide. Ask locally for directions or a guide.

One local, no-name restaurant on the beach prepares seafood dishes during the day. Rumors say a 330-hectare project that will include an 18-hole golf course and a luxury hotel is on the way.

To find Piaxtla you must first get to the railway junction town of Dímas (see above). A rutted, dirt road leads southwest from Dímas to Barras de Piaxtla. A high-clearance vehicle is recommended; during times of heavy rain this road may be impassable without 4WD.

Rancho Las Moras

About 30 minutes (21 km) northeast of the city by car, this exclusive guest ranch offers all-inclusive vacations in a 150-year-old mezcal (cousin to tequila) hacienda set on 3,000 acres. Recreational activities include horseback riding, tennis, nature hikes, and swimming in the ranch pool. Among other ranch facilities are a menagerie of exotic animals (including llamas, miniature ponies, and peacocks) and a whitewashed chapel overlooking the surrounding countryside.

Six guest rooms ("villas") in the main 19th-century building with original carved wooden doors, some salvaged from haciendas elsewhere, cost well into our exclusive category—if you have to ask, you can't afford it (US$200-400 range)—but include all meals served on the hacienda's dining terrace.

Transportation from Mazatlán International Airport is provided by Rancho Las Moras, or, if you have your own transportation, they will send directions upon confirmation of your reservation. For further information or reservations, contact Rancho Las Moras, Av. C. Sábalo 204, Suite 6, Mazatlán, Sin. 82110 or 9297 Siempre Viva Rd., Suite 15-474, San Diego, CA 92173, tel. (69) 16-5044, fax 16-5045.

Concordia

Founded by Spanish grandée Francisco de Ibarra as a mission pueblo in 1565, and later expanded as a silver mining center, this mountain hamlet lies 45 km east of Mazatlán on scenic Mexico 40. Much of the town (pop. 26,000) looks the same as it did 200 years ago, with cobblestoned streets and tile-roofed stucco homes, though development along the highway is less charming.

The hilly town boasts the state's oldest standing church, **Iglesia de San Sebastián.** Built in the baroque style 1705-85, the pink stone portico is its most striking feature. The giant rocking chair on the town plaza symbolizes Concordia's major claim to fame, furniture-making, which has been a local industry since the 17th century. Most of the furniture is made with Mexican pine from Durango and Chihuahua, but a local tree called *guanacostle,* with a very large trunk and characteristics similar to ebony, is also used in some furniture crafting, as is cedar imported from Ecuador and Colombia. The town is also well known for ceramics. Both Mexican and gringo tourists flock here to buy pottery and furniture.

Tepuxtla, 24 km (15 miles) northwest of Concordia via paved road, is famous for handforged *machetes.*

Practicalities: Budget accommodations are available near the highway at **Hotel Rancho Viejo,** tel. (696) 8-0290, a relaxed place with a sweet older couple running the show. Rooms are simple and clean, and a shaded patio is lined with rocking chairs and other locally made furniture items. To find the hotel, turn right under the bridge and then follow the road underneath the highway. **Restaurant El Granero,** near the Iglesia de San Sebastián, has the best local food. There are also several dubious-looking *loncherías* on the highway.

A PEMEX station is on the highway near the town entrance.

Mexico 40, the highway between Mazatlán and Durango, becomes increasingly steep and winding beyond Concordia.

Copala

Copala, 21 km (13 miles) east of Concordia along Mexico 40, was founded in the same year as neighboring Concordia, but is even more quaint as virtually all of the buildings are in the rustic provincial-colonial style. Built over cliffs, ravines, and steep lower Madrean slopes (elev. 2,300 feet/690 meters), the town's whitewashed

Copalá

houses, tiled roofs, and narrow, cobblestoned streets are vaguely reminiscent of Tuscany.

The baroque **Iglesia de San José** was begun in 1740 and completed in 1775, by which time the town's population had swelled to 10,000 on the success of local silver mines. During the brief 1860s reign of Maximilian, the French kept a garrison here. Current residents number around a thousand; electricity arrived only in the 1970s.

A sketch map of the town from Daniel's Restaurant outlines a walking tour that will take you past the church and plaza, old courthouse, bullring, and jail to a viewpoint over the town.

Practicalities: Posada San José, on the small town plaza opposite the church, houses guests in a 400-year-old building that served as headquarters for the Butter Copala Mining Company until the early 1940s. Each of the cozy rooms has two beds and private bath; shoestring rates (US$8-10). Downstairs is the **Butter Company,** a restaurant serving inexpensive standard Mexican fare for breakfast, lunch, and dinner.

Daniel's Restaurant, tel. (696) 85-4225, near the town entrance from Mexico 40, is a rambling eatery that caters to bus tourists. Owned by Daniel Garrison, a booster of local restoration and tourism, the restaurant allows buses to park in the large lot in front since Copala's streets are too narrow for bus traffic. Besides good Mexican specialties (perhaps over-billed as "the best Mexican food in Mexico"), the restaurant is famous for banana-coconut cream pie. The dining room is open daily 9 a.m.-5 p.m. Daniel's also has a few rooms for rent for US$10 a head.

Capilla de Taxtle

Shown simply as "El Taxtle" on some maps, this village perched on the mid-level western slopes of the Sierra Madre Occidental has one primary attraction, the anomalous German-style **Motel Villa Blanca** on the west side of Mexico 40, about 18 km north of Copala. The quaint, budget-priced rooms are decorated with German and Mexican antiques. From the roof of the inn you can see all the way to Mazatlán and the Pacific coast. Parking space is also available for self-contained campers and RVs. Meals available. Rates: US$35 per night including three meals (mostly German food), or US$15 s, US$25 d without meals.

The area around the inn is suitable for long walks with views of surrounding mountains and

Nuestra Señora del Rosario

valleys. Away from the highway, local wildlife includes white-tailed deer, coyote, fox, wild turkey, and jaguarundi.

Rosario

Forty-four km (27 miles) southeast of Mazatlán via Mexico 15 on the way to Teacapán, Rosario is a nondescript town on the banks of the Río Baluarte; like many towns in northwestern Mexico, it went through a boom-and-bust cycle with the discovery and exhaustion of local silver and gold deposits.

The town's 18th-century **Templo de Nuestra Señora del Rosario** contains a large and gilded baroque altar. Opposite the church stands a 1990-vintage statue of Our Lady of Rosario with hand outstretched and mouth open as if singing. An inscription partially translates as "Rosario, you gave birth to us and raised to all the world the song of Mexico." The late Mexican *cantadora* Lola Beltrán, a Rosario native and probably the most famous Mexican female vocalist of the 20th century, supposedly posed as a model for the figure. Beltrán died in 1996 at the age of 64; after lying in state at the Bellas Artes in Mexico City and then the Teatro Angela Peralta in Mazatlán, she was buried in the town cemetery.

Three or four decent hotels in the shoestring range are available in Rosario. **Hotel San Angel,** tel. (695) 2-1199, a modern-looking brick place near the south end of town, represents perhaps the best value, with a/c rooms, a restaurant, and bar. Rates: US$10 s, US$12 d; add US$2/3 for TV.

Laguna El Caimanero and Playa Caimanera
West of Rosario via a 30-km (18.6-mile) partially paved road lies **Laguna el Caimanero,** also known as Laguna del Huizache, an estuarial lagoon formed near the mouth of the Río Baluarte. Along the way are several farms cultivating mangoes, coconuts, and other fruits and vegetables. Although shrimp farming around the lagoon has impacted on precious waterbird habitat to some extent, birding along the shores of the lagoon remains superb. Follow the road beyond Agua Verde to arrive at **Playa Caimanera,** a so-so beach backed by 32 km (20 miles) of sand dunes and a string of *palapa* restaurants. Sea turtles lay eggs along the beach in late summer and early fall.

Teacapán
This off-the-beaten-track destination is slowly gaining in popularity but is still little known—even among people who vacation yearly in Mazatlán, 107 km (66 miles) to the north.

The main attraction here is 80 km (35 miles) of inland mangrove-lined estuarial waterways, including Laguna El Caimanero, Laguna Los Cerritos, Laguna Agua Grande, Estero Teacapán, and Estero Puerto del Río. Snook, mackerel, and bay snapper fishing is said to be excellent in the area; nonanglers like to visit for the natural environment and overall *tranquilidad.*

The 41-km (25.4-mile), two-lane, paved road between Escuinapa del Hidalgo (the junction with Mexico 15) and Teacapán passes between pretty lagunas Grande and Los Canales, both with plenty of waterfowl, as well as through plantations of mango, papaya, sugarcane, casava, and coconut; according to the state government, there are over three million coconut palms in this area.

Several Pacific beaches, including **Playa Las Cabras, Playa Los Angeles** (also called Playa Angel), and **Playa La Tambora,** can be visited via

sandy side roads that branch off the Escuinapa-Teacapán road. La Tambora is the cleanest of the three; the turnoff for this beach is about 35 km from the highway (follow signs to Lupita's and Big River RV). It's not unusual to see dolphins swimming relatively close to the beach. Tambora features a good beach break that builds to tremendous proportions during tropical storms.

The town of Teacapán itself offers little more than a collection of boxy stucco buildings clustered around a tiny plaza. A short walk west will take you to the edge of a sand-encircled peninsula that looks like something plucked from the South China Sea, complete with colorful fishing boats and waving coconut palms. *Pangas* can be chartered for cruises around the lagoon in search of tree iguanas, crocodiles, tropical birds (including the flamingo-like roseate spoonbill), and dolphins.

Kayaking or canoeing is excellent in these environs. One can put in at Teacapán and follow **Estero Teacapán** south till it curves around the peninsula in the opposite direction and joins **Estero Agua Grande,** which then leads north to **Laguna Agua Grande,** a journey of around 30 km (18.6 miles).

A more ambitious alternative would be to cut east from Estero Teacapán just below **Isla La Palma,** then follow **Estero Puerto del Río** 45 km south until it feeds into massive **Laguna Agua Brava** in the state of Nayarit. Camping is possible on islets and high shores along the way; bring plenty of food, drinking water, and insect repellent.

Accommodations: Rancho Los Angeles Teacapán Ecológico, on Playa Los Angeles, tel. (695) 3-2550 is a new motel/resort offering comfortable a/c rooms with private hot-water showers, plus a pool, trampoline, restaurant, horse rental, sand volleyball courts, and *palapa* beach bar. It's run on the all-inclusive plan: US$35 pp per day covers lodging, food, and all activities except horseback riding. Ecological tours of the lagoons by *panga* can also be arranged at extra cost.

The shoestring-priced **Hotel Denisse,** built around a small courtyard on the Teacapán plazuela, offers clean rooms with ceiling fans (no a/c) and good bathrooms. Rates: US$15 s/d, or US$10 per night if booked by the week. You can write in advance for reservations to Hotel Denisse, Calles R. Buelna y Morelos, Teacapán, Sin. 82560. The management can arrange *panga*

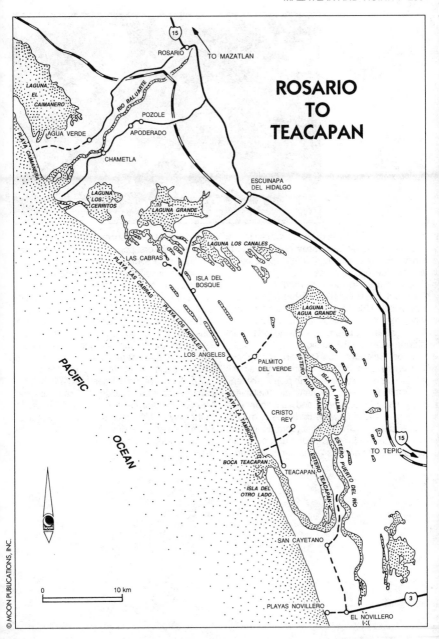

ROSARIO TO TEACAPAN

TO MAZATLAN

ROSARIO

LAGUNA EL CAIMANERO

RIO BALUARTE

POZOLE

AGUA VERDE

APODERADO

CHAMETLA

PLAYA CAMARONERA

ESCUINAPA DEL HIDALGO

LAGUNA LOS CERRITOS

LAGUNA GRANDE

LAGUNA LOS CANALES

LAS CABRAS

ISLA DEL BOSQUE

LAGUNA AGUA GRANDE

PLAYA LAS CABRAS

PLAYA LOS ANGELES

LOS ANGELES

PALMITO DEL VERDE

ESTERO AGUA GRANDE

ISLA LA PALMA

PACIFIC OCEAN

PLAYA LA TAMBORA

CRISTO REY

TO TEPIC

BOCA TEACAPAN

TEACAPAN

ESTERO PUERTO DEL RIO

ESTERO TEACAPAN

ISLA DEL OTRO LADO

SAN CAYETANO

0   10 km

PLAYAS NOVILLERO

EL NOVILLERO

© MOON PUBLICATIONS, INC.

cazonero, *Teacapán*

JOE CUMMINGS

trips. If the Denisse is booked up, you can stay at the shoestring **Motel Gratos** or **Motel Santa Cruz** in Escuinapa (around US$8-11), but they're a very poor second choice.

Camping: On the side road to Playa La Tambora, **Big River RV Park** has full RV/trailer hookups for US$8 per night, tent sites for somewhat less. You can also camp on the beach for free or at nearby **Lupita's,** a private *palapa* picnicking area, for US$2 a night.

Food: Restaurant La Tambora and **Cabaña El Cerezo,** both at Playa Tambora, serve fresh seafood and cold beer beneath *palapa* shelters.

Simple, fresh seafood meals are available at rustic cafes in Escuinapa and Teacapán. One local specialty is *tamales barbones* or "bearded tamales," in which *masa* (corn dough) flavored with fish broth is folded around garlic, onions, *chiles anchos asados,* cumin, and a peeled and deveined shrimp with the head on so that the "whiskers" poke out. Pineapple tamales are another local delicacy to look for.

Shops around Teacapán's plazuela sell chilled young coconuts, very refreshing in hot weather. *La tuba,* a fiery fermented and distilled palm juice, is available for US$0.15 per *trago.*

Transportation: Transportes de Escuinapa runs second-class buses between Mazatlán and Teacapán several times a day for US$2.50 each way. Both Escuinapa and Teacapán have PEMEX stations with Magna Sin and diesel.

An alternative way to head south from Teacapán without backtracking to Escuinapa and Mexico 15 is to ferry across Estero Teacapán to the Nayarit fishing village of San Cayetano. From here you can catch a bus through El Novillero east to Acaponeta farther south on Mexico 15.

BOB RACE

THE STATE OF CHIHUAHUA

Although Mexico City's *chilangos* might not agree, in many ways Chihuahua—Mexico's largest state—has functioned as the country's spiritual heartland during the post-Spanish era. As Mexico slowly forged a separate identity for itself, Chihuahua stood by as instigator and protector of Mexican sovereignty, serving variously as refuge for national hero Benito Juárez during the Mexican War of Reform, as headquarters for the resistance government during the French occupation, as the last state to recognize Porfirio Díaz's dictatorial rule, and as home to Pancho Villa and his triumphant División del Norte during the Mexican Revolution. In fact the revolution was born when Francisco I. Madero crossed from El Paso into Chihuahua in 1910.

Around 80 separate Amerindian tribes inhabited what is now the state of Chihuahua at one time or another, including the famous Paquimé of Casas Grandes, a ruined city that has been linked to the Anasazi and Pueblo Indian cultures of the U.S. Southwest. Most of Chihuahua's peaceful tribes died out in the face of Spanish conquest or were absorbed by Mexican culture. A major exception are the reclusive Tarahumaras, a sub-

stantial number of whom still live in traditional villages in the Sierra Madre Occidental.

In the late 17th century, the more violent Plains Indians began venturing south from the Rocky Mountains to attack Chihuahuans—natives and immigrants alike. For 200 years (roughly 1686 to 1886), Chihuahua bore the brunt of Comanche and Apache raids on Mexico; in the U.S. such attacks occurred over a period less than half as long. According to local mythology, "wild" Apaches ("Apache," incidentally, comes from *apachu,* the Zuni word for "enemy") are still living a clandestine existence in the northwestern Sierra Madre Occidental.

In the imagination of many Mexicans, Chihuahua plays a role similar to that played by Texas in the American psyche: It's huge (12.51% of Mexico's total area); it's perceived as "bold and rugged"; and it's identified with a frontier ethos that is as important a part of modern Mexico's spiritual heritage as the place held by Texas mythology in U.S. culture. The Texas symbol that resonates most in the U.S. is the Alamo; for Chihuahua and Mexico it's Francisco "Pancho" Villa, leader of the only foreign army ever to

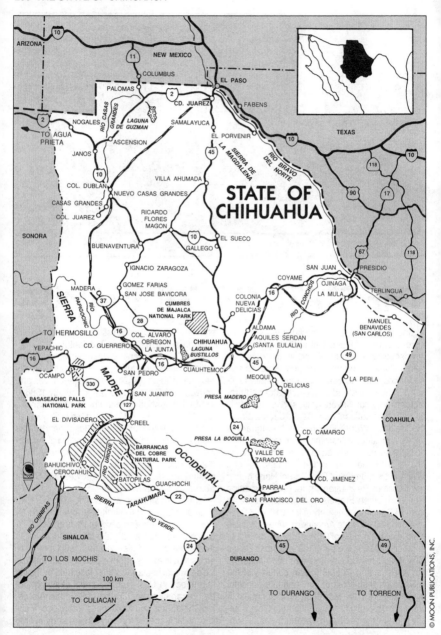

invade the continental United States. Both symbols are associated with tragic outcomes, all the better to keep the memory alive and poignant.

Like Texas, Chihuahua today is a wealthy state, with the fourth highest per-capita ownership of automobiles among the states of Mexico (after Mexico D.F., Baja California Norte, and Baja California Sur). Around a fifth of the nation's *maquiladoras* (twin-plant or in-bond manufacturing facilities) have been established here, although the largest export commodities remain timber and wood products from the Sierra Madre.

The state's second largest occupation is cattle ranching, which produces Angus, Hereford, and Charolais cattle for domestic and U.S. beef markets. Chihuahua and Sonora maintain a constant rivalry over which state produces the best beef. (Sound familiar, Texans and Kansans?) Chihuahua also produces a very tough rodeo steer, a direct descendant of the *criolla* breed brought to the New World by the Spanish four centuries ago. Because it is capable of running for nearly 10 hours straight, it is highly prized by U.S. pro-rodeo associations.

Texans like to brag about how big their ranches are, but historically Chihuahua had even bigger ranches than the Lone Star state's famous King spread. The largest, the Terrazas hacienda, at its peak encompassed over 20 million acres, an area equal to Switzerland, Belgium, Holland, and Denmark combined. American publishing tycoon William Randolph Hearst owned the 875,000-acre Babícora Ranch (centered around modern-day Gómez Farías), which ran 20,000 head of Hereford and 22,000 sheep. Following the Mexican Revolution, some of the larger ranches were expropriated by the Mexican government and divided into 30- to 50-acre *ejidos* under the collective ownership of mestizo peasants.

Many powerful ranching families managed to keep parts of their ranches intact, however, and today the state has a more sympathetic outlook on land ownership and free enterprise than most other states in Mexico. While most of the rest of the country has continued to support one-party, PRI rule, rebellious Chihuahuans elected a PAN governor in 1992 for a six-year term.

Geography

Roughly half the size of Spain, Mexico's largest state stretches across a remarkably varied terrain of desert, grasslands, chaparral, river valleys, and high mountains. Towering over the southwestern quarter of the state is the vast Sierra Madre Occidental, a green citadel of 2,700-meter (9,000-foot) peaks, sparkling rivers, and gaping chasms. The northeastern half is covered by the desert scrublands, low mountains, alluvial fans, and *bolsones* (salt lakes) of the Chihuahuan Desert—North America's largest desert. Wedged between highlands and desert, occupying about a quarter of the state's center, are the *llanos*—a section of grass basins and low wooded sierras—and the rolling hills of the *llomería*.

Pancho Villa and his troops, 1914

CIUDAD JUÁREZ

INTRODUCTION

Largest city in the state (pop. 1.2 million), fourth largest in Mexico, and probably the largest border city in the world, Ciudad Juárez is a bursting metropolis that sits 1,128 meters (3,760 feet) above sea level on the Río Bravo/Rio Grande, at the edge of the Chihuahuan Desert where the states of Chihuahua, New Mexico, and Texas meet. For most visitors to Mexico it's merely a border crossing—a very large and daunting one with a maze of city streets fanning out in all directions. For residents of neighboring El Paso it's a destination in its own right for food, nightlife, shopping, and greyhound and horse racing.

When visiting Ciudad Juárez, keep in mind it has the highest consumer price index in Mexico. For most American and Canadian visitors, shopping remains a bargain, but accommodations and food typically cost more than anywhere else in Mexico. Part of the reason for this is the city's overall affluence, but what really boosts prices is the fact that the city is virtually in the middle of nowhere; transportation adds a premium to most costs. Many everyday consumer items are U.S. goods brought in from El Paso. In spite of the relatively high cost of living, the city has Mexico's fifth highest U.S. expatriate population—more than 28,000 at last count.

Culturally Juárez has always followed its own path. Juárez Straight American Whiskey has been produced here since 1909 at a distillery founded by two Kentucky entrepreneurs and run by Mexicans since the post-WW II era. The 1940s' zoot-suited *pachuco* culture emanated out of Juárez, and today the city's artists and scholars are at the forefront of the new *fronteriza* culture that blends Latin and American pop cultures to produce such hybrids as Spanish-language rap music and hyper-real photography. On the darker side, the city has become one of the capitals for Mexico's drug culture, with regard to both use and trafficking. The murder rate—most of it narco-related—is estimated to be one of the highest in the country. But crimes against tourists—even petty theft—are rare.

History

Ciudad Juárez (pronounced WHAH-res) is the oldest town along the entire U.S.-Mexico border. New Spain's Rodríguez-Chamuscado expedition mapped a convenient river crossing and mountain pass here in 1581, though Cabeza de Vaca may have stopped here on his epic journey as early as 1527. The crossing was dubbed El Paso del Norte ("Northern Pass") and soon became an important relay point for Spanish colonization northward. Later, Anglo-American opportunists coming from the east used the pass to continue west to California through what is today Mexican territory.

Lured by Indian stories of gold in the mountains of New Mexico and West Texas, Don Juan de Oñate led a group of several hundred Spaniards across the Chihuahuan Desert to the pass in 1598. De Oñate found no substantial gold or silver deposits in the area (though legend persists he may have stashed a vast treasure in the so-called "Lost Padre Mine" in nearby mountains), but he brought back word that the area was suitable for long-term settlement, with a mild climate and year-round water.

Sixty-one years after de Oñate came north, Franciscan friar García de San Francisco was sent to El Paso del Norte to establish a mission. On Dec. 8, 1659, at a site that is now in downtown Ciudad Juárez, Fray García constructed a simple adobe mission dedicated to Nuestra Señora de Guadalupe. It was one of the first churches dedicated to that patron, and became the first successful mission among the area's Manso Indians. The mission introduced agriculture and livestock to the Indians and constructed irrigation canals to divert water to the fields. Among other agricultural accomplishments, the friar planted vineyards in the valley and supplied missions of the region with wine. The village that grew up around the mission became an important stop on the Camino Real or "Royal Road," which extended between Chihuahua City and Santa Fe and later became known as the Chihuahua-Santa Fe Trail—the very first road in North America. This route is now followed by Mexico 45 (the Pan-American

MYSTERY DOG

Typically standing no higher than 13 cm (5.1 inches) at the shoulder and weighing from one-half to three kilograms (one to six pounds), the Chihuahua is the world's smallest dog breed. Though dog fanciers the world over are familiar with its short, pointed ears and large, round eyes, the reasons that the diminutive canine shares the name of the Mexican state and city are lost to history. Legend says the pre-Cortesian natives of Mexico bred the Chihuahua's ancestors, a claim for which there is no archaeological evidence. Another theory says the breed was brought by the conquistadors from Spain, but again, no records have been found to confirm or refute this idea.

Since breeding tiny dogs was popular in imperial China, perhaps the most plausible explanation is that the Chihuahua accompanied the wave of Chinese immigrants who landed on Mexico's Pacific coast in the 19th century. Since many Chinese worked as miners and farmers in the northwestern states of Sonora and Chihuahua, it's possible that, as the breed multiplied, the miniature dogs from this area of Mexico became associated with 19th-century Chihuahua (which to North Americans at the time was much better known than Sonora).

Today the Chihuahua as a "pure" breed has been all but lost in its namesake state. While Chihuahua has plenty of dogs, few can be considered true Chihuahuas, and state residents today show no particular interest in the breed. In Mexico the dogs are known as *chihuahueños* while the human residents of the state are *chihuahuenses* and only the city and state are known as Chihuahua. When speaking Spanish in Chihuahua, try to keep these straight, as using the terms incorrectly could be taken as an insult by some *chihuahuenses*.

The first Anglo-Americans began moving into the area in 1827, and by the late 1840s five small Anglo settlements had been established north of the Río Bravo. One settlement, Franklin, became the political anchor for what is today El Paso, Texas. Immediately following the loss of New Mexico and Texas to the U.S. via the 1848 Treaty of Guadalupe Hidalgo, the U.S. Army established Fort Bliss on the north side of the Río Bravo, which became the border between the two countries.

The Mexican side of El Paso del Norte continued to grow and prosper until civil war struck both sides of the border. In the U.S., the Confederates briefly occupied Fort Bliss, while on the Mexican side, Benito Juárez and his liberal reformists made El Paso del Norte the provisional capital of Mexico while awaiting the outcome of Mexico's War of Reform. Almost immediately following the reformists' 1861 victory, the French invaded Mexico and the Juárez government remained in exile in El Paso del Norte until they were able to return to Mexico City in 1867. In honor of Benito Juárez's local tenure, the city's name was changed from El Paso del Norte to Ciudad Juárez in 1888.

Today Ciudad Juárez is still capitalizing on its location, now the junction of three major interstate highways (I-25, I-10, and Mexico 45) and several railways. Rail and truck shipping are a major source of income, along with revenue from 13 industrial parks skirting the city's perimeters. The city also serves as an important regional education center, with four major colleges and universities: Universidad Autónoma de Ciudad Juárez, Instituto Tecnológico de Ciudad Juárez, Instituto Tecnológico de Monterrey (a branch of the original ITM), and Universidad Autónoma de Chihuahua.

SIGHTS

Ciudad Juárez doesn't have a lot to see in terms of traditional "tourist attractions," but if you find yourself stuck here for the day you'll have more than a few ways to pass the time. The city's parks, museums, and markets make it a fairly pleasant city to visit once you have your bearings.

Misión Nuestra Señora de Guadalupe
Facing the west side of Plaza Principal (also called Plaza de Armas) between the Palacio

Highway) south of the border and by US Interstate 25 north of the border.

In 1690 another mission, Ysleta del Sur, was founded nearby to receive Tigua and Piro refugees from the Pueblo Indian Revolt in Ysleta, New Mexico. As Villa Paso del Norte's strategic importance increased, the Spanish built a military garrison near Ysleta del Sur to defend the pass against Apache raids.

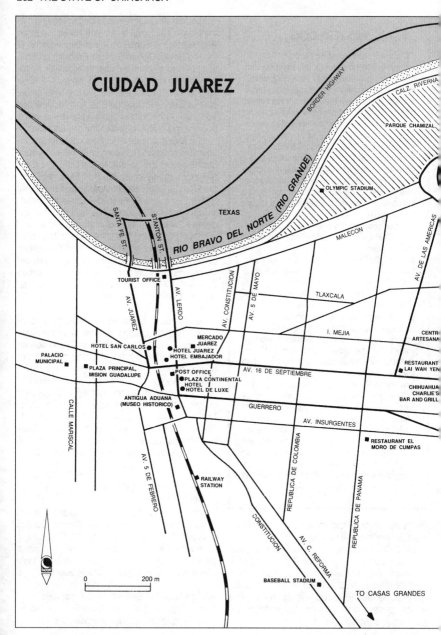

CIUDAD JUAREZ

BORDER HIGHWAY

CALZ. RIVERNA

PARQUE CHAMIZAL

OLYMPIC STADIUM

SANTA FE ST.

STANTON ST.

TEXAS

RIO BRAVO DEL NORTE (RIO GRANDE)

MALECON

AV. DE LAS AMERICAS

TOURIST OFFICE

AV. LERDO

AV. JUAREZ

AV. CONSTITUCION

AV. 5 DE MAYO

TLAXCALA

I. MEJIA

CENTR
ARTESANA

HOTEL SAN CARLOS

MERCADO
JUAREZ

PALACIO
MUNICIPAL

PLAZA PRINCIPAL,
MISION GUADALUPE

HOTEL JUAREZ
HOTEL EMBAJADOR

POST OFFICE

RESTAURANT
LAI WAH YEN

AV. 16 DE SEPTIEMBRE

PLAZA CONTINENTAL
HOTEL
HOTEL DE LUXE

CHIHUAHUA
CHARLIE'S
BAR AND GRILL

ANTIGUA ADUANA
(MUSEO HISTORICO)

GUERRERO

AV. INSURGENTES

CALLE MARISCAL

AV. 5 DE FEBRERO

REPUBLICA DE COLOMBIA

RESTAURANT EL
MORO DE CUMPAS

RAILWAY
STATION

CONSTITUCION

AV. C. REFORMA

REPUBLICA DE PANAMA

0   200 m

BASEBALL STADIUM

TO CASAS GRANDES

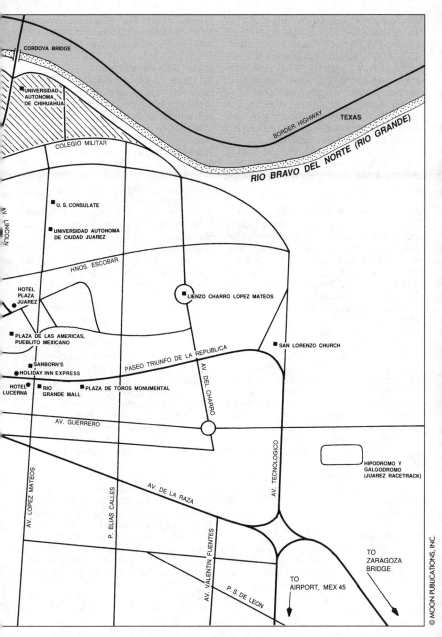

Municipal and Mercado Cuauhtémoc, off Calle Mariscal downtown, this humble stone church is dwarfed by the modern cathedral next door.

The original mission was built under the direction of Fray García de San Francisco between 1668 and 1670 and has been restored numerous times. To appreciate Guadalupe's historic charm, you must enter the church, walk halfway down the center aisle, and look up to see the superb handcarved vigas (wooden roof beams) and *coro* (choir mezzanine). The pine vigas appear almost as beautiful and fresh as they must have looked over 300 years ago, when the Manso Indians carved the floral and pine cone designs.

Museo Histórico de Ciudad Juárez

This INAH-sponsored museum in the recently restored Antigua Aduana (Old Customs) building, on Av. 16 de Septiembre between Av. Juárez and Av. Lerdo, is perhaps the city's most important cultural center. The building's central hall hosts temporary, rotating exhibits on history, archaeology, or anthropology, while rooms surrounding the hall contain the museum's permanent collection.

The first room (Sala 1) begins with Chihuahuan prehistory, including displays on the Conchos, Tobosos, Tepehuanes, Sumas, and Jumanos, while the second room (Sala 2) is entirely devoted to the Paquimé culture. Rooms three and four (Salas 3 and 4) continue with the Spanish conquest, Mexican independence, and the Virreinato; followed by the Epoca Nacional and the history of the Chamizal (Sala 5); La Apachería and the Porfiriato (Salas 6, 7, and 8); and the Mexican Revolution (Salas 8 and 9).

American and European films are presented twice a week in the museum's auditorium. The museum is open Tues.-Sun. 10 a.m.-6 p.m.; admission is free.

Museo de Arte

Sponsored by the Instituto Nacional de Bellas Artes, this small museum in the former PRONAF center (now called Plaza de las Américas) houses rotating contemporary art exhibits of varying quality. Museum hours are Tues.-Sun. 10 a.m.-6 p.m.; free admission.

The Cine Club Francés screens French films for the public (free admission) at the Museo de Arte every Sunday evening at 7:30 p.m.

Museo de la Revolución

On the second floor of Pueblito Mexicano in Plaza de las Américas, this small commercial operation is devoted to the 1910-20 Mexican Revolution, with a heavy emphasis on local hero Francisco Villa. Displays include weaponry, period clothing, historic photos (many of them taken by foreign journalists), and newspapers from the era. Open Tues.-Sun. 10 a.m.-10 p.m.; admission US$0.50.

Parque Conmemorativo Chamizal

The flood plains encompassed by this 700-acre park were once a serious bone of contention between the U.S. and Mexican governments. Because the Río Bravo-Rio Grande—the natural border between the two countries—occasionally changed course (thus taking huge chunks of land away from one country or the other), neither side was able to establish a mutually agreeable border until 1963, when the two governments agreed to build a concrete channel from which the river could not stray.

At the time of the agreement this meant an 823-acre gain for Mexico, most of which was converted into this national park. Chamizal is a local favorite for long-distance walkers and joggers who savor its shady trees, neat landscaping, and overall tranquillity. Other assets include a huge field of basketball courts near Av. Malecón, a swimming pool, an exposition center, and a soccer stadium used by the Cobras, a first-division pro team since 1987.

The park's **Museo de Antropología e Historia,** open Tues.-Sun. 9 a.m.-7 p.m. (free admission), contains a small collection of artifacts and the usual revolution-era photos, but the museum's real attraction is behind the building itself—a garden with ponds, flowers, trees, and large-scale reproductions of sculpture from ancient Mayan, Aztec, Toltec, Zapotec, Mixtec, Teotihuacán, Olmec, Tarascan, Totonac, and Huastec cultures. Although some of the reproductions are unfortunately deteriorating, a tour of the garden makes a nice stroll.

The park is closed to outside traffic in July, when it's used for Formula 3 racing. Horse cart rides are available in the park year-round for US$1.60 pp.

ACCOMMODATIONS

Although Ciudad Juárez's hotels can be a bit pricier than hotels elsewhere in Mexico, quality is generally higher than average as well. Efficient service is the norm, and much of the plumbing and fixtures used in hotel construction comes from north of the border.

Shoestring
Two downtown spots, **Hotel Juárez,** Av. Lerdo Nte. 143, tel. (16) 12-9985 and **Hotel Correo,** Av. Lerdo Sur 250, tel. (16) 15-0875, offer basic but adequate rooms. Rates: US$8-12.50 s, US$9-12.50 d. On Av. Juárez near the bridge, **Hotel San Carlos,** tel. (16) 15-0419, is a basic, two-story brick building. Rates: US$12 s, US$13 d; we got the impression you could negotiate the room rates further downward. Farther east but still downtown, **Motel Mi Ranchito,** Paseo Triunfo de la República 5825, tel. (16) 13-2029, is okay for a cheap night's sleep. Rates: US$7.80-10.50 s/d.

Budget
Visitors who want to be within walking distance of the Av. Juárez tourist strip, both municipal markets, and the Plaza Principal might consider the **Hotel Embajador,** at the corner of Av. F. Villa and Av. 16 de Septiembre, tel. (16) 12-0048. Once among the fanciest hotels in the city, the seven-story Embajador is faded a bit now, but good value. Rooms have TV, a/c, and phone. Rates: US$19.50 s, US$24.75 d.

Another good buy in the same price range is the clean and efficient, 140-room **Motel Chula Vista,** at the corner of Av. del Charro and Paseo Triunfo de la República on the east side of town, tel. (16) 17-1468, fax 18-6288. This is a good location for road departures south out of the city, yet still within easy driving or city bus distance of the downtown area. All rooms come with a/c and TV, and on the premises are a pool, restaurant, and bar.

On Av. Lerdo, near the Stanton Street Bridge to El Paso on the northwestern edge of town, are two aging places: **Hotel Santa Fe,** tel. (16) 14-0270 and **Hotel Impala,** tel. (16) 12-0431.

Both feature a/c and TV. The Impala is the nicer of the two and has a few rooms with kitchenettes. Rates: around US$21-23 s, US$26-28 d. In the center of Av. Lerdo, not far from Mercado Juárez, is the better-value **Plaza Continental Hotel,** tel. (16) 15-0084, fax 14-0531, formerly Hotel Continental, which offers 65 rooms with direct-dial phones and TV, plus parking. Rates: US$18-25.

On the same street and also near Mercado Juárez, the three-story **Hotel De Luxe,** Av. Lerdo Sur 300 (at Galeana), tel. (16) 15-0082, is another fair deal. Facilities include 68 clean rooms, piped-in ambient music, piano bar, nightclub, cafeteria, a/c, and fake grass courtyard. Rates: US$16.50 s, US$18 d.

Inexpensive
Racetrack enthusiasts or those needing to make a quick highway getaway might choose the tidy, 118-room, motel-style **Hotel Villa del Sol,** Paseo Triunfo de la República Sur 339, tel. (16) 17-2424 or 17-3030. It's near the Juárez Racetrack, the airport, and Mexico 45 South. This is one of the only hotels in this price range in town with a swimming pool. Rates: US$32 s, US$37 d.

The popular 175-room **Hotel Plaza Juárez,** Av. Lincoln at Coyoacán, tel. (16) 13-1310, fax 13-0084, has the advantage of being within walking distance of Plaza de las Américas. Facilities include a gym, travel agency, and pool. Rates: US$58 s/d. **Hotel Colonial Las Fuentes,** nearby at Av. Lincoln and Av. de las Américas, tel. (16) 13-5050, fax 13-4081, is equally well located and well maintained. All 219 rooms come with TV, a/c, minibar; there's also a pool, restaurant, and bar. Rates: US$42.75 s/d.

Moderate
The city's top-deck cruise is the **Hotel Lucerna,** at Paseo Triunfo de la República 3976 (corner of Av. López Mateos), tel. (16) 13-3232, fax (16) 13-3778, U.S./Canada tel. (800) LUCERNA. The Lucerna offers 138 fully equipped rooms, a heated pool, two bars, a disco, and a gourmet French restaurant. It's part of an independent, three-hotel chain whose other properties are in Mexicali and Tijuana. Rates: US$64.25 s, US$69 d.

Expensive
Next to Sanborn's Department Store on Paseo Triunfo de la República, the relatively new five-

star **Holiday Inn Express,** tel. (16) 29-6000, gives the Lucerna a run for its money, with 148 luxury rooms, a gym, pool, and coffee shop. Rates: US$84 s/d.

FOOD

Ciudad Juárez has hundreds of places to eat, from sidewalk taco stands to elegant dining rooms in restored Porfiriato mansions. In spite of the city's location adjacent to El Paso, its first McDonald's (at Av. López Mateos and Paseo Triunfo de la República) only opened in 1992.

Mexican

Chihuahua Charlie's Bar & Grill, Paseo Triunfo de la República 2525, tel. (16) 13-9940, is the northernmost outpost (in Mexico, that is) of the famed Grupo Anderson chain. Charlie's features a menu of original recipes based on such familiar Chihuahua standards as *carne asada* and *queso fundido,* along with fresh seafood (tequila shrimp and *huachinango a la veracruzana* are specialties) and homemade tortillas. Moderate prices. Open daily 8 a.m.-1 a.m.; live music Wednesdays and Sundays.

Degá Restaurant Bar, Av. 16 de Septiembre 1559, tel. (16) 14-6490, occupies a large, turn-of-the-century casa with a pleasant, understated decor. Degá offers a number of standard Mexican *platillos,* plus several daily specials. Very attentive service. Moderate to expensive. Open daily for lunch and dinner.

El Burrito Cristósomo is at the corner of Av. V. Guerrero and Av. de la Huerta, opposite Río Grande Mall (no phone). It's a simple but very popular stand-up diner with some of the city's best burritos and quesadillas. Inexpensive. Open 24 hours.

The bottom floor of the everyday-style **Mercado Cuauhtémoc,** off Calle Mariscal south of the Palacio Municipal, houses several inexpensive *loncherías,* the most popular of which are **Doña Chole** and **Cafetería Chávez.** It's a good spot for breakfast, lunch, or snacks; strolling *trovadores* entertain. Inexpensive. Open daily 7 a.m.-7 p.m.

Restaurant El Moro de Cumpas, Av. Insurgentes at Calle de la Raza, tel. (16) 13-8778, specializes in *comida norteña,* including *cabrito,*

carne asada, pollo asado, and *barbacoa.* Inexpensive to moderate. Open daily 11 a.m.-midnight.

Pueblito Mexicano (no phone), part of the Plaza de las Américas shopping center, holds a number of clean, inexpensive snack bars serving tasty tacos, *tortas,* and other *antojitos,* along with *licuados* and *dulces.* Open daily 10 a.m.-9 p.m. On the first floor of Pueblito Mexicano is **Restaurant Viva México,** tel. (16) 29-0156. The walls of the large, circular dining room are painted to look like a colonial cityscape in silhouette—kind of corny—but the food is very dependable and very Mexican, and the clientele is more local than gringo. The attached Cantina El Atorón serves "Pancho Villas" and *vampiros,* two typical Chihuahuan cocktails. Moderate prices. Open Mon.-Thurs. 8 a.m.-2 a.m., Fri.-Sat. 8 a.m.-3 a.m.

Steak

Las Brasas Restaurant Bar specializes in USDA prime beef and seafood. Two locations: Av. 16 de Septiembre and Anahuac, tel. (16) 12-8681, and Av. de las Américas and Mejía tel. (16) 13-6848. Moderate prices. Open daily 11 a.m.-11 p.m.

Restaurant Nuevo Martino, Av. Juárez 643, tel. 16-12-3370, is in the heart of the Av. Juárez bar-restaurant-disco strip. This venerable establishment is known for steak Milanesa (Mexico's version of chicken-fried steak) and Spanish brochette—skewered chunks of beef, onions, tomatoes, and green peppers served over Spanish rice. Moderate to expensive. Open daily 11 a.m.-midnight.

Restaurant Parrilla del Río, Av. Lincoln 1194, opposite Pueblito Mexicano, tel. (16) 13-0642, is generally considered to have the best Chihuahua-style steaks in town. Moderate to expensive. Open daily noon-11 p.m.

Miscellaneous

With at least eight branches throughout the city, **Café de Europa** and its wonderful pastries, ice cream, pizza, and espresso are never very far away. A convenient branch for most tourists is the one on Av. 16 de Septiembre near the intersection with Av. Juárez. Inexpensive to moderate. Open daily 7 a.m.-11 p.m.

Restaurant Lai Wah Yen is at Av. de las Americas 276 (at Av. 16 de Septiembre), tel. (16) 13-1291. This restaurant and the Shangri-La across the street try to outdo each other in opulent, Chinese banquet-style ambience; LWY has the edge. Moderate prices. Open daily noon-1 a.m.

Sanborn's, Paseo Triunfo de la República at Av. López Mateos (opposite Hotel Lucerna), tel. (16) 16-9203, is an old standby that serves a reliable menu of Mexican, American, and continental dishes at reasonable prices. Inexpensive to moderate. Open daily 7:30 a.m.-10 p.m.; special *almuerzo* buffet served 7:30 a.m.-1 p.m.

SHOPPING

Ciudad Juárez has two main shopping districts: the traditional area surrounding the cathedral and municipal markets near the intersection of Av. 16 de Septiembre and Av. Juárez; and the newer, flashier strip along Av. de las Américas, which caters to day-trippers from El Paso.

The government-sponsored **Centro Artesanal,** on Av. Lincoln opposite the Plaza de las Américas (formerly PRONAF), carries an extensive selection of quality ceramics—including some one-of-a-kind pieces—plus clothes, woodcarvings, masks, basketry, and other craft media, all of it handmade. Ample parking is available at Plaza de Américas opposite; several other upscale handicraft shops are in the vicinity.

In the Plaza de las Américas itself, the newish **Pueblito Mexicano** features a collection of small shops—a *farmacia, dulcería* (with sweets from all over Mexico), duty-free *perfumería,* photo studio where you can pose in old-fashioned Mexican clothing, and dozens more that haven't opened yet—around a simulated, enclosed (and a/c) town plaza. This is a major stop for the daily Border Jumper trolley-bus from El Paso.

Farther south in the same general area, **Sanborn's,** Paseo Triunfo de la República at Av. López Mateos, carries a small but high-quality selection of Mexican crafts, as well as English-language books and magazines, maps, and pharmaceuticals. Sanborn's *cafetería* is popular.

Closer to the real thing is the **Mercado Juárez,** Av. 16 de Septiembre at Av. Melgar, in the city's older shopping district. This funky, two-story market building is filled with vendors selling handicrafts, fruits, piñatas, clothes, foodstuffs,

silver, Mexican curios (my favorite, chess sets in which the opposing sides represent *federales* vs. revolutionaries, or conquistadors vs. Indians), and leather—some of it at good prices. Outside along one side of the building is a half-gentrified section with open-air cafes, restaurants, and ice-cream parlors.

More traditional yet is the three-floor **Mercado Cuauhtémoc,** off Calle Mariscal south of the cathedral. The ground floor is taken up with cheap *loncherías,* fresh meats, and *queso asadero* from Villa Ahumada. On the upper floors you'll find an assortment of live chickens, doves, parrots, fruits, flowers, medicinal herbs, and lucky buddhas (with crosses and other charms inside). East of the market, extending three or four blocks, is an outdoor market consisting mostly of fruit and vegetable vendors, while Calle Minas behind the market is lined with *carnicerías* (butcher shops) and various other *tiendas.*

A more mixed shopping venue, popular among tourists as well as locals, is **Av. Juárez,** which runs from the Puente Santa Fé border crossing south to Av. 16 de Septiembre. Small shops along the avenue offer Mexican-made boots, untaxed liquors, Cuban cigars, kitschy souvenirs, clothing, and a myriad of other items meant to please everyone, from the *campesino* with only a few pesos to spend, to first-time American visitors bent on emptying their pockets.

Ciudad Juárez has several modern shopping malls, the largest of which is **Río Grande Mall,** Paseo Triunfo de la República at Av. López Mateos. Shoes are among the best mall buys.

Many El Paso residents visit Ciudad Juárez regularly to take advantage of lower prices on pharmaceuticals. **Farmacias Catedral de Juárez** has three branches open 24 hours, the most conveniently located of which is at Av. López Mateos Nte. 372, tel. (16) 13-8988.

ENTERTAINMENT

Bars and Discos

For locals as well as tourists, Av. Juárez is the city's major entertainment center—a place where you can wander past an assortment of night spots designed for every budget and proclivity. Although this avenue is lined with bars and small discos, none really live up to the town's former wild reputation—especially since they close everything down at midnight, purportedly to curb teenage alcoholism in Juárez.

At the southern end of the avenue is a cluster of ranchero bars that feature dancing to live *norteña* music. Although this end of the avenue puts out a rough image, the clubs with cover charges (usually around US$2) are generally pretty safe. **El Sinaloense,** on Av. Juárez just north of 16 de Septiembre, usually has the best bands.

Another bar rich in local tradition is the 1920s-vintage **El Kentucky Club,** Av. Juárez 629 (between Tlaxcala and Colón), tel. (16) 14-9999; look for the building's tile front and chrome doors (the sign in front says "Kentucky Cantina"). Housed in a building that has been a cantina or bar for nearly 150 years, the Kentucky features a pretty carved wooden bar and loads of history. One of the more colorful stories of the origin of the margarita says it was invented here when a Mexican bullfighter was drinking tequila in the traditional Mexican way—straight shots sandwiched between a pinch of salt and a squeeze of lime. When his female companion requested a more "ladylike" drink, the bartender improvised a cocktail of lime juice, tequila, and Controy—and named the drink after her. Marilyn Monroe reportedly celebrated her quickie Mexican divorce from playwright Arthur Miller by buying everyone a round of drinks at the Kentucky Club. El Kentucky's wood-paneled ambience still attracts a few regulars.

Another long-running place is the amazing **Cavern of Music**—also called Las Glutas Bar—near the intersection of Av. Juárez and Ignacio Mejía. The bar's entrance is built to look like the mouth of a cave. The women's room at Las Glutas has a famous statuette of Adam with movable fig leaf—lift the leaf and flashing lights go on in the bar.

The **Mariachi Bar** on Av. Juárez, as its name suggests, is the place to go to hear live mariachi music. **¡Ajuaa! Restaurant and Bar** on Av. Juárez is a new cigar bar featuring *puros* from Mexico, Jamaica, Honduras, and Cuba.

Behind the plaza area—in perfect irony, not far from the cathedral—is "Boy's Town," the Juárez red-light district. Warning: a sign that reads "ladies bar" doesn't mean it's a bar for ladies; on the contrary, it's a bar for men looking for ladies.

North of Calle Mejía on Av. Juárez are the more "modern" bars and discos. Of the many discos, the most popular are **Noa Noa Disco** (owned by famous romantic singer Juan Gabriel), at Av. Juárez and Calle M. Martínez near the Woolworth store; **Sarawak Disco,** Av. Juárez 645; and **Cosmos Discotheque,** 1.5 blocks from the Santa Fe Bridge. **Crazytown,** opposite Cosmos, is popular with visiting weekend gringos. **Bar Mariachi,** two blocks from the bridge, has live mariachi music and no cover charge.

Just opposite the bridge is a cluster of other bars and discos that cater almost exclusively to an El Paso crowd, including **Alive, La Playa, Spanky's, Copa Cabana,** and **Manhattan.** The next couple of streets west of Av. Juárez, particularly Calle Mariscal, are devoted to go-go bars. These do not, as promised by street touts, feature topless or nude dancers, but young women dressed in bikinis. Topless dancing is illegal in Ciudad Juárez.

Shuttle: The cities of El Paso and Juárez run a free **Fiesta Shuttle Service** along Av. Juárez every hour on the hour 8 p.m.-2 a.m. You can park your vehicle at 325 S. Santa Fe St. in El Paso and the shuttle will take you to and from the following locations: Alive, Cosmos, Copa Cabana, Restaurant Florida, La Playa, Mariachi Bar, The Sub, Spanky's, Manhattan Disco, Restaurante Nuevo Martino, and Superior.

Radio

For the best of border radio, tune in 105.1 FM, a bilingual station that plays a vigorous mix of *norteña*-style *cumbias, rancheras,* and *boleros.* For more esoterica, listen to Juárez's XEWR-AM 1110, where you can catch tunes by Mexican bands like Los Teen Tops and Rebeldes de Rock. You can also listen to El Paso's liveliest FM radio station, KBNA ("K-Buena") at FM 97.5 and AM 920. Bilingual DJs on KBNA play a great mix of *norteña,* South Texas R&B, soul, and other jumpin' music.

RECREATION

Bullfights

Each summer, four bullfights are held in Juárez at the **Plaza de Toros Monumental** on Av. 16 de Septiembre, beside Rio Grande Mall a bit east of Plaza de las Américas. Seating up to 17,000, Monumental is the world's fourth-largest bullring and a major stop on the professional *corridas* circuit. The annual season runs April-Sept.; the first *corrida de toros* takes place around Easter and then three more *corridas* are held on four Sundays before Labor Day. These are real Spanish-style bullfights in which the bull may be killed by the matador.

Admission costs US$7-15 depending on the seat, while parking costs US$1; rent cushions for US$0.30. The city's older ring, Plaza Balderas (downtown at Av. Francisco Villa), is now used only for concerts and other events. Check with the Tourist Information Center, tel. (16) 14-0123, or the El Paso Convention and Visitors Bureau for the latest scheduling.

Charreadas

Two *charro* rings, **Lienzo Charro López Mateos** (Av. del Charro between Av. Hnos. Escobar and Paseo Triunfo de la República) and **Lienzo Charro Baca Gallardo** (Carretera Panamericana Km 13) host Mexican rodeo events off and on year-round—usually on Sundays and national festivals. Mexican rodeos are held here most Sundays between April and October at 4 p.m. or so. Admission is about US$3.

Racing and Off-Track Betting

The **Hipódromo y Galgódromo de Ciudad Juárez** (Juárez Racetrack), off Av. Vicente Guerrero to the east of Plaza de las Américas, is primarily a *galgódromo* (dog track) and features greyhound racing Wed.-Sat. at 8 p.m. year-round; horse races are occasionally held during the summer. Seats in the a/c general admission section cost US$0.50, while the Jockey Club section upstairs runs US$3. The advantages to Jockey Club seating are giant-screen replay and table service for food and beverages. A bar downstairs offers off-track betting and sports book, TV tables for watching several races and sports events, and full food and beverage service. The racetrack operates shuttle buses to and from several of the city's major hotels.

The **Juárez Turf Club,** downtown just a block south of the Santa Fe Bridge on the east side of Av. Juárez, allows El Pasoans to walk over Santa Fe Bridge and wager on live horse and greyhound races—as well as a range of televised North American sports events—without going all the way out to the track. Facilities include a full bar, multiscreen TV for off-track betting and sports, and betting counters. Open daily 10 a.m.-midnight.

INFORMATION AND SERVICES

SECTUR has maintained an on-again, off-again **tourist office** in the Unidad Administrativa Municipal (UAM) just across the border from the U.S. on Av. Colegio Militar between Av. Juárez and Av. Lerdo. More reliable is the **Coordinación Estatal de Turismo** (State Office of Tourism),

Plaza and Church of El Paso del Norte, as sketched by William Emory in the 1850s

in the Presidencia Municipal (City Hall) at Av. Francisco Villa and Av. Malecón, tel. (16) 15-2301 or 14-0607. It's open daily 8 a.m.-7 p.m.

The **U.S. consulate** is at Av. López Mateos 924 (just north of the Universidad Autónoma de Ciudad Juárez), tel. (16) 13-4048, after-hours El Paso tel. (915) 525-6066. Open Mon.-Fri. 8 a.m.-4:30 p.m. In El Paso, the **Mexican consulate** is at 910 E. San Antonio St., tel. (915) 533-3644.

Ciudad Juárez has the usual telephone offices and hotel phone systems, but if you need to make an international call, it may be less expensive to walk across the Santa Fe Bridge to downtown El Paso and use the U.S. system. Many Juárez residents take advantage of a bank of **phone booths** only a few meters beyond the U.S. customs station.

The local **Green Angels** unit, tel. (16) 14-6692 or 14-0670, is based at the tourism office.

GETTING THERE

Air

Regional carrier **TAESA,** Av. de la Raza 5385, locales 59, 62, 63, Centro Comercial Plaza Grande, tel. (16) 29-2368, fax (16) 29-2370, fields flights to and from Mexico City, Tijuana, and Zacatecas.

Aero California, Av. de la Raza 6108-2, tel. (16) 18-3399, has nonstop flights to and from Torreón, plus connecting flights to/from Culiacán, Guadalajara, La Paz, Ciudad Obregón, Los Mochis, Los Angeles, Mazatlán, and Mexico City.

Aeroméxico, Av. Lincoln 759, tel. (16) 13-8719, offers nonstop flights between Ciudad Juárez and Chihuahua, Hermosillo, Mazatlán, Mexico City, and Torreón.

The airport is 18.5 km (11.5 miles) from the city center—about a half-hour by car or taxi. The standard taxi fare is US$10; a *colectivo* costs US$5 pp. Or you can hop a blue-and-white bus marked "Aeropuerto" on the sides for US$0.30.

Bus

Built in 1991, the city's impressive Central de Autobuses, at the intersection of Paseo Triunfo de la República and Av. López Mateos (near the Plaza Río Grande shopping center and Plaza

de Toros Monumental), features a left-luggage service, moneychanger, post office, long-distance telephone counter, customs check (for buses arriving from the U.S.), and sparkling clean *cafetería* serving pizzas, burgers, *tortas,* and *flautas.*

Because Ciudad Juárez is a major transportation junction, buses depart to virtually anywhere in Mexico from this station. **Turistar** has higher-class *ejecutivo* service to Chihuahua (US$19, seven daily departures), Torreón (US$36, three daily departures), Guadalajara (US$64, two daily departures), Durango (US$39, one daily departure), and Mexico City (US$68).

Omnibus de Mexico operates first-class buses to and from Chihuahua (US$13, every hour 6 a.m.-9 p.m.), San Luis Potosí (US$51, four daily departures), and Zacatecas (US$44, four daily departures).

Chihuahuenses has hourly departures to Chihuahua (US$13) and El Paso (US$5), plus twice-daily buses to Mazatlán (US$47); **Estrella Blanca** runs similar routes for slightly lower fares.

TNS offers once-daily first-class departures to Hermosillo (US$29) and Guaymas (US$37).

Turismos Rápidos operates bus services that connect with Greyhound lines in El Paso and continue on to Los Angeles for US$40, to Denver for US$45, and to Albuquerque for US$25. You can also ride one of their buses to El Paso for US$5. Departures leave every hour; tickets can be purchased at the Greyhound kiosk in the station.

Other stateside departures are provided by **Transportes del Norte,** which operates daily buses to and from Los Angeles (US$35), Albuquerque (US$15), and Denver (US$69).

Several smaller, regional companies offer regular second-class bus service from the Central de Autobuses to towns within the state of Chihuahua; a typical second-class fare to Chihuahua is around US$4-6.

Border Jumper

The El Paso-Juárez Trolley Co., El Paso tel. (915) 544-0061, operates this trolley-style bus between downtown El Paso and Juárez. The trolley departs from the El Paso Civic Center and makes 10 stops along a circular route via the Cordova Bridge, Plaza de las Américas, Puebli-

DRIVING FROM CIUDAD JUÁREZ TO CHIHUAHUA

Motorists have a choice of three different routes between Ciudad Juárez and Chihuahua's state capital —depending on how much you want to see vs. how much time you have.

Mexico 45, modern-day heir to the Camino Real (Oñate's 1598 *entrada*) and the Chihuahua-Santa Fe Trail, takes the more direct southerly angle straight through the Chihuahuan Desert. A four-lane toll road from Juárez to just north of Chihuahua speeds road progress considerably; the toll is very reasonable compared to tolls in the Monterrey corridor or further south in Central Mexico. Around 13 km (eight miles) south of the airport is a federal checkpoint; if you don't have a temporary import permit you won't be allowed to drive any farther. The entire Ciudad Juárez-Chihuahua stretch is 354 km (219.5 miles) long and takes most drivers around 3.5 hours to complete—not counting rest or lunch stops.

The second and longest route—much more scenic but nearly twice as long as the first—involves driving west on Mexico 2 to Janos (261 km/162 miles from Ciudad Juárez), then south along Chihuahua 10 through the eastern foothills and floodplains of the Sierra Madre Occidental. Along the way are several areas of interest: Casas Grandes (Paquimé ruins, Mormon colonies), Madera on Chihuahua 37 (proto-Anasazi ruins, Madrean woodlands), and Cuauhtémoc at the junction of Chihuahua 16 and 23 (Mennonite camps). The whole route runs 736 km (456 miles) and really should be planned with at least one and preferably two overnight stays along the way.

A compromise between the two routes that would take in a visit to the Casas Grandes area—but leave out Maderas and Cuauhtémoc—would follow the previous route as far as Buenaventura, 82 km (51 miles) southeast of Nuevo Casas Grandes, then continue east instead of south to the small junction town of Ricardo Flores Magón (54 km/33.5 miles from Buenaventura), where you can pick up a new two-lane tollway shortcut southeast to Mexico 45. The latter highway passes through Las Varas and Providencia before joining Mexico 45, roughly 60 km (37 miles) north of Chihuahua. An overnight in Casas Grandes is recommended if you do the latter route.

Visitors traveling by intercity bus can choose the quicker Mexico 45 route by taking an express or executive-class bus in Ciudad Juárez. Those with more time may take the longer Mexico 2-Chihuahua 10 route by riding buses bound for Nuevo Casas Grandes, spending a night or two in the Casas Grandes area, then boarding a southward-bound bus from there to Chihuahua or points beyond.

to Mexicano, Silver Castle (arts and crafts), Rio Grande Mall, Holiday Inn Express, Chihuahua Charlie's, and Mercado Juárez before returning to El Paso via the Santa Fe Bridge. The fare is $10 pp roundtrip. Trolleys run Nov.-March, daily 9 a.m.-4 p.m. (every hour); April-Oct., Sun.-Tues. 9 a.m.-4 p.m. and Wed.-Sat. 9 a.m.-5 p.m. A free shuttle service to the Civic Center terminal is available from the following El Paso hotels: Paso del Norte, Holiday Inn (Sunland Park), El Paso Airport Hilton, Howard Johnson Lodge, Embassy Suites, Radisson Suite Inn.

The Chihuahua Charlie's stop is only about two blocks west of the Central de Autobuses, so the Border Jumper is a viable alternative to the Chihuahuenses bus (which costs the same but leaves from El Paso's downtown bus terminal). The main clientele for the Border Jumper, however, are El Pasoans on daytime shopping excursions.

Border Taxis

Quick trips across the border are the specialty of a number of El Paso taxicab companies, including **Texas Cab,** tel. (915) 562-0033, **Border Taxi,** tel. (915) 565-1440, and **Yellow Cab,** tel. (915) 533-3433. A short trip between downtown El Paso and downtown Ciudad Juárez costs around US$10-13; the fare from the Mexican side is about the same. You'll find a taxi stand near the Stanton Street Bridge.

Train

The División del Norte train No. 8 offers first-class seats to Mexico City with stops in Chihuahua, Jiménez, Torreón, Zacatecas, Aguascalientes, and Querétaro. Between Zacatecas and Mexico City, second-class seats are also available.

Although the fare between Ciudad Juárez and Chihuahua is only US$7.50, few people choose to take the División del Norte between the two cities since it involves a 10 p.m. departure from Juárez with a 3:15 a.m. arrival in Chihuahua (for a comfortable 9:30 a.m. arrival in Mexico City).

The Tren Mixto, Región Norte, offers mixed passenger-cargo service between Ciudad Juárez and La Junta, with stops in Nuevo Casas Grandes and Madera. Passenger space is inconsistent, however, and you can't count on getting a ticket unless you inquire at least four days ahead of your intended departure. The train leaves Ciudad Juárez daily except Sunday at 7 a.m., arriving in La Junta between 10 p.m. and midnight depending on the cargo. In the reverse direction the train leaves La Junta at 10:30 a.m. and arrives in Ciudad Juárez around 1 a.m. In either direction, arrival times in Nuevo Casas Grandes and Madera are in the midafternoon. Fares are under US$10 for any destination along the line.

Border Formalities

Mexico's customs and immigration station at Ciudad Juárez is large and efficient. If you're planning to stay more than 72 hours you'll need a tourist card. If you plan to drive beyond the federal checkpoint 13 km (eight miles) south of the airport, you'd better stop for a temporary auto-import permit.

GETTING AROUND

Taxi

Ciudad Juárez taxis operate from *sitios* or stands throughout the city; they can also be flagged down on the street. Typical fares: Av. Juárez to downtown El Paso, US$9; downtown Ciudad Juárez to Central de Autobuses, US$7.

Bus

City buses cost US$0.20. As elsewhere in Mexico, the terminating destination is marked over the windshield. Any bus taken west along Av. 16 de Septiembre ends up downtown on either Av. Juárez or Av. Lerdo; any bus taken east on Av. Malecón ends up going south on Av. Lincoln or Av. de las Américas. Using these two routes—which together form a circuit around the city's commercial heart—you can get to most areas of historical or shopping interest.

Driving

The most heavily used bridge crossing is the Santa Fe Bridge (called both Puente Juárez and Puente Santa Fé on the Mexican side), which costs US$1.95 for vehicles, US$0.50 for pedestrians. This bridge allows one-way vehicular traffic into Ciudad Juárez; in the reverse direction motorists use the parallel Stanton Bridge.

The traffic along the Santa Fe and Stanton Street Bridges is intense; a better alternative for motorists visiting Ciudad Juárez is the Cordova Bridge (called Puente de las Américas on the Mexican side), which has an exit directly off highway I-10 east on the U.S. side. This bridge takes you through Parque Chamizal to the junction of Av. de las Américas, Av. Lincoln, and Av. Malecón, three streets that will take you almost anywhere in the city.

If your goal is to reach Mexico 45 as quickly and easily as possible, your best bet is to use the new Santa Teresa border crossing, which puts you west of Ciudad Juárez on Mexico 2 between Km 22 and 23. Mexico 2 links with Mexico 45 just southeast of the city. Coming from I-10 east, you can also cross at the

AUTO RENTAL AGENCIES IN CIUDAD JUÁREZ

Alpri Rent-A-Car
Av. Lincoln and Calle Coyocan
tel. (16) 16-0876

Avis
Av. 16 de Septiembre Ote. 999
tel. (16) 14-0019 or (800) 7-0643

Budget
Av. de las Americas Nte. 545
tel. (16) 11-2844

Dollar Rent-A-Car
Paseo Triunfo de la República 3976
tel. (16) 11-0435

Hertz
Paseo Triunfo de la República 2408-2
tel. (16) 33-0732

Monaco Rent-A-Car
Paseo Triunfo de la República 4404-2
tel. (16) 13-2727

Zaragoza Road Bridge (near Ysleta del Sur), about 16 km (10 miles) east of downtown Ciudad Juárez. This crossing, too, connects with Mexico 45 via Mexico 2.

Fuel

PEMEX stations with Magna Sin are plentiful throughout the city as well as along the city outskirts at Mexico 2 and Mexico 45.

Auto Rental

At last count Ciudad Juárez had 10 car rental agencies; several are along Paseo Triunfo de la República. Avis and Budget also have counters at Juárez International Airport. Rates are a uniform US$24 per day plus US$0.12 per km for standard VW bugs; US$43.50 per day plus US$0.16 per km for a Nissan Tsuru II (Sentra); US$56 per day plus US$0.33 per km for a Mercury Topaz.

Flat-fee, unlimited-km rentals are sometimes available by the week; Avis International, U.S. tel. (800) 331-1212, often has the best weekly deals on Mexico rentals.

VICINITY OF CIUDAD JUÁREZ

Villa Ahumada

About a third of the way between Ciudad Juárez and Chihuahua, Villa Ahumada is famous throughout the state for *queso asadero* ("griller's cheese"), *crema* (a thick cream somewhat similar to American sour cream), and *chorizo* (Mexican sausage). Shops selling these foodstuffs line the highway through town.

Because several good restaurants are also found along the highway, Villa Ahumada is a popular lunch stop for travelers coming from the south. The better ones are **Restaurant Oscar's, Restaurant El Paisano,** and **Restaurant El Oasis.** The Oasis is open 24 hours and is attached to a 24-hour PEMEX. Between here and Chihuahua, 241 km (150 miles) to the south, there is only one other gas station, in El Sueco, so be sure to top off if you're down a half tank or more.

Villa Ahumada is also the junction for the toll *(cuota)* and free *(libre)* highways south toward El Sueco. The free road is roughly 65 km (40 miles) longer than the toll highway.

Palomas (Rodrigo M. Quevedo) and Columbus

The little town opposite Columbus, New Mexico, is the only official border crossing between Mexico and New Mexico. Known variously as Palomas, Puerto Palomas, and Rodrigo M. Quevedo (its official name), the town is little more than a relay point for agricultural goods—mostly chile products—produced in the Ascensión *municipio.* Millions of kilograms of chiles—including cayennes (about a quarter of the crop), jalapeños, long greens, fresh reds, yellow hots, and serranos—cross the border here each year.

Like every town along the U.S.-Mexico border, Palomas is larger than its U.S. counterpart, though in this case that's not saying much. Palomas does have a tidy little *placita* with an attractive, twin-towered stone church, **Nuestra Señora de Guadalupe,** alongside. *Las Fronteras,* a bilingual newspaper representing Palomas and Columbus, is circulated in both towns.

Across the border, the near-ghost town of **Columbus** is known among U.S.-Mexico history buffs as the only place in the continental U.S. to be invaded by foreign troops, thanks to Pancho Villa. After U.S. president Woodrow Wilson declared American support for the Carranza presidential candidacy in Mexico, Francisco "Pancho" Villa (Carranza's sworn enemy) retaliated by attacking the 13th U.S. Cavalry at Camp Furlong near Columbus on March 9, 1916. The U.S. forces were able to repel Villa's troops (killing 150 of an estimated 500 Villistas in the process), but during their retreat the Mexicans stopped in Columbus for a looting and window-shooting spree that left several U.S. civilians dead. President Wilson ordered a "punitive expedition" into Mexico the next day.

Led by Gen. John "Blackjack" Pershing, the expedition entered Mexico on March 15, 1916 with 4,800 troops, plus airplanes and motorized military vehicles (the first time either were used in U.S. warfare). Although Pershing and company got as far south as Parral, Chih., they never captured Villa and left Mexico empty-handed on Feb. 5, 1917. It was the last mounted U.S. Cavalry expedition in U.S. military history. Politically, the action was a disaster, as it bolstered Villa's moral standing among Mexicans and forced President Carranza to sever relations with the U.S. government.

Practicalities: Though few travelers choose to spend the night in either Columbus or Palomas, the latter has one inexpensive hotel—**Hotel San Francisco,** Av. 5 de Mayo 910, US$20-24 per night—and three *clase económica* places that run about US$10-15 a night. A decent place to eat in Palomas is **Pancho Villa** (open daily 11 a.m.-midnight), just a stone's throw from the border crossing at the back of a variety store.

Mexico 23 leads south 35 km (21.7 miles) from Palomas to a junction with Mexico 2 called **Tres Caminos,** where there's a PEMEX station with Magna Sin (between Km 112 and 113) and several cafes.

In Deming, 32 miles north of Columbus, you can choose among: **Deming Motel,** 500 W. Pine, tel. (505) 546-2661, US$28-36; **Days Inn,** 1709 E. Spruce, tel. (505) 546-8813, US$42 s/d; and **Holiday Inn,** I-10 East, exit 85, tel.(505) 546-2661, US$59 s/d. There are also three RV parks/campgrounds in Deming: **81 Palms RV Resort,** 2800 W. Pine, tel. (505) 546-7434, and **Little Vineyard RV Park & Resort,** 2901 E. Motel Dr., tel. (505) 546-3560, both with full hookups for US$11-12 daily, and **Low-Hi RV Ranch,** call for directions, tel. (505) 546-4058, where two-way sites are just US$6, boondocks US$1.

NUEVO CASAS GRANDES TO CUAUHTÉMOC

CASAS GRANDES–
NUEVO CASAS GRANDES

These twin towns at the confluence of the Casas Grandes and Piedras Verdes Rivers are supported by extensive agriculture on the surrounding river plains. Both rivers originate in the Sierra Madre Occidental; the Río Casas Grandes is the largest of all waterways flowing eastward from the sierra. From here it flows northward into the Chihuahua Desert, divides into several channels, reunites, and empties into Laguna de Guzmán, a *bolsón* that averages around a meter deep year-round.

The area's 1,463-meter (4,845-foot) altitude, gently sloping hills, and plentiful water sources make it well-suited to farming. Groups of Mormon immigrants settled the area between 1885 and 1912 to avoid a U.S. ban on polygamy (see "Colonia Juárez," below, for more information on the Mormon colonies). Though many Mormons returned to the U.S. during the Mexican Revolution years, a number stayed behind and introduced modern farming techniques—including the cultivation of slopes, hitherto not practiced in Northern Mexico—that have contributed much to local prosperity.

Apples and peaches are the principal local cash crops (U.S. pie-maker Sara Lee is a major purchaser), sustaining five major fruit packers *(empacadoras)* and employing hundreds of residents. The area is also known for producing the nation's best turkey; over a half million are produced yearly and distributed throughout the republic.

The main commercial center for the area is prosperous Nuevo Casas Grandes, which started in 1898 as a railway station on the La Junta rail line and today is a collection of agricultural supply stores, modest hotels for business travelers and the occasional tourist, banks, restaurants, PEMEX stations, and other sundries needed to support a town of 44,000 people. Though surrounded by rolling, grassy hills, the town itself—with its wide avenues spread over a flat plain—gives the impression of a town in the American Southwest more than a typical Mexican town.

Set amid rolling hills and fruit orchards six km southwest of Nuevo Casas Grandes is "Old" Casas Grandes, a quaint, shady farming community of 6,000 that has been quietly neglected since being bypassed first by the rail line and more recently by the national highway. With the slowly increasing notoriety of the nearby Paquimé ruins—the most important archaeological site in all of Northern Mexico—the town obviously hopes to benefit from the trickle of tourists driving through town on their way to see the archaeological zone. A school on the plaza is being converted into a museum that will contain local antiquities.

Dividing the two towns is the lovely Río Casas Grandes, lined with *alamo* (cottonwood) trees whose leaves change from deep green in spring and summer to bright copper in fall and winter.

CASAS
GRANDES -
MADERA

= GENERAL RUINS ZONE

0   25 km

Accommodations

Most of Nuevo Casas Grandes' hotels are lined up along Av. Juárez, which is parallel to Chihuahua 10.

Shoestring If you're just passing through, the simple, **Motel Los Arcos,** tel. (169) 4-4260, right on the highway south of town has a few standard rooms and a few others under renovation that may cost more when finished. Rates: US$10.60 s, US$12 d.

Shoestring/Budget: Hotel Paquimé, Av. Juárez 401, tel. (169) 4-4720, is a good choice if you plan to stop over for sightseeing, as the staff is very knowledgeable about the area. Altogether there are 45 rooms. Some are recently renovated and have phones, satellite TV, ceiling fans, a/c, and heat. Others are older with fewer amenities. Security parking is provided below the building. Rates: US$13 s, US$14 d for the older rooms; US$17 s, US$20 d for the renovated rooms.

Budget: Friendly 57-room **Motel Piñon,** Av. Juárez 605, tel. (169) 4-0166, fax (169) 4-0847, is similar but has a small pool and courtyard parking. All rooms have a/c, heat, and TV. A small collection of Paquimé artifacts is on display in the lobby; information on local sightseeing is readily dispensed. Rates: Posted room rates start at US$22, but "tourist discounts" of US$17 s, US$19.50 d, US$22 t, and US$25 q are readily available. Just north of Motel Los Arcos on the highway (called Av. Colón here) is **Motel Las Fuentes,** tel. (169) 4-5402, with a pool and 55 rooms around a courtyard. It's neither as quiet nor as clean as the Piñon. Rates: US$18 s/d.

Inexpensive: Top of the heap is the modern, 124-room **Motel Hacienda,** Av. Juárez 2603, tel. (169) 4-1046, fax (169) 4-4818, toward the north end of town. The clientele here is mostly businesspeople, and many of the staff are bilingual. Rooms have full amenities, and the motel has a pool. Rates: US$32 s, US$37 d, including tax.

RVs: Motel Los Arcos offers a few RV/trailer spaces with full hookups for US$10 per night.

Food

Several modest restaurants are on Av. Juárez in the vicinity of Hotel Paquimé, Motel Piñon, and Motel Hacienda (all of these hotels have their own restaurants as well). Some are of the fast-food variety, such as **Pecos Pizza,** next to El Bandido Pub and popular with a younger crowd. **Restaurant Constantino,** Av. Juárez 400, has been serving Mexican and regional cuisine in a casual coffee shop-style ambience for over 35 years.

The most notable eating spot in town is **Restaurant Malmedy,** tel. (169) 4-1025, a unique Belgian-Mexican restaurant housed in a turn-of-the-century, Mormon-built brick-and-wood house at the north end of Av. Juárez. Belgian-born chef Philippe Gentges has worked in Mexico for nearly a decade. Married to a local woman, he now prepares a toothsome selection of continental-style beef, chicken, and fish dishes, all from original recipes. During warmer weather a few outside tables make for pleasant dining. Malmedy is open daily noon-11 p.m.

Restaurant Dinno's, Calle Constitución (paralleling Av. Juárez to the east) at Calle Minerva, serves pizza and Mexican dishes but is especially popular for breakfast. For steak, town opinion is split between Restaurant Malmedy and **Restaurant El Herradero,** Av. Juárez 2610.

Fresh tamales—your choice of *chile colorado* (pork in chile sauce), *chile verde con queso* (cheese and green chiles), or *dulce* (sweet corn)—are available for US$0.25 each at **Tamales El Centro,** Av. Juárez 1010. The tiny shop also sells fresh *masa* by the kilo and *champurrado* (a drink of hot chocolate mixed with thick corn flour) to go.

When you're in the mood for ice cream, go straight to **Helados Bing,** on Av. Juárez near the corner of Av. 6 de Marzo.

Shopping

Casas Grandes-style pottery can be perused or purchased at small shops in Nuevo Casas Grandes or Casas Grandes Viejo, or you can go straight to the source and try your luck at Mata Ortíz. The selection isn't necessarily any greater in Mata Ortíz, as most potters complete only a few pieces per month; many are bought by dealers as soon as they're finished.

Money

Banamex and **Banca Serfín,** both near the intersection of 5 de Mayo and Av. Constitución, feature ATMs.

Transportation

Most people visit Casas Grandes as part of the Ciudad Juárez-Chihuahua loop, some combining

CASAS GRANDES POTTERY

Juan Quezada, who started the renaissance of the Casas Grandes or Paquimé-style ceramic pottery in Mata Ortíz, is known throughout the international art world for his exquisite ceramic work. Rather than resort to mere reproduction, Quezada accomplished a rare indigenous art revival in which the resulting pots are deemed an authentic, artistic step forward in a style that lay dormant for at least 600 years.

Although his mother was an active potter, Quezada's interest in Casas Grandes pottery began when he found original Paquimé shards in the surrounding valley as a child. After collecting and studying Casas Grandes form and design for over 20 years, he started making pots of his own design—using the originals as stylistic points of departure.

One of the more remarkable aspects of Casas Grandes pottery is the abstract "maze" design painted on the outside, wherein an unpainted area ("negative space" in art terms) can follow an uninterrupted path along the vessel's exterior. Original Paquimé pottery left the lower portion of the vessels unpainted, while the typical Quezada design does away with the circular band that terminated designs along the lower area of the vessel, thus allowing the design to move across the entire surface. For the viewer, tracing the mazes from beginning to end is a hypnotic exercise.

Collectors now recognize four basic types of Casas Grandes/ Paquimé pottery. The Ramos Poly design—for which Juan Quezada is famous—involves design repetition, positive-negative color reversal, the outlining of brighter colors with black lines, and the incorporation of abstract mazes over the entire vessel. In Ramos Negra (also called *barro negra*), the entire vessel has a polished black surface. Carretas Poly—the most common original style —is similar to Ramos Poly except that it has a lower border and less design repetition. Villa Ahumada Poly is a name given to taller pots with lower borders.

Pottery has become an important cottage industry in Mata Ortíz. Potters still work entirely without the use of wheels or kilns. To fire the pots, they place the raw vessels on an inverted bucket, bury the whole thing in dried cow chips, and set the chips aflame. The better potters are very picky about the cow chips they use, choosing only black, grain-free manure in order to attain the correct temperature.

Quezada produces seven or eight pots a month, each one a masterpiece that can fetch from several hundred dollars for a smaller piece to as much as US$4,000 for a large piece on the international market. A few years ago, Japan's Fuji Corporation had a contract to buy everything Quezada produced within a circumscribed period. Other skilled potters in Mata Ortíz tend to produce work in the US$30-200 range.

ERIN DWYER

this leg with an extended trip from Chihuahua into the Barranca del Cobre (Copper Canyon) area.

If seeing the state capital isn't an important part of your itinerary, a more original plan would be to bypass Chihuahua entirely by heading straight south from Casas Grandes to Cuauhtémoc—where the Chihuahua al Pacífico train can be met for the rail journey to the coast. Or you can head directly west from Cuauhtémoc to Basaseachic Falls via Mexico 16.

Buses: Caballero Azteca, Estrella Blanca, Futura, Elite, and **Omnibus de Mexico** operate from the bus terminal in the center of town. Most buses run along a north-south route; typical fares to Ciudad Juárez or Agua Prieta are US$7, to Chihuahua US$9.

Train: You can catch a train from Nuevo Casas Grandes to Madera and La Junta (a junction for the Chihuahua al Pacífico train) every other day, but it's mostly for cargo. If you're bent on taking this ride, show up at the station a couple of days ahead of time and make a few inquiries as to how the load looks.

Taxis: Fares in Nuevo Casas Grandes are reasonable. A taxi from the bus terminal to the Av. Juárez hotel area costs about US$2.30.

Driving: Nuevo Casas Grandes is 315 km (195 miles) from El Paso/Ciudad Juárez; the average drive time is three to four hours. From Douglas/Agua Prieta it's just 211 km (131 miles), but since Mexico 2 is in fairly poor condition between Agua Prieta and Janos, the trip takes about three hours. If road conditions improve, this could be a two-hour trip.

Nuevo Casas Grandes has four PEMEX stations with Magna Sin; including a 24-hour PEMEX on Av. Colón. The Barrio PEMEX at Av. Juárez and Jiménez offers car washes and oil changes. Heading out of town, you'll find a full-service PEMEX station 52 km south of Nuevo Casas Grandes on Chihuahua 10—seemingly in the middle of nowhere—on the way to Buenaventura.

Between Nuevo Casas Grandes and Ciudad Juárez, both Janos and Ascensión have PEMEX stations.

Paquimé

PAQUIMÉ ARCHAEOLOGICAL ZONE

Long before Mormons or Mexicans arrived in the Río Casas Grandes area, an ancient, little-understood Amerindian culture built a large adobe city called Paquimé on the banks of the river. Spanish explorer Francisco de Ibarra and his scribe Baltasar de Obregón came upon the abandoned city in 1565 during a survey of Northern Mexico. Their chronicles comment that the city contained "buildings that seemed to have been constructed by the Ancient Romans. It is marvelous to look upon." The ruins of the multistory pueblo so impressed later visitors that the area became known as "Casas Grandes" or "Big Houses" throughout Mexico. Architecture and artifacts at Paquimé suggest the culture lasted nearly 800 years and exhibited a unique blend of Anasazi-Pueblo Indian and Mesoamerican characteristics. The citizens of Paquimé are also thought to have practiced the first agriculture in northwest Mexico.

The city must have looked very different when Ibarra and Obregón visited—just 225 years after

its abandonment—than it did 400 years later during its first excavation. Although the ruins were briefly explored by Swiss-American ethnologist Adolph Bandelier in the 1890s, Paquimé remained relatively neglected until Sept. 1958, when Arizona's Amerindian Foundation received authorization from Mexico's INAH to carry out a three-year research project. Continuing research is currently being conducted by resident British archaeologist R.B. Brown.

History

Centered in a 221,000-square-km area covering northwestern Chihuahua and northeastern Sonora, with Paquimé as its focal point, the Casas Grandes culture is known to have existed as early as A.D. 700 and is thought to have reached its apex during the 11th to 14th centuries. In addition to being Northern Mexico's first agriculturists, the citizens of Paquimé traded in obsidian, turquoise, shells, quetzal feathers, and peyote with Anasazi and Mesoamerican groups—thus developing a crossroads between the cultures of the American Southwest and those of Southern Mexico. Archaeological evidence shows Mesoamerican influence in the city's ballcourt games, copper ornamentation, and Quetzalcoatl cult, while the general architecture is obviously related to Anasazi-Pueblo Indian styles (in which direction the architectural influence flowed has yet to be determined), though somewhat more advanced. The presence of seashells also indicates contact with communities living along the Sea of Cortez coast.

At its peak, Paquimé may have been linked to hundreds of satellite villages extending from Mesa Verde, Colorado, to Mexico City, a vast area known as "Oasis America" among Mexican anthropologists. The culture is thought to have begun stagnating by the late 13th century, and evidence suggests that Paquimé proper was razed by marauding tribes from the north around 1340 (an alternate theory blames an accidental but all-consuming fire). Mass migrations away from the city, similar to those among the Anasazis of Arizona and New Mexico, may also have occurred—although where these people may have gone is a complete mystery. The uncanny parallels between the Anasazi and Casas Grandes cultures is fertile research territory as yet relatively unexplored.

Architecture and City Planning

The archaeological zone, seven km southwest of Nuevo Casas Grandes via Chihuahua 18, currently extends 123 acres from the banks of the Río Casas Grandes southward, about two-thirds of which have been excavated. Outlines of Paquimé structures occur over 88 acres and are thought to have encompassed 1,780 rooms that were inhabited by as many as 2,200 people. Unexcavated sites outside the zone continue as far south as Laguna Babícora (near Madera), as far north as Janos, and as far west as Nacori Chico, Sonora, with the Río Casas Grandes as the eastern boundary.

Early Paquimé houses were round and semisubterranean (similar to the "kivas" of the U.S. Southwest), but designs later evolved into rectangular structures with two to four floors, complete with sewage systems, water systems, and kitchens. Walls of rammed earth (adobe) are 1-1.5 meters (3-4.5 feet) thick. These thick walls were fashioned not from adobe bricks but from raw adobe tamped into forms and covered with plaster. As indicated by the construction of the bottom floors (in most instances the only floors visible today), some buildings may originally have contained up to five floors. The partial remains of fourth floors can be seen in places.

Rooms were fitted together with complex, right-angled, jigsaw-puzzlelike precision, with as many as 16 interior walls per room. Every doorway is shaped like a thick "T," with a maximum height of 1.3 meters (4.3 feet) so that it was necessary for the inhabitants to pass slowly, one person at a time, through them. The top crossbar of the T-door was narrower than the bottom vertical so that residents could carry things in their arms from room to room. Most likely this door design was a means of defense, preventing invading enemies from moving quickly through the buildings; the complex, mazelike room layout may also have been defense related.

The majority of rooms had heating stoves and windows for ventilation, and many also show wall niches where religious idols may have been placed. Some of the community's dead—possibly family heads—were buried (usually in the fetal or flexed position common to burial customs in all Mesoamerican cultures) in corners of bottom-floor rooms along with offerings of turquoise adornments, pottery, and obsidian points.

Unique interior stairways of cedar and adobe differentiate Paquimé architecture from that of the Anasazis, who used movable ladders rather than permanent stairways. Another major difference between Anasazi and Paquimé building design is that the bottom floors of Anasazi-Pueblo structures were solid bodies that served solely as a base for upper floors, while the bottom floors of Paquimé houses had functional rooms with exterior doors.

The comparative sophistication of Paquimé architecture to Anasazi-Pueblo may be explained by the fact that for most of its history the Casas Grandes culture lived in less defensive, more secure circumstances. Because they needed to be able to retract their simple ladders from the ground when under attack, the Anasazis never developed stairs or ground-floor rooms.

Water in Paquimé was directed from a spring eight km northwest of the city via meter-deep open pipes or aqueducts made of stone slabs. The water was stored in 10-meter-deep stone wells, from which it could be directed at will from house to house via another set of stone pipes or used to irrigate nearby fields. A waterwheel excavated in one unit reached a water table 14 meters below the surface—a hydraulic engineering feat unequaled elsewhere in the Americas before that time. In the fields, water flow was also controlled by means of a system of earthen walls, terraces, and dams.

That the Paquimé culture developed a highly efficient social organization in which everyone worked for the community is demonstrated by evidence of labor specialization. Sotol (a liquor made from a type of agave), for example, was produced in a special section of the city where large ovens were used to bake the agave hearts. Another section was used for the raising of the resplendent quetzal *(Pharomachrus mocinno)*, whose long, iridescent plumage was highly revered in Mesoamerican cultures. Using ceramic spindles, Paquimé weavers created fabrics from cotton and natural fibers, along with plain and brocaded bags, underskirts, hairbands, and serapes.

Other specialized city structures included ball courts, ceremonial plazas, and military emplacements. The city's primary ceremonial monument is a stone cross with five-meter arms lying flat on the ground and surrounded by four circular platforms, each seven meters in diameter and one meter high. The arms of the cross are aligned with the points of the compass, suggesting it was used by Paquimé shamans for astronomic or agricultural-cycle predictions.

An excavated ball court in the shape of a double "T" or capital "I" lies 70 meters west of the cross and is similar to those of the Toltec period, which are found farther south. A highly ornate copper pendant, molded by the lost-wax process into the shape of a turtle with rattlesnake motifs on the reverse, was found on this court. A second, smaller ball court can be seen in another part of the ruins. Other monuments include an offering platform and various other platforms of unknown function.

Pottery

A major hallmark of Casas Grandes culture was a sophisticated ceramics tradition that produced delicate, multicolored pots made without a potter's wheel. When Norwegian explorer Carl Lumholz visited the site in the 1890s, he described the ceramicware he found buried in the dust between the walls as "far superior in quality and decoration to anything now made in Mexico." Highly prized for their mazelike decorations, agate-polished surfaces, and smooth-curved bottoms that miraculously keep the pots upright, Paquimé pots were traded throughout pre-Cortesian Mexico and the U.S. Southwest. Some of the more elaborate pieces were fashioned in human or animal figures, yet still functioned as pots. Hopi ceramics bear a certain resemblance, though the Casas Grandes tradition is older.

Original Paquimé pots (also called "Casas Grandes" pottery) are priceless collector's items; a revived Casas Grandes style emanating from the nearby village of Mata Ortíz is also very collectible (see "Mata Ortíz and Hacienda San Diego," below for more information).

Visiting The Ruins

To reach the main archaeological zone, drive six km from Av. Juárez in Nuevo Casas Grandes to Casas Grandes, then turn left onto a one-km dirt road signed "Ruinas Paquimé." The ruins are open to the public daily 10 a.m.-5 p.m.; admission is US$1.30 except Sunday, when it's free.

From the entrance road the ruins look more diminutive than might be expected, so you really have to wander through them to gain a full appreciation for their size and complexity. Because of the mazelike layout, visitors sometimes become temporarily lost in the larger structures.

The recently established Central Cultural Paquimé next to the ruins contains a museum open Tues.-Sun. 10 a.m.-5 p.m. The exhibits, labeled in Spanish only, give plenty of detail about Paquimé history and culture, including a display of rare Paquimé jewelry and a collection of Paquimé musical instruments—sea snail trumpets, whistles, hand rattles, and guiros. Atop the center is a platform for viewing the layout of the ruins, though it's not really high enough to see much. Admission to the museum is free with a paid admission to the ruins.

Other Sites

Trips to other nearby sites, such as the secluded cave dwellings at **Valle de las Cuevas** (including "Cueva de la Olla," a cave with a huge, floor-to-ceiling corn urn made of mud-coated, coiled grass) along Río Piedras Verdes, can be arranged through local guides. Although some sites can be reached within two hours' drive of Casas Grandes, others involve hikes lasting from a half day to four days. Ask at the home studio of potter Manuel Olivas, who lives at the southern edge of "old" Casas Grandes, just before Km 9 on the left side of Chihuahua 71 (en route to Colonia Juárez). Señor Olivas is very knowledgeable about local Paquimé sites and petroglyphs; the back wall of his workshop is painted with a large map showing many of the principal spots.

Hotel Paquimé or Motel Piñon in Nuevo Casas Grandes can also arrange archaeological tours of the area.

COLONIA JUÁREZ AND VICINITY

This small farming community set in the verdant Río Piedras Negras valley, 27 km (16.7 miles) southwest of Nuevo Casas Grandes via Chihuahua 18 (17 km/10.6 miles from the Paquimé ruins turnoff), is one of two Mormon colonies in Mexico.

American members of the Church of Jesus Christ of Latter-Day Saints (or the Mormon Church) originally founded eight colonies in Chihuahua and Sonora following the 1880s' passage of the Edmunds-Tucker Act prohibiting polygamy (plural marriage) in the United States. Although not all of the original colonists were members of polygamous marriages, as one Mormon sister said in 1885, "We came willingly because we had to, for Uncle Sam got cross because there were so many of us women." By the turn of the century 5,000 Mormon colonists were living in Chihuahua and Sonora.

Founded in 1886 on the birthday of Benito Juárez (hence the town's name), Colonia Juárez was the Mormons' second Mexican colony; Colonia Díaz, Chih., founded the year before, was abandoned in 1912 and burned to the ground shortly thereafter. All eight colonies were eventually abandoned during the Mexican Revolution; five were resettled by less than a quarter of the original numbers, and of these only two colonies have survived to this day. The other, Colonia Dublán, has become a virtual northern suburb of Nuevo Casas Grandes.

Fruit farming has been the economic mainstay of Colonia Juárez; the colony operates its own fruit-packing cooperative, Empacadora Paquimé. The Mormons introduced cheesemaking to Northern Mexico at least 20 years before Chihuahua's Mennonites, although over the years dairy production has taken a back seat to agriculture.

The town's charming, Mormon-built brick homes feature sloped roofs—distinguishing them immediately from the flat-roofed homes of their Mexican neighbors—and are surrounded by plentiful shade trees and flower gardens. Besides a Mormon temple and a few small stores, the town boasts the **Academía Juárez**, a K-12 school founded by the Mormons in 1904. The school's English-Spanish bilingual curriculum fulfills requirements for U.S. as well as Mexican high-school diplomas and is probably one of the most successful bilingual programs in the U.S., Canada, or Mexico.

An annual average of over 80% of the Academy's students go on to college or university, many of them at UNAM and ITM. School facilities include a main classroom building of brick, a well-equipped high-school gym (several of Mexico's Olympic basketball players have been A.J. grads), and a soccer field. To the casual visitor, the school gives the impression of a high school out of a 1950s' U.S. suburb—tidy and immaculate grounds, with kids in pressed jeans and short-sleeved, collared shirts. George Romney, governor of Michigan, was born and raised in Col. Juárez.

Mata Ortíz and Hacienda San Diego

Mata Ortíz, a unique village of dirt streets and dark brown adobe buildings, originally grew up around a prospering U.S.-owned lumber mill placed next to the Ciudad Juárez-La Junta rail line by Enrique Creel and Canadian entrepreneur F.S. Pearson in 1907. Then known as "Pearson," the village boasted the second largest sawmill in North America; raw timber from Madera was shipped here, milled, and then sent on by rail to Ciudad Juárez for transshipment throughout the United States. Many of the railroad ties used during construction of the Chihuahua al Pacífico railway were also made here. In addition to the sawmill, Pearson contained a couple of hotels, a hospital, and several bars.

Hacienda San Diego

JOE CUMMINGS

Pearson died on the *Lusitania* when it went down in 1917.

Canadian and American interests fled during the 1910-20 revolution and the mill closed, but the little antique train station continued to service trains along the Ciudad Juárez-La Junta line until the line closed. In 1925 the Mexican government renamed the town Mata Ortíz in honor of a Mexican army officer who fought off Apache marauders in the area during the late 1800s. A few older residents still call the village by its original name, and the main grocery supplier in Mata Ortíz is called "Abarrotes Pearson."

One man, Juan Quezada, started the Mata Ortíz pottery tradition—a colorful revival of the polychromatic Casas Grandes style. With the construction of nearby Mexico 2 in the early 1980s, collectors from California and Arizona and other potters who had heard about Juan's work came pouring in. Virtually every Mata Ortíz resident today—about 300 in all—is involved in the pottery renaissance. A smaller number dabble in cattle ranching and farming, and several picturesque *ranchitos* are located along the Río Piedras Verdes, which runs alongside the village. Pottery can be bought at the source from many of the households in Mata Ortíz—look for people firing pots behind their homes.

Juan Quezada's home usually has the largest selection—many of them made by his relatives—but there are several other potters in town whose work is worth collecting. One is Nicolás Ortíz Estrada, who specializes in fashioning pots in the shape

of owls, rabbits, javelina, coyotes, snails, and turtles. The work of the better potters starts at around $40 a pot and peaks at around $300 (select pieces may cost much more), but you can also buy nice decorative pots for as little as US$5. Even if you're not looking to buy pottery, Mata Ortíz is an interesting place to wander around.

About 11 km from Colonia Juárez along the road to Mata Ortíz are the ruins of **Hacienda San Diego,** once part of the vast Luis Terrazas estate. Built 1902-04, the main building dominates the surrounding valley and features a sandstone facade with an iron-pillared terrace and engraving ("LT"). Terrazas's San Diego holdings are now *ejido* lands; the former grain-storage buildings and workers' quarters are inhabited by *ejidatarios*. The main building is under INAH stewardship but is decaying badly.

Practicalities: Posada de las Ollas, founded by an American anthropologist who wrote his master's thesis on Mata Ortíz, offers four small rooms—simple but clean—with shared bath for US$39 s, US$59 d. Rooms are fan-cooled in summer, warmed by electric space heaters in the winter. Rates include three meals served family style in a separate adobe structure with a stone fireplace. Reading materials on Mata Ortíz are available in a pleasant sitting area. A large patio area is also used as a gathering spot on warm evenings. For further information or reservations, contact Mike Williams, 4201 E Camelback Rd. #21, Phoenix, AZ 85018, tel. (602) 952-8304.

The village has a couple of small *tiendas* where limited supplies are available. **Takería La Pasadita,** south of the old railway station in a neighborhood known as Barrio Porvenir, serves basic meals of burritos and tacos.

Getting There: To reach Hacienda San Diego or Mata Ortíz by car, follow the dirt road heading southeast from Colonia Juárez between the narrow bridge and the Juárez Academy. Mata Ortíz is 19.8 km (12.3 miles) from the Academy via this road. Hacienda San Diego is reached 8.8 km (5.5 miles) before Mata Ortíz.

MADERA

Founded in 1906 by the Sierra Madre Land and Lumber Co. as a lumber transshipment point along the Chihuahua-La Junta railway, Madera ("Wood") still bases much of its livelihood on the timber industry. The town sits right at the start of the pine belt, on the lower slopes of the Sierra Madre Occidental at an elevation of almost 2,000 meters (6,500 feet). The area enjoys mild summers and crisp winters—perfect for year-round hiking.

An estimated 500 pre-Paquimé cave and cliff dwellings, many of which have barely been explored, are found within a 100-km (62-mile) radius of the town. Most are difficult to find without the services of a guide, which can be arranged in Madera through Motel Real del Bosque or possibly one of the other motels in town. All sites require some mountain hiking to reach—any-

where from a half-hour's walk over fairly level cliff rock to three hours' up-and-down slogging across ravines, slippery scree, and steep slopes. A few sites can be reached only by rock climbers.

At the Hotel Real del Bosque, the **Museo de la Momia** holds a small private collection of Paquimé ceramics, metates, and other protohistoric objects, plus a well-preserved Indian mummy from one of the nearby caves.

Arroyo Sirupa (Cañon Huápoca)

The main concentration of cave and cliff dwellings is west and southwest of Madera along a tremendous gorge (arroyo or *barranca*) formed by the Sirupa and Papigochi Rivers. From here north, for a distance of around 60 km along the river, are scattered adobe remains tucked away in rock clefts; some seem virtually unreachable, so precarious are their positions relative to terra firma. Whether the original inhabitants used ladders to reach these homes isn't known—but no evidence of ladders has so far been found. Many doors show T-shaped openings reminiscent of those at Paquimé.

One of the easiest sites to find (though a guide is still highly recommended) is the **Complejo Anasazi** or Anasazi Complex, 46 km west of Madera via a gravel-and-dirt logging road. After 11 km this road meets Campo 3, a logging settlement, then jogs south for 35 km before reaching the Complejo Anasazi area (if you come to El Paraje, you've gone too far on the first road). The ruins here are some of the best-preserved

El Nido de las Aguilas

JOE CUMMINGS

cliff dwelling sites in Northern Mexico—far better than the more accessible Cuarenta Casas site north of Madera. Archaeologists have dated the ruins to around A.D. 800, a bit older than the ruins today visible at Paquimé (earlier structures at Paquimé were presumably built over). The name is speculative; informed guesses as to the identity of the original Río Sirupa inhabitants vary from Mogollon to Anasazi to early Paquimé.

Wedged into the upper portion of a sheer cliff, suspended in time and space over the river gorge, is the most impressive site at Complejo Anasazi, **El Nido de las Aguilas** ("Eagle's Nest"). A few paintings remain on the adobe interior, along with broken *manos* and *metates,* potsherds, original roof beams, and storage urns for corn. The cliff itself forms the eastern face of a huge rock point jutting out into the gorge; around on the western side is the long **Cueva de la Serpiente,** which contains 14 well-preserved dwellings, some with two stories.

Reaching either of these sites requires a strenuous hike of about an hour from the logging road. A passage supposedly links the two sides of the bluff; the author, not knowing of such a passage, had to hike around the yoke of the cliff to reach both sides—probably the most difficult and dangerous part of the venture. If the passage exists and if you can find it, use it.

Another 16 km southwest via the same road (66 km from Madera) is **Cueva Grande,** a cave of 50 meters (164 feet) depth with a small waterfall near the entrance. The adobe dwellings inside this cave are numerous but little explored since the site requires a long hike across the Barranca Sirupa.

The area west of Madera toward the Sonora state border is one of the last habitats of the *carpintero grande (Campephilus imperialis)* the world's largest woodpecker—whose continued existence is endangered by heavy logging. Other rare and endangered species thought to live in the area include Mexican wolf, black bear, puma, and possibly jaguar.

A useful topographic map for negotiating Arroyo Sirupa—as well as Valle de las Cuevas farther north—is the INEGI 1:250,000 Madera H12-9. While none of the ruins described above are marked on the map, the Sirupa and Piedras Verdes Rivers are clearly marked, as are the gravel and dirt roads.

Cuarenta Casas

Less famous than Paquimé but more well known than the Arroyo Sirupa sites is the Cuarenta Casas ("Forty Houses") complex in **Arroyo del Garabato,** northwest of Gómez Farías off Chihuahua 23 and just north of the village of El Vallecillo. Explorer Carl Lumholz, during his 1898 Northern Mexico expedition, was the first European to note this site.

The numerous cave dwellings (around 40, hence the name) are similar in style to the ground dwellings at Paquimé. As these ruins are frequently visited by area residents, virtually nothing remains in terms of projectiles, potsherds, or other artifacts, and the ruins themselves are not very well preserved since they have been inhabited by various nomadic groups since their initial construction a thousand or more years ago.

To reach Cuarenta Casas, take the only paved road northwest out of Gómez Farías to Las Varas, then continue northwest on a newly paved road to just beyond El Vallecillo—ask someone in the village for directions to the ruins if you're traveling on your own. A one-km, unpaved access road leads to a parking lot, from where a footpath descends into Arroyo del Garabato to the caves.

The dirt road continues northwest over the Continental Divide to Nacori Chico, Son., via Tres Ríos—an interesting off-highway route between Chihuahua and Sonora. Four-wheel drive isn't necessary but a vehicle with high road clearance is recommended.

Accommodations

Shoestring: Motel Maras, Calle 5 at Juárez (no phone), has plain rooms catering to transient loggers. Rates: around US$8-12 a night. **Cabañas El Prado,** Calle 3 2006 (no phone), has seven rustic rooms with kitchenettes. Rates: US$13 s/d, US$16 t.

Budget: In the center of town, **Hotel San Pedro,** Calle 5 2001, tel. (157) 2-0384, **Hotel Alpino,** Calle 3 at Ojinaga, tel. (157) 2-0384, and **Hotel Mirmay,** Calle 3 at Guerrero, tel. (157) 2-0277, offer basic two-star accommodations. Rates: US$15-20 s/d.

Inexpensive: Hotel Real del Bosque, tel. (157) 2-0538, fax (157) 2-0066, just off Chihuahua 37 at the south entrance to Madera, has large, comfortable, heated rooms with TV. The bilingual manager is very helpful and can arrange guided visits to nearby archaeological sites as well as Sierra Madre hunting trips for goose, duck, wild turkey, white-tailed deer, and mule deer. Rates: US$35 s/d.

Food
The restaurant at Hotel Real del Bosque is very good for Mexican food, steaks, and the local specialty: fresh rainbow trout from nearby Presa Piñitas. If you're doing your own cooking, you can buy fresh trout from truck vendors along Calle 3 in town for US$3-4 per kilo.

Ostionería y Pescadería Boquilla, Calle 3 at 5 de Mayo, is a fair choice for inexpensive *antojitos,* breakfasts, and seafood. Along Calle 1, in the vicinity of the plaza and post office, are several *taquerías.*

Basic hotels and restaurants are also available in nearby Gómez Farías.

Tours
Remarkable Journeys, P.O. Box 31855, Houston, TX 77231-1855, tel. (713) 721-2517 or (800) 856-1993, operates a once-a-year tour called "Ancient Cultures of Northern Mexico" that focuses on the art and archaeology of Paquimé, Cañon Huápoca, Cuarenta Casas, and other sites in the Sierra Madre. Led by Joe Orr, a knowledgeable specialist in Northern Mexican archaeology and rock art, the trip lasts nine days and costs US$1,395 pp, including all transportation, lodging, and meals out of El Paso.

Transportation
Bus: Direct buses are available between Madera and Chihuahua, Cuauhtémoc, and Gómez Farías. From Ciudad Juárez your best bet is to take a bus to Gómez Farías and switch to a Madera-bound bus there.

Train: A train intended primarily for cargo runs from Nuevo Casas Grandes to Madera and La Junta (a junction for the Chihuahua al Pacífico train) every other day. Ask at the station a couple of days in advance as to your chances for getting a seat.

Driving: From the north, Madera is reached via Chihuahua 10 and Chihuahua 65. The turnoff for the latter is at San José Bavícora just south of Gómez Farías. From Cuauhtémoc to the south, Mexico 16/Chihuahua 16 via La Junta is the short-

est route (and has the least traffic), although many people take the longer and more heavily traveled Chihuahua 28 route through Colonia Alvaro Obregón because the road surface is a bit better.

CUAUHTÉMOC

Cuauhtémoc sits in the center of Chihuahua's scenic *llanos,* an area of plains and rolling hills. Surrounded by flourishing farmlands (the local apples are said to be Mexico's best), this town of 150,000 inhabitants has prospered from supplying its hard-working Mennonite neighbors with farm machinery and everyday consumer goods. It's also an important transportation junction where highways Mexico 23 and Mexico 16 meet the Chihuahua al Pacífico rail line.

Although there is little of tourist interest to see in the town, the Mennonite *campos* north of Cuauhtémoc are easily reached by road, and Basaseachic Falls is within an short day's drive. See "Parque Nacional Cascada de Basaseachic (Basaseachic Falls National Park)" in the Sierra Tarahumara ("Copper Canyon") section below. Visitors traveling the Barranca del Cobre-Casas Grandes loop can also use Cuauhtémoc to bypass the city of Chihuahua, proceeding directly north to Madera or Casas Grandes, or westward to the Barranca del Cobre.

Accommodations
Few travelers choose to overnight in Cuauhtémoc unless they're waiting for the train or have simply run out of daylight en route to Chihuahua.

Shoestring: *Clase económica* hotels in town include **Hotel Cuauhtémoc,** Av. Morelos 306, and **Hotel del Norte,** Calle Reforma 302. Rates: US$10-15 a night.

Budget: The place most geared toward tourists—with maps and information—is the **Motel Tarahumara Inn,** Av. Allende at Calle 5, tel. (141) 1-1919, fax (141) 2-4865, offering pleasant rooms with a/c, heating, and satellite TV. The Inn can arrange tours to nearby attractions, including the Mennonite camps, the Barranca del Cobre, and Basaseachic Falls. Car rentals are also available through the hotel. Rates: from US$19 s, US$24 d. On the opposite corner of Av. Allende and 5, the similarly priced and slightly older **Hotel Union,** tel. (141) 2-1114, has more character but fewer services. Also on Allende are the three-story **Hotel Princesa,** tel. (141) 2-0783, and **Hotel Plaza,** tel. (141) 2-4112, both offering budget rooms with heat and a/c.

On Mexico 23 at Km 3, just north of the Mexico 16 junction along the northwestern outskirts of town, is the modern, efficient, and very good value **Motel del Camino,** tel. (141) 1-0088, fax (141) 1-0146. Rooms are clean and fairly new. This is probably the best choice for the motorist passing through on the way north to Madera or Casas Grandes, or southeast to Chihuahua. The motel also has a good coffee shop. Rates: US$25 s/d.

Inexpensive: Hotel Rancho La Estancia, Apdo. Postal 986, Chihuahua, Chih., tel. (16) 12-2282, fax (16) 5-5297, is 20 km north of Cuauhtémoc via Mexico 23, then 12 km west on a gravel road into the Sierra Madre foothills at 2,160 meters (7,200 feet). Operating primarily as a resort, Rancho La Estancia offers a private landing strip, heated pool and sauna, horseback riding, and guided hunting/fishing trips to nearby Laguna Bustillos. Rates: US$50 s/d.

Food
Near the Hotel Princesa and Hotel Plaza on Mexico 16 in town, **Restaurant-Cafetería El Den** provides a standard diner atmosphere and good, inexpensive Mexican food. Many local ranchers meet here for coffee every morning. Two of the nicest restaurants in town are **Equs Restaurant-Bar,** Av. Allende 1310, and **Restaurant La Cueva,** Av. Guerrero 423, both of which serve Mexican and international cuisine. Near La Cueva at Av. Guerrero 317, **Restaurant Rancho Viejo** is locally renowned for steaks. The popular **La Fama,** near the plaza, serves tasty and inexpensive Mexican *antojitos.*

Transportation
The westbound **Chihuahua al Pacífico** train departs Cuauhtémoc at 9:15 a.m.; eastbound, the train departs at 6:25 p.m. **Rápidos Cuauhtémoc** operates buses to and from Chihuahua hourly 5 a.m. to midnight; the fare is US$2.60 one-way.

Motorists have a choice of two highways between Cuauhtémoc and Chihuahua: the free road through the small towns of Trias, Riva Palacio, and Bustillos; and the faster, more direct toll road (US$3). The free road winds around sharp but well-marked curves through scenic rolling hills and apple orchards.

Although most maps mark the road between Cuauhtémoc and Colonia Alvaro Obregón as Mexico 23, signs along the highway read Chihuahua 65. This highway joins Mexico 16 west of Cuauhtémoc.

Cuauhtémoc has several PEMEX stations.

THE MENNONITE CAMPS

Chihuahua's famous *campos menonitas* are concentrated to the north and south of Cuauhtémoc, although there are communities as far north as Madera and as far west as La Junta. Altogether the Mennonites number around 15,000. Most of them speak a Low German dialect and maintain a strict adherence to the Mennonite faith.

The most accessible camps are strung out along the 42-km (26-mile) section of Chihuahua 23 between Cuauhtémoc and Alvaro Obregón to the north. This stretch features around 20 Mennonite communities, each one numbered rather than named (e.g., Campo 3, Campo 5, etc.). Surrounded by cultivated fields, each community is inhabited by around 20 families (not untypically with nine or 10 children each), whose peaked-roof, wood-frame-and-adobe houses line one long, usually unpaved street parallel to the highway.

Don't visit the *campos* expecting to find the buggies and black suits common among Pennsylvania's Mennonites. Except for their red cheeks and blond hair, most Chihuahua Mennonites look very much like any other Mexican farmers. Men typically wear jeans, boots, and cowboy hats or John Deere gimme caps. Some of the women wear distinctive, colorful print dresses, and most cover their heads with scarves topped by straw hats. The rare business sign appears in German. Gleaming farm machinery in the fields and Ford pickups parked next to tidy white houses give the impression of a rural farming community in the U.S. Midwest.

History of the Mennonites
Around 9,000 Mennonites first arrived in Mexico from Canada in 1921, but the sect got its start in 15th-century Friesland (an island district of northern Holland) as pacifistic "Silent Communities" or

"Communities of the Cross" led by ex-Catholic priest Simons Menno (1492-1559). Constantly persecuted for their ascetic socio-religious practices and refusal to volunteer for military service, the group moved from Friesland to Prussia, Russia, and Canada before they were forced to leave Canada for declining to serve in the Canadian army during WW I.

In 1921 Canadian leaders of the sect met with Mexican president Alvaro Obregón, who allowed them to immigrate to Mexico with exemptions from military duty and the swearing of allegiance, while giving them the right to enter and leave the country at will and the authority to establish and administer their own schools without government interference. Many Mexican citizens protested that this allowed them all the benefits of citizenship with few of the corresponding responsibilities, but Obregón wisely saw the Mennonite immigration as an opportunity to upgrade Mexican farming techniques and raise the standard of living in Chihuahua. Unquestionably, the Mennonites have been more of an asset than a liability to Mexico.

Cheese

The Mennonites' most famous product is *queso menonita* or Mennonite cheese, known as *queso chihuahua* or Chihuahua cheese outside the state. It's typically a mild white cheddar. Although the Mennonites weren't the first to produce cheese in Mexico (the Mormons of Colonia Juárez began production in the 1890s), they've been curding it since the 1920s and their cheese is widely considered the nation's best.

Hence no visit to the *campos* is complete without a visit to a *quesería*. Altogether around 200 cooperative members deliver 22,500 liters of milk daily to two major *queserías* which produce about two tons of cheese per day. The cheese factory in Campo 6.5 is open to the public for tours every day except Sunday. Another cheese factory in Campo 2B is also open to the public.

Practicalities

Virtually everything in the *campos,* including the cheese factories and restaurants, is closed on Sundays, when many of the residents are cloistered in church or at their homes. For more activity, it's best to visit Mon.-Saturday.

Hotel Rancho La Estancia, 10 km (6.2 miles) from Chihuahua 65 via a turnoff between Km 20 and 21 (near Campo 6), has the only tourist accommodations in the area, save for hotels and motels in Cuauhtémoc.

Peter's, 12.8 km (eight miles) north of Cuauhtémoc on Mexico 23, is a Mennonite-run trailer park with full hookups for US$12 per night, tent camping for less. You can reserve a space in advance by writing to Peter's at Apdo. Postal 401, Cuauhtémoc, Chihuahua.

Restaurant El Duff, on the west side of the highway near Campo 22, serves Mexican and Mennonite food for breakfast, lunch, and dinner daily except Sunday. **Doña Maria's,** opposite the cheese factory in Campo 2B, can prepare home-cooked Mennonite meals with a day or two's advance notice. Mennonite cooking is similar to Dutch or West German cuisine.

OJINAGA TO ALDAMA

For travelers heading for Chihuahua from points east of El Paso, Ojinaga provides a convenient Mexico gateway as it avoids the hassles of crossing at El Paso/Ciudad Juárez and is a much more direct route. Highway US 67 leads directly to Presidio, the Texas side of the border, from US 90 (which in turn links San Antonio, Del Rio, Marathon, Alpine, Marfa, and El Paso). Out-of-state visitors sometimes combine a trip to Texas's Big Bend National Park with a visit to Chihuahua.

OJINAGA

Named in honor of Manuel Ojinaga, former governor of Chihuahua and military commander who was killed while defending western Chihuahua against the French, this border town of 45,000 is primarily an agricultural center for the fertile flood plains of the Río Conchos and Río Bravo (Rio Grande). Over 300 years old, it was originally founded as a Spanish presidio (hence the name of the Texas town on the opposite river bank) with the ungainly moniker Nuevo Real Presidio de Nuestra Señora de Betleña y Santiago de Las Amarillas de La Junta de los Ríos Norte y Conchos ("New Royal Garrison of Our Lady of Bethlehem and St. James on the Banks of the Junction of the Ríos Grande and Conchos"), later shortened to Presidio del Norte.

The surrounding river plains are the oldest continually cultivated farmlands in North America. When the Spanish arrived in the 16th century, they were astonished to find "advanced" Amerindians living in adobe houses and cultivating their own food. The Patarabueyes, about whom little is known except that they seem to have been a Pueblo Indian group, had apparently been farming this land since at least A.D. 1200. By the late 1600s the Patarabueyes had been missionized and, due to Spanish mistreatment and Mescalero Apache pressure, they disappeared by the 19th century.

Today, principal crops here include cotton, wheat, and beans. The Chihuahuan Desert also provides material for local cottage industries inherited from the former native inhabitants—rope and twine called *istle* made from lechugilla *(Agave lechugilla)*, bootleg liquor from sotol *(Dasylirion wheeleri)*, wax from candelilla *(Euphorbia antisyphilitica)*, and herbal remedies from a number of other desert plants. Local *botánicas* still trade in these herbs.

Ojinaga was once notorious as a conduit for contraband drugs coming from the Mexican interior, but state and local police have largely wiped out the drug trade in recent years and the town is now safe for foreign visitors. The local *tránsitos* (traffic police) are helpful to visiting motorists and will even provide free escort services for lost drivers as well as emergency automotive repairs.

In midsummer, Presidio/Ojinaga is one of the hottest areas in either Texas or Mexico. In July or August it's not unusual for afternoon temperatures to reach or exceed 40° C (104° F).

Crossing the Border

The border crossing to "O.J.," as it's known to many Texas residents, has been expanded and modernized. It's open Mon.-Fri. 7:30 a.m.-9 p.m., Sat.-Sun. 8 a.m.-4 p.m. If you're planning to stay more than 72 hours you'll need a tourist card, and if you're planning to drive to Chihuahua you'll need a temporary auto-import permit—both are available at the border station. Mexican vehicle insurance can be obtained at **La Junta Travel,** tel./fax (915) 229-4621 or (800) 847-8305, in Presidio at the junction of US 67 and O'Reilly St. just before crossing the border.

If you're driving, after you cross the bridge into Ojinaga just go straight ahead until you see an "Ojinaga Centro" sign; there are two, the first pointing to Av. Morelos, the second to a wide street called Calle Trasviña y Retes. Either one will lead to Calle Zaragoza, where you should turn left to reach the main plaza area. In this area you'll find most of the restaurants, bars, and pharmacies patronized by visiting foreigners—there are really only a few as Ojinaga isn't a major tourist stop.

Accommodations

Budget: Hotel y Motel Rohana, downtown at Calle Juárez and Trasviña y Retes, near the plaza, tel. (145) 3-0078, is a quaint 43-room hotel with high ceilings and tiled floors. Facilities include a secure parking lot, an upstairs bar, and an attached restaurant popular among border-hoppers for quail and other border specialties. Rates: around US$20 s, US$25 d. **Motel Diana,** Av. Justo Sierra at Blvd. Libre Comercio, tel. (145) 3-1645, has 80 rooms, slightly higher rates and less atmosphere. On the Presidio (Texas) side, **Three Palms Inn,** US 67, tel. (915) 229-3611, has clean, basic rooms and a popular coffee shop with steaks and good Tex-Mex food. Rates: US$25. The Three Palms also offers a few RV hookups.

Inexpensive: Motel Ojinaga, Blvd. Libre Comercio and Morelos, tel. (145) 3-0191, is a more modern place on the main highway toward Chihuahua (about five blocks from the bridge). All 80 rooms have phone, TV, and a/c; a pool, restaurant, bar, and disco are on the premises. Rates: US$40-50.

Food

Restaurant Los Comales, opposite the Presidencia Municipal at Calle Zaragoza 106, serves Mexican breakfasts, combo platters, and *carnes a la parrilla* (grilled steak) from 8 a.m. to midnight. **Chuco's,** a big green building at Av. Trasviña y Retes and Calle 13, is a popular gringo stop for beer and Mexican food and claims to stay open 365 days a year. **Mini-Chuco's** out front serves burritos, *barbacoa, asado, tortas, chile colorado, nachos americana,* tacos, and fajitas in a casual outdoor dining area.

Clean and inexpensive **La Fogata,** Calle Juárez 6, tel. (145) 3-0604, serves *cabrito* (barbecued kid goat) and has an English-speaking owner. **Cafetería El Puente,** a block from the bridge, offers inexpensive *comida corrida* specials daily 12:30 p.m.-5 p.m.

Shopping and Services

Low-cost dentistry is available at several clinics in town; the local *farmacias* also do a good business with visiting Texans. At **Dulcería La Joya,** Calle Juárez 11, you can buy traditional Mexican candies at wholesale and retail prices, plus colorful piñatas. The bilingual *International/Internacionale* newspaper, published across the river but available on both sides, is priced in both U.S. and Mexican currency.

Transportation

By Train: Ojinaga-Chihuahua passenger rail service was discontinued some years ago. A group of Texas investors recently purchased the rights to a railway route that runs from Dallas's Union Station to Presidio. They've also bought several Pullman cars and reportedly have plans to launch a regular passenger service within the next year or two. Without a corresponding rail link with the Chihuahua al Pacífico on the Mexican side, however, it remains to be seen whether this project will succeed.

By Bus: Transportes Chihuahuenses operates eight buses per day to Chihuahua (US$7.30). The town provides short- or long-term security parking in a large, fenced lot in the middle of town (at Calle Hidalgo and Calle de la Paz) for motorists wishing to take the bus to Chihuahua or beyond.

By Car: Driving time to Chihuahua is around three hours (238 km/147.5 miles). Gasoline is available in town; if you're heading west toward Chihuahua, be sure to top off here (or in Presidio), as the next PEMEX station is 209 km (129.5 miles) away in Aldama.

By Taxi: A *chuco* or collective taxi, in this case a blue and white Chevy Suburban, plies a route from in front of Presidio's MB Supermarket to Ojinaga's main plaza every half hour or so for US$2 each way. You could also arrange a private taxi in the same areas for US$5 each way.

SAN CARLOS (MANUEL BENAVIDES)

An island in the desert about 27.5 km (17 miles) south of the Río Bravo/Rio Grande, San Carlos sits 4,300 feet above sea level in a green, spring-fed arroyo. The Spanish constructed a presidio here in 1772 but departed 10 years later, leaving behind small acequias (stone-lined irrigation canals) that still flow beside some streets. The surrounding Sierra Rica was mined for copper, lead, and zinc in the 1800s (hence its name, "Rich Mountain Range"), but since then commerce has become limited to small-scale farming and ranching. Today the town's official post-Revolution name is Manuel Benavides, though most people still refer to it as San Carlos. Modern Mexican maps tend use the newer name.

The attached Cañon de San Carlos makes a fine hiking destination. Temperatures tend to run 8° C (15° F) cooler than in Ojinaga. With directions from locals along the way, you could mountain-bike to San Carlos from Paso Lajitas (opposite the Texas town of Lajitas near Big Bend National Park); expect an elevation gain of approximately 1,200 feet. **Desert Sports,** tel. (915) 371-2727 or toll free tel. (888) 989-6900, in Terlingua, Texas, rents bikes for $25 per day.

Tours

Several companies operate soft adventure tours to San Carlos from the small Texas towns of Lajitas and Terlingua at the western edge of Big Bend National Park. Lajitas-based **San Carlos Excursions,** tel. (915) 424-3221, operated by experienced Mexican-American guide Kiko Garcia, runs all-day GMC Suburban trips to San Carlos from the Lajitas Trading Post every Saturday, Sunday, and Monday at 10 a.m., returning at 6:30 p.m. In addition to cruising the town, Kiko leads a hike through Cañon de San Carlos that takes in a hot springs, wax factory, and 150-year-old aqueduct. After lunch the group goes to Cañon de las Pilas to cool off in a waterfall. The cost is $65 pp for two to three people (two-person minimum), including lunch; four or more people pay just $50 pp and there's a 20% discount for seniors. Similar trips can also be arranged in Lajitas and Terlingua through **Big Bend River Tours,** tel. (800) 545-4240, **Lajitas Stables,** tel. (915) 424-3238, **Big Bend Birding Expeditions,** tel. (915) 371-2356, and **Desert Sports,** tel. (915) 371-2727 or toll free tel. (888) 989-6900.

Accommodations

La Gloria Bed and Breakfast offers accommodations in a modern four-bedroom, three-bath house near the mouth of Cañon de San Carlos. Rates of $40 pp include dinner and breakfast. Transportation from Lajitas must be arranged separately; La Gloria can provide roundtrip transportation for $75 in a pickup truck (two passengers) or for $100 in a van (up to nine passengers). For further information call Rick Page or Gloria Rodríguez in Lajitas at (915) 424-3203.

Getting There

You can easily drive yourself to San Carlos by crossing the border at Presidio/Ojinaga, then proceeding 30 km (19 miles) south along Chihuahua Hwy. 18, and then bearing east onto a graded gravel road (signed "Manuel Benavides") another 63 km (39 miles) to San Carlos. Not counting the time it takes to cross the border and clear through Ojinaga, this drive takes about two hours.

More adventurous drivers with sturdy, high-clearance vehicles can use the same route the Lajitas tours use, straight across a shallow river ford near Paso Lajitas (a Mexican village opposite Lajitas), then about nine miles southwest on a rutted dirt road till it ends at the aforementioned gravel road. At this junction, turn left and continue southeast another eight miles or so to San Carlos. Ask in Lajitas for explicit directions to the river ford. Strictly speaking it's illegal to cross the border where there are no immigration/customs inspectors (the same goes for Boquillas del Carmen in Coahuila), but as far as we know, no one has ever been prosecuted for crossing here in either direction. This may change as "Operation Rio Grande"—the latest effort to halt illegal immigration into the U.S.— takes effect, so ask around before trying. If the tours are still operational, you can assume it's okay to cross.

CONTINUING TOWARD CHIHUAHUA

Continuing southeast from Ojinaga on Mexico 16, you'll soon come to **Cañon de Peguis,** where the Río Conchos has cut a scenic, 2,000-foot-deep gash into the high desert floor. The canyon is about 31 km (19 miles) northeast of Coyame. Vehicles can be parked at the well-marked *mirador* (viewpoint) at the side of the highway near the canyon. A trail leads from the parking area down to the canyon edge.

The small town of **Coyame,** 87 km (54 miles) west of Ojinaga on Mexico 16, is best known for its mineral springs and for one of the last sotol distilleries in Chihuahua. A kilometer south of town by dirt road are the little-visited **Grutas de Coyame** or Coyame Grottoes—15 limestone caverns with plenty of stalactites, stalagmites, and crystal formations.

Villa de Aldama, most often known simply as Aldama, is a farming center 22 km (13.6 miles) northeast of Chihuahua. It was originally founded as Misión Santa Ana de Chinarras by Jesuit padres in 1717. The mission church's two-story baroque facade is being restored, and other historic provincial-colonial architecture is under renovation as well—with the intention of at-tracting weekend and holiday visitors from the state capital. **Hotel Los Pedales** offers two-star accommodations here for US$14-18, and Al-dama's PEMEX station is usually stocked with Magna Sin.

CHIHUAHUA (CITY) AND VICINITY

Capital of Mexico's largest state, Chihuahua (pop. 516,000) serves a dual role as state ad-ministrative center and commercial hub for tim-ber, cattle ranching, and mining. Set near the junction of the Chuvíscar and Sacramento Rivers, on a high-desert plain ringed by moun-tains, the urban landscape blends ordinary-look-ing Mexican commercial districts with a stately Porfiriato town center and a wealthy residential quarter of renovated Victorian mansions at the southwest edge of the city.

Most foreign visitors to the city come either to conduct business with the industrious Chi-huahuans or to embark on (or disembark from) the Chihuahua al Pacífico rail journey across the Sierra Madre Occidental. Although not tra-ditionally considered a tourist destination, the city has a number of historical sights worth see-ing, including the Pancho Villa museum (Quinta Luz), the regional museum (Quinta Gameros), and the Centro Cultural Chihuahua.

Climate and Seasons
At an elevation of 1,410 meters (4,700 feet) and surrounded by desert, Chihuahua has a very dry climate. The only precipitation of note—less than 10 cm (3.9 inches) per month—falls July-September.

June, when daytime highs average 30.5° C (87° F), is generally the warmest month of the year, while January is the coolest month with evening lows of around 1-4° C (34-40° F). Occa-sional northern winds in the winter will force the thermometer below freezing and add a wind-chill factor (light snow isn't unknown); hence the best overall time to visit Chihuahua is March-November.

MEXICAN CALENDAR KING

One of Chihuahua's least known but most in-fluential native sons was Jesús Helguera (1910-1971), who is today considered one of the foremost representatives of popular art in Mexico. As a painter, Helguera was a master of composition and light, and the traditional scenes he chose as his subjects—dark-eyed women carrying handmade *ollas* through tidy Mexican markets in shawl and peasant dress, or hand-some *charros* preparing their silver-saddled steeds—evoked tranquility, harmony, dignity, respect, and a pride in Mexican culture. His oil paintings came to symbolize Mexican life for many art lovers—much as Norman Rockwell's art at one time embodied life in the U.S.—and they became highly sought after for use on post-WW II Mexican calendars. Through this medium of distribution, his work established an ideal aesthetic of *mestizaje* that has been imitated by Mexican calendar artists ever since. Helguera calendars and paintings are now considered collectors items in Mexico.

HISTORY

In 1707 Spaniard Juan Holguín registered a claim on a silver mine at Santa Eulalia (present-day Aquiles Serdán), on the banks of the Río Chuvíscar about 18 km southeast of the current state capital. Other rich silver veins were dis-covered in the area and several small mining settlements soon sprouted; one near the con-fluence of the Chuvíscar and Sacramento Rivers was made a *cabecera* (district seat) of Nueva Vizcaya in 1709. The local Tarahumaras called the site *chihuahuara,* meaning "place where sacks are made." Under Spanish control the town was named San Francisco de Cuellar.

The Jesuits soon arrived and established San Francisco de Cuellar as a religious cen-ter, building a Colegio de Loreto de la Com-pañía de Jesús in 1718 and the Templo de San Francisco in 1724. By this time the name had been changed again, to San Felipe Real de Chihuahua. Apache raids held back further development in the area until the late 1800s. Along with Indian attacks, Chihuahua had to contend with the Mexican independence struggle, during much of which Chihuahua remained loyal to the Spanish crown. Padre Miguel Hidalgo y Costilla, the father of Mexican independence, was captured by Royalist forces, convicted of treason and heresy by the Holy Office of the Inquisition, and executed in Chihuahua in July 1811. Following independence the government chose to delete the Spanish parts of the name for the city, leaving only the native "Chihuahua."

During the 1840s' Mexican-American War, the city was briefly occupied by U.S. troops, an event described as "pallid compared to the terror inspired by an Apache raid." With the shooting of Chiricahua Apache chief Victorio by a Tarahumara scout in 1880, Chihuahua enjoyed a brief period of relative peace until the 1910-20 Mexican Revolution. In 1910 Pancho Villa and his División del Norte army took the city and based themselves there for the duration of the revolution. As the national political scene deteriorated, Villa became a regional warlord, controlling much of Northern Mexico. His *quinta* or manor is now a museum.

Chihuahua's prosperity peaked in the 1920s, after which the economy weathered decades of nationalization and misgovernment to become a major Northern Mexico capital. Manufacturing has recently begun supplementing Chihuahua's traditional dependence on timber, mining, and cattle. The Ford Motors plant at the city's Complejo Industrial turns out around 4,000 autos per year for both national and international markets. Zenith. Motorola, and Data General also have manufacturing facilities in the area.

SIGHTS

Catedral de San Francisco

Also known as Catedral Metropolitana de Chihuahua, this important religious edifice on the city's Plaza de Armas (Calle 2 and Libertad) was begun in 1724 as the "Parroquía de Nuestra Señora de la Regla de San Francisco de Asís" and built in stages through 1826. In 1891 the church attained cathedral status with the creation of a separate Chihuahua Diocese.

The twin-towered facade, sculpted in quarried pink stone, features the 12 apostles in late baroque style—complete with a profusion of foliage, flowers, and fruit. Inside is a large 1920-vintage altar of Carrara marble beneath three naves arranged in typical cruciform fashion. A side chapel contains the **Museo de Arte Sacro** (Museum of Sacred Art), dedicated in 1984 and featuring Mexican religious paintings (including works by Cabrera, Páez, Alcíbar, and Antonio de Torres) from the 18th century.

Opposite the cathedral entrance on the Plaza de Armas stands a bronze statue of the 1709 founder of Chihuahua, Don Antonio Deza y Ulloa.

an 1843 lithograph of Chihuahua

COLECCIÓN CENTRO DE ESTUDIOS

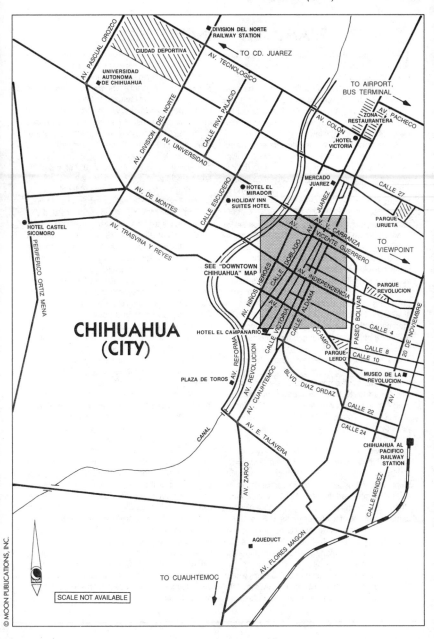

FRANCISCO "PANCHO" VILLA

Born Doroteo Arango in San Juan del Río, Dur., in 1877 (1879 according to some sources), the man most of the world knew as Pancho Villa spent much of his life in Durango until, at age 16, he killed a man who had raped his younger sister. Little record exists of the next four or five years of his life, during which time he changed his name to Francisco Villa to evade the law.

By the time he was 20, Villa had moved northward to Chihuahua, working on and off as a miner in Parral while selling stolen cattle in Chihuahua (official government biographies list his occupation then as "wholesale meat-seller"). In 1899 he returned to mining, this time in Santa Eulalia near Chihuahua, but he soon tired of the laborer's life and added bank robbery to cattle rustling and murder on the list of crimes for which he was wanted by the Díaz government.

Villa's Robin Hood story began after he established himself and his bandit followers in the sierras in 1900 (officially, the years 1900-09 are "unaccounted for") and became a legendary hero to the poor for skillfully evading the Porfiriato's oppressive *rurales* for nearly a decade. In 1910 Villa and his men came down from the hills to join Francisco I. Madero's revolutionary forces, thereby making a historical transition from *bandidos* to *revolucionarios*. The charismatic figure was able to recruit an army of thousands, including a substantial number of Americans, some of whom were made captains in the División del Norte. Villa even created one squadron made up entirely of Americans under the leadership of Capt. Tracey Richardson, a man who apparently fought with many different insurgent armies around the world at that time.

Following Madero's short-lived victory and assassination, Villa remained in command of his División del Norte army in resistance—along with Coahuila's Venustiano Carranza and Sonora's Alvaro Obregón—against the 1913-14 Victoriano Huerta dictatorship. Around this time Villa also became something of a folk hero in the U.S., and Hollywood filmmakers as well as U.S. newspaper photographers flocked to Northern Mexico to record his battle exploits—many of which were staged for the benefit of the cameras.

Villa's forces were based in Chihuahua, where Villa ruled over Northern Mexico like a warlord. Villa financed his army by stealing from the endless cattle herds in Northern Mexico and selling beeves north of the border, where he found plenty of U.S. merchants willing to sell him guns and ammunition. Faced with a stagnant economy, he issued his own money; if merchants refused to take it, they risked being shot. Executions, which Villa often ordered on a whim; were usually left to his friend Rodolfo Fierro, best known by his nickname "El Carnicero" ("the Butcher"). In true Robin Hood style, he broke up the vast land holdings of local *hacendados* and parceled it out to the widows and orphans of his fallen soldiers.

During *fiestas* the mustachioed legend would dance all night with female camp followers, although he didn't drink. When Emiliano Zapata insisted Villa join him in a toast when their two armies met outside Mexico City in December 1914, Villa gagged on a swig of brandy. He was an avid swimmer and would run to stay in shape. According to one of Villa's last surviving widows, he officially married 26 times.

A split among the revolutionary leaders soon pitted Villa against Obregón and Carranza. When the U.S. government came out openly in support of the Carranza presidency, Villa retaliated by raiding U.S border towns, most notably Columbus, New Mexico. On the U.S. side of the border, Villa's image plummeted while many in Mexico saw Villa as an avenger of decades of *yanqui* oppression. Despite his popularity, the combined forces of Carranza and Obregón defeated the Villistas in one battle after another. After two U.S. Army "punitive expeditions" into Mexico in 1916 and 1919 failed to rout Villa, the Mexican government accepted his surrender and retired Villa on a general's salary to Canutillo, Durango. In 1923 he was assassinated while returning from bank business in Parral, Chihuahua.

Today Villa is remembered with pride by most Mexicans for having led the most important military campaigns of the constitutionalist revolution, in which his troops were victorious as far south as Zacatecas and Mexico City, east as far as Tampico, and west as far as Casas Grandes. Because of Villa's Columbus escapade and subsequent evasion of U.S. troops, he is also often cited as the only foreign military personage ever to have "successfully" invaded continental U.S. territory. When speaking with Mexicans—especially *norteños*—about Villa, don't underestimate the respect his name still garners in Mexico.

Centro Cultural Chihuahua

Cattle baron and ex-governor of Chihuahua Don Luis Terrazas had this palatial mansion at Calle Aldama and Ocampo (a brief walk from Plaza de Armas) built in 1889 as his home. In typical Spanish style, the two-story stone building forms a rectangle of huge rooms around a central patio finished with fine tile flooring, ironwork banisters, and a stone fountain.

Since Terrazas's death, the building has been used as a monastic cell, boardinghouse, IMSS (Mexican social security) state headquarters, and now as a cultural and educational institution owned by Grupo Chihuahua, an association dedicated to maintaining regional identity through the support of Chihuahuan art and culture. All the stonework, woodwork, and ironwork have been beautifully restored and reconstructed to original specifications.

In addition to the grand *fin-de-siglo* architecture—an attraction in itself—the second floor of the Centro Cultural houses a high-quality, permanent collection of Paquimé pottery. Other rooms in the building contain rotating displays on the region's art, anthropology, and archaeology. A noticeboard on the ground floor posts information on cultural events to be held at the center and elsewhere in the city. Entry to the building—and all exhibits—is free. Open daily 10 a.m.-2 p.m. and 4-7 p.m.

Museo de la Revolución (Quinta Luz)

Of the several small museums dedicated to Francisco "Pancho" Villa throughout the state of Chihuahua, this is the most complete. During the Mexican Revolution, this 50-room *quinta* (manor) served as Villa's home and headquarters for his revolutionary army, the División del Norte. After the revolution Villa retired to the Parral area farther south, but following his 1923 assassination, the government awarded the mansion to his only legal wife, Luz Corral de Villa (Pancho was known to have had at least 22 common-law wives or mistresses).

Señora Luz restored several rooms to their original 1910 decor and allowed visitors in for brief tours before she passed away in 1981. Since then the Mexican army has taken possession of the building and turned it into a full-scale museum displaying an array of Villa's personal effects, historical photographs, revolu-

tionary weaponry, and the bullet-riddled black Dodge in which Villa was assassinated.

The museum, located at Calle Decima 300 and Méndez on the southeastern side of town, is open daily 9 a.m.-1 p.m. and 3-7 p.m.; admission is US$0.65. Although it's a 13- to 14-block walk, the museum can be reached on foot from the downtown Plaza de Armas area in about 30 minutes. You could stop at the Museo Regional along the way, breaking the trip into two neat halves.

Quinta Gameros (Centro Cultural Universitario or Museo Regional)

Built 1907-10 by wealthy miner Manuel Gameros, this is one of the preeminent examples of French art nouveau in North America; note the *fin-de-siglo* stained glass and skylights. Several of the rooms contain authentic, original art-nouveau furnishings (including a dining room decorated completely in this style), a living room that's basically Louis XV with art-nouveau influences, and an impressive, art-nouveau bathroom. Other galleries in the museum house traveling exhibits of modern art and photography.

The museum is at Paseo Bolívar and Calle 4. Hours are Tues.-Sun. 10 a.m.-2 p.m. and 4-7 p.m. Tuesday through Saturday, admission is US$1.35 adults, US$0.65 students with ID; on Sunday, admission costs US$0.95 adults, US$0.45 students with ID. To get there from the downtown area, follow Calle 4 southeast from behind the cathedral (about a 20-minute walk).

Aqueduct

This impressive, five-km-long, 15-meter-high *acueducto* of stone arches was built by the Spanish 1751-86 to carry water from nearby Presa Chuvíscar to the city. Until 1969 it served as the city's main water supply. The best-preserved section is between Calle 32 and Av. Zarco.

Government Buildings

Chihuahua has several turn-of-the-century buildings used by the government in the downtown area. The three-story, rectangular **Palacio de Gobierno** on Calle Aldama (facing diminutive Plaza Hidalgo) was built toward the end of the 19th century. In its central courtyard, a red light bulb over the Altar de la Patria (Fatherland Altar) burns perpetually to honor Padre Miguel Hidalgo y Costilla, who met his death in front of a firing squad on

COURTESY MUSEO DE LA REVOLUCIÓN, CHIHUAHUA

Villa crying at the grave of President Madero

this spot on 30 July 1811. The interior walls feature murals depicting the history of Chihuahua, as painted by muralist Aarón Piña Mora.-Thematic highlights of the mural include Pancho Villa on horseback; Emiliano Zapata naked except for a bandolero; Cabeza de Vaca and Estebanico on their legendary journey across Texas and Mexico; the discovery of gold in the state in 1567 and subsequent exploitation of the Tarahumaras; 18th-century incursions of the Apaches; the building of the cathedral; Padre Hidalgo in the Chihuahua dungeon; and a panel showing Benito Juárez flanked by Abraham Lincoln and Simón Bolívar.

Before his execution, Padre Hidalgo was kept prisoner in a *calabozo* or "dungeon" (actually a tower room) in the **Palacio Federal** at Av. Juárez and Av. Carranza. A verse of compassionate thanks written in charcoal by Hidalgo to his jailers is preserved in bronze and displayed. The Palacio Federal was originally built as the Colegio de Loreto de la Compañía de Jesús in the 18th century.

The **Palacio Municipal,** facing the Plaza de Armas, was designed by English architect Alfred Giles (who also designed many historic buildings in Texas) and erected in 1906 to house the Casa de Cabildo or town council; the Sala de Cabildos contains what is reportedly one of the world's largest conference tables.

Plaza Hidalgo
This small, leafy plaza opposite the Palacio de Gobierno contains a bronze statue of Padre Hidalgo delivering his famous *grito* (shout for independence), surrounded by four other revolutionary heroes in bronze: José María Morelos, Juan Aldama, Mariano Jiménez, and Ignacio Allende. Plaza Hidalgo has the city's best selection of shoeshine kiosks.

ACCOMMODATIONS

Chihuahua has a good selection of places to stay in all budget categories, and a large percentage of hotel staffers are Spanish-English bilingual.

Shoestring
A perennial favorite with folks watching their pesos is **Hotel San Juan,** Calle Victoria 823 (a couple of blocks southwest of Plaza de Armas), tel. (14) 10-0035, fax (14) 10-2683, an older hotel with 61 rooms around a courtyard. The tile entrance is beautiful; the rooms are not. In fact, they are worn out and a bit seedy, but each has heating and private bathroom. The San Juan has its own restaurant and bar. Rates: US$4.60 s, US$5.30 d, US$7 t, plus US$1.33 for each additional person up to five.

A few doors down from the San Juan toward the plaza, **Hotel Nuevo Reforma** (some signs say just Hotel Reforma), Calle Victoria 809, tel. (14) 12-5800, is a better low-budget choice these days. Spacious rooms surround a faded double-staircase atrium courtyard. A simple and inexpensive coffeeshop is attached. Rates: US$6 with one bed, US$7.50 with two twin beds, US$7 with a king bed, US$8 with two double beds, US$9 with four twin beds, plus US$3 per additional person for as many more as you can stuff into a room.

Similar in price but with less character (and no restaurant/bar) are **Hotel María Dolores,** Calle 9 #917 (at Av. Niños Heroes), tel. (14) 10-4770, and **Hotel Carmen,** Av. Juárez at Calle Decima 4, tel. (14) 15-7096.

Farther south downtown, a Casa de Hués-

CALLE 13

HOTEL
MARIA DOLORES

AV. REFORMA

CANAL

AV. REVOLUCION

AV. REVOLUCION

HOTEL
AVENIDA

EDIFICIO AGUSTIN
MELGAR

CENTRO DE LAS
ARTESANIAS
DEL ESTADO

PALACIO
FEDERAL

PALACIO
DE GOBIERNO

CALLE JULIAN CARRILLO

AV. NIÑOS HEROES

AV. JUAREZ

CALLE LIBERTAD

AV. V. CARRANZA

PLAZA HIDALGO

MERCADO DE
ARTESANIAS

AV. VICENTE GUERRERO

MOTEL POSADA
TIERRA BLANCA

CALLE 5

CALLE ALDAMA

AH CHILES
TACOS Y SALSA
PIZZA DE REY

HOTEL
PALACIO DEL SOL

SORIANA

PLAZA LIBERTAD

CALLE VICTORIA

CALLE 7

HOTEL SANTA
REGINA

BANAMEX

BANCA
SERFIN

**DOWNTOWN
CHIHUAHUA**

CALLE 5

MERCADO
REFORMA

AEROMEXICO

CALLE 3

AL SUPER

BANCOMER

CATEDRAL DE
SAN FRANCISCO
AND PLAZA DE ARMAS

IBANCA

AV. INDEPENDENCIA

CALLE
DOBLADO

CALLE LIBERTAD

AV. OCAMPO

HOTEL
SAN FRANCISCO

LA PARILLA

CALLE 2

AV. JUAREZ

HOTEL NUEVO
REFORMA

CALLE VICTORIA

CALLE ALDAMA

CENTRO
CULTURAL
CHIHUAHUA

CALLE ALLENDE

CALLE 4

HOTEL
CARMEN

HOTEL
SAN JUAN

CASA DE HUESPEDES

MI CAFE

CALLE 12

CALLE OJINGA

CALLE MORELOS

AV. OCAMPO

CALLE DE LA LLAVE

LOS OLIVOS
RESTAURANT

MUSEO
REGIONAL

PASEO BOLIVAR

CALLE 10

MOON

SCALE NOT AVAILABLE

© MOON PUBLICATIONS, INC.

pedes, Calle 12 #209 (between Victoria and Libertad), offers eight basic rooms with clean shared bathroom. The management is friendly and many of the tenants are long-term renters. Rates: US$4.

On Calle Gómez Farías between Calle 2 and Independencia, east of the plaza a few blocks, the two-story **Hotel Cortez** occupies an old stucco building in a residential neighborhood. Picture a slightly seedy Hollywood apartment building. The smallish, relatively clean rooms surround a courtyard and have private hot-water bathrooms. Rates: US$6.50 s, US$7.30 d.

Budget

In this price range you begin to see a/c and off-street parking. **Hotel Santa Regina,** Calle 3 #107, tel. (14) 15-3889, fax (14) 10-1411, is a two-story downtown hotel featuring clean rooms of moderate size with TV, phone, and a/c. This is definitely one of the better values in the town center. There's parking downstairs and credit cards are accepted. Rates: US$19 s, US$21 d, US$24 t, US$25 q. Also good is **Hotel El Campanario,** Blvd. Díaz Ordaz at Privada de Libertad, tel. (14) 15-4545, which has clean, comfortable. and modern rooms and a decent *cafetería*. Rates: US$16-19.

Friendly **Hotel Avenida,** Av. V. Carranza 1101, tel. (14) 15-2891, is popular with middle-class Mexican businesspeople. Rooms have TV, direct dial phones, a/c, and heating. There are free purified water dispensers on every floor. The hotel doesn't have its own parking lot, but parking can usually be arranged nearby. Credit cards accepted. Rates: US$26-30.

Another four-star, downtown favorite is the friendly and efficient 106-room **Motel Posada Tierra Blanca,** Av. Niños Héroes 100, tel. (14) 15-0000, fax 14-1663, opposite the more expensive Hotel Palacio del Sol. Rooms have a/c, color TV, and direct dial phones. Other amenities include a secure parking lot and swimming pool. Rates: US$31 s, US$32 d.

Grand old dame **Hotel Victoria,** Av. Juárez at Colón in the city's "Zona Rosa," was at one time the biggest and most popular hotel in Chihuahua. The owners have placed the "Vic" on the market.

Inexpensive

Two-story motel-style **Hotel El Mirador,** Av. Universidad 1309, tel. (14) 13-2205, fax (14) 13-

8906, Mexico toll-free tel. (800) 9-0475, U.S. toll-free tel. (800) 782-9422, is a Best Western affiliate and features comfortable a/c rooms and an outdoor pool. Rates: US$36.50-45.50 weekdays; as low as US$25 weekends.

On the way into Chihuahua from Ciudad Juárez via Mexico 45 (south of the Ford plant, north of Av. Vallarta), the motel-style **Hotel Parador San Miguel,** Av. Tecnológico 7901, tel. (14) 17-0303, fax (14) 17-1500, looks fairly ordinary from the outside but is a spotlessly clean, well-run establishment. Nice touches include arched brick ceilings in the rooms and local folk art in the coffee shop and other public rooms. All rooms have satellite TV, heating and a/c, and phones. Another plus: You can leave your vehicle and store your luggage here at no charge while taking the Chihuahua al Pacífico train ride. Rates: US$36 s, US$40 d.

A bit lower in cost, and popular with Americans and Canadians because it's on the highway and has parking space for RVs/trailers, is **Motel Nieves,** Av. Tecnológico at Ahuehuete, tel. (14) 13-2516. The simple rooms surround a pool and parking lot. Rates: US$33 s, US$36 d.

Next door to Chihuahua's huge bus terminal, the six-story **Hotel Central Palace,** Priv. Gral. Roberto Fierro 8017, tel. (14) 29-1929, offers clean, modern rooms with phone, TV, carpet, and a/c. Facilities include a bar, restaurant, coffeeshop, and disco. Credit cards accepted. Rates: US$36-43.

Moderate

Four hotels in this category (plus one slightly more expensive) compete for upper-class business travelers and better-heeled tourists. All accept credit cards. Heating, a/c, satellite TV, telephones, and security parking are standard.

A very good choice for downtown location is the efficient and comfortable, 132-room **Hotel San Francisco,** Victoria 409 (close to the Plaza de Armas), tel. (14) 16-7770, fax (14) 15-3538, Mexico toll-free tel. (800) 1-4107, U.S./Canada toll-free tel. (800) 847-2546. This hotel is often full so reservations are advised. Rates: US$52 s, US$64 d; weekend specials as low as US$40 are sometimes available.

If the Hotel San Francisco is full, a second downtown choice is the high-rise, 190-room **Hotel Palacio del Sol,** at Av. Independencia

116 (off Perif. Ortíz Mena, two blocks north of the Plaza de Armas), tel. (14) 15-6000, fax (14) 15-9947, Mexico toll-free tel. (800) 1-4007, U.S./Canada toll-free tel. (800) 852-4049. Because of its size, many tour groups use this hotel. One of the nicer features: VCRs and videos available for loan. Rates: US$51 s, US$61 double.

The **Holiday Inn Suites Hotel,** Calle Escudero 702 (between Av. Independencia and Av. Universidad, northwest of downtown), tel. (14) 14-3350, fax (14) 14-3313, gets high marks for its suites with refrigerators, fully equipped kitchens, IDD phones with data ports, VCR with free movies, and complimentary continental breakfast. The hotel also has two heated pools, a sauna, and jacuzzi. Rates: US$80 s/d.

For quick access to Mexico 45, another good choice is the upscale motel-style **Hotel Casa Grande,** Av. Tecnológico 4702, tel. (14) 19-6633, fax (14) 19-3235, Mexico toll-free tel. (800) 1-4222, U.S./Canada toll-free tel. (800) 343-6344. The spacious rooms have IDD phones and all the amenities. Hotel facilities include a tennis court, pool, travel agency, and business center with fax, copy, and secretarial services. Rates: US$55-72.

Moderate/Expensive

Hotel Castel Sicomoro, Perif. Ortíz Mena 411 (on the extreme west side of town), tel. (14) 13-5445, fax (14) 13-1411, is a modern five-star hotel with a pool and disco but little else to recommend it. Its location toward the Complejo Industrial makes it popular with visiting factory execs. Rates: US$60-85 s/d.

RV Parks

Chemaju Trailer Park, Av. Tecnológico 6505, tel. (14) 13-2516, has 23 spaces with electricity and water for US$10 per night. Motel Nieves (see "Inexpensive" hotels above) has a few RV spaces as well.

FOOD

Inexpensive restaurants are abundant around Plaza de Armas, along Calle Aldama, along Av. Niños Héroes, and in Plaza Libertad, a pedestrian mall created by closing off Calle Libertad to vehicular traffic between Av. Independencia and Av. J.N. Santos.

In Mercado Reforma (off Av. Niños Héroes west of the Plaza de Armas) are several inexpensive *loncherías* open for breakfast and lunch. The area around Mercado Reforma is also dotted with inexpensive *taquerías* and street vendors, especially at night when the daytime markets close and the streets are packed with snackers. Chihuahua's most popular street food is *barbacoa,* pit-cooked head of sheep or cow.

Mexican

Ah Chiles Tacos y Salsa, Calle Aldama, between Calle 7 and Av. V. Guerrero, is a fast-food style place with good tacos of all kinds, plus a substantial salsa bar. Open daily 10 a.m.-10 p.m.

Cafetería Dega, on the ground floor of Hotel San Francisco, is a very clean and efficient coffee shop with an extensive menu of Mexican and regional specialties (plus a few American dishes) at moderate prices. The huge weekend breakfast buffet costs just US$5 and includes custom omelettes. Open daily 7 a.m.-11 p.m.

La Casa de los Milagros, Victoria 812 (near the San Juan and Nuevo Reforma Hotels), tel. (14) 37-0693, occupies a restored colonial with indoor and outdoor (courtyard) seating. This cafe and gallery is the nicest addition to Chihuahua's culinary scene in a long time. Live folk music most evenings. Open Sun.-Thurs. 5 p.m.-midnight, Fri.-Sat. 5 p.m.-1:30 a.m.

Chihuahua Charlie's Bar and Grill, Av. Juárez 3329, tel. (14) 15-7589. was once a hot spot among young Chihuahuans, but of late it seems to have lost favor with just about everyone. The menu features a number of regional dishes made from original recipes. Moderate prices. Open daily 11 a.m.-1 a.m.

Mi Café, Calle Victoria 1000, tel. (14) 10-1238, is a modern, coffee shop-style place specializing in *pollo o lengua en mole,* and *machaca en chile colorado,* as well as inexpensive to moderately priced breakfasts and *comida corrida.* Open daily 7 a.m.-11 p.m.

At **La Parilla,** Calle Victoria 420 (opposite Hotel San Francisco), tel. (14) 15-5953, the house specialty is Chihuahuan-style *carne al carbón* (charcoal-grilled steak). Also on the menu are a splendid array of Northern-style tacos and *antojitos,* including *cebolletas* (grilled spring onions) and *frijoles norteños.*

Pistaco's, Agustín Melgar 2116 (one block from Av. Tecnológico), tel. (14) 13-7657, serves *pozole, menudo, carnitas,* and a grand selection of tacos of all kinds. Inexpensive. Open daily 5 p.m.-midnight.

More Upscale
The city's compact "Zona Restaurantera" at the north end of Av. Juárez is lined end-to-end with upscale restaurants. The coming and going of chefs and local trends makes it difficult to single out the "best," and the district seems to have lost local patronage over the last couple of years.

La Calesa, Av. Juárez at Av. Colón, tel. (14) 16-0222, offers a good selection of steaks and international and Mexican food. Open daily 1 p.m.-midnight. **La Olla,** Av. Juárez 331, tel. (14) 14-7894, serves classic Mexican cuisine in a converted 19th-century brewery decorated with empty wine bottles and copper brewing vats. Open daily for lunch and dinner.

Japanese
The best of Chihuahua's several Japanese restaurants is **Restaurant Japonés y Barra de Sushi (Yaki Niku Barra de Sushi),** Centro Comercial Plaza Vallarta, Av. Tecnológico, tel. (14) 19-4619. The sushi bar is well run. Japanese expatriates living in Chihuahua dine here. Moderate to expensive. Open Wed.-Sun. noon-10 p.m.

Vegetarian
El Bocado del Sol, Calle Libertad 1910, is a typical combination of natural food/herb shop with vegetarian lunch fare. **Los Olivos Restaurant Vegetariano,** Calle de la Llave 202 (between Calle 2 and 4 near the Museo Regional), tel. (14) 10-0161, is a charming, casual spot with a varied vegetarian menu of Mexican and international dishes. Open 8 a.m.-5 p.m.

Other
Visitors staying on the city's northern outskirts at one of the hotels or motels along Av. Tecnológico will find several fast-food places (Pizza del Rey, Ricky's Tacos, KFC, Ah Chiles Tacos y Salsa, and Burger King) in the **Plaza Vallarta** shopping center near Hotel Casa Grande.

Restaurant Woolworth, Plaza Libertad (Calle Libertad pedestrian mall) opposite the cathedral, serves a mix of Mexican standards and American coffee shop fare. It's reliable, popular, and inexpensive; open daily 8 a.m.-9:30 p.m. **Pizza del Rey,** near Ah Chiles Tacos y Salsa on Calle Aldama, makes decent pizza and is a favorite hangout for young Chihuahuans.

Groceries
In downtown Chihuahua the best area for grocery shopping is a complex of small streets (generally referred to as **Mercado Reforma,** the name of the largest open-air market here) between Av. Juárez and Av. Niños Héroes, where a number of open-air markets and grocery stores can be found. This area has superseded the much-touted Mercado Juárez on Av. Juárez and Calle 25, which isn't as busy as it used to be.

Mercado Reforma itself has every foodstuff imaginable. The smaller **Mercado Combate,** between Calle Doblado and Niños Héroes around the corner from Mercado Reforma, has beautiful vegetables and a good assortment of Mennonite cheeses. Nearby are two well-stocked grocery stores: **Soriana,** on Av. Independencia and Niños Héroes; and **Al Super,** on Av. Juárez.

On the city bypasses, **Plaza Vallarta** on Av. Tecnológico and **Futurama Leones** on Perif. Ortíz Mena have supermarkets.

ENTERTAINMENT

Industrious Chihuahua seems to go to bed earlier than other Mexican cities of similar size, so you won't find much to do after dark. Following, however, are a few suggestions.

Behind Club de los Parados on Av. Juárez is a popular outdoor bar called **Jardín Carta Blanca** (don't look for a sign; you won't find one). It's known locally as "La Cervecería" ("The Brewery"). Inexpensive beer and cocktails (including *vampiros*) are served in what looks like an American-style drive-in; *trobadores*—both mariachi and *norteña*—provide the music. A similar place, **La Alameda,** can be found on Av. Colón at Canal.

In a similar vein but more upscale is **Taberna La Cervecería,** Av. Juárez 3333, tel. (14) 15-8380. Done up with huge copper vats and crusty brick walls to look like an old brewery, the Taberna serves light and dark Carta Blanca beer on tap, plus good Mexican *botanas.*

Several of the city's five-star hotels have bars and discos. One of the liveliest is the Hotel San Francisco's **Bar Los Primos,** which features live music nightly. **Club 21,** Av. Juárez at Calle 43, is a posh newer disco that attracts a younger crowd.

Several modern **cinemas** showing first-run European and American films are located downtown near the Palacio de Gobierno around Av. V. Carranza. The **Alliance Française Mexique (Alianza Francesa de Chihuahua),** at Calle Aldama 430, tel. (14) 16-1491, occasionally screens French films.

Also check the Centro Cultural Chihuahua (see "Sights," above, for location) for occasional art and music events.

RECREATION

Bullfights
The 8,000-seat **Plaza de Toros Esperanza,** off Av. Reforma next to the western end of the canal, holds occasional *corridas de toros* on Sundays at 4 p.m. in summer. Bullfighting isn't nearly as popular here as in Ciudad Juárez.

Shopping
Plaza Libertad, the pedestrian mall along Calle Libertad opposite the cathedral and Plaza de Armas, is flanked by watch and jewelry shops, booteries, Mexican versions of Sears and Woolworth, and various other specialty shops and department stores.

USEFUL CHIHUAHUA TELEPHONE NUMBERS

State Tourist Office	29-3421
Red Cross	11-2211, 12-1558
State Hospital	15-9000
Federal Highway Police	17-9513
Green Angels	17-8972
Chihuahua al Pacífico Station	10-3751, 10-5643
Chihuahua Area Code	14

For a greater selection of Mexican boots, cruise the back-to-back **boot shops** along Av. Ocampo between Aldama and Juárez. Boot prices are very low compared to those in the United States.

El Quinto Sol, Río de Janeiro 524, tel. (14) 14-3165, carries a quality collection of Mexican furniture and decorative accessories, including antique doors, wagons, and carts, and Talavera ceramics from Puebla.

Mercado de Artesanías, Calle Victoria 506, is a large, touristy curios store with crafts from all over Mexico. Some good buys can be found if you take time to wade through the kitsch. **Centro de las Artesanías del Estado,** on Av. Juárez between Guerrero and Carranza, is similar.

INFORMATION AND SERVICES

Tourist Offices
Downtown, the most convenient source of information is the state tourism office in the Edificio Agustín Melgar at Calle Libertad and Calle 13, tel. (14) 16-2436 or 29-3421. Hours are Mon.-Fri. 8 a.m.-7 p.m.

Post and Telephone
Chihuahua's central post office is in a huge turn-of-the-century building at the corner of Calle Libertad and Av. V. Carranza. Hours are Mon.-Fri. 9 a.m.-6 p.m., Sat.-Sun. 9 a.m.-noon. You'll find operator-staffed long-distance TelMex offices at Av. V. Carranza 1403 and at the Central Camionera; both are open daily 9 a.m.-9 p.m.

Money
Several *casas de cambio* lie along Aldama near the intersection with Independencia; the huge **Ibanca Centro de Cambio** (just north of Calle 2 on the east side of Aldama) is open 24 hours and features drive-in booths and a walk-in section. Another Ibanca branch is on the east side of Av. Juárez south of Gómez Marín, opposite Calle 25.

TRANSPORTATION

Air
Chihuahua's airport, 22 km northeast of the city, has a restaurant called **Wings** upstairs, a snack

bar downstairs, several car rental places, and an ATM that takes cards on the Plus system.

Lone Star Airlines, at the airport, tel. (14) 20-9155, Mexico toll-free tel. (800) 817-1932, U.S./Canada toll-free tel. (800) 877-3932, recently began flying Chihuahua to/from Dallas (Mon.-Sat.; US$196 roundtrip, US$285 one-way) and to/from El Paso (Sun.-Fri.; US$96 roundtrip, US$110 one-way). It remains to be seen how long this service lasts; Lone Star is known for short-lived experimental routes like this.

Aeroméxico, Paseo Bolívar 405, tel. (14) 15-6303, operates regular nonstop flights between Chihuahua and Ciudad Juárez, Ciudad Obregón, Culiacán, El Paso, Hermosillo, Los Mochis, Mexico City, Monterrey, and Torreón.

Aero California, Perif. Ortíz Mena 1809, tel. (14) 37-1022, flies nonstop to/from Tijuana and Mexico City only. **Mexicana,** at the airport, tel. (800) 325-0990 in Mexico, fields nonstops to/from Hermosillo and Monterrey, with connections to several other major Mexican cities. **TAESA,** Av. Jiménez 1204, tel. (14) 16-5146, flies daily to/from Ciudad Juárez and Mexico City.

Airport Transportation: Fares for shuttle vans and taxis into the city from the airport are strictly controlled at the airport. A *colectivo* costs US$4.66-8.50 depending on the distance, while a private taxi costs US$11-12.50.

Bus

Chihuahua's cavernous Terminal Central de Autobuses—also still called Central Camionera (its old name)—is at the southeastern outskirts of the city on Av. Juan Pablo II, the road to the airport. This ultramodern edifice houses all kinds of services, including a pharmacy, restaurant, *casa de cambio,* left-luggage facility (a steep US$0.33 an hour), telephone office, snack bars, sundries shops, and a telecommunications center. City buses (US$0.20) from Av. Niños Héroes downtown (marked "C. Camionera") go to the bus terminal; in the reverse direction they end up along Av. Juárez. From the airport take buses numbered E-179.

The main bus line for in-state travel is **Estrella Blanca,** tel. (14) 12-4987, which runs buses to Creel (US$9, eight times daily), Cuauhtémoc (US$3, every half-hour 6 a.m.-6:30 p.m.), and La Junta (US$5, every half-hour 6 a.m.-6:30 p.m.). Less frequent buses run deeper into the Sierra

Tarahumara, including Cusárare, Batopilas, Basihuare, and Guachochi, each for US$9-11. Tickets for Estrella Blanca buses can be purchased at the line's city ticket office, Av. R.F. Magón at Calle 44, tel. (14) 18-8659.

Transportes Chihuahuenses, tel. (14) 12-0101, runs longer routes on better buses; destinations include Ojinaga (US$7, seven times daily), Ciudad Juárez (US$12, three times daily), Parral (US$7, 13 times daily), Durango (US$20, eight times daily), Torreón (US$15, 19 times daily), San Luis Potosí (US$34, six times daily), Zacatecas (US$28, 18 times daily), and Mexico City (US$49, two times daily).

Omnibus de México, tel. (14) 15-0665, operates first-class buses to/from Ciudad Juárez (US$12, three times daily), Guadalajara (US$12, once daily), Ojinaga (US$7, once daily), Reynosa (US$34, once daily), Saltillo (US$24, once daily), and Mexico City (US$49, once daily).

Turistar, tel. (14) 15-6282, specializes in *ejecutivo* service to/from Ciudad Juárez (US$17, three times daily), El Paso (US$25, twice daily), Torreón (US$20, once daily), Monterrey (US$33, once daily), and Guadalajara (US$55, once daily). Turistar also has its own first-class waiting lounge.

Train

Chihuahua has two separate railway stations: one for the **Chihuahua al Pacífico,** Calle Méndez at Calle 24, tel. (14) 15-7756; the other for **División del Norte,** Av. División del Norte, tel. (14) 13-0093.

On its run between Ciudad Juárez and Zacatecas via Chihuahua, the División del Norte train offers first-class, reserved seating only. At Zacatecas, second-class seats to Mexico City become available. The fare between Ciudad Juárez and Chihuahua is only US$7.50, but the schedule is inconvenient. The southbound train leaves Juárez at 10 p.m. and passes through Chihuahua at 3:15 a.m. (arriving in Mexico City at 9:30 a.m.). The northbound train leaves Chihuahua for Juárez at 1:20 a.m. Southbound from Chihuahua, fares are as follows: to Torreón, first class US$9; to Zacatecas, first class US$18/second class US$10; to Aguascalientes, US$20/$11; to Querétaro, US$24/$13; to Mexico City, US$31/$18. At the División del Norte station in Chihuahua, a cafe serves burgers and standard Mexican dishes.

JOE CUMMINGS

Bahuichivo train station

The Chihuahua al Pacífico train, one of the main tourist objectives for visitors to the city of Chihuahua, runs between Chihuahua and Los Mochis, Sin., on the Sea of Cortez coast. Since the entire trip takes around 13 hours and the best scenery occurs between Cuauhtémoc and El Fuerte, travelers taking the train for sight-seeing purposes should consider breaking the trip into shorter segments. This can be done by spending the night somewhere along the line, or by taking the train only as far as El Fuerte (or vice versa)—a rail journey of around 11 hours.

First-class (only) Chihuahua al Pacífico fares out of Chihuahua include Creel US$19, Divisadero US$22, Posada Barrancas US$23, Bahuichivo US$25, Témoris US$28, El Fuerte US$36, and Los Mochis US$41. Depending on length of journey, add 12-17% for stopovers (maximum of two permitted on one ticket); children ages 5-11 are eligible for a 50% discount on all fares. Fares are of course subject to change.

Scheduling and conditions for the Chihuahua

al Pacífico are discussed in more detail in the Sierra Tarahumara section of this book.

The second-class "Chihuahua-Sufragio-Los Mochis" line departs Chihuahua daily at 8 a.m., arriving in Los Mochis sometime before midnight. Fares are less than a third of the ordinary Chihuahua al Pacífico fares, but this line (nick-named the *pollero*) is crowded and slow.

Train tickets can be purchased at the station an hour before scheduled departure, but tickets for the Chihuahua al Pacífico are more easily booked in advance through a travel agency authorized to sell FNM tickets. In Chihuahua two agencies have this authorization: **Quezada Tours,** Calle Aldama 316-4, tel. (14) 15-7141, fax (14) 15-7606; and **Viajes Línea Nueva,** Centro Commercial Plaza Campestre, Perif. Ortíz Mena 211, tel. (14) 15-8416, fax (14) 15-8930. Viajes Línea Nueva also has an office in the Hotel Castel Sicomoro.

Driving
Chihuahua is 374 km (232 miles) from Ciudad Juárez via the Mexico 45 tollway, typically 3.5 to four hours by car (not allowing time for getting lost in Ciudad Juárez).

If you're driving south toward Durango, Zacatecas, and Mexico City, and don't plan to stop over in Chihuahua, stick to Av. Tecnológico and follow signs for Mexico 45. Several motels and PEMEX stations are available along this road. If you're coming from Ciudad Juárez and plan to bypass the city on your way to Cuauhtémoc or Creel, turn west (right) on Periférico de la Juventud, a loop that leads around the western outskirts of Chihuahua to Mexico 16.

If you're driving in from Ojinaga (238 km/147.5 miles/three hours) on Mexico 16, you'll enter the city limits near the airport and intercity bus terminal; to get downtown, take a right on Av. Pacheco, which heads north and intersects with Av. 20 de Noviembre and Av. Juárez in the city.

Fuel: You'll find PEMEX stations throughout Chihuahua, especially along the various bypass roads encircling the city.

Getting Around
Bus: Chihuahua has a comprehensive city bus system that costs US$0.25 for one-way rides any-where in the city. You can catch city buses to the airport (marked "Aeropuerto") and bus terminal (marked "C. Camionera") along Av. Niños Héroes.

AUTO RENTAL AGENCIES IN CHIHUAHUA

Ansa Renta de Autos
Hotel Castel Sicimoro
tel. (14) 14-2171

Avis
Av. Universidad 2749
tel. (14) 13-1782, 14-1999, or
(800) 7-0643

Budget
Av. Independencia 1205
tel. (14) 16-0909, 16-0404

Continental
Av. Reforma 601-B
tel. (14) 16-9995

Dollar Rent-A-Car
Av. Colón and Av. Reforma
tel. (14) 14-3907, 14-4228

Hertz
Aeropuerto Internacional
tel. (14) 16-6473, 15-7818

Numero Uno Autorentas
Blvd. Díaz Ordaz 222
tel. (14) 13-8833
and Hotel Palacio del Sol
tel. (14) 20-5555

Taxi: Major taxi stands can be found next to the Plaza de Armas on Av. Juárez and near the Mercado Reforma on Av. Niños Héroes. Taxis also hang around all the larger hotels. Fares within the downtown area are around US$2-2.50, between the downtown and the Terminal de Autobuses US$3, and to the airport US$4. Return fares from the airport are much higher.

VICINITY OF CHIHUAHUA

Santa Eulalia (Aquiles Serdán)
Although it's only 15-20 minutes by car from the capital, the state's second mining settlement (founded 1707) retains the charm of "old Chihuahua." Some parts of town have been restored; some parts are still in ruins.

The town is seven km (4.3 miles) from Mexico 45 via Chihuahua 245, 18 km (11 miles) total from Chihuahua. At the town entrance, follow the road along the arroyo to the left and park a few blocks ahead. Then wander the narrow cobblestoned streets to view pastel-colored, one-story colonials, an old church, and village-style shops. Local bands play live music in the plaza on Sundays.

A working silver mine that dates to its 1652 discovery by Capt. Diego del Castillo still supports the town by providing lesser minerals. To finance his armies during the Mexican Revolution, Pancho Villa invaded the district several times and took over the mines. A small museum at the **Casa de la Cultura** displays historic photos, rocks, mining ore, various other rocks, mining tools, and prehistoric objects. Open daily 8:30 a.m.-noon and 2:30-6 p.m.

Visitors to town often eat at **El Mesón de Santa Eulalia,** near the plaza, tel. (14) 16-6089, especially on Sundays when the restaurant features a large Mexican buffet. Open Thurs.-Sat. 1-10 p.m., Sunday for Mexican buffet 10 a.m.-3 p.m.

monument to local miners, Santa Eulalia

JOE CUMMINGS

RVs: The streets aren't wide enough for most RVs, so park your rig near the town entrance and walk in.

Parque Nacional Cumbres de Majalca

This oasis northwest of Chihuahua protects 11,790 acres of stony peaks, rock formations, oak and evergreen forests, and canyons cut by streams feeding into the Chuvíscar and Sacramento Rivers. Opportunities for hiking, canyoneering, and rock climbing are plentiful, and wilderness camping is permitted. Summer, when natural sources of water are most abundant and the canyons are most attractive, is the best time for backpacking the park. The contrast between the cool greenness of the *cumbres* (peaks) and the surrounding Chihuahuan Desert can be striking.

Basic lodging is available in park cabins or in motels on Mexico 45 nearby. The turnoff for the park is 30 km (19 miles) north of Chihuahua via Mexico 45; then it's 40 km northwest on a gravel road.

CHIHUAHUA TO PARRAL

Motorists have a choice of two routes to Parral (Hidalgo del Parral) from Chihuahua. The first is Mexico 45, which now features a 113-km (70-mile) section of four-lane tollway as well as the original 301-km (187-mile) two-lane free road that zigzags to Parral via Camargo and Jiménez. The quicker and more direct route is Mexico 24, which meets Mexico 16 about 30 km southwest of Chihuahua and descends 182 km (112 miles) almost straight south (via Valle de Zaragoza) to Parral, a distance savings of 119 km (75 miles). The longer Mexico 45 route allows stopovers in Delicias, Camargo, or Jiménez, while Mexico 24 runs through mostly unpopulated *lomerías*.

Ciudad Delicias

This prosperous town halfway between Chihuahua and Ciudad Camargo on Mexico 45 benefits from nearby **Presa Francisco I. Madero,** a Río San Pedro/Conchos impoundment that irrigates surrounding fields of vinifera, watermelon, corn, wheat, oats, peanuts, cotton, green chiles, and beans. The sizable lake at Presa Madero is reportedly a productive bass fishery as well as a site for duck, goose, and dove hunting.

The area competes with Cuauhtémoc for the "best Mexican apple" title; earlier this century the Hacienda de las Delicias developed the Red and Golden Delicious apples now famous in North America. Wineries in the area produce wines that, while not as famous as those from Zacatecas or Baja California, are nonetheless quite drinkable.

Meoqui, nine km north of Delicias on Mexico 45, is a historic mining settlement of the same era as Santa Eulalia and Aldama. A hot springs nearby is channeled into two rustic *balnearios* (spas): **El Delfín** and **Junta de los Ríos.**

Accommodations and Food: Motel El Dorado, Av. 6 Ote. at Calle 2 Nte., tel. (14) 2-1377, and **Hotel Baeza,** Calle 2 Nte. 309, tel. (14) 2-1000, both offer clean rooms at budget rates (around US$20). The **Hotel Casa Grande,** Av. 6 Ote. 601, tel. (14) 4-0404 or (800) 1-4222, offers spacious, modern rooms with all the amenities at inexpensive rates (from US$40). Several places to eat can be found along Calle 2 Nte. in the vicinity of the latter two hotels, including **Cafe Paris, La Cebolla Grill,** and **Pizzería Orsini's.**

Ciudad Camargo

Another prosperous little Camino Real town, Camargo is supported by a mix of farming, cattle ranching, and textile production; much of the wheat grown in the Delicias-Camargo area is also milled here. The **Iglesia de San Francisco de los Conchos,** 21 km southeast of town via the paved road to Presa La Boquilla, is a 17th-century mission church with a two-story, folk-baroque facade.

Although it's in the middle of the Chihuahuan Desert, rivers and springs keep the area sufficiently watered and provide residents and visitors with a variety of recreational possibilities. And at an altitude of 1,632 meters (5,440 feet), Camargo's summer climate is milder than that of the surrounding plains. **Ojo Caliente Pascualeño,** a *balneario* 20 km (12.5 miles) southwest of town, offers hot mineral baths and swimming. Other *balnearios* nearby include **Los Filtros,** at San Francisco de Conchos, and **Ojos Calientes de Santa Rosalía,** nine km northeast.

Presa La Boquilla (Lago Toronto), a huge lake formed by the impoundment of the Río Conchos 29 km (18 miles) southwest of Camargo, is stocked with catfish, black bass, perch, and bluefish and is popular for swimming, boating, and fishing. The dam is an important source of hydroelectric power for much of Chihuahua.

Accommodations and RV Parking: The well-run **Villa del Charro Motel y Trailer Park,** 5.3 km (3.3 miles) south of town, tel. (146) 2-2221, has 45 spaces with full hookups, plus showers, a convenience store, and propane. The attached motel has eight basic rooms at shoestring rates.

Ciudad Jiménez
At the junction of Highways 45 and 49, Ciudad Jiménez is a regional transportation hub, as well as a center for cattle, cotton, and wheat production. Historical attractions include the 18th-century **Parroquía de Santo Cristo de Burgos** and a turn-of-the-century **municipal market** constructed of iron.

Motel Florido, Av. Juárez at 20 de Noviembre, tel. (154) 2-0186, has budget rates, while **Motel Las Pampas,** on Mexico 45, tel. (154) 2-1041, offers budget-to-inexpensive rates and a restaurant. For a quick bite to eat, **Pollos Guamuchil** on the highway is a good choice.

Valle de Allende
Twenty-five km east of Parral on Mexico 25, then south six km, this beautiful area of fruit and nut orchards is a favorite weekend spot for Parral residents, who come to bathe at the *balnearios* near the entrance to town. The older haciendas along the river are attractive, as is the 17th-century **Iglesia de Nuestra Señora del Rosario** with its arches and octagonal window.

HIDALGO DE PARRAL

One of the oldest towns in Chihuahua, Parral (pop. 88,000) owes its existence to the founding of La Negrita mine in 1631 and nearly 200 mines founded since then. Now called La Prieta, the founder mine as well as several others were working until the mid-1980s, when low precious metal prices and reduced local ore supplies made mining no longer profitable. Since then Parral's economy has had a tough go of it, though the 1991 establishment of a General Motors automotive plant brought more jobs to town.

Farming and ranching contribute to the economy, though the town is too high and dry for intensive agriculture. The area reportedly produces some of the best pecans in the world—according to locals, something about the angle of the sun results in nuts with thin, easy-to-crack shells and plump, orange meat.

Residents are proud not only of their pecans but of the town's distinctive history. Wedged in a valley between the Sierra Madre Occidental foothills and the high central Chihuahuan Desert, in a relatively isolated part of Mexico, Parral has developed its own distinctive culture and accent. In fact, the particularly thick version of Chihuahuan Spanish spoken here can lead to minor communication difficulties even for those who know Mexican Spanish well.

Once you're off the highways (Mexico 45 and 24, which intersect here), the funky, hidden charms of downtown Parral become apparent. Crossed by nine small bridges, the crooked Río Parral snakes through a collection of shops and hotels that look like they've been kept in a glass case since the 1940s or '50s. Tourists are relatively rare, and the townspeople are happy to give directions (often necessary as the streets seem to follow a particularly distorted pattern) or to hold forth on a little town history.

All of the town sights can be explored on foot in a single afternoon. In addition to several historic churches, Parral is host to a small museum dedicated to Pancho Villa, who spent the final chapter of his life here.

As in the city of Chihuahua, the climate in Parral is mild most of the year. The occasional north wind can bring near-freezing temperatures to the valley Dec.-March.

Sights
Virtually everything of any size or beauty in Parral was built with mining money. The **Catedral de San José** is renowned for the diamond-shaped masonry motif on its walls and for a striking interior containing a large baroque altar of pink marble with gilt edges. Interred in the altar are the remains of Don Juan Rangel de Viesma, Parral's founder. Miners began constructing the church in 1846 and completed it in 1854; pillars supporting the roof are decorated with chunks of ore from nearby mines. Formerly a *parroquía,* the church attained cathedral

status in 1992 with the assignment of a bishop to the area.

The building opposite the cathedral was designed by a French architect and was originally a hotel. It was constructed in 1906 for the wealthy Alvarado family, who later presented it to Pancho Villa. Villa's body was brought here immediately following his 1923 assassination. The building is mostly empty now, save for a store selling decorative items in one of the large ground-floor rooms; inside, the original pressed-tin ceiling can be seen.

Nearby, at the corner of Calle P. de Verdad and Riva Palacio, is **Palacio Alvarado,** an 1899-1903 mansion constructed in Byzantine-baroque style. A tortured-looking face sculpted over the door is said to represent an Indian miner at work. Founder of the Mina La Palmilla, one of the world's richest silver mines, Don Alvarado was so wealthy he offered to pay off Mexico's national debt—but Díaz refused. Scions of the Alvarado family still live in the building.

The **Templo de la Virgen de Fátima,** on a hill overlooking the city near Mina La Prieta, was built almost entirely of metals taken from local mines. Instead of pews, the church features short, square pillar-stools fashioned in the shape of claim boundary markers; the walls and pillar sides show tiny ore chunks from area mines, including gold, silver, zinc, and lead. Finished in 1956, the interior of the church is said to resemble the chapels built into caverns in some of the larger mines.

The town's oldest continually functioning church, the **Templo del Rayo,** was built in the 17th to 18th centuries and is unremarkable except for its extremely tall and narrow profile. Older but abandoned is the tiny and plain 17th-century **Templo de San Tomás** at the south edge of the city.

To commemorate the town's 350th anniversary in 1980, Parral residents erected a bronze statue of founder Don Juan Rangel de Viesma in the town plaza. A colonial-style *kiosco* is also a rather recent addition to the plaza.

Villa Memorials

In 1920, after 10 years of fighting in the Mexican Revolution, Francisco "Pancho" Villa retired—with a lifetime general's pay—to a ranch in Canutillo, 80 km southeast of Parral. Accompanied by his entourage of Dorados ("Golden Ones"), Villa frequently made trips to Parral for banking and other errands. On 20 July 1923, the last day of his life, Villa had picked up a consignment of gold with which to pay his Canutillo ranch staff and was driving through the city in his black Dodge roadster when a group of seven riflemen fired 150 shots (in just two minutes) into his car.

To this day it's not known for certain who ordered the killing. The assassins were given light prison sentences, leading many people to believe that someone in the Mexican government—possibly Pres. Alvaro Obregón himself or president-to-be P.E. Calles—gave the order simply because ex-*bandido* Villa had become an embarrassment to post-revolutionary Mexico.

The **Museo de General Francisco Villa,** upstairs in the local library, contains colorful murals depicting battle scenes, old photos, old newspaper cuttings, pieces of Villa's coffin, weapons, and a death mask of Villa that was found in Redford College in El Paso. A German furniture-maker is said to have made the mold of Villa's face from which the bronze death mask was cast and then smuggled it out of Mexico. Outside on the sidewalk is a starburst-shaped bronze plaque where Villa's car ran into a tree after being riddled with bullets; it is the final in a series of bronze historical plaques marking Villa's last-day route through the city. The fusillade was fired from the building directly opposite the library-museum. The museum is open Mon.-Fri. 9 a.m.-8 p.m., Saturday 9 a.m.-1 p.m.; admission is free.

Villa's grave in the **Panteón Municipal** is a source of mystery nearly as piquant as that shrouding his assassination. Three years after Villa's burial, someone exhumed the body and removed Villa's head. Most Mexicans believe a long-time rumor that says the decapitation was performed by an American adventurer on behalf of an eccentric Chicago millionaire who collected the skulls of historic figures. As if this weren't bizarre enough, three years following the decapitation the federal government ordered Villa's body moved to Mexico City so that it could be interred in the Tomb of Illustrious Men.

Local residents, however, will tell you that their mayor had the body shifted in the graveyard a meter or so to the right of the marked grave and replaced with another body to prevent any more of Villa's body parts from being taken. It was this decoy body, they insist, that was later taken to Mexico City! Whether Villa's headless body is still in the ground or not, his tall, stately tombstone remains in place and people still lay flowers on the grave. To the right of Villa's headstone is the grave of his son Miguel, who died in a Mexican Air Force crash in 1950 at age 30.

Accommodations

Parral has a number of very similar, older downtown hotels that are perfectly adequate for a night or two. Each has an attached restaurant.

Shoestring: Best value of the lot is the 1940s-style **Hotel Acosta,** Calle Barbachano 3, tel. (152) 2-0657 or 2-0221, just off the downtown square. Spacious, high-ceilinged rooms—some with original tile floors—come with TV, a/c (but no heat), and private bath. A rooftop terrace offers good views of the city. Rates: US$9 s, US$11 d, US$12 t, and US$13 q, including tax.

The friendly and efficient **Hotel Turista,** Plazuela Independencia 12, tel. (152) 3-4100 or 3-4024, fax (152) 3-4024, has well-worn but clean rooms with TV, a/c, heat, and phone. The manager and staff are very knowledgeable about local sights; some English is spoken. Rates: US$11 s, US$13 d, US$15 t. **Hotel San José,** Calle S. Méndez 5, tel. (152) 2-2453, fax (152) 2-2712, is similarly priced and has off-street parking.

Toward the downtown area along Av. Independencia (the main access road into town) is **Motel Las Nogales,** with basic rooms that are okay in a pinch but definitely not a first choice even in the shoestring range. Rates: US$10 s, US$13 d.

Budget: A bit farther along the same road, next to the PEMEX station, the low-rise, American-style **Motel El Camino Real,** Av. Independencia, tel. (152) 3-0202, fax (152) 3-0262, has rooms with TV, a/c, and heat, plus a swimming pool, sauna, restaurant, and courtyard parking. This one tends to fill up by early evening. Rates: in the US$21-25 range.

Around the corner from the Camino Real, next to the bus terminal, modern-looking **Hotel Los Arcos,** Calle Dr. Pedro de Lille 13, tel. (152) 3-0597, fax (152) 3-0537, has similarly priced rooms.

Food

Your best bets in Parral are the traditional restaurants attached to the older downtown hotels.

One of the nicer ones is the **Restaurant La Parroquía,** attached to the Hotel San José.

The breakfast and lunch specials at the restaurant attached to the Hotel Turista are tasty and inexpensive. A well-prepared, complete *comida corrida* at the Turista costs less than US$2 and is better than the usual US$2 *comida corrida* in other Mexican cities.

Cabrito al Pastor El Asadero, on the road into town from Mexico 24, has very good *pollo asado,* roasted over a wood fire, as well as *cabrito.*

Mercado Hidalgo, across from the Plaza Principal, has a couple of decent *loncherías.*

Transportation

Buses: Several lines operate buses between Parral and towns in Chihuahua and Durango. Between the city of Chihuahua and Parral, a variety of classes is available: second class for around US$6 (depending on the bus line); first class for US$7; and *ejecutivo* for US$17. **Futura** runs buses to Chihuahua (nine times daily, US$7), Juárez (nine times, US$19), Durango (eight times, US$13), and Guachochi (twice, US$3), while **Chihuahuense** goes to Chihuahua (four times daily, US$17), San Luis Potosí (twice, US$30), Zacatecas (once, US$23), Torreón (three times, US$10), and Monterrey (once, US$21). **Estrella Blanca** and **Omnibus de México** offer similar first-class services.

Driving: Via Mexico 24, the Chihuahua-Parral drive takes around two to three hours. At the junction for Valle Zaragoza, 62 km (38.4 miles) north of Parral, you'll find a couple of basic hotels and restaurants as well as a PEMEX station (Nova only). Magna Sin is available in Parral.

Parral offers a nifty back-door entrance into Sierra Tarahumara country for motorists. Follow Mexico 24 west from Parral 32 km (19.8 miles), then bear right onto recently paved Chihuahua 23 and follow signs to Samachique (Samachic), about 270 km (167 miles) from this junction. Gasoline is available along the way in Guachochi and other villages. Samachique is on the Batopilas-Creel road. For more details, see the Batopilas or Creel sections of this book.

It's also possible to drive from Parral across the Sierra Madre to the Pacific coast near Culiacán via Mexico 24. The road is paved for 140 km (86.8 miles) only as far southwest as

Guadalupe y Calvo. Following Guadalupe y Calvo is an unpaved, partially graded section for 85 km (52.7 miles) until Santiago de los Caballeros, after which it's another 75 km (46.5 miles) to Mexico 15. Nova (leaded) gasoline is available at a couple of towns along the way.

Stick to the main road all the way—some of the side tracks lead to areas where opium and marijuana are grown illegally.

For details on the Mexico 45 route between Parral and Durango, see "Durango to Parral" in the Durango chapter.

SIERRA TARAHUMARA ("COPPER CANYON")

The Sierra Tarahumara, one of the highest and most rugged sections of the Sierra Madre Occidental, is also one of Mexico's premier attractions, yet remarkably few foreigners seem to have heard of it. Few maps of the area, in fact, even include the name "Sierra Tarahumara," a term used to designate a 64,000-square-km (25,000-square-mile) zone that is the traditional (though not the original) homeland of Mexico's 50,000 Tarahumaras. Although the Tarahumaras are by far the most numerous Amerindians in the sierra, the region is also inhabited by Pimas (northwest), Guarojillos (west), and Tepehuanes (south).

The Canyons

People who know of the area may be more familiar with the term "Copper Canyon," which is often loosely applied to one of the sierra's most salient geographical features: its vast network of canyons. Cut into the sierra by the Chínipas, Candameña, Urique, Tararécua, Septentrión, Batopilas, and Verdes Rivers (among others), these canyons represent North America's largest canyon system; at least four canyons here (each

over 1,800 meters/5,900 feet deep) are deeper than Arizona's Grand Canyon (1,425 meters/4,654 feet at Hopi Point) according to standard canyoneering measures. Not to put too fine a point on it; none of the Sierra Tarahumara canyons are as wide as the Grand Canyon—most are deep and relatively narrow by comparison (though wide enough that you can't see rim to rim in the larger ones). Together they have nearly four times the volume of the Grand Canyon.

"Copper Canyon," a translation of the Spanish "Barranca de Cobre," refers to a canyon section formed by the Río Urique that extends eastward from the Río Urique/Río Tararécua junction as far south as Puente Humirá, where the Creel-Batopilas road crosses the Río Urique. It's a bit confusing since the section of the Río Urique southward from the Urique/Tararécua junction is termed "Barranca de Urique" or "Urique Canyon" even though it's basically a continuation of the same canyon. Although most of the individual canyons have their own names (usually named after the rivers that form them), locals often refer to the entire canyon system as "las Barrancas del Cobre." Some maps

SIERRA TARAHUMARA CANYONS

NAME	DEPTH	RIVER LEVEL	MUNICIPIO
Batopilas	1,800 meters (5,905 feet)	700 meters (2,290 feet)	Batopilas
Candameña	1,640 meters (5,380 feet)	900 meters (2,952 feet)	Ocampo, Uruachi
Chínipas	1,600 meters (5,249 feet)	400 meters (1,312 feet)	Chínipas
Del Cobre	1,300 meters (4,265 feet)	1,000 meters (3,280 feet)	Boycoyna, Urique Guachochi
Oteros	1,520 meters (4,986 feet)	700 meters (2,296 feet)	Maguarichi, Uruachi
Sinforosa	1,830 meters (6,003 feet)	700 meters (2,290 feet)	Guachochi, Batopilas
Urique	1,879 meters (6,135 feet)	500 meters (1,640 feet)	Urique, Batopilas

JOE CUMMINGS

burro driver, Batopilas

refer to the entire region as "Parque Natural Barrancas del Cobre" or "Copper Canyons Natural Park," an honorary appellation that has bestowed no public facilities (and no special protection) on the area except for one campground near Creel. In fact, the Sierra Tarahumara canyonlands do not appear on any official government lists of protected areas in Mexico, much to the chagrin of those of us who consider these lands an absolute national treasure.

"Cobre," incidentally, refers to the color of the canyon walls more than to the fact that copper may have been mined here. Gold and silver, however, have been mined in vast quantities over the centuries, along with turquoise and amethyst. Although insufficient ore remains to interest large mining concerns, perhaps hundreds of small-time gold prospectors still manage to eke out a living in the canyons.

Most visitors to the Sierra Tarahumara traverse the area by train, catching glimpses of three magnificent canyons along the way: Septentrión (Témoris area), Urique (Bahuichivo to El Divisadero), and Tararécua (El Divisadero to Creel, with glimpses of Barranca del Cobre in the distance). Of those who take the time to descend into the canyons—whether on foot or by motor vehicle—most end up in the Cobre, Tararécua, Batopilas, and Urique Canyons, each one a world unto itself. A hardy few make it as far as the Barranca de Sinforosa in the extreme southeast portion of the sierra.

Climate and Seasons

The Sierra Tarahumara region harbors two distinct climatic zones, one in the highlands and another at the canyon bottoms, with various gradations between. In the highlands the weather is mild April-Oct., with warm but not hot days (18° C/65° F to 24° C/75° F) and cool, crisp nights. From mid-November to April, nighttime temperatures drop considerably, often hitting the freezing point (or lower) in the early morning hours. Winter snowfalls in the highlands are not uncommon, though they don't usually cover the ground for very long. Occasional heavy rains mid-July to mid-September are normal, sometimes to the extent that unpaved roads become impassable. The average monthly precipitation during these months is 13.5 cm (5.3 inches), with a total year-round average of around 63 cm (25 inches).

Down at the canyon bottoms temperatures are subtropical year-round. The hottest time of year is May-July, before the summer monsoon arrives; afternoon temperatures frequently break 40° C (104° F). Once the rains begin, daytime maximums drop several degrees but afternoons can still be almost intolerable for some visitors. The rivers and streams reach their highest levels this time of year, hence you can't count on crossing them whether hiking or driving. Monthly and yearly averages for precipitation are around 20% lower than in the highlands.

Timing Your Visit: If you're only planning to stay in the highlands or along canyon rims, any time of year is good for a visit, though you run the greatest risk of rain and cloudy skies July-September. Whatever the time of year, come prepared for warm days and cold nights.

For canyoneers, the optimum time to visit is immediately after the monsoon, i.e., late Sept.-Oct., when water is plentiful and the canyons are greenest. Winters are also very pleasant,

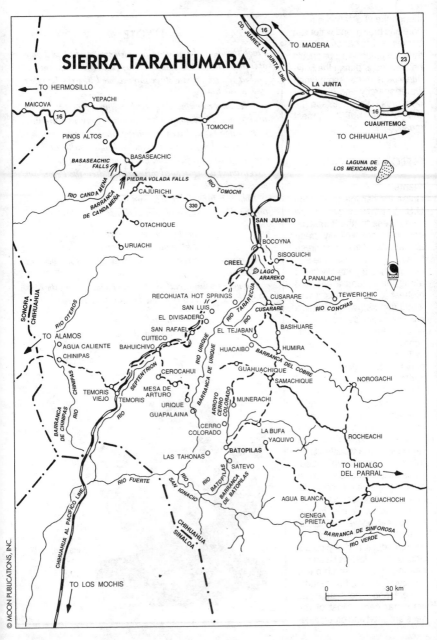

though the vegetation is more bare and brown, and water can be scarce. The one time of year that canyon-bottom trips should be avoided is during the May-June peak hot season, when water scarcity and high temperatures combine to sap the will of all but the most masochistic.

FLORA AND FAUNA

Plants

Unlike the canyonlands of the U.S. Southwest, which are mostly desertic, the Barrancas del Cobre are typically green and wooded. Mixed evergreen forests of ponderosa pine and Douglas fir are generally found along the upland areas and highest canyon rims (over 2,000 meters), with piñon-live oak-juniper woodlands at slightly lower mountain/rim elevations (500-1,500 meters). Sierra Tarahumara forests are superlative on two counts: They contain the largest stands of old-growth forest in the Americas; and they produce more pine and oak than any other area in the world.

The undergrowth of the lower piñon-oak woodlands (or "Madrean evergreen" woodlands) also includes a number of scrub species, succulents, and short cacti such as hedgehog, catclaw, cane cholla, prickly pear, agave, and yucca.

Just below the rims on canyon slopes, arid-tropical deciduous thorn forests begin appearing; look for scrub oaks, mesquite, agave, bromeliads, bursera, and various large and columnar cacti. Most of the trees are short and drought-de-

PEYOTE

I took Peyote in the mountains of Mexico, and I had a dose of it that lasted me two or three days with the Tarahumara, and at the time those three days seemed like the happiest days of my life.

I had stopped tormenting myself, trying to find a reason for my life, and I had stopped having to carry my body around.

I realized that I was inventing life, that that was my function and my raison d'être, *and that I suffered when my imagination failed, and Peyote gave it to me.*

A human being stepped forward and drew the Peyote out of me with a blow.

I made it into real shreds, and the cadaver of a man was torn to shreds and found torn to shreds, somewhere.

rai da kanka da kum
a kum da na kum vönoh
Granting that this world is not the reverse of the other and still less its half,

this world is also a real machinery of which I have the controls, it is a true factory whose key is inborn humor.

sana tafan tana
tanaf tamafts bai
—Antonin Artaud,
The Peyote Dance

the earliest known sketch of Lophophora williamsii, *from* Botanical Magazine, *1847*

SIERRA TARAHUMARA BIOTIC COMMUNITIES

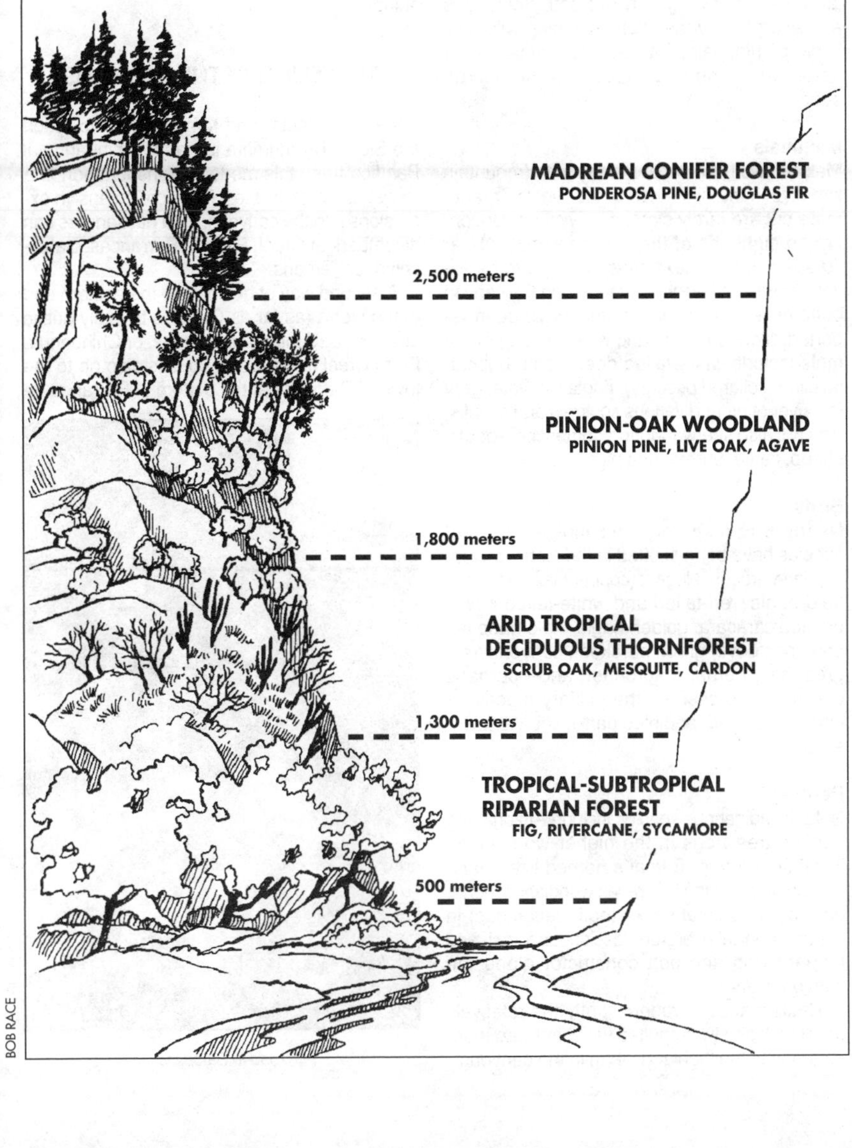

MADREAN CONIFER FOREST
PONDEROSA PINE, DOUGLAS FIR

2,500 meters

PIÑION-OAK WOODLAND
PIÑION PINE, LIVE OAK, AGAVE

1,800 meters

**ARID TROPICAL
DECIDUOUS THORNFOREST**
SCRUB OAK, MESQUITE, CARDON

1,300 meters

**TROPICAL-SUBTROPICAL
RIPARIAN FOREST**
FIG, RIVERCANE, SYCAMORE

500 meters

BOB RACE

ciduous, dropping their leaves during long periods between rains. For this reason the canyons generally appear most lush in October, following the late summer rains.

Down on the canyon floors bordering the rivers are sections of tropical-subtropical riparian forests showing a mix of both deciduous and evergreen vegetation, including wild figs, liana, orchid, palm, bamboo, sycamores, river cane, and various grasses and thornscrub species.

Mammals

Mexican wolf, black bear, and puma (mountain lion) live in the highlands of the Sierra Tarahumara but are rarely sighted by visitors. Unconfirmed sightings of the Mexican grizzly bear *(Ursus horribilis mexicanus),* thought to be extinct, have also been reported. Along the canyon bottoms jaguar and jaguarundi have been reported. More common and wide-ranging mammals include white-tailed deer, coati, bobcat, javelina (collared peccary), ringtail, coyote, gray fox, river otter, and various squirrels and skunks. You will also see wandering domestics—goats, sheep, cattle, burros, and pigs.

Birds

Nearly 300 migratory and indigenous bird species have been spotted in the sierra, including eared trogon, elegant (coppery-tailed) trogon, bald eagle, red-tailed and white-tailed hawk, crested caracara, golden eagle, Aplomado falcon, Inca dove, green parakeet, canyon wren, great blue heron, roadrunner, and—perhaps the most impressive—the military macaw, a large green, red, and blue parrot seen at lower elevations.

Reptiles

Notable indigenous species include Arizona and canyon tree frogs in the higher woodlands; Tarahumara frog, Ditmar's horned lizard, and alligator lizard in the piñon-oak woodlands; beaded lizard and coral snake (both venomous) in the arid-tropical evergreen/deciduous forest; and leopard frog and boa constrictor along the canyon rivers.

Rattlesnakes—predominantly the relatively small rock and twin-spotted varieties—are more common in the highlands than in the canyons.

Fish

The Tarahumara build stone chutes in canyon streams to catch channel and flathead catfish and freshwater eel for food. Among other common fish species found in the sierra are carp, mullet, tilapia, Mexican stoneroller, molly, and shiner.

TRAVELING IN THE CANYONS

The most popular and romantic way to reach the Sierra Tarahumara is via the Chihuahua al Pacífico train; this mode of transportation is a tourist attraction in itself. For more extensive excursions into the canyons, train passengers can disembark at Creel, Posada Barrancas, Bahuichivo, or Témoris.

A second way of getting into the eastern end of the sierra (as far as Creel) is by daily public bus from La Junta, Cuauhtémoc, or Chihuahua. From Creel thrice-weekly buses also go to the town of Batopilas at the bottom of Barranca de

road to Batopilas

Batopilas. This mode of transportation limits you to the Barranca del Cobre and Barranca de Batopilas, unless of course you strike out on foot for other canyons.

Driving your own (or a rented) vehicle offers the most flexibility and the widest range of potential destinations. Inherent problems are the scarcity of fuel (and relative unavailability of unleaded gas) in the Sierra Tarahumara, the overall lack of mechanical assistance, and the rough road conditions.

Roads are gradually improving in the area; ordinary sedans with a full tank of gas (when unleaded is necessary, fill up with Magna Sin in La Junta or Creel) can now get as far as Creel and Cusárare. For other destinations, vehicles best suited for Sierra Tarahumara road travel will have high road clearance, rugged chassis, heavy-duty tires, and either the capacity to burn leaded gas or a spare fuel tank. Four-wheel drive would be a definite plus, especially for crossing sandy, muddy, or stream-filled arroyos.

With an off-highway vehicle you can reach all of the same towns accessible by rail (since a dirt road roughly parallels the track as far south as Témoris), as well as the Batopilas, Urique, Septentrión, and Sinforosa Canyons (not to mention dozens of villages along a fairly extensive network of unpaved roads southeast of the rail line).

Army squadrons on patrol are common throughout the Sierra Tarahumara, and you may see units of 25 or more men in green bivouacked outside towns and villages such as Creel, Batopilas, Urique,. Bahuichivo, Cerocahui, Témoris—really just about anywhere. The army presence is part of the Mexican government's stepped-up efforts to interdict drug trafficking in the sierra. At most the soldiers are a minor inconvenience to sierra travelers—if you're driving in the area you may have to undergo brief searches—while many people feel they have brought a new sense of security to the region.

Hiking

The Chihuahua al Pacífico train journey through the Sierra Tarahumara canyons is spectacular, but to really experience this great wilderness you've got to walk around in it. The variety of terrain is simply astounding—from cool, resin-scented pine forests to sand-fringed, bamboo-curtained rock pools filled with turquoise spring water.

As the entire canyon region is crisscrossed with footpaths created by the Tarahumaras for walking (or running) from one *ranchería* to another, the Sierra Tarahumara's hiking potential is limited only by your hiking stamina and your capacity to carry provisions. This latter concern is the most important, as outside of the canyon-bottom towns of Urique and Batopilas, and the few towns along the canyon rims, no provisioning sources are available along the way. Tarahumara settlements almost invariably operate at a subsistence level, hence to attempt to rely on Tarahumara pueblos for food and water (except in emergencies) would place an unreasonable burden on their livelihoods.

You can avoid loading yourself down with food and water by using larger canyon or mountain towns as bases for day-hikes, by hiring a guide with pack burros, or by signing up with an organized backpacking tour. It is not advisable to consider setting off on a multiday backpacking trip on your own, unless you're going with someone who knows the area very well. Even with Mexican topo maps, people tend to get lost on long hikes because of the many intersecting trails. Another danger is running across a clandestine marijuana field whose tenders may be less than happy to see you.

During a recent October I joined a six-day guided trek that used a spectacular "new" (to outsiders) canyon crossing route from Batopilas to Urique. Along the way we passed three pot fields, one recently harvested and two with 10- to 12-foot plants still waving in the breeze. This is not the kind of trip to do without a local guide who knows the area well and who knows which families along the way are *sembrando* (growing).

Guides and Outfitters

Many Sierra Tarahumara trails link canyon rims with canyon rivers below. These rim-to-river hikes typically take one easy day to descend and one strenuous day—or an easier day and a half—back up. For a typical three- or four-day, rim-to-river roundtrip, a local guide is usually sufficient.

The better, more experienced guides—Tarahumara or mestizo—charge US$20-30 a day, plus the cost of food. More casual guides, i.e., someone who knows the territory but hasn't necessarily led many (or any) backpacking trips be-

CHIHUAHUA AL PACÍFICO RAIL JOURNEY

Known as the "Q" line among FNM officials or the "Copper Canyon train" among tourists, Mexico's Chihuahua al Pacífico is the most spectacular train ride in North America in terms of both scenery and sheer engineering marvels. Some railroad buffs have gone so far as to claim it the world's most scenic railroad line under 1,000 km.

What makes this 674-km (418-mile) rail line between Mexico's Altiplano and the Sea of Cortez coast so awe-inspiring is the way it winds through a conifer-forested Sierra Madre canyon complex four times larger than the Grand Canyon, then drops 2,400 meters (8,000 feet) onto the tropical-arid coastal plains. Along the way the railway passes over 37 bridges, threads 86 tunnels, and crosses the Continental Divide three times.

The most sensational section is around Témoris (Km 707), where three levels of bridges, tunnels, and viaducts all converge into a canyon formed by the Río Septentrión. Looking over this scene from one of the rail cars is like finding yourself miniaturized and magically transported into an elaborate toy train setup. Between Km 688 and 708 the railway threads 16 tunnels carved into the edge of the canyon.

History

The mountains and canyons of the Sierra Madre Occidental have been a major transportation challenge ever since the mid-19th century, when road and rail engineers began seeking a way to link the fertile Chihuahua plains (and the American Midwest) with a west-coast shipping route. The Chihuahua-Topolobampo route was first conceived by American railway engineer and utopian impresario Albert Kinsey Owens when he arrived in Mexico in 1861. After choosing Bahía Oguira (Topolobampo) as the western rail terminus, Owens formed a Mexican-American company in 1863 to design the project and was granted a contract by the Mexican government to build a railway between Piedras Negras and Topolobampo, with branch lines to Mazatlán, Alamos, and Ojinaga.

After Owens failed to produce sufficient funds to begin construction, his contracts were taken over by Foster Higgins and his Rio Grande, Sierra Madre, and Pacific Railway Company. Higgins and company completed a 259-km railway between Ciudad Juárez and Casas Grandes in the state of Chihuahua in 1898 before throwing in the towel.

Along came entrepreneur Enrique Creel and his Kansas City, Mexico, and Orient Railroad, who completed a Casas Grandes-La Junta line between 1910 and 1914. Creel also started the Ojinaga-Chihuahua-Creel section of the railroad but left it unfinished in 1914 due to revolutionary attacks along the route. Although Creel is often given credit for the entire Chihuahua al Pacífico line, the truth is that he only established the least challenging sections at the line's eastern end.

In the early years the Chihuahua-Creel stretch took two or three days (four hours today); the train would stop anywhere along the line for passengers and it is said that 90% of the trains derailed at least once per journey. Passengers helped lever the cars back onto the tracks and stopped to chop wood along steeper grades to fire up enough steam to get the train over the top.

By the turn of the century various small American and Mexican companies had extended a rail line east from Topolobampo to El Fuerte and in 1927-28 the Mexican government finished the Chihuahua-Ojinaga section begun by Creel. This left a gap of around 260 km (161 miles) in the most difficult Sierra Tarahumara terrain, with an elevation change of roughly 2,100 meters (7,000 feet). In 1940 the government nationalized the railway companies at both ends of the line and in 1953 announced plans to complete the route.

After 18 years of tunneling and laying track, the gap was finally closed in Nov. 1961, almost exactly 100 years after Albert Owens had pronounced his vision. The final construction tab was over US$100 million. The Chihuahua al Pacífico train became part of the Ferrocarriles Nacional de México system in 1987.

Until the 1992 paving of the Chihuahua-Hermosillo highway, the Chihuahua al Pacífico line was the only commercially viable land route across the Sierra Madre Occidental. The train remains the most direct route from central and northeastern Mexico to the nation's deepest port, Topolobampo.

Train Highlights

From Los Mochis, the Chihuahua al Pacífico moves from sugarcane fields and truck farms along the coastal plains to the chaparral of the Sierra Madre Occidental foothills near El Fuerte. East of Loreto (Km 791), lower mountain valleys cloaked in oak, juniper, piñon, and agave rise along either side of the line.

As the elevation increases, ponderosa pine and Douglas fir begin appearing as the line moves from Madrean evergreen woodland to montane conifer forest. With increasing elevation, scenic tributary canyons or arroyos break into the main canyons cut by the Fuerte and Septentrión Rivers as mean annual precipitation rises to as high as 114 cm (45 inches) in the upper heights. About 75% of this rain falls between July and September, making late September or early October an especially beautiful time of year to make the trip.

Other landmarks and points of interest along the way include:

*Km 942 **Topolobampo,** western terminus of the line

*Km 921 **Los Mochis,** bustling commercial center where most train tourists board or disembark

*Km 882 **Sufragio,** rail junction with FNM's Del Pacífico line (north-south service between Nogales/Mexicali and Guadalajara)

*Km 805 **Puente del Río Fuerte,** at 491 meters (1,637 feet), the longest bridge along the line

*Km 748 **Puente de Chínipas,** the highest rail bridge (106 meters/355 feet above the Río Chínipas) along the route

*Km 707-8 **Témoris,** three parallel levels of track curving around one another

*Km 703 **Placa Conmemorativa,** marking the spot where crews working from both ends of the line finally met in 1961

*Km 665 **Bahuichivo,** jumping-off point for road trips to Cerocahui and Urique

*Km 662 **Cuiteco.** Between here and Km 647 are nine tunnels totaling 1,504 meters (4,933 feet) and five bridges totaling 641 meters (2,103 feet).

*Km 639 **Puente de la Laja** (212 meters long, 65 meters high), the first bridge in Mexico built with reinforced concrete beams

*Km 622 **Divisadero,** a major sightseeing stop for sweeping views over the Barranca del Cobre (Copper Canyon), one of six major canyons in the Sierra Tarahumara

*Km 592 **El Lazo,** where the line makes a 360-degree loop over itself, first over and then under a rail bridge

*Km 583 **Los Ojitos,** the highest point (2,421 meters/8,071 feet) along the line

*Km 564 **Creel,** Barranca del Cobre's tourist headquarters and starting point for trips to Cusárare and Batopilas

*Km 562 **Continental Tunnel** (1,260 meters/4,133 feet long), so named because it pierces the Continental Divide

*Km 531 **San Juanito,** a lumber town (elev. 2,400 meters/8,000 feet) that typically registers the coldest annual temperatures in Mexico

*Km 451 **La Junta,** where the Chihuahua al Pacífico is joined by the Bosques de Chihuahua freight line, a major carrier of timber from the northern Sierra Madre Occidental; a major rail workshop for the Q line is located here

*Km 401 **Cuauhtémoc,** agricultural trade center for Chihuahua's Mennonite colonies

*Km 268 **Chihuahua,** capital of the state of Chihuahua and a rail junction where separate lines (carrying mostly freight) continue to Ojinaga (connecting with the Atchison, Topeka, and Santa Fe railroad in Presidio, Texas) and Ciudad Juárez (connecting with the Southern Pacific, Union Pacific, and Atchison, Topeka, and Santa Fe railways in El Paso, Texas)

Train Riding Tips

When the trains run on time, it really doesn't matter whether you travel westbound or eastbound, as the most spectacular points (Divisadero, Témoris) are reached in midafternoon in either direction. If the westbound train (No. 74) is running late, however, you risk not seeing Témoris—which is scheduled for a 4:30 p.m. arrival going west, 11:11 a.m. going east—in the winter when the sun sets early. Hence if your main objective is the train ride itself (as opposed to stopping over in the Sierra Tarahumara for a few days), the journey is best taken from the western end. Although many people start the trip in Los Mochis, it is just as well begun in El Fuerte since the scenery isn't that spectacular until well east of El Fuerte.

Overall, the best views are seen from the south side of the train, i.e., the left side westbound or the right side eastbound. Since the train windows are rarely kept clean enough for an unobstructed view, passengers often crowd onto the small platforms between cars for a look at the passing scenery.

(continues on next page)

CHIHUAHUA AL PACÍFICO RAIL JOURNEY
(continued)

Wear clothes you don't mind getting dirty if you anticipate standing between cars—the dust and diesel soot outside may not be noticeable at first but they have a definite cumulative effect.

There is no checked baggage for personal items (unless you're dealing with FNM's cargo department), but overhead space is ample for most bags. Seats—arranged four across in pairs—usually recline in first-class cars and there's plenty of leg room. If the train isn't full, you can easily change cars when necessary (e.g., when the a/c or heating system in your car isn't working properly).

Food service is available but you'll do better to bring your own snacks along. A styrofoam-boxed (and unrefrigerated) sandwich with Coke costs around US$4. Beer and soft-drink service is more dependable.

The Chihuahua al Pacífico train suffered several armed robberies in 1993, but by early 1994 state judicial police working with federales and the Mexican army managed to bring all such incidents to a halt. Since then armed guards—either police or soldiers, sometimes uniformed, sometimes in civilian clothes—have accompanied every train trip, both first- and second-class.

For details on Chihuahua al Pacífico fares, see the "Transportation by Train" section under "Los Mochis." For departure and arrival times, see the Transportation Appendix. Advance train reservations can be made by writing to the Jefe, Depto. Reg. Pasajeros, Ferrocarriles Nacional de Mexico, Apdo. Postal 46, Chihuahua, Chihuahua. Tickets are also available at each train station along the line an hour before departure.

---

fore, charge as little as US$10-15 a day. Make sure you get some kind of recommendation from other local residents for whomever you're considering. These prices do not include food, and you are expected to provide food for your guide as well as for yourselves. Never pay in advance except as is necessary for the purchase of supplies—and you'll do better to make these purchases yourself.

Pack burros cost an extra US$5-10 per day and each can carry around 45 kilos (100 pounds). Riding mules or horses may be available for certain segments on an hourly basis (figure around US$3-4 per hour). Prices per beast of burden should include all saddlery. For burros this means an *aparejo,* a pack-saddle made with a frame of *zacate* (wild fig tree) covered with leather, as well *cascateles,* pairs of square wooden crates for holding cargo fastened to the *aparejo.* For small groups of five trekkers or less, it's best to keep five or 10 gallons of water stored away in plastic jugs that can be carried by burro; these can be topped off at canyon streams along the way.

Guides can often be contacted through hotels or guesthouses in Creel, Cerocahui, Bahuichivo, Batopilas, and Urique. The larger, package-tour-oriented hotels charge the most

for guide services—US$50 or more per day, of which the guide may receive only a percentage.

For longer, more extensive backpacking trips, an organized group trek is highly recommended. Typically these involve 5-10 paying customers along with an experienced guide and a small local staff who take care of portage and cooking. Currently one of the most knowledgeable and most reliable of the Sierra Tarahumara outfitters—and the one with the greatest variety of trips—is **Remarkable Journeys,** P.O. Box 31855, Houston, TX 77231-1855, tel. (713) 721-2517 or (800) 856-1993. Remarkable Journeys offers four different canyon trekking itineraries of nine to 10 days duration, plus three hotel-based trips of nine days each, one nine-day Semana Santa trip, and two eight-day train-based trips. Shorter custom train trips are also available. Most trips start in Chihuahua and work out to cost about US$95 per day, including all transportation, most meals, guide service, water, hotel, and pack animals. For camping portions of the trekking itineraries, you bring your own tent and sleeping bag—or they can be rented from Remarkable Journeys.

Wilderness Expeditions, P.O. Box 40092, Tucson, AZ 85717, tel. (602) 882-5341, offers a variety of more specialized trekking tours to the

Sierra Tarahumara, including six-day Christmas and Easter trips for US$650-760 pp and a rugged "Unknown Tarahumara" trip to a non-Christian Tarahumara area (US$750 pp). Customized itineraries are also available.

For those with more time than money, a good approach is simply to turn up in Creel or Cerocahui and ask around. Weeklong trips can be thrown together on the spur of the moment—when enough visitors express an interest—through Casa de Margarita's in Creel. These are generally the most inexpensive organized treks in the region and can be customized according to the tastes and hiking skills of the participants. See the "Creel" section for more detail on the kinds of trips offered.

Mountain Biking: Wildhare's Booze & Adventure in El Paso, tel. (915) 532-4117, leads four mountain biking trips per year into the canyon. Prices run around US$350 pp for five- to six-day itineraries.

Maps

In the INEGI-distributed topo map series, the 1:250,000-scale "San Juanito" map covers most of the upper Sierra Tarahumara (as far south as Batopilas and Urique) and is good for general trip planning and off-highway driving. For serious hikers, more detail is available in eight different 1:50,000 maps which, put together, cover approximately the same territory as the San Juanito map with a bit extra on the southern end. These maps are *usually* available for purchase at the Tarahumara mission store (Artesanías Misión) in Creel (sometimes one or more of them may be out of stock), but to be on the safe side, check with the INEGI office in Hermosillo, Son. (see "Services and Information" under "Hermosillo" for the address), if you have a chance on your way to the Sierra Tarahumara. Buy whatever maps you need there. These maps are not infallibly accurate. In fact some of the trail and village placement is obviously quite off. Nonetheless, they're the best cartographic sources available; it would be crazy to take more than a day-hike without the appropriate map.

Another useful map to have for general orientation is the "Sierra Tarahumara-Barrancas del Cobre" map issued by the International Map Co. (University of Texas at El Paso, Box 400, El Paso, TX 79968-0400). It can be ordered by mail or purchased at the mission store in Creel. I've also seen it for sale in the Terlingua Trading Co. bookstore/gift shop, tel. (915) 371-2234, in Terlingua, Texas (on the outskirts of Big Bend National Park). This simple but accurate map shows most towns and major villages, major rivers, many roads (some with kilometer distances), and the Chihuahua al Pacífico railway. Several well-known villages such as Guahuachique, Tewerichi, Guadalupe, and Guapalaina are oddly missing from the map, even though they appear on SECTUR's Chihuahua state map.

Other Considerations

Accommodations: Although the Chihuahua state tourist office doesn't list them, every town that has a train station has at least one place to stay, often a rustic hotel or guesthouse that costs US$7-10 per night for a spartan room with *baño colectivo*. Simple meals can usually be ordered with a couple of hours' advance notice. It isn't necessary to stay in the highly visible, US$80-plus-per-night, all-inclusive tourist hotels, though they are definitely more comfortable. Specific hotels and guesthouses in all price categories are cited under the appropriate destination sections below.

Camping: Although most of the sierra's annual precipitation falls in the late summer, a danger of flash floods in arroyos (streambeds or gullies) is present year-round. *Never* camp in an arroyo. Almost any flat area on high ground will make a suitable campsite. Shallow caves and rock overhangs are common along some trails, though you may find yourself sharing space with Tarahumaras on the move from one part of the sierra to another. Wilderness etiquette demands you offer something to eat or drink to camp companions as a gesture of courtesy.

Except in the early summer, when a two-season or even summer-weight sleeping bag will suffice from rim to river, you'll need a good three-season bag rated to around -4° C (25° F)—possibly with an insulating liner for cold nights—to cover all elevations.

Getting Around: Local buses are available between the larger towns and villages, but usually run only once a day or perhaps no more than two or three times per week. If you're driving your own vehicle, note that the PEMEX station in Creel now has Magna Sin (unleaded).

Nonhikers

If for some reason you're not able to hike in the canyons, and you don't have your own vehicle, you can still enjoy the scenery. At most of the highland hotels in Creel or Posada Barrancas, you can arrange for day or overnight visits by vehicle. Or you can take a train tour.

Train Tours

For those with more money than time, several U.S. and Mexican tour operators organize package tours in conjunction with the Chihuahua al Pacífico railway. One company that continually receives the best reports and has the most flexible itineraries is **Columbus Travel,** 900 Ridge Creek Lane, Bulverde, TX 78163, tel. (800) 843-1060, fax (830) 885-2010. Columbus operates basic trips of 4-10 nights, in addition to customized trips of virtually any length for individuals or small groups. Most tours allow the option of choosing Los Mochis, Chihuahua, El Paso, or Presidio (Texas) as gateways.

Currently, Columbus's basic trips out of Chihuahua or Los Mochis range from about US$799 (four nights/five days) to US$1,679 (10 nights/11 days) pp; El Paso or Presidio departures cost roughly US$80-100 more. The company can also arrange hiking, burro, and backpacking trips in the Barranca del Cobre area.

Balderrama Tours at Hotel Santa Anita in Los Mochis offers a couple of economical, no-frills package trips. A two-night/three-day package includes roundtrip rail tickets between Los Mochis and Creel, overnight stops in Cuiteco and Creel, and all meals (except lunch in Creel) and transfers for US$140 pp. A two-day package only goes as far as Divisadero, with one overnight stop in Cuiteco, plus all meals and transfers, for US$110.

Hotel Colinas in Los Mochis advertises mid-price packages of US$325-360 s, US$485-510 d for four nights/five days. The price includes rail transportation, tours, hotel, and some meals.

The ultimate in comfortable train transit along the Chihuahua al Pacífico, if you can afford it, is operated by **South Orient Express,** 16800 Greenspoint Park Dr., Suite 245 North, Houston, TX 77060-2308, tel. (713) 872-0190 or (800) 659-7602, fax (713) 872-7123. This company offers two types of private railcar services on the C-P line: the South Orient Express (SOE),

which operates October through mid-April only, and the Vagón Superior Privado (VSP), which runs year-round. The SOE employs stainless steel Budd railcars dating to the 1940s and '50s, including dome dining cars, vista dome cars, an observation car, and a parlor car. All cars are a/c and full bar service is available in each. During the season, the SOE departs weekly from Chihuahua and Los Mochis with stops in El Fuerte and Creel. Fares range from US$1,640 quadruple occupancy for a three night, four-day itinerary to US$1,999 single occupancy on the seven-night, eight-day itinerary; these prices include roundtrip airfare from Tucson, all meals, non-alcoholic beverages (alcoholic beverages available at extra cost), hotels in Chihuahua, Divisadero, and Los Mochis, plus guides for sightseeing along the way.

The VSP uses similar cars but without domes. Departures from the Chihuahua end of the railway are scheduled each Monday, Thursday, and Saturday, while from Los Mochis departures occur on Tuesday, Friday, and Sunday. Stopovers are permitted in Cuauhtémoc, Creel, Divisadero, Bahuichivo, or El Fuerte. One of the main advantages of the VSP is that you can book one-way tickets (US$148 pp), and these can sometimes be purchased on the day of travel. Independent (nonguided) tours that include roundtrip airfare from Tucson, all meals, nonalcoholic beverages, and hotel in Los Mochis, Divisadero, Cerocahui, Creel, and Chihuahua, are available on VSP cars from US$679 quadruple occupancy in the summer to US$1,849 single occupancy in the fall. Subtract US$210 from these tour prices if you don't want air transportation from Tucson.

CREEL

Named for railroad tycoon Enrique Creel, this overgrown logging village of around 3,600 residents is the most popular base for extended Sierra Tarahumara explorations. It's at Km 564 (counting from Chihuahua) along the Chihuahua al Pacífico rail line at an altitude of 2,338 meters (7,668 feet), the second-highest stop along the line (San Juanito to the north is 10 meters higher).

Spreading across a wide, gently sloping arroyo, Creel is a strange mix of frontier town and tourist haven, a place where vaqueros riding horses meet gringos in Ford Broncos at the same intersection. Although wags may say it's getting too touristed for its own good, the truth is that most of the time Creel's attention remains focused on logging. During the fall and spring peak seasons, however, the little town does teem with foreigners, most of whom use Creel as a base for excursions in the surrounding forests as well as to three nearby canyons: Barranca de Tararécua, Barranca del Cobre, and Barranca de Batopilas.

For vistas of the town, climb the hill (elev. 2,410 meters/7,905 feet, about 72 meters/236 feet above Creel) west of the rail station to the cement Cristo Rey statue. The lower Cerro Chapultepec, east of Av. López Mateos, offers a view that requires less legwork.

Surrounding Creel are several Tarahumara settlements and mission villages consisting of timber houses, cave dwellings, and small corn and vegetable plots. Other attractions include **Valle de los Hongos** ("Valley of Mushrooms"), an area of mushroom-shaped rock formations

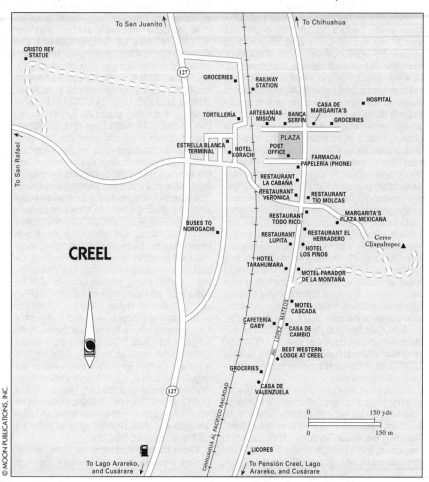

about three km south of Creel, and **Lago Arareko,** a scenic, horseshoe-shaped lake ringed by huge boulders and pine woodlands seven km south of Creel off the road to Cusárare.

Accommodations

Creel basically offers three types of accommodations: small, traditional hotels oriented toward Mexican visitors or small-timers in the logging business; guesthouses for hikers and backpackers on shoestring budgets; and a couple of motels for package tourists and travelers seeking Creel's most comfortable rooms.

Shoestring: The old backpacker's standby, **Casa de Margarita's,** tel./fax (145) 6-0245, enjoys a lively atmosphere in which travelers from all over the world exchange word-of-mouth information—sometimes dubious, sometimes brilliant—on what to see and where to go in Mexico, Latin America, and beyond. Accommodations range widely from narrow dorm beds to a comfortable three-bed "penthouse" with hot shower. No matter which part of Margarita's compound you stay in, your stay includes breakfast and dinner, served family-style in a rustic but cozy dining area next to the kitchen—there's also a table right in the kitchen. A bemused Margarita often presides over the whole scene herself, making sure everyone gets a bed and everyone gets a meal. Tours to nearby villages and into the canyons are available at very reasonable prices. About the only drawback to staying at Margarita's is that during peak season—Oct.-Dec. and March-May—when the place is full, you may have to wait up to 30 minutes to get a seat at mealtime. Mexican children often meet incoming trains to lead disembarking passengers to Margarita's, which stands near the northeast corner of the main plaza, next to a church, on Av. López Mateos. Rates: US$2.60 pp in a dorm with shared hot-water shower; US$4-5.30 pp in two- to four-bed rooms with shared facilities; US$6.60 pp in two- and three-bed rooms with private hot-water shower.

Farther south along Av. López Mateos are a trio of other budget lodgings. Margarita's is a better deal, but if it's full—or if you find the "scene" to be too much—then you may want to try one of these. Two-story **Hotel Los Pinos,** next to Restaurant El Herradero, has 11 simple rooms with hot-water showers but no heat. Rates: US$13 s/d, US$20 t,

US$26 q. Opposite the more expensive Parador de la Montaña is **Hotel Tarahumara,** tel. (145) 6-0252, where we were quoted two completely different sets of room rates on two separate visits. Basic rooms come with private hot-water showers but not heat. As best we could tell, rates run just US$3 s, US$6 d, and then leap to US$13 for t or q. Long-running **Casa de Valenzuela** is an older place with eight clean, sparsely furnished rooms with private hot-water shower but no heat. It's run by a kindly older woman, and the place has such a homey feel that staying here would probably approximate living with a Mexican family. Rates: US$5 pp.

Newer **Cabañas Berti's,** set back a bit from Av. López Mateos, tel. (145) 6-0086 or in Chihuahua (14) 18-4960, offers small rooms with private hot-water shower, plus off-street parking. Some rooms have fireplaces. Like Margarita's, Berti's pushes inexpensive local tours. Rates: US$8 s, US$10 d, US$16 t, US$21 q. **Pensión Creel,** at the south end of Av. López Mateos (No. 61), tel. (145) 6-0071, fax (145) 6-0200, offers 11 rooms in a rustic stone building about 800 meters (a half mile) from the plaza and train station. Some rooms sleep two persons while a few sleep up to four. Rates include a breakfast of tepid coffee and cold eggs; a kitchen is also available where guests may cook for themselves. A large dining/sitting room with a fireplace contains an information board with bus and train schedules, local maps, and information on nearby hikes. Mountain bikes and some camping equipment are available for rent. Interior parking. Except for the occasional budget tour group, this place is often empty, possibly because of its distance from the town center or the rather indifferent management. Rates: US$5 pp.

Shoestring/Budget: Next door to the small bus terminal, above the railroad tracks, **Hotel Korachi,** tel. (145) 6-0207, offers eight simple, clean rooms with shared bath. Only the hallways are heated, so in peak cold weather you might suffer a bit if you don't have a warm sleeping bag to throw over the bed. Rates: US$9 s, US$13 d, US$16 t, and US$20 q. In back of the hotel are 14 cabins with private baths and small woodstoves; rates slightly higher at US$13 s, US$16 d, US$20 t, US$22 q.

Shoestring-to-Inexpensive: Near the train station, **Posada de Creel** (formerly the Hotel

Chavez), tel. (145) 6-0142, U.S./Canada tel. (817) 558-9979, features multibed common rooms (US$5-8 pp), 11 refurbished rooms with shared bathrooms, and 10 rooms with private bath (US$25 pp).

Budget: Margarita's Plaza Mexicana, on Calle El Fido Batista Caro (off Av. López Mateos), tel./fax (145) 6-0245, is a relatively new annex to Margarita's with 26 modern, comfortable rooms around a courtyard. All rooms have private hot-water showers and heating. An attached restaurant serves more upscale Mexican food than at the original Margarita's. Rates of US$29-33 include a large breakfast.

Budget/Inexpensive: A couple of doors down from the Korachi, directly across from the train station, is the similar **Hotel Nuevo,** tel. (145) 6-0022, which offers standard rooms (US$20 s, US$24 d/t), larger deluxe rooms with fireplaces (US$33 d/t/q), and "cabins" (actually rooms in a row house with stone and wood trim) with TV and heat (US$40). Nonfunctioning baths and toilets are attached to the rooms; a better *baño colectivo* is down the hall. Astonishingly, the Hotel Nuevo accepts credit cards—or at least they did at last pass.

Inexpensive: Motel Parador de la Montaña, Av. López Mateos 41, tel. (145) 6-0075, Chihuahua tel. (14) 10-4580, Chihuahua fax (14) 15-3468, offers spacious rooms with private bath and heat (but cold tile floors). A restaurant, comfortable lounge, and secure parking lot are on the premises. Rates: US$40. Next door to the Parador, **Motel Cascada Inn,** Av. López Mateos 49, tel. (145) 6-0253, fax (145) 6-0151, has large, comfortable rooms with TV, private bath and heating. The motel also has a parking lot and a restaurant/bar. Rates: US$39 s, US$41 d, US$53 t, US$62 q.

Moderate: The relatively new **Best Western Lodge at Creel,** Av. López Mateos 61, tel. (145) 6-0071, fax (145) 6-0082, Mexico toll-free tel. (800) 9-0475, U.S./Canada toll-free tel. (800) 528-1234, features 27 rooms in separate cabins of three to four rooms each. Every room has two double beds, a woodstove, TV, coffeemaker, tub/shower, and a small wooden porch. When booked up, this hotel sends its overflow guests to Pensión Creel, hardly a reasonable substitute. Rates of US$62 d (plus US$5 per each extra guest) include breakfast.

Camping

About three km (two miles) south of Creel in an area known as **Complejo Ecoturístico Arareko** you are permitted to camp for a fee of US$3.30. This area is near Lago Arareko, within the Tarahumara *ejido* of San Ignacio de Arareko. Water and trash service are supposedly available, but a recent letter from a reader warned: "There is no water available—outhouse facilities were primitive (at best) and the Rarámuri vendors were a constant fixture when we camped there; nice people but you could not blow your nose without a small person or mother/children observing from nearby and selling trinkets all the time. I appreciate that they need to make a living, but it makes it a trying experience to camp out there."

Creel has no RV parks, but self-contained rigs can park in the Parador or Cascada Inn lots for a nominal fee.

Food

Creel's simple eateries are concentrated along Av. López Mateos between the plaza and the Cascada Inn. **Restaurant Veronica** (the sign says "Vero") serves good *antojitos,* breakfasts, sandwiches, and *comida corrida,* and is popular with locals as well as tourists. The similar **Restaurant La Cabaña** features a wide menu selection, including spit-roasted chicken along with the usual *antojitos.* At either of these restaurants you should be able to eat well at very moderate prices. **Restaurant Lupita** is virtually a carbon copy of the foregoing, as is **Cafetería Gaby,** except that the latter is only open during the day for breakfast and lunch. **Restaurant El Herradero** is a simple *antojitos* and *carne asada* place.

Popular among tourists is the well-decorated **Restaurant Tío Molcas,** which serves a similar range of *antojitos* at slightly higher prices. **Restaurant Todo Rico,** a small, five-table place that's very popular with locals, serves very good quesadillas and okay pizza.

El Caballo Bayo, Av. López Mateos 25, is an American-owned restaurant and bar (the only bar in town) with international cuisine and courtyard dining. It's one of the more pricey places to eat in town, although it's still moderately priced and beer is cheap.

A couple of small grocery stores can also be found along Av. López Mateos.

Information and Services
On the plaza, Jesuit-sponsored **Artesanías Misión** sells maps and books about the Sierra Tarahumara, as well as quality Tarahumara crafts. All proceeds go to a local hospital.

Money: Despite what other guidebooks might say, traveler's checks can easily be cashed at Banca Serfín. The *tienda de licores* on Av. López Mateos will also cash travelers checks. Farther south on López Mateos, a relatively new *casa de cambio* called **Nuevo Horizonte Internacional** has good rates for TCs and can also arrange Visa cash advances.

Post: The town post office is on the plaza, opposite the mission store.

Telephone: Papelería Cristo Rey de Todo, on Av. López Mateos a few doors south of the plaza, has efficient long-distance phone service.

Tours
Most of the hotels and guesthouses in town can arrange guided or independent tours to surrounding areas. Prices often depend on how many people are going on a tour. Since Margarita's gets more walk-in business than anyone else, you're more likely to be able to put together a small group and save money. Margarita's standard tours include: Cusárare and Lake Arareko, five hours, US$6.50 pp; Barranca de Tararécua and hot springs, US$6.50 (plus US$1.25 to enter the springs); Cascada de Basaseachic and Barranca de Candameña, 10 hours (three-hour drive, plus three-hour hike to the waterfall), US$16 pp; La Bufa, 10 hours, US$16; Divisadero, seven hours of driving and hiking, US$8. All of these prices suppose a minimum of four people. Longer trips can be arranged on a custom basis.

Best Western Lodge at Creel does tours to Arareko and Cusárare for US$13 pp; to Recohuata Hot Springs for US$20; to Barranca de Urique for US$20; to Batopilas for US$65; and to Basaseachic for US$48.

Buses
Estrella Blanca operates the main intercity bus service in Creel; the small terminal is next to Hotel Korachi above the train tracks. To or from Chihuahua, the four-hour bus trip costs US$8.50, with seven departures per day. Other Estrella Blanca destinations along the same route in-

Tarahumara children

JENNIFER BARTLETT

clude Cuauhtémoc (US$6), La Junta (US$4), and San Juanito (US$1.50). Estrella Blanca also goes to Guachochi daily at 5 p.m. for US$2.60.

On Tuesday and Saturday at 11 a.m. a bus leaves for Norogachi (US$6.40) from a small office on a street that runs parallel to and between Av. López Mateos and the highway.

Buses to Batopilas leave Tuesday, Thursday, and Saturday at 7 a.m. from the plaza for US$8 per seat. The trip takes five to six hours. Tickets can be purchased in advance from Artesanías Rarámuri on Av. López Mateos, next to Restaurant El Herradero.

Train
The first-class Chihuahua al Pacífico train passes through Creel in both directions daily. The southwestbound train (No. 74) arrives from Chihuahua around 12:25 p.m.; the northeastbound train from Los Mochis (No. 75) arrives around 3:14 p.m. A chalkboard in the Creel station gives the latest estimated departure times for trains;

unlike at many train stations in Mexico, the staff is good about keeping the chalkboard up to date. First-class fares to/from Chihuahua cost US$19 adult, half that for $6 children under six.

The slower and more crowded second-class *pollero* costs just US$3 and runs on Tuesday, Thursday, and Saturday. The schedule has the train arriving from Chihuahua at 2 p.m., and from Los Mochis at 5 p.m., but it isn't unusual for this train to run up to two hours late. This train used to be called the "Tarahumara" till someone pointed out the offense the name might cause the Tarahumara people. It's now officially called the Chihuahua-Sufragio-Los Mochis line.

Tickets go on sale at the station a half hour before departure, or you can simply buy your ticket on the train. Even in the high tourist season it's not usually necessary to buy tickets in advance; we've never seen either train fill up completely.

Driving

The drive to Creel along Mexico 16 from La Junta, Cuauhtémoc, or Chihuahua is fairly smooth all the way. The Creel PEMEX station pumps Nova and Magna Sin. Beyond Creel the road is paved all the way to San Rafael (around 55 km), after which only rugged vehicles with off-highway capabilities should continue. A highway branching off to Cusárare is paved all the way to Samachique and Guachochi, and beyond to Hidalgo de Parral. Another road, unpaved, splits off near Samachique and continues all the way to Batopilas and Satevó.

EXCURSIONS FROM CREEL

Before deciding on which hikes or day-trips take, it's a good idea to talk to other travelers who have been in the sierra awhile for personal recommendations—Margarita's and Pensión Creel are good places to get this kind of word-of-mouth information. After talking to a few people, you may be able to customize your own trips, hiring burros, guides, and cooks as needed.

For hikers the topo map to have is the Creel G13A22 1:50,000-scale quadrangle, usually available at the Tarahumara mission store on the plaza (or from the INEGI office in Hermosillo, Sonora).

Longer, multiday trips can be arranged either on your own, using other Sierra Tarahumara towns (such as Cusárare, Batopilas, Cerocahui, or Urique) as springboards, or through local hotels and guesthouses. See the "Tours" section under "Creel" for examples.

Complejo Ecoturístico Arareko

Good destinations for day-trips include placid **Lago Arareko** (five km from the south edge of town) and **San Ignacio de Arareko,** a Tarahumara mission village only two km east of Pensión Creel. The villagers here plant corn and beans, and raise goats. **Valle de los Hongos** ("Valley of Mushrooms") and **Cueva de Sebastián** are short walks from the mission. The latter is a cave inhabited by an extended Tarahumara family and is open to the public. Although it seems rather zoolike in concept, the family seems happy to receive visitors and show them around. As these are now part of the Complejo Ecoturístico Arareko, there is a small admission charge to the area.

A further 3.5 km northeast of San Ignacio is **Valle de los Monjes** ("Valley of Monks"), a set of peculiar rock formations that look vaguely like hooded, robed monks. A dirt road continues on from San Ignacio 16 km (10 miles) via the tiny hamlet of Gonogochi to the rim of a medium-sized canyon formed by the Río Conchos.

Accommodations: At the edge of Lago Arareko, **Cabaña Segórachi,** tel. (145) 6-0126, managed by Complejo Ecoturístico Arareko, is a cooperative now 100% owned by Rarámuris. The large chalet-style cabin sleeps up to 16 and features a full kitchen, fireplace, four full bathrooms, and a small boat dock. A rowboat supposedly comes with the cabin. Also managed by the cooperative, the similar **Cabañas Batosárachi,** off the lake in a wooded area, has space for 70 people, heat, electricity, hot water, full baths, and shared eating and kitchen facilities. Stays at either place cost US$5 pp. With advance planning these cabins could make a good place for a long-term visit to the area; both would need a good cleaning first, however, as they aren't very well maintained. Bookings can be made at the Complejo Ecoturístico Arareko office in Creel, on Av. López Mateos next door to Farmacia Cristo Rey, not far from the plaza.

Recohuata Hot Springs

A more challenging trip from Creel would be the trek to Recohuata Hot Springs in Barranca de Tararécua, about 10 km south of Lago Arareko via logging roads—study a topographic map before setting out and don't go without a compass. You may also be able to reach the springs by following the river all the way from the lake through the canyon, but for this you will definitely need a guide who knows the arroyo. The canyon rim near the hot springs (about a 45-minute walk) can be reached by off-highway vehicle from Creel or Cusárare if you prefer doing it the easy way. Creel's hotels and guesthouses can also arrange guided treks to this canyon and hot springs.

San Juanito

From the smell of wood smoke to the stacks of timber in all directions, you'll know this small town 30 km north of Creel is almost totally dedicated to the lumber business. Few visitors stop here except for fuel (PEMEX with Nova only) or groceries. In addition to a Banamex, the town has several grocery stores and *cafeterías*, an Estrella Blanca bus terminal, a train station on the Chihuahua al Pacífico line, and the rustic **Motel Posada del Cobre,** where rooms are available for about US$10 a night. One of the town peculiarities is that a number of residents have converted abandoned railcars into homes, complete with flower gardens out front.

A gravel road leads 70 km northwest from San Juanito to Basaseachic Falls. For anyone wishing to visit the falls by vehicle from Creel, this is a quicker route than doubling back all the way to Mexico 16 near La Junta, in spite of the fact that Mexico 16 is a paved highway.

Boycona

Fourteen km northeast of Creel, this is another logging town much like San Juanito, and a good supply point for road excursions to the Tarahumara pueblos of **Sisoguichi** and **Panalachi.** These lie 19 km and 38 km, respectively, southeast of Boycona via a winding, unpaved road. Both have become popular as places to attend Tarahumara Semana Santa festivals. Even better for the latter is **Tewerichic** (spelled "Tehuerichi" on some maps), a mission village about 2.5 to three hours farther southeast on a bad

dirt road. The village lies in a splendid valley of canyons and cliffs along the Río Conchos.

El Tejabán

Like Divisadero on the railway line to the west, El Tejabán commands one of the best canyon views—in this case of the famed Barranca del Cobre or "Copper Canyon" itself—in the sierra. Unlike Divisadero there's no train coming through two to four times a day, no crowds of souvenir vendors—and no easy access. The unpaved, often ungraded road to El Tejabán requires a sturdy, high-clearance vehicle and a determined sense of direction.

The view here is rim to rim. Hikers can avail themselves of several trails winding down into the canyon, along the canyon bottom, and up the other side. Aside from a relatively minor tourism industry, the area draws income from **Mina La Purísima,** a very important complex of several mines along the Río Urique below, yielding amethyst, turquoise, gold, silver, and copper. Four different owners share all the mines; a Canadian enterprise is currently exploring three of the tunnels.

A small hot springs called **El Ojito** is a 1.5-hour hike from the rim, while the village of **Guaicabo,** toward the bottom of the canyon on the other side of the river from El Tejabán, can be reached on foot in 2.5 hours. The best way to cross the river at the bottom is to use the *canastilla,* a basket suspended from a wire cable worked with pulleys. A two-day hike will bring you to **Munérachi,** or you can reach **Batopilas** in three days. Both of these destinations are described further on in this book. A more adventurous route would take you southwest to the Tarahumara village of **Guahuachique,** from where you could hike or hitch a ride along a dirt road east to Samachique, continuing by road to Batopilas, or go west to the Barranca de Urique. Local guides can be arranged at the Hotel El Tejabán or in Guaicabo.

Accommodations: Hotel El Tejabán, at the end of the road from Cusárare, tel. (146) 2-4442 in Camargo, is an 18-room limestone-block lodge perched at 2,200 meters (7,200 feet) on the canyon rim. A huge restaurant at the center of the complex offers a wraparound view of the canyon. Spacious, well-appointed rooms with fireplace and satellite TV cost US$60 pp with three meals, while a cabaña with jacuzzi and sitting room costs a flat US$213 for up to six persons including meals for the first two guests, other meals charged pp. There are also two 20-bed dorms, one for men and one for women, that cost US$16 pp with meals, US$10.60 pp if you bring your own food.

The hotel provides guides down to the river at no charge. ATVs and mountain bikes are available for rent, or you can even hire the hotel's small plane. The hotel van will pick up guests with reservations in Creel at no charge.

Getting There: Assuming you have a rugged vehicle, you can drive to El Tejabán on your own except in the wet season (July-Sept.), when the road may become impassable. The signed turnoff is 23.5 km (14.7 miles) from the Creel junction. The road, mostly surfaced in caliche (broken limestone), winds through pretty pine forests along the way but don't get too distracted or you may become lost. There are two major forks along the way; at the first one you should bear right, and at the second bear left. Aside from these there are many smaller detours that either fade out or reconnect with the main trunk. You'll avoid lots of dead-ends and torturous splits if you stick to the more well-worn, wider road—sometimes this may require a little scouting. The road eventually crests at around 2,400 meters (8,000 feet), then drops down onto Mesa Colorada, where you'll cross an airstrip 22.5 km (14 miles) from the highway. You'll arrive at the hotel gate at 25 km (15.5 miles). Total drive time is about two hours.

You can walk to the lodge from Cusárare in one day.

Cusárare

A Tarahumara name meaning "Place of Eagles," Cusárare is a collection of native *ranchitos* fanning out from a scenic gorge formed by the Arroyo de Cusárare. The main village is centered around an 18th-century mission church of minor interest.

One of the region's most popular day-hikes is to **Cusárare Falls** via a trail from the Copper Canyon Sierra Lodge, the area's only tourist accommodations. From the lodge parking lot, the trail heads west parallel to a stream, about an hour's leisurely walk each way. The trail crosses the stream three times but is fairly easy to follow.

Along the way are several sandy "beaches" (the water is cold but swimmable in summer), huge boulders, and shady idylls. Local Tarahumaras use the same trail and you're likely to come across a few basket-and-trinket vendors. Keep an eye out for the eared trogon, a small, iridescent, orange-feathered bird related to the sacred quetzal of the Aztecs.

The falls themselves are 30 meters (98 feet) high and very broad, but not thundering; when the water is low you can walk across the top of the falls and peer into the stream below. For the best view of the falls, look for a path that leads past the falls on your left. Sometimes a park entry fee of US$1 is collected by a local Tarahumara *ejidatario* standing on the trail with a book of tickets.

Other short hikes in the area can be made to the **Cueva Pintada** (a rock shelter with polychromatic pictographs of undetermined age)—a 40-minute roundtrip walk that passes Tarahumara *ranchitos*—and to **Cusárare village,** about an hour roundtrip on foot (2.5 km/1.5 miles upstream if you follow the stream in the opposite direction from the falls). Ask at the lodge for a key to the mission church before setting off for the village. Beyond Cusárare the trail continues east for three to four km to the bucolic Tarahumara hamlets of Gomírachi and Chochípachi. Tarahumara children will sometimes volunteer to serve as guides for these short hikes for an expected tip of around US$0.40 per visitor.

Guides for the longer hike to Recohuata Hot Springs can be arranged through the Copper Canyon Sierra Lodge at a cost of US$10-13 per day per guide. Horseback trail rides can also be arranged for US$4 per hour per horse plus an additional US$4 per hour per guide. The trek to Recohuata takes three to five hours each way and includes a 300-meter (thousand-foot) descent into the Barranca de Tararécua. The hot springs—just a bit warmer than the average air temperature—flow from the canyon's north wall near the headwaters of the Río Tararécua and are piped into a primitive concrete bathhouse smelling of sulfur and mineral salts. According to John Fayhee's whimsical Tararécua chronicle, a better, lesser-known hot spring is only a half day's hike downstream. Beyond this point the canyon is filled with boulders that are very difficult to negotiate.

Excursions to **El Tejabán,** a *ranchería* and hotel overlooking the Barranca del Cobre, usually involve a four-hour drive along logging roads, then an hour's hike into the canyon. Although the view over the canyon from El Tejabán is one of the sierra's most beautiful, it's probably not worth the eight-hour roundtrip drive unless you plan to make it an overnight camping trip or stay at the hotel there; see "El Tejabán," above for more information.

Accommodations: The **Copper Canyon Sierra Lodge** (formerly the Sierra Madre Lodge, and known locally as Cabañas Cañon del Cobre) is the only place to stay in Cusárare. Built of logs and other native materials, the 23-room lodge is delightfully quiet and rustic, and is staffed by Tarahumaras from the local *ejido* (the lodge sits on *ejido* lands). Each room has a small woodstove (and supply of wood), a couple of kerosene lanterns, a private bathroom with hot shower, and comfortable furnishings.

Rooms are generally offered only as part of an eight-night trip that starts with one night in Chihuahua at Hotel Palacio del Sol, then two nights at the Sierra Lodge, three nights at the Riverside Lodge in Batopilas, another night at the Sierra Lodge, and the final night in Chihuahua again. During high season (mid-December to mid-January and mid-March to mid-May) the cost is US$1,045 pp double occupancy. In July and August the price drops to US$795. Twelve-day itineraries are available for US$1,295 pp. These trips run every Saturday and Monday year-round except for the month of June when the lodge is closed. When space is available, walk-ins are welcome for US$175 s, US$250 d per night. Rates—whether for the multiday schedules or for walk-ins—include all ground transportation (including Chihuahua-Creel-Chihuahua train tickets), all meals, guided excursions, and lodging.

For information or reservations, contact **Copper Canyon Lodges,** 2741 Paldan Dr., Auburn Hills, MI 48326, in Mexico tel. (145) 6-0179, fax 6-0036, in the U.S./Canada tel. (810) 340-7230 or (800) 776-3942, fax (810) 340-7212.

Camping: The area has no campgrounds, but you might try asking for permission to camp in the *ejido* near the Cueva Pintada, or else simply pitch a tent in the woods along the trail to the falls.

Transportation: Unless you have reservations to stay at the Copper Canyon Sierra Lodge (in which case you'll be met at the train station and driven to the lodge), you'll have to arrange your own transportation or hike the three km from the Creel-Guachochi highway junction at Km 112. Buses to Batopilas or Guachochi will drop passengers off at this junction. Cusárare is 23 km from Creel via the road to Batopilas, though the lodge (and trailhead for the Cusárare Falls hike) is beyond the turnoff for Cusárare off the main road. It's possible to hitchhike but you can't count on catching rides in both directions on the same day. A taxi from Creel costs US$20 one-way.

BATOPILAS

In a turn of phrase more suitable for a travel brochure than a realistic appraisal, a 1992 issue of *National Geographic Traveler* attempted to evoke Batopilas with "Imagine Tahiti, Treasure Island, hidden away in the bottom of the Grand Canyon . . . " You'll be hard pressed to find anything obviously reminiscent of Tahiti or Treasure Island in Batopilas, although there's probably more potential for adventure here than anywhere in Tahiti or the Society Islands. Perhaps it was the tropical fruit—mangoes, papayas, oranges, bananas, avocados—growing here that infected the writer's imagination. Gold is mined in the Batopilas area, but it's mostly of the "green" variety, the cultivation and trade of which is a source of local cash, though this doesn't mean that Batopilas is an unsafe place to visit as long as you stay aloof from the trade. About half the population of 1,150 is of Tarahumara descent.

The first vehicle road to Batopilas was constructed only around 18 years ago, but the town chronology goes back over 350 years. Spanish *adelantados* (advance guard) arrived in 1632 and found pure silver on the river banks. Because river currents polished it to a smooth white finish, the Spaniards called it *plata nevada* ("snowy silver") and soon established a mine called Mina Nevada and a town called San Pedro de Batopilas (the latter a corruption of the Tarahumara description *bachotigori,* meaning "near the river"). Native silver masses weighing up to 200 kilos apiece weren't unusual in the early years. After the Spanish left, Mexicans and

Batopilas rooftops

Americans took over the mines and added many more, the biggest of which were the turn-of-the-century holdings of Alexander Shepherd's Batopilas Mining Company.

Batopilas's historical legacy shows in the town's late 19th-century architecture, but the ambience is much sleepier than it must have been during the silver-mining heyday. Mule trains with dubious cargo from nearby villages put in for supplies, and a few prospectors still pay with gold or silver nuggets from clandestine mines. Horses are as common as cars or trucks, and the streets are cobbled in flagstone. Travelers with flexible schedules often find themselves lingering in Batopilas for longer than originally planned in order to savor the history and atmosphere, and to explore the many trails fanning out from the town. The elevation of 462 meters (1,515 feet) is quickly left behind in steep climbs toward the canyon rim.

A carpenter next to Plaza Constitución at the south end of town makes custom Tarahumara-style sandals—tire strips laminated with leather and tied to the ankle with a long leather thong.

One of the most important local festivals is the **Fiesta de la Virgen de Carmen,** celebrating the town's patron saint, on July 6th. Semana Santa is also big, though it's mostly celebrated in the Mexican style with only a few Tarahumara flourishes.

Hacienda San Miguel
Alexander Shepherd administered his silver empire from this site on the east side of the Río Batopilas, about a kilometer northeast of the town center. His Hacienda San Miguel lies in brick ruins, among which are the remains of an assay office, refectory, boardinghouse, corral and stables, machine shop, iron foundry, ingot mill, and amalgamation sheds. At one time an 800-meter aerial tram linked canyon slopes on both sides of the river. Much of the current attraction is botanic and exploring the ruins is a bit of a jungle walk. Several large fig trees grow on the compound walls and the tallest building is overgrown with a huge bougainvillea, while shorter trees and plants occupy the remainder of the grounds. Someone has reconstructed one of the property's smaller buildings for use as a living space.

You must cross the bridge (originally built by Shepherd and company) at the north entrance of town to reach the ruins. The front gate to the hacienda is usually open during the day—ask in town first to make sure.

Church
In the middle of town is an older church with ore fragments studding the lower interior walls—a telltale sign that it was built by miners. Along one wall is a Christ-in-a-box used annually for Easter processions, and in a niche on the opposite wall is a black saint, San Martín de Torres.

Aqueduct and Dam
This functioning stone marvel was built by Shepherd and company nearly a hundred years ago to provide a constant water supply for the town and to generate hydroelectric power. Batopilas still relies on the structure for its main water supply (several *ranchitos* north of town irrigate their crops via the aqueduct) and in 1988 hydroelectric capabilities were reinstalled. A walk north along the trail below the aqueduct leads to the simple stone dam across the Río Batopilas, a great spot for cooling off on a hot day. For more detail on this outing, see "Hikes from Batopilas," below.

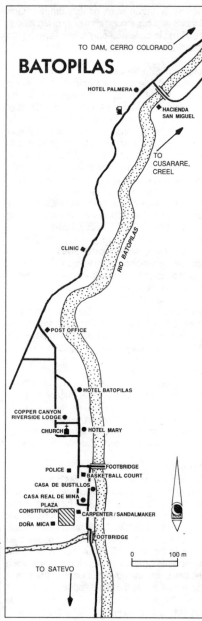

BATOPILAS

TO DAM, CERRO COLORADO

HOTEL PALMERA ●

● HACIENDA
SAN MIGUEL

TO
CUSARARE,
CREEL

RIO BATOPILAS

CLINIC ●

● POST OFFICE

● HOTEL BATOPILAS

COPPER CANYON
RIVERSIDE LODGE ●
CHURCH ✝ ● HOTEL MARY

POLICE ■ ● FOOTBRIDGE
■ BASKETBALL COURT
CASA DE BUSTILLOS
CASA REAL DE MINA ■
PLAZA
CONSTITUCION ● CARPENTER / SANDALMAKER
DOÑA MICA ■
● FOOTBRIDGE

0   100 m

TO SATEVO

© MOON PUBLICATIONS, INC.

Satevó

One of the premier local attractions is this impressive, triple-domed mission church 6.5 km (four miles) south of Batopilas in the heart of Barranca de Batopilas. It's an easy half-day roundtrip hike now that the road—part of the Camino Real—has been graded. Along the way you'll pass a quaint footbridge across the river as well as impressive views of the church and canyon in the distance.

The church is about 14 meters (48 feet) high from its base to the top of the naves. A single bell tower extending another four meters or so holds bells dated 1801, 1720, and 1630, plus others on which the dates are obscured. A long, shaky ladder inside the church leads to a *coro* overlooking the interior, and another ladder—short and shaky—leads into the bell tower. Climb with extreme caution. Still in use by the small Satevó community, the church features white-washed walls stained with berry juice to signify Christ's blood. Crypts beneath the flagstone floor reportedly hold the remains of Jesuit padres. The church is often locked on weekdays—you'll have to ask someone at the nearby general store to unlock it.

A few years ago an overimaginative writer (Batopilas tends to get the pens working overtime) dubbed the Satevó church the "Lost Cathedral," but evidence suggests the church was never a cathedral (which requires the presence of an archbishop) and it was certainly never "lost" in the sense that locals and visitors didn't know of its existence—especially since it's on a branch of the Camino Real, Mexico's most well-known historical thoroughfare. The date of construction is indeed a mystery, but architectural styles suggest it was probably erected in the 17th century and may have been the original site of San Pedro de Batopilas. Since Jesuit records were often destroyed by the Franciscans when they took over church administration in the 18th century, the exact dating of the church will probably never be known—though if it had been a cathedral, not even the jealous Franciscans could have kept this secret from present-day historians.

The graded road to Satevó makes a hot and dusty walk—if you plan to walk, best go in the morning before it heats up. Traffic along the road to Satevó is almost nil, but you can hire a truck to drop you off at the church for around US$5 if you prefer not to walk both ways. Cold soft drinks are available at a small store near the church.

Semana Santa

As Barranca de Batopilas is a stronghold for less-assimilated Tarahumaras, the nearby villages are good places to observe Semana Santa celebrations (see the special topic "The Tarahumaras" for details on this festival and for visiting guidelines).

Accommodations

Little Batopilas has eight places to spend the night, six of them quite basic but adequate for most hikers.

Shoestring: Friendly **Hotel Palmera,** near the bridge and north entrance to town, features seven clean rooms with hot-water showers. A small garden in front makes a pleasant sitting area. The main drawback to staying here is that it's a fairly long walk to the center of town. Rates: US$8 s/d per night.

Next south along the road into the center of Batopilas, over a local general store in a big white building, is **Hotel Chula Vista,** which offers unkempt rooms with dirty linen. To be avoided at all costs, this place is used mainly as a brothel. Rates: US$4.60 pp.

On the east side of the plaza that doubles as a basketball court, **Casa de Señora Monse** (also known as Casa de Bustillos) is a favorite backpackers' hangout mainly because the owner-manager, Sra. Monse Bustillos, speaks some English. She also sells Tarahumara artifacts and can arrange meals (including vegetarian) for US$3 per meal. Guests share a cold-water bath or bathe in the river behind the house. Lately the rooms have not been very well maintained. Rates: US$2.60 pp.

A few doors south from Monse's and also backing onto the river is the better **Casa de Señora Juana,** where six basic but clean rooms come with attached private cold-water bathrooms. Rates: US$6 s, US$10.60 d in one-bed rooms with private bath; US$7.30s, US$12 d, US$17.30 t, and US$20 q in two-bed rooms.

The nearby **Hotel Mary** (also known as Hotel Parador), opposite the town church, offers clean, simple rooms; the collective bathrooms sometimes have hot water. Some people like this

hotel and use it time after time, others find the service rather lacking. Rates: US$5 s/d. **Hotel Batopilas,** three blocks north of the plaza opposite the massive Riverside Lodge, has small, plain rooms with cold-water shared bath. Like Hotel Mary, this one has both fans and detractors. Rates: US$5 pp.

Budget: The town's best value, dollar for dollar, is the relatively new and well-run **Casa Real de Mina de Acanasaina,** just north of Plaza Constitución, tel. (145) 6-0624 or 6-0632. This thick-walled, 100-year-old former *casona* contains five capacious rooms with private hot-water bath, plus one room with shared bath. Each room comes with two large beds and a floor fan. Another plus is the attached Restaurant Astrid Estefania. Rates: US$13 s, US$20 d, US$26 t, US$32 q.

Copper Canyon Riverside Lodge

Occupying a huge block in the center of town is the two-story Copper Canyon Riverside Lodge (also known locally as Hotel Hacienda Batopilas), originally built around 1890 as a hacienda for a wealthy Mexican family and now a pet project of tour impresario Skip McWilliams. Batopilas has been called "wonderfully weird" and this hotel fits that description perfectly. It's a time-warp oasis in a remote corner of Mexico, inspired perhaps by A.R. Shepherd's Hacienda San Miguel. Mozart and Patsy Cline, emanating from a tape system in the parlor, drift across interior courtyards planted with kumquat and avocado trees. The parlor itself is furnished with Porfiriato antiques and sports a ceiling fresco depicting a whimsical history of Batopilas.

Other public areas include a Mexican-style prayer room, roof terrace, open-air dining room, and library containing historical literature and maps. Guest rooms, most of them with small colonial-style terraces overlooking the streets below, are large, comfortable, and well-furnished, with attached hot-water bathrooms. Although the kitchen, dining rooms, and parlor are electrified, the guest rooms are lamp-lit. The hotel does not take walk-in guests and only books rooms in conjunction with an eight-day package that includes accommodations in Cusárare and Chihuahua (see "Cusárare," above, for details on the package). Once you've sprung for the package deal, it's possible to book extra nights in Batopilas.

Food

Overall the best restaurant in town is the Casa Real de Minas' **Restaurant Astrid Estefania**, which serves good standard Mexican fare. The only problem is the restaurant may not be open when there are no guests in the attached hotel.

Though usually empty, **Restaurant Quinta Patio** at Hotel Mary features a simple menu of *antojitos* that cost US$2-3 pp. Local legend **Doña Mica** serves home-cooked, ranchero-style meals on the front porch of her house (also known as Michaela's) south of the town's smaller plaza

THE BATOPILAS MINING COMPANY

Since 1632 more than 300 mines, claims, and veins have been worked in the Batopilas district; most of them were established at an elevation of 700-1,200 meters. The Nuestra Señora del Pilar mine, founded around 1730, yielded 40,000 pesos a week for nearly 30 years. Mining subsided immediately after the Spanish expulsion in 1820, but new mines were started by Mexicans in 1842.

In 1861 American John Robinson bought an older property of two mines thought to be worked out. Robinson was completing a tunnel between the two mines when he came upon a blind vein that came to be known as La Veta Grande or "Great Vein," a major source of native silver. Transportation of the raw ore to Chihuahua for processing seemed prohibitively expensive, however, and Robinson sold the so-called San Miguel Tunnel to Alexander Robey Shepherd for US$600,000 in 1880.

Shepherd had been the last governor of Washington, D.C. before the U.S. government removed him from office (and banished the D.C. governorship altogether) in the 1870s for alleged corruption in public works. (The accusations were never proven, and, due to Shepherd's efforts to upgrade Washington's public works, the U.S. government canceled its plans to move the U.S. capital to St. Louis.) Following the purchase of the tunnel, Shepherd moved to Batopilas with his family and soon filed over 350 other claims in a 31-square-km area, with total underground workings encompassing 120 km. His holdings were consolidated as the Batopilas Mining Company, and this town at the bottom of a deep canyon soon became one of the wealthiest spots in Mexico.

Shepherd wisely constructed his own amalgamating/retorting facility and foundry at his Hacienda San Miguel on the river, and between 1880 and 1906 approximately 20 million ounces of silver were extracted from the company mines. At the 1893 Chicago World's Fair, silver ore from his mines took first place in the competition with a solid silver mass weighing 172 kilograms (380 pounds). Shepherd's company cast the processed silver into bars weighing 30 kilograms each, then loaded them two per mule into monthly bullion trains that transported at least 50 and often 100-200 silver bars on the backs of 30-100 mules to the Banco Minero in Chihuahua. Pancho Villa once stole US$38,000 in silver bars from one of the company's mule trains, a deed that forever tainted Villa's reputation among gringo miners.

Most of the buildings standing in Batopilas today were constructed during the 1890s heyday of the Batopilas Mining Company. At the time, it took eight days to reach the town from Chihuahua—three days by rail and five on muleback—but Shepherd and company managed to ship in an incredible variety of cultural and technological accoutrements in spite of the town's remoteness. Hence Batopilas became one of the first places in North America (the second in Mexico) to have electricity. A local "Ladies Society" also restored the old church and hosted concerts, theater, dances, and even occasional operas.

By the time Shepherd died in 1902, the town's population had grown from 400 to around 5,000 (it is now around 600). The hydroelectric facility he installed on the river was restored in 1988 and once again powers the town, and his original aqueduct still provides the local water supply.

Shepherd's sons ceased operations in 1920, by which time the lion's share of the ore had already been extracted. At their peak, Shepherd's mines were the wealthiest in the world, paying around US$1 million in dividends per year. Other miners made unsuccessful attempts to get the mines going again as late as the 1940s.

Grant Shepherd, one of Alexander Shepherd's sons, has written *The Silver Magnet* (New York: E.P. Dutton, 1938), a detailed account of the Shepherd mining business and town history. Though a number of common Spanish words are strangely misspelled (e.g., chile and tequila), the book gives a good idea of what life in Batopilas must have been like at the turn of the century. Photos in the book show Batopilas hasn't changed much—at least physically—since 1895.

on a winding side street. It's best to let her know a few hours in advance if you want to dine on her front porch—sometimes you'll be offered a choice, but most often it's potluck. Vegetarians can request her famous *sopa de papas y queso* (potato-cheese soup) or *enfrijoladas* (cheese-stuffed corn tortillas bathed in a bean sauce). Señora Monse and Sra. Juana can arrange meals at their guesthouses as well.

Other than the above, your best bets are the local grocery stores, of which there are few. Locally grown fruits and vegetables are reasonably priced, while just about everything else is costly due to the long distances supplies must travel. A horse that costs US$300 in Creel, for example, goes for US$1,000 in Batopilas.

Batopilas is a dry town, so alcoholic beverages can't legally be consumed, bought, or sold (the Riverside Lodge and Casa Real de Minas are exceptions, but only for guests). A bootleg can of Tecate—the only beer available, under the table at certain stores—costs US$1. Lechugilla, a strong contraband liquor made from the succulent of the same name, is surprisingly expensive at nearly US$10 per liter.

Transportation

Half the attraction in coming to Batopilas is the scenic road trip from Creel. Before this 135-km (84-mile) road was completed 18 years ago, a branch of the Camino Real—little more than a steep, winding path—was the only way in and out. The road was paved for around 60 km (47 miles), as far as the junction to **Samachique,** a lumber settlement roughly halfway to Batopilas. The remaining 75 km (46.5 miles) is winding, unpaved gravel. Just before Samachique a paved highway splits off and heads southeast to Guachochi (90 km/56 miles from the junction) and onward to Mexico 24, which leads to Hidalgo del Parral. Past Samachique, the Creel-Batopilas road worsens considerably but the canyon scenery becomes very dramatic.

Descending into Barranca de Batopilas, the road then passes two small villages, the all-Tarahumara **Basigochi** and the mixed Tarahumara and mestizo **Quírare** (Kírare). The best view along the road comes after Quírare, where you can see deep into the canyon as the vegetation passes from cottonwood to oak to mesquite. Look for **Cerro El Pastel** ("Cake Hill"), named for its

alternating layers of pink and white volcanic rock, on the left. A few kilometers beyond Quírare the road arrives at **La Bufa,** a scenic Río Batopilas crossing and site of a former silver mine, made obvious by the mounds of slag covering a nearby cliff. Mexicans and foreigners alike seem fond of debating the origin of the word "bufa" since in Spanish it's an uncommon word; it derives from the same Latin root as the Italian *buffa* and French *bouffant* and can refer to anything with a billowing appearance, e.g., a monk's cowl, a tall hairdo, a pig's bladder, or a wineskin. On your right you should be able to make out the Camino Real winding along the side of the canyon; this path is still used by Tarahumaras and prospectors, since for travel by foot or mule train it reaches the top more quickly than the newer vehicle road.

By car or truck, the road takes about five hours from Creel to Batopilas or vice versa. Needless to say, neither fuel nor mechanical assistance are available along the way (although you can buy Nova and Magna Sin from barrels—at an elevated price—in Batopilas). Many of the curves along the way are blind and feature steep, unguarded drops; this is not a road for squeamish drivers. Eventually—possibly within the next couple of years—the road will be paved all the way to Batopilas.

Buses to Batopilas leave from Creel Tuesdays, Thursdays, and Saturdays at 7 a.m., usually arriving around noon or 1 p.m. (or later—depending on the passenger load and number of stops); the fare is US$8. The return bus to Creel leaves on Mondays, Wednesdays, and Fridays at the same hour but arrives in Creel at 11 a.m. or noon; the ride uphill is faster than downhill because the driver doesn't have to pamper the brakes as much. The bus can be crowded and slow but is quite a cultural experience.

Hitchhiking can be very difficult along this road; if you're going to try it, early morning (5-7 a.m.) is the best time to start at either end. After 8 or 9 in the morning you can forget it.

Information

Batopilas has no banks or moneychangers, so bring plenty of cash; U.S. dollars are negotiable at most stores and hotels.

The ancient post office gets very little business and most people take their own mail to Creel or give it to friends or relatives going there.

The town has a small clinic that can handle minor medical problems but not much else.

You may occasionally see armed soldiers in town when the Mexican army sweeps through Batopilas and the surrounding area to make a show of marijuana trade suppression. Although searches of foreign visitors are rare these days, if you cheerfully cooperate with the search things will go smoothly and quickly.

HIKES FROM BATOPILAS

The INEGI topographic map to have for extensive canyon forays in the area is the Batopilas 1:50,000 quadrangle (G13A41).

Several moderate hikes north of town can be taken without a guide. If you've just arrived, consider warming up to the territory with the relatively easy walks to Hacienda San Miguel and Satevó described above.

Aqueduct Trail

A pleasant half-day's outing can be made along the aqueduct north of town to the old dam. Actually there are two trails, one that runs below the aqueduct most of the way, another along the top of the aqueduct itself. The lower trail—a much-used section of the Camino Real—is shadier and more scenic, and it crosses a couple of small waterfalls formed by runoff from the aqueduct into the Río Batopilas. Walking across or through these falls isn't a problem most of the year, but if the flow is heavy (usually during the July-Sept. rainy season), you'll have to use the trail on top of the aqueduct.

Along the way you'll pass nearby the Porfirio Díaz Mine (2,340 meters/7,800 feet long), above the aqueduct near the bridge—be sure to bring a flashlight along if you plan to explore this or other tunnels on the way. You'll also pass a few *ranchitos* that irrigate their fruit orchards directly from the aqueduct—farmers will sometimes offer oranges, avocados, or papayas for sale to passing hikers. Swimming is possible in places where the aqueduct meets the river.

The lower trail parallels the aqueduct most of the way, then rises gently over it at a place where the stone structure pierces a large boulder—an amazing engineering feat. At this point the lower trail is still paved with large stones left over from

hiking between Batopilas and Urique

the days when the Camino Real was a major thoroughfare. Occasionally you'll meet mule trains, men on horseback, or Tarahumaras on foot carrying cargo in or out of the canyon.

At a leisurely pace it's about an hour's walk from the Río Batopilas bridge to the dam at the mouth of the aqueduct. Some of the best swimming spots in the river are found here. Beyond the dam, the trail turns westward from the river into the Arroyo Cerro Colorado and then continues northward to the villages of Cerro Colorado and Munérachi, and eventually across the Barranca del Cobre to El Tejabán, where it meets a logging road to Cusárare.

Cerro Colorado-Munérachi

The Camino Real-aqueduct trail described above can be continued through the lovely Arroyo Cerro Colorado to the Mexican village of Cerro Colorado and the Tarahumara village of Munérachi. Bring plenty of drinking water along, as this can be a hot day's slog.

From the dam the trail hooks left to the tiny village of Las Juntas (it's hard to miss, but you can use the village of Casas Colorados on the river's opposite side as a landmark) and climbs along the canyon's left side. From Las Juntas, follow the trail parallel to the canyon stream for about three hours to reach Cerro Colorado (a total of four hours from Batopilas). The trail crosses the stream several times along the way, providing opportunities to soak tired feet; in times of high water it may be necessary to detour to a higher trail parallel to the stream (there's one on each side of the stream). Along the way you'll pass a couple of smaller Mexican villages settled by small-time prospectors who practice placer mining. Keep an eye out for *tahonas,* rustic hand- or river-powered mills used to grind gold ore. In Cerro Colorado, a small store sells beverages and a few groceries.

Munérachi is another two to three hours upstream along Arroyo Cerro Colorado and Arroyo Munérachi (which branches northeast from Arroyo Cerro Colorado about an hour's walk from Cerro Colorado). Very little in the way of supplies is available in Munérachi, so don't come this far unless you're self-contained.

If you decide to make this an overnight hike from Batopilas, you can camp on the outskirts of Cerro Colorado or ask at the store about a room to rent in the village.

Beyond Munérachi it isn't advisable to continue without a guide because of the rugged terrain, number of intersecting trails, and relative lack of village life. With a guide, it's possible to reach El Tejabán to the north with another three days' hike through canyon and high forest country, or you can head west (via Cerro Colorado) to the town of Urique at the bottom of the Barranca de Urique in one day. This is the most popular way to do the "canyon crossing" though hardly the most adventurous since parts of the trail have been widened into logging or mining roads. Another option is to hike back to Cerro Colorado via Santa Rita, a small village below a mesa that affords outstanding views of Barranca de Batopilas.

Other Trails

The Batopilas area is honeycombed with footpaths through shady arroyos clouded with parrots and butterflies, along precipitous canyon walls, to crystal, sand-fringed springs, and over mountain peaks. **Arroyo las Minas** (north of town) and **Arroyo Huinolito** (just south) are two of the more challenging all-day hikes.

A popular two- to four-day hike (depending on which of at least four routes you choose) crosses the **Barranca de Urique** from Batopilas to the town of Urique. One of the least used but most scenic (and challenging) of these goes via **Mesa San José** to the south of Batopilas. A branch path off this trail leads to **Mesa Yerbaniz,** an outcropping that juts out over Barranca de Batopilas and affords unparalleled views of the town and river. The latter could be visited on a long day-hike from Batopilas and back, or you could camp there for a night or two before returning. Guides are highly advised for these ascents south of town as the trails are neither obvious nor easy.

Twelve km northeast of Batopilas is the logging settlement of **Yaquivo,** where you can pick up a logging road to **Guachochi** (via Agua Blanca), a junction town for "back door" exits from the Sierra Tarahumara to Parral. **Agua Blanca** can also be used as a gateway for backpacking trips into the deep, little-explored **Barranca de Sinforosa.**

Aside from the well-traveled Cerro Colorado routes described above, these trips really should not be attempted without the guidance of someone who knows the territory. Besides the danger of getting lost or injured in a remote spot, there's the added risk of stumbling onto a pot or poppy patch, which can get you in trouble with either the growers or the *federales* if your timing is bad.

If you backtrack towards Creel to **Samachique,** you'll find several trails in that vicinity worth exploring. **Guahuachique,** about 20 km northwest of Samachique, is one of the better places in the canyonlands to attend a Tarahumara Semana Santa. From Guahuachique you could continue north to Barranca del Cobre and across to El Tejabán, or you could continue west to Barranca de Urique and cross to Divisadero. Few people have hiked this area and guides are a must.

Guides: Ask at any of the hotels or guesthouses in Batopilas for guide services. Depending on the skill and popularity of the guides, you can expect to pay US$20-30 a day per guide (a bit higher than most other places in the sierra because of the tourist trade), plus around US$10 a day for each pack animal. Anyone in Batopilas who charges less is probably not very experienced. You must bring all your own food as well as food for your guides. Water is available from streams along the way but you should bring along some sort of water purification system, either a filter or chemicals.

If you can afford to spend more, you might consider letting an outfitter like Remarkable Journeys or Columbus Tours handle all arrangements. Although more expensive than doing it yourself, it's virtually guaranteed that things will proceed more smoothly and there will be less of a risk margin. You'll also avoid the bane of all self-directed guide arrangements in the canyonlands—when the trek is over and the guide pleads for more payment than was originally agreed to. Sometimes the request for more money is reasonable, i.e., when unexpected guide expenses have arisen, but most of the time this is simply a technique for fleecing inexperienced canyon trekkers.

Guachochi and the Barranca de Sinforosa

This large Tarahumara mission pueblo in the eastern sierra is sometimes visited by road travelers using the "back door" route in or out of the Sierra Tarahumara via Parral. It's also at the northern outskirts of the Barranca de Sinforosa, one of the deepest canyons in North America and relatively unexplored. You can drive as far as Ciénega Prieta at the canyon's edge via a dry-weather road. Local radio station XTAR, "La Voz de la Tarahumara" (Voice of the Tarahumara), often broadcasts details on *raríparos* (Tarahumara ball games) held in the early days of summer. These are usually organized up to a month in advance by a *choaqueame* or game director. One popular spot for local *raríparos* is nearby flat-topped Mesa de Payeguachi, where a typical game route covers six km of ravines, meadows, forests, and rocky areas.

Barranca de Sinforosa: With a guide from Guachochi you could make any of several descents into 1,830-meter (6,000-feet) deep Sinforosa, named for a defunct ranch near the confluence of the Verde and Guachochi Rivers toward the canyon's east edge. One of the better hikes follows a trail from Agua Blanca to **Huérachi** on the banks of the Río Verde, a six- or seven-hour walk via an area on the northern rim known as Cumbres de Huérachi. In nine km

this trail drops 1,830 meters in elevation, possibly the greatest elevation change in the shortest distance of any walkable route in the canyons. You might also hike to little-known **Cascadas de Rosalinda,** a stepped falls with a height of 80 meters (262 feet). At present two of the most knowledgeable guides in Guachochi are Luis Holduín and Rayo Bustillos.

Practicalities: Basic rooms are available at **Hotel Melina,** tel. (154) 3-0255, and **Hotel Chaparro,** tel. (154) 3-0055, for US$6-10 per night. The **Hotel Oprimel,** which shares a building with the bus ticket office, isn't bad either and is even cheaper.

A paved road northwest out of Guachochi leads to the Napuchi/Samachique junction (90 km/55.8 miles), about midway between Batopilas and Creel. A dry-weather road also heads west to Agua Blanca, than northwest to Yaquivo, which is about a 12-km hike from Batopilas.

A PEMEX station in Guachochi now carries Magna Sin as well as Nova.

EL DIVISADERO ~ POSADA BARRANCAS

These two stations just minutes apart on the Chihuahua al Pacífico rail line are major stopovers for tour groups doing the rail circuit. The train always stops at El Divisadero ("The Viewpoint") for 15 minutes to allow passengers to look over the rim into the junction of the Barranca del Cobre, Barranca de Urique, and Barranca Tararécua. Souvenir and food vendors crowd the platform at El Divisadero whenever a train arrives.

Unless you're staying at one of the hotels here, hiking in the area is limited by the unavailability of provisions, as this area is geared more toward hotel tourists than backpackers. Possible treks would include trips down to the Río Urique or across to the Tarahumara settlement of Pamachi on the other side—a vigorous day's hike along a good trail. Short day-hikes can also be taken along and below the rim here to a heavily touristed Tarahumara cave dwelling. From here the trail continues to the canyon bottom. Guides can be contacted at the Hotel Mansión Tarahumara nearby, though they're not absolutely necessary for a one-day descent and return. A guided trip to the river at the bottom of the canyon by

canyon rim, El Divisadero

horse or on foot costs US$20. The hotel also offers two-hour horseback tours along the rim for US$10 pp.

Accommodations

Hotels at both stations are a bit pricey, no doubt due to the "priceless" canyon views and lack of competition. Camping is certainly possible, though you'll have to search a bit to find spots that won't be trammeled by sightseers.

Shoestring: By far the most economical place to stay is the friendly, family-run **Casa de Huéspedes Díaz,** a short walk from the Posada Barrancas station in a hamlet called Areponapuchic. It offers four very basic but clean rooms in a concrete building with a shingle roof. All rooms are heated by woodstoves. You can walk to the canyon rim in 15 minutes or so. To reach the guest house from the station, turn right past the church, then left by a cemetery. Rates: US$13 per room with two double beds and shared hot-water shower, or you can bunk in a nine-bed room for US$6.50 a head.

Moderate: On the canyon rim near the Posada Barrancas station is the moderately priced **Rancho Posada,** part of the Balderrama chain based in Los Mochis. The large rooms have tile floors, wood-beam ceilings, fireplaces, terraces, and private baths. Meals available. Rates: US$50 s, US$60 d, US$65 t not including meals. Add US$8 for breakfast, US$16.50 each for lunch and dinner. For information or reservations, contact the Hotel Santa Anita, Apdo. Postal 159, Los Mochis, Sin. 81200, tel. (68) 18-7046, fax (68) 12-0046, U.S./Canada tel. (800) 896-8196.

Expensive: A bit farther away from the station hustle-bustle is the 46-room, medieval castle-style **Mansión Tarahumara,** tel. (14) 16-2672, fax (14) 16-5444 in Chihuahua. Although this hotel isn't built directly on the rim like its rivals, panoramas of the canyon are a short walk away. Rates include three meals a day; jacuzzi suites available (July-April). Guide services and horseback trail rides are available for US$8-9. The Mansión Tarahumara will also store excess luggage if guests decide to go on overnight hiking excursions. Rates: US$72 s, US$96 d, US$132 t, US$153 for a private cabin with king size bed and jacuzzi. Add US$16 each for children under 11.

Premium: Posada Mirador, a relatively new 30-room hotel under the same management as Rancho Posada, is perched just below the rim against the canyon wall near the original hotel. All rooms come with two double beds, private bath, heating, and a balcony with tremendous canyon views. Three meals a day are included. Rates: US$120 s, US$165 d, US$175-233 for suites sleeping up to four. For information or reservations, contact the Hotel Santa Anita, Apdo. Postal 159, Los Mochis, Sin. 81200, tel. (68) 18-7046, fax (68) 12-0046, U.S./Canada tel. (800) 896-8196.

Five minutes south by train at El Divisadero station is the well-designed, **Hotel Divisadero Barrancas,** Apdo. Postal 661, Chihuahua, Chih. 31238, tel. (14) 15-1199 or 56-0099, fax (14) 15-6575 in Chihuahua, where the 50 rooms all have private bath and fireplace. Three meals a day are included. The tastefully decorated lobby/bar has large, picture-window canyon views. Credit cards are accepted. Mountain bikes and horses are available for rent. Rates: US$84 s, US$124 d, US$169 t, US$213 q.

(continues on page 342)

JOE CUMMINGS

THE TARAHUMARAS

The semi-native inhabitants for whom the Sierra Tarahumara is named have been the subject of heavy doses of myth and romanticization ever since 1902, when Norwegian explorer Carl Lumholz pronounced the Tarahumara "many times better off, morally, mentally, and economically, than his civilised brother." More recent writings have described the Tarahumaras as "Neolithic noblemen" or "selfless and innocent people" living a Walden Pond sort of existence.

The truth is that very, very few non-Tarahumara can claim any sort of in-depth knowledge of these people or their culture. Modern-day Jesuit missionaries, who have found their way back into the mountains where the Tarahumara originally fled to avoid missionization and Spanish slavery, probably know them best. But even the missionaries associate only with "baptized" Tarahumaras or those amenable to conversion and assimilation into the Mexican mestizo culture; the more culturally resistant "gentiles" have retreated ever more deeply into the mountains and canyons of the Sierra Tarahumara, holding off dire predictions of cultural extinction that have been repeated with increasing frequency over the last hundred years. Fame-seeking anthropologists have also found an ever-tightening cult of secrecy which the Tarahumaras have developed in reaction to keen outside interest.

The latest threats to the Tarahumara culture are various proposals to expand logging in the western Sierra Tarahumara.

Naming and Language

The Tarahumara have always called themselves Rarámuri, "The Runners" (the term is also sometimes translated "those who walk correctly through life," though this is a bit of a stretch), to differentiate themselves from more sedentary Amerindian groups. "Tarahumara" is actually a Spanish corruption of the native term. Mestizo locals sometimes call Tarahumaras *"tohuises,"* while the Tarahumara in return call Mexicans *"chabochis."* Both those terms carry pejorative connotations (thumbing their noses at the mestizo epithet, a Tarahumara musical group from Batopilas calls itself "Los Tohuises del Norte").

Their language, Rarámuri, belongs to the Uto-Aztecan linguistic family and can be divided into three main dialects roughly corresponding to the deeper canyons and mountain ridges between

Bahuichivo and Batopilas (sometimes referred to as the Baja Sierra Tarahumara), the area northeast of Río Batopilas, and the area north of Río Urique. The standard reference work on the language is *Diccionario Rarámuri-Castellano* by D. Brambila (published by Mexico City's Obra Nacional de la Buena Pensa), usually available at Creel's Artesanías Misión.

Abodes and Way of Life

When the Spanish arrived in the early 1500s, the Tarahumaras occupied the fertile *llanos* and *llomerías* of central Chihuahua. To evade Jesuit missionaries and Spanish exploitation, they gradually abandoned their homelands and moved west into the Sierra Madre Occidental's rugged mountains and canyons, where they have remained for 400 years, preferring to maintain an aloof subsistence rather than integrate into the Spanish or Mexican economies.

JOE CUMMINGS

raising the Judas effigy, Semana Santa

Today around 62,000 Tarahumaras (Northern Mexico's second largest native tribe after San Luis Potosí's Huastecas) are scattered within a 67,000-square-km (26,000-square-mile) section of the Sierra Madre Occidental—an area often referred to as the Sierra Tarahumara—in 25 of Chihuahua's 67 *municipios*. They tend to live apart from other Mexicans in out-of-the-way places, including caves, cliffsides, or small wood-and-stone houses in secluded meadows. Jesuit padres divide their communities into "pueblos" (those settlements with churches), and "ranchos" (those without churches). To the Tarahumara, all ranch and farm groupings are simply *betechi* or *beterachi*, "places to live" in Rarámuri.

Except where Tarahumaras are working for timber or mineral concerns, their settlements tend to be small, usually only a few families, at most 20 households. Many settlements are seasonal, since traditionally the Tarahumaras live in highland caves or cabins along the canyon rims during the summer, and move to lowland houses and canyon bottoms in the winter. To ensure a constant water supply for drinking, washing, cooking, and irrigation, they have a preference for streamside habitations.

Self-sufficient farming and ranching have allowed at least some portion of Tarahumara society to survive without assimilation into the local timber and mineral industries. Tarahumara agriculture is said to be one of the most complex and productive systems of native agriculture anywhere in the world. Their crops may be raised anywhere between 300 and 2,700 meters (1,000 and 9,000 feet), from canyon bottoms to mountain peaks.

Fields along river plains are fertilized with manure in the *barbecho* or "moving corral" rotation method, while on steep canyon slopes the Tarahumaras employ swidden ("slash-and-burn") methods. The latter involves cutting Madrean woodlands in Nov.-Dec., setting aside the timber to dry for fuel, burning the brush in late spring, and then planting crops in the ashen, nitrogen-rich soil as the rains arrive in June. Land processed thus is fertile for two or three years, after which it is unfarmable for the next 5-10 years; hence new plots must be sought out, cut, burned, and planted in serial fashion. A third technique, *trinchera* ("trench") farming, uses stone walls arranged stepwise along steep slopes to form terraces where crops can be planted along flat planes.

Corn is the Tarahumaras' major crop and the major constituent of the Tarahumara diet. Just about every household maintains at least one *milpa* or

cornfield, where they plant up to six principal strains, including blue, yellow, red, and white corn. Many local corn varieties are said to come from rare pre-Cortesian, nonhybrid strains. Other important crops are beans, squash, peaches, apples, and potatoes.

Tarahumaras supplement their mostly vegetable-legume-grain diet by raising cattle, pigs, goats, and sheep, all of which are kept as much for their fertilizing manure as for their hides, wool, or meat. In some traditional cave dwellings these animals may be kept in "basements" created by inserting simple timber floors between the human and animal living spaces. Other sources of protein include freshwater fish trapped in streams and rivers, deer and small game, and—in hard times—lizards, toads, insects, berries, and fungi. The Tarahumaras' vast knowledge of herbs, roots, and other medicinal/culinary plants has hardly been cataloged.

Traditional dress for Tarahumara men includes a short, white muslin skirt, a billowy, white or flower-print shirt *(zaraza)* with huge sleeves, and a long red cotton headband. Some men walk (and run) barefoot while others wear sandals with a single leather thong that passes between the toes from the sole and wraps around the ankle. In or near mestizo villages and towns, many Tarahumara men dress in the typical ranchero fashion with boots, jeans, plaid shirt, and straw cowboy hat. Women wear long dresses, long-sleeved blouses, and head scarves—all made from colorful print material.

Running

One aspect of the Tarahumara way of life that easily lends itself to myth and lionization is the tradition of long-distance running. Walking and running are still the main modes of transportation among the Tarahumara, whose resting heart rates and blood pressure reportedly run around 20% below "normal." Even at a walking pace Tarahumara typically cover canyon territory three times faster than any non-Tarahumara. When running for sport, a Tarahumara can cover 65 km (40 miles) of rough canyon and mountain terrain (up to 97 km/60 miles on flat terrain) in six to eight hours; when hunting, good runners are supposedly capable of chasing deer to the point where the animals collapse of exhaustion.

It is common knowledge (confirmed by the writings of Carl Lumholz) that before the Creel-Batopilas road was built, Tarahumara men carried the mail on foot between Chihuahua and Batopilas at the bottom of the Barranca Batopilas, a journey of

(continues on next page)

THE TARAHUMARAS
(continued)

300 miles each way. The mail carrier took six days to complete the route in one direction, rested for just one day, and started back the other way.

Another oft-repeated story describes how in the 1968 Mexico City Olympics the Mexican government fielded two Tarahumara men in the marathon (41.8 km/26 miles) competition. The Tarahumaras didn't even place, however, as they reportedly complained about being made to run in shoes and for having to run a distance so short it was hardly worthy of real runners.

The Tarahumaras have their own homegrown running event beside which the modern marathon pales. In *rarjíparo* (or *rarahipa*), teams of two to 12 male runners kick a 10-cm (four-inch) ball made of solid madrone wood up and down boulder-studded slopes, through thick pine forests, across streams and gullies, and over fences for up to two days without stopping—all this at altitudes of up to 2,400 meters (8,000 feet). All the players carry for sustenance during the game are small bags of toasted, ground maize—called *pinole* in Spanish, *kobishi* in Rarámuri—which they mix with water from canyon streams to form a nutritious paste. When stuck in a crevice or stream, the ball may be dislodged using a stick the players' companions carry for this purpose; otherwise the ball cannot be moved forward except with the feet. Tarahumara women have their own version called *dowérami*, in which two interlocked hoops of lechuguilla fiber are flipped along a course with sticks. Spectators bet on which team will kick the ball across the finish line first. Physicians who have examined the runners immediately following the end of the race have found diastolic blood pressure readings of zero, rising to 60-80 after a few minutes of rest.

Although visitors to the Sierra Tarahumara will rarely have the opportunity (or the stamina) to observe one of these races (try Guachochi), it's not uncommon to see individual Tarahumaras trotting up or down narrow, steep mountain paths and carrying loads—sometimes as large as the carriers—slung from the forehead by a tumpline.

Another native sport enjoyed by the Tarahumaras is *najarapuami*, a type of wrestling match that uses original grappling and throwing techniques. *Najarapuami* plays an important role in Tarahumara Semana Santa celebrations.

Beliefs and Rites

As is common among traditional societies throughout world history, shamans and priests are the highest authorities and most important source of political power in the community; in post-Cortesian times this power has come to focus on the Jesuit padre. But like native peoples throughout the Americas, the Tarahumaras have woven strands of their pre-Christian belief systems into the missionary religions, creating a hybrid that is neither one nor the other (or both, depending on your viewpoint). Most Tarahumaras identify Tata Dios (God the Father, also called Onorúame) with the sun and the Virgin Mary with the moon; both are often the objects of offerings of food and *tesgüino* (a thick, fermented corn beverage).

The *tesgüinada,* or *tesgüino* drinking session, is an integral part of all religious celebrations. *Tesgüino* (called *suguiki* in Rarámuri) is made by soaking dried corn kernels in water and leaving them to sprout in a dark place. The sprouted corn is hand-ground into a paste, which is then boiled with a local grass seed (*basiáwi* or brome grass) and fermented for a day or so. The resulting low-alcohol beverage must be drunk within two to three days (after which it will spoil), which perhaps has something to do with why so much *tesgüino* is consumed in so short an interval at the typical *tesgüinada.* Gourd cups called *hueja* are dipped into pots of *tesgüino* day and night until the brew is finished and virtually everyone participating has passed out from drunkenness.

Another psychoactive substance used far less frequently and less extensively by the Tarahumaras is peyote, a Chihuahuan Desert cactus known as *híkuli* among the Tarahumaras and as *Lophophora williamsii* to Western botanists. A complex set of ritual taboos restrict its ingestion to Tarahumara shamans and pickers of the cactus, although it may also be applied externally for various afflictions, including snakebite and rheumatism, and may in rare cases be administered internally as a last resort for seemingly incurable diseases. According to anthropologist John G. Kennedy, peyote is widely feared by Tarahumaras as a substance with an independent soul that can "see." Among those remote villages that still count peyote as an important religious sacrament, a yearly journey is made to certain desert ridges between Ojinaga and La Perla in eastern Chihuahua to gather the cactus.

Semana Santa: The most important religious ceremony of the Tarahumara calendar is Semana Santa ("Holy Week"), the week leading to and including Easter Sunday. Much has been written about the "standard" Tarahumara customs and ceremonies during Semana Santa, but the truth is that every part of the Sierra Tarahumara seems to celebrate the week differently. What they all have in common is music, dance, and *tesgüino;* where they differ most is in costuming and roles assigned during the religious dramas enacted on the Friday and Saturday before Easter Sunday.

This differentiation must have come about because Spanish padres originally taught Christianity to the Indians by acting out religious dramas based on biblical stories; since the Tarahumaras passed on their own myths this way, they quickly adopted and adapted the new Christian myths. But after the Jesuits were expelled from Mexico in 1767, the dance-dramas continued to evolve in relative isolation from Catholic influences, hence each village was able to develop its own style.

In spite of all the North American attention directed toward the ritual battles (described below), the true religious heart of Semana Santa is probably the Holy Thursday enactment of the Passion along the *via dolorosa* or "sorrowful way" beneath temporary arches—made from tree branches and saplings in mountain pueblos or simply represented by three wooden crosses in canyon pueblos—to the village church. A framed picture of the Virgin of Guadalupe, accompanied by a woman carrying a censer filled with burning copal (Mexican incense), may also be carried in the procession to the accompaniment of violins, flutes, guitars, drums, and whirl rattles *(matracas).*

The social side of the celebrations begins in earnest on Friday. In many canyon areas the common dramatic thread is a ritual battle between evil and good, as represented by the Pharisees *(fariseos)* and the soldiers *(soldados).* The Pharisees, often daubed with white clay paint, carry wooden swords or guns and a white flag. The soldiers, who may be dressed in traditional Tarahumara garb or in ordinary Mexican clothes, carry wooden spears and a red flag (to protect the Virgin of Guadalupe from the mocking Pharisees). The Pharisees, some wearing head feathers or diabolic horns, come running into the village on Friday afternoon, get drunk, scare young children, laugh inside the church, and in general create mayhem. Chasing them around the village—between *tesgüino* bouts—are the soldiers.

This continues until the middle of the night, when the two sides join in drunken wrestling matches or *najarapuami* (in some villages *najarapuami* has been banned due to the high number of past injuries), all the while accompanied by live music. The wrestling and drinking continue all night; late Saturday morning, the ritual chase-dancing becomes more organized and culminates in the appearance of a straw Judas effigy displaying a huge wooden phallus. The Pharisees parade the Judas around the church environs until the soldiers capture the effigy, lash it to a stake, spear the figure into a pile of straw, and then set fire to it.

This is but one way in which the Friday-Saturday drama may be celebrated. Instead of *fariseos,* other villages may role-play *pintos* (Norogachi), *mulatos* (Tónachi), or *moros* (Samachique) in opposition to the *soldados.* An interesting confusion of didactic myths seems to be taking place here, mixing representations of the struggle between Pharisees and Christians in the Bible, Moors and Christians in Spain, and mestizos and Amerindians in Mexico. On top of everything else, in biblical literature the soldiers and Pharisees are on the same (evil) side, yet somehow they've become opposed in Tarahumara mythology.

In other areas no struggle between good and evil is enacted, although participants may costume themselves similarly. In Cerocahui the celebration focuses on *matachine* dancers, and the whole affair is more like that of an all-night country dance. In Creel and other logging towns, local mestizos participate together with the Tarahumaras, and the fiesta is more reminiscent of an ordinary Mexican Semana Santa. In some places—Divisadero-Posada Barrancas, for example—Semana Santa activities are organized expressly for visiting tourist groups.

Another important festival for the Tarahumaras is Fiesta Guadalupana, held on 12 Dec. in honor of the Virgin of Guadalupe. Characterized by all-night *matachine* dances inside pueblo churches, this celebration is less touristed than Semana Santa (though most Tarahumara Semana Santa celebrations are relatively unexploited compared to Patzcuaro's Day of the Dead, for example).

(continues on next page)

THE TARAHUMARAS
(continued)

Notes for Visitors
When you are traveling in the Sierra Tarahumara, remember you are a guest in a region to which the Tarahumaras moved hundreds of years ago first and foremost because they wanted to be left alone. Above all, be sure to respect their sense of privacy, which extends to their simple dwellings and to any fenced areas nearby. Never attempt to enter a Tarahumara home or cross a fence around a home without asking permission first. The same goes for photos of the people or their homes—always ask permission first and if refused, move on.

The Coordinación Estatal de la Tarahumara, a state office that oversees Tarahumara affairs, offers these guidelines for visitors attending Semana Santa or Fiesta Guadalupana celebrations:

Do:
• Act with the same respect you'd like other people to show toward your own religious celebrations.

• Obey all indications from the Tarahumaras or their authorities about taking photos, trespassing in reserved places, time to stay or leave, etc.

• Keep a discreet distance at every moment during the celebration of "La Fiesta."

Don't:
• Participate in processions, dances, or rites. Keep apart.

• Take places inside the churches assigned to the authorities or to the Tarahumaras themselves.

• Make any comments, play music, or take photos that would distract or interrupt the celebration.

• Go dressed as if you were going on a picnic. This religious celebration, although different, is holy.

Food
The only places serving food in the area are the four hotels and the collection of daytime food vendors at El Divisadero station. The latter serve tacos, quesadillas, and other snacks to locals as well as tourists who disembark from the train every day, hence they generally set up around scheduled train arrival times, then pack up after the trains have left.

Transportation
The paved road south from Creel crisscrosses the railway all the way to both station settlements. This road is in fairly good condition, the main hazards being the sometimes blind railroad crossings (switch off your engine to listen for oncoming trains).

CUITECO

Only 12 minutes north of the Bahuichivo station by train, Cuiteco offers a rail stopover that's less frequented than Bahuichivo, El Divisadero, Posada Barrancas, or Creel. The village itself has little to see other than a small, 300-year-old mission chapel. A small village store carries a limited selection of foodstuffs.

The area from here south (Cuiteco, Bahuichivo, Cerocahui, Urique, Témoris, Chínipas) is sometimes called "Baja (Lower) Sierra Tarahumara." When you're driving to Cuiteco or beyond from the north, note that the pavement ends a couple of kilometers north at San Rafael so the road south can be rough. The river crossing here can be particularly tricky since you must drive upstream for about 180 meters (600 feet) before completing the crossing. It's best to get out of your vehicle and scout the stream first to find the route with the least rocks and shallowest water. From here southward the road is very rugged; fuel, even Nova, is scarce.

Accommodations
Shoestring to Inexpensive: Hotel Cuiteco (Cuiteco Casitas Hotel) has basic rooms at inexpensive rates including four meals, and shoestring-priced dormitory beds where college students from Sinaloa come for a Sierra Tarahumara experience. Rates: US$40 rooms; US$10 dorm bunk. Reservations can be made through the Hotel Santa Anita in Los Mochis, Apdo. Postal 159, Los Mochis, Sin. 81200, tel. (68) 18-7046, fax (68) 12-0046, U.S./Canada tel. (800) 896-8196.

BAHUICHIVO

The next station south on the Chihuahua al Pacífico line, Bahuichivo is a good jumping-off point for longer excursions into the Barranca de Urique; food supplies are available along the way in Bahuichivo, Cerocahui, and Urique.

Accommodations
Shoestring: A ramshackle lumber village extends eastward from the Bahuichivo station. The gray concrete **Hotel Camino Real** and red concrete **Hotel Viajero** both have spartan rooms for rent for around US$5 a night. Slightly better are the rooms for rent (US$9) at **Restaurant Daniela.**

Food
Restaurant Daniela serves typical Mexican plates; three or four other cafes serve basic potluck fare. A couple of stores stock canned food, *pinole* (ground roasted corn that can be mixed with water to form an edible gruel), and a few fresh fruits and vegetables brought up from the canyon floors.

Transportation
There is a daily bus to Cerocahui, 1.5 hours away, for US$2.50 pp. Bahuichivo recently got its first PEMEX station

CEROCAHUI

This highland Tarahumara pueblo (elev. 1,500 meters/5,000 feet) of around 800 inhabitants was founded as a Jesuit mission in 1680 by Padre Juan María de Salvatierra—the same priest who 17 years later founded Baja California's first mission in Loreto. The sandstone mission church is one of the most attractive in the Sierra Tarahumara. A small plant powers the town 8-11 p.m. only.

Several small-scale gold mines are still functioning in the area, including the Mina Sangre de Cristo an hour away. One of the easiest and most scenic hikes from Paraíso del Oso Lodge (see "Accommodations," below) is to nearby **Cueva de las Cruces,** a Tarahumara burial cave painted with 51 crosses. The cave itself is little more than a large, curved depression in

the side of a cliff, but the trail to the cave passes through a fertile valley where *trinchera* ("trench" or terrace) farming was practiced centuries ago, then follows a beautiful stream flanked by grass that looks as if it were manicured by fairy-tale illustrators. On the way back you can hike over a plateau with views of the valley instead of back-tracking along the stream. A half-dozen other canyon and cave hikes are available in the vicinity of the Paraíso del Oso.

Accommodations
Shoestring: On the pueblo's small plaza is an unsigned *casa de huéspedes* known as **Feo's,** which offers basic rooms at rock-bottom rates (US$3 pp per night). Around the corner from Feo's is a better *casa de huéspedes* called **Rarámuri** (also unsigned), where better rooms with private hot-water bath cost a few dollars more (US$7) **Rancho del Oso,** behind the more expensive Paraíso del Oso Lodge (see below), features tent sites costing US$5 and dorm rooms with breakfast for US$9.

Inexpensive: Hotel Mesa de Arturo, on the mesa of the same name on the road to Urique about an hour from Cerocahui, offers pentagonal-shaped wooden cabins in a forested area. Each cabin has a private hot-water shower and a woodstove and can sleep up to six. Rates: US$53 per night.

Expensive: North of town on the way to Bahuichivo (12 km/7.4 miles from the railway station) is **Paraíso del Oso Lodge,** a top choice among hikers and backpackers who have come to explore Barranca de Urique and the highlands near Cerocahui. Comfortable, kerosene lamp-lit rooms have woodstoves and hot showers, and the lodge has a large dining room with fireplace and a small library of classic literature on the Sierra Madre; hiking maps and a detailed bird list are available on request. Three meals a day and roundtrip transportation from the railway station are included. Guided trips to the bottom of the canyon, Cerro Gallegos on the canyon rim, Témoris (timed so that rail buffs can observe trains passing through the most spectacular portion of the Chihuahua al Pacífico line), or the mining town of Piedras Verdes are available from the lodge for modest fees, as are local horseback trail rides using what is purportedly the finest saddlestock in the canyons. Unguided hik-

JOE CUMMINGS

tahona

ing is also possible in the area. Rates: US$92 s, US$115.50 d, US$146 t, US$169 q. For reservations or more information, contact Paraíso del Oso, c/o P.S. Travel, 8838 Viscount Blvd., Suite C, El Paso, TX 79925, tel. (915) 598-6188 or (800) 432-5152, fax (915) 595-5944.

Expensive/Premium: Hotel Misión, next to the mission church, is a 32-room, Balderrama-owned hotel with pleasant lodge-style rooms, some with fireplaces or woodstoves. Rates are available with or without three meals a day; free transportation to/from the Bahuichivo train station is provided. Rates: US$107 s, US$153 d, US$199 t including three meals; subtract US$38 pp for room rates without meals. Make reservations through Hotel Santa Anita in Los Mochis, Apdo. Postal 159, Los Mochis, Sin. 81200, tel. (68) 18-70f46, fax (68) 12-0046, U.S./Canada tel. (800) 896-8196.

Transportation
Both Hotel Misión and Paraíso del Oso provide van transportation from the railway station for guests with reservations. Public buses bound for Piedras Verdes or Urique meet the trains as well, and these will take you to Cerocahui and Paraíso del Oso Lodge for around US$2.

If you're driving to Cerocahui from the north, you'll find paved road roughly parallel to the railway as far as San Rafael (about 1.5 hours from Creel), after which the road is unpaved and deteriorated for the stretch through Cuiteco, then looks a bit better as it heads south from Bahuichivo to Cerocahui. Over the next couple of years the San Rafael-Cerocahui portion of the road will be upgraded. There is now a PEMEX in Bahuichivo; barrel Nova is available in Cerocahui.

URIQUE

At the bottom of the Barranca de Urique on the banks of Río Urique, this town was the first place in the Sierra Tarahumara officially named by the Spanish, who somehow found their way here toward the end of the 16th century. One of the larger *municipios* in Chihuahua, Urique covers 3,968 square km and has a population that is 75% Tarahumara, 25% mestizo.

The town itself consists mostly of century-old, pastel-painted adobe buildings with tin roofs and dirt floors—Batopilas is a metropolis by comparison—many of which grow oranges, mangoes, avocados, and guavas in small orchards out back. As in Batopilas, a more clandestine crop is rumored to be under cultivation farther away from town. Burros and horses are a common sight on the main street. Like Cerocahui, the town has electric power 8-11 p.m. only.

Several gold mines, some dating to the Spanish colonial period, are still in operation in the area, but people are very close-mouthed about their location since many are worked without claims. One old fellow I met near Cerocahui takes around 45 kilos of ore per day from an abandoned mine, packs it by burro to his *tahona* (ore mill) on the river, and extracts US$2-3 in gold for each day's labor.

Several places are suitable for swimming in the Río Urique near town, as well as for pleasant day-hikes along the river in either direction. About two hours south of town on foot is a splendid sandy beach along the river next to **Piedra Agujerada** ("Pierced Rock"), a huge rock formation that looks like a giant conquistador head. A deep river pool here is great for swimming, and the beach would make a nice campsite for a few days.

Guapalaina, a Tarahumara pueblo a few kilometers south of Urique on the river, is a popular spot for Mexicans to watch the Tarahumara Semana Santa celebrations. Cerro La Ventana, a brightly colored, 1,800-meter (5,900-foot) peak, looms over town to the northeast. With a high-clearance vehicle you can easily drive from Urique to Guapalaina.

Accommodations and Camping
Shoestring: Three small, rustic hotels offer basic rooms along the town's main drag. The best is **Hotel Cañon de Urique,** a one-story adobe building housing rooms with private bath. Hot water is available in the morning and evening only. Rates: US$5.30 s/d.

Upstream from town about 750 meters is a gringo-owned house offering campsites in a mesquite grove in front of the house, as well as more secluded sites in a bouldered area behind the house; US$2 pp. They also rent a nicely furnished stone and wood cabin in back by the week. For information or reservations, call Tom, Keith, or Cenovio in Chihuahua at (14) 13-4581.

Food
Of the town's three unimpressive cafes, the friendly **Restaurant Plaza** is the best and features a pleasant garden sitting area in back. A meal—whatever's on the hearth that day—costs around US$3.

Hikes from Urique
A number of one- to three-day hikes can be taken out of Urique either along nearby arroyos (Mezcalerita, Hacienda, Cañitas, Camuchines, and La Higuera, to name a few) or along the river itself. If you follow the river a few kilometers in either direction you'll come to Tarahumara villages. Particularly scenic is the walk north along the river and across a suspended footbridge to Guadalupe Coronado.

The popular Urique-Batopilas hike can be accomplished in two to four days depending on the route taken. Several routes are possible, the easiest being the southern route via Guapalaina, but the most spectacular and challenging route goes via Mesa San José. Because of all the in-

tersecting trails and the possibility of inadvertently running across a pot patch, it's best to engage the services of a guide for the crossing. The typical cost for a guided Guapalaina-Batopilas trip, including a pack burro, is US$60 for two persons; food costs extra, and can be bought in several *tiendas* in town or brought with you. Inquire at Hotel Cañon de Urique, at Restaurant Plaza, or in Guapalaina.

In years past, Guadalupe Coronado (north of town across the river) and Guapalaina (south of town on the same side of the river) have hosted well-attended Semana Santa fiestas.

For hikes in the Urique area you should use the Batopilas 1:50,000 topo map (G13A41).

Transportation
The same padre (Salvatierra's successor) who built the Cerocahui mission church also had a tunnel cut through canyon rock to connect Cerocahui and Urique by road. The result is a trip with spectacular views, equal or superior to anything seen on the Creel-Batopilas road.

The Bahuichivo-Urique bus costs US$4.60 pp and meets the Chihuahua al Pacífico train (Chihuahua-bound No. 73) at around 12:15 p.m. each day. If the train is late, the bus usually waits. In the opposite direction the bus leaves Urique at 7 a.m. The second train of the day is met by a bus going to Piedras Verdes rather than Urique—be sure to ask before boarding (this bus leaves Piedras Verdes at 7 a.m.). The Bahuichivo-Urique bus trip takes five to six hours.

TÉMORIS AND CHÍNIPAS

These two mining towns at the southwestern edge of the Sierra Tarahumara are on the unpaved road to Alamos, Sonora. Témoris is also a station on the Chihuahua al Pacífico rail line and is a favorite spot for rail buffs who come to marvel at the design and construction of three levels of railway bridges, tunnels, and viaducts, all converging into the Barranca de Septentrión. The original town a few kilometers northwest is sometimes called "Témoris Viejo" or "Old Témoris."

Before the railway was built, Chínipas was the main staging point for traversing the canyon country for nearly 400 years; along the Río Chínipas is one of the largest Spanish aqueducts (around 48 km long) in Mexico. Downstream from Chínipas along the river is the little-explored Barranca de Chínipas, one of the sierra's deeper canyons.

Practicalities

Basic hotel accommodations are available in Témoris. In **Agua Caliente,** a few km north of Chínipas, there's a guest house with hot showers and toilets. If you plan to hike in the area, you'll need the INEGI topo map Témoris G12B39.

The road from Bahuichivo to the northeast continues as far as Témoris, where another road heads northwest to Chínipas (2.5 hours from Témoris) and from there all the way to Alamos (six hours from Chínipas under good conditions). You have to ford the Río Chínipas along this route; during the dry months it's only about two feet deep. This road is often impassable during the July-Sept. monsoon season. Nova gasoline is available in both Chínipas and Témoris.

PARQUE NACIONAL CASCADA DE BASASEACHIC (BASASEACHIC FALLS NATIONAL PARK)

This rugged, 14,300-acre area along the northern edge of the Sierra Tarahumara achieved national park status in 1981, making it the only part of the sierra thus protected. An accident of topography in which the Arroyo Basaseachic meets the Barranca de Candameña, cut by the Río Candameña, has created the park's centerpiece, the Cascada de Basaseachic (also spelled Basaseachi). The second highest waterfall in Mexico, third highest in North America, and 26th highest in the world, Basaseachic drops 246 meters (806 feet) according to the most conservative measurement; Mexico's national park service says 299 meters/980 feet, while AAA and the state of Chihuahua claim 310 meters/1,020 feet. While the canyon itself is pristine by most standards, logging and overgrazing threaten areas along the fringes of the park.

The average elevation along the canyon rim is 2,000 meters (6,560 feet) and yearly rainfall averages around 65 cm (25 inches), most of it occurring during late summer. The best time to see the falls is at the end of the rainy season (late September, early October) when the water

JOE CUMMINGS

Cascada de Basaseachic

volume is greatest. For hiking, winter is best since the areas surrounding the top and base of the falls are safer and more accessible.

At least five other cascades, including impressive Piedra Volada, are within the park boundaries, as are several trails in and out of Barranca de Candameña. The main trails are marked—a bit of a shock if you've just been hiking in the Urique, Cobre, or Batopilas canyons. A kilometer-long trail that descends from near the top of the falls to the base takes about 45 minutes down, 90 minutes up. Although the falls are impressive from the lookout points opposite, you really need to hike down to the base to appreciate the scale and to revel in the misty pine forests along the way.

The park has two main entrances: one at the southeast end of the park off Chihuahua 330 (the road from San Juanito) and one at the northern end off Mexico 16 (the Chihuahua-Hermosillo highway). Near the southeast entrance are two marked *divisaderos* or viewpoints with cross-canyon vistas of the waterfall. Divisadero I is a short walk from the parking lot while Divisadero II is a 20-minute, winding descent (a stiff 30 minutes coming back up) below Divisadero I. From Divisadero I you can reach the top of the falls along a 1.2-km trail, or descend to a rock gap called La Ventana, "The Window," where you can look across at the falls from a medium distance. If you continue descending along this same trail you'll reach the bottom of the falls, 2.2 km (1.4 miles) from Divisadero I.

All of these trails can also be reached from the north entrance parking lot. The trail to the top of the falls from this lot is shorter than the one from Divisadero I, while the Ventana and bottom linkups are longer. Next to the north entrance parking lot, several food vendors sell *antojitos* during the day.

Other highlights include fascinating rock formations and an abundance of birdlife. At its deepest point, Barranca de Candameña measures 1,640 meters (5,280 feet).

Cascada de Piedra Volada
Southwest of Basaseachic in a branch off the main canyon, Cascada de Piedra Volada ("Balancing Rock") falls 453 meters (1,486 feet) to the canyon floor, ranking as Mexico's tallest waterfall and the 11th tallest in the world. Because of the structure of the canyon walls at the falls, Piedra Volada is difficult to reach and wasn't fully explored or measured until 1995, when Mexican canyoneers rappelled down nearby cliffs. The only vantage point from which to get even a partial view of the falls without the use of cables is **Cerro de la Cornoa,** about an hour's drive plus an hour's walk from the highway junction to the park's southeast entrance. Ask in San Lorenzo for directions or hire a San Lorenzo guide—the going rate for a tour to Cerro de la Cornoa is US$25 pp.

Accommodations
Shoestring: At the park's north entrance, one of the souvenir/food vendors rents a small two-bed room in back of his shop; simple evening meals can be arranged. Rates: US$10 per night.

Between Km 262 and 263 on Mexico 16 (7.2 km/4.5 miles east of the San Juanito road junction), **Villas Alpiñas** rents adobe cabins, each with three beds and fireplace. The owners can arrange guided trips in the area. This is a better bargain than Motel Alma Rosa's more expensive rooms (see below). Rates: US$13.

Shoestring/Inexpensive: Outside the park at Km 278 on Mexico 16 (1.3 km/0.8 mile from the northern park access road) in the highway hamlet of Alma Rosa, **Motel Alma Rosa** offers small shoestring-priced rooms facing the highway. All have private showers and small fireplaces. Rates: US$12 per night. Behind the motel are larger, more modern cabins in the inexpensive category—a bit overpriced for what are essentially simple rooms. Only two of the rooms have fireplaces, albeit large ones. Rates: US$37. The Alma Rosa has an attached cafe with decent Mexican fare.

Also in Alma Rosa, **Hotel Nena** has stark cement cells with low ceilings—definitely a last resort. Rates: US$8 pp. Several other unsigned places in Alma Rosa also rent rooms.

Budget: In a settlement called **San Lorenzo,** off the access road to the south entrance for Basaseachic Falls National Park, several large, two-story log cabins are for rent. Each cabin has a kitchen, a fireplace, three bedrooms, a hot-water shower, and kerosene lamps. Wood for the fireplace is supplied for free. The helpful and friendly family that rents the cabins can advise on what to see in the area or arrange guides in the Barranca de Candameña area. There is also a good, secure campground here; see "Camping," below for details. Rates: US$33 for two people, US$67 for six people, US$87 for six, or US$100 for eight people. For information or reservations (usually not necessary), contact Lobo Turismo y Aventura, Av. Francisco Villa 3700-10 A, Chihuahua, Chih. 31200, tel. (14) 21-2656.

Accommodations Farther Afield
Other places to stay in the general vicinity include five-room *casa de huéspedes* in Maycoba ("Maicova" on some maps) on Mexico 16, 85 km (53 miles) northwest of the park, and the very basic **Hotel Las Brisas** in the lumber town of Yécora, another 47 km west along the same highway.

None of these lodgings have telephones. The nearest phone is in Cajurichic, a small town just off Mexico 330, 14 km (8.7 miles) south of the Mexico 16/Mexico 330 junction.

Camping
Basaseachic Falls National Park has perhaps the best public campgrounds in Northern Mexico. A well-maintained, no-fee Zona de Camping

near the two *divisaderos* features tent sites, barbecue pits, trash barrels, water spigots, and outhouses set amid small pines and junipers.

A better, private campground can be found in **San Lorenzo**, before you reach the park campgrounds off the same access road. Well-spaced sites in a wooden area have fire rings, and the US$8-per-vehicle fee includes wood for campfires. Facilities include well-maintained bathrooms with toilets, hot-water showers, and potable water. The proprietors plan to add an RV area with water, sewage, hot-water shower, and laundry room in a large area separate from both the cabins and campground; all three areas are separated by hundreds of meters. When open, RV sites will cost US$12 per day. Another main advantage to the San Lorenzo campground is that there's always someone around, while the park campground has no one supervising on a daily basis.

Transportation

Mexico 16—paved all the way from Chihuahua or Hermosillo—is the main access route for the park, which is 200 km (124 miles) west of Cuauhtémoc, 305 km (189 miles) west of Chihuahua, and 372 km (230.6 miles) east of Hermosillo. The highway section between Basaseachic and La Junta follows a scenic arroyo, with especially beautiful rock formations in the Km 200s.

Magna Sin gasoline is available in La Junta. About halfway between La Junta and Basaseachic, at around Km 217 (60 km/37 miles northwest of Basaseachic), the lumber town of Tomochi offers a small hotel, groceries, and a PEMEX with Magna Sin. Tomochi is also the nearest "wet" town (where alcoholic beverages can be purchased) to Basaseachic. Another PEMEX station can be found in **Cahuisori,** at Km 281 on Mexico 16 west of the park.

For visitors coming from Creel or elsewhere in the heart of the Sierra Tarahumara, the most convenient access is via 107-km (66-mile) Chihuahua 330—most of which is gravel-surfaced—from San Juanito. The latter town is 30 km (18.6 miles) north of Creel via Chihuahua 127; the total 137-km (85-mile) trip from Creel to Basaseachic takes three to four hours. This road cuts off at least an hour from the longer Creel-La Junta-Basaseachic route.

The turnoff for San Lorenzo and the southwestern park entrance is 93 km/58 miles from San Juanito; the eight-km (five-mile) access road is paved.

Buses running between Hermosillo and Chihuahua via Mexico 16 will stop at Basaseachic on request.

URUACHI

Around 56 km (35 miles) south of Basaseachic, the quaint little town of Uruachi has the only road entrée into Barranca de Oteros, a canyon formed by the Río Oteros. Home to Tarahumaras at its northern end, Guarojillos to the south, at its greatest depth this canyon measures 1,520 meters (4,986 feet). At the bottom of the canyon below Uruachi is a huge cluster of *huertas* (orchards), collectively known as **La Finca** ("The Farm"), with roughly 25,000 trees bearing oranges, limes, avocados, mangos, guavas, and bananas. Sugarcane and peanuts are also grown near the canyon bottom.

The Spanish founded Uruachi in 1736 as a base from which to mine gold, and as in other areas of the Sierra Tarahumara, there's enough trace gold left to support a small mining community. Fruit and vegetable cultivation is an even more important source of local income. In addition to the fruits named above, it's likely that some *mota* fields are tucked away in hard-to-reach corners of the canyon.

Because of its midlevel elevation of around 1,200 meters (3,900 feet), Uruachi has a mild year-round climate, not as hot in summer as the canyon bottoms, and not as cold in winter as the canyon rims. It shares certain similarities with both Batopilas and Urique, although the town's 1,500 residents seem even more relaxed and traditional. The town architecture consists of numerous hundred-year-old, two-story adobe buildings with tin roofs—a few of them with wooden balconies along the second floor—lined up along narrow streets. A small plaza planted with orange trees surrounds a wooden *kiosco*.

On the road that branches off Mexico 330 and leads to Uruachi, you'll pass several smaller pueblos, beginning with **Cajurichi,** which has a grocery store, barrel gas, and a whitewashed old church that contains a wooden image of the Virgen de Aranzazu brought from Spain in the 17th or 18th century. The only other place we've seen this image is in San Luis Potosí's 18th-century Capilla de Aranzazu. The church also holds around a half dozen older religious paintings, perhaps dating to the 18th and 19th centuries.

Beyond Cajurichi the road begins a serpentine winding as it descends into the canyon bit by bit. Around 34 km (21 miles) from the south entrance to Basaseachic you'll reach the small corn-growing village of **Calaveras.** Just four miles short of Uruachi is another farming settlement, **Tabletas.**

Another dirt road branches off the road to Uruachi and leads seven km to the Tarahumara pueblo of **Otachique.** Nearby are viewpoints over the Barranca de Charuyvo, where there are several rock shelters with Amerindian rock art, and cliff dwellings similar to those in the vicinity of Madera. Local guides to these sites can be hired at the Hostal de Otachique in Otachique, in Uruachi, or in San Lorenzo. Just outside Otachique is an airstrip that's 2.6 km (1.6 miles) long and 15 meters wide, the biggest in the sierra.

Not far from Uruachi, the Tarahumara village of **Jicamorachi** is reputed to have a better-than-average Semana Santa celebration, plus a mission church that's supposed to one of the first established in the Sierra Tarahumara.

In Uruachi, electric power is generated nightly around 7 p.m.-10:30 p.m.

The town celebrates the feast day of Santa Rosa de Lima, the local *santo patronal,* on the 30th of August each year.

Accommodations and Camping

Shoestring: On Calle Mineros in Uruachi, several places post "Cuartos a Renta" signs. The best guest house we found was a two-story place painted bright green, with six clean and spacious rooms and 24-hour hot water for US$8 per room. Other places in town cost US$6.60-8 per room. A small, family-run **cafe** opposite the green guest house is clean and friendly.

Budget: In Otachique, **Hostal de Otachique,** tel. (145) 6-0650, offers 10 log cabins on 80 acres next to a lake. These are very similar to the cabins in San Lorenzo, next to Basaseachic Falls National Park. All cabins have kitchens. Rates: from US$30 d.

Camping: At the bottom of Barranca de Oteros, almost directly below Uruachi, **Campamento La Finca** is a simple, private campground run by Lobo Turismo y Aventura. In order to camp there you must make arrangements with Lobo in advance. See the Basaseachic Falls National Park section for contact information.

Transportation

It takes about 2.5 hours to drive the unpaved road that runs off Mexico 330 south of Basaseachic, 56 km away. Reportedly the government will be cutting a brand new road between Alamos and Uruachi sometime in the future. If that ever happens, it may present a better alternative western gateway to the Sierra Tarahumara than the current Alamos-Chínipas route.

Unfortunately there is no regularly scheduled public transportation to Uruachi, but it probably wouldn't be too difficult to hitch a ride along the road.

BOB RACE

THE STATE OF DURANGO

Though only the fourth largest state in Mexico (behind Chihuahua, Sonora, and Coahuila), Durango provides an even deeper study in contrast than its neighbors to the north because it contains both the heavily forested mountains of the Sierra Madre Occidental to the west and the Bolsón de Mapimí—the starkest section of the Chihuahuan Desert—to the east. Between the two are sections of plains and valleys irrigated by the Colorado, Tamazula, Los Remedios, Aguanaval, Tunal, Mezquital, and Nazas Rivers, where cotton, pecans, grapes, oregano, wheat, chiles, and safflower are cultivated in abundance.

Durango's portion of the Sierra Madre Occidental (here called the Sierra Tepehuanes) produces some 2.5 million cubic meters of timber each year, nearly twice Chihuahua's output and over a quarter of the national production. Cattle ranching is also an important means of livelihood for Durangueños, who specialize in raising hardy rodeo steers.

The entire state population totals only 1.4 million, about a third of whom live in the capital. Although the population is predominantly mestizo, a small colony of Mennonites near Santiago Papasquiaro in the north produces renowned apples, cheese, and cured meats. The state's southern corner, where the Sierra los Huicholes spreads across the junction between Durango, Nayarit, and Jalisco, is inhabited by some 4,000 Huichol, along with several thousand Coras, Tepehuanes, and Mexicaneros.

In Mexico the state has a reputation for rough living and still has relatively few paved highways. Notorious revolutionary hero Pancho Villa was born in San Juan del Río in central Durango (110 km/68 miles northwest of the capital) in 1877. As in Chihuahua, Villa is a potent regional symbol and one does not speak disapprovingly of the man. According to Mexican legend, Villa once made a pact with the Devil in a cave north of the city of Durango to relinquish his soul in return for "mastery over men."

Climate

Durango has a climate similar to that of western Chihuahua, except that temperatures tend to be a bit cooler due to the gradual ascension of the Altiplano from north to south. Along the central plains May is the hottest month, with temperatures in the 30s C (90s F). In this area the monsoon season extends June-Sept., during which time an average 56 cm (23 inches) of precipitation falls on the plains; in the mountains rainfall reaches as high as 100 cm (40 inches) per annum. Scant precipitation also occurs in January and February.

The eastern, desertic third of the state bordering Coahuila and Zacatecas is much drier, with annual rainfall of less than 25 cm (10 inches) and summer temperatures exceeding 38° C (101° F).

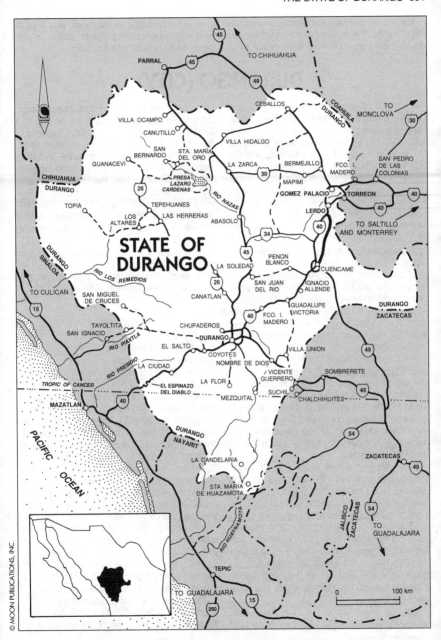

STATE OF
DURANGO

© MOON PUBLICATIONS, INC.

Much as in Chihuahua's Sierra Tarahumara, the climate of the western sierra varies tremendously from canyon bottom to mountain peak.

Overall the best time for mountain visits is fall or early spring. Light snow in the mountains isn't uncommon in January and February.

DURANGO (CITY)

Francisco de Ibarra founded the settlement of Guadiana (named for a river that flowed from Spain's central plateau to the Atlantic coast) in 1563 but later that year changed the name to Durango in honor of his home village in the Spanish province of Vizcaya. Durango became an important outpost of Nueva Vizcaya, the largest province in Nueva España (covering what is now Durango, Sinaloa, Sonora, and Chihuahua), but friction between the Spanish settlers and local Tepehuanes and Acaxes restricted early development of the area.

A particularly bloody confrontation on the plains of Cacaria in 1616 resulted in the deaths of 15,000 natives. Because of local hostilities, between 1679 and 1738 each Durango governor carried out his term in Parral, Chihuahua, some 411 km to the north. By the mid-18th century, when the Indian "threat" was deemed manageable, colonial construction in Durango continued in earnest.

A substantial boost in Durango's fortunes occurred after English timbermen founded the lumber and mining camp of El Salto on the nearby slopes of the Sierra Madre Occidental around the turn of the century. The English built a railway between El Salto and Mexico City and by the early 1900s Durango had become an important transshipment point for lumber and minerals taken from the sierra.

Now officially named Victoria de Durango, the city has grown to a population of 600,000 and sits 1,893 meters (6,209 feet) above sea level in the Valle del Guadiana. Looming over the city is the Cerro de Mercado, a mountain of iron ore first discovered by Vázquez de Mercado in 1532 but "forgotten" until 1828, when iron production first began. Considered one of the largest iron deposits in the world, the mountain produces over 300 tons of iron daily and is estimated to continue production at this rate for at least a century.

The city serves as an important transportation junction since it sits at the crossroads of

Mexico 40 (connecting the Pacific port of Mazatlán with Torreón, Saltillo, and Monterrey) and Mexico 45 (Durango to Mexico City). Because of the city's historic architecture, most of which dates to the 17th and 18th centuries (including around a dozen historic churches spanning gothic to neoclassic styles), the Mexican government has declared Durango a national monument. It is a city best seen on foot, since its moderate charms tend to be missed when driving through on the main boulevards linking Mexico 40 and 45.

Among film buffs, Durango is famous as a location setting for over a hundred motion pictures, most of them in the "western" genre (see the special topic "Durango on Film").

SIGHTS

Catedral Basílica Menor
(Catedral de Durango)
The city's premier example of *virreinato* architecture, the Catedral Basílica Menor is the third religious structure to have been built on this site. The first was a 1571 parish church that was destroyed by fire in 1631; the second an ill-conceived twin-towered church that had to be demolished because it was in danger of toppling.

Construction on the current edifice—on Av. 20 de Noviembre facing the Plaza de Armas—began in 1691 and was completed in 1770. Reflecting the evolution of Mexico's grand baroque period, the principal facade has four Tuscan-style columns on the lower *portada,* six Solomonic-style columns on the upper *portada,* and bas-relief that prefigures the ultrabaroque style seen in the Catedral de Zacatecas. The building plan originally followed classic cathedral design with five naves in a cruciform with a central dome. Two more domes were later added in front.

The cathedral's interior was altered from the neoclassical style so that the choir—originally in the center of the church like the *coros* of cathedrals

Catedral
de Durango

ERIN DWYER

in Mexico City and Puebla—has been moved to the back. On display is a rare gilded *sillería* (clerical pew) dating to 1737, the only other example of which can be found at Mexico City's San Ildefonso. A collection of paintings chronicling Durango's bishops dates from the 17th century.

Legends: Almost hidden in shadow at the back of the eastern nave is a heavy wooden confessional that is the subject of a chilling local legend. According to most versions of the story, Spaniard Juan Pérez de Toledo made a pact with a satanic emissary for his soul in exchange for money and women. Later, as his resultant excesses almost wore him out, he decided to renounce the pact before he died. Just as he was about to receive pardon for his sins from a priest at the confessional, Satan appeared and pinned the priest to the wall. At the same moment Pérez was reportedly struck down by a beam of light that left a strange odor of sulfur. The community has abandoned the confessional since 1738, the year of the reported incident.

Another legend associated with the cathedral is that of *la monja de la catedral*. In the mid-19th century a French soldier sought asylum in the cathedral after deserting the Napoleonic army, which at the time had invaded Mexico. A nun *(monja)* stationed at the church fell in love with the Frenchman and the two made plans to marry. Before celebrating their nuptials, however, they decided that the soldier should return to France and seek pardon for his crime of desertion; when he came back to Durango the nun would leave the nunhood and the two would marry. On his way back to France the soldier was captured by his countrymen in Mexico and executed.

Not knowing of his fate, the nun climbed to the tower balcony nightly to await her lover's return until she finally died of heartbreak. To this day, Durangueños swear that an apparition of the nun can be seen in the middle balcony of the west tower each night at sunset. If you want to see for yourself, the best vantage point is a spot next to the entrance of the Hotel Plaza Catedral on Calle Constitución, along the west side of the cathedral. Gaze at the middle balcony of the nearest tower and you should be able to make out the apparition—or trick of the light, or whatever it is.

Casa del Conde Suchil

Built 1760-70 in typical Spanish style by a Spanish count, this large colonial jewel features a Churrigueresque facade, along with magnificent tile floors and wood paneling in the interior. The building, at Calle 5 de Febrero and Madero near the plaza, now contains a bank (the best place to see the restored interior) and several shops.

Templo del Sagrado Corazón

This 19th-century church on Calle 5 de Febrero between Progreso and Saucos is a well-preserved example of the Mexican gothic style. The fortresslike structure is enlivened by its arched windows, stained glass, and a *rosetón* carved of native stone over the main entrance.

Museo de las Culturas Populares

At Juárez Nte. 302, at the corner of Gabino Barreda, this new museum opened in late 1996 and contains a modest collection of exhibits on regional basketry, ceramics, food preparation, and textiles. Open daily 10 a.m.-6 p.m.

Edificio Central de La Universidad Juárez

Originally a Jesuit convent dating to the 16th century, this two-story colonial building of native stone at Calle Constitución and Pino Suárez (near the plaza) was transformed into the Insti-

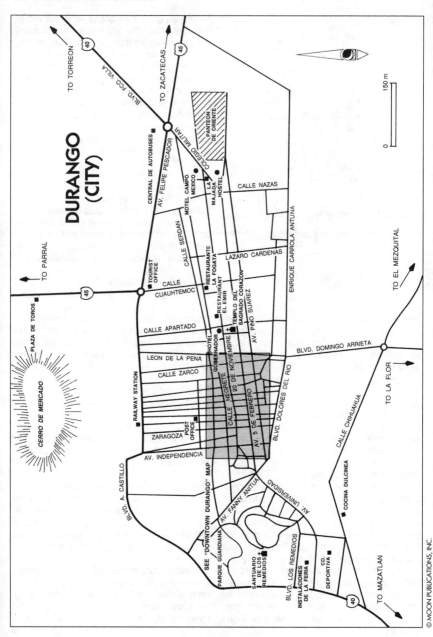

DURANGO (CITY)

TO TORREON
TO ZACATECAS
BLVD. FCO. VILLA
TO PARRAL
TO EL MEZQUITAL

150 m
0

CERRO DE MERCADO
PLAZA DE TOROS

CENTRAL DE AUTOBUSES
AV. FELIPE PESCADOR
COLEGIO MILITAR
PANTEON DE ORIENTE
MOTEL CAMPO MEXICO
LA MAJADA HOSTEL
CALLE NAZAS
CALLE SERDAN
LAZARO CARDENAS
ENRIQUE CARROLA ANTUNA

TOURIST OFFICE
CALLE CUAUHTEMOC
RESTAURANTE LA FOGATA
Restaurant EL EMIR
TEMPLO DEL SAGRADO CORAZON

CALLE APARTADO
HOTEL GOBERNADOR
AV. PINO SUAREZ

LEON DE LA PENA
CALLE ZARCO
20 DE NOVIEMBRE
CALLE NEGRETE
BLVD. DOMINGO ARRIETA
TO LA FLOR

RAILWAY STATION
AV. 5 DE FEBRERO
BLVD. DOLORES DEL RIO

ZARAGOZA
POST OFFICE
CALLE CHIHUAHUA

AV. INDEPENDENCIA
BLVD. A. CASTILLO
SEE "DOWNTOWN DURANGO" MAP
AV. FANNY ANITUA
AV. UNIVERSIDAD
COCINA DULCINEA

PARQUE GUARDIANA
SANTUARIO DE LOS REMEDIOS
BLVD. LOS REMEDIOS
INSTALACIONES DE LA FERIA
CD. DEPORTIVA
TO MAZATLAN

© MOON PUBLICATIONS, INC.

tuto Juárez in 1856. In 1956 it became the Universidad Juárez del Estado de Durango (Juárez State University) with a variety of academic departments, including law, medicine, accounting, business administration, art, music, sociology, and others. Murals with contemporary social themes are painted over stairway landings.

Teatro Ricardo Castro

Constructed in 1901 as Teatro Principal and renamed for a Durango native who was an illustrious pianist and composer, this neoclassical-style theater was renovated in 1990 to prepare for a visit by Pope John Paul II. The interior, which features beautiful tile and marble flooring, is used for visiting theatrical, music, and dance performances as well as ongoing film programs. The theater is at the corner of Av. 20 de Noviembre and Bruno Martínez.

Santuario de Los Remedios

On the summit of a hill of the same name, this is the oldest surviving church in Durango. Established in 1640, the austere stone edifice built in the style of a fortress served not only as a place of worship but also as protection against raids by Apaches and other Indians.

A legend attributes construction of the church to a miraculous apparition. According to the legend, a shepherd caring for his animals on the hill spied a tiny woman carrying some mud on a tray toward the summit. When asked what she was doing, the woman replied that she wanted to build a church at the top of the hill. The shepherd pointed out that she would need a large quantity of mud to build a church, far more than she was carrying. Her response was, "If you don't believe I can do it, go tell the *cura* (parish priest) that the Virgen de los Remedios would like him to build a church atop the hill."

Convinced by her words and manner, the shepherd paid a visit to the priest, who dismissed the old man as crazy. Some weeks later the shepherd returned to the hill and saw the Virgin carrying small stones up the hill with the intention of building the church from small stones. The shepherd tried once again to convince the parish priest of the existence of the Virgin and

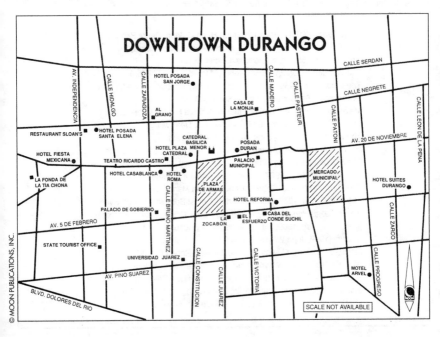

DURANGO ON FILM

Durango's heyday as a location setting for Hollywood westerns began in the 1950s, when producer/director Robert Jacks (of later *Zorba the Greek* fame) found the terrain perfect for his 1955 *White Feather,* a film starring Robert Wagner, Hugh O'Brien, and Debra Paget about gold prospectors encroaching on Indian territory. This film and the following year's *The Tall Men* (featuring Clark Gable, Robert Ryan, and Jane Russell) put Durango on movie screens for the next 30 years; the trend slowed in the 1980s following the decline of the western film genre. Relatively recent major productions in the Durango area have included *Romancing the Stone, Power, The Old Gringo, Revenge, Fat Man and Little Boy,* and *First Knight.*

In the U.S., the late John Wayne was the actor (and director) most associated with films shot in Durango, though Burt Lancaster and Robert Ryan turned up almost as often. Sam Peckinpah directed two groundbreaking films in Durango, *The Wild Bunch* and *Pat Garrett and Billy the Kid.* Many Mexican-produced films have also used Durango for location shooting; in Mexico, it's Rodolfo de Anda whom viewers most associate with the state.

Directors from both countries favor Durango for three reasons. First, it's sparsely populated, with few paved roads or power lines in sight, making it especially suitable for movies with pre-20th century themes. Second, the weather is consistently sunny most of the year and the quality of the light is said to be especially photogenic. Finally, wages are low in this state because of the lack of other industries, so labor—and acting extras—are inexpensive even by Mexican standards.

More than 116 motion pictures have used Durango for location shooting. Of the many Mexican productions, several used B-grade U.S. actors (e.g., *El Mal,* made in 1965 with Glenn Ford and Stella Stevens) but were released only in the Spanish-speaking world. Others, such as *Guns for San Sebastian* (a 1967 Mexico/Italy/France co-production starring Anthony Quinn and Charles Bronson) were produced for international release.

The following list includes some of the more notable films shot partially or entirely in Durango, along with the year of filming (rather than year of release) and major stars:

White Feather (1954, Robert Wagner, Hugh O'Brien, Debra Paget)
The Tall Men (1955, Clark Gable, Robert Ryan, Jane Russell)
Comanche (1955, Dana Andrews, Linda Cristal)
The Wonderful Country (1958, Robert Mitchum, Julie London)
The Unforgiven (1959, Burt Lancaster, Audrey Hepburn, Audie Murphy)
Geronimo (1961, Chuck Connors, Kamala Devi)
Major Dundee (1964, Charlton Heston, Richard Harris, James Coburn)
The Sons of Katie Elder (1965, John Wayne, Dean Martin)
The War Wagon (1966, John Wayne, Kirk Douglas)
Hour of the Gun (1966, James Garner, Robert Ryan, Jason Robards)
The Scalphunters (1967, Burt Lancaster, Shelley Winters, Telly Savalas)
Day of the Evil Gun (1967, Glenn Ford, Arthur Kennedy)
Five Card Stud (1968, Robert Mitchum, Dean Martin, Inger Stevens)
The Wild Bunch (1968, William Holden, Ernest Borgnine, Robert Ryan)
A Man Called Horse (1968-69, Richard Harris, Dame Judith Anderson)
The Undefeated (1969, John Wayne, Rock Hudson)
Chisum (1969, John Wayne, Bruce Cabot, Forrest Tucker)
Lawman (1970, Burt Lancaster, Lee J. Cobb, Robert Duvall)
Big Jake (1970, John Wayne, Maureen O'Hara, Richard Boone)
Buck and the Preacher (1971, Sidney Poitier, Harry Belafonte, Ruby Dee)
Something Big (1971, Dean Martin, Brian Keith, Honor Blackman)
Kid Blue (1971-72, Dennis Hopper, Warren Oates, Peter Boyle)

still from The Sons of Katie Elder

The Wrath of God (1972, Robert Mitchum, Frank Langella, Rita Hayworth)
Pat Garrett and Billy the Kid (1972-73, Kris Kristofferson, Bob Dylan, James Coburn)
Cahill, U.S. Marshal (1972-73, John Wayne, George Kennedy)
The Deadly Trackers (1973, Richard Harris, Rod Taylor)
The Devil's Rain (1975, Ernest Borgnine, Eddie Albert, Ida Lupino)
The Return of a Man Called Horse (1975, Richard Harris, Gale Sondergaard)
The Great Scout and Cathouse Thursday (1975-76, Oliver Reed, Lee Marvin, Kay Lenz)
Who'll Stop the Rain (1977, Nick Nolte, Michael Moriarty, Tuesday Weld)
Goin' South (1977, Jack Nicholson, Mary Steenburgen)
Eagle's Wing (1978, Martin Sheen, Harvey Keitel)
Cattle Annie and Little Britches (1979, Burt Lancaster, Rod Steiger, Amanda Plummer)
Caveman (1980, Ringo Starr, Barbara Bach, Dennis Quaid)
Romancing the Stone (1983, Michael Douglas, Kathleen Turner, Danny DeVito)
Power (1985, Richard Gere, Julie Christie, Gene Hackman)
The Old Gringo (1988, Jane Fonda, Gregory Peck)
Revenge (1988, Kevin Costner, Anthony Quinn, Sally Kirkland)
Fat Man and Little Boy (1988, Paul Newman, John Cusack)
First Knight (1995, Sean Connery, Richard Gere)

was again rebuffed. Returning a third time to the hill, the shepherd found the Virgin binding the small stones one on top of another with the mud. This time, after some pleading, the sacerdote and his entourage visited the hill, immediately recognized the Virgin as genuine, and set about building a church in her honor.

Today few visit the Santuario de los Remedios except to take advantage of the sweeping city views. The hill is southwest of the town center, across Blvd. Dolores del Río from the end of Av. 20 de Noviembre.

Movie Sets

Villa del Oeste: One of the oldest movie sets *(escenario)* still visible is the Villa del Oeste (also known as Rancho Howard) near Km 10 north of Durango on Mexico 45. Originally built from scratch as a "typical" Old West town, the town was later occupied by squatters until bit by bit it became an actual village. Access to Villa del Oeste is privately controlled and protected by a locked gate; sometimes it's open, sometimes not, and you might have to pay an entrance fee of a few pesos. A bar has recently been added and horse rentals are sometimes available.

Chupaderos: Just a bit farther north along Mexico 45 at Km 14 is the more accessible Chupaderos, an actual Mexican village "discovered" by John Wayne. It was turned into a movie set and used for more Hollywood westerns than any other Durango location. Driving through Chupaderos, you'll note the striking juxtaposition of Mexican peasants sitting on the porches of Old West-style buildings that have been added to the village over the years.

Los Alamos: Currently the most intact local set is one constructed to represent the town of Los Alamos, New Mexico, for the filming of *Fat Man and Little Boy,* a 1989 motion picture about the development of the atom bomb starring Paul Newman. The large set includes several wooden military-style barracks, a water tower, and a log cabin where Newman stayed during the location shooting. To find the latter you must walk along a short trail from the set's center to a bluff overlooking a canyon cut by the Ríos Chico, Los Arcos, and Tunal. It's an easy hike to the bottom of the canyon a hundred meters or so below for a swim.

The *Fat Man* set is 29 km south of Durango on the road to La Flor (follow Blvd. Domingo Arrieta

"midget card" for The Treasure of the Sierra Madre

south out of town). It's worth the short trip for the canyon views alone, but there has been talk of turning the set into a police training center.

Film Office: The state has its own office dedicated to assisting filmmakers in Durango. The **Dirección Estatal de Cinematografía,** Calle Hidalgo Sur 408 (in the same building as the state tourism office), tel. (18) 11-2139 or 11-1107, also organizes group tours of local film sets. A smaller branch office is at the corner of Av. Felipe Pescador and Calle Cuauhtémoc, tel. (18) 11-5681.

ACCOMMODATIONS

Durango has a good variety of places to stay in all price ranges, including several in historic colonial buildings. Occasionally when a movie production is in town the better rooms may be booked up by film crew and actors, but this is a much less common occurrence than it was during the 1950s to '70s heyday of Durango westerns.

Shoestring

Durango has a **Villa Deportiva Juvenil** (youth hostel) at Av. Heróico Colegio Militar s/n, tel. (18) 17-2216. Unlike hostels in many Mexican cities, this one is conveniently located just a few blocks from the main bus terminal and a short bus ride from the city center. An inexpensive *cafetería* is on-site. Rates: US$1.40 per night per bed.

One of the best deals in town is the 100-year-old, colonial-style **Posada Durán,** Av. 20 de Noviembre Pte. 506, tel. (18) 11-2412, near the Plaza de Armas. Spacious rooms with spartan furnishings and private baths surround an interior courtyard. Rates: US$10 s, US$12 d, US$15 t. Nearby **Hotel Posada San Jorge,** Calle Constitución Sur 102, tel. (18) 13-2557, offers economic rooms in a two-story colonial building. Rates: US$10 s, US$11.50 d, US$12.50 t. Near the cathedral, **Hotel Roma,** Av. 20 de Noviembre Pte. 705, tel. (18) 12-0122, has rooms in a similar two-story colonial. Rates: US$13.50 s, US$15.50 d, US$16.75 t, US$18 q.

The one-star **Hotel Prince,** Calle Juárez Sur 502, tel. (18) 11-9258, offers basic but adequate rooms with private bath. Rates: US$6.50 s, US$8 d, US$12 t. Small **Motel Arvel,** Calle Progreso Sur 104, tel. (18) 12-5333, has decent rooms with black and white TV (add US$2 for color TV), as well as off-street parking. Rates: US$11 s, US$12 d, US$12.50 t, US$13.50 q.

Budget

Around the corner from the Posada Durán is the similarly historic but better furnished **Hotel Plaza Catedral,** Calle Constitución 216 Sur tel. (18) 13-2480. Rates: US$15 s, US$16 d, US$20 t. Also known as the Durango Hotel, the four-story **Hotel Suites Durango,** Av. 5 de Febrero Ote. 103, tel. (18) 11-5580, has large rooms with private bath. Breakfast is included in the rates of US$14.50 s, US$17.50 d, US$20.50 t, US$22-27 suites. The two-story, semimodern **Hotel Reforma,** Av. 5 de Febrero at Madero, tel. (18) 13-1622, lacks charm but has fairly comfortable rooms with private bath and phones. Rates: US$9 s, US$15.50 d, US$21.75 t.

In the restored colonial section of Calle Negrete near the cathedral and several good restaurants, **Hotel Posada Santa Elena,** tel. (18) 12-7818, offers surprisingly economical rooms with TV and telephone. Rates: US$16 s, US$18.50 d, or US$23 for a three-person suite. The six-story **Hotel Casablanca,** Av. 20 de Noviembre Pte. 811, tel. (18) 11-3595, fax (18) 11-4704, also has a convenient downtown location, as well as a parking garage (a block from the hotel) and a/c rooms. Rates: US$20 s, US$22 d.

Motel Campo Mexico Courts, Av. 20 de Noviembre at Colegio Militar, tel. (18) 18-7744, fax (18) 18-3015, is a favorite overnight stop for gringos because it's close to Mexico 40, the highway northeast to Torreón and Monterrey. (The main sign out front reads "Mexico Motel.") Rooms have satellite TV, a/c, and phone; many have refrigerators. Facilities include a swimming pool, restaurant, and bar with lots of photos of famous and not-so-famous movie actors who filmed in the area. Rates: from US$26 for a standard single to US$30 for a superior double.

Inexpensive

The four-star **Hotel Fiesta Mexicana,** Av. 20 de Noviembre at Independencia downtown, tel. (18) 11-9880, is completely decorated in traditional but elegant Mexican style. Rooms have a/c, heat, TV, and phone, and breakfast is included. Rates: US$30 s, US$35 d—quite reasonable considering the facilities and central location. Near the Motel Campo Mexico Courts, **Motel Los Arcos,** Av. Colegio Militar Ote. 2204, tel./fax (18) 18-7777, has large rooms surrounding a secure parking lot. Rates: US$30 s, US$35 d, US$41 t.

Moderate/Expensive

The top choice for business travelers, filmmakers, and upscale tourists is the efficient **Hotel Gobernador,** Av. 20 de Noviembre Ote. 257, tel. (18) 13-1919, fax (18) 11-1422. Housed in a former prison that has been completely made over into a modern yet atmospheric four-star hotel, the Gobernador offers all the amenities, including a/c, heat, satellite TV, direct-dial phones, and the city's nicest coffee shop and best hotel pool. Rates: US$60-123 s/d (depending on size and location), including tax.

RV Parks

The **Motel Campo Mexico Courts,** Av. 20 de Noviembre at Colegio Militar, tel. (18) 18-7744, fax (18) 18-3015, has around a dozen RV spaces with full hookups for US$5 a night. Some outlets are 220V, so check before plugging in.

FOOD

Durangueños take pride in their cuisine and pleasure in eating; the city's restaurants offer some of the best and most *típico* food in Northern Mexico. A famous local specialty is *caldillo durangueño*, a thick soup made with small pieces of dried venison (or beef) and chile strips. *Gorditas*, thick corn tortillas stuffed with a choice of beans, cheese, *picadillo* (chopped meat-and-chile salad), egg, potatoes, and other fillings are also popular. Other local delicacies include *asado de puerco* (pork in a sauce of tomatillo and *chile verde*), *quesadilla durangueña* (flour tortillas filled with melted cheese and chorizo), *calabaza/biznaga cubierto* (crystallized squash or barrel cactus—eaten as sweets), and *dulces de almendra* (almond sweets).

Mescal, a potent liquor made from hearts of maguey in the mountains of southern Durango, is available for around US$8 per liter in the city or US$4 in mountain villages where it's distilled. The smoothest distillate is a variety locally known as *mescal tepemete*.

If you're not sure exactly where you want to eat, take a stroll down Calle Negrete near the cathedral; on and off this street are a number of restaurants and cafes in restored colonial buildings.

Mexican and Regional

At the southwest edge of the city near the Ciudad Deportiva, **Cocina Dulcinea,** Calle Río Yaqui, tel. (18) 13-2316, is one of the most authentic eateries in Durango. This small, family-run spot is said to prepare the city's best *caldillo durangueño* and *gorditas.* A delicious *comida corrida* in the afternoon sells for US$2.30. Local mescal is available on request. Open daily 9 a.m.-5 p.m.

La Fonda de la Tía Chona, Calle de Nogal 110 (near the Hotel Fiesta Mexicana), tel. (18) 11-7748, is a slightly upscale restaurant in a restored colonial mansion decorated with traditional Mexican art and artifacts. The menu—a mix of regional dishes as well as Mexican standards—changes periodically and is recited by the waiters, so you'll need to use your best restaurant Spanish to feed well. Prices are moderate and the food is very good. Open Mon.-Sat. 11 a.m.-11 p.m., Sunday 11 a.m.-6 p.m.

Casa de la Monja, Calle Negrete Pte. 308 (near Calle Madero), tel. (18) 11-7162, serves well-prepared *carne a la tampiqueña* and fish in the atmospheric courtyard of an 18th-century hacienda. Moderate. Open daily 1-11 p.m.

Restaurant El Kilo, Km 10, Mexico 40, tel. (18) 18-1992, specializes in preparing *birria, barbacoa,* and *carnitas* sold by the kilo, accompanied by fresh tortillas. Inexpensive. Open daily 8 a.m.-11 p.m.

Ultramarinos Finos, Calle Libertad at Fpe. Pescador, tel. (18) 17-1843, is a recommended stop for quick and cheap *tortas,* burritos, *molletes,* quesadillas, *taquitos,* and *hamburguesas,* plus delicious juices and *licuados.* Open daily 8 a.m.-8 p.m.

Steak

Popular **La Majada,** Av. 20 de Noviembre Ote. (across from Motel Campo Mexican Courts), tel. (18) 18-4828, serves Durango and American-style steaks, including *arrachera* (known farther north as fajitas) and *medalión durangueño. Cabrito al carbón* is also a house specialty. Breakfast buffet served till noon. Moderate to expensive. Open daily 7 a.m.-midnight.

Restaurante La Fogata, Calle Cuauhtémoc at Negrete, tel. (18) 17-0347, offers Durango-style *carne asada* and *arrachera* by the kilo, plus domestic and imported wines. Moderate prices. Open daily noon-11 p.m.

International

A short walk from the Hotel Gobernador, **Restaurante El Emir,** Av. 20 de Noviembre Ote. 510, is an immaculate, a/c restaurant specializing in Lebanese, Mexican, and continental dishes. Moderate to expensive. Open Tues.-Sat. noon-9 p.m.

Corleone Pizza, Calle Constitución Nte. 114 (a few blocks north of Calle Negrete), tel. (18) 13-3128, features a funky wine-cellar decor popular with the local university crowd. The menu offers a wide variety of pizza in two basic sizes, plus cocktails, beer, wine, pasta, and salads. Moderate prices. Open daily noon-midnight.

Just west of Calle Hidalgo (a few doors from Hotel Posada Santa Elena), **Sloan's Restaurant Bar,** Calle Negrete Pte. 1003, tel. (18) 12-2199, occupies a huge restored colonial. This is Durango's most upscale restaurant and serves steaks and continental and Mexican food. Moderate to expensive. Open daily 6 p.m.-midnight.

Seafood
Playa Azul Restaurant-Bar is an inexpensive seafood chain with branches at Av. Colegio Militar 312, Calle Chihuahua 1450, Calle Constitución 241, and Calle Madero Sur 508. Open daily 10 a.m.-9 p.m.

Coffee Shops
La Zocabón and **El Esfuerzo** are on Av. 5 de Febrero Pte. near the southeast corner of the Plaza de Armas. These two cafes offer inexpensive breakfasts for around US$1.20-2. El Esfuerzo is the nicer of the two; here you'll almost always find a group of middle-aged Mexican men sipping coffee and smoking endless cigarettes while engaged in deep discussion. Both places are open 8 a.m. till late.

Hotel Gobernador, Av. 20 de Noviembre Ote. 257, has a moderately priced restaurant/coffee shop popular for business breakfasts and lunches. Breakfasts here—whether American, Mexican, or continental—are the best in Durango. *Pan dulce* is available from 7 a.m. till they run out (usually around 8:30 a.m.). Open daily 7 a.m.-midnight.

Vegetarian
Al Grano, Calle Negrete Pte. 804 (at Zaragoza), features vegetarian versions of typical Mexican dishes, including *gorditas, tostadas de ceviche,* and *mole verde,* plus "hamburgers" and sandwiches, all made with soy or gluten meat substitutes. The attached store sells whole wheat bread, yogurt, and other natural foods. Inexpensive. Open Mon.-Sat. 8 a.m.-8 p.m.

Samadhi Comida Vegetariana, Calle Negrete Pte. 403 (at Calle Madero), tel. (18) 11-6227, is similar, with gluten and soy-based Mexican dishes, breads, yogurt, etc. Inexpensive. Open daily 8 a.m.-10 p.m.

RECREATION AND ENTERTAINMENT

Clubs and Music
The bars at Sloan's, Corleone Pizza, and other restaurants in the area of Calle Negrete and Calle Constitución are popular with *durangueños* of all ages. Tía Chona's has recently opened **La Cantina de Tranquilino** at Calle Nogal 113, opposite the restaurant, with intentions of offering mellow live jazz.

Hoping for pickup gigs, mariachi and *norteña* musicians hang out along Av. 20 de Noviembre between the Hotel Reforma and the Posada Durán. *Norteña* music is very big in Durango; the Mexican disco scene really hasn't hit the city (yet).

Day of the Dead in a country cemetery, Durango

JOE CUMMINGS

Shopping

Durango is known for its wool sarapes, leather boots, *charro* clothing, and Tepehuán crafts, all of which can be found inside or near the **Mercado Municipal** (Mercado Gómez Palacio) between Avenidas 20 de Noviembre and 5 de Febrero (with main entrances on Calles Patoni and Pasteur).

Fancier boutiques near the Plaza de Armas and on the lower floor of the plaza's grand *kiosco* carry consumer goods from all over Mexico and abroad.

Charreada

Durango is big on Mexican rodeo, with no less than five *charro* rings in town. *Charreadas* are held year-round, usually on alternating Saturdays. Check with the tourist office for the latest schedule.

Festivals

The **Feria de la Fundación de la Ciudad de Durango** (the Founding of Durango Fair) takes place annually during the second week of July, preceded the previous week by—and merging with—the **Feria Agricola, Ganadera, Forestal, Industrial y Comercial** (Agricultural, Ranching, Forestry, Industrial, and Commercial Fair).

Together the two fairs produce a number of expositions and activities revolving around the display of regional skills in ranching, farming, technical/trade affairs, and sports. Many live musical performances, folkloric dancing, and regional handicraft exhibits are also held, making this one of the largest urban festivals in Mexico. Fair events are centered at the Instalaciones de la Feria and in the adjacent sports arena in Durango's southwest corner, though many activities are scattered

throughout the city. If you would like to attend the festivities, be sure to book a hotel room at least two months in advance. The state tourist office (see "Information," below) can provide an up-to-date schedule of events and venues.

During the **Days of the Dead** (Días de los Muertos, Nov. 1-2), the huge Panteón de Oriente, off Av. Colegio Militar at the city's east end, is resplendent with flowers and other offerings to the deceased.

INFORMATION

Tourist Offices

The **Dirección Estatal de Turismo,** Calle Hidalgo Sur 408, tel. (18) 11-2139, distributes information on hotels and tourist attractions in the state of Durango. Some of the staffers speak good English.

Maps

Topographic maps of Durango, Zacatecas, and Chihuahua are available for US$3 a sheet at the **INEGI office,** Av. Felipe Pescador Ote. 706, tel. (18) 12-8230, fax (18) 14-1783.

TOURS

For visitors interested in wilderness travel, Durango is a state well worth considering. The state's wilderness areas have been so little explored that roads, hotels, camping areas, and other services are limited. An experienced guide can take you to places in the Sierra Madre Occidental, for example, that you would never find on your own (unlike in western Chihuahua, where the sierra is fairly well traveled).

At the moment the widest variety of itineraries is available from **Pantera Excursiones,** Apdo. Postal 670, Durango, Dgo. 34001, tel. (18) 25-0682 or 25-2030, U.S./Canada tel. (800) 487-4783. Operated by Walter Bishop, the bilingual, bicultural son of a former British consul to Durango, Pantera Excursiones leads tours all over the state, including trips to the Zona de Silencio, Mapimí, the Sierra Madre, and the Sierra Tarahumara in Chihuahua. Some itineraries focus on mountain biking, others on trekking or camping; groups are kept to a maximum size

---

DURANGO TELEPHONE NUMBERS

Local Police	11-2162, 17-5406
Highway Patrol	14-3621
Green Angels	11-5681
State Tourist Office	11-2139
State Cinematography Office	11-1107
Red Cross	17-3444
General Hospital	11-9115
Durango Area Code	18

AUTO RENTAL AGENCIES IN DURANGO

Auto Rentas Numero Uno
Av. 20 de Noviembre Ote. 1010
tel. (18) 17-0284
Airport
tel. (18) 17-0345

Renta de Autos Laguna
Av. 20 de Noviembre Ote. 1406
tel. (18) 18-8660

---

of 15 clients. Rates are very reasonable and include the leadership of experienced, ecologically sensitive guides, support vehicles, food, and all land transportation.

Another agency, **Viajes Anamar,** Calle Negrete 1204 Pte., tel. (18) 11-4271, fax (18) 12-5080, specializes in trips to the Zona de Silencio.

TRANSPORTATION

Air
Aeroméxico, Calle Juárez Sur 201, tel. (18) 11-2652, has direct flights between Durango and Culiacán, Guadalajara, Mazatlán, Mexico City, Monterrey, and Torreón.

Aero California, Av. 20 de Noviembre 1410, tel. (18) 17-7177, flies to Durango direct from Guadalajara and Tijuana, as well as from other cities with connections.

Mexicana, Saavedra Sur 317, tel. (18) 13-1619 or 13-6299, fields weekly direct flights to/from León, Zacatecas, and Chicago.

Airport Transportation: The airport is 26 km northeast of downtown Durango off Mexico 40; a *colectivo* costs US$5, a taxi US$7 for the half-hour trip.

Bus
Durango's huge bus station—holding many *loncherías*—is at the junction of Av. Colegio Militar and Av. Felipe Pescador near Mexico 40. **Turistar,** tel. (18) 18-3781, runs *ejecutivo* buses to/from Mexico City (US$38), Monterrey (US$25),

Mazatlán (US$16), Tijuana (US$55), and Mexicali (US$55). **Omnibus de México,** tel. (18) 18-3361, operates Mercedes buses daily to/from Ciudad Juárez (US$30), Chihuahua (US$18), Mexico City (US$26), and Zacatecas (US$8.50).

Transportes Chihuahuenses, tel. (18) 18-3781, and **Transportes del Norte,** tel. (18) 18-3061, combine services for first-class buses to/from Aguascalientes (US$13), Monterrey (US$17), Mazatlán (US$9), and Houston (US$46).

Less expensive first- and second-class buses on smaller lines such as **Estrella Blanca,** tel. (18) 18-3241, and **Transportes Frontera,** tel. (18) 18-3499, offer once-daily services to/from Mexico City (US$24), Mazatlán (US$8), Torreón (US$6.50), Chihuahua (US$16), Monterrey (US$20), Saltillo (US$14), and Zacatecas (US$7).

Driving
A new toll *autopista* to Gómez Palacio speeds drive time between the two cities to 2.5 hours.

Getting Around
Bus: A good city bus system circulates Durango's main streets for US$0.15 per trip. Perhaps the most useful is the line that runs between the Central de Autobuses and El Centro (downtown) along Av. 20 de Noviembre, the city's main east-west artery. Most hotels and sights worth visiting are within easy walking distance of this line.

Taxi: Taxi stands are concentrated in the downtown area and at the larger hotels. A taxi anywhere in the downtown area costs US$2-3, to the outer fringes of the city US$4. Although most trips are meter-measured, taxis can be hired on a time basis for US$7 an hour. Beyond five hours, it might be more economical to rent a car (around US$50 per day).

Driving: The traffic in Durango moves fairly well and most streets are well marked. Parking in the downtown area near the cathedral can be a problem, especially during the daytime, so you may want to consider leaving your vehicle at your hotel and getting around town by bus or taxi.

Fuel: PEMEX stations are numerous, especially along the bypass roads such as Av. Felipe Pescador (north edge of town), Av. Colegio Militar (east), and Calle Chihuahua (southwest).

AROUND THE STATE

DURANGO TO MAZATLÁN

The 318-km section of Mexico 40 that extends between Durango and Mazatlán (in Sinaloa) through the Sierra Madre Occidental is one of Mexico's most scenic drives—a sinuous mountain road past stupendous cliffs and valleys and through blooming tropical jungle and tall ponderosa forests. It is not a drive to take lightly, however, and motorists should carry all the spare parts, including tires and belts, that might be needed to remedy automotive problems along the way. No repair facilities are available between the two cities.

Mexico 40 begins climbing into the sierra around 40 km west of Durango. **Cabañas El Soldado** at Km 43 near Agua Blanca offers cab-

B. TRAVEN, MYSTERY AUTHOR

No literary work is more identified with the Mother Range than *The Treasure of the Sierra Madre,* B. Traven's novel of greed and betrayal set in 1920s' Northern Mexico. Although Traven published over a dozen novels and short story collections around the world before his death in 1969, *Treasure* has survived the vagaries of literary fashion via John Huston's brilliant 1948 motion picture version, which featured a grizzled Humphrey Bogart in the starring role (along with Walter Huston and Tim Holt). Huston won two Oscars for his direction and screenwriting of the film, which featured the often misquoted line "I don't have to show you any stinking badges!" spoken by a Mexican *bandido* leader— yet another of Hollywood's many contributions to the *bandido* stereotype.

Like the novel, the film tracks a trio of down-on-their-luck Americans from Tampico's waterfront boardinghouses to a moral (and politically allegorical) denouement somewhere in Durango's Sierra Madre Occidental. So real were Traven's geographical descriptions (and Huston's film, which was shot on location in Northern Mexico) that fans of the novel continue to debate the location of the fictional mine.

No less mysterious was Traven's past, a story he concealed from his American publishers while he was alive and writing novels, short stories, essays, and movie scripts in English, German, and Spanish. His first novel, *The Death Ship,* appeared in Germany in 1926, and it wasn't until 1933—by which time his books were selling millions in Europe— that Alfred Knopf offered to publish a few titles in the United States. Called "one of the neglected geniuses of 20th-century American literature," Tra-

ven assiduously avoided all contact with the press and lived a secluded life in Mexico until his death in 1969.

A 1966 dust-jacket biography claimed that B. Traven had been born Traven Torsvan in Chicago in 1890, had shipped out of San Francisco as a cabin boy on a tramp freighter around 1900, and then had jumped ashore in Mazatlán in the 1920s. Following Traven's death, however, a carefully researched BBC documentary revealed a more intriguing past. According to information obtained from Scotland Yard and FBI files, Berick Traven Torsvan was born in a Polish district of Germany, where he spent part of his later youth as an actor. During WW I he wrote revolutionary literature under the pen name "Ret Marut"; when the war ended he accepted a government office in the short-lived Bavarian Socialist Republic.

After the BSR was overthrown, Traven was sentenced to death but managed to escape a roomful of condemned prisoners and join the disaffected legions drifting through postwar Europe. Somewhere in Europe he boarded a Norwegian freighter that ended up in 1920s' Tampico. Traven spent the rest of his life in Mexico, mostly in the state of Tamaulipas, where he took up his literary career.

Among Traven's other novels, *The White Rose* is perhaps the most ambitious. Set in turn-of-the-century Northern Mexico, the compelling story follows the rise and decline of the hacienda system. It is especially notable for its clear-eyed interpretation of pre-WW II U.S.-Mexican relations, wherein both sides made long-range political errors that are only now beginning to be rectified.

CHRIS HUMPHREY

colonial ruins near Tayoltita

Venceremos, after which it is generally traversable only in dry weather and in high-clearance (preferably 4WD) vehicles. About 100 km (62 miles) north is the former mining town of **San Miguel de Cruces,** a good jumping-off point for canyon-sierra explorations. Las Quebradas is so steep and rugged that not a single Spanish mission was ever established in the area.

Tayoltita

A turnoff at Santo Domingo, about halfway between Mexico 40 and San Miguel de Cruces, leads west to Tayoltita, the earliest mining site in the state and a potential base for exploring some of the most remote and quaint towns in the sierra. Founded in the 17th century, Tayoltita (also locally called Tayolta) is still a serious mining town of 8,000 inhabitants, most of whom derive their livelihoods directly or indirectly from Minas de San Luis, a complex of five local mining sites that produce over 100,000 ounces of gold and silver each year. Marijuana and opium poppy fields in the area also supplement local incomes. Although Tayoltita is the oldest settlement in this sierra, a better place to see colonial and postcolonial architecture is nearby **San Dimas,** which lies over a ridge 18 km south of town on the road to Contra Estaca. In San Dimas around 150 residents live amid tile-and-stucco ruins in surreal surroundings that could have come from Juan Rulfo's *Pedro Páramo.*

Practicalities: Sra. María Rivera operates a small, simple guest house in Tayoltita at Calle Parroquía 10, next to a church. Clean, sparse rooms with communal bathroom cost US$5 pp. Several cafes in town serve unremarkable Mexican food.

The road from San Miguel to Tayoltita is very bad and the town can be more easily reached via a gravel road from San Ignacio, Sinaloa, just 33 km northeast of Mexico 15 between Culiacán and Mazatlán. From San Ignacio it's an 80-km, six-hour drive to Tayoltita along the scenic Río Piaxtla. This latter road, though slow, can be traversed by any high-clearance vehicle Dec.-April. During periods of rain, *vados* are often too deep to cross. Daily buses go from San Ignacio to Tayoltita when conditions permit. Back on the Durango side, buses run from El Salto to San Miguel de Cruces and Tayoltita several times a week, leaving at 8 a.m. from either end and tak-

ins for rent as well as horseback rides in the surrounding forest. **Parque Natural El Tecuán** at Km 57 is a public park with picnic tables and grills, set amid mountain pines and meadows. Moderately priced cabins with fireplaces, gas stoves, and hot water can also be rented here; for information or reservations, contact the Durango DIF (Desarollo Integral de la Familia) at tel. (18) 12-2344.

Further on near Km 105, **Cabañas Mil Diez,** near the village of Mil Diez, rents private cabins oriented toward hunting vacations.

Región de las Quebradas

Four-wheelers can use a logging road running north off Mexico 40 around 15 km before El Salto (about 85 km/53 miles west of Durango) to explore an area of the Sierra Madre Occidental called "Las Quebradas" ("The Breaks"); the name derives from the huge canyons slashed into the mountains by the Ríos Quebrada del Salto, El Varal, Tabillas, Miravalles, and Las Paridas. The road is fairly good as far as the village of Unidos

ing seven to eight hours as far as San Miguel, then another 8-10 hours to Tayoltita.

Easiest of all is to fly with **Aerolineas Centauro,** tel. (18) 17-9704, from Durango airport. Centauro operates two five-passenger Cessnas per day Mon.-Sat. for US$40 each way. The flights leave Durango at 7 a.m.; it's best to book a seat two or three days in advance. The 75-minute flight crosses some of the most breathtaking canyon country in North America, and the landing is not for the faint of heart. Centauro also fields one flight a day to/from San Ignacio, Sin., for US$18 each way.

El Salto

This rough-and-tumble timber town 95 km west of Durango has little to recommend a stop unless your vehicle needs gas. The surrounding area, however, is beautiful and at 2,610 meters (8,230 feet) above sea level, summers are mild and winters crisp. Hiking along the nearby Río Quebrada del Salto might be a rewarding pastime, and longer hikes into the sierra and nearby *barrancas* (deep canyons) can be taken with local guides.

Basic, shoestring accommodations are available near the rustic bus terminal in El Salto at **Hotel Los Pinos** (US$9 s, US$11.50 d).

West of El Salto

Around 26 km west of El Salto is an area known as **Mexiquillo** that is famous for unusual mushroom-shaped rock formations similar to those found near Creel in the Sierra Tarahumara. After another 20 km or so begins **El Espinazo del Diablo** ("The Devil's Backbone"), a winding, nine-km stretch of road along a narrow mountain ridge. Heavy rains have been known to turn the road in this area into barely passable mud, but the vistas are unsurpassed. Basic services are available in nearby **La Ciudad.** You can hike from El Salto to La Ciudad in three to four days following a railway line that was never put into operation, passing two waterfalls with swimming holes and the villages of Mil Diez and Mexiquillo along the way.

Beyond El Espinazo del Diablo the sierra begins its descent toward the Pacific coast. Two historic towns worth visiting along the western slopes of the sierra are **Copala** and **Concordia** (see the relevant entries in the Sinaloa chapter).

SOUTHERN DURANGO

Nombre de Dios

"Name of God," 52 km southeast of Durango via Mexico 45, was one of the first Spanish settlements in Nueva Vizcaya. Durango's first religious edifice, the Templo de San Francisco, was built here in 1557; the structure was long ago destroyed by fire.

The town's main claim to fame these days is the production of mescal, a high-proof liquor distilled from the boiled and mashed hearts of the maguey (agave) plant. You can see mescal being made at the edge of town.

West of town about four km via Mexico 45 is a scenic, sabino-lined stretch of the Río Mezquital known as **Los Salones,** a favorite local picnicking and swimming spot. On a nearby tributary of the river is **El Saltito,** a 20-meter waterfall and spring.

Suchil and Chalchihuites

On the Durango-Zacatecas border 40 km southeast of Nombre de Dios, the tiny town of Suchil was once a mining center. Now it's notable for its abandoned haciendas and the nearby ruins at Chalchihuites.

Positioned almost precisely on the Tropic of Cancer, where the sun turns around at equinox, the ruins of Chalchihuites are thought to have been an astro-religious observatory built by the Teotihuacán culture. Now little more than a row of stone columns, Chalchihuites was the northernmost outpost of Mesoamerica and a major trade center and military outpost.

Although the ruins themselves aren't that impressive to the casual visitor, the volcanic scenery of the surrounding Sierra Sombrerete may enchant.

Mezquital

On the banks of the scenic Río Mezquital, this town 82 km southeast of Durango at the southernmost extreme of the Sierra Madre Occidental is even more famed than Nombre de Dios for mescal production. Most of the distilling actually takes place in nearby Tepehuán villages in the canyon formed by the Río Mezquital; there are also a few villages on the lower slopes of the sierra.

According to local legend, little-studied Amerindian cliff dwellings nearby were once inhabited by a race of pygmies. A more likely explanation is that the low-ceilinged structures were used for grain storage, but so far they haven't been properly excavated.

Thermal springs at nearby **La Joya** are the site of a *balneario* with three pools, a restaurant, and inexpensive cabins. As there are no hotels or guesthouses in Mezquital, this might be the best staging point for hiking and backpacking into what is probably the most unexplored section of the Sierra Madre Occidental.

Huichol Country (Huicholitos)

South of Mezquital, the mountains become steeper and less accessible. The major Huichol settlement in the state of Durango, **Santa María de Huazamota** (on some maps this is spelled "Huayamota," like the river), is best reached by private plane, although it may also be possible to hike there from La Candelaria, around 60 km southwest of Mezquital via a network of gravel roads and dirt tracks. From La Candelaria, accomplished backpackers with a local guide could make their way south another 20 km or so along the Río Huaynamota (also known as Río Jesús María) to Huazamota. Trucks run frequently between Huazamota and Mezquital, and it's easy to hitch rides—inquire at the INI (Instituto Nacional

BOB RACE

Huichol yarn painting

Indígenas) office in Durango, Calle Hidalgo Sur 311, tel. (18) 11-5277.

Huazamota is a good place to become accustomed to Huichol country, as it's a mixed mestizo and Huichol town. Hiking in the surrounding countryside is *not* advisable alone or even in groups without a guide, as the Huichol have been known to exhibit rude, even violent behavior toward outsiders. They might feel, for example, no compunction about spitting on your sleeping bag or tent, or snatching away a pointed camera. *Always* ask permission before taking photos of a Huichol—payment is often expected. Though their behavior may be unpleasant, one has to admire their fierce determination to be left alone and their willingness to act on it—unlike, for example, the somewhat gentler Tarahumara.

For guide services from the city of Durango, inquire at Pantera Excursiones (see "Tours" in the Durango section, above, for details). Guides may also be available through the INI or in Huazamota itself.

DURANGO TO PARRAL

Mexico 45 runs more or less straight north from Durango to Parral (in Chihuahua) for 412 km (256 miles). High-desert scenery and light traffic make this a pleasant drive; this is also the route most buses between Durango and Chihuahua use (from Parral, Mexico 24 continues north to Mexico 16, less than 50 km west of Chihuahua).

El Palmito

Along the way motorists can turn west at La Zarca (about halfway between Durango and Parral on Mexico 45) to reach **Presa Lázaro Cárdenas** at the top of Río Nazas (better known to many gringo anglers as Lake Palmito). The lake sits amid mountain scenery at 1,500 meters (4,900 feet), and it's a good fishing spot for black bass, carp, crappie, mojarra, catfish, and tilapia. "Pancho's" has a few rustic cabins at the lake for rent, plus plenty of space for camping. El Palmito, the village at the east end of the lake, has a small hotel, a PEMEX station, and a couple of *tiendas* (but no ice). Local wildlife includes puma, deer, bighorn sheep, gray fox, coyote, wild turkey, quail, and various waterfowl.

HUICOT CULTURES

The southern end of the Sierra Madre Occidental, near the junction of the states of Durango, Nayarit, Jalisco, and Zacatecas, is the northernmost limit of Mexico's remnant Mesoamerican cultures as principally represented by the Tepehuán (numbering 17,600), Huichol (14,800), and Cora (10,200), as well as smaller groups such as the Tepecano of Azqueltán and the Nahua of San Pedro Jícora, Durango. All belong to the Uto-Aztecan ethnolinguistic family and share a common mythology based on key legends concerning the sun, fire, flood, and corn.

The Huicholes have stimulated the most outside interest because of their strong ritual traditions. Although they are to a large degree a Christianized group, the Huichol *mara'akames* or shamans are careful to keep Christian rites separate from Huichol rites so as not to contaminate them. Oddly enough, there is no single word for "tradition" in the Huichol language, the closest being the Huichol word for "journey" or "trip," since for the Huicholes tradition involves a series of offerings made at various sacred sites near and far. Water is one of the most important ritual components, so caves containing springs are particularly revered.

Corn, deer, and peyote (a hallucinogenic cactus) form a mystic trinity in the Huichol tradition. The first two components of the trinity are available in their Sierra Madre mountain homelands, but for peyote the Huicholes must make annual pilgrimages to Real de Catorce, San Luis Potosí, in order to gather the cactus tops; the pilgrimage is usually performed between October and January (when there is no corn to tend) by individual groups from each of the five major *rancherías* in the Sierra los Huicholes. A sacred deer hunt is held in May, followed by the *maíz tostado* ("toasted corn") ceremony in June.

Mexico's Instituto Nacional Indigenista identifies the Huichol/Cora/Tepehuán cultural network by the acronym Huicot, using parts of the names of these three principal tribes. The Mexican government's Proyecto Huicot, created for the development of these communities, focuses on training and assistance in agriculture, education, sanitation, and communications.

Northwestern Sierra

Sixty-nine km (43 miles) north of Durango, Mexico 26 splits northwest from Mexico 45 to **Canatlán** and **Santiago Papasquiaro,** two towns noted for apple cultivation—a tradition started by Mennonite colonists early in the 20th century. A small museum in Canatlán's Escuela Mariano Valleza exhibits Amerindian artifacts, including arrow points and ceramics found in the area. The community of **Guatimape,** 49 km (30.4 miles) northwest of Canatlán via Mexico 26, is a center for local Mennonite *campos.* Several small hotels in Canatlán and Santiago Papasquiaro offer adequate, inexpensive rooms.

Twenty-two km (13.6 miles) northwest of Santiago Papasquiaro a paved road heads west from Mexico 26 into the Sierra Tepehuanes. Average sedans can make it as far as **Los Altares,** 45 km (30 miles) west of Mexico 26, a scenic drive that passes a couple of thermal springs. Beyond Los Altares the road deteriorates to gravel and then to dirt; 4WD vehicles can make it all the way to the end of the road at **Topía,** a possible staging point for hikes into canyons formed by the Tamazula and Sianori Rivers. An adventurous east-to-west sierra-and-canyon crossing from Topía to **Coloma,** a village near the Sinaloa state border, would take about a week of serious up-and-down hiking; guides may be available in Topía.

Mexico 26 continues 52 km north of Santiago Papasquiaro to the sierra town of **Tepehuanes,** once a center for Tepehuanes but now a timber center inhabited mainly by mestizos. Tepehuanes has a PEMEX station (Nova only) and three small, basic hotels.

Canutillo

Francisco "Pancho" Villa chose this small town (pop. 2,090) at 1,890 meters (6,199 feet) in the sierra foothills for his retirement following an illustrious career of banditry and revolution. His retirement was cut short by a fusillade of bullets fired into his car in nearby Parral in 1923 (see "Hidalgo de Parral" in the Chihuahua chapter for details).

A small museum in Villa's retirement hacienda displays photos and memorabilia from his life. Canutillo is just off Mexico 45, 131 km north of Presa Lázaro Cárdenas, or about 85 km south of Parral. If the doors are locked, take a look around for the caretaker, who will gladly open them for visitors.

NORTHEASTERN DURANGO

Gómez Palacio

Founded in 1898, this commercial center forms a corner of the Región Lagunera urban triangle that includes larger Torreón and smaller Lerdo. Bringing cotton to market from surrounding farms is the town's main life support; Levi Strauss and Co. has a large plant here.

For culture as well as superior hotel selection, most visitors passing through the region opt for neighboring Torreón, just across the border in Coahuila (see the Coahuila chapter for information). If you stop in Gómez Palacio, the only sight of mild interest is the **Casa de la Cultura** at Calles Berlín and Rosas in Colonía Campestre. Included in the complex are a small history museum and a contemporary art museum with rotating exhibits; both are open Tues.-Sun. 9 a.m.-1 p.m. and 4-7 p.m.

Accommodations and Food: The best hotel in town is the four-star **Hotel Posada del Río,** Av. Fco. Madero Sur at Juárez downtown, tel. (17) 14-3399, fax (17) 14-7483. The budget-priced rooms (US$30 s/d) have a/c, satellite TV, phones, and private bath.

Several smaller hotels along Av. Fco. Madero in the shoestring range include: **Motel La Siesta,** Av. Madero Nte. 320, tel. (17) 14-2840; **Motel La Cabaña,** Av. Madero Nte. 1630, tel. (17) 14-1678; and **Hotel Monarrez,** Av. Madero at Centenario, tel. (17) 14-1199.

The **Quinta Colima Trailer Park,** three blocks east of the Renault plant, has RV slots with full hookups.

Clean and efficient **Restaurant Martin's,** Blvd. Alemán at Victoria, tel. (17) 14-7541, offers a good menu of Mexican standards as well as breakfasts and a few American selections. Open daily 7 a.m.-midnight.

Mapimí

The Misión de Mapimí was founded in 1598 by Jesuit padres but the surrounding territory was so inhospitable that development in the surrounding area gradually shifted toward the Región Lagunera (Gómez Palacio, Lerdo, and Torreón), where irrigation was possible.

Today the town of Mapimí ("rock on the. hill"), 64 km northwest of Gómez Palacio on Mexico 30, isn't a worthwhile stop in itself except to see the nearby 320-meter (1,050-foot) suspended bridge, **Puente Colgante de Ojuela.** Said to be the longest such span in the Americas, the bridge was built of iron and wood in 1892 on the west side of the Sierra de la Bufa to allow mining trains to ford a deep gorge. Most mining in the area was suspended by the 1920s; the ruins of stone houses at the old mining settlement can still be seen on a hillside not far from the bridge. A few Japanese firms maintain large chicken farms in the area.

Ask in Mapimí for a local guide who can arrange day-trips to the bridge and to the **Grutas de La Lágrima,** a set of picturesque caverns in the nearby Sierra del Rosario. Pantera Excursiones in Durango (see "Tours" under "Durango (City)") also offers small group tours to the Mapimí region.

There are a couple of Mexican cafes in Mapimí.

El Bolsón de Mapimí and La Zona de Silencio

Roughly centered on an area straddling meridian 104 and parallel 27 near the heart of the arid Bolsón de Mapimí (at the three-way intersection of the Chihuahua, Durango, and Coahuila state borders), the so-called "Zone of Silence" is one of the most remote desert areas in all of Mexico. The name derives from the common assumption that radio signals can neither be sent nor received within the zone, a notion that is easily disproved by anyone who carries a radio into the area.

The area surrounding the zone is a favorite destination for mineral collectors due to the abundance of exceptional samples of agate, selenite, calcite, and meteorite chunks. Meteorites are said to fall here almost every day of the year. Whether this is true or not, the zone's exceptionally clear air makes it an excellent place to observe nighttime meteor showers.

Two of the largest ferrous (iron-containing) meteorites ever discovered fell to earth in the zone. But the most notorious meteorite landing here was 1969's "Allende meteorite" (named for a nearby ranch), said to be the most thoroughly

UFOS, MISSILES, AND SECRET CITIES

Among the many *zoneros*, a small following of UFO cultists claim that the *zona de silencio* is a landing site used as a "safe haven," free from radar detection or other terrestrial interference, for extraterrestrial spaceship repairs or other necessary ground contact. A Mexican association, El Centro de Investigación de Antropología Cósmica de la Escuela Filosófica Lumen (Research Center of Cosmic Anthropology from the Philosophical School of the Light), believes that an ancient race of tall, yellow Maya from the lost civilization of Tulum-Balaam live directly below the Reserve in a city called Magnetotzen (Magnet Land)—and that desert hills here are actually hidden pyramids. Both groups suspect that the UNESCO research station in the Bolsón de Mapimí is actually some kind of cover for extraterrestrial—or subterranean—contact.

All zone-heads agree that the unexplained 1970 crash here of an Athena missile fired from Green River, Utah (with an intended White Sands Missile Range, New Mexico, touchdown nearly a thousand miles north)—as well as the perennial landing of an unusually high number of meteorites in the zone—is an indication that something out of the ordinary is going on in the Zona de Silencio.

The Athena missile crash is particularly perplexing because the 70-ton projectile totally disappeared from U.S. radar screens before leaving Utah airspace. Reports of a strange ball of fire in the sky from a nearby ranch resident led authorities to the vicinity of the crash site, but it took nearly three weeks for scientists in jeeps and helicopters to find the exact location, a large crater (formed by the missile's nose cone, which was carrying radioactive cobalt) in a sand dune just 600 meters from the Chihuahua-Durango line. One of many unanswered questions about the crash is why a missile (and its associated launch mechanisms) with lunar target capabilities could veer from such a short course as the Utah-New Mexico route without detection. Mexican sources have suggested that the Athena crash was engineered by NASA to give U.S. scientists an excuse to scrutinize the mysterious Zona de Silencio more closely.

So otherworldly is the zone that NASA officials had previously considered training American astronauts here to simulate lunar landings. (A training site in Mexico's Desierto del Pinacate in Sonora was later selected instead.) Rocket scientist Wernher von Braun supposedly flew a private plane here several times in 1969-70 with the idea of locating a radio-telescope in the zone because of the lack of radio interference.

investigated piece of cosmic debris in the history of extraterrestrial geology. German and American researchers dated this chunk of carbonaceous material—which entered the earth's atmosphere with a supersonic thunderclap and greenish glow—at over five billion years old, more ancient than anything in our own solar system. *Scientific American* (August 1971) concluded that the meteorite consisted of "virgin planetary material" dating to the primordial cosmic explosion that created the universe. These and subsequent findings forced scientists to alter then-current "big bang" theories which had dated the origin of the physical universe at least a half-billion years later.

According to a growing number of occult groups and mystics, the Zona de Silencio forms part of the Earth's "belly-button chakra," a powerful energy source traced by the planet's 27th parallel. Believers in this "Mystery Parallel" point out that it intersects the Caribbean's Bermuda Triangle, Egypt's Great Pyramids, and Tibet's mythical Shambhala in the Himalayan cordillera. Local residents refer to such occultists as *zoneros* or *silenciosos*, a group that includes many Mexican nationals. *Zoneros* hold regular conferences and overnight meetings in the area during which they may claim to see and hear beings from other worlds.

Locals find the zone-heads perplexing but are happy to serve as guides in the area. A local *corrido* sums up the way they feel about the so-called "zone":

> *Amigos que quede claro*
> *Que no hay Zona de Silencio*
> *Y les invito a conocer*
> *Este bonito desierto*

> *Friends, let it be clear*
> *That there is no Zone of Silence*
> *And I invite you to know*
> *This beautiful desert*

Biosphere Reserve: A few kilometers east of the Zona de Silencio is something of more tangible value—the best preserved section of Chihuahuan Desert bolsón in Mexico. Gopherus flavomarginatus, the largest land turtle in North America, is native to the area; it is said to have descended from a species of sea turtle that lived here a hundred million years ago, when the region was under a vast Cretaceous Period sea that geologists call the Sea of Thetis. Flavomarginatus lives up to 200 years and may weigh as much as 20 kilograms (44 pounds). To protect this exceptional (and endangered) tortoise as well as a number of other endemic fauna and flora, the United Nations—in cooperation with the Mexican government—declared 160,000 hectares of the Bolsón de Mapimí as a Biosphere Reserve in 1976 as part of its "Man and Biosphere" (MAB) program. To date, the program encompasses around 280 reserves in 70 countries worldwide.

A UNESCO-funded research station, the **Laboratorio del Desierto del Instituto de Ecología,** has been established in the Mapimí ejido of San Ignacio to study bolsón ecology.

Getting There: The best way to reach the Zona de Silencio and Biosphere Reserve is by vehicle. Drive north from Gómez Palacio about 120 km (or south from Jiménez 110 km) along Mexico 49 to a gravel road heading east from the highway just south of the small town of Ceballos. This road passes through the heart of the Reserve and leads to the "Punta de Triño" ("Triad Point") where the states of Durango, Chihuahua, and Coahuila meet—a point usually considered the center of the Zona de Silencio—about 55 km from Mexico 49. If you see any little green men or such, please send detailed descriptions!

BOB RACE

THE STATE OF ZACATECAS

An inland state in north-central Mexico, Zacatecas sits high on the Altiplano—the central plateau between the Sierra Madres Occidental and Oriental—at an average elevation of around 2,400 meters (7,800 feet). Long before the Spanish entered the region in the 1530s, the Aztecs and other Amerindian cultures had been extracting silver (which they valued over gold) in the area.

Today the state's sparse population still depends primarily on the mining of gold, silver, and other minerals at higher elevations, along with ranching (statewide) and limited agriculture in the state's southern and central regions. Many of Mexico's best fighting bulls are bred and raised at the haciendas of San Mateo, Malpaso, and Trancoso.

The vaquero (cowboy) tradition in Zacatecas has a stronger Mexican flavor than farther north, as indicated by the change of hat style from the curly-brimmed, Texas-style Stetson to the broader- and flatter-brimmed *sombrero* with tassels dangling from the back of the crown. *Charrería,* which is said to have originated in the state, is particularly robust in Zacatecas, meaning that opportunities to attend *charreadas* or to purchase saddlery and *trajes de charros* (*charro* suits) are plentiful.

Zacatecas produces 40% of the country's silver and is also the country's top cultivator of chiles and beans.

ZACATECAS (CITY)

Perched at an altitude of 2,496 meters (8,200 feet), in a high river gorge between two arid peaks, the state capital is Mexico's second highest city (after Tolula) and one of its major cultural treasures. Its steep, cobbled streets are lined with colonial architecture constructed of *cantera rosa* (pink sandstone)—including the single best example of Churrigueresque cathedral architecture in all of Mexico. And the city's museums are endowed with some of the best collections of both colonial and modern art in the country.

According to the prestigious *Artes de México,* the city enforces Mexico's most advanced urban preservation laws and "for many reasons could be considered our most beautiful urban area." A citizens group called Cultural Patronage of Zacatecas formed in 1941 to focus attention on cultural preservation; in 1965 the Committee for the Protection and Preservation of Monuments and Historic Regions in the State of Zacatecas moved many utility cables underground and removed all advertising boards from the central city. The latter group has won 76 out of 77 law-

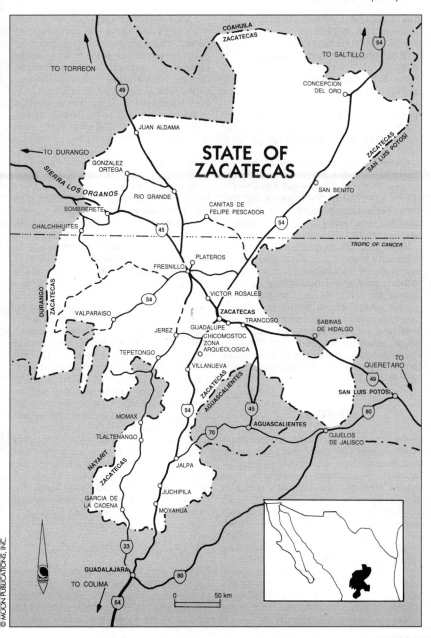

TO TORREON

TO DURANGO

SIERRA LOS ORGANOS

COAHUILA
ZACATECAS

TO SALTILLO

CONCEPCION
DEL ORO

JUAN ALDAMA

GONZALEZ
ORTEGA

RIO GRANDE

SOMBRERETE

CHALCHIHUITES

STATE OF
ZACATECAS

ZACATECAS
SAN LUIS POTOSI

SAN BENITO

CANITAS DE
FELIPE PESCADOR

TROPIC OF CANCER

PLATEROS

FRESNILLO

DURANGO
ZACATECAS

VALPARAISO

VICTOR ROSALES

ZACATECAS
TRANCOSO

SABINAS
DE HIDALGO

JEREZ

GUADALUPE
CHICOMOSTOC
ZONA
ARQUEOLOGICA

TEPETONGO

VILLANUEVA

TO
QUERETARO

SAN LUIS POTOSI

ZACATECAS
AGUASCALIENTES

MOMAX

TLALTENANGO

NAYARIT
ZACATECAS

AGUASCALIENTES

OJUELOS
DE JALISCO

JALPA

GARCIA DE
LA CADENA

JUCHIPILA

MOYAHUA

GUADALAJARA

TO COLIMA

0   50 km

© MOON PUBLICATIONS, INC.

suits filed against developers who sought to alter the urban plan. In 1993 the city was made a UNESCO World Heritage Site.

Of the republic's 31 states, Zacatecas, with its museums, archeological zones, and historical monuments (ex-conventos, casas históricas, capillas, and templos), continually ranks in the top 10 in Mexican national tourist visitation, often exceeding figures for Chiapas, Guanajuato, and Jalisco. Yet the city of Zacatecas has remained oddly anonymous among international tourists.

Because of its authentically pre-modern cityscape, Zacatecas was chosen as one of the location settings for U.S.-produced The Old Gringo, a film starring Gregory Peck and Jane Fonda that speculated about San Francisco journalist Ambrose Bierce's disappearance in Mexico during the 1910-20 revolution.

Within the capital município limits, according to Mexico's latest census, live around 150,000 people, though if you take into account the surrounding urban sprawl that connects the city to Guadalupe, Trancoso, and Ojocaliente, that number swells to around 300,000. A unique aspect to Zacatecas is that, unlike most sizable Mexican cities, there is virtually no border of poverty around the city. And along with a strong respect for tradition, Zacatecans display a definite taste for chic in their fashionable dress and tony downtown shops.

HISTORY

Before the entrada, Amerindian groups living in what is now the state of Zacatecas included the Zacatecos (from zacatl or "grass," and tecatl or "people"), Guachichiles, Pames, and Tepehuanes. Although missionaries were mining for souls in Zacatecas as early as the 1530s, silver drew the Spanish to the area in considerable numbers after Juan de Tolosa found a rich vein at the foot of Cerro de la Bufa in 1546. Initially called "Las Minas de Nuestra Señora de los Zacatecas," the city became the third richest in Nueva España by the mid-17th century, when it was supplying at least 20% of Spain's mineral wealth from the Americas. The first four millionaires in the New World—as measured in real dollars today—lived in Zacatecas.

A social hierarchy of criolla mine owners living in the city, cattle ranchers in surrounding haciendas, military officers in nearby presidios, and Indian workers literally at the bottom—extracting silver ore in deep mine shafts day and night—developed early in the city's evolution. The overall prosperity also provided an infrastructure for the establishment of Zacatecas as an important spiritual headquarters for the Catholic missionization of all Spanish-held areas to the north. Most religious architecture in the city dates to the Seraphic Order's founding of the influential Propaganda Fide de Nuestra Señora de Guadalupe during the 18th century; other Catholic sects that based their northern missionary efforts in Zacatecas included the Franciscans, Jesuits, Dominicans, and Augustines.

Silver mining remained strong throughout the 19th and early 20th centuries, interrupted only by the civil wars of the mid-19th century and the 1910-20 Mexican Revolution. On 23 June 1914, Pancho Villa and his División del Norte "liberated" the city from Huerta's troops in a famous revolutionary battle known as "La Toma de Zacatecas." Villa's pillaging left the city without water, lights, medicine, authorities, or police; Zacatecans called 1915 the "Year of Hunger."

Silver from the nearby Mina El Bote continues to be one of the city's major sources of income, supplemented by ranching, viticulture, the arts, and tourism. Although the citizens jealously guard their architectural heritage, they aren't antidevelopment. Outside the city, Grupo Modelo, producers of Corona and several other Mexican beers, recently built the largest brewery in Latin America, expanding their national capacity by nearly 50% and importing fermentation and aging tanks from Germany, bottling equipment from Italy, cooling equipment from England, and motors from the United States. The brewery has attracted a huge bottle-top plant as well as one for aluminum cans.

CLIMATE

Because of the city's high elevation, temperatures tend to be milder than elsewhere in Northern Mexico. April-Aug. are the warmest months, although daytime temperatures rarely rise beyond 26° C (80° F). Any time of year evenings

*an 1830 engraving
of Zacatecas by
Carlos Nebel*

can be chilly, so be sure to bring a jacket or sweater. Rain is negligible Oct.-May, while even during the June-Sept. rainy season monthly precipitation seldom exceeds 8.9 cm (3.5 inches).

SIGHTS

Walking is the best way to see the city, as the narrow streets and switchback curves may be confounding to motorists who don't know the city well. When Spanish architects designed the layout in the 17th and 18th centuries, they couldn't follow the typical grid pattern and instead allowed the Arroyo de la Plata's steep and angled topography to create a city full of twists, turns, and uneven planes—imagine an M.C. Escher drawing brought to life. Sudden ascents and descents of the cobbled street and walkway surfaces, sharp bends, and narrow, steep alleys are commonplace, providing a visual surprise at almost every corner and an overall surrealist perspective to the city. Bring sturdy walking shoes.

In the older part of the city, wedged into the space between Cerro de la Bufa and Cerro del Grillo, the architecture consists of broad planes of stone assembled in cubistic forms with baroque ornamentation. Development moved down the valley from Cerro de la Bufa in a southwesterly direction from here, so that the buildings become more modern in style from east to west. Early Tlaxcalteca masonry skills have been inherited by today's Zacatecan stonemasons, who

are among the most talented in Mexico.

As in San Luis Potosí, many buildings originally built in the 18th-century in a neo-Hispanic baroque style had their facades remodeled in the neoclassical style during the late 19th and early 20th centuries.

Catedral de Zacatecas

Originally constructed as Capilla de Santo Cristo in 1707, then redone as a *parroquía* in 1718, the current cathedral was begun in 1729 and was finally consecrated in 1752. Cathedral status was bestowed in 1859 with the creation of a Zacatecas diocese. The entire construction was carried out in pink sandstone, a typical medium for Zacatecan architecture ever since.

The three-tiered main facade is considered a masterpiece of baroque design, with its intensive floral ornamentation resembling cake frosting artfully squeezed from a *pastelero's* tube onto 18 Solomonic columns. A huge *rosetta* over the heavy wooden doors contains stained glass. Surmounting the facade is a Christ figure presiding over six apostles and six church fathers on baroque pedestals. The cluster of dense foliage above Christ represents God and the mysticism of the Holy Trinity.

A large, classical stone crucifix dominates the north facade, while the south facade features the richly carved Virgen de los Zacatecas, both impressive works of stonemasonry. Symmetrical, tile-domed towers—each containing 16 belfries—are identical in design and coloring even though they're a hundred years apart in construction (north tower 1785, south tower 1904). The stone interior of the cathedral—worked over during the Reform—is relatively bare.

The cathedral faces Av. Hidalgo, between the Plaza de Armas and the Mercado González Ortega.

Templo de Santo Domingo
Next door to the Pedro Coronel museum, at the junction of Calles Villalpando and Dr. Hierro, is the city's most well-endowed church. Built by

the Jesuits 1746-49 and modified by the Dominicans after the Jesuit expulsion in 1767, Santo Domingo has a more impressive interior than the Catedral de Zacatecas, with eight gilded baroque *retablos,* original wooden-plank flooring, and religious paintings by Francisco Martínez in the sacristy.

Ex-Templo de San Agustín
At the southern end of Calle Miguel Auza at Callejón del Lazo, this former Augustinian church and convent is thought to have been

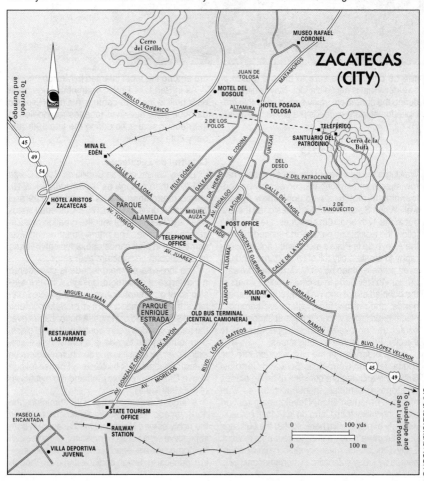

*Zacatecas cathedral,
1843*

DE HISTORIA DE MÉXICO CONDUMEX

designed by Andrés Manuel de la Riva, the architect of Guanajuato's La Valenciana. One of the state's oldest religious structures, the church was begun in 1590, consecrated in 1617, and renovated in 1782 to produce a unique octagonal, neo-Hispanic baroque cupola over the nave. Following the Reform, the property was sold first for use as a gaming house and hotel in 1863 and then again to the U.S. Presbyterian Society of Missions in 1882. Later the structure was used as a community hall, again as a hotel, then as a warehouse, and finally as a bishopry, its main function today.

The Presbyterians destroyed the beautiful baroque facade in front and replaced it with a plain white wall. Fortunately, a striking Churrigueresque side facade remains intact; it depicts St. Augustine in the garden of his house during his conversion, flanked by six empty or partially empty niches. The restored interior courtyard is decorated with stone masonry of note and contains a few historical exhibits, including sketches of the original facade.

The building is open Mon.-Fri. 10 a.m.-2 p.m. and 4-7 p.m., Saturday 10 a.m.-4 p.m. Admission is free.

Teatro Calderón

This huge, three-story theater (each story four meters/13 feet tall), opposite Mercado González Ortega on Av. Hidalgo, opened in 1832 and remains one of the city's most important cultural centers. Extensive reconstruction in 1891 gave the building a neoclassical style with art nouveau and beaux arts undertones. The authenti-

cally restored interior remains faithful to 19th-century theater design. The theater is named for Jalisco poet/playwright Fernando Calderón.

Operated today by the Universidad Autónoma de Zacatecas (U.A.Z.), the theater regularly hosts drama, music, and dance performances in its main hall, as well as lectures, round-table discussions, readings, theater workshops, and dance classes in smaller ancillary rooms.

Plaza de Armas

The large, empty plaza is more notable for the buildings that surround it than for the flagstone space itself. Facing the west side of the plaza (adjacent to the Hotel Continental Plaza) is the neoclassical **Palacio de Justicia,** originally the mansion of a Basque mine owner named Manuel de Rétegui. It's more commonly known as the "Palacio de la Mala Noche" ("Palace of the Bad Night"), after Rétegui's Mala Noche mine. According to local legend, the mine received its name because its principal lode was unearthed one night while Rétegui sat in his mansion contemplating suicide after having exhausted all his funds on mineral exploration. A side door to the mansion opens onto Callejón de Veyna—a level above the plaza—supposedly put in place to allow Don Manuel to come and go unnoticed from the mansion's second floor. Actually this pedestrian alley is typical of *callejones* that connect upper and lower street levels throughout the city. The building's large interior courtyard is open to the public.

On the east side of the plaza, the sober, 18th-century **Palacio de Gobierno** has been remod-

CHRIS HUMPHREY

Teatro Calderón

eled to exhibit the flattened window pilasters typical of the post-neoclassical or republican style. In the interior courtyard is a mural by Antonio Pinto Rodríguez depicting the city's history.

Mercado Jesús González Ortega ("El Mercado")

Opposite the south side of the cathedral, this 1886-vintage municipal market is one of the most splendid of its type in Mexico. The beaux-arts-style building was designed so that the upper level, opening onto Av. Hidalgo, was to be used as the main sales area while the lower level, opening onto Calle Tacuba on the opposite side, could be used as a warehouse. Large-scale, wrought-iron columns serve as *portales* along the upper level, which is now filled with posh boutique-style shops. The Tacuba level is occupied by two restaurants specializing in regional cuisine.

Adjacent to the market building is a widened *callejón* known as **Plaza Goitia,** where outdoor musical performances are frequently held.

Museo Pedro Coronel

The former Jesuit Colegio y Seminario de San Luis Gonzaga (established 1616) two blocks northwest of El Mercado on Plaza de Santo Domingo (adjacent to Templo de Santo Domingo) houses one of the country's best private art collections. All of the museum's pieces are works accumulated by Zacatecas painter and sculptor Pedro Coronel (1923-85), who, before his death, bequeathed his estate to the city. Most of the collection is on display here, while a smaller portion is exhibited at the Museo Francisco Goitia (see entry below).

Opened to the public in 1983, this extremely well-curated, not-to-be-missed museum contains hundreds of works—many of them gifts of the artists—by Pablo Picasso, Salvador Dali, Marc Chagall, Georges Braque, Jean Cocteau, Henry Moore, Victor Branner, Joan Miró, Antonio Saura, Alexander Calder, Robert Motherwell, Josef Albers, and George Segal, as well as paintings and sculptures by Coronel himself. Highlights include a large series of works by Goya (including *La Tauromaquía* and *Los Proverbios*), exquisite 18th-century architectural prints by Venetian architect Gian Battista Piranesi, and an entire room dedicated to the etchings of William Hogarth.

Separate rooms off the main upper colonnade contain displays of Greek and Roman sculpture dating 200 B.C.-A.D. 200; traditional art from Thailand, Burma, Cambodia, China, Japan, Tibet, Sri Lanka, India, Persia, and Egypt; a small African mask collection; excellent pre-Cortesian sculpture from the *culturas de occidente* (Colima, Jalisco, Nayarit, and Michoacán); lesser Mayan art from the Yucatán Peninsula; Mexican and Guatemalan masks; and 18th-century Mexican religious art.

Students of Spanish literature may be interested in the **Biblioteca Elías Amador** on the ground floor near the entrance. The valuable, 25,000-volume collection contains the bulk of the city's historical literary sources, including writings from most of the original convents dating from the 16th-19th centuries.

The museum is open Mon.-Wed. and Fri.-Sat. 10 a.m.-2 p.m. and 4-7 p.m., Sunday 10 a.m.-5 p.m.; it's closed on Thursday. Admission is US$1.30.

Antiguo Templo y Convento de San Francisco and Museo Rafael Coronel

In 1593 the Franciscans established a convent on this site, from which they sent missionary expeditions to New Mexico, Arizona, Colorado, and Texas. The adjacent church, oldest in the city, was completed at the end of the 17th century and features a baroque facade with triple-tiered Solomonic columns. The Jesuits eventually took over church and convent until the Jesuit expulsion in 1767, after which the property was abandoned. Mostly roofless, the ruins of the former Templo de San Francisco have been landscaped to create a pleasant, parklike atmosphere that makes exploring the ruins especially enjoyable.

Opened to the public in 1990 after years of neglect, the convent today contains a collection of nearly 4,000 Mexican masks donated by Zacatecan painter Rafael Coronel (brother of Pedro Coronel). A plaque near the entrance carries a quotation from Mexican writer Miguel Covarubias that summarizes the organizing principles for the curatorship of the masks: "The mask poses strange powers of suggestion over the imagination. It represents the synthesis and essence of deity, diabolism, death, and heroism." The well-labeled (in Spanish) exhibits provide a good overall introduction to basic Mexican mask types.

The main galleries on the convent's second floor display masks used to represent demons, *pascolas* (deer hunts), *moros y cristianos* (Moors and Christians), animals, death, and *pastorales* (the suffering on the journey to Bethlehem in order to view the infant Christ) in traditional ritual and dance. A smaller gallery on the ground floor houses a collection of pre-Hispanic ceramics, and another houses marionettes from Mexico, Indonesia, India, Burma, and China.

The museum and church are about a kilometer northeast of the Plaza de Armas—follow Av. Hidalgo till it becomes Calle Juan de Tolosa; once past the Fuente de los Conquistadores, bear right at the fork, and the church-convent complex will soon appear on the left. Also on the premises are a museum-operated cafe and gift shop. The museum and facilities are open Thurs.-Tues. 10 a.m.-2 p.m. and 4-7 p.m., Sunday 10 a.m.-5 p.m.; closed Wednesdays. Admission is US$1.30.

Museo Francisco Goitia (Goytia)

In an ex-governor's mansion encircled by rose gardens, this museum houses nearly a hundred years' worth of paintings, silkscreens, and sculptures by six 19th- and 20th-century Zacatecan artists: Francisco Goitia, Pedro Coronel, Rafael Coronel, Manuel Felguérez, Julio Ruelas, and José Kuri Breña.

The museum, at Calle Gral. E. Estrada 102 (on the west side of Parque Enrique Estrada), is open Tues.-Sun. 10 a.m.-1:30 p.m. and 5-8 p.m.; admission is US$1.30.

Museo Zacatecano

Housed in the former Casa de Moneda de Zacatecas, a small two-story hacienda that served as the city's mint for over a hundred years (1802-1905), this new museum displays over a hundred works of Huichol folkcrafts and magico-religious art, beautifully enlarged photos of the Huichols from the 1940s, a collection of nearly 200 *retablos* from the 16th-19th centuries, and some examples of colonial ironwork, including a rather intimidating chastity belt. Labeling is minimal, and mostly in Spanish.

The museum is at Dr. Hierro 301 (just across from Ex-Templo de San Agustín), tel. (492) 2-9021. Open Wed.-Sun. 10 a.m.-5 p.m.; admission is US$1.40.

Gardens

Jardín Juárez, a leafy and quiet garden plaza tucked away at the southern end of Calle Miguel Auza, just beyond the U.A.Z. rectory, was fashioned in 1857 and offers a nearly hidden refuge from the city's stony streets. A passageway off the garden through the neoclassic, 19th-century **Mesón de Jovito** leads to another small garden, **Jardín de la Madre** (more commonly known as Jardín Morelos).

Farther northwest in the same direction is the considerably larger **Alameda** (full name "Alameda Trinidad García de la Cadena"), Zacatecas's counterpart to New York's Central Park. During spring, this long, rectangular expanse of trees and monuments dedicated to illustrious local figures becomes a daily venue for *trobadores* performing *mañanitas* or morning songs.

The **Parque Enrique Estrada** (also known as the Parque González Ortega because a statue of the Zacatecan hero stands in the park), off Av. González Ortega between the Museo Goitia and the aqueduct, is even larger and more wooded.

Acueducto del Cubo

At the east edge of Parque Enrique Estrada, across Av. González Ortega, is an impressive stone aqueduct with flying buttresses begun by the Spanish and finished during the early years of the independent republic. The aqueduct continued to carry water from the Arroyo de la Plata until early this century.

Cerro de La Bufa

La Bufa (named for its billowing shape, from the same Latin root that generates the word "bouffant") towers over Zacatecas and provides the widest possible view of the city. It can be reached on foot via Calle del Angel (east of the Mercado González Ortega), by car via a road that winds around to the summit, or by *teleférico* (cable car) from the lower Cerro del Grillo on the northwest side of town.

Several bloody battles were fought on the hill, including confrontations between the Royalists and *insurgentes* during the struggle for Mexican independence, between conservatives and liberals during the War of Reform, and between the Villistas and Huertistas during the Mexican Revolution.

Scattered monuments on the summit bear witness to these and other historical events. The **Santuario del Patrocinio** (also known as the Capilla de Nuestra Señora de los Zacatecas) was built in 1728 to honor the city's patron saint, embodied in a highly venerated image known as the Virgen del Patrocinio. The Virgen dates to the first La Bufa chapel, which was built in 1548; the chapel has been restored many times, most recently in 1967. Every 3-15 Sept., thousands of worshipers and *matachine* dancers climb La Bufa in pilgrimage to the sanctuary. The climax of the celebration occurs on 8 Sept., when the Virgen is carried from the sanctuary to the Catedral de Zacatecas below.

In front (to the west) of the sanctuary, the **Museo de la Toma de Zacatecas** chronicles Pancho Villa's victory over Huerta's forces, a decisive battle in the Mexican Revolutionary campaign. Inaugurated in 1984 in commemoration of the battle's 70th anniversary, the simple muse-

um contains weapons, uniforms, newspaper clippings, photos, and a miniature model of the battle. The museum is closed on Mondays; admission is US$0.70. The **Plaza de la Revolución,** on the other side of the sanctuary, commemorates the same event in a larger context. Nearby are equestrian statues of the three *caudillos* who led the revolutionary division: Francisco "Pancho" Villa, Felipe Angeles, and Pánfilo Natera.

Farther east on the road to the summit is the **Mausoleo de los Hombres Ilustres,** a collection of tombs where famous Zacatecans are interred. The **Observatorio Meteorológico,** a functioning weather observatory, sits on the edge of the summit facing town. A small restaurant on the premises offers simple Mexican fare.

Teleférico Zacatecas and Mina El Edén

A Swiss-built *teleférico* (cable car) system carries passengers between the two hills on either side of the city in about eight minutes, a trip that affords panoramic views of the cityscape below.

The main cable car station is on the Cerro del Grillo side off Paseo Díaz Ordaz, a short but

teleférico

steep walk from the Plaza de Armas area.

The station is linked via a two-car tramway with the **Mina El Edén,** a former silver mine which began operations in 1583 and closed in the 1960s. Most of the silver that built the city came from El Edén, an ironic name given the severe working conditions. When the tram is running, visitors can ride to the end of the tracks (1.6 km/one mile), then walk about 400 meters through the mine shafts with a tour guide to view rickety wooden ladders, rope bridges, and a subterranean chapel. The mine shafts are lit with bare light bulbs 12:30-7:30 p.m.; when the tram isn't running you can walk in on your own. The shaft maintains a constant temperature of 12° C (54° F). A discotheque built into the mine is open at night.

Tickets for both the tramway and cable car cost US$0.65 each way; both run daily 10 a.m.-6 p.m.

ACCOMMODATIONS

Zacatecas doesn't have a huge variety of accommodations, but the selection is more than adequate. Several historic buildings downtown contain simply furnished, reasonably priced hotels. Rooms tend to be drafty in the cooler months and heating may not be adequate; ask the management for the loan of a space heater *(calentador)* if your room is uncomfortably cold. Or wear more clothes! These places are built around courtyards; for maximum quiet, request a room off the street.

Shoestring
Zacatecas has two youth hostels (all ages welcome): **Villa Deportiva Juvenil I,** Parque del Encantado 103, tel. (492) 2-1801, a 70-bed facility five minutes south of the train station; and **Villa Deportiva Juvenil II,** Av. de los Deportes 100, tel. (492) 2-9377, a 100-bed hostel adjacent to the west side of Estadio Francisco Villa, quite a distance east of the city center. Both charge US$1.60 per bed.

Near the aqueduct and former bullring, **Hotel del Parque,** Av. González Ortega 302, tel. (492) 2-0479, rents simple but adequate rooms. Avoid streetside rooms as there's some traffic noise and a disco across the way. There is no sign out

front—look for the gold letters "HP" on the glass door of a modern building south of Hotel Quinta Real and Parque Enrique Estrada on the right (west) side of the road. Rates: US$6.50 s, US$8 d.

Simple rooms are also available at **Hostal del Ángel,** Calle 1 de Mayo 211 (behind the cathedral and Mercado González Ortega), tel. (492) 2-5026 (around US$9); **Hotel Río Grande,** Calz. de la Paz 513, tel. (492) 2-9876; and **Hotel Conchita,** Av. López Mateos 401, tel. (492) 2-1494 (US$7 s, US$8.50 d). The latter two are in the vicinity of the city bus terminal; the Conchita is the nicer of the two.

Out on Mexico 45 east of the city, **Motel El Convento,** tel. (492) 2-0849, is convenient for highway travelers and a restaurant is attached. Rates: US$11 s, US$12 d, US$13 t.

Budget
The 18th-century **Hotel Condesa,** Av. Juárez 5 (downtown off Av. Hidalgo), tel. (492) 2-1160, looks impressively historic on the outside. Inside it's less than inspiring but livable. Rooms have private baths. Rates: US$14 s, US$16 d. Housed in an 18th-century mansion on the opposite side of Av. Juárez from Hotel Condesa is **Posada de los Condes,** tel. (492) 2-1412 or 2-1093, where the rooms are better and the moderately priced cafe receives high marks. Rates: US$16 s, US$21 d.

In the 19th-century building next door to the Teatro Calderón on Av. Hidalgo, **Posada de la Moneda,** tel. (492) 2-0881, has decent rooms with carpeting, TV, and phones. Because of its location near the cathedral, this hotel is often full. Rates: from US$24 s. Northeast of the plaza and cathedral toward the Museo Rafael Coronel, **Hotel Posada Tolosa,** Calle Tolosa 811, tel. (492) 2-5105, offers 37 clean, modern rooms, each with TV and phone, in an old house reminiscent of the Hostal del Vasco. There is a small parking garage in back. Rates: US$18 s, US$22.50 d, US$25 t.

Motel del Bosque, on Paseo Díaz Ordaz, Cerro del Grillo (near the tramway and cable car lines), tel. (492) 2-1034 or 2-0745, offers aerial views of the city and clean rooms with TV, phone, and private bath. The road to the motel is steep. Rates: US$17.50 s, US$22 d.

In a quiet corner of the historical district, just off the east end of the Alameda, **Hostal del**

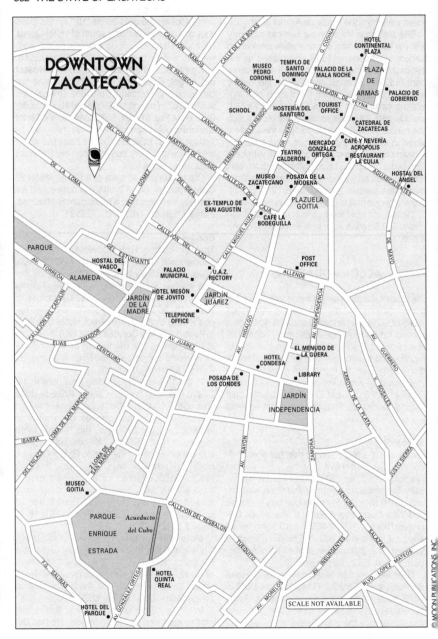

DOWNTOWN ZACATECAS

CALLEJÓN RAMOS
CALLE DE LAS BOLAS
G. CODINA
HOTEL CONTINENTAL PLAZA
DE PACHECO
MUSEO PEDRO CORONEL
TEMPLO DE SANTO DOMINGO
PALACIO DE LA MALA NOCHE
PLAZA DE ARMAS
SERDÁN
CALLEJÓN DE VEYNA
PALACIO DE GOBIERNO
DEL COBRE
LANCASTER
SCHOOL
HOSTERÍA DEL SANTERO
TOURIST OFFICE
CATEDRAL DE ZACATECAS
MÁRTIRES DE CHICAGO
DR. HIERRO
CAFÉ Y NEVERÍA ACRÓPOLIS
DE LA LOMA
FELIX GOMEZ
FERNANDO VILLALPANDO
TEATRO CALDERÓN
MERCADO GONZÁLEZ ORTEGA
RESTAURANT LA CUIJA
DEL IDEAL
CALLEJÓN DE LA CAJA
MUSEO ZACATECANO
POSADA DE LA MODENA
HOSTAL DEL ÁNGEL
DE AGUASCALIENTES
EX-TEMPLO DE SAN AGUSTÍN
PLAZUELA GOITIA
CALLE MIGUEL AUZA
CAFÉ LA BODEGUILLA
CALLEJÓN DEL LAZO
DE MAYO
PARQUE
DEL ESTUDIANTE
POST OFFICE
AV. TORREÓN
ALAMEDA
HOSTAL DEL VASCO
PALACIO MUNICIPAL
U.A.Z. RECTORY
ALLENDE
CALLEJÓN DEL CAPULÍN
AMADOR
JARDÍN DE LA MADRE
HOTEL MESÓN DE JOVITO
JARDÍN JUÁREZ
AV. INDEPENDENCIA
ELÍAS AMADOR
CENTAURO
TELEPHONE OFFICE
AV. JUÁREZ
AV. HIDALGO
EL MENUDO DE LA GÜERA
AV. GUERRERO
IBARRA
LOMA DE SAN MARCOS
HOTEL CONDESA
LIBRARY
V. ROSALES
DEL ENLACE
2 LOMA DE SAN MARCOS
POSADA DE LOS CONDES
JARDÍN INDEPENDENCIA
AV. RAYÓN
ARROYO DE LA PLATA
ZAMORA
JUSTO SIERRA
MUSEO GOITIA
CALLEJÓN DEL RESBALÓN
F.G. SALINAS
PARQUE ENRIQUE ESTRADA
Acueducto del Cubo
TUEQUITO
VENTURA DE SALAZAR
AV. GONZÁLEZ ORTEGA
HOTEL QUINTA REAL
AV. INSURGENTES
BLVD. LÓPEZ MATEOS
HOTEL DEL PARQUE
AV. MORELOS

SCALE NOT AVAILABLE

© MOON PUBLICATIONS, INC.

Vasco, tel. (492) 2-0428, provides 18 spacious rooms (some with kitchenettes) with phone, TV, and heating in a restored 17th-century house. The courtyard contains a small but charming dining area. The kitchenettes do not come with utensils and not all the kitchen stoves work. Rates: US$28 s, US$33 d, US$39 t, including tax.

Inexpensive

East of the city on Mexico 45, beyond Motel El Convento on the right, **Hotel Parador Misión del Real,** tel./fax (492) 3-4282, has good rooms with heating, a/c, phones, and satellite TV. Free shuttle service is provided to and from the airport; car rental is also available on the premises. Rates: US$38 s, US$45 d.

West of (and overlooking) the city, **Hotel Aristos Zacatecas,** on Loma de la Soledad off Mexico 45, tel. (492) 2-1788, has rooms with all the amenities, and each one has a private terrace with city view. Facilities include a heated pool, sauna, restaurant, and convention rooms. Rates: US$35 and up. On the way to Guadalupe, five-story **Hotel Don Miguel,** Blvd. López Mateos at Calle del Plomo, tel./fax (492) 4-1002, has 141 rooms with all the international amenities. Ask for a room in back to avoid highway noise. Rates: US$34-38 s/d.

Moderate

Opposite the Plaza de Armas on Av. Hidalgo, in the heart of the historical district, **Hotel Continental Plaza Zacatecas,** tel. (492) 2-6183, fax (492) 2-6245, Mexico toll-free tel. (800) 9-0229, is housed in an 18th-century baroque-neoclassical building that has been restored inside and out to offer 116 spacious but unheated rooms. On the premises are two restaurants (one overlooking the plaza), a bar, gift shop, beauty salon, and underground valet parking garage. Rack rates start at US$56 s/d.

The modern, five-story **Zacatecas Holiday Inn,** Blvd. López Mateos at Callejón del Barro (east of the old bus terminal), tel. (492) 2-3311, fax (492) 2-3415, Mexico toll-free tel. (800) 4-4040, has clean, well-maintained rooms with satellite TV, a/c, and individually controlled heating. Facilities include a coffee shop, indoor pool, and travel agency with car rental. Rates: US$60-74 s/d/t.

Moderate/Expensive

Atmospheric **Hotel Mesón de Jovito (Jobito),** tel./fax (492) 4-1722, Mexico toll-free tel. (800) 4-40-00, occupies a restored 19th-century hacienda that once served as a boardinghouse for visiting merchants; the restoration is beautiful and the building is adjacent to tranquil Jardín Juárez. There are 31 elegant standard suites for US$58 s/d, plus five master suites with jacuzzi for US$85. Service is top-notch, and a restaurant and bar are attached.

Expensive

A former bullring near the Acueducto del Cubo is now one of Mexico's most interesting hotel experiments. **Hotel Quinta Real Zacatecas,** Av. Rayón 434, tel. (492) 2-9104, fax (492) 2-8440, Mexico toll-free tel. (800) 3-6015, U.S./Canada toll-free tel. (800) 445-4565, offers 46 deluxe suites (10 with jacuzzis) and public areas that have been built into and onto the Antiguo Plaza de Toros de San Pedro, reportedly the second oldest bullring in the western hemisphere (first opened in 1866). On the premises are a restaurant, bar, art gallery, antique shop, and silver shop. Rates: US$95-100.

RV Parks and Camping

Tent camping is permitted at the Villa Deportiva Juvenil I (see "Shoestring," above) at no charge. **Motel Del Bosque** has six RV spaces with full hookups for US$7 a night, but bigger rigs might have trouble making the steep grade and tight turns on the Paseo Díaz Ordaz.

Morelos RV Park, 6.5 km (four miles) northwest of the city at the junction of Mexico 45 and Mexico 49, has 40 spaces with full hookups for US$8-12 per night. The adjacent restaurant is a popular road stop.

FOOD

Although local restaurants don't offer the range of cuisines found in San Luis Potosí, Zacatecans take gastronomy seriously and are keen to recommend places to eat. Common local specialties include *sopa de tortilla, carne adobada, enchiladas zacatecanas, pipián ranchero* (rich, pumpkin-seed sauce served over chicken), and *asado de boda* (a kind of pork mole). As in San

Luis Potosí, *colonche,* an alcoholic beverage distilled from fermented cardón fruit juice, is occasionally seen. Zacatecan mezcal, however, is more popular. Zacatecan wines—especially those made from a vinifera hybrid of Carignan and cabernet sauvignon varietals—are among the best in Mexico.

In the *centro histórico,* men riding burros slung with large terra-cotta jars sell *aguamiel,* a refreshing drink made from unfermented maguey extract.

Regional

Near the Mercado González Ortega, **Hostería del Santero,** Callejón del Santero 109, tel. (492) 4-0561, is a casual spot with inexpensive *almuerzo,* free *botanas* with beverage orders in the afternoon, and, in afternoon and early evening, regional specialties such as *asado de boda, parrillada Zacatecana, quesos fundidos, sopa de tortilla, enchiladas zacatecanas, pozole, tamales y atole,* and *gorditas.* Open daily 11 a.m.-7 p.m.

La Cantera Musical Fonda y Bar, tel. (492) 2-8828, is on the bottom floor of the Mercado González Ortega facing Tacuba. Housed in the market's former warehouse area, La Cantera features a casual, festive atmosphere and a large menu of regional dishes for around US$4 per entree. House specialties include *mole rojo a la zacatecana* and *asado de boda jerezano,* made with pork, cumin, bay leaves, and oranges. *Menudo, pozole,* and *atole* are always available; tortillas are handmade on the premises. Open daily 9 a.m.-11 p.m.

Restaurant Bar La Cuija, tel. (492) 2-8275, is on the bottom floor of the Mercado González Ortega, a couple of doors down from La Cantera. A bit more formal, but only a little more expensive than La Cantera, La Cuija is associated with the Cacholá winery and features an extensive menu of fish, beef, and chicken dishes, along with a few Italian dishes and a selection of Zacatecan wines. Open daily 1 p.m.-midnight. Live guitar trio Thurs.-Saturday.

National

Los Candiles Restaurant, Continental Plaza, Av. Hidalgo, has a light and airy atmosphere that's a nice change from the typically dark interiors of many Zacatecas restaurants. The food—Mexican standards, *carne asada,* seafood, and continental—and service are very good. The daily buffet, served 1-6 p.m., is a good value. Open daily 7 a.m.-11 p.m.

Cenaduría Los Dorados, Plazuela de Garefa 1314, tel. (492) 2-5722, is on the street just south of Ex-Convento de San Francisco/Museo Rafael Coronel. The restaurant specializes in *pozole verde* and *antojitos.* Open daily 1 p.m.-1 a.m.

Unpretentious little **Las Comales,** opposite the cathedral on Av. Hidalgo, serves inexpensive *antojitos* and *comidas corridas.* Open Mon.-Sat. 8 a.m.-10 p.m.

El Menudo de la Güera, Plaza Genaro Codina 114, has been in business for 40 years, and serves the city's best *menudo.* In the evening, *pozole* is served with tostadas. Open daily noon-midnight.

International

Ristorante Borsalino, Dr. Hierro 404, tel. (492) 4-2727, serves a range of Italian dishes at reasonable prices and offers a decent wine selection. Open daily 1-11 p.m.

Restaurant Garufa, Jardín Juárez 135 (adjacent to Mesón del Jovito), is a chic new Argentine restaurant specializing in grilled steaks made from huge, imported cuts of beef, plus pasta and chicken dishes. Family atmosphere. Moderate to expensive. Open daily 2-11 p.m.

Restaurante Las Pampas, Av. López Mateos 123 (at Colegio Militar), tel. (492) 2-1008, specializes in charcoal-broiled steaks and chicken. Open daily noon-midnight.

Restaurant La Plaza, Hotel Quinta Real, tel. (492) 2-9104, is built into the former Plaza de Toros de San Pedro. This very elegant restaurant features a menu of original recipes based on Mexican and international standards. Very expensive. Open daily for breakfast, lunch, and dinner.

Zacatecas Grill, on Blvd. López Mateos in Colonia Florida, east of city center, tel. (492) 3-3029, is known for its Pacific seafood and fresh cuts of beef from local *ganaderías.* Pricey. Open Mon.-Sat. noon-midnight, Sunday noon-8 p.m.

Other

Café La Bodeguilla, Callejón de la Caja (formerly Calle de San Agustín) 103, just above Av. Hidalgo, has a pleasant, small interior dining area, a bar, and outside tables that have become very popular with the local trendsetters lately. The kitchen produces Spanish-style tapas and tortillas (Spanish appetizers and omelettes), along with tasty grilled baguette sandwiches called *bocadillos*—great for light meals. Open daily noon-1 a.m.

A Zacatecas institution, **Café y Nevería Acrópolis,** on the northwest corner of the Mercado González Ortega facing Av. Hidalgo, tel. (492) 2-1284, is a coffeeshop popular for breakfasts, sandwiches, Mexican *antojitos*, pastries, ice cream, and 12 kinds of espresso, cappuccino, and other coffee drinks. Open daily 8 a.m.-10 p.m.

La Terraza, upper floor of Mercado González Ortega facing east, has a great location, but the uninspired menu of burgers, sandwiches, and malts wouldn't attract a soul if it weren't for the view of Calle Tacuba below. Open daily 11 a.m.-9:30 p.m.

Off Calle Allende #116 is a corridor lined with inexpensive *loncherías* mixed in with beauty salons and luggage vendors. Near the old bus terminal are several more *loncherías*.

RECREATION AND ENTERTAINMENT

Bullfights and *Charreadas*

In Zacatecas the first *fiestas bravas* were recorded in 1593, making the city one of Mexico's oldest bullfight venues. Several bullrings have come and gone in the interim, including the stately Plaza de Toros de San Pedro, recently transformed into the Hotel Quinta Real.

The main stadium is now contained in the **Instalaciones de la Feria,** midway between Zacatecas and Guadalupe off Av. López Mateos. Adjacent to the Instalaciones is a large *charro* ring *(lienzo charro)* where *charreadas* are held regularly throughout the year. For a current schedule of *corridas,* inquire at the tourist office on Av. Hidalgo.

Bars and Discos

The **Bar Pirame** and **Bar El Botarel,** in the Continental Plaza Zacatecas and Quinta Real Hotels, respectively, are good places for a quiet drink. The **Centro Nocturno El Grillo** in the Holiday Inn features live dance music Wed.-Sat. nights.

Bar Arcano, downstairs at Hidalgo 114, is a favorite lounging spot for local nightowls and

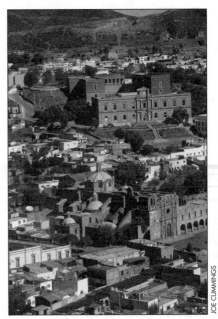

JOE CUMMINGS

Zacatecas from above

features live jazz, blues, and bossa nova Mon.-Saturday. No cover.

At the summit of Cerro del Grillo, on Paseo Díaz Ordaz next to the cable car station, the popular **Discoteque de Elefante Blanco,** tel. (492) 2-7194, is open for dancing Thurs.-Sat. 9 p.m.-2 a.m. The defunct Mina El Edén, a short distance southwest on Paseo Díaz Ordaz, contains a disco called **El Malacate,** tel. (492) 2-3000, which is open the same days and hours as the Elefante Blanco.

Callejonadas

Zacatecas has a tradition of small fiestas held in pedestrian alleys *(callejones)* and most often taking place on Saturdays. The typical *callejonada* features music (especially brass-band *conjuntos*), folkloric dancing, food, and speeches evoking civic pride. Many attendees wear clay cups dangling from red ribbons around their necks; the cups are periodically filled with local mezcal which is drunk to ward off the chilly Zacatecas nights. Inquire at the tourist office on Av. Hidalgo to learn of any upcoming alley parties. Plaza Goitia, the enlarged *callejón* next to El Mercado, is a frequent venue.

Shopping

Zacatecas is famous for its silver crafts fashioned from ore extracted from nearby Mina El Bote, and the downtown areas are dotted with silver shops. **Artesanías y Platería Real de Angeles,** near the cathedral at Callejón de G. Farias 97, has a good selection and good prices.

The **Centro Platero Zacatecano,** tel. (492) 3-1007, in the ex-hacienda de Bernández, 20 minutes east of the city by car, is a silversmithing school where you can observe artisans at work and also buy silver pieces. The Centro maintains a storefront in the Mercado González Ortega downtown as well. To find the school, follow Av. López Mateos (Mexico 45/49) east until it becomes Blvd. México, then continue along this *avenida* until it ends at a T-intersection. Turn left on Restauradores and continue north along Mina la Cantera till you see signs for the Centro Platero Zacatecano. The center is open to the public Mon.-Sat. 10 a.m.-6 p.m.

Zacatecas is also known for its distinctive sarapes, which feature bold black-and-red stripes trimmed with black-and-white, geometric-patterned borders. Leatherwork—belts, saddles, boots, etc.—is another regional specialty. In the Mercado González Ortega, **La Espuela de Oro** sells *piteado* saddles (embroidered with *pita,* a hemplike agave fiber), *charro* suits, hats, sarapes, silver *espuelas* (spurs), leather jackets, and other items associated with the state's vaquero tradition.

Wine is another good buy in Zacatecas. The **Cacholá** label is quite drinkable, especially the ruby cabernet (made from a grape that's a cross between cabernet sauvignon and Carignan). Other local labels include **Solera del Bodequiero, Puerta de Hierro,** and **Flor del Altiplano.** A typical bottle of Zacatecan wine costs just US$5 at one of the wine shops in the Mercado González Ortega. By prior arrangement, you can also visit the Cacholá winery in Valle de las Arsinas, Guadalupe, at Km 634 Mexico 45 (at the junction of Mexico 45 and Mexico 49, about 27 km/16.5 miles east of Zacatecas). Inquire at Restaurant La Cuija, which is partially owned by the Cacholá winery, about a visit; or contact Cacholá Wines, Carretera Panamericana Km 634, Valle de las Arsinas, Guadalupe, tel. (492) 4-1555.

Events

During Semana Santa (March or April), the city celebrates the **Festival de Zacatecas en la Cultura** with a 10-day program of culturally focused exhibits, conferences, and performances held in city plazas and gardens, at the Teatro Calderón, and in the museums.

For three days each August, Zacatecanos celebrate **La Morisma,** a richly costumed reenactment of the defeat of the *moros* (Moors) by the *cristianos* (Christians). Originally the ritual was developed by Spanish missionaries to inspire faith among Mexico's Amerindians, but it's now a Mexican tradition in the states of Puebla, Michoacán, Tlaxcala, Mexico D.F., and Zacatecas. The strongest and most elaborate Morisma tradition, however, is practiced in Zacatecas. The annual venue for the event is El Bracho, a large field in the northeast section of the city where the turbaned Moors meet the helmeted Christians in a mock battle. Before being given lead roles in the performance, participants must train for years at the Cofradía de San Juan Bautista (Brotherhood of St. John the Baptist), a Zacatecas association devoted to the preservation of La Morisma. Earned according to merit, service, and seniority, actors' roles make up a dramatic hierarchy of princes, pages, shield-bearers, soldiers, officers, and so on. The battle ends with the capture and beheading of the Moorish king and is followed by musical performances and merrymaking. La Morisma begins on the last Friday of August.

Two weeks in September are devoted to the **Feria de Zacatecas,** which celebrates the founding of the city and pays homage to the city's patron saint, the Virgen del Patrocinio. Ranching, farming, and handicraft exhibitions are held at various places around the city, and the Teatro Calderón hosts a special series of musical and theatrical performances, as well as bullfights and other sporting events. For out-of-town visitors, the most colorful aspect of the annual *feria* is the *matachine* processions to the Santuario del Patrocinio on Cerro de la Bufa (see the "Cerro de la Bufa" entry above for details).

INFORMATION AND SERVICES

Tourist Offices
The **Dirección Estatal de Turismo** operates a small information office opposite the cathedral at Av. Hidalgo 606, where sketch maps and brochures are available. Someone usually is on hand who speaks English. The main office, tel. (492) 4-0393 or 4-0552, is on Prolongación González Ortega next to the railway station. The federal **SECTUR** delegation is at Blvd. López Mateos 923-A, tel. (492) 2-6750.

Books and Maps
The City of Zacatecas, published by the state in 1991, is a glossy 150-page book with high-quality color photos and good background and sightseeing information. Available either in Spanish or English at various gift shops and museums, the book is rather expensive at US$20-30 (depending on where you purchase it).

The bilingual Zacatecas map issued by Centro Regional Zacatecas (Blvd. López Mateos 504) is the best of the locally available maps for sightseeing. Also good is *Guía Forasteros Centro Histórico Zacatecas,* produced by Guías Turísticas Banamex.

Post Office
The *correo* on the north side of Calle Allende between Hidalgo and Tacuba is a convenient location for visitors staying in or visiting the historical district.

Money
Banamex, Hidalgo 132, has an ATM that takes most major credit/debit cards. **San Luis Divisa,** Independencia 82, opposite Jardín Independencia, is a *casa de cambio* with good rates; they'll also cash travelers checks. **Viajes Mazzocco,** Enlace 115, Col. Sierra de Alicia, tel. (492) 2-5902, is the local American Express rep with all the usual services, including emergency check-cashing, TC replacement, and mail-holding.

ZACATECAS TELEPHONE NUMBERS

Local Police	2-0180
Highway Patrol	4-5500
Green Angels	2-4008
State Tourist Office	4-0393
Red Cross	2-3005
Emergencies	06
Zacatecas Area Code	492

GETTING THERE

Air
Mexicana, Mercado González Ortega, Av. Hidalgo, tel. (492) 2-7470 or 2-3248, flies nonstop to Zacatecas from Chicago, Denver, Los Angeles, Mexico City, San Jose, San Francisco, and Tijuana.

TAESA, Av. Hidalgo 305, tel. (492) 2-0050, operates direct flights to/from Aguascalientes, Guadalajara, Chicago, Mexico City, Morelia, and Morelia, with connections from Los Angeles.

Zacatecas's airport is 25 km (15.5 miles) southwest of the city, a US$10 taxi ride, or US$3 in a *colectivo.*

Bus
Most interstate buses use the Central Camionera on Terrenos de la Isabelica, off the *anillo periférico* (ring road). **Transportes Chihuahuenses, Futura,** and **Transportes del Norte** operate first-class buses to/from Aguascalientes (US$4, 12 times daily), Chihuahua (US$25, 10 times daily), Ciudad Juárez (US$36, four times daily), Durango (US$8, 10 times daily), Mexico City (US$19, four times daily), Matamoros (US$22, once daily), and Monterrey (US$13, five times daily).

Estrella Blanca/Camiones de los Altos has less expensive second-class buses to many of the same cities as the above companies—including Ciudad Juárez, Chihuahua, Durango, Guadalajara, Monterrey, Nuevo Laredo, Saltillo, and San Luis Potosí—plus Fresnillo (US$4) and Mazatlán (US$15).

Omnibus de México operates from the old bus terminal at Blvd. López Mateo 719 and serves San Luis Potosí, Durango, Guadalajara, and Torreón with fares similar to those posted by Transportes del Norte.

Train
The city railway station is just south of the junction of Av. González Ortega and Blvd. López

Mateos. *El División del Norte* stops in Zacatecas on its daily run between Mexico City and Ciudad Juárez. The conditions/reliability nowadays on this line are such that it should only be considered by hardcore railfans or the very impecunious.

Driving

A four-lane tollway, Mexico 49D, links León Guzmán (just south of Torreón) and Zacatecas in three separate sections, each with its own toll gate; the total toll for the entire 386-km (239-mile) route is around US$8. The original free road runs parallel to the tollway much of the way and is not much slower.

If you take the free road, drive cautiously along the stretch of Mexico 49 through Fresnillo (61 km/37.8 miles northwest of Zacatecas), as the federal highway police are very vigilant in enforcing the 30 kph (18.6 mph) speed limit through town.

Southeast of Zacatecas on Mexico 49 between Guadalupe and Trancoso (about 14 km east of Guadalupe), the 24-hour **Santa Monica Centro de Descanso** offers Magna Sin, ice, a restaurant, clean restrooms, and an auto parts shop. Beyond Trancoso the Altiplano grasslands along Mexico 49 are studded with robust yucca trees, prickly pear, and agave; Mexico's strongest fighting bulls are bred and raised in this area.

GETTING AROUND

Bus

Zacatecas's *centro histórico* can easily be navigated on foot. Of the several city bus lines, most useful are the Ruta 7 between the central district and Blvd. López Mateos, and the Ruta 8 bus between downtown and the Central Camionera.

Taxi

Taxicabs around town cost US$1-2 in the central district, US$2-2.50 for destinations along the Zacatecas-Guadalupe strip.

Driving

With its winding, steep, one-way streets, Zacatecas is not the easiest city to drive in. Fortunately, most streets are marked with names and one-way arrows, so with a little fortitude (and a map), you should be able to find your way around without too much aggravation. If sightseeing is your main objective, however, you'd do best to park your vehicle and see the city on foot.

Zacatecas has two car rental agencies: **Budget,** Blvd. López Mateos 108, or at the airport, tel. (492) 2-9458; and **Arrendadora Número Uno,** Blvd. López Mateos 201, or at the airport, tel. (492) 2-0974.

AROUND THE STATE

GUADALUPE

If you have a spare half day to spend while in Zacatecas, don't miss the opportunity to visit this colonial town only five km (three miles) east of the state capital.

Adjacent to the main plaza is the **Ex-Convento de Guadalupe,** originally founded in 1707 by Franciscan friar Antonio Margil de Jesús as a center for the propagation of Catholicism in northern Nueva España. Restored and maintained by Mexico's INAH, the former convent now contains the **Museo de Arte Virreinal de Guadalupe,** a repository for the finest collection of viceregal art outside Mexico City. Among the paintings on display are works by Ibarra, Antonio de Torres, Miguel Cabrera, and Andrés López. In the convent's upper cloister is a striking series of 14

Templo de Guadalupe

CHRIS HUMPHREY

oval-framed Cabrera paintings depicting scenes from the life of the Virgin Mary. The museum is open Tues.-Sun. 10 a.m.-4:30 p.m.; admission is US$1.70.

The baroque facade of the attached **Templo de Guadalupe** is in good condition and features a unique set of tripartite columns known as *tritósilas*. The choir contains heavy, opulently carved wooden chairs backed with holy portraits. Even more impressive is the convent's 19th-century **Capilla de Nápoles,** with its gilded dome and plasterwork and wood-parquet floor. On the main altar a figure of the Virgin Mary sculpted in Naples sits on an ornate domed pedestal.

The **Museo Regional de Historia,** in a former orphanage annexed to the convent, contains Huichol artifacts and a collection of horse carriages, antique cars, railway cars, and other transportation-related exhibits. Hours are the same as for the Museo Virreinal but admission is free.

Getting There: Guadalupe is linked to Zacatecas by Calz. López Mateos (Mexico 45/49); the five-km stretch between the two towns has developed so that they have really become part of one metropolitan unit. **Transportes de Guadalupe** runs frequent red-and-white buses from the Alameda in Zacatecas to central Guadalupe for US$0.21 each way.

JEREZ DE GARCÍA SALINAS

More commonly known simply as **Jerez,** the town was originally established in 1565 as a military post along the Camino Real and is today known for its authentic provincial-colonial architecture. It sits at an elevation of 1,980 meters (6,500 feet), about the same as San Miguel de Allende, and has a pleasant year-round climate. Horse-mounted vaqueros are a common sight in the clean, cobbled streets lined with simple one-story colonials. In the evening the main plaza becomes a venue for a traditional Mexican courtship ritual wherein single men sitting on benches flirt with young women circumambulating the plaza.

Sights

Antique churches include the 18th-century **Vieja Parroquía de la Inmaculada Concepción** and the 19th-century **Santuario de la Soledad**. The restored **Teatro Hinojosa,** facing the south side of the main plaza, is reportedly an exact replica of Washington, D.C.'s Ford Theater, where U.S. president Abraham Lincoln was assassinated. Both structures were inspired by the Paris Opera.

Jerez was the home of renowned poet Ramón López Velarde. Velarde's house is now a museum displaying memorabilia from his life and career.

Accommodations

Shoestring: Rooms in the US$6-8 range are available at three small hotels on the Plaza Principal: **Hotel Jardín,** Plaza Principal Pte. 5, tel. (494) 5-2026; **Hotel Plaza,** Plaza Principal Sur 9, tel. (494) 5-2063; and **Hotel Central,** Plaza Principal Sur 10, tel. (494) 5-2483. The Hotel Jardín has an attached restaurant and bar.

Budget: Seven-story **Leo Hotel,** on the road in from Mexico 54, tel. (494) 5-2001, fax (494) 5-4415, has modern rooms with a/c, heating, satellite TV, and phones. On the premises are a restaurant, bar, coffee shop, disco, and pool. Rates: US$23 s, US$29 d.

Food

A number of decent restaurants are strung out along Av. E. Carranza-Suave Patria, a broad avenue that crosses the north side of Plaza Principal. Among these are **Restaurant La Luz, El Bohemio Hostería,** and **El Patio Jerezano. Cenaduría Galvan,** Comercio 7, just north of the Parroquía, is also good. Burritos are a popular snack and can be found at **Burritos Olguin,** corner of López Velarde and Alameda Sur, and at **Burritos La Palma,** Calle La Palma 14-B.

Shopping

Jerez is well known for the cultivation of roses and for *cuero piteado,* leather embroidered with a cactus fiber. Several shops carry embroidered saddles, lariats, bridles, *chaparreras,* and boots—handcrafted ranching accoutrements collectively known as *talabartería.*

Events

Beginning on Holy Friday in April, the town celebrates the 10-day *Fiesta de la Primavera* with bullfights, cockfights, flower shows, agricultural and ranching expositions, and other diversions.

Getting There

Línea Zacatecas Jerez operates second-class buses between Zacatecas and Jerez several times daily. If you're driving from Zacatecas, take Mexico 54 south for 23 km (14 miles), then turn west at Malpaso and follow the signed, paved road 26 km (16 miles) to Jerez.

LA QUEMADA (CHICOMÓSTOC)

These enigmatic ruins south of the capital off Mexico 54 represent perhaps the northernmost outpost of Mesoamerican culture. Carbon dating suggests the site was inhabited A.D. 350-950, although by whom continues to be debated. Various theories have called it a Teotihuacano enclave, a Toltec emporium, a Tarasco bastion, a Caxcán center, or simply an independent development by an as-yet-to-be-identified Amerindian group. Scholars believe a spiderweb of stone and clay roads once emanated from La Quemada for a radius of 170 km, linking a mosaic of transitional cultures between the peaceful northern pueblos and martial Mesoamerica. The site may have been closely associated with Chalchihuites farther north near the Durango state line. The hilltop site is surrounded by a valley where the Quemada culture cultivated corn, beans, squash, maguey, amaranth, tomatoes, and nopal.

The ruins consist of several sets of circular, cylindrical, and rectangular monuments made of brick and stone, all perched on a barren hill overlooking the Valle de Villanueva. It is estimated that around 15% of the original structures were pillaged by the Spanish, who used the stone materials for colonial construction projects. One of the more remarkable designs is the so-called **Salón de las Columnas** (Room of Columns), a set of 11 two-meter-high (6.5-feet-high) brick columns. The Huicholes of Zacatecas hold a highly secret peyote ceremony here a few days prior to the spring equinox each year, during which time the site is closed to the public.

Another set of stone structures is known as the **Juego de Pelota** ("Ball Court") and was

La Quemada

used for the famous Mesoamerican ritual ball game known as far north as Casas Grandes in Chihuahua and as far south as Honduras. The function of the **Pirámide Votiva** ("Votive Pyramid"), at the northern edge of the site, remains a puzzle.

Much of the confusion regarding the function or sociological role of La Quemada owes to the variety of structures that make up the site. It is now known that the current structures were erected in distinct eras and that the nucleus of the masonry in some cases predates outer layers of construction. The majority of the remnants visible today pertain to the last period of occupation and constitute a fortified ceremonial center similar to those erected in Mesoamérica during the so-called *epiclásico* period (A.D. 600-900).

Evidence is still not sufficient to ascertain whether this region became the adopted home of agricultural colonists originating from the south or whether seminomadic northern groups took up a more sedentary lifestyle here, or both. Without a doubt the growth of a stable rural population was necessary in order to maintain a governing group that directed the evolution of such a complex ceremonial center.

It is evident that something grave happened in the valley and caused a generalized process of retreat that ended in the abandonment of the site between A.D. 900 and 950. From the Ciudadela, in the extreme north of La Quemada, to the Salón de las Columnas in the south, signs of fire have been observed in almost all the roofed spaces of the area. Famine has also been postulated.

A new visitors center, designed by a talented Mexican architect, offers interpretive exhibits. The ruins and visitors center are open to the public daily 10 a.m.-5 p.m. except during Huichol pilgrimages; admission is US$2 except on Sundays, when it's free.

Getting There
There is no public transportation serving the ruins. A nine-km (5.6-mile) paved access road runs east off Mexico 54, 47 km (29 miles) south of Zacatecas.

PLATEROS

Seven km (4.3 miles) northeast of the silver-mining center of Fresnillo, at about 2,225 meters (7,300 feet), this small town revolves around pilgrimages to its **Santuario de Plateros.** The 18th-century church contains two highly revered images—El Señor de los Plateros (the patron saint of silversmiths) and El Santo Niño de Atocha (the Christ child as a pilgrim)—that are objects of pilgrimages throughout the year.

The Santo Niño in particular is thought to have the power to grant requests and perform miracles. Written on walls next to native paintings are personal testimonials such as, "I give thanks to El Santo Niño de Atocha for having miraculously opened the doors of work after I was out of a job for eight months."

SOMBRERETE AND VICINITY

Midway between Durango and Fresnillo on Mexico 45, Sombrerete has the state's second largest collection of colonial architecture. Founded in 1155 and named for a nearby hill that resembled a type of Spanish hat worn in the 16th century, the town's main attractions include the 18th-century baroque **Parroquía de San Juan Bautista,** the 17th-century **Templo de Santo Domingo,** and the 16th-century Franciscan **Convento de San Mateo.**

Sierra Los Organos

Twelve km (7.4 miles) northwest of Sombrerete via Mexico 45, then five km (three miles) northeast by dirt road, Los Organos consists of 25 square km of monolithic igneous rock formations named for their resemblance to organ pipes. John Wayne used the sierra as a backdrop in some of his films; in return for the cooperation of villagers in nearby San Francisco de los Organos, Wayne donated a picnic site with grills and tables near the formations. The labyrinthine valleys and canyons carved by erosion between the formations would be interesting to explore, while the rocks themselves must be one of the world's great undiscovered rock-climbing sites. There are plenty of flat places among the rocks suitable for camping, and enough texture for handholds to entertain even the most experienced gravity rebels. Paths through the curvy terrain would also make good mountain biking. Nearby are the friendly nearby villages of Dorotea Arango and Agua Zarca.

BOB RACE

THE STATE OF SAN LUIS POTOSÍ

San Luis Potosí hovers over the hazy cultural and geographic border between Northern and Southern Mexico. Encompassing full measures of the dry, windswept plains of the Altiplano, the mist-encircled mountains of the Sierra Madre Oriental, and the moist, tropical valleys of the Región Huasteca (most of the state lies below the Tropic of Cancer), the state comes close to providing a microcosm of everything—except beaches—that Mexico has to offer: modest pre-Cortesian ruins, jungles, high desert, indigenous arts and culture, an exceptionally varied cuisine, colonial architecture, and a genuine hospitality that comes from having been virtually ignored by mainstream tourists.

The state has also been largely isolated from the rest of Mexico. Despite heavy Spanish activity along the Gulf of Mexico coast, a road to the state capital from Tampico was only completed in 1854, followed by a railroad spur from Mexico City in 1890. After that, virtually no major transportation improvements were made before Mexico 57 (from Piedras Negras) was inaugurated in 1930.

Today the state provides a sometimes startling contrast between modern (the capital) and traditional (the rest of the state). Even the highway into the capital from the airport is paralleled by cart tracks. On a per capita basis, the state has the third lowest number of households with electricity in the country (after Oaxaca and Chiapas). About 12% of the population is Amerindian, mostly Pames, Huastecs, and Nahuatls, who for the most part are concentrated in the Región Huasteca.

Mountainous and landlocked, but centrally located, the state serves as an important transportation hub for rail and road connections between North and South. Mining—principally for silver, gold, copper, lead, zinc, antimony, arsenic, and quicksilver—is still a significant source of local income, along with petroleum from the Ebano and Limón oilfields. Other key industries include beer, furniture, textile, flour, and leather production.

SAN LUIS POTOSÍ (CITY)

One of the most pleasant state capitals in Mexico, the 400-year-old city of San Luis Potosí offers a moderate year-round climate, plenty of historic architecture, and a spate of great restaurants. Few foreigners seem to know that San Luis is an excellent choice for those looking to explore urban Mexico—both modern and historic—at its best; the historical district is small enough to cover on foot and most of it is conveniently closed to vehicular traffic, making it even easier for pedestrians to get around.

Nicknamed "The City of Gardens," San Luis has at least one *jardín* or garden plaza in each of its seven original districts *(los siete barrios).* Although most famous for its outstanding examples of neo-Hispanic baroque churches, the city's architecture is predominantly neoclassical and republican, much like that of older Mexico City districts. According to the 1995 national census, the city's current population is estimated to be around 550,000. In the political arena, San Luis Potosí has been a key stronghold for PAN opposition to Mexico City rule.

HISTORY

Before the Spanish *entrada,* the present city site in the Valle de San Luis was thought to have been an Amerindian settlement called Tangamanga, inhabited by the seminomadic Guachichiles (an Aztec name meaning "red-painted," describing the way the Guachichiles—possibly related to the Huastecs—painted their hair red). Franciscan missionaries under Fray Diego de la Magdalena passed through in the mid-1500s and established a small Guachichil pueblo in 1583. The community was supplemented by the 1590 import of Tlaxcalteca set-

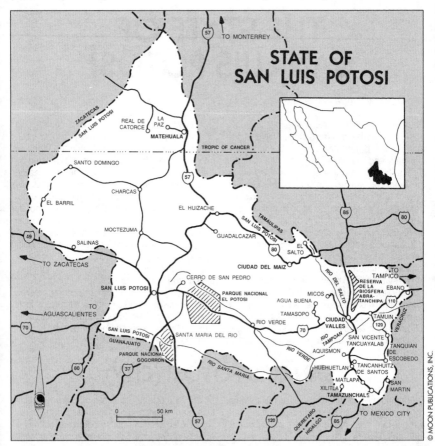

© MOON PUBLICATIONS, INC.

tlers—a pattern followed throughout Northern Mexico in which the cooperative Tlaxcaltecas served as model *indígenas* for less docile Amerindian groups.

The pueblo might have faded into obscurity if a large silver vein hadn't been discovered at nearby Cerro de San Pedro in 1592. More Spanish immediately moved in and expanded the town, designing the basic city plan as seen in downtown San Luis Potosí today. The city took the grand title Real San Luis Minas de Potosí; "San Luis" in honor of then-Viceroy of Mexico Luis de Velasco, "Minas de Potosí" for a rich mine in Bolivia. The vein failed to produce as prodigiously as its Bolivian namesake, but ranching and trade filled the gap and prosperous San Luis received official *ciudad* status in 1656. By the 18th century, the city had been declared a regional capital for northeastern Nueva España, with jurisdiction over Coahuila, Nuevo León, Tamaulipas, Louisiana, and Texas. During this era, when San Luis was considered the third most important city in Mexico, many of the city's historic baroque churches were built.

Immediately following independence from Spain in 1824, the city was named capital of the new state of San Luis Potosí. Under Mexican president Benito Juárez, it also twice served as the provisional capital of Mexico—once in 1863 as Juárez was fleeing French forces in Mexico City, and again in 1867 when Juárez returned to San Luis to sign an execution order for Emperor Maximilian.

Under Porfirio Díaz, San Luis Potosí was linked to the national railway network and became the richest city in Northern Mexico. Liberals opposed to the Díaz regime held a seminal meeting here in 1901, and in 1910 revolutionary Francisco I. Madero devised his Plan de San Luis while incarcerated in San Luis's municipal prison. Upon his release from jail, Madero headed to San Antonio, Texas, where his revolutionary plan was unveiled. The plan announced that Díaz had been illegally elected and proclaimed Madero the rightful president of the republic, thus sparking the 1910-20 Mexican Revolution.

In the late 1930s, San Luis was a capitalist island in socialist Mexico, and the only state not to enforce the antireligion laws set in motion by Calles and continued by Cárdenas. During this period the state was more or less ruled by a rebel general of Indian descent named Saturnino Cedillo, who waged guerrilla warfare against the federal government from the hills surrounding the capital. Cedillo wasn't himself a practicing Catholic, but he once said, "Perhaps I do not believe in all this religion myself, but the poor people want it, and I am going to see that they get what they want." As a result, the Calles-Cárdenas years didn't break the city's economy quite as much as it did that of many other state capitals in Mexico, and when the more moderate policies of later administrations were put into effect San Luis was in a good position to begin benefitting almost immediately.

Although San Luis Potosí's stature as an economic powerhouse has been somewhat eclipsed by the rise of Monterrey in Nuevo León to the north, perhaps the city's major achievement has been its capacity to modernize while maintaining a strong sense of culture and tradition.

CLIMATE

Just about any time of year is good for a visit to San Luis Potosí. At 1,880 meters (6,170 feet) above sea level, the city has been compared to Jerusalem or Athens for its typically clear, blue skies. Average annual precipitation is just 36 cm (14 inches), with most rain falling between May and October.

The average monthly temperature from hottest to coolest months varies by less than eight degrees Celsius (15 degrees Fahrenheit), from 20.6° C (69° F) in April to 12.8° C (55° F) in January. The occasional northern wind sends temperatures toward freezing for a few days here and there in December and January, though minimum temperatures seldom drop below 2.4° C (36° F). April and May—before the rains start—are the warmest months, but temperatures rarely exceed 29° C (85° F).

SIGHTS

Although colonial-era architecture can be seen in several quarters throughout the city, San Luis Potosí's main **historical district** is concentrated in the center of the city, in an area bounded by Calle Independencia to the west, Av. Obregón to the north, Av. Constitución to the east, and Calle Abasolo to the south. Several of the streets in this district have been closed to vehicular traffic, making it an especially pleasant and safe area to explore on foot. For peoplewatching, the best time is early evening when antique street lamps are lit (electrically) and the plazas and narrow streets are full of Potosinos out for an evening stroll.

Plazas, Parks, and *Jardines*

San Luis Potosí is blessed with a large number of plazas, many of which are called *jardines* (gardens) because they are so heavily planted. Because of the city's benevolent climate, they are all well visited and are excellent places to observe Mexican public life.

Jardín Hidalgo (Plaza de Armas), the city's premier plaza, is in the center of the historical district at Calles Los Bravo, Zaragoza, Madero/M.J. Othón, and 5 de Mayo. A large *kiosco* in the center hosts live musical performances on weekends and holidays. The plaza is flanked on the east by the Catedral Santa Iglesia (see "Churches," below) and by the republican-style **Palacio Municipal,** which was built in 1838 and once served as a bishop's residence. The Salón de Cabildos, on the second floor, is decorated with mytho-religious paintings by Italian artist Erulo Eroli.

SEVEN GARDENS FOR SEVEN BARRIOS

Each of the seven traditional neighborhoods in San Luis Potosí has its own *jardín* or garden plaza around which the local festival life revolves.

Jardín de Tequisquiapan: Av. V. Carranza

Jardín de Santiago: Av. de la Paz

Jardín de San Miguelito: Vallejo amd Gral. Fuero

Jardín de Tlaxcala: Cición and Eje. Vial

Jardín de San Sebastián: Av. Constitución and Sevilla

Jardín de San Juan de Guadalupe: Calle S.J. de Dios Peza

Jardín del Montecillo: Azteca and M.J. Othón

The **Casa de la Virreina,** built in 1736 but extensively remodeled in the 19th century, faces the north side of the plaza. Originally this building must have been done in the neo-Hispanic baroque style but it is now thoroughly neoclassic/republican. Once the residence of Doña Francisca de la Gándara, Mexico's only *virreina* (or vicereine, the female equivalent to viceroy), it is now occupied on the ground floor by a popular cafe.

On the west side of Jardín Hidalgo stands the imposing, full-block-square **Palacio de Gobierno,** which was constructed in the neoclassic style between 1798 and 1816 to serve as the seat of government for all of northeastern Mexico (it now serves as the state capitol). In the Sala Juárez on the second floor are wax figures of President Juárez refusing Princess Salm Salm's request for a stay of execution for deposed Emperor Maximilian.

The **Plaza de los Fundadores** ("Founders Plaza") at Obregón, D. Carmona, V. Carranza, and Aldama, commemorates the spot where the original city was established. It is flanked by the Capilla de Loreto (see "Churches," below) and several other historic buildings but is otherwise lacking in character or ambience. This is a favorite venue for local political demonstrations.

Fronting the Templo de San Francisco between Calles Guerrero, Galeana, and Vallejo is the **Plaza de San Francisco,** a long, narrow, and shady plaza that's a favorite with benchsitters. Largest of all the central downtown plazas is the **Alameda Juan Sarabia,** a large rectangular park between Av. Universidad and Calle M.J. Othón that has the same dimensions as Mexico City's Alameda. Criss-crossed with diagonal paths, it's a popular jogging venue.

The patriarch of parks in San Luis Potosí is **Parque Tangamanga,** a 411-hectare (1,015-acre) section of greenery southwest of the city center, off Diagonal Sur and Av. Tatanacho. Its wooded grounds feature walking paths, benches, playgrounds, small-scale carnival-style rides, a 4,000-seat amphitheater, two lakes, a planetarium, a convention center, two museums, and various athletic courts. On weekends and holidays food vendors set up along some of the paths. The park proved so popular that a Parque Tangamanga II was built on the north side of the city, off Mexico 49.

JOE CUMMINGS

Templo del Carmen

Churches

Just as each of the city's seven traditional *barrios* is associated with a garden plaza of its own, each has its own major church as well. The impressive variety of styles can be attributed to the fact that, as a regional capital for northern expansion in the 17th-19th centuries, the city hosted almost every conceivable Christian sect—including Augustines, Carmelites, Johnists, and Jesuits—each of which built its own churches and convents. Only Mexico City and Guadalajara compare.

Catedral Santa Iglesia: Most often known simply as *la catedral,* this most important of churches stands on the east side of Jardín Hidalgo. Constructed as a *parroquía* between 1670 and 1730, the cathedral's most outstanding feature is its neo-Hispanic baroque facade, which features four Carrera-marble apostles (replicas of Roman originals) along with Solomonic columns and twin bell towers.

Around the time that cathedral status was bestowed on the church (1866), the interior was entirely redone in a blend of Byzantine and neoclassical styles. Italian artisans carved the wooden *coro* and the San Sebastian statue, which, like the apostle sculptures on the facade, is a replica of Bernini's original at the Basilica of St. John Lateran in Rome. Original vice-regal paintings hang on the walls. In recognition of its historical value, the cathedral was declared a National Monument in 1935.

Templo del Carmen: This church at Av. Constitución and Calle M.J. Othón was begun in 1749 and consecrated in 1764 by the Carmelites, an ascetic monastic sect most known for their vow not to wear shoes. An atrium, designed to accommodate large numbers of Amerindian worshipers in the open air, once extended from the facade into present-day Plaza del Carmen. The single tower, forbidden in Carmelite churches, was built with the palms-up complicity of local clerical authorities. Most impressive is the central portion of the facade, which represents *churrigueresco* detail rivaled in the north only by the cathedral in Zacatecas. A side entrance, dedicated to San José (St. Joseph), employs the shell motif common to late baroque.

As in the Catedral Santa Iglesia, gilded altars inside are done in neoclassical style. The *altar mayor* or main altar was designed by Francisco Eduardo Tresguerras (1759-1833), an architect, painter, sculptor, poet, and musician who was the most influential Mexican artist of his era. Paintings in the sacristy include works by Francisco Antonio Vallejo (1713-56).

Templo de San Francisco: Facing leafy Plaza de San Francisco, this 1680s-vintage church dedicated to St. Francis has a simple baroque facade and asymmetric towers built of pink sandstone. Inside, the sacristy is considered one of the best surviving examples of interior baroque architecture in San Luis Potosí. Several examples of 18th-century art, including paintings by renowned artists Miguel Cabrera and Antonio de Torres, are on display in the sacristy. A ship-inspired crystal chandelier hanging from the dome above the nave was a donation from a parishioner who survived a shipwreck. The rest of the interior, as in most baroque churches in the city, was remodeled in the neoclassic style during the Reform. The original convent and cloister—which once extended into Calle Galeana—also fell victim to the Reform.

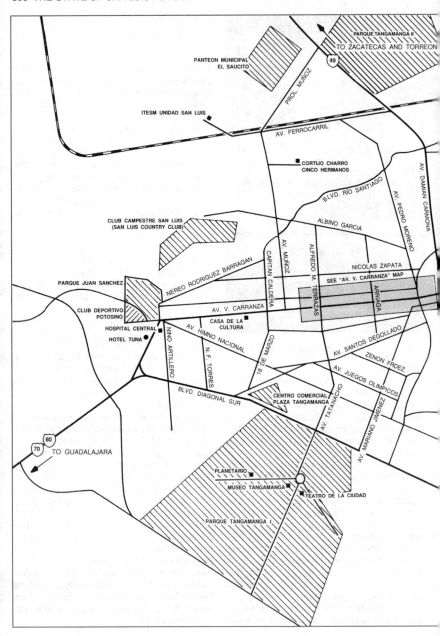

80
57
TO AIRPORT, MOTEL EL MESQUITE,
PARADOR TURISTICO EL POTOSI,
MATEHUALA, AND SALTILLO

AV. 20 DE NOVIEMBRE

BLVD. RIO SANTIAGO

AV. LA PAZ

V. LA PAZ

EJE VIAL

AV. MEXICO

MERCADO 16 DE SEPTIEMBRE

MERCADO REPUBLICA

SAN LUIS POTOSI (CITY)

MERCADO HIDALGO

E "HISTORICAL DISTRICT WNTOWN)" MAP

RAILWAY STATION

MANUEL JOSÉ OTHON

70

ALAMEDA

CENTRO TAURINO POTOSINO

AV. UNIVERSIDAD

GLORIETA JUAREZ

TO CD. VALLES AND TAMPICO

PLAZA DE TOROS FERMIN RIVERA

VILLA DEPORTIVA JUVENIL (HOSTEL)

HOTEL CENTRAL

HOWARD JOHNSON PLAZA

CAJA DEL AGUA

HOTEL ARIZONA

CENTRAL CAMIONERA

HOTEL MARIA DOLORES

HOTEL REAL D'MINAS

TEMPLO DE SAN SEBASTIAN

MOTEL SANDS

MOTEL LA POSADA

AV. JUAREZ

CONSTITUCION

5 DE MAYO

RANCHO DEL CHARRO

SANTUARIO DE GUADALUPE

TEMPLO DE SAN JUAN DE GUADALUPE

HOLIDAY INN

57

BLVD. DIAGONAL SUR

TO SANTA MARIA DEL RIO,
CENTRO VACACIONAL GOGORRON,
QUERETARO, AND MEXICO CITY

0   1 km

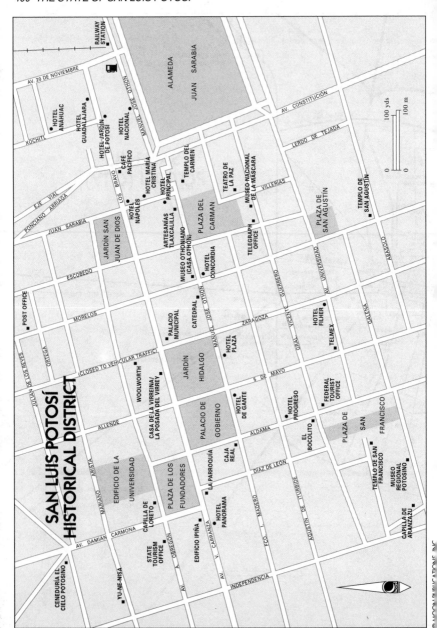

SAN LUIS POTOSÍ
HISTORICAL DISTRICT

Capilla de Loreto: Built in 1700 by the Jesuits, this chapel next to the Edificio de la Universidad on the northwest end of Plaza de los Fundadores (Av. Obregón and Av. D. Carmona) contains one of the few surviving Jesuit *retablos* (altar pieces) in Mexico (most were destroyed following Jesuit expulsion from the New World in 1767). Though simple (only two Solomonic columns, one tower), the facade is considered the best of all those executed by the Jesuits in Mexico.

Behind the Capilla de Loreto is another Jesuit chapel, Capilla del Sagraria, which dates to 1675 but is of less architectural interest. A large stone cross between the two chapels commemorates the founding of the city.

Templo de San Agustín: The Augustines established themselves at the current city site in 1599 and built a convent and church on this spot in 1615. The current church, near the intersection of Calles Morelos and Abasolo, was erected in the mid-18th century; the Churrigueresque tower is the exterior's most striking feature. Inside, the main altar dates to the same period but is neoclassical in style. Older, baroque religious paintings hang in the sacristy.

Templo de San Sebastian: Originally founded by the Augustines in 1603, the current church was rebuilt between 1708-75. The baroque facade features Solomonic columns between two simple, asymmetric towers. The pink limestone arches and pilasters in the interior were installed earlier this century.

Santuario de Nuestra Señora de Guadalupe: South of the main historical district on Av. Juárez, Colonia Guadalupe, the city's principal Guadalupana church was consecrated in 1772 on a spot where Spanish captain Francisco de Castro y Mampaso had built a small Virgen de Guadalupe shrine in 1656. During the French era, troops occupied the church and the image of the Virgen de Guadalupe was taken to the cathedral for safekeeping. The much-revered image was destroyed in a fire and replaced by a new image in 1838 (though many locals maintain the original is still kept in the sacristy), and it wasn't until 1871 that the church itself was restored. The sanctuary's twin towers are the tallest in San Luis Potosí and are thus visible from almost anywhere in the city. The facade exhibits an interesting mix of baroque and neoclassical elements.

Other Historic Architecture

Most of the older buildings in downtown San Luis Potosí date to the late-18th and 19th centuries and represent the neoclassical and republican styles. The earlier neoclassical commercial or governmental architecture typically features two stories of arch-topped windows with iron-grille balconies on elaborately carved pedestals. Windows on both floors are flanked by prominent, rounded columns. The next stage in Potosino architecture (mid-19th century) retained the second-floor window pedestals and grillwork but flattened the tops of the windows.

By the end of the 19th and beginning of the 20th centuries, all curves—including window pedestals and columns—were replaced by rectangles in the "republican" style. Facing the west side of Plaza de los Fundadores, the **Edificio Ipiña** represents the late neoclassic/early republican style, with arched *portales* along the ground floor and rectangular windows on the second.

One of the only secular baroque-style buildings in the city is the **Caja Real** (also rendered "Real Caja"), on the corner of Calles Madero and Aldama in the heart of the historic district. Built in the late 18th century as the treasury for the Spanish Crown's *quinto* (the fifth of all mining profits owed to the Crown), it features a truncated corner entrance with massive carved wooden doors, Potosino-style window pedestals, and an interior patio with fountain. The large doorway and spacious interior were designed to allow mules or other pack animals to enter with their cargo of ore. Caja Real is used today as an adjunct building for the Universidad Autónoma de San Luis Potosí.

The unique **Caja del Agua** ("Water Case"), whose rotund, cone-tipped profile appears on official stationery as the symbol of San Luis Potosí's state government, sits in a small park at the northern end of Av. Juárez (at Calle Miguel Barragán), six blocks south of Calle Galeana in the historic district. Originally erected in 1832, the elaborate structure served as a container for water piped in from the Cañada del Lobo via an aqueduct. The huge "lid" is made of glass tiles and topped by a sculpted pinecone. When the reservoir was functional, Potosinos drew water from the eight ornate ducts around the Caja's lower circumference.

The late 19th-century **Teatro de la Paz,** beside the Templo del Carmen and opposite the Museo de la Máscara, features a classical Greek facade (complete with columns and a peaked roof) and wall mosaics by artist Fernando Leal. Modeled after the Paris Opera, the U-shaped interior holds 1,450 seats. The attached Sala German Gedovious contains rotating visual art exhibits.

Museo Regional Potosino
Established in 1952 in a 16th-century former Franciscan convent, this regional museum contains a good collection of pieces outlining the state's archaeology, anthropology, and history. One of the museum's better exhibits features ceramics from the Zapotec, Mixtec, Huastec, Totonac, and Mexica cultures. The Huastecs, like the Olmecs and Mayas, practiced cranial deformation, binding the skull so that it projected upwards; two such skulls are displayed.

In the room dedicated to the Huastec culture, the most intriguing item is the 1.5-meter tall "El Adolescente," found at El Consuelo (Tamuín). Dated to the Huastec postclassic era (A.D. 900-1500), the figure is carved in sandstone with a network of glyphs engraved on the shoulders, wrists, right lower torso, and right leg. One of the shoulder glyphs represents Quetzalcóatl, the sacred plumed serpent. Another figure on display stands around 1.75 meters and features a two-sided design representing a shaman or priest on one side and a skeleton on other. The piece is unlabeled, but perhaps illustrates the shaman's ritual control of life and death. The figure here is an excellent replica of the original, which stands in the Museo de Antropología in Mexico City.

Other rooms contain viceregal artifacts, the most impressive of which can be found upstairs in the attached **Capilla de Aranzazu.** Constructed in the mid-18th century as a private Franciscan chapel, the chapel is dedicated to the Virgin of Aranzazu. The latter word is reportedly Basque for "among thorns"; according to legend, a priest found a figure of the virgin among *zazus* or thorns. The chapel architecture is typical late baroque on a small scale; particularly notable is the plasterwork along the inside of the cupola. Religious paintings from the 18th and 19th centuries adorn the walls.

The museum is at Calle Galeana 450, around the corner from the Templo de San Francisco. It's open Tues.-Fri. 10 a.m.-1 p.m. and 3-8 p.m., Saturday 10 a.m.-noon, and Sunday 10 a.m.-1 p.m. Admission is free.

**Museo Nacional de la Máscara
(National Museum of Masks)**
Housed in a beautiful, neoclassical 19th-century building with late baroque undertones, this museum is devoted to the history, description, and display of Mexican masks. Though not as well labeled as its counterpart in Zacatecas, the collection here is quite good and represents virtually all aspects of mask typology. Classrooms in the building are also used to teach maskmaking and other arts.

The museum is at Calle Villerías 2 (on the opposite side of the same building that contains the main post office). Open Tues.-Fri. 10 a.m.-2 p.m. and 4-6 p.m., Sat.-Sun. 10 a.m.-2 p.m. Free admission.

Museo Othoniano (Casa Othón)
One of Mexico's foremost poets and dramatists, Manuel José Othón (1858-1906) was born and schooled in San Luis Potosí. His literary work is today considered among the best ever to have appeared in the Spanish language. *Norteños* consider Othón one of their own since he spent most of his life living and working in San Luis Potosí, Tamaulipas, Coahuila, Durango, and Nuevo León.

Othón's birth house at Calle M.J. Othón 225 (two blocks east of the Jardín Hidalgo) has been made into a museum containing a simple collection of furnishings, letters, and mementos of the Othón family. Occasional readings, lectures, and literary events are held in the house. The house is open to the public Mon.-Fri. 10 a.m.-2 p.m. and 4-6 p.m. Free admission.

Centro Taurino Potosino
Known in English as the Bullfighting Center of San Luis Potosí, the Centro Taurino is housed in a two-story, whitewashed building adjacent to the Plaza de Toros Fermín Rivera at the corner of Av. Universidad and Calle Triano. San Luis Potosí is one of Mexico's premier *fiesta brava* venues, and a small museum inside the Centro Taurino contains one of the most complete

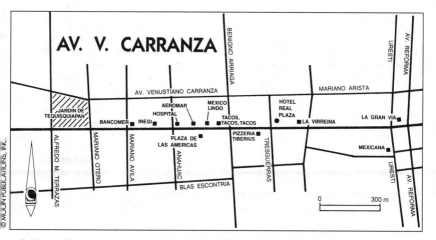

collections of *tauromaquía* memorabilia in the country, including *banderillas, trajes de luces, capotes,* famous bulls' heads, poster art, and historical photographs. The museum has posted hours of Tues.-Sat. 11 a.m.-1:30 p.m. and 5:30-7:30 p.m., but in reality it only seems to be open on bullfight days and during the annual Feria Taurino in November.

The adjacent **Plaza de España** displays bronze sculptures of famous matadors, including one of Manolete donated by a Spanish sculptor. The most prominent space in the plaza, however, is given to a figure of hometown hero Fermín Rivera. The fountain in the middle is a replica of Seville's Fuente de los Fardes.

Casa de la Cultura

Built as a republican-style mansion at the beginning of this century, the large, two-story *casa* is situated on spacious, landscaped grounds away from *el centro*. A setting for a variety of cultural events held throughout the year, the building also contains a number of exhibit rooms with permanent displays of regional art and archaeological discoveries. Highlights include the Huastec exhibit on the ground floor and the Potosino handicrafts exhibit (including rebozos and *cajas de rebozos*) on the second floor. The galleries are open Tues.-Fri. 10 a.m.-2 p.m. and 4-6 p.m., Saturday 10 a.m.-2 p.m. and 6-9 p.m., Sunday 10 a.m.-2 p.m.; there is a small admission fee.

Museo Regional de Arte Popular and Casa de Artesanías

These two museums are housed in joined quarters in the Parque Tangamanga (see "Plazas, Parks, and *Jardines,*" above). The exhibits include regional ceramics, rebozos and *chales* (handwoven shawls), woodcarvings, textiles, and other handicrafts from the state of San Luis Potosí and beyond. Open Tues.-Fri. 10 a.m.-2 p.m. and 4-6 p.m., Sat.-Sun. 10 a.m.-2:30 p.m.; admission free.

Cerro de San Pedro

Eight km (five miles) east of the city via Mexico 70, then 19 km (12 miles) north, this large hill was the source of the area's original wealth—silver. A virtual ghost town was left behind when various mining companies, including the American Smelting and Refining Co., abandoned the mines earlier this century. A couple of small chapels of some historic interest can be seen.

ACCOMMODATIONS

Shoestring

The **Villa Deportiva Juvenil,** tel. (48) 18-1617, in the CREA complex just southwest of Glorieta Juárez on Diagonal Sur, has 72 beds (US$2 per night) with lockers, plus a *cafetería*. It's conveniently located within walking distance of the Central de Autobuses and is a short bus or taxi ride (about two km) from the railway station via

Av. Universidad. Reservations are taken up to 15 days in advance.

Across the narrow Jardín Escontria from the Hotel Guadalajara is the grungy but adequate **Hotel Jardín de Potosí,** on Calle Los Bravo, tel. (48) 12-3152. Rates: US$8 s, US$8.60 d, US$10 t, US$11.30 q. A block farther south, **Hotel Nacional,** Calle M.J. Othón 425, tel. (48) 12-2550, has rock-bottom rooms with *baño colectivo.* Rates: US$5. Also in this area are the similarly priced **Hotel La Terminal,** tel. (48) 12-2142, and **Hotel María Elena,** both within walking distance of the railway station and historical district.

Best of the *clase económica* hotels in the vicinity of the railway station is the clean **Hotel Guadalajara,** Calle Jiménez 245, tel. (48) 12-4612, only a couple hundred meters from the station. Rooms have private baths. Rates:US$13 s/d. Around the corner, the friendly and efficient **Hotel Anáhuac,** Calle Xochitl 140, tel. (48) 12-6505, fax (48) 14-4904, offers clean rooms; small extra charge for TV or parking. Rates: US$9 s, US$10.40 d.

In the historical district downtown are several inexpensive hotels in quaint 19th-century buildings. In addition to providing atmosphere coupled with low prices, these locations allow budget-conscious visitors to explore the city's museums and architecture on foot, thus saving money on buses and taxis. **Hotel Progreso,** Calle Aldama 415 (diagonally opposite the Plaza de San Francisco), tel. (48) 12-0367, is among the least expensive and is housed in a handsome building; rooms have high ceilings, balconies, and wood floors. Rates: US$12 s, US$15 d. **Hotel Principal,** Calle J. Sarabia 145 (just north of the Templo del Carmen), tel. (48) 12-0784, is neither handsome nor historic, but spartan and adequate. Rates: US$10-12.

Facing the south side of Jardín Hidalgo, **Hotel Plaza,** tel. (48) 12-4631, is a two-star bargain with simple, uninspiring rooms around a courtyard. Rates: US$10.50 s.

Budget

The 48-room **Hotel Filher,** Av. Universidad at Zaragoza, tel. (48) 12-1562, has a historic facade and fairly well-kept if small rooms. A restaurant is attached and overnight parking may be arranged. Rates: US$16 s, US$19 d, US$21 t. The public areas of historic **Hotel de Gante,** Calle 5 de Mayo 140 (a block south of the Jardín Hidalgo), tel. (48) 12-1492, are furnished with kitschy 1950s' moderne; corner rooms are really big. No parking. Rates: US$15 s, US$17 d.

In the historical district at Calles Morelos and M.J. Othón, the quaint **Hotel Concordia,** tel.(48) 12-0666, offers 96 modern rooms with TV in a historic building that was probably designed to have fewer rooms. Downstairs is a cozy bar-restaurant decorated with art prints; free parking is available in a garage across the street. Rates: US$21 s, US$23.60 d.

The more modern, six-story **Hotel Nápoles,** Calle J. Sarabia 120 (near the fabulous Café Pacífico), tel. (48) 12-8419, costs about the same as the Concordia and features a restaurant, bar, car rental, and parking (US$1.30 a day). Just south of the Nápoles, the similarly modern, 11-story **Hotel María Cristina,** Calle J. Sarabia 110, tel. (48) 12-9408, has rooms with a/c; hotel facilities include a pool, parking, and rooftop restaurant. Rates: in the US$20-30 range.

The efficient, 10-story **Hotel Panorama,** Av. Carranza 315, tel. (48) 12-1777, fax (48) 2-4591, Mexico toll-free tel. (800) 4-8001, is one of the easier downtown places to reach by car from the north since it's near the end of the wide, two-way Av. D. Carmona. Spacious rooms come with a/c, carpeting, satellite TV, and mini-bar; rooms on the upper floors have good views of

Huastec effigy vase

the city skyline. Facilities include a parking lot, travel agency, car rental, coffee shop, restaurant, and pool. Rates: US$33 d.

West of the historical district, in the city's small *zona rosa* at Av. V. Carranza 890 (at Calle Tresguerras), the supermodern, 14-story **Hotel Real Plaza**, tel. (48) 14-6055, fax (48) 14-6639, has spacious rooms with a/c, satellite TV, and heavily tinted windows. Amenities are similar to those at the Hotel Panorama. Parking is available in the basement. Rates: US$35 d.

Several hotels and motels are strung out along Mexico 57 near the huge, multilayered traffic circle known as Glorieta Juárez, at the east edge of the city. This area would be a good choice for motorists on their way to Santa María del Río, Querétaro, or Mexico City. On the other hand, there's absolutely nothing of interest within walking distance of the area (except for auto dealerships), so this is a bad choice if you've come to see the city.

Least expensive is the imitation colonial-style **Motel Sands**, a kilometer southeast of the circle, tel. (48) 18-2533. Rooms have phones, TV, and private bath (but no a/c). Rates: US$21 s, US$25 d. Similar in price and conditions are two places closer to the Glorieta and bus terminal on Av. Torres: **Hotel Arizona**, Torres 158, tel. (48) 18-1848, and **Hotel Central**, Torres 290, tel. (48) 22-1444. The Arizona is the nicer of the two.

Just a bit farther southeast on the highway, **Motel La Posada**, tel. (48) 18-2088, has similar rooms at similar prices but caters to truckers. Facilities include a 24-hour restaurant and pool.

At Km 13 on Mexico 57, at the northeastern edge of town on the way to/from the airport, Matehuala, and Saltillo, **Motel El Mesquite**, tel. (48) 31-1972, has fair rooms plus a restaurant, pool, and trailer park. Rates: US$20-24.

At the south end of town on the loop that links Mexico 80 South and Mexico 57 South, **Motel Colonial**, Diagonal Sur 340, tel. (48) 15-2206, offers three-star rooms in the US$22-30 range.

Inexpensive

About a kilometer south of the Glorieta Juárez, **Hotel Real d'Minas**, tel. (48) 18-2616, fax (48) 18-6915, has rooms with all the amenities. Rates: US$35-50. On the east side of the highway closer to Glorieta Juárez is the newly renovated **Howard Johnson Plaza**, tel. (48) 22-1995, fax

(48) 22-0550, formerly the Cactus Hotel, where rooms have a/c, satellite TV (with video), and phones. A trailer park is also on the premises. Rates: US$44 s/d.

Inexpensive/Moderate

At the extreme west end of the city, between the Glorieta González Bocanegra (near the university) and the highway to Aguascalientes and Guadalajara, is the older but popular **Hotel Tuna Best Western**, Calle Dr. M. Nava 200, tel. (48) 13-1260, fax (48) 11-1415, eight km from downtown. Rooms have satellite TV and ceiling fans; a few come with kitchenettes. Other facilities include a pool and parking lot. Rates: US$45-55 s, US$50-60 d, US$60-70 t.

Moderate

Most of the city's upper-end hotels are clustered south of the Glorieta. The **Hotel María Dolores**, tel. (48) 12-5116, fax (48) 22-0602, Mexico toll-free tel. (800) 4-8016, has 213 rooms with all the modern amenities, plus 16 master suites with jacuzzis. On the premises are two swimming pools, a restaurant, coffee shop, bar, nightclub, and disco. Rates: from US$55.

Five km southeast of the circle (Km 420) is the top-rank **Holiday Inn**, tel. (48) 18-1312, fax (48) 18-6105, formerly Hostal del Quijote, where nicely furnished rooms have a/c, satellite TV, video, phones, and refrigerators. On the well-landscaped grounds are a heated pool, lighted tennis court, restaurant, coffee shop, and secure parking area. Rack rates: US$60-75.

Expensive

The city has a new *gran turismo* hotel, the **Westin San Luis Potosí Hotel**, Real de Lomas 1000 (off Mexico 80 South at the southwestern edge of the city), tel. (48) 25-0125, U.S./Canada tel. (800) 228-3000. Very well-appointed rooms, spacious public areas, a pool, fitness center, and a long list of other amenities make this a top choice among visiting business executives. Rack rates: from US$85.

RV Parks

Motel El Mesquite (see "Budget," above) offers 200 RV spaces with full hookups for US$10 a night. Eighty spaces at the **Howard Johnson Plaza** (see "Inexpensive," above) come with electrical/water hookups only and cost US$12-13, hence they're usually empty.

FOOD

If one of your objectives in visiting Mexico is to sample authentic regional cuisines, you could hardly find a better place than San Luis Potosí's state capital. Potosinas are extremely proud of their local cooking, whether waxing eloquent over the roast corn or fresh *papitas* (potato chips) sold at every other street corner in pedestrian areas, or praising an elaborate dish of *fiambre potosino* (chicken, beef tongue, and pig's feet, marinated in vinaigrette and served cold on a platter of vegetables).

Typical *cocina potosina* is delicately spiced and features lots of vegetables. The state's most famous dish is *enchiladas potosinas*, in which the tortilla *masa* is mixed with *chile colorado* to form small, delicate, reddish tortillas which are then folded over a ricotta-like cheese with a strip of chile or *salsa jitomate* (chile-tomato sauce) and garnished with chopped onion. In another popular dish, *tacos Camila* (named for the famous *fritanguera* or "fryer" who popularized it), corn tortillas are rolled in tomato sauce, stuffed with cheese, then lightly fried and served under a mound of lettuce, cooked potatoes, carrots, green beans, and crumbled cheese. You may also see *tacos potosinos,* which are similar to *tacos Camila*—small corn tortillas rolled into loose, flattened tubes filled with the same ricotta-like cheese (or occasionally chicken), then lightly fried in a chile-tomato salsa and covered with cooked green beans, potatoes, and carrots, and sometimes a little *chorizo* and extra *queso fresco*.

Another typical Potosino dish is *asado de boda,* a "wedding stew" made with a *chile ancho* base in which bits of pork and various spices are simmered together and served with rice. It differs from the Zacatecan version in the richer spicing. *Nopalitos*—strips of prickly pear pads (spines removed) pickled with salt, onion, and garlic—make a tasty *ensalada potosina* when tossed with sliced tomato, oregano, cilantro, vinegar, and oil. The typical Potosino meal begins with a complimentary *botana* of pickled tripe (or pork entrails) and vegetables. Many Potosino dishes are served with a thin, red, heated table salsa.

The Altiplano's abundant cactus is also employed in *queso de tuna,* a very common sweet in which cardón fruit juice is boiled to a syrup, then heated directly over a fire to form a dense, caramel-like mass the color of *café con leche.* Once you acquire a taste, *queso de tuna* can be quite addictive (fortunately it's a very inexpensive habit). Yet another use for cactus is the equally addictive *colonche,* cardón fruit juice fermented until it produces its own alcohol.

The Huastec influence on the city has made tamales of all kinds very popular, especially in winter, when many restaurants serve them with hot *atole.*

Cocina Potosina
While in many cities it can be a struggle to find authentic regional cuisine, in San Luis Potosí you'll likely find more *potosina*-oriented restaurants than anything else.

El Bocolito, corner of Calles Guerrero and Aldama, opposite the Hotel Progreso downtown, is a small, student-run diner offerng cheap and filling regional specialties, including the namesake *bocolitos* (small round corn cakes made with local herbs and cheese, and served with black beans). Open Mon.-Sat. 11 a.m.-11 p.m.

Cenaduría El Cielo Potosino, Calle J. de los Reyes 400-A, tel. (48) 14-2428, is a casual and very inexpensive diner-style eatery downtown. It lacks any kind of atmosphere, but is often cited as the most "typical" of the city's *cocinas.* In addition to the Potosino *antojitos* described above, El Cielo specializes in savory *pozole* and *menudo.* Open 11 a.m.-midnight daily.

The 24-hour **Café Pacífico,** corner of Calle Los Bravo and Av. Constitución, next to Hotel Nápoles downtown, has a high ceiling supported by iron pillars and hung with ceiling fans. It's popular with people from nearly all social strata. The dining room is clean, service is fast and efficient, the food is good, and prices are low (most *antojitos* cost US$1.50-3). *Cocina huasteca con enchiladas* is a house specialty, along with *enchiladas potosinas, tacos potosinos, tacos Camila, atole, pozole, cabrito adobado,* and all manner of regional and national breakfasts (served anytime). Don't confuse the Café Pacífico with the Restaurant Mariscos Pacífico opposite.

Next to the Hotel Panorama, **La Parroquía,** Av. Carranza 303, tel. (48) 12-6681, is more upmarket than the Café Pacífico but just as popular. This 20-year veteran specializes in regional cooking along with a wide range of other Mexican cuisines. The *café con leche* is excellent, and can be ordered with fresh *pan dulce* in the morning (better order before 8:15 a.m. or so, when they usually sell out). Open daily 7 a.m.-midnight.

Other Regional and National
El Herradero, Mexico 57, Km 12, south of Motel La Posada, tel. (48) 18-5139, is a huge log cabin-style place featuring American cuts of beef, *cabrito,* and hearty *norteña* cuisine. Live music some nights. Open daily noon-midnight.

At **La Posada del Virrey,** on the north side of Jardín Hidalgo in the historic Casa de la Virreina, tel. (48) 12-7055, regular patrons linger long over coffee to discuss the issues of the day. The menu at this cafe/bar/restaurant is a Mexican/Potosino blend; the *botanas* section is very popular. Open daily 7:30 a.m.-midnight.

Restaurant La Silla, Km 402, Mexico 57 South (near the hotel-motel cluster), tel. (48) 18-5668, specializes in *norteña* cuisine, particularly *carnes al carbón.* Open daily noon-midnight.

Tacos, Tacos, Tacos, Carranza 1016A, is a small but very good and very clean taco shop next door to México Lindo. Open daily noon-midnight.

International
La Gran Vía, Av. V. Carranza 560, Zona Rosa, tel. (48) 12-2899, is a very elegant restaurant in a restored colonial (Maximilian-era) mansion with courtyard. It serves highly rated Spanish and international cuisine. Open daily 1 p.m.-1 a.m. (last order taken at 7:30 p.m.).

Restaurante La Virreina, Av. V. Carranza 830, tel. (48) 12-3750, is a bit farther west along the same avenue as La Gran Vía. This restaurant is also housed in a restored mansion and has a reputation as one of the city's better restaurants. The menu is mostly continental but includes a few regional dishes. Open Mon.-Sat. 1-11 p.m.

Vegetarian
El Manantial, Calle Bolivar at Madero, just west of downtown, tel. (48) 12-8099, is a combina-

tion natural foods shop and vegetarian food bar. You'll find yogurt, whole-grain breads, soy products, and so on. Open Mon.-Sat. 10 a.m.-7 p.m.

In the northwestern corner of downtown, **Yune-nisa,** Calle Arista at Independencia, tel. (48) 14-3631, is similar to El Manantial, with a small eating area inside a natural foods store. Open daily 9 a.m.-6 p.m.

Other
Pastelería La Noria, two doors west of the Hotel Panorama on Av. V. Carranza, is a large bakery well stocked with many kinds of *pan dulce* and *pasteles.* Open Mon.-Sat. 7 a.m.-6 p.m.

Woolworth, corner of Hidalgo and Obregón in the historical district, tel. (48) 12-8880, has good bargains in breakfasts, Mexican standards, soups, and *tortas.* Open daily 8 a.m.-9:30 p.m.

Fast-Food: Opposite the Hotel Real Plaza on Av. V. Carranza is a **Burger King.** Other burger and sandwich joints can be found along Av. V. Carranza west of Hotel Real Plaza. Branches of **Helados Tucky-Tucky,** an ice-cream chain, are all over town. San Luis Potosí has several good pizza/pasta places, including **Pizzería Nápoles,** Av. V. Carranza 775C, and **Pizzería Tiberius,** Cordillera del Sur 310.

RECREATION AND ENTERTAINMENT

Bullfights
Along with Mexico City and Aguascalientes, San Luis Potosí is one of Mexico's bullfighting capitals and hence is one of the best places in the country to view the *sombra y sol* spectacle. The main *corridas de toros* venue is the large and well-designed **Plaza de Toros Fermín Rivera** (named for a famous Potosino matador), on Av. Universidad approximately a kilometer east of the historical district (a kilometer west of Glorieta Juárez). Adjacent to the bullring in the Centro Taurino Potosino is an exhibit of historic artifacts connected with regional *tauromaquía* (see "Sights" earlier in this section for details). Tickets, ranging in cost from US$5 for general admission on the *sol* (sun) side to US$16 for reserved *sombra* (shade) or US$23 in a reserved box, can be purchased at the bullring ticket office or through the state tourist office on Av. V. Carranza.

The main bullfighting season runs May-Sept., although bullfights are also held in association with several of the city's larger festivals year-round. Most notable of these is **La Feria Taurino,** a festival devoted to bullfighting held the third week of November. During the festival, *lidias de toros* are held daily and the city fills with bullfight fans from all over Mexico and abroad.

Charreadas

Local *charro* associations practice and compete in three *charro* rings in or near the city. **Cortijo Charro Cinco Hermanos** is in the northwest section of the city, off Av. Muñoz between Blvd. Río Santiago and Av. Ferrocarril; while **Rancho del Charro** is off Av. Juárez near the Santuario de Guadalupe, south of downtown. The third ring, **Lienzo Charro La Pila,** is south of town a few kilometers on Mexico 57 (on the way to Santa María del Río). You can usually count on finding a *charreada* at one of these venues at least every other Sunday year-round. Ask at the tourist office for the latest schedule.

Discos and Bars

While the early part of the week is usually quiet, the city's discotheques fill up Thurs.-Sun., beginning around 11 p.m. The main dance clubs are: **Arusha,** Prol. Muñoz 105, tel. (48) 17-4230; **Coliseum,** on Mexico 57 south at Km 2; **Dulcinea,** Holiday Inn, Mexico 57 South, tel. (48) 18-1312; **Museum Discoteque,** Av. Carranza 763; and **Oasis,** Hotel María Dolores, Mexico 57 South, tel. (48) 12-5116.

Local bands play live *norteña* and Mexican pop at **Centro Nocturno El Jardín,** Calle Pedro Moreno 833, and **Bar Jaguar,** Hotel Panorama, Av. V. Carranza 315, tel. (48) 12-1777.

For a quiet drink, try the atmospheric **Bar Pinín** on Calle de A. Iturbide east of Calle Aldama in the historical district.

Cinemas

Along Av. V. Carranza are three movie houses, from east to west: **Cine Othón** (#140), **Cine Avenida Vistarama** (#790), and **Cine Las Americas** (#1055); the standard bill features a combination of Latin American and U.S. movies. First-run American movies are also frequently shown at the new **Multicinemas Tangamanga** in the Plaza Tangamanga mall.

SHOPPING

Market District

Callejón Hidalgo, a section of Calle Hidalgo, north of Calle Los Bravo in the historical district, has been transformed into a pedestrian walkway lined with middle-class and upscale shops selling watches, jewelry, shoes, and clothes. Almost every evening, especially on weekends, the *callejón* is packed with shoppers and window-shoppers. Once you pass Calle Guajardo, walking north, the fancy stores give way to vendors with more inexpensive, everyday wares. Smaller streets off Hidalgo are also jammed with sometimes interesting shops; **Abarrotes Uruapan,** at Calle Salazar 125 (a block east of Hidalgo opposite the post office), sells fresh-roasted, fresh-ground coffee.

Eventually Hidalgo leads to the **Mercado Hidalgo,** a traditional municipal market with clothes, fruits, and vegetables downstairs, *comedores* upstairs. Surrounding the market is an array of vendors, cobblers, and taco stands. The best time for a stroll through the market area is just after sunset, when downtown residents do their daily shopping. Opposite the south entrance of the market, on Calle M. Mier y Terán, are several shops that sell Potosino handicrafts. Among these, **La Estrella** has the best selection of *chales* and rebozos; a good-quality, everyday rebozo here costs US$35-50. This shop accepts major credit cards.

If you turn right on Av. Reforma north of Mercado Hidalgo, you'll come to Av. 16 de Septiembre, which leads farther north to **Mercado República** (Reforma and 16 de Septiembre) and **Mercado 16 de Septiembre** (16 de Septiembre and Serdán). Both are typical municipal markets.

Arts and Crafts

A good place for regional as well as national handicrafts is **Tlaxcalilla Artesanías,** at Plaza del Carmen 325 (opposite the Templo del Carmen) in the historical district. In business since 1973, Tlaxcalilla offers a broad range of curios, carpets, rebozos, Huastec musical instruments, and clothing.

México Lindo, Av. Carranza 1016, carries a tasteful selection of *artesanías mexicanas* from central and southern México. Two other shops along this same stretch of Av. Carranza, **El Camanche Antiguedades** and **La Casa de Artesano,** are in a similar vein.

Shopping Centers

For modern consumer goods, one of the best venues is the large **Plaza Tangamanga,** opposite the park of the same name (off Diagonal Sur). The mall has nearly 200 store sites (though not all have been leased yet), including a **Sears, Comercial Mexicana supermarket,** and **Sanborn's department store.** The latter has a small but high-quality arts and crafts department, plus a section with English-language books and magazines.

EVENTS

April: Semana Santa (the week before Easter) is celebrated with much style in San Luis Potosí. Good Friday is the climax of the week when an elaborate reenactment of the Passion of Christ is performed in the Barrio de San Juan de Guadalupe in the early morning. Later that same day, hooded celebrants walk through the downtown streets carrying important holy images from local churches in a silent, torchlit procession known as the Procesión del Silencio. Held annually since 1954, this procession is famous throughout Mexico and abroad for its solemn beauty.

Francisco Gonzales Bocanegra

May: The **Festival de Arte Primavera Potosina** runs for 10 days in the middle of the month and involves the whole city in a celebration of art and culture. Local, national, and international artists participate in symphony concerts, live theater, and folkloric and contemporary dance performances around the city. Expositions of visual arts, cinema, and handicrafts are also organized.

August: In the latter part of the month, the **Feria Nacional Potosina** (FENAP) is organized around a series of bullfights, *charreadas,* cockfights, and other sporting and cultural events. The highlight of the festival is the **Maraton Internacional Tangamanga** (International Tangamanga Marathon), which has been held yearly since 1983 and attracts athletes from all over Mexico as well as abroad. The 42-km (26-mile) footrace begins in Parque Tangamanga (with the first 10 km within the park itself) then circles through the streets and gardens of the Siete Barrios, ending near the starting point in Parque Tangamanga. Contact the tourist office (see "Information," below) for more information.

October: Performers from the Región Huasteca, along with music and dance scholars from around the country, gather for the **Festival de Música y Danza de la Huasteca** during the first half of the month.

December: In 1854 San Luis native Francisco González Bocanegra composed the Mexican national anthem, selected from a nationwide competition sponsored by the Santa Anna government. To encourage other local composers to follow Bocanegra's example, the **Homenaje a Compositores Potosinos,** held during the first half of December, celebrates Potosino composers and their compositions with a series of musical performances centered at the Teatro de la Paz.

INFORMATION AND SERVICES

Tourist Offices

The **Coordinación General de Turismo,** housed in an impressive Porfiriato-era building at Av. Obregón 520 (between Av. Independencia and Av. Damián Carmona), tel. (48) 12-2357, has a good selection of maps and brochures containing tourist information for city and state.

ERIN DWYER

SAN LUIS POTOSÍ
TELEPHONE NUMBERS

Local Police 12-5583, 12-5324
Highway Patrol. 12-6128, 18-2961
Green Angels 14-0906, 12-2178
State Tourist Office. 12-6203
Red Cross. 15-3322
U.S. Consulate. 17-2501, 17-2557
San Luis Potosí Area Code. 48

The **SECTUR** office at Calle Guerrero 14, tel. (48) 14-0906, has some of the same information but is less well staffed.

Maps
The state tourist office (see above), in conjunction with the local hotel association, produces useful Spanish-language tourist maps for the city, the Región Huasteca, and the Altiplano sections of the state.

Topographic maps for the state of San Luis Potosí and adjacent states may be obtained from the knowledgeable staff at the **INEGI** office at Av. Carranza 1138, tel. (48) 17-8280 or (800) 4-8510. Open Mon.-Fri. 9 a.m.-9 p.m.

U.S. Consulate
A U.S. consulate is located at Calle Fco. de P. Mariel 103 (off Av. V. Carranza southwest of the Hotel Real Plaza), tel. (48) 17-2501 or 17-2557. The office is open Mon.-Fri. 9 a.m.-1 p.m. and 4-7 p.m.

Post Office
The main downtown post office is at Calles Salazar and Morelos, a short walk north from the historical district but very difficult to reach by vehicle since the streets around the post office are narrow and congested.

GETTING THERE

Air
San Luis Potosí is well connected by air via Guadalajara, Monterrey, and Mexico City. Mexico City is less than an hour away by plane, making for short flight connections to other cities.

Aero California, at Plaza Gigante Tangamanga, tel. (48) 11-8054, offers nonstop flights to Mexico City.

Aeroméxico, Av. V. Carranza 1160-2, tel. (48) 18-7371, operates daily nonstop flights to/from Durango, Guadalajara, Mexico City, and Monterrey, with connections via Mexico City to/from many other cities in the U.S. and Mexico. Aeroméxico flies nonstop daily between Monterrey and San Antonio, hence San Antonio-Monterrey-San Luis Potosí flights are easily arranged.

Mexicana, Av. Carranza 1525-101, tel. (48) 13-3399, fields direct flights to/from Mexico City, Monterrey (with connections to San Antonio), and Guadalajara, plus the usual array of connections through Mexico City.

Aeromar, Av. Carranza 1030, tel. (48) 13-0559, flies daily to/from Mexico City. The Aeromar office also handles ticketing and reservations for United Airlines, although United doesn't yet have flights to San Luis Potosí.

Airport Transportation: The airport is 20 km northeast of city center via Mexico 57. Taxis to/from the airport usually cost around US$10-13 while a *colectivo* is US$4.50 pp.

Bus
The Central Camionera, south of Glorieta Juárez on Diagonal Sur (about two km east of the city center), has a post office, *cafetería,* and two separate departure/arrival sections for first- and second-class buses. San Luis Potosí is a major transportation hub, so buses to nearly every corner of Mexico leave round the clock.

In McAllen, Texas, there's a new **Central de Autobuses** at Beech and N. Main where you can get a first-class Mercedes Benz bus with a/c and TV to San Luis Potosí for US$27.50; there is one departure daily and the trip takes about five hours.

From San Luis, **Omnibus de México** operates to Ciudad Juárez (US$46, seven times daily), Chihuahua (US$34, four times daily), Durango (US$15, three times daily), Torreón (US$19, six times daily), Monterrey (US$16, three times daily), Mexico City (US$14, seven times daily), Tampico (US$14, three times daily), and Zacatecas (US$5.60, six times daily).

Turistar has first-class/*ejecutivo* buses to Zacatecas (US$6, once daily), Nuevo Laredo (US$32, once daily), Mexico City (*ejecutivo,*

US$18, twice daily), and Monterrey (*ejecutivo*, US$22, once daily), with Greyhound connections in Monterrey to San Antonio (US$16), Austin (US$26), Houston (US$34), and Dallas (US$38).

Estrella Blanca offers cheaper fares west and north to Durango (US$14, once daily), Aguascalientes (US$6, hourly), Matehuala (US$5, hourly), Reynosa (US$ 19, once daily), Matamoros (US$17, once daily), Monterrey (US$15, hourly), Piedras Negras (US$25, three times daily), Ciudad Acuña (US$27, once daily), Mexico City (US$13, hourly), Nuevo Laredo (US$22, once daily), Juárez (US$45, once daily), and Torreón (US$18, once daily). Estrella Blanca also goes east to Ciudad Valles (US$9, once daily) and Tampico (US$13, once daily). **Omnibus de Oriente** goes to Río Verde (US$15, twice daily), Ciudad Victoria, Tamuín, Ciudad Valles, and smaller towns in the Región Huasteca.

Transportes Tamaulipas operates first-class buses to Nuevo Laredo (US$24.50, three times daily), McAllen (US$21, six times daily), Monterrey (US$16, eight times daily), and Matehuala (US$6, once daily). Matehuala is the town you want if you're headed for Real de Catorce. Little **Noroeste** runs three buses daily to Charcas on the Altiplano for US$3.

Services to the eastern part of the state and southern Tamaulipas are covered by **Vencedor Río Verde,** which offers hourly departures to Río Verde and Ciudad Valles from 4:25 a.m. to midnight for US$5 and US$9.30, respectively. This line also operates seven buses a day to Tamazunchale (US$12) and Tampico (US$14).

Autobuses Roja and **Autobuses Potosinos** operate hourly buses during the day and evening to Centro Vacacional Gogorrón and Santa María del Río for a few dollars each.

Train

A major railway junction, San Luis Potosí has separate stations for passengers and cargo, plus a number of sidings and workshops for the servicing of trains. The west-east Aguascalientes-Tampico line meets the north-south Nuevo Laredo-Mexico City and Monterrey-Mexico City lines at the main railway station just north of Alameda Juan Sarabia at Av. 20 de Noviembre and Calle M.J. Othón. This station is notable for its murals by Mexican artist Fernando Leal.

On the *Mexico City-Monterrey-Nuevo Laredo* line, both first- and second-class cars are available between Nuevo Laredo and Mexico City. A second-class ticket to/from Monterrey costs US$5.60, first-class US$10. Advance tickets can be purchased at the station daily 4:30-6 p.m., or one hour in advance of departure. The complete Nuevo Laredo-San Luis Potosí trip takes roughly 15 hours, an overnight trip.

El Regiomontano runs between Mexico City and Monterrey, with a connection to Piedras Negras via Saltillo. The northbound train (No. 71) stops in San Luis Potosí at 12:01 a.m., the southbound (No. 72) at 3:45 p.m. First-class reserved fares (not including extra sleeper charges) are: Monterrey US$10; Saltillo US$7; Mexico City US$9.50; second-class seats cost about 45% less. Advance tickets may be purchased at the San Luis Potosí railway station daily 11 a.m.-12:30 p.m. Rumors persist that FNM may be discontinuing the *Regiomontano* line—check with the tourist office for the latest.

The second-class *El Huasteco* operates between San Luis Potosí, Ciudad Valles, and Tampico. Number 353 departs San Luis Potosí at 8 a.m., arriving in Tampico 11-12 hours later. In the reverse direction, No. 354 runs on the same schedule. Tickets cost US$5 through to Tampico, about half for Ciudad Valles, and may be purchased an hour before departure. Remember, all this is subject to change according to the whims of FNM.

Driving

If you're heading south to Mexico City on Mexico 57 and don't wish to stop over in San Luis Potosí, take the *libramiento oriente* turnoff near San Elias (northeast of San Luis Potosí). This bypass saves at least 45 minutes of driving time over the old route through the eastern edge of the city.

GETTING AROUND

Bus

San Luis Potosí has a very well-designed and well-maintained city bus system. (*AIM* newsletter—produced by Americans living in Mexico—once pronounced it "the cleanest and brightest we have ever seen.") Small, modern buses that run up and down Av. V. Carranza are very useful for east-west trips across towns.

To get from the railway station to Glorieta Juárez, take a Ruta 9, 10, or 11; these three numbers are also good for trips between the historical district (catch the bus at the western edge of the Alameda on Calle M.J. Othón) and the bullring. Ruta 9 also stops at the main bus terminal, so this is the bus to take from the terminal to reach the historical district.

Taxi

Taxis in San Luis Potosí are reasonably priced. A cab between the Central Camionera and *el centro,* for example, costs around US$2.

Driving

For the most part, city streets are well marked. Driving in the historical district can be a bit harrowing, since some streets are blocked off to vehicular traffic while many others allow traffic in one direction only. For drivers unfamiliar with the territory, this can mean a lot of time spent driving in circles. Visiting motorists would do well to leave their vehicles at their hotels and explore this district on foot. RVers should forget about trying to navigate the historical district in their rigs; the charming streets are simply too narrow for large wheelbases.

Car Rental: National, tel. (48) 28-2062, has a concession at the airport office. Rates are higher than normal for a city of this size, which indicates that most business and leisure travelers to San Luis don't normally rent vehicles. Perhaps this is because the buses and taxis are so cheap and convenient.

Huastec shell ear-disk

BOB RACE

NORTH OF SAN LUIS POTOSÍ

Northern Mexico's Altiplano reaches its highest elevations in the northern quadrant of the state, known as the Altiplano Potosino. Though arid and desertic, the region is high enough that milder temperatures prevail. The desert flora, with yuccas predominating, can be impressive.

Outside the state capital, the Altiplano's main attractions are clustered to the north in the mining area around Matehuala.

MATEHUALA AND VICINITY

The third largest city in the state is merely a quick gas or motel stop for most visitors on their way to the state capital or heading west to the historic mining town of Real de Catorce. Travelers going to Real de Catorce by bus have no choice but to break their journey in Matehuala, since no direct buses travel from San Luis Potosí to Real.

The town's name comes from a Guachichil phrase meaning "Don't come." One can imagine the conquistadors interrogating the locals in Spanish or Náhuatl: "What's this place called?" "Don't come." The conquistadors ignored the warning and exploited gold and silver ore found in the area. Mining is still important to the local economy, although the largest mines quit producing earlier this century. La Paz gold and silver mines, about 10 km (six miles) southwest of town, were founded in 1864 and local residents still work them. The production of *ixtle,* a fiber used to make rope, baskets, shoes, and other household goods, is another means of livelihood in Matehuala.

Street life in Matehuala revolves around the **Plaza Principal,** which is flanked by 19th-century architecture such as the Templo de San Salvador.

Several motels in town (including the Capri, Oasis, and Las Palmas) can arrange six-hour sightseeing trips to Real de Catorce.

Accommodations

Shoestring: In downtown Matehuala are some small, old, and cheap hotels that aren't very convenient for motorists (lack of parking, narrow streets) but are good for backpackers since they're within walking distance of the plaza and local bus terminals. Though very plain, the most atmospheric of these is the **Hotel Matehuala,** Calle Bustamante Ote. 134, tel. (488) 2-0680, a colonial-style place with rooms around a courtyard. Upstairs rooms have private baths, downstairs rooms share common bathrooms and are less expensive. Rates: US$8-10 upstairs; US$6 downstairs. Similarly priced, very basic rooms are also available at: **Hotel Monterrey,** Calle Hidalgo Sur 212, tel. (488) 2-0796; **Casa de Huéspedes Amina,** Calle Negrete 306, tel. (488) 2-2620; **Hotel Alamo,** Calle Guerrero 116, tel. (488) 2-0017; and **Hotel María Esther,** Calle Madero 111, tel. (488) 2-0714. The latter is close to the Transportes Tamaulipas terminal, not far from the plaza, and has a homelike atmosphere.

Budget: Most of Matehuala's hotels and motels are strung along Mexico 57 east of town and are oriented toward motorists—especially motorists carrying U.S. dollars. From the north, the first you'll see on the highway is the attractive **Motel Hacienda,** at Km 620, tel. (488) 2-0065, which has very comfortable, modern rooms, some edging up into our "inexpensive" price category. Rates: US$30-40 depending on amenities. Just south of the Hacienda are the less expensive **Motel El Pedregal,** tel. (488) 2-0054, **Motel La Mansión,** tel. (488) 2-0704, and **Motel El Parador de San Miguel,** tel. (488) 2-0174, all of which offer adequate motel rooms for US$18-22. These are Mexican trucker favorites.

The next batch of motels south along the highway near Km 617 fall in the US$25-35 range, including **Motel Oasis,** tel. (488) 2-3362, **Motel Capri,** tel. (488) 2-0171, **Hotel Parador Misión del Real,** tel. (488) 2-3148, and **Motel El Dorado,** tel. (488) 2-0174. All offer decent a/c rooms; El Dorado also has a pool.

Budget/Inexpensive: For just a few dollars more, the pick of the pack at this end of town is the well-run **Motel Las Palmas Midway Inn,** a bit north of the El Dorado at Km 617, tel. (488) 2-0001 or 2-3620, fax (488) 2-1396. Las Palmas is oriented toward Real de Catorce visitors and has a pool, mini-golf course, RV spaces with full hookups, and a good restaurant. Lodging options include economy rooms (US$31-36 s/d),

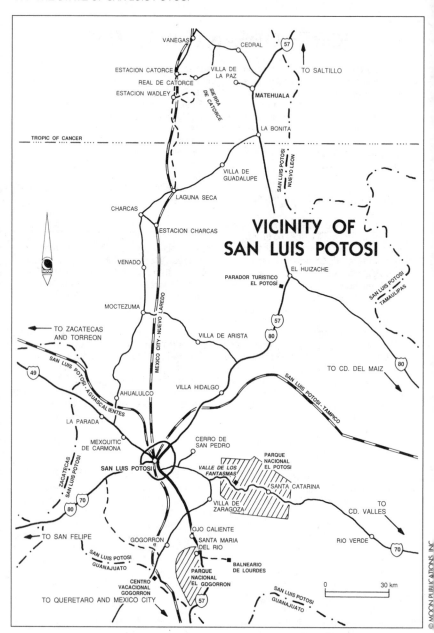

VANEGAS
CEDRAL
57
TO SALTILLO

ESTACION CATORCE
VILLA DE
LA PAZ
REAL DE CATORCE
ESTACION WADLEY
MATEHUALA
SIERRA DE CATORCE

LA BONITA

TROPIC OF CANCER

SAN LUIS POTOSI NUEVO LEÓN

VILLA DE
GUADALUPE

LAGUNA SECA
CHARCAS

ESTACION CHARCAS

VICINITY OF
SAN LUIS POTOSI

VENADO

EL HUIZACHE
PARADOR TURISTICO
EL POTOSÍ

SAN LUIS POTOSI TAMAULIPAS

MOCTEZUMA

MEXICO CITY - NUEVO LAREDO

TO ZACATECAS
AND TORREON

57
80

VILLA DE ARISTA

80
TO CD. DEL MAIZ

49

SAN LUIS POTOSI- AGUASCALIENTES

VILLA HIDALGO

SAN LUIS POTOSI - TAMPICO

AHUALULCO

LA PARADA

MEXQUITIC
DE CARMONA

CERRO DE
SAN PEDRO

PARQUE
NACIONAL
EL POTOSI

ZACATECAS
SAN LUIS POTOSI

SAN LUIS POTOSI

70

VALLE DE LOS
FANTASMAS
SANTA CATARINA

VILLA DE
ZARAGOZA

TO
CD. VALLES

80

TO SAN FELIPE

GOGORRON

OJO CALIENTE
SANTA MARIA
DEL RIO

RIO VERDE

70

SAN LUIS POTOSI
GUANAJUATO

BALNEARIO
DE LOURDES

CENTRO
VACACIONAL
GOGORRON

PARQUE
NACIONAL
EL GOGORRON

0   30 km

TO QUERETARO AND MEXICO CITY

57

SAN LUIS POTOSI
GUANAJUATO

SAN LUIS POTOSI

© MOON PUBLICATIONS, INC.

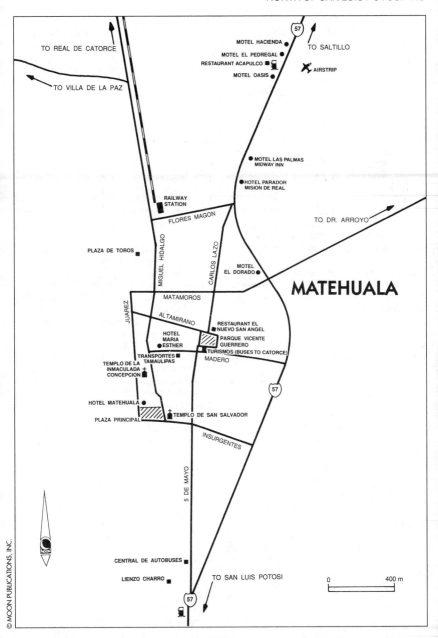

TO REAL DE CATORCE

TO VILLA DE LA PAZ

MOTEL HACIENDA

MOTEL EL PEDREGAL

RESTAURANT ACAPULCO

MOTEL OASIS

57

TO SALTILLO

AIRSTRIP

MOTEL LAS PALMAS
MIDWAY INN

HOTEL PARADOR
MISION DE REAL

RAILWAY
STATION

FLORES MAGON

TO DR. ARROYO

PLAZA DE TOROS

MIGUEL HIDALGO

CARLOS LAZO

MOTEL
EL DORADO

MATEHUALA

MATAMOROS

JUAREZ

ALTAMIRANO

RESTAURANT EL
NUEVO SAN ANGEL

HOTEL
MARIA
ESTHER

PARQUE VICENTE
GUERRERO

TURISMOS (BUSES TO CATORCE)

TRANSPORTES
TAMAULIPAS

MADERO

TEMPLO DE LA
INMACULADA
CONCEPCION

HOTEL MATEHUALA

PLAZA PRINCIPAL

TEMPLO DE SAN SALVADOR

57

INSURGENTES

5 DE MAYO

CENTRAL DE AUTOBUSES

LIENZO CHARRO

TO SAN LUIS POTOSI

0   400 m

57

© MOON PUBLICATIONS, INC.

rooms with a/c and TV (US$37-44 s/d), and RV spots (US$10). English magazines are sold in the lobby, and the hotel rents bicycles for US$6.50 per four hours.

Food

The ground floor of **Hotel María Esther** houses the very inexpensive **Restaurant La Reyna,** which serves a good *comida corrida.* **Restaurant El Nuevo San Angel,** on the plaza downtown, is clean and offers dependable Mexican fare.

Taquería El Pueblo, next to the Turismos bus office on Plaza Vicente Guerrero, specializes in *pozole, menudo,* tacos, *gorditas,* and other *antojitos.* **Pan Panchita,** a few doors east of the Hotel María Esther, sells *pan dulce, bolillos,* and other Mexican baked goods. Many shops downtown sell *natillas, cajetas,* and other goat-milk sweets.

On the highway, the **Oasis** and **Las Palmas** motels have good, reasonably priced restaurants open 7:30 a.m. till late. **Restaurant Matehuala** and **Restaurant Acapulco,** practically side-by-side next to the PEMEX station near the north end of town, are slightly less expensive and generally reliable.

Transportation

Bus: Matehuala's Central de Autobuses is at the south end of town, where Av. 5 de Mayo meets Mexico 57 (about 1.5 km from town center). Services include a snack bar and long-distance-phone counter.

Transportes Tamaulipas, the most useful regional line, operates six buses a day to Real de Catorce for US$2 each way. **Turismos** on Plaza Vicente Guerrero also runs buses between Matehuala and Catorce. Buses to/from San Luis Potosí and Monterrey depart nine times daily and cost US$5.70 and US$10, respectively, each way. Transportes Tamaulipas also runs five buses per day to McAllen, Texas, for US$18. This bus line has its own small terminal downtown near the plaza.

Similar services to Monterrey, McAllen, and San Luis Potosí are provided by **Autobuses del Noreste** and **Transportes Frontera.** The latter also runs buses to Saltillo (US$7) and Nuevo Laredo (US$19) five times daily. **Autobuses Blancos** provides similar services, plus Ciudad Acuña (US$22) and Piedras Negras (US$21) three times daily.

Driving: If you're coming from the north, you'll cross the Tropic of Cancer just before Km 167 on Mexico 57. A **Green Angels** station at Blvd. Carlos Lazo 101, tel. (488) 2-0858, is just off the highway. The PEMEX station toward the north end of town on the highway sells Premium. Farther south toward San Luis Potosí, at Km 100, is a large PEMEX station with Premium and a restaurant.

To Real de Catorce

It takes about 1.5 hours to drive from Matehuala to Real de Catorce (or 2.5 hours by bus). The route first takes you 27 km (16 miles) northwest through Cedral via a paved two-lane road, then winds 25 km (15.5 miles) southwest into the Sierra de Catorce along a wide, bumpy, cobblestone road that's practically a work of art in itself. This latter road skirts several abandoned mines and semi-abandoned villages and passes a *mirador* with wide-ranging views of the plains below.

Between Matehuala and Real de Catorce (19 km/12 miles west of Mexico 57), the friendly little town of **Cedral** is supported by spring-irrigated agriculture and locally quarried onyx. Founded in the 18th century, Cedral has a pleasant plaza surrounded by ash and walnut trees, a parish church, and several *tiendas* where groceries, ice, and beer are available. Local culinary specialties include *chorizo* and *cabrito guisado de Cedral* (kid goat stuffed with olives and cracklings, covered with *chile ancho* paste, and stewed in its own blood).

Practicalities: Hotel Plaza, on the plaza, has spartan rooms for around US$5-8 per night. The nearest PEMEX station is in Matehuala. **Transportes Tamaulipas** buses from Matehuala stop in Cedral briefly on the way to Real de Catorce. If you're getting off in Cedral for any reason, the Matehuala-Cedral bus fare is US$0.75.

REAL DE CATORCE AND VICINITY

Surrounded by rolling hills and desert valleys, this historic ex-mining town sits at a cool 2,756 meters (9,039 feet) above sea level. Three peaks standing taller than 3,000 meters (9,840 feet)—**El Lucero, El Barco,** and **La Leona**—border the Real de Catorce plateau.

In its semi-ghost town state, Real's windswept, cobblestone streets and stone-block buildings would make the perfect set for a Sergio Leone western; the town has in fact appeared in several Mexican cowboy films. Gabriele Salvatores, Italian director of the Oscar-winning *Mediterraneo,* used Real de Catorce for location shooting in his 1992 film, *Puerto Escondido.*

Today the town has less than a thousand full-time residents, most of whom make their living as independent prospectors working the abandoned mines for a few pesos a week or by catering to the tens of thousands of pilgrims who come yearly to worship at the Parroquía de la Purísima Concepción, which contains a highly revered St. Francis shrine. The town's remoteness has kept it in a uniquely preserved state that attracts

a trickle of tourists, mostly Potosinos visiting on weekends and holidays. A very small—and fluctuating—artists' colony is located here. About 30 foreigners live in the immediate area (some in the *pueblo de fantasma* or "ghost town" over the tunnel) full time.

Real de Catorce is also a traditional pilgrim center for the Huichol rancherías of Nayarit, Durango, Jalisco, and Zacatecas. The Huicholes visit the area every spring to gather *Lophophora williamsii,* the hallucinogenic cactus more commonly known in Mexico as peyote (or híkuri among the Huicholes). Although peyote is available in other parts of Northern Mexico, for the Huicholes only the plants collected from sacred Wírikuta (the Huichol name for the Catorce plateau as well as for the spiritual state

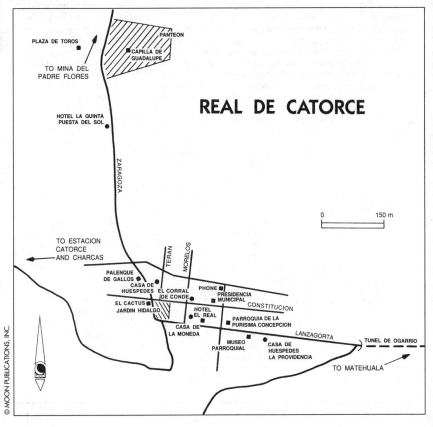

REAL DE CATORCE

JOURNEY TO WIRIKUTA

The arduous physical pilgrimage the Huicholes make to the desert outside Catorce each year in search of peyote is accompanied by an equally demanding spiritual journey. Of the several pilgrimages Huicholes undertake to different parts of central and Northern Mexico, this is the most important since the outcome to a large degree predetermines tribal destiny for the coming calendar year.

Although from a geographical perspective, the *peyoteros'* destination is Catorce's high-desert plains, their more esoteric, inner journey traverses a parallel, nonphysical dimension known as Wirikuta. Wirikuta, which is also one of the Huichol names for peyote, can only be penetrated upon completion of the rituals performed at Real de Catorce.

Crucial to the accurate performance of such rituals are the services of a *mara'akame,* the Huichol shaman charged with the responsibility of leading the annual peyote pilgrimage for each *ranchería* community. The great wisdom and simplicity of the *mara'akame* are believed to make him the only one who can percieve the magico-religious Kauyumari or blue deer, an entity considered an elder brother of the Huicholes and the most important temporal representative of their gods. Only Kauyumari—along with his faithful companion Tatehauri, the Huichol fire god—knows the Huichol destiny.

The journey begins when peyote pilgrims travel by truck to a designated spot at the edge of the desert outside Catorce, then walk several hours to a sacred peyote-gathering spot. Costuming is important; the *peyoteros* wear clean clothes and decorate their flat-brimmed hats with squirrel tails and colored bird feathers—preferably those of the turkey.

Starting with the day before their departure for Catorce, pilgrims reduce their food intake as much as possible, drink only water, refrain from all sexual activity, and do not speak unnecessarily. Once a set of routine preparatory rituals has been completed, a fire is lit and all participants enter a period of contemplation, followed by a session during which each man confesses all of the sexual encounters he has had throughout his life. An appointed younger man uses a stick to strike their legs and goad them into confessing, until one by one, amid much joking and laughter, they unravel their tales of sexual experience. Couples show no jealousy or resentment upon hearing of affairs, and children make fun of the old and vice versa. For each incident, one knot is tied in a rope, and at the end the rope is hurled into the fire.

After the confessions the *peyoteros* line up facing Wirikuta's mythical portals, the "door where the clouds collide," while the *mara'akame* passes his sacred feathers over their bodies, one by one, and asks Kauyumari to help them cross into the other world. As they walk across the "threshold," each pilgrim is thought to have passed from a profane to a sacred state.

Once in Wirikuta, the pilgrims proceed to two lakes, one considered "the mother of all waters" and a smaller one called "the mother of all children," where they leave offerings of wool-embroidered cloth squares ("yarn paintings"), deer blood, feathers, and other sacred objects. At this point the *mara'akame* anoints the heads of the *peyoteros* with sacred water from each lake, after which the participants collect water in goatskin bags to bring home for sprinkling on their cornfields, livestock, and family members as a blessing from Wirikuta.

Finally they approach a plateau where another sacred boundary line is crossed, then wait in a line while the *mara'akame* scans the horizon for the blue deer. The "blue deer" or Kauyumari is, in fact, the bluish-tined peyote cactus. If it isn't spotted, they must return home empty-handed. Once the shaman sees it, he leads the group to the first bunch of cactus, slices off the tops into button-shaped segments, and offers one to each pilgrim. The *peyoteros* sing their thanks to Kauyumari and leave offerings at the spot where the blue deer first appeared to the *mara'akame.*

They continue around the plateau, carefully slicing the tops from the sacred plant in such a way that the plant can regenerate and they will be able to harvest it again. In the last couple of decades, the cactus has become more scarce due to what the Huicholes call "urban robbery"—habitat loss caused by excess human interference as well as the improper gathering of peyote by non-Huichol—acts which profane and pollute this sacred area.

At night they again gather around a fire, eat, and all night long sing songs of gratitude and homage to the deeds of the gods and creatures of the earth. The next day the *peyoteros* return to their communities with enough peyote to carry them through the year's ceremonies.

attained during a peyote pilgrimage) are considered appropriate for their rituals. Some say the Huichol peyote cult and San Francisco pilgrims are proof that Real de Catorce is one of the earth's "power spots."

Except during the first week of October, when St. Francis pilgrims throng the streets, Real saturates the visitor with a tranquil, lost-world feeling. Stargazers will find very clear skies virtually year-round. Visit during the week and you'll have practically the whole town to yourself. Be sure to bring warm clothes if you plan to visit Nov.-March, when evenings can be cold. Any time of year, the steep, cobblestone streets will be easier to negotiate if you wear sturdy shoes or boots.

History

Several legends regarding the origin of the town's name ("Kingdom of the Fourteen") circulate. The most repeated story claims that 14 bandits once headquartered themselves here, while another says 14 soldiers died defending a Spanish encampment from Amerindian attacks. Yet another recounts that 14 travelers discovered silver while spending the night here.

It isn't known precisely when the first silver lode was discovered, though Spanish records indicate that ore was extracted here in 1773 by *afromestizo* Ventura Ruíz. In 1779 the town was officially established under the name "Real de Minas de Nuestra Señora de la Limpia Concepción de Guadalupe de los Alamos de Catorce" ("Mining Kingdom of Our Lady of the Immaculate Conception of Guadalupe from the Cottonwoods of Catorce"). By the end of the 18th century it was one of the most prosperous *reales de minas* in Nueva España, with 15,000 inhabitants working the mines or servicing the miners. In 1822 an Englishman brought the first steam boiler ever used in Mexican mines to pump water from flooded shafts. This same joint Mexican-British venture was later the first in Mexico to use dynamite to blast tunnels, the most famous of which is the Túnel de Ogarrio, which provides the main access to the town from the east.

By the late 19th century Real de Catorce had paved streets, electric lights, a municipal water system, a bullring, a cockfighting *palenque,* and its own silver-coin mint. At their peak the local mines produced US$3 million in high-grade silver annually. Around the turn of the 20th century—by which time the richest veins had been used up—the price of silver dropped precipitously. At the lower prices, the smaller, harder-to-work lodes weren't worth mining on a large scale, resulting in a general cutback in production. Mineral exploration stopped completely with the outbreak of the Mexican Revolution in 1910, after which the town slipped into near oblivion.

A regeneration of sorts begin in the 1950s when a few Mexicans and American expats began visiting the town, sometimes staying for a few weeks or months of high-desert solitude. Such visits have accelerated ever so slightly in recent years.

Sights
Parroquía de la Purísima Concepción: The simple neoclassical exterior of this church in the center of town belies its sumptuous, late baroque interior. Constructed in 1814 by French architect Jean Crusot, the typical Latin cross floor plan features a unique mesquite-wood floor made from coffin lids. The principal object of interest of most *peregrinos,* however, is the small San Francisco image in one of the side altars.

French architect Jean Crusot designed the Parroquía de la Purísima Concepción in Real de Catorce in 1814.

Devotees of Purísima Concepción's San Francisco cult believe that the image has the power to answer prayer requests and to cleanse believers of sin. The origin of the cult is uncertain but it dates to at least as far back as Real's abandonment, 1905-10, when former residents of the town began making annual pilgrimages to "pay" for fulfilled requests. Locks of hair cut from the heads of pilgrims in penance, or in return for the granting of a request, are attached to tin *retablos* in the bell tower. Pilgrims numbering in the tens of thousands arrive during the week of 4 Oct., the feast day for St. Francis.

Casa de la Moneda: The old mint, opposite the church, dates to the early 1860s. To conform to the sloping terrain, the neoclassical structure features three floors on one side, two on another.

Other Historic Structures: A native-stone *palenque de gallos,* built in 1789 for cockfighting matches, still stands on the west side of town. It's occasionally used for outdoor musical and theatrical performances by artists from the state capital. About a kilometer north of the main plaza, beyond the Hotel Puesta del Sol on the left-hand side of the road, is a stone **bullring** from the same era. On the other side of the road more or less opposite the old bullring is the town *panteón* or walled cemetery. The small Guadalupe chapel on the cemetery grounds was built in 1775.

Museo Parroquíal: On the street leading into town from the tunnel, a one-room museum houses a small collection of dusty historical mementos. Admission is US$0.15; hours are erratic.

Túnel de Ogarrio: Real de Catorce is accessed from the east via an impressive 2.3-km tunnel through solid rock; the tunnel was started in 1897 and finished in 1901.

Hiking and Riding

When you run out of things to see in town—it won't take long—consider hiking or horseback riding in the surrounding area. One of the more popular walks is to **Cerro Quemado,** an elephant-shaped hill sacred to the Huichol around 1.5 hours from town on foot. Nearby villages—some more ruined and abandoned then Catorce—can also be visited. You can rent horses in town for US$3.30 an hour, plus US$3.30 for an equestrian guide. Inquire at any of the hotels or restaurants.

Further afield and more challenging would be a desert walk. One of the more scenic pieces of high desert surrounds the town of **Estación Wadley,** southwest of town toward Estación Catorce and Charcas. To get there, take a jeep from Real de Catorce to Estación Catorce, where you can catch a bus to Estación Wadley, a total road journey of about 2.5 hours. Jeeps to Estación Catorce can be hired in front of Miguel's market in Real de Catorce for US$2 pp. Buses from Estación Catorce to Estación Wadley leave frequently 7 a.m.-6 p.m. All the usual precautions concerning desert hiking apply; you might also consider taking along a guide from Estación Wadley or Estación Catorce—someone who knows the area.

Accommodations

Real de Catorce now has several reliable places to stay. On weekends it tends to fill up with visitors from the state capital, so come on a weekday if you want to be sure of a room.

Shoestring: During festivals, several homes open as temporary *casas de huéspedes* and offer rooms for as little as US$3 per night. The least expensive place to stay that's open year-round is the **Casa de Huéspedes** on Calle Terán, off Calle Constitución. It offers eight simple but nicely kept rooms with shared hot water bath in an old stone complex. Rates: US$3.30 pp. On another small street off Calle Constitución, two-story **Hospedaje Familiar** has similar rates but doesn't have quite the charm of the *casa* on Calle Terán.

On Calle Lanzagorta, the road leading from the tunnel into town, you might easily miss seeing the **Casa de Huéspedes La Providencia,** on the left before the museum. Rooms are furnished basically but are clean and have private hot-water showers. Meals can be ordered in the cozy kitchen/dining room at the front of the house. Rates: US$6.50 s to US$10.60 d, depending on room size and number of beds (add 20% during festivals).

Budget: In the center of town east of Jardín Hidalgo, in a nicely restored colonial mansion on Calle Morelos, is the simple but atmospheric **Hotel El Real,** tel. (488) 2-3733 or, in Matehuala, (488) 2-2593. Its high-ceilinged rooms are furnished with rustic antiques and have attached bathrooms. The hotel's roof terrace affords terrific views of the surrounding town. The only drawback to this hotel is that the unheated rooms can get very chilly during cold-weather months. A small dining room downstairs offers à la carte Mexican and Italian meals. Rates: US$15.30 with one double bed, US$19 for two double beds. When the 13 rooms in the older building are full, guests are sent to a newer 14-room building a couple of blocks away, where the rates are US$22 s, plus US$5.30 per extra person (add 20% during holidays).

Around the corner from the Hotel El Real in an old house is a well-decorated inn called **El Corral de Conde.** El Corral features three huge suites that can sleep up to four each or can be divided into six rooms. By prior arrangement a large kitchen can be included in the deal. For reservations or further information, call (488) 2-3733—yes, the same number as for El Real; this is the only phone in Real de Catorce so far. Rates: from US$30 d.

North of town toward the bullring and cemetery, **Hotel La Quinta Puesta del Sol,** on Calle del Cemeterio, tel. (488) 7-02-81 in Matehuala, sits on a hillside overlooking the scenic valley of Barranca El Voladero. The hotel offers 20 original rooms with private bathrooms, plus new, more expensive rooms in an annex separate from the original rooms. Rates: from US$21 s, US$27 d. Fixed-price meals in the hotel dining room cost US$2-3 for breakfast, US$4-5 lunch, US$3-4 dinner.

Long-Term: With a little asking around, you should be able to find simple rooms or houses for rent by the week or month. Up in the "ghost town" over the tunnel, old stone houses without power or running water rent for just US$20-40 a month, while in Catorce itself a house with a shower and kitchen can be had for US$150 a month. Ask at Hotel El Real for further information on house rentals.

Food

The most reliable place to eat in town is the dining room at **Hotel El Real,** as it's the only place that seems to be open daily year-round. Last time we passed through, a French woman was managing the restaurant, which serves Italian food, Mexican food, and pizza. As in many out-of-the-way destinations in Mexico, food service can be slow. On the wall of the restaurant is an interesting oil painting of a Huichol peyote ritual.

Eucalipto, up a steep street to the west of Jardín Hidalgo, features an eclectic menu of mostly Italian dishes but is open only on weekends. By rural San Luis Potosí standards it's rather pricey but the food is good. Another place open only on weekends, **La Paz,** is around the corner from El Real and serves Mexican, European, and American dishes. Prices are moderate and the place is popular when open.

A cafe called **El Cactus,** opposite Jardín Hidalgo, also features an eclectic menu and is especially popular for breakfast. It usually closes around 6 p.m., or at least it did when we visited.

Information and Services

There's only one phone in town, in a store near El Corral de Conde on Calle Constitución. The number is (488) 2-3733 and service is available Mon.-Sat. 9 a.m.-2 p.m. and 5-8 p.m., Sunday 9 a.m.-noon. At times this phone may be nonfunctioning for as long as one or two weeks; during a recent fiesta it was down for three weeks.

Transportation

Bus: From Matehuala, **Transportes Tamaulipas** and **Turismos** operate at least six buses per day to Real de Catorce for US$2. These buses stop in Cedral, so if you miss a Matehuala departure you may be able to get another bus on to Cedral in time for the Cedral-Real departure.

Mini-van: Several of the highway motels in Matehuala can arrange for mini-van transportation (or six-hour tours) to Real de Catorce. Prices are negotiable depending on the number of passengers and how long the driver is needed in Real de Catorce; it's possible to arrange pickup on another day.

Driving: Negotiating the cobblestone road between Cedral and Real de Catorce is like riding on a continuous carpet of *topes* (Mexican speed bumps)—but the scenery makes up for the slow pace. Toll-takers at the entrance to the Ogarrio tunnel collect a US$1 toll. Since the tunnel can only accommodate traffic in one direction, a radio telephone system—staffed at each end of the tunnel—is used to regulate the change of direction at regular intervals. Hence arriving motorists may have to wait at one end for 20 minutes or so until the direction is reversed.

Motorists with sturdy, high-clearance, 4WD vehicles can also arrive or depart via a dirt track that runs 10 km (6.2 miles) west from Real de Catorce to the Estación Catorce railway depot, then roughly 50 km (31 miles) south, parallel to the railway, to a paved road that continues southwest 19 km (11.7 miles) to Charcas. From Charcas it's 101 km (62.6 miles) south to Mexico 49, the highway between Zacatecas and San Luis Potosí.

Recently there has been talk of putting in a paved highway between San Luis Potosí and Catorce using the Charcas route.

Charcas

Few tourists, whether Mexican or foreign, ever make it to Charcas, the oldest town in the Altiplano Potosino. Founded as a Franciscan mission in 1574, it soon developed into one of Northern Mexico's "Reales de Minas." Like Real de Catorce, it was a town built of native rock, with twisted cobblestone streets and a stone church, the difference being that Charcas is still an im-

portant mining center. An 18th-century convent and *parroquía*—containing the patroness of miners, the Virgen de Charcas—stand near the plaza; a festival held at the beginning of September honors the Virgin. The townspeople have converted a 16th-century *alhóndiga* or granary into a school.

Four km (2.5 miles) south of town via a gravel road are the **Grutas de la Cueva Azul** ("Blue Cave Grottoes"), a series of caverns with bluish stalagmite/stalactite formations.

Practicalities: The **Roma, Paris,** and **Rosas** Hotels offer simple lodging for under US$12.

Charcas is 63 km (39 miles) southwest of Mexico 57 (at La Bonita, which is 19 km/11.7 miles south of Matehuala), or 101 km (62.6 miles) north of Mexico 49. Gasoline supplies are spotty along this entire 164-km (101.6-mile) stretch, so be sure to fill up in San Luis Potosí or Matehuala. Buses to Charcas are available in Matehuala and San Luis Potosí.

SOUTH OF SAN LUIS POTOSÍ

The Altiplano Potosino continues southeast beyond the state capital as far as the Río Santa María Valley, where it gradually begins to merge with the more lush and tropical Región Huasteca. Along the river itself, within 60 km of the capital, are several *balnearios* as well as the renowned handicraft center of Santa María del Río. Mexico 57D, the 45-km tollway through the valley, offers a smooth, divided surface until just past Santa María del Río, where it merges with the older two-lane Mexico 57 to Mexico City. Within the next few years the tollway will extend another 35 km to the San Luis Potosí-Guanajuato state line.

PARQUE NACIONAL EL GOGORRÓN

Covering 25,000 hectares of the Valle de Gogorrón, this national park established in 1936 is embraced by two mountains: the taller, rockier Bernalejo and the smaller Cuesta. Both are blanketed with an intriguing floral mix of pines and cactus. Camping is permitted, although outside the Gogorrón *balneario* no public facilities are available.

The **Centro Vacacional Gogorrón** (Calle M.J. Othón 100 in San Luis Potosí, tel. (48) 12-3636) is a large *balneario* at the western edge of the park. Facilities include thermal baths, moderately priced cabins (from US$33 pp), a restaurant, swimming pools, and landscaped gardens. If you just want to use the "Roman baths," it's US$2.60 a day.

Getting There

Access to the Centro Vacacional Gogorrón is 55 km (34 miles) south of San Luis Potosí—25 km south via Mexico 57 and then 30 km on the road to Villa de Reyes. Buses are available from the Central Camionera in San Luis.

The national park extends westward from the town of Santa María del Río. Trails can be accessed from either this town or from the village of Gogorrón on the other side. Guided burro trips may be available in Santa María del Río—check with the Motel Puesta del Sol.

SANTA MARÍA DEL RÍO

San Luis Potosí's most famous handicraft product, the rebozo, hails from this charming town 45

THE REBOZO

Originating in Persia and India, the rebozo or Mexican shawl was introduced to the Spanish during the Moorish conquest of Spain, then brought to Mexico by the Spanish. While the garment was called a *chal* in Spain (*shal* in the Orient, "shawl" in the Anglo world), Mexicans invented their own word, rebozo, from the verb *arrebozarse,* "to cover oneself with a cape or coat." Over the years the Mexican shawl lengthened, narrowed, and borrowed influences—including ikat or tie-dye weaving techniques—from shawls brought from China, the Philippines, and India aboard Mexico's Manila galleons in the 16th and 17th centuries. A 1582 royal decree forbidding the wearing of indigenous clothing by *mestizas, mulatas,* and *negras* furthered quickened the rebozo's rate of adoption among non-Amerindian, non-Spanish women.

It takes one to two months to complete a top-quality silk rebozo approximately one meter wide and 2.5 meters long (3.3 feet by eight feet). The best rebozos are fine enough to be pulled through a wedding ring. Such quality typically costs over US$300. Less expensive silk or cotton rebozos—still of high quality—go for around US$100. In Santa María del Río, rebozos are often presented inside handmade, inlaid cedar boxes as wedding gifts. The *chal,* a thicker shawl made of wool or synthetic fabric, is usually less expensive than a rebozo.

rebozo weaving

JOE CUMMINGS

km south of the state capital. One of the most typical of all Mexican clothing accessories, these delicately woven shawls adorn the shoulders of aristocrats and peasants alike throughout the country and are a de rigueur part of every Potosina's wardrobe.

Although several regions in Mexico have their own rebozo styles, colors, and weaving techniques, those made in Santa María del Río are the most coveted. The state government considers the preservation of this *artesanía* so important to regional culture that since 1953 it has sponsored the **Escuela de Artesanías,** housed in a section of the Gobierno Constitucional del Estado off the larger of the town's two plazas. Visitors are welcome to observe the artisans working at traditional *telares de cintura* or "belt looms," in which the loom is tied to a post or wall hook and stretched around the backs of the weavers with a wide belt. Other handicrafts, particularly marquetry (wood inlay) and basketry, are also taught at the school.

Santa María del Río, founded in 1589 as a Franciscan mission, has a number of modest but historic structures, including the **Templo de Carmen** (dedicated in 1764). Colonial-era stone houses with wooden door and window frames are common. The town has two plazas: the large **Plaza Principal** in front of the Gobierno Constitucional del Estado, and a smaller one that's diagonally linked with the first. **El Arquillo,** an old aqueduct bordered by walnut trees, can be followed to a 15-meter (45-foot) waterfall along the Río Santa María, a favorite local picnic spot.

Farther west, the low Sierra Bernalejo is the beginning of Parque Nacional Gogorrón, an area suitable for camping and hiking.

Accommodations
Shoestring: For the most economical accommodations in town, try the basic **Casa de Huéspedes Jardín,** Calle Jardín Unión 7, tel. (485) 3-0310, and **Hotel Santa María,** Calle Bautista 24, offer simple lodging. Rates: US$8-12.

Budget: At the north end of town near the highway, **Motel Puesta del Sol,** México-Piedras Negras Hwy. Km 140, tel. (485) 3-0059, has comfortable a/c rooms. Rates: US$22-25.

Food
Motel Puesta del Sol has a fair restaurant that's usually empty except on weekends and holidays. Around the smaller of the town's two plazas are a number of restaurants and cafes. One of the local specialties is *campechana,* a sweet, crispy pastry.

Shopping
Near the main square are several shops selling rebozos—for cash only. They can also be purchased at the Escuela de Artesanías, although the school sometimes has a short supply. A fine-quality rebozo costs around US$100, though versions made of synthetic materials are priced as low as US$30-40, while a top-drawer shawl may cost as much as US$300. Traditionally speaking, bright colors are considered more suitable for younger women, muted colors for older. Ask at the school or at one of the shops for a demonstration of the many ways to wear the rebozo.

Santa María del Río is also known for wood furniture, inlaid cedar boxes *(cajas de rebozo)*

used to store Mexican shawls, reed baskets, and *ixtle* bags, all of which can be found in shops around town.

Events
During the first half of August, Santa María del Río celebrates the **Feria del Rebozo** along with the feast day of the Virgen de la Asunción.

Transportation
Bus: The **Potosinos** bus line operates second-class buses hourly between San Luis Potosí and Santa María del Río for less than US$3. In Santa María del Río these buses arrive and depart alongside the town's smaller plaza.

Driving: A four-lane tollway speeds motorists 45 km south from San Luis Potosí to Santa María del Río in half an hour. Near the town entrance off the highway is a PEMEX station.

BALNEARIOS

Approximately 48 km (30 miles) south of San Luis Potosí on Mexico 57, then 11 km (6.5 miles) east on a partially paved road, is **Balneario de Lourdes,** on the Río Santa María, tel. (48) 25-1434 in San Luis Potosí. Formerly the Hacienda La Labor del Río, this resort features hotel accommodations, a restaurant, mineral baths, a swimming pool, squash courts, horseback riding, and a restaurant. Beyond the resort is a plant where mineral water is bottled. Rates start at US$20 pp including three meals and use of all facilities. Lourdes is closed Jan.-Feb. each year.

The **Balneario Ojo Caliente,** a resort with a rustic motel, thermal baths, and three swimming pools, is accessed by a dirt road approximately 30 km south of San Luis Potosí via Mexico 57 on the way to Santa María del Río. The resort's namesake village of Ojo Caliente is regionally famous for *gorditas* and, on weekends, *carnitas.*

REGIÓN HUASTECA

Covering parts of Tamaulipas, San Luis Potosí, Veracruz, and Hidalgo, the Región Huasteca encompasses a lush area of mountains, valleys, and coastal plains that are the ancestral homelands of the Huastecs. The Huastecs inhabited

this part of Mexico long before the *entrada* and have imbued the region with a unique culture that is a hybrid of mestizo and *indio* ways.

Abundant rivers and streams along with fertile soils produce a bounty of fruits (particularly cit-

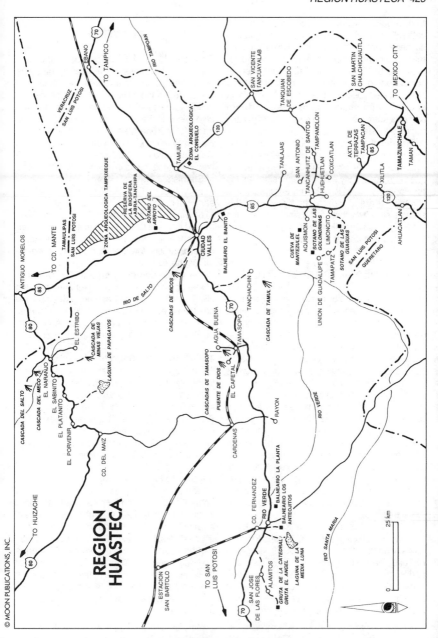

rus), vegetables, coffee, sugarcane, and dairy cattle. For the visitor, a combination of natural scenery—waterfalls, lakes, cloud forests, mountains—and indigenous culture makes the region one of Mexico's most attractive destinations. Adding to the allure is the fact that few foreigners—aside from a handful of American art students who make pilgrimages to Edward James's surrealist retreat—seem to know of the region's existence.

The regional weather is most pleasant in the fall, winter, and early spring when temperatures are moderate. At lower altitudes the weather in late spring and early summer can be hot, as the humid valleys tend to hold in the tropical heat. Cane fields are also put to the torch during this season, an activity that adds a smoky haze to the landscape. Although it can rain any time of year, the rains are heaviest in late summer.

PARQUE NACIONAL EL POTOSÍ

Roughly 70 km (43.5 miles) east of San Luis Potosí via Mexico 70, surrounding the small town of Santa Catarina, this national park incorporates 2,000 hectares (4,940 acres) of the wooded Valle de los Fantasmas ("Valley of the Ghosts"), including a major portion of the Cañada Grande watershed—the origin of numerous streams that feed into the Río Verde.

The diverse forest, in which pine and live oak dominate, can be seen from the highway; at its highest points the highway passes through sections of cloud forest where even the mesquite trees are draped with ball moss. The vegetation becomes more lush as you move east. In the highlands you can sometimes spot the bright green plumage and yellow-and-black, canoe-shaped bill of the **emerald toucan.** Even if you don't see one, you might be able to hear its low, nasal barking.

Public facilities and access to the park are virtually nil. To explore the area, try taking the dirt roads north from Mexico 70 toward the villages of Armadillo de los Infante (west of Santa Catarina) and Portrero de Santa Gertrudis (east of Santa Catarina). Take care if you're driving; in some stretches the winding mountain roads can become obscured by fog without warning.

RÍO VERDE

Situated 135 km (83.7 miles) east of the state capital on the banks of the river of the same name, Río Verde has an agreeable climate and is a center for the cultivation of corn, beans, avocado, and especially oranges. Dairy cattle are also raised in the area. The town is considered part of "La Zona Media," the gateway to the Región Huasteca, and as you're driving through, your car radio may begin picking up radio stations with broadcasts in Huastec dialect instead of Spanish.

Founded in 1617, Río Verde sports an assortment of colonial-era buildings, including the 1761-vintage **Templo de Santa Catarina Mártir** next to Plaza Constitución in the town center. Two-wheeled *solkis* (horse carts) provide transportation around town, enhancing the bygone-era atmosphere.

On weekends the **Mercado Colón,** three blocks south of the plaza, bustles with shoppers filling string bags with fresh produce and local cheeses. Several rustic *balnearios* with thermal spas are near town, including Los Anteojitos, La Planta, San Diego, and Palma Larga.

Train Trip to San Bartolo

From Río Verde you can take a short but scenic train trip 45 km (28 miles) north to San Bartolo. The train leaves Río Verde each day at 9 a.m., arriving in San Bartolo about an hour later, then returns to Río Verde at 1 p.m. The Río Verde railway station is a little over a kilometer west of Plaza Constitución; take Calle Potosinos west to the railbed, then follow the tracks north to the station.

Laguna de La Media Luna

This half-moon-shaped lake, fed by thermal springs and encircled by pines, has very clear water at a constant 20° C (84 ° F), and hence is a favorite local destination for snorkelers and scuba divers. Lots of small fish as well as turtles can be seen. The lake measures 300 meters (980 feet) long and 70 meters (230 feet) wide at its widest point; near the major spring source the depth reaches around 36 meters (118 feet), though the average depth elsewhere is 25 meters (82 feet).

During the week the lake is virtually deserted. A free campground features picnic tables and tent sites. The turnoff for the lake is three km (1.8 miles) west of Río Verde on Mexico 70, after which an 11-km (6.8-mile) dirt road paralleling an irrigation canal leads southwest to the lake. If you would like to dive and need equipment, **Media Luna Dive Shop** in Rio Verde, tel./fax (487) 2-0625, can oblige.

Gruta de La Catedral/Gruta El Angel

To reach these caves drive 11 km (6.8 miles) west of Río Verde on Mexico 70, then southwest 15 km (9.3 miles) to the village of Alamitos. In Alami-

tos you can arrange for a guide to lead you for an hour on foot to the Gruta de la Catedral, named for a large cavern with formations said to resemble a pulpit, altar, and pews; a hole in the ceiling sprays light onto the scene. Seventy meters beyond is the Gruta del Angel, where stalagmite formations in five chambers resemble angels.

Accommodations

Shoestring: In town your best bet is either **Hotel Plaza,** tel. (487) 2-0100, next to Plaza Constitución (US$11-15), or the slightly nicer **Hotel Río,** Calle Hidalgo 700 on Plaza Constitución, tel. (487) 2-3072, fax (487) 2-3079 (US$12-15). **Hotel Santan-**

© MOON PUBLICATIONS, INC.

der, a block north of Plaza Constitución, tel. (487) 2-0900, offers small, clean rooms with private bath around an open courtyard. Rates: US$6.50 s, US$10 d, US$12 t, US$13 q. Cheapest place in town is the **Hotel Morelos,** Calle Morelos 246, with 27 spartan but adequately clean rooms with shared hot-water shower. Rates: US$3-4.

Budget: The very comfortable 73-room **Motel María Dolores,** at Km 127.5 on Mexico 70, tel. (487) 2-0516, not far from the town entrance. Spacious rooms at the María Dolores come with all the amenities and cost US$18 s, US$21 d, US$24 t, US$26 q.

Food
Near the Mercado Colón are several restaurants of varying quality. *Enchiladas rioverdenses,* a variation on the *potosina* and *huasteca* styles, are a local specialty. Fresh-squeezed orange juice is very inexpensive. **Restaurant González,** just south of Plaza Constitución, is clean and serves a variety of *antojitos.*

Transportation
From Río Verde's bus terminal, **Oriente** runs first-class buses to/from San Luis Potosí (US$4.50, seven times daily), Tampico (US$9, four times), Matamoros (US$17, four times), Reynosa (US$18, four times), and Mexico City (US$12, twice daily). Regional specialist **Vencedor** runs hourly second-class buses between Río Verde and Xilitla (US$4.50), Ciudad Valles (US$4.50), and Tamazunchale (US$8).

RÍO VERDE TO CIUDAD VALLES

Cascadas de Tamasopo
Near the village of Tamasopo between Río Verde and Ciudad Valles are a number of *cascadas* or waterfalls that can be reached by car. For Cascadas de Tamasopo, take the road north marked for Tamasopo and Agua Buena off Mexico 70, 77 km (47.7 miles) east of Río Verde. The falls are two km north of the village of Tamasopo via a paved road. They begin as one cascade at the 20-meter level, then split into three 15-meter cascades that tumble into a five- to seven-meter-deep, turquoise green river pool suitable for swimming. You can dive from a cement platform into the river or swing into the pool via a rope.

The river that feeds the falls is the Río Tamasopo, while the river the falls flow into is the Río Damián Carnoma, which in turn falls into the Río Gallinas via 105-meter **Cascada de Tamul,** described below.

Follow the Río Damián Carnoma or parallel roads in either direction to find other pools. Two km farther north, for example, a side road leads to **El Trampolín** ("The Diving Board"), a wooded area with small cascades and idyllic springs. At the bottom of a gorge that's a 15-minute walk from the El Cafetal railway station (three km by dirt road from Tamasopo) is **Puente de Dios** ("Bridge of God"), where the river has carved a rock bridge between two rock hills. Turquoise-blue waters sparkle in rounded pools to either side of the bridge. A short waterfall connects the two pools, and several small cascades trickle down surrounding rock walls.

Practicalities: The basic, shoestring **Hotel Cosmos** in Tamasopo has rooms with fan and hot water for US$6.50 s, US$8 d.

A *balneario* near the Tamasopo cascades charges US$0.70 per day to pitch a tent in a clean camping area shaded by fruit trees. A small *palapa*-roofed restaurant at the *balneario* offers good home-cooked *cocina potosina.*

The falls are least crowded during the week. If you like crowds, visit Tamasopo during the colorful sugarcane festival, held in mid-March each year.

Cascadas de Micos
Named for the monkeys *(micos)* once seen frequently in the area, this series of five falls feeds into a deep pool in the Río El Salto. To get there, go seven km (4.3 miles) west of Ciudad Valles on Mexico 70 and then take a posted dirt road north for 18 km (11 miles). The last couple of kilometers require vehicles with high road clearance; otherwise you'll have to walk.

Cascada de Tamul
The largest and most impressive waterfall in the state, Tamul is fed by the Río Gallinas and plummets 105 meters (344 feet) into the Río Tampoán, a wide river in a lush *cañada.* During rainy periods the Tampoán spreads up to 300 meters (980 feet) wide.

The only safe way to approach the falls is by boat along the Río Tampoán from Tanchachín. An unpaved road to Tanchachín starts 25 km

(15.5 miles) west of Ciudad Valles on Mexico 70, then proceeds south for 18 km (11 miles) to the village. Ask around for someone who will pilot a *lancha* up the river to the falls, a journey of two hours. The downriver return trip takes only 45 minutes. The best time to visit the magnificent Cascada de Tamul is during the drier months (Oct.-June).

CIUDAD VALLES

The state's second most populated city, Valles was founded on the banks of the Río Valles in 1533 by Nuño de Guzmán, who named the site Villa de Santiago de los Valles de Oxitipa. Little

of historical note remains and today the town is a center for ranching, light manufacturing, and the processing and shipping of coffee, sugar, and oranges.

Although the town offers little to see or do, Valles makes a convenient headquarters for visits to nearby waterfalls, *balnearios,* ruins, and Huastec villages. And, even though its population is at least half mestizo, the town is considered the capital of Huastec culture. According to no less an authority than the owner of Discos Corasón, Mexico's foremost producer of folkloric audio recordings, Ciudad Valles is to Mexican folk music (especially *huapangos* and *son huasteco*) what Nashville is to American country and western music.

© MOON PUBLICATIONS, INC.

LA CULTURA HUASTECA

The Huastec civilization developed along the Gulf of Mexico coast over a period of 6,000 years and flourished along river systems west of Tampico for some 2,500 years (1000 B.C.-A.D. 1500) before being suppressed by the Spanish conquest. The Huastecs may have been the first agriculturists in Mexico, and developed "culture" (as defined by the emergence of art, religion, and social organization) contemporaneously with Mesoamerican cultures as far south as Guatemala and Honduras.

Today visible Huastec archaeological sites are found as far north as Río Soto la Marina, as far west as Tamuín and Aquizmón, and as far south as El Tajín. According to historians, Huastec art and social organization reached its apex between 300 B.C. and A.D. 900, an era anthropologists call the "classic period" or "Pánuco III." Following the scheme generally used to classify pre-Cortesian cultures in Mexico, the years 1000-300 B.C. are deemed preclassic Huastec, while the period A.D. 900-1500 is labeled postclassic Huastec. Archaeological excavation and restoration of Huastec sites have been scant, because Mexico City-based authorities have given higher priority to Aztec and Mayan sites in Central and Southern Mexico.

Huastec woman

Linguistically related to the Mayans and Toltecs, the Huastecs nonetheless developed along a separate track. During the classic period, Huastec influence in Mesoamerica was so great that several other indigenous groups adopted Huastec deities. Unlike other Mesoamerican groups, the Huastecs originally erected circular buildings of worship, which were usually dedicated to Quetzalcóatl, the Plumed Serpent. This architecture was later co-opted by the Aztecs, who also took Tlazoltéotl (the goddess of love) and Xochiquetzal (the god of flowers). It has been theorized that the Huastecs may have founded the great city-state of Teotihuacán in Central Mexico, later taken over by the Aztecs.

The Aztec name for the Región Huasteca was Cueztlán ("place of platforms"). Huastec temples were painted with murals in black, ocher, coffee-brown, red, and white, and adorned with beautiful sandstone sculptures—predominantly masculine and feminine figures, birds, and serpents. During the postclassic period, Huastec religious architecture converted to rectangular plans similar to those customary among the Mayans and Aztecs.

The Huastecs preferred brightly colored clothes and jewelry, and painted their coiffures red and yellow. According to records compiled by the Spanish, the Aztecs considered the Huastecs to be sexually promiscuous. In the 15th century the Aztecs began a 60-year military campaign against the peace-loving Huastecs in an attempt to conquer them.

When the Spanish arrived in the 16th century, the million-strong Huastecs entered into an alliance with them in hopes that the new arrivals would help them defend their homelands against Aztec conquest. Unfortunately, the cruel Nuño de Guzmán was put in charge of the Región Huasteca, and the "alliance" led to the almost complete destruction of the Huastec culture, via Guzmán's introduction of the slave trade. By the end of the 16th century only about 100,000 Huastecs remained in the region.

Today approximately 91,000 Huastecs live in southeast San Luis Potosí, northern Veracruz, northeastern Hidalgo, and southern Tamaulipas. In their own language they call themselves Tenec and their traditional homelands Tenec-Bichou. Although their days of building ritual platforms are long gone, the Huastecs still hold fast to tradition, preferring to live in simple thatched-roof homes in isolated rural communities where they can farm, hunt, and practice their own customs. Due to the historical and continuing influence of missionaries, they are largely Christianized, but like indigenous peoples elsewhere in Mexico they've blended Christian and Amerindian elements into a syncretic belief system.

Arts and Crafts

The Huastecs once made beautiful ceramics. Exquisite pots dating to around 1000 B.C. feature tripod feet and incised eyes and mouths; by 50 B.C, Huastec pottery featured polychromatic (orange, red, and brown) animal shapes. Huastec handicrafts today are limited to basketry, reed mats, functional pottery, traditional clothing, and other items sometimes seen in local markets, along with a variety of harder-to-find folk and ritual utensils that aren't usually offered for sale.

Modern Huastec men cut their hair and dress much like the average rural Mexican. As is common with ethnic minorities around the world, it is the women who tend to wear the most traditional clothing. Most striking is the *petob,* an arrangement of their own hair interwoven with thick skeins of wool in green, orange, pink, and cherry-red, sometimes with a cloth pinned behind the head. A skirt of solid white or black fabric is held in place with a striped red-and-blue fabric belt.

A diamond-shaped tunic, called a *quechquémal* (*quisquem* or *cayem* in the Huastec language), made of white cotton embroidered with flowers, double crosses, animals (especially ducks, chickens, rabbits), and other figures from nature is worn over the shoulders and torso. Persons knowledgeable about *quechquémal* patterns can identify their village of provenance. In the premissionary days, the skirt and tunic would have been the full costume, but puritanical *misioneros* have influenced the Huastec women to wear solid or floral-print blouses beneath the *quechquémal.*

A bag embroidered with similar patterns is often worn over the shoulder. Known as a *talega,* this bag is used to carry a baby's gourd bottle, combs, and other items. Among Huastecs it's a common wedding gift offered by *madrinas* (godmothers).

Music and Dance

The Huapango or *son huasteco potosino,* popular well beyond the Región Huasteca itself, cannot be considered a pure Huastec musical form but is nonetheless a traditional part of modern culture in the Región Huasteca. Afro-Cuban rhythms have joined Huastec melodic motifs to become part of the general folkloric repertoire of Mexico. Marked by fast rhythms and high singing with prolonged falsettos, the typical Huapango is played by two standard violins, a *jarana* (a small, five-stringed guitar), a wooden flute, a small, indigenous three-stringed violin, a 29-string harp, and *maracas, casacabeles,* and other rhythm instruments. The term "Huapango" comes either from the Spanish "fandango" or the Náhuatl *huapantlico* ("on the platform").

Other popular song/dance forms include the *valona* and *décima,* both of which are typically performed by urbanized Huastecs at private functions (weddings, christenings, birthdays, patron saint days) using violins and guitars. More folk than folkloric, *valones* and *décimas* are quite danceable and incorporate a type of improvisational poetry that involves verbal jousting on stage. Musicians who play this type of music call themselves *poesilleros* or poets rather than *músicos.*

Another traditional but more rural dance, *las varitas* ("the twigs," a reference to sacro-medicinal botanicals used by Huastec shamans), is commonly performed during the feast of San Miguel Arcángel, the Huastecs' main patron saint. In this dance, Huastec men dressed in white hold knives in one hand, bells and ribbons in the other, while performing movements and gestures in imitation of various forest creatures; the dance is accompanied by violin and flute music. In Aquismón, a similar dance called *zacamsón* is performed to the accompaniment of violin, harp, and guitar.

Food

While Huastecan culinary influences have reached restaurants in the state capitals of San Luis Potosí and Tamaulipas, in the Región Huasteca itself the best place to try local specialties is among the vendor stands set up at the weekly *tianguis* or at festivals. Corn is an important local crop and thus a major ingredient in local cuisine. Sugarcane extract—cheap and abundant—is fermented and distilled to produce a fiery contraband *aguardiente,* which is drunk in copious amounts during important religious festivals.

One of the most famous Huastecan foods is the *zacahuil,* a huge tamal made with corn dough soaked in a deep red *chile chino* or *chile pequín* sauce, stuffed with pork or chicken, wrapped in banana leaves, and baked in a wood-fired oven. *Zacahuiles* can reach up to two meters (six feet) long and are especially available during festivals. A similar snack food, the *bolim,* looks a bit like a *zacahuil* but is much smaller and is always stuffed with either chicken or turkey. Another local source of protein is *acamayas* or freshwater shrimp. *Palmito,* or heart of palm, is cooked to a smooth consistency and served as a snack or appetizer with tostadas.

Other popular fiesta foods include the *bocol*—a *gordita de maíz* (thick corn tortilla) filled with cheese, beans or potatoes—and *guiso borracho* ("drunken stew"), a sumptuous stew made with a variety of meats, fruits, and vegetables marinated beforehand in *pulque* (fermented maguey extract) and served in bowls or on crisp tostadas. Cafes (especially in Río Verde and Ciudad del Maíz) sometimes serve *guiso borracho.*

The main business and shopping district is along Calles Abasolo and Hidalgo west of the highway through town. Here you'll find the small **Mercado Municipal** and a few handicraft vendors. Classier shops are found along Calle Hidalgo, the more straightforward places along Calle Independencia.

Visits to two sugar mills *(azucareros)* outside of town—**Plan de Ayala** and **Plan de San Luis**—can be arranged through the larger hotels.

Museo Regional Huasteca

This small museum off Blvd. Sur (Mexico 70/85 in town) near the Glorieta Hidalgo contains exhibits of ceramics and other Huastec artifacts. Although the posted hours are Mon.-Fri. 9 a.m.-1 p.m. and 4-8 p.m., the actual opening times are more erratic. Admission is free.

Puente Tampoán

Built 1936-39, this steel bridge over the wide Río Tampoán south of Ciudad Valles is an engineering marvel in itself, but the main reason to stop here is to watch the ongoing excavation of river sand. In the shallow waters below the bridge, workers shovel accumulated sand into canoes, then paddle the sand to shore where it's loaded into trucks. This keeps the river flowing while providing a cheap source of material for local cement factories.

Reserva de la Biosfera Abra-Tanchipa

One of Northern Mexico's newest and smallest biosphere reserves protects 21,464 hectares extending north of Ciudad Valles and east of Mexico 85 in the state's relatively undeveloped northeastern corner. Two spurs of Sierra Madre Oriental—Sierra Abra and Sierra Tanchipa—act as a meteorological barrier between the warm, supermoist Gulf coastal plains and the cool, arid Altiplano, mingling climatic influences from both regions to produce cloud-forest conditions. Because of the relative lack of human habitation, the federal government has been able to dedicate nearly 80% of the reserve to a nucleus zone devoted to scientific research activities, with only the outer 20% in private or *ejido* hands.

Temperatures vary little from a mean 24° C, while annual rainfall averages 107 cm (42 inches)—a perfect environment for 300 species of plants, including epiphytes, bromeliads, orchids, and a unique tropical oak *(Quercus oleoides)*. Another extraordinary arboreal species found in the Abra-Tanchipa's thick forests is the giant ficus, a very tall wild fig tree. Jaguar, tigrillo, ocelot, puma, whitetail deer, javelina, and the endangered boa constrictor are among the reserve's notable fauna. Some 17 Huastec archaeological sites and a half dozen little-explored caves are in the area.

So far there is no official public access to the reserve, although a drive north along Mexico 85 will allow western views. Check with the tourist office in Ciudad Valles for any visitor programs that may have been established since this writing.

Accommodations

As in many towns and cities in Mexico, hotels located on the highway cost more than those downtown and typically offer more amenities.

Shoestring: A couple of blocks off the highway toward downtown, the two-story **Hotel Rex,** Calle Hidalgo 418, tel. (138) 1-0411, fax (138) 2-3335, has rooms with or without TV. Rates: around US$8.50 s, US$10.50 d without TV; US$11.50 s, US$14 d with TV. **Hotel Condesa** lies across from the Palacio Municipal on Calle Juárez, in a pink and green building constructed in 1934. The rooms are clean and have fans and shared bath. Rates: US$6 s, US$6.50 d. The 57-room **Hotel Piña,** Calle Juárez 210, tel. (138) 2-0183, fax (138) 2-4461, has basic rooms as well as fancier rooms with fan, TV, and phone; a/c available for US$3 extra. Rates: US$8.50 s, US10.50 d basic; US$11.50 s, US$14 d with amenities. On Mexico 85 (Blvd. México-Laredo), **Hotel San Fernando,** tel. (138) 2-0184, offers plain but clean, medium-sized rooms with a/c, phone, hot water, and satellite TV at bargain prices. A 24-hour restaurant and parking lot are attached. Rates: US$14 s, US$14.50 d.

Budget: Hotel Quintamar, on Mexico 70 on the way into town from San Luis Potosí, tel./fax (138) 2-3224, is a small, modern, three-story place where rooms have a/c, phone, carpeting, and color TV. A restaurant/bar is on the premises. Rates: around US$32. Fifteen km (11 miles) east of town on Mexico 70 (on the way to Tampico), the sugar-cooperative-owned **Hotel Balneario Taninul,** tel. (138) 2-0000 or 2-4414, offers quiet landscaped grounds, a terrace with rocking chairs, a good restaurant, a tennis court, and a pool fed by hot mineral springs. You'll find hiking trails nearby, including one to the source of the Río Coy. This is a good place to get away and relax. Rates: US$26 s, US$31 d.

Budget/Inexpensive: East along Mexico 70 and then south on Mexico 85 (Blvd. México-Laredo) into the heart of town, the delightful **Hotel Valles,** tel. (138) 2-0050, is a worn but clean and friendly place with 10 acres of tropical landscaping and a pool. Cozy rooms with private bath, a/c, cable TV, phone, and minibar are available in a newly renovated wing or the old classic wing. Rates: US$30-35 s, US$31-41 d, US$41-47 t.

Inexpensive: South of Hotel Valles on Mexico 85 (Blvd. México-Laredo) is **Posada Don Antonio,** tel. (138) 2-0066, fax (138) 2-3048, a renovated, colonial-style hotel with a variety of comfortable a/c rooms with TV and phones, plus a pool, coffeeshop, and restaurant/bar. Rates: US$37-47.

RV Parks

El Bañito Trailer Park, 9.6 km (six miles) south of town on Mexico 85, tel. (138) 2-0608, offers 60 slots with full hookups (most also have patios) for US$7 a day, or US$6 a day for stays longer than a month. On the spacious grounds are two thermal-fed pools, a recreation room, mini-market, and restaurant.

Hotel Valles also has 25 RV slots with full hookups for just US$5 per night.

Food

The shopping area downtown holds several small eateries, including Calle Hidalgo's **Bonanza Restaurant y Cafetería** (open 24 hours) and **Principal,** both of which serve Mexican standards.

On the Mexico 70/85 boulevard through town are some larger restaurants such as **El Asadero,** a specialist in *carnes al carbón.* The quick and easy **Pollo Loco,** between the Mexico 70 and 85 junction and the traffic circle (Glorieta Hidalgo), has chicken-beans-tortillas combos.

Restaurant del Bosque, attached to the Hotel Valles, has good food and service, and is one of the only places in town that accepts credit cards. A few Huastecan specialties are available such as *enchiladas huastecas* which are very similar to *enchiladas potosinas* except that they

come with a piece of fried chicken (or a pork chop) and black beans instead of pinto beans.

A coffee shop attached to the Posada Don Antonio serves reasonably priced Mexican, Lebanese, and Huastecan food, including tasty *bocoles* (*gorditas* filled with cheese) with *nopalitos* (strips of cooked or pickled prickly pear cactus) and *jamón* (ham).

Events

During the third week of March, Valles sponsors the **Feria Nacional de la Huasteca Potosina** (FENAHUAP), a big fair with ranching, agricultural, and cultural expositions. This is a good time of year to hear *son huasteco* and other regional folk music.

Friendly town residents open their homes to outsiders during the **Days of the Dead,** 1-2 Nov., inviting visitors as well as neighbors in to see their home altars, and to share tamales and tea. Street processions feature altars festooned with hundreds of orange or yellow marigolds; the best receive awards.

Information

The **Coordinación General de Turismo,** Morelos 5, second floor of the Edificio Magdalena downtown, tel. (138) 2-4252, fax (138) 1-0290, can help with questions visitors might have about where to go in the Región Huasteca or how to get there.

Transportation

Bus: Valle's main bus terminal is at the southern edge of town (around three km from the town center) off Mexico 85. The first-class **Omnibus de México** operates to/from San Luis Potosí (US$9, four times daily), Mexico City (US$11, three times daily), and Guadalajara (US$19, twice daily). **Omnibus de Oriente** has service to/from Ciudad Victoria (US$7, three times daily), Tampico (US$4, eight times daily), Reynosa (US$16, three times daily), Tamuín (US$1, five times daily), Río Verde (US$5, five times daily), and Xilitla (US$2, five times daily). The **Potosinos** and **Huasteco** lines handle second-class buses all over the state as well as to Tampico, Guanajuato, and Veracruz, while **Transportes Vencedor** handles all the main villages of the Huastec region.

Train: The San Luis Potosí-Tampico *El Huasteco* stops in Ciudad Valles at 1 p.m. daily. Second-class (only) seats cost just US$2.50 one-way.

EL CONSUELO (TAMUÍN)

Of the region's 527 Huastec archaeological sites, the **Zona Arqueológica El Consuelo** is the most well known and the most accessible; many other sites are on private lands. Excavated in 1946, El Consuelo ("The Consolation") covers 17 hectares and features a number of stepped ceremonial platforms. When first discovered, the stucco walls of the platforms featured ancient paintings that have since worn away. Tombs in which corpses in fetal positions faced east were also discovered on the grounds. One of the more remarkable discoveries here was the sculpted figure known as "El Adolescente," now in Mexico City's National Museum of Anthropology (a replica can be seen in San Luis Potosí's Potosino Regional Museum). The iconography and dating of the figure suggests that the Huastecs formed a Quetzalcóatl cult before the Aztecs.

*Huastec
adolescent
sculpture (from
El Consuelo)*

BOB RACE

The entire complex faces more or less east, so for photography it's best to arrive in the morning. From the top of the largest platform you can just make out two mounds to the west about three km (two miles) in the distance. On private lands, these mounds are actually two large, overgrown pyramids, the larger of which, known as Cantóc, may be the largest unexplored pyramid in the western hemisphere. Neither has ever been open to the public or excavated.

Accommodations: Hotel Tamuín, Leandro Valle 10, tel. (138) 8-0515 or 8-0571, offers comfortable rooms with a/c, satellite TV, phone, laundry service, and secure parking at budget rates (around US$22).

Getting There: The ruins are six km (3.7 miles) south of Tamuín, which is 28 km (17 miles) east of Ciudad Valles (or 51 km/31.6 miles west of Ebano) via Mexico 70. It is also possible to reach El Consuelo from Tancanhuitz de Santos via Tanquián de Escobedo and San Vicente Tancuayalab, but this southern route is often rough; the road is often riddled with huge potholes every hundred meters or so, forcing motorists to drive slowly most of the way. If you're driving from Mexico 85 south, it's much quicker to drive all the way north to Ciudad Valles and then proceed east on Mexico 70 to Tamuín, then south to the ruins.

SOUTH OF CIUDAD VALLES

Mexico 85 heads south from Ciudad Valles into the cultural heart of the Región Huasteca. The scenery is lush, with wooded valleys interspersed with sugarcane fields and orange orchards, plus smaller farms of avocado, papaya, mango, bananas, pineapple, breadfruit, and guava. High on the slopes west of the road are a number of small coffee plantations.

Fresh-roasted coffee—whole bean or ground in hand mills on the spot—can be purchased in local markets for only US$3 per kilo. Unfortunately, soft world coffee prices (along with three uncharacteristic winter freezes during the last 15 years) have discouraged coffee production in recent years and have wiped out several of the more financially vulnerable operations.

Practicalities: For local color, market days are the best time to visit Huastec towns and villages. Most take place on Fridays, Saturdays, or Sundays; thus weekends are generally the best time to explore the area. **Transportes Vencedor** is the region's main bus line, with routes between Ciudad Valles (also, in some cases, San Luis Potosí) and every town in the area.

Tancanhuitz de Santos

Also known simply as Tancanhuitz ("Place of the Flower of Love") or Ciudad Santos, this is one of the region's larger Huastec centers. Four km (2.5 miles) east of Mexico 85, the town straddles a *cañada* formed by the Arroyo Huehuetlán, which divides the population into a Náhuatl section on the north side of the stream, Huastec on the south. It is the second most developed Huastec town (after Tamazunchale) in the area, with lots of satellite dishes attached to the largely Mexican-style houses.

Public life revolves around the 18th-century **Parroquía de San Miguel Arcángel** (feast day 29 Sept.). A *tianguis* or open-air market is held every Sunday; here you'll find *quechquémetls,* shoulder bags, baskets, and other handicrafts.

Surrounding villages with more traditional Huastec lifestyles include Huehuetlán, Coxcatlán, and San Antonio. **Huehuetlán** is well known for a unique dance-drama ritual performed only in this village during pre-Lenten weekends of February-March, on Day of the Dead (1-2 Nov.), and on 12 November, feast day for the village's patron saint Diego de Alcalá. In Huastec dialect the dance is called "Kamal," the name of the Huastec god of fire in whose honor the performance is given, while local Spanish-speaking Mexicans call the dance "Huehue" after the village. Performed since the Spanish *entrada,* the all-male dancers wear loincloths and paint their bodies in vivid colors (one separate color or combination of colors over the entire body of each dancer), then dance to music performed by an instrumental ensemble consisting of *quinta* (a small guitarlike instrument), violin, and *jarana* (also small and guitarlike). The performance tells the story of how the Huastecs abandoned the practice of human sacrifice.

Twenty-five km (15.5 miles) east of Mexico 85 on the main road is the smaller Huastec town of **Tampamalón,** a quaint sugarcane center with thatched-roof homes and an old church.

Practicalities: Although Tancanhuitz can easily be visited from Ciudad Valles as a day-trip, modest, shoestring-priced lodging is available in town at **Hotel Casa Colorado,** not far from the main bus stop. A room with a bed, fan, and private bath goes for US$8 s, US$9 d. **Vencedor** operates buses between Tancanhuitz, Ciudad Valles, and San Luis Potosí.

Aquismón

More interesting and slightly more off the beaten track than Tancanhuitz, the *município* of Aquismón is almost entirely Huastec, although the *cabecera* or capital town is mixed. A new plaza planted with almond trees and Indian laurels is the site for a weekly *tianguis* held on Saturdays. *Pilón,* blocks of raw sugar wrapped in cane bundles, is a good buy. As in Tancanhuitz, the town's annual *fiesta patronal* takes place on 29 September.

Several all-Huastec villages near Aquismón can be visited, including the nearby **Tanquimé** (Tancuimé)—follow the dirt road just north of the plaza about 2.5 km (1.5 miles) until you reach an area of traditional thatched-roof homes. Other villages on the mountain slopes west of Aquismón are harder to reach but worth seeking out. A dirt road leads west a few km to the **Cueva de Mantezulel,** a seldom-visited limestone cave. The latter is known locally as the "Cueva del Sol" or Cavern of the Sun; it's a small opening high on a hillside with a large chamber below and can be entered without technical gear.

Practicalities: The small **Hotel San Cosme,** Calle Juárez 7, offers simple, shoestring-priced rooms with *baño colectivo* (US$5 s, US$6.50 d). Rooms at the **Hotel La Mansión,** on the main road through town, are also basic and shoestring priced, but are larger and cleaner, with two double beds, a fan, and private hot-water bath (US$12 s/d). **Vencedor** operates buses between Ciudad Valles and the highway turnoff for Aquismón (less than US$2); from there you can hop a *colectivo* the last few kilometers into Aquismón (US$0.50).

Sótano de las Golondrinas

Seven km southwest of Aquismón on foot or about 30 km (18.6 miles) by road (23 km/14 miles of unpaved road from Mexico 85), this huge pit cave is one of Mexico's major caving challenges. Named for the thousands of swifts *(golondrinas)* that inhabit the *sótano* (literally "cellar"), the cave has a mouth measuring 60 meters (197 feet) in diameter, plunges to over 350 meters (1,148 feet) in depth, and has a floor that covers six acres. A tunnel off the floor has been explored to a length of four km (2.5 miles).

In addition to the swifts commonly seen flying from the cave at sunset, the cave also hosts a large number of colorful parakeets. The Huastecs believe that the "Earth Owner" lives in the cave. Nearby is the smaller **Sótano de las Guaguas.**

Special equipment and careful preparation are necessary to even begin to explore Las Golondrinas. The state tourist office in San Luis Potosí may be able to recommend local guides and caving associations that can arrange a descent. The Aquismón municipality office also has information on the *sótano.*

If all you want is a peek down into the pit, seek out a small ranch owned by Alejandro Santiago and family right below the Sótano. The Santiagos keep a registry book that visitors to the cave are expected to sign. One of the Santiago brood can lead you to the best place to peer in, a ledge on the north side of the opening. Gringo base jumpers have reportedly parachuted into the pit from here. You can also ask the Santiagos for permission to camp near the ranch.

About 45 minutes walk along a nearby trail is another, smaller pit cave with a 35-meter shaft leading to a huge cavern. One of Alejandro's sons will gladly lead visitors there for a small tip.

Las Pozas (La Casa de Inglés)

Bizarre metal and reinforced concrete sculptures rising out of the jungle near Xilitla—visible only to those willing to leave the highway—are the Región Huasteca legacy of a visionary Englishman who, in the 1930s and '40s, mingled with Salvador Dali, Aldous Huxley, Picasso, Magritte, Max Ernst, and others involved in the early surrealist movement. Born in Scotland in 1907 as the grandson of King Edward VII, Edward James studied literature at university and published a number of poems, plays, and short stories before embarking on world travel. While exploring Mexico in 1945 in the company of his Pima Indian friend Plutarco Gastelum, James found the retreat he was looking for in Xilitla and in 1949 began building this 80-acre forest idyll next to a spring and waterfall.

Later, while living at his Xilitla estate, James erected a number of linked pavilions, walls, walkways, and steps leading nowhere, surrealistic iron or cement sculptures (a set of oversized sculpted hands supposedly represent Dali's right hand, front and back), a 60-foot concrete imitation of a bamboo grove, and other "constructions." James died in 1984 and his works are now decaying and somewhat overgrown; some are obviously unfinished. Of the 36 structures on the estate—many with names ("The House with a Roof Curved like a Whale," "Parrot House," and "Tank like an Eye," among others)—only one was intended for human habitation.

Between 1962 and 1984 James employed 40 local men and spent US$5 million on the project. Gastelum, who served as foreman for most of the construction, died in 1992. Some Mexican and American journalists add the title "Sir" before James's name, unaware that he was never knighted.

The complex has a sort of hideous beauty, but the best part of visiting Las Pozas is simply walk-

Las Pozas

ex-Convento de San
Agustín, Xilitla

JOE CUMMINGS

ing through the lush grounds, viewing the orchids and other tropical vegetation, and sitting beside the cool falls that run along one side of the estate; these falls were channeled by James into a series of clean pools suitable for swimming. They can be approached from the bottom near the entrance to the estate or via a set of steps that loops through the estate to the top of the falls.

The part of the James estate that contains the falls represents about half the original property and is open to the public daily. Allow an hour or two to explore the buildings, stairs, and waterfalls. During rainy spells the stairs and pathways can become very slippery; also take care on the higher exposed constructions—especially with children. A small entry fee is collected at a kiosk near the entrance, where you'll find a small snack bar with a few tables.

Another section of the estate is now owned by an American and is closed to the public. In the nearby town of Xilitla, Gastelum's James-inspired home has been converted to a bed and breakfast.

Getting There: To reach Las Pozas, take Mexico 120 west off Mexico 85 (26 km/16 miles south of the turnoff for Tancanhuitz) and head southwest 12.5 km (7.8 miles) to a graded dirt road on the right, just before a small bridge. Follow this road about a kilometer to a fork in the road and bear left; this branch leads to Las Pozas.

Xilitla

The name of this town means "place of *cozole*" (a type of local freshwater crab) in Náhuatl. One of the earliest settlements in the Región Huasteca, Xilitla was founded in the 1550s by the Augustine sect, who in 1557 constructed the convent of **San Agustín de la Gran Xilitla.** The convent's high, thick, flagstone walls didn't deter local native attacks, and the convent was completely sacked in 1585. Today the convent chapel serves a population of 14,000 and the ancillary rooms are used for community services.

Perched on a precipitous hill at 1,050 meters (3,440 feet) above sea level, the town's steep, narrow streets lead you into what seems like a tiny mountain kingdom. One sizable house on the edge of town was obviously designed by Edward James (see above). The climate is temperate and rains tend to fall year-round.

On Sundays a *tianguis* or open-air market behind the chapel offers coffee, copal (a type of incense), *piloncillo* (cones of raw sugar), tobacco, and *zacahuil* (huge Huastecan tamales), among the usual inexpensive consumer goods. Many vendors also set up on the sidewalks on weekends, the better to catch all the visitors from surrounding villages who come to browse and shop.

Eighteen km (9.3 miles) farther along Mexico 120 is the smaller Huastec village of **Ahua-catlán.** Back on Mexico 85, a few km south of the Mexico 120 junction, **Axtla de Terrazas** is well known for its **Fiesta Huasteca** held annually on 24-25 November; it's a celebration of Huastec culture through music, dance, and food.

Accommodations and Food: Several small hotels in town offer rooms for US$4.50-8. The best-looking place is the **Hotel Ziyaquetzas** on the plaza, where the small clean rooms have private bath.

El Castillo, a block from the plaza at Ocampo 105, tel. (136) 5-0038, fax (136) 5-0055, is a bed and breakfast in the former home of Plutarco Gastelum, Edward James's construction foreman and friend. The architecture is a blend of Mexican, English and Moorish styles, and each of the six rooms is almost as unique and bizarre as Edward's jungle lair. All rooms are spacious and offer views of the surrounding jungle and town. A delicious Mexican breakfast with plenty of fresh local coffee is included in the inexpensive-to-moderate rates (US$40-75, depending on the location). Even if you don't stay here, the house is worth a visit to witness the unique style and bizarre architecture of each room. One of the inn's assets is a huge common room filled with Huastecan artifacts and books on art and culture. You can also use the VCR here to view a video documentary entitled "Builder of Dreams," about Edward James and produced by Avery and Lenore Danziger, who manage El Castillo. The Danzigers can arrange hiking guides, horseback riding, car tours, river outings, and transportation to and from the airport in Tampico. Room reservations and travel arrangements can be made through their U.S. agent, Cooper Travel Service, tel. (800) 776-3138.

La Casa Vieja, a yellow and blue adobe on the plaza, serves several pasta dishes as well as burgers, espresso, and excellent desserts. In the vicinity of the plaza you'll find several other inexpensive cafes and restaurants.

Transportation: Xilitla is 15 km (9.3 miles) southwest of Mexico 85 via Mexico 120. **Vencedor** provides second-class bus service between here and other towns in the Región Huasteca, including Ciudad Valles.

Take care on the steep, narrow streets if you're driving. The best strategy is to park as soon as you're at or near the top of the hill and finish exploring the town on foot. RVers with rigs over 20 feet long may want to park at the bottom of the hill.

Tamazunchale

A municipal *cabecera* (capital) and significant regional trade center, this town on the Río Moctezuma is not that interesting except on Sundays, when a large *tianguis* or open-air market convenes; look for two local specialties—live river shrimp and *chile pequin.* Getting here is more than half the fun, as the scenery is impressive.

The **Fiesta de Todos los Santos** (All Saints Fiesta, Day of the Dead) on 1-2 Nov. is particularly well celebrated here.

Many nearby rivers and streams add increased lushness to an already green area; in several mountainous spots the streams form pools deep enough for swimming. Two km outside town is the *balneario* of **Poxtapa,** in a wooded area with showers, changing rooms, grills, and a snack bar. Entrance is by donation.

If you want to get a better look at the countryside and its inhabitants, you can hike from nearby Agua Zarca (13 km southwest at Km 26 on the highway to Mexico City) to Xilitla in two days. If you need a guide, English-speaking Rodolfo ("Rudy") Reyes charges about US$20 a day; he can be contacted through the Hotel Tamazunchale.

Accommodations: Tamazunchale has almost as many hotels as Ciudad Valles, although the standards are by and large a bit lower. Several *clase económica* places in the US$8-12 range are found along Av. 20 de Noviembre, the main commercial strip, including **Hotel González,** at #301, tel./fax (136) 9-1136; **Hotel Mirador,** at #62, tel. (136) 9-1136; and **Hotel Tropical,** at #404, tel. (136) 2-0041. Cheaper still is the basic **Casa de Huéspedes Lorenzo Sandoval** at Calle Hidalgo 413. The newly renovated, three-story **Hotel Tamazunchale,** Av. 20 de Noviembre 122, tel. (136) 2-0496, fax (136) 2-0389, offers small but comfortable and clean, budget-priced rooms with a/c and satellite TV. Other amenities include 24-hour private parking, laundry service, and a restaurant. Rates: US$24 s, US$31 d.

Transportation: Several bus companies with San Luis Potosí, Hidalgo, and Veracruz routes serve the town.

BOB RACE

THE STATE OF COAHUILA

Officially named Coahuila de Zaragoza, Mexico's third largest state—after Chihuahua and Sonora—shares borders with Texas, Chihuahua, Durango, Nuevo León, Zacatecas, San Luis Potosí (just a pinch, squeezed between Zacatecas and Nuevo León), and Tamaulipas. The Spanish first explored the area in 1570 and established a colonial settlement at Saltillo in 1577, although early expansion was severely limited by natives whom the Spanish described as "bellicose and indomitable."

The Coahuilteca tribes—who have left behind a considerable legacy of rock art in the state—were later dominated by Lipan Apache raiders who invaded the region from the north. Throughout the 17th century constant friction flared between the Coahuiltecas, Apaches, and Spanish, but by the early 19th century the area had been "tamed" and colonization continued in earnest.

Despite large tracts of land classified as desert because of scant rainfall, Coahuila has an extensive river system that allows for year-round cultivation of vinifera, olives, cotton, and other agricultural products. As elsewhere in northeastern Mexico, cattle ranching is also a major economic activity.

Travel highlights include the lofty, forested Sierra del Carmen in the northwest, colonial Saltillo in the southeast, and the pristine *bolsón* environments near Cuatrociénegas in the center. Because they're among the least busy along the U.S.-Mexico frontier, Coahuila's well-equipped border crossings at Piedras Negras and Ciudad Acuña are favorite Mexico gateways for repeat visitors from the U.S. and Canada.

Information

The Coahuila state government is very pro-tourism and has overseen the production of five excellent map guides covering six regions (Frontera, Sureste, Laguna, Centro, Desierto, and Carbonífera); these are available at tourist offices in Saltillo, Arteaga, Parras de la Fuente, Ciudad Acuña, Piedras Negras, Monclova, Nueva Rosita, and Torreón. Each map guide contains a state highway map, a regional map, and a number of city maps with descriptions of tourist attractions.

The state has also posted tourist information map-boards in major cities. These enlightened steps, as well as the overall fine maintenance of state highways, go a long way toward making out-of-state visitors feel welcome.

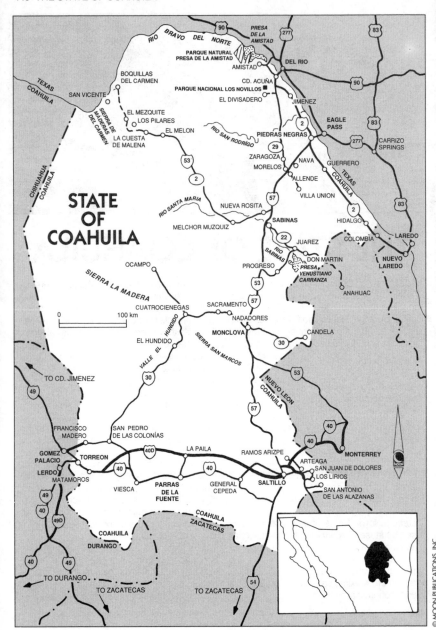

© MOON PUBLICATIONS, INC.

NORTH OF SALTILLO

CIUDAD ACUÑA

The smaller of the state's two border gateways, Ciudad Acuña (pop. 56,000) was founded as a military encampment on the Río Bravo (Rio Grande) in 1877. By the 1880s the military was replaced by ranchers who ignobly named the spot Congregación Las Vacas ("Cow Congregation"). In 1912 the town was renamed for noted revolutionary Saltillo poet Manuel Acuña, although locally some people still refer to the town by the nickname "Las Vacas." This is also the name of an arroyo that runs along the north edge of town, feeding into the Rio Grande.

Today, though still a farming and ranching center, Acuña has also taken on a few *maquila* (in-bond plant) facilities which have managed not to disrupt the town's quiet nature too much. It's just large enough to be of varied interest to the casual border-hopper, yet small enough (and remote enough) to have escaped the sleaze of transborder metropolises like Ciudad Juárez and Nuevo Laredo. The town enjoys a particularly amiable relationship with Del Rio, its U.S. twin across the border.

Another claim to fame for Del Rio-Acuña is that two famous radio figures broadcast their shows from a "pirate" radio station, XER, on the Mexican side of the border. The first was Dr. John R. Brinkley, the infamous goat gland surgeon of the 1930s; the second was rock 'n' roll DJ Wolfman Jack in the late '50s and early '60s. The facility was set up so announcers could operate out of a Del Rio studio while the 500,000-watt transmitter was located in Acuña, thus circumventing FCC licensing. The station's antenna boosted the transmission power to an astounding one million watts, providing a signal that reached all the way to Canada. Mexican radio still rules the airwaves in south Texas.

Former University of Texas student Robert Rodríguez chose Acuña for the location shooting of his film *El Mariachi,* a cult favorite produced for a budget of $7,000, and for its much higher-budget Hollywood sequel *Desperado,* starring international Latin heartthrob Antonio Banderas. Portions of the motion pictures *Lone Star* and *Like Water For Chocolate* were also filmed in Ciudad Acuña.

The town's social center is shady Plaza Benjamin Canales, named after another revolutionary hero and located just on the other side of the International Bridge. On warm evenings, the streets come alive with food vendors and evening strollers. Though not especially geared toward gringo shoppers, several *artesanías* and liquor stores can be found along Av. Hidalgo near the bridge.

Lake Amistad

Nineteen km northwest of Acuña, **Presa de la Amistad** ("Friendship Dam") came about after the governments in the U.S. and Mexico, through the International Boundary and Water Commission (IBWC), agreed to build a dam across the Río Bravo (Rio Grande). This site was chosen since it's just below the confluence of the Río Bravo/Rio Grande, Pecos River, and Devils River—giving humans control over three rivers at once and providing water conservation, flood control, hydroelectric power, and recreation.

With a surface area that varies between 65,000 and 89,000 acres and a shoreline of 1,200-1,600 km (744-990 miles), the Amistad is a favorite spot for swimming, boating, and fishing, although the facilities on the Mexican side of this huge lake can't compete with those on the Texas side, which is managed by the U.S National Park Service. To fish on either side, you'll need a valid fishing permit.

Bulls and Horses

Acuña's bullring, **Plaza de Toros La Macarena,** is on Libramiento Oriente (West Bypass), not far from the International Bridge. The *charro* ring, **Lienzo Charro El Potrero,** is in the northwest corner of town on Calle California, off Blvd. López Mateos. Check with the tourist office for a current schedule of *charreadas* and *corridas de toros.* Bullfights generally only take place during occasional festivals.

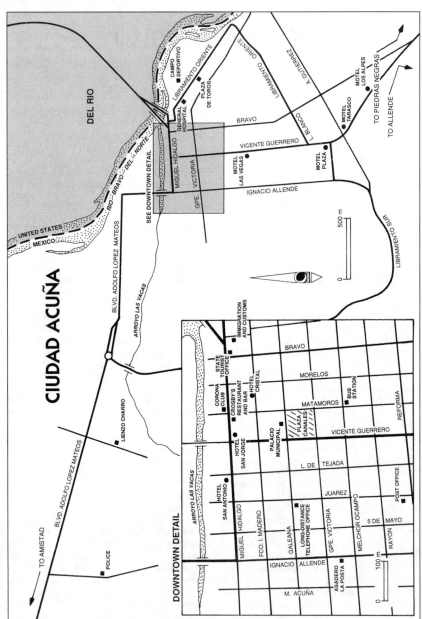

CIUDAD ACUÑA

DEL RIO

UNITED STATES
MEXICO

RIO BRAVO DEL NORTE

TO AMISTAD

BLVD. ADOLFO LOPEZ MATEOS

ARROYO LAS VACAS

LIENZO CHARRO

POLICE

SEE DOWNTOWN DETAIL

MIGUEL HIDALGO
GPE. VICTORIA

GENERAL HOSPITAL
CAMPO DEPORTIVO
LIBRAMIENTO ORIENTE
PLAZA DE TOROS
LIBRAMIENTO ORIENTE
A. GUTIERREZ

BRAVO
VICENTE GUERRERO
MOTEL LAS VEGAS

IGNACIO ALLENDE

L. BRAVO

MOTEL TARASCO
MOTEL LOS ALPES
MOTEL PLAZA

TO PIEDRAS NEGRAS
TO ALLENDE

LIBRAMIENTO SUR

0   500 m

DOWNTOWN DETAIL

ARROYO LAS VACAS

IMMIGRATION AND CUSTOMS
STATE TOURIST OFFICE
CORONA CLUB
CROSBY'S RESTAURANT AND BAR
HOTEL CRISTAL

BRAVO
MORELOS
MATAMOROS

PLAZA CANALES
PALACIO MUNICIPAL
HOTEL SAN JORGE

VICENTE GUERRERO

BUS STATION
REFORMA

HOTEL SAN ANTONIO

L. DE TEJADA

JUAREZ

POST OFFICE

MIGUEL HIDALGO
FCO. I. MADERO
GALEANA
LONG-DISTANCE TELEPHONE OFFICE
GPE. VICTORIA
MELCHOR OCAMPO

5 DE MAYO

IGNACIO   ALLENDE

ASADERO LA POSTA

RAYON

M. ACUÑA

0   100 m

© MOON PUBLICATIONS, INC.

Parque Nacional de los Novillos

One of Mexico's smallest (42 hectares) and oldest national parks (established in 1940), Los Novillos is centered around a cool arroyo resplendent with prickly pear, oaks, cottonwoods, and willows. A small *balneario,* fed by the Río San Diego (a tributary of the Río Bravo) is popular in summer. The park has day-use facilities only (no overnight camping permitted). Park access is 45 km south of Acuña off Mexico 29.

Accommodations

Budget: Downtown over a Mexican curios shop, **Hotel San Jorge,** Calle M. Hidalgo 165 (at Av. V. Guerrero), tel. (877) 2-5070, is conveniently located two blocks from Plaza Canales. Rooms have carpet, phones, TV, a/c, heat, and private hot-water showers. Rates: US$19-22 s/d. The newer **Motel Tarasco,** Obregón 150 (just off Mexico 57 and convenient for road travel south), tel. (877) 2-6483, is a two-story motel painted white with blue trim. The simple, large, clean rooms have a/c, heat, TV, and phone. Parking is available in back. Rates: US$19 s/d. Others in this price range include **Motel Plaza,** Av. V. Guerrero 2010, tel. (877) 2-2869, on the way out of town toward Saltillo and Piedras Negras (US$16 s, US$22 d); **Hotel Cristal,** Calle Madero at Morelos downtown, tel. (877) 2-6463 (US$14 s, US$20 d); and **Motel Las Vegas,** Guerrero at Villaldama, tel. (877) 2-5483 (US$19 s/d).

Moving up a notch in comfort, the friendly ranch-style **Motel Los Alpes,** on Av. V. Guerrero southeast of the Motel Tarasco, tel. (877) 2-6231, fax (877) 2-6139, has clean, well-maintained rooms with a/c and satellite TV, plus a pool and parking. Like the Plaza and Tarasco, this is a good choice for quick exits from town on the way south. Rates: US$25-28 s/d. The nicest rooms downtown are available at the three-story **Hotel San Antonio,** Calle Hidalgo at Lerdo, tel./fax (877) 2-5108. Rates: US$33 s/d.

Food

The favorite hangout for gringo border-hoppers is **Crosby's Restaurant & Bar,** Av. Hidalgo Ote. 195, tel. (877) 2-2020, just a few blocks from the International Bridge. Since the 1930s, Crosby's has drawn a curious mix of Coahuilan cowboys, Texas ranchers, and tourists, and it's still going strong. House specialties include *cabri-*

to, Portuguese-style chicken, frog legs, roast quail, fresh bass from Presa de la Amistad, and the usual border platters. The walls are decorated with old black-and-white photos of Mexico, bass trophies, and handpainted tile. It's open daily 9 a.m.-midnight.

Another outstanding choice is **Asadero La Posta,** Calle Allende 350 (south off Hidalgo eight blocks from the bridge). La Posta specializes in fajitas, *queso fundido, queso con chile,* and *carne asada.* On weekends the upstairs room occasionally hosts live *norteña* music. Open daily 8 a.m.-11 p.m.

Also on Av. Hidalgo, diagonally opposite Crosby's, is the **Corona Club,** which is really more of a drinks and *botanas* (appetizers) place then a full-fledged restaurant. This is where the long opening sequence for *Desperado*—the part that included the brilliant ensemble acting between Steve Buscemi, Cheech Marin, and Quentin Tarantino—was filmed. Walking into the Corona you can imagine yourself sliding into Antonio Banderas's boots as you blast the bad guys into the wood-paneled walls.

Festivals

Every 25 Oct., the twin cities of Del Rio (Texas) and Ciudad Acuña celebrate the **Fiesta de la Amistad** or Friendship Festival, with parades, games, music, dancing, and speechmaking.

Carnaval, in February, is typically celebrated only in seacoast towns, but Ciudad Acuña uses the proximity of Presa de la Amistad as an excuse to celebrate the pre-Lenten festival (this is one of the few border towns—perhaps the only—to do so). See the "Mazatlán" section in the Sinaloa chapter for a general idea of what goes on during Carnaval; Acuña's is of course a much smaller affair.

Shopping

Artículos de Tradición Mexicana, Guerrero at 2 de Abril (in the vicinity of the Motel Plaza and Motel Tarasco), tel. (877) 2-0188, carries a good selection of Mexican tiles, brick, and ceramics, and can design and make wrought iron.

Information

The state tourist office, tel. (877) 2-4070, at the border station (opposite the offices of immigration and customs) has informative, annotated maps of the region and state. The Ciudad Acuña border crossing is open 24 hours.

Transportation

Unlike at some border towns, here it's not easy to walk between the U.S. town (Del Rio) and the Mexican one (Acuña); from city limit to city limit it's 4.8 km/three miles. Instead, most visitors drive, catch public buses, or take taxis. Parking lots on Las Vacas St. in Del Rio charge US$2 to park all day.

Bus: Buses pass along Del Rio's Las Vacas St. regularly on the way to Ciudad Acuña and cost US$0.50 each way. In Acuña the **Terminal de Autobuses** is at the corner of Calle Matamoros and Ocampo, three blocks west and four blocks south of the bridge. Passenger buses leave frequently for Saltillo (US$16-17), Mexico City (US$44-59), Monterrey (US$16-18), and Piedras Negras (US$2.50).

Taxi: A taxi from Del Rio (Las Vacas St.) costs US$6 one-way; taxis coming the opposite way will ask for more, but you shouldn't pay over US$8-9. Cab companies on the Del Rio side provide free parking if you hire one of their taxis.

Driving: Arreola's Insurance, near the bridge on Spur 239 in Del Rio, tel. (830) 775-3252, is an agent for Sanborn's and can arrange Mexican auto insurance for longer journeys south of the border.

In Del Rio, two routes lead to the border crossing: the old way via Spur 277 (Garfield St., which turns into Las Vacas St. toward the border), and a new, faster bypass that extends southeast and then south from Gibbs downtown. The bridge toll costs $1.25 per vehicle.

PIEDRAS NEGRAS

Nearly double the size of Ciudad Acuña, with a population of around 100,000, Piedras Negras is Coahuila's main border crossing. Its name, "Black Rocks," refers to a stratum of coal exposed by erosion in the area.

The local economy is supported by cattle ranching, twin-plant manufacturing, and coal extraction. Coal-burning power plants near Nava and Allende, about 54 km southwest of Piedras Negras, produce 12% of the power for the entire country; the coal is mined near Piedras Negras

and shipped 20 km by fast conveyor belts to a coal depot, where it's unloaded and taken to the plants. Piedras Negras is also an important transportation hub because of the railway that runs south to Saltillo.

Although Piedras Negras is the closest border town to San Antonio, Texas (142 miles via US 57/I-35), the town gets far fewer tourists than Nuevo Laredo. The many shops in the plaza area near the bridge are not particularly tourist-oriented so bargains are plentiful. The **Mercado Municipal** on Calle Zaragoza (one block west and two blocks south of the bridge) is full of handicrafts as well as housewares.

Across the Río Bravo is Eagle Pass, Texas (pop. 24,000), virtually a suburb of Piedras Negras. The Mexican newspaper *Zócalo* serves both towns.

Based on a novel by Laura Esquivel and directed by her husband Alfonso Arau, the 1992 Mexican film *Like Water For Chocolate (Como Agua para Chocolate)* was shot on location in Piedras Negras and Eagle Pass. Parts of John Sayles's 1996 *Lone Star* were also filmed here.

Small-game hunting (rabbit, hare, quail, dove, duck, goose, javelina) and fishing are popular area pastimes. Sports enthusiasts congregate at the local **Club de Caza, Tiro y Pesca** ("Hunting, Shooting, and Fishing Club") on Calle Ocampo between Calles Mina and Dr. Coss.

Accommodations

Hotels and motels in Piedras Negras are geared toward motorists; all have ample parking, usually in a motel-style courtyard.

Shoestring: Hotel Reforma, Calle Campo 108 (near the train station), tel. (878) 2-0390, is a basic, two-story whitewashed place with plain rooms and private hot-water showers. Rates: US$9 s, US$13 d. **Hotel Miranda,** tel. (878) 2-0205, a small, two-story inn on Av. E. Carranza near Calle Veracruz, just outside the town center, has tidy but simple rooms. Rates: from US$13. A cheap downtown place is the basic but adequate, two-story **Hotel Santos,** Calle Allende at Hidalgo (a block north of the market), tel. (878) 2-1968. Rates: US$12/15 s/d.

Budget: Autel Río, Calle Padre de las Casas 121, tel. (878) 2-7064, is an American-style motel in the heart of town (only two blocks from the bus terminal and within walking distance of

TO CIUDAD ACUÑA

PIEDRAS NEGRAS

UNITED STATES

PALACIO MUNICIPAL
UNIDAD DEPORTIVA MUNICIPAL
SEE DOWNTOWN DETAIL
ABASOLO
MATAMOROS
CALLE ALLENDE
PLAZA DE TOROS
MOTEL CALIFORNIA
MINA
HOTEL REFORMA
POST OFFICE
CLUB DE CAZA, TIRO Y PESCA
MOTEL 57
CUSTOMS
RAILWAY STATION
AV. E. CARRANZA
AV. PROGRESO FUENTE
MOTEL DEL SOL
NEZAHUALCOYOTL
RIO BRAVO

GRAL. R. CEPEDA
AV. HEROICO COLEGIO MILITAR
AV. A. LOPEZ MATEOS
AV. LAZARO CARDENAS
LAREDO

FIDEL VILLARREAL
LIENZO CHARRO
CASABLANCA INN
VICENTE SUAREZ
DR. ARMANDO TREVINO FLORES
MINA

0   600 m

© MOON PUBLICATIONS, INC.

MINA

TO ALLENDE   TO GUERRERO
57   2

DOWNTOWN DETAIL

CALLE JIMENEZ
STATE TOURIST OFFICE
CALLE PADRE DE LAS CASAS
CALLE XICOTENCATL
POLICE
ABASOLO
ARTESANIAS FONART
PLAZA PRINCIPAL
CALLE JUAREZ
EL OSCAR DRIVE INN
CALLE ZARAGOZA
MATAMOROS
MORELOS
INEGI
HOTEL SANTOS
LONG - DISTANCE TELEPHONE OFFICE
CALLE CUAUHTEMOC
SAM'S
MERCADO MUNICIPAL ZARAGOZA
CALLE TERAN
RESTAURANT - BAR MODERNO
AUTEL RIO
CALLE HIDALGO
CALLE ALLENDE
BUS STATION
0   150 m

Restaurant-Bar Moderno and the border. It offers clean, secure rooms with a/c, heat, TV, and phones. Rates: US$25 s, US$28 d. A step up in class is the newer **Motel del Sol,** Av. E. Carranza 1239, tel. (878) 3-2324, fax (878) 3-4586, which features clean rooms with a/c, TV, and phone, plus parking and a restaurant. Rates: US$26 s, US$33 d, US$39 t, US$44 q.

Along Mexico 57 (Av. Lázaro Cárdenas) on the southern fringes of town are several motels with a/c, heat, and TV, including the two-story adobe-style **Casablanca Inn,** a Holiday Inn property, tel. (878) 3-0646, fax (878) 3-0050. Rates: around US$31 s, US$35 d. Others in this price range include **Motel 57,** tel. (878) 2-7744, fax (878) 2-4870, and **Motel California,** tel. (878) 2-2453, both on Av. E. Carranza near Veracruz. Rates: around US$24-31.

Inexpensive: Toward the top of the heap is **Hotel Posada Rosa,** Calle San Luis at Sinaloa (two blocks northwest of Av. E. Carranza), tel. (878) 2-7024. Its well-kept, modern rooms have a/c, heat, TV, and phones. Other facilities include a clean swimming pool, tennis court, nightclub, restaurant, and coffee shop. Rates: US$38-45 s/d.

In Eagle Pass: On the Texas side of the river, decent budget-priced rooms are available at **Eagle Pass Inn,** four miles north of town on US 277, tel. (830) 773-9531. Rates: US$28-35. **La Quinta Motor Inn,** 2525 Main St., tel. (830) 773-7000, has larger, nicer rooms at inexpensive/moderate rates (US$45-60).

Food

Piedras Negras's most famous institution is the **Restaurant Bar Moderno,** three blocks west and two blocks south of the International Bridge on Calle Morelos between Calle Terán and Allende (the old entrance, now closed, faces Allende). Established in 1934 (and originally called the Victory Club), the Moderno is supposedly the spot where cook Ignacio "Nacho" Anaya searched a near-empty pantry for something to feed a late-night party of hunters and came up with tortilla chips topped with melted cheese and sliced jalapeños—the birth of nachos.

You know you're in for something different when you walk in and find a large green Buddha statue at the end of the entrance hallway. Though the Moderno remains a citadel of Tex-Mex cuisine,

the dining room and adjacent bar are elegant, with uniformed, starched-shirt waiters and clean white tablecloths. Nachos and other border dishes, including frog legs, *chalupas,* and *arracheras* (fajitas), are prominently featured, along with steak, Mexican standards, and seafood. The waiters all speak English but at least half the clientele on any given night is Mexican. If nothing else, stop in for a drink; you haven't done the Tex-Mex border until you've been to the Moderno. Open Mon.-Fri. 11 a.m.-midnight, Saturday till 1 a.m.; live music and dancing most nights after 9 p.m.

Yes, there are other places to eat in town besides the Moderno. **Sam's,** Calle Terán at Padre de las Casas, a half block north of Autel Río, is a clean and efficient 24-hour coffee shop with a good selection of Mexican and American standards. The reasonably clean **Restaurant Los Arcos,** Calle Morelos at Matamoros, offers cheap Mexican breakfasts plus an extensive selection of *antojitos.* Along the north side of Plaza Principal next to the International Bridge is a row of snack booths open only in the daytime during cool weather; later during summer months. Next to the plaza is the clean and inexpensive **El Oscar Drive Inn,** a classic takeout (or eat-in) joint with giant burgers and *antojitos.*

Recreation

Plaza de Toros Monumental Arizpe, on the north side of Av. López Mateos between Calles Mexicali and Tepic (about two km from the bridge); and **Lienzo Charro Oscar González Ramos,** off Calle V. Suárez in Colonia Tecnológico (about 5.5 km from the bridge), hold bullfights and Mexican rodeos periodically—usually during the summer. Check with the state tourist office in town for the latest schedules.

Local residents picnic, hunt, and fish at the nearby San Diego, Santo Domingo, San Rodrigo, San Antonio, and Escondido Rivers. **Rio Grande Rancho Hunting Resort,** P.O. Box 1143, Eagle Pass, TX 78853, tel. (830) 773-4444, off Mexico 2 between Piedras Negras and Nuevo Laredo, offers hunting vacations for dove, quail, duck, goose, sandhill crane, and Rio Grande wild turkey.

Events

Each October the town organizes an "International Day of the Nacho and Nacho Cookoff," an event that attracts around 3,000 visitors to the main plaza, to sample "experimental" nachos topped with shrimp, octopus, caviar, and other nontraditional items. Contact the state tourist office in Piedras Negras or the Eagle Pass Chamber of Commerce for details.

Shopping
The **Mercado Municipal** on Calle Zaragoza, one block west and two blocks south of the bridge, is full of handicrafts and housewares. Nearby **Mosaicos El Aguila** carries a good selection of Talavera tiles and sinks.

Information and Services
Tourist Services: The **state tourist office,** Calle Hidalgo at Abasolo, tel. (878) 2-0876, can answer questions about travel in Piedras Negras and Coahuila. They can also summon the local **Green Angels** unit which is based at Calle Guadalupe 307, tel. (878) 3-0137. The **Eagle Pass Chamber of Commerce,** 400 Garrison St., P.O. Box 1188, Eagle Pass, TX 78852, tel. (830) 773-3224, also offers information on Piedras Negras.

Maps: The Piedras Negras **INEGI office,** on Calle Cuauhtémoc between Calles Matamoros and Juárez, carries topographic maps for Coahuila, Tamaulipas, and Nuevo León. For excursions into northwestern Coahuila (the Sierra del Carmen area), ask for the 1:250,000 maps H13-9, H14-7, and H13-12 (1:50,000 scale maps are also available but the larger-scale maps are sufficient for most purposes). Hours are Mon.-Fri. 8 a.m.-3 p.m.

Telephone: A *caseta de larga distancia* can be found at the corner of Xicoténcatl and Padre de las Casas.

Transportation
Bus: The town's small bus terminal, Calle Allende at Cuauhtémoc, is used more for cargo than for passenger services. **Autobuses Blancos** and **Autobuses El Aguila** handle all passenger services, with buses to Mexico City (US$42 second class, US$54 first class, three times daily), Monterrey (US$14/16, three times daily), Saltillo (US$13/16, 12 times daily), and Torreón (US$17/18, four times daily).

Train: The *Regiomontano* train #182 leaves Piedras Negras at 7:30 a.m. and arrives in Saltillo at 4:30 p.m.; in the reverse direction, #181 leaves Saltillo at 8:15 a.m. and arrives in Piedras Negras at 5:15 p.m. The fare is US$8.50 for a reserved seat, or US$4.50 in unreserved second class. The train has not been very popular since it's three hours slower than the bus (nine hours versus six hours), and rumors say the passenger service may be discontinued. The trip is scenic, however, and for those with time to spare the train might be preferable to the bus.

Driving: Traffic at the border is usually light, and driving through Piedras Negras is a fairly straightforward undertaking. Avenida Lázaro Cárdenas leads southwest to the junction of Mexico 2 (for Nuevo Laredo or Ciudad Acuña) and Mexico 57 (for Saltillo and Monterrey). Mexican vehicle insurance can be arranged in Eagle Pass, Texas, at **Capitol Insurance,** 1115 Main, tel. (830) 773-2341.

Crossing the Border: The Piedras Negras crossing is open 24 hours. Bridge toll at the border is US$2 for vehicles, US$0.50 for pedestrians.

SOUTH TOWARD SALTILLO

Mexico 57, the highway between Piedras Negras and Saltillo, was almost entirely resurfaced in 1992, so it's fairly smooth going all the way for the moment. Traffic is usually light, and the scenery is classic Altiplano terrain, marked by mesquite, yucca, sotol, maguey, and cholla amid rolling hills and valleys. Fuel is available along the way in Nueva Rosita, Sabinas, and Monclova; the longest stretch without gasoline is Monclova-Saltillo (192 km/119 miles).

Sabinas
At the heart of the Región Carbonífera, the municipality of Sabinas (138 km/85.5 miles south of Piedras Negras) is the nation's third largest coal producer. The town also serves as a supply center for nearby vegetable, wheat, corn, and barley farms irrigated by the Río Sabinas.

Because it offers an adequate array of fuel, food, and lodging, Sabinas is the best place along the highway to break a journey between the border and Saltillo.

Practicalities: Motel Tres Caminos, just off Mexico 57 near the north end of town, tel. (861) 3-0389, has clean, reasonably priced a/c rooms and a pool. Inexpensive rooms are available near the plaza downtown at **Hotel Santa Clara,** Av. Independencia near Calle Lamadrid, tel. (861) 2-1231. Good food is available at **Restaurant La Carreta** and **Restaurant Guadalajara,** both on the highway in the vicinity of Motel Tres Caminos.

The state maintains an **Infotur** office with material on Coahuila at Km 122, about 20 km north of Sabinas on Mexico 57.

Presa Venustiano Carranza

Also known as Lake Don Martín, this 180-square-km impoundment of the Río Sabinas is 70 km (44 miles) east of Sabinas via Coahuila 22. The take here includes trophy-sized striped bass, robalo, catfish, and carp. At **Campo Rumanía** at the northwest end of the lake, you'll find a few rustic cabins for rent, a restaurant, and camping space. Similar facilities are available along the north-east shore of the lake at **Don Martín.** Boats can be launched in several places around the lake's perimeter.

To get to the lake from Sabinas, take the left fork at Motel Tres Caminos and look for the sign marked "Don Martín." Follow the sign to a church on the right, turn left, and then it's about 60 km to the lake via a paved road.

The lake can also be reached from the east by following highway Nuevo León 1 southwest out of Nuevo Laredo 67 km (41.5 miles) to Anahuac, then heading 62 km west on the only paved road in that direction.

Melchor Múzquiz

Thirty-five km (21 miles) west of Nueva Rosita via Coahuila 2, Melchor Múzquiz (pop. 30,000) is the center of Mexico's largest coal-producing region with an output equal to half the nation's coal reserves. Ensconced at the edge of Sierra Hermosa de Santa Rosa, the area is also rich in silver, zinc, lead, and fluorite, and is a center for cattle ranching. In spite of local industry, Múzquiz is a fairly traditional Northern Mexican town.

The Spanish established a military garrison called Santa Rosa here as early as 1735, the only legacy of which is the 18th-century baroque **Templo de Santa Rosa de Lima** at the north-east corner of the main square (Plaza de Armas).

Nearby attractions include the scenic **Balneario La Cascada,** fed by the Río Santa María, and the Kikapú ("Kickapoo") settlement at **El Nacimiento.** In August each year the Kikapú display their handicrafts (including leather and suede garments) at the **Feria Oasis del Norte** in Melchor Múzquiz. If you plan to visit El Nacimiento (37 km/23 miles west of Múzquiz via Coahuila 2), note that although "El Nacimiento" is the official state government name for the village, the Kikapú settlement is usually called "La Ranchería" by local mestizo Mexicans, who generally reserve the name "El Nacimiento" for another village settled by Seminoles eight km south. The Kikapú themselves refer to their village as "Colonia de los Kikapú." About 500 individuals live in the village most of the year; during the summer they move to a ramshackle settlement eight miles south of Eagle Pass, Texas, off FM 1021.

Accommodations: In the center of town, 2.5 blocks northwest of the Plaza de Armas, the **Hotel María Isabel,** tel. (861) 6-0368, has simple shoestring rooms with private bath (US$12-15). Two hotels on the eastern outskirts of town off Coahuila 2, **Hotel Los Angeles,** tel. (861) 6-0300, and **Motel La Mina,** tel. (861) 6-1212, offer decent budget-priced rooms (around US$20); the Los Angeles has a small swimming pool.

Getting There: The simplest way to reach Múzquiz is via Mexico 57 to Nueva Rosita, then 35 km (22 miles) northwest on Coahuila 2. You can also come via the village of Boquillas del Carmen, 260 km (160 miles) northwest on the other side of the Sierra del Carmen on the Texas-Mexico border, just opposite Texas's Big Bend National Park. Twice a week around 8 a.m. a bus leaves Boquillas for Melchor Múzquiz; the seven-hour trip costs US$8.

Monclova

Few motorists stop in Monclova since the Coahuila 50 loop enables drivers who are following Mexico 57 to Saltillo or Piedras Negras to skirt the town entirely.

The town served as the provincial capital of Coahuila y Texas from 1811-24, when Saltillo took the honor. American Harold R. Pape established the local steel industry in the 1940s and Monclova now supports what is reportedly the largest steel foundry on the North American continent. The **Harold R. Pape Museum-Library,** on the highway through town just south of the IMSS hospital, hosts rotating exhibits of various national and international artists; works by

Dali, Picasso, Orozco, and Cuevas have been shown here.

Accommodations: Though tourism in Monclova is practically nil, business travelers support around a dozen hotels. The place of choice is the **Hotel Chula Vista,** tel. (863) 1-0211, which sits on a hill overlooking Monclova on Calle Valparaíso, just off the highway through town. Rooms have all the amenities at budget rates starting at US$30 per night. Several hotels on or just off Av. V. Carranza in the center of town near the Plaza Principal and Plaza Alonso de León also offer rooms in the budget range. These include: **Hotel Ilbac, Hotel Viena, Hotel San Cristobal, Hotel Olimpia,** and **Hotel Noruega.**

Information: A state tourist office next to the firehouse at Blvd. Harold R. Pape (Mexico 57 in town) and Calle Madero, tel. (863) 5-3290, distributes information on state and local attractions as well as tips on food and lodging.

Driving: Motorists heading to Torreón, Durango, or Mazatlán will save time and distance by taking Mexico 30 southwest from Monclova. Although not in the best condition, this route is more direct than hooking through Saltillo. Traffic is light all the way to San Pedro de las Colonias, 65 km (40 miles) northeast of Torreón, where the highway connects with Mexico 40 onward to Durango and Mazatlán.

Vicinity of Monclova

Around 30 km south of Monclova, Mexico 57 cuts through **Cima de la Muralla** ("Top of the Wall"), a scenic mountain pass in the Sierra San Marcos halfway between Guadalupe and Monclova.

East of Monclova, Mexico 30 threads 140 km (87 miles) through the scenic Sierra La Gloria and Sierra Pájaros Azules to meet Nuevo León 1, the toll-free highway between Nuevo Laredo and Monterrey.

SIERRA DEL CARMEN

This beautiful but little-known, little-explored limestone and volcanic mountain range in Coahuila's northwest corner spills over the U.S.-Mexico border into Texas's Big Bend National Park, where it is known as the Dead Horse Mountains. On the Mexican side, the highest and most pristine section of the mountain range, an area known as

the **Sierra de Maderas del Carmen** (also called Sierra las Maderas or simply "Las Maderas") is entirely volcanic, with two peaks over 2,900 meters (9,500 feet), at least seven peaks over 2,500 meters (8,200 feet), and 10 times as much terrain over 1,500 meters (5,000 feet) as Big Bend's Chisos Mountains.

Although the area was heavily logged in the late 1940s and early '50s, dense groves of Douglas fir, ponderosa pine, aspen, and Arizona cypress can still be seen at higher elevations, along with grassy, flowered meadows and clear streams similar to those found across the border in the Chisos. Some of the prettiest meadows are found in the Maderas's high *cañones,* including Cañon Cinco, Cañon del Oso, and Cañon de la Media Luna. The area is home to hundreds of animal species, many rare. The Sierra del Carmen white-tailed deer, for example, lives only in the Sierra del Carmen and Chisos Mountains.

Park Status

Since the 1930s, Mexican and U.S. government officials have been talking about establishing an international park that would encompass Big Bend and parts of the Sierra del Carmen, thus protecting over 1.5 million acres of pristine "mountain islands in a desert sea." Recent meetings between U.S. National Park Service directors and their Mexican counterparts in Mexico City have been more fruitful than in the past, mainly because proposals on Mexican lands are finally proceeding according to Mexican terms. Participants are hopeful NAFTA trade will encourage U.S. technological support for the development of the park—especially in the villages of Boquillas del Carmen and San Vicente on the Río Bravo border. At the moment tariffs on U.S. goods and services are too costly for Mexico to consider such support.

Coahuila's state government was so confident that the international park would become a reality in 1990 that "Parque Internacional del Río Bravo" appeared on 1990 state maps (the label has been deleted from the map's most recent version). Weary of waiting for international authorities to come to an agreement, the Coahuila state government is already working toward the establishment of a state park and has set aside 37,000 acres of the Sierra del Carmen as a natural sanctuary.

PROPOSED PARQUE INTERNACIONAL DEL RIO BRAVO

UNITED STATES

UNITED STATES / MEXICO

TERLINGUA

PANTHER JUNCTION

DEAD HORSE MOUNTAINS

STUDY BUTTE

LAJITAS

BIG BEND NATIONAL PARK

RIO GRANDE VILLAGE

BOQUILLAS DEL CARMEN

PASO LAJITAS

CHISOS MOUNTAINS

SIERRA DEL CARMEN

MEXICO

CASTOLON

RIO GRANDE / RIO BRAVO DEL NORTE

SAN VICENTE

SANTA ELENA

PROPOSED MEXICAN NATIONAL PARK

SIERRA DE SANTA ELENA

MOON

SIERRA DE SAN VICENTE

⸺ · · · ⸺ = BOUNDARY OF PROPOSED PARQUE INTERNACIONAL DE RIO BRAVO

TO SABINAS

NOT TO SCALE

© MOON PUBLICATIONS, INC.

State and federal officials in Mexico are currently developing guidelines for El Proyecto Reserva de la Biosfera Santa Eleña-Sierra del Carmen ("the Santa Eleña-Sierra del Carmen Biosphere Reserve Project," more commonly known on the U.S. side simply as "the Santa Eleña Project"). The intention is to establish a 1.5-million-acre preserve roughly divided between the states of Chihuahua and Coahuila. If approved, the reserve will extend 200 miles eastward from a point on the Rio Grande near Redford, Texas, and would coincide with the Texas borders of the Big Bend Ranch State Park, Big Bend National Park, and Black Gap Wildlife Management Area, covering the Sierra del Carmen in

Coahuila as well as the Sierra Rica in Chihuahua. The projected reserve would thus protect about 50% more land than the combined territory of the three protected areas on the Texas side. The Mexican plan is then to apply for UNESCO biosphere status in combination with the Big Bend area, forming an international reserve exceeding 2.5 million acres—nearly 4,000 square miles.

At the moment both Sierra Maderas del Carmen and Santa Eleña Canyon are denoted as *áreas de protección de flora y fauna silvestre,"* loosely translated as "wildlife sanctuaries," which means hunting is forbidden in these areas. The World Bank recently granted one million pesos to the Mexican government for the purpose of preserving these valuable environmental assets.

Much of the sierra remains in private hands—some choice highlands are owned by a former Coahuila state governor—or is occupied by *ejidos,* agricultural peasant collectives. U.S. park rangers cross the Rio Grande frequently to attend *ejido* meetings to ensure cooperation in the development of a Sierra del Carmen biosphere reserve.

THE KIKAPÚ OF EL NACIMIENTO

Originally hailing from Wisconsin and Michigan, the Kikapú ("Kickapoo") were driven south in the 18th and 19th centuries by westward-moving Europeans. In 1775, Spain's Charles III gave them permission to settle in the colonial province of Coahuila y Texas in return for defending the area against Comanche and Apache raids. By the late 1800s, many of those on the Texas side were banished to Oklahoma reservations. Some were able to flee to Northern Mexico and were given land by the Mexican government. Like the legendary Seminoles, a number of Kikapús came north again to serve as scouts with the U.S. Cavalry in Texas.

Today a core of around 500 Kikapú choose to live together and follow a semitraditional lifestyle at two seasonal settlements on either side of the Texas-Coahuila border. They speak an Algonquin dialect as their first language, pidgin (or "broken") Spanish as a second. Those who read and write Kikapú use a syllabary devised by the Cherokee Sequoyah. Their oval-shaped, windowless winter homes in Mexico are built of hackberry, bald cypress, or sycamore wood, with low, dome-shaped roofs. Summer houses feature a rectangular plan with wooden posts supporting airy walls of sotol, a desert succulent.

For the most part the Kikapú dress in a style similar to that of other Mexican peasants. The main difference is in the way females wear their hair; young girls plait their hair in three braids, often joined on top of the head in a topknot. After puberty, women switch to one long braid.

The Kikapú belief system revolves around nature spirits presided over by Kitzihiat, the "Great Spirit." Subordinate to Kitzihiat is Wisaka, the creator of the cosmos. The most common regular religious practice among the Kikapú is the preparation and possession of *misami* or medicine bundles which serve as sacred talismans for warding off evil. *Misami* contents are closely guarded secrets; they usually include a variety of dried plants, roots, and herbs, plus occasional human and animal parts. Wrapped in white cloth and covered by the skin of a two-point buck, the bundles are usually around 60 cm (two feet) long and 15 cm (six inches) wide.

Although the Kikapú employ peyote for medicinal, nonritual purposes only, they sometimes gather a surplus of the cactus to sell to the Oklahoma Kikapú and other Amerindians who use the hallucinogenic substance ritually, since northwestern Coahuila is a primary source of the plant.

Mexican lithograph of the Kikapú in 1865

Accessing the Sierra

Coahuila 2 extends 120 km (74.5 miles) north-west from Nueva Rosita (15 km/nine miles north of Sabinas) as far as the mining village of **La Cuesta de Malena** at the foot of the great Sierra de Maderas del Carmen. The Maderas del Carmen can be reached by continuing west about 22 km beyond La Cuesta via a gravel road, then turning northeast onto a dirt road that leads to the ranchería of **Los Pilares.** From Los Pilares you will have to continue on foot to reach the heart of the Maderas del Carmen. Most hikers make a base camp at **Cañon de la Media Luna,** at 1,680 meters (5,500 feet), from where they hike up to over 2,700 meters (9,000 feet).

The terrain here is rugged and remote and hikes shouldn't be undertaken without a guide; it may be possible to hire a guide and pack burros in La Cuesta or Boquillas del Carmen. Because no camping facilities or marked trails exist, skills in wilderness camping and orienteering are a minimum requirement. INEGI topographic maps H13-9 (Manuel Benavides) and H13-12 (San Miguel) would be useful for general navigation.

Boquillas del Carmen: Beyond La Cuesta, a 55-km (34-mile) gravel road leads all the way to Boquillas del Carmen on the Río Bravo opposite Big Bend National Park. Boquillas is a popular destination for Big Bend visitors who cross by ferry for the day. The nondescript village has a souvenir shop/cafe known as **Falcón's,** with a few tables and a kitchen offering burritos and cold beer. A real bar up the street has a pool table and is well-stocked with tequila and other liquors—including fiery sotol (US$1 per *probita*).

Should you choose to spend the night in Boquillas, rustic **Buzzard's Roost** offers simple accommodations for US$10 a night including breakfast. Like the locals, you'll have to bathe at a pipe from the hot springs near the river. Twice a week around 8 a.m. there's a bus to Melchor Múzquiz (see above).

Fuel: Gasoline (Nova only) is available from barrels in La Cuesta and Boquillas at elevated prices. The best approach is to top off in Nueva Rosita and carry enough extra fuel so that you can make it all the way to Los Pilares and back without depending on local supplies.

Public Transportation: Rumored changes in the area include the proposed extension of power lines across the river from Texas to supply Boquillas with electricity, a public car ferry across the river, and/or a bridge between Big Bend's Rio Grande Village campgrounds and Boquillas del Carmen. For now, simple rowboat ferries are the only means of communication and transportation between the two sides of the river near Rio Grande Village (US$2 roundtrip). When you land on the Mexican side of the river, the locals will try to sell you a US$4 burro ride for the three-quarter-mile walk into the village—if you've never ridden a burro, here's your chance. Less expensive is the pickup "taxi" service, which costs US$2 pp roundtrip or US$4 for the whole truck. Or simply walk.

Tours from Big Bend

The easiest and safest way to experience the grandeur of the Sierra del Carmen is to hire a guide on the Texas side. Marcos Paredes, a Big Bend park ranger, leads occasional four- or five-day treks into the mountains on horseback and foot; for information contact **Far Flung Adventures,** P.O. Box 31, Terlingua, TX 79852, tel. (915) 371-2489, or contact Paredes directly by calling (915) 477-2223 or (915) 371-2469. The Panther Junction Information Center at **Big Bend National Park,** tel. (915) 477-2251, can also provide information on exploring the sierra.

CUATROCIÉNEGAS

Founded in 1800, the small town of Cuatrociénegas (pop. 8,500) is famous as the birthplace of Venustiano Carranza, who initiated the Plan de Guadalupe, thus terminating the dictatorial rule of Victoriano Huerta. The house where Carranza was born is now the **Museo Casa de Carranza** (on Calle Zaragoza facing Plaza Zaragoza), with six rooms of exhibits chronicling his life.

In the middle of town near the plaza are some good examples of homogeneous pre-1930 northeastern Mexico architecture, including the *presidencia municipal, parroquía,* and railway station. The **Parroquía de San José,** a 19th-century neo-gothic and neoclassical design, sports the only wooden tower of its kind.

Cuatrociénegas is seemingly in the middle of nowhere, a Chihuahuan Desert outpost 740 meters (2,430 feet) above sea level and nearly surrounded by the Sierra de San Marcos and Sierra de La Fragua, two spurs of the Sierra Madre Oriental. It's geographic isolation has made the valley a "biological island" somewhat like the Galapagos.

The town's name means "four *ciénegas*," referring to an uncommon desert feature west of the Sierra Madre Oriental: desert wetlands consisting of interlinked freshwater pools and surface streams that look almost like manmade canals. South of town are several such wetlands—beautiful reed-and-grass-lined streams feeding into crystal-clear, turquoise-green pools. The principal water source for the marshes is a series of thermal springs in the Sierra de San Marcos. The springs are assisted by an intricate system of subterranean passageways that funnel ground water beneath the mountains. At one time such desert wetlands were common in west Texas, but ranchers and farmers there destroyed or depleted all of them.

During the rainy season, springwater from the *ciénegas* mixes with rainwater to form shallow lakes called *bolsones,* the largest of which is **Laguna Grande.** Another interesting *bolsón* feature here is the presence of extensive gypsum dunes. Gypsum is dissolved in the springwaters, and as the water evaporates and the lakes shrink, crystallized gypsum is left behind. At the edges of the basin this powdered gypsum is blown into dazzling white dunes 6-10 meters (18-30 feet) above the desert floor. The most beautiful dune group, **Los Arenales,** consists of a stand of pure white gypsum—the only one of its kind in the country—in front of the Sierra de San Marcos near Laguna de Churice.

Southwest of Cuatrociénegas via Mexico 30 in **Valle El Hundido** are several rock-art sites thought to have been painted by Coahuiltecas, the area's original inhabitants.

The limestone mountain range northwest of town, **Sierra de la Madera,** peaks at around 3,000 meters (9,800 feet) and features pine and oak highlands.

La Reserva Biosfera de Cuatrociénegas

The desert marshes support a surprising variety of plants and creatures; there is more aquatic diversity here than in all other North American deserts combined. One unique resident is *Terrapene coahuila,* the world's only aquatic species

of box turtle (called *tortuga de bisagra* or "hinge turtle" in Spanish). In spite of its aquatic abilities, this turtle is very sedentary, carrying out all its daily activities within an average 12.4-square-meter area. Though it's mainly nocturnal, the turtle may occasionally be seen in daylight after a hard rain. Your best chance of seeing one is at Laguna de los Burros. Another turtle here is the endemic *Trionix ater,* or whiteshell turtle.

Half of the 16 fish species found in the *ciénegas* are endemic, among them the *cichlid,* a perchlike freshwater fish that feeds on snails and organic bottom debris.

Among the marshes are splendid examples of such Chihuahuan Desert standards as mesquite, yucca, ocotillo, saltbush, lechugilla, creosote bush, and desert Christmas cactus (*tasajillo rojo* in Mexico). A yellow flower endemic to the area, *Dyssodia gypsophilia* ("gypsum-loving dogweed") is so rare it has no common name.

The same springs that feed the marshes have formed natural pools or *pozas* at nearby **El Mojarral, Poza Azul, Pozas de Becerra,** and

JOE CUMMINGS

Poza Azul, Cuatrociénegas

Pozas de Escobedo, to name but a few of the estimated 200 *ciénegas* thought to exist in the valley. Some of these pools are as deep as 13.5 meters (45 feet). Water temperatures in the *pozas* measure 20-28° C (68-82° F) in winter, 20-32° C (68-90° F) in summer. Until 1994, when the Mexican government declared the *pozas* part of a 150,000-hectare *area de protección de flora y fauna silvestre* (wildlife sanctuary) to better conserve the area's biological riches and natural resources, the pools were used as public *balnearios* or bathing resorts. The pools are now being allowed to return to their natural state. In 1995 federal protection was upgraded to biosphere reserve.

Visiting the *Pozas:* Diving, snorkeling, or just floating around in the warm, ultraclear pools is a real treat. The larger pools closest to town—found between Kms 9 and 23 to the southwest toward Torreón—are fenced off and you must have a permit and a guide to visit them. These can be arranged at the Dirección de Ecología, in the Palacio Municipal in Cuatrociénegas. So far there are no specific fees for permits or guide services but you are encouraged to make a donation to help fund the protection of these aquatic treasures. The office also can help plan other activities in the area, such as mountain biking and hiking.

Accommodations and Food

Motel Santa Fé, tel. (869) 6-0425, sits on Mexico 30 at the eastern entrance to town and offers modern rooms with private bath for US$20 s, US$23 d, US$27 t. That's a little overpriced considering what you get but there's virtually no competition. The Santa Fé management is very helpful with information on the area and can arrange guides. The **Hotel Ibarra** on Calle Zaragoza doesn't cost much less but can only be described as adequate.

Restaurant El Doc, on Plaza Zaragoza in the center of town, serves standard Mexican fare. **Pollos Villareal,** also on the plaza, specializes in *pollo asado al carbón,* while nearby **Tacos Alheli** covers the taco crowd. The town is famous for sweets made from nuts and honey, which can be bought in local shops.

A local winery, **Bodega Ferriño,** has been producing simple table wine since 1860.

Tours

In cooperation with the local Dirección de Ecología, the **Texas Parks and Wildlife Dept.** offers five-day nature tours to Cuatrociénegas for around US$725 pp, including roundtrip transportation from McAllen, Texas, all lodging, and most food. For further information call (800) 841-6547 in the U.S. or Canada.

Turismo e Investigación del Desierto Mexicano, Calle Antonio Navarro 70, Quinta Trinidad, Saltillo, Coahuila 25000, tel. (84) 14-9690, or 382 Treeline Park #613, San Antonio, TX 78209, tel. (210) 283-5142, also arranges Cuatrociénegas trips.

Getting There

Cuatrociénegas lies 83 km (51.5 miles) west of Monclova and 186 km (115 miles) northeast of San Pedro de las Colonias—at the edge of the Región Lagunera, near Torreón—via Mexico 30, a two-lane paved highway. A small bus office on the plaza fields buses to and from Monclova, Saltillo, Monterrey, and Torreón. There is one PEMEX station in town.

SALTILLO AND VICINITY

For visitors approaching from the north via Mexico 57, Saltillo seems to rise out of nowhere—a Mexican combo plate ringed by desert mountains. Pastel-colored, 18th- and 19th-century stone buildings with arched doorways and iron grillwork are typical of the slightly hilly downtown area and make Coahuila's oldest city the strongest example of colonial Mexico in the northeast.

Though Saltillo is only an hour or so by car from Monterrey, N.L., to the east, its pace of life is much slower and more traditional. The city's 400-year history is preserved in its central Spanish-style grid layout, with modern districts well away from the center along Blvd. Carranza to the north and Blvd. Fundadores to the east. For borderhoppers not inclined to spend their time among the high-rises of Monterrey or the kitsch of border towns, Saltillo is a good place to find "Old Mexico" within a half day's drive of the Rio Grande.

History

Once densely populated by Guachichil and Borrado Indians, the Valle de Saltillo saw its first Spaniards in 1577. That year the governor of Nueva Vizcaya established a supply point here for *conquista* expeditions along the road from Zacatecas to Texas and Louisiana. The settlement was originally called Santiago del Saltillo del Ojo de Agua, and its first residents dedicated themselves to the capture and sale of Amerindian slaves for use in Spanish mines—a practice then condoned by the mission system. The natives responded with rebellions and attacks, destroying the first Franciscan mission in 1582 and forcing Spanish colonists to flee south.

At the beginning of the 17th century, the viceroy sent a group of "civilized" Tlaxcaltecas to found San Esteban de Nueva Tlaxcala as an example to local natives. By this time European diseases and Apache attacks had weakened native resistance to outsiders, and the Tlaxcaltecas were able to grow wheat, build flour mills, and establish vineyards and cattle ranches. Eventually San Esteban expanded east to include the old settlement at nearby Saltillo. In 1824 Saltillo was made the capital of the state of Coahuila y Texas, which included the present-day states of Texas, Coahuila, Tamaulipas, and Nuevo León.

In 1847 a decisive battle in the Mexican-American War occurred 10 km south of Saltillo at Buena Vista, where a U.S. force of 4,500 led by Gen. Zachary Taylor defeated Santa Anna's battalion of over 20,000. Saltillo remained the capital of Coahuila but declined in importance as Mexico lost many of its northern territories to the United States.

Benito Juárez brought the National Archives here during his opposition to the 1862-67 French intervention. Saltillo slumbered through the remainder of the 19th century until a railway from the border transformed the city into an important transportation junction. The economy's traditional ranching and farming base has more recently been supplemented by Chrysler and General Motors automotive plants just east of the city.

Climate

At 1,590 meters (5,216 feet) above sea level, Saltillo enjoys a dry but mild climate year-round. The highest average daily temperature, 22.5° C (72.5° F), occurs in June and July; the lowest, 12° C (53.6° F), in January. The occasional winter north wind will drop temperatures to near freezing for a day or two, but sunny days are the norm even then.

August and September are the wettest months, with an average monthly precipitation of four cm (1.5 inches) and 4.5 cm (1.75 inches), respectively—hardly enough to impinge on a vacation.

SIGHTS

The charms of the city's narrow, colonial-style streets are best seen on foot. You'll find a convenient downtown parking lot off Calle G. Victoria near the intersection with Calle Xicoténcatl. One of the best streets for native turn-of-the-century architecture—some of it restored and some in an advanced state of decay—is Calle General Cepeda. Excellent examples of Mexican republican or neoclassical architecture include

SALTILLO

TO MONCLOVA

TO MONTERREY

BLVD. ISIDRO LOPEZ

BLVD. NAZARIO S. ORTIZ GARZA

■ LIENZO CHARRO PROF. ENRIQUE GONZALEZ

BLVD. VITO ALESSIO ROBLES

● RESTAURANT PRINCIPAL

● EUROTEL PLAZA HOLIDAY INN

● IMPERIAL DEL NORTE MOTOR HOTEL

BLVD. CARRANZA

TO TORREON

PERIF. LUIS ECHEVERRIA

■ LIENZO CHARRO EL RAYITO

● INSTITUTO TECNOLOGICO DE SALTILLO

AV. UNIVERSIDAD

● UNIVERSIDAD AUTONOMA DE COAHUILA

■ STATE TOURIST OFFICE

TO PLAZA DE TOROS →

JESUS VALDES SANCHEZ

SALVADOR GONZALEZ LOBO

● SUPERMERCADO SORIANA

HOTEL LA TORRE

● TOURIST OFFICE (CASETA COSS)

● HOTEL CAMINO REAL

PALACIO MUNICIPAL

BLVD. FCO. COSS

■ CIUDAD DEPORTIVA

BLVD. DE LOS FUNDADORES

57

● OKEY INN

MADERO

● CRUZ ROJA

● HOTEL PREMIER

● MOTEL LA FUENTE

● MOTEL CORONA NORTE

JUAN ALDAMA

CARDENAS

PASEO DE LA REFORMA

PARQUE ALAMEDA ZARAGOZA

R. ARIZPE

CASTELAR

MUNICIPAL LIBRARY

TO CENTRO DE CONVENCIONES AND MATEHUALA

● RAILWAY STATION

CARLOS SALAZAR

SEE "DOWNTOWN SALTILLO" MAP

● BASEBALL FIELD

PERIF. LUIS ECHEVERRIA

SAN LORENZO

CALZ. A. NARRO

PEDRO ARANDA

MARIANO ABASOLO

DE LA FUENTE

● POLICE

FELIPE J. MERY

● HOTEL RANCHO EL MORILLO

■ BUS STATION

PERIF. LUIS ECHEVERRIA

● BASEBALL FIELD

54

0   1 km

© MOON PUBLICATIONS, INC.

Tecnológico de Saltillo (one of the country's first architecture schools), the **Palacio Gobierno,** and the **Teatro de la Ciudad Fernando Soler.**

Catedral de Santiago de Saltillo

Construction on Mexico's northernmost example of Churrigueresque (or "ultra-baroque") architecture began in 1745 and continued through 1800, with the addition of the tower 1893-97. Originally built as a parochial church dedicated to the city's patron saint (Santiago or St. James), the structure was criticized as being "of a size that exceeds the necessities of a population as small as Saltillo's." The archdiocese disagreed, and the establishment of a bishop's office here in 1891 conferred cathedral status. Now a focus of city and state pride, the cathedral has been restored, preserved, and documented as thoroughly as any church in Mexico.

The ornate baroque facade, elaborate porticos, and wooden doors (carved in the late 1700s and featuring images of saints Peter and Paul) are the most striking exterior features. A shell motif, symbolic of St. James the Elder (Santiago), is reproduced several times in the exterior decoration, predominantly over doorways. Inside, the neoclassical main altar features a statue of Santiago flanked by smaller statues of Christ and the Virgin Mary. More impressive baroque side altars, built between 1745 and 1800 and dedicated to the Sacred Heart and San José, respectively, are at opposite ends of the lateral arms of the cathedral's cruciform floor plan. The engraved silver front on the San José altar has been exhibited at New York's Metropolitan Museum of Art. Several viceregal-style sacred paintings by Don José de Alcíbar are hung on the cathedral walls.

Attached to the cathedral is the **Capilla del Santo Cristo,** which contains a highly revered wooden crucifix carved in Spain and brought to Saltillo in 1608.

Two festivals associated with the cathedral include Saltillo's patron saint day on 25 July, and the even bigger **Novenario de Santo Cristo** on 6 Aug., when pilgrims from all over the state come to pay homage to the Spanish crucifixion in the *capilla.* Semana Santa and Christmas are also impressively celebrated here.

The cathedral faces the Plaza de Armas at Calle Hidalgo and Juárez.

Museums

Centro Cultural Vanguardia, Hidalgo 231, is a large churchlike Victorian structure built in 1906 by the Purcells, an English mine-owning family. *Vanguardia* newspaper now maintains it as an art museum and children's library, although the main attraction for most people remains the building itself. The outside of the building is made of stone, while the inside is almost entirely paneled in wood and features antique mirror-topped fireplaces, ornate brass lighting fixtures, and period furniture. Free admission.

Housed in the restored 19th-century Colegio de San Juan Nepomuceno, **Museo de la Aves,** Bolívar at Hidalgo, tel. (84) 14-0167 or 14-0168, displays approximately 1,800 stuffed birds (representing 70% of all Mexican species) in realistic natural settings with state-of-the-art lighting and climate control. It's open Tues.-Sat. 10 a.m.-6 p.m., Sunday 11 a.m.-6 p.m.; admission US$0.70 for adults, US$1.40 for a family of seven or fewer, US$0.25 students and children under 12.

Instituto Coahuilense de Cultura (formerly Museo CAVIE), in a stately 19th-century colonial at the corner of Calle Juárez and Hidalgo (diagonally opposite the cathedral), hosts rotating exhibits by local and regional artists. Open daily 9:30 a.m.-7 p.m.; admission free.

The **Ateneo Fuentes** (Fuentes Athenaeum), on Calle E. Carranza on the Universidad Autónoma de Coahuila campus, displays a permanent collection of works by accomplished Mexican and international painters in a Mexican art deco building. Open daily 9:30 a.m.-7 p.m.; admission free.

Parque Alameda Zaragoza

This large and very nicely landscaped park covering eight blocks at the west end of Calle G. Victoria is a good spot to while away an hour or two. It dates to 1920 and is one of the most beautiful parks in the country outside Mexico City.

An equestrian statue of the park's namesake, Ignacio Zaragoza, stands in the Alameda's center. Zaragoza was a hero at the Battle of Puebla of 5 May 1862 (celebrated annually in the Fiesta del Cinco de Mayo), in which Mexican troops repulsed French military invaders.

Plazas

Plaza de Armas and **Plaza de Nueva Tlaxcala,** separated by the Palacio de Gobierno west of the cathedral, are large squares empty except for the occasional stroller or shutterbug trying for an angle on the cathedral.

The real action is at **Plaza Acuña** (two blocks north of Plaza de Armas via Calle Allende), a small, leafy square with benches and food vendors next to bustling Mercado Juárez. The plaza is named for Manuel Acuña, a famous Saltillo poet who killed himself at age 23.

ACCOMMODATIONS

Shoestring
Saltillo's lowest-priced hotels are found downtown between the Alameda and Plaza de Armas.

Hotel Bristol, Aldama Pte. 405, tel. (84) 10-4337, is entered through a small budget shopping center. The reception area looks much more dismal than the rooms, which are surprisingly quiet considering the location. Decent rooms come with TV and private bath. Rates: US$8 s, US$9 d in one-bed rooms; US$11 d, US$12 t, US$13 q in two-bed rooms.

Even cheaper are a couple of basic places along nearby Calle Flores (near the west side of Plaza Acuña): the twin **Hotel Jardín,** tel. (84) 12-5916, and **Hotel De Avila** (same telephone and ownership). Rates: around US$8-11 s/d. Farther south along Calle Flores, **Hotel Hidalgo** looks promising but is mainly a short-time hotel used by hookers and their clients.

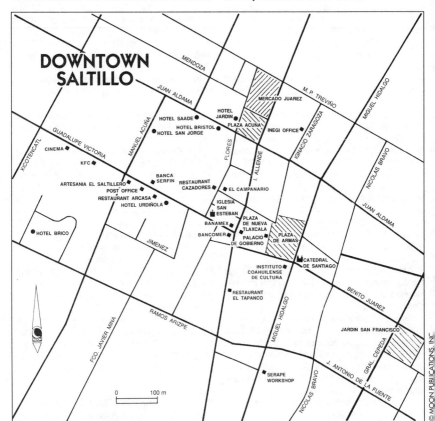

A bit farther south is the charmless and well-worn **Hotel Brico,** Calle Ramos Arizpe 552, tel. (84) 12-5146, with relatively clean rooms. Rates: US$8 s/d in a one-bed room; US$9 d, US$11 t, US$12 q in a two-bed room.

Budget

Probably the best deal in town is the colonial-style **Hotel Urdiñola,** Calle Victoria 211, tel. (84) 14-0940, not far from the Plaza de Armas and convenient to downtown shopping and eating. The tidy, well-maintained rooms surround an interior courtyard. A small coffeeshop is attached. Rates: US$15 s, US$17 d.

The well-located, four-story **Hotel Saade,** Calle Aldama Pte. 397 (between Calles Acuña and Flores), tel. (84) 12-9220, fax (84) 12-9129, offers 71 rooms with TV, phone, a/c, and heat. Facilities include off-street parking, a restaurant, and a travel agency. Rates: US$16 s, US$19 d. Centrally located **Hotel Premier,** Calle Allende Nte. 508, tel. (84) 12-1050 or (800) 8-4444 for reservations, offers good rooms with a/c and TV. Rates: US$22 s, US$25 d.

Hotel Rancho El Morillo (Apdo. Postal 304, Saltillo, Coah.), tel. (84) 17-4078, fax (84) 14-1975, offers 14 spacious rooms in a restored hacienda on wooded grounds. Amenities include a pool, chapel, ping-pong tables, a tennis court, volleyball court, and dining room with *comida casera* ("home cooking"). Rates: US$22 s, US$26 d, US$28 t, US$30 q. El Morillo is off Periférico Luis Echeverría Sur at Calle Obregón, about three km (two miles) southwest of downtown Saltillo.

At the western outskirts of town on Blvd. Fundadores (a good location if you're driving to/from the south, e.g., Matehuala or San Luis Potosí), **Motel La Fuente,** tel. (84) 30-1599, fax (84) 30-1497, is a well-kept, one-story courtyard motel with a pool, tennis court, and restaurant. Rooms come with TV, a/c, and heat. Rates: in the US$23-33 range. Nearby **Motel Corona Norte,** tel. (84) 30-2229, is similar and has spacious rooms, some with jacuzzi. Rates: US$16-21 s/d. Another place geared to motorists is the new **OKey Inn,** Blvd. Fundadores Km 4, tel. (84) 30-1300 or 30-1084, which has large rooms with a/c, TV, phone, and heat. Rates: US$16 s/d, US$19 t, US$22 q.

Hotel La Torre, tel. (84) 30-0600, six km southeast of town on Mexico 57, has modern rooms in a tower complex with good mountain views. Junior suites are available (at inexpensive rates). On the premises are a swimming pool and tennis courts. Rates: US$27 s/d, US$40 junior suite.

Budget/Inexpensive

Most of Saltillo's better hotels are found along Blvd. V. Carranza (Mexico 40 North) and Blvd. Fundadores (Mexico 57 South). To find the latter boulevard from the city (or from Mexico 40), follow signs reading "Matehuala."

At the northern edge of town, the two-story **Imperial del Norte Motor Hotel,** Blvd. V. Carranza 3800, tel. (84) 15-0011, fax (84) 16-7543, is a friendly spot with quick Mexico 40 access and renovated rooms with color TV, a/c, heat, phones, and carpet. Facilities include pool, restaurant, volleyball court, fax service and parking. Rates: US$33-39 s/d; economy rooms (without a/c and carpet) US$17.

Inexpensive

Tall, white **Hotel San Jorge Best Western,** Calle Aldama at Acuña downtown, tel. (84) 12-2222, U.S. toll-free tel. (800) 635-4456, offers large rooms (no a/c) and a heated pool. Rates: US$40 s on weekends; US$45 s, US$52 d weekdays.

Moving toward the north end of town, the **Eurotel Plaza Holiday Inn,** Blvd. V. Carranza 4100 (about 4.8 km/three miles from downtown Saltillo), tel. (84) 15-1000, Mexico toll-free tel. (800) 0-0999, offers modern rooms with satellite TV, a/c, and heating. Facilities include a travel agency, restaurant, car rental, and indoor pool. Rates: US$48 s/d.

Moderate

A popular choice among visiting North American business travelers is the relaxed but efficient, five-star **Hotel Camino Real,** situated on quiet, nicely landscaped grounds on Blvd. Fundadores six km southeast of town, tel. (84) 30-0000, fax (84) 30-1030, U.S./Canada reservations tel. (800) 722-6466. Rooms, arranged in separated ranch-style buildings, come with refrigerator/bar, satellite TV, a/c, and telephone. Facilities include a cozy bar, restaurant, coffee shop, putting green, two lighted tennis courts, and a well-maintained, heated pool. Rates: US$55-65 s/d.

RV Parks

The **Imperial del Norte Motor Hotel** provides around a half dozen RV sites with full hookups for US$10, plus plenty of parking without hookups for overflow RVers. **Hotel Camino Real** also maintains a number of RV and trailer spaces with full hookups. Rates vary with the season but are generally in the US$10-15 range. For addresses and telephone numbers, see the hotel listings above.

Self-contained RVs and campers are also permitted to park—for no charge—at the Centro de Convenciones parking lot on Blvd. Fundadores (Mexico 57).

FOOD

Saltillo cuisine is very much in the *norteña* style, with an emphasis on *carnes al carbón* (charcoal-grilled steaks), *cabrito, guisada, machaca,* flour tortillas, and milk-based pastries and sweets. Among Mexicans the city is perhaps most famous for *pan de pulque,* bread made with fermented maguey extract. This delicacy can be hard to find outside people's homes, since the best *pulque* (known as *pulque casera* or "house pulque") is circulated privately. If you're interested in tasting some, ask at a local *panadería*—try **Panadería La Crema,** just south of Hotel San Jorge on Calle Acuña—or take a day-trip to Ramos Arizpe, where it's most common (see "Around Saltillo," below).

Restaurant Principal, Calle Allende Nte. 702, tel. (84) 14-3384, specializes in *carne asada* and *cabrito.* In the vicinity of the cathedral and Plaza de Armas, **Restaurant Arcasa,** next door to Hotel Urdiñola on Calle G. Victoria, serves a tasty and inexpensive *comida corrida,* plus a variety of tacos and *tortas.* Around the corner on Calle Flores (between Victoria and Ocampo), **Café Victoria** specializes in moderately priced Mexican standards, cheap breakfasts, burgers, and sandwiches. The cafe also offers fax and long-distance phone service. The a/c **Restaurant Cazadores,** a bit farther south on the same street, has a similar menu but isn't as popular.

The outdoor tables in front of **Mercado Juárez** facing Plaza Acuña are pleasant and vendors serve inexpensive *antojitos;* if nothing

else, it's a good spot to watch plaza life while sipping a *refresco* or beer.

For something more elegant, try **El Tapanco,** Calle Allende Sur 225 (a block and a half south of the Plaza de Armas), a converted 17th-century house with courtyard and fountain. The varied menu offers both international and Mexican standards for lunch and dinner Mon.-Saturday.

El Campanario, Ocampo 338-2 (in an old building on Plaza San Esteban) is a small place with traditional Mexican dishes and a friendly staff trying to draw a young, artsy crowd. It's open Mon.-Sat. noon-10 p.m.; live music on Thurs.-Sat. evenings.

Homesick Americans can stop in at **KFC** or **Dunkin' Donuts** on Calle Victoria. A string of other American-style fast-food places (including **Wendy's**) can be found along Blvd. Carranza northeast of Blvd. Fco. Coss.

BULLFIGHTS AND *CHARREADAS*

Saltillo's **Plaza de Toros Armillita** is on Av. Jesús Valdés Sánchez (Coahuila 10), the old road to Arteaga, about four km (2.5 miles) east of the Ciudad Deportiva. Summer is the usual bullfight season.

escaramuzas

The local *charro* association holds *charreadas* in two different rings: the **Lienzo Charro El Rayito (Dr. Carlos Cárdenas V.),** off Blvd. Ortiz Garza in the northeastern section of the city; and the easier-to-find **Lienzo Charro Prof. Enrique González,** on Mexico 40, three km (two miles) north of Periférico Luis Echeverría Norte. The tourist offices in town should be able to provide current *corrida* and *charreada* schedules.

SHOPPING

When the Tlaxcaltecas established the colony of San Esteban de Nueva Tlaxcala in the early 1600s, they brought with them the art of weaving sarapes—multihued, multipurpose blankets associated with the stereotypical *campesino* (Mexican peasant). One of the best places to shop for sarapes, rugs, and handwoven wool or cotton items is **El Saltillero,** Calle G. Victoria Pte. 469, just two blocks west of the Plaza de Armas. Sarapes here start at US$8 for a basic souvenir model and reach over US$100 for top-quality, all-wool original designs; a fairly nice one costs about US$27. The traditional Saltillo sarape is a bright, rainbow-colored pattern with a diamond in the center—usually the one that looks most "touristy" to the untrained eye. Sarapes and *jorongos* (a sarape with a hole in the middle for the head) in muted earth tones are a more recent development. El Saltillero also carries a broad range of other regional and Mexican crafts.

Other places to try include **El Sarape de Saltillo,** Hidalgo 305, and the several curios shops along Calles Victoria and Ocampo. You can also visit a **sarape workshop** on the east side of Calle Hidalgo, just south of Calle Ramos Arizpe downtown.

Botas Recio, Allende Nte. 701, tel. (84) 12-1237, fax (84) 12-8222, claims to be the largest boot store in Mexico. The shop also sells other leather goods, western clothing, hats, belts, and buckles. **Saltillo Silver Factory,** across from Hotel Urdiñola, has a large selection of silver crafts. It's only open Mon.-Sat. 4:30-7 p.m. At **Mercado Juárez** (north end of Plaza Acuña) you'll find many of the same crafts as at the curios shops but at lower prices.

INFORMATION AND SERVICES

Tourist Offices
Coahuila's main tourist office, **Fomento Turístico,** is on the 11th floor of the Torre Saltillo at Blvd. Luis Echeverría 1560, tel. (84) 16-9221, 15-2162 or 15-2174; open Mon.-Fri. 9 a.m.-3 p.m. and 5-9 p.m. A small branch office called **Caseta Coss** is on Blvd. Fco. Coss at Acuña, a block west of Blvd. V. Carranza. Both offices distribute high-quality information on Saltillo and the surrounding state; several of the staffers speak English.

Post Offices
Saltillo's post offices seem to be better located and easier to find than in most Mexican cities of comparable size; hence if you have mail business to take care of, this is a good city in which to get it accomplished. Perhaps the most convenient branch is the small post office in a building next door to the Caseta Coss tourist office at Blvd. Fco. Coss and Acuña. In the center of town, another convenient post office branch is on Calle G. Victoria near Hotel Urdiñola.

Maps
Saltillo's INEGI office, conveniently located downtown on Calle Zaragoza (two blocks north of the cathedral), carries topographic maps for Coahuila, Nuevo León, and Zacatecas.

Language Study
The **Instituto Mexicano-Norteamericano de Relaciones Culturales de Saltillo** offers Span-

SALTILLO TELEPHONE NUMBERS

Local Police	14-4550
Fire	15-4244
Highway Patrol	15-5122
Green Angels	14-3175, 15-4129
State Tourist Office	15-4504, 12-4050
Red Cross	14-3333
University Hospital	12-3000
Saltillo Area Code	84

ish classes for US$8.92 per hour, with a 25-hour minimum. Contact IMARC, P. Cárdenas Pte. 840, Saltillo, Coah., tel. (84)14-8422, fax (84) 12-0653.

The language department of the **Universidad Autónoma de Coahuila** receives U.S. college groups studying for credit but also offers 90-hour courses (minimum three persons) for US$255. The department will also arrange lodging in private homes for maximum immersion. Contact Profesora María del Refugio Cárdenas, Departamento de Idiomas, Universidad Autónoma de Coahuila, Hidalgo y González Lobo, Col. República, Saltillo, Coah., tel. (84) 16-5143, fax (84) 16-5083.

GETTING THERE

By Air
With the Monterrey behemoth so close, few airlines serve Saltillo directly. In fact the only regularly scheduled commercial passenger flights to Saltillo are those from Mexico City operated daily by both **TAESA,** Europlaza Mall, Blvd. Carranza 4120, tel./fax (84) 15-6202, and **Mexicana,** Europlaza Mall, tel. (84) 15-0353.

Aeropuerto Plan de Guadalupe is 13 km north of Saltillo (via Mexico 40) in Ramos Arizpe.

By Bus
The **Central Camionera Saltillo** is on Periférico Luis Echeverría Sur at Calle Libertad, about two km south of the city center. **Transportes Monterrey-Saltillo,** tel. (84) 17-0243, has a monopoly on buses to/from Saltillo, with departures every 30 minutes between 5 a.m. and 9 p.m. for US$2.50 ordinary class, US$6 *ejecutivo.* **Transportes del Norte,** tel. (84) 17-0902, operates buses to Torreón (US$9, four times daily), Chihuahua (US$37, twice daily), and Ciudad Victoria (US$12, twice daily). **Autobuses El Aguila,** tel. (84) 17-0135, specializes in service to border towns, including Acuña (US$14, three times daily), Piedras Negras (US$13, five times daily), Monclova (US$6, 10 times daily), plus long-distance services to San Luis Potosí (US$12, six times daily), Matehuala (US$7, eight times daily), Zacatecas (US$12, seven times daily), and Guadalajara (US$23, seven times daily).

Connections with Greyhound add service to Houston (US$33) and Dallas (US$43) once daily.

By Train
The first-class *Regiomontaño* connects Saltillo with Monterrey (US$2), San Luis Potosí (US$7), and Mexico City (US$15). Although the Monterrey-Saltillo fare is relatively cheap, that segment takes two hours and 15 minutes, twice as long as the bus. To San Luis Potosí (around five hours) and Mexico City (12 hours), sleeping berths and private cabins are also available for extra charges.

Driving
Savvy motorists heading for the interior of Mexico from the Texas border use Saltillo as a gateway rather than Monterrey; traffic tie-ups are fewer and there are no toll charges along the way (so far).

GETTING AROUND

By Bus
Buses marked "Camionera-Centro" ply back and forth between the bus terminal and downtown Saltillo; other buses connect the *centro* with Blvd. Fundadores (for the convention center and La Fuente, La Torre, and Camino Real Hotels) and Blvd. V. Carranza (Imperial Motor Hotel, Eurotel Plaza, and Lienzo Charro Prof. Enrique González). City bus fare is US$0.24.

By Taxi
Taxicabs are plentiful downtown near Plaza Acuña and at the larger hotels. A typical ride within the downtown area costs around US$1.70; to the city outskirts US$5-7 depending on the distance. Taxis can be hired by the hour for US$5.

Driving
With a map it's fairly easy to find your way around the city. Narrow streets in the older downtown district aren't a problem for the average sedan, truck, or van; motorists driving large RVs may want to park on the larger avenues at the edges of town, then use public transportation (or walk) downtown.

The city has devised a system of pentagonal, numbered street signs that are intended to help motorists reach their destinations more easily.

Signs marked "1," for example, lead to Blvd. V. Carranza and Mexico 40 East, while those marked "23" lead to Mexico 54 and Calle M. Abasolo. With so many different options, however, it's difficult to associate numbers with destinations unless you're a long-term visitor or resident.

AROUND SALTILLO

Ramos Arizpe

Only 12 km northeast of Saltillo via Mexico 40, Ramos Arizpe became a virtual city suburb with the opening of the Aeropuerto Plan de Guadalupe, the only commercial airport serving the Saltillo area. The town is regionally famous for *pulque,* an alcoholic beverage made with fermented maguey (agave) extract, and for *pan de pulque,* bread made with pulque. If you've had trouble finding this substance, look no further than the **Pulque Restaurant** on Calle Gral. Charles between Morelos and Ocampo, three blocks south of Arizpe's Plaza Principal.

Other local attractions include the nearby *balneario* at **Ojo Caliente,** and the abandoned **Hacienda de Santa María** four km northeast of town.

Arteaga

The foothills of the Sierra Madre Oriental, rising east of Saltillo along the Nuevo León border, are little explored by out-of-state visitors but are highly favored by Saltillo residents, many of whom have built vacation cabins in the area. A good starting point for an excursion into the mountains (here called the Sierra de Arteaga) is the small ranching and farming town of Arteaga, 17 km (11 miles) east of Saltillo via Mexico 57. Flanked by picturesque Arroyo Seco and Arroyo Blanco, Arteaga is known for the production of apples and handicrafts, particularly ceramics. A small state tourist office on Mexico 57 just west of town toward Saltillo has ample information on the area.

Farther east and southeast, narrow paved roads off Mexico 57 ascend the sierra to **El Parque Forestal El Chorro, El Cañon de la Roja,** and the quaint mountain villages of **Los Lirios, San Juan de Dolores,** and **San Antonio de las Alazanas.**

WEST OF SALTILLO

PARRAS DE LA FUENTE

Founded in 1578 as Santa María de las Parras, this town of 26,000 makes a convenient midway stopover on Mexico 40 between Saltillo (146 km/90.5 miles east) and Torreón (152 km/94 miles west). Underground streams sourced in the Sierra Madre Oriental reach the surface as springs at Parras, which is known as the Oasis de Coahuila for its many pecan, walnut, fig, date, and avocado orchards. It's also considered the "cradle of North American viticulture," since the first winery established anywhere in the Americas was founded in Parras in 1593 by Spain's Marqués de Aguayo. By the time the Aguayo winery closed its doors in 1898, winemaking had become one of Parras's cultural hallmarks; the area is still an important winemaking center. Parras's other claim to fame is that the republic's first president after the Mexican Revolution, Francisco I. Madero, was born here.

The 100- and 200-year-old architecture in the center of town is remarkably well preserved, making Parras one of the most attractive towns in all of Northern Mexico, yet very few tourists seem to know about it. It's also a remarkably friendly town, perhaps because it receives so few foreign visitors. At an elevation of 1,520 meters (4,985 feet), the town enjoys a relatively mild climate year-round.

Wineries

Vinifera is cultivated in many fields surrounding Parras, while in town several wineries maintain bodegas (storage and distribution facilities) where wines may be tasted and purchased. Most of the wine produced in Parras is oriented toward a low-price, Old World Mexican market that favors sweet wines, sherry, and port. Typical of the genre is **Fábrica de Licores y Vino El Vesubio,** Calle Madero 36, which bottles *jerez dulce* (sweet sherry), *tinto semiseco* (semidry table wine), *moscate dulce* (muscatel), *sangre de* *cristo* ("blood of Christ," a heavy red table wine), and even *uva con nuez,* a pecan-infused brandy. Other bodegas in town with similar fare include **Vinos Caseros Santo Madero,** Calle Ocampo near Fco. I. Mina, and **Vinos Caseros Fuantos,** Degollado on the Alameda.

By international standards, the only producer of fine wines in the area is **Casa Madero,** in the ex-Hacienda de San Lorenzo about five km north of town on the road to La Paila. Established in 1597, it's the oldest functioning winery in the Americas, and the vintners take this legacy seriously. Varietals from Casa Madero include chardonnay, cabernet sauvignon, and—their best—a merlot. Casa Madero also produces two very good reserve brandies—approaching cognac in style and substance and probably the best brandies in Mexico—plus a unique white (clear) brandy labeled Blanco Total. Visitors are welcome to visit the stately grounds;

wines and brandies may be sampled and purchased in a large tasting room on the premises. Open daily 9 a.m.-5 p.m. For information call (842) 2-0111.

Other Sights and Activities

Madero's family home, **Recinto Madero,** Calle 16 de Septiembre at Alameda del Rosario, has been turned into a small museum chronicling the revolutionary leader's life.

More interesting perhaps is the **Museo del Vino,** which contains exhibits on the crushing, fermenting, and aging processes used in local winemaking. The museum is housed in the 300-year-old **Hacienda de Urdiñola,** a few km north of town off Coahuila 125, the road to La Paila.

The **Iglesia y Colegio de San Ignacio Loyola,** Treviño at Madero (near the northeast corner of the Plaza de Armas), contains rare religious paintings from the 16th and 17th centuries.

Accommodations

Shoestring: The town's least expensive hotel is the simple **Hotel Parras,** Calle Ramos Arizpe at Reforma (near the main plaza), tel. (842) 2-0644, where rooms are spartan. Rates: around US$5-10. Better is the **Hotel La Siesta,** Calle Acuña 9, tel. (842) 2-0374, where well worn but spacious and clean rooms have TV and phone. Rates: US$8 s, US$12 d, US$17 t, US$ 20 q.

Budget: Hostal El Farol, Treviño 22 (near the corner of Ramos Arizpe), tel. (842) 2-1113, is a big step up in quality and a huge leap up in atmosphere. Large rooms in a historic building surround an interior courtyard, and the old hotel bar is a genuine classic. Parking is available in back. Rates: US$13 s, US$20 d, US$26 t, US$35 q.

For about the same price as the El Farol—less if there are more than two in your party—the best place to stay downtown is the well-run and well-maintained **Hotel Posada Santa Isabel,** Calle Fco. I. Madero 514, tel. (842) 2-0572, a block west of the plaza in an old adobe typical of Parras architecture. Large, comfortable, and clean rooms surround a courtyard. Amenities include a small pool, security parking, and a low-key cafe/restaurant serving good Mexican food. Rates: US$19 s, US$21 d US$24, US$27 q.

Inexpensive: Outside of town is Parras's most famous hostelry, **Rincón del Montero Hotel & Resort** (Apdo. Postal 37, Parras, Coah.), 22.5 km (14 miles) south of Mexico 40 on Coahuila 125, tel. (842) 2-0540, fax (842) 2-2347. Situated on 57 shady acres, the resort features a nine-hole golf course, tennis courts, horseback riding, a spring-fed pool, restaurant, bar, and spacious rooms with kitchenettes. Rates: from US$37. Twelve RV spaces with full hookups and showers are available for US$10 per night.

Food

Restaurant El Colonial, facing the south end of Plaza de Reloj on Calle Madero, is a diner-like spot with good regional and Mexican standards. **Restaurant La Rueda** (formerly Restaurant Maracay), on Calle Ramos Arizpe near Vinos Caseros Santo Madero, serves good and inexpensive *platillos típicos.* **El Rincón del Recuerdo,** Calle Cayuso 10 (south of Plaza de Reloj and the Parroquía de Santa María de las Parras), serves traditional Mexican food in a 200-year-old building.

Restaurant El Tiburón, on Reforma between Madero and Arizpe, and **Chávez Cocina Económica,** next door, offer quick, cheap *antojitos.*

Parras is famous for *dulces* (sweets) made from cactus fruit *(tuna),* pecans, and honey; downtown you'll find at least a half dozen *dulcerías.* One of the best and most typical is **Dulcería Regionales de la Rosa,** on Reforma between Calles Ramos Arizpe and Madero.

Events

For those interested in wine culture, the best time of year to visit Parras is during the **Festival de la Vendimia** ("Vintage Festival"), which coincides with the annual grape harvest in August. In addition to free-flowing wine, the festival proudly purveys a seemingly unending supply of regional *dulces* and other foods made with Parras's bountiful supply of figs, dates, walnuts, and pecans.

Information

Parras has an informative state tourist office, tel. (842) 2-0876, north of town on Coahuila 125.

Transportation

The main bus terminal (Central de Autobuses) is downtown on Calle Ramos Arizpe near Calle Melchor Múzquiz, about two blocks east of Plaza de Reloj. Buses leave six times daily to Torreón (US$4.60) and eight times daily to Saltillo (US$3.45).

TORREÓN AND VICINITY

Mexican, American, British, and French interests founded Torreón as a rail center in 1887. It's the largest of the Región Lagunera cities and an important cotton, wheat, vinifera, mining, and dairy farming center. In spite of being well within the borders of the Chihuahuan Desert, this area has managed—with irrigation help—to become one of Northern Mexico's economic strongholds.

Torreón attained official city status in 1897, at which time engineers carefully laid out an urban plan. What was intended to be a "modern and very practical" community has turned out to be an attractive and livable city of 507,000 residents. Wide avenues with palm-lined medians in the city center give the impression of what Pasadena, California, might have looked like if it

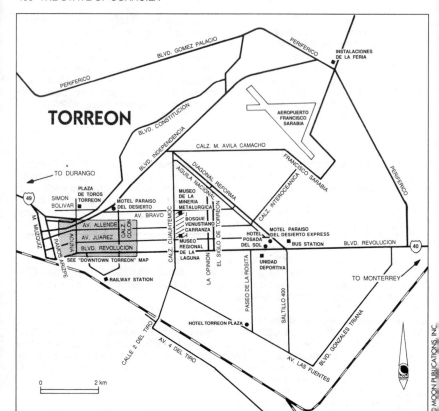

Parks

Perhaps Torreón's most impressive assets are its large and leafy parks, which provide an easy respite from summer heat and a refuge for migrating birds. Food and beverage vendors hawk their wares on warm evenings and on weekends, adding a festive atmosphere.

The city's largest park, **Bosque Venustiano Carranza,** covers 30 square blocks bordered by Av. Juárez, Av. Bravo, Calz. Cuauhtémoc, and Calle Juan Pablo in the middle of the city. Large casuarinas, fan palms, and other trees provide shady paths for walkers and joggers,

had been built by Europeans, while several downtown parks and plazas contribute splashes of green to the cityscape.

and benches are distributed throughout for more sedentary park visitors and kissing couples. The park also contains a small zoo, pool, theater, children-oriented amusement park, and the **Museo Regional de la Laguna.** This INAH-sponsored museum (open daily 10 a.m.-5 p.m.) houses permanent exhibits on regional archaeology; a collection of Mesoamerican ceramics; ethnographic displays from Coahuila, Oaxaca, Puebla, Hidalgo, Chiapas, Chihuahua, and Guerrero; a small library; and occasional traveling exhibits. Toward the north end of the park and less interesting (at least to nongeologists) is the **Museo de la Minería,** which contains exhibits on various minerals native to the region.

Second in size is six-block-square **Alameda Zaragoza,** west of Bosque V. Carranza between

Calles Ortega and Guerra off Av. Juárez. Smaller yet is the **Plazuela Juárez,** farther west between Calles Corona and Galeana off Av. Morelos, where a statue of Benito Juárez always seems to have a bird sitting on its guano-crowned head.

Accommodations

Built within the last two decades, most of Torreón's hotels are modern, boxy affairs. If you're planning on stopping over to see some of the city, one of the downtown hotels would be a good choice since driving in and out of the city from Mexico 40 and Mexico 49 can be an ordeal; conversely, if you're just passing through and need a place to sleep, a hotel or motel on the outskirts of the city might be more suitable. Downtown hotels are considerably less expensive than highway motels. Locally quarried marble is liberally used in the older hotels.

Shoestring: Basic but adequate lodgings are available at the two-story **Hotel Galicia,** facing the east side of Plaza de Armas on Calle Cepeda, tel. (17) 16-1111, and at **Hotel Arriaga,** a block east at Av. Hidalgo and Calle Cepeda, tel. (17) 16-1055. The Galicia is a bit nicer than the Arriaga. Rates: US$8-10. At Av. Morelos and Treviño, six-story **Hotel del Paseo,** tel. (17) 16-0303, has a marble-floored lobby, adequate

rooms, a small restaurant, and parking at nearby Hotel Río Nazas (same owners). Rates: US$12 s, US$15 d.

Shoestring-to-Inexpensive: On the east end of town near Mexico 40, **Hotel Posada del Sol,** on Blvd. Revolución two blocks west of Diagonal Reforma, tel. (17) 20-3121, offers accommodations to suit a wide range of pocketbooks. Choose from newly remodeled rooms with TV and phone (US$19 s/d); cheaper cabañas with no TV or phone (US$11.50 s, US$12 d); and higher priced suites (US$40).

Budget: Most of the better hotels downtown are found in the vicinity of the Plaza de Armas on Av. Morelos or Av. Juárez. The six-story **Hotel Calvete,** Av. Juárez at Calle Corona, tel. (17) 16-1010, has good rooms with a/c and TV, as well as a parking garage a block away. Rates: US$21-27 s/d.

The well-worn but clean and comfortable nine-story **Hotel Río Nazas,** tel. (17) 16-1212, fax (17) 12-6177, near Hotel del Paseo, has a/c, TV, phones, a basement parking garage, and a restaurant/bar. The hotel celebrated its 50th anniversary in 1996, as the antique elevator will confirm if you get stuck between floors. The marble lobby is fitted with chandeliers, a fountain, and murals of local grape harvest scenes. Rates: US$16-23 s/d.

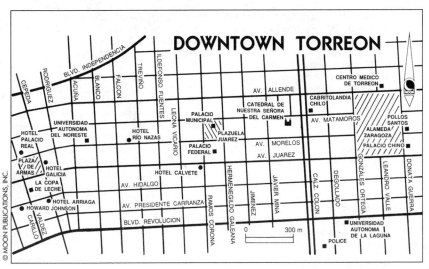

A block and a half southwest of the Plaza de Armas, recently remodeled **Howard Johnson,** Hidalgo Pte. 1353, tel. (17) 16-9652, fax (17) 16-9699, features a marble lobby and comfortable rooms with a/c, TV, and mini-bar—a bargain. Rates: US$24 s/d, US$27 junior suite, US$32 full suite.

On the east side, **Motel La Villa,** on Diagonal Reforma just north of Av. Juárez (about five blocks northwest of Blvd. Revolución/Mexico 40), tel. (17) 20-1512, offers standard, a/c rooms around a parking lot and pool. Rates: US$26-28.50 s/d.

The friendly **Motel Campestre,** Blvd. Miguel Alemán Ote. 251 (next to a PEMEX station west out of town on Mexico 49/40), tel. (17) 14-2781, fax (17) 14-0743, is technically within Gómez Palacio city limits, but it's actually closer to downtown Torreón. Rooms surround a pool and parking lot. Rates: in the US$22-25 range.

Inexpensive: The city's top downtown hotel is the **Hotel Palacio Real,** tel. (17) 16-0000, fax (17) 16-8608, a stately, nine-story, European-style hotel facing the north side of Plaza de Armas. Completing the effect is the hotel's atmospheric **Café de Paris** on the ground floor. Rooms have all the amenities, and hotel facilities include a swimming pool, disco, travel agency, car rental, parking garage, restaurant, and bar. Rates: US$48 s/d; US$51 s/d in the remodeled section.

Very near Motel La Villa on Diagonal Reforma is **Motel Paraíso del Desierto Express** (formerly Motel Paraíso del Camino), tel. (17) 13-9930, tel./fax (17) 20-0333, Mexico toll-free tel. (800) 1-7017, where pleasant rooms with a/c, refrigerator, TV, and phone surround a pool and parking lot. Rates: US$42 s/d.

Moderate: A bit east from the center of town yet not quite on the outskirts is **Hotel Torreón Plaza** (formerly Hotel del Prado), on Paseo de la Rosita two km south of Blvd. Revolución, opposite the Club Campestre La Rosita (Rosita Country Club), tel. (17) 21-2424, fax (17) 21-2958. The plush rooms have servibars, a/c, satellite TV, and other amenities, and the hotel has a pool, restaurant, coffee shop, and disco. A large buffet breakfast is included in the rates (US$71 s/d).

On the west side of town near Mexico 49, **Motel Paraíso del Desierto,** Blvd. Independencia at Jiménez, tel. (17) 16-1122, is the motel equivalent of the downtown Palacio Real, offering spotless, modern rooms with a/c, refrigerators, satellite TV, and phones, plus a pool, internet service, breakfast buffet, security parking, and coin laundry. Rates: US$62-66 s/d.

RV Parks

RVers and campers may park their rigs in the **Motel Campestre** lot and pay a nominal fee for the use of showers in unoccupied rooms. See also the Gómez Palacio section in the Durango chapter for details on the Quinta Colima Trailer Park.

Food

Prosperous Torreón supports restaurants of every menu and budget. Many inexpensive and medium-priced eateries can be found along Av. Morelos between Hotel Río Nazas and Plaza de Armas, including the popular *cafetería* at **Benavides Farmacia,** just east of the Río Nazas at Av. Morelos and Calle Treviño. The Benavides menu features Mexican standards, inexpensive breakfasts, sandwiches, soups, and salads; it's open 7 a.m.-9 p.m. Another good spot for breakfast or an afternoon coffee is **La Copa de Leche,** on Calle Carrillo a half block south of the Plaza de Armas.

El Granjero, on Av. Morelos between Calle L. Vicario and Calle Corona, is a typical natural-foods grocery with a small vegetarian cafe and bakery attached. Another good bakery—and one where you can get coffee as well as pastries (a rarity outside Mexico City)—is **Cafetería y Pastelería Star Cake,** Av. Hidalgo Pte. 274, three blocks south of Plazuela Juárez.

Palacio Chino, Donato Guerra Sur 25, is a decent and inexpensive Chinese restaurant specializing in Cantonese cuisine. **Pollos Santos,** Calle D. Guerra (Calle 16) at Av. Morelos (facing the east side of Alameda Zaragoza), is a popular outdoor fried-chicken place that serves beer. **Cabritolandia Chilo,** Av. Matamoros at Calz. Colón (about four blocks east of Plazuela Juárez), specializes in *cabrito al pastor* (spit-roasted kid goat). **Restaurant Regio,** Blvd. Independencia at Calle 16, is an old standby for American-style steaks, *carne asada,* and *cabrito al pastor.*

Festivals and Events

Bullfights are periodically held at the **Plaza de Toros Torreón,** Calle Blanco at Av. Simón Bolívar (northeast of Av. Independencia). The state tourist office should have a current schedule, or you could stop by the bullring itself for a look at posted schedules.

The city's biggest annual celebration is the **Feria del Algodón y Uva** ("Cotton and Grape Fair") held each September, usually the second and third week of the month. Parades, exhibits, concerts, dances, and various other activities take place at different venues around town, although the main events are held at the Instalaciones de la Feria at the intersection of Periférico Norte and Mexico 30 on the city's northern outskirts.

Services

The city post office is in the large, virtually unmarked Palacio Federal facing Av. Juárez between Calles Corona and Galeana.

Torreón's radio station 96.3 FM is one of the most progressive stations in Northern Mexico, with a varied format of jazz, world music, and regional styles.

Transportation

By Air: Aero California, Blvd. Independencia Ote. 15, offers nonstop flights between Torreón and Ciudad Juárez, Durango, Guadalajara, Tijuana, and Mexico City. **Aeroméxico,** Blvd. Independencia Ote. 565, tel. (17) 12-4406, flies nonstop to/from Ciudad Juárez, Chihuahua, Culiacán, Durango, Guadalajara, Mazatlán, Mexico City, and Monterrey. **Lone Star Airlines,** tel. (17) 12-4406, flies nonstop to Dallas and Del Rio.

Torreón's **Aeropuerto Internacional Francisco Sarabia** is right on the northeastern edge of town, about 15 minutes by car from the city center. Taxis cost US$2.50 from downtown Torreón, while *colectivos* are US$0.50 pp.

By Bus: The modern **Central de Autobuses de Torreón** is near the eastern end of Av. Juárez off Av. Presidente Carranza. **Omnibus de México, Futura, Chihuahuenses,** and **Transportes del Norte** serve most large cities in Northern Mexico as well as Mexico City and Guadalajara. For intercity travel within the state, **Transportes Frontera, Autobuses Blanco,** and **Autobuses El Aguila** provide most bus services. Some sample first-class bus fares: Chihuahua, US$15; Ciudad Juárez, US$27; Mazatlán, US$19; México City US$46; Monterrey US$12; Tijuana US$65.

Around town, city buses ply main east-west Avenidas Revolución, Juárez, and Allende, and north-south Calle Ramos Arizpe, Calz. Colón, and Calz. Cuauhtémoc.

By Train: The División del Norte trains arrive at and depart from the FNM railway station at the southern end of Calle Galeana (about five blocks south of Blvd. Revolución). This line runs from Ciudad Juárez to Mexico City; both first-class and second-class seats are available between Ciudad Juárez and Torreón. The fare is US$16 for first-class, US$9 for second-class, and the trip takes 14 hours. To Mexico City fares are US$12 second class, US$22 first.

By Car: Torreón is laid out like a large grid broken into partial grids separated by diagonal boulevards to form a large triangle (if this sounds confusing, it's nothing compared to the street configuration itself). Calzada Cuauhtémoc bisects the peak of the triangle formed by Blvd. Independencia and Diagonal (Blvd.) Reforma, while Blvd. Revolución forms the triangle's base. When driving across these diagonals from one "shard" of the triangle to another, it's very easy to become lost. Keep a map handy; without one you're liable to spend an inordinate amount of time driving in angled circles.

Adding to the confusion is a system of one-way streets and a decided lack of signs pointing the way in or out of the city from Mexico 40 or 49. Remember that Calle Ramos Arizpe is the way out of the city toward Mexico 49 North (actually west at this point), while the way in (south/east) is via Calle Melchor Múzquiz one block west. Another hint: heading out of town toward Mexico 49, follow signs for "Durango" even if you're heading south (e.g., to Zacatecas). At the east end of town, accessing Mexico 40 East is somewhat easier. Use the *periférico* (bypass) that arches north over the city to go from Mexico 49 to Mexico 40.

Car Rental: Cars can be rented from travel agencies at the Palacio Real and Río Nazas Hotels, as well as from **Numero Uno Autorentals** at Morelos and Degolindo, tel. (17) 12-0990. Since Torreón doesn't get many tourists, rental volume is low and rates tend to be higher than average.

Viesca

Set amid a desert oasis of sand dunes and date palms, Viesca (77 km/47.5 miles east of Torreón) looks like a scene plucked from *Beau Geste* or an Indiana Jones epic. In fact the local dune field known as Dunas de Bilbao was used as a backdrop for the David Lynch sci-fi film *Dune*. *Dátiles* (dates) are a primary agricultural product of the area, along with cotton, corn, and wheat. The town itself has just over 3,400 inhabitants and was named for the first governor of the former Province of Coahuila y Texas, San José de Viesca y Bustamante.

Each July Viesca residents celebrate the **Feria Regional de Aniversario** in honor of the town's 1830 founding. No accommodations are available in Viesca but food is available from cafes off Av. Hidalgo (Mexico 40) and from vendors near the town plaza.

BOB RACE

BOB RACE

THE STATE OF NUEVO LEÓN

Of the five Northern Mexican states that border the U.S., the smallest is Nuevo León, which shares only a 19-km (12-mile) sliver of border with Texas. With a literacy index above 95%, Nuevo León has one of Mexico's top three most educated populations (along with the Federal District and Baja California), largely due to the influence of its state capital, Monterrey. In many ways the whole state is but a capital suburb, trading labor and raw materials for Monterrey money and initiative. Of all the stockbrokers licensed in Mexico since 1975, two thirds have been based in Nuevo León.

Under Spanish rule, the territory was called Nuevo Reino de León and was a colonial backwater devoted to cattle ranching. Hostile natives prevented regional development until the end of

Spain's tenure in Mexico, after which the state had to deal with years of border disputes and war with the Republic of Texas and the U.S. before the industrialization of Monterrey at the turn of the century brought a sudden measure of prosperity.

Today most of the state's population is concentrated in the Monterrey metropolitan area, which includes the surrounding municipalities of San Nicolás de los Garza, San Pedro Garza García, Ciudad Guadalupe, Gen. Escobedo, Santa Catarina, and Apodaca. The state's second most populated region is the agricultural zone around Allende, Montemorelos, and Linares in the southeast. Currently the nation's biggest producer of citrus, the Allende-Linares area is also a major source of sorghum, alfalfa, corn, wheat, cattle, pigs, and poultry.

MONTERREY AND VICINITY

The self-titled Sultana de Norte ("Sultan of the North") sits on the Río Santa Catarina flood plain, 539 meters (1,765 feet) above sea level and surrounded on all sides by distinctive peaks of the Sierra Madre Oriental. The saddlelike profile of **Cerro de la Silla** ("Saddle Hill")—often considered a symbol of the city—rises to the east; to

the south is **Loma Larga** ("Long Slope"), to the west **Cerro de las Mitras** ("Bishop Hats Hill"), and to the north **Cerro del Topo Chico** ("Little Mole Hill").

Over the last century the city has become Mexico's industrial capital due to its strategic location (at a mountain pass near the U.S. bor-

GLASS AND BEER

Two companies exemplify Monterrey's aggressive economy and demonstrate how Mexico is moving ahead with an updated international trade agenda. Vitro, a maker of glass and household appliances and one of the city's first major manufacturers, purchased failing American company Anchor Glass in 1989, introduced new (and more advanced) technology to the company, and turned it into a profit-maker. More recently the firm entered into equal-partner (not *maquila* or in-bond) ventures with Whirlpool, Ford, and Dow Corning to sell glass components to those companies. As a result, Vitro is now Mexico's largest industrial group and the nation's first multinational; more than half its sales are in U.S. dollars.

Visa, a consortium owned by the Garza Sada clan, is doing so well with the Cervecería Cuauhtémoc and other endeavors that it now owns a major share in Bancomer, Mexico's second largest bank. The company has also recently modernized its barley cultivation, harvesting, and processing to compete with the U.S. beer industry. The only thing protecting the current Mexican market from a U.S. beer invasion is high tariffs; with a drop in tariffs virtually guaranteed by the NAFTA accords, Visa executives know Mexican beer doesn't stand a chance against the American giants unless production can be stepped up.

Before the oil boom of the 1970s, Monterrey also claimed an astonishing 25% of Mexico's GNP and nearly a third of its exports. With such a strong footing in the world of commerce, it's no surprise that the Partido Acción Nacional (PAN) has a firm grip on the city and surrounding state. Local workers belong to company-sponsored unions that provide inexpensive housing, daily commuter transportation, and a variety of leisure activities, from weekend baseball to beach vacations, making the average PRI-subsidized labor union look shabby by comparison.

Monterrey is unique in its strict enforcement of local littering and seat-belt laws. And 100% of the city's wastewater is now treated before being returned to the Río Santa Catarina; Monterrey is in fact the first—and so far the only—major metropolitan city in Mexico to treat all of its wastewater.

der); well-developed transportation connections; access to petroleum, coal, natural gas, and other nearby natural resources; and its skilled and highly educated workforce. The city is also an important supply-and-market center for nearby ranching, agriculture, and poultry production, as well as the site of a large military base. Yet another important source of metropolitan revenue is the steady influx of tourists and investors from Texas. A new tollway has brought San Antonio within 4.5 hours' drive instead of six.

According to Mexico's 1995 census, 2.6 million people live in the Monterrey metropolitan area; the city's chamber of commerce claims that the number tops out at three million. Either figure makes it the nation's third largest metro area after Mexico City and Guadalajara. Restricted to Monterrey city limits, the population numbers just over a million.

Often described as the nation's most forward-looking city, Monterrey has the country's largest number of colleges, universities, and institutes of technology on a per capita basis and owns over 20% of Mexico's computers.

HISTORY

Monterrey was founded on the banks of the Río Santa Catarina in 1596 by a group of 700 Spaniards. These settlers had fled Mexico City because the Inquisition suspected them of adhering to Judaism—an offense then punishable by death. The settlers named the colony in honor of the Viceroy of Nueva España, Gaspar de Zúñiga Acevedo, Conde de Monterrey.

Franciscan missionaries arrived in 1603 but had little success in converting the native Amerindian population, and by 1672 the colony had only 685 inhabitants. It wasn't until the beginning of the 18th century that the natives were sufficiently "pacified" to allow movement into the valley's more fertile areas. After minerals were discovered in the surrounding mountains in 1715, trade with booming Zacatecas to the south increased, the population mushroomed to 3,000, and a Jesuit college was founded.

Monterrey's development, however, suffered a serious setback when a major flood in 1752 in-

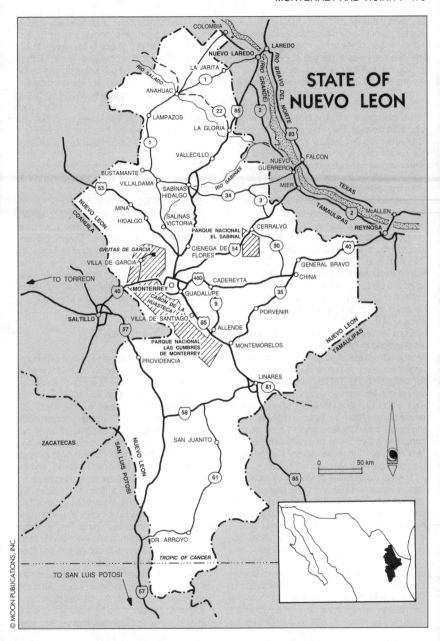

STATE OF NUEVO LEON

COLOMBIA
LAREDO
NUEVO LAREDO
LA JARITA
RIO SALADO
ANAHUAC
LAMPAZOS
LA GLORIA
VALLECILLO
BUSTAMANTE
VILLALDAMA
SABINAS HIDALGO
MINA
HIDALGO
SALINAS VICTORIA
GRUTAS DE GARCIA
VILLA DE GARCIA
TO TORREON
SALTILLO
MONTERREY
GUADALUPE
CAÑON DE LA HUASTECA
VILLA DE SANTIAGO
PARQUE NACIONAL LAS CUMBRES DE MONTERREY
PROVIDENCIA
ALLENDE
MONTEMORELOS
LINARES
SAN JUANITO
DR. ARROYO
TO SAN LUIS POTOSI
ZACATECAS
SAN LUIS POTOSI
NUEVO LEON
RIO BRAVO DEL NORTE (RIO GRANDE)
FALCON
NUEVO GUERRERO
MIER
TEXAS
McALLEN
REYNOSA
TAMAULIPAS
RIO SABINAS
PARQUE NACIONAL EL SABINAL
CIENEGA DE FLORES
CERRALVO
GENERAL BRAVO
CHINA
CADEREYTA
PORVENIR
NUEVO LEON TAMAULIPAS
NUEVO LEON COAHUILA

0 50 km

TROPIC OF CANCER

© MOON PUBLICATIONS, INC.

undated the town and almost totally destroyed the fragile economy. Many Monterrey residents left for better climes in neighboring Tamaulipas, and the area was in danger of losing its entire population. But the opening of nearby Mina de la Iguana in 1757 attracted a new wave of settlers.

In 1792 a major turning point for the city's fortunes arrived with the establishment of a Monterrey bishop's office. The civic-minded second and third bishops, Fray Rafael José Verger and Don Ambrosio de Llanos y Valdés, arranged for the construction of a number of important public works, including an aqueduct to ensure a steady water supply for the city.

Just as things were looking rosy for Monterrey, another major disaster struck in the shape of the 1836 partition of Texas from Mexico, an event that led to a drastic decline in local commerce. A decade later, before the city had time to recover from Texas independence, the Mexican-American War erupted. On 8 Oct. 1846, after a three-week battle in which the Mexicans used the Obispado as a fort, 6,200 U.S. troops under the command of Gen. Zachary Taylor took control of the city and remained as an occupation force until 8 July 1848.

Once the war was over and the U.S. had granted statehood to Texas, however, Monterrey wisely took advantage of its proximity to the world's largest economy as both endpoint and relay point for burgeoning U.S.-Mexico trade. If revenge was ever a Monterrey intention, it took form during the U.S. Civil War (1860-66), when Monterrey profited heavily from the traffic of supplies and armaments to the Confederacy (an ironic position, considering that Texas originally seceded from Mexico in part because slavery had been declared illegal in all Mexican territories).

The industrialization of Monterrey took place rapidly between 1882 and 1910. Using national and international (especially U.S.) capital, Monterrey entrepreneurs first constructed a railroad between Monterrey and the border in 1882, a major boost for U.S.-Mexico trade. Next they built one of the world's largest breweries (Cervecería Cuauhtémoc, 1890), a huge iron and steel foundry (Fundidora de Fierro y Acero Monterrey, 1901), a major cement plant (Fábrica de Cementos Hidalgo, 1906), and a state-of-the-art glass factory (Fábrica de Vidrios y Cristales, 1909, today Vitro). These four industries be-

came the cornerstones of Monterrey's modern economy and remain so today.

The founding of Cervecería Cuauhtémoc was probably the most profound event in Monterrey's entire history. Besides making and selling an ocean of beer, the brewery spawned the first plants in Mexico to produce glass and cardboard on a mass scale. Another company established in response to the brewery's needs—in this case for caps and cans—was the Mexican steel giant, Hylsa, which nowadays specializes in ultrathin steel sheets.

After the Mexican Revolution, the city's population exploded, rising from 88,000 in 1920 to 333,000 by 1950, and exceeding 2.5 million 40 years later. In spite of its size, the city has the highest per capita standard of living in Mexico today; televisions (an admittedly one-sided measure) are in 60% of the homes. Despite the peso crisis of 1995, all indicators point to increasing prosperity for Monterrey residents; the city has added banking, financial, and information services to its traditional industrial base with the intention of further diversifying the economy.

CLIMATE

Chamber of commerce and tourist brochures published in Monterrey readily confess that when it comes to climate, this is a city of extremes. The mean temperature in July is 27° C (81° F), with daytime highs climbing into the 30s C (90s F), sometimes higher. The most uncomfortable months are August and September, when humidity rises along with temperatures. During these months the occasional inversion layer holds suspended particulates over Monterrey, and the surrounding mountains are cloaked in haze.

If you plan to travel to Monterrey during the winter months, don't expect balmy weather. Though winters tend to be mild, the occasional *norte* blows across the Great Plains, down through Texas, and right into the Valle de Monterrey, forcing residents to don gloves and overcoats for a week or so at a time.

Monterrey's mean annual precipitation is 49.6 cm (19.5 inches). As in South Texas, May and September are typically the rainiest months.

In terms of weather, the best overall months to visit Monterrey are October, March, and April, when it's usually dry, sunny, and temperate. Second best are May, June, and November.

SIGHTS

El Obispado (Bishop's Palace)

Construction of Monterrey's most striking pre-Revolutionary structure, at the west end of Av. Padre Mier, began in 1787 as a residence for Don Fray Rafael José Verger, the city's second bishop. Fray Rafael died before its completion in 1797, and the massive domed building was used as a service annex by the local diocese until 1819, when it was converted into military barracks. During the 1846 U.S. invasion, Mexican soldiers used it as a fort because of its strategic hill position overlooking the city; Pancho Villa later made it his temporary headquarters during revolutionary campaigns in northeastern Mexico. The late British author Graham Greene pronounced El Obispado "as beautiful as anything out of the Middle Ages."

El Obispado was declared a Colonial Monument by the Mexican government in 1932 and now houses the **Museo Regional de Nuevo León.** Among the displays contained in the

El Obispado

BOB RACE

museum's eight rooms are a small collection of pre-Hispanic artifacts from northeast Mexico, an exhibit on the Spanish hacienda era, 18th- and 19th-century religious art (mostly of local provenance), and exhibits on Mexican independence and the 1910-20 revolution, focusing on roles played by Nuevo León citizens.

The museum is open daily 10 a.m.-5 p.m.; admission is US$1.30 Mon.-Sat., free on Sunday. Even if you're not interested in the museum, El Obispado's grounds are worth visiting for views over the city. Laid out along the slopes below the Bishop's Palace is **Colonia Obispado,** a neighborhood of huge mansions built in the 1940s and '50s.

Catedral de Monterrey

Facing Plaza Zaragoza (the south end of the Gran Plaza), the Monterrey Cathedral is similar in overall design to the cathedral in Saltillo, with an ornate, late baroque facade flanked by two towers of asymmetric height. Construction began in 1770 under Franciscan supervision, and the main structure—including the facade—was completed in 1791. The shorter clock tower was added in 1817 (the clock itself, made in Mexico City, dates to 1786), and the neoclassical bell tower was fashioned in 1899. Cathedral status was bestowed in 1833.

The somewhat austere cruciform interior contains several altars and 19th-century religious paintings. The lower section of the main altar is adorned with a mural painted by Mexican muralist Angel Zárraga in 1945. Depicting the life of the Virgin Mary, this is one of the few public works of art that Zárraga—who was quite popular in France and Spain—executed in Mexico.

Barrio Antiguo

Behind the Catedral de Monterrey, the "Old Neighborhood" consists of 15 blocks bordered by Río Santa Catarina along the south, Calle Dr. Coss to the west, Calle Matamoros to the north, and Calle Naranjo to the east. Representing the best-preserved parcel of 18th-, 19th-, and early 20th-century architecture in the city, the colonial-style casas here are a mix of residences, warehouses, art studios, and antique shops—Monterrey's equivalent of Manhattan's Soho. Since 1988 the district's architectural integrity has been protected by its state-recognized status as a "historical preserve." In summer, the city sponsors live outdoor music and theater in the neighborhood.

Along with the Bishop's Palace and the cathedral, one of the most impressive examples of viceregal architecture in Monterrey is the Barrio Antiguo's **Casa del Campesino,** Calle Mina 1101 (between Ocampo and Abasolo, three blocks east of the cathedral). Originally built as a resi-

dence for the governor of Nuevo Reino de León province around 1750, it was converted into the city's first hospital in 1791 and is now used by various agrarian organizations. The building covers an entire city block, surrounding three patios with high-ceilinged rooms in the typical colonial style. The building's largest room, a neo-gothic auditorium, contains a classic Mexican Revolutionary mural painted in the 1920s.

19th- and 20th-Century Architecture

With its modern glass-and-steel skyscrapers and neat suburban tract homes, Monterrey looks more like an American city than any other city in Mexico. Or to be more specific, more like a Texas city;

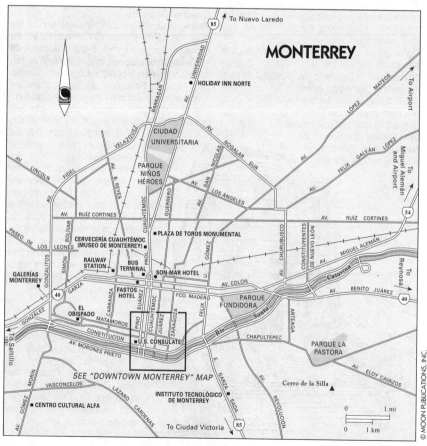

© MOON PUBLICATIONS, INC.

Monterrey is only 142 miles from Laredo, 304 miles from San Antonio, and is closer to Dallas than to Mexico City—the influence shows.

Even the city's 19th-century downtown has U.S. roots, due to the prominence of the work of architect Alfred Giles. Though born in London in 1853, Giles emigrated to the U.S. and established his career in San Antonio, Texas.

During the 1890s, at the beginning of Monterrey's industrialization, Giles was contracted to design the **Banco Mercantil** (corner of Morelos and Zaragoza), **Edificio La Reynera** (Morelos and Parás), **Casino Monterrey** (Zuazua and Abasolo), **Arco de la Independencia** (Av. Pino Suárez and Calz. Madero), and the house of Don Joel Rocha (today the **Centro Cultural de Monterrey,** Av. Padre Mier 545), as well as many other buildings that have since been razed. Designed in beaux arts style, these elegant turn-of-the-century buildings are similar to some of the structures seen in downtown San Antonio, several of which were also Giles endeavors.

Moving west from the downtown area (toward the Obispado) and chronologically into the 20th century, the *colonias* (neighborhoods) of **Mirador** (built in the 1920s) and **María Luisa** ('30s-'50s) contain many *neocolonial* (the Mexican term for Victorian and Georgian styles) houses that could have been taken from any number of cities in the southeastern United States.

Southwest of downtown Monterrey, the newer **Del Valle** district (part of **San Pedro de Garza García,** the wealthiest municipality in all of Mexico) has drawn its inspiration from Texas and the U.S. Southwest with modern, boxy, flat-roofed homes mixed with peaked-roof two-story bungalows, often with Chevy/GMC Suburbans parked in their driveways. In Monterrey this housing style is sometimes referred to as "neo-McAllen" (a descriptor that raises that south Texas city's architectural status considerably). Except for the preponderance of surrounding trees, the rows of satellite dishes sprouting from virtually every rooftop make residential Del Valle look like a satellite tracking station at first glance; Calz. Del Valle, the district's main avenue, could almost pass for a Dallas suburb.

Gran Plaza

Sometimes referred to as "Macroplaza" for its size, the Gran Plaza actually joins several small-er plazas and parks into a lengthy north-south pedestrian corridor running parallel to Calles Zuazua and Zaragoza from Av. 5 de Mayo to the river. Carried out between 1980 and 1985, the project severed several east-west avenues, including Morelos, Padre Mier, Matamoros, Ramón, and 15 de Mayo.

At the south end of the plaza toward the river looms the huge, concrete-and-glass **Nuevo Palacio Federal,** built in 1973. Just north of the federal building is the oldest plaza section, **Plaza Zaragoza,** flanked by the cathedral and Barrio Antiguo to the east, and the 19th-century downtown to the west. Opposite Calle Ocampo from the cathedral, the relatively new **Museo de Arte Contemporáneo de Monterrey** (see the separate MARCO entry for a description) faces the 1930s' **Círculo Mercantil Mutualista** and modern **Condominio Acero** on the west side of the plaza; together with the Nuevo Palacio Federal, the three buildings form a wall of concrete, glass, and steel around the south end of the Gran Plaza.

In the middle of this end of the plaza stands a 70-meter-high, 12.5-meter-wide, 1.8-meter-deep vertical slab known as the **Faro del Comercio** ("Lighthouse of Commerce"). Designed by celebrated Mexican architects Luis Barragán and Raúl Ferrera, the structure was erected in 1984 as part of the ambitious Gran Plaza project and is Mexico's tallest monument. A green laser beam projected from the top of the red, prismatic tower focuses on different city symbols, including El Obispado, Cerro de la Silla, and the Palacio de Gobierno. Beneath this section of the Gran Plaza is a subterranean shopping center and parking lot.

Northward, about halfway up the plaza on the east side, the **Teatro de la Ciudad** is one of Mexico's premier theatrical venues. Facing the theater on the opposite side of the plaza is the huge, angular **Torre Administrativa,** built in 1984 as headquarters for the state congress and other state government bodies. On the plaza between the Teatro de la Ciudad and Torre Administrativa, the simple **Parque Hundido** offers passersby a retreat from the sharp angles and glaring surfaces of modern Monterrey with trees, benches, modern sculptures, and a fountain.

Farther north in the plaza is the **Explanada de los Héroes,** a large, empty square flanked by stone fountains and balustrades decorated with urns and masks in the Greek style. Monuments to revolutionary heroes Juan Zuazua, Antonio Villareal, Pablo González, Benito Juárez, and Miguel Hidalgo y Costilla break up the space toward the north end. The plaza ends at the impressive turn-of-the-century **Palacio de Gobierno.**

Basílica de la Purísima

Designed by renowned Mexican architect Enrique de la Mora, this church is considered one of the most significant modern religious structures in Mexico if not all of Latin America. A 19th-century *templo* on the site was demolished in 1942 to make way for Mora's 1946 project, which is based on a system of parabolic shells—a technique now copied around the world.

The slender, 43-meter bell tower bears a terra-cotta sculpture of the Immaculate Conception executed by sculptor Adolfo Laubner in 1946 and fired by the famous Ladrillos Monterrey brickworks. It is purportedly the largest terra-cotta sculpture on the American continent. The church's three facades feature 15-meter parabolic arches surmounted by onyx window frames. The striking bronze *Christ and the Apostles* sculpture over the principal facade was done by German sculptor Herbert Hoffman Ysenbourg.

During the day, the interior of the church is bathed in natural light filtered through modern stained-glass windows fashioned by Mexican, German, and American artists. Modern religious paintings of the Virgin of Guadalupe, San Felipe, the Four Evangelists, Santa Teresita, and others hang on the walls.

Sitting on the main altar is the most sacred religious image in Monterrey, the **Virgen Chiquita** or "Little Virgin." A crude wooden image standing only 17 cm (6.6 inches) high, the Virgen Chiquita was originally housed in a small chapel (on the same site as the current basilica) built in the mid-1700s by a Tlaxcalteca woman known 's "La Zapatera" (the "Shoemaker"). According to legend, the great flood of 1756 receded from the city when La Zapatera brandished the little image before the floodwaters. During his 1990 visit to Mexico, Pope John Paul II bestowed sainthood on the Virgen Chiquita, thereby officially recognizing the miracle.

The basilica is on the corner of Av. Hidalgo Pte. and Serafín Peña, west of Av. Pino Suárez. Barrio de la Purísima, the surrounding neigh-

borhood, dates to the turn of the century and features many neoclassical-style residences known for their conservative inhabitants.

Basílica del Roble

Another church associated with a mythic holy image, the Basílica del Roble is at Calle Juárez and 15 de Mayo, a few blocks south of the Mercado Juárez. According to legend, in 1592 Franciscan Padre Andrés de León came upon an oak tree *(roble)* that bore an image of the Virgin Mary on its trunk. Believing it to be an omen, he founded a mission nearby; the settlement of Monterrey was established four years later. In 1853 the Iglesia del Roble was built on the spot, and in 1963 it was given basilica status. To many Monterreienses it is the city's "mother church" because of its associations with the city's founding.

The church resembles a Roman temple, with a peaked roof and portico supported by marble-tiled columns. A colorful mosaic over the main door depicts the legend of the Virgen de Roble ("Virgin of the Oak Tree"). Inside are three large, column-supported naves; the main altar is crowned by an ornate bronze *baldaquín* (altar canopy) similar to those found in Italian basilicas.

Museo de Historia Mexicana

The modern-looking Museum of Mexican History opened in 1994 and features a number of permanent and temporary exhibits that are considerably enhanced by creative lighting, videos, interactive modules, sound effects, and multi-image screens. The permanent exhibits include a huge room devoted to Ancient Mexico, with a high-quality display of pre-Cortesian ceramics, stone carvings, and scale replicas of the ruins at La Venta, Teotihuacán, Monte Albán, Palenque, Chichén Itzá, and Paquimé. Another room focuses on Revolution-era Mexico with an exhibit of an early 20th-century railcar and train engine (with old films running inside), turn-of-the-century clothing, and early machinery tracing the mechanization of modern Mexico. Besides the exhibit *salas,* the museum contains a cinema, cafeteria, gift shop, and library.

The museum is open Tues.-Thurs., 11 a.m.-7 p.m., and Fri.-Sun. and holidays 11 a.m.-8 p.m. Admission varies according to the day of the week: Tuesdays free; Wed.-Fri. US$1.30; Saturday US$0.65, Sunday US$0.13. Students with

ID get a 50% discount except on Sunday, when they are admitted free. Admission is free all the time for children under 12 and seniors of *la tercera edad,* "the third age," meaning over 60. The museum is at Calle Dr. Coss Sur 445, tel. (8) 345-9898.

Museo de Arte Contemporáneo de Monterrey (MARCO)

This US$11 million museum, designed by Mexican architect Ricardo Legorreta, opened in 1991. Set around a central courtyard, the two-story building contains a permanent collection of contemporary Mexican and Latin American art, plus traveling exhibits. The MARCO shop carries a very good collection of books on Mexican art, plus a few posters and quality handicrafts. Also on the premises are a *cafetería* and courtyard cafe.

The museum faces the east side of the Gran Plaza at Zuazua and Ocampo. Hours are Tuesday, Thurs.-Sat. 11 a.m.-7 p.m., Wednesday and Sunday till 9 p.m., closed Monday. Admission is US$1.20, free for students and children under 6; Wednesday admission is free for everyone. For further information call (8) 342-4820.

Museo de Monterrey and Salón de Fama (Cervecería Cuauhtémoc)

Dating to the 1890s, the original brick warehouse of the Cervecería Cuauhtémoc, Av. Universidad Nte. at Av. Luis Mora, has been converted into an art museum containing exhibits of contemporary Latin American art. The museum's collection of over a thousand works includes such masterpieces as "El Maizal" by Gerardo Murillo, "El Grande de España" by Diego Rivera, "El Lanceado" by José Clemente Orozco, and "La Mujer Dormida" by David Alfaro Siqueiros. Temporary exhibits have featured works by Henry Moore, Alberto Giacometti, Frida Kahlo, Rufino Tamayo, Pablo Picasso, and other superstars of the art world. Two large copper brewing vats hang through the museum's upper floor, the only beer-related exhibit. A cafe on the upper floor offers coffee and snacks. The museum is open Tuesday, Thurs.-Sun. 11 a.m.-8 p.m., Wednesday 10 a.m.-8 p.m. Admission is free.

Outside the warehouse, in a shaded corner of the grounds, is a pleasant outdoor beer garden that's open in warm weather. In a small cement, steel, and glass structure in the west section of

the grounds is the **Salón de Fama,** Monterrey's Sports Hall of Fame. One room is dedicated entirely to the evolution of Mexican baseball, while two other rooms contain trophies, uniforms, autographed pictures, and other artifacts from a variety of sports played in Mexico. Hours are Tues.-Fri. 9 a.m.-8 p.m., Sat.-Sun. 10:30 a.m.-6 p.m.; free admission. Free tours of the brewery works themselves can be taken Mon.-Fri. 9:30 a.m.-3:30 p.m. or Saturday 9:30 a.m.-3 p.m. The Museo de Monterrey is within walking distance of the "Cuauhtémoc" Metro station.

Museo Metropolitano

Housed in a striking, 1818-vintage building next to the Hotel Monterrey Clarion on Zaragoza, this historical museum was inaugurated in 1989 and contains various exhibits on the historical and cultural evolution of northeastern Mexico. Artifacts on display range in date from the pre-Hispanic era to Monterrey's period of industrialization. One room is also set aside for temporary displays of painting, sculpture, and other visual arts. Hours are Tues.-Sun. 8 a.m.-6 p.m.; admission is free.

Centro Cultural Alfa

Located in posh San Pedro Garza García, the Centro Cultural Alfa is funded by the nonprofit arm of an industrial consortium and devoted to expositions of the sciences. The complex's most striking architectural feature is the Pabellón El Universo or "Universe Pavilion," a building in the shape of a huge, toppling cylinder. Among the facilities are an exploratorium-type exhibit, planetarium, aquarium, aviary, garden containing pre-Cortesian art, and Omnimax theater. For the most part, the offerings are oriented toward children rather than adults.

The center is open Tues.-Fri. 3-9 p.m., Saturday 2-9 p.m., and Sunday noon-9 p.m. Admission is US$2. Occasionally the center sponsors morning and evening events with different hours and admission charges.

To reach the CCA from downtown Monterrey, follow Av. de la Constitución west along the river on Av. Gómez Morín and turn south (left), then continue on Av. Gómez Morín to Av. Roberto Garza Sada; the CCA is left on R.G. Sada (look for the Pabellón El Universo). Free shuttle buses to the CCA are provided from the Alameda on Av.

Pino Suárez in the city center every hour Tues.-Fri. and every half-hour Sat.-Sunday.

La Pastora Zoo

This zoo, founded in 1985, houses over 300 species of animals from Africa, Asia, Europe, and the Americas in regular indoor-outdoor exhibits, plus a wooded area containing species native to the region. A recreational lake with paddleboats is connected to a circuit of artificial streams. A miniature train circulates throughout the facility, and there are several snack bars. The zoo is east of central Monterrey off Av. Eloy Cavazos, in Guadalupe near Río La Silla. Open daily 9 a.m.-7 p.m. For information, call (8) 337-1388.

Instituto Tecnológico de Monterrey

A group of local engineers led by Don Eugenio Garza Sada founded this citadel of higher education in 1943, and it soon distinguished itself for academic excellence in Mexico. Among the campus buildings is the boldly designed 1988 **Edificio de Tecnología Avanzada** (Advanced Technology Building), which consists of two eight-story wings linked by a lower three-story building and "tilted" in opposite directions so that they form a 60-degree angle between them—purportedly a reflection of the Cerro de la Silla and a modern representation of a classic Mesoamerican ceremonial motif. From a distance they look like half-toppled skyscrapers.

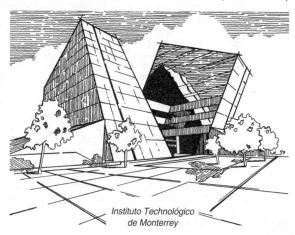

Instituto Tecnológico de Monterrey

ITM is now the mother campus for the Instituto Tecnológico de Estudios Superiores (ITESM), a system with 26 campuses in 25 cities around Mexico with a total enrollment of 48,000 (the Monterrey campus enrolls around 1,500). The campus also participates in visiting scholar/professor programs with 27 foreign universities. ITM's strongest programs are in engineering, business administration, "informatics" (computer science), food sciences, natural sciences, and education. Since 1990, ITESM has developed a system of "hallmark courses" designed to balance the sciences with studies in the humanities for the purpose of developing values, improving communication skills, and fostering a "spirit of enterprise."

Among other sports programs, ITM sponsors a collegiate American-style football team, the Borregos (Bighorn Sheep).

ITM is southeast of the Río Santa Catarina and city center off Av. E. Garza Sada.

Cintermex

One of the largest facilities of its kind in Latin America, the Centro Internacional de Negocios Monterrey (International Trade Center of Monterrey), also known as Cintermex, was inaugurated by Pres. Carlos Salinas in 1991 following the signing of the North American Free Trade Agreement. In addition to 40,000 square meters of first-class exhibit space, the center contains a section with posh retail shops, a bank, and secretarial services. A modern Holiday Inn stands adjacent. The entire complex was built on the former site of an old foundry that contained Latin America's first blast furnace.

City officials and local investors hope that, in the wake of NAFTA, rapidly increasing trade will make Cintermex an important focus of Mexican national and international trade.

Cintermex is in the Parque Fundidora, east of the city center via Av. F.I. Madero. The "Parque Fundidora" Metro station is within easy walking distance.

BOB RACE

ACCOMMODATIONS

Shoestring

Several of the city's least expensive hotels are found in the general vicinity of the busy intersection of Av. Colón and Av. Universidad, near the bus and train stations. This location is also convenient to the "Cuauhtémoc" Metro station and the Museo de Monterrey (Cervecería Cuauhtémoc), as well as city bus lines to anywhere in the city. None of these hotels have parking lots, so they're more practical for visitors using public transportation than for the self-propelled.

Least expensive of all is the **Villa Deportiva Juvenil,** tel. (8) 343-0808, a 400-bed youth hostel in the Parque Fundidora near Cintermex on Av. Madero Antiguo (east of downtown). You must have a Hostelling International (AYH/IYH) membership or be willing to sign up on the spot. Downtown Monterrey is only 10-15 minutes west of the hostel by city bus or Metro (use the "Parque Fundidora" Metro station). Rates: US$2 per bed.

Many shoestring places are on Calle Amado Nervo, two blocks west of, and parallel to, Av. Pino Suárez. **Hotel Amado Nervo** Calle Amado Nervo 1110, tel. (8) 372-3590, fax (8) 372-5488, and **Hotel Nuevo León** Calle Amado Nervo 1007 (on the corner of Calz. Madero), tel. (8) 374-1900, both offer spartan rooms with private bath. Rates: US$8-12. A bit higher in price is the well-kept and quiet, four-story **Hotel Posada** Calle Amado Nervo 1138 (at Reforma), tel. (8) 372-2467. Rooms are small but clean and come with TV, phone, and private bath. Rates: US$12 s, US14 d. The cheaper but spartan three-story **Hotel Virreyes,** Calle Amado Nervo Nte. 902, tel. (8) 374-6610, offers plain but large rooms with no TV or phone; the staff seems friendly and helpful. Rates: US$7-11. Nearby **Hotel Reforma** (formerly Hotel America), Av. Universidad Nte. 1114, tel. (8) 375-3268 or 375-7068, has plain but not-very-quiet rooms in the same price range.

Budget

In the US$15-35 range are several good hotel choices, including some that are in or near the Zona Rosa—the shopping/eating/hotel district west of the Gran Plaza. The top choice here is **Hotel Colonial,** Av. Hidalgo Ote. 475, tel. (8) 343-6791, fax (8) 342-1169, an older building in the heart of the Zona Rosa. All rooms are clean and offer a/c, TV, phones, and carpeting. A parking lot is attached to the hotel and you'll find a restaurant downstairs. Be sure to book ahead for this popular hotel. Rates: US$26 s, US$31 d.

El Paso Autel, Calle Zaragoza Nte. 901 (at Calle R. Martínez, about 10 blocks north of the Zona Rosa), tel. (8) 340-0690, fax (8) 344-4647, is a clean, well-run place with a/c, TV, pool, restaurant, and basement parking. Rates: US$21 s/d. About the same distance west of the Zona Rosa, near the Basílica de la Purísima, is the equally pleasant and similarly priced **Hotel Los Reyes de Monterrey,** Av. Hidalgo Pte. 543, tel. (8) 343-6168, fax (8) 345-0329. Facilities include a restaurant/bar and ample parking. Neither of these hotels are well located if you plan to sightsee on foot.

The reliable, five-story **Son-Mar Hotel,** Av. Colón at Av. A. Reyes Nte., tel. (8) 375-4400, fax (8) 372-5077, Mexico toll-free tel. (800) 8-3382, near the "Cuauhtémoc" Metro and main bus stations, has large a/c rooms and a restaurant/bar; parking is available. Rates: US$23 s/d, US$30 t. Also in this general vicinity, **Hotel Jandal,** Av. Cuauhtémoc Nte. 825 (between Arteaga and Salazar), tel. (8) 372-3172, fax (8) 374-4495, has small but pleasant rooms with a/c, phones, and satellite TV, plus attached restaurant and parking. Rates: US$19-23 s/d. The efficient seven-story **Hotel Fastos,** Av. Colón Pte. 596 (across from the bus terminal), tel. (8) 372-3250, fax (8) 372-6100, has modern, well-kept rooms

with a/c, TV, and phone. Night owls may like the Fastos for its 24-hour restaurant. Rates: around US$21-26. South of the "Cuauhtémoc" Metro station is the modern, no-frills **Hotel Soles,** Calle Jiménez Nte. 1120 (east of Av. Cuauhtémoc), tel. (8) 375-0776, which has a/c rooms and parking. Rates: US$12-18.

Budget/Inexpensive

The cozy **Hotel Royalty,** Av. Hidalgo Ote. 402, tel. (8) 340-2800, fax (8) 340-5812, Mexico toll-free tel. (800) 8-3093, is squeezed between the lofty Ambassador and Ancira Hotels in the Zona Rosa. Rooms have all the amenities; spacious suites are available. A pool and parking are on the premises. Rates: US$39 s/d on weekdays, US$26 weekends; suites US$53.

Facing the Gran Plaza is the imposing **Hotel Monterrey Gran Plaza,** Zaragoza at Morelos, tel. (8) 343-5120, fax (8) 344-7378, Mexico toll-free tel. (800) 8-3240, U.S./Canada toll-free tel. (800) 432-9605. Rooms have TV, phone, voice mail, minibar, electronic safe, and hairdryer; some have better views of the plaza than others. Higher-priced suites available. Complimentary breakfast buffet. Rates: US$32-39 s/d; suites US$69.

In Parque Chipinque, atop Meseta de Chipinque overlooking southwestern Monterrey, **Motel Chipinque,** tel. (8) 378-1100, offers rooms with satellite TV. Facilities include a restaurant, pool, and tennis courts. Rates: US$35.

North of downtown, off Mexico 85 at Km 15.5 (just south of the Infotur office and Saltillo bypass), the comfortable, motel-style **Hotel Nueva Castilla,** tel. (8) 376-6770, has rooms with a/c, heat, phones, and satellite TV around a parking lot and pool. Rates: US$30-45.

Inexpensive

The 193-room **Hotel Río,** Av. Padre Mier at Garibaldi (a few blocks northwest of the Zona Rosa), tel. (8) 344-9040, fax (8) 345-1456, Mexico toll-free tel. (800) 8-3009, U.S. toll-free tel. (800) 432-2520, has full amenities, including a pool, gym, and parking. It's popular with tour groups from Texas. Rates: US$40-56. For about the same rates you can stay at the much newer and more up-to-date, 176-room **Fiesta Inn Monterrey Valle,** Av. Lázaro Cárdenas Ote. 327, San Pedro Garza García, tel. (8) 389-8989, fax (8) 363-6895. Rooms come with all the amenities, including phones with dataports. A restaurant and bar are downstairs.

Moderate/Expensive

Three of Monterrey's hotels have earned *gran turismo* ratings, while six boast five-star ratings, more than any other city in Northern Mexico. In this era of peso deflation, these comfortable establishments aren't really high-priced from a dollar perspective. Although tourists make up a significant portion of the guests at these hotels, the majority are business travelers. Because most business travel takes place during the week, all of the hotels listed below run regular weekend specials with discounts of 40-50% below rack rates. To get the best rates, always ask about possible discount programs; even during the week you should be able to get a "corporate" discount.

Starting at a mere five stars, the stately and historic **Gran Hotel Ancira Radisson Plaza,** Ocampo Ote. 443, tel. (8) 345-7575, fax (8) 344-5256, Mexico toll-free tel. (800) 9-0090, U.S./Canada toll-free tel. (800) 333-3333, was built in 1911 in the beaux-arts style and augmented in 1952 in the then-fashionable "Streamline" (California deco) style. A local anecdote featuring this hotel tells how Pancho Villa, upon arrival in Monterrey with his troops during the Mexican Revolution, entered the spacious Ancira lobby on horseback—one of the deeds that no doubt helped earn him the epithet "Centaur of the North." At the moment operated by the Radisson chain, Ancira's elegant rooms come with a/c, heat, satellite/video TV, minibars, and direct dial phones. Rooms on the executive floor include major domo service, daily newspaper, and use of the executive center. Rates: US$65-78 s/d standard; US$78-91 executive floor.

In the exclusive Contry residential neighborhood close to ITM, the newish, four-star **Holiday Inn Express,** Av. E. Garza Sada, tel./fax (8) 329-6000, offers pleasant modern-colonial architecture and rooms with balconies and all the amenities. Complimentary breakfast every morning and complimentary beer in the early evening. Rates: US$75-85.

Expensive

For location and service, Monterrey's best *gran turismo* is **Hotel Ambassador Camino Real,** Av. Hidalgo Ote. 310 in the Zona Rosa, tel. (8) 340-3690, fax (8) 345-1984. The spacious, international-class rooms have a/c, heating, refrigerators, satellite/video TV, and 24-hour room service. Hotel facilities include security valet parking, a heated pool, indoor tennis court, a health club, two restaurants, a coffee shop, and bar. Rates: US$96-110; suites US$190-469.

Around the corner, between Hotel Colonial and Sanborn's, is the subdued **Santa Rosa Suites Hotel,** tel. (8) 342-4200, fax (8) 342-3344, a quiet, executive-oriented place where each spacious, well-decorated junior suite is equipped with a CD players, TV, coffeemaker, mini-bar, and two phones. Rates: US$90-103 rack; as low as US$45 on weekends. On the small plaza opposite Santa Rosa Suites, the relatively new **Howard Johnson Hotel Plaza Suites Monterrey,** Corregidora Ote. 519, tel. (8) 319-0900, fax (8) 319-0990, offers 276 attractive rooms and suites, with amenities including an indoor pool, gym, business center with secretarial service, and travel agency. Rates: US$80-99; as low as US$67 on weekends.

Fiesta Americana Monterrey, Av. Vasconcelos Ote. 300 (near Lázaro Cárdenas), tel. (8) 363-3030, fax (8) 363-4322, is a landmark unto itself, not far from the Centro Cultural Alfa in the San Agustín neighborhood of San Pedro Garza García. This huge, modern hotel has the largest number of rooms in Monterrey (307), with the usual international-class amenities plus a heated indoor pool, outdoor tennis court, spacious public areas, and courtyard with waterfall. Rates: from US$80 s/d.

At last pass, the Holiday Inn chain (Mexico toll-free reservations tel. 800-0-0999) had three properties in Monterrey. On the north side of the city toward Mexico 85, **Holiday Inn Monterrey Norte,** Av. Universidad Nte. 101, tel. (8) 376-2400, fax (8) 332-0565, features 198 rooms each with a/c, refrigerator, satellite/video TV, and phone. Other amenities include a pool, two lighted tennis courts, and free airport shuttle (most hotels in Monterrey charge a fee for airport transportation). Rates: US$100 rack; as low as US$75 weekends. The 198-room **Holiday Inn Crowne Plaza,** downtown at Av. Constitución Ote. 300, tel. (8) 319-6000, fax (8) 344-3007, has five-star rooms with the usual amenities, plus a heated indoor pool, outdoor tennis court, health club, and disco. Rates: US$100-110.

RV Parks

Hotel Nueva Castilla has spaces with electrical/water hookups for RVs, campers, or trailers at US$10 d, US$1 each additional person.

Bahía Escondida Resort, tel. (8) 385-1112, is 36 km (22 miles) south of Monterrey on Presa Rodrigo Gómez (commonly called "Presa de la Boca") near Santiago. The resort offers sites with electrical/water hookups for US$10 per night, plus a restaurant, tennis courts, and barbecue grills. Normally the resort is open only to members, but they will usually accept nonmember RVers on a space-available basis.

FOOD

As you would expect from Mexico's third largest city, Monterrey has a wide variety of restaurants and cafes. Nuevo León is prime ranching country, so local specialties include many beef dishes. Among the most typical are *agujas asadas a las brasas* (charcoal-broiled spare ribs), *machacada con huevos* (dried beef, eggs, and *salsa picante* mixed together and served with flour tortillas), *carne soasada* (dried meat marinated in lime juice, baked till it turns a golden hue, and served as an appetizer or snack), and *cortadillo norteño* (cuts of beef stewed in a spicy tomato sauce).

Many vendors and small restaurants specialize in Monterrey-style *tacos al carbón* (often simply called *taquitos*), a plate of small, open corn tortillas topped with a shredded *carne asada* and served with a variety of salsas; a local theme for several *taquito* restaurants revolves around waitresses and cooks dressed as *monjas* or Catholic nuns! In the Zona Rosa a section of Av. Hidalgo has been turned into an open pedestrian mall where several taco stands are open nightly.

Goat also occupies a special place in Nuevo León cuisine, and the classic *cabrito al pastor* (kid goat spit-roasted over mesquite coals) is found in many Monterrey restaurants.

Burgers, fried chicken, and other fast food are amply available at U.S. franchises like **Carl's Jr.** (Colonia Del Valle, Colonia Contry), **Burger King** (Las Torres, Colonia Villa los Pinos), **Kentucky Fried Chicken** (13 locations, including Alameda, Cuauhtémoc, Cumbres, Tecnológico, San Agustín, Centro, Del Valle, Madero, Contry), **Wendy's** (Zona Rosa, Del Valle, Cintermex),

McDonald's (Gonzalitos, Garza Sada, Walmart Las Torres, Walmart Miguel Alemán, Santa Catarina, Escobedo, Linda Vista, Galerías Monterrey, Gómez Morín, Del Valle, Tecnológico), and **Chili's Grill & Bar** (Las Torres, Plaza Kinta, Anahuac, Cumbres).

Those on a tight budget will find the cheapest eats downtown at the huge *lonchería* section in the west end of **Mercado Colón**, at Avenidas Juárez and Constitución. **Mercado Juárez** (ten blocks north at Av. Juárez and Aramberri) also has a substantial collection of *loncherías*.

Though many hotels offer bottled or filtered water, the tap water in metropolitan Monterrey is considered potable.

Regional

Restaurant Avenida, Av. Los Angeles Ote. 412, San Nicolás de los Garza, tel. (8) 351-0961, is well northeast of the city center. But this *cabrito* house is worth a mention since it serves *pollo al carbón* (charcoal-grilled chicken) as well as goat and *carne al carbón*. Inexpensive to moderate.

Restaurant Los Castores, Calle Gonzalitos Sur 325, tel. (8) 346-2939, specializes in *machacada con huevos* and other local-style *almuerzos,* plus *carnes al carbón* and *cabrito*. Inexpensive to moderate.

Restaurant El Pastor del Norte, is a no-frills eatery thought by many to serve the best *cabrito al pastor* in the city. *Carne asada* is also on the menu. There are two locations: Calz. Madero Pte. at Av. A. Reyes, tel. (8) 374-0480, and Calz. Madero Pte. at Av. S. Bolívar, tel. (8) 346-8954. Both are west of Av. Cuauhtémoc and open daily noon-midnight. Inexpensive to moderate.

El Rey de Cabrito, Av. Constitución Ote. 817 (at Calle Dr. Coss, behind MARCO), tel. (8) 345-3232, is a three-story restaurant convenient to the Zona Rosa and Gran Plaza. It's another strong contender for the local *cabrito* crown and is our particular favorite. The masculine decor includes plenty of mounted trophy heads. There are two other branches: Av. Gonzalitos Sur 455, tel. (8) 333-3885, and Av. Constitución Pte. 2210. Open daily, 11 a.m.-midnight. Inexpensive to moderate.

Las Monjitas, Calle Galeana 1018 (off Hidalgo pedestrian mall, Zona Rosa), is one of the better *taquito* places with staff dressed as nuns. Nearby on Hidalgo is the similar **La Parroquía.** Both are inexpensive.

GETTING YOUR GOAT

The art of breeding, herding, and eating goats came to Nuevo León with early Spanish settlers—most likely either Basques or Sephardic Jews—who were originally introduced to the animals by their Moorish conquerors from North Africa prior to the 16th century. Like arid North Africa, Northern Mexico has turned out to be perfect goat country, and no one else in the world relishes goat cuisine like Monterreienses.

By far the most common goat dish in Monterrey is *cabrito al pastor,* kid goat roasted whole on an iron spit angled toward (but not directly over) a fire pit filled with glowing mesquite coals. Before cooking, the *cabrito* is marinated in a mixture of herbs and spices for up to eight hours; the marinade used by each *cabrito* house is a closely guarded secret. At least 15 restaurants in Monterrey specialize in *cabrito al pastor,* not to mention the many other eateries that list the dish on their menus.

All parts of the goat, including the head *(cabecita)* and internal organs, may be served. Diners order by the cut; most popular because of the abundance of meat are the *pierna* (leg) and *paleta* (shoulder). *Cabrito guisado* is a thick stew of shredded *cabrito* and slightly spicy *salsa jitomate* (tomato sauce). Also cherished but harder to find outside restaurants that specialize in goat are *cabrito en su sangre* (cabrito stewed in its own blood), *machitos* (cooked goat tripe rolled into flour tortillas with *salsa picante*),

and *fritada de cabrito* (fried, ground goat blood cooked with pieces of goat meat). More appetizing to the average visiting gringo are *glorias,* chewy candy made from nuts and/or seeds cooked with sweetened goat's milk.

The prime season for goat-eating is May-Oct., when fresh *cabrito* is available. Other times of year, frozen *cabrito* or older goats—not nearly as tasty—may be substituted.

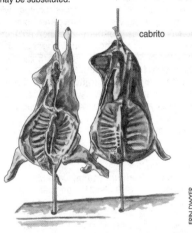

cabrito

ERIN DWYER

El Tío Restaurante, Av. Hidalgo at México, Colonia Obispado, tel. (8) 346-2818, has been in business since the 1930s. This colorful, colonial-style establishment has a garden dining area with trees, fountains, and a waterfall, and it's one of the best places in the city for an introduction to the regional cuisine. House specialties include *carne asada, cabrito al pastor,* and *fritada de cabrito,* but Mexican standards and international dishes are included on the menu. Moderate to expensive. Open daily 1 p.m.-midnight.

National
Casa del Maíz, Abasolo 870 (between Diego de Montemayor and Dr. Coss), tel. (8) 340-4332, is an artsy coffee shop/restaurant in the Barrio Antiguo specializing in dishes from Mexico City and Veracruz. Inexpensive.

The indoor/outdoor **Cenaduría San Marcos,** Av. Bosques Del Valle 110, Plaza Londres (near Alfa Cultural Center in the Garza García district), tel. (8) 378-9797, serves *pozole* (hominy soup) and other *antojitos*—all *muy típico.* Open daily 7 a.m.-midnight.

Restaurant Amado Nervo, Calle Amado Nervo Nte. 1110, serves inexpensive *milanesa, chuletas,* enchiladas, tacos, *tortas,* quesadillas, *chilaquiles, comida corrida, licuados, aguas frescas,* and Mexican breakfasts. Open 24 hours a day—a boon to those staying in the district's budget hotels.

Restaurant La Fe Palenque, Av. Morones Prieto 2525 (a kilometer east of Av. Gonzalitos), tel. (8) 345-1347, offers nightly mariachis, folkloric dancing, and cockfights as the main draw. The festive amphitheater-style restaurant serves standard *platillos mexicanos.* Moderate. Open daily 1 p.m.-1 a.m.; shows begin at 5 p.m.

La Fonda de San Miguel, Av. Morelos Ote. 924, tel. (8) 342-9687, is a casual restaurant/bar in the Barrio Antiguo that specializes in *botanas*. Moderate. Open daily noon-midnight.

El Molino Restaurante, Av. Bosques del Valle 110, Colonia Bosques del Valle, tel. (8) 356-5612, is a somewhat upscale Mexican restaurant in an old house with high ceilings. The menu features such creative dishes as *crepas de flor de calabaza* (squash-flower crepes), *pulpos al ajillo* (octopus in garlic sauce), and *huachinango a la tikin-chik* (Yucatán-style red snapper). Several regional dishes, such as *agujas norteñas* (Northern-style short ribs) and *cabrito*, are also on the menu. *Mangos al tequila* is one of several tasty desserts. Expensive. Open daily 1 p.m.-midnight.

Plazuela de los Antojitos, Centro Comercial Galerías Monterrey, Av. González Garza, is a huge mall in western Monterrey; one wing is occupied by a reasonably priced food court where several vendors sell Mexican food. Open daily 11 a.m.-8 p.m.

International

La Cabaña Regiomontaña, Calle Matamoros Pte. 318, tel. (8) 342-4813, originally opened in 1953. This coffeeshop-style place is a favorite local venue for a broad cross-section of Monterrey residents. In spite of the restaurant's name, the menu features a range of inexpensive and moderately priced continental, American, and Mexican dishes. The neighborhood is less than inspiring. Open Sun.-Thurs. 11 a.m.-1 a.m., weekends 11 a.m.-2 a.m.; live music 2-5 p.m. daily.

Das Bierhaus is a popular chain serving German standards in a beer-hall ambience. Of the six locations, the most conveniently located include: Calle Escobedo Sur 580, Centro; Av. Hidalgo and Rayon, Centro; Av. Revolución Sur 800, Col. Contry; and Av. E. Garza Sada 2408, near ITM. Moderate to expensive.

Restaurant Luisiana, Av. Hidalgo Ote. 530, Zona Rosa, tel. (8) 343-1561, is a Monterrey institution close to the Ancira, Monterrey, and Ambassador Hotels. The Luisiana combines reliable continental and American cuisine with impeccable service and an elegant decor. Expensive. Open daily noon-midnight except Christmas Day and New Year's Day.

Coffee Shops

No-nonsense, American-style *cafeterías* have become an institution in Monterrey. Four chains—Sanborn's, Benavides, Vip's, and Martin's—dominate the scene. All are good values any time of day but are especially popular for *desayuno* and *almuerzo*. The similar menus feature a wide list of Mexican and American dishes along with soups, salads, pasta, and sandwiches. All are open around 7 a.m.-10 p.m.

Benavides, a *farmacia*-attached chain, has the lowest prices overall. Locations: Morelos and Escobedo, Zona Rosa; Av. Pino Suárez Sur 602, Centro; Mississippi Pte. 129, Colonia Del Valle; Av. Vasconcelos Pte. 404, Bosques del Valle; Paseo de la Victoria 2200, Colonia Las Cumbres; Gonzalitos 625, Galerías Monterrey; Av. Garza Sada Sur 2410, Colonia Roma; Calz. Madero Pte. 3350, Madero.

Martin's is very good, but mostly limited to the suburbs. Locations: Av. E. Garza Sada, Contry; Alejandro de Rodas 3102, Las Cumbres; Av. Lincoln at Gonzalitos, Lincoln.

Sanborn's is pricier than the others but the food is generally tastier and more creative. The Zona Rosa branch has a separate bakery area with counter stools, good for a quick pastry and coffee. Locations: Calle Escobedo 920, Zona Rosa; Real San Agustín Sur 614, next to Hotel Fiesta Americana, Plaza San Agustín; Gonzalitos 625, Galerías Monterrey.

Vip's has the most efficient service of the chains. Locations: Av. Hidalgo Ote. 402, Zona Rosa; Av. E. Garza Sada 1711, Tecnológico; Av. Universidad and Colón, Universidad; Av. San Pedro 110, Del Valle.

Galería Café, Morelos Ote. 902, tel. (8) 342-5071, is around the corner from Casa del Maiz in the Barrio Antiguo and offers good espresso drinks and a few snacks. It's open 24 hours, but 1-4 a.m. is the busiest time.

Asian

La Cocina de Honan is the only Chinese restaurant chain in Mexico that specializes in spicy Hunan cuisine. At several locations, including 15 de Mayo Pte. 710 (between Villagrán and Alvarez), tel. (8) 342-2666; Av.Tecnológico Filósofos 207, tel. (8) 387-3891; and Av. Morelos 359, Plaza Mexico, tel. (8) 342-6699. Open Sun.-Thurs. noon-11 p.m., Fri.-Sat. noon-11:30 p.m.

El Dragón Chino is a large, banquet-style Chinese restaurant serving reliable Cantonese and Mandarin cuisine at three locations: Santa Rosa: Calle Escobedo Sur 928 (between Morelos and Hidalgo), Centro Comercial Patio; Av. Vasconcelos Pte. 65, Del Valle; and Río Pánuco at Técnicos, Tecnológico. Each is open daily 11 a.m.-11 p.m. **Gran Plaza,** Calle Escobedo Sur 480, tel. (8) 342-0457, is similar to El Dragón Chino; open daily noon-11 p.m.

Hei Sei Sushi Bar, Av. Real San Agustín 222, Residencial San Agustín, tel. (8) 363-1086, is a reasonable facsimile of a real sushi bar, with plenty of fresh fish. Try the Tampico Roll (sort of a Mexican version of the California Roll). Open daily 1-11 p.m.

Pizza

Pizzas Josephino's and Pizza Hut make the most reliable pizzas in town; Josephino's is slightly less expensive.

Pizzas Josephino's: Zaragoza Sur 840, Gran Plaza; Av. Hidalgo Pte. 1612, Obispado; Calle Escobedo Sur 930, Patio Santa Rosa; Padre Mier and Av. Cuauhtémoc, Centro; Humberto Lobo 520, Plaza San Pedro, Del Valle.

Pizza Hut: Av. Pino Suárez 725, Centro; Calz. Madero and Guadalajara, Madero; Av. Universidad Nte. 320, Universidad; Av. Vasconcelos at Bosques del Valle, Del Valle.

Vegetarian

Monterrey's vegetarian restaurants all fall into the typical Mexican mold, i.e., natural-foods stores with small cafe areas attached. Offerings include whole-grain breads, yogurt, salads, soups, and standard Mexican dishes using soy and gluten for meat substitutes.

Try **La Naranja,** Calle Filósofos 207, Pasaje Tecnológico, tel. (8) 358-4737; **Mana Vegetariano,** Av. Vasconcelos 143, Colonia Del Valle, tel. (8) 378-4815; **Restaurant Vegetariano,** Calle Ocampo at Av. Cuauhtémoc (northeast corner); or **Señor Natural,** Calle Escobedo Sur 713, Centro, tel. (8) 344-5768.

Groceries

Supermarkets are abundant in the suburbs, but noticeably lacking in the city itself. On the north side of town, the large **Soriana** chain has a branch at Av. A. Reyes and F. Bartolomé. An-other Soriana can be found at Calle Humberto Lobo and Capellanéa in Colonia Del Valle. **Gigante** has a branch near ITM at Av. E Garza Sada 699, Colonia Florida. Downtown you'll find several daily markets with fresh produce.

ENTERTAINMENT

Bullfights

Although the *fiesta brava* is not as popular in Monterrey as in some parts of Mexico, there are ample opportunities to view bullfighting. The main venue, **Plaza de Toros Monumental,** tel. (8) 374-0450, is just east of Av. Universidad (also known as Av. A Reyes here) at Priv. del Prado, north of the Arco de la Independencia. Originally built in 1937 and renovated in the '70s, this concrete-and-steel stadium has a retractable roof so that the *sombra y sol* can take place in any kind of weather. The season runs during May and December; tickets (US$6.50 average) are available through the Infotur office next to the Gran Plaza. Events are typically held on Sundays at 4:30 p.m. except during the occasional festival, when a three-day *corrida* may be scheduled.

MONTERREY'S WHEEL OF FORTUNE

Of the many traditions and customs that distinguish Monterrey from other Mexican cities, one unique one is the "Sorteo Tec," a municipal lottery that began in 1947 with the raffling of a 1947 Lincoln sedan. The Sorteo has escalated to four raffles a year in which the first prize is a newly built, fully decorated and furnished, a/c house with two new cars in the garage and a pool. Second prize is a new car—recent offerings have included Dodge Ram Chargers and Chrysler New Yorkers.

The money earned by the lottery supports around 25% of the students enrolled in the ITESM university system; tickets cost up to US$100 each (yes, foreigners may participate). Many of the autos raffled off in the Sorteo Tec are supplied by local auto factories. Mercedes Benz recently joined the award lineup; in 1994 the German auto manufacturer opened a Monterrey plant that produces 2,000 vehicles per year.

If you're in town on a weekend during the season when no *corridas* are scheduled at Plaza Monumental, you may be able to attend one at the **Plaza de Toros Cuauhtémoc** in Guadalupe, a suburb east of Monterrey. The Cuauhtémoc ring is within walking distance of the "Expo Guadalupe" metro station, a 20-minute ride from downtown Monterrey. Typical ticket prices here are US$3.30 on the sun side, US$8 for shade. The Infotur staff will have the current Cuauhtémoc schedule.

Cadereyta (33 km/20.5 miles east of the city via Mexico 40) also has a *plaza de toros,* worth a try should both the Monterrey and Guadalupe rings be inactive when you visit.

Charreadas

Monterrey has several *charro* associations that practice *charrería* in various locations around the city. The premier venue for the sport is **Cortijo San Felipe** in the Garza García district. Inquire at the Infotur office for schedules and *lienzo charro* locations.

Theater

The arts are heavily subsidized in Monterrey and the city has the best live theater resources outside Mexico City. Since 1988 the city has been the permanent home of the Muestra Nacional de Teatro (under the auspices of the Instituto Nacional de Bellas Artes and the Consejo Nacional de la Cultura y Arte), and has been a three-time host (alternating with Guanajuato) of the internationally renowned Festival Internacional Cervantino, considered the most significant dramatic arts festival in Latin America.

Major theatrical venues include: **Teatro de la Ciudad,** Matamoros at Zuazua (near the Gran Plaza), tel. (8) 343-8975; **Teatro Monterrey,** Av. Constitución at P. Díaz, Centro, tel. (8) 343-6466; **Teatro Calderón,** Juárez at Tapia, Centro, tel. (8) 375-1220; **Teatro del Maestro,** Washington Pte. 802, Centro, tel. (8) 375-1320; **Teatro Montoya,** Aramberri at Villagrán, tel. (8) 342-1497; and **Aula Magna,** Universidad Autónoma de Nuevo León, Av. 5 de Mayo between Juárez and Colegio Civil, Centro, tel. (8) 342-4507.

For the latest theatrical offerings, check the "Teatro" page in the "Gente" section of *El Norte,* or inquire at Infotur.

Bars and Discos

All the major hotels have nightclubs, although these are not as heavily frequented by local clubgoers as in most other Northern Mexican cities.

Outside the hotels, both locals and tourists make plenty of noise at **Señor Frog's,** in Plaza Fiesta San Agustín, Av. L. Cárdenas at Real de San Agustín; and **Iguanas Ranas,** Plaza Versailles Cumbres, off Paseo de la Victoria in Colonia Las Cumbres. One of the more interesting bars downtown is **La Fonda de San Miguel,** Av. Morelos Ote. 924 in the Barrio Antiguo, tel. (8) 342-9687. The San Miguel features live folk and jazz music Wed.-Sat. evenings.

Several low-key bars and late-night cafes, often art-themed, can be found in the Barrio Antiguo along Padre Mier east of Dr. Coss. Among these are **Café Arte** and **Galería Café.**

Among the most popular discos are **Onix,** E.C. Livas Pte. 201; **Koko Loco,** Av. Pino Suárez Sur 849; **Kaos,** Av. E. Garza Sada; and **S.S.,** Río Orinoco Ote. 105.

Cinema

Monterrey is the movie-viewing capital of Northern Mexico, and local movie houses show a remarkable number of first-run foreign (including American) films. The "Cine" page of the "Gente" section in *El Norte* daily newspaper provides a comprehensive list of what's showing around town, along with cinema addresses and starting times. Admission prices are a bit higher than elsewhere in Mexico, about US$2.

The **Alliance Française,** Av. 20 de Noviembre Sur 651, Colonia María Luisa, tel. (8) 342-4805, screens French films on Saturday nights at 6 p.m.; admission is free. The auditorium at **MARCO** occasionally shows foreign art films.

RECREATION

Parque Ecológico Chipinque

Atop Meseta de Chipinque at 1,500 meters (4,920 feet), this forested park 20 km (12 miles) southwest of downtown Monterrey is always a few degrees cooler than the city below and as such is an especially popular picnic spot during hot summer months. Only 300 of the park's 1,625 hectares are open to the public; the remainder is left untouched to protect native flora and fauna.

When the air is clear you'll have good aerial views of Monterrey. Walkers and hikers will find 15 km of foot trails. The restaurant/bar at the Motel Chipinque is a good spot for pre-sunset drinks, but take care on the drive back down, especially after dark.

Other Parks

The Río la Silla, which runs east and south of the city, is a favorite waterway for local canoe enthusiasts. Canoes can be rented at the beautiful, 108-hectare **Parque La Pastora** on the banks of the river in Guadalupe (follow Av. Chapultepec southeast off Av. Revolución).

Parque Canoas, southeast of the city on Av. E. Garza Sada (past the Av. Revolución junction), is a small, shady park with canoes for rent on the same river.

Tennis

Visitors can play tennis for hourly rates at **Chipinque Racquet Club,** Av. Lázaro Cárdenas 97, Residencial San Agustín, tel. (8) 335-3376, and **Sierra Madre Tennis Club,** Prol. de los Angeles 617, Colonia Jerónimo Siller, tel. (8) 378-4770. Several of the larger hotels in the city also have courts.

SHOPPING

For many Canadian and American visitors, shopping is the name of the game in Monterrey. Just about anything available in Mexico City (or San Antonio, Texas, for that matter) can be found in the markets, shops, department stores, and malls dotting the cityscape.

Shopping Areas

Many Mexican-made, fully licensed, designer goods—Ralph Lauren Polo, Calvin Klein, Gucci, Louis Vuitton, etc.—are sold in shops in the Zona Rosa, especially along the **Av. Hidalgo** pedestrian mall. These kinds of items are also available in the various shopping centers in well-to-do San Pedro Garza García, southwest of the city.

Of the larger shopping plazas for which the city is famous, the most impressive are the **Mall Del Valle,** off Av. Vasconcelos in the posh Del Valle area; **Galerías Monterrey,** off Av. González Garza, west of the Gonzalitos loop; and **Plaza Fiesta San Agustín,** opposite the Hotel Fiesta Americana off Av. Lázaro Cárdenas. The latter contains over 100 shops and department stores, including JCPenney, Sears, and Sanborn's, along with a huge multicinema.

The Zona Rosa branches of **Vip's** and **Sanborn's** have good magazine sections with plenty of English-language reading material (Vip's is better organized).

Markets

Filling an entire block between Avenidas Juárez and Cuauhtémoc (east-west) and Calle Ocampo and Av. Constitución (north-south), **Mercado Colón** is a traditional urban Mexican market with

Galerías Monterrey

JOE CUMMINGS

row upon row of vendors purveying live birds, herbs, fresh-dressed *cabrito,* inexpensive pottery, kitchen utensils, curios, fruits, vegetables, baskets, and *artículos religiosos.* In the vicinity of this market, especially along Calle Ocampo between Juárez and Cuauhtémoc, are many small shops selling inexpensive clothes, umbrellas, and household goods; on the north side of Ocampo is a smaller market called **Mercado San Luis.** Farther north from here on Av. Juárez, between Calles Aramberri and Ruperto Martínez, is **Mercado Juárez,** another large market with many of the same items as Mercado Colón.

Arts and Crafts
A good spot for regional handicrafts is **Casa de las Artesanías de Nuevo León,** Dr. Coss at Allende, tel. (8) 345-5817, which offers a large selection of glass, ceramics, copper, brass, leather, and carved wooden items.

Carapán, Av. Hidalgo Ote. 305 (opposite Hotel Ambassador), tel. (8) 345-4422, is worth checking out for its tasteful assortment of rugs, homespun cottons, handblown glass, silver, and other arts and crafts selected for their high quality. The **Sanborn's** at Galerías Monterrey and at Plaza Fiesta San Agustín have small but high-quality *artesanía* sections that include Talavera ceramics, among other pieces. The Zona Rosa Sanborn's also stocks arts and crafts, though the selection is not as good as at the aforementioned branches.

Other handicraft shops in downtown Monterrey include **Quetzal Artesanías,** Dr. Coss Sur 1217, Centro, tel. (8) 342-0049; **Mercado Indio,** Simón Bolivar Nte. 1150, Mitras Centro, tel. (8) 348-5020; and **Unión de Artesanos de Nuevo León,** Morelos between Zaragoza and Escobedo, Zona Rosa, tel. (8) 75-1705.

World-renowned crystal glass producer **Kristaluxus** has a factory outlet at Calle José María Vigil 400 in Colonia del Norte, tel. (8) 351-6396, where crystal can be purchased at discounted prices. The plant also invites visitors to have a look at glass-producing processes; guided tours are available at 10:30 a.m. Mon.-Sat. The shop is open Mon.-Fri. 9 a.m.-6:30 p.m., Sunday 9 a.m.-2 p.m.

Pharmacies
Monterrey is well equipped with modern *farmacias,* with locations throughout the city. **Farmacia**

Las 24 Horas Benavides, opposite the Hospital Civil at Av. Madero Pte. 3350, tel. (8) 345-1435, is open round-the-clock.

EVENTS

Monterrey's biggest annual event is the two-week **Feria de Primavera** or "Spring Fair" in April (beginning Palm Sunday), when a number of commercial expositions, parades, concerts, and sports events are held at various venues around the city.

Perhaps of more interest to foreign visitors is the **Northern Mexican Fair** ("Feria del Norte de México"), held in conjunction with the traditional **Fiesta Guadalupana** during the second week of December. One of the most impressive religious processions takes place at the Basílica de Roble, culminating in an all-night mass on 12 Dec. (the feast day of the Virgin of Guadalupe). Other highlights of the fair include handicrafts, agricultural exhibits, and *norteña* food and culture.

INFORMATION AND SERVICES

Tourist Offices
The main branch of the state tourist office is on the fourth floor of Edificio Kalos at Av. Constitución and Zaragoza (at the south end of the Gran Plaza), tel. (8) 340-1080. For everyday inquiries, the smaller **Infotur** office at Dr. Coss and Padre Mier, along the east side of the Gran Plaza, is more than sufficient. It's open Tues.-Sun. 10 a.m.-5 p.m.

Infotur has two toll-free telephone numbers for information on Monterrey and Nuevo León: (800) 8-3222 in Mexico; (800) 235-2438 from the U.S./Canada.

Media
English-language newspapers available at the Zona Rosa hotels or at most Sanborn's and Vip's department stores include the *Mexico City News, USA Today, Laredo Times,* and *Wall Street Journal.*

Mexico's highest-quality Spanish-language newspaper, *El Norte,* is published in Monterrey. Even if your Spanish is minimal, *El Norte* is a good source of information on local cultural events, often listed in easy-to-follow columns.

MONTERREY TELEPHONE NUMBERS

Local Police	342-9188
Highway Patrol	343-0173
Green Angels	340-2113
State Tourist Office	340-1080
Infotur	345-0870
Red Cross	342-1212
U.S. Consulate	345-2120
Monterrey Area Code	8

What to Do, Where to Go in Monterrey is a very informative monthly pamphlet published by the state that highlights concerts, cultural and sporting events, and museum exhibits. It's distributed free at a number of places around the city, including most tourist and business hotels.

Standard Monterrey television consists of eight channels—three from Mexico City, plus five local networks. Many residents also use satellite dishes to receive U.S. stations. The city boasts 45 radio stations, with a higher-than-usual number of Top 40-style formats.

Maps
Good city maps of Monterrey are difficult to find. At Sanborn's and Vip's you can purchase the *Guia Roji* map, which is very detailed and in its latest version pinpoints most landmarks, monuments, tourist attractions, and parks, as well as streets and neighborhoods. Infotur distributes free sketch maps that depict the main avenues for cross-city traffic and are useful for general touring. What this city sorely needs is a map similar to those once published by HFET or those now published in the neighboring state of Coahuila.

Monterrey's INEGI office, Av. Revolución 3000, Edificio Torre del Sur, tel. (8) 369-4810, carries topographical maps for all of northeastern Mexico.

Immigration Office
If you've somehow made it as far as Monterrey without a tourist card or other immigration documents, you can make yourself legal at the city immigration office at Edificio Manchester, Morones Prieto 2110, tel. (8) 343-1523 or 343-1571. Open Mon.-Fri. 8:30 a.m.-2:30 p.m.

Money
As elsewhere, the best banks for foreign exchange are **Banca Serfín,** Av. Hidalgo Pte. 330 and at the airport; **Banamex,** Av. Padre Mier Ote. 102; and **Bancomer,** Av. Padre Mier Ote. 480.

Several *casas de cambio* are in downtown Monterrey and in the Del Valle and San Agustín districts. The greatest concentration is along Av. Ocampo Ote. near the Zona Rosa, where you'll find the convenient **Casa de Cambio Monterrey, Casa de Cambio Toledo,** and **Casa de Cambio Cadeca.** Hours of operation are generally around 9 a.m.-7 p.m.

American Express has an office at Av. Padre Mier Pte. 1424, tel. (8) 345-2628 or 343-0460, where you can report lost/stolen traveler's checks or receive a cash advance on an American Express card.

Post and Courier
The city's main post office is at Av. Zaragoza and Washington downtown. **U.S. Mail,** Isaac Garza Ote. 2112-A, Col. Obrera, tel. (8) 342-0389, maintains post office boxes in McAllen, Texas. **DHL** has four offices in Monterrey but only one phone number to keep it simple; call (8) 318-0418 for the nearest location.

GETTING THERE

By Air
Because of its role as Mexico's economic center, air services to Monterrey are extensive. The best choice from most of the continental U.S. is **Continental,** Galerías Monterrey, tel. (8) 333-2622, Mexico toll-free tel. (800) 537-9222, U.S. toll-free tel. (800) 523-3273, which operates nonstop flights to/from Houston, with connections to many other U.S. cities as well as Vancouver.

For Texans, **Aeroméxico,** Av. Padre Mier and Av. Cuauhtémoc, tel. (8) 343-5560, is more convenient, with nonstop flights from San Antonio, McAllen, and Houston. Aeroméxico also flies nonstop to Monterrey from Chihuahua, Culiacán, Guadalajara, Mexico City, Piedras Negras, San Luis Potosí, Tampico, and Torreón.

Mexicana, Av. Hidalgo Pte. 922, tel. (8) 380-7300, flies direct to Monterrey from Chihuahua, Culiacán, Guadalajara, Mazatlán, Mexico City, Monclova, San Luis Potosí, and Tampico, with

492 THE STATE OF NUEVO LEÓN

connections to/from Durango, La Paz, Los Angeles, San Francisco, and Tijuana.

Local airline **Aviacsa/Aero Exo,** Calle Humberto Lobo 660, Col. Del Valle, tel. (8) 336-4400, fields flights to/from Mexico City, Guadalajara, Tijuana, Las Vegas, Houston, and Chicago.

Airport Transportation: Aeropuerto Internacional Mariano Escobedo is 25 km (14.8 miles) northeast of the city center via Mexico 54, around 40 minutes by car. The standard *sitio* taxi fare out to the airport is US$12, while a *colectivo* costs US$3.50 pp. Better—if you don't have much luggage—are the green VW Eco-Taxis, which charge according to meter readings. A ride to the airport from downtown Monterrey in an Eco-Taxi should cost US$6-7 if taken during off-commute hours. Buses also run between the main downtown bus terminal and the airport several times a day for less than US$1.

By Bus
Autotransportes Elite, Transportes del Norte, Estrella Blanca, Futura, Noroeste, Autobuses Blanco, Omnibus de México, Turistar and **Transportes Frontera** offer several buses per day to/from Nuevo Laredo on the Texas border for around US$6-8.50 each way, as well as buses to/from Matamoros (US$10), Tampico (US$16-26), San Luis Potosí (US$16), Torreón (US$12-16), and Zacatecas (US$12-14). Estrella Blanca, Turistar, and Transportes del Norte also operate buses to/from Chihuahua for US$24-33 one-way.

Buses to Monterrey can be booked through **Greyhound** in Texas for links with Transportes del Norte from San Antonio (US$25), Houston (US$30), Austin (US$35), and Dallas (US$40). For scheduling details, contact a Greyhound ticket agency anywhere in the United States. From McAllen's new Central de Autobuses at Beech and N. Main, a first-class Mercedes Benz bus to Monterrey with a/c and TV costs US$11.50.

For service to/from Piedras Negras, you'll want **Autobuses Blanco,** which operates four buses a day for US$16 each way. This company also has buses to Cuatrociénegas (US$8.50).

Transportes del Norte, Frontera, and **Turistar** have frequent departures to Saltillo, for US$2.50-2.60 ordinary class, US$4 *ejecutivo*.

Towns and villages in Coahuila, San Luis Potosí, and Tamaulipas—e.g., Ciudad Victoria (US$9), and Monclova (US$5-6)—are served by **Noreste, Futura,** and **Autobuses Blanco.**

Bus Terminal: Monterrey's large and busy Central de Autobuses, Av. Colón near Av. Universidad, tel. (8) 375-3238, has all the usual services, including a pharmacy, lockers, photocopy machine, and *cafetería.* Several city bus lines terminate here; the "Cuauhtémoc" and "Central" Metro stations are within walking distance.

CONSULATES IN MONTERREY

Austria: Río Orinoco Pte. 105, tel. (8) 356-9015

Canada: Av. Andromeda, tel. (8) 382-7714

Colombia: Monte Palatino Nte. 120, Col. Fuentes de Valle, tel. (8) 363-5957

Dominican Republic: Av. Lázaro Cárdenas Pte. 2475, Col. San Agustín, tel. (8) 378-6227

Ecuador: Calz. del Rosario 286, tel. (8) 338-4203

France: Padre Mier at E. Carranza, Centro, tel. (8) 335-1784

Germany: E. Carranza 1215, Col. Palo Blanco, tel. (8) 335-1784

Great Britain: Priv. Tamazunchale 104, Col. del Valle, tel. (8) 378-2565

Honduras: Av. Insurgentes 1717, Col. Santa María, tel. (8) 333-3984

Italy: Dr. Coss Sur 465, Centro, tel. (8) 344-3250

Netherlands: Av. Morelos Ote. 867, Centro, tel. (8) 342-5055

Nicaragua: Profra. Rosa Gómez Sur 250, Centro, tel. (8) 338-5377

Panama: Pedro Quintanilla 390, Col. Chepe Vera, tel. (8) 346-3371

Peru: Loma Alta 606, Col. Loma Larga, tel. (8) 340-4244

Sweden: Blvd. Díaz Ordaz 200, tel. (8) 346-3090

United States: Calle Constitución Pte. 411, Centro, tel. (8) 345-2120 (after hours tel. 8-344-5261)

By Train

Two *primera especial* trains to Monterrey from the U.S.-Mexico border are available. **El Tamaulipeco** operates between Matamoros and Monterrey via Reynosa. The one-way fare of US$6.35 from Matamoros or US$4.70 from Reynosa includes a box lunch and soft drinks served by uniformed train employees. Second-class seats are no longer available on this line and it remains to be seen how much longer the Tamaulipeco will continue operations, considering that buses along this route are much faster. The trip takes around 6.5 hours from Matamoros, 2.5 hours from Reynosa.

You can also ride a train to Monterrey from Piedras Negras via Saltillo on *El Regiomontaño*. See the "Piedras Negras" section for details on this train between the border and Saltillo. From Saltillo the train takes 2.5 hours and costs US$3. From Monterrey, *El Regiomontano* leaves at 6:15 p.m. and continues southward to San Luis Potosí (US$9) and Mexico City (US$18).

Railway Station: The impressive Monterrey railway station, off Av. Colón west of the bus terminal, has gift shops, a *casa de cambio,* clean restrooms, schedule boards (rare in Mexico), and a restaurant. The nearest Metro station is "Central."

Driving

Nuevo León 1 (from Colombia), Mexico 85 (from Nuevo Laredo or Ciudad Victoria), Mexico 54 (from Ciudad Miguel Alemán), and Mexico 40 (from Reynosa or Saltillo) all converge at Monterrey. The new eight-lane bridge, warehouse, and customs complex at Colombia is mainly used by cargo-carrying traffic as a way to bypass the congested Nuevo Laredo crossing. If you plan to follow Nuevo León 1 rather than Mexico 85 to Monterrey, the Colombia crossing is quicker and more efficient than the Nuevo Laredo crossing. Count on around 3.5 hours between Colombia and Monterrey, more if you slow down to look at historic Bustamante and Villaldama.

The Mexico 85-D tollway begins 69 km (43 miles) south of Nuevo Laredo and costs a stiff US$11.75 for the 165-km (102-mile) ride; the speed limit is 110 kph (68 mph), which makes the total Nuevo Laredo-Monterrey driving time (including those stretches not covered by the tollway) about two hours. From San Antonio the driving time is around 4-4.5 hours. There has

been some discussion of lowering the toll since the tollway is very much underused—for dollar-holders the toll was effectively cut in half when the peso plunged in 1995. The original two-lane *libre* (toll-free) road is in good condition but truck traffic can be heavy at times; count on around three to four hours.

The shortest way to Monterrey from the border is from the crossing at Roma, Texas, via Ciudad Miguel Alemán and Mier, Tamps., a distance of 171 km (106 miles) along Mexico 54; from Nuevo Laredo it's 230 km (143 miles) total, from Colombia 299 km (186 miles). When traffic is light, the Roma-Monterrey route can be done in about three hours.

Approaching Downtown Monterrey: Coming from the north via **Mexico 85** or **Nuevo León 1,** the quickest way downtown is to take the "Monterrey Via Rápida" bypass off the highway (Nuevo León 1 merges with Mexico 85 14 km/8.7 miles north of the city), then follow signs for "Zona Centro" to Av. M. Barragán, which becomes Av. Cuauhtémoc, then Av. Universidad, before merging with Av. Pino Suárez downtown.

From the northeast (**Mexico 54**) there is no bypass, so stay with Mexico 54 till it becomes Blvd. Miguel Alemán, then Calz. Madero; Madero leads into the heart of downtown via Av. Colón. From Cadereyta/Reynosa, **Mexico 40 East** becomes Av. Benito Juárez, then merges with Calz. Madero and Av. Colón as above.

From **Mexico 54 South** (Montemorelos, Ciudad Victoria), the highway becomes Av. E. Garza Sada, which leads directly across Río Santa Catarina to Av. Constitución; turn left on Constitución to reach the city center.

From Saltillo (**Mexico 40 West**), follow "Centro" signs for a fairly smooth transition to downtown Monterrey via Blvd. Díaz Ordaz.

GETTING AROUND

By Metro

Monterrey has an elevated tramway/subway called "Metrorrey," more commonly known simply as "El Metro," one of only three such systems in Mexico. The first line—Línea 1, or the yellow line—was inaugurated in 1991 and runs 17.5 km (10.8 miles) from San Bernabé (northwest of the city proper) to Exposición ("Expo Guadalupe," east of the city). It was financed by a combination of private and public funds, and its most outstanding feature so far is the cavernous steel-and-plexiglass "Cuauhtémoc" Metro station near the intersection of Av. Colón and Av. Cuauhtémoc. The newer and so far much shorter line—Línea 2 or the green line (also referred to as El Metro Subterráneo)—was completed in 1994 and runs north-south from Gral. Anaya (north-central Monterrey) to Zaragoza (Plaza Zaragoza/Gran Plaza). Línea 2 runs entirely underground and will eventually be extended farther north to San Nicolás and farther south to Garza García.

The two lines meet at the Cuauhtémoc station. Línea 2—the green line—is more useful for the average sightseer as it carries passengers to within walking distance of Cervecería Cuauhtémoc (Museo de Monterrey), Plaza Zaragoza, MARCO, and the Barrio Antiguo.

Cheaper than taxis but more expensive than city buses, the Metro moves at an average 36 kph (by comparison the average auto in Monterrey does 25 kph, the average bus 17 kph) and carries 90,000 passengers a day, a figure well below that carried by Mexico City's subway but higher than Guadalajara's. When the Metro is running smoothly, it only takes around 20 minutes to run the longer yellow line—a considerable time savings over any other mode of transportation. Cars are clean and air-conditioned.

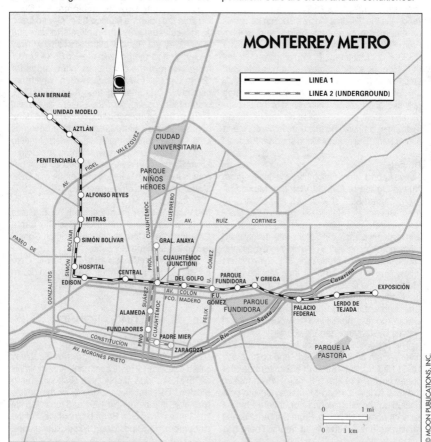

© MOON PUBLICATIONS, INC.

Ticket cards are dispensed from machines in each station in various peso denominations; the shortest journey—between two consecutive stations—costs US$0.25. In total there are 23 stations. The more stations you traverse in a single trip, however, the cheaper the fare. A four-station trip, for example, costs US$0.75.

By Bus

An extensive city bus system covers the metropolitan area, with main routes along Av. Cuauhtémoc-Av. Alfonso Reyes (south-to-north), Av. M.L. Barragán-Av. Pino Suárez (north-to-south), Av. Colón (east-to-west and west-to-east), Av. Constitución (east-to-west), and Av. Morones Prieto (west-to-east). Most of downtown Monterrey is within walking distance of points along these routes. One-way fares run US$0.24

By Taxi

As usual, taxi *sitios* (stands) are concentrated around the bus and train terminals, major hotels, and market areas. The average hire (e.g., from the bus or train terminal to the Zona Rosa) for a large taxi from one of the *sitios* is US$1.50-2 per trip. A less expensive alternative is to take one of the metered "Eco-Taxis," green VW bugs that burn only unleaded gas (hence the name) and cost around US$1.50 for the same trip. Eco-Taxis must be flagged down on the street—outside of the city center they are sometimes few and far between.

Driving

Although Monterrey is not the easiest of cities to drive in, it's not nearly as difficult as, for example, Torreón, Zacatecas, or Guanajuato. City streets are wide and mostly well marked, and there are few of the diagonals that make the traditional Spanish grid so maddening; in fact the city plan is closer to that of a large American city than a typical Mexican city.

Still, as with any large city, you should plan your routes with a map before setting out from point A to point B. Several city streets bear the family name of the local Garza Sada technocratic dynasty, a fact which leaves many Mexican as well as gringo motorists racking their brains to distinguish one Garza Sada (Francisco, Roberto, and Eugenio are three of them) from another.

Blue-and-white signs point the way to tourist attractions in and around the city. Unfortunately, they're not always in place from start to finish and may leave you stranded (as the El Obispado signs left the author); don't count on them.

Street Numbers: The central point for the city street-numbering system is the southwest corner of the Mercado Juárez at Av. Juárez and Aramberri; streets running east and west of Juárez are Ote. and Pte., respectively, while those to the north and south are Nte. and Sur. Thus Av. Hidalgo Ote. 310 is, theoretically, three blocks east of Juárez; the system isn't perfect but it serves as a good general guideline.

Rush Hours: Monterrey's heaviest traffic generally occurs 8:30-9 a.m., 1-2:30 p.m., and 6-7:30 p.m. To avoid delays and frustration, avoid driving during these times of day when you have a choice.

Traffic Laws: The four-lane section of highway that forms Av. Constitución (along the Río Santa Catarina at the south edge of downtown Monterrey) has separate speed limits for each lane, an absurd idea that almost no one pays any attention to! Note, however, that a law requiring the use of seat belts in Monterrey is enforced.

Parking: Except in the Zona Rosa, parking isn't much of a problem. In the Zona Rosa, a convenient 24-hour parking lot is off Av. Hidalgo Ote., just west of the Hotel Ambassador; fees are very reasonable. Beneath the Gran Plaza is another large pay lot.

Auto Rental: Several auto rental agencies have offices in the Zona Rosa along Av. Hidalgo Ote., near the Hotel Ambassador.

TOURS

From San Antonio

Alamo Coaches, in San Antonio, Texas, tel. (210) 271-0047, offers a convenient three-day shopping/sightseeing tour of Monterrey and Saltillo. The tour departs San Antonio at 5:45 a.m. Friday morning and arrives just after noon in Monterrey for hotel check-in (usually the Hotel Río). In the afternoon the tour continues to Cañon de la Huasteca, the Basílica del Roble, and the Palacio de Gobierno. On Saturday the tour moves on to Saltillo to see the Catedral de Saltillo and market square, and on Sunday returns to San Antonio with a shopping stop in Nuevo Laredo. The trip costs US$99 pp including transportation, site tours, and lodging. All tour leaders are bilingual.

City Tours
In Monterrey itself, **Osetur,** tel. (8) 347-1599, leads half-day tours of the city (departing 9 a.m. from behind the Gran Hotel Ancira) and nearby attractions (departing 1:30 p.m. from behind the Ancira). The tours run daily Tues.-Sun. except on Sunday afternoons; each day involves a different itinerary for a total of 11 possible tours. All tours cost US$6-8.50 depending on the itinerary. Sample city destinations include the Gran Plaza, Kristaluxus, Cervecería Cuauhtémoc, and Galerías Monterrey; Monterrey-vicinity tours might include Cola de Caballo ("Horsetail Falls"), Centro Cultural Alfa, or the Grutas de García. **Gray Line Monterrey,** tel. (8) 369-6472, offers similar tours.

Private city tours with a bilingual car and driver can be arranged through the more tourist-oriented hotels for about US$25 a day; tours to Cola de Caballo or the Grutas de García will cost around US$6-7 more.

VICINITY OF MONTERREY

Parque Nacional Las Cumbres de Monterrey
The most extensive national park in Mexico, Las Cumbres covers 246,500 hectares (609,000 acres) at the northern end of the Sierra Madre Oriental near Monterrey. The limestone moun-

AUTO RENTAL AGENCIES IN MONTERREY

Alal
Airport
tel. (8) 344-7002
Hidalgo Ote. 400
tel. (8) 344-5500

Auto Rentas Ejecutivas
Escobedo Sur 1013
tel. (8) 345-8019

Avis
Airport
tel. (8) 369-0834
Galeana Sur 1050 (at Ocampo)
tel. (8) 344-6580

Berim del Norte
Matamoros Pte. 210
tel. (8) 344-2937

Budget
Airport
tel. (8) 369-0819
Hidalgo Ote. 433
tel. (8) 340-4100

Centenario
E. Carranza (south of Hotel Ambassador)
tel. (8) 344-6463, fax (8) 342-0065

Century Rent a Car
Diego de Montemayor Sur 224
tel. (8) 342-0439

Dollar Rent-A-Car
Gran Hotel Ancier
tel. (8) 345-1060
Airport
tel. (8) 369-0897

Hertz
Airport
tel. (8) 369-0822
Hotel Ambassador
tel. (8) 345-6195
Garibaldi Sur 814
tel. (8) 344-8065
Hotel Río
tel. (8) 345-6136, fax (8) 340-1547

Mazda Rente Un Auto
Airport
tel. (8) 343-0549
Ocampo Ote. 379
tel. (8) 342-9868

National
Escobedo at Hidalgo
tel. (8) 344-6363
Airport
tel. (8) 369-0940

tains, some reaching over 3,000 meters (9,800 feet), are cut with numerous streams that provide water for the city of Monterrey and form major canyons, including La Huasteca, San Juan Bautista, Santa Catarina, and La Mielera. Several of metropolitan Monterrey's most popular recreation areas—Horsetail Falls, Cañon de la Huasteca, Grutas de García, and Meseta de Chipinque—fall within park boundaries.

Since national park status in Mexico does not forbid human habitation or exploitation (with the proper permission only), don't go to these places expecting untrammeled wilderness. Still, with some effort you can find satisfying wilderness areas near the main attractions.

This area is honeycombed with over 500 known limestone caves, some of which offer the best caving experiences in North America. Permission to explore many of the caves is difficult to obtain; if interested, your best bet is to work through a caving association in Texas.

Cascada Cola de Caballo

"Horsetail Falls" is 42 km (26 miles) southeast of Monterrey via Mexico 85; the turnoff is three km (two miles) south of Villa de Santiago. The last few kilometers of road wind through an attractive wooded area.

Because the park is around 2,000 meters (6,500 feet) above sea level, temperatures tend to be several degrees lower than on the plains below; a near-constant mist from the falls keeps the surrounding area green and lush. Osetur, a Monterrey tour operator, manages the nicely landscaped grounds, which include picnic tables with grills alongside streams formed by the falls. The 25-meter (82-foot) falls themselves are about 500 meters (550 yards) from the ticket booth at the entrance, along a stone path that can become slippery with spray at times. Stone steps climb alongside the falls to about a third of its height. Another trail farther to the side goes to the summit of the falls.

On summer weekends and holidays the park can become thick with city residents escaping the heat; come early in the day to beat the crowd. The falls are practically deserted in winter yet still a worthwhile visit for the misty mountain atmosphere.

Entry to the park is US$1.30. You can ride a horse to the top of the falls for US$3, or a horse

Cascada Cola de Caballo

JOE CUMMINGS

cart for US$2.60; horses for general riding can be hired for US$5 per hour.

A small, free parking lot is at the entrance to the falls, about 50 meters beyond the Motel Cola de Caballo entrance. The motel charges US$1.30 to park in its lot. The motel itself is in a state of disrepair and not a recommendable place to stay.

Beyond the falls, the road continues past a few mountain villages to the less-visited **Cascada Chipitín,** one or two hours away via a dirt road. Watch for animals and pedestrians along this road.

Villa de Santiago

Santiago began as a hacienda established in the fertile Valle de Guajuco, in the foothills of the Sierra Madre Oriental, in 1650. By the beginning of the 18th century, the hacienda had grown to "Villa" status and its cobbled streets and simple colonial buildings are now a local tourist attraction. Most of the architecture dates to the 1800s but several *casas*—particularly along Calle Morelos off the town plaza—were built as early as 1745.

The clean and friendly **Restaurante Las Palomas** on the plaza serves typical regional cuisine.

Santiago is 36 km (22 miles) south of Monterrey via Mexico 85. To reach the plaza from the main exit off Mexico 85, follow signs marked "Palacio Municipal" near the entrance to town.

Cañon de La Huasteca

Sixteen km (10 miles) west of Monterrey via Mexico 40, this steep-walled canyon was once used by Spanish settlers as well as local Amerindians as a refuge from marauding Apaches. Dramatic rock wall formations caused by erosion, as well as native petroglyphs and pictographs, attract visitors from all over the northeast. One cavelike formation is known as "Cueva de la Virgen" because at certain times of day, light from a crack in the wall projects an image of the Virgin Mary onto another wall.

In Mexico the canyon is famous for its use as a location setting for the film *Cuando Lloran los Valientes* ("When the Valiant Cry"), starring Mexican movie idol Pedro Infante as the legendary *regiomontaño* bandit Agapito Treviño. Treviño, known as "El Caballo Blanco" for his white mount, used the canyon to hide from pre-Revolutionary soldiers in pursuit.

To explore this area on foot, obtain a copy of INEGI's G14-7 (Saltillo) topographical map.

Grutas de García

Among the largest known caverns in Mexico, the Grutas de García are eight km (five miles) east of Villa de García, which is 41 km (25 miles) west of Monterrey off Mexico 40 (on the way to Saltillo). The main entrance measures 12 meters (39 feet) tall by 15 meters (49 feet) wide. Passages through the caves—16 caverns in all—are lighted so that visitors can admire crystalline formations with names like Mano del Muerto ("Hand of Death") and Teatro (named for is heavy, curtainlike shapes). A cable car runs nearly a kilometer from the parking area to the caves, which are 1,110 meters (3,700 feet) above sea level in the side of Cerro del Fray ("Friar's Mountain").

The caves are open daily 8 a.m.-4 p.m. An entry fee of US$3.40 for adults, US$2 for children, covers admission, cable-car ride, 90-minute

tour, and use of a children's playground and swimming pool near the parking area.

The narrow and winding road between Villa de García and the caves is not suitable for RVs. Villa de García itself was founded in 1577, but the standing architecture dates to the mid- to late-19th century.

Villaldama

A Franciscan mission was established here in 1690 on the mission road between Zacatecas and San Antonio; following the discovery of nearby gold and silver veins, a town named San Pedro de Villaldama was settled in 1826. Local mines were abandoned after American mining interests fled the violence of the 1910-20 Mexican Revolution.

Of minor interest is the neoclassic **Ex-Templo de San Pedro de Boca de Leones,** a church built at the beginning of the 19th century on the site of the original Franciscan mission. The building is now used as a cultural center. Calle de Rangel Frías joins the two town plazas and is lined with examples of typical regional architecture.

Villaldama is 91 km (56.4 miles) north of Monterrey via Nuevo León 1.

Bustamante

Seventeen km (10.5 miles) farther north along Nuevo León 1, Bustamante began as Misión San Miguel de Aguayo, founded in 1686 by Tlaxcaltecas from Saltillo. The traditional houses—of which few are left—feature walls of adobe and brick topped by peaked, thatched roofs. Another local style is characterized by long, shallow pilasters that run alongside windows and doors from foundation to roof.

On Calle Independencia near the town plaza, the art deco **Hotel Ancira,** built in the 1950s as a residence, doubles as a simple lodge and town bus terminal.

Six km (3.7 miles) south via a gravel road are the **Grutas de Bustamante,** a little-explored network of caves. One of the largest, Gruta del Palmito, is 45 meters (150 feet) wide, 30 meters (100 feet) high, and 160 meters (525 feet) long.

Cerralvo

Roughly halfway between Monterrey (152 km/71 miles southwest) and the Texas border, Cerralvo is the oldest town in Nuevo León. Founded as a mining community named Ciudad de León in 1577, the town was renamed in 1629 after the 15th viceroy of Nueva España, the Marqués de Cerralvo. Several buildings in town date to the early 1600s, including the partially ruined **Antigua Casa de la Moneda** (the Old Mint) on Calle Mina. As in Bustamante, the elongated door and window pilasters are typical of regional colonial architecture during the 17th and 18th centuries.

The **Antiguo Hospital** on the corner of Calles Hidalgo and Zaragoza was constructed at the end of the 18th century in a grand "C" shape around a central patio. The unique entrance facade features a floral-carved stone arch extending over short columns that are mounted on large stone pedestals.

Good food and lodging are available at **Hotel El Paso,** Calle Morelos Ote. 617. Several blocks west at Calle Morelos Pte. 222, **Restaurant Noreste** offers regional cooking.

Parque Nacional El Sabinal: Just southeast of Cerralvo off Mexico 54, this eight-hectare (20-acre) national park preserves old stands of sabinos (Montezuma bald cypress) along a scenic arroyo, forming a cool, wooded oasis in this arid region. Birding is excellent during the winter months, and picnic tables and grills are available for public use.

Linares

This town 83 km (51.5 miles) southeast of Monterrey, at the junction of Mexico 85 and Mexico 58, is the center of the state's "Zona Naranjera," where most of northeast Mexico's *naranjas* (oranges) are grown.

Citrus cultivation was introduced to the area by American Joseph Robertson at the beginning of the century, but the town has been around since its founding in 1712 by Spanish soldiers. Linares attained official city status and Nuevo León's first bishopry in 1777. The **Catedral de San Felipe Apostol** on the town plaza was built in 1779; a cupola and tower were added in 1805 and 1853. Several other 18th- and 19th-century structures can be found in the vicinity of the plaza. A modern building of interest is the post-revolutionary, neo-Aztec **Botica Morelos** at Morelos and Madero, facing the plaza's west corner.

Near Los Altares, 32 km (20 miles) west of Linares via Mexico 58, is scenic **Cañon de Santa Rosa,** on whose vertical rock walls the sculptor Federico Cantú has carved a 650-square-meter (7,000-square-foot) relief.

In Linares, the **Hotel Guidi** (Av. Morelos between Allende and Zaragoza) offers adequate rooms for shoestring rates (US$15-20), while budget-priced **Hotel Plaza Mira** (Calle Hidalgo at Juárez) is a bit nicer (US$25-30). Both have attached restaurants. **Restaurante Cabritos,** Av. Suárez between Hidalgo and Allende, serves its namesake, while **Restaurante El Herradero,** Calle P. Salce at Independencia, concentrates on *carne asada.*

BOB RACE

THE STATE OF TAMAULIPAS
INTRODUCTION

HISTORY

Meaning "High Mountains" in a Huastec dialect, Tamaulipas was inhabited by descendants of the Olmec culture when the first Spanish navigators explored the upper Gulf of Mexico coast five years before the Conquest. In 1516 Hernández de Córdoba sailed from Cuba and entered the mouth of the Río Pánuco, only to turn back upon sighting Huastec villages along the river banks.

A more extensive exploration of the coast was carried out by Capt. Alfonso Alvarez de Piñeda, who followed the course of the Río Bravo (Rio Grande). Alvarez named this wide waterway Río de las Palmas because it was profusely lined with native sabal palms (virtually the only wild palms left today are in the Sabal Palm Grove Sanctuary near Brownsville on the U.S. side). Alvarez was killed by Huastecs while exploring the Río Pánuco in 1519. Later explorations of the Tamaulipan coast continued to focus on the

mouths of the Bravo, Soto la Marina, and Pánuco Rivers.

Under Spanish rule the area became known as the Province of Pánuco. Spain's *empresario* program, which encouraged the colonization of Northern Mexico, Texas, and Louisiana by offering generous land grants, attracted Capt. José de Escandón to what is now northern Tamaulipas. Escandón, who had arrived in the New World at age 15 as a cavalry soldier, was commissioned in 1746 to survey the lands between Tampico and the Río San Antonio. In 1748, after obtaining permission to distribute land grants in the Río Bravo area, he helped establish 23 settlements in this region, including the present-day towns of Laredo, Dolores, Mier, Camargo, Reynosa, San Fernando, Soto la Marina, and Ciudad Victoria. Under Escandón's governorship the province's name was changed to Nuevo Santander; this name held through Mexican independence but was changed to Tamaulipas following Texas secession in 1836.

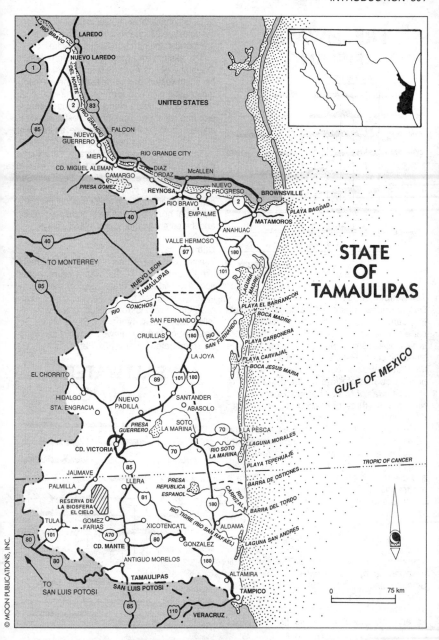

STATE OF TAMAULIPAS

FRESHWATER FISHING

(WHEN TO FISH)

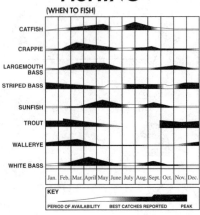

	Jan.	Feb.	Mar.	April	May	June	July	Aug.	Sept.	Oct.	Nov.	Dec.
CATFISH												
CRAPPIE												
LARGEMOUTH BASS												
STRIPED BASS												
SUNFISH												
TROUT												
WALLERYE												
WHITE BASS												

KEY

PERIOD OF AVAILABILITY   BEST CATCHES REPORTED   PEAK

Tamaulipas Today

Due to the abundance of water, farming (cotton, cereals, tobacco, sugarcane, coffee) and cattle ranching are the prime inland economic activities, while fishing and shrimping predominate along the coast. Petroleum and natural gas from the Pánuco Basin near Tampico is also an important source of state revenue, as are the *maquiladoras* of Nuevo Laredo, Reynosa, and Matamoros—three of Mexico's largest border communities.

During Spanish rule, Tamaulipas became the cradle of cattle ranching in North America and today the ranchero culture arches over virtually everything Tamaulipan, from the music (polka and *chotis* in the north, *huapango* in the south) to the traditional Tamaulipan costume of fringed chamois and calfskin.

LAND AND SEA

Tamaulipas boasts 430 km (267 miles) of Gulf coastline, cut by the Bravo, Guayalejo, Pánuco, Soto la Marina, and San Rafael Rivers. The intersection of river and sea has created an extensive network of estuaries, lagoons, *bocas,* beaches, and saltmarshes that make the Tamaulipas coast of considerable interest to naturalists. Along the coast are 23 inhabited islands, seven of which are found in the northern Laguna Madre.

The eastern escarpment of the Sierra Madre Oriental extends northwest-southeast through the southwestern part of the state, where it meets the coastal plains to form several unique environments, including cloud forest and Tamaulipan tropical/subtropical thorn forest. Latitude is another contributor to the landscape, as the lower third of the state falls below the Tropic of Cancer.

Tamaulipas borders the state of Veracruz to the south, the Gulf of Mexico to the east, Texas to the north, and the states of Nuevo León and San Luis Potosí to the west. Geoculturally, the state can be divided into three major regions: the semi-industrial north, the sparsely populated coast, and the primarily agricultural inland valleys.

Climate

The northern part of the state has a climate much like that of South Texas, with a warm, humid coastline and a temperate, semidry *matorral* inland with scattered rain year-round. To the southeast, the climate is tropical/subtropical with rain falling mostly in summer. The Sierra Madre Oriental region to the southwest is warm and semidry, moderated by moist Gulf breezes from the

SALTWATER FISHING

(WHEN TO FISH)

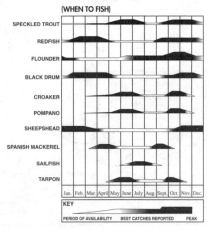

	Jan.	Feb.	Mar.	April	May	June	July	Aug.	Sept.	Oct.	Nov.	Dec.
SPECKLED TROUT												
REDFISH												
FLOUNDER												
BLACK DRUM												
CROAKER												
POMPANO												
SHEEPSHEAD												
SPANISH MACKEREL												
SAILFISH												
TARPON												

KEY

PERIOD OF AVAILABILITY   BEST CATCHES REPORTED   PEAK

east and protected from the interior desert by high peaks to the west. In most of the state you can expect high June-Sept. temperatures.

RECREATION

Beaches
The best beach areas in the state are, from north to south, **Bagdad, El Mezquital, El Barrancón, Carbonera, La Pesca, Tepehuaje, Barra de Ostiones, and Barra del Tordo.** They all share a broad, flat profile—much like beaches along the Texas Gulf Coast but with fewer crowds. Facilities are limited to *palapas* and trash receptacles.

Fishing and Crabbing
The state hosts more than 20 annual fishing tournaments and maintains over 50 *parques turísticos* on its lakes, rivers, and beaches. Among the lakes frequented by keen anglers are **Vicente Guerrero, Falcón, Gómez, Caballero, Méndez, San Lorenzo,** and **Real de Borbón,** all of which primarily contain freshwater bass (striped, black) and catfish.

Saltwater anglers will find lagoon fishing along the Tamaulipan coast to be especially productive. In the calm, easily accessible "flats"—shallow, sandy lagoons on the leeward side of the barrier islands *(barras)*—anglers can hook flounder, sheepshead, croaker, redfish, and speckled trout. The lagoons also support populations of saltwater crabs. All you need for a crabbing expedition is a length of twine equal to the water's depth, crab bait (chicken meat is recommended), and a hand net; net the crab *before* you pull it from the water or it'll release the bait.

Surf casting on the Gulf-facing beaches and islands is a bit more challenging and offers a wide variety of redfish, speckled trout, black drum, whiting, and sandtrout. Offshore catches include marlin, sailfish, yellowfin tuna, kingfish, yellowjack, tarpon, amberjack, pompano, and red snapper; you'll need to launch your own boat—or hire a local boat—to take advantage of this fishery.

Hunting
The most popular hunting areas are found near Miguel Alemán, Reynosa, Matamoros, San Fernando, Padilla, Ciudad Victoria, Soto la Marina, and Ciudad Mante. White-winged dove *(paloma alas blancas,* in season mid-August to November) is the favorite game of *tamaulipecos,* followed by quail and wild turkey *(codorniz* and *guajalote,* same season as dove), white-tailed deer *(venado de cola blanca,* December to mid-January), and goose and duck *(ganzo* and *pato,* mid-October to mid-February).

NUEVO LAREDO

Mexico's quintessential border town receives more daily visitors from the north than any other city along the U.S.-Mexico border (Tijuana has slightly higher vehicle counts but proportionately more passers-through). Partially this is due to the city's location only 2.5 hours from one of the 10 largest cities in the U.S. (San Antonio, Texas); another reason is that the city offers a well-developed downtown with everything from elegant dining to street vendors to cut-rate liquor stores, plus two leafy public plazas, all within walking distance of the International Bridge.

Although Nuevo Laredo's population of 274,000 has outpaced that of "Old" Laredo's 120,000, the two cities are closely linked by culture and economics. Holidays as culturally distinct as Washington's Birthday and Mexican Independence Day are celebrated on both sides of the border, and the twin cities share a single pro baseball team, Los Tecolotes de los Dos Laredos, which plays in both Mexican and American minor leagues.

Tariff and customs revenues collected at Nuevo Laredo are greater than at any other port of entry in Mexico, and along with Ciudad Juárez and Tijuana, Nuevo Laredo is one of the most important business centers along La Frontera. The *maquila* industry that plays such an important role in other large border towns is integrated here into a more diverse area economy that includes import-export operations, transportation, cotton farming, cattle ranching, and tourism.

HISTORY

Laredo began when *empresario* Don Tomás Sánchez established a colony on the north bank of the Río Bravo in 1755. In honor of his sponsor José de Escandón, who hailed from Laredo, Spain, Sánchez named the settlement Villa de San Agustín de Laredo. Founded as the first nonmissionary, nonmilitary Spanish settlement in North America, the town served as a center for the continent's first cattle ranches.

In the early 1800s the city found itself caught between two wars of national liberation—first Mexico's fight for independence from Spain (throughout which most Laredo residents remained Spanish loyalists), then Texas's struggle for independence from Mexico. When neither of the newly formed republics of Texas and Mexico would provide protection against marauding bandits and Apaches, Laredo joined the states of Tamaulipas, Coahuila, and Nuevo León in declaring their own "Republic of the Río Grande" in 1840. Laredo was made the capital of the new republic, which lasted only 10 months before Mexican troops brought the area back under Mexican rule.

In 1845, when the Republic of Texas was annexed to the U.S., Laredo was again abandoned in a no-man's land between the two countries, since the U.S. and Mexico disagreed over the boundary line between Texas and Mexico. The Treaty of Guadalupe Hidalgo, signed at the end of the Mexican-American War, established the Río Bravo (Rio Grande) as the border; those Laredo residents who wanted to remain Mexican citizens moved across the river and established Nuevo Laredo in 1848.

In the late 1800s the founding of two new railroads made the two Laredos a major transportation link between the U.S. and Mexico. The Texas-Mexican Railway connected the city with the deepwater port of Corpus Christi on the Texas Gulf coast, while the Missouri Pacific joined the midwestern U.S. with Mexico's national railway and Mexico City.

The city's transportation role was further strengthened when the Pan-American Highway (Mexico 85) was completed in 1935, establishing a continuous roadway between Laredo and the Panama Canal via Mexico and Central America. Another boost to the local economy arrived during the U.S. Prohibition years, when Texas residents began slipping over the border to the Cadillac Bar and other Nuevo Laredo watering holes for a legal drink, thus introducing tourism to the area. By the end of WW II, Nuevo Laredo was one of the most prosperous cities in Mexico.

SIGHTS

As Nuevo Laredo is a relatively new city by Mexican standards, it offers virtually no sights of historical interest. For Texas residents it's a place to shop and party on weekends and holidays, though most visitors never get farther than a few blocks down Av. Guerrero, the main tourist strip that runs directly south from the bridge.

If you're just going for the day, it's easy to walk over International Bridge No. 1 from downtown Laredo near Hotel La Posada—you can park your vehicle in the free lots off Laredo's Zaragoza St., below Riverdrive Mall. Those who are driving across will use International Bridge No. 2. Parking in downtown Nuevo Laredo is tight but pay lots are available.

Parque Arqueológico Morelos

This park three blocks east of International Bridge No. 1, between Calles Bravo and 15 de Junio, exhibits some 50 replicas of historical sculptures representing the seven major pre-Cortesian cultures in Mexico and Mesoamerica. Many have been copied from artifacts at Mexico City's famous Museum of Anthropology as well as from the Mayan ruins of Chichén Itzá and Teotihuacán.

Plazas

Three plazas strung out north to south along Av. Guerrero are the focus of public life in Nuevo Laredo: **Plaza Juárez,** two blocks from the bridge at Calles Victoria and Galeana; **Plaza Hidalgo,** Av. Guerrero at Calle González; and **Plaza México,** Av. Guerrero at Independencia. Plaza Hidalgo is the largest of the three and serves as city center, flanked by the Palacio Federal on the east and various restaurants and hotels to the west.

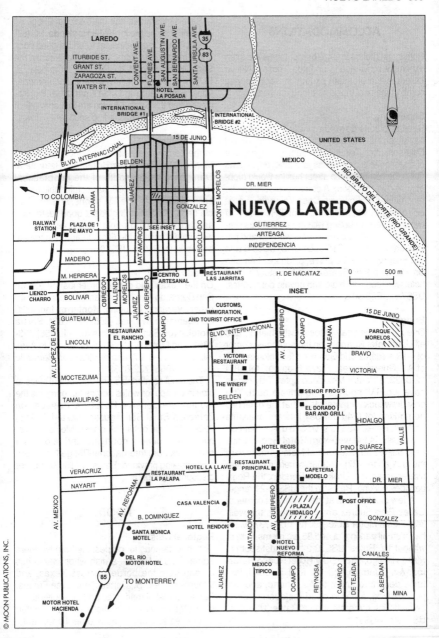

ACCOMMODATIONS

Hotels and motels in large border towns are often expensive by Mexican standards. Those in Nuevo Laredo are a pleasant exception, representing some of the best bargains along the border.

Shoestring

Several places downtown near Plaza Hidalgo have rooms for only US$5 a night (Hotel Calderón, Hotel Texas, Hotel Sam's), but most are of questionable cleanliness and function; anyone not in the company of a street hustler would probably be denied a room. A couple of places can be recommended, however. **Casa Valencia**, a *casa de huéspedes* opposite the Hotel Rendón in a two-story yellow building with green trim, has simple but reasonably clean rooms with fan and private bath. Rates: US$6 s, US$7 d, US$9 d with TV. Friendly **Hotel La Llave**, on Juárez between Dr. Mier and Pino Suárez, is a two-story budget hotel with rooms with a/c and private bath. Rates: US$7 s, US$8.50 d.

Budget

One of the best deals in town is the friendly and efficient **Hotel Rendón,** on the southeast corner of Calles Juárez and González (two blocks west of Av. Guerrero near Plaza Hidalgo), tel. (87) 12-0532, a classic Mex-deco hotel. Tidy rooms have a/c, TV, phones, and private bath. The only drawback for motorists is that the hotel has no parking lot (24-hour pay lots are available nearby). Rates: US$16 s, US$18 d. Another border classic is the well-worn **Hotel Regis**, Calle Pino Suárez 3013 (corner of Matamoros toward the bridge), tel. (87) 12-9035, where rooms offer similar amenities. Unlike the Rendón, the Regis provides parking. Rates: in the US$19-21 range.

A few blocks west, at the northwest corner of Calles Pino Suárez and Ocampo, is the well-kept **Fiesta Motor Hotel,** tel. (87) 12-4737, which has a small parking lot and 35 a/c rooms, with or without TV. Rates: US$20-22 s/d. Just south of Plaza Hidalgo, three-story **Hotel Nuevo Reforma,** Av. Guerrero 822, tel. (87) 12-6250, features decent rooms with TV, phone, and a/c, plus parking, a bar, a good restaurant, and a semiattractive marble lobby. Rates: US$22 s, US$26 d, US$31 t.

Seven km south of the International Bridge on Av. Reforma, the **Motor Hotel Hacienda,** tel. (87) 17-0000, has relatively quiet rooms, a good pool, and a restaurant. Rates: US$26 s/d. Nearby, the **Santa Monica Motel,** Av. Reforma at Candela, tel. (87) 14-2116, offers fair two-star accommodations. Rates: around US$17 s/d. Both the Hacienda and the Santa Monica are in a convenient location for motorists heading south out of town.

Inexpensive

In the same area as the Hacienda and Santa Monica, **Del Río Motor Hotel,** Av. Reforma at Obregón (five km south of the international Bridge), tel. (87) 14-3666, has comfortable rooms each with a/c, satellite TV, phone, and two double beds. Amenities include a good restaurant and two swimming pools. The hotel is within walking distance of the Gigante and Soriana supermarkets. Rates: US$40.

Laredo, Texas

On the Texas side of the border just off I-35 on San Bernardo Ave. are several motels in the inexpensive range, including: **Monterrey Inn,** 4820 San Bernardo Ave., tel. (956) 722-7631; **Siesta Motel,** 4109 San Bernardo Ave., tel. (956) 723-3661; and **Motel 6,** at 5310 San Bernardo Ave., tel. (956) 725-8187, and at 5920 San Bernardo Ave., tel. (956) 722-8133.

The most comfortable and convenient place to stay in Laredo for walks across the border is the moderate/expensive **Hotel La Posada,** on Zaragoza St. at San Agustín Plaza, tel. (956) 722-1701. Laid out in the classic Mexican colonial style around a courtyard and pool, it's a short walk from International Bridge No. 1. Security parking provided. Rates: US$60-90 (senior discount available).

FOOD

Regional Cuisine

The most famous food specialty from Northern Tamaulipas is fajitas—a dish whose fame has spread from the border, across Texas, and throughout the U.S., Canada, and even Europe. Fajitas consist of marinated and mesquite-grilled skirt steak served with flour tortillas, grilled onions, salsas, and various other condiments.

EL DORADO BAR & GRILL

Nuevo Laredo has been a favorite eating and drinking spot for South Texans since the 1920s Prohibition, and the longest running border joint of them all is alive and well under its latest moniker, El Dorado Bar & Grill, tel. (87) 12-0015. Originally established in 1922 as a combination casino and restaurant named El Caballo Blanco, the restaurant was purchased by New Orleans native Mayo Bassan in 1926. Bassan renamed it the Cadillac Bar and introduced a Creole style of cooking—including dishes such as roast quail, fried soft-shelled crab, red snapper *en papillote,* and braised frog legs—that influenced restaurant cuisine throughout the Rio Grande region. He later added *cabrito* and several Northern Mexican standards to the menu.

Bassan's most famous innovation was the Ramos gin fizz (listed on the current drink menu as "New Orleans gin fizz"), a sweetish cocktail made with frothy egg whites and gin. The house drink list encompasses 99 items, including such antiques as sherry and egg, absinthe frappe, Sazerac, and the "popper," a savory tequila concoction served in a large shot glass with a loud flourish—in which a white-jacketed waiter slams the glass onto the bar (or table), then stands back while you down the drink in one swallow.

In 1958 Bassan turned the Cadillac Bar over to his Texan son-in-law Porter Gardner, who operated the restaurant until his retirement in 1980. Gardner left the Cadillac to his employees and it was eventually sold to the Longoria family, who changed the name to El Dorado Bar & Grill in 1992. A franchise operated in the U.S. under the name "Cadillac Bar" has no relation to the original Nuevo Laredo location other than the name and a drink called the "slammer," inspired by the original Cadillac's popper.

Nothing much has changed at the legendary Belden and Ocampo location (two blocks south and one block east of the bridge); the El Dorado has the same white-coated waiters, the same piano-player, the same funky smell you'd expect from a 70-year-old bar, and the same menu featuring quail, *cabrito,* frog's legs, and Mexican standards. The sturdy wooden bar, with not a blender in sight, is still the restaurant's greatest asset. The large, guarded parking lot in back of the restaurant is useful for downtown shopping sprees; as long as you eat or drink at El Dorado, parking is free. The restaurant is open daily 10 a.m.-11 p.m.

They are most often cooked and served while on a picnic outing, but you can buy them by the kilo in several Nuevo Laredo restaurants.

The easiest to find is **Restaurant La Palapa,** Av. Reforma 3301, tel. (87) 14-0068, not far from the Hacienda and Del Río hotels; it's open daily for dinner and is slightly upscale. **Las Jarritas** (formerly Las Tablitas), H. de Nacataz 2002 (at the corner of Calle Degollado east of Plaza Hidalgo downtown), tel. (87) 12-8890, also specializes in fajitas, as well as *queso flameado* (Mexican-style cheese fondue); it's open daily noon-midnight. Both restaurants serve acclaimed *carne asada,* norteña-style steak.

Goat *(cabrito)* is also popular in the Nuevo Laredo area. The original source of the northern tradition of naming at least one goat eatery "Principal" in every town is the Cantú-family-owned **Restaurant Principal,** Av. Guerrero 624 (just north of Calle Dr. Mier), tel. (87) 12-1301—look for the skewered *cabritos* roasting *al pastor* in the window. This clean, inexpensive restaurant also serves *pollo asado, carne asada,* and *machitos* (goat-tripe burritos), with *frijoles rancheros* (ranch-style beans) on the side. The Principal is open daily for lunch and dinner. The nearby **Restaurant Bar Nuevo León,** Av. Guerrero 508 (just north of Calle Pino Suárez), tel. (87) 12-1660, is another authentic *norteña* place with *cabrito al pastor,* fajitas, and *machitos.* Open daily 8 a.m.-midnight.

A bit more upscale is **El Rincón del Viejo,** Calle González 4834, tel. (87) 12-2523, near Parque Mendoza. Regional dishes, including *cabrito al pastor,* are served in an inside dining room as well as in a courtyard dining area where tables are arranged along shallow ponds. El Rincón is open for lunch and dinner daily.

El Dorado Bar & Grill (see the special topic), formerly the Cadillac Bar, is a border classic.

National

For tacos of all kinds, Nuevo Laredo's most renowned restaurant is **Restaurant El Rancho,**

Av. Guerrero 2134 (just north of Av. Lincoln), tel. (87) 14-8753, also known as **Su Majestad El Taco** ("His Majesty the Taco"). In addition to a huge selection of tacos, El Rancho specializes in *carnitas, pozole, birria estilo Jalisco* (Jalisco-style stew), *carne asada,* and a wider-than-average selection of Mexican beers. Open daily 11 a.m.-midnight.

México Típico, Av. Guerrero 9 (between Mina and Canales), tel. (87) 12-1525, is the place to go for traditional Mexican atmosphere, mariachis, and an extensive menu of national standards, plus a few regional specialties (such as *carne asada a la tampiqueña,* one of the restaurant's best dishes). Open daily for breakfast (served till midnight), lunch and dinner.

For quick Sinaloa-style barbecued chicken with beans, tortillas, and salsa, stop at **El Pollo Loco,** Av. Guerrero 2454 (just north of Carranza) or Calle Matamoros 702 downtown.

Breakfast
Another regional specialty, *machacado con huevo* (dried beef with eggs) is available at two inexpensive coffee shops on the north side of Plaza Hidalgo. **Cafetería Modelo,** on the northeast corner of Ocampo and Dr. Mier, is the cleaner of the two and offers pastries as well as egg breakfasts. Both *cafeterías* are open for breakfast, lunch, and dinner.

If you plan on making your own breakfast and need to stock up on coffee, search out **Café Bola de Oro,** Calle Matamoros 444 (at Hidalgo), not far from the international bridges. Bola de Oro roasts and grinds several varieties of fresh coffee.

Seafood and International
Mariscos Mandingo, Calle Obregón 1307, tel. (87) 13-1205, bills itself as "a little corner of Veracruz in Nuevo Laredo"—the restaurant specializes in fresh *huachinango* (red snapper) as well as other fish and shellfish from the Gulf.

Popular with border-hopping gringos are two elegant restaurants near the international bridge: **Victoria Restaurant and Bar,** on the northwest corner of Victoria and Matamoros, tel. (87) 12-0895; and **The Winery Pub and Grill,** Calle Matamoros 308 (between Victoria and Belden), tel. (87) 12-8895. Both restaurants serve a variety of continental, American, and Mexican dishes and are open daily 11 a.m.-11 p.m.

ENTERTAINMENT

Racing and Sports Book
Nuevo Laredo Downs, Hipódromo-Galgódromo Nuevo Laredo, tel. (87) 12-3802, Texas tel. (956) 726-0549, is 11 km (seven miles) south of town off Mexico 85 and features greyhound racing Wed.-Fri. and horse racing on weekends. The funky **Nuevo Laredo Turf Club,** Calle Bravo at Ocampo (only a block from the bridge), offers off-track and sports betting on U.S. and Mexican sports events in a bar setting.

Bullfights
The 9,000-seat **Plaza de Toros Lauro Luis Longoria,** 4111 Av. Monterrey (off Mexico 85 just past the Nuevo Laredo airport), presents Sunday bullfights once a month between late February and mid-July. Tickets cost from US$5 (general admission on the sunny side of the ring) to US$20 (first row reserved seats on the shady side). In Nuevo Laredo, you can purchase tickets

matachine *dancers, Nuevo Laredo*

at the Tecolotes de Los Dos Laredos office at Calles Obregón and Gutiérrez, tel. (87) 12-7102, and at Restaurant El Rancho. On the Laredo side they can be purchased at Narvaez Beef Store and Talamas Music Hall. Or you can buy them the day of the *corrida* at the Plaza de Toros; the box office opens at 10 a.m. For scheduling information, contact the Nuevo Laredo state tourist office next to the International Bridge or call the Laredo Convention and Visitors Bureau in Laredo, Texas, tel. (956) 722-9895 or (800) 292-2122 (outside Texas).

Discos

Nuevo Laredo's discos are crowded with bouncing bodies on weekends. **Vivanti's,** tel. (87) 15-3120, opposite the Del Río Motor Hotel, and **Firenze's,** two blocks down from Vivanti's, get a mix of young people from both sides of the border. Also popular with locals and gringos alike is **Freedom,** Degollado at Jalisco, tel. (87) 15-5383. The newest hot spot for college students from Texas is **Señor Frog's,** Ocampo 531, tel. (87) 13-3031. All are open Wed.-Sun. till 2 a.m.

Radio

A Tejano station in Laredo, 92.7 FM, broadcasts a good variety of border music and can be picked up on either side of the border.

SHOPPING

One of Nuevo Laredo's major tourist draws—for Mexicans as well as foreigners—is that it offers the best shopping anywhere along the U.S.-Mexico border. In large part this is due to its position at the head of the Pan-American Highway; all cargo heading north or south passes through Nuevo Laredo, a major convenience for wholesale buyers and sellers.

Tourist-oriented gift shops line the north end of Av. Guerrero near the bridge. Except for liquor and cigarettes (which cost about the same anywhere in town), prices aren't always that good, so it pays to shop around. Overall, the best selection and prices are at the **Nuevo Mercado de la Reforma,** a collection of around 100 shops taking up an entire block on the west side of Av. Guerrero (look for a red sign reading "MERCADO"). The **New Juárez Market,** a small mall at Av.

Guerrero and Calle Bravo with around 10 shops, is also good. Most of the shops in both of these malls accept credit cards. **Pochteca Artesanías,** in New Juárez Market, tel. (87) 12-6990, stocks a good selection of clay vases, pottery, decorative accessories, lamps, and furniture.

For handicrafts alone, your best bet is **Mercado M. Herrera,** a collection of around 50 shops at Calles Ocampo and Hidalgo (1.5 blocks east of Av. Guerrero). The **Centro Artesanal,** Av. Guerrero at M. Herrera a few blocks farther south, also offers arts and crafts for sale.

La Mansión, Av. Guerrero 206, has very good prices on picture frames, whether ready-made or custom. Including glazing and matting, prices run as much as 80% cheaper than in the U.S. or Canada. La Mansión also sells handicrafts, patio furniture, and planters.

Marti's, Calle Victoria 2923 (at Av. Guerrero), is a boutique specializing in custom-designed clothes, high-end furniture, and handicrafts—with boutique prices to match. **Curiosidades Nelly,** Av. Guerrero 2328 and 2610, stocks a large variety of ceramics, including Talavera pottery.

If you're looking for Saltillo tile or the smaller handpainted Mexican tiles and sinks, the best place to shop for them along the entire border is **Marmoles y Materiales Treviño,** Calle Degollado 1452 (nine blocks east of Av. Guerrero on the road that connects with International Bridge 2). Prices here often beat even shops in the interior of Mexico, simply because of the volume business Treviño does.

For custom-made furniture, you can't beat **Luis Median Custom Furniture,** Calle Anahuac 3351; Medina even offers faux crackle finishes to achieve the antique look.

Cem-Pochtecatl, in Mercado Los Arcos at Ocampo and Belden (a block east of Av. Guerrero, opposite El Dorado Bar & Grill), has a few good deals on well-selected baskets, antiques, and furniture. Other good spots for curios nearby on Calle Ocampo include **Casa Mañana, Don Juan Gifts,** and **San Miguel.**

Reyes, on the east side of Av. Guerrero just south of Calle Hidalgo, offers boots, saddles, and other handmade leather goods at decent prices. **La Casa del Café,** Matamoros at Hidalgo, sells whole or fresh-ground coffee beans by the kilo at excellent prices.

INFORMATION AND SERVICES

The **state tourist office,** tel. (87) 12-0104, just to the west of International Bridge No. 1, has a list of Nuevo Laredo hotels and a few informational brochures. On the U.S. side of the border, the **Laredo Convention and Visitor's Bureau,** tel. (956) 722-9895 or (800) 292-2122 (outside Texas), works closely with the Mexican side and can provide information on both Laredos. They have an office in the Laredo Civic Center at 2310 San Bernardo Ave. as well as an information center in El Mercado at Flores and Hidalgo, near Laredo's Hotel La Posada.

Nuevo Laredo's main **post office** is in back of the Palacio Federal, just east of Plaza Hidalgo. The **INEGI office,** Calle Chilapa 2549, Colonia Guerrero, tel. (87) 15-5974, carries topographical maps for Tamaulipas, Coahuila, and Nuevo León. The **American consulate** is at Av. Galeana and Madero (about 12 blocks south of the bridge), tel. (87) 14-0696, after-hours Laredo tel. (956) 763-1315.

TRANSPORTATION

By Air
Mexicana, tel. (87) 12-2211, serves Nuevo Laredo with daily nonstop flights to/from Mexico City and Guadalajara. Taxis between the Laredo airport and Nuevo Laredo run US$6.50 pp.

Bus
The busy Nuevo Laredo bus terminal is at the corner of Calle Anahuac and Av. América, tel. (87) 14-0334. Facilities include left-luggage service and a *cafetería.* Futura buses run between the terminal and the Greyhound bus depot at Matamoros and San Bernardo Ave. in downtown Laredo; fare is US$3. You can also buy through-fares for trips to other cities in the U.S. and Mexico.

Omnibus de México handles first-class buses to/from Saltillo (US$11), Aguascalientes (US$27), and Guadalajara (US$35). **Turistar, Elite,** and **Futura** have first-class and *ejecutivo* buses to/from Ciudad Victoria (US$17-23), San Luis Potosí (US$33), Mexico City (US$40-54), Guadalajara (US$35-47), Monterrey (US$12), and

Zacatecas (US$23). Elite also has first-class departures for Mazatlán (US$42), Durango (US$29), Torreón (US$21), Saltillo (US$11), and Tampico (US$25).

Less expensive second-class buses to towns and cities in Tamaulipas and Nuevo León are operated by **Transportes Frontera, Tamaulipas Noreste,** and **Aguila.**

City Buses: The most useful lines for getting around Nuevo Laredo run north and south along Guerrero, Juárez, and López de Lara between the city bus depot at Matamoros and Belden and the Central Camionera off Av. López Lara.

Taxis: Cabs are abundant but not inexpensive. A taxi from the Central Camionera to Plaza Hidalgo, for example, costs about US$8. A taxi across the bridge between Nuevo Laredo and Laredo (from the northernmost end of Av. Guerrero and Water St.) costs US$5.

Train
Passenger service out of Nuevo Laredo is operated on the Mexico-Monterrey-Nuevo Laredo line (sometimes called the **Aguila Azteca** or "Aztec Eagle"), which reportedly hasn't missed a day of service since the Mexican Revolution. Train No. 2 departs Nuevo Laredo at 6:55 p.m. and makes stops in Monterrey, Saltillo, San Luis Potosí, San Miguel de Allende, and Querétaro before reaching Mexico City at 7 a.m. the next day.

The fare between Nuevo Laredo and San Luis Potosí is US$8 second class, US$14 first; other one-way fares include Monterrey US$2.85/

NUEVO LAREDO TELEPHONE NUMBERS

Police	12-3737
Highway Patrol	14-1284
Red Cross	12-0949
State Tourist Office	12-0104
Club Cruz Ambar (medical emergencies)	12-8954
U.S. Consulate	14-0696
after hours	(512) 763-1315 in the U.S.
Nuevo Laredo Area Code	87

$5, Saltillo US$4/$7, San Miguel de Allende US$9.75/$17.40, and Mexico City US$13/$23.

Advance tickets can be purchased at the FCN railway station at Av. López de Lara and Calle Gutiérrez.

Driving
Traffic in Nuevo Laredo isn't all that bad as long as you avoid the bridge during ordinary commute hours and on Sunday afternoons. There's a convenient parking garage in the same building as The Winery Pub and Grill, at Matamoros and Belden near the bridge. Note that Av. Guerrero merges with Av. Reforma just south of Calle Campeche, about five km (three miles) from the bridge, and Av. Reforma in turn merges with Mexico 85 South.

If you're only using Nuevo Laredo as a Mexico gateway and don't plan to stop over, you can avoid the city altogether by using the relatively new Puente Internacional Solidaridad (Solidarity International Bridge) at Colombia, N.L., 40 km (25 miles) west of both Laredos. From Colombia it's a short drive to Mexico 2 (which leads northwest to Piedras Negras, southeast to Nuevo Laredo) and Nuevo León 1 (south to Lampazos, Bustamante, and Monterrey).

Onward to Monterrey: An 85-km (53-mile), four-lane toll highway from Nuevo Laredo to Monterrey is only nine miles shorter than the old road but shortens the drive from an hour and a half to about an hour. The speed limit is 110 kph (68 mph), one of the highest in Mexico. The toll is also a record-breaker—$11.75 each way.

Mexican Vehicle Insurance: If you don't already have Mexican insurance (highly recommended), you can purchase a temporary auto policy in Laredo, Texas, at **Bravo Insurance,** 2112 Santa Ursula, tel. (956) 722-0931, fax (956) 723-3657.

Border Formalities
The Nuevo Laredo and Colombia crossings are open 24 hours. Bridge tolls run about US$2 in either direction, US$0.35 if you're on foot, (depending on the value of the peso).

THE RIVER HIGHWAY

Known as La Carretera Ribereña or "The River Highway," the 330-km (205-mile) stretch of Mexico 2 that runs parallel to the Río Bravo (Grande) from Nuevo Laredo to Matamoros passes through the most historic section of the state. Early Spanish land grants for farms and ranches along the river plains that eventually became the province (and later the state) of Nuevo Santander, and then the states of Tamaulipas and Texas, have endured through centuries of wars, revolution, and Apache attacks. While the larger border cities of Nuevo Laredo, Reynosa, and Matamoros today reflect a modern, hybridized Mexican-American culture, the smaller towns along the river are proud guardians of their Hispanic heritage.

Straight through, the drive takes around 3.5 hours; count on a half day if you plan to stop along the way. This is a route best chosen by motorists with the time to explore; visitors in a hurry or relying on public transportation will be better off using the faster US 83 on the American side.

GUERRERO VIEJO AND FALCON DAM

The original town of Guerrero was founded in 1750 under the Spanish *empresario* plan. Native son José Bernardo Gutiérrez de Lara (1774-1841) served as the first Tamaulipas state governor and later as the first Mexican ambassador to the United States. The whole town of 4,000 packed up and relocated in 1953 when the Falcon Dam flooded the town with the impounded waters of the Río Bravo.

Many of the original buildings in Guerrero Viejo (Old Guerrero) can be seen when the lake level drops. Guerrero Viejo is 32 km (20 miles) north of Nuevo Guerrero (or 85 km/52.5 miles southeast of Nuevo Laredo)—watch for a small "Guerrero Viejo" sign on the east side of the road at about Km 163, then drive 30 km (18 miles) east on a rocky road through several open gates. What can be seen of the old town, when the lake level permits, are the tops of several sandstone buildings, including the 1750-vintage **Nuestra Señora del Refugio** parish church, the outlines of the plaza and remains of the plaza *kiosco*, cobblestone streets, and the walls of the former Hotel Flores. The plaster from these buildings has washed away to reveal the masterful masonry beneath.

Near Nuevo Guerrero, on the southwest edge of the 87,000-acre lake, is a *parque turístico* with facilities for camping, fishing (black, white, and striped bass; crappie; and catfish), boating, and picnicking (grills, tables, and trash receptacles). Falcon State Park on the U.S. side also has facilities for tent camping (US$6 per night) and RVs (water and electricity, US$9), plus screened shelters (US$15), picnic areas, and a boat launch.

MIER

This quiet town of 6,000 is 19 km (11 miles) farther south along Mexico 2. Founded in 1752 near a low-water crossing known as Paso del Cántaro, Mier's narrow sandstone architecture, narrow cobbled streets, old churches, and plazas haven't changed much since the Nuevo Santander era. On one side of a large shady plaza is **Nuestra Señora de la Purísima Concepción de Mier,** designed by Spanish-German architect Enrique Portcheller in 1798. Using his trademark blend of Spanish and French Creole styles, Portscheller designed many of the larger 18th-century buildings in Roma and Rio Grande City across the border. Near the highway junction is **Capilla San Juan,** a nicely restored chapel built in 1752.

Among Republic of Texas historians, Mier is infamous as the execution site of 17 Texas independence fighters in 1842. Captured by Mexican troops during an unsuccessful raid north of the Río Bravo, 176 Texans were on their way to Mexico City when they made an unsuccessful escape attempt near Salado, Texas. Upon their recapture, they were taken to Mier and forced to draw beans from a pot. The 17 rebels who drew black beans (10% of the band of 176 rebels) were executed on the spot.

Accommodations and Food
Few tourists spend the night here, but simple rooms costing less than US$20 per night are available at **Motel Barrera,** Terán at America, and **Hotel Garza,** Palacios at Morelos. Slightly nicer and pricier is **Motel Asia,** Obregón at Matamoros.

Libations and Mexican food can be taken at **Restaurante La Mansión** or **Restaurante Casa del Sol,** both on Calle Allende.

CIUDAD MIGUEL ALEMÁN

Fifteen km (9.5 miles) southeast of Mier along Mexico 2, Ciudad Miguel Alemán has little to interest the visitor in terms of history or architecture. Its chief draw is that it's on one end of the fastest road route between the border and Monterrey (see "Getting There" in the Monterrey section for more details).

A suspension bridge built in 1927—the only one over the Río Bravo/Rio Grande and a National Historical Landmark in both countries—links the small Mexican town with Roma, Texas (on the opposite side of the river within walking distance). Residents of Roma come to Ciudad Miguel Alemán to eat Mexican food and shop for curios.

On the outskirts of town, off Mexico 2, is **Balneario Santa Lucia,** a rustic resort with thermal baths and pools.

In mid-March the local chamber of commerce hosts a "Winter Texan" fiesta for all the American and Canadian snowbirds who spend their winters across the river in the Rio Grande Valley. Avenida Hidalgo is closed off to vehicular traffic to allow vendors and strolling mariachis to create a festive atmosphere.

Practicalities

Ciudad Miguel Alemán has its own state tourist office on Av. Hidalgo, not far from the bridge. A PEMEX station in town pumps Magna Sin. At Km 1 on Mexico 2 (on the southwestern outskirts of town), **Motel California** has adequate rooms at budget rates (US$15-21 per night).

The Roma-Ciudad Miguel Alemán border crossing is open 24 hours. Mexican vehicle insurance can be purchased at Roma's **Guerra Insurance,** corner of Franklin and US 83, tel. (956) 849-1261.

CAMARGO

Along with Mier, this is another of the more historic towns along Mexico 2. Founded in 1749, Camargo (pop. 7,000) has always been relatively prosperous; during the 19th century, steamboats plied the Río Bravo (Rio Grande) between the town and the river's mouth at the Gulf of Mexico. Today Camargo is a center for farming, ranching, and brickmaking; many brick buildings are found around town, interspersed with older pastel-colored adobe and stucco houses. A local quarry, the source for the molded bricks used in Portscheller buildings throughout the lower Rio Grande corridor, still supplies local brickmasons. Camargo is also the birthplace of Tex-Mex *cumbia* king Fito Olivares, best known for his dance hit "Juana La Cubana."

The oldest section of the tidy downtown near the main plaza (**Plaza Hidalgo**) has charming, narrow streets. Tall Washington palms surround the plaza, where a block of three buildings (including the 18th-century **Palacio Municipal**) to one side have been nicely restored for use as local government offices. On another side of the plaza is **Parroquia de Nuestra Señora de Santa Anna,** a small, single-towered, 18th-century church. The church is the focus of much celebrating each year on 26 July, the town's patron saint day.

On the opposite bank of the river is **Rio Grande City,** Texas, originally founded as the Spanish colony of Carnestolendas in 1768. In 1852, following the end of the Mexican-American War, an army of Mexicans and Texans who were dissatisfied with national governments on both sides convened in Rio Grande City and led an unsuccessful attack on Mexican troops in Ca-

margo in an attempt to establish a "Republic of the Sierra Madre" in Northern Mexico.

Practicalities

Tourists are a rare sight in Camargo but the local citizens are friendly. A shop at one side of the plaza stocks liquors and curios. Should you become hungry while visiting, the clean, a/c **Restaurant Miramar** (a block southwest of the plaza) offers seafood, tacos, and Mexican standards.

Camargo is 24 km (15 miles) southeast of Ciudad Miguel Alemán. Just outside of Camargo on Mexico 2 toward Ciudad Miguel Alemán, a roadside booth collects a US$1 toll even though Mexico 2 doesn't widen or improve in either direction along this stretch!

The Camargo-Rio Grande City border crossing is open weekdays 7:30 a.m.-9 p.m., weekends 8 a.m.-4 p.m.

PRESA MARTE R. GÓMEZ

Also known as Presa del Azúcar ("Sugar Lake"), this impoundment of the Río San Juán is 24 km (15 miles) southwest of Camargo via a paved road. An old favorite with Texan anglers, Gómez still produces a fair number of largemouth bass as well as crappie, dagger, and catfish.

Practicalities

The lake has facilities for fishing, boating, and camping, plus a restaurant that serves Mexican food and freshwater fish under outdoor *palapas*. Simple rooms and cabins with kitchenettes can be rented on the lake at **El Azúcar Motel,** tel. (897) 2-2196 or 2-1703 in Ciudad Miguel Alemán, which also has a restaurant, bar, pool, boat ramp, rental boats, ice, and a few RV spots with full hookups.

Also in the vicinity, but not as well equipped as El Azúcar, are the similarly priced **Motel Loma Vista** and **Motel Ess.** Other camping, fishing, and boating facilities are available nearby.

GUSTAVO DÍAZ ORDAZ

Continuing southeastward 32 km (20 miles) south of Camargo, the next town along Mexico 2 is nondescript Gustavo Díaz Ordaz, a small cot-

Los Ebanos ferry

JOE CUMMINGS

ton- and sorghum-farming center. The town's claim to fame is the unique *chalán* or vehicle ferry, which has made daily runs across the Río Bravo to and from Los Ebanos, Texas, since 1954 and is the only such service anywhere along Mexico's borders.

To use the ferry or to watch it in action, take Av. Hidalgo, the main street into Díaz Ordaz from the highway, then turn right at the sign marked "El Vado Los Ebanos" and follow this street past the plaza (about 2.9 km/1.8 miles from the highway) until it becomes a dirt road. From the plaza it's 2.2 km (1.4 miles) to the ferry crossing. The ferry runs daily 8 a.m.-4 p.m. and costs US$1.50 per auto; only three cars can cross at a time. Pedestrians may ride for US$0.50 pp. There are immigration checks on both sides of the river.

The state government has tentative plans to replace the unique Vado Los Ebanos ferry with a bridge at some point in the future.

Accommodations
The two-star **Motel San Miguel,** Calle Morelos 220, offers adequate shoestring-priced rooms (around US$14 per night).

REYNOSA

This modern, industrial city of 300,000 is the least interesting of the larger border towns in the touristic sense but is an important business destination due to its *maquilas* and huge PEMEX facility.

The second Escandón settlement on the Río Bravo, the city was founded in 1749 as Nuestra Señora de Guadalupe de Reynosa and became an important post for salt trade in early Nuevo Santander. A flood in 1800 destroyed the town and forced the residents to move to the current site (hence the lack of historical sights). Directly across the river is the small town of Hidalgo, Texas, which is about 16 km (10 miles) south of larger McAllen.

Reynosa's main square, market, and cathedral sit atop a small *meseta* or rise, about a kilometer from the bridge via Calle Zaragoza. A traditional iron *kiosco* and antique street lamps enhance **Plaza Hidalgo,** which is bounded by Calles Zaragoza, Juárez, Hidalgo, and Morelos. Between the bridge and the square along Zaragoza and Allende are a string of tourist-oriented shops, *casas de cambio,* restaurants, bars, discos, and hotels. Despite the city's urban veneer, it's not that unusual to see the occasional burro cart downtown.

Museo Histórico de Reynosa, on the northeast corner of Ortega and Allende, contains a few displays chronicling the city's founding and development. Flanking the city are several industrial parks and one of Mexico's largest petrochemical refineries.

Accommodations
Shoestring: Hotel Nuevo León, on Calle Díaz (near Hotel Rey), tel. (892) 2-1310, offers simple but unimpressive rooms. Rates: US$8-14 s/d.

Budget: Among the better downtown choices is the well-located **Hotel Rey,** Calle Díaz between Méndez and Madero, tel. (892) 2-6232, where clean rooms come with a/c and TV. Similar in price and features is **Hotel San Miguel,** tel. (892) 2-2170, on Av. Colón between Mina and Terán.

More upscale accommodations are available at the four-star **Hotel San Carlos de Reynosa,** Calle Hidalgo Nte. 970, tel. (892) 2-1280, where the large a/c rooms have TVs and phones. Rates: US$22-36. Another four-star choice is **Hotel Virrey,** Blvd. Hidalgo (Mexico 40) at P. Balboas, tel. (892) 3-1050, four km (2.5 miles) southwest of the International Bridge. Rooms have all the amenities plus private terraces, and a pool is on the grounds. Rates: US$24 s, US$35 d. Both the San Carlos and the Virrey have their own restaurants.

One of Reynosa's better accommodations deals is **Motel Engrei,** at Km 104 on Mexico 40, tel. (892) 3-1730, seven km (4.3 miles) southwest of the bridge on the outskirts of town. The rooms are well maintained and have a/c, phones, and satellite TVs. On the premises are a pool, tennis court, and restaurant (open daily 7 a.m.-11 p.m.) Rates: US$16-20 s, US$20-25 d.

McAllen, Texas: Across the river in McAllen, hotel and motel rates are the highest in the Rio Grande Valley. The best bargain is in nearby San Juan (west of McAllen proper) at the family-owned, budget/inexpensive **San Juan Hotel,** 125 US 83 Business, tel. (956) 781-5339. The simple rooms are in a restored 1800s' house. Rates: US$22-25 s, US$28-40 d. At the upper end, the place to stay is the **Doubletree Club Hotel (Casas de Palmas),** 100 N. Main, tel. (956) 631-1101 or (800) 274-1102, fax (956) 631-7934, where rooms in a 1918-vintage colonial-style inn rent for moderate rates (US$60-80).

RV Parks

Reynosa has nothing catering to the RV/camper crowd, but Texas's Rio Grande Valley, just across the river, is a national RV headquarters.

From Mission east to Brownsville is a string of over a hundred RV parks. In the McAllen area, you'll find **Ashworth Trailer Park,** Ash and 6th, tel. (956) 686-0221; **Casa de Mobile,** 2022 11th St., tel. (956) 686-1836; **Citrus Valley RV Park,** State 107 and Rooth, tel. (956) 383-8189; **Hand-**ke's **Mobile Park,** Taylor Rd., tel. (956) 686-3076; and **VIP Motel & RV Park,** 3501 US 83, tel. (956) 682-8384. Rates run around US$10-13 per night. Dozens more RV parks are in the nearby communities of San Juan, Mission, Pharr, Alamo, and Penitas—many of these have the lowest rates in the valley. If you're interested in learning more about South Texas and the Rio Grande Valley, read Moon's *Texas Handbook.*

Food

Reynosa bears the distinction of having the largest number of restaurants per capita in the state of Tamaulipas. Many of them are along Calles Zaragoza, Aldama, and Allende in the town's *zona rosa* or tourist district. **Sam's Restaurant & Bar,** Allende at Ocampo, tel. (892) 2-0034, is famous throughout the area for its inexpensive steak dinners, Mexican platters, and border specialties such as quail. The pricey **La Cucaracha,** Aldama at Ocampo, tel. (892) 2-0174, is a border-hopper's favorite for Mexican and continental cuisine.

La Fogata, a large, fancy piano bar/restaurant at the corner of Matamoros and Chapa, features an upstairs outdoor dining area as well as indoor dining downstairs. The menu is heavy on steak and other grilled meats.

Gorditas are a regional specialty, and the place to try them is **Las Gordas de Don Vicente,** Calle Zaragoza Ote. 223, tel. (892) 2-7484. *Cabrito* and *carne asada* are house specialties at **Restaurante El Pastor,** Calle Juárez Nte. 710, tel. (892) 2-4191.

Fried-chicken lovers will find seven branches of **Pollos Frito Buenos Aires** in town: Díaz at Guerrero, Blvd. Hidalgo, Ramírez at Guadalajara, Ramírez at Nayarit, Prol. Paris at G.L. Velarde, Balboa at Río Mante, and Blvd. L. Cárdenas at Paraguay.

Two hotel eateries worth mentioning include the restaurant attached to the **Motel Virrey,** which is popular for *cabrito, carne asada,* and Gulf shrimp; and the **Café San Carlos,** the Hotel San Carlos's bustling coffee shop—good for breakfasts. (See "Accommodations," above, for locations.)

Entertainment

Bullfights: Though Reynosa is not a big town for the *fiesta brava,* the Plaza de Toros Monumental

516 THE STATE OF TAMAULIPAS

off Matamoros and Zapata, about 10 blocks west of the main plaza, hosts occasional *corridas*. Check with the tourist office in town for scheduling.

Bars: Among the several bars in the *zona rosa* catering to gringos, the most classic hangouts are **La Pequeña Holanda** (aka Dutch's), Calle Ocampo Nte. 1020 (look for the windmill out front), and **Mission Bar,** on Morelos facing the plaza. **Treviño's Bar,** in a gift shop of the same name near the International Bridge, usually has mariachis. A classic Mexican cantina worth checking out if you're game is **El Quijote Botanas Bar** at the corner of Allende and Zarzamora.

Near Sam's on Allende, west of Ocampo, is a string of dance clubs popular with young McAllen residents as well as local Reynosenses on weekends: **La Roca, XO Club, Fiesta Mexicana, Alaskan,** and **Lambada.** Around the corner on Ocampo is another dance spot, **Video Bar Disco El Cielo.**

Shopping
The usual vendors and souvenir shops line the tourist streets near the bridge. **Mercado Zaragoza,** a block southwest of Plaza Hidalgo off Calle Hidalgo at Matamoros, is a large market with handicrafts. Other curios shops can be found along a section of Calle Hidalgo blocked off for pedestrians for a block in either direction off Matamoros.

Information and Services
Tourist Offices: SECTUR has an office at Calle Oaxaca 360, Colonia Rodríguez, tel. (892) 2-4660. A state tourist office also is attached to the immigration/customs office at the International Bridge.

Money: The greatest concentration of *casas de cambio* is along Calle Hidalgo near the plaza.

Getting There
Air: Aeroméxico, Av. Guerrero 510 (at Portes Gil), tel. (892) 2-9014, operates daily flights to/from Mexico City. Taxis between downtown Reynosa and the airport, 15 km southeast of city center, cost US$10; a *colectivo* is US$5.

Bus: Reynosa's Terminal de Autobuses is off Calle Colón west of Mina. **Valley Transport Company** (VTC) and **Transportes Monterrey-Cadereyta-Reynosa** buses run between the McAllen and Reynosa terminals for US$3 each way.

Autotransportes Elite, Transportes Frontera, Omnibus de México, Transportes del Norte, and **Transportes Tamaulipas** all offer several buses per day between Reynosa and Monterrey for around US$6 each way.

Transportes Frontera and **Transportes Tamaulipas** offer long-distance buses to cities throughout San Luis Potosí and Tamaulipas, as well as to Mexico City and Querétaro. Service to Zacatecas, Guadalajara, Durango, Chihuahua, and other points west is provided by **Omnibus de México** and **Transportes del Norte.**

Train: El Tamaulipeco runs between Reynosa and Monterrey for US$4.70 first class; there is no longer second-class service along this route.

Driving: The traffic in Reynosa can be thick during commute hours (early morning, midafternoon, early evening), especially at the junction of Mexico 2 and Mexico 40. The city has an extensive system of one-way streets, and not all of them are marked, so take special care when driving.

For **Green Angels** assistance, call (892) 2-1119.

If you're heading toward Reynosa from the U.S. and need Mexican vehicle insurance, one of the oldest and most reliable agencies along the entire border is **Sanborn's Mexican Insurance,** 2009 S. 10th in McAllen, tel. (956) 686-0711, fax (956) 686-0732. In Hidalgo you can also arrange a Sanborn's insurance policy at **Patty's Insurance,** 309 S. Bridge, tel. (133) 843-2863.

Border Formalities: The Reynosa bridge crossing is open 24 hours.

Getting Around
City Bus: Buses and *colectivos* link all sections of the city; most have their destinations prominently displayed on a marquis over (or whitewashed onto) the windshield. Fares are US$0.12-0.24.

Taxi: Cabs are plentiful in the Plaza Hidalgo area, near the International Bridge, and at upscale hotels. Count on around US$2 for a downtown hop, US$5 between the bridge and the junction of Mexico 2 and Mexico 40.

Auto Rental: Underscoring the city's importance as a business destination, Reynosa has more car rental agencies than any other city

AUTO RENTAL AGENCIES IN REYNOSA

Avis
Hidalgo Nte. 370, Centro
tel. (892) 2-1237 or (800) 7-0643
Blvd. Morelos 1230, Col. Rodríguez
Aeropuerto Internacional Lucio Blanco
tel. (892) 2-1237

Hertz
Km 103, Mexico 2, Col. El Anhelo
tel. (892) 3-9933
Aeropuerto Internacional Lucio Blanco
tel. (892) 3-0040

Dollar
Juárez Nte. 1050
tel. (892) 3-0020
Aeropuerto Internacional Lucio Blanco
tel. (892) 2-3330

Budget
Blvd. Morelos 275
tel. (892) 2-5693
Aeropuerto Internacional Lucio Blanco
tel. (892) 3-0196

along the border. See the accompanying "Auto Rental Agencies in Reynosa" list.

BETWEEN REYNOSA AND MATAMOROS

East of Reynosa, Mexico 2 veers away from the Río Bravo (Rio Grande) and passes through the farming centers of Río Bravo and Ramírez before returning to the river at Matamoros. The rich alluvial soils of the Río Bravo plains were virtually ignored until the turn of the century, when river levees and underground irrigation systems were developed. Before that, periodic floods made farming along the river a risky proposition. Also, although the soils were intrinsically rich, the naturally high evaporation rate made it almost impossible to farm the flood plains without irrigation. As a result of controlled watering and mild year-round temperatures, the area now enjoys a 330-day growing season and is an important truck-farming center.

The spread-out town of **Río Bravo,** 16 km (10 miles) southeast of Reynosa, has several small hotels, including the shoestring **Hotel Río,** Madero 709; the budget **Hotel Papagallo,** Calle 5 de Febrero Sur 105; and the inexpensive **Hotel La Mansión,** Madero at Galeana, and **Hotel Posada San José,** Calle 5 de Mayo 203. Restaurants, including several fast-food places, are abundant along the town's main avenues.

A gravel road north off Mexico 2, 32 km (20 miles) east of Reynosa, leads north 13 km (eight miles) to the tiny community of **Nuevo Progreso,** opposite Progreso, Texas. The latter is linked to US 83 by paved road. On the Mexican side, **Restaurant Arturo's** is a favorite border hop for quail and other game platters. The bridge at this crossing is open weekdays 7:30 a.m.-9 p.m., weekends 8 a.m.-4 p.m.

MATAMOROS

History

Founded under the Escandón *empresario* plan as San Juan de los Esteros Hermosos in 1765, Matamoros was originally a cattle ranching colony. In 1820, the port of Bagdad was established at the nearby mouth of the Río Bravo (Grande) and the town quickly became a regional trade center. Renamed Matamoros in 1826 in commemoration of Mexican independence hero Mariano Matamoros, it's one of only four cities in Mexico whose names are preceded by the honorific "H," which stands for the English equivalent of "Heroic, Loyal, and Unconquered" (hence Mexican traffic signs in the area read "H. Matamoros").

Following the annexation of Texas, the U.S. government established Fort Taylor on the Texas side of the river in 1846, thus sparking the Mexican-American War. After Mexican troops attacked the post and killed its commander, Maj. Jacob Brown, it was renamed Fort Brown. Several other battles in this brief war were fought in the area, until Mexico surrendered its border claim a few months after the establishment of the fort. In Matamoros, Mexican troops quartered themselves at Casa Mata; Matamoros was briefly occupied before war's end in 1848. Both Gen. Zachary Taylor and Gen. Mariano Arista were heroes at battles fought at Brownsville;

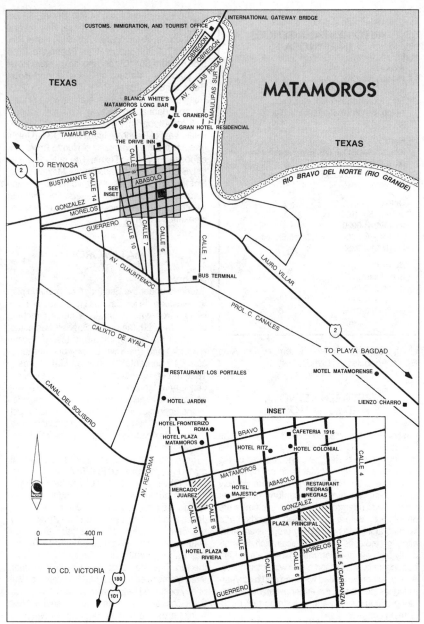

INTERNATIONAL GATEWAY BRIDGE

CUSTOMS, IMMIGRATION, AND TOURIST OFFICE

OBREGON
OBREGON

AV. DE LAS ROSAS

TAMAULIPAS SUR

TEXAS

MATAMOROS

BLANCA WHITE'S
MATAMOROS LONG BAR

NORTE

EL GRANERO
GRAN HOTEL RESIDENCIAL

TEXAS

TAMAULIPAS

THE DRIVE INN

CALLE 8

TO REYNOSA

2

BUSTAMANTE

CALLE 14

ABASOLO

SEE
INSET

GONZALEZ

MORELOS

RIO BRAVO DEL NORTE (RIO GRANDE)

GUERRERO

CALLE 10

CALLE 7

CALLE 6

CALLE 1

AV. CUAUHTEMOC

LAURO VILLAR

BUS TERMINAL

CALIXTO DE AYALA

PROL. C. CANALES

2

TO PLAYA BAGDAD

CANAL DEL SOLISERO

RESTAURANT LOS PORTALES

MOTEL MATAMORENSE

HOTEL JARDIN

LIENZO CHARRO

0   400 m

MOON

AV. REFORMA

INSET

HOTEL FRONTERIZO
ROMA

HOTEL PLAZA
MATAMOROS

BRAVO

CAFETERIA 1916

HOTEL RITZ

HOTEL COLONIAL

MATAMOROS

ABASOLO

CALLE 4

MERCADO
JUAREZ

HOTEL
MAJESTIC

RESTAURANT
PIEDRAS
NEGRAS

CALLE 10

CALLE 9

GONZALEZ

PLAZA PRINCIPAL

TO CD. VICTORIA

HOTEL PLAZA
RIVIERA

CALLE 8

CALLE 7

CALLE 6

MORELOS

CALLE 5 (CARRANZA)

180

101

GUERRERO

© MOON PUBLICATIONS, INC.

LOWER RÍO BRAVO CORRIDOR

The U.S.-Mexico borderlands contain some of the richest and most diverse natural environments in either country. With more species per square kilometer than anywhere in the United States, the lower Río Bravo (Rio Grande) corridor in particular represents a fortuitous cross section of Gulf coastal plains, Río Bravo river delta, and Tamaulipan inland plains—a unique blend of humid, subtropical conditions and brush country.

Ten biotic communities have been identified in the area: Tamaulipan thorn forest, upper valley flood forest, *barretal,* upland thornscrub *(matorral),* mid-delta thorn forest, mid-valley riparian woodland, woodland potholes and basins, coastal brushland potholes, sabal palm forest, and *loma* (coastal clay) tidal flats.

These habitats together support over 115 unique vertebrate species, including four of the six remaining wildcat species in the U.S. and Mexico—the cougar, bobcat, and the endangered **ocelot** and **jaguarundi.** Fifty years ago the Río Bravo plains were also home to the jaguar and the margay cat, but these may have since disappeared from the area. These habitats also provide important nesting and migratory grounds for around 400 bird species, since this is where two North American migratory paths—the Central and Mississippi flyways—converge.

both generals went on to become presidents in their respective countries.

The city prospered during the American Civil War by supplying Confederate troops in Texas via the port of Bagdad, thus avoiding the Union stockade along the Texas Gulf coast. Bagdad didn't last because of the almost continuous onslaught of hurricanes, bandits, and pirates. In 1904 the St. Louis, Brownsville, and Mexico railway was routed to Brownsville, thus reestablishing Matamoros's importance as a commercial center.

Matamoros Today

The area now supports over 80 *maquiladoras,* and a Union Pacific rail terminus has replaced the old St. Louis, Brownsville, and Mexico line. The Gateway International Bridge joins Brownsville

and Matamoros (pop. 363,000) and leads to the clean and well-lit Av. Alvaro Obregón, which is lined with bars, restaurants, and souvenir shops. To get a feel for nontourist Matamoros, walk a few blocks down Obregón and make a left at Calle 5 (Carranza) or 6, which lead to the **Plaza Principal,** the main public square. Day or night, this is the city's downtown heart.

Museo Casa Mata

Built in 1845 to defend Mexico from invading U.S. soldiers, this former military quarters contains exhibits of local historical artifacts, Huasteca ceramics, and weapons from the Mexican Revolution era. It's at the corner of Guatemala and Santos Degollado (take Calle 1 south to Santos Degollado and make a left). Open Tues.-Sun. 9:30 a.m.-5:30 p.m.; admission free.

Accommodations

Shoestring: Rock bottom rates are offered at **Hotel Colonial,** Calle 6 at Matamoros, tel. (88) 16-6418, an older hotel with atmosphere and street noise; no parking lot. Rates: US$5 s, US$6 d. Several of the city's cheaper, one-star hotels are found along Calle Abasolo downtown, including **Hotel Majestic,** Abasolo at Calle 9, tel. (88) 13-3680, **Hotel El Rey,** Abasolo at Calle 14, tel. (88) 12-0144, and **Hotel Mexico-Frontera Norte,** Abasolo at Calle 9, tel. (88) 12-0856. These have basic rooms (no a/c) with private baths, but little besides price to recommend them. Rates: US$6.50-12.

Quieter, less central, and about the same price is the string of budget motels along Av. Lauro Villar (Mexico 2), the road southeast toward Playa Bagdad. Two of the better choices on this avenue are the **Fontana Motel** at Km 3, tel. (88) 16-4123, and **Motel Matamorense,** Av. Lauro Villar at Voz de la Frontera, tel. (88) 13-3095. Both motels have a/c and parking lots. Rates: US$12-16.

Budget: Hotel Ritz, Calle 7 at Matamoros, tel. (88) 12-1190, fax (88) 13-0279, is a classic border hotel with a fountain lobby and 90 large rooms with a/c, heat, TV, phone, and fax service. A restaurant and parking lot are attached. Rates: US$26-35. If the Ritz is full, three-story **Hotel Fronterizo Roma,** nearby at Calle 9 and Bravo, tel. (88) 16-0573, has similar rates and amenities but doesn't have quite the charm. Yet another in the same class is **Hotel Plaza Riviera,** Calle 10 at Morelos downtown (two blocks from Mercado Juárez), tel. (88) 16-3998.

Out on Av. Lauro Villar at Fco. Villa, **Hotel Road Runner,** tel. (88) 13-2613, has rooms with a/c, cable TV, and phones. The Road Runner also has a pool, restaurant, and parking lot. Rates: US$19-32.

Inexpensive: The efficient **Hotel Jardín,** Calle 6 at Bilbao, tel. (88) 17-0737, fax (88) 17-0722, toward the south end of town and Mexico 180, has very good rooms with a/c, heat, satellite TV, phones, and refrigerators. The hotel also has a restaurant and room service. Rates: US$44-46. Four-story **Hotel Plaza Matamoros,** Calle 9 at Bravo, tel. (89) 16-1696, is across the street from Hotel Fronterizo Roma and features a nice marble lobby and comfortable rooms with TV, phone, a/c, heat, and fridge. A restaurant is attached. Rates: US$40 s, US$47 d, US$51 t.

Inexpensive/Moderate: Top of the heap is the **Gran Hotel Residencial Matamoros** (formerly the Del Prado), on the east side of Calle 5 near El Granero, tel. (88) 13-9440 or 13-9492. Conveniently located within walking distance of several of the city's best restaurants, this colonial-style hotel has a spacious lobby with a dramatic entrance and modern rooms catering to visiting business executives, plus a pool amid landscaped grounds. Rates: US$50-59.

Camping: Self-contained campers and tenters will find plenty of space on the beach in the vicinity of Playa Bagdad, 38 km (23.5 miles) east of town via Mexico 2 (see "Recreation," below). An official camping area with showers and toilet (bring your own toilet paper) costs US$1.30 per vehicle.

Accommodations In Brownsville, Texas
Budget: On the U.S. side, one of the least expensive places is **Motel 6,** off US 77/83 at the FM 802 exit, tel. (956) 546-4699. Rates: around US$30 s. Just a bit more expensive is the nearby **Best Western Rose Garden Inn,** 845 US 77/83 N, tel. (956) 546-5501. Rates: US$35-45.

A couple dozen apartment complexes in Brownsville take winter Texans for a few weeks or months at a time (rates are much lower than at the hotels). The **Brownsville Tourist Information Center,** US 77/83 at FM 802, tel. (956) 541-8455, maintains a list of these and can assist with reservations.

RV Parks: Like the rest of Texas's Rio Grande Valley, Brownsville is well equipped for RV and mobile-home drivers. Most of the RV parks are scattered throughout an area east of town, off Boca Chica Blvd. and Minnesota Ave. (FM 313). Several reputable parks that belong to the Brownsville Recreational Vehicle and Mobile Home Association (which represents approximately 1,900 RV spaces) include: Autumn Acres Trailer Park, 5034 Boca Chica, tel. (956) 546-4979; Citrus Gardens Trailer Park, 2225 S. Dakota, tel. (956) 546-0527; Crooked Tree Campland, 605 FM 802, tel. (956) 546-9617; Four Seasons RV & MH Park, 6900 Coffee Port, tel. (965) 831-4918; Los Amigos Trailer Park, 3350 Boca Chica, tel. (956) 542-8292; Paul's RV Park, 1129 N. Minnesota, tel. (956) 831-4852; Río RV & MH Park, 8801 Boca Chica, tel. (956) 831-4653; Stagecoach RV Park, 325 FM 802, tel. (956) 542-8488; Tip-O-Tex, 6676 N. Frontage, tel. (956) 350-4031; and Trailer Village, 5107 Boca Chica, tel. (956) 546-8350. Rates tend to be a uniform $10-12 nightly, $100 monthly, $200-225 for three months, $450 for six months.

Food
As in Nuevo Laredo, *cabrito* and *carne asada* are specialties here. Matamoros also prides itself on serving the best tacos along the border. Along Calle 5 are several inexpensive outdoor taco places popular with locals.

One of the nicer taco huts is **El Granero,** just south of Blanca White's Matamoros Long Bar on Av. Obregón near the intersection of Calle Gardenias. In a diminutive, a/c building, El Granero's kitchen turns out over a dozen kinds of moderately priced tacos (among the best are smoked chicken, *rajas poblanas,* and *carne asada*), all served with *frijoles a la charra* and three kinds of salsas in a very clean, low-key atmosphere. El Granero is open Tues.-Sun. 11 a.m.-10 p.m.

Blanca White's Matamoros Long Bar, Av. Obregón 49 (just north of El Granero at Gardenias), tel. (88) 12-1859, is another outpost in the ubiquitous Grupo Anderson chain. As usual, the menu features dishes inspired by local recipes but turned out with an original flair. Unlike the typically rowdy Anderson restaurants found at Mexican beach resorts, Blanca White's has both good food and a fairly restrained ambience. It's open daily noon-midnight.

Nearby at Calle Obregón and Las Rosas is the airy, fern-style **Oscar's Café,** with a broad selection of Mexican, American, and continental dishes. Oscar's is open daily for breakfast, lunch, and dinner. The clientele is a mix of border-hoppers and businesspeople.

Dark and velvet-lined, **The Drive Inn,** Calle 6 at Hidalgo, tel. (88) 12-0022, has been a border institution since 1916. Steak, seafood, continental and Mexican choices are well represented on the menu; some border aficionados swear by the place while others abhor it.

Restaurant Frontera, Bravo at Matamoros, tel. (89) 13-2440, serves inexpensive *antojitos* and juicy fajitas. **Gambrinos Restaurant,** a half block down on Matamoros is similarly good.

Moderately priced **Restaurant Piedras Negras,** across the street from the Teatro de la Reforma on Calle 6 between Abasolo and González (near Plaza Principal), comes highly recommended locally for steak, *carne asada,* and huge Mexican breakfasts.

Out toward the Hotel Jardín on the east side of Calle 6 at Calle J.S. El Cano, the straightforward **Restaurant Los Portales,** tel. (88) 12-3338, specializes in *cabrito* and *carne asada,* served with *frijoles rancheros,* for lunch and dinner daily.

Breakfasts: For hearty *desayunos* and *almuerzos,* Matamoros has several downtown coffee shops worth trying. One of the more popular ones—day or night—is the **Cafetería 1916,** Calle 6 at Matamoros, near the Hotel Colonial; the menu covers just about all the standards. Farther north on Calle 6 at Galeana is the equally popular **Cafetería El Faro.** Several other *cafeterías* are located in the vicinity along Calles 6 and 7.

For something different, scan the local markets for *micharro,* the sweet, gelatin-like kernels of the sabal texana or sabal palm—a delicacy that's becoming increasingly difficult to find.

Entertainment

Bullfights and *Charreadas:* Matamoros has a Plaza de Toros at the southern outskirts of town off Av. Reforma. Local *charro* associations practice and compete at the **Lienzo Charro La Costeña,** also south of town on the highway. Check with the Matamoros tourist office at the International Bridge or with the Brownsville Convention and Visitors Bureau in Brownsville, Texas, for scheduling information. Bullfight season generally runs May-Sept., while *charreadas* are held year-round.

Theater: The city's historic **Teatro de la Reforma,** built in 1864 and recently restored to all its original glory (and then some), hosts ballet, live theater, and other highbrow entertainment. The theater is on the east side of Calle 6 between Abasolo and González, near Plaza Principal.

Bars: Matamoros's main restaurant and bar area, or *zona rosa,* extends southeast from the bridge to the main plaza at Calle 5 (Carranza) and González. **Blanca White's Matamoros Long Bar** (see "Food" in this section) is well stocked and well serviced, a very reliable choice, if a bit pricey by Mexican standards. The clientele is a mix of well-heeled locals and gringos. On the same street, the more local **Garcia's,** Av. Obregón 2, tel. (88) 13-1566, features live Latin music most nights.

The lobby bar and disco at **Gran Hotel Residencial** are popular on weekends, as is **Gerry's Sports Bar** at the Hotel Ritz.

Festivals: One of the oldest and biggest events of the year, **Días de los Charros** ("Charro Days" in Brownsville) is a cross-border celebration involving both Brownsville, Texas, and Matamoros. A local version of the pre-Lenten festival (à la Carnaval and Mardi Gras), it's held for three days in late February at various venues in each city and features parades, costume balls, food, music, and dancing.

Diez y Seis or Mexican Independence Day (16 Sept.) is also big in both cities; on the weekend nearest the 16th they cooperate for **Fiesta Internacional,** a bicultural weekend of fireworks, parades, and *mucho* celebration. For scheduling details on either event, contact the Brownsville Chamber of Commerce, U.S. tel. (956) 542-4341.

Día de Nuestra Señora del Refugio, the city's patron saint day (4 July), is confined to the Mexican side and features a pageant of *matachine* and other folk dances.

Radio: For some great border radio, tune in 96.1 FM (KIWW), a Tejano station received on both sides of the river. Bilingual DJs play a hot mix of Tex-Mex, *norteña,* and Tejano pop.

Shopping

Though not as popular a shopping venue as Nuevo Laredo, Matamoros sees many Texans looking for quick south-of-the-border bargains. The shops along Av. Obregón are not the cheapest, since they cater to day tourists who don't venture very far into town, but some of their folk art is decent. **Bárbara de Matamoros,** 40 Av. Obregón, is one of the better shops along the main tourist drag.

Two large markets in town carry a wide selection of Mexican arts and crafts and are more susceptible to negotiation. **Mercado Juárez,** stretching across Abasolo and Matamoros between Calles 9 and 10 (about three blocks east of the plaza), is the biggest; a smaller version is on Bravo between Calles 8 and 9. Friendly Johnny Garza at **Jhonny's Place,** on Calle 8 between Bravo and Bustamante, tel. (88) 12-4110, has one of the better selections of curios in town. Inexpensive Mexican furniture can be found at **Mueblería José Gutiérrez,** on Calle Herrera between Calles 8 and 9 (no phone). For good-quality, well-priced wrought iron, **Fabricaciones Metálicas Ríos** on Calle 6 Sur, tel. (88) 17-4644, is the place to go.

Liquor is much cheaper in Matamoros than on the U.S. side, typically 50% lower. It's also duty-free, as long as you don't bring back more than a quart within a 30-day period.

Playa Bagdad

Formerly known as "Playa Lauro Villar," this Gulf of Mexico beach 38 km (23.5 miles) east of Matamoros stretches north some 16 km to the mouth of the Río Bravo near the abandoned port of Bagdad. This is one of the most pleasant coastal recreation areas along the Gulf, and only a small portion of it has been developed. *Palapas* (US$1.30 per day) extend for a couple of hundred meters north and south of the road's end, with a modest seafood restaurant at the north end. Freshwater showers are available, as is a first-aid clinic and parking lot (also US$1.30 all day).

Windsurfing is tops all along the Gulf shore and, except in storm conditions, the beach is suitable for swimming. Camping is permitted north or south of the public area.

Surf casting is fair anywhere along the beach, and anglers also have the option of fishing in an inland lagoon. The best saltwater fishing in the area is 22 km (13.6 miles) south via the sandy coastal flats at the *escolleras* (jetties), beyond the fishing village of Conchillal (eight km/five

miles south). This is also where the best surfing action is.

Getting There: The highway to the beach from Matamoros is in fairly good condition all the way. If you don't have your own vehicle, you can catch one of the blue-and-white *colectivos* that run from Plaza Allende (Plaza Principal) downtown all the way to Playa Bagdad three or four times daily.

Information

The **state tourist office,** at Puerta México (the customs-immigration building next to the International Bridge), tel. (88) 12-3630, distributes brochures, maps, and information on local sights and activities. A limited amount of information on Matamoros can also be obtained at the **Brownsville Information Center,** at the junction of FM 802 and US 77/83, tel. (956) 596-3721 or (800) 626-2639 outside Texas. It's open Mon.-Fri. 8:30 a.m.-5 p.m., Saturday 8 a.m.-5 p.m., Sunday 9 a.m.-4 p.m. The **U.S. Consulate** is at Calle 1 #232, tel. (89) 16-7271, after-hours tel. (956) 638-7027 in Brownsville.

Getting There

Air: Aeroméxico, Av. Obregón 21, tel. (88) 13-0701, has daily nonstop flights to/from Guadalajara and Mexico City. The airport is 12 km (7.5 miles) south of town off Mexico 180; taxis cost US$9, *colectivos* are US$3.50, and buses from the Central de Autobuses are US$0.24.

Bus: The city's Central de Autobuses is off Calle Canales between Calle Aguilar (Calle 2) and Calle 1. The main regional bus lines are **Línea**

MATAMOROS TELEPHONE NUMBERS	
Police	16-0700
Highway Patrol	17-0134
Green Angels	12-3630
State Tourist Office	12-3630
Cruz Roja (medical emergencies)	12-0044, 16-6562
U.S. Consulate	16-7270, 16-7271
after hours . . . (512) 638-7027 in the U.S.	
Matamoros Area Code	89

AUTO RENTAL AGENCIES IN MATAMOROS

Budget
Av. A. Obregón 33-A (and airport)
tel. (89) 13-4880

Dollar
Av. A. Obregón 10
tel. (89) 12-3854

Reyes Rent a Car
Gran Hotel Residencial
tel. (89) 12-2553

Azul, Oriente, Noreste, and **Transportes Frontera,** which serve cities and towns throughout the states of Tamaulipas, Nuevo León and San Luis Potosí.

Futura and **Transportes del Norte** have daily *ejecutivo* buses to Monterrey for US$10-13 each way. Transportes del Norte also operates first-class buses to Tampico for US$12.

Buses to Matamoros from Brownsville leave frequently throughout the day from the **Greyhound/Valley Transit Co. (VTC)** station at 1305 E. Adams, tel. (956) 546-2264. The fare is US$3.

Train: El Tamaulipeco takes 6.5 hours to complete its daily run between Monterrey and Matamoros, with a stop in Reynosa. Reserved first-class fares for the journey (available Sat.-Mon.) are US$2 Matamoros-Reynosa, US$4.50 Reynosa-Monterrey, US$6.50 Matamoros-Monterrey.

Driving: Matamoros is one of the easier border cities to drive through because of its wide, well-planned avenues, which link the border crossing directly with Mexico 2 and Mexico 180.

To reach Mexico 2 east (to Playa Bagdad) from the International Bridge, follow Av. Obregón south and bear left onto Calle 2 (Blvd. Lauro Villar) at the sign marked "A Playa Bagdad." Blvd. Lauro Villar becomes Mexico 2 within a couple of kilometers.

For Mexico 180 south (to La Pesca and Tampico), stay on Av. Obregón until it merges with Calle 6, which becomes Av. Reforma south of Calle Canales; Av. Reforma eventually turns into Mexico 180.

The Matamoros bridge border crossing is open 24 hours.

SOUTH OF MATAMOROS

The 504-km (312-mile) coastal route between the Texas border and the Gulf port of Tampico is scenic and lightly trafficked. Mexico 101 leads southeast from Matamoros through San Fernando, then links with Mexico 180, which zigzags farther south via Aldama to Tampico. Along the way several roads branch east off Mexico 101 and Mexico 180 to the vast Laguna Madre and Gulf of Mexico shores, where you'll find mile after mile of undisturbed *loma* tidal flats, saltmarshes, and sandy beaches.

Although there has long been talk of developing a modern megaresort somewhere along this stretch, so far the entire coast has been blissfully neglected by mass tourism. Birding, beaching, windsurfing, surfing, and fishing are superb in many spots but are best enjoyed by self-contained visitors who travel with their own shelter and supplies. The only hotels north of Tampico are in La Pesca, San Fernando, Aldama, and Barra del Tordo. The typical *laguna* branch road terminates at a local fish camp, not always the most attractive of places but a source for minimal supplies.

AROUND LAGUNA MADRE

Playa El Mezquital

This broad beach area on a long barrier peninsula wedged between the Gulf of Mexico and vast Laguna Madre has many similarities to Padre Island National Seashore along the Texas coast except that it's even more remote from human intervention. Although there are no facilities to speak of, access to both Gulf and Laguna Madre beachcombing, fishing, and camping is superb for well-equipped visitors.

The turnoff for El Mezquital is 21 km (13 miles) south of Matamoros off Mexico 180, after which it's another 57 km (35 miles) on a paved surface to the coast. The scenic road bridges the

Río El Tigre (the first of two Río Tigres along the coast) and the north end of the Laguna Madre. Vehicles equipped for sand-flats driving can continue south some 60 km (37 miles) or more along the peninsula.

Other names for this barrier peninsula include "Punta La Capilla" and "Barra San José."

Isla Las Malvinas

Largest of the seven inhabited islands in Laguna Madre, Isla Las Malvinas (pop. 237) measures approximately one kilometer from northeast to southwest and about 350 meters across. Fishing is the island's main livelihood and most households are concentrated along the calmer western shore in the villages of **Las Malvinas,** at the north, and **Puntilla Norte,** at the south. The island has no roads to speak of and no electric power.

The only way to reach Las Malvinas is by boat—launch your own or charter locally in El Mezquital. Basic supplies are available on the island, which would make a good base for exploring other bay islands and fishing the productive Boca Madre cut. This is also an excellent place to test the effectiveness of your mosquito repellent.

San Fernando (Fernando de Presas)

This small town on Mexico 180, where the highway crosses the Río San Fernando, is a popular restaurant and fuel stop for long-distance motorists. It's also a staging point for excursions to the Laguna Madre beaches of El Barrancón, Carbonera, and Carvajal, and for hunting trips in the *matorral* surrounding the Río Conchos. In the center of town near the plaza are several buildings that date to the mid-19th century, including the **Palacio Municipal, Mercado Hidalgo,** and stone **Iglesia de San Fernando.** The latter is very much in the style of the San Antonio missions in South Texas.

Accommodations: Several budget-priced motels along or near the highway offer basic but comfortable lodgings. One of the better choices in town is **Motel La Serena,** Calle Zapata, tel. (894) 4-02-65, which offers clean a/c rooms and a swimming pool. Rates: US$16-22. **Motel La Hacienda,** at the north end of town at Km 174, tel. (894) 4-0499, has similar facilities for around US$5 less. Clustered in this same area along

the highway are **Hotel San José,** Km 173, tel. (894) 4-1729, **Hotel Las Palomas,** Km 178, tel. (894) 4-0485, and **Hotel Paso Real,** Km 172, tel. (894) 4-1036, all in the US$15-22 range.

RV Park: Attached to the Motel La Serena is **La Serena RV Park,** with full hookups for US$11 per night.

Food: Of the several highway eateries, only **El Granero Grill** is open 24 hours. Other highway spots include **Pollo Frito Buenos Aires, El Esfuerzo, Davila,** and **Boca de Catán.**

Hunting Resorts: El Tejón, outside San Fernando off Mexico 180, hosts hunters shooting for white-winged dove, quail, duck, and goose along the Río Conchos. Facilities include landscaped grounds, a restaurant, pool, and tackle shop. Farther southwest near the village of Criullas (39 km/24 miles south on Mexico 180, then west about 25 km/15.5 miles), **La Loma** specializes in quail and white-winged dove. For information on either resort, contact Sunbelt Hunting & Fishing, P.O. Box 3009, Brownsville, TX 78520, tel. (800) 876-4868.

East of town 40 km (25 miles) on Lago La Nacha, a natural lake fed by the Río Conchos, is the **Laguna Vista,** a hunting and fishing resort with a/c rooms, restaurant, and pool. For further information contact Laguna Vista, P.O. Box 44, Combes, TX 78535, tel. (956) 421-4401 or (800) 274-4401.

Playa El Barrancón and Playa Carbonera

Almost any road heading east from Mexico 180 between Matamoros and San Fernando leads to the Laguna Madre western shore. Most are unpaved and lead to saltmarshes—great sites for birding.

Along this shore, intrepid beachgoers and sportfishers can ferret out at least two sandy beaches, both of which are suitable for camping and lagoon fishing. **Carbonera** is the most accessible; a paved road leads east from the town of San Fernando all the way to the lagoon shore, a distance of about 52 km (32 miles). From Carbonera an unpaved road continues south to **Playa Carvajal,** a beach at the tip of Punta Barranco Amarillo where the estuarial Laguna El Catán branches west off the Laguna Madre. Both beaches have *palapas,* picnic tables, cooking grills, and trash receptacles; Carbonera also has an area set aside for camping.

To find **El Barrancón** you must make an eastward turn off Mexico 180 about 18 km (11 miles) north of the Mexico 180/Mexico 97 junction, just three km south of the small town of Alfredo V. Bonfil. The first road is paved as far as Santa Rita (about 23 km/14 miles), after which it forks into two dirt roads. Take the left fork for El Barrancón. Beach facilities include *palapas,* grills, tables, and trash bins; camping is permitted.

SOTO LA MARINA AND LA PESCA

La Pesca ("Fish") is the name generally given to an area at the mouth of the Río Soto la Marina, where river and sea meet to form a network of estuarial lagoons. Starting with the southernmost extension of the Laguna Madre, named *lagunas* include La Sal, Almagre, Tulosa, Santa Rita, Contadero, Chovenosa, and Morales. These lagoons, along with the Gulf and the wide Río Soto la Marina itself, offer a seemingly endless variety of venues for fishing, boating, birding, and simple enjoyment of the estuarial environment.

For years there has been talk of establishing a government-funded, Cancún-style resort here, but for now the area safely remains a sleepy backwater with a bit of seasonal fishing and small-scale tourism. Perhaps the area's saving grace is that, though beautiful in its own right, the Gulf tidal flats don't fit the palm-fringed, crystal-sands image required to compete with Mexico's Pacific or Caribbean coastal resorts. A more realistic objective would be the condotel-style development found at South Padre Island along Texas's south coast, though many frequent visitors would rather see La Pesca preserved the way it is today.

The small town of La Pesca, a jumble of unfinished or decaying breeze-block architecture near the end of the 54-km (34-mile) paved road from Soto la Marina, is the least attractive aspect of the area. Visitors normally stay in vacation homes or small resorts along the estuary, or else they camp on the beach well away from town. The beach at the end of the road has *palapas,* wooden shelters, trash receptacles, and a breakwater jetty. Another road continues north behind the dunes for a couple of kilometers before giving way to hard-packed sand.

Soto la Marina is the main supply center for La Pesca visitors and residents. One of the original Escandón settlements dating to the mid-18th century, the town's main historical claim is that it hosted northeastern Mexico's first printing press, installed and operated by Bostonian J. Samuel Bangs in 1816.

Geography and Wildlife
Typified by barrier islands, barrier peninsulas (or *barras*), and coastal lagoons, the topography surrounding La Pesca is similar to that found all the way along the Gulf coast from Galveston Island, Texas, to Tampico. The major differences are that the Mexican portion is much less developed and the average temperatures significantly milder, thus allowing for a greater variety of flora and fauna to flourish.

Barra Soto la Marina: Extending northward from La Pesca nearly 200 km (124 miles), this thin wedge of sand and tidal clay separates the Gulf of Mexico from the Laguna Madre. The entire length of the Gulf side is sandy beach—one of the longest on the North American continent. The beach is backed by a coastal dune ridge, which is held in place by salt-tolerant vegetation such as sand verbena and red or black mangrove. On the lagoon side of the dunes are coastal grasslands and saltmarshes of varying width; in some places the dunes extend all the way across the *barra,* while in others the land behind the dune ridge is submerged by wash-over channels.

Laguna Madre: Separating Barra Soto la Marina from the mainland, this vast, shallow, brackish lagoon is fed by freshwater from the Soto la Marina, El Carrizo, and Conchos Rivers mixed with saltwater from the Gulf of Mexico. Because of the greater number of rivers emptying into Mexico's Laguna Madre, the average salinity is significantly lower than that of Texas's Laguna Madre. The lagoon's median depth is around a meter (three feet); in some places the lagoon barely covers the tidal flats underneath.

Silting near the mouth of the Río Soto la Marina has created a land bridge across the *barra,* thus dividing the Laguna Madre from the Laguna Morales to the south.

Fauna: The aquatic interplay of rivers, lagoon, tidal flats, marshes, wash-over channels, and Gulf waters produces a perfect environment for the spawning, foraging, and nursing of fish and shellfish species. Many local species spawn in one area, nurse in another, and feed in yet another, participating in a cycle that wouldn't be viable anywhere else. Redfish, for example, spawn in the Gulf but spend most of their lives in the lagoons; young shrimp nurse in the lagoons but move into the Gulf as adults.

Manatees are sometimes seen at the mouth of the Soto la Marina river in the fall (when they begin migrating toward the Yucatán Peninsula for the winter), while roseate spoonbills, pelicans, marsh hawks, snow geese, and other colorful waterfowl often frequent the edges of the lagoons and marshes in winter. Easy to spot are white pelicans, which attain wingspans of up to three meters (nine feet), and the frigate bird, whose wingspan is often 2-2.5 meters (seven to eight feet).

Occasionally visitors may catch glimpses of bottle-nosed, spotted, or bridled dolphins swimming close to shore. Sea turtles—including the loggerhead, hawksbill, green sea turtle, giant leatherback, and Kemp's (Atlantic) ridley, were once common but due to overharvesting are now rarely seen near shore.

Climate

La Pesca is just north of the Tropic of Cancer (but farther south than the Florida Keys), which means mild temperatures most of the year. The average low for January is 10.5° C (51° F), while the average high for the same month is 21° C (70° F). In July, La Pesca temperatures range from 24-34° C (76-93° F). In general, summer highs in the area are two or three degrees lower than in Matamoros or Nuevo Laredo.

Average annual precipitation in the area is around 65 cm (25 inches), or about half the average rainfall in Miami. September is the wettest month, averaging around 13 cm (five inches) of rain. The hurricane season begins in May, peaks in August and September, and fades out by the end of October, but most of the *barra* suffers little or no damage during tropical storms or hurricanes—just rain and high winds (there's only a one-in-eight chance of a hurricane striking this far south in any given year). With an eye to the weather, the best time of year for a visit is Oct.-May.

On hot summer weekends and extended holidays, crowds fill the central beach area at La Pesca. April's Semana Santa, in particular, is a time to avoid if enjoying the beach is your primary objective.

El Sabinito Ruins

Twenty km west of Soto La Marina on the road to Ciudad Victoria in Ejido Sabinito are the circular stone ruins of a pre-Cortesian ceremonial site, possibly proto-Huastecan. From the *ejido* a rough unpaved road leads 4-5 km uphill to the ruins. A guide can be arranged through any of the resorts at La Pesca.

This is just one of dozens of such ceremonial plazas scattered throughout the hilly semitropical area of southern Tamaulipas, all of them covered with vegetation and little studied at the present time due to the Mexico City bias toward Mesoamerican archaeology. This bias continues despite the fact that Tamaulipas was the cradle of the earliest civilization—as marked by agriculture—in Mexico.

Accommodations

Most of the places to stay in the area are strung out along the Río Soto la Marina, off the south side of the road before you reach the town of La Pesca itself. All have their own piers or boat launches and can arrange fishing trips. There is no telephone service in the area but some places maintain reservation/information lines in Reynosa, Soto la Marina, Tampico, or McAllen, Texas.

The budget-priced **Hotel Villa del Mar,** located on the estuary just before La Pesca between Km 43 and 44, tel. (132) 7-0610, offers 15 well-worn but clean rooms with hot water and a/c. Rates: US$16 s/d, US$20 t, US$22 q. Villa del Mar also has RV spots for self-contained rigs for US$5-7 and a pleasant *palapa* sitting area by the river.

A hundred meters east of Km 44 is **La Marina del Río Campo Turista,** tel./fax (892) 7-0699 in Reynosa, U.S. tel. (956) 630-0138, U.S. fax (956) 630-6206, an eight-room Mediterranean-style lodge with a/c, TV, a restaurant, and pool. Rates are on the high side of the budget category (US$31 for two double beds, US$37 for three beds, US$44 for four beds) but include meals. La Marina has the best all-around reputation for comfort and service in the area, as well as the best boat-launching facilities. Nearby is the budget, 24-room **Hotel La Pesca,** tel. (12) 13-1333 in Tampico, which has exceptionally well-kept grounds—quite an accomplishment given the fast-growing flora along the estuary. All rooms have three beds, a/c, and hot water. Hotel La Pesca has its own fishing dock and is popular with visiting anglers. Rates: US$16 weekdays, US$20 on weekends.

La Gaviota Trailer Park, on the estuary at Km 48, U.S. tel. (956) 380-1240, has full hookups for US$5-8, tent spaces for US$5, a private pier, *palapas,* and barbecue pits. Recently added hotel rooms are available at prices ranging from budget to moderate. (Basic rooms on the first floor go for US$22-40; kitchenettes on the second floor rent for US$60.)

In the same vicinity is **Campo La Pesca del Río,** U.S. tel. (956) 632-6849 or (800) 331-0479, a 20-room, Mediterranean-style, hunting-and-fishing lodge with 20 rooms for US$10 pp; no restaurant or kitchen facilities are available. It's getting very run-down and is in need of renovation; the a/c works in only a few rooms. It's also known as Hotel La Pesca and La Pesca Lodge. Fishing trips are offered for US$40 per day.

Moderately-priced **Hacienda El Contadero,** tel. (131) 4-1477, Monterrey tel. (8) 333-0800, Monterrey fax (8)-333-2901, is on the opposite side of the river; you'll have to take a ferry ride to get there. The Hacienda has 30 rooms with TV, phones, and a/c. Facilities include a pool, *palapa* restaurant and bar. Rates: US$62 d, US$77 t.

Camping: Most of the resorts along the river will allow tent camping on their grounds for a nominal fee. Camping on the beach is free.

Soto la Marina: Should you find yourself in need of lodging in Soto la Marina, try the budget-priced **Hotel María Cristina,** tel. (11) 7-0051, or **Hotel Chicago,** tel. (11) 7-0193. Both are near the junction of Mexico 180 and the road to La Pesca, and both offer fair rooms with a/c for US$16-21 s/d.

Food

All of the resorts have restaurant service. In La Pesca itself are several well-stocked mini-markets and a couple of basic seafood places; ice is readily available. A greater selection of groceries is available in Soto la Marina. Out on the highway in Soto la Marina, a/c **Restaurant Tampico** serves good seafood and *antojitos.*

Recreation

Fishing: Most visitors to La Pesca are interested in trying their luck with the area's namesake. Among the gamefish species common to the Laguna Madre are redfish, black drum, flounder, sheepshead, speckled seatrout, skipjack, and striped mullet. Several of these are also found on the Gulf side, along with pompano, mackerel, manta ray, seabass, shark, corvina, tarpon, sand trout, and, farther offshore, grouper, bonito, kingfish, red snapper, marlin, and sailfish. A variety of oysters and crabs make their home among the island's intertidal zones. Crabs are especially plentiful, with perhaps 20 species commonly seen.

Even at its most crowded, La Pesca has plenty of room for every angler. Any of the resorts mentioned under "Accommodations," above, can arrange guided fishing trips by boat, although there is no guide industry comparable to that in Port Isabel/South Padre Island north of the border. A couple of local fishing associations organize annual fishing tournaments, most notably the international tournament hosted by the Club Tiro, Caza y Pesca Tamatán through Hotel La Pesca in mid-November.

Boating: Trailered or cartopped boats can be launched at any of the resorts mentioned above. Shallow, flat-bottomed boats are best for river or lagoon boating. Boating in Gulf waters should only be undertaken by persons experienced in open-sea boating, as salvage and rescue services are scarce.

Surfing: The surf near the beach jetty is very good at times, comparable to wave action in Port Aransas, Galveston Island, and other Texas surfing destinations where artificial hard shores are available. In general, the best times of year for surf are spring and late summer/early fall.

Windsurfing: Novices will find the Laguna Madre or Laguna Morales perfect for working on turns or for long sails in one direction; the mouth of the Río Soto la Marina offers stronger breezes suitable for intermediate boardsailors, while the Gulf has stronger winds yet and offers the added surf challenge.

Hunting: Inland from the estuarial system are hunting areas for white-winged dove, quail, duck, goose, wild turkey, wild boar, and white-tailed deer. Most of the resorts can advise and arrange hunts; contact **Hotel La Pesca** or **Campo la Pesca del Río** for information. Hunting regulations in Mexico are very strict; be sure to read the section on hunting in the On the Road chapter of this book. Going through a Mexican hunting broker is the simplest way to clear the necessary red tape.

Getting There

Air: La Pesca has its own 2,070-meter (6,800-foot) airstrip for small planes. If arriving pilots buzz the strip once or twice, someone will drive out to provide taxi service.

Bus: Between Soto la Marina and La Pesca there is only one slow bus daily—count on a three- to four-hour ride and a US$1 fare. Buses to Soto la Marina leave frequently from Matamoros (US$8, hourly), Reynosa (US$8, hourly), Ciudad Victoria (US$3, seven times daily), and Tampico (US$6.50, hourly).

Driving: Due to the road conditions and the number of towns encountered along the way, it's nearly a full day's drive from Matamoros (254 km/157.5 miles) or Tampico (279 km/173 miles) to La Pesca, four to five hours from Ciudad Victoria (180 km/111.5 miles), and about an hour from Soto la Marina (54 km/33.5 miles)—if you obey the speed limits and make stops for food and gas along the way. (The state tourist office claims it only takes two hours from the border, a time record that would surely mean violating speed limits the entire way.) From any direction, it's two-lane highway all the way; the last leg between Soto la Marina and La Pesca was recently upgraded but retains an extensive middle section of rolling hills with tight curves.

Ciudad Victoria to Soto la Marina: The 1.5-to two-hour, 121-km (75-mile) drive from Ciudad Victoria to Soto la Marina along Mexico 70 is particularly scenic; the eastern half of the Victoria-Soto road passes through the rolling Sierra Tamaulipas and some of the state's best examples of Tamaulipan thornforest. Here you can truly begin to make sense of the "tropical/arid" description geographers have bestowed upon this type of terrain. Mexico 70 is heavily patched in places but overall is in fair condition; traffic is light. You'll pass several ranches along the way; **Rancho El Cone** near Km 80 features a small roadside restaurant in a stone house.

Fuel: La Pesca has one PEMEX station, near the estuarial fishing harbor. Fuel is also available in Soto la Marina.

SOUTH TO TAMPICO

Beaches North of Tampico

South of Soto la Marina, several roads branch east off Mexico 180 to coastal zones with flat, sandy beaches much like those found farther north. The turnoff for **Playa Tepehuaje** is 56 km (35 miles) south of Soto, from which it's 40 km (25 miles) by paved road to the beach. *Palapas*, tables, grills, and trash collection are provided by the state. By this point, you've left the Tropic of Cancer behind and are firmly within tropical Mexico.

Well off the beaten track, **Barra de Ostiones** (also known as El Brasil) is the next beach south, 98 km (61 miles) south of Soto and then 36 km (22 miles) east via a gravel road. Facilities are nil but there is plenty of space for camping; the small Río Carrizo empties into the Gulf here, providing an estuarial zone of interest to naturalists.

About 18 km south of Barra de Ostiones along the coast is **Barra Vicente** (also called Rancho Nuevo), the only known area where the endangered Atlantic ridley sea turtle still nests and lays eggs in any sustainable numbers. At one time the Atlantic ridley nested all along the western Gulf coast (in 1947, a film recorded some 40,000 ridleys laying eggs at Rancho Nuevo), but its numbers have been in drastic decline over the last 30 years. Since 1978 a team of Mexican and U.S. marine biologists have been attempting to restore the population by habituating the turtles to new nesting areas.

Barra del Tordo is 50 km (31 miles) northeast of Aldama, which is 148 km (92 miles) south of Soto la Marina. This long stretch of mostly undeveloped beach at the mouth of the Río Carrizal is popular on hot weekends and on holidays. Facilities include a long line of *palapas*, picnic tables, restrooms, and plenty of room for free camping. Between April-Oct. **Hotel Playa Azul,** a mediocre restaurant-hotel concession at the mouth of the Río Carrizal estuary, may be open. Relatively clean rooms are available at shoestring/budget rates (US$14 with fan, US$19 with a/c). During Semana Santa the beach is thick with food vendors.

Small fishing boats are available for rent year-round for trips up the scenic Río Carrizal. Francisco Haces, tel. (956) 350-4986 in Brownsville, or (12) 13-1426 in Tampico, operates a fishing resort on this river.

South of here at the mouth of the Río Tigre (San Rafael), where it feeds into the **Laguna San Andrés,** is a fishing lodge called **Pelifinos** with rooms overlooking the river. For information on rates and reservations, contact Trips Unlimited, Route 1, Box 81M, San Benito, TX 78586, tel. (956) 399-8800. A rock reef offshore offers interesting diving possibilities.

Aldama

Originally founded as Presas del Rey in 1790, Aldama today is a ranching, farming, and hunting center that serves as a supply and staging point for excursions to Barra del Tordo, Rancho Nuevo, Barra de Ostiones, and **Presa República Española.** The latter is a reservoir 40 km (25 miles) north of town with facilities for camping and fishing (large black bass are plentiful).

Aldama is known by gastronomes throughout the state for *barbacoa* and cheeses, especially *queso panela* (often served grilled). The town has also earned a reputation for skillfully made saddles, *chaparreras,* and other leather vaquero gear.

A turnoff from Mexico 180 at Km 29, south of Aldama, leads about 19 km (12 miles) to three large cenotes, or water-filled limestone sinkholes in the hills. The cenotes are connected via an underground system of streams and caverns. The largest, **Posa Zacatón,** plunges to 800 meters (2,600 feet) and is said to be the deepest such sinkhole in the world. Cliffs surrounding Posa Zacatón are too steep to allow entry unless you bring ropes to rappel down to the water. A small group of Americans died a few years ago exploring the tunnels off Zacatón with scuba gear. **Posa Verde** is more accessible and is a popular spot for swimming on weekends and holidays. Turtles, birds, and other fauna are plentiful in the area. Reddish floating islands move around on the surface of the cenotes in the wind.

Practicalities: On the highway near the PEMEX, **Hotel Hacienda,** tel. (127) 8-1415, offers nine very basic rooms at shoestring rates (US$8 s, US$9 d). In town at Méndez and Reforma, the similarly priced and much better **Hotel Rancho Viejo,** tel. (127) 4-0184, has large, clean rooms (US$8.50 s, US$10.50 d).

Restaurante Las Trojas and **Restaurante Los Motivos,** both near Km 35 on the highway, feed passing motorists.

At Presa República Española, **El Paraíso Fishing & Hunting Lodge,** tel. (12) 13-1426 in Tampico or (956) 350-4816 in Brownsville, Texas, and **Campo Española,** James Mayo, 505 Martin St., Monroe, LA 71292, tel. (318) 323-8612, offer a/c lodging and meals.

century plant

TAMPICO

Modern Tampico is a curious mixture of upscale shopping malls and seedy waterfronts, classy suburban homes and downtown blocks whose air of romantic decay, though often compared to New Orleans, is perhaps more reminiscent of a monsoon-blasted South China Sea port.

Surrounded on three sides by water—the Gulf of Mexico to the east, the Río Pánuco to the south, and a patchwork of lagoons to the west—Tampico is most of all a mariner's city. The second oldest and largest port in Mexico (after Pajaritos, Veracruz), the Río Pánuco harbor handles over 10% of all offshore cargo in the country. Sea freight lines terminate in the U.S. at Galveston, Texas, and New Orleans, Louisiana (for transshipment of Mexican goods by road throughout the U.S. and Canada), and to various ports in Europe.

Considerable shipping traffic also moves between Tampico and other ports in Mexico's "Faja de Oro" or "Gold Belt" for oil production, which extends from the central Tamaulipas coast southeast to Campeche. Annexed neighbor city Ciudad Madero is home to the biggest PEMEX facility in Northern Mexico; an oil pipeline runs northwest from Madero through Ciudad Victoria to Cadereyta for use by industrial giant Monterrey. Despite local industry, the city itself is surprisingly clean.

Including Ciudad Madero, metropolitan Tampico currently counts 545,000 inhabitants and is the nation's eighth largest metro area. The city's principal livelihood remains the storage, refining, and shipping of oil (centered in Ciudad Madero), with transportation, chandlery, textiles, food processing, military service, and fishing close behind. Shrimp—in addition to being harvested by offshore Gulf trawlers—are raised in the many lagoons that dot the inland landscape.

Both short-term visitors and longer-term snowbirds will be glad to hear that Tampico has Mexico's second lowest consumer price index among the country's 35 largest cities.

HISTORY

Exploration and Settlement

Spanish conquistadors came upon the confluence of the Río Pánuco, Río Tamesí, and Gulf of Mexico—the site for today's Tampico—early in their Gulf coast explorations. Explorer Alfonso Alvarez de Piñeda, who surveyed much of the upper Gulf, met his demise at the hands of Huastec Indians when probing the Río Pánuco in 1519. *Misionero* Fray Andrés de Olmos had more peaceful contact with Huastecs living on the south bank of the Río Pánuco (at present-day

19th-century Mexican engraving of Tampico's harbor

Ciudad Cuauhtémoc) in 1530, 1532, and 1544. It wasn't until 1554, however, that Franciscan friars were able to establish the *ranchería* of Villa de San Luis de Tampico on the north shore. It was populated by a mix of Spaniards and Tlaxcaltecas from the settlement of San Esteban de Pánuco (present-day Pánuco, Veracruz) farther southwest; this colony, along with the newer *ranchería*, was razed by pirate Sir Laurent Graff—known as "Lorencillo" among the Spanish—in 1684.

French mariners, Spaniards, indigenous tribes, and pirates battled over control of the estuarial harbor throughout the remainder of the 17th and 18th centuries, preventing permanent settlement by any single group until late in the northern *empresario* program. Antonio López de Santa Anna finally transferred a sizable chunk of land (which he had been granted in return for his successful campaign against Emperor Agustín de Iturbide) to ranchers along the north bank of the Río Pánuco in 1823. At the time, a Huastec settlement called Tampico sat on the south bank; thus the new settlement was named Santa Anna de Tampico. American troops occupied the city in 1847 during the Mexican-American War, and when Santa Anna fell in 1854, the unpopular dictator's name was quickly removed. Tampico was also briefly occupied by the French during France's 1862-63 naval invasion.

Growth and *La Bonanza Petrolera*

Fishing and chandlery were the primary occupations for the remaining 19th and early 20th centuries. Because of the abundance and high quality of crabs harvested in the huge estuarial system, Tampico soon earned the nickname Puerto Jaiba or "Crab Port." The town also offered a secure harbor for ships moving along the Gulf coast between Mexico and the United States.

Crabbing quickly took a back seat following the discovery of petroleum in the Pánuco Basin in 1911. During the early years of oil exploration in the 1910s and '20s, Tampico was a boomtown that attracted workers, speculators, and hangers-on from all over the Western world. American and British companies flocked to the area and flooded Northeastern Mexico with U.S. dollars, turning Tampico into the "New Orleans of Mexico." During the city's prenationalization heyday, a quarter of all the crude petroleum extracted in the world came from Tampico. In the 1920s the city was so far ahead of the rest of Mexico in terms of technology and modernization that the nation's first commercial airliner left the ground not from Mexico City or Monterrey but from Tampico.

Nationalization and Diversification

Largely due to an oil workers' strike in Tampico, Mexican president Lázaro Cárdenas expelled all foreign companies and nationalized mineral resources in the mid-1930s. The city's short-lived glory faded as the new Petróleos Mexicana (PEMEX) failed to maintain the quality and growth of regional oil exploitation. When the oil boom of the 1970s boosted the city's fortunes again, Tampico's city government wisely used the windfall to diversify the economy, improving and extending local infrastructure for manufacturing, food production, and shipping.

Although a preponderance of Tampiqueñas still work in PEMEX-related jobs, the city is no longer entirely oil-dependent. Altamira, 20 km to the north, is scheduled to be developed into perhaps the most important cargo port in Latin America.

SIGHTS

Plazas and Historical Buildings

The city's heart is the **Plaza de Armas,** bounded by Calles Fray Andrés de Olmos, Colón, Carranza, and Mirón. Surrounded with palms, the plaza's huge, tile-domed *kiosco* frequently hosts live mariachi or marimba music on Sundays. Any day of the week—unless it's raining—the park is packed with people strolling or sitting. Facing the north side of the plaza is the imposing **Catedral de Tampico,** built in 1931 on the site of an earlier 1823-vintage church, with money donated by an American oil mogul.

Two blocks southeast, at Juárez and Madero, the slightly smaller **Plaza de la Libertad** dates to the turn of the century and is flanked by Porfiriato-era, beaux arts-style architecture—the prime example of which is the **Correos y Telégrafos** building on the north side. On the west side of the Plaza, at Madero and Juárez, the **Hotel Posada del Rey** bears the typical wrought-iron balconies of the era that have inspired comparisons with New Orleans.

TAMPICO

TO SOTO LA MARINA

HOTEL POSADA DE TAMPICO
PLAZA TRES ARCOS
PLAZA CRYSTAL
LIVERPOOL

AV. TAMAULIPAS
BLVD. COSTERO
PLAYA MIRAMAR
GULF OF MEXICO

AV. UNIVERSIDAD
LOPEZ MATEOS

AGUA DULCE
FRANCITA
AV. HIDALGO
EJERCITO MEXICANO
CUAUHTEMOC

AV. OBREGON

CALLE 1 DE MAYO
BUS TERMINAL
MUSEO DE LA CULTURA HUASTECA

RIO PANUCO

HOTEL CAMINO REAL
LAGUNA DEL CARPINTERO

70

SEE INSET

TO CD. VALLES

TO VERACRUZ
180

INSET

HOTEL CAPRI
A. OBREGON
V. CARRANZA
F.A. OLMOS
ALTAMIRA

DR. MATIENZO
MENDEZ
S. J. INES DE LA CRUZ
S. DIAZ MIRON
HOTEL IMPALA

PLAZA DE ARMAS

B. JUAREZ
ADUANA
LOPEZ DE LARA

HOTEL LA PAZ
20 DE NOVIEMBRE
COLON
F. I. MADERO
HOTEL INGLATERRA
CAFE Y NEVERIA ELITE
SUPER CREAM
HOTEL MONTE CARLO

RIBERA
HOTEL BUENA VISTA
HOTEL MUNDO
HOTEL TAMPICO

HOTEL JALISCO
HOTEL PLAZA
HOWARD JOHNSON
CAFE MUNDO
RESTAURANT LA GRAN MURALLA CHINA

MARKET
HOTEL POSADA DEL REY
RESTAURANT INSURGENTES

PLAZA DE LA LIBERTAD
VIPS
A. SERDAN

SALON PALACIO
PORTAS GIL

0   100 m

RIO PANUCO

HOTEL REGIS
H. DEL CANONERO

RAILWAY STATION

ADUANA

© MOON PUBLICATIONS, INC.

Tampico's downtown architecture shows Spanish-French Creole influence.

ALEX PETERSON

Museo de la Cultura Huasteca

The little-known Huastec Culture Museum, in the Instituto Tecnológico de Ciudad Madero, houses the best exhibits on the history and archaeology of the Huastec civilization outside Mexico City. Displays include extensive examples of Huastec ceramics, architecture, painting, clothing, copper and shell crafts, lapidary arts, and sculpture. The museum is at Calle 1 de Mayo and Juana Inés de la Cruz in Ciudad Madero, tel. (12) 12-6339. It's open Mon.-Fri. 10 a.m.-5 p.m., Saturday 10 a.m.-1 p.m.; admission is free.

Waterfront

Visitors interested in the maritime realm may want to explore the Río Pánuco riverfront along the southwestern edge of downtown Tampico, parallel to the rail line. Like many waterfronts around the world, Tampico's projects a classically seedy atmosphere, characterized by cheap taco bars, bustling markets, street vendors, seamen's hotels, and congested traffic—in fact the waterfront looks much like it did during the 1948 production of *The Treasure of the Sierra Madre,* parts of which were filmed on location here.

The best streets for exploration are Héroes del Cañonero and Ribera where they cross Méndez, Aduana, Juárez, Olmos, and Colón. The occasional whiff of Chinese incense wafting down the narrow streets comes from the home altars of buildings inhabited by descendants of Chinese merchants and workers who arrived 80 years ago. It's okay to wander around this area during the day, but at night it can be a tad rough.

At the south end of Calle Aduana on the waterfront (two blocks south of the Plaza de la Libertad) is the **Aduana Marítima,** a huge brick Victorian built in 1880 as the city's first customs house; it's considered one of the best preserved constructions from the Porfiriato Era.

Puente Tampico

This graceful, ultramodern suspension bridge, completed in 1988, arches high over the Río Pánuco to link the states of Tamaulipas and Veracruz—and Northern Mexico with Southern Mexico. At the south end of the bridge you are actually farther south than the northern tip of the Yucatán Peninsula. Before the bridge was built, southbound travelers had to cross the wide river by ferry or take the long way around west of Laguna Chairel.

From northeast Tampico, Av. López Mateos leads to the bridge, which affords a bird's-eye view of the river and city—it's worth the US$2 bridge toll.

ACCOMMODATIONS

Because of the city's relatively low cost of living, hotels in Tampico typically cost less than hotels and motels in comparably sized Mexican cities. Weekend room rates are often lower than weekday rates.

Shoestring

Several tattered hotels near the waterfront on Calles H. de Cañonero and Ribera cater to merchant mariners, transient oil workers, and a few intrepid budget travelers. Among these are **Hotel Monterrey,** H. de Cañonero Pte. 515, tel. (12) 12-4371, **Hotel Buena Vista,** H. de Cañonero Ote. 112, tel. (12) 12-2946, and **Hotel Progreso,** H. de Cañonero Ote. 218, tel. (12) 12-3913. Rooms cost US$3-7 and are very basic (hot water is usually unavailable). They're secure for male visitors, but solo female travelers might find their occupations misconstrued and hence would best avoid these hotels.

A gem floating in the middle of the colorful but congested market area on the waterfront is the clean and efficient, pink, six-story **Hotel Jalisco,** Calle La Paz Pte. 120, tel. (12) 12-2924, which offers plain, comfortable rooms with TV, a/c, and hot water. Rates: US$6.50 s, 8.50 d. The nearby four-story **Hotel La Paz,** Calle La Paz Nte. 307, tel. (12) 14-0382, is similar. Rates: US$10s, US$11.50 d, plus US$1.25 for each additional person.

Hotel Regis, Madero Ote. 605, tel. (12) 12-0290, has clean, cheap, small rooms with fans and private bath. Rates: US$6.50 s, US$8 d, US$9 t, US$10.50 q.

North of the Plaza de Armas in the center of town are a couple of other cheap hotels: **Hotel Capri,** Calle Juárez Nte. 202, tel. (12) 12-2680, and **Hotel Nuevo León,** Calle Aduana Nte. 107, tel. (12) 12-4370. The Capri is the least expensive at just US$5 per night for spartan rooms with fan and bath—and only one bed each, suggesting this is a brothel; the Nuevo León adds TV and charges a couple of dollars more.

Shoestring/Budget

Moving up a large notch, the friendly **Hotel Tampico,** Calle Carranza Ote. 513 downtown, tel. (12) 19-0057, is a grand old dame that has seen better days but is nonetheless atmospheric and well located for sightseeing and restaurants. Spacious, plain rooms have private hot-water showers and TV. The ballroom on the first floor is often used for private parties, so the higher your room is, the quieter your stay is likely to be. The hotel has its own security parking lot in back, and an inexpensive restaurant. Rates: US$13-16 s/d.

Budget

Although it has no parking lot (24-hour pay parking can be arranged at nearby lots), the historic and well-run **Hotel Posada del Rey,** Calle Madero Ote. 218 (on the Plaza de la Libertad), tel. (12) 14-1024, has small but comfortable rooms with TV and a/c. This is one of Tampico's best hotel values under US$25; ask for an inside room *(habitación interior)* to avoid the street noise below. Rates: US$17s, US$19 d. A room with a balcony on the plaza costs US$2 more.

Practically next door to the Posada del Rey, the friendly and efficient **Howard Johnson Hotel Tampico** (formerly the Hotel Colonial), Calle Madero Ote. 210, tel. (12) 12-7676, fax (12) 12-0653, offers recently remodeled rooms with a/c and TV. The hotel has a restaurant and parking and is a real bargain. Rates: US$26 s, US$28 d. Up the street from HoJo's, the **Hotel Plaza,** Madero Ote. 204, tel. (12) 12-1784, fax (12) 12-6680, has rooms with atmosphere. Rates: US$14-19.

On Calle Díaz Mirón near the Plaza de Armas are two traditional favorites among business travelers and middle-class Mexican tourists. **Hotel Impala,** Calle Mirón 220, tel. (12) 12-0990, fax (12) 12-0684, offers sheltered parking and 83 comfortable, spacious rooms with a/c and TV. Rates: US$19 s, US$23 d (if you belong to Sanborn's Mexico Club you may receive a further 20% discount).

Nearby **Hotel Mundo,** Díaz Mirón Ote. 413, tel. (12) 12-0360, fax (12) 12-6553, offers 50 clean rooms with a/c, phone, and TV, plus a coffeeshop and parking. Rates: US$21 s, US$24.50 d.

Inexpensive

Ten-story **Hotel Monte Carlo,** Av. López de Lara Nte. 107 (a block west of the Hotel Tampico), tel. (12) 14-1093 or (800) 5-7070 for reservations, has recently remodeled and moved up in service and facilities. Large comfortable rooms have a/c and TV; an elegant restaurant and a parking lot are attached. Rates: US$53 for two double beds.

Hotel Inglaterra, Calle Mirón Ote. 116 (opposite the Plaza de Armas), tel. (12) 19-2857, fax (12) 14-0556, is rated at five stars by the state government (to be taken with a grain of salt). A Best Western property, it features basement parking, a restaurant, sauna, and completely remodeled rooms with all the amenities—a/c, TV, phone, mini-bar/refrigerator. Rates: US$53 s/d.

Moderate

For true five-star luxury it's necessary to move away from downtown Tampico to the newer sections of the city. About two km northwest of downtown, the efficient **Camino Real,** Av. Hidalgo 2000, tel. (12) 13-8811, has 100 well-appointed rooms on tropical landscaped grounds. Facilities include TV, satellite TV, video, phones, a restaurant, coffee shop, car rental agency, travel agency, and swimming pool, plus tennis and golf course privileges at a local country club. Rates: US$63 s/d on weekends, US$80 on weekdays. The 44-room **Holiday Inn Hotel and Suites,** Ejército Mexicano 1435, tel. (12) 16-9070, is similarly priced and comfortable.

Farther out along Av. Hidalgo beyond the Plaza Crystal shopping center (about seven km/four miles northwest of downtown), **Hotel Posada de Tampico,** tel. (12) 28-0515, has 130 modern rooms, a pool larger than the Camino Real's, a lighted tennis court, a putting green, and a restaurant and disco. Rates: US$77 s/d.

RV Parking

Motorists with RVs or campers may park overnight in the airport parking lot for a small fee.

FOOD

Tampico's seafood restaurants are much admired by Mexicans from Matamoros to Veracruz. Known throughout Mexico as "Puerto Jaiba" ("Crab Port"), the city harvests around 20 different species of crab from the rivers, lagoons, and Gulf. For Tampiqueñas the favored method of preparing crabs is simply to boil them whole in salted water to produce *jaiba al natural,* which is cracked and eaten with flour tortillas and special salsas of lime, chile, and garlic. Another popular dish is *jaiba relleno,* crab shells stuffed with shredded flounder, shrimp, or striped mullet.

Striped mullet *(lisa)* is also commonly served as ceviche, in which small pieces of the raw fish are marinated in lime juice, onions, cilantro, chile, and tomatoes, and eaten as a *botana* or snack. Shrimp *(camarón)* is as common as crab, and

comes boiled, barbecued, or fried, or in *empanadas de camarón* (shrimp turnovers), *tortas de camarón* (shrimp sandwiches), and *tamales de flor de calabaza y camarón* (steamed with squash flowers inside a wrapper made of banana leaves instead of the usual corn husks).

The city is also widely known for *carne asada a la tampiqueña,* often called "Steak Tampico" or "Tampico Filet" on English-language menus. Much favored by *mexicanos* and gringos alike, this dish consists of thin, butterflied fillets of beef quickly seared and served with *enchiladas verdes,* pickled chiles, *frijoles a la charra,* and a square of grilled cheese (usually *panela*), with salsa and cubed avocado (or guacamole) on the side—the original Mexican combination plate. It was probably this dish—carried in the memories of U.S. oil workers returning home in the 1930s—that introduced Americans to Mexican food (and the famous Mexican "combination platter") on a large scale. In authentic *tampiqueña,* the beef is *not* marinated first like fajitas.

Many of the foregoing dishes can be sampled inexpensively at streetside vendors in the market area along Calle P.J. Méndez between Calles 20 de Noviembre and Colón, near the Recinto Fiscal (customs area). Tacos, for example, cost just US$0.25 apiece here, US$0.40 elsewhere in the city.

For higher quality but still moderately priced *cocina típica,* you'll find numerous restaurants—several of them unique—in the area between Hotel Tampico and Plaza de la Libertad.

Seafood

Restaurant Jardín Corona, Av. Hidalgo 1915 (a block south of the Hotel Camino Real), tel. (12) 12-4245, is at the upper end of the scale in price and ambience. This marble-floored eatery offers fresh seafood in a variety of ways—baked, broiled, fried, and steamed—plus steak platters and Mexican standards. Moderate to expensive. Open daily noon-11 p.m.

Restaurant-Bar Pikio, Playa del Mirador (south end of Playa Miramar near the mouth of the Río Pánuco), is one of two seafood restaurants parked near the outer harbor. Pikio specializes in tasty *brocheta de pescado adobado,* chunks of marinated fresh fish barbecued on skewers. Moderately priced. Open Wed.-Sun. 11 a.m.-8 p.m.

Regional

The *café y nevería* (coffee and ice-cream shop), a downtown Tampico tradition, usually serves far more than just coffee and ice cream. Open long hours, the shops attract a steady clientele throughout the day by offering inexpensive, filling meals and a place to hang out for an hour or two with friends.

Café y Nevería Elite, Calle Díaz Mirón Ote. 211, tel. (12) 12-0364, is popular with a broad cross section of office workers, politicos, and coffee dreamers. It offers an assortment of Mexican and seafood dishes, including delicious *brochetas de camarón* and stuffed crab, as well as breakfasts. Inexpensive to moderate. Open daily 7:30 a.m.-11 p.m.

Café Mundo, López de Lara at Mirón, tel. (12) 14-1831, is old, funky, and open 24 hours. The Mundo is especially popular with students and workers, and its inexpensive menu covers the gamut from *desayuno* to *torta milanesa.*

Café-Nevería El Globito, Calle Andrés de Olmos, at one corner of the Plaza de Armas, is also open 24 hours and is strong on ice cream and fruit drinks; it's a bit cheaper than the Elite.

Restaurant Insurgentes, Calle Mirón between Av. López de Lara and Calle Aduana, is a popular, inexpensive spot serving good *enchiladas huastecas* and seafood. Open daily noon-11 p.m.

Established in 1897, the once-rowdy **Restaurant-Bar Salón (Saloon) Palacio,** Aduana at H. de Cañonero Ote. (near Plaza de la Libertad), tel. (12) 12-1877, has been somewhat tamed by tourism. The cantina, which appears in the Tampico bar scenes in *The Treasure of the Sierra Madre,* has recently been remodeled inside and out, retaining the marble floors and brass-and-wood bar. The menu—a cross-section of *mariscos, carne asada a la tampiqueña,* and other Tampico specialties including *huachinango* (red snapper) stuffed with shrimp and crab—is a reasonable value given the historic surroundings. Moderate. Open Mon.-Sat. 11:30 a.m.-midnight.

Restaurant La Troya, at Hotel Posada del Rey, Calle Madero 218, tel. (12) 14-1024, is a popular, reasonably priced hotel eatery specializing in seafood and *gringas* (burritos filled with cheese and chorizo). Balcony tables overlook the Plaza de la Libertad. Open daily 11 a.m.-11 p.m.

Chinese

Tampico is known to have the best Chinese restaurants along Mexico's entire Gulf coast. Several are found along Av. Hidalgo (Mexico 80/180) in the vicinity of the Camino Real and Posada de Tampico.

La Gran Muralla China, at Av. Hidalgo 5201, tel. (12) 28-1919, and at Av. López de Lara Sur 107 downtown, tel. (12) 12-4759, specializes in high-quality seafood prepared in the Southern Chinese style with just a bit of Mexican influence. Moderately priced. Open daily noon-midnight.

Imperio Chino, Blvd. Hidalgo 3302 (near the Hotel Camino Real), tel. (12) 13-1277, is a huge, banquet-style place with a menu to match. Moderately priced. Open daily noon-11 p.m.

Other

A number of American-style fast-food places, including **Pollo Loco, Super Cream del Camino, Super Burger Hidalgo,** as well as the American chains **KFC, McDonald's, Burger King,** and **Pizza Hut** are lined up along Av. Hidalgo. Two shopping centers on Hidalgo, **Plaza Crystal** and **Tres Arcos,** have well-stocked food courts with good Mexican food.

Super Cream is worth a special mention because it's one of the few sit-down bakeries—and one of the few to serve coffee—in Northern Mexico. The downtown location, on Calle Carranza a block west of Hotel Tampico (between Calle Aduana and Av. López de Lara), is open daily 7:30 a.m.-10 p.m.

Vip's, at the corner of Aduana and Madero facing Plaza de la Libertad, offers its usual clean and modern American-Mexican coffeeshop atmosphere. Prices are reasonable.

ENTERTAINMENT

Bars and Dance Clubs

Tampico has a swinging nightlife, although many of the bars, cantinas, and *salones* downtown are frequented by men only. **La Tasca,** attached to the Restaurant La Troya in the Hotel Posada del Rey, is an exception and is reasonably atmospheric, as is the long, stool-less bar at the **Salón Palacio** (see "Food," above).

Turning up the heat a bit, the **Centro Nocturno Tropicana,** Av. López de Lara Sur 111 downtown, features a mix of live and recorded Latin dance music nightly. Out on Av. Hidalgo are a couple of discos, including **Close Up Discotheque,** Edificio Maraboto, Av. Hidalgo, and **El Porvenir,** Av. Hidalgo 1403, tel. (12) 13-0562.

Popular with a young, post-teen crowd are **Byblomania Video-Bar,** Calle Byblos 1, **Iguanas Rock,** Av. Universidad 500, and **La Cigarra,** Calle Morones Prieto 202. La Cigarra hosts occasional live music.

Radio
Tune in 94.5 FM (broadcast from Poza Rica, Veracruz) for an invigorating blend of *norteña* and *tropicale* music.

RECREATION

Tampiqueñas count themselves lucky to live in a city that is practically surrounded on all sides by lagoons, rivers, and the Gulf of Mexico, creating abundant opportunities for fishing, swimming, boating, and other aquatic activities.

Laguna del Carpintero
This lagoon in the middle of the city provides public facilities for picnicking, swimming, waterskiing, or simply strolling along the water's edge. A small zoo and children's park are also on the premises. Certain sections of the shoreline are still under development and will reportedly feature water slides and other more elaborate diversions at some point in the future.

Playa Miramar
Known locally simply as "La Playa," this 10-km (six-mile) stretch of packed sand washed by Gulf surf is northeast of Tampico proper at the edge of Ciudad Madero. *Palapas* (with wooden chairs beneath) line the length of the central beach, which is backed by a stand of casuarina trees and seafood kiosks. A few run-down concrete beach hotels of 10-20 rooms each stand well back from the beach toward the north end. By all appearances, the water along most of Playa Miramar seems amazingly clean considering the proximity of the harbor entrance and PEMEX facility.

Driving on the beach is permitted; the main part accessible by vehicle extends 3.7 km (2.3 miles). At its southeast end, near the mouth of the Río

Pánuco, the beach ends at a long concrete pier suitable for fishing or strolling. At the north end, the sand becomes too loose for driving and hence this is the nicest area for lounging around. *Palapas* at the north end rent for US$2 a day; a large *palapa* restaurant offers fresh seafood.

The central part of the beach—where the *palapas* are—becomes crowded with Mexican families on warm-weather weekends and holidays. Tampiqueñas practically headquarter themselves here all week to celebrate Semana Santa. During the fall and winter, though, you'll have the place almost all to yourself.

Framed by grassy dunes and beach houses (some of them abandoned), the beach continues for several kilometers north. A poor, broken-asphalt road on the landward side of the dunes meanders for a few kilometers, after which you must continue by foot. This area is worth exploring for its natural flora (prickly pear, live oak, verbena, casuarina), less-visited beaches, and cleaner water.

Getting There: From downtown Tampico it's 15 km (nine miles) to Playa Miramar. If you're driving, simply follow Av. López de Lara from Tampico till it becomes Av. Obregón, which in turn leads through Ciudad Madero (past the huge PEMEX facility and naval base) to the beach. *Colectivos* and *taxis de ruta* labeled "Tampico-Playa" run back and forth along this route, as does the No. 24 city bus.

Laguna Tamiahua
Across the state line in the state of Veracruz, this huge estuarial lagoon paralleling the coast is known for fishing and shrimping, as well as for uninhabited islands, mangroves, and wildlife. Buses to Naranjos, Ver., will drop passengers off in Horconcitos near the north end of the lagoon, where boats can be rented; or you can ride all the way to Naranjos and switch to a Tamiahua-bound bus. Motorists can drive themselves to the lagoon via Mexico 180 South. The town of Tamiahua, at the south end of the lagoon, is the main supply center.

SHOPPING

Tampico doesn't have much of interest in the way of traditional markets or handicrafts, but for Mexicans in the region it's highly prized for its modern malls and shopping plazas. The **Plaza Tres Arcos** and **Plaza Crystal** malls, next to one another on Blvd. Hidalgo toward the Posada de Tampico and airport, are stuffed with upscale stores. (Cinemas Gemelos, in the latter, shows recently released American films for only US$2 admission.)

Across from Plaza Crystal on Blvd. Hidalgo is **Liverpool,** a plush, Macy's-style department store with imported foods (on the second floor) and a small handicrafts section.

EVENTS

March/April: Throughout these two months both Tampico and its neighbor, Ciudad Madero celebrate a string of festivals, beginning with **Carnaval** (see "Festivals and Events" in the On the Road chapter for details on this holiday) the week before Lent.

During the third week of April, Tampiqueñas celebrate the **Aniversario de la Repoblación de Tampico** with art, culture, and sporting events. A special emphasis is placed on folkloric dancing, and the city hosts a regional conference on *huapango,* a traditional dance indigenous to southern Tamaulipas's Región Huasteca. This festival more or less merges with Semana Santa, which involves fireworks and *matachine* processions centered at Playa Miramar in Ciudad Madero.

December: Día de la Virgen de Guadalupe, 12 Dec., attracts many *indígenas* from the southern part of the state who come to worship and dance at various churches dedicated to Guadalupe, including the Catedral de Tampico on Plaza de Armas.

Other: The city honors the Virgen de San Juan de los Lagos twice a year, on 2 Feb. (Candelaría) and 15 Aug. (Ascension Day), at the Iglesia Nuestra Señora de Guadalupe.

INFORMATION AND SERVICES

Tourist Office
The **Oficina de Atención Turística,** 20 de Noviembre Nte. 218, tel. (12) 12-2668, distributes hotel brochures, a Spanish-language tourist newspaper, and a city map.

**TAMPICO
TELEPHONE NUMBERS**

Police	12-1437
Highway Patrol	28-0542
Green Angels	13-8578
State Tourist Office	12-2668
Red Cross	12-1333
U.S. Consulate	13-2217
Tampico Area Code	12

Telephone
Hotel Posada del Rey houses a convenient, 24-hour LADA office where long-distance national and international calls may be paid for with a credit card (Visa, MasterCard, or American Express).

U.S. Consulate
Tampico has a U.S. consular post at Av. Hidalgo 2000, tel. (12) 13-2217, next to the Hotel Camino Real. The consulate is open Mon.-Fri. 9:30 a.m.-1:30 p.m.

GETTING THERE

Air
Aeroméxico, Plaza Tres Arcos, tel. (12) 17-0656, operates nonstop flights daily to/from Monterrey and Veracruz, with connecting flights to/from Ciudad Juárez, Chihuahua, Culiacán, Durango, Guadalajara, Mexico City, and Torreón in Mexico, as well as Houston, San Antonio, and McAllen, Texas in the United States. **Mexicana,** Av. Universidad 700-1, tel. (12) 13-9600, has nonstop flights to/from Mexico City, Monterrey, and Veracruz.

Aeropuerto Francisco Javier Mina, tel. (12) 28-0572 or 28-0571, is nine km northwest of downtown Tampico off Mexico 80/180, about 15 minutes by car. A taxi to central Tampico will cost around US$4, while a *colectivo* will run around US$3.50.

Bus
Tampico's **Centro de Autobuses** is on Calle Zapotal and Av. López Mateos (off Av. Ejército Mexicano), 2.4 km (1.5 miles) east of Av. Hidalgo.

Autobuses de Oriente (ADO) operates first-class buses to/from Matamoros (US$14, three times daily), Monterrey (US$16, five times), and San Luis Potosí (US$14, six times). To/from Veracruz, first-class buses cost US$22 and run 10 times daily.

Omnibus de Mexico has buses to/from Mexico (US$17, seven daily), Ciudad Valles (US$5, one daily), Saltillo (US$20, one daily), and Torreón (US$26, one daily).

Transportes Mante has second-class buses to/from Monterrey (US$16, six daily), Soto la Marina (US$6, four daily), and Ciudad Victoria (US$7, seven daily).

Vencedor Río Verde has cornered the market on second-class buses between Tampico and Río Verde (US$8, once daily), Xilitla (US$7, once daily), and San Luis Potosí (US$14, four daily). **Del Norte** runs first-class buses to Río Verde (US$10, seven daily) and San Luis Potosí (US$13, five daily)

Train
El Huasteco, a second-class train between San Luis Potosí and Tampico, costs US$4.50 each way and takes around 11 hours (for scheduling information, see the San Luis Potosí "Getting There" section). The railway station, tel. (12) 12-8471, faces the Río Pánuco waterfront on the southwestern edge of downtown Tampico.

Driving
From the southern outskirts of Matamoros to Tampico is about a six-hour drive under normal road conditions. Avenida Hidalgo slices into the northwest corner of the grid at a diagonal and links the downtown district with Mexico

80/180 North and the airport. Avenida López Mateos links Mexico 80/180 North with Mexico 180 South via Puente Tampico over the Río Pánuco. If you're heading toward San Luis Potosí, you'll want Av. Universidad, which leads to Mexico 110/70 West.

GETTING AROUND

Taxis de rutas and *colectivos* circulate all over town, especially along main thoroughfares Hidalgo, López de Lara, Obregón, and López Mateos. The standard passenger fare for these is around US$0.25. The city bus system costs a bit less but is more complicated. Taxis in the downtown district cost US$3-4 per trip.

Driving
Tampico's neat downtown grid is easy to follow, but the one-way street system that keeps traffic moving so well also sometimes forces newcomers to drive around in circles in order to reach a given destination.

More than in any other city in Northern Mexico, local residents tend to run red lights with regularity. Whether on foot or in your own vehicle, always look both ways before entering an intersection.

Car Rental
Four agencies handle the demand for rental vehicles: **National,** Av. Hidalgo 2000-A, tel. (12) 13-5434 or 17-0402; **Dollar,** international airport, tel. (12) 28-0587; **Avis,** international airport, tel. (12) 28-0585; and **Budget,** Av. Hidalgo 3400, tel. (12) 13-6961.

CIUDAD VICTORIA AND VICINITY

Tamaulipas's state capital was founded in 1750 as Santa María de Aguayo under José de Escandón's *empresario* program. In 1825 it was made state capital and the name was changed to honor Mexico's first president, Guadalupe Victoria. In 1846 the city was briefly occupied by U.S. troops during the Mexican-American War, and it also played a key role in the 1910-20 Mexican Revolution.

Today this bright, clean, and prosperous little city at the intersection of Mexico 101, 70, and 85, shadowed to the west by the Sierra Gorda, has a population of 244,000, most of whom are supported by government service, education, construction, and manufacturing, or by supplying surrounding farms and ranches. One of the premier local crops is henequen, an agave plant used to make twine, burlap bags, floor mats, and upholstery interiors. The city is also known for leather crafts, especially the *cuera tamaulipeca,* a fringed chamois jacket with white calfskin patterns on the shoulders and cuffs and the state coat of arms on the back. Other Victoria products include furniture fashioned from *ebano* (Texas ebony), mesquite, pine, and palm.

Situated at nearly 300 meters (980 feet) above sea level, Ciudad Victoria is blessed with a mild climate most of the year; the occasional summer heat wave or winter freeze are departures from the norm. Hunting, fishing, and nearby El Cielo Biosphere Reserve are major local attractions for Mexican and foreign visitors alike.

In October the city holds an **Exposición Agricola, Ganadera, Comercial, Industrial y Turística,** a large state fair of sorts that features events and exhibits having to do with farming, ranching, trade, industry, and tourism.

SIGHTS

Museo de Antropología e Historia
In the rectory of the Universidad Autónoma de Tamaulipas downtown on Av. Colón, this small museum contains the usual photos from the revolutionary era, along with pre-Hispanic artifacts (mostly ceramics and arrowheads) and early portraits of noteworthy men of local provenance. It's open Mon.-Fri. 8 a.m.-7 p.m.; admission is free.

Parque Recreativo Tamatán
This huge pastoral park at the southwestern edge of town along the Río San Marcos contains a playground, zoo, artificial lake, and *lienzo charro,* along with acres of woods.

Paseo Méndez
Of the three public plazas in town, this is the largest and leafiest. Open-air theatrical and musical performances are occasionally held here. The *paseo* is at Calles 5 de Mayo and Rosales, just west of the tourist office.

ACCOMMODATIONS

Shoestring
Best of the lower-priced places is the tidy **Hotel Posada Don Diego,** on Calle Juárez between Calles 9 and 10, tel. (131) 2-1279. Basically furnished, small rooms with satellite TV, attached baths, and ceiling fans, surround a courtyard in the colonial style. The hotel has its own parking lot (it's one of the only places under US$35 that does) and **Restaurant La Carolina.** Rates: US$8-11 s/d; with a/c, add US$2.

Facing Plaza Hidalgo just a block off Blvd. J.B. Tijerina (the main north-south avenue through town), the well-located **Hotel Los Monteros,** Calle Hidalgo Ote. 962, tel. (131) 2-0640, offers a quiet, classic Mex-deco interior around two courtyards. The downstairs restaurant is good. The hotel doesn't have a parking lot but free parking can be arranged at a 24-hour pay lot around the corner. Rates: US$8 s/d, US$13 t.

Hotel San Juan, Calle Colón Nte. 427 (north of the Hotel Santorín), tel. (131) 2-7993, has more spartan rooms, and no parking. Rates: US$5 s/d with one bed, US$5.50 s/d with two beds, and US$10 t/q.

One of the best deals in town if you don't mind dorm-style accommodations is the **Hostal de Escandón,** Calle Juan B. Tijerina Sur 143, tel. (131) 2-9004 or (131) 2-2010. It's mostly intended for students going to university in Victoria, but anyone can stay here when there's space. The staffers are friendly. Rooms are clean, gender-segregated by floor, and come with bunks, reading lamps, and private bathrooms. Rates include three meals a day (making it an even better deal), served communally at wooden benches and tables in the center of the first floor courtyard—a good place to practice Spanish with the students. Air-conditioned rooms are available for a few dollars more but do not include meals. Parking is available for just US$0.50 per day. Rates: a one-person room costs US$11.50, two-person room US$8 pp, three-person room US$6.50 pp, and a four-person room US$6 pp.

Bus travelers can overnight at **Hotel Savi,** next to the bus station on Carrera Torres, tel. (131) 6-9270, fax (131) 6-7045. The basic but relatively clean rooms have a/c, TV, and oversoft beds. Rates: US$12 s, US$15 d. There are several other basic hotels near the bus terminal but they can't be recommended—they're cheap but not at all clean. Better to take a city bus into town and find someplace nicer for the same price.

CIUDAD VICTORIA

INSET

© MOON PUBLICATIONS, INC.

At the north end of town where Mexico 85 North meets the *periférico,* **Motel Jardín,** tel. (131) 6-1555, has 15 run-down rooms and is recommended only as a last resort. Rates: US$9-11.50.

Budget

Hotel Fiesta Plaza, Juárez (Calle 14) 401, tel. (131) 2-1761, one block from the Palacio de Gobierno, is a clean and quiet place where rooms come with a/c, heat, phone, and satellite TV. On the premises are a parking lot and coffee shop. Rates: US$17 s, US$20 d, US$22 t/q including tax.

Several motels on the northern and northeastern outskirts of town offer convenient lodging for motorists. At the north end of town off Mexico 85, the **San Antonio Motel,** tel. (131) 6-2616, has clean and comfortable a/c rooms around a pool and parking lot. Rates: US$28 s, US$31 d, US$33 t, US$37 q. On the northeast edge of town, the well-run **Paradise Inn,** Km 1 on Mexico 101 (the highway from Matamoros), tel. (131) 6-8181, fax (131) 6-8371, has similar amenities. Rates: US$31.75-35 s/d. The nearby two-story **Motel La Villa,** tel. (131) 6-8011, was being remodeled as we went to press. Rooms have a/c, heat, phone and TV. Rates: US$19-US$22 s/d; prices may go up when renovations are completed. The San Antonio, Paradise, and La Villa all have attached restaurants and free parking.

Down on the southern edge of town off Mexico 85, the heavily advertised **Motel Panorámico,** tel. (131) 2-5999 or 2-5506, sits on a hill overlooking the city. Rooms have a/c, phones, satellite TV, and in-house video. Facilities include a pool and restaurant. Rates: US$28-32 s/d.

Inexpensive

Next door to the Hotel Los Monteros on Hidalgo is the busier (and noisier) **Hotel Sierra Gorda,** tel. (131) 2-2010, fax (131) 2-9799. The staff is very helpful with tourist information. Well-worn but ample-sized rooms feature a/c, phones, and satellite TV. Be sure to request an inside room if you're bothered by street noise. The Sierra Gorda has no parking facility of its own but a pay lot is attached to the hotel. Rates: US$35-38 s/d.

On the west side of the plaza is the nine-story **Hotel Everest,** Av. Colón 126, tel. (131) 2-4050, fax (131) 2-1443, Mexico toll-free tel. (800) 5-

8165, where 85 modern rooms come with a/c, satellite TV, in-house video, and phones. Unlike the foregoing hotels, the Everest offers free underground parking. Other facilities include elevators, a tobacco shop, barber shop, dry cleaning, and laundry. Rates: US$37 s, US$40 d.

The modern **Best Western Hotel Santorín,** Av. Colón Nte. 349 (two blocks north of Plaza Hidalgo), tel. (131) 2-8066, fax (131) 2-8342, offers comfortable rooms with all the amenities. Nonsmoking rooms are available on request, and the hotel has its own parking garage, a National Car Rental office, travel agency, restaurant, and lobby bar. Rates: US$32 s, US$35 d, US$39 t, US$44 q.

Motel Las Fuentes, Km 227 on Mexico 85, tel. (131) 2-5655, fax (131) 2-5570, provides large and comfortable rooms with a/c, mini-bar, TV, and phone. Amenities include free parking and an attached restaurant. Rates: US$39-41.50.

RV Parks

The **Victoria Trailer Park Resort,** on the Mexico 85 bypass one km (0.6 mile) west of the Mexico 101 intersection, tel. (131) 2-4824, has 150 sites with full hookups on 10 acres. Slots are US$10 per night per rig for two persons, plus US$1 extra for use of a/c and US$2 for each additional person (discount for longer stays). Shower facilities are available.

At the junction of Mexico 85 North and the *periférico,* the **Motel Jardín** has a small trailer park with 10 RV sites with full hookups for US$7 per night, plus showers and toilets. Highway noise would definitely be a problem here.

FOOD

Gorditas Estilo Doña Tota has become famous throughout the state and there are now three branches in town. The original—a funky eatery with photos of old-time Mexican actors on the walls—is at Av. Berriozábal 1748 between Calles 5 and 6. Other branches are at Calle Juárez Ote. 205 and Calz. Luis Caballero 520. All serve the trademark *gorditas* (thick tortillas stuffed with shredded beef, *nopales,* and scrambled egg) along with *nopalitos con salsa* (strips of prickly pear cactus served with salsa) and quesadillas. Prices are low.

cuera
tamaulipeca

ERIN DWYER

entrepreneur skilled at providing efficient and high-quality food service at low prices.

Moving upscale a bit, the semi-elegant and long-running **Restaurant El Granero,** Carrera Torres Ote. 509, tel. (131) 2-6155, serves Mexican and international cuisine; house specialties include *carne asada* and seafood. **La Posta Plaza,** Calle Zaragoza 701 (at Calle 11), tel. (131) 2-1444, has a similar menu but is decidedly classier (and more expensive) with its fountain and garden dining areas.

Just north of the San Antonio Motel on the east side of Blvd. Tamaulipas, **El Mesquite Grill,** tel. (131) 2-6155, is a reliable restaurant with a Mexican and international menu. A large breakfast buffet is served daily, and delicious cookies (not the usual bland *pan dulce*) come with breakfast coffee orders. On Sunday *cabrito* is available.

INFORMATION AND SERVICES

Tourist Office
The **Dirección General de Turismo,** Calle Rosales 272, tel. (131) 2-1057, fax (131) 2-1111, is the head tourist office for the state and a good source of information on Ciudad Victoria and vicinity, Mon.-Fri. 8:30 a.m.-3:30 p.m. and 6-8:30 p.m.

Maps
INEGI, Calle 22 #601 (at Carrera Torres), tel. (131) 14-1033, carries topographic maps of northeastern Mexico, including sheets with El Cielo Biosphere Reserve.

Radio
Victorenses are proud of their Tamaulipan heritage, and the university-sponsored "Radio

Near Plaza Hidalgo are several inexpensive and moderately priced restaurants, including the U.S.-style **Daddy's Restaurant,** at Av. Colón Nte. 148 (next door to the Hotel Everest), tel. (131) 2-4050. Daddy's menu features a broad range of steaks, seafood, burgers, sandwiches, salads, soups, and Mexican standards. Down the street a bit, **El Patio Mexicano,** Colón Sur 124, tel. (131) 2-6871, serves good Mexican platters amid a traditional Mexican decor; breakfast specials include a fruit plate, coffee, juice, eggs, and beans for US$2.75.

The humble and popular **Café Canton,** Calle Colón 114 (two doors north of El Patio Mexicano), provides a decent *comida corrida* for US$2.50-3, as well as inexpensive Mexican breakfasts. The home-style enchiladas and *entomatadas de pollo* are particularly good here. If the lack of Chinese food in a place with a Chinese name surprises you, it's because this is what's known in Mexico City as a *café chino,* or "Chinese cafe"—an eatery established by a Chinese

CIUDAD VICTORIA TELEPHONE NUMBERS	
Police	2-0195
Highway Patrol	6-4779
Green Angels	2-1057
State Tourist Office	2-1067
Red Cross	6-2077
Ciudad Victoria Area Code	131

Tamaulipas," 107.9 FM, plays *mucho* local and regional music (with no advertising).

Shopping

Artesanía Tamaulipeca, Calle 16 at Rosales (near the Centro Cultural), tel. (131) 2-1954, carries a selection of regional handicrafts, including the *cuera tamaulipeca.* A smattering of folk crafts is also available at (and around) the **Mercado Municipal,** Calle Díaz (Calle 7) at Av. Morelos.

Along the south end of Calle Madero (Calle 17), a pretty divided boulevard with trees shading the median, a number of modern shops and boutiques offer a variety of purchasing possibilities.

GETTING THERE

Air

Aeromar, Carrera Torres at Abasolo, tel. (131) 6-9191, fields one daily nonstop flight to/from Mexico City. In the past, Aeroméxico has also operated flights between Matamoros and Ciudad Victoria, but for the time being all flights now operate via Mexico City. **Aero California,** Guerrero 9 (at Bravo), tel. (131) 5-1850, has daily nonstop flights to/from Mexico City and Matamoros.

The airport is 20 km (12.5 miles) east of town off Mexico 70. A *colectivo* to the airport from the city center costs US$3, a private taxi US$10.

Bus

The Central Camionera is at the east end of Carrera Torres where it meets the *libramiento de tránsito pesado* (an inner ring road for bus and truck traffic). All the major bus companies based in Reynosa, Matamoros, Tampico, and San Luis Potosí operate buses hourly to Ciudad Victoria for US$7-9 first class. Buses to/from Mexico City cost around US$25. **Transportes Tamaulipas** has frequent first-class buses to/from Monterrey (US$9), Monclova (US$14.50), and Nuevo Laredo (US$15). **Transportes del Norte** buses ply between Ciudad Victoria and Torreón (US$21), while **Oriente** goes to Tula (US$4) and San Luis Potosí (US$9).

Train

Travel to Monterrey and Tampico by train takes twice as long as by bus, but it's cheaper and the scenery is better. **Del Golfo** No. 171 departs Tampico at 7:45 a.m. and arrives in Ciudad Victoria around 1 p.m., then continues on almost immediately to Monterrey, arriving there at 6:45 p.m. In the opposite direction, No. 172 leaves Monterrey at 7:45 a.m. and arrives in Ciudad Victoria at 1 or 1:30 p.m., then departs at 1:50 p.m. for Tampico, with a 6:45 or 7 p.m. arrival on the coast. The fare for either leg is just US$2.50 (second class only).

The railway station is at the west end of Av. Hidalgo at Calle Carranza (Calle 22).

Driving

The city's central portion is laid out in the same neat grid designed by city planners in 1895. From the north, Mexico 85 turns into Blvd. Tamaulipas, which then becomes Blvd. J.B. Tijerina through the city proper. A ring road around the city is well marked and leads to Mexico 101 South (for San Luis Potosí), Mexico 101 North (to Reynosa), Mexico 70 East (for Soto la Marina), and Mexico 85 South (for Ciudad Mante and Tampico).

PEMEX stations are plentiful in town as well as along the highway junctions on the outskirts.

Auto Rental

Cars can be rented at **National,** tel. (131) 6-2275, and at **Car Rental Islas Aruba,** tel. (131) 5-1877, both at Best Western Hotel Santorín. Prices are higher than average.

VICINITY OF CIUDAD VICTORIA

Presa Vicente Guerrero

An impoundment of the Soto la Marina, Corona, Pilón, and Purificación Rivers, 47,000-hectare Presa Guerrero is known as one of the best bass-producing lakes—possibly *the* best—in Mexico. The main supply and lodging center for the lake is **Nuevo Padilla,** 54 km (33.5 miles) northeast of Ciudad Victoria via Mexico 101 (about 200 km/124 miles/four hours southwest of Reynosa). The original town of Padilla, founded by José de Escandón in 1749, appears in historical footnotes as the place where Mexican emperor Agustín de Iturbide was executed in 1824. The town was flooded when the dam was constructed in 1970; during periods of low water you can catch glimpses of old Padilla architecture above the water near the mouth of the Río Purificación. The original highway (Mexico 101) was also inundated; a new road now curves around the north end of the lake to Nuevo Padilla, where Mexico 101 continues southward.

Villa de Casas, on the southern end of the lake off Mexico 70 (44 km/27 miles east of Ciudad Victoria), is another lakeside center where a *parque turístico* offers picnic tables, grills, and *palapas.*

Along the undeveloped east shore of the lake is **Rancho La Lajilla,** designated a "protected natural area" by the state of Tamaulipas because of its exemplary flora (primarily Tamaulipan thornforest) and fauna (including the endangered jaguar). Hunting for quail, white-winged dove, wild turkey, and white-tailed deer in season is permitted in the area.

Along untouched sections of nearby rivers, especially along the Río Corona, venerable Montezuma bald cypress (*sabina* or *ahuehuete* in Mexico) and Texas ebony *(ebano)* grow in abundance.

Fishing: The large lake offers many different types of shore terrains from which to hook catfish, tilapia, and several varieties of largemouth bass; the lake record is held by a lunker weighing over 7.2 kilograms (16 pounds). Recommended tackle includes medium-action rods, 17- to 20-pound test monofilament line, large plastic worms, slab spoons, spinners, and buzz baits. Fish are generally biting year-round, though Dec.-Feb. are considered the best months for trophy-sized bass, April-June for sheer numbers.

A limited supply of bait and tackle, along with simple accommodations and food, are available in Nuevo Padilla and Villa de Casa. Several lakeside fish camps also offer lodging, food, and fishing (and/or hunting) packages that can be booked through Texas offices. The typical one-night, two-day package for a Texas-affiliated lodge includes a comfortable a/c room, meals, and an English-speaking fishing guide for US$180 pp. At more rustic Mexican-run camps you usually pay as you go, with separate (and lower) fees for lodging, food, and guide.

At the northeast end of the lake near where old Mexico 101 was submerged, one of the premier facilities is **Big Bass Lodge** (on the lake) and its associated **Club Exclusivo** (inland). Each has a hotel, pool, restaurant, and bar; Big Bass also has a private airstrip and boat ramp (guests at one lodge may use the facilities at either). Three-day fishing packages are US$175-200, and minimum room-and-meals packages are US$85 pp per day. For information or reservations, contact Big Bass Tours, 1418 Beech St., Suite 122, McAllen, TX 78501, tel. (800) 531-7509, fax (956) 687-8514. Big Bass Tours sponsors an annual Big Bass Fishing Tournament at Presa Guerrero in October.

Also on the northeast end of the lake, **Hacienda Alta Vista,** P.O. Box 1511, Harlingen, TX 78551, tel. (956) 423-2234, offers a 35-room hotel, full RV hookups, pool, jacuzzi, private airstrip, boat-launching facilities, and similar multiday fishing packages.

Around the northwest edge of the lake, on the north bank of the Río Purificación (east of Nuevo Padilla), **Campo El Sargento** has 20 rooms, RV slots with full hookups, a restaurant/bar, pool, private airstrip, and boat ramp. Rates for room and board only are US$75 per day, while fishing packages are US$175 per day. Hunting packages are also available. For further information or reservations, call or write Sunbelt Hunting and Travel, P.O. Box 3009, Brownsville, TX 78520, tel. (956) 546-9101 in Texas or (131) 2-4356 in Padilla.

The nearby **Campo La Reforma,** tel. (131) 2-5611 in Ciudad Victoria, has simple cabins and fishing guides. A bit farther south near Padilla Viejo (Old Padilla), at the mouth of the Río Purificación, the Mexican-operated **El Pelicano,** tel. (131) 2-1550 in Ciudad Victoria, has five cabins, a restaurant, full hookup RV sites, a boat ramp, and moderately priced package deals. **La Tortuga,** just south of Padilla Viejo on the lake, has a few simple cabins and RV sites with full hookups.

Toward the southwest end of the lake, on the north bank of the Río Corona, **La Isla,** P.O. Box 3763, Brownsville, TX 78520, tel. (800) 327-3574, features a 12-room lodge, two-way RV hookups, showers, pool, *palapa* bar, gravel airstrip, and hunting/fishing packages.

At the south end of the lake (actually along the Río Villa de Casas, which feeds into the lake) are five fish camps of varying costs; signs in the town of Villa de Casas point the way to each. Closest to Casas is **Chato's,** which features several cabins, a pool, rustic restaurant/bar, boat launch, and parking for RVs and trailers. **Croix,** west of Chato's, and **Chico's,** to the east, offer places to camp, RV parking, and boat launches, but that's about it. Southwest of Croix, **El Dorado,** L&J Outdoor Tours, P.O. Box 4906, McAllen, TX 78502, tel. (131) 2-3024 in Ciudad Victoria, (956) 631-3665 or (800) 533-8687 in the U.S., has a lodge with 10 a/c units, full-hookup RV sites, showers, toilets, restaurant/bar, pool, and boat ramp; hunting/fishing packages are available.

Northeast of Villa de Casas on a separate road is **Campo Charly Morris** (a.k.a. Victoria Bass Club; contact L&J Outdoor Tours), with several a/c cabins, a restaurant/bar, and hunting/fishing packages.

El Chorrito

The most important religious pilgrimage site in northeastern Mexico, El Chorrito ("Little Stream") is a shrine to the Virgen de Tepeyac, whose image appears in a votive-like cave formation. The formation itself is at the rear of a *templo-gruta*, a large, domed chapel with a volcanic cave at the rear; skeptics will note that the image looks as if it has had the temporal assistance of a sculptor. The site is doubly sacred because it is also the source of a spring which feeds into slender El Chorrito waterfall, set amid lush surroundings and impressive valley and mountain views.

Annual pilgrimages and *matachine* dance processions to honor the Virgen del Chorrito are held 17-19 March, then again during April's Semana Santa, and yet again for Fiesta Guadalupana (12 Dec.). An average 50,000 pilgrims visit the shrine every year. The village of El Chorrito has several shops selling shrine paraphernalia, as well as a few places to eat; during festival times the enterprising villagers set up trailer parks, *palapa* restaurants, and more souvenir stalls.

Getting There: El Chorrito is 25 km (15.5 miles) west of El Tomaseño (near Villa Hidalgo), which is 77 km (48 miles) northwest of Ciudad Victoria via Mexico 85 (or 78 km south of Linares, N.L.).

Reserva de la Biosfera El Cielo

About 50 km (31 miles) south of Ciudad Victoria is North America's northernmost cloud forest, a rare area of extreme biodiversity known as El Cielo ("The Sky"). Because of its scientific value, in 1985 the Mexican government declared 144,530 hectares (360,000 acres) of land surrounding El Cielo in the Sierra de Cucharas (a subrange of the Sierra Madre Oriental) to be a Biosphere Reserve. The following year the United Nations added the reserve to its "Man and the Biosphere" program.

The reserve drapes over the southern end of Sierra de Guatemala, part of the larger Sierra Madre Oriental. El Cielo represents a transition zone between tropical and temperate zones that has produced four basic ecosystems: **tropical caducifolia jungle** in the eastern third of the reserve, at an elevation of 200-800 meters (650-2,600 feet); **mesophilic montane forest** or **cloud forest** (*bosque de niebla* in Spanish), an area covering about 18% of the reserve that receives rain around six months a year and produces a fantastic variety of flora—including over 30 types of orchids—at an elevation of about 800-1,400 meters (2,600-4,600 feet); **pine-oak forest** over about a third of the reserve at 1,400-2,400 meters (4,600-8,000 feet); and **chaparral-matorral** on the sierra's lower western slopes, an arid area of dwarf oaks and heaths.

Throughout El Cielo—but especially in the cloud forest belt and along the Río Sabinas—a unique and profuse mixture of flora grow side by side, including native palms, North American cacti, cedars, tropical orchids, oaks, ferns, lianas, Spanish moss, acacias, willows, cottonwoods, poplars, four species of sugar maples (twice the number found in New England!), sweet gums, dahlias, roseapples, and magnolias.

Both neoarctic and neotropical animal species inhabit the reserve, among them jaguar, ocelot, *temazate* (red deer), white-tailed deer, gray fox, and black bear, plus 21 species of amphibians, 60 reptiles, and 40 bats. Bird counts have confirmed 255 resident bird species (including quetzal, elegant trogon, collared forest falcon, crested caracara, chachalaca, curassow, blue-crowned motmot, warbling vireo, amethyst-throated hummingbird, and ferruginous pygmy owl) and 175 migratory bird species, or roughly half of all bird species known in Mexico.

Just over half of the reserve lies in the *municipio* of Jaumave, with smaller portions divided among Gómez Farías, Llera, and Ocampo.

TO CD. VICTORIA (50 km)
101
TO CD. VICTORIA (50 km)

TO TULA

JAUMAVE

SAN LORENZO
PADRON Y JUAREZ
85
CARAMBANCHEL

JOYA DE MOLINA
NOGALES
20 DE ABRIL

**RESERVA
DE LA BIOSFERA
EL CIELO**

LOS TANQUES

JOYA DE SALAS
JULILO
EL ENCINO
LA LIBERTAD
EL PORVENIR
(LA PERRA)
LAS CALABASAS
EL AZTECA

ALTA CIMA
LA MORITA
LA NORIA
SAN JOSE
GOMEZ FARIAS
EL ELEFANTE
SABINAS

EL REFUGIO

EL PARQUE

TO CD.
MANTE

0   10 km

85
TO TULA

▨ =PINE - OAK FOREST
◩ =CHAPARRAL - MATORRAL
▥ =TROPICAL CADUCIFOLIA JUNGLE
▤ =MESOPHILIC MONTANE FOREST / CLOUD FOREST

© MOON PUBLICATIONS, INC.

Around 2,500 Mexicans still reside on lands within the reserve—many are lumber workers from the southern states of Michoacán and Hidalgo who came to work for timber concessions in the 1960s—but the government prefers that they leave on their own rather than be forced out. Newcomers are permitted to settle but not to raise crops or domestic animals, which means hardly anyone is interested in settling this part of the sierra nowadays. Solar panels are being distributed free or at low cost to reduce the reliance on firewood for heat.

Visiting El Cielo: The reserve is closed to the general public but permission to visit may be granted on a case-by-case basis. Permission is usually granted as long as visitors are accompanied by guides registered with the government. Permits may be requested in person at the Dirección de Ecología office on the eighth floor of the Torre del Gobierno in Ciudad Victoria, tel. (131) 2-3242.

Gómez Farías is very much the main base from which most visitors enter the reserve. Gómez itself is lush and tropical, and so famous for its mangoes that a mango is emblazoned on the city insignia. Here and in nearby La Morita you'll find lots of mango juice, mango jelly, mango ice cream, and mango pie for sale, even out of season. There are other ways to access the reserve, but only the eastern entrée from Gómez is open to non-scholars.

From Gómez a rough 4WD road winds up to Alta Cima at the base of the cloud forest. There is also a steep 10-km foot trail cut through the jungle that leads to Alta Cima—a route preferred by birders. An *eco-tienda* called **La Fé** in Alta Cima sells books about El Cielo, some crafts, and homemade foods, while **Hotel El Pino** has a few rustic cabins for rent. You can make day-hikes into the forest from here or from San José, further into the heart of the reserve about two hours hike from Alta Cima. You can also swim at El Nacimiento, a pool at the headwaters of the Río Frío—but you'll probably need a guide to find it. Guides for hikes in the reserve can be hired through La Fé at a cost of around US$5 per six km, e.g., a hike of 12 km would cost US$10 per guide, shorter hikes less.

Most of those applying for permits are researchers and students. Government-sponsored facilities available for use in the reserve include a laboratory, cabins, dorms, and a kitchen at **Canindo Research Station,** at 1,300 meters (4,300 feet) in the middle of the cloud forest. There is a charge of US$10 pp per day (US$3 for students and professors) to use the cabins—plus a good deal of red tape to work through in Ciudad Victoria. At La Fe in Alta Cima, burros and mules can be arranged as pack animals and riding stock to reach Canindo.

In San José, a small *ejido* less than a kilometer beyond Canindo, local resident José Barrones has a two-room guest house where you can stay without all the red tape, for about the same cost.

Six buses a day go from Ciudad Mante to Gómez Farías, which is 11 km west of Mexico 85. The nearest hotel is in Mante.

During the rainy season, May-Oct., El Cielo's cloud forest layer is almost perpetually veiled in mist.

Tours: Tamaulipas Travel, Calle Rosales 272, Ciudad Victoria, Tamps., tel. (131) 2-1057, fax (131) 2-7002, can arrange full tours to El Cielo Biosphere Reserve at reasonable cost.

Rancho Cielito

On the banks of the scenic Río Sabinas, at the eastern edge of El Cielo, this private, 150-acre ranch is popular among birders and naturalists. The river is lined with Montezuma bald cypress and offers several good swimming areas. Simple accommodations and campsites are available. For further information, write Larry Loff at Texas Southmost College, Brownsville, TX 78520, or call Jack Berryman, tel. (956) 546-5131 in Texas.

Ciudad Mante

Few travelers stop off in Ciudad Mante, a sugarcane center southeast of Ciudad Victoria about halfway to Ciudad Valles, S.L.P. Visits to either of two active sugar mills south of town may be arranged through almost any hotel in town.

Ciudad Mante serves as a supply point for excursions to two nearby lakes. **Presa Ramiro Caballero,** 25 km (15.5 miles) east of Ciudad Mante via Mexico 80, then four km south on a dirt road, is a favorite local camping and fishing spot. The 7,000-acre **Presa San Lorenzo,** about 48 km (30 miles) northeast of Ciudad Mante (127 km/79 miles southeast of Ciudad Victoria), near the town of Xicoténcatl (about midway between Mexico 85 and Mexico 81), turns out a fair number of largemouth bass. The state provides grills, *palapas,* tables, two boat ramps and camping areas. At least two lakeside fish camps with accommodations are currently being developed under American auspices.

Accommodations: Several hotels in town provide basic shoestring-priced lodging. Cheapest (around US$8-13 a night) are: **Hotel California,** Km 9, Mexico 85; **Hotel Riestra,** Av. Juárez Pte. 317; and **Hotel Jardín,** Calle Galeana Nte. 103. The nicer **Motel Río,** Blvd. González at Azuceña, tel. (123) 2-2020, fax (123) 2-1995, provides clean, medium-sized rooms with a/c, TV, phone, and hot water around a tennis court, pool, and parking lot. Rates: US$12-16. The shoestring/budget **Hotel Monterrey,** Calle Juárez Ote. 503, tel. (123) 2-2712, is a three-story place offering clean rooms with a/c, TV, phone, and hot water. Other facilities include parking and a restaurant. Rates: US$13 in a smaller room, US$20 in a very large one.

The most comfortable place in town is the budget-priced **Hotel Mante,** Av. Guerrero at Sidar, tel. (123) 2-0990, which has four-star rooms with a/c, phone, and TV, plus parking, pool, restaurant, and bar. Rates: US$31-35.

Tula

Founded in 1617 by Franciscan missionaries, Tula is the state's oldest town and the first place in southwestern Tamaulipas that begins to show Huastec influence. Many 18th- and 19th-century buildings have survived, and there are minor Huastec ruins in the nearby *ejidos* of **La Laguna, Potrero de Palma, El Coronel,** and **Las Pintas.**

Tula is known for handcrafted leatherwork, including *cueras tamaulipecas.* The city's **Centro Artesanal** is housed in a two-story, 19th-century building in the old section of town.

If you're coming from Ciudad Mante to the east, the last 48 km (30 miles) from Ocampo to Tula is breathtaking. The road, a mix of gravel and pavement, is in fair to good condition and winds up into the mountains—through tropical jungle, cloud forest, and pine forest—then down into the dryer western side toward Tula.

Accommodations: Two places in town provide shoestring-priced rooms. The **Hotel Rossana,** Calle Hidalgo 7-B, tel./fax (123) 6-0177, features basic rooms around a pleasant open courtyard. Rates: US6.50 s, US$8 d. **Hotel Mesón de Mollinedo,** Calle Morelos 1, tel. (123) 6-0045, provides simple but very tidy stone-floored rooms with rustic handmade furniture. This one feels a bit like Margarita's in Creel minus all the tourists. Rates: US$9 for one to three people, US$10.50 for four.

Food: The local cuisine has more in common with that of San Luis Potosí than with Tamaulipan styles. Specialties include *enchiladas tultecas* (chile-dipped tortillas smothered with cheese, *chorizo,* lettuce, onions, tomatoes, and *chile pequín* sauce), *pipián* (a currylike preparation of chiles and pumpkin seeds), tamales, *nopalitos,* and *atole.* Regional cooking is available at **Restaurante Tulteco,** Km 40 on Mexico 101 on the outskirts of town. **Restaurant Colonial,** near the Hotel Mesón and Hotel Rossana, serves Mexican standards as well as a few local dishes.

Restaurant Wendy (I'll bet Dave Thomas doesn't know about this), on the main road, is an inexpensive *antojitos* place full of locals.

emerald toucanet

ERIN DWYER

RESOURCES
BOOKLIST

DESCRIPTION AND TRAVEL

Bowden, Charles. *The Secret Forest*. Albuquerque: University of New Mexico Press, 1993. A captivating social, historical, and ecological evocation of the Sonoran tropical deciduous forest surrounding Alamos, Sonora. Includes numerous color photos.

Burleson, Bob, and David H. Riskind. *Backcountry Mexico: A Traveler's Guide and Phrase Book*. Austin: University of Texas Press, 1986. Part guidebook, part anthropological study of Northern Mexico with useful tips on backcountry travel.

Greene, Graham. *Another Mexico*. New York: Viking Press, 1939. The esteemed British author's account of his famous journey to Chiapas and back contains chapters on Nuevo Laredo, Monterrey, and San Luis Potosí. Greene's incandescent prose and keen insight into people and places makes up for his general lack of appreciation for Mexico. Like many of Greene's essays on Mexico, the books focuses on Catholicism more than almost any other social aspect.

Hancock, Richard. *Chihuahua: A Guide to the Wonderful Country*. Norman, OK: University of Oklahoma Press, 1978. This hard-to-find, out-of-print book has good historical notes on some of the state's smaller towns.

Lumholz, Carl. *New Trails in Mexico*. Tucson: University of Arizona Press, 1990. A re-publication of Lumholz's classic 1912 volume on Sonora's Papagueria (Tohono O'odham homelands) with historic photos and sketches. Contains marvelous descriptions of the native medicinal uses of such common Sonoran Desert plants as saguaro and greasewood, even snippets of Papago songs.

Morris, Mary. *Nothing to Declare: Memoirs of a Woman Traveling Alone*. Boston: Houghton Mifflin, 1988. Mostly a very personal journey but sprinkled with insights into daily Mexican life.

Nelson, Mike. *Mexico from the Driver's Seat*. Oak Park, MI: Scrivener Press, 1991. A collection of Nelson's humorous, homespun columns from the *McAllen Monitor, Mexico City News,* and other periodicals, based on his extensive motor travels around Mexico researching road conditions for Sanborn's Mexican Insurance. Although cheaply produced, with many typesetting gaffes, Nelson's unique and infectious prose levels the myths about driving in Mexico.

Nelson, Mike. *More than a Dozen of Mexico's Hidden Jewels*. McAllen, TX: Hidden Books, 1995. This slim 36-page booklet offers details on many off-the-beaten-track spots, most of them in Northern Mexico, which Nelson visited while researching Sanborn's Insurance "travelogs".

Pfefferkorn, Ignaz. *Sonora: A Description of the Province*. Tucson: University of Arizona Press, 1989. Originally published in German in 1794-95 and translated into English by Theodore Treutlein in 1949, this complete description of northern Sonora (including present-day southern Arizona) was written by a German Jesuit missionary who spent a decade among the Pima and Papago Indians prior to the Jesuit expulsion in 1767.

Wallace, Dillon. *Beyond the Mexican Sierras*. Chicago: McClury & Co., 1910. Well-written, humorous account of the author's travels along Mexico's Pacific coast at the turn of the century.

HISTORY AND POLITICS

Cabeza de Vaca, Alvar Nuñez. *Cabeza de Vaca's Adventures in the Unknown Interior of America*. Albuquerque: University of New Mexico Press, 1983. The classic account of Cabeza de Vaca's nine-year journey on foot through the American Southwest and Northern Mexico.

Herzog, Lawrence A. *Where North Meets South: Cities, Space and Politics on the U.S.-Mexico Border*. Center for Mexican American Studies, University of Texas at Austin, 1990. Sociologist Herzog postulates a new urban paradigm, the "transfrontier metropolis." The text focuses mostly on the San Diego-Tijuana area, with plenty of demographic and economic statistics and maps to illustrate the author's points.

Llosa, Alvaro Vargas, Carlos Alberto Motaner, and Plinio Apuleyo Mendoza. *Manual of the Perfect Latin American Idiot*. Madrid: Plaza & James, 1997. Co-authored by a Peruvian journalist, Cuban novelist, and Colombian journalist, this best-seller throughout Latin America has recently been released in English. This Latin intellectual tag team explodes the persistent myth that Latin America is currently experiencing a free-market revolution, detailing how closed markets are for the most part merely moving from the public to private sector through government-business cronyism. They argue that in addition to continuing inefficiency, the danger posed by such closed-market capitalism is that it is creating a powerful populist opposition and weakening the case for the free market in Latin American countries. Mexico and the Salinas years form a perfect example of their basic thesis.

Reavis, Dick J. *Conversations with Moctezuma: Ancient Shadows over Modern Life in Mexico*. New York: William Morrow & Co., 1990. This collection of observations by an American foreign correspondent living in Mexico is full of insider information on political and social organization in modern Mexico, with special reference to Monterrey and the 1988 presidential election.

ART AND CULTURE

Artaud, Antonin. *The Peyote Dance*. New York: Farrar, Straus & Giroux, 1976. An interesting piece of participatory anthropology in which the notorious founder of *théâtre de cruel* dares to live the Tarahumara myths in the face of possible insanity. Much of this work was in fact written from a Paris asylum upon Artaud's return to France after spending eight months with Tarahumara shamans.

Bierhorst, John. *The Mythology of Mexico and Central America*. New York: William Morrow, 1990. A good introduction to Mexican mythology, with passages on Yaqui, Mayo, Tarahumara, Cora, and Huichol myths among others.

Gershman, Suzy, and Judith Thomas. *Born to Shop Mexico*. New York: Bantam Books, 1989. Delightful shopping guide written by two very savvy Texas women. Includes sections on border towns.

Parks, Walter P. *The Miracle of Mata Ortíz: Juan Quezada and the Potters of Northern Mexico*. The Coulter Press, 1993. This large-format paperback contains a detailed history of the Chihuahuan potters village of Mata Ortíz, copious descriptions of pottery styles, an annotated list of the village's main potters, and a selection of color and black-and-white illustrations.

Paz, Octavio. *The Labyrinth of Solitude: Life and Thought in Mexico*. New York: Grove Press, 1961. Paz has no peer when it comes to expositions of the Mexican psyche, and this is his best work.

Stewart, Omer. *Peyote Religion: A History*. Norman, OK: University of Oklahoma Press, 1987. The most authoritative book on the subject of peyote in North America gathers together research from all quarters, including a thorough history of peyote use in Northern Mexico, where the cactus originated. Complete with maps, tables, and historical citations.

NATURAL HISTORY

"Biotic Communities of the American Southwest—United States and Mexico," *Desert Plants,* Vol. 4, Nos. 1-4. Superior, AZ: University of Arizona Press (for the Boyce Thompson Southwestern Arboretum), 1982. A carefully team-researched study of Greater Southwest biomes with plenty of detail on northwestern Mexico (including Durango and Chihuahua). Although it's tough going, this is a definitive work for those with a serious interest in the typology of Mexican vegetation.

Davis, L. Irby. *A Field Guide to the Birds of Mexico and Central America.* Austin: University of Texas Press, 1972. A good supplement to the Peterson guide (see below).

Ives, Ronald L. *Land of Lava, Ash, and Sand: The Pinacate Region of Northwestern Mexico.* Tucson: Arizona Historical Society, 1989. Edited by Karen J. Dahood. This collection of excerpts from the prolific writings of Ronald Ives (1919-82), who specialized in environmental research on northwest Mexico, presents an admirable synthesis of the geography, geology, meteorology, volcanology, history, and anthropology of the Pinacate region.

Peterson, Roger Tory, and Edward L. Chalif. *A Field Guide to Mexican Birds.* Boston: Houghton Mifflin, 1973. Despite being a bit outdated, this is still the most popular and useful guide to birding in Mexico.

Simon, Joel. *Endangered Mexico: An Environment on the Edge.* San Francisco: Sierra Club Books, 1997. As the title makes explicit, this book is intended to send out a loud note of alarm for Mexico's environment. This it does quite well, particularly in its coverage of Mexico City. What it sorely lacks is a global context for environmental issues in Mexico. It would have been instructive, for example, to compare Mexico's environmental record with that of other developing countries; within the latter context Mexico fares better than average. In comparison with the U.S., for example Mexico is producing far less per-capita greenhouse emissions and consuming far fewer non-recyclables. Still, this book should be read by anyone concerned with environmental policy in Mexico.

Steinhart, Peter. *Two Eagles/Dos Aguilas: The Natural World of the United States-Mexico Borderlands.* Berkeley: University of California Press, 1994. Pre-publication material for this book, which examines the borderlands as a "distinct province of the hemisphere," looks very good. Includes excellent photography by Tupper Ansel Blake.

Wauer, Roland H. *A Naturalist's Mexico.* College Station, TX: Texas A&M University Press, 1992. Although only 65 pages are devoted to Northern Mexico (plus 14 pages on Isla Tiburón), this anecdotal, travelogue-style narrative of Mexico's natural environment is a good read. Birding activities receive more emphasis than other aspects of the author's Mexican explorations, so those with a keen interest in Mexican birds will enjoy this book most.

FICTION

Esquivel, Laura. *Como Agua para Chocolate (Like Water for Chocolate).* New York: Doubleday, 1993 (available in either Spanish or English language versions from the same publisher). See "Film and Video," below for a description of the magical story.

McCarthy, Cormack. *All the Pretty Horses.* New York: Knopf, 1992. Reclusive El Paso resident McCarthy has written a string of striking novels which have led critics to crown him as "the new William Faulkner." This is his most accessible, a succinct yet powerful narrative of a boy's coming of age along the Texas-Mexico border. The descriptions of locales in Northern Mexico are so accurate they suggest the author actually visited all the places he writes about in the book.

McCarthy, Cormack. *The Crossing.* Vantage, 1995. The second in McCarthy's so-called "border trilogy" takes place almost entirely within Northern Mexico. Once again the descriptions of Mexican settings are excellent, although this time the story of misspent revenge is less compelling.

FOOD

DeWitt, Dave, and Nancy Gerlach. *The Whole Chile Pepper Book.* Boston: Little, Brown and Co., 1990. By the editors of *Chile Pepper* magazine, this compendium of fact, lore, and recipes is the definitive culinary guide to chiles.

Peyton, James W. *The Cuisine of Northern Mexico.* Santa Fe: Red Crane Books, 1990. A good introduction to the border cuisines of Sonora, Chihuahua, Coahuila, and Nuevo León, complete with 150 easy-to-follow, mouthwatering recipes.

SPORTS AND RECREATION

Franz, Carl, with Steve Rogers. *RV Camping in Mexico.* Santa Fe: John Muir Publications, 1989. A bit out of date, but the introductory chapters would be useful for anyone planning their first RV trip to Mexico.

Lehman, Charles. *Desert Survival Handbook.* Phoenix: Primer Publishers, 1990. A no-nonsense guide to desert survival techniques that ought to be part of every pilot's or coastal navigator's kit.

Oleksak, Michael, and Mary Oleksak. *Béisbol: Latin Americans and the Grand Old Game.* Indianapolis: Masters Press, 1991. The best reference on baseball south of the border.

Wyatt, Mike. *The Basic Essentials of Sea Kayaking.* Merrillville, IN: ICS Books, 1990. A good introduction to sea kayaking, with tips on buying gear, paddling techniques, safety, and kayak loading.

THE TARAHUMARAS

Since most books on the Tarahumaras were written 20 or more years ago, it's difficult to judge how authoritative or relevant any of them are with respect to today's Tarahumaras. On top of that, descriptions of customs and ceremonies differ so completely from book to book that it almost seems as if the author-researchers are describing different tribes—and in a way they are, since there is no "standard" Tarahumara group.

Bennett, Wendell, and Robert Zingg. *The Tarahumara: An Indian Tribe of Northern Mexico.* Glorieta, NM: Rio Grande Press, 1976. Republished from the original 1835, pioneering work, this is the best source on mid-19th century Tarahumara life.

Fayhee, M. John. *Mexico's Copper Canyon Country.* Evergreen, CO: Cordillera Press, 1989. Humble and humorous, this anecdotal guide gives a good feel for what Sierra Tarahumara hiking and backpacking is all about, although details on transportation and accommodations are out of date.

Fontana, Bernard L. *Tarahumara: Where Night Is the Day of the Moon.* Flagstaff, AZ: Northland Publishing, 1979. A nicely photographed, large-format work containing some of the most current (but far from up-to-date) anecdotal research on the Tarahumaras. Both the text and photographs (by John P. Schaefer) refer to the highland Tarahumaras east of the Continental Divide, an area peripheral to the geographic and cultural heart of the Sierra Tarahumara.

Kennedy, John C. *The Tarahumara of the Sierra Madre: Survivors on the Canyon's Edge.* Asilomar Press, 1996. Kennedy's cultural assessment of the Tarahumara is well worth reading.

Kennedy, John C., and Raúl López. *Semana Santa in the Sierra Tarahumara: A Comparative Study of Three Communities.* Berkeley: University of California Press, 1981. A good source for understanding the cultural variation among different Tarahumara villages.

Lumholz, Carl. *Unknown Mexico: Explorations and Adventures Among the Tarahumara, Tepehuane, Cora, Huichol, Tarasco, and Aztec Indians,* volumes 1 and 2. New York: Charles

Scribners & Sons, 1902. A pioneering piece of research by the legendary Norwegian ethnologist. Information on the Sierra Tarahumara is mostly contained in volume 1.

Pennington, Campbell W. *The Tarahumar [sic] of Mexico: Their Environment and Material Culture.* Salt Lake City: University of Utah Press, 1963. Considered by many to be the seminal work on Tarahumara culture.

Roca, Paul M., Spanis Jesuit Churches in Mexico's Tarahumara. Tuscon: University of Arizona Press, 1970. Contains thorough coverage of Jesuit missions in the sierra, including many not mentioned in this guidebof

OTHER RESOURCES

FILM AND VIDEO

El Mariachi. Directed by 23-year-old Robert Rodriguez, at the time a UT-Austin film student, and produced in Ciudad Acuña, Coah. on a budget of US$7,000, this 1992 film stars Carlos Gallardo as a young guitarist mistaken for a hit man in the world of *narcotraficantes.* The unique combination of a poetic tone with in-your-face realism had critics jumping out of their seats. In Spanish with English subtitles; available on video.

Desperado. Also known as *El Mariachi 2.* Hollywood gave Rodriguez at least 10 times the budget of his original flick to direct what is very nearly a remake of *El Mariachi,* except that this time the trigger-happy guitarist is portrayed by heart-throb Antonio Banderas, the soundtrack features Los Lobos, and Quentin Tarantino makes a surprise appearance in the classic opening bar sequence. 1995. Available on video.

Like Water for Chocolate (Como Agua para Chocolate). Based on Laura Esquivel's succulent novel and adapted for the screen by her director/husband Alfonso Arau, this 1992 film is one of the most successful transitions of Latin American literature's magic realism to the screen. The story takes place during the Mexican Revolution years in the vicinity of Piedras Negras, Coah., where the film was shot on location. Tita, the youngest of three daughters, is condemned by tradition to taking care of her mother in old age rather than marrying the man she loves; the novel follows the way in which she sublimates her romantic passions in the kitchen.

In the book, each chapter begins with a recipe containing classic border motifs. The title is a Mexican expression that describes a passion akin to boiling water ready for the addition of ingredients to produce hot chocolate. Distributed in the U.S. by Miramax (producers of *Enchanted April, Mediterraneo*). In Spanish with English subtitles, available on video.

Lone Star. Although set almost entirely in south Texas, John Sayle's 1996 film starring Chris Cooper, Elizabeth Peña, Kris Kristofferson, and Matthew McConaughey, hit a new watermark in terms of the quality of feature films about the Mexican border area. As critic Roger Ebert began his four-star review of the film, "*Lone Star* contains so many riches it humbles ordinary movies," and concluded, "the best work yet by one of our most original and independent filmmakers." Focusing on dramatic interaction between Texans of Anglo, African, Mexican, and Seminole descent in a fictionalized but very realistic Texas border county, the film presents the cultural cross-fertilization and conflict inherent in *la frontera* better than any other cinematic attempt to date. Though most of the action was filmed in Eagle Pass, Texas, small sequences were shot in Ciudad Acuña. The soundtrack contains several classic *norteña* tunes. Available on video.

LANGUAGE STUDY

Dictionaries and Phrasebooks

One of the best dictionaries of a portable size for the Spanish student is the paperback *University of Chicago Spanish-English, English-Spanish Dictionary,* which emphasizes New World usages and contains useful sections on grammar and pronunciation. If even this small volume is too large for your backpack, the *Collins Gem Dictionary: Spanish-English, English-Spanish* comes in a tiny 4 by 3.25 by 1-inch size with a sturdy plastic cover and over 40,000 entries.

Berlitz's *Latin-American Spanish For Travellers* is a small phrasebook divided by topics and situations (e.g., Grammar, Hotel, Eating Out, Post Office) that some people find very helpful. Not all of the phrases and terms it contains are used in Mexico but it's better than nothing.

One of the best references for off-the-road adventurers is Burleson's and Riskind's *Backcountry Mexico: A Traveler's Guide and Phrase Book* (University of Texas Press). Although it's rather bulky for carrying in a backpack, it contains many words and phrases that could be of value to hikers and campers if studied before taking an extended backcountry trip.

If you're serious about getting deep into Mexican Spanish, the best available reference is the 1,200-page *Diccionario de Mejicanismos,* by Francisco J. Santamaria (Mexico City: Editorial Porrúa, 1983). This is the only disctionary we found that contained, for example, a definition for *cocol* (ringlet), a word that apparently doesn't exist in any other contemporary Spanish dialect.

Advanced Spanish students may be able to improve their command of idiomatic Spanish with Frances de Talavera Berger's *¡Mierda!* (Plume: New York). Subtitled *The Real Spanish You Were Never Taught in School,* the book's copious *vulgarismos* or slang expressions have a decidedly scatological slant and should probably be aired in public only after practice with a trusted native speaker.

Courses

Those who plan to spend an extended period of time in Northern Mexico should seriously con-

sider enrolling in an intensive Spanish course. Night classes at an adult community school or summer university courses are a fine introduction, but the most time-and-cost-effective study program is one that immerses you in the language and culture within Mexico. The *Centro de Idiomas* in Mazatlán is a long-running private language school with reasonable rates, and there are a couple of newer language programs in Saltillo (see the "Information" sections for those cities in this book).

In the U.S., excellent eight- to 10-week Spanish summer programs are open to the public at the University of California, Berkeley (Department of Spanish & Portuguese, Dwinelle Hall, University of California, Berkeley, CA 94720, tel. 510-642-6000); and at the San Antonio branch of Mexico's Universidad Nacional Autonoma de Mexico (600 Hemisfair Park, P.O. Box 830426, San Antonio, TX 78283, tel. 210-222-8626). Many other colleges and universities in the U.S. and Canada offer similar summer intensives. In investigating a program, be sure to ask what type of Spanish—Latin American or Castilian—will be taught.

USEFUL INTERNET SITES

Borderlands Encyclopedia

www.utep.edu/border/
This site, sponsored by the University of Texas at El Paso, provides a set of good internet links for many different aspects of the U.S.-Mexico border area, including culture, trade, and politics.

Don Pato's Gay Mexico

http://donpato.simplenet.com/mexico/
Reports on the gay entertainment scene in several different cities in Mexico, including Tijuana and Ensenada, but of general interest to almost anyone interested in Mexican nightlife.

Eco Travels in Latin America

www.planeta.com
A rich site with information on officially protected areas in Mexico and elsewhere in Latin America, as well as regularly updated files on ecologically related news.

Guía Roji
www.guiaroji.com.mx
Excellent on-line atlas of Mexico City with maps of Guadalajara and Monterrey soon to come.

Mexican Embassy
www.quicklink.com/mexico/ingles/ing.html
Carries information posted by the Mexican foreign service regarding visas and other immigration matters, with links to other government sites.

Mexico Net Guide
www.mexguide.net
Miscellaneous information about Mexico with many links to other Web sites.

Mexico Online
www.mexonline.com
Carries much general information on Mexico in many categories, plus hot links to other sites.

NaftaNet
www.nafta.net
Information pertinent to the North American Free Trade Agreement.

Newspapers
www.mediainfo.com
Gateway to over 2,500 on-line newspapers around the world, including some from Mexico.

Olsen Currency Converter
www.olsen.ch/
For fast quotes on exchange rates for all international currencies, including the Mexican peso.

Quick Aid
www.quickaid.com
Supplies international airport information and flight schedules.

Sanborn's Mexican Insurance
www.hiline.net/sanborns/index/html
Contains ample information on Mexican vehicle insurance plus tips on driving in Mexico.

Secretaría de Turismo (SECTUR)
www.mexico-travel.com
Well-constructed home page for Mexico's Ministry of Tourism, organized by region and by state.

SEMARNAP
www.semarnap.gob.mx
Website for the Mexican government agency concerned with environmental matters.

U.S. Embassy
www.internet.com.mx/embassy
Contains the home page for the U.S. Embassy in Mexico City, with information on consular services to U.S. citizens as well as State Department warnings.

University of Texas Map Library
www.lib.utexas.edu/libs/PCL/
Stocked with maps of Mexico of various kinds.

World Health Organization
www.who.ch/
Provides the latest information on health situations around the world; includes daily press releases on disease outbreaks.

GLOSSARY

abarrotes—groceries

aduana—customs service

antojitos—literally "little whims," quick Mexican dishes like tacos and enchiladas

aparejo—burro saddle

arroyo—canyon, dry wash, or stream

atole—thick, flavored corn beverage popular in San Luis Potosí and southwestern Tamaulipas

autopista—freeway

bahía—bay

balneario—spa or bathing resort, usually associated with natural springs

barrio—neighborhood

basura—trash or rubbish; the sign No Tire Basura means "Don't throw trash."

boca—literally "mouth," a geographic term describing a break in a barrier island or peninsula where sea meets lagoon

bolsón—desert depression where rainwater collects

cabecera—*municipio* capital, roughly equivalent to a county seat

calle—street

callejón—alley or lane

cañon—canyon

cardón—*Cereus pringelei,* the world's tallest cactus

casa de huéspedes—guesthouse

cerro—hill or mountain

cerveza—beer

charreada—Mexican-style rodeo

charro/charra—horseman/horsewoman

CONASUPO—Compañía Nacional de Subsistencias Populares (National Company for Popular Subsistence)

Churrigueresque—*churrigueresco* in Spanish, named for Spain's Churriguera family of architects, a late baroque style in neo-Hispanic churches and cathedrals characterized by heavy ornamentation

cigarro—cigarette

colectivo—van or taxi that picks up several passengers at a time for a standard per-person fare, much like a bus

comedores—small diners, often near bus stations or in municipal markets

comida corrida—fixed-price afternoon meal

correo—post office

corrida de toros—"running of the bulls" or bullfight

COTP—Captain of the Port

curandero—traditional healer

D.F.—Distrito Federal (Federal District), a special federal entity that grants Mexico City an administrative status similar to that of a state

desertland—biotic community with an average annual precipitation of 25 cm (10 inches) or less

efectivo—cash payment

ejido—collectively owned agricultural lands

ensenada—cove or small bay

FONART—Fondo Nacional para el Fomento de las Artesanías (National Foundation for the Development of Arts and Crafts)

FONATUR—Fondo Nacional de Fomento del Turismo (National Foundation for Tourism Development)

forest—biotic community dominated by trees over 15 meters (49 feet) in height, usually with a closed and/or multilayered canopy

Gral.—abbreviation for "General" (rank)

grassland—biotic community dominated by grasses and/or other herbaceous vegetation

gringo—Mexican slang for Caucasian foreigner

hectare—equal to 2.74 acres

IMSS—Instituto Mexicano del Seguro Social (Mexican Social Security Institute)

INAH—Instituto Nacional de Antropología e Historia (National Institute of Anthropology and History)

indios—Mexicans of predominantly Amerindian descent

ISSSTE—Instituto de Seguridad y Servicios Sociales para Trabajadores del Estado (Security and Social Services Institute for Government Workers)

laguna—lagoon, lake, or bay

llano—plains

lleno—full

lomerías—hilly desert grasslands of southern Chihuahua and northern Durango

maguey—agave or century plant; maguey extract is often fermented and distilled to produce alcoholic beverages, including mescal and tequila

maquiladora (maquila)—a "twin-bond" or "in-plant" manufacturing enterprise where foreign components may be imported and assembled, then exported to a foreign country, free of customs duties in each direction; now that NAFTA has been enacted, the *maquiladora* may become extinct.

malecón—waterfront promenade

mescal/mezcal—alcoholic beverage distilled from maguey extract

mariscos—literally "shellfish," but often used as a generic term for seafood

matachine—a type of religious dance procession popular in the north

mochila—knapsack or backpack (*mochilero:* backpacker)

municipio—the next administrative unit below the state, Mexico's equivalent to a county

mercado—market

nopal, nopales—prickly pear cactus; with the spines removed it is commonly served as a side dish—parboiled or grilled—throughout the north; *nopalitos* are strips of cooked or pickled nopal.

palacio municipal—literally "municipal palace," equivalent to city or county hall in the U.S.

palapa—thatched, umbrellalike shade shelter or roof

panadería—bakery

parrada—bus stop

PAN—Partido Acción Nacional, the main opposition party to the ruling Partido Revolucionario Institucional (PRI)

PEMEX—Petróleos Mexicanos (Mexican Petroleum)

periférico—highway loop or bypass

peyote—*Lophophora williamsii*, a hallucinogenic cactus used for religious rituals among certain Amerindian cultures

pensión—boardinghouse

playa—beach

plaza—town square

plazuela—smaller plaza

pre-Cortesian—a reference to Mexican history before the arrival of the Spanish conquistador Hernán Cortés, i.e., before 1518; other terms with the same meaning include "pre-Columbian" and "pre-Hispanic"

punta—point

Porfiriato—the period during which Porfirio Díaz was president of Mexico, when many foreigners purchased land and established businesses in Mexico

presidio—military garrison

PRD—Partido Revolucionario Democrático, a close second behind PAN in effective electoral opposition to the PRI

PRI—Partido Revolucionario Institucional

Prol.—an abbreviation for "Prolongación," an extension of an older avenue/boulevard

puro—cigar

ramal—branch road

ranchería—a collection of small ranching households, most often inhabited by *indios*

ranchito—small ranch

rebozo—traditional handwoven Mexican shawl; the best are made in the state of San Luis Potosí.

refresca—soda or soft drink

retablo—altarpiece; also, a devotional carving (usually tin or wood) presented as a shrine offering

sarape—traditional all-purpose blanket; the most famous are from Saltillo

scrubland—biotic community dominated by shrubs and/or multistemmed trees generally under 10 meters (31 feet)

SECTUR—Secretaría de Turismo (Secretariat* of Tourism)

SEDESOL—Secretaría de Desarrollo Social (Secretariat* of Social Development)

SEMARNAP—Secretaría del Medio Ambiente, Recursos Naturales y Pesca (Secretariat* of the Environment, Natural Resources, and Fishing)

s/n—*sin número* or "without number," used for street addresses without building numbers

Solomonic—an architectural term applied to Spanish baroque columns—common on 17th- to 18th-century church facades—with spiral motifs

tahona—wooden mill for grinding ore to separate gold; sometimes hand operated, sometimes powered by burro or waterwheel

tianguis—open-air market

tienda—store

tinaja—pool or spring

topes—speed bumps

trago—slang for a "swallow," i.e., a quick drink

ultramarinos—delicatessen/liquor store

viceregal—*virreinal* in Spanish; a reference to the 300-year period (1521-1821) when a Spanish viceroy ruled Mexico as Nueva España; as a historical term, "viceregal" is often synonymous with "colonial."

woodland—biotic community dominated by trees not exceeding 15 meters (49 feet) in height with an open (or interrupted) single-layer canopy

*can also be roughly translated as "Ministry"

SPANISH PHRASEBOOK

PRONUNCIATION GUIDE

Consonants

c   as c in cat, before a, o, or u; like s before e or i
d   as d in dog, except between vowels, then like th in that
g   before e or i, like the ch in Scottish loch; elsewhere like g in get
h   always silent
j   like the English h in hotel, but stronger
ll like the y in yellow
ñ   like the ni in onion
r   always pronounced as strong r
rr trilled r
v   similar to the b in boy (not as English v)
y   similar to English, but with a slight j sound. When y stands alone it is
    pronounced like the e in me.
z   like s in same
b, f, k, l, m, n, p, q, s, t, w, x as in English

Vowels

a   as in father, but shorter
e   as in hen
i   as in machine
o   as in phone
u   usually as in rule; when it follows a q the u is silent; when it follows an h or g
    its pronounced like w, except when it comes between g and e or i, when it's also
    silent

NUMBERS

0	cero	11	once	40	cuarenta
1	uno (masculine)	12	doce	50	cincuenta
1	una (feminine)	13	trece	60	sesenta
2	dos	14	catorce	70	setenta
3	tres	15	quince	80	ochenta
4	cuatro	16	diez y seis	90	noventa
5	cinco	17	diez y siete	100	cien
6	seis	18	diez y ocho	101	ciento y uno
7	siete	19	diez y nueve	200	doscientos
8	ocho	20	veinte	1,000	mil
9	nueve	21	viente y uno	10,000	diez mil
10	diez	30	treinta		

DAYS OF THE WEEK

Sunday — *domingo*
Monday — *lunes*
Tuesday — *martes*
Wednesday — *miércoles*

Thursday — *jueves*
Friday — *viernes*
Saturday — *sábado*

TIME

What time is it? — *¿Qué hora es?*
one o'clock — *la una*
two o'clock — *las dos*
at two o'clock — *a las dos*
ten past three — *las tres y diez*
six a.m. — *las seis de mañana*
six p.m. — *las seis de tarde*
today — *hoy*

tomorrow, morning
  — *mañana, la mañana*
yesterday — *ayer*
day — *día*
week — *semana*
month — *mes*
year — *año*
last night — *anoche*

USEFUL WORDS AND PHRASES

Hello. — *Hola.*
Good morning. — *Buenos días.*
Good afternoon. — *Buenas tardes.*
Good evening. — *Buenas noches.*
How are you? — *¿Cómo está?*
Fine. — *Muy bien.*
And you? — *¿Y usted?*
So-so. — *Más ó menos.*
Thank you. — *Gracias.*
Thank you very much. — *Muchas gracias.*
You're very kind. — *Muy amable.*
You're welcome; literally, "It's nothing."
  — *De nada.*
yes — *sí*
no — *no*
I don't know. — *Yo no sé.*
it's fine; okay — *está bien*
good; okay — *bueno*
please — *por favor*
Pleased to meet you. — *Mucho gusto.*
excuse me (physical) — *perdóneme*
excuse me (speech) — *discúlpeme*
I'm sorry. — *Lo siento.*
goodbye — *adiós*

see you later; literally, "until later"
  — *hasta luego*
more — *más*
less — *menos*
better — *mejor*
much — *mucho*
a little — *un poco*
large — *grande*
small — *pequeño*
quick — *rápido*
slowly — *despacio*
bad — *malo*
difficult — *difícil*
easy — *fácil*
He/She/It is gone; as in "She left," "He's
  gone" — *Ya se fue.*
I don't speak Spanish well.
  — *No hablo bien español.*
I don't understand. — *No entiendo.*
How do you say . . . in Spanish?
  — *¿Cómo se dice . . . en español?*
Do you understand English?
  — *¿Entiende el inglés?*
Is English spoken here? (Does anyone
  here speak English?)
  — *¿Se habla inglés aquí?*

TERMS OF ADDRESS

I — *yo*
you (formal) — *usted*
you (familiar) — *tú*
he/him — *él*
she/her — *ella*
we/us — *nosotros*
you (plural) — *vos*
they/them (all males or mixed gender)
   — *ellos*
they/them (all females) — *ellas*

Mr., sir — *señor*
Mrs., madam — *señora*
Miss, young lady — *señorita*
wife — *esposa*
husband — *marido* or *esposo*
friend — *amigo* (male), *amiga* (female)
sweetheart — *novio* (male), *novia* (female)
son, daughter — *hijo, hija*
brother, sister — *hermano, hermana*
father, mother — *padre, madre*

GETTING AROUND

Where is . . . ? — *¿Dónde está . . . ?*
How far is it to . . .?
   — *¿A cuánto queda . . . ?*
from . . . to . . . — *de . . . a . . .*
highway — *la carretera*
road — *el camino*
street — *la calle*
block — *la cuadra*
kilometer — *kilómetro*

mile (commonly used near the
   U.S. border) — *milla*
north — *el norte*
south — *el sur*
west — *el oeste*
east — *el este*
straight ahead — *al derecho* or *adelante*
to the right — *a la derecha*
to the left — *a la izquierda*

ACCOMMODATIONS

Can I (we) see a room?
   — *¿Puedo (podemos) ver un cuarto?*
What is the rate? — *¿Cuál es el precio?*
a single room — *un cuarto sencillo*
a double room — *un cuarto doble*
key — *llave*
bathroom — *lavabo* or *baño*
hot water — *agua caliente*

cold water — *agua fría*
towel — *toalla*
soap — *jabón*
toilet paper — *papel higiénico*
air conditioning — *aire acondicionado*
fan — *ventilador*
blanket — *frazada* or *manta*

PUBLIC TRANSPORT

bus stop — *la parada del autobús*
main bus terminal
   — *terminal de buses*
railway station
   — *la estación de ferrocarril*
airport — *el aeropuerto*
ferry terminal
   — *la terminal del transbordador*

I want a ticket to . . .
   — *Quiero un boleto a . . .*
I want to get off at . . .
   — *Quiero bajar en . . .*
Here, please. — *Aquí, por favor.*
Where is this bus going?
   — *¿Adónde va este autobús?*
roundtrip — *ida y vuelta*
What do I owe? — *¿Cuánto le debo?*

DRIVING

Full, please (at gasoline station).	With four-wheel drive?
— *Lleno, por favor.*	— *¿Con doble tracción?*
My car is broken down.	It's not passable — *No hay paso.*
— *Se me ha descompuesto el carro.*	traffic light — *el semáfora*
I need a tow. — *Necesito un remolque.*	traffic sign — *el señal*
Is there a garage nearby?	gasoline (petrol) — *gasolina*
— *¿Hay un garage cerca?*	gasoline station — *gasolinera*
Is the road passable with this car (truck)?	oil — *aceite*
— *¿Puedo pasar con este carro*	water — *agua*
(esta troca)?	flat tire — *llanta desinflada*
	tire repair shop — *llantera*

AUTO PARTS

fan belt — *banda de ventilador*	gasket — *empaque, junta*
battery — *batería*	filter — *filtro*
fuel (water) pump —	brakes — *frenos*
bomba de gasolina (agua)	tire — *llanta*
spark plug — *bujía*	hose — *manguera*
carburetor — *carburador*	starter — *marcha, arranque*
distributor — *distribuidor*	radiator — *radiador*
axle — *eje*	voltage regulator — *regulado de voltaje*
clutch — *embrague*	

MAKING PURCHASES

I need . . . — *Necesito . . .*	Can I see . . . ? — *¿Puedo ver . . . ?*
I want . . . — *Deseo . . .* or *Quiero . . .*	this one — *ésta/ésto*
I would like . . . (more polite)	expensive — *caro*
— *Quisiera . . .*	cheap — *barato*
How much does it cost? — *¿Cuánto cuesta?*	cheaper — *más barato*
What's the exchange rate?	too much — *demasiado*
— *¿Cuál es el tipo de cambio?*	

HEALTH

Help me please. — *Ayúdeme por favor.*	drugstore — *farmacia*
I am ill. — *Estoy enfermo.*	medicine — *medicina, remedio*
pain — *dolor*	pill, tablet — *pastilla*
fever — *fiebre*	birth control pills — *pastillas*
stomache ache — *dolor de estómago*	*anticonceptivas*
vomiting — *vomitar*	condoms — *preservativos*
diarrhea — *diarrea*	

FOOD

menu — *lista, menú*
glass — *vaso*
fork — *tenedor*
knife — *cuchillo*
spoon — *cuchara, cucharita*
napkin — *servilleta*
soft drink — *refresco*
coffee, cream — *café, crema*
tea — *té*
sugar — *azúcar*
purified water — *agua purificado*
bottled carbonated water — *agua mineral*
bottled uncarbonated water — *agua sin gas*
beer — *cerveza*
wine — *vino*
milk — *leche*
juice — *jugo*
eggs — *huevos*
bread — *pan*

watermelon — *sandía*
banana — *plátano*
apple — *manzana*
orange — *naranja*
meat (without) — *carne (sin)*
beef — *carne de res*
chicken — *pollo*
fish — *pescado*
shellfish — *mariscos*
fried — *a la plancha*
roasted — *asado*
barbecue, barbecued — *al carbón*
breakfast — *desayuno*
lunch — *almuerzo*
dinner (often eaten in late afternoon)
    — *comida*
dinner, or a late night snack — *cena*
the check — *la cuenta*

TRANSPORTATION
APPENDIX

AIRLINES SERVING NORTHERN MEXICO

* = nonstop flights available

Note: All routes are subject to change; call the airlines for the latest information. Listed are all flights within Northern Mexico, plus La Paz, Guadalajara and Mexico City, along with international connections.

AERO CALIFORNIA (U.S./CANADA TEL. 800-237-6225)

Flights from:

Chihuahua to Ciudad Obregón, Culiacán, Guadalajara, La Paz, Los Mochis, Mazatlán, Mexico City*, and Tijuana*

Ciudad Juárez to Ciudad Obregón, Culiacán, Guadalajara, La Paz, Los Angeles, Los Mochis, Mazatlán, Mexico City, and Torreón*

Ciudad Obregón to Chihuahua, Ciudad Juárez, Ciudad Victoria, Guadalajara, Los Mochis*, Matamoros, Mexico City, Monterrey, San Luis Potosí, Tijuana, Torreón, and Tucson

Ciudad Victoria to Chihuahua, Ciudad Juárez, Ciudad Obregón, Culiacán, Guadalajara, Hermosillo, La Paz, Los Mochis, Matamoros*, Mazatlán, Mexico City*, Monterrey, Tijuana, and Torreón

Culiacán to Chihuahua, Ciudad Juárez, Ciudad Victoria, Guadalajara*, Hermosillo, La Paz*, Los Angeles*, Los Mochis*, Mexicali, Matamoros, Mexico City*, Monterrey, San Luis Potosí, Tijuana*, Torreón, and Tucson

Durango to Guadalajara*, La Paz, Los Angeles*, Los Mochis, Mexico City, Tijuana*, and Torreón*

Hermosillo to Chihuahua, Ciudad Victoria, Culiacán, Guadalajara, La Paz*, Los Angeles*, Los Mochis*, Matamoros, Mexico City, Monterrey*, San Luis Potosí, Tijuana*, and Tucson*

La Paz to Chihuahua, Ciudad Juárez, Ciudad Victoria, Culiacán*, Durango, Guadalajara*, Hermosillo*, Los Angeles*, Los Mochis*, Matamoros, Mazatlán*, Mexico City, Monterrey, San Luis Potosí, Tijuana*, Torreón, and Tucson

Los Angeles to Culiacán*, Durango*, Guadalajara, Hermosillo*, La Paz*, Los Mochis, Mazatlán*, and Torreón

Los Mochis to Chihuahua, Ciudad Juárez, Ciudad Obregón*, Ciudad Victoria, Culiacán*, Durango, Guadalajara*, Hermosillo*, La Paz*, Los Angeles, Matamoros, Mexico City*, Monterrey, San Luis Potosí, Tijuana,* Torreón, and Tucson

Matamoros to Chihuahua, Ciudad Juárez, Ciudad Obregón, Ciudad Victoria, Culiacán, Guadalajara, Hermosillo, La Paz, Los Mochis, Mazatlán, Mexico City, Monterrey, Tijuana, and Torreón

Mazatlán to Chihuahua, Ciudad Juárez, Ciudad Victoria, Guadalajara*, La Paz*, Los Angeles*, Matamoros, Mexico City*, Monterrey, San Luis Potosí, Tijuana, and Torreón

Monterrey to Ciudad Obregón, Ciudad Victoria, Culiacán, Guadalajara, Hermosillo*, La Paz, Los Mochis, Matamoros, Mazatlán, Mexico City*, San Luis Potosí, and Tijuana

San Luis Potosí to Chihuahua, Ciudad Juárez, Ciudad Obregón, Culiacán, Hermosillo, La Paz, Los Mochis, Mazatlán, Mexico City*, Monterrey, Tijuana, and Torreón

Tijuana to Chihuahua*, Ciudad Juárez, Ciudad Obregón, Ciudad Victoria, Culiacán*, Durango*, Guadalajara*, Hermosillo*, La Paz*, Los Mochis*, Matamoros, Mazatlán, Mexico City, Monterrey, San Luis Potosí, and Torreón

Torreón to Ciudad Juárez*, Ciudad Obregón, Culiacán, Durango*, Guadalajara*, La Paz, Los Angeles, Los Mochis, Mazatlán, Mexico City*, and Tijuana*

Tucson to Ciudad Obregón, Culiacán, Guadalajara, Hermosillo*, La Paz, and Los Mochis

AEROLITORAL (U.S./CANADA TEL. 800-531-7921)

Flights from:

Chihuahua to Culiacán*, Los Mochis*, Monterrey*, San Luis Potosí, and Torreón*

El Paso to Chihuahua*, Hermosillo, and Monterrey

Hermosillo to Chihuahua*, Ciudad Juárez*, Ciudad Obregón*, Culiacán*, Los Mochis, Monterrey, San Antonio, McAllen, Tampico, Torreón, and Tucson*

McAllen (Texas) to Durango, Guadalajara, Monclova, Monterrey*, San Luis Potosí, Tampico, and Torreón

Monterrey to Chihuahua*, Ciudad Obregón, Durango, Guadalajara*, Los Mochis, McAllen*, Monclova*, Piedras Negras*, San Antonio*, San Luis Potosí*, Tampico,* Torreón*, and Tucson

San Antonio to Monclova* and Monterrey*

Tucson to Hermosillo*, Chihuahua, Ciudad Obregón, and La Paz

AEROMÉXICO (U.S./CANADA TEL. 800-237-6639)

Flights from:

Charlotte (North Carolina) to Mexico City

Chihuahua to Atlanta, Ciudad Juárez*, Ciudad Obregón*, Culiacán*, Durango, El Paso*, Guadalajara, Guerrero Negro, Hermosillo*, Houston, La Paz, Los Angeles*, Los Mochis*, Mazatlán, McAllen (Texas), Mexico City*, Monclova, Monterrey*, San Antonio, San Luis Potosí, Tampico, Torreón, and Tucson

Cincinnati (Ohio) to Mexico City

Ciudad Juárez to Chihuahua*, Ciudad Obregón, Culiacán, Durango, Guadalajara, Guerrero Negro, Hermosillo*, Houston, La Paz, Mazatlán*, Mexico City*, Monterrey, San Antonio, San Luis Potosí, Tampico, Tijuana, Torreón, and Tucson

Ciudad Obregón to Ciudad Juárez, Chihuahua*, Culiacán*, Durango, El Paso, Guadalajara*, Hermosillo*, La Paz*, Los Mochis, Mazatlán, Mexico City, Monterrey, San Luis Potosí, Tijuana, Torreón, and Tucson

Ciudad Victoria to Guadalajara and Mexico City*

Culiacán to Chihuahua*, Ciudad Juárez, Ciudad Obregón*, Durango*, El Paso, Guadalajara*, Hermosillo*, Mexico City*, Monclova, Monterrey, San Antonio, San Luis Potosí, Tampico, Tijuana, Torreón*, and Tucson

Daytona (Florida) to Mexico City

Durango to Ciudad Juárez, Ciudad Obregón, Chihuahua, Culiacán, Guadalajara*, Hermosillo, Houston, Los Angeles, Mazatlán*, McAllen, Mexico City*, Monclova, Monterrey, San Antonio, San Luis Potosí*, Tampico, Tijuana, and Torreón*

El Paso to Ciudad Obregón, Chihuahua*, Culiacán, Guadalajara, Hermosillo, La Paz, Los Mochis, Mexico City, Monterrey, and Torreón

Greensboro (North Carolina) to Mexico City

Guaymas to Hermosillo, La Paz*, Los Angeles, Mexico City, and Tucson*

Hermosillo to Chihuahua*, Ciudad Juárez*, Ciudad Obregón*, Culiacán*, Durango, El Paso, Guadalajara*, Guaymas, Guerrero Negro*, La Paz*, Los Mochis*, Mazatlán, Mexicali*, Mexico City*, Monclova, Monterrey, San Antonio, San Luis Potosí, Tampico, Tijuana*, Torreón, and Tucson*

Houston to Ciudad Juárez, Chihuahua, Durango, La Paz, Mazatlán, Mexico City*, Monclova, Monterrey*, San Luis Potosí, Tampico, and Torreón

(continues on next page)

AIRLINES SERVING NORTHERN MEXICO
(continued)

La Paz to Ciudad Juárez, El Paso, Houston, Los Mochis*, Mexico City*, Monterrey, San Antonio, Tijuana*, and Tucson

London (Gatwick) to Monterrey

Los Angeles to Durango, Mazatlán, Monterrey, San Luis Potosí, and Torreón

Los Mochis to Ciudad Juárez, Ciudad Obregón, Chihuahua*, El Paso, Guadalajara*, Guerrero Negro, Hermosillo*, La Paz*, Mazatlán*, Mexico City, Monterrey, San Antonio, Tijuana*, Torreón, and Tucson

Madrid to Monterrey, Tijuana, and Torreón

Matamoros to Guadalajara and Mexico City*

Mazatlán to Ciudad Juárez*, Ciudad Obregón, Chicago, Chihuahua, Durango*, Guadalajara*, Guerrero Negro, Hermosillo*, Houston, La Paz*, León/El Bajio, Los Angeles, Los Mochis*, Mexico City*, Monclova, Monterrey*, San Antonio, San Luis Potosí, Tampico, Tijuana*, Torreón*, and Tucson

McAllen (Texas) to Chihuahua, Durango, Guadalajara, Mexico City, Monclova, Monterrey*, San Luis Potosí, Tampico, and Torreón

Memphis (Tennessee) to Mexico City

Mexicali to Ciudad Obregón, Culiacán, Hermosillo*, Los Mochis, Mexico City, and Tucson

Mexico City to Atlanta*, Austin (Texas), Baltimore, Boston, Ciudad Juárez*, Ciudad Obregón, Ciudad Victoria*, Charlotte, Chicago, Chihuahua*, Cincinnati, Cleveland, Colorado, Dallas/Ft.Worth*, Durango*, El Paso, Ft. Lauderdale, Greensboro (North Carolina), Guaymas, Guerrero Negro, Hermosillo*, Houston*, La Paz*, London-Gatwick, Los Angeles*, Los Mochis, Madrid*, Matamoros*, Mazatlán, McAllen (Texas), Memphis, Mexicali, Miami*, Monclova, Monterrey*, Nashville, New Orleans, New York*, Paris*, Philadelphia, Phoenix*, Raleigh (North Carolina), Reno, Reynosa*, Richmond (Virginia), Salt Lake City, San Antonio, San Francisco, San Luis Potosí*, Seattle, Tampa, Tampico, Tijuana*, Torreón*, and Tucson

Miami to Mexico City*, Monterrey, and Torreón

Monclova to Chihuahua, Culiacán, Durango, Guadalajara, Hermosillo, Houston, Mazatlán, McAllen, Mexico City, Monterrey*, San Antonio*, San Luis Potosí, Tampico, Tijuana, and Torreón

Monterrey to Amsterdam, Atlanta, Ciudad Juárez, Ciudad Obregón, Chihuahua*, Culiacán*, Durango, El Paso, Guadalajara*, Hermosillo, Houston*, La Paz, London, Los Angeles, Los Mochis, Madrid, Mazatlán*, McAllen* (Texas), Mexico City*, Miami, Monclova, New Orleans, New York, Paris, Phoenix, Piedras Negras*, San Antonio*, San Diego, San Luis Potosí*, Tampico*, Tijuana, Torreón, and Tucson

Nashville to Mexico City

New Orleans to Guadalajara, Mexico City, and Monterrey

New York to Mexico City*, and Monterrey

Oklahoma City to Mexico City

Orlando to Guadalajara, Mexico City*, and Monterrey

Paris to Guadalajara, Mexico City*, Monterrey, Tijuana, and Torreón

Philadelphia to Mexico City

Phoenix to Guadalajara, Mexico City*, and Monterrey

Piedras Negras to Monterrey* and Tampico

Pittsburgh to Mexico City

Raleigh (North Carolina) to Mexico City

Reno to Mexico City

Reynosa to Mexico City

Salt Lake City to Mexico City

San Antonio to Ciudad Juárez, Chihuahua, Culiacán, Durango, Guadalajara, Hermosillo, Houston, La Paz, Los Mochis, Mazatlán, Mexico City, Monclova*, Monterrey*, San Luis Potosí, Tampico, and Torreón

San Diego to Guadalajara, Mexico City, and Monterrey

San Francisco to Mexico City

San Luis Potosí to Ciudad Juárez, Ciudad Obregón, Chihuahua, Culiacán, Durango*, Guadalajara*, Hermosillo, Houston, La Paz, Los Angeles, Mazatlán, McAllen (Texas), Mexico City*, Monclova, Monterrey*, San Antonio*, Tijuana, and Torreón

Seattle to Mexico City

Tampa to Mexico City

Tampico to Ciudad Juárez, Chihuahua, Culiacán, Durango, Guadalajara, Hermosillo, Houston, Mazatlán, McAllen (Texas), Mexico City, Monclova, Monterrey*, San Antonio, and Torreón

Tijuana to Ciudad Juárez, Ciudad Obregón, Chihuahua, Culiacán, Durango, Guadalajara*, Hermosillo*, La Paz*, Los Mochis*, Mazatlán*, Mexico City*, Monclova, Monterrey, Paris, San Luis Potosí, and Torreón

Torreón to Ciudad Juárez*, Ciudad Obregón, Chihuahua*, Culiacán*, Durango*, El Paso, Guadalajara*, Guerrero Negro, Hermosillo, Houston, Los Angeles, Los Mochis, Madrid, Mazatlán*, McAllen (Texas), Mexico City*, Miami, Monclova, Monterrey*, Paris, San Antonio, San Luis Potosí, Tampico, Tijuana, and Tucson

Tucson to Ciudad Juárez, Ciudad Obregón, Chihuahua, Culiacán, Guaymas, Guerrero Negro, Hermosillo*, La Paz, Los Mochis, Mazatlán, Mexicali, Mexico City, Monterrey, and Torreón

Washington, D.C. to Mexico City

AERO EXO (U.S./CANADA TEL. 800-237-6396)

Flights from:

Guadalajara to Monterrey* and Tijuana

Las Vegas to Monterrey*

Mexico City to Monterrey*

Monterrey to Guadalajara*, Las Vegas*, Mexico City*, and Tijuana

Tijuana to Guadalajara*, Mexico City, and Monterrey*

ALASKA AIRLINES (U.S./CANADA TEL. 800-426-0333)

Flights from:

Los Angeles to Mazatlán*

Mazatlán to Los Angeles*, San Francisco*, and Seattle-Tacoma

San Francisco to Mazatlán*

Seattle-Tacoma to Mazatlán

(continues on next page)

AIRLINES SERVING NORTHERN MEXICO
(continued)

CONTINENTAL (U.S./CANADA TEL. 800-523-3273)

Flights from:

Houston to Brownsville/So. Padre Island/Matamoros*, Mazatlán*, Mexico City*, and Monterrey*

Mazatlán to Houston*, with connections to many other U.S. cities

Monterrey to Houston*, with connections to many other U.S. cities

MEXICANA AIRLINES (U.S./CANADA/PUERTO RICO TEL. 800-531-7921)

Flights from:

Chicago to Guadalajara*, Mazatlán, Mexico City*, and Zacatecas

Chihuahua to Durango, Guadalajara, Hermosillo*, Mexico City, and Monterrey*

Ciudad Juárez to Durango, Guadalajara, Hermosillo*, Monterrey, and Tampico

Ciudad Obregón to Hermosillo*

Ciudad Victoria to Chicago, Los Angeles, and Mexico City*

Durango to Chicago*, Chihuahua, Ciudad Juárez, Guadalajara*, Mexico City*, Monterrey, Tampico, Torreón*, and Zacatecas

Guadalajara to Chicago*, Chihuahua, Ciudad Juárez, Denver*, Durango*, Los Angeles*, Mazatlán*, Mexicali*, Mexico City*, Miami, Monterrey*, Montreal, New York, Nuevo Laredo*, Saltillo, San Francisco*, San Jose*, San Luis Potosí*, Tampico, Tijuana*, and Torreón*

Hermosillo to Chicago, Chihuahua*, Ciudad Juárez*, Ciudad Obregón*, Culiacán*, Guadalajara, Guerrero Negro*, La Paz*, Mazatlán, Mexicali*, Mexico City*, Monterrey, San Luis Potosí, Tampico, and Torreón

La Paz to Hermosillo*, Mazatlán*, and Monterrey

Los Angeles to Ciudad Victoria, Guadalajara*, Mazatlán, Mexico City*, Monterrey, San Luis Potosí, Tampico, Torreón, and Zacatecas*

Mazatlán to Chicago, Denver*, Guadalajara*, Hermosillo, La Paz*, Los Angeles, Mexico City*, Miami, Monterrey*, San Luis Potosí, Tampico, and Torreón*

Mexicali to Ciudad Obregón, Culiacán, Guadalajara*, Hermosillo*, Mexico City, Monterrey, San Luis Potosí, Torreón, and Zacatecas

Mexico City to Chicago*, Chihuahua, Ciudad Victoria*, Culiacán, Durango*, Guadalajara*, Hermosillo*, Los Angeles*, Mazatlán*, Mexicali, Miami, Monclova, Monterrey*, Montreal*, New York*, Nuevo Laredo*, Saltillo*, San Antonio*, San Francisco, San Jose, San Luis Potosí*, Tampico*, Tijuana*, Tokyo, Torreón, and Zacatecas*

Miami to Guadalajara, Mazatlán, Mexico City, Tampico, and Zacatecas

Monclova to Mexico City, Monterrey*, San Luis Potosí, and Tampico

Monterrey to Chihuahua*, Culiacán*, Durango, Guadalajara*, Hermosillo, La Paz, Los Angeles, Los Mochis, Mazatlán*, Mexicali, Mexico City*, Monclova*, San Francisco, San Luis Potosí*, Tampico*, Tijuana, Torreón*, and Zacatecas

Montreal to Guadalajara, Mexico City*, and Tampico

New York to Guadalajara, Mexico City*, and Tampico

Nuevo Laredo to Guadalajara* and Mexico City*

Saltillo to Guadalajara and Mexico City*

San Antonio to Mexico City*

San Francisco to Guadalajara*, Mexico City, Monterrey, San Luis Potosí, Tampico, Torreón, and Zacatecas

San Jose (California) to Guadalajara*, Mexico City, Torreón, and Zacatecas

San Luis Potosí to Hermosillo, Los Angeles, Mazatlán, Mexico City*, Monterrey*, San Francisco, and Tijuana

Tampico to Chicago, Guadalajara, Los Angeles, Mazatlán, Mexico City*, Miami, Monterrey*, Montreal, New York, Oaxaca, San Francisco, Tijuana, and Zacatecas

Tijuana to Guadalajara*, Los Angeles*, Mexico City*, Monterrey, San Luis Potosí, Tampico, Torreón, and Zacatecas

Tokyo to Mexico City

Torreón to Durango*, Guadalajara*, Los Angeles*, Mazatlán*, Mexicali, Mexico City, Monterrey*, San Francisco, San Jose (California), Tampico, and Tijuana

Zacatecas to Chicago*, Denver*, Guadalajara, Los Angeles*, Mexicali, Mexico City*, Miami, Monterrey, San Francisco, San Jose*, Tampico, and Tijuana*

TAESA (U.S./CANADA TEL. 512-725-8414)

Flights from:

Chicago to Ciudad Juárez*, Durango, Guadalajara*, Mexico City, and Zacatecas*

Chihuahua to Mexico City*

Ciudad Juárez to Chicago*, Durango*, Mexico City, and Zacatecas*

Durango to Chicago, Ciudad Juárez*, and Mexico City

Hermosillo to Mexicali* and Mexico City

Saltillo to Mexico City*

Zacatecas to Chicago*, Ciudad Juárez*, Mexico City, and Tijuana

RAILWAY SCHEDULE

Arrival/departure for the following rail lines may change at any time. Only major first- and second-class routes are listed.

To follow routes, read downward on the left time column, and upward on the right time column to return (e.g., depart on Train No. 1 from Guadalajara at 9:30 a.m.; arrive Nogales at 10:50 a.m. To return, depart on Train No. 2 from Nogales at 2:30 p.m.; arrive Guadalajara at 7:00 p.m.)

EL PACÍFICO (SPECIAL 1ST-CLASS RESERVED), GUADALAJARA/NOGALES/GUADALAJARA

	TRAIN NO. 1		TRAIN NO. 2	
Depart	9:30 a.m.	Guadalajara	7:30 p.m.	Arrive
	1:35 p.m.	Tepic	12:30 p.m.	
	5:30 p.m.	Mazatlán	7:15 a.m.	
	8:44 p.m.	Culiacán	4:26 a.m.	
	11:45 p.m.	Sufragio	1:15 a.m.	next day
next day	1:58 a.m.	Navojoa	11:28 p.m.	
	2:57 a.m.	Ciudad Obregón	10:24 p.m.	
	4:55 a.m.	Empalme	8:40 p.m.	
	6:45 a.m.	Hermosillo	6:45 p.m.	
	8:25 a.m.	Benjamin Hill*	4:44 p.m.	
	11:20 p.m.	Caborca	2:37 p.m.	
	1:10 p.m.	Puerto Peñasco	12:20 p.m.	
Arrive	4:55 p.m.	Mexicali	9:00 a.m.	Depart
		Connecting to:		
Depart	9:45 a.m.	Benjamin Hill*	4:10 p.m.	Arrive
Arrive	2:30 p.m.	Nogales	2:00 p.m.	Depart

CHIHUAHUA AL PACÍFICO (SPECIAL 1ST-CLASS RESERVED), LOS MOCHIS/CHIHUAHUA/LOS MOCHIS

	TRAIN NO. 73		TRAIN NO. 74	
Depart	6:00 a.m.	Los Mochis	7:50 p.m.	Arrive
	6:43 a.m.	Sufragio	6:59 p.m.	
	7:26 a.m.	El Fuerte	6:15 p.m.	
	11:11 a.m.	Témoris	4:30 p.m.	
	12:12 p.m.	Bahuichivo	3:32 p.m.	
	1:30 p.m.	Posada Barrancas	2:10 p.m.	
	1:35 p.m.	Divisadero	1:45 p.m.	
	3:14 p.m.	Creel	12:26 p.m.	
	6:25 p.m.	Cuauhtémoc	9:15 a.m.	
Arrive	8:50 p.m.	Chihuahua	7:00 a.m.	Depart

CHIHUAHUA-LOS MOCHIS (TARAHUMARA) (2ND CLASS), LOS MOCHIS/CHIHUAHUA/LOS MOCHIS

	TRAIN NO. 75		TRAIN NO. 76	
Depart	7:00 a.m.	Los Mochis	10:25 p.m.	Arrive
	8:45 a.m.	Sufragio	9:25 p.m.	
	9:40 a.m.	El Fuerte	8:42 p.m.	
	1:45 p.m.	Bahuichivo	5:25 p.m.	
	3:30 p.m.	Posada Barrancas	3:25 p.m.	
	3:58 p.m.	Divisadero	3:10 p.m.	
	5:00 p.m.	Creel	2:00 p.m.	
Arrive	11:25 p.m.	Chihuahua	8:00 a.m.	Depart

EL REGIOMONTANO (SPECIAL 1ST-CLASS RESERVED OR SLEEPER), MEXICO CITY/MONTERREY/MEXICO CITY

	TRAIN NO. 71		TRAIN NO. 72	
Depart	6:00 p.m.	Mexico City	10:00 a.m.	Arrive
next day	00:01 a.m.	San Luis Potosí	3:45 a.m.	next day
	5:44 a.m.	Saltillo	10:00 p.m.	
Arrive	8:10 p.m.	Monterrey	7:50 p.m.	Depart

EL COAHUILENSE (2ND CLASS) SALTILLO/PIEDRAS NEGRAS/SALTILLO

	TRAIN NO. 181		TRAIN NO. 182	
Depart	8:15 a.m.	Saltillo	6:55 p.m.	Arrive
Arrive	5:35 p.m.	Piedras Negras	9:15 a.m.	Depart

EL TAMAULIPECO (RESERVED SEAT AND 2ND CLASS), MONTERREY/MATAMOROS/MONTERREY

	TRAIN NO. 141		TRAIN NO. 142	
Depart	10:30 a.m.	Monterrey	4:00 p.m.	Arrive
	3:05 p.m.	Reynosa	11:05 a.m.	
Arrive	4:00 p.m.	Matamoros	9:20 a.m.	Depart

DIVISIÓN DEL NORTE (SPECIAL 1ST-CLASS RESERVED* OR 2ND CLASS), MEXICO CITY/CIUDAD JUAREZ/MEXICO CITY

	TRAIN NO. 7		TRAIN NO. 8	
Depart	8:00 p.m.	Mexico City*	9:30 a.m.	Arrive
	11:30 p.m.	Querétaro*	5:40 a.m.	next day
next day	6:30 a.m.	Aguascalientes*	10:30 p.m.	
	9:30 a.m.	Zacatecas*	8:05 p.m.	
	5:10 p.m.	Torreón	12:00 p.m.	
	9:20 p.m.	Jimenez	7:40 a.m.	
next day	1:20 a.m.	Chihuahua	3:15 a.m.	next day
Arrive	6:45 a.m.	Ciudad Juárez	10:00 p.m.	Depart

NUEVO LAREDO-MONTERREY-MEXICO CITY (SPECIAL 1ST-CLASS RESERVED* OR 2ND CLASS), MEXICO CITY/NUEVO LAREDO/MEXICO CITY

	TRAIN NO. 1		TRAIN NO. 2	
Depart	9:00 a.m.	Mexico City*	7:00 p.m.	Arrive
	12:56 p.m.	Querétaro*	2:42 p.m.	
	2:35 a.m.	San Miguel Allende*	1:09 p.m.	
	5:10 p.m.	San Luis Potosí*	10:05 a.m.	
	11:55 p.m.	Saltillo	2:35 a.m.	next day
next day	2:20 a.m.	Monterrey	11:30 p.m.	
Arrive	7:20 a.m.	Nuevo Laredo	6:55 p.m.	Depart

EL TAMAULIPECO (SPECIAL 1ST CLASS RESERVED), MONTERREY/MATAMOROS/MONTERREY

	TRAIN NO. 141		TRAIN NO. 142	
Depart	10:30 a.m.	Monterrey	4:00 p.m.	Arrive
	2:40 p.m.	Reynosa	11:25 a.m.	
Arrive	5:10 p.m.	Matamoros	9:20 a.m.	Depart

INDEX

ARCHAEOLOGICAL SITES

FESTIVALS

---

mines: Chihuahua 326, 332; San Luis Potosí 413; Zacatecas 381
missions: Ciudad Juárez 261-264; Sonora 150-151, 155, 156, 160, 161
Moctezuma: 161
Monclova: 448-449
moneychangers: 123-125
Monterrey: 471-496
mordida: 105, 131-132
mosquitoes: 118-119, 136
motels: *see specific place*
motorcycles: 100-101
movie locations: 356-358, 417
movies: Monterrey 488
Munérachi: 326, 334-335
museums: Ciudad Juárez 264; Ciudad Valles 432; Chihuahua 295; Cosalá 217; Durango 353; Guadalupe 389; Harold R. Pape Museum-Library 448-449; Madera 283; Monterrey 478-479; Museo Arqueológico, Mazatlán 225; Museo Casa de Carranza 452; Museo Casa Mata 519; Museo Costumbrista de Sonora 194; Museo de Antropología e Historia 540; Museo de Arte de Sinaloa 213; Museo de Arte Contemporáneo de Monterrey (MARCO) 479; Museo de Arte Virreinal de Guadalupe 389; Museo de General Francisco Villa 307; Museo de Historica Mexicana 478-479; Museo de la Cultura Huasteca 533; Museo de La Lucha Obrera 158; Museo de la Minería 466; Museo de la Revolución 295; Museo de los Seris 173; Museo de los Yaquis 189; Museo Francisco Goitia 379; Museo Nacional de la Máscara 402; Museo Pedro Coronel 378; Museo Pimiera Alta Historical Society 151; Museo Regional de la Laguna 466; Museo Rafael Coronel 379; Quinta Gameros 295; Reynosa 514; Saltillo 457; San Luis Potosí 402-403; Sonora 164-165; Torreón 466; Zacatecas 378, 379-380
music: 63-66

N
Nacimiento: 448
Naco, Arizona: 155
Nacozari de García: 160-161
NAFTA: 30, 37-38
narcotics trafficking: 64-65, 215
Navojoa: 191-192
newspapers: 126

NATIONAL PARKS

Basaseachic Falls: 346-348
Cumbres de Majalca: 305
El Gogorrón: 422
El Pinacate: 136-139
El Potosí: 426
Las Cumbres de Monterrey: 496-497
Los Novillos: 443

nightclubs: *see specific place*
Nogales, Arizona: 151-152
Nogales, Sonora: 152-154
Nombre de Dios: 366
Nuevo Laredo: 503-511
Nuevo León: 471-499
Nuevo Padilla: 544-545
Nuevo Progreso: 517

O
Oasis America: 21-22
observatories: Zacatecas 380
occult: 369-370; *see also* legends
oil: 531
Ojinaga: 288-289
on-line services: 129-130
orange groves: 499
Otachique: 349
Othón, Manuel José: 402

P
Pacífico Brewery: 229
Palomas: 273-274
Panalachi: 326
Pape, Harold: 448-449
Paquimé Archaeological Zone: 278-281
parasailing: Mazatlán 243
Parque Arqueológico Morelos: 504
Parque Commemorative Chamizal: 264
Parque Ecológico Chipinque: 488-489
Parque Nacional Cascada de Basaseachic: 346-348
Parque Nacional Cumbres de Majalca: 305
Parral: 306-309
Parras de la Fuente: 463-465
Parroquía de la Purísima Concepción: 419-420
Parroquía de Santo Cristo de Burgos: 306
PEMEX: 106-108

ABOUT THE AUTHOR

JOE CUMMINGS has written about travel and culture for nearly two decades. Attracted to geographical extremes, he took his his first in-depth journeys to the river deltas and rainforests of Southeast Asia, where he worked as a Peace Corps volunteer (Thailand) and university lecturer (Malaysia), and later contributed to acclaimed guidebooks on Thailand, Malaysia, Singapore, Burma, Laos, Indonesia, and China.

Joe became infatuated with desert terrains while exploring the Sierra del Carmen and Chihuahuan Desert reaches of Texas's Big Bend Country for Moon's *Texas Handbook*. His love of South Texas border culture, including *norteña* music and food, eventually spilled over into Mexico, where he has undertaken intensive Spanish language courses and lived with a Mexican family. For Moon he has also written *Baja Handbook* and *Cabo Handbook* and is co-author of *Mexico Handbook*. After covering more than 50,000 miles of Mexican roads by car and four-wheel drive, he recently became a full-time resident of Mexico and is building a home there.

Joe continues to receive accolades for his guidebooks work, including a 1995 Lowell Thomas Travel Journalism Gold Award. When not on the road, Joe likes to kayak, snorkel, and read/re-read Graham Greene, B. Traven, and Alvaro Mútis novels.

NOTES

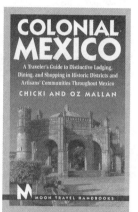
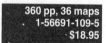

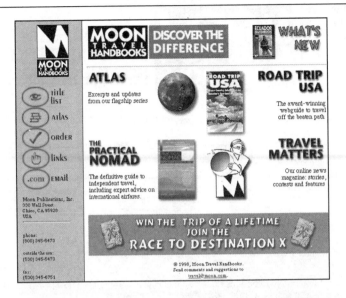

www.moon.com

Enjoy our travel information center on the World Wide Web (WWW), loaded with interactive exhibits designed especially for the Internet.

ATTRACTIONS ON MOON'S WEB SITE INCLUDE:

ATLAS
Our award-winning, comprehensive travel guides cover destinations throughout North America and Hawaii, Latin America and the Caribbean, and Asia and the Pacific.

PRACTICAL NOMAD
Extensive excerpts, a unique set of travel links coordinated with the book, and a regular Q & A column by author and Internet travel consultant Edward Hasbrouck.

TRAVEL MATTERS
Our on-line travel zine, featuring articles; author correspondence; a travel library including health information, reading lists, and cultural cues; and our new contest, **Destination X,** offering a chance to win a trip to the mystery destination of your choice.

ROAD TRIP USA
Our best-selling book, ever; don't miss this award-winning Web guide to off-the-interstate itineraries.

Come visit us at: **www.moon.com**

LOSE YOURSELF IN THE EXPERIENCE, NOT THE CROWD

For 25 years, Moon Travel Handbooks have been the guidebooks of choice for adventurous travelers. Our award-winning Handbook series provides focused, comprehensive coverage of distinct destinations all over the world. Each Handbook is like an entire bookcase of cultural insight and introductory information in one portable volume. Our goal at Moon is to give travelers all the background and practical information they'll need for an extraordinary travel experience.

The following pages include a complete list of Handbooks, covering North America and Hawaii, Mexico, Latin America and the Caribbean, and Asia and the Pacific.To purchase Moon Travel Handbooks, check your local bookstore or order by phone: (800) 345-5473 M-F 8 am.-5 p.m. PST or outside the U.S. phone: (530) 345-5473.

"An in-depth dunk into the land, the people and their history, arts, and politics."
— *Student Travels*

"I consider these books to be superior to Lonely Planet. When Moon produces a book it is more humorous, incisive, and off-beat."
— *Toronto Sun*

"Outdoor enthusiasts gravitate to the well-written Moon Travel Handbooks. In addition to politically correct historic and cultural features, the series focuses on flora, fauna and outdoor recreation. Maps and meticulous directions also are a trademark of Moon guides."
— *Houston Chronicle*

"Moon [Travel Handbooks] . . . bring a healthy respect to the places they investigate. Best of all, they provide a host of odd nuggets that give a place texture and prod the wary traveler from the beaten path. The finest are written with such care and insight they deserve listing as literature."
— *American Geographical Society*

"Moon Travel Handbooks offer in-depth historical essays and useful maps, enhanced by a sense of humor and a neat, compact format."
— *Swing*

"Perfect for the more adventurous, these are long on history, sightseeing and nitty-gritty information and very price-specific."
— *Columbus Dispatch*

"Moon guides manage to be comprehensive and countercultural at the same time . . . Handbooks are packed with maps, photographs, drawings, and sidebars that constitute a college-level introduction to each country's history, culture, people, and crafts."
— *National Geographic Traveler*

"Few travel guides do a better job helping travelers create their own itineraries than the Moon Travel Handbook series. The authors have a knack for homing in on the essentials."
— **Colorado Springs** *Gazette Telegraph*

MEXICO

"These books will delight the armchair traveler, aid the un-
decided person in selecting a destination, and guide
the seasoned road warrior looking for lesser-known
hideaways."

—Mexican Meanderings Newsletter

"From tourist traps to off-the-beaten track hideaways,
these guides offer consistent, accurate details without
pretension."

—Foreign Service Journal

Archaeological Mexico	**$19.95**
Andrew Coe	410 pages, 27 maps
Baja Handbook	**$16.95**
Joe Cummings	544 pages, 46 maps
Cabo Handbook	**$14.95**
Joe Cummings	272 pages, 17 maps
Cancún Handbook	**$14.95**
Chicki Mallan	270 pages, 25 maps
Colonial Mexico	**$18.95**
Chicki Mallan	360 pages, 38 maps
Mexico Handbook	**$21.95**
Joe Cummings and Chicki Mallan	1,200 pages, 201 maps
Northern Mexico Handbook	**$17.95**
Joe Cummings	590 pages, 69 maps
Pacific Mexico Handbook	**$17.95**
Bruce Whipperman	580 pages, 68 maps
Puerto Vallarta Handbook	**$14.95**
Bruce Whipperman	330 pages, 36 maps
Yucatán Handbook	**$16.95**
Chicki Mallan	470 pages, 52 maps

LATIN AMERICA AND THE CARIBBEAN

"Solidly packed with practical information and full of significant cultural asides that will enlighten you on the whys and wherefores of things you might easily see but not easily grasp."

—*Boston Globe*

Belize Handbook	**$15.95**
Chicki Mallan and Patti Lange	390 pages, 45 maps
Caribbean Handbook	**$16.95**
Karl Luntta	400 pages, 56 maps
Costa Rica Handbook	**$19.95**
Christopher P. Baker	780 pages, 73 maps
Cuba Handbook	**$19.95**
Christopher P. Baker	740 pages, 70 maps
Dominican Republic Handbook	**$15.95**
Gaylord Dold	420 pages, 24 maps
Ecuador Handbook	**$16.95**
Julian Smith	450 pages, 43 maps
Honduras Handbook	**$15.95**
Chris Humphrey	330 pages, 40 maps
Jamaica Handbook	**$15.95**
Karl Luntta	330 pages, 17 maps
Virgin Islands Handbook	**$13.95**
Karl Luntta	220 pages, 19 maps

NORTH AMERICA AND HAWAII

"These domestic guides convey the same sense of exoticism that their foreign counterparts do, making home-country travel seem like far-flung adventure."

—*Sierra Magazine*

Alaska-Yukon Handbook	**$17.95**
Deke Castleman and Don Pitcher	530 pages, 92 maps
Alberta and the Northwest Territories Handbook	**$17.95**
Andrew Hempstead and Nadina Purdon	530 pages, 72 maps,
Arizona Traveler's Handbook	**$17.95**
Bill Weir and Robert Blake	512 pages,54 maps
Atlantic Canada Handbook	**$17.95**
Nan Drosdick and Mark Morris	460 pages, 61 maps
Big Island of Hawaii Handbook	**$15.95**
J.D. Bisignani	390 pages, 23 maps
British Columbia Handbook	**$16.95**
Jane King and Andrew Hempstead	430 pages, 69 maps

Colorado Handbook	**$18.95**
Stephen Metzger	480 pages, 59 maps
Georgia Handbook	**$17.95**
Kap Stann	370 pages, 50 maps
Hawaii Handbook	**$19.95**
J.D. Bisignani	1,030 pages, 90 maps
Honolulu-Waikiki Handbook	**$14.95**
J.D. Bisignani	380 pages, 20 maps
Idaho Handbook	**$18.95**
Don Root	610 pages, 42 maps
Kauai Handbook	**$15.95**
J.D. Bisignani	320 pages, 23 maps
Maine Handbook	**$18.95**
Kathleen M. Brandes	660 pages, 27 maps
Massachusetts Handbook	**$18.95**
Jeff Perk	600 pages, 23 maps
Maui Handbook	**$14.95**
J.D. Bisignani	410 pages, 35 maps
Montana Handbook	**$17.95**
Judy Jewell and W.C. McRae	480 pages, 52 maps
Nevada Handbook	**$18.95**
Deke Castleman	530 pages, 40 maps
New Hampshire Handbook	**$18.95**
Steve Lantos	500 pages, 18 maps
New Mexico Handbook	**$15.95**
Stephen Metzger	360 pages, 47 maps
New York City Handbook	**$13.95**
Christiane Bird	300 pages, 20 maps
New York Handbook	**$19.95**
Christiane Bird	780 pages, 95 maps
Northern California Handbook	**$19.95**
Kim Weir	800 pages, 50 maps
Oregon Handbook	**$17.95**
Stuart Warren and Ted Long Ishikawa	588 pages, 34 maps
Pennsylvania Handbook	**$18.95**
Joanne Miller	448 pages, 40 maps
Road Trip USA	**$22.50**
Jamie Jensen	800 pages, 165 maps
Southern California Handbook	**$19.95**
Kim Weir	720 pages, 26 maps
Tennessee Handbook	**$17.95**
Jeff Bradley	530 pages, 44 maps
Texas Handbook	**$18.95**
Joe Cummings	690 pages, 70 maps
Utah Handbook	**$17.95**
Bill Weir and W.C. McRae	490 pages, 40 maps

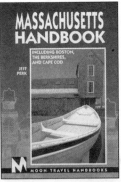

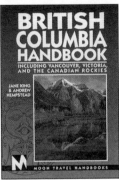

Washington Handbook	$19.95
Don Pitcher	870 pages, 113 maps
Wisconsin Handbook	$18.95
Thomas Huhti	590 pages, 69 maps
Wyoming Handbook	$17.95
Don Pitcher	610 pages, 80 maps

ASIA AND THE PACIFIC

"Scores of maps, detailed practical info down to business hours of small-town libraries. You can't beat the Asian titles for sheer heft. (The) series is sort of an American Lonely Planet, with better writing but fewer titles. (The) individual voice of researchers comes through."

—Travel & Leisure

Australia Handbook	$21.95
Marael Johnson, Andrew Hempstead, and Nadina Purdon	940 pages, 141 maps
Bali Handbook	$19.95
Bill Dalton	750 pages, 54 maps
Bangkok Handbook	$13.95
Michael Buckley	244 pages, 30 maps
Fiji Islands Handbook	$13.95
David Stanley	280 pages, 38 maps
Hong Kong Handbook	$16.95
Kerry Moran	378 pages, 49 maps
Indonesia Handbook	$25.00
Bill Dalton	1,380 pages, 249 maps
Japan Handbook	$22.50
J.D. Bisignani	970 pages, 213 maps
Micronesia Handbook	$14.95
Neil M. Levy	340 pages, 70 maps
Nepal Handbook	$18.95
Kerry Moran	490 pages, 51 maps
New Zealand Handbook	$19.95
Jane King	620 pages, 81 maps
Outback Australia Handbook	$18.95
Marael Johnson	450 pages, 57 maps
Philippines Handbook	$17.95
Peter Harper and Laurie Fullerton	670 pages, 116 maps
Singapore Handbook	$15.95
Carl Parkes	350 pages, 29 maps
Southeast Asia Handbook	$21.95
Carl Parkes	1,000 pages, 203 maps

South Korea Handbook	**$19.95**
Robert Nilsen	820 pages, 141 maps
South Pacific Handbook	**$22.95**
David Stanley	920 pages, 147 maps
Tahiti-Polynesia Handbook	**$13.95**
David Stanley	270 pages, 35 maps
Thailand Handbook	**$19.95**
Carl Parkes	860 pages, 142 maps
Vietnam, Cambodia & Laos Handbook	**$18.95**
Michael Buckley	730 pages, 116 maps

OTHER GREAT TITLES FROM MOON

"For hardy wanderers, few guides come more highly recommended than the Handbooks. They include good maps, steer clear of fluff and flackery, and offer plenty of money-saving tips. They also give you the kind of information that visitors to strange lands—on any budget—need to survive."

—US News & World Report

Moon Handbook	**$10.00**
Carl Koppeschaar	141 pages, 8 maps
Moscow-St. Petersburg Handbook	**$13.95**
Masha Nordbye	259 pages, 16 maps
The Practical Nomad: How to Travel Around the World	**$17.95**
Edward Hasbrouck	575 pages
Staying Healthy in Asia, Africa, and Latin America	**$11.95**
Dirk Schroeder	197 pages, 4 maps

MOONBELT

A new concept in moneybelts. Made of heavy-duty Cordura nylon, the Moonbelt offers maximum protection for your money and important papers. This pouch, designed for all-weather comfort, slips under your shirt or waistband, rendering it virtually undetectable and inaccessible to pickpockets. It features a one-inch high-test quick-release buckle so there's no more fumbling around for the strap or repeated adjustments. This handy plastic buckle opens and closes with a touch but won't come undone until you want it to. Moonbelts accommodate traveler's checks, passports, cash, photos, etc. Size 5 x 9 inches. Available in black only. **$8.95**

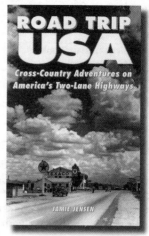

THE PRACTICAL NOMAD

✈ TAKE THE PLUNGE

"The greatest barriers to long-term travel by Americans are the disempowered feelings that leave them afraid to ask for the time off. Just do it."

✈ TAKE NOTHING FOR GRANTED

"Even 'What time is it?' is a highly politicized question in some areas, and the answer may depend on your informant's ethnicity and political allegiance as well as the proximity of the secret police."

✈ TAKE THIS BOOK

$17.95   576 pages

With experience helping thousands of his globetrotting clients plan their trips around the world, travel industry insider Edward Hasbrouck provides the secrets that can save readers money and valuable travel time.
An indispensable complement to destination-specific travel guides, *The Practical Nomad* includes:

> **airfare strategies**
> **ticket discounts**
> **long-term travel considerations**
> **travel documents**
> **border crossings**
> **entry requirements**
> **government offices**
> **travel publications**
> **Internet information resources**

WHERE TO BUY MOON TRAVEL HANDBOOKS

BOOKSTORES AND LIBRARIES: Moon Travel Handbooks are distributed worldwide. Please contact our sales manager for a list of wholesalers and distributors in your area.

TRAVELERS: We would like to have Moon Travel Handbooks available throughout the world. Please ask your bookstore to write or call us for ordering information. If your bookstore will not order our guides for you, please contact us for a free catalog.

> **Moon Travel Handbooks**
> **P.O. Box 3040**
> **Chico, CA 95927-3040 U.S.A.**
> **tel.: (800) 345-5473, outside the U.S. (530) 345-5473**
> **fax: (530) 345-6751**
> **e-mail: travel@moon.com**

IMPORTANT ORDERING INFORMATION

PRICES: All prices are subject to change. We always ship the most current edition. We will let you know if there is a price increase on the book you order.

SHIPPING AND HANDLING OPTIONS: Domestic UPS or USPS first class (allow 10 working days for delivery): $4.50 for the first item, $1.00 for each additional item.

Moonbelt shipping is $1.50 for one, 50 cents for each additional belt.

UPS 2nd Day Air or Printed Airmail requires a special quote.

International Surface Bookrate 8-12 weeks delivery: $4.00 for the first item, $1.00 for each additional item. Note: We cannot guarantee international surface bookrate shipping. We recommends sending international orders via air mail, which requires a special quote.

FOREIGN ORDERS: Orders that originate outside the U.S.A. must be paid for with an international money order, a check in U.S. currency drawn on a major U.S. bank based in the U.S.A., or Visa, MasterCard, or Discover.

TELEPHONE ORDERS: We accept Visa, MasterCard, or Discover payments. Call in your order: (800) 345-5473, 8 a.m.-5 p.m. Pacific standard time. Outside the U.S. the number is (530) 345-5473.

INTERNET ORDERS: Visit our site at: www.moon.com

ORDER FORM

Prices are subject to change without notice. Be sure to call (800) 345-5473,
or (530) 345-5473 from outside the U.S. 8 a.m.–5 p.m. PST for current prices and editions.
(See important ordering information on preceding page.)

Name: _____ Date: _____

Street: _____

City: _____ Daytime Phone: _____

State or Country: _____ Zip Code: _____

QUANTITY	TITLE	PRICE

Taxable Total_____

Sales Tax (7.25%) for California Residents_____

Shipping & Handling_____

TOTAL_____

Ship: ☐ UPS (no P.O. Boxes)   ☐ 1st class   ☐ International surface mail

Ship to: ☐ address above   ☐ other _____

_____

Make checks payable to: **MOON TRAVEL HANDBOOKS**, P.O. Box 3040, Chico, CA 95927-3040
U.S.A. We accept Visa, MasterCard, or Discover. **To Order**: Call in your Visa, MasterCard, or Discover number,
or send a written order with your Visa, MasterCard, or Discover number and expiration date clearly written.

Card Number: ☐ **Visa**   ☐ **MasterCard**   ☐ **Discover**

☐ ☐ ☐ ☐ ☐ ☐ ☐ ☐ ☐ ☐ ☐ ☐ ☐ ☐ ☐ ☐

Exact Name on Card: _____

Expiration date:_____

Signature: _____

U.S.~METRIC CONVERSION

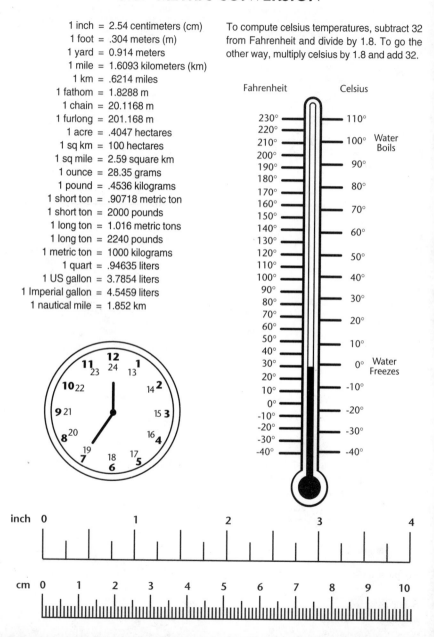

1 inch = 2.54 centimeters (cm)
1 foot = .304 meters (m)
1 yard = 0.914 meters
1 mile = 1.6093 kilometers (km)
1 km = .6214 miles
1 fathom = 1.8288 m
1 chain = 20.1168 m
1 furlong = 201.168 m
1 acre = .4047 hectares
1 sq km = 100 hectares
1 sq mile = 2.59 square km
1 ounce = 28.35 grams
1 pound = .4536 kilograms
1 short ton = .90718 metric ton
1 short ton = 2000 pounds
1 long ton = 1.016 metric tons
1 long ton = 2240 pounds
1 metric ton = 1000 kilograms
1 quart = .94635 liters
1 US gallon = 3.7854 liters
1 Imperial gallon = 4.5459 liters
1 nautical mile = 1.852 km

To compute celsius temperatures, subtract 32 from Fahrenheit and divide by 1.8. To go the other way, multiply celsius by 1.8 and add 32.